Elections in Africa

A Data Handbook

Edited by

DIETER NOHLEN
MICHAEL KRENNERICH
and
BERNHARD THIBAUT

OXFORD
UNIVERSITY PRESS

OXFORD
UNIVERSITY PRESS

Great Clarendon Street, Oxford OX2 6DP

Oxford University Press is a department of the University of Oxford.
It furthers the University's objective of excellence in research, scholarship,
and education by publishing worldwide in

Oxford New York

Athens Auckland Bangkok Bogotá Buenos Aires Cape Town
Chennai Dar es Salaam Delhi Florence Hong Kong Istanbul Karachi
Kolkata Kuala Lumpur Madrid Melbourne Mexico City Mumbai Nairobi
Paris São Paulo Shanghai Singapore Taipei Tokyo Toronto Warsaw

with associated companies in Berlin Ibadan

Published in the United States
by Oxford University Press Inc., New York

First published 1999

British Library Cataloguing in Publication Data
Data available

Library of Congress Cataloging in Publication Data
Data available

ISBN 0-19-829645-2

3 5 7 9 10 8 6 4 2

Typeset by IPW, Heidelberg
Printed in Great Britain
on acid-free paper by
Biddles Ltd., Guildford and King's Lynn

Acknowledgements

This handbook is part of a continuous scientific work on elections, electoral systems and political development in different world regions realized at the Institute of Political Science of the University of Heidelberg since the 1960s, when Dolf Sternberger and Bernhard Vogel initiated a voluminous research project on 'The Election of Parliaments and other State Organs'. The first result of this project was the publication of *Die Wahl der Parlamente* (1969), a two-volume book containing documentation and analyses of the electoral development of all European countries. In 1978 a second, two-volume book was published on Africa under the subtitle *Politische Organisation und Repräsentation in Afrika*, principally authored by Franz Nuscheler and Klaus Ziemer. In the same year Dieter Nohlen published his *Wahlsysteme der Welt*, a systematic handbook on electoral systems of the world. In the late 1980s a multinational research group directed by Dieter Nohlen began a new stage of the larger project (though under a different label), now working on parliamentary and presidential elections in Latin America and the Caribbean. The result was published in 1993 in German (*Handbuch der Wahldaten Lateinamerikas und der Karibik*) and in Spanish (*Enciclopedia Electoral Latinoamericana y del Caribe*). Building on the experience of this data handbook which had received a strong impulse from the numerous democratization processes in Latin America, and under the impetus of political regime changes in Africa, we began in 1994 to conceptualize another project with the aim of compiling an as complete as possible systematic documentation of electoral data of African countries since independence. Further steps will include an updated and reworked edition of the handbook on Latin America and, finally, a similar volume on Asia, which both will be published by Oxford University Press. For the realization of this plan the help of many people and organizations has been, and still remains, indispensable.

For invaluable financial support in the preparation of this handbook we are indebted to the *Deutsche Forschungsgemeinschaft* (DFG). Earlier related projects were also supported by the Volkswagen Foundation, the Alexander von Humboldt Foundation and the Interamerican Institute for Human Rights (San José, Costa Rica). On behalf of the DFG, Helga Hoppe has administered the project in the most confident and competent way. Important academic support came from Max Kaase, whose energetic recognition of the relevance and the viability of our plans has helped a lot in decisive moments of our work.

To participate as an author in projects like this one is neither easy nor fun. There is little room to give one's contribution an individual profile. Instead there are many inconvenient guidelines to be followed and many time consuming questions and comments of the editors to be dealt with before one has completed a chapter that from a distant point of view does not count very much in one's bibliographical record. We are therefore more than grateful to our authors for their constant readiness to cooperate and for their patience in awaiting the final publication of their contributions. Helga Fleischhacker and Christof Hartmann have not only participated as authors but have also provided important assistance in the process of data collection and standardization of the information presented in this handbook.

The help we and our authors received from many colleagues and from scientific and political institutions with regard to country specific research problems as well as with regard to administrative and logistical questions went far beyond professional standards. We are grateful to the Institute of Political Science at the University of Heidelberg, the Max Planck Institute for Comparative Public Law and International Law in Heidelberg, the Institute of African Affairs in Hamburg, the International Foundation for Electoral Systems in Washington, the Friedrich Ebert Foundation and the Konrad Adenauer Foundation. In a number of African countries, electoral offices have done a lot to improve our documentation of legal electoral norms and election results.

Finally, we would like to thank Dominic Byatt, Amanda Watkins and the editorial staff of Oxford University Press for helpful advice and technical support.

The editors — Heidelberg, December 1998

Contents

Notes on Editors and Contributors

Editors

DIETER NOHLEN is Professor of Political Science at the University of Heidelberg and a well known expert on electoral systems, regime change and democratization processes and development studies with a focus on Latin America. He received the Max Planck prize for internationally outstanding research in 1991. His numerous books include *Wahlsysteme der Welt* (1978; Spanish edition 1981), *Sistemas electorales y partidos políticos* (3rd edition 1998), *Electoral systems and Party Systems* (1996). He is also coeditor of an eight-volume Handbook of the Third World (with F. Nuscheler, 3rd edition 1991–1994) and editor of a seven-volume Encyclopedia of Political Science (1992–1998).

MICHAEL KRENNERICH is a research associate at the Institute for Political Science at the University of Heidelberg where he studied Political Science, Philosophy and Public Law (Ph.D. 1996). For his doctoral dissertation he received the 1997 prize of the Association for European Research on Central America and the Caribbean. In recent years he has been engaged in consulting activities in the field of electoral reforms in Latin America, Africa, Asia and Eastern Europe. He has published numerous articles on political development and elections in various world regions and is author of a book on elections and civil wars in Central America (1996).

BERNHARD THIBAUT is a research associate at the Institute for Political Science at the University of Heidelberg where he studied Political Science and Sociology (M.A. 1991, Ph.D. 1996). For his doctoral dissertation he received the 1998 ADLAF-prize of the German Association for Latin American Studies for the best thesis on Latin America. His has published numerous articles on institutional aspects of democratic transition and consolidation in Latin America and other world regions and is author of a book on presidentialism and democracy in Latin America (1996).

Contributors

DIRK AXTMANN holds a master's degree in Political Science from the University of Heidelberg and is Ph.D. candidate at the German Orient Institute in Hamburg. He is an expert on political development in Algeria where he conducted several field studies.

MATTHIAS BASEDAU is a Ph.D. candidate at the University of Heidelberg where he obtained a master's degree in Political Science in 1995 and is currently conducting research on the conditions of stability and instability of political regimes in Southern Africa.

GOSWIN BAUMHÖGGER is in charge of the Southern African region at the Institute of African Affairs in Hamburg (Germany) and has also considerable experience relating to the region of East Africa. He has written extensively on most of the countries of both regions, with the main emphasis on domestic and foreign policies and regional integration processes. Baumhögger holds a Ph.D. in Social Sciences and has been specializing in contemporary African history for a very long time. He is author and co-author of several books and editor of documentations and a bibliography.

PETRA BENDEL is managing director of the Institute for Regional Studies at the University of Erlangen-Nürnberg (Germany). She holds a master's degree (1992) and a Ph.D. (1996) in Political Science from the University of Heidelberg and has served as a research fellow at the same University as well as at the Institute for Iberoamerican Studies in Hamburg. She has published numerous articles on democratization processes, elections and party systems in Latin America and on problems of civilian society in emerging democracies. She has edited a book on Central America (1993) and is author of a book on Party Systems in Central America (1996).

STEFAN BRÜNE is a senior researcher at the German Overseas Institute, Hamburg, and Professor of Political Science and Social Geography at the University of Osnabrück (Germany). He also serves as a consultant for the Federal Ministry for Economic Cooperation and Development. Coeditor of a German yearbook and a review on Third World issues, he has also taught at the Universities of Addis Abeba, Leipzig and written on political and economic development in the Horn of Africa, EU-ACP relations, French

African politics and the evaluation of development cooperation. His current research focuses on information and communication technologies in developing countries.

ANA CATARINA CLEMENTE-KERSTEN studied Political Science, Economics and Public Law at the University of Heidelberg and gained her master's degree in 1994. Currently a Ph.D. candidate at the same university she is conducting research on the politics of decentralization in Portugal and also working as a freelance for a German radio station.

CURTIS F. DOEBBLER is an international lawyer based in Khartoum, Sudan. He holds a Ph.D. and is advisor to the government of Sudan on human rights and advised the National Constitutional Committee drafting the 1998 Constitution. He is also counsel to private Law Offices in Khartoum and a part-time lecturer at Khartoum University (Sudan).

ULF ENGEL teaches 'Politics in Africa' at the Institute of African Studies at Leipzig University (Germany). He is a freelancer with the Institute of African Affairs (Hamburg) and holds a Ph.D. in Political Science (University of Hamburg). He has written on Germany's Africa policy as well as political developments in Southern and Eastern Africa (particularly on South Africa and Zimbabwe). His field of research includes state and society in Africa, democratization and conflict prevention. He is author of *The Foreign Policy of Zimbabwe* (Hamburg 1994) and coeditor of several books on African politics.

WOLFGANG FENGLER holds a master's degree in Political Science and Statistics from the University of Augsburg (Germany) and has worked on numerous research and consulting projects on African politics and development issues for institutions such as World Bank, the German Ministry of Defence and the Centre d'Etudes d'Afrique Noire (CEAN) in Bordeaux (France). He was observer of the Tanzanian parliamentary and presidential elections in 1995 and is founder and director of Ebenhausen based consulting agency Africa Consulting. He has published a number of articles on elections and political development in Tanzania and is author of a book on political conflicts in Tanzania (1997).

HELGA FLEISCHHACKER is a research fellow and Ph.D. candidate at the Institute for Political Science of the University of Heidelberg. She holds degrees in Political Science (University of Munich, Germany) and Public Administration (Post-Graduate School of Administrative Sciences, Speyer). Her current research focuses on political parties in Africa.

FLORIAN GROTZ is a research fellow and Ph.D. candidate at the University of Heidelberg. His current research focuses on electoral systems and party system development in post communist Eastern Europe and on institutional aspects of democratic transition and consolidation. He has published articles on elections and electoral systems in Eastern Europe.

CHRISTOF HARTMANN studied Political Science, History and International Law and holds a master's degree (1994) and a Ph.D. (1998) from the University of Heidelberg. He has worked on regime change and democratization, development issues and conflict resolution in Sub-Saharan Africa. He is author of a book on the international dimension of political transitions in Benin, Côte d'Ivoire, Kenya and Uganda (1999).

DIRK HARTMANN is a graduate student of Political Science at the University of Heidelberg. He is working on the politics of ethnicity in Kenya and Uganda where he has conducted several field studies.

HANSPETER MATTES is a senior fellow at the German Orient Institute in Hamburg. He holds a Ph.D. from the University of Heidelberg and has published extensively on politics and development in the Middle East. He teaches at the University of Hamburg and is coeditor of a German yearbook on the Middle East.

ANDREAS MEHLER is research associate at the Institute of African Affairs (Hamburg), with regional responsibility for Cameroon, Central African Republic and Chad. He holds a Ph.D. in Political Science (University of Hamburg) and has written on violent conflicts, elections and democratization processes in Africa south of the Sahara. He has worked as a consultant (in collaboration with electoral commissions; civic education programs) and as an election observer. Mehler is author of a book on the democratic transition in Cameroon (1993) and coeditor of several volumes on African politics.

MICHAEL MEIER is currently representative of the Friedrich Ebert Foundation in Addis Abeba, Ethiopia. He held formerly the same position in Senegal before. He holds degrees in African Studies and Economics (Free University of Berlin) and in Development Policies (German Institute for Development Policy Berlin).

HEIKO MEINHARDT is a research associate at the Institute of International Relations in Hamburg (Germany) and holds a Ph.D. (1997) in Political Science of the University of Hamburg (Germany). He is a research fellow and lecturer at the Institute for International Affairs of the same University and also teaches regular courses on African countries for the German Foundation for International Development. Meinhardt has conducted numerous field studies in Southern Africa and published numerous articles on African politics as well as a book on political transition and democratization in Malawi (1997). Currently he is working on a book on external determinants of African democratization processes.

JUAN MONTABES is Professor of Political Science at the University of Granada (Spain). He has spent various academic and research stays at the Universities of Florence (Italy), Harvard (USA), Rabat (Moroco) and Tunisia. As editor, he has directed and participated in the publication of the books *Explosión demográfica, empleo y trabajadores emigrantes en el Mediterráneo Occidental—Demographic Explosion, Employment and Immigrant Workers throughout the Western Mediterranean* (1993) and *El Magreb tras la crisis del Golfo* (The Maghreb after the Gulf Crisis). From June 1992 to April 1994 he was member of the Spanish Delegation for the Euro-Arab University.

SHAHEEN MOZAFFAR is Associate Professor of Political Science at Bridgewater State College and Research Fellow of the African Studies Center at Boston University. He has written on the colonial state, ethnic politics and democratic transition in Africa, and is currently working on a comparative study of constitutional designs and electoral systems in Africa's emerging democracies.

MARÍA A. PAREJO FERNANDEZ is a research associate of the Department of Political Science at the University of Granada (Spain).

ANDREW REYNOLDS is assistant professor in the Department of Government and International Studies at the University of Notre Dame. He has written extensively on issues of democratization and constitutional design in Southern African and consulted on issues of electoral system design in South Africa, Indonesia, Liberia, Sierra Leone, Jordan and Fiji. His books include *Electoral Systems and Democratization in Southern Africa* (1998), *Elections and Conflict Management in Africa* (co-editor, 1998), *The International IDEA Handbook of Electoral System Design* (co-author, 1997) and *Election '94 South Africa: An Analysis of the Campaigns, Results and Future Prospects* (editor, 1994).

MATTHIAS RIES holds a master's degree in Political Science and History from the University of Heidelberg (1995). He is a Ph.D. candidate at the same University and a scholar of the Friedrich Ebert Foundation. His research focuses on the 'Oslo-Accord' and on the conditions of sustainability of the Israeli-Palestine negotiation process. He works for several NGO's in the general field of Middle East affairs.

MANUELA RÖMER is currently working as a radio-journalist for the European News-Network-Provider 'BLR/Radiodienst' in Munich. She holds degrees in Political Science, Sociology and Slavonic Studies (Ludwig-Maximilians-Universität München, Germany).

SIEGMAR SCHMIDT is currently Associate Professor for Political Science at Trier University. His main fields of research include political systems/democratic transitions in Africa, economic reform and structural adjustment as well as comparative foreign policies of Western states. He has just finished a longer comparative study dealing with German foreign policies promoting democracy and human rights in Africa and Eastern Europe. He is author of a book on the role of black trade unions in the political transition of South Africa.

TILO STOLZ has studied Political Science, History and Public Law at the University of Heidelberg (Germany). Since 1995 he has been a graduate student of Political Science at the University of Massachusetts at Amherst (US). He has worked as a Program Assistant for the Regional Bureau for Africa of the United Nations Development Program. His current research focuses on the democratization processes in Kenya, Malawi, Tanzania and Zambia.

DANIEL STROUX has studied Political Science at the University of Munich, Germany. Since 1992, he has focused research and field studies on transition processes in Africa with Congo-Zaire and the Great Lakes Region becoming his main region with respective publications. He has worked as a consultant in international cooperation, among other for the European Commission. More recently, he founded the Munich based Bureau for Institutional Reform and Democracy BIRD, which consults on Democracy Building and Conflict Prevention.

REGINA WEGEMUND holds a degree in Political Science and Oriental Studies from the University of Hamburg and is a freelance of the Institute of African Affairs (Hamburg). She has worked on political, economic and social development in Northern, Western and Central Africa and has published numerous articles on the political system of Mauritania and the Sahel states. She is author of book on political ethnicity in Mauritania and Senegal (Hamburg 1991).

Technical Notes

The data in this handbook are presented in the same systematic manner for all countries in order to provide electoral statistics in line with internationally established standards of documentation. The tables in the country chapters are organized in ten parts:

2.1 Dates of National Elections, Referendums and Coups d'Etat: In table 2.1 we present a survey of all (direct) election dates as well as institutional interruptions by coup d'état.

2.2 Electoral Body: In order to provide for a comparative overview over the evolution of the electoral body, data on population size, registered voters and votes cast are summarized in table 2.2. Whereas tallies on registered voters and votes cast are drawn from tables 2.5, 2.6, 2.7 and 2.9, the population data generally follows UN documentation. Other sources are named in a footnote. Where information was not available, this is indicated by a long hyphen (—).

2.3 Abbreviations: Abbreviations and full names of political parties and alliances emerging in tables 2.6, 2.7 and 2.9 are presented in alphabetical order. Where the full name of a political party or alliance could not be identified, this is indicated by a long hyphen (—).

2.4 Electoral Participation of Parties and Alliances: Electoral participation of political parties and alliances is presented in chronological order including the years and number of contested elections; in bicameral systems only the number of elections to the Lower House is indicated. Only those parties are included which appear in tables 2.6, 2.7 and 2.9. Where total numbers could not be provided, only those parties which gained representation in Parliament (table 2.8) could be included.

2.5; 2.6; 2.7; 2.9 Distribution of votes in National Referendums, Elections to Constitutional Assembly, Parliamentary and Presidential Elections: In these tables we aim to provide for the most exhaustive documentation of total numbers and percentages of electoral participation in every balloting since independence (or the last pre-independence elections). The percentages given in the tables refer to: votes cast as a percentage of registered voters; invalid and valid votes as a percentage of votes cast; party votes as a percentage of valid votes. The purpose of national referendums is indicated in a footnote whenever the relevant information could be obtained. In some cases, those political parties or candidates who secured only few votes in elections (e.g. less than 0.5%) were subsumed in a residual category (Others). Where exact data were not available, this is indicated by a long hyphen (—). Where there was no information applicable, because the political party did not take part in a particular election, this is indicated by a short hyphen (–). As far as exact data were available, the regional distribution of votes is presented in subtitles following the respective chapter. Those tables do not follow a rigid format in order to meet different exigencies like the number of regions or electoral districts.

2.8 Composition of Parliament: In general, table 2.8 presents the number of directly elected seats. In some cases we found it necessary to differentiate between directly elected seats and indirectly elected or appointed seats as well as between directly elected seats and the total of seats distributed. Where this is the case explanations are given in a footnote. Where there was no information applicable, because the political party was not represented in Parliament in that particular term, this is indicated by a short hyphen (–).

2.10 List of Power Holders: In table 2.10 we provide information on the succession in the executive branch of the political system. In principle, a survey of both Heads of State and Heads of Government are given, who are, however, in many cases identical. As a rule, Prime Ministers are only mentioned it they are effective Head of Governments (i.e. in semi-presidential and parliamentary systems).

ELECTIONS AND ELECTORAL SYSTEMS IN AFRICA

by Dieter Nohlen, Michael Krennerich and Bernhard Thibaut*

1. Historical Overview

Elections have been an integral part of African politics since political independence. Between 1950 and 1998, Africa was witness to 18 elections to constitutional assemblies, 186 presidential elections and 311 parliamentary elections. In addition, there were 115 referendums. It is, however, clear from the contributions in this handbook that elections in African countries take place with a wide range of frequencies and under very difficult political conditions. The competitive character and the political function of elections vary widely, depending on the country and the phase of political development.

1.1 Elections in the Pre-colonial and Colonial Era

The idea of voting was not completely foreign to pre-colonial Africa. In some traditional societies, leaders were chosen by 'election' in as much as a choice was made between several individuals through a process of consultation (see Hayward 1987). It should be remembered, however, that the range of choice and degree of participation in these selection processes was in general very limited. Competitively oriented systems with the direct participation of the complete adult population were exceptional. When these did occur, it was usually in the form of a decision at a local level which could be made at a face-to-face meeting. Such systems cannot simply be scaled up to nation states and elections with direct mass participation. Although they are often viewed as a basis for a democratic culture, they do not represent a pool of political experience which is relevant for a national electoral policy. Such policy first became important in the British and French colonies after the Second World

---

* Many thanks to Christof Hartmann and Florian Grotz for their comments on earlier versions and valuable research assistance.

War. The colonial authorities not only imported the concept of national elections with the associated electoral legislation and organization, they also exerted direct or indirect influence on the formation of political parties.

After Second World War, the French and British colonies went through a type of political development which—although manifest in very different ways—led them through numerous steps to internal autonomy and finally to independence. Although elections had taken place previously in some colonial areas, it was only through this post-war development that the electoral processes and the right to vote became widely distributed (see Sternberger/Vogel/Nohlen/Landfried 1978). The colonial powers gave way to the participatory demands of the local elites, which then in turn used the elections to mobilize support against colonial rule. As far as the colonial powers were concerned, the elections after the Second World War served to 'take the wind out of the sails' of African nationalists and those critical of colonial policy. In addition to this, the elections were—as in the case of the French colonies—part of a policy of assimilation, under the auspices of which the French overseas territories even gained representation in the Republic's Parliament for a short period. Towards the end of the colonial era, elections became a constitutional tool used to lead colonies into independence, and/or to pre-structure the post-colonial development of the new African states in the interest of the old colonial powers. It would be erroneous to interpret national elections after the event as the expression of 'colonial generosity' by benevolent colonial rulers. They were much more a result of political struggle. The demand for elections and an extension of the right to vote was closely tied to demands for participation, self-determination and the independence of the African states, and proved to be one of the most effective weapons available to anti-colonial movements in and outside Africa. It was only in the context of growing opposition to colonial rule at home and abroad that the French and British governments introduced the general right to vote in the 1950s and 1960s. With a few exceptions (e.g. Uganda), the universal suffrage came into use in each country's last parliamentary election before independence.

Although each African state had a different electoral and political history behind it at the moment of independence, they all had one thing in common: Universal, equal, direct and secret elections had only been introduced immediately before independence, if at all. There is no question of any democratic voting tradition already being rooted in the population or in the new political elite. The colonial powers had been authoritarian and repressive for long periods. In addition, the French colonial administrators in particular exerted wide-ranging and manipulative influence on the electoral process. 'In this respect the French colonial electoral experiences created a legacy of abuse that lived on after independence' (Hayward 1987: 8). The Belgian and later the Portuguese colonies also achieved independence without the slightest experience of the art and craft of electoral politics.

1.2 Elections in the Independence Era

As the majority of the African states attained independence at the end of the 1950s and in the 1960s, most of them were equipped with liberal-democratic constitutions which, to a greater or lesser extent, reflected the essentials of the constitutional systems used by the former colonial powers. The imported constitutional regulations hardly ever worked as they had in their countries of origin, however. The constitutions were either soon withdrawn, fundamentally modified by the new rulers or simply ignored. This development was strongly reflected in the electoral arena.

In most states, the first governments were results of the last multi-party elections held before independence. In most cases, however, the bases for competitive electoral politics were undermined *de facto* or removed *de iure* at the start of the post-colonial era. The new rulers no longer saw elections as powerful tools of political emancipation to be used against the colonial powers, or as a resource 'which could be used by rival factions among the indigenous elites—especially the younger activists who wished to replace their older, and often more conservative, competitors' (Collier 1982: 33). Instead, elections were to be used to secure the power of the new elites which had (even before independence, in some cases) achieved a position of hegemony, or at least to assert a hegemonial claim. Competition was not in the interest of the new elites, and was visibly understood as a threat to political stability, development and national unity[1]. With the exception of Botswana, Gambia and Mauritius, almost all African states introduced a one-party state in the short or medium term. Some states did not even hold further multi-party elections before introducing a one-party system. Others—like Benin, Burundi, Congo, Kenya, Madagascar, Senegal, Sierra Leone, Somalia,

---

[1] In this sense, the new governments demonstrated continuity with their colonial forebears who had, in the final years of their rule, only supported the validity of democratic principles as long as these were in their interest. The principle of this limited government was not only a contradiction to African tradition, but also stood in opposition to the philosophy and practical reality of colonial government.

Swaziland, and Zambia—did so, but the elections were usually far below the competitive standards seen today.

1.3 Elections in the One-Party State

The introduction of the single-party system grew out of the extension of the governing party's hegemony, the marginalization and obstruction of opposition parties, the co-optation of opposition leaders and/or the constitutional abolition of multi-partyism and the banning of opposition parties. Only in Tanzania was the governing regime able to achieve 'a peaceful transition to a one-party system through the ballot box'. Kenneth Kaunda, in Zambia, attempted to follow the Tanzanian example—without success. It was not possible to completely politically neutralize the opposition in the elections held under the first Zambian Republic (1964–1972), and the governing regime finally resorted to a constitutional introduction of the one-party system, the banning of opposition parties and co-optation offers to opposition politicians. With a few exceptions (e.g. Tanzania and Zambia), the transition to one-party regimes was not even preceded by any serious intra-party discussion process. Often, the change was justified using the arguments for African 'one party democracy' which had been developed and given substance by national leaders like Julius K. Nyerere (Tanzania), Kwame Nkrumah (Ghana) or Sekou Touré (Guinea). These argued that the monopoly of power had been historically legitimized by the struggle for independence and that the one-party system was appropriate to the African political–cultural tradition as well as being necessary for national unity, political stability and in order to reach socioeconomic development targets.

In political practice, the one-party system met with only limited success in its efforts towards national integration. Against the background of politicized ethnicity, it did contribute somewhat to the preservation of the nation. In fact, however, the call for 'national unity' served mostly to secure the hegemony of the ruling elite which distanced itself visibly from the population. The identification of the ruling party with the complete nation was always part of the political program, but was never reality. Most of all, the one-party system was never able to drive socioeconomic development or build up an effective state structure. Self-interest, nepotism and corruption soon left their marks on the African state.

Despite the promises of internal democracy, all one-party states were governed with increasing and irreversible authoritarianism (Ansprenger 1997). This often involved the distillation of political power into personal power, transforming one-party rule into one-man rule. This tendency was strengthened institutionally by the creation of presidential constitutions and the extension of presidential competence soon after independence (Thibaut 1998). Many states held direct presidential elections under one-party systems, but these were without exception non-competitive. One candidate was invariably offered, usually the leader of both the governing party and the state. In some countries—e.g. Algeria, Djibouti, Egypt, Sudan, Tanzania and Zambia—voters were able to make not only Yes votes but also No votes against the single candidate. Otherwise, the non-competitive elections were not formally capable of removing a President.

Many political leaders were able to govern throughout the entire one-party phase, up to the (re-)introduction of multi-party systems in the 1990s: e.g. Kenneth Kaunda in Zambia (1964–1991), Hastings K. Banda in Malawi (1964–1994), Aristides M. Pereira in Cape Verde (1975–1991) and Manuel Pinto da Costa in São Tomé and Príncipe (1975–1991). Others even remained in power after a transition to multi-party democracy, such as Felix Houphouët-Boigny in Côte d'Ivoire (1960–1993), Hassan Gouled Aptidon in Dijbouti (since 1977) and France A. René in the Seychelles (since 1977). If a change in leadership did occur under a one-party system, it took place through mechanisms other than elections. In a few cases, the President resigned voluntarily, such as Léopold S. Senghor in Senegal (1981), Ahmadou Ahidjo in Cameroon (1982) and Julius K. Nyerere in Tanzania (1985). More often, the President died through accident or natural causes, e.g. Omar Bongo in Gabon (1967), Jomo Kenyatta in Kenya (1978), Hourari Boumedienne in Algeria (1978), Agostinho Neto in Angola (1979), Sekou Touré in Guinea (1984) and Samora Machel in Mozambique (1986). In both these situations, the presidency was usually assumed by a hand-picked successor who was sometimes confirmed by intra-party vote. One exception is Guinea, where the military assumed power after Touré's death. Most often, a change in government occurred via military coup d'état, where the one-party system was on occasion replaced by a military regime. The coup against Nkrumah in Ghana (1966) attracted particular attention, as he had seemed to enjoy wide popular support until then. Military coups led to the fall of one-party governments in Burundi, Chad, Congo (Brazzaville), Guinea-Bissau, Liberia, Madagascar, Mali, Mauritania, Niger, Rwanda, Togo and Uganda, among others.

As in the presidential elections, the initial parliamentary elections under one-party rule allowed no form of competition (with the exception of Tanzania). Single-member constituencies offered only the official candidate for election, while multi-member constituencies had their official party list. Such 'classical' non-competitive parliamentary elections took place—at least for some period—under one-party systems, for example, in Algeria, Benin, Burundi, Cameroon, Cape Verde, CAR, Chad, Comoros, Congo (Brazzaville), Côte d'Ivoire, Djibouti, Equatorial Guinea, Gabon, Guinea, Madagascar, Malawi, Mali, Mauritania, Niger, Rwanda, Senegal, Somalia, Togo and Zaire.

Semi-competitive parliamentary elections, in which the voter could choose between several candidates approved by the state party, were rare at first. The pioneer of this form in Africa was Tanzania. In the Tanzanian parliamentary elections of 1965, two ruling-party candidates were allowed to compete for the voters' mandate in each single-member district. Semi-competitive single-party elections were later introduced in a modified form in Kenya (1969) and Zambia (1973). As Africa felt a small 'draught of change' in the late 1970s and Senegal, Ghana, Nigeria, Burkina Faso and Uganda allowed multi-party elections, some authoritarian regimes introduced (temporarily) one or another variant of the semi-competitive one-party election (multiple candidates or competitive lists from the ruling party; semi-open primaries etc.). Among these nations were Sudan (1974), Algeria (1977), Zaire (1977 and again in 1987), Malawi (1978), Mali (1979), Seychelles (1979), Côte d'Ivoire (1980), Sierra Leone (1982), Togo (1985), Ethiopia (1987), CAR (1987), Comoros (1987) and Cameroon (1988)[2].

Even in cases of semi-competitive single-party elections, the voter had little or no influence on the question of who would rule or how. The one-party system gave the voter no say in the question of the national leadership or overall policy directions. The elections were far more intended to secure the power of the ruling elite. In this sense, they fulfilled various functions which were expressed more or less strongly according to the country and phase of political development. Elections served to provide national and international legitimacy for the one-party system. They gave the population the opportunity to demonstrate ceremonially their loyalty to the government. In addition, the elections made it easier for the authoritarian rulers to reward their own clientele through

---

[2] The years shown here refer to the first semi-competitive single-party elections for Parliament. In Uganda, Idi Amin's coup d'état took place before semi-competitive elements could be introduced in the parliamentary elections planned for 1971.

the distribution of usually lower-level political positions, to balance the interests of competitive client networks and, should the situation arise, to co-opt political opponents and critics. Elections also gave the national leadership a mechanism to recruit new members of the elite with complete control over the selection of the candidates and to clear out dead wood from the governing group.

Over and above this, the elections served to inform the electorate of the government's development targets and to mobilize the nation's support in order to achieve them. Dissatisfaction with the government's performance, on the other hand, could be channeled into the elections without threatening the stability of the regime. Semi-competitive single-party elections made it easy for the national leadership to lay the responsibility for development deficits at the door of particular party factions or politicians and to draw attention away from genuine areas of conflict (like the growing social divide between rich and poor farmers in Kenya, for example). From the electorate's point of view, elections made possible the removal of unpopular politicians—if not Heads of State and Government, than at least parliamentarians and occasionally ministers. The electoral turnover of parliamentarians was sometimes quite high in some countries (e.g. Kenya, Tanzania, Zambia, Sierra Leone). The popularity of representatives depended greatly on their ability to secure as many government resources for their home region as possible, and on their readiness to defend their clientele against the predications of the central administration (see Nuscheler/ Ziemer 1980). In the best cases—in Kenya, for example (see Barkan/ Okumu 1978)—the elections did actually offer some meaningful avenues for linking the bulk of the population with the political process.

Semi-competitive single-party elections became a much-discussed method of guaranteeing a minimum of competition and accountability in systems where an opposition party was not part of the picture. Some thought that they represented a genuine African variant of democratic elections—or, in the words of Chazan (1979) an 'African-derived formula for constructive popular representation'. Others saw this type of election as the start of an incremental process leading to true competitive elections (Sklar 1983). Neither assumption stood the test of time. In most cases, the restrictive limits placed on intra-party dissent and 'participation from below' soon became obvious, and the authoritarian, manipulative character of the elections was revealed. Semi-competitive single-party elections did not prove to be the start of an incremental process which would lead to a democratization of the political system. Usually, the political opening was short-lived. The semi-competitive single-party elections were as a rule not the forerunners of a political democratization, but rather an attempt to hinder this. Indeed, the majority of states which held elections of this type are still not democratically governed (even when a multi-party system is now formally in place).

1.4 Surviving Multi-Party Elections

In the light of the above, it is hardly remarkable that in those states which formally retained multi-party systems after independence, cases arose where either election results which threatened the hegemony of the ruling party were nullified (Lesotho 1970) or a change of government was prevented by a military coup (Sierra Leone 1967). On the other hand, it is far more remarkable that some states remained true to the principle of multi-party elections (Botswana, Mauritius, Gambia up to 1994) and that some countries temporarily returned to multi-party systems after military coups or periods of one-party rule: Ghana (1969, 1979), Nigeria (1979, 1983), Upper Volta (1970, 1978), Senegal (1978), Uganda (1980), Central African Republic (1981) and Sudan (1986).

Many opinions have been expressed concerning this somewhat puzzling state of affairs. Some commentators see these cases as proof of Africa's not extinguished desire for plural democracy. Others see them as exceptions which prove the rule that it is difficult to establish competitive multi-party systems in Africa. This argument might be strengthened by the observation that many multi-party elections had a very restricted competitive character. This was very clear in the two- and three-party systems in Nigeria and Senegal, which were obviously imposed 'from above'. In addition, until the 1990s only Botswana, Gambia, Mauritius and later Senegal held multi-party elections over longer periods. Otherwise, plural elections led at best to the creation of new civil governments which, as in the independence era, were not followed by subsequent multi-party elections. Military coups ensured that these did not take place. With this in mind, the question of the re-introduction and abolition of multi-party elections in states like Ghana, Nigeria, Sudan, Uganda, Upper Volta and the CAR is best discussed with reference to the political role of the military.

Those leading military coups in Africa often assumed power with the promise that they would be taking the reins of power only provisionally—to guide the country through a political or economic crisis—and would be returning to their barracks as soon as they had done their 'duty to the nation'. Most of these promises were not kept. They took lasting power, and attempted with greater or lesser success to institutionalize military regimes. In the face of strong criticism of their legitimacy, a handful of military regimes were nonetheless willing to allow elected civilian governments to run the official business of the country. In these cases, however, it was clear that the civilian governments were 'on test'. All the multi-party experiments introduced by military governments in the 1970s and 1980s were quickly cancelled, either because of continuous political or economical crises, or because of the power games of individual military leaders. The deep mistrust of competitive electoral politics and the readiness to intervene displayed by the military could not be dissipated through the short-term re-introduction of multi-party elections—indeed, this often strengthened such tendencies.

Even in research, multi-party elections were generally viewed with skepticism until the 1990s. The opinion was often expressed that questions of political power as well as programmatic and ideological policy orientation were not really determined by elections, even under the conditions of an officially sanctioned contest for public office (see Cohen 1983, Chazan 1992). For this reason, no noteworthy increase in the amount of scientific research into voting took place in Africa despite the temporary return to multi-party elections. '(C)onditions for the introduction and regulation of competitive politics in Africa raised little interest' (Cowen/ Laakso 1997: 731). Accountability and political legitimacy were, as before, seen more in the form of informal representation and the ability of civil society to curb the hegemony of the state[3]. This situation did not change until the democracy wave of the 1990s prompted a veritable flood of elections and electoral studies of wide-ranging quality.

1.5 Multi-Party Elections in the 1990s

Although post-colonial development was shaped for long periods by autocratic, personality-led one-party systems and military regimes, 1989 saw the beginning of a comprehensive phase of democratic reforms. Multi-party systems were formally introduced in the majority of African states and multi-party elections took place with notable regularity. The fact that several parties were (once again) represented at the elections

---

[3] Thus, Chazan (1982) and Fatton (1987) saw the revaluation of *formal* participation through the reintroduction of multiparty elections (in Ghana and Senegal) as yet another attempt by the ruling classes to regain control over the civil population, which was manifesting decreased submissiveness through *informal* participation.

did not, however, necessarily mean that the elections were free and fair—and thus actually competitive[4]. The question as to whether the elections were 'free and fair—or at least acceptable' (Elklit/ Svenson 1996) was frequently the subject of heated debate. It must be remembered here that the technical and logistical problems of the multi-party elections in the 1990s were tremendous. In addition, the 'political playing field' generally had not yet been leveled. The rules for the electoral process were usually a subject for negotiation between the incumbent rulers and their political opposition, often under the influence or pressure of international players.

In view of the organizational and political shortcomings which still characterized most African elections, it was necessary to examine each election individually in order to ascertain whether any irregularities were the result of systematic action and whether the will of the voter had been significantly distorted. The results of many elections were disputed. Against this background, the international electoral observation which had begun with the large-scale employment of electoral observers and monitors in the founding elections in Namibia (1989) became very important. The United Nations' role in Namibia was not only that of observer, but of supervisor, and the organization later took on a similar function in Angola (1992), Eritrea (referendum 1993), Mozambique and South Africa (both 1994). Alongside the UN, a whole series of other international organizations, national governments and non-governmental organizations sent electoral observation teams into Africa (see Engel/ Hofmeier/ Kohnert/ Mehler 1996). On occasion, they also provided electoral assistance. In addition to these international groups, national teams of observers were also active. In some cases (e.g. Zambia 1996), these teams delivered a damning verdict on the election.

The assessment of elections was often hotly debated. Even the electoral observers could not always agree on their findings, to say nothing of the politicians involved. Declaring an election to be 'free and fair' was in itself a political act, not least because it had political consequences—for example with reference to the reactions of international

[4] In the social sciences the concept of competitiveness of elections has different bearing. In a narrow sense it refers to the range of electoral competition between candidates and parties and is only one of various criteria (regularity, inclusiveness, competitiveness, efficacy) of democratic elections. Following a wider understanding the concept of competitiveness reveals the democratic character of an election and is used as an equivalent term for 'free and fair', 'classical' or just 'democratic elections'. In this sense competitive elections allow the voters to choose the political power holders under the conditions of 'voter's freedom' and 'fair-multi-party-competition'. For a more concrete definition of the broad term used here, see Krennerich (1996*b*, 2000).

donors. If we leave aside those states which have not yet held elections in the 1990s (Democratic Republic of Congo, Eritrea, Rwanda, Somalia), the materials available (see the reference list for the appropriate country) suggest the following preliminary groupings[5]:

1) States which have held competitive elections for some time. These include Mauritius (since 1967), Botswana (since 1969) and, with reservations, Senegal (since 1978). Gambia must be excluded from this group following the military coup of 1994.

2) States which have held exclusively competitive elections since their democratic opening in the 1990s. These include Namibia (1989, 1994), Cape Verde (1991, 1996), São Tomé and Príncipe (1991, 1996), Benin (1991, 1996), Seychelles (1993, 1998), as well as, with reservations, Madagascar (1992, 1996), Mali (1992, 1997) and Lesotho (1993, 1998). All these states have already completed more than one electoral period since (re-)democratization. In the Republic of South Africa, Malawi and Mozambique (all 1994) and, with reservations, Liberia (1997), only competitive 'founding elections'[6] have taken place to date. The 'second elections' (Bratton 1998) are still approaching.

3) States which held competitive founding elections as part of the democratization wave in the 1990s, but which have not experienced competitive second elections. This group includes Angola (founding elections 1992), Congo (Brazzaville) (1992), Burundi (1993), the CAR (1993), Guinea-Bissau (1994) and Sierra Leone (1996). In these countries, the process of democratization was interrupted before the end of the first electoral period. Two countries represent special cases: Zambia (1991, 1996) held second elections which cannot be considered fair and free. In Niger a competitive presidential election (1993) and two

---

[5] Except in the case of parliamentarian systems, the election years (in brackets) refer to presidential elections only.

[6] The concept of *founding elections* has been borrowed from Latin American studies. It describes a situation where '*for the first time after an authoritarian regime, elected positions of national significance are disputed under reasonably competitive conditions*' (O'Donnell/ Schmitter 1986: 57). With reference to Africa, the concept has been applied in various ways. There is no consensus as to whether all inaugural multi-party elections should be considered founding elections, or only those which are judged free and fair. There is also disagreement as to whether the concept should be applied to all national elections, or only those which directly or indirectly select the chief political executive. In the latter case, presidential elections are primarily meant, and parliamentary elections only come into question in cases where the Head of Government is not directly elected (Ethiopia, Lesotho, South Africa and initially Namibia). For both interpretations, compare Mehler (1994) with Bratton (1997, 1998) or Bratton/van de Walle (1997).

competitive parliamentary elections (1993, 1995) were followed by a military coup and subsequent semi-competitive presidential and parliamentary elections under non-democratic conditions (1996).

4) States whose first multi-party elections after democratization were not up to the usual standards assumed for competitive elections, but whose second elections were considered free and fair. Members of this group are Ghana and the Comoros. Although the 1992 presidential election in Ghana was disputed and the parliamentary elections of 1993 were the subject of a boycott, the Ghanaian elections of 1996 can certainly be termed competitive. A tendency of improving electoral standards can also be stated with regard to the second presidential elections in the Comoros.

5) States which in the 1990s have held only semi-competitive multiparty elections—in other words, elections which have not reached a democratic standard: Algeria, Burkina Faso, Cameroon, Chad, Côte d'Ivoire, Djibouti, Equatorial Guinea, Ethiopia, Gabon, Guinea, Kenya, Mauritania, Nigeria, Tanzania, Togo and Tunisia. Morocco (since 1962), Egypt (since 1976) and Zimbabwe (since 1980) are also basically members of this group.

6) States whose elections—at least officially—were not the scene of inter-party competition. This heterogeneous category includes the no-party elections in Uganda (most recently in 1996), Swaziland (1993, 1998) and Sudan (1996).

Before 1989, changes of government through elections were a rare exceptions in Africa. Electoral victory for the ruling party was a forgone conclusion, *de facto* or *de iure*. In fact, the only change of government to occur via electoral process was that in Mauritius in 1982. Interestingly, most of the multi-party elections held in the 1990s were also won by incumbent parties or presidential candidates. This can partly be attributed to the fact that, in most countries in Africa, the electoral playing field is not yet technically or politically leveled enough for genuinely free and fair elections. Semi-competitive multi-party elections are rather difficult for the opposition to win. The structure of the party system in each country exerts a further influence: In many African countries there are political parties which, because of their historical, ethnic or regional base, enjoy a built-in majority. The notorious weakness of the (often divided) opposition is another factor.

This makes it even more significant that so many of the founding elections held since 1989 have led to a change of regime: in Cape Verde, São Tomé and Príncipe, Benin, Zambia, Mali, Congo (Brazzaville), Madagascar, Niger, Lesotho, Burundi, the CAR, the Republic of South Africa and Sierra Leone[7]. Namibia (1989) is a special case as the country actually became independent only in 1990. Although only a few second elections led to an opposition victory (Benin, Madagascar), it can be stated that competitive elections have established themselves in the 1990s as an alternative to undemocratic methods of obtaining and holding political power.

The establishment of competitive elections in some African states has obviously not led to a complete restructuring of the forms of winning and maintaining power on that continent. Firstly, the risk of coup d'état is still a real one (although it has become more difficult in the current international environment to putsch one's way to enduring power in Africa)[8]. Secondly, most of the elections cannot be said to have attained democratic standards. Thirdly, even where competitive elections have taken place, the elected rulers are not shy to use authoritarian methods to remain in power. Frederick Chiluba's government in Zambia is a much discussed example. From a sociological point of view, and with a few prominent exceptions (e.g. South Africa), competitive elections in Africa have only just begun to dissolve the social restrictions controlling access to power. Even under competitive conditions, political power remains mostly in the grasp of a relatively small group of people, who not infrequently enjoy personal, familial, economic, social and/or ethnic connections. It must therefore be assumed that in some countries—even under a democratic system—the political elites and counter-elites will remain small and exclusive bodies, relatively well screened against ingress from 'below'.

Nonetheless, the fact that elections in Africa can lead to a change in government at all remains one of the most significant innovations since the start of the 1990s. Moreover, there is a growing sense among political elites and masses alike that competitive elections are the only legitimate way to choose national leaders. Notably, with the exception of

---

7 In some cases, transitional governments had already partly or completely disempowered authoritarian Presidents. Exceptions include Zambia, Burundi, Lesotho, the CAR and Malawi.

8 Successful coups in Nigeria (1993), Burundi (1993), Gambia (1994) and Niger (1996) must be seen in the context of unsuccessful attempts in Lesotho (1994), São Tomé and Príncipe (1995), the Central African Republic (1995), in Comoros (1996), and Sierra Leone (1997/8). Furthermore, the coup-regimes in Gambia and Niger felt themselves forced to hold elections, although these cannot be considered free and fair. Elections are scheduled for 1999 in Nigeria.

Angola (1992), Burundi (1993), Mali (1997) and recently Lesotho (1998), the results of most competitive multi-party elections have been accepted by the losers. Semi-competitive multi-party elections, in contrast, have often been disputed by the loser. Not infrequently, some opposition parties have refused to contest elections of this type, complaining that the electoral conditions were not free or fair enough[9]. Other parties decided to take part rather than sacrifice all their political influence, taking the risk of becoming part of a democratic facade hung in front of a basically authoritarian regime by the incumbents. In return, they hoped to be able to extend the political opening process and push for a genuine democratization.

The system of competitive elections tends to have a positive effect not only on the legitimacy of the government, but also on the opposition—although the deeply rooted (and for a long period politically reinforced) culture of intolerance towards the opposition in Africa is by no means a thing of the past. For decades, under the one-party system, the opposition was reviled as the essence of division, feuding and enmity. Nonetheless, it is now the case that political opposition parties compete for political power and are usually represented in Parliament. This is a major qualitative innovation, even if electoral competition in Africa's political and cultural context has more to do with personalities than programs. And although competitive elections may politicize the existing (often officially taboo) ethnic identities and/or sharpen political conflict (extreme examples: Burundi and Angola), they can also teach much about dealing with political opponents in a democratic way. This is especially true when elections are combined with voter education campaigns and the main political players keep to basic democratic rules.

It is difficult to measure empirically the level of legitimacy which the electorate attribute to elections. The voter turnout—at least under democratic conditions—can be used as the first reference point, but care should be taken in the interpretation. Firstly, the voter turnout can be influenced by a series of technical and logistical factors. Additionally, participation in or abstention from an election do not necessarily indicate support for or disapproval of elections and political parties as such. The

---

[9] The following elections have been fully or partly boycotted by the opposition: Parliamentary elections in Cameroon (1992), Djibouti (1992), Equatorial Guinea (1992), Comoros (1993, second round, 1996), Ghana (1992), Mauritania (1992), Congo (Brazzaville) (1993, second round), Ethiopia (1995), Zimbabwe (1995), Niger (1996), Zambia (1996) and Mali (1997); presidential elections in Burkina Faso (1991, 1998), Djibouti (1993), Togo (1993), Côte d'Ivoire (1995), Equatorial Guinea (1996), Zimbabwe (1996), Zambia (1996), Mauritania (1997), Mali (1997) and Cameroon (1997).

individual motives of voters and non-voters are numerous and complex. It is nonetheless conspicuous that many competitive elections have enjoyed turnouts of more than 75%, or even in cases 85% or 95% (of registered voters). Examples include Mauritius, Botswana, Namibia, Seychelles, South Africa, Malawi, Guinea-Bissau and Mozambique, Liberia as well as Angola (1992) and Burundi (1993). In other states, however, a comparatively small portion of the electorate cast their votes in competitive elections. This was especially the case in the Sahel states of Mali and Niger (with regard to the competitive elections 1993/95), in Senegal, where the turnout dropped dramatically over the course of the 1990s; in São Tomé and Príncipe and Benin, where the turnout only started to rise again at the latest elections. In Zambia, the turnout for the much-discussed founding elections in 1991 was even lower than that at the semi-competitive second elections five years later. The turnout at semi-competitive multi-party elections is much more difficult to interpret than at competitive elections, because the voter's freedom and range of choice is restricted and the official data are not always reliable. However, low voter turnout is often linked to electoral boycott by opposition parties. Obviously, there also differences within the group of semi-competitive multi-party elections. Low turnouts, for instance, in Burkina Faso, Chad, Djibouti, Mauritania (up to 1997), Togo and Zimbabwe contrast with high official figures in, for example, Equatorial Guinea, Ethiopia, Gabon, Tanzania and Tunisia.

In closing, it is important to note that even in the context of the wave of liberalization and democratization since 1989 and the introduction of multi-party elections almost throughout the continent, there is still a great diversity of electoral experience in Africa. The democratic quality and political meaning of multi-party elections vary, sometimes considerably. This diversity is now even visible in the political and institutional framework of voting, including the electoral systems themselves.

2. Electoral systems in independent Africa

2.1 Parliamentary Electoral Systems

It is well known that in the process of decolonization in Africa during the 1950s and 1960s the basic institutional features of the new independent countries' polities were largely conditioned, if not determined, by their colonial background. The general institutional framework laid down in the independence constitutions often closely resembled that of the respective mother countries. Important political institutions had been implemented already in the areas where a gradual expansion of internal self-determination had taken place in the pre-independence era. This was especially true for the parliamentary electoral systems. In the British as well as in the French part of Africa territorial legislatures and direct elections under conditions of universal suffrage had been introduced by the colonial powers.

In all countries arising from the British Empire (with the exception of the Seychelles, where independence was achieved only in 1976) the plurality system in single-member districts was a key element of the polity after independence. A modification of the British system was introduced in some countries insofar as it provided for a certain number of nominated Members of Parliament in addition to the elected members. Besides, in some countries parliamentary elections on the basis of individual candidacies were held not in single-member districts but in multi-member districts[10], e.g. in Swaziland (from 1967 to 1972) and Mauritius (continuously since independence)[11]. Note, however, that in Mauritius the plurality system was introduced against the advice of the British administration whose representatives would have preferred a PR system because of the ethnic structure of the country.

At the time when universal suffrage and territorial legislative elections were introduced in the French colonies in Africa by the *Loi Cadre* in 1956 the National Assembly elections of the Fourth Republic were held under an absolute majority system in multi-member districts with closed and blocked party lists; only in the Paris region was a PR system applied[12]. In the African colonies generally a plurality system in multi-member districts with closed and blocked party lists was introduced. In a considerable number of cases the last territorial legislature elected before the final achievement of independence became the first regular national Parliament of the new country and the first post-independence elections were already held under the conditions of a *de facto* single-party regime. The strong majoritarian effects of the electoral system contributed to this tendency in some countries where the parties or alliances leading the independence process turned out as dominant or even hegemonic

[10] It should be kept in mind, however, that in the United Kingdom the plurality system has been applied uniformly in single-member districts in the whole country only since 1950 (Nohlen 1978: 160).

[11] In Mauritius a few additional seats are allocated to 'best losers' (see country chapter).

[12] It is well known that France belongs to the relatively rare category of countries where the electoral system has been changed very often in the course of regime changes or even within one and the same constitutional order (Nohlen 1990: 165ff.).

political forces in multi-party legislative elections (e.g. Djibouti, Gabon, Madagascar).

When the three African countries with a Belgian colonial background became independent in 1960 and 1962, two (Burundi and Rwanda) introduced a PR system with preferential voting in multi-member districts similar to, though not identical with, the one used in Belgium, whereas in the Republic of Congo a plurality system with open lists was applied. In these countries the legislative elections held shortly before independence were the first elections under universal suffrage and the respective institutional rules had been designed in the context of independence negotiations.

In the Portuguese colonies which gained independence after the Portuguese revolution of April 1974 elections were held neither in the pre-independence era nor in the early phases of post-colonial development. With the exception of Guinea-Bissau (parliamentary elections in 1976 and in 1984) direct national elections did not take place before the 1990s. In all countries parliamentary elections have been held exclusively under PR in constituencies of diverse size, as in Portugal. In Angola and Mozambique constituencies are predominantly large while in the island states (Cape Verde, São Tomé and Príncipe, Guinea-Bissau) most constituencies are of small size.

Institutional development in the field of electoral systems in the post-independence era in large parts of Africa is marked much more by continuity than by change. This is especially true for the countries with a British colonial background. In the vast majority of these countries the plurality system in single member constituencies has survived all political transformations and was not only used in multi-party elections but also—with different political functions—in the periods of single-party rule where semi-competitive elections with elements of intra-party competition easily could be arranged on the basis of this system.

In the context of the democratization of political systems since the early 1990s the plurality system has been maintained nearly everywhere in anglophone Africa. Only Namibia, South Africa, Sierra Leone and Liberia introduced proportional representation: In all cases a highly pure PR under which parliamentary seats are allocated at national level. These four countries have, however, a historical and institutional background quite dissimilar to the rest of anglophone Africa. Only Sierra Leone became independent in the larger context of decolonization in Africa after the second world war. Liberia never was a colony, South Africa left its colonial status already in 1910 whereas Namibia became independent only in 1990.

In Liberia as well as in Sierra Leone, the introduction of pure PR was strongly related to problems of electoral administration after the end of a civil war. Voter registration was much easier to realize under the conditions of PR at the national level than at the constituency level because of the immense migration produced by the civil wars. Besides, the complexities (and related conflicts) of constituency design could be avoided. In both countries it seems not unlikely that the plurality system will be reintroduced when these special conditions of the founding elections do not hold any longer. In South Africa and Namibia genuine political motivations were more important for the introduction of pure PR, although technical considerations played a role too. In both countries the design of the electoral system was part of the negotiations in the process of transition from an apartheid regime to liberal democratic politics. In the end, all political forces which participated in these negotiations felt the necessity for a highly representative Constitutional Assembly in order to promote national integration. Therefore, relatively early a broad consensus was achieved between the main political players that the electoral system should produce a high degree of proportionality and encourage inclusiveness and integration by representing all social and political groups in Parliament[13]. However, especially in the Republic of South Africa the 'lack of constituency representation' which accompanies PR systems with closed regional or national lists is widely regarded as a drawback of the electoral system. In recent reform debates the introduction of an adapted or modified version of the German mixed member proportional system, which combines single-member constituencies with the principle of proportional representation is often regarded as a possible solution (Krennerich/ de Ville 1997).

In francophone Africa institutional development in the field of electoral systems has been more diverse than in the anglophone parts of the continent. However, in most cases basic decisions that were made in the context of the independence process—that is, shortly before or shortly after the achievement of national sovereignty—were not altered drastically. The then established basic type of electoral system (which was a majority system in most countries) has remained untouched, institutional reforms have signified more or less a move from one subtype to another. With regard to these countries, several paths of institutional development can be distinguished.

---

[13] In South Africa the objective of proportional representation has even been given constitutional status. The constitution stipulates that the electoral system for the National Assembly 'results, in general, in proportional representation'.

(1) Continuity: Two countries (Djibouti and Tunisia) have maintained the plurality system in multi-member districts with closed and blocked party lists in the period of single-party rule as well as under multi-party elections since the early 1990s. In both countries this institutional continuity is a main reason for the lack of parliamentary representation of opposition parties since the return to multi-party politics and (apart from supposed manipulations of the electoral process) the most important barrier against full democratization of the political system. With regard to Tunisia this observation holds notwithstanding the fact that since 1993 19 seats in the 163-member Parliament are allocated to 'best losers'.

(2) Toward plurality or absolute majority in single-member and/or small multi-member constituencies: In the majority of the francophone countries (Cameroon, Central African Republic, Chad, Congo Brazzaville, Côte d'Ivoire, Gabon, Mali, Mauritania, Morocco, Togo) non-competitive and partly semi-competitive elections under the one-party regimes established soon after the achievement of independence took place under the formal rules of the plurality system in single-member districts and in some cases also in small multi-member districts. When multi-party elections were reintroduced this electoral system remained unchanged in Morocco and Côte d'Ivoire. In Cameroon a modified type of the absolute majority formula with closed and blocked party lists is now applied in the multi-member constituencies. In the other countries mentioned above recent multi-party elections have been held under the absolute majority system in single-member districts and/or small multi-member districts with party lists.

(3) Toward PR in small constituencies: Benin and Burkina Faso have a certain tradition of PR which was established in the decade after the achievement of independence and has been revitalized in the 1990s. In Benin the plurality system in multi-member constituencies with party lists was replaced by a pure PR system with national party lists before the parliamentary elections in 1964 which were, however, the last competitive elections in the country until the democratic transition the country experienced in 1990. For the elections of 1991 a PR system with medium-sized constituencies was established. In Burkina Faso a PR system in medium-sized constituencies was introduced for the elections of 1970 and (with some modifications) again for the elections of 1978. The same system was applied in the first elections of the fourth republic in 1992. In both countries constituencies were reduced in size between the first and the second multi-party elections. The proportionality of votes and seats is thus limited by the high natural threshold connected to small

constituency size. A similar observation holds for Equatorial Guinea where PR in predominantly small constituencies was introduced before the elections of 1993 which ended the period of single-party rule.

(4) Toward PR in medium-sized and large constituencies: In Niger as well as in Algeria all parliamentary elections from independence until the 1990s took place under the conditions of single-party rule and were held according to the inherited plurality system in multi-member districts. When multi-party politics were introduced in Niger by the constitution of 1992 a PR system with medium-sized and large constituencies was established and has been maintained by the constitution of 1996 following the military intervention of the same year. In Algeria initial plans to introduce a PR system in the context of the transition of 1989–1991 were abandoned and an absolute majority system was established instead on the basis of the (erroneous) assumption that it would be easier under this system to prevent an electoral victory of the Islamic Salvation Front in the elections of 1991. The elections of 1997 were held more or less according to the initial ideas of 1989 under PR in predominantly medium-sized and large constituencies.

(5) Toward segmented systems: Senegal and Guinea have moved from plurality systems with closed and blocked national lists applied in the respective periods of single-party rule to parallel systems that were introduced in the context of democratic transition in the 1990s[14]. In Guinea one third of the parliamentary seats is allocated in single-member constituencies according to plurality while two thirds are allocated according to PR at the national level. In Senegal one half of the seats is allocated by plurality in single-member and multi-member constituencies (with closed and blocked lists) and the other half according to PR at the national level.

Madagascar does not fit in any of these broad categories. At the time of independence parliamentary elections were not held under the plurality system but under PR in predominantly small and medium-sized constituencies[15]. After the end of the single-party regime established in the 1970s the first elections of the Third Republic in 1993 were held under a PR system in predominantly small constituencies. However, before the second parliamentary elections that were held in May 1998, a new electoral system was introduced combining single-member districts with plurality vote on the one hand and two-member constituencies with

[14] In Senegal a PR system had been used from 1977 onwards for the distribution of seats between the three existing parties.

[15] However, a special provision of the electoral law stipulated that any list which gained more than 55% of the valid votes would get all the seats of the respective constituency.

closed and blocked party lists where seats are allocated according to a PR formula (binominal system) on the other hand.

Turning to the countries with a Belgian colonial background, elections have been a rather rare event during the last decades and only limited institutional change can be observed. Burundi moved from the Belgian style PR system (preferential voting with party lists in multi-member constituencies) which was applied in the elections of 1961 to a plurality system in single-member districts with party lists composed of four candidates and preferential voting in the elections of 1965. The semi-competitive elections of 1982 were held with preferential voting between two candidates presented by the regime party in any single-member district. The multi-party elections of 1993 were held according to PR with closed and blocked lists in constituencies of variable size. In Rwanda the inherited Belgian system of PR with preferential voting in multi-member districts applied until the elections of 1969. Preferential voting was applied also in the semi-competitive elections under single-party rule in 1981, 1983 and 1988 when voters could chose between two officially nominated candidates for every seat in the Parliament.

Table 1 gives an overview of the parliamentary electoral systems which are currently in use in African countries. A more detailed description of the electoral systems can be found in the appendix of this chapter and of course in the country chapters of this handbook. By and large the distribution of countries in the table underscores the lasting significance of colonial background. To tell the story in other words: Institutional traditions that were established before or shortly after the achievement of independence remain influential in most of the countries. The special conditions which may help to explain exceptions like Liberia and Sierra Leone have already been commented on above. With regard to the countries with PR in small or medium-sized constituencies (e.g. Cape Verde, Benin, Burkina Faso) it is remarkable that constituency sizes have been reduced in the course of the 1990s so that these systems produce strong majoritarian effects.

Only in a small number of African countries has a possible reform of the electoral system been on the political agenda in the context of the opening and/or democratization of former authoritarian political regimes since the early 1990s. In many cases the formal electoral rules that had been applied under the one-party regime or in pre-authoritarian periods respectively were maintained virtually without any discussion. Exceptions are Mali and Benin, where debates on an electoral reform were intense at some time but resulted in only minor reforms. The limited significance of electoral reforms in Africa is all the more remarkable as—in contrast to other world regions—majority systems still predominate the political landscape of the continent.

Table 1: Parliamentary Electoral Systems and Colonial Background

Electoral system	Countries with colonial background			Others
	British	**French**	**Portuguese**	
Plurality in MMC	Mauritius[a]	Djibouti[b]		
Plurality in SMC	Botswana Gambia Ghana Kenya Lesotho Malawi Swaziland Tanzania Uganda Zambia Zimbabwe	Côte d'Ivoire Madagascar[c]		Ethiopia
Absolute majority in SMC and/or MMC (party lists)	Sudan	Cameroon CAR Chad Comoros Gabon Mali Mauritania Togo		
PR in small MMC (majoritarian effect)		Benin Burkina Faso Equatorial Guinea	Cape Verde Guinea-Bissau São Tomé and Príncipe	
Segmented systems	Seychelles	Guinea Senegal		
PR in medium and large MMC		Niger	Angola Mozambique	
Pure PR	Sierra Leone			Liberia Namibia South Africa

[a] Individual candidacies; additional 'best loser' seats.
[b] Closed and blocked party lists.
[c] 78 out of 150 seats are allocated according to a binominal system.

In the scientific community, issues of constitutional engineering and, more specifically, the design of electoral systems, have received much attention within the broader context of studies on the transition to and the consolidation of new democracies in Third World regions and former communist countries. Although most of these studies have referred much more to Latin America and to Eastern Europe than to Africa (Lijphart 1991 and 1992, Nohlen/Kasapovic 1996, Sartori 1994) a number of scholars have revitalized the old, if not classical, discussion on the relative merits of majority versus PR systems[16] under the social, ethnic and political conditions of African countries. Reynolds (1995*a*, 1995*b*) has argued for the mainstream opinion that in plural societies with multiple ethnic divisions which are common in southern Africa PR is better suited than a majority formula to provide for a fair political representation of different social groups and to stimulate politics of compromise which are regarded as an indispensable prerequisite of national integration and democratic consolidation in these societies.

Barkan (1995) has argued against this view and stood up for the Westminster plurality system widely used in anglophone Africa, notwithstanding the strong criticism that has been raised against this system already in the early post-independence era. According to Barkan the plurality system in single-member districts is superior to PR under the conditions of agrarian societies because it allows for a closer relationship between voters and representatives and thus entails better possibilities of holding the latter accountable to the former. Empirically, Barkan has tried to show that supposed merits of PR with regard to the proportionality of electoral results in a number of southern African countries have been less relevant than one would expect theoretically and that the plurality system in single-member districts has produced satisfying results in this respect. On the other hand, he argues, the plurality system produces much better results than PR when it comes to a comparison of the 'quality' of representation (Barkan 1995: 113).

Obviously, questions of institutional engineering should always be discussed on solid empirical grounds and with explicit reference to concrete cases with their specific configuration of institutional and socio-political structures. In debates on electoral system, however, there is often a tendency to contrast one specific type of majority system (e.g. the plurality-system in single-member districts) with the broad category of PR on a rather theoretical level and with only limited reference to historical experience and little awareness of the numerous possibilities to combine technical elements of electoral systems in a way which may help to compensate, at least partially, supposed deficiencies of a certain

[16] For a critical evaluation of this debate see Krennerich/ Lauga (1998).

system without abandoning it altogether (for instance, PR may be combined with personal representation in single-member districts as in the electoral systems of Germany, New Zealand and Venezuela). Besides, there certainly is still a lack of empirically based knowledge about the political effects of electoral systems in African countries (both with regard to structural aspects of political representation in the party system and with regard to the quality of the relationship between voters and representatives) which should keep us from formulating all too general statements on the 'most appropriate' or 'optimal' electoral system for African countries.

Nevertheless, available historical evidence lends considerable support to a rather critical evaluation of majority systems in Africa. As one of the authors of this chapter has pointed out (Nohlen 1996: 105ff.) majority systems may produce or exacerbate certain problems of political representation in ethnically segmented societies. Among these problems are especially the risks of: (a) a non-representation of ethnic minorities which do not have regional strongholds; (b) an accentuation of regional hegemonies when ethnic groups are dominant in different regions, and thus the transformation of regional electoral strongholds of different parties into a territorial cleavage; (c) the exaggeration of the majority in parliamentary terms compared to votes so that opposition parties may be virtually eliminated while ethnic dominance is transformed into political hegemony[17]; (d) the emergence and stabilization of a dominant or even hegemonic party system without any chance of alternation or even effective opposition[18].

All in all, majority representation in segmented societies runs the risk not only of exaggerating ethnic conflicts but also of sharpening ethno-regional polarization. The above cited considerations should, however, not be taken as general propositions on the effects of majority systems in Africa. Rather, they should be taken as a guideline for systematic efforts to analyze such effects on the bases of the empirical data presented in this handbook.

A solid comparative evaluation of specific electoral systems in Africa with regard to their political effects as well as with regard to the political

---

[17] The results of the parliamentary elections of 1993 and 1998 in Lesotho, which have produced much political frustration, may be taken as an example how the winning party can totally dominate the Parliament due to the electoral system.

[18] To be sure, predominant party systems may emerge and exist also under the conditions of PR. An example is Namibia. However, in cases like this the predominant party has no extra advantages connected to the electoral system (here: pure PR). The likelihood of 'manufactured majorities' (in contrast to 'earned majorities') is much lower than under a majority system.

conditions under which they operate is in our view important in two respects. First, it will enhance our understanding of at least some of the problems associated with political development in new African democracies and, eventually, enable political scientists to consult in a sensible and effective way in national debates on institutional reform that may emerge in one or another country of the region. Second, the African experience will enrich the empirical bases of scientific discussions on the relevance, the substance and the operating conditions of institutional factors in political development. Both points apply not only to the study of parliamentary electoral systems but also to the study of presidential electoral systems.

2.2 Presidential Electoral Systems

Most African countries with a constitutional form of government based at least formally on competitive elections have a presidential or semi-presidential system of government[19]. The predominance of presidentialism in Africa—usually with constitutionally powerful Presidents whose political position often is additionally strengthened by the lack of an institutionally well represented opposition—again is closely related to the circumstances under which the countries became independent or developed in the early phase of their post-colonial history. In many cases the undisputed role of a charismatic leader of the independence movement (e.g. Jomo Kenyatta in Kenya, Julius Nyerere in Tanzania, Kenneth Kaunda in Zambia, Kwame Nkrumah in Ghana) set the stage for the creation of a politically strong Head of State and impeded the establishment of effective checks and balances.

In the anglophone countries the shift from the inherited Westminster system to a presidential form of government often complemented the emancipation from ceremonial remnants of colonialism and the adoption of a republican constitution which unified the functions of the Chief of Government and the Head of State. Most of the francophone countries started independence with a constitution built after the model of the French Fifth Republic which foresaw the co-existence of a directly elected President and a Prime Minister responsible to the National Parliament. However, in practice and often as well in constitutional form the President quickly assumed full political power. In the course of

[19] For definitions and discussions of the different types of government see Shugart/Carey (1992), Sartori (1992), Mainwaring (1992), Thibaut (1998).

political development in the post-independence era presidentialism was a constant feature in phases of democratic and non-democratic (single-party or military authoritarian) government.

In recent transitions toward polities based on the division of power and periodical competitive elections the constitutional choice between presidential, semi-presidential and parliamentary systems of government generally has not been a relevant issue in Africa, notwithstanding intense debate on this subject with regard to other world regions like Latin America and Eastern Europe (Nohlen/ Fernández 1991, 1998; Linz/ Valenzuela 1996; Thibaut 1996; Mainwaring/ Shugart 1997; Taras 1997). Today, parliamentary systems *strictu sensu* can be found only in Ethiopia, Botswana, Lesotho and Mauritius. In South Africa the President, who unifies the functions of both Head of State and Government is elected by the Parliament but cannot be removed by it on political grounds. In all other countries of the region with a constitutional form of government the President is directly elected. In contrast to Central and Eastern Europe, there are only very few cases of a directly elected but constitutionally weak President in Africa (Cape Verde, São Tomé and Príncipe).

Direct presidential elections have been a common feature of African politics since the 1960s. However, until the early 1990s presidential elections in most countries were organized as plebiscites which allowed voters at best to say 'Yes' or 'No' to a single official candidate. Under the political conditions of the one-party state no electoral competition at all was allowed to take place with regard to the question who should hold the highest political office of the nation—unlike in parliamentary elections where semi-competitive elements (in the form of primaries at the local level or through the presentation of several officially admitted candidates) were accepted in some countries.

Against this historical background the holding of competitive presidential elections has been an outstanding event in the opening of authoritarian political regimes and one-party systems since the late 1980s. In comparison to multi-party parliamentary elections presidential elections gained importance by the fact that they were directly linked to the question of whether the institutional transition of the political system would be accompanied by a substantial transfer of power from the former authoritarian ruler (who ran for re-election in most cases) to a representative of the opposition. In many countries the first multi-candidate presidential elections since independence were held in this context.

Thus, questions regarding the specific procedural rules under which presidential elections are held, the interrelation or coincidence between presidential and parliamentary elections and the possible consequences of electoral systems and electoral cycles for the overall development of the party system (Nohlen 1991; Shugart/ Carey 1992; Jones 1996) can now be discussed with reference to African cases and political scientists much more than in the past will need to integrate African experiences in their research on the related questions.

Table 2 presents a comparative view of basic aspects of the procedural framework for direct presidential elections in African countries. Without attempting to enter into substantial discussions on the possible political effects of different institutional settings a few rather descriptive observations regarding the historical evolution and current tendencies of procedural norms applied in presidential elections are in order.

With regard to the electoral system there is a clear predominance in Africa of the absolute majority system (or majority run-off) with a second round between the two strongest candidates if the required majority of 50% plus one of valid votes cast is achieved in the first round (*ballotage*). In 29 out of 37 countries listed in the table this system (which has been criticized by some political scientists for its supposed polarizing and/or disorganizing effects on the party system; see Jones 1996) is in use. A plurality system is applied only in Cameroon, Malawi and Zambia, whereas in the remaining countries various forms of qualified majorities are required. Most African countries have not experimented with different presidential electoral systems but have maintained the system chosen when direct presidential elections were held for the first time (note, however, that in many countries of the continent only one or two multi-candidate presidential elections have taken place since independence). Gambia, Tanzania and Togo originally held competitive presidential elections under the relative majority formula and introduced the absolute majority system only before the most recent elections. Only a very few countries have moved in the opposite direction from majority run-off to the plurality system: Equatorial Guinea and Zambia[20]. In Nigeria a variety of complex electoral formulas has been tried over the years with the aim of providing for a certain amount of electoral legitimacy of the President throughout the country and across different ethnic groups without polarizing the electorate.

---

[20] Worldwide there seems to be a trend toward the absolute majority formula in direct presidential elections. Since the 1980s this system has replaced the plurality system also in number of Latin American countries (e.g. Uruguay, Colombia) and it is applied throughout Eastern Europe with the exception of Slowenia.

Table 2: Basic Features of Direct Presidential Elections

Country	Pluralist elections[a]	Concurrency[b]	Term (years)	Consecutive terms	Required majority	Further procedure	Last election	Strongest candidate[b]
Algeria	1	no	5	two	50% + 1	ballotage	1995	61.0
Angola	1	no	5	two	50% + 1	ballotage	1992	49.6
Benin	4 (2)	no	5	two	50% + 1	ballotage	1996	35.7
Burkina F.	2 (1)	no	7	no limit	50% + 1	ballotage	1991	100.0
Cameroon	2	no	7	two	plurality	—	1997	92.6
Cape Verde	2	no	5	two	50% + 1	ballotage	1996	92.1[g]
CAR	2 (1)	no	6	two	50% + 1	ballotage	1993	37.3
Chad	1	no	5	two	50% + 1	ballotage	1996	43.8
Comoros	2 (1)	no	5	no limit	50% + 1	ballotage	1996	21.3
Congo (Br.)	1	no	5	two	50% + 1	ballotage	1992	35.9
Côte d'Ivoire	2	no	5	no limit	50% + 1	2nd round, plurality	1995	96.0
Djibouti	1	no	6	two	50% + 1	ballotage	1993	60.7
Equ. Guinea	2 (1)	no	7	two	plurality	–	1996	97.8
Gabon	1	no	7	two	50% + 1	ballotage	1993	51.2
Gambia	4	no	5	two	50% + 1	ballotage	1996	55.8
Ghana	3 (2)	yes	4	two	50% + 1	ballotage	1996	57.4
Guinea	1	no	5	two	50% + 1	ballotage	1993	51.7
Guinea-B.	1	no	5	two	50% + 1	ballotage	1994	46.2
Kenya	2	yes	5	two	qualified[e]	ballotage	1997	40.1
Liberia	2	yes	6	two	50% + 1	ballotage	1997	75.3
Madagascar	4 (2)	no	5	two	50% + 1	ballotage	1996	36.6
Malawi	1	yes	5	two	plurality	—	1994	47.2
Mali	2	no	5	two	50% + 1	ballotage	1997	87.4
Mauritania	2	no	6	no limit	50% + 1	ballotage	1997	91.0
Mozambique	1	yes	5	two	50% + 1	ballotage	1994	53.3
Namibia	1	yes	5	two	50% + 1	repetition	1994	76.3
Niger	2	no	5	two	50% + 1	ballotage	1996	52.2
Nigeria[d]	3 (2)	no	4	—	qualified	2nd round	1993	58.4
São Tomé	2	no	5	three	50% + 1	ballotage	1996	41.4
Senegal	4	no	7	two	qualified[f]	plurality	1993	58.4
Sierra Leone	1	yes	5	two	55%	ballotage	1996	35.8
Sudan	1	no	5	n.a.	50% + 1	ballotage	1996	75.7
Tanzania	1	yes	5	three	50% + 1	ballotage	1995	61.8
Togo	2	no	5	two	50% + 1	ballotage	1993	96.5
Uganda	1	no	5	two	50% + 1	ballotage	1996	74.2
Zambia	3 (1)	yes	5	two	plurality	–	1996	68.9
Zimbabwe	2	no	6	no limit	50% + 1	ballotage	1996	92.7

General note: In Botswana, Eritrea, Ethiopia, Lesotho, Libya, Mauritius, Morocco, South Africa and Swaziland no direct presidential elections have been held since independence. In Congo DR, Egypt, Rwanda, Somalia and Tunisia only single-candidate elections have been held. Recent presidential elections in the following countries were boycotted by the opposition: Burkina Faso (1991, 1998), Djibouti (1993), Togo (1993), Côte d'Ivoire (1995), Equatorial Guinea (1996), Zimbabwe (1996), Zambia (1996), Mauritania (1997), Mali (1997) and Cameroon (1997).

[a] Number of multi-candidate presidential elections held since independence. Number in parenthesis indicates elections held before the current period of political development.

[b] 'Yes' means: Both presidential and parliamentary elections must be held on the same day regularly (not incidentially) i.e. the President and the Parliament have the same electoral period.

[c] At most recent presidential elections (first round).

[d] Information on procedural rules refers to 1993 elections.

[e] Plurality nationwide and at least 25% in at least five out of eight regions.
[f] Besides the number of votes must amount to at least 25% of the total number of registered voters.
[g] Elections were open for competing candidates but neither contested nor boycotted.

In the vast majority of African countries presidential and parliamentary electoral periods differ from one another. With the exception of Ghana, Liberia, Kenya, Malawi, Mozambique, Namibia, Sierra Leone, Tanzania and Zambia presidential elections are held separately from parliamentary elections. Political scientists have noted that under these institutional conditions differing majorities in the executive and the legislature ('divided government') and related problems of governability seem more likely to arise than in systems where presidential and parliamentary elections are temporarily and, eventually, with regard to technical rules, closely linked to one another. However, recent political development in Africa does not provide for sufficient empirical data to allow for an evaluation of the relevance of the different timing of presidential and parliamentary electoral periods. The party systems of most countries are so unstructured and weak that theoretical concepts which build upon the experience of other world regions should be applied only very carefully in the African context. In practice, African Presidents are only in rare cases effectively checked by the legislature. Multi-partyism often has not yet led to a significant rise of the parliamentary representation of the opposition and problems of 'divided government', that is, institutional conflicts between the executive and a legislature controlled by the opposition, have rarely been virulent (e.g. in Niger before 1995, in Madagascar in some instances since 1992, in São Tomé and Príncipe since 1994, in Benin from 1993 to 1996).

African Presidents tend to have a slightly longer term of office than most of their counterparts in other world regions (the medium period is 5.4 years, in the Americas and the Caribbean 4.7 years, in Asia as well as in Europe 5.1 years respectively). In a number of francophone countries the presidential term of office has recently been prolonged (Côte d'Ivoire, Gabon, Cameroon). With regard to re-election most African constitutions provide for a limit of two consecutive terms (i.e.: one immediate re-election); São Tomé and Príncipe as well as Tanzania allow for three terms; in Burkina Faso, the Comoro Islands, Côte d'Ivoire, Mauritania and Zimbabwe there are no limits at all.

All in all, restrictions to re-election are lower in Africa than in Latin America but rather similar to those in Europe and in Asia (see Nohlen/ Grotz/ Krennerich/ Thibaut 2000). In some cases, however, the respective restrictions have to be interpreted against the background that

Presidents have been in office already for several decades (Hassan Gouled of Djibouti, Omar Bongo of Gabon, Gnassingbe Eyadéma of Togo) and/or did hold the office for a prolonged period under a single-party regime before the introduction of competitive presidential elections in the 1990s (Paul Biya of Cameroon, Didier Ratsiraka of Madagascar, Jerry Rawlings of Ghana). These Presidents are still or again in office because the constitutional norms regarding re-election are new and not applied retroactively. It remains to be seen in which cases these norms outlive future presidential elections. In Namibia the possibility interpreting the respective Article of the Constitution in such a way as to allow President Sam Nujoma (in office since 1989) to run for a third term is discussed, reasoning that for his first term he was elected indirectly by Parliament. In some other countries, where the President in office is backed by a dominant legislative majority, discussions of a possible reform of constitutional norms regarding re-election are likely to emerge.

3. Electoral Statistics

To compile statistical electoral data for African countries is no easy task. In comparison to regions like Europe and the Americas reliable and consistent data are much more difficult, if at all, to obtain, especially if one tries to establish time series which cover the period since independence. The availability of electoral statistics varies between countries and between different time periods of the electoral history or the character of prevailing political regimes respectively.

For the elections held in the context of the independence process a more or less complete and reliable documentation was often produced by administrative services that had long been established by the colonial powers. These elections received much attention from social scientists of the time. For this period the compilation of Sternberger/ Vogel/ Nohlen/ Landfried (1978) remains the most valuable secondary source[21]. In the period(s) of authoritarian single-party rule neither national authorities

[21] The volume, mainly authored by Franz Nuscheler and Klaus Ziemer, contains statistical data and historical information for national parliamentary and presidential elections as well as for pre-independence elections for territorial legislatures and, in the case of the French colonies, for territorial representatives to the French National Assembly. We have decided to document only the last pre-independence elections in this handbook insofar as they are relevant for an understanding of post-independence political development (e.g. with regard to the structure of the party system).

nor the public within and outside the countries were particularly interested in an exact and detailed documentation of electoral processes and election results. Officially, often only vague statements regarding voter turnout and the degree of approval of the candidates presented by the regime were published. Where parliamentary elections had a semi-competitive character (e.g. Kenya, Tanzania), additionally, the amount to which office holders running for re-election were beaten by their competitors, was made public and received some attention.

Naturally, the multi-party elections held in African countries since the early 1990s generally have received much attention from the domestic public as well as from external observers and statistical data as well as information regarding the legal and administrative framework of electoral processes generally are more accessible than in past, not least because of the efforts of international organizations which have observed these elections. However, in many countries much needs to be done to improve the administrative organization and statistical documentation of electoral processes.

The chance to obtain a more or less complete and largely reliable documentation of election results tends to be relatively good in countries where a special (at best permanent) administrative entity with the task of organizing elections exists and where this electoral authority enjoys a minimum amount of independence *vis à vis* other state organs, especially the executive. However, even where responsibilities for the administration of elections are clearly defined (which was rarely the case during the last decades and has yet to become a matter of course in the polities of the region) data are often inconsistent between different sources (e.g. in Benin data published by the National Office for Statistics differ from those available at the Ministry of the Interior), between different levels of documentation (e.g. regional and national) and internally (e.g. because of counting errors). Even one and the same administrative unit may publish differing data at different time points or in different media. Apart from the general lack of financial, technical and human resources in the administrative bodies of many African countries simple errors in typing and/or transmission may account for such inconsistencies[22]. But there are certainly also cases where inconsistencies between election

---

[22] For instance, as a consequence of administrative problems with regard to voter registration the number of registered voters is a potentially unreliable figure in many countries of the region. This is reflected in the strong divergence of data (often not more than arbitrary estimations) provided by different units of administration as well as in fluctuations between different elections which definitely go beyond the increase (or decrease) that could be expected from the general demographic development.

results published at different time points and/or by different sources are a consequence of manipulations by the responsible authorities. Another problem—of minor importance—is related to systematic deviations of officially provided electoral data from international standards. For instance, in some countries, the vote share of parties or candidates is given not as a percentage of valid votes but as a percentage of votes cast. In such cases the authors of this handbook recalculated the data on the bases of absolute figures whenever these were available.

Only in a small number of countries are reliable data for all or most national elections readily available. An outstanding example is Botswana where the Supervisor of Elections is obliged by the constitution to submit a report on each election to the minister responsible for the elections within a relatively short time (usually a few months). The minister in turn has to table the report in Parliament within seven days after the beginning of its next session. In Madagascar the complete results of almost all national elections since independence have been published in the official journal of the republic and in the Seychelles the Electoral Commissioner, an authority established by the constitution of 1993, effectively takes care that election results are easily accessible within as well as outside the country through the world wide web and provides information on the legal and administrative framework of elections.

The usefulness of official journals or gazettes varies considerably with regard to the search for statistical electoral data. In some countries election and referendum results are generally published, in others only presidential elections are considered important enough to justify an official publication. Sometimes only decisions of the Supreme or Constitutional Court on actions of invalidation because of supposed manipulations are published. Often, official journals are published only occasionally and it is very difficult for the scholar to get access to a complete edition even within the respective country. As some of the authors of this handbook report in their country chapters even insisting consultation of responsible authorities does not bring about the desired results, be it because of the already mentioned administrative problems African developing countries have to cope with or because of a certain mood of non-transparency which seems to be imbedded in the administrative culture of many states, probably as a result of longstanding authoritarian rule. In the case of some francophone countries (e.g. Djibouti, Togo) requests addressed to the local embassy of France turned out as a more effective way to obtain electoral data than any efforts to establish contacts with state organs.

Generally, results of presidential elections are more easily available than data for parliamentary elections in African countries. A complete documentation of the results of parliamentary election is especially difficult to obtain in those countries where an absolute majority or plurality system in single-member districts is applied. Often, only the names and party affiliation of the winning candidates are published on the bases of provisional results. However, improvements of the electoral administration during the last years have led to a more complete and reliable documentation of electoral data in a considerable number of countries. International organizations like the International Foundation of Electoral Systems (IFES) or the International Parliamentary Union (IPU) have done much to improve the transparency of election processes and results in Africa as well as in other world regions, but remain, in the end, dependent on the cooperation of national authorities.

Apart from official publications the authors of this handbook had to rely on statistical and background information provided by local newspapers and international publications like *Africa Research Bulletin*, *Keesing's Record of World Events*, *African Contemporary Records*, *Politique Africaine*, *Marchés Tropicaux et Méditerranéens*, *Jeune Afrique* as well as regionally specialized documentation services. A number of internet-sources (for example, Wilfried Derksen's Electoral Websites: www.agora.stm.it/elections/election.htm, and IPU's Parline Database: www.ipu.org/parline-e/parline.htm) are quite helpful with regard to the most recent elections but provide for many African countries only incomplete results. The Association of African Election Authorities (AAEA) which was founded within the IFES in 1994 hopefully will become a reliable international source of electoral statistics and legal documents relevant for electoral processes and lay as well the bases for the introduction of international standards of electoral administration and documentation in its member countries.

4. Bibliography

Ansprenger, F. (1997). *Politische Geschichte Afrikas im 20. Jahrhundert.* (2nd edn.). München: Beck.

Barkan, J. D. (1995). 'Elections in Agrarian Societies'. *Journal of Democracy*, 5/3: 106–124.

— (1997). 'African Elections in Comparative Perspective', in United Nations (ed.), *Elections: Perspectives on Establishing Democratic Practices.* New York: United Nations, 1–29.

Bratton, M. (1997). 'Deciphering Africa's Divergent Transitions'. *Political Science Quarterly*, 112/1: 67–93.

— (1998). 'Second Elections in Africa'. *Journal of Democracy*, 9/3: 51–66.

— and Walle, N. van de (1997). *Democratic Experiments in Africa: Regime Transitions in Comparative Perspective*. New York: Cambridge University Press.

Centre d'Etude d'Afrique Noire (1978). *Aux Urnes l'Afrique! Elections et pouvoirs en Afrique noire*. Paris: Pedone.

Chazan, N. (1979). 'African Voters at the Polls: A Re-examination of the Role of Elections in African Politics'. *Journal of Commonwealth and Comparative Politics*, 17: 136–158.

— (1982). 'The New Politics of Participation in Tropical Africa'. *Comparative Politics*, 14: 169–189.

— (1992). 'Democratic Fragments: Africa's Quest for Democracy', in S. N. Eisenstadt (ed.), *Democracy and Modernity*. Leiden: Brill, 111–142.

Clark, J. F., and Gardinier, D. E. (eds.) (1998). *Political Reform in Francophone Africa*. Boulder, Col.: Westview Press.

Cohen, D. L. (1983). 'Elections and Election Studies in Africa', in Y. Barongo (ed.), *Political Science in Africa: A Critical Review*. London: Zed Press, 72–93.

Collier, R. B. (1982). *Regimes in Tropical Africa*. Berkeley, Cal.: University of California Press.

Conac, G. (ed.) (1993). *L'Afrique en transition vers le pluralisme politique*. Paris: Economica.

Cowen, M., and Laakso, L. (1997). 'An Overview of Election Studies in Africa'. *The Journal of Modern African Studies*, 35/4: 717–744.

Elklit, J. (ed.) (1997). *Electoral Systems for Emerging Democracies. Experiences and Suggestions*. Copenhagen: Min. of Foreign Affairs, Danida.

— and Svensson, P. (1996). 'When are Elections Free and Fair—or at least Acceptable?'. Paper presented on the Workshop on Democratization: The Status of Today's Empirical Theory, Nordic Political Science Triennial Meeting, Helsinki, Finland, 15–17 August 1996.

Engel, U., Hofmeier, R., Kohnert, D., and Mehler, A. (eds.) (1994). *Wahlbeobachtung in Afrika.* Hamburg: Institut für Afrika-Kunde.

— (eds.) (1996). *Deutsche Wahlbeobachtung in Afrika*. Hamburg: Institut für Afrika-Kunde.

Fatton, R. Jr. (1987). *The Making of a Liberal Democracy: Senegal's Passive Revolution, 1975–1985*. Boulder, Col.: Lynne Rienner.

Fleischhacker, H., Krennerich, M., and Thibaut, B. (1996). 'Demokratie und Wahlen in Afrika und Lateinamerika: Bilanz der neunziger Jahre', in *Jahrbuch Dritte Welt 1997*. München: Beck, 93–107.

Hayward. F. M. (1987) (ed.). *Elections in Independent Africa*. Boulder, Col.: Westview Press.

Hermet, G., Rose, R., and Rouquié, A. (1978) (eds.). *Elections Without Choice*. London: Macmillan.

Horowitz, D. L. (1991). *A Democratic South Africa? Constitutional Engineering in a Divided Society*. Berkeley: Univ. of California Press.

Hyden, G. (1994). 'Political Representation and the Future of Uganda', in H. B. Hansen and M. Twaddle (eds.), *From Chaos to Order. The Politics of Constitution-Making in Uganda*. Kampala: Fountain Publ., 180–192.

International Institute for Democracy and Electoral Assistance (1997). *Voter Turnout from 1945 to 1997: A Global Report on Political Participation*. Stockholm: International IDEA.

Jinadu, L. A.(1997). 'Matters Arising: African Elections and the Problem of Electoral Administration'. *African Journal of Political Science*, 2/1, 1–11.

Jones, M. (1996). *Electoral Laws and the Survival of Presidential Democracies*. Notre Dame, Ind.: University of Notre Dame Press.

Joseph, R. (1997). 'Democratization in Africa after 1989. Comparative and Theoretical Perspectives'. *Comparative Politics*, 29: 363–382.

Krennerich, M. (1996*a*). 'Electoral Systems: A Global Overview', in J. de Ville and N. Steytler (eds.), *Voting in 1999: Choosing an Electoral System*. Durban: Butterworths, 7–18.

— (1996*b*). *Wahlen und Antiregimekriege in Zentralamerika*. Opladen: Leske & Budrich.

— (2000). 'Competitiveness of Elections', in R. Rose (ed.), *International Encyclopedia of Elections*. Washington, D.C.: Congressional Quarterly (forthcoming).

— and de Ville, J. (1997). 'A Systematic View on the Electoral Reform Debate in South Africa'. *Verfassung und Recht in Übersee*, 30/1, 26–41.

— and Lauga, M. (1998). 'Diseño versus política. Observaciones sobre el debate internacional y las reformas de los sistemas electorales', in D. Nohlen and M. Fernández (eds.), *El presidencialismo renovado*. Caracas: Nueva Sociedad, 69–82.

Lijphart, A. (1990). 'Electoral Systems, Party Systems and Conflict Management in Segmented Societies', in R. A. Schrire (ed.), *Critical Choices for South Africa*. Cape Town: Oxford University Press, 2–13.

— (1991). 'Constitutional Choices for New Democracies'. *Journal of Democracy*, 2: 72–84.

— (1992). 'Democratization and Constitutional Choices in Czech-Slovakia, Hungary and Poland'. *Journal of Theoretical Politics*, 4/2: 207–223.

— (1994). *Electoral Systems and Party Systems*. Oxford: Oxford University Press.

Mackenzie, W. J. M. (1958). *Free Elections. An Elementary Textbook*. London: George Allen and Unwin.

Mackie, T. T., and Rose, R. (1991). *The International Almanac of Electoral History. Fully Revised Third Edition*. Houndsmill/ London: Macmillan.

— (1997). *A Decade of Election Results: Updating the International Almanac*. Glasgow: Centre for the Study of Public Policy, University of Strathclyde.

Mainwaring, S. (1993). 'Presidentialism, Multipartism, and Democracy: The Difficult Combination'. *Comparative Political Studies,* 26/2: 198–228.

— and Shugart, M. S. (eds.) (1997). *Presidentialism and Democracy in Latin America.* Cambridge: Cambridge University Press.

Mehler, A. (1994). *'Gründungswahlen' und 'Fassadenwahlen'. Plädoyer und Skizze für eine künftige Wahlforschung in Afrika südlich der Sahara*. IAK-Diskussionsbeiträge, 1. Hamburg: Institut für Afrika-Kunde.

Meyns, P., and Nuscheler, F. (1993). 'Struktur- und Entwicklungsprobleme von Subsahara-Afrika', in D. Nohlen and F. Nuscheler (eds.), *Handbuch der Dritten Welt. Band 4: Westafrika und Zentralafrika*. Bonn: Dietz, 13–129.

Nohlen, D. (1978). *Wahlsysteme der Welt*. München/ Zürich: Piper.

— (1990). *Wahlrecht und Parteiensystem*. Opladen: Leske & Budrich.

— (1991). 'Presidencialismo, sistemas electorales y sistemas de partidos. Reflexiones para América Latina', in D. Nohlen and M. Fernández (eds.), *Presidencialismo versus parlamentarismo. América Latina.* Caracas: Nueva Sociedad, 51–70.

— (ed.) (1993). *Enciclopedia Electoral Latinoamericana y del Caribe.* San José, Costa Rica: Instituto Interamericano de Derechos Humanos.

— (1996). *Elections and Electoral Systems.* Delhi: Macmillan India.

— and Fernández, M. (eds.) (1991). *Presidencialismos versus parliamentarismo. América Latina.* Caracas: Nueva Sociedad.

— and Fernández, M. (eds.) (1998). *El presidencialismo renovado. Instituciones y cambio político en América Latina.* Caracas: Nueva Sociedad.

— and Grotz, F., Krennerich, M., and Thibaut, B. (2000). 'Appendix: Electoral Systems in Independent Countries', in R. Rose (ed.), *International Encyclopedia of Elections*. Washington, D.C.: Congressional Quarterly (forthcoming).

— and Kasapovic, M. (1996). *Wahlsysteme und Systemwechsel in Osteuropa.* Opladen: Leske & Budrich.

— and Nuscheler, F. (eds.) (1992–1995). *Handbuch der Dritten Welt.* (8 volumes). Bonn: Dietz.

— and Picado, S., and Zovatto, D. (eds.) (1998). *Tratado de Derecho Electoral Comparado de América Latina.* Mexico: FCE *et al.*

Nuscheler, F., and Ziemer, K. (1980). *Politische Herrschaft in Schwarzafrika. Geschichte und Gegenwart.* München: Beck.

O'Donnell, G., and Schmitter, P. C. (1986). *Transitions from Authoritarian Rule.* Baltimore: John Hopkins University Press.

Quantin, P. (1998). 'Pour une analyse comparative des élections africaines'. *Politique Africaine* 69: 12–28.

Reynolds, A. (1995*a*). 'Constitutional Engineering in Southern Africa'. *Journal of Democracy*, 6/2: 86–97.

— (1995*b*). 'The Case for Proportionality'. *Journal of Democracy*, 6/4: 117–124.

— (1998). *Electoral Systems and Democratization in Southern Africa.* Oxford: Oxford University Press.

Rose, R. (ed.) (2000), *International Encyclopedia of Elections.* Washington, D.C.: Congressional Quarterly (forthcoming).

— and Massawir, H. (1967). 'Voting and Elections: A Functional Analysis'. *Political Studies*, 15/2: 173–201.

Sartori, G. (1994). *Comparative Constitutional Engineering.* Basingstoke: Macmillan.

Shugart, M. S., and Carey, J. M. (1992). *Presidents and Assemblies.* Cambridge: Cambridge University Press.

Sklar, R. L. (1983). 'Democracy in Africa. *African Studies Review*, 26/3–4: 11–24.

Sisk, T. D., and Reynolds, A. (eds.) (1997). *Elections and Conflict Resolution in Africa*. Washington D.C.: United States Institute for Peace Press.

Sternberger, D., Vogel, B., Nohlen, D., and Landfried, K. (eds.) (1978). *Die Wahl der Parlamente und anderer Staatsorgane. Band II: Politische Organisation und Repräsentation in Afrika*, by Franz Nuscheler, Klaus Ziemer *et al.*. Berlin/ New York: Walter de Gruyter.

Taras, R. (1997) (ed.). *Postcommunist Presidents.* Cambridge: Cambridge University Press.

Thibaut, B. (1996). *Präsidentialismus und Demokratie in Lateinamerika.* Opladen: Leske & Budrich.

— (1998). 'Präsidentielle, parlamentarische oder hybride Regierungssysteme? Institutionen und Demokratieentwicklung in der Dritten Welt und in den Transformationsstaaten Osteuropas'. *Zeitschrift für Politikwissenschaft*, 8/1, 5–37.

Wiseman, J. A. (1990). *Democracy in Black Africa. Survival and Revival.* New York: Paragon House.

— (1992). 'Early Post-Redemocratization Elections in Africa'. *Electoral Studies*, 11/4: 279–291.

— (ed.) (1995). *Democracy and Political Change in Sub-Saharan Africa.* London/ New York: Routledge.

Young, T. (1993). 'Elections and Electoral Politics in Africa'. *Africa*, 63/3: 299–312.

Appendix: Basic Features of Parliamentary Electoral Systems in Africa

Country	Year	Electoral system	Elected seats	Constituencies Number	Size(s)	Mean size	Level(s) of seat allocation	Electoral formula	Rose-Index
Algeria	1997	PR in MMC	380	48	4-24	7.9	constituency	Hare quota and largest remainder; 5%-threshold	85.8
Angola	1992	PR in five-member constituencies with additional national list	220:			n.a.			94.1
			90	18	5		constituency,	d'Hondt	
			130	1	130		nation	Hare quota, largest remainder	
Benin	1995	PR in MMC	84	18	3-6	5.3	constituency	Hare quota, greatest average	72.1
Botswana	1994	Plurality system in SMC	40	40	1	1	constituency	Plurality	87.2
Burkina Faso	1997	Majority system in SMC and PR in MMC	111	45	1-11	2.5	constituency	Hare quota, greatest average (plurality in SMC)	77.6
Cameroon	1997	Majority system in SMC and MMC	180	—	1-7	—	constituency	SMC: plurality; MMC: absolute majority with elements of a bonus system and PR	86.6
Cape Verde	1995	PR in MMC	72	19	2-13	3.8	constituency	d'Hondt	91.8
CAR	1998	Absolute majority system in SMC	109	109	1	1	constituency	Absolute majority	n.a.
Chad	1997	Absolute majority system in SMC and MMC	125	59	1-	2.9	constituency	Absolute majority	72.8
Comoros	1996	Absolute majority system in SMC	43	43	1	1	constituency	Absolute majority	n.a.
Côte d'Ivoire	1995	Plurality system in SMC and MMC	175	157	1-4	1.1	constituency	Plurality	79.8
Djibouti	1997	Plurality list system in MMC	65	5	4-37	13	constituency	Plurality	78.6
Egypt	1995	Absolute majority system in TMC	444	222	2	2	constituency	Absolute majority	n.a.
Equatorial Guinea	1993	PR in MMC	80	18	—	4.4	constituency	Hare quota, smallest remainder; 10%-threshold	84.8
Ethiopia	1995	Plurality system in SMC	547	547	1	1	constituency	Plurality	96
Gabon	1996	Absolute majority system in SMC	120	120	1	1	constituency	Absolute majority	n.a.

—

Country	Year	Electoral system	Elected seats	Constituencies Number	Size(s)	Mean size	Level(s) of seat allocation	Electoral formula	Rose-Index
Gambia	1997	Plurality system in SMC	45	45	1	1	constituency	Plurality	73.8
Ghana	1996	Plurality system in SMC	200	200	1	1	constituency	Plurality	86.2
Guinea	1995	Segmented system	114:			n.a.			91
			38	38	1		constituency,	Plurality	
			76	1	76		nation	Hare quota, largest remainder	
Guinea-Bissau	1994	PR in MMC	102	29	1-6	3.5	constituency	d'Hondt (plurality in SMC)	82.7
Kenya	1997	Plurality system in SMC	210	210	1	1	constituency	Plurality	—
Lesotho	1998	Plurality system in SMC	80	80	1	1	constituency	Plurality	74.8
Liberia	1997	Pure PR	64	1	64	n.a.	nation	Hare quota, largest remainder	96.8
Madagascar	1998	Plurality system in SMC and PR in TMC	150	121	1-2	1.2	constituency	SMC: Plurality; TMC: Hare quota with greatest average	—
Malawi	1994	Plurality system in SMC	177	177	1	1	constituency	Plurality	97
Mali	1997	Absolute majority system in MMC	147	55	—	2.6	constituency	Absolute majority	88.2
Mauritania	1996	Absolute majority system in SMC and PR in TMC	79	53	1-2	1.5	constituency	SMC: absolute majority; TMC: unspecified quota, 10%-threshold	79
Mauritius	1995	Plurality system in MMC	70						68.5
			62	21	2-3	3.0	constituency,	Plurality	
			8	n.a.	n.a.		community	'best loser'	
Morocco	1997	Plurality system in SMC	325	325	1	1	constituency	Plurality	84.2
Mozambique	1994	PR in MMC	250	11	11-54	22.7	constituency	d'Hondt ; 5%-threshold	85.7
Namibia	1994	Pure PR	72	1	72	n.a.	nation	Hare quota, largest remainder	98.7
Niger	1996	PR in MMC (plus minority SMC)	83:				constituency		86.7
			75	8	4-14	9.4		Hare quota, largest remainder	
			8	8	1	n.a.		Plurality	
São Tomé & Principé	1998	PR in MMC	55	7	5-13	7.9	constituency	d'Hondt	92.6
Senegal	1998	Segmented system	140:						83.6
			70	30	1-5	2.4	constituency	Plurality	
			70	1			nation	Hare quota, largest remainder	

Country	Year	Electoral system	Elected seats	Constituencies Number	Size(s)	Mean size	Level(s) of seat allocation	Electoral formula	Rose-Index
Seychelles	1998	Segmented system	34			n.a.			73.5
			25	25	1		constituency,	Plurality	
			9	1	9		nation	Hare quota; 10%-threshold	
Sierra Leone	1996	PR in one MMC	68	1	68	n.a.	nation	Hare quota, largest remainder; 5%-threshold	88.4
South Africa	1994	Pure PR (Party share of	400:					STV-droop quota, largest remainder	98.8
		400 seats is determined at	200	9	4-34	22.2	constituency,		
		national level)	200	1	200	n.a.	nation		
Sudan	1996	No-party absolute majority system in SMC	275	275	1	1	constituency	Absolute majority	n.a.
Swaziland	1998	No-party plurality system in SMC	55	55	1	1	constituency	Plurality	n.a.
Tanzania	1995	Plurality systemin SMC	232	232	1	1	constituency	Plurality	74.2
Togo	1994	Absolute majority system in SMC	81	81	1	1	constituency	Absolute majority	—
Tunisia	1994	Plurality system in MMC	163:						90.4
		(plus compensatory	144	25	2-10	5.8	constituency,	Plurality	
		national list)	19	1	19	n.a.	nation	Hare quota, greatest average	
Uganda	1996	No-party plurality system in SMC	214	214	1	1	constituency	Plurality	n.a.
Zambia	1996	Plurality system in SMC	150	150	1	1	constituency	Plurality	73.7
Zimbabwe	1995	Plurality system in SMC	120	120	1	1	constituency	Plurality	83.1

Abbreviations: SMC = single-member constituency; TMC = two-member constituency; MMC = multi-member constituency; PR = Proportional Representation; m. = mean size of constituencies; r. = range of constituency sizes; n.a. = not applicable. '—' = data not available.

ALGERIA

by Dirk Axtmann

1. Introduction

1.1 Historical Overview

Since independence from France (Treaties of Evian, 1962) and up to 1989, Algeria's political history has been characterized by the single-party system of the National Liberation Front *(Front de Libération Nationale*, FLN), formally fixed in the 1963 and 1976 Constitutions as well as in the 'National Charters' of 1976 and 1986. The real power, though, remained in the hands of the President and an emerging technocratic class. Moreover, since Lieutenant Houari Boumedienne had backed Ahmed Ben Bella's investiture as first Algerian President (1962–1965), this 'state-class' was intimately linked to the army. The military take-over by Boumedienne in 1965 confirmed the army as the decisive force in Algerian politics up to our days.

In the 1960s and 1970s Algeria embarked on a socialist development strategy (land-reform, nationalization of the oil-industry, 'agricultural revolution'), maintaining an Arabic and Islamic orientation. In the 1980s, however, the economic situation deteriorated dramatically, revealing harsh imbalances in the development of the different economic sectors and high dependence on fluctuating prices of crude oil on world-markets. In the political realm, demands for more political freedom and the growing importance of cultural demands on the part of the Berber minority and fundamentalist Islamic groups, especially among young Algerians, showed the increasing delegitimation of the ruling (FLN-) state class.

The constitutional amendments (November 1988) carried out after the riots in October 1988, and the new constitution of 1989 (both approved by referendum) officially abolished the FLN-monopoly in Algerian politics; political parties were permitted to constitute freely; a remarkably free press emerged; the constitutional position of the Parliament was strengthened, and the role of the military was formally limited to defense tasks. As the newly legalized Islamic Salvation Front (FIS) took a clear advance over the FLN during the first round of the legislative elections on 26 December 1991 and was about to gain the overall majority in the second round, the army interrupted the electoral process on 11 January 1992. The military ousted President Chadli Bendjedid (President 1979–1992), handed power to a newly created collegial government, the 'High Committee of State' under Mohamed Boudiaf (killed in June 1992) and subsequently to the Minister of Defense Liamine Zéroual who was invested as transitional President in January 1994. A 'Transitional Council', composed of representatives from political parties, civil society and public authorities, was appointed to serve as Parliament in the meantime. Since the suspension of the FIS and the declaration of the state of emergency (March 1992) Algeria has experienced an ongoing and escalating confrontation between security forces and clandestine Islamist groups, which is reported to have cost about 80,000 human lives until early 1998 among security forces, Islamists, civilians and even foreign residents. In January 1995 several opposition parties—among them FIS-representatives—signed the 'Rome-Platform' in which they called for a dialogue between government and opposition—including the FIS—as an alternative to the regime's 'policy of eradication' of the Islamist underground.

In the meantime the army-backed government tried to broaden its legitimacy by organizing a series of elections. Even with the major opposition parties calling for an electoral boycott, the presidential elections of 16 November 1995 turned out to be an impressive confirmation of Liamine Zéroual; a victory obviously boosted by Algerians' wish for political stability. One year later opposition parties denounced the anti-democratic character of the new constitution approved by referendum on 26 November 1996 and the massive manipulation in the run-up to this referendum. This constitution has again strengthened the role of the President and created an upper chamber, the *Conseil de la Nation*, (one third appointed by the President) which controls parliamentary decisions.

Like other parties the moderate Islamist *Mouvement de la Société Islamique-Hamas* (MSI-Hamas), serving as a junior-partner in Zéroual's government, was obliged to modify its name (now *Mouvement de la Société pour la Paix* MSP) and program so as to match the new Party Act (1997) banning parties based 'exclusively on regional and religious characteristics'. These provisions have to be considered as an additional obstacle deliberately put up to weaken the opposition parties rooted in the mainly Berber-populated regions. The overwhelming victory of the newly created *Rassemblement National Démocratique* (RND), considered close to President Zéroual, in the 5 June 1997 legislative elections has provided the President with a majority in the National People's Assembly. In spite of criticism by the Algerian opposition as well as by international observers concerning widespread electoral fraud, the announced return to elected institutions has been accomplished with the municipal and regional elections of 23 October 1997, and the subsequent investiture of the *Conseil de la Nation* on 25 December 1997.

1.2 Evolution of Electoral Provisions

The evolution of electoral provisions reflects the major distinction between the periods from 1962 to 1988/1989 (single-party system) and after 1989 (political liberalization and emergence of a destabilizing (Islamist) majority).

The suffrage was of 21 years for the election of the Constitutional Assembly in 1962 and was reduced to the age of 19 for the 1963–1964 polls. Since 1976 the right to vote is attributed to every Algerian aged 18 and more. As for the eligibility, the age of 23 years/ 25 years entitled every Algerian to stand as a candidate for Parliament in 1964/ 1977 respectively. In 1980 the minimum age was brought to 30 years to be finally reduced again to 28 years before the legislative elections in 1991.

The principles of universal, equal, direct and secret suffrage were applied for the electoral consultations from 1962 onwards. However, the parliamentary (national, regional and municipal) as well as the presidential polls and referendums until the 1980s must be characterized as non-competitive elections. The FLN's exclusive right to nominate the candidates for the parliamentary elections was laid down in the constitutions of 1963 and 1976. The candidates were not necessarily members of the FLN but could well come from civil organizations affiliated to the single-party (e.g. organizations of veterans/ trade unions). According to the Electoral Act of 1976 the majority of the candidates had to be 'workers' or 'peasants'. However, the majority of parliamentarians were state officials, functionaries and teachers. The parliamentary elections of 1977 (the first since 1964) introduced semi-competitive elements, since voters could choose out of three candidates for each parliamentary seat, presented by the FLN in the constituencies. Voters had to cancel one or several candidates' names, without the possibility of adding others, and actually made use of this, though limited, opportunity to manifest their discontent with candidates placed on top of the single list.

For the elections to the Constitutional Assembly in 1962 and the parliamentary elections in 1964, a plurality system was applied in 15 constituencies (corresponding to the 15 regions [*wilayat*]). For the parliamentary elections of 1977, 1982 and 1987 the same system was used in constituencies based on the 161 (since 1984: 229) *dairat* (administrative entities between municipalities and regions). The number of seats was 196 for the Constitutional Assembly in 1962 and 138 for the *Assemblée Populaire Nationale* in 1964. With the Electoral Act of 1976 the number of seats was extended to 261 for the 1977 polls and subsequently increased to 281 (1982) and 295 (1987) due to the growth of population. Presidential elections were run by one candidate nominated by the FLN to be elected in universal, equal, direct and secret vote by relative majority. The presidential term was of six years (since 1979: five years) without any limitation of terms.

The promulgation of the Party Act (5 July 1989) and of a new Electoral Act (7 August 1989) paved the way for the first competitive elections in 1990/ 1991. The Electoral Act (EA) aroused much concern among the newly created parties and civil society associations in the run-up to the 1990 (regional and municipal) elections. It passed through several modifications and amendments before the 1991 parliamentary poll, intended to avoid a possible electoral victory for the FIS. Thus the proportional system initially stipulated by the EA was afterwards modified to an absolute majority system in April 1991.

In the run-up to the parliamentary elections of 26 December 1991 the number of constituencies was brought to 542 and subsequently to 430 single-member constituencies, clearly over-representing the southern Saharan and rural regions supposed to be more loyal to the former single party FLN. Proxy-voting, which traditionally allowed registered voters (less likely the wife) to vote in place of his/her spouse as well as other family members, was reduced from five possible proxy-votes authorized by the EA of 1989 to three (1990) and finally to one (1991). Proxy-voting was supposed to benefit mainly the FIS because of presumably more patriarchal family structures in its electorate.

1.3 Current Electoral Provisions

Sources: Constitution of the People's Democratic Republic of Algeria (28 November 1996); Ordonnances No. 97-07; 97-08 (6 March 1997) (Electoral Act); Ordonnance No. 97-09 (Party Act) and Executive Decree No. 97-423 (precising the elections for the *Conseil de la Nation*)

Elected national institutions: President of the Republic, elected for a five-year term; one direct re-election allowed; 380 members of the lower chamber of Parliament (*Assemblée Populaire Nationale*), elected for a five-year term; 144 members of the *Conseil de la Nation* (upper chamber) serving for a six-year term (renewal of half of its members every three years).

Suffrage: The principles of universal, equal, direct and secret suffrage are applied. Every citizen who has reached the age of 18 is entitled to vote. Voting is not compulsory, but in order to vote Algerians have to register with the electoral list of their municipality, the list being updated every year. Algerian citizens living permanently abroad can register with the Algerian diplomatic missions or their municipality of origin. Proxy-voting is possible for one person.

Nomination of candidates
- *presidential elections*: Every Algerian citizen of Muslim religion, aged 40 or more is eligible for presidency. The application for candidature has to be accompanied by a document certifying the Algerian nationality of the candidate's spouse. The candidate has to certify his participation in the revolution of 1 November 1954 (if born before July 1942), respectively to certify that his parents were not involved in acts hostile to the revolution (if born after July 1942). Finally the candidate has to prove by signature the support of 600 elected members of parliamentary assemblies or of 75,000 individuals registered on electoral lists and coming from at least 25 regions.
- *elections to the National People's Assembly* (*APN*): Every Algerian citizen who has reached the age of 28 and has accomplished military service is eligible. Members of the army and of other security forces as well as persons holding higher positions in the administration are not entitled to candidature while occupying the respective function (and one year after leaving it). Candidates have to figure on a list established by one or several parties or on an independents' list, each list giving as many names as seats to be allotted plus three substitute candidates. An independents' list requires the backing of at least 400 registered voters per constituency for every seat to be filled.
- *elections to the Council of the Nation* (*Conseil de la Nation*): Candidature is open to every Algerian, aged 40 or older, who is elected member of a regional assembly (*Assemblée Populaire de la Wilaya)* or of a

municipal assembly (*Assemblée Populaire Communale*). In addition, the same incompatibilities as established for the APN apply.

Electoral system
- *presidential elections*: Absolute majority system. If no candidate receives more than 50% of the votes cast a second ballot is held among the two leading candidates.
- *elections to the National People's Assembly*: Proportional representation list system at the regional level (*wilayat*). Technical elements: *48 constituencies of differing size (four to 24 seats per constituency; 17 constituencies with 4–5; 22 constituencies with 6–10; eight constituencies with 11–16; one constituency with 24 seats (Algiers); number of seats per constituency is dependent on the population size of the respective region: one seat per 80,000 inhabitants (residual: 40,000 inhabitants). Minimum of four seats for the regions with less than 350,000 inhabitants; eight seats are reserved to the Algerian Community abroad). *Closed party lists. *Single vote. *Hare quota and largest remainder formula. *5%-threshold at constituency level.
- *elections to the Council of the Nation*: One third of the 144 seats is appointed by the President, two thirds (96—two per region) are indirectly elected by and among the members of regional and municipal assemblies (*Assemblées Populaires Communales, Assemblées Populaires de wilaya*) assembled in electoral colleges at departmental level.

1.4 Comment on the Electoral Statistics

Generally speaking, official sources such as the *Journal Officiel de la République Algérienne* (JORA) or the semi-official *El-Moudjahid*, as well as secondary literature (particularly the *Annuaire de l'Afrique du Nord* ANN), daily newspapers (e.g. *Le Monde*) or international news agencies provide valid information on the electoral consultations in Algeria. Sometimes, and particularly in the early years of the Algerian Republic, the data displayed in the governmental bulletin JORA and those published by international newspapers or agencies differ slightly. The following tables are based, as far as possible, on the official results figuring in JORA. Parliamentary elections in the authoritarian period (1962–1989), apparently of little political importance, were not documented in JORA (except for the Constitutional Assembly elections in 1962). In these cases the author has referred to results reported by International News Agencies like APF and to data found in secondary literature, especially ANN.

2. Tables

2.1 Dates of National Elections, Referendums and Coups d'Etat

Year	Presidential elections	Parliamentary elections	Elections for Constitutional Assembly	Referendums	Coups d'état
1962			20/09[a]	01/07	
1963	15/09			08/09	
1964		20/09			
1965					19/06
1976	10/12			27/06 19/11	
1977		25/02			
1979	07/02				
1982		05/03			
1984	12/01				
1986				16/01	
1987		26/02			
1988	22/12			03/11	
1989				23/02	
1991		26/12[b]			
1992					11/01
1995	16/11				
1996				28/11	
1997		05/06			

[a] Algerian voters were called to ratify a Bill constituting and authorizing the Constitutional Assembly to nominate a provisional government, to pass laws and to work out the constitution.

[b] Only the first round of this legislative poll was held. The fundamentalist FIS being about to take a clear advantage in the scheduled second round, the army forced President Chadli Bendjedid to retreat from his office and established a collegial government the 'High Committee of State'. The results of the first round were nullified, the scheduled second round of the elections was cancelled.

2.2 Electoral Body 1962–1997

Year	Type of election[a]	Population[b]	Registered voters		Votes cast		
			Total number	% pop.	Total number	% reg. voters	% pop.
1962	CA	11,236,000	6,504,033	57.9	5,528,428	85.0	49.2
1962	Ref	11,236,000	6,549,736	58.3	6,017,680	91.9	53.6
1963	Pr	11,460,000	6,581,340	57.4	5,850,133	88.9	51.1
1963	Ref	11,460,000	6,391,818	55.8	5,287,229	82.7	46.1
1964	Pa	11,690,000	6,091,991	52.1	5,177,631	85.0	44.3
1976	Pr	16,516,000	8,352,147	50.6	8,107,485	97.1	49.1
1976	Ref	16,516,000	7,940,978	48.1	7,290,671	91.2	44.1
1976	Ref	16,516,000	8,076,834	48.9	7,504,696	92.9	45.4
1977	Pa	17,030,000	7,960,000	46.7	6,037,537[c]	75.8	35.5
1979	Pr	18,105,000	7,888,875	43.6	7,490,479	94.9	41.4
1982	Pa	19,862,000	8,990,820	45.3	6,420,330	71.4	31.5
1984	Pr	21,173,000	10,154,715	48.0	9,776,952	96.3	43.3
1986	Ref	22,497,000	10,954,063	48.7	10,502,524	95.9	46.7
1987	Pa	23,124,000	11,322,680	49.2	9,889,100	87.3	43.0
1988	Ref	23,758,000	12,572,043	52.9	10,435,046	83.0	43.9
1988	Pr	23,758,000	13,060,720	55.0	11,634,139	89.1	49.0
1989	Ref	24,374,000	13,170,137	54.0	10,401,548	79.0	42.7
1991	Pa	25,680,000	13,258,554	51.6	7,822,625	59.0	30.5
1995	Pr	27,600,000	15,965,280	57.8	11,965,280	74.9	43.4
1996	Ref	29,183,032	16,434,527	56.3	13,114,477	79.8	44.9
1997	Pa	29,830,370	16,767,309	56.2	10,999,139	65.6	36.9

[a] CA = Constitutional Assembly; Pa = Parliament (National People's Assembly); Pr = President; Ref = Referendum.

[b] Population data are UN estimations as published in the Penn World Tables except for 1995 (*Nahost Jahrbuch*), 1996 and 1997 (World-Factbook).

[c] Author's calculation from participation rate and number of registered voters.

2.3 Abbreviations

AHD 54[a]	'Ahd 54/ '*Pledge*' 54
AJL	Alliance pour la Justice et la Liberté / Alliance for Justice and Freedom
ALP [a]	Algerian Liberal Party
ANDI	Alliance Nationale des Démocrates Indépendants / National Alliance of Independent Democrats
ANR	Alliance Nationale Républicaine / National Republican Alliance
APUA	Association Populaire pour l'Unité et l'Action / Popular Association for Unity and Action
BN	Bloc National / National Block
EL	Ecologie et Liberté / Ecology and Liberty
FAD	Front des Algériens Démocrates / Front of Algerian Democrats
FAAD	Front pour l'Authenticité Algérienne Démocratique / Front for Algerian Democratic Authenticity
FDU	Front du Djihad pour l'Unité / Djihad ('*Holy war*') Front for Unity
FDUN	Front du Djihad pour l'Unité Nationale / Djihad ('*Holy war*') Front for National Unity
FFP	Front des Forces Populaires / Popular Forces' Front
FFS[b]	Front des Forces Socialistes / Socialist Forces' Front
FGI	Front des Générations de l'Indépendance / Independence Generations' Front
FIS	Front Islamique du Salut / Islamic Salvation Front
FLN	Front de Libération Nationale / National Liberation Front
FNB	Front National Boumédièniste / National Boumedienist Front
FNIB	Front National Islamique Boumédieniste / National Islamic Boumedienist Front
FSN	Front du Salut National / National Salvation Front
GD	Génération Démocratique / Democratic Generation
HEH [a]	*Hizb el-Haq*/ Parti du Droit / Party of Law
MA [a]	Mouvement Amel/ Amel ('*work*') Movement
MAJD	Mouvement Algérien pour la Justice et la Démocratie / Algerian Movement for Justice and Democracy
MDA[b]	Mouvement pour la Démocratie en Algérie / Movement for Democracy in Algeria
MDRA[b]	Mouvement Démocratique pour le Renouveau Algérien / Democratic Movement for an Algerian Renewal
MEN	Mouvement de l'Entente Nationale / Movement of the National Entente
MFAI	Mouvement des Forces Arabo-Islamiques / Movement of the Arab-Islamic Forces
MJD[b]	Mouvement de la Jeunesse Démocratique / Democratic Youth Movement
MNI	Mouvement de la Nahda Islamique / Islamic Nahda ('*renaissance/rebirth*') Movement

MN	Mouvement En-Nahda / Nahda (*'renaissance/rebirth'*) Movement
MNHFA	Mouvement National des Hommes et Femmes Algériens
MNJA	Mouvement National de la Jeunesse Algérienne / National Movement of Algerian Youth
MNND	Mouvement National pour la Nature et le Développement/ National Movement for Nature and Development
MPA	Mouvement du Peuple Algérien / Algerian People's Movement
MRI	Mouvement de la Risala Islamique / Movement for the Islamic Risala (*'mission'*)
MSA	Mouvement Social pour l'Authenticité / Social Movement for Authenticity
MSI-Hamas	Mouvement de la Société Islamique-'Hamas' / Islamic Society Movement-'Hamas' (*'religious enthusiasm'*)
MSP	Mouvement de la Société pour la Paix / Movement for a Peaceful Society
OFARIL	Organisation des Forces de l'Algérie Révolutionnaire Islamique Libre / Organization of the Forces of Free Revolutionary Islamic Algeria
PAHC	Parti Algérien pour l'Homme Capital / Algerian Party of the Essential Man
PAJP	Parti Algérien pour la Justice et le Progrès / Algerian Party for Justice and Progress
PI	Parti de l'Intégrité / Party of Integrity
PJS	Parti de la Justice Sociale / Social Justice Party
PLJ	Parti Libérateur Juste / Liberal Just Party
PNA	Parti National Algérien / Algerian National Party
PNDS	Parti National Démocratique Socialiste / Socialist National Democratic Party
PNSD	Parti National pour la Solidarité et le Développement / National Solidarity and Development Party
PPD	Parti Progressiste Démocrate / Democratic Progressive Party
PR[b]	Parti Républicain/ Republican Party
PRA	Parti du Renouveau Algérien / Party of Algerian Renewal
PRP	Parti Républicain Progressiste / Republican Progressive Party
PSD	Parti Social-Démocrate / Social Democratic Party
PSL	Parti Social Libéral / Liberal Social Party
PST[b]	Parti Socialiste des Travilleurs / Workers' Socialist Party
PT[b]	Parti des Travailleurs / Workers' Party
PUAID	Parti de l'Union Arabe Islamique Démocratique / Party of Democratic Islamic Arab Union
PUP	Parti de l'Unité Populaire / People's Unity Party
RA	Rassemblement Algérien / Algerian Rally
RABI	Rassemblement Algérien Boumédieniste et Islamique / Algerian Boumedien Islamic Rally
RAI	Rassemblement Arabo-Islamique / Arab-Islamic Rally

RCD	Rassemblement pour la Culture et la Démocratie / Rally for Culture and Democracy
RJNA	Rassemblement des Jeunes de la Nation Algérienne / Algerian Nation's Youth Rally
RNA	Rassemblement National Algérien / Algerian National Rally
RNC	Rassemblement National Constitutionnel / National Constitutional Rally
RND	Rassemblement National Démocratique / National Democratic Rally
RNP	Rassemblement National pour le Progrès / National Rally for Progress
RUN	Rassemblement pour l'Unité Nationale / Rally for National Unity
UDIA	Union Démocratique Islamique Arabe / Democratic Islamic Arab Union
UDL	Union pour la Démocratie et les Libertés / Union for Democracy and Freedom
UFD	Union des Forces Démocratiques / Union of Democratic Forces
UFP	Union des Forces pour le Progrès / Union of Forces for Progress
UPA	Union du Peuple Algérien / Union of the Algerian People

General note: After promulgation of Law No. 89-11 (5 July 1989) which stipulated the right of parties and political associations to work and organize freely in full respect of the 1989 constitution, some 60 parties applied for registration. With regard to the great variety of party names, which often scarcely differ from one another, we cannot exclude that certain parties have run for both multi-party elections with their name slightly modified each time or even between the polls. So one and the same political group may figure under two or even three different labels.

[a] The parties' acronyms given in Algerian official sources mostly follow the French spelling. Exceptions: AHD 54 ('Pledge' 54), HEH (*Hizb el-Haq* / Party of Law), ALP (Algerian Liberal Party) and MA (*Mouvement Amel*) are presented in official sources according to the Arabic/ English spelling; a presentation we have adopted for this listing as well.

[b] Some of the parties operated clandestinely before being legalized by the 'Party Act' of 1989. This concerns: FFS, founded on 3 September 1963 (secession from the FLN under 'historical leader' Hocine Ait Ahmed); the MDA was founded on 20 May 1984 by Ahmed Ben Bella in Paris; the MDRA was founded in the aftermath of the October 1988 riots and has a historical precursor (MDRA) in 1967–70; the MJD claims to have worked since 19 June 1965 (ousting of Ben Bella as President); PR represents the former *Parti Algérien du Peuple* (founded in 1990, organized since 24 May 1983) changed name in 1990; PST is successor to the *Trotzkist Groupement Communiste Révolutionnaire* (founded in 1974); PT: ex-OST/ *Organisation Socialiste des Travailleurs* (OST since October 1988), founded in 1979 as *Comité de Liaison des Trotzkistes*.

2.4 Electoral Participation of Parties and Alliances 1962–1997

Party / Alliance	Years	Elections contested Presidential	Parliamentary
FLN	1962, 1963, 1964, 1976, 1977, 1979, 1982, 1984, 1987, 1988, 1991, 1997	5	7[a]
AHD 54	1991	0	1
AJL	1991	0	1
ALP	1991, 1997	0	2
ANDI	1991, 1997	0	2
APUA	1991	0	1
ANR	1997	0	1
EL	1991	0	1
FAAD/ FAD [b]	1991, 1997	0	2
FDU/ FDUN [b]	1991, 1997	0	2
FFP	1991, 1997	0	2
FFS	1991, 1997	0	2
FGI	1991	0	1
FIS	1991	0	1
FSN	1991	0	1
GD	1991	0	1
HEH	1991	0	1
MAJD	1991, 1997	0	2
MDA	1991	0	1
MDRA	1991	0	1
MJD	1991, 1997	0	2
MNI/ MN [b]	1991, 1997	0	2
MRI	1991	0	1
MSA	1991, 1997	0	2
MSI/MSP [b]	1991, 1995, 1997	1	2
OFARIL	1991	0	1
PAHC	1991	0	1
PAJP	1991, 1997	0	2
PJS	1991, 1997	0	2
PNA	1991	0	1
PNSD	1991, 1997	0	2
PPD	1991	0	1
PR	1991, 1997	0	2
PRA	1991, 1995, 1997	1	2
PRP	1991, 1997	0	2
PSD	1991, 1997	0	2
PSL	1991, 1997	0	2
PST	1991, 1997	0	2
PUP	1991, 1997	0	2

[a] The number includes the participation in the elections for the Constitutional Assembly 1962.

Party / Alliance	Years	Elections contested	
		Presidential	Parliamentary
PUAID	1991	0	1
RABI	1991	0	1
RAI/ RA [b]	1991, 1997	0	2
RCD	1991, 1995, 1997	1	2
RJNA	1991	0	1
RNA	1991, 1997	0	2
RNP	1991	0	1
RUN	1991	0	1
UDL	1991, 1997	0	2
UFD	1991	0	1
UFP	1991	0	1
BN	1997	0	1
FNB	1997	0	1
MA	1997	0	1
MEN	1997	0	1
MNJA	1997	0	1
MNND	1997	0	1
MPA	1997	0	1
PLJ	1997	0	1
PNDS	1997	0	1
PT	1997	0	1
RNC	1997	0	1
RND	1997	0	1

[b] Some parties changed their names in March 1997 due to the modified Party Act prohibiting parties based exclusively on religious items/ regional characteristics. This concerns (in brackets the new acronym): *MSI-Hamas* (MSP), MNI (MN), FAAD (FAD), RAI (RA), FDU (FDUN).

2.5 Referendums 1962–1996

Year	1962[a] Total number	%	1963[b] Total number	%
Registered voters	6,549,736	–	6,391,818	–
Votes cast	6,017,680	91.9	5,287,229	82.7
Invalid votes	25,565	0.4	16,173	0.3
Valid votes	5,992,115	99.6	5,271,056	99.7
Yes	5,975,581	99.7	5,166,195	98.0
No	16,534	0.3	104,861	1.9

[a] Approval of 'Self-Determination' accorded in the Evian Treaties.
[b] Approval of the constitution elaborated by the Constitutional Assembly.

Year	1976 (27/06)[a] Total number	%	1976 (19/11)[b] Total number	%
Registered voters	7,940,978	–	8,076,834	–
Votes cast	7,290,671	91.8	7,504,696	92.9
Invalid votes	42,068	0.6	25,007	0.3
Valid votes	7,248,603	99.4	7,479,689	99.7
Yes	7,130,033	98.4	7,407,626	99.0
No	118,508	1.6	67,683	1.0

[a] Approval of the 'National Charter' 1976.
[b] Approval of the new Constitution of 1976.

Year	1986[a] Total number	%	1988 Total number	%
Registered voters	10,954,063	–	12,572,043	–
Votes cast	10,502,524	95.9	10,435,046	83.0
Invalid votes	74,102	0.7	312,940	3.0
Valid votes	10,689,926	99.3	10,122,106	97.0
Yes	10,508,863	98.3	9,341,429	92.3
No	181,063	1.7	780,677	7.7

[a] Approval of the 'enrichment' of the National Charter. For this referendum 'valid votes' in official sources do not include the valid votes cast abroad. The 10,689,926 valid votes comprise the 10,428,422 votes cast in Algeria and 261,504 abroad which the official source (*JORA)* displays separately. Accordingly the 10,508,863 Yes votes have to be split into 10,258,934 (Algeria) and 249,929 (abroad) votes, the No-votes into 169,488 (Algeria) and 11,575 (abroad).

Year	1989[a]		1996[b]	
	Total number	%	Total number	%
Registered voters	13,170,137	–	16,434,527	–
Votes cast	10,401,548	79.0	13,114,477	79.8
Invalid votes	473,110	4.6	359,363	2.7
Valid votes	9,928,438	95.5	12,755,114	97.3
Yes	7,290,760	73.4	10,945,321	85.8
No	2,637,678	26.6	1,809,793	14.2

[a] In the referendums of both 1988 and 1989 the electorate was asked to approve the major institutional modifications in the aftermath of the October 1988 riots which formally ended FLN-monopoly in Algerian polity, guaranteed fundamental democratic rights and allowed the emergence of a multi-party system. Yes: approbation of the constitutional amendments to the 1976 Constitution (03/11/1988) and the Constitution of 1989 (23/02/1989) respectively; No: rejection.
[b] Approval of the Constitution of 1996. Contrary to the overall tendency the only two regions voting by majority 'no' were the mainly Berber-populated *wilayat* of Béjaïa (70.5% 'no') and Tizi-Ouzou (64.4% 'no'), the participation rate (33.0% and 25.3% respectively) being additionally clearly inferior to the national average.

2.6 Elections for Constitutional Assembly[a]

1962	Votes		Seats	
	Total number	%	Total (196)	%
Registered voters	6,328,415	–		
Votes cast	5,302,294	83.8		
Invalid votes	16,290	0.3		
Valid votes	5,286,004	99.7		
FLN (Yes votes)[b]	5,267,324	99.7	196[c]	100
No votes[b]	18,680	0.4	–	–

[a] The elections to the Constitutional Assembly (20 September) were organized as a referendum on the attributions and the term of office of the assembly. Yes (FLN): approbation of the bill (Ordonnance No. 62-011), according to which the newly established assembly was to nominate a provisional government, to pass laws and to elaborate the Constitution and approval of the FLN-list for the Constitutional Assembly. No: rejection of the bill
[b] One party elections. The voters were presented a single list which they could approve or reject.
[c] Of the 196 seats 180 were reserved to Arab Algerians, 16 seats to Algerian citizens of European (French) origin.

2.7 Parliamentary Elections 1964–1997

Year	1964	
	Total number	%
Registered voters	6,091,991	–
Votes cast	5,177,631	85.0
Invalid votes	12,785	0.3
Valid votes	5,164,846	99.8
FLN (Yes votes)	4,493,416[a]	87.0[a]

[a] Sources indicate only the number of Yes votes. No information is available as to the qualification of the remaining votes.

Detailed data for the 1977, 1982 and 1987 elections are not available. Voting, however, meant automatically voting for a list established by the FLN. The data for registered voters and votes cast are reported in table 2.2.

Year	1991[a]		1997	
	Total number	%	Total number	%
Registered voters	13,258,554	–	16,767,309	–
Votes cast	7,822,625	59.0	10,999,139	65.6
Invalid votes	924,906	11.8	502,787	4.6
Valid votes	6,897,719	88.2	10,496,352	95.4
RND	—	—	3,533,434	33.7
FIS	3,260,222	47.3	—	—
MSI Hamas/ MSP [b]	368,697	5.4	1,553,154	14.8
FLN	1,612,947	23.4	1,497,285	14.3
MNI/ MN [b]	150,093	2.2	915,446	8.7
FFS	510,661	7.4	527,848	5.0
RCD	200,267	2.9	442,271	4.2
ANR	—	—	208,379	2.0
PT	—	—	194,493	1.9
MDA	135,882	2.0	—	—
PRA	67,828	1.0	197,262	1.9
MNJA	—	—	97,875	0.9
MEN	—	—	83,939	0.8
RA	—	—	79,554	0.8
PRP	4,872	0.0	65,371	0.6
MAJD	27,623	0.4	61,829	0.6
RNC	—	—	55,553	0.5
MJD	8,902	0.1	54,929	0.5
MA	—	—	53,621	0.5
UDL	9,298	0.1	51,090	0.5
PSL	9,272	0.1	36,374	0.4
Others	221,891[c]	3.2	327,412[d]	3.1
Independents	309,264	4.5	459,233	4.4

[a] Results of first round only. The second round was cancelled.

[b] Due to the new Party Act prohibiting any use of Islam for 'political purposes' a number of parties had to adapt their names: Thus the *Mouvement de la Nahda Islamique* (MNI) renamed itself *Mouvement Ennahda* (MN); the *Mouvement de la Société Islamique* (MSI-Hamas) was now called MSP (*Mouvement de la Société pour la Paix*).

[c] PNSD 48,208; PSD 28,638, MDRA 10,934; RAI 10,824, AJL 9,898, RABI 9,037, UFD 8,853, PUP 7,731, PUAID 7,283, ANDI 6,867, GD 6,726, FSN 6,575, APUA 6,455, PST 6,464, EL 5,558, UFP 4,184, FDU 3,899, FGI 3,860, PR 3,668, FAAD 3,600, ALP 2,934, PAHC 2,698, AHD 54 2,490, PPD 2,380,RNA 2,045, HEH 1,476, MSA 1,225, PAJP 1,222, PJS 1,186, FFP 1,067, RUN 933, OFARIL 930, RJNA 928, PNA 816, MRI 188, RNP 111.

[d] ALP, ANDI, BN; FAD, FDUN, FFP, FNB, MNND, MPA, MSA, PAJP, PJS, PLJ, PNDS, PNSD, PR, PSD, PST, PUP, RNA. Exact data are not available for these parties.

2.8 Composition of Parliament 1964–1997

Since the parliamentary elections until 1987 were single-party elections the FLN held always 100% of the seats (absolute numbers: 1964: 138, 1977: 261, 1982: 281, 1987: 295).

The multi-party elections of 1991 were nullified after the first round and the Parliament never took office. However, according to the results of the first round, 232 of a total of 430 seats would have to be distributed as follows: FIS: 188 (43.3%), FFS: 25 (5.8%), FLN: 16 (3.7%), Independents: 3 (0.7%).

On 18 March 1994 an interim Parliament was established for the transitional period with 200 members who were appointed according to the 'National Platform' (January 1994) for a three-year term (1994–1997) from 31 parties (MSI-Hamas, PRA [each 5 seats], ALP, ANDI, APUA, FDU, FFP, FGI, FNIB, FSN, HEH, MAJD, MFAI; MJD, MNHFA, MNND, MSA, PI, PNDS, PNSD, PPD, PSL, PUP, RAI, RJNA, RNA, RUN, UDIA, UDL, UFD, UPA [each 2 seats]), a number of civil society organizations (85 seats) and members of state organs (30 seats). 17 of the 200 seats which had been reserved for opposition groups remained vacant as these parties refused to participate in the government-led transition process.

Year	1997[a]	
	Seats	%
	380	100
RND	156	41.0
MSP	69	18.2
FLN	62	16.3
MN	34	8.9
FFS	20	5.3
RCD	19	5.0
PT	4	1.0
PRP	3	0.8
PSL	1	0.3
UDL	1	0.3
Independents	11	2.9

[a] Composition of Parliament after final correction by the *Conseil Constitutionnel*, cf. *El-Watan* (18/06/1997).

2.9 Presidential Elections 1963–1995

1963	Total number	%
Registered voters	6,581,340	–
Votes cast	5,850,133	88.9
Invalid votes	22,515	0.4
Valid votes	5,827,618	99.6
Ahmed Ben Bella (FLN)	5,805,103	99.6
No votes	22,515	0.4

1976	Total number	%
Registered voters	8,352,147	–
Votes cast	8,107,485	97.1
Invalid votes	87,663	1.1
Valid votes	8,019,822[a]	98.9
Houari Boumedienne (FLN)	7,976,568	99.5
No votes	43,242	0.5

[a] Official figure. Votes for Boumedienne and No votes add up to 8,019,810.

1979	Total number	%
Registered voters	7,888,875	–
Votes cast	7,809,438	99.0
Invalid votes	23,803	0.3
Valid votes	7,785,635[a]	99.7
Chadli Benjedid (FLN)	7,736,697	99.4
No votes	48,938	0.6

[a] The given number corresponds to the sum of Yes and No votes (authors calculation).

1984	Total number	%
Registered voters	10,154,715	–
Votes cast	9,776,952	96.28
Invalid votes	56,322	0.58
Valid votes	9,720,630[a]	99.42
Chadli Benjedid (FLN)	9,664,168	99.42
No votes	56,462	0.58

[a] The given number corresponds to the sum of Yes and No votes (authors calculation).

1988	Total number	%
Registered voters	13,060,720	–
Votes cast	11,634,139	89.08
Invalid votes	264,835	2.28
Valid votes	11,369,304	97.72
Chadli Benjedid (FLN)	10,603,067	93.26
No votes	766,237	6.74

1995	Total number	%
Registered voters	15,965,280	–
Votes cast	11,965,280	74.9
Invalid votes	345,748	2.9
Valid votes	11,619,532	97.1
Liamine Zéroual	7,088,618	61.0
Mahfoud Nahnah (MSI-Hamas)	2,971,974	25.6
Saïd Sadi (RCD)	1,115,796	9.6
Noureddine Boukrouh (PRA)	443,144	3.8

2.10 List of Power Holders 1962–1998

Head of State[a]	Years	Remarks
Ahmed Ben Bella	1962–1965	Elected by the Constitutional Assembly on 20 September 1962. Took office on 26 September 1962. Ousted from power as a consequence of a regime internal conflict between himself and Boumedienne.
Houari Boumedienne	1965–1978	Took office on 19 June 1965 after military coup.
Rabah Bitat	1978–1979	Interim President after Boumedienne's death (27 December 1978).
Chadli Bendjedid	1979–1992	Constitutionally elected President. Took power on 7 February 1979. Two times confirmed in the office. The army forced him to resign on 11 January 1992 in reaction to the first round of the parliamentary elections.
High Security Council/ High Comittee of State	1992–1994	Collegial executive, presided by Mohamed Boudiaf from 16 January 1992 until his assassination on 29 June 1992; by Ali Kafi from then on until 31 June 1994.
Liamine Zéroual	1994–	Appointed by the High Committee of State on 31 June 1994. Confirmed in the office in the elections of 1995.

[a] Until 1979 the President was single head of the executive.

Head of Government[a]	Years	Remarks
Mohamed Abdelghani	1979–1984	Took office on 08 March 1979
Abdelhamid Brahimi	1984–1988	Took office on 22 January 1984
Kasdi Merbah	1988–1989	Took office on 05 November 1988
Mouloud Hamrouche	1989–1991	Took office on 09 September 1989
Sid Ahmed Ghozali	1991–1992	Took office on 08 June 1991
Belaïd Abdessalam	1992–1993	Took office on 19 July 1992
Rédha Malek	1993–1994	Took office on 21 August 1993
Mokdad Sifi	1994–1995	Took office on 11 April 1994
Ahmed Ouyahia	1995–1998	Took office on 31 December 1995
Smaïl Hamdani	1998–	Took office on 14 December 1998

[a] The office of a 'chief of government' was created in 1979 under the Constitution of 1976. He remained in a weak position compared with the competencies of the President, who presides over the cabinet, 'incarnates the principle of national unity', is Commander-in-Chief of the armed forces, and defines the foreign policy. Since 1988 the Prime Minister has been responsible to the Parliament, but still invested by the President to whom he was responsible as well. The Constitution of 1997 confirmed this institutional model.

3. Bibliography

3.1 Official Sources

Journal Officiel de la République Algérienne (JORA), 1962 ff., various issues.
Journal Officiel de l'Etat Algérien (JOEA), 1962, various issues.
'Constitution of the People's Democratic Republic of Algeria' (10/09/1963).
'Constitution of the People's Democratic Republic of Algeria' (22/11/1976). Amended by Law No. 79-06 (07/07/1979). Amended by Décret No. 88-223 (5/11/1988).
'Constitution of the People's Democratic Republic of Algeria' (23/02/1989).
'Transitional Platform' (26/01/1994).
'Constitution of the People's Democratic Republic of Algeria' (28/11/1996).
Electoral Act: 'Ordonnance No. 62-010/1962 (16/07/1962)'. *JOEA*, 2: 14–15.
Electoral Act: 'Lois No. 63-305/ No. 63-306 (20/08/1963)'. *JORA*, 58: 826–828.
Electoral Act: 'Ordonnance No. 76-113 (29/12/1976)'. *JORA*, 3/1977: 26–29 (amended by 'Ordonnance No. 77-2 (30/01/1977)'. *JORA*, 11: 162.)
Electoral Act: 'Loi No. 80-08 (25/10/1980)'. *JORA*: 1144–1155.
Electoral Act: 'Loi No. 89-13 (07/08/1989)'. *JORA*, 32: 718–730 (amended by 'Loi No. 90-06 (27/03/1990)'. *JORA*, 13: 373–375; 'Loi No. 91-06 (02/04/1991)'. *JORA*, 1991: 390–393; 'Loi No. 91-07 (03/04/1991)'. *JORA*, 15: 396–438; 'Loi No. 91-17 (15/10/1991)'. *JORA*, 48: 1542–1547; 'Loi No. 91-18 (15/10/1991)'. *JORA*, 49: 1550–1587; 'Décret Exécutif No. 95-202 (29/07/1995)'. *JORA* 42: 6–7.
Electoral Act: 'Ordonnance No. 97-07'. *JORA*, 12: 3–22; 'Ordonnance No. 97-08'. *JORA* 12: 22–23 (design of constituencies and number of seats to be allocated); 'Décret Présidentiel No. 97-58' (06/03/1997). *JORA*, 12: 29–32; 'Décret Exécutif No. 97-423 (11/11/1997)'. *JORA* 75: 10–13 (precising the elections for the *Conseil de la Nation*).
Party Act: 'Loi No. 89-11 (05/07/1989)'. *JORA*, 27: 604–607.
Party Act: 'Ordonnance No. 97-09'. *JORA*, 12: 24–28.

3.2 Books and Articles

'Annuaire de l'Afrique du Nord'; Paris: Ed. du CNRS, published annually.
Aoued, A. (1987). *Constitutional Law of Algeria: Texts and Contents*. Glasgow: Royston.

Bachir, Y. C. (1990). 'Le multipartisme en Algérie. Une nouvelle donnée constitutionelle'. *African Journal of International and Comparative Law*, 2/3: 440–455.

Bendourou, O. (1989). 'La nouvelle constitution algérienne du 28 février 1989'. *Revue du droit public et de la science politique en France et à l'étranger*, 105/5: 1305–1328.

Benheddi, Z. (1990). 'Les élections de 1990 en Algérie et la victoire du Front islamique de Salut'. *Hérodote*, 58-59: 104–110.

Biegel, R. (1996). 'Die algerischen Präsidentschaftswahlen vom 16. November 1995'. *Orient*, 37/2: 265–279.

— (1997). 'Die algerischen Parlamentswahlen vom 5. Juni 1997. Die demokratische Erneuerung bleibt auf der Strecke'. *KAS-Auslandsinformationen*, 13/8: 26–45.

Bitar, M.-C. (1990). 'Les lendemains d'un scrutin'. *Les Cahiers de l'Orient*, 2: 1–12.

Brule, J. C., and Fontaine, J. (1997). 'Géographie de l'islamisme politique en Algérie. Essai d'interprétation à partir des élections de 1990 et 1991'. *Bulletin de l'Association des Géographes Français*, 74 (Espaces du monde arabe): 83–96

Cherrad, S.-E. (1992). *Elections municipales et législatives en Algérie: les scrutins du 12 juin 1990 et du 26 décembre 1991*. Montpellier: Université Paul Valéry.

Djeghloul, A. (1990). 'Le multipartisme à l'algérienne'. *Monde Arabe. Maghreb-Machrek*, 127: 194–210.

Djerbal, D. (1997). 'Les élections législatives du 5 juin en Algérie. Enjeux politiques, logiques et acteurs'. *Monde Arabe. Maghreb-Machrek*, 157: 149–161.

Entelis, J. P. (1992). *State and Society in Algeria*. Boulder, Col.: Westview Press.

— (1996). 'Civil Society and the Authoritarian Temptation in Algerian Politics: Islamic Democracy vs. the Centralized State', in A. R. Norton (ed.), *Civil Society in the Middle East*. Vol. II. Leiden/ New York/ Köln: E. J. Brill, 45–86.

Faath, S. (1990): *Algerien. Gesellschaftliche Strukturen und politische Reformen zu Beginn der neunziger Jahre*. Hamburg: Deutsches Orient-Institut.

Fontaine, J. (1990). 'Les élections locales algériennes du 12 juin 1990. Approche statistique et géographique'. *Monde Arabe. Maghreb-Machrek*, 129: 124–140.

— (1992a). 'Les élections législatives algériennes. Résultats du premier tour (26 décembre 1991)' *Monde Arabe. Maghreb-Machrek*, 135: 155–165.

— (1992b): 'Quartiers défavorisés et vote islamiste à Alger'. *Revue du monde musulman et de la Méditerranée*, 65: 141–164.

— (1996). 'Algérie: Les résultats de l'élection présidentielle. 16 novembre 1995'. *Monde Arabe. Maghreb-Machrek*, 151: 107–118.

— (1997). 'Algérie: Les élections législatives du 5 juin 1997 en Algérie. Résultats et évolution des forces politiques'. *Monde Arabe. Maghreb-Machrek*, 157: 161–180.

Gourdon, H. (1977). 'Citoyen, travailleur, frère: la deuxième constitutionnalisation du système politique algérien'. *Annuaire de l'Afrique du Nord 1976*, 99–121.

— (1997). 'La Constitution algérienne du 28 novembre 1996'. *Monde Arabe. Maghreb-Machrek*, 156: 36–48.

Kapil, A. (1990): 'Algeria's Elections show Islamist Strength'. *Middle East Report*, 20: 31–36.

— (1991). 'Portrait statistique des élections du 12 juin 1990. Chiffres-clés pour une analyse'. *Les Cahiers de l'Orient*, 3: 41–63.

— (1994). 'Algeria', in F. Tachau (ed.), *Political Parties of the Middle East and North Africa*. London: Mansell, 1–68.

Lajoie, J.-L. (1989). 'La troisième constitution algérienne. L'abandon de la référence socialiste, ou le citoyen contre le militant-travilleur'. *Revue du droit public et de la science politique en France et à l'étranger*, 105/5: 1329–1350.

Leca, J., and Vatin, J. C. (1977). 'Le système politique algérien'. *Annuaire de l'Afrique du Nord 1976*, 15–80.

Purtschet, C., and Valentino, A. (1966). *Sociologie électorale en Afrique du Nord*. Paris: Presses Universitaires de France.

Rulleau, C. (1989). 'La nouvelle constitution algérienne une volte-face complète'. *Les Cahiers de l'Orient*, 14: 157–169.

Salah Bey, Anisse (1964). 'L'Assemblée nationale constituante algérienne'. *Annuarie de l'Afrique du Nord 1962*: 115–125.

Seddon, D. (1990). 'Elections in Algeria'. *Review of African Political Economy*, 1990: 70–73.

Sutton, K. (1992). 'Political Changes in Algeria. An Emerging Electoral Geography'. *The Maghreb Review*, 17/1-2: 3–27.

— and Aghrout, A. (1992). 'Multi-Party Elections in Algeria: Problems and Prospects'. *Bulletin of Francophone Africa*, 2: 61–85.

Tahar, T. (1990). 'Le pluralisme dans la Constitution Algérienne du 23 février 1989 à travers le pouvoir exécutif'. *African Journal of International and Comparative Law*, 2/3: 298–313.

Yousfi, M. (1991). 'Modes de scrutin, loi et stratégies électorales'. *Revue algérienne des sciences juridiques, économiques et politiques* (Alger), 29/4: 769–790.

Zartman, W., and Habeeb, W. M. (eds.) (1993). *Polity and Society in Contemporary North Africa*. Boulder, Col.: Westview Press.

ANGOLA

by Ana Catarina Clemente-Kersten

1. Introduction

1.1 Historical Overview

Angola became independent on 11 November 1975 after 14 years of armed and unarmed resistance to Portuguese colonial rule. The three major independence movements (MPLA—*Movimento Popular de Libertação de Angola*; the regionally based FLNA—*Frente Nacional de Libertação de Angola* and the mainly Ovimbundu UNITA—*União Nacional da Independência Total de Angola*) signed the Alvor Agreement on the transition and independence of Angola with Portugal in January 1975. The independence day was set to be the 11 November 1975 and a provisory coalition government with the three independence movements would be empowered. Due to political divergence the accord broke down in February and a civil war started between the MPLA supported by Cuba and the Soviet Union, and the UNITA supported by South Africa and the USA. The 11 November 1975 MPLA took over power and declared the independence of the People's Republic of Angola, institutionalizing a Marxist–Leninist one-party system with Agostinho Neto as Head of State. José Eduardo dos Santos succeeded President Neto and during the following 13 years the war continued between UNITA and MPLA; in the north the *Frente de Libertação do Enclave de Cabinda* (FLEC) fought for the independence of the oil-rich Cabinda enclave. In 1985 the American congress repealed the Clark amendment from 1975 thus legalizing US-military help to the UNITA.

As part of the Namibian peace accords with South Africa, Angola and Cuba signed the Tripartite Agreement on 22 December 1988. This included the withdrawal of Cuban troops from Angola and the establishment of the UN Angola Verification Mission (UNAVEM I) to supervise the procedure. Negotiations with representatives of the Angolan government and the UNITA began in April 1990 in Portugal. After 12 months the Bicesse Accords were signed on the 30 May 1991 in Lisbon by President dos Santos and UNITA leader Jonas Savimbi. The treaty included a cease-fire agreement and the implantation of a multi-party system with monitored elections, putting an end to 16 years of civil war. The MPLA mandate extended only up to the elections and for a period of 18 months. A Joint Commission (*Comissão Conjunta Político-Militar*, CCPM) composed of the United Nations, the government, UNITA, and three observer nations (Portugal, Russia and the USA) was created to organize the elections and the UN established the UNAVEM II, to monitor the cease-fire, the confinement of troops to assembly areas, their eventual demobilization and to observe the electoral process. A National Council of the Opposition was built by 13 opposition parties in October 1991 to be heard in matters of electoral legislation, which led to the removal of institutional barriers to the registration of new parties. It was extremely difficult to propagate a consolidated party program in the few months remaining, nevertheless 18 parties ran for Parliament and 11 candidates for President. The elections of 1992 were held peacefully and orderly, which demonstrated an enormous will of the population for the maintenance of peace. Both parliamentary and presidential elections gave the MPLA the majority and confirmed the regional party division (UNITA in the south, MPLA in the north, FNLA in Uige and Zaire-province, and PRS in Lunda Norte and Lunda Sul). UNITA and seven further parties refused to accept the electoral results and called for new elections. The UN mission, however, declared the election fair and free and set the second round of the presidential elections to take place within the legal time, as no candidate gained absolute majority. UNITA generals left the Unified Command of the Armed Forces and thus broke the peace agreement. The run-off presidential election was never accomplished since UNITA left the political scene and started a devastating war soon occupying large parts of the territory. The new multi-party Parliament started without the UNITA deputies and the peace talks arranged by the UN in Addis Abeba 1993 were interrupted and then constantly postponed by the UNITA.

A cease-fire was finally established with the Lusaka Protocol signed on the 20 November 1994 between UNITA and MPLA. It comprehended a Government of National Unity and Reconciliation (GURN) with the inclusion of UNITA nominees in the Cabinet and a special status for Savimbi. But key issues such as the extension of state administration throughout the country, freedom of movement, future policies of the GURN and the control of the diamond region delayed the peace process. After having categorically rejected the office of Vice-President offered by the MPLA in August 1996, Savimbi later demanded the position of principal adviser to the President along with supervisory power over several ministries. After various postponements and an official visit of UN Secretary-General Kofi Annan to Angola in March 1997, the Joint Commission agreed on giving Savimbi the status of leader of the opposition and special privileges, including access to the Cabinet. In April, 70 UNITA deputies took their seats in the National Assembly and the GURN finally took place on 11 April 1997. UNITA had four of 29 ministers and seven of 58 vice-ministers as well as numerous provincial government officials. The composition and the program of the GURN were not determined by the results of the elections held in 1992, but by the economic and military power of the two main opponents Savimbi and dos Santos backed up by major economic (oil and diamonds) international interests in the region.

The solution of problems such as demobilization, administration throughout the country and restructuring the economy depended on the will of the parties to cooperate and respect the accords made. The failure to do so, and the missing spirit of conciliation and national unity at the level of central government thus led to the outbreak of new hostilities in Angola since late 1998.

1.2 Evolution of Electoral Provisions

The principles of universal, equal, direct and secret suffrage were applied for the first elections held since independence in 1992. Every Angolan citizen of 18 years or over was eligible for voter registration.

1.3 Current Electoral Provisions

Sources: Constitution of the Republic of Angola, 1992; Lei Eleitoral No.5/92.

Elected national institutions: President of the Republic, National Assembly with 223 elected members. (The number of elected deputies was reduced to 220 for the 1992 elections due to organizational difficulties collecting the suffrages of Angolan communities abroad.) Regular term of office: five and four years respectively. Vacant seats are filled according to the order of preference appearing on the respective party list. The President shall not be re-elected for three consecutive terms of office.

Suffrage: The principles of universal, equal, direct and secret suffrage were applied. Every Angolan citizen 18 years of age and older, whether resident in Angola or abroad, is entitled to register as a voter.

Nomination of candidates
- *presidential elections*: Eligible for candidature as President of the Republic are native Angolan citizens over 35 years of age enjoying full civil and political rights and having resided in Angola for the six months previous to the date of the election. The candidates must be presented by the legally constituted political parties or coalitions of parties or by a minimum of 5,000 registered voters.
- *parliamentary elections:* Angolan citizens of 18 years and over in full enjoyment of their civil and political rights are eligible for candidature as deputy to the Parliament. Citizens who have acquired Angolan nationality are eligible seven years after the acquisition.

Electoral system
- *presidential elections*: Absolute majority system. If no candidate obtains more than 50% of the valid votes a run-off election will take place within a period of 30 days after the publication of the results of the first scrutiny.
- *parliamentary elections*: Proportional representation system: *223 member Parliament (reduced to 220 in 1992) composed of 130 deputies elected at national level from one national constituency and 90 deputies from Angola's 18 provincial constituencies on the basis of five deputies per province. Three deputies are to be chosen from one constituency for the Angolan communities abroad (two deputies for the African region and one for the rest of the world). *Closed party lists; *single vote; *in the multi-member constituencies at the provincial level the d'Hondt method is applied, at national level the Hare quota is used; remaining seats are distributed on the basis of the largest remainder.

1.4 Comment on the Electoral Statistics

The official statistics from 1992 are complete and reveal the importance of obtaining and processing accurate electoral data. The absolute figures are taken from official documents (see 3.1). The percentages were calculated by the author. The major difficulty resides in obtaining accurate population data. The census of 1992 is not complete due to the civil war situation.

2. Tables

2.1 Dates of National Elections, Referendums and Coups d'Etat

Year	Presidential elections	Parliamentary elections	Elections for Constitutional Assembly	Referendums	Coups d'état
1992	29–30/09	29–30/09			

2.2 Electoral Body 1992

Year	Type of election[a]	Population	Registered voters		Votes cast		
			Total number	% pop.	Total number	% reg. voters	% pop.
1992	Pr	10,000,000[b]	4,828,468	48.3	4,401,339	91.2	44.0
1992	Pa	10,000,000[b]	4,828,468	48.3	4,410,575	91.3	44.1

[a] Pa = Parliament (National People's Assembly); Pr = President.
[b] UN estimation.

2.3 Abbreviations

AD-Coligação[a]	Angola Democrática
CNDA	Convenção Nacional Democrática de Angola
FDA	Forum Democrático Angolano
FLEC	Frente de Libertação da Enclave de Cabinda
FNLA	Frente Nacional de Libertação de Angola
FpD	Frente para a Democracia
MDIA-PCN	Movimento de Defesa dos Interesses dos Angolanos - Partido de Consciência Nacional
MPLA[b]	Movimento Popular de Libertação de Angola
PAI	Partido Angolano Independente
PAJOCA	Partido da Aliança Juventude Operária e Camponesa de Angola
PAL	Partido Liberal Angolano
PDA	Partido Democrático Angolano
PDLA	Partido Democrático Liberal de Angola
PDPA	Partido Democrático Pacífico de Angola
PDP-ANA	Partido Democrático para o Progresso de Aliança Nacional Angolana

PLD	Partido Liberal Democrático
PNDA	Partido Nacional Democrático de Angola
PNEA	Partido Nacional Ecologista de Angola
PRA	Partido Reformador Angolano
PRD	Partido Renovador Democrático
PRS	Partido de Renovação Social
PSD	Partido Social Democrático
PSDA	Partido Social Democrático Angolano
UDA	Partido de Unificação Democrática de Angola
UNITA	União Nacional da Independência Total de Angola

[a] The coalition was formed by FpD, MDIA-PCN, PDPA, UDA, PAL and PNEA. The PDPA left the coalition in November 1992.

[b] From 1977 to 1991 the official designation was MPLA-PT Partido do Trabalhador.

2.4 Electoral Participation of Parties and Alliances 1992

Party / Alliance	Year	Elections contested	
		Presidential	Parliamentary
AD-Coligação[a]	1992	1	1
CNDA	1992	0	1
FDA	1992	0	1
FNLA	1992	1	1
MPLA	1992	1	1
PAI	1992	0	1
PAJOCA	1992	0	1
PDA	1992	1	1
PDLA	1992	1	1
PDP-ANA	1992	0	1
PLD	1992	1	1
PNDA	1992	1	1
PRA	1992	1	1
PRD	1992	1	1
PRS	1992	0	1
PSD	1992	1	1
PSDA	1992	0	1
UNITA	1992	1	1

[a] The coalition was formed by FpD, MDIA-PCN, PDPA, UDA, PAL and PNEA. The PDPA left the coalition in November 1992.

2.5 Referendums

Referendums have not been held.

2.6 Elections for Constitutional Assembly

Elections for Constitutional Assembly have not been held.

2.7 Parliamentary Election 1992

1992	Total number	%
Registered voters	4,828,468	–
Votes cast	4,410,575	91.3
Invalid votes	458,310	10.4
Valid votes	3,952,265	89.6
MPLA	2,124,126	53.7
UNITA	1,347,636	34.1
FNLA	94,742	2.4
PLD	94,269	2.4
PRS	89,875	2.3
PRD	35,293	0.9
AD Coligação	34,166	0.9
PSD	33,088	0.8
PAJOCA	13,924	0.4
FDA	12,038	0.3
PDP-ANA	10,608	0.3
PNDA	10,281	0.3
CNDA	10,237	0.3
PSDA	10,217	0.3
PAI	9,007	0.2
PDLA	8,025	0.2
PDA	8,014	0.2
PRA	6,719	0.2

2.7 a) Parliamentary Elections 1992, Regional Distribution of Votes

1992 (absolute numbers)							
	MPLA	UNITA	FNLA	PLD	PRS	Others[a]	Total
Cabinda	7,448	1,544	209	28	58	308	9,595
Zaire	20,240	16,353	20,053	1,131	548	5,597	63,922
Uige	136,167	79,277	13,292	8,645	6,039	19,054	262,474
Luanda	531,294	140,959	30,883	4,328	5,188	39,213	751,865
K. Norte	102,213	6,658	2,929	748	900	5,045	118,493
K. Sul	220,086	61,099	2,983	5,303	3,363	13,264	306,098
Malange	185,935	26,201	2,783	5,130	4,127	14,071	238,247
Lunda N.	77,694	8,844	2,274	1,246	18,673	9,847	118,578
Benguela	181,730	260,655	3,100	15,869	5,433	19,664	486,451
Huambo	61,146	289,283	1,361	20,722	4,593	17,002	394,107
Bié	36,598	204,930	839	12,790	2,572	8,531	266,260
Moxico	66,344	27,290	1,931	3,264	6,264	8,344	113,437
K. Kubango	26,693	87,808	533	2,616	1,214	3,871	122,735
Namibe	42,458	15,374	759	1,314	656	3,139	63,700
Huila	245,952	100,219	3,698	8,987	5,437	21,632	385,925
Cuneme	90,233	4,714	1,006	712	1,473	4,820	102,958
Lunda S.	37,309	2,681	995	541	22,811	4,998	69,335
Bengo	54,586	13,747	5,114	895	526	3,217	78,085
Total	2,124,126	1,347,636	94,742	94,269	89,875	201,617	3,952,265

[a] PRD, PAJOCA, PAI, PDLA, PSDA, PDP-ANA, PRA, CNDA, PNDA, PDA, FDA, PSD, AD-Coligação.

1992 (percentages)	MPLA	UNITA	FNLA	PLD	PRS	Others	Total[a]
Cabinda	77.6	16.1	2.2	0.3	0.6	3.2	100
Zaire	31.6	25.6	31.3	1.8	0.9	8.7	100
Uige	51.9	30.2	5.1	3.3	2.3	7.3	100
Luanda	70.7	18.7	4.1	0.6	0.7	5.2	100
K. Norte	86.3	5.6	2.5	0.6	0.8	4.3	100
K. Sul	71.9	19.9	1.0	1.7	1.1	4.3	100
Malange	78.0	11.0	1.2	2.2	1.7	5.9	100
Lunda N.	65.5	7.5	1.9	1.1	15.7	8.3	100
Benguela	37.4	53.6	0.6	3.3	1.1	4.0	100
Huambo	15.5	73.4	0.3	5.3	1.2	4.3	100
Bié	13.7	77.0	0.3	4.8	1.0	3.2	100
Moxico	58.5	24.1	1.7	2.9	5.5	7.4	100
K. Kubango	21.7	71.5	0.4	2.1	1.0	3.2	100
Namibe	66.7	24.1	1.2	2.1	1.0	4.9	100
Huila	63.7	26.0	1.0	2.3	1.4	5.6	100
Cuneme	87.6	4.6	1.0	0.7	1.4	4.7	100
Lunda S.	53.8	3.9	1.4	0.8	32.9	7.2	100
Bengo	69.9	17.6	6.5	1.1	0.7	4.1	100
Total	53.7	34.1	2.4	2.4	2.3	5.1	100

[a] Due to rounding the added total of the percentages is not always 100.

2.8 Composition of Parliament 1992

1992	Seats	%
	220	100
MPLA	129	58.6
UNITA	70	31.8
PRS	6	2.7
FNLA	5	2.2
PLD	3	1.4
PRD	1	0.5
AD-Coligação	1	0.5
PSD	1	0.5
PAJOCA	1	0.5
FDA	1	0.5
PNDA	1	0.5
PDP-ANA	1	0.5

2.9 Presidential Election 1992[a]

1992	Total number	%
Registered voters	4,828,468	–
Votes cast	4,401,339	91.2
Invalid votes	460,455	10.5
Valid votes	3,940,884	89.5
José Eduardo dos Santos (MPLA)	1,953,335	49.6
Jonas Malheiro Savimbi (UNITA)	1,579,298	40.1
Alberto Neto (PDA)	85,249	2.2
Roberto Holden (FNLA)	83,135	2.1
Honorato N'Lando (PDLA)	75,789	1.9
Luís dos Passos (PRD)	58,121	1.5
Pedro João Bengui (PSD)	38,243	1.0
Simão Cacete (AD-Coligação)	26,385	0.7
Daniel Júlio Chipenda (PNDA)	20,646	0.5
Anália de Victória Pereira (PLD)	11,475	0.3
Rui de Victória Pereira (PRA)	9,208	0.2

[a] Only first round held.

2.9 a) Presidential Elections 1992: Regional Results

1992 (absolute numbers)						
	Santos	Savimbi	Neto	Holden	Others	Total
Cabinda	7,652	1,594	54	116	187	9,603
Zaire	19,260	18,226	696	23,299	4,007	65,488
Uige	116,247	100,414	10,390	13,455	26,663	267,169
Luanda	532,568	171,743	4,942	22,697	19,682	751,632
K. Norte	92,671	9,690	2,461	2,519	6,368	113,709
K. Sul	188,089	74,381	9,739	1,677	21,652	295,538
Malange	163,303	41,650	6,553	1,934	21,654	235,094
Lunda N.	86,203	12,879	5,143	1,275	11,707	117,207
Benguela	158,259	294,972	8,753	2,841	28,537	493,362
Huambo	57,380	326,551	1,808	736	14,644	401,119
Bié	32,907	230,480	1,505	417	9,268	274,577
Moxico	60,359	34,209	5,743	1,271	12,013	113,595
K. Kubango	22,117	93,078	1,742	442	4,646	122,025
Namibe	36,540	18,197	1,543	551	4,858	61,689
Huila	199,089	121,656	14,574	3,032	36,305	374,656
Cuneme	76,374	8,731	5,454	680	7,057	98,296
Lunda S.	53,313	4,617	2,919	696	7,124	68,669
Bengo	51,004	16,230	1,230	5,497	3,495	77,456
Total	1,953,335	1,579,298	85,249	83,135	239,867	3,940,884

1992 (percentages)	Santos	Savimbi	Neto	Holden	Others	Total[a]
Cabinda	79.7	16.6	0.6	1.2	1.9	100
Zaire	29.4	27.8	1.1	35.6	6.1	100
Uige	43.5	37.6	3.9	5.0	10.0	100
Luanda	70.9	22.8	0.7	3.0	2.6	100
K. Norte	81.5	8.5	2.2	2.2	5.6	100
K. Sul	63.6	25.2	3.3	0.6	7.3	100
Malange	69.5	17.7	2.8	0.8	9.2	100
Lunda N.	73.5	11.0	4.4	1.1	10.0	100
Benguela	32.1	59.8	1.8	0.6	5.8	100
Huambo	14.3	81.4	0.5	0.2	3.7	100
Bié	12.0	84.0	0.5	0.2	3.4	100
Moxico	53.1	30.1	5.1	1.1	10.6	100
K. Kubango	18.1	76.3	1.4	0.4	3.8	100
Namibe	59.2	29.5	2.5	0.9	7.9	100
Huila	53.1	32.5	3.9	0.8	9.7	100
Cuneme	77.7	8.9	5.5	0.7	7.2	100
Lunda S.	77.6	6.7	4.3	1.0	10.4	100
Bengo	65.8	21.0	1.6	7.1	4.5	100
Total	49.6	40.1	2.2	2.1	6.1	100

[a] Due to rounding the added total of the percentages is not always 100.

2.10 List of Power Holders 1975–1998

Head of State	Years	Remarks
Agostinho Neto	1975–1979	Neto declared the independence of the People's Republic of Angola and became President as head of the MPLA on 11 November 1975. Simultaneously Holden Roberto (FNLA) and Jonas Savimbi (UNITA) declared the independence of the Democratic People's Republic of Angola. Neto died on 10 September 1979.
José Eduardo dos Santos	1979–	The Central Committee of the MPLA-PT elected dos Santos as successor to Agostinho on 21 September 1979. In 1992 dos Santos was democratically elected President, but the second round of the election did not take place due to the civil war situation.

Head of Government	Years	Remarks
Lopo do Nascimento	1975–1978	Appointed by the President on 14 November 1975. The office of the Prime Minister was eliminated in December 1978 after a major re-structuring of the party and its new orientation as a Marxist-Leninist Party.
Fernando França Van-Dunem	1991–1992	Appointed by the President on 20 July 1991. The office of the Prime Minister was created following the change towards a multi-party system in 1991.
Marcolino José Carlos Moco	1992–1997	Appointed by the President on 27 November after the elections.
Fernando França Van-Dunem	1997–	Appointed by the President on 11 April 1997. The GURN was officially empowered after the Lusaka Protocol.

3. Bibliography

3.1 Official Sources

Constituição da República de Angola, 1992.

Lei Eleitoral. No.5/92.

Security Council Resolution 1106 (1997) on Angola'.

3.2 Books, Articles and Electoral Reports

Aguirree, M. (1993). 'Construire la paix civile, de l'Angola au Cambodge. Douteux paris sur les 'combattants de la liberté''. *Le Monde diplomatique*, May, 21.

Anstee, M. J. (1993). 'Angola. The Forgotten Tragedy'. *International Relations*, 9/6: 495–511.

— (1996). *Orphan of the Cold War. The Inside Story of the Collapse of the Angolan Peace Process, 1992–93*. Basingstoke: Macmillan.

Bacelar, R. (1991). 'Les appuis de l'UNITA'. *Le Monde diplomatique*, June, 12.

Beaudet, P. (1991). 'Espoirs de paix a Luanda, extreme tension en Afrique du Sud, L'Angola au hasard de la réconciliation'. *Le Monde diplomatique*, June, 12.

Becker, J. (1988). *Angola, Mosambik und Zimbabwe. Im Visier Südafrikas*. Köln: Pahl-Rugenstein.

Birmingham, D. (1992). *Frontline Nationalism in Angola and Mozambique.* London: James Currey

Bornholdt, L. (1991). 'Politische und gesellschaftliche Kräfte in Angola'. *KAS-Auslandsinformationen*, 6: 32–36.

Brittain, V. (1992). 'Une réconciliation imposée par les puissances extérieures, Fragile transition démocratique en Angola'. *Le Monde diplomatique*, May, 23.

— (1993). 'When Democracy is Not Enough: Denying Angola's Electoral Result'. *Southern Africa Report*, 8/3-4: 41–46.

— (1995). 'Comment reconstruire l'état et la société? Les défis de l'après-guerre en Angola'. *Le Monde diplomatique*, October, 21.

— and Watkins, K. (1994). 'La souveraineté menacée des états de l'Afrique australe. Impossible réconciliation en Angola et au Mozambique'. *Le Monde diplomatique*, February, 26.

Diederichsen, T. (1993). *Angola - oder wie man mit Wahlen einen Krieg verlieren kann*. Hamburg: Institut für Afrika-Kunde.

Eduardo Modlale Foundation, Holland Commitee on Southern Africa, and Africa Studies Centre (1992). *Democratization in Angola*. Seminar, Leiden (Netherlands), 18 September, Amsterdam/ Leiden.

James, W. M. (1992). *A Political History of the Civil War in Angola 1974–1990*. New Brunswick: Transaction Publ.

Maier, K. (1996). *Angola: Promises and Lies.* London: Serif.

Meyns, P. (1992). 'Vom antikolonialen Befreiungskampf zu externer Destabilisierung und internem Bürgerkrieg', in R. Hofmeier and V. Matthies (eds.), *Vergessene Kriege in Afrika*. Göttingen: Lamuv, 61–96.

Minter, W. (1994). *Apartheid's Contras. An Inquiry into the Roots of War in Angola and Mozambique.* Johannesburg: Witwatersrand University Press.

Morel, E. *et al*. (1997). *Angola*. Paris: Montechrestin.

Pereira, A. W. (1994). 'The Neglected Tragedy: the Return to War in Angola, 1992–3'. *The Journal of Modern African Studies*, 32/1: 1–28.

Pössinger, H. (1992). 'Angola—ein Neuanfang?', in P. Meyns (ed.), *Demokratie und Strukturreformen im portugiesichsprachigen Afrika*. Freiburg: Arnold Bergstraesser Institut, 97–117.

Tvedten, I. (1992). 'US Policy Towards Angola Since 1975'. Journal of Modern African Studies, 30/1: 31–52.

— (1993). 'The Angolan Debacle'. *Journal of Democracy*, 4/2: 108–118.

— (1997). Angola: Struggle for Peace and Reconstruction. Boulder, Col.: Westview Press.

United Nations (1995). *The United Nations and the Situation in Angola, May 1991–February 1995.* New York: United National Department of Public Information.

Venâncio, M. (1994). *The United Nations, Peace and Transition. Lessons from Angola*. Lisbon: IEEI.

Vines, A. (1995). *Angola and Mozambique: The Aftermath of Conflict*. London: Research Institute for the Study of Conflict and Terrorism.

Witzel, R., and Wagner, I. (1978). 'Angola', in D. Sternberger, B. Vogel, D. Nohlen and K. Landfried (eds.), *Die Wahl der Parlamente und anderer Staatsorgane. Band II: Politische Organisation und Repräsentation in Afrika,* by Franz Nuscheler, Klaus Ziemer *et al.*, Berlin/ New York: Walter de Gruyter, 461–490.

Wright, G. (1997). *The Destruction of a Nation: United State's Policy Towards Angola since 1945*. London: Pluto Press.

BENIN

by Christof Hartmann

1. Introduction

1.1 Historical Overview

Since independence, Benin, then called Dahomey, has gone through numerous regime changes. Between 1960 and 1972 the Heads of State changed 10 times, but rarely according to constitutional procedures, and six times as a result of military coups. However, only the takeover of Mathieu Kérékou's military regime in 1972 led to a real change of power through the installation of a Marxist–Leninist military-dominated one-party system. In the context of the virtual economic and political collapse of this regime, a coalition of civil society forces and exiled politicians used a national conference in February 1990 to stage a 'democratic' *coup de force* and to set up a transitional government. Presidential and legislative elections in 1991 inaugurated this second democratic experiment.

The beginning of electoral politics after World War II did not imply—in contrast to the majority of French colonies—the assertion of one dominant political leader. The country was rather divided into three spheres of influence (largely corresponding to the traditional royalties). Three political leaders, Hubert Maga, Magan Apithy and Justin Ahomadegbe had formed political parties in the 1950s and managed to monopolize the political decision-making process in their regions. When Dahomey gained an autonomous status as a part of the *Communauté Française* after a referendum in September 1958, this tripartite basic structure had thus already emerged. However, the leaders proved unable to build a stable interregional coalition at the national level where persistent competition between the three political forces (not diverging political or ideological agendas) led to the permanent exclusion of one party and institutional deadlock. Until 1972, virtually every possible alliance and every possible institutional design (regime type, party system, electoral system) had been tried and found wanting.

The parliamentary system of the *Communauté*-inherited Independence Constitution survived only a few months before being replaced by a strong presidential system which still allowed multi-party competition but *de facto* suppressed it. By virtue of an electoral system which attributed all seats to the winning list, the presidential and parliamentary elections in 1960 and 1964 resulted in a one-party Parliament with the party's candidate as elected President. The military's bid to organize presidential elections in 1968 and 1970 failed because of extremely low participation rates and internal troubles, leading to military assignments of civil Presidents or civil-military pacts like the Triumvirate of 1970, where the three leaders agreed on a division of power and a rota system. The planned multi-party parliamentary elections in 1968 and 1970 did not take place, and the new constitution, which was ratified by a referendum in 1968, was suspended after the annulled presidential elections. Only in the five years until 1965 did the political parties gain some influence but even then they relied on the insurmountable ethnic-regional blocs. The only change in Dahomey's tripartite party system consisted in the changing nomenclature. Attempts to create a viable one-party system failed just like political projects on a non-tribal and non-regional basis in the face of the clientelist pressure from the three powerful regional networks.

The military's intervention which was initially justified by internal strife and political instability marked the end of constitutional government which had lost its significance anyway. In the end, neither the army nor the great bulk of the population saw any alternative to a full and permanent assumption of power by the armed forces. The astonishing consolidation of the military regime of Mathieu Kérékou from 1972 onwards is to be explained by the removal of the previous political class and a radically changed international context which improved the economic situation in the country. Instead of holding elections which would have buttressed the ethnic-regional networks, the military government chose the Marxist–Leninist option to secure internal and external legitimacy. By 1975 the country was ruled by a socialist one-party system and was given a new name, People's Republic of Benin. The military-controlled government elaborated a new socialist constitution in 1977 and organized parliamentary elections for the *Assemblée nationale révolutionnaire* (ANR) every five years from 1979 onwards. The party list of the *Parti de la Révolution Populaire du Bénin* (PRPB) included quotas for every important social, political and religious group. Since the beginning of the 1980s, the economic crises and growing corruption gradually undermined the legitimacy of the Kérékou regime which could maintain power only by repressing students' and teachers' protests and the activities of the clandestine *Parti Communiste Dahoméen* (PCD).

In February 1990, a national conference gathering the important social and political forces organized by the regime to secure loyalty and discuss some constitutional modifications laid the foundation for a new radical constitutional change to a democratic presidential system. Even if Kérékou retained his presidential functions, real power was switched to a transitional government which prepared a new democratic constitution (ratified by referendum in December 1990) and parliamentary and presidential elections in 1991. The so-called *renouveau démocratique* meant in many regards a return to the institutions and problems of the 1960s. The new constitution was nearly identical with the one of 1968. The revolutionary and peaceful character of the transition process which removed the military from power for the first time since 1963 and allowed the first competitive multi-party elections since 1959, made Benin a praised pioneer of the African democratic movement. The resulting party system, however, was again very much based on the ethnically structured blocs of the pre-1972 period, the tripartite model being replaced by a much more fragmented and fluctuating system with 32 parties and party lists, on the occasion of the 1995 parliamentary elections. The return of the former socialist president Mathieu Kérékou as a now democratically elected president in March 1996 and the high acceptance of the democratic institutions, particularly the conflict-mediating Constitutional Court, by all actors, can, however, be considered as evidence for the beginning of democratic consolidation.

1.2 Evolution of Electoral Provisions

Regulations concerning electoral laws and electoral systems have been laid down in the different constitutions as well as in ordinary laws and decrees. The legal framework for the first elections of the *renouveau démocratique* had already been formulated by the Constitutional Committee of the National Conference and the electoral laws were adopted by the transitional Parliament *Haut Conseil de la République* in December 1990.

Since independence the President is elected for five years and, unlike the constitutions in the 1960s (unlimited re-election), the current regulations provide for only one re-election. The mandate of the deputies has been reduced from five to four years. Since 1991 the Constitutional Court is charged with the final announcement and validation of the election results. After the parliamentary and presidential elections of 1995 and 1996, the court eventually used its prerogatives to annul results and (in the case of the parliamentary elections) to order by-elections in two constituencies. Parliamentary and presidential elections in 1995 and 1996 were organized by an independent electoral commission.

Ever since the first elections after independence, the principles of universal, equal, direct and secret suffrage were applied. The Beninese living abroad could take part in the presidential elections of 1991, but not in 1996.

In the case of the presidency eligibility was circumscribed by strict age limits (in the 1960s: 35 years, 1990: 40 years). In order to rule out the candidature of the ancient Presidents in 1968, the military government had to resort to extra-constitutional measures by prohibiting ancient Presidents and Heads of Government from being candidates. In 1990, the same problem arose and had to be resolved in the constitution which prescribes an age limit of 70 years, a clause which was so disputed that the constitutional referendum offered two yes options, one maintaining and one eliminating the age limit. Independent candidature has not only been possible but has become the regular feature of presidential elections since 1968. Every citizen of 25 years is eligible for a parliamentary mandate. In the case of parliamentary elections the electoral systems practiced since 1960 made independent candidatures impossible.

With regard to the electoral system, in 1960 and 1964, the electoral law prescribed the direct election of President and Vice-President/ Head of Government as top candidates of the party list winning the parliamentary elections by a plurality. Since 1968 an absolute majority is required for the direct election of the President, if necessary with ballotage between the two leading candidates. During the Marxist–Leninist period the Head of State was designated by the elected members of the revolutionary Parliament.

For parliamentary elections, until 1964 Benin relied on plurality systems in multi-member districts. Since 1964 the Parliament has been elected according to a proportional representation system, providing the following technical elements: *Constituencies: In 1959 the 70 seats were distributed in five constituencies; from 1960 up to 1989 there was only one national constituency. In 1991 each of the six departments formed one constituency; each list had to present candidates in every constituency. *Form of candidacy and voting: Closed party lists were applied, where the voter has only one single vote (no independent candidates). *Allocation of seats: In 1959 the winning lists obtained all seats in the five respective constituencies; in 1960 the list winning a relative majority gained all mandates in the national constituency; in 1964 proportional representation was introduced with a PR formula (Droop-quota). As only one list presented candidates, however, the system did not work in practice. The 'socialist' elections allowed only approval, abstention or refusal of one party list. With the *renouveau démocratique* (1991) proportional representation was reintroduced with six constituencies, Hare quota and greatest remainder formula, and without legal electoral thresholds.

1.3 Current Electoral Provisions

Sources: Constitution of the Republic of Benin, 1990, Electoral Laws *loi* 94-013, *loi* 94-015, *loi* 94-030 and *loi* 95-015; Decisions of the Constitutional Court DCC 34-94 and DCC 96-002.

Elected national institutions: President of the Republic and National Assembly (84 members). Regular terms of office: five years (President), four years (Parliament). A person cannot hold office as President for more than two terms. In the case of the National Assembly, no by-elections are held. Vacant seats are filled through appointments from the respective party list.

Suffrage: The principles of universal, equal, direct and secret suffrage are applied. Every citizen who has reached the age of 18 has the right to vote and is entitled to be registered as a voter. In principle, Beninese citizens living abroad have the right to vote if they register at their embassies.

Nomination of candidates
- *presidential elections*: Every citizen aged between 40 and 70 years, holding Beninese citizenship for a minimum of 10 years and living in the country for a minimum of one year.
- *parliamentary elections*: Every citizen who has reached the age of 25 is eligible if he has had citizenship for 10 years and has lived in the country for one year; independent candidature is not allowed.

Electoral system
- *presidential elections*: Absolute majority system. If no candidate receives more than 50% of the votes cast the two best placed candidates are admitted for a second ballot.
- *parliamentary elections*: Proportional representation list system at the *prefecture*-level; *18 constituencies with extremely low numbers of mandates (ten constituencies with three/four mandates, only one constituency with more than six mandates). *Closed party lists (parties are obliged to present lists in every constituency): *Single vote. *Hare quota and greatest average. *No legal electoral threshold exists.

1.4 Comment on the Electoral Statistics

The following tables are based on official statistics, partly on secondary sources which have used official sources. Because of their limited political relevance the elections of the 1960s, 1970s and 1980s are seldom and incompletely documented. The tables are based on Ziemer (1978), and various editions of Africa Research Bulletin (October 1979, June 1984).

Since the *renouveau démocratique* we find very well elaborated material which even allows regional breakdowns but unfortunately lacks reliability. The official and detailed figures of the National Statistic Institute (INSAE) rarely correspond with the figures that are officially announced by the legitimated political (government) or legal (Constitutional Court) institutions. As a rule the official figures are cited, even if they do not allow regional specifications. The practice of the Constitutional Court—for example during the last presidential elections—to annul considerable percentages of votes is unfortunately not documented in the text or appendix of the respective decisions. The percentages given in the following tables are calculated by the author according to the standards of the data handbook.

2. Tables

2.1 Dates of National Elections, Referendums and Coups d'Etat

Year	Presidential elections	Parliamentary elections	Elections for Constitutional Assembly	Referendums	Coups d'état
1958				28/09	
1959		02/04			
1960	11/12	11/12			
1963					28/10
1964	19/01	19/01		05/01	
1965					29/11 22/12
1967					16/12
1968	05/05[a] 28/07[b]			31/03	
1969					10/12
1970	09–29/03[c]				
1972					26/10
1979		20/10			
1984		10/06			
1989		18/06			
1990				02/12	
1991	10/03 (1st) 24/03 (2nd)	17/02			
1995		28/03[d]			
1996	04/03 (1st) 18/03 (2nd)				

[a] Annulled by the military government.
[b] Actually a plebiscite for the designated candidate.
[c] Suspended by the military government.
[d] By-elections (as ordered by the Constitutional Court) in two constituencies on 28 May 1995.

2.2 Electoral Body 1958–1996

Year	Type of election[a]	Population[b]	Registered voters		Votes cast		
			Total number	% pop.	Total number	% reg. voters	% pop.
1958	Ref	1,725,000	775,170	44.9	431,407	55.7	25.0
1959	Pa	1,830,000	—	—	369,995	—	—
1960	Pr/Pa	1,934,447	971,012	50.8	689,233	71.0	35.6
1964	Ref	2,300,000	1,051,614	45.7	968,229	92.1	42.1
1964	Pr/Pa	2,300,000	1,055,910	45.9	995,929[g]	94.3	43.3
1968	Ref	2,571,000	1,126,155	43.8	922,050	81.9	35.9
1968	Pa	2,571,000	1,138,388	44.2	295,667	27.0	11.5
1968	Pr	2,571,000	1,140,378	44.4	828,076	72.6	32.2
1970	Pr	2,686,000	997,226[c]	37.1	565,347	56.7	21.0
1979	Pa	3,331,210	1,582,910	47.5	1,275,461	80.6	38.3
1984	Pa	3,825,000	1,987,173	51.9	1,851,044	93.2	48.4
1989	Pa	4,591,000	2,200,815	47.9	1,892,701[g]	86.0	41.2
1990	Ref	4,736,000	2,056,353[d]	43.4	1,308,451	63.6	27.6
1991	Pa	4,855,000	2,069,343	42.6	1,069,367	51.7	22.0
1991	Pr (1st)	4,855,000	2,091,488	43.0	1,177,666	56.3	24.2
1991	Pr (2nd)	4,855,000	2,052,638	42.3	1,315,123	64.1	27.1
1995	Pa	5,219,000	2,531,120	48.5	1,922,553	75.8	36.8
1996	Pr (1st)	5,340,311	2,517,970[e]	47.2	2,211,677	87.8	41.4
1996	Pr (2nd)	5,340,311	2,524,262[f]	47.3	1,958,855	77.1	36.7

[a] Pa = Parliament (*Assemblée Nationale*); Pr = President; Ref = Referendum.

[b] Population data are based on UN Population official estimates. Official census in November 1960: 1,934,447, in October 1979: 3,331,100 and in February 1992: 4,855,349. UN official estimates for the years 1989–1991 are not very probable in the light of the 1992 census. For lack of other figures we nevertheless cite the UN figures, for 1991 we take the census data from February 1992. 1995 figures are UN official estimates, 1996 figures are based on information of the national election commission CENA, Cotonou.

[c] Elections took place only in five out of six *départements*.

[d] This figure includes the Beninese living abroad.

[e] On 26 February 1996 the National Electoral Commission, CENA, decided to exclude citizens living abroad from participating in the elections even if they had already registered.

[f] As in 1991 the Constitutional Court gives differing figures of registered voters for the respective first and second rounds of the presidential elections.

[g] Number of valid votes.

2.3 Abbreviations

ADD	Alliance pour la Démocratie et le Développement
ADP	Alliance pour la Démocratie et le Progrès
API	Alliance Politique des Indépendants
ARC	Alliance pour le Renouveau Civique
ASD	Alliance pour la Social - Démocratie
BGLD	Bâtisseurs et Gestionnaires de la Liberté et du Développement
BSD	Bloc pour la Social Démocratie
FARD-Alafia	Front d'Action pour le Renouveau Démocratique
FDDM	Forum pour la Démocratie le Développement et la Moralité
All. Caméléon	Alliance Caméléon
MDPS	Mouvement pour la Démocratie et le Progrès Social
MNDD	Mouvement National pour la Démocratie et le Développement
MSUP	Mouvement pour la Solidarité, l'Union et le Progrès
NCC	Notre Cause Commune
PCB	Parti Communiste du Bénin
PDD	Parti Démocratique Dahoméen
PDU	Parti Dahoméen de l'Unité
PNDD	Parti National pour la Démocratie et le Développement
PNSP	Parti National pour la Solidarité et le Progrès
PNT	Parti National du Travail
PPD	Parti pour le Progrès et la Démocratie
PRD	Parti du Regroupement Dahoméen (1959)
PRD	Parti du Renouveau Démocratique (since 1991)
PRPB	Parti de la Révolution Populaire du Bénin
PS	Parti du Salut
PSD	Parti Social Démocrate
RAP	Rassemblement Africain pour le Progrès et la Solidarité Nationale
RB	Renaissance du Bénin
RDD	Rassemblement Démocratique Dahoméen
RDL-Vivoten	Rassemblement des Démocrates Libéraux – Vivoten
RDP	Rassemblement pour la Démocratie et le Panafricanisme
RDT	Rassemblement pour la Démocratie et le Travail
RND	Rassemblement National pour la Démocratie
RNJP	Rassemblement National pour la Justice et la Paix
UDD	Union Démocratique Dahoméenne
UDES	Union Démocratique pour le Développement Economique et Social
UDFP	Union Démocratique des Forces du Progrès
UDRN	Union pour la Démocratie et la Reconstruction Nationale
UDRS	Union Démocratique pour le Renouveau Social
UDS	Union pour la Démocratie et la Solidarité Nationale
ULD	Union pour la Liberté et le Développement
UNDP	Union Nationale pour la Démocratie et le Progrès

UNSP	Union Nationale pour la Solidarité et le Progrès
URP	Union Républicaine du Peuple
UTD	Union pour le Travail et la Démocratie

2.4 Electoral Participation of Parties and Alliances 1959–1996

Party / Alliance	Years	Elections contested	
		Presidential[a]	Parliamentary
PRD	1959	0	1
RDD	1959	0	1
UDD	1959, 1960	1	2
PDU	1960	1	1
PDD	1964	1	1
PRPB	1979, 1984, 1989	0	3
ADP	1991, 1995	0	2
ASD	1991, 1995	0	2
BGLD	1991	0	1
BSD	1991	0	1
MDPS	1991	0	1
MNDD	1991, 1995	0	2
MSUP	1991, 1995	0	2
NCC	1991, 1995	0	2
PNDD	1991, 1995	0	2
PNT	1991, 1995	0	2
PRD	1991, 1995	0	2
PSD	1991, 1995	0	2
RDL-Vivoten	1991, 1995	0	2
RND	1991, 1995	0	2
UDES	1991	0	1
UDFP	1991, 1995	0	2
UDRN	1991, 1995	0	2
UDRS	1991	0	1
UDS	1991, 1995	0	2
ULD	1991, 1995	0	2
UNDP	1991, 1995	0	2
UNSP	1991, 1995	0	2
URP	1991	0	1
ADD	1995	0	1
API	1995	0	1
ARC	1995	0	1
FARD-Alafia	1995	0	1
PCB	1995	0	1
PNSP	1995	0	1
PPD	1995	0	1

Party / Alliance	Years	Elections contested	
		Presidential[a]	Parliamentary
PS	1995	0	1
RAP	1995	0	1
RB	1995	0	1
RDP	1995	0	1
RDT	1995	0	1
RNJP	1995	0	1
UTD	1995	0	1

[a] Since 1968 presidential candidates are independent candidates; even if they belong to existing parties, they do not represent parties.

2.5 Referendums

	1958		1964	
	Total number	%	Total number	%
Registered voters	775,170	–	1,051,614	–
Votes cast	431,407	55.7	968,229	92.1
Invalid votes	3,198	0.7	619	0.1
Valid votes	428,209	99.3	967,610	99.9
Yes	418,963	97.8	966,292	99.8
No	9,246	2.2	1,318	0.2

Year	1968		1990	
	Total number	%	Total number	%
Registered voters	1,126,155	–	2,056,353	–
Votes cast	922,050	81.8	1,304,870	63.6
Invalid votes	3,221	0.3	39,887	3.1
Valid votes	918,829	99.7	1,264,983	96.9
Yes (Total)	847,212	92.2	1,179,266	93.2
Yes (incl. age-clause)	–	–	926,860	73.3
Yes (without age-clause)	–	–	252,064	19.9
No	71,617	7.8	85,717	6.8

2.6 Elections for Constitutional Assembly

Elections for Constitutional Assembly have not been held.

2.7 Parliamentary Elections 1959–1995

Year	1959		1960	
	Total number	%	Total number	%
Registered voters	—	–	971,012	–
Votes cast	—	—	689,233	71.0
Invalid votes	—	—	6,982	1.1
Valid votes	366,995	—	682,251	98.9
UDD	162,574	43.9	213,572	31.3
PRD	144,038	38.9	–	–
RDD	63,383	17.2	–	–
PDU	–	–	468,679	68.7

Year	1964		1979	
	Total number	%	Total number	%
Registered voters	1,055,910	–	1,582,910	–
Votes cast	—	—	1,275,461	80.6
Invalid votes	—	—	5,410	0.4
Valid votes	995,929	—	1,270,051	99.6
PDD	995,929	100	–	–
PRPB-Yes	–	–	1,248,613	98.3
PRPB-No	–	–	21,438	1.7

Year	1984		1989	
	Total number	%	Total number	%
Registered voters	1,987,173	–	2,200,815	–
Votes cast	1,851,044	93.1	—	—
Invalid votes	5,119	0.3	—	—
Valid votes	1,845,925	99.7	1,892,701	100
PRPB-Yes	1,811,808	98.2	1,695,860	89.6
PRPB-No	27,720	1.5	164,665	8.7
PRPB-Abstention	6,397	0.3	32,176[a]	1.7[a]

[a] Author's calculation.

Year	1991		1995[a]	
	Total number	%	Total number	%
Registered voters	2,069,343	–	2,536,234	–
Votes cast	1,069,367	51.7	1,922,553	75.8
Invalid votes	39,350	3.7	43,361[b]	2.4
Valid votes	1,030,017	96.3	1,876,192	97.6
UDFP-MDPS-ULD	194,213	18.9	–	–
RB	–	–	212,428	14.6
UDFP	–	–	21,093	1.4
RND	124,392	12.1	28,455	1.9
PNDD-PRD	120,705	11.7	–	–
PRD	–	–	225,175	15.4
ARC-PPD-PNDD	–	–	39,149	2.7
NCC	104,347	10.1	82,898	5.7
PSD-UNSP	101,348	9.8	–	–
PSD	–	–	111,756	7.7
FDDM-UNSP	–	–	44,752	3.1
MNDD-MSUP-UDRN	86,556	8.4	–	–
MNDD	–	–	28,993	2.0
MSUP-UDRN	–	–	15,006	1.0
UDS	72,899	7.1	71,061	4.9
RDL-Vivoten	57,852	5.6	63,152	4.3
ADP-UDRS	38,684	3.8	–	–
ADP	–	–	35,896	2.5
ASD-BSD	35,700	3.5	–	–
ASD	–	–	20,266	1.4
UNDP	31,601	3.1	37,563	2.6
UDES	25,893	2.5	–	–
URP-PNT	20,490	2.0	–	–
UTD-PNT	–	–	25,571	1.8
BGLD	15,337	1.5	–	–
FARD-Alafia	–	–	89,919	6.2
PCB	–	–	48,021	3.3
RAP	–	–	37,690	2.6
ADD	–	–	36,370	2.5
API	–	–	28,162	1.9
RNJP-PS	–	–	23,232	1.6
Alliance Caméleon	–	–	21,960	1.5
RDP	–	–	21,027	1.4
RDT-PNSP	–	–	20,939	1.4

[a] In 1995 five other lists obtained less than 1%. The order of the parties in the table illustrates the continuities of parties and alliances between the two elections.
[b] Including invalidation by the Constitutional Court.

2.8 Composition of Parliament 1959–1995

Year	1959 Seats	%	1960 Seats	%	1964 Seats	%	1979 Seats	%
	70	100	60	100	42	100	336	100
UDD	11[a]	15.7	–	–	–	–	–	–
PRD	37[a]	52.8	–	–	–	–	–	–
RDD	22	31.4	–	–	–	–	–	–
PDU	–	–	60	100	–	–	–	–
PDD	–	–	–	–	42	100	–	–
PRPB	–	–	–	–	–	–	336	100

[a] After the election PRD and UDD agreed to divide the seats of one constituency, so that the final composition was the following: UDD 20; PRD 28; RDD 22.

Year	1984 Seats	%	1989 Seats	%	1991 Seats	%	1995 Seats	%
	196	100	200	100	64	100	83	100
PRPB	196	100	200	100	–	–	–	–
UDFP-MDPS-ULD	–	–	–	–	12	18.8	–	–
RB	–	–	–	–	–	–	21	25.3
RND	–	–	–	–	7	10.9	0	0.0
PNDD-PRD	–	–	–	–	9	14.1	–	–
PRD	–	–	–	–	–	–	19	22.9
ARC-PPD-PNDD	–	–	–	–	–	–	3	3.6
NCC	–	–	–	–	6	9.4	3	3.6
PSD-UNSP	–	–	–	–	8	12.5	–	–
PSD	–	–	–	–	–	–	8	9.6
FDDM-UNSP	–	–	–	–	–	–	2	2.4
MNDD-MSUP-UDRN	–	–	–	–	6	9.4	–	–
MNDD	–	–	–	–	–	–	1	1.2
UDS	–	–	–	–	5	7.8	5	6.0
RDL-Vivoten	–	–	–	–	4	6.3	3	3.6
ADP-UDRS	–	–	–	–	2	3.1	–	–
ADP	–	–	–	–	–	–	1	1.2
ASD-BSD	–	–	–	–	3	4.7	–	–
ASD	–	–	–	–	–	–	1	1.2
UNDP	–	–	–	–	1	1.6	1	1.2
URP-PNT	–	–	–	–	1	1.6	–	–
FARD-Alafia	-	–	–	–	–	–	10	12.0
PCB	–	–	–	–	–	–	1	1.2
RAP	–	–	–	–	–	–	1	1.2
ADD	–	–	–	–	–	–	1	1.2
All. Caméleon	–	–	–	–	–	–	1	1.2
RDP	–	–	–	–	–	–	1	1.2

2.9 Presidential Elections 1968–1996

Hubert Maga (PDU 1960) and Magan Apithy (PDD 1964) were automatically elected President as heads of their respective party list.

1968 (May)	Total number	%
Registered voters	1,138,388	–
Votes cast	295,667	27.0
Invalid votes	8,275	2.8
Valid votes	287,392	97.2
Basile Adjou	241,273	84.0
Urbain Karim da Silva	19,319	6.7
Eustache Prudencio	11,359	3.9
Paul Hazoumé	11,091	3.9
Jean-Baptiste Vierin	4,350	1.5

1968 (July)	Total number	%
Registered voters	1,140,378	–
Votes cast	828,076	72.6
Invalid votes	3,269	0.4
Valid votes	824,807	99.6
Emile-Derlin Zinsou	630,018	76.4
No-Votes	194,789	23.6

1970	Total number	%
Registered voters	997,226	–
Votes cast	565,347	56.7
Invalid votes	18,223	3.2
Valid votes	547,124	96.8
Justin Ahomadegbé	200,092	36.6
Magan Apithy	176,828	32.3
Hubert Maga	152,551	27.9
Emile-Derlin Zinsou	17,653	3.2

1991 (First round)	Total number	%
Registered voters	2,091,488	–
Votes cast	1,177,666	56.3
Invalid votes	19,340	1.6
Valid votes	1,158,326	98.4
Nicéphore Soglo	419,787	36.2
Mathieu Kérékou	315,079	27.2
Albert Tevoedjré	165,174	14.3
Bruno Amoussou	66,053	5.7
Adrien Houngbedji	53,187	4.6
Moise Mensah	39,984	3.4
Sévérin Adjovi	30,710	2.7
Bertin Borna	18,578	1.6
Idelphonse W. Lemon	11,517	1.0
Assani Fassassi	10,393	0.9
Gatien Houngbedji	10,272	0.9
Robert Dossou	9,641	0.8
Thomas Goudou	8,041	0.7

1991 (Second round)	Total number	%
Registered voters	2,052,638	–
Votes cast	1,315,123	64.1
Invalid votes	10,417	0.8
Valid votes	1,304,706	99.2
Nicéphore Soglo	881,205	67.5
Mathieu Kérékou	423,501	32.5

1996 (First round)	Total number	%
Registered voters	2,517,970	–
Votes cast	2,211,677	87.8
Invalid votes	45,980	2.1
Annulled votes (CC)	494,673	22.4
Valid votes	1,671,024	75.5
Nicéphore Soglo	596,371	35.7
Mathieu Kérékou	567,084	33.9
Adrien Houngbedji	329,364	19.7
Bruno Amoussou	129,731	7.8
Pascal Fantodji	17,977	1.1
Leandre Djagoue	15,418	0.9
Lionnel A. Agbo	15,079	0.9

1996 (Second round)	Total number	%
Registered voters	2,542,262	–
Votes cast	1,958,855	77.1
Invalid votes	20,026	1.0
Annulled votes (CC)	34,750	1.8
Valid votes	1,904,079	97.2
Mathieu Kérékou	999,453	52.5
Nicéphore Soglo	904,626	47.5

2.9 a) Presidential Elections 1991–1996: Regional Results

1991, first round (absolute numbers)							
	Ouémé[b]	Atlant.[b]	Mono[b]	Zou[b]	Borgou[b]	Atacora[b]	Total[a]
Soglo	37,107	193,388	33,215	128,819	12,416	10,083	419,787
Kérékou	6,567	19,139	11,381	19,375	126,747	127,769	315,079
Tevoedjere	110,099	36,900	5,753	5,838	2,013	1,899	165,174
Amoussou	2,060	4,644	56,686	1,991	278	339	66,053
Adrien Houngbedji	31,817	8,789	3,365	5,680	649	1,588	53,187
Mensah	1,900	16,428	15,888	4,395	292	347	39,894
Adjovi	5,530	11,459	5,333	5,657	710	1,165	30,710
Borna	3,187	4,276	2,734	3,195	923	4,169	18,578
Lémon	2,257	4,568	2,004	1,711	303	454	11,517
Fassassi	2,512	2,645	2,157	2,163	362	495	10,393
Gatien Houngbedji	2,793	2,793	1,325	1,117	763	1,419	10,272
Dossou	1,439	2,807	3,239	1,148	464	454	9,641
Goudou	2,365	1,666	1,231	1,175	652	919	8,041

[a] Total sum includes votes obtained from voters abroad.

[b] Regional breakdown follows Benin's six *departements* (from South to North) Ouémé, Atlantique, Mono, Zou, Borgou, Atacora.

1991, first round (percentages)							
	Ouémé	Atlant.	Mono	Zou	Borgou	Atacora	Total
Soglo	17.7	62.5	23.0	70.7	8.5	6.7	36.2
Kérékou	3.1	6.2	7.9	10.6	86.5	84.6	27.2
Tevoedjere	52.5	11.9	4.0	3.2	1.4	1.3	14.3
Amoussou	1.0	1.5	39.3	1.1	0.2	0.2	5.7
A. Houngbedji	15.2	2.8	2.3	3.1	0.4	1.1	4.6
Mensah	0.9	5.3	11.0	2.4	0.2	0.2	3.4
Adjovi	2.6	3.7	3.7	3.1	0.5	0.8	2.7
Borna	1.5	1.4	1.9	1.8	0.6	2.8	1.6
Lémon	1.1	1.5	1.4	0.9	0.2	0.3	1.0
Fassassi	1.2	0.9	1.5	1.2	0.2	0.3	0.9
G. Houngbedji	1.3	0.9	0.9	0.6	0.5	0.9	0.9
Dossou	0.7	0.9	2.2	0.6	0.3	0.3	0.8
Goudou	1.1	0.5	0.9	0.6	0.4	0.6	0.7

1991, second round (absolute numbers)							
	Ouémé	Atlant.	Mono	Zou	Borgou	Atacora	Total[a]
Soglo	197,281	324,408	114,196	218,797	5,943	11,352	881,205
Kérékou	19,622	23,710	25,902	22,524	160,407	166,170	423,501

[a] Total sum includes votes obtained from voters abroad.

1991, second round (percentages)							
	Ouémé	Atlant.	Mono	Zou	Borgou	Atacora	Total
Soglo	91.0	93.2	81.5	90.7	3.6	6.4	67.5
Kérékou	9.0	6.8	18.5	9.3	96.4	93.6	32.5

1996, first round (absolute numbers)[a]							
	Ouémé	Atlant.	Mono	Zou	Borgou	Atacora	Total
Soglo	64,511	309,052	75,301	263,856	37,461	16,867	767,048
Kérékou	57,569	78,211	43,576	60,106	229,130	236,677	705,269
Houngbedji	227,093	85,844	33,936	24,631	8,081	7,854	387,439
Amoussou	14,575	18,398	103,419	9,902	4,696	1,861	152,851
Fantodji	3,083	3,190	10,640	1,738	919	1,798	21,368
Djagoue	3,952	3,262	4,183	2,392	2,101	1,335	17,225
Agbo	3,375	2,994	4,095	2,383	2,711	2,556	18,114

[a] Figures of the National Electoral Commission CENA—as published in *La Nation* (Cotonou), 11/03/1996—which include the votes later annulled and differ from figures given in table 2.9. The Constitutional Court did not give regional breakdowns of annulled votes.

1996, first round (percentages)							
	Ouémé	Atlant.	Mono	Zou	Borgou	Atacora	Total[a]
Soglo	17.2	61.7	27.4	72.3	13.1	6.3	37.1
Kérékou	15.4	15.6	15.8	16.5	80.4	88.0	34.1
Houngbedji	60.7	17.1	12.3	6.7	2.8	2.9	18.7
Amoussou	3.9	3.7	37.6	2.7	1.6	0.7	7.4
Fantodji	0.8	0.6	3.9	0.5	0.3	0.7	1.0
Djagoue	1.1	0.7	1.5	0.6	0.7	0.5	0.8
Agbo	0.9	0.6	1.5	0.6	0.8	1.0	0.8

1996, second round (absolute numbers)[a]							
	Ouémé	Atlant.	Mono	Zou	Borgou	Atacora	Total[a]
Soglo	104,444	355,385	95,200	307,258	44,761	18,372	925,420
Kérékou	230,440	150,269	122,706	76,262	264,167	244,240	1,088,084

[a] Figures of the National Electoral Commission CENA which include the votes later annulled and differ from figures given in table 2.9. The Constitutional Court did not give regional breakdowns of annulled votes.

1996, second round (percentages)							
	Ouémé	Atlant.	Mono	Zou	Borgou	Atacora	Total[a]
Soglo	31.2	70.3	43.7	80.1	14.5	7.0	46.0
Kérékou	68.8	29.7	56.3	19.9.	85.5	93.0	54.0

2.10 List of Power Holders 1960–1998

Head of State and Government	Years	Remarks
Hubert Maga	1960–1963	Presidential election 31/12/1960.
Christophe Soglo	1963–1964	Military coup 28/10/1963.
Sourou Migan Apithy	1964–1965	Presidential election 19/01/1964.
Tahirou Congacou	1965	Military coup 29/11/1965.
Christophe Soglo	1965–1967	Military coup 22/12/1965.
Alphonse Alley	1967–1968	Military coup 16/12/1967.
Emile Derlin Zinsou	1968–1969	Plebiscite election 28/07/1968 (Zinsou designated by military government).
Paul Emile de Souza	1969–1970	Military coup 10/12/1969.
Hubert Maga	1970–1972	Civil-military 'pact' including rota-system of three leading politicians 07/05/1970.
Justin Ahomadegbé	1972	Regular rotation after two years 07/05/1972.
Mathieu Kérékou	1972–1990	Military coup 26/10/1972.
Mathieu Kérékou/ Nicephore Soglo	1990–1991	National Conference installs transition government Nicéphore Soglo as Head of Government, Kérekou remaining President 01/03/1990.
Nicéphore Soglo	1991–1996	Presidential election 24/03/1991.
Mathieu Kérékou	1996–	Presidential election 18/03/1996.

3. Bibliography

3.1 Official Sources

République du Bénin and Commission Electorale Nationale Autonome (1996). *Elections presidentielles de Mars 1996. Recueil de textes fondamentaux*. Cotonou (incl. Constitution of 03/12/1990 and various electoral laws)

République du Bénin, Ministère du Plan et de la Restructuration Economique and Institut National de la Statistique et de l'Analyse Economique (INSAE) (1991). *Resultats des élections referendaires, legislatives, présidentielles*. Cotonou, Mars 1991

— (1995). *Elections legislatives, 1995. Statistiques des resultats definitifs*. Cotonou

— (1996). *Elections presidentielles de 1996. Deuxième tour. Resultats provisoires*. Cotonou

Fondation Friedrich Naumann (1994). *Les actes de la Conférence Nationale*. Cotonou: Editions ONEPI

— (1995). *Recueil des decisions de la Cour Constitutionnelle, Vol.1 1991–93, Vol.2 1994*. Porto Novo: Editions JORB

3.2 Books and Articles

Adamon, A. D. (1995a). *Le renouveau démocratique au Bénin. La conférence nationale des forces vives et la période de transition*. Paris: L'Harmattan.

— (1995b). *Le renouveau démocratique au Bénin. Les élections de la période de transition*. Porto Novo: Editions du JORB.

Adjahouinou, D. (1994). 'L'observation des elections de fevrier-mars 1991 au Benin'. *Afrika-Spectrum,* 29/2: 217–226.

Africa Research Bulletin, various volumes and numbers.

Ali Yérima, A. R. (1995). 'Comment fortifier les institutions démocratiques béninoises'. *Afrique Démocratie et Développement,* 6/6: 43–52.

Allen, C. (1989). 'Benin', in *idem et al.*, *The Congo, Burkina Faso*. London/New York: Pinter, 1–144.

— (1992). 'Restructuring an Authoritarian State. "Democratic Renewal" in Benin'. *Review of African Political Economy,* 54: 42–58.

Bakary, T. D. (1992). 'Des militaires aux avocats: une autre forme de coup d'état, "La conference nationale souveraine"'. *Geopolitique Africaine,* 15/2: 1–6.

Bako-Arifari, N. (1995). 'Démocratie et logique du terroir au Benin'. *Politique Africaine,* 59: 7–24.

Banégas, R. (1995). 'Mobilisations sociales et oppositions sous Kérékou'. *Politique Africaine*, 59: 25–44.

— 'Marchandisation du vote, citoyenneté et consolidation démocratique au Bénin'. *Politique Africaine* 69: 75–87.

Cabanis, A., and Martin, M. L. (1992). 'Note sur la constitution béninoise du 2 decembre 1990'. *Revue juridique et politique (Le Vesinet),* 46/1: 28–37.

Cornevin, R. (1981). *La République populaire du Benin*. Paris: Maisonneuve/Larose.

Daloz, J.-P. (1992). 'L'itinéraire du pionnier—sur l'évolution politique béninoise'. *Politique Africaine,* 46: 132–137.

Decalo, S. (1997). 'Benin. First of the New Democracies', in J. F. Clark and D. E. Gardinier (eds.), *Political Reform in Francophone Africa*. Boulder, Col.: Westview Press, 43–61.

Dix, H. (1996). 'Präsidentschaftswahlen in Benin 1996'. *KAS-Auslandsinformationen,* 12/5: 45–50.

Dossou, R. (1993). 'Le Bénin: Du monolithisme à la démocratie pluraliste, un témoignage', in G. Conac (ed.), *L'Afrique en transition vers le pluralisme politique*. Paris: Economica, 179–197.

Eboussi-Boulaga, F. (1993). *Les conférences nationales. Une affaire à suivre*. Paris: Karthala.

Fondation Friedrich Ebert (1993). *Le processus de la democratisation en Afrique de l'Ouest - Le cas du Bénin: Bilan et perspectives*. Cotonou.

Gbegnonvi, R. (1995). 'Les legislatives de mars 1995'. *Politique Africaine,* 59: 59–69.

Glélé, M. A. (1969a). *Naissance d'un état noir. L'évolution politique et constitutionnelle du Dahomey, de la colonisation à nos jours*. Paris: LGDP.

— (1969b). *La République du Dahomey*. Paris: Ed. Berger-Levrault.

— (1993). 'Le Bénin', in G. Conac (ed.), *L'Afrique en transition vers le pluralisme politique*. Paris: Economica, 173–177.

Godin, F. (1982). *Bénin 1972-82: logique de l'état africain*. Paris: L'Harmattan.

Hartmann, C. (1996). 'Benin: Die Rückkehr des Chamäleons. Bekommen Afrikas gestürzte Diktatoren eine zweite Chance?'. *blätter des informationszentrums 3.Welt,* 218: 4–6.

— (1999). *Externe Faktoren im Demokratisierungsprozeß. Eine vergleichende Untersuchung afrikanischer Länder*. Opladen: Leske & Budrich.

Heilbrunn, J. R. (1993). 'Social Origins of National Conferences in Benin and Togo'. *Journal of Modern African Studies,* 31/2: 277–299.

Houngbedji, A. (1994). 'Le renouveau démocratique du Bénin. Genèse, enjeux et perspectives'. *Revue Juridique et Politique (Le Vesinet),* 48/1: 17–26.

Institut des Droits de l'Homme et de Promotion de la Démocratie, and Fondation Konrad Adenauer (1994). *Modes de scrutin et financement des campagnes electorales dans une démocratie pluraliste*. Cotonou.

Iroko, F. (1994). 'Review of the First Free Elections Held in Benin. Thoughts and Reflections', in W. Jung and S. Krieger (eds.), *Culture and Democracy in Africa South of the Sahara*, Mainz: von Hase & Koehler, 163–170.

Kérékou, M. (1995). *Préparer le Bénin du futur. Reflexions d'un citoyen sur le devenir du pays*. Porto-Novo: Presses du CPPS.

Kohnert, D., and Preuß, H.-J. (1992). 'Vom Camarade zum Monsieur. Strukturanpassung und Demokratisierung in Benin'. *Peripherie,* 46: 47–70.

Kohnert, D. (1996). 'Zur Kluft zwischen Verfassungsgebung und Verfassungswirklichkeit im Demokratisierungsprozeß Benins'. *nord-süd-aktuell,* 10/1: 73–84.

Laloupo, F. (1993). 'La conference nationale du Benin: Un concept nouveau de changement de regime politique'. *Année africaine 1992-93*, 89–114.

Lavroff, D. G. (1978). 'L'évolution constitutionnelle de la République Populaire du Bénin: la constitution de 1977'. *Année africaine 1977*, 128–59.

Magnusson, B. (1996). 'Benin: Legitimating Democracy. New Institutions and the Historical Problem of Economic Crisis. *L'Afrique Politique 1996*, 33–54.

Martin, M. L. (1986). 'The Rise and "Thermidorization" of Radical Praetorianism in Benin', in J. Markakis and M. Waller (eds.), *Military Regimes in Africa*. London: Frank Cass, 58–81.

Mayrargue, C. (1996). '"Le caméléon est remonté en haut de l'arbre": le retour au pouvoir de M. Kérekou au Bénin'. *Politique Africaine*, 62: 124–131.

Nwajiaku, K. (1994). 'The National Conferences in Benin and Togo Revisited'. *Journal of Modern African Studies,* 32/3: 429–447.

Olodo, A. K. (1978). 'Les institutions de la République Populaire du Bénin'. *Revue juridique et politique (Le Vesinet),* 32/2: 759–792.

Paraiso, A. (1980). 'La loi fondamentale et les nouvelles institutions de la République Populaire du Bénin'. *Penant,* 769: 288–306 and 770: 403–440.

Raynal, J. J. (1991). 'Le renouveau democratique beninois. Modèle ou mirage'. *Afrique contemporaine*, 160: 3–25.

Robinson, P. T. (1994). 'The National Conference Phenomenon in Francophone Africa'. *Comparative Studies of Society and History*, 34/2: 575–610.

Ronen, D. (1975). *Dahomey. Between Tradition and Modernity*. Ithaca, N.Y.: Cornell UP.

— (1978). 'People's Republic of Benin: the Military, Marxist Ideology and the Politics of Ethnicity', in J. Harbeson (ed.), *The Military in African Politics*. New York: Praeger, 93–122.

Rumpf, W. (1996). 'Eine Wahlbeobachtung in Benin'. *Internationales Afrikaforum,* 32/3: 285–289.

Toulabor, C. (1993). 'Paristroika et revendication démocratique', in D. C. Bach and A. A. Kirk-Greene (eds.), *Etats et Sociétés en Afrique Francophone*. Paris: Economica, 119–135.

Vittin, T. E. (1991). 'Bénin. Du "système Kérékou" au renouveau démocratique', in J.-F. Médard (ed.), *Etats d'Afrique noire*. Paris: Karthala, 93–115.

Westebbe, R. (1994). 'Structural Adjustment, Rent Seeking, and Liberalization in Benin', in J. A. Widner (ed.), *Economic Change and Political Liberalization in Sub-Saharan Africa*. Baltimore: John Hopkins University Press, 80–100.

Ziemer, K. (1978). 'Benin (Dahomey)', in D. Sternberger, B. Vogel, D. Nohlen and K. Landfried (eds.), *Die Wahl der Parlamente und anderer Staatsorgane, Band II: Politische Organisation und Repräsentation in Afrika*, by Franz Nuscheler, Klaus Ziemer *et al.*, Berlin/ New York: Walter de Gruyter, 491–542.

BOTSWANA

by Goswin Baumhögger

1. Introduction

1.1 Historical Overview

Characterized by the absence of a significant nationalist movement and, thus, a much less antagonistic nationalist struggle than was the rule elsewhere in Africa, the poverty-stricken and politically conservative society of Botswana was subjected to a rapid process of social and political change within a relatively short period after independence (30 September 1966). This resulted in the transformation of tribally based societies with distinct group identities into a centrally organized state structure, headed by an executive President indirectly elected by the members of the relatively small Parliament. While the President presides at meetings of the Cabinet exclusively appointed from among members of Parliament, government business in Parliament is administered by the leader of the house. This function is exercised by the Vice-President, a presidential appointee holding the post of Minister of Finance and Development Planning since 1969/ 70 as well. Considerable power is also exercised by the Minister of Presidential Affairs and Public Administration.

The transformation process before independence had been initiated and initially controlled by the colonial power Great Britain, which had encouraged the formation of a moderate, conservative and non-racial political party—the Botswana Democratic Party (BDP, founded in 1962)—to inherit the post-colonial state, in preference to other potentially contesting forces which were systematically incapacitated by the special favors accorded to the BDP. Among them were the traditional chiefs as well as the Botswana People's Party (BPP, founded in 1960) which the colonial power assessed as being too radical due to its involvement in nationalist policies of neighboring South Africa. The BPP remained peripheral in the long run also because of its internal rivalries leading to several splits. These gave birth, among others, to the

Botswana Independence Party (BIP, 1964) and also the Botswana National Front (BNF, 1965).

The BDP overwhelmingly won the pre-independence elections of 1965 (80% of the votes), much of its dominant position being owed to the personality of its President Sir Seretse Khama. He could count, among others, on the trust of the traditional chiefs having been the main link and line of contact between the colonial state and the people under the British indirect rule system. Although Khama had been forced to renounce all claims to the chieftainship of the biggest Tswana group, the Bamangwato in the central part of the country, after having been exiled from 1950 to 1956 because of his marriage to a white woman, he still enjoyed the charismatic reputation of a chief without being exposed to the oftentimes compromising responsibilities of this office. Khama thus became the first President of the country which, by holding free and competitive elections every five years, earned a reputation of being a multi-party democracy with unparalleled political stability as well as economic success (due to the discovery of vast diamond deposits). Although the political institutions which had been imposed from above have remained comparatively weak, political parties were legitimized as the sole contestants for political office in preference to the once very powerful traditional chiefs who were relegated to an advisory role in the House of Chiefs and had their powers reduced significantly, particularly with regard to their traditional rights to allocate land and control mineral concessions.

A new challenge to the dominant position of the BPD arose at the first post-independence elections (1969), when the influential Bathoen II, ex-Chief of the Bangwaketse, became the driving force of the BNF which was thus able to entrench itself in the Bangwaketse area in the southern part of the country, although its original orientation had been more suitable for gaining support in urban areas. The BNF immediately established itself as the second biggest political party, leaving behind the BPP and the BIP both of which rapidly developed into regionally based marginal parties in the North East and North West respectively. Nevertheless, the BNF was not able to make too much of an impact until 1984, while the real breakthrough came 10 years later when it polled 37% of the votes and managed to overcome the disadvantages of the majority system for the first time by gaining about one third of the elected parliamentary seats thus putting the notion of a dominant party system into question.

While much of the success of the BNF owed to its appeal to the rapidly growing urban electorate, another contributing factor was the death of Sir Seretse Khama in 1980. Although the succession by Quett—now Sir Ketumile—Masire was a smooth one, as he had been one of the co-founders of the BDP and its first Secretary-General as well as the country's Vice-President since independence, he did not command quite the same respect (belonging to the minority Bangwaketse community) and integrative capacity as Khama. Nevertheless, the BDP was able to hold its position for some time still. Its long-time reputation of a relatively clean government was, however, considerably weakened in the wake of a corruption scandal in 1992 which resulted among others in the forced resignation of the then Vice-President and the Secretary-General of the BDP from their government positions. In addition, albeit not totally unrelated to this, a serious internal conflict between modernizers or technocrats based in the Cabinet on the one hand and the old party guard on the other exposed an amount of disunity which again had quite some impact on the reputation of the BDP as a united political force, making it rather vulnerable at the time of the election in 1994. The shock of the election result—an all-time low of only 55% of the votes—resulted in a number of reforms (some of them relating to electoral procedures) designed to take the wind out of the BNF's sails. After a referendum on some of the resulting constitutional amendments, Sir Ketumile Masire announced his wish to retire, which he did on 31 March 1998, with Vice-President Festus Mogae succeeding him according to the amended constitution.

1.2 Evolution of Electoral Provisions

Starting with the first general election in 1965, one and a half years ahead of independence, the principles of universal adult as well as equal, direct and secret suffrage have been applied, in combination with the plurality system in single-member constituencies. The number of constituencies has been increased from 31 (1965) to 32 (1974), 34 (1984) and 40 (1994) respectively. There is no direct election for the office of the executive President which is instead linked to the election of members of the National Assembly.

1.3 Current Electoral Provisions

Sources: The electoral law relating to parliamentary elections was promulgated in 1968 as the Electoral Act 1968 (No. 38 of 1968), and relating to presidential elections a year later: Presidential elections (Supplementary Provisions) Act 1969 (No. 41 of 1969). Both have been amended several times since, the former by the following Acts: No. 49 of 1969, No. 8 of 1974, No. 15 of 1977, No. 50 of 1977, No. 17 of 1979, No. 29 of 1981, No. 16 of 1984, No. 18 of 1988, No. 20 of 1989, and No. 10 of 1993, the latter by Act No. 14 of 1977 and No. 14 of 1979. The most recent update including all amendments to the Electoral Act up to 1993 is '[Republic of Botswana]: Electoral. Chapter 02:07. Dated 31st December, 1993'; the date has since been rectified to 31 August 1994.

Furthermore, the electoral system has been laid down in the constitution: Botswana Independence Order, including Schedule 2: The Constitution of Botswana [Statutory Instrument 1966 No.1171 UK]. The constitution, too, has been amended several times, but only the amendments contained in Acts No. 43 of 1969, No. 28 of 1972, No. 24 of 1973, No. 1 of 1983, No. 22 of 1987, No. 27 of 1992, No. 16 and No. 18 of 1997 relate directly to provisions with regard to the electoral system.

Elected national institutions: The legislature consists of the President and a National Assembly with 40 directly elected members. Another four 'specially elected' members are chosen by the elected members from a list of four candidates each, presented by the President as well as any elected member of the National Assembly. In addition, there are *ex-officio* members of the National Assembly: the Attorney General, the Speaker (in case he is not an elected member) and since 1974 the President (prior to that he had to be an elected member). The maximum life of the National Assembly is five years.

In addition, there is a House of Chiefs which is not directly elected. It comprises eight *ex-officio* members, being the chiefs of the principle tribes as laid down in the constitution (the relevant section is, however, under review). Another four members are elected by sub-chiefs of other tribes from among their own number, and those 12 members elect an additional three 'specially elected' members. The tenure of office corresponds with the life of the National Assembly.

The President, too, is only indirectly elected. Prospective candidates have to be nominated prior to the nomination of parliamentary candidates who have to indicate their preference for a particular presidential candidate on the nomination paper for their own candidature. The presidential candidate who commands the support of more than one half of the newly elected members of the National Assembly is declared President, holding office for the duration of Parliament. A constitutional amendment passed in 1997 limits the tenure of office to an aggregate period not exceeding 10 years, while prior to this there had been no restriction.

Suffrage: All registered voters are entitled to vote. The qualifications for being registered are: The person must be a citizen of Botswana, must have attained the age of 18 years (prior to a constitutional amendment passed in 1997 it used to be 21 years), and must have been born in Botswana or resided in Botswana for a continuous period of at least 12 months preceding the date of application. Persons are entitled to be registered in the constituency where they have their principal residence or in the constituency where they were born (if they do not have a residence). The lack of provisions for postal votes has resulted in the disenfranchisement of voters living outside the country, but this was rectified by a constitutional amendment passed in 1997.

Nomination of candidates: Parliamentary candidates must have been registered as voters and must command a sufficient knowledge of speaking and reading English to take an active part in the proceedings of Parliament. A constitutional amendment passed in 1997 reduced the qualifying age from 21 to 18 years. The nomination has to be supported by at least nine validly registered persons, and candidates must pay a deposit which is lost if they win less than 5% of the votes. Exempted are members of the House of Chiefs and those who hold a public office. In addition also, those persons are exempted who hold any office the functions of which involve responsibility for the conduct of any elections to the Assembly or the compilation or revision of any electoral register for the purpose of such elections.

With regard to the qualification for election as President, the candidate must have attained the age of 30 years, must be qualified to be elected as a member of the National Assembly and has to be a citizen by birth (those persons who became citizens prior to the amendment of the Citizenship Act in 1982) or by descent (persons who had to register as a citizen because they were born outside Botswana, although the father was a Botswana citizen at that time).

Electoral system: Plurality system in 40 single-member constituencies. Each elector has one vote. The actual voting is done by using counters (i.e. small discs) with different voting colors allotted to candidates of particular parties. In the polling booth, the counter is put into a ballot envelope which is then sealed by the voter, while the unused counters are put into discard boxes. The ballot envelope is then dropped into the ballot box placed in front of the presiding officer. The winner of the majority of votes in a constituency is declared to be elected; if there is only one candidate, no polling is conducted.

1.4 Comment on the Electoral Statistics

Data for national elections are readily available and exceptionally reliable. The Supervisor of Elections is obliged by the constitution to submit a report on each election to the minister responsible for the elections. This is usually done within a relatively short time (a few months). The minister in turn has to table the report in Parliament within seven days of the beginning of its next session. The Independent Electoral Commission, which was provided for as a successor to the Supervisor of Elections by a constitutional amendment passed in 1997, will presumably face similar obligations with regard to compiling and publishing reports.

The data presented here have been drawn from those reports, with only minor corrections in two cases: in 1984 the election for one constituency had to be repeated a few weeks after the general elections because of an election petition, and in 1994 the election in one of the constituencies had to be postponed for a month due to the death of one of the candidates a few days before the general elections. The results of the latter by-election have been included, while in the case of the 1984 by-election only the allocation of seats has been corrected accordingly. The data have, however, some shortcomings with regard to voter participation. The voters' rolls have so far been inflated because of frequent double registration regularly resulting in somewhat lower figures of voter participation than is actually the case. The use of a computerized system during the elections of 1994 has clearly made an impact on this. Because of the system of discs used for voting instead of ballot papers, there seem to be only very few invalid votes; in any case, the official statistics have never given any numbers of invalid votes at all.

2. Tables

2.1 Dates of National Elections, Referendums and Coups d'Etat

Year	Presidential elections	Parliamentary elections[a]	Elections for Constitutional Assembly	Referendums	Coups d'état
1965		01/03			
1969		18/10			
1974		26/10			
1979		20/10			
1984		08/09			
1987				26/09	
1989		07/10			
1994		15/10			
1997				04/10	

[a] As from 1969, communal elections have been held on the same day as parliamentary elections.

2.2 Electoral Body 1965–1994

Year	Type of election[a]	Population[b]	Registered voters		Votes cast		
			Total number[c]	% pop.	Total number[d]	% reg. voters[e]	% pop.
1965	LA	559,000	189,000	33.8	140,788	80.4	25.2
1969	NA	629,000	156,533	24.9	76,858	54.7	12.2
1974	NA	650,000	236,872	36.4	64,011	31.2	9.8
1979	NA	879,000	243,483	30.8	134,496	58.4	17.0
1984	NA	1,043,000	301,815	32.1	227,756	77.6	24.2
1989	NA	1,237,000	367,069	31.1	250,487	68.2	21.1
1994	NA	1,468,000	370,179	27.9	283,375	76.6	21.4

[a] LA = Legislative Assembly, NA = National Assembly.

[b] Estimation according 1965–1974: Statistical Yearbook, UNESCO; 1979–1994: figures calculated according to the census figures of 1981 and 1991.

[c] Numbers in italics: registered voters in contested constituencies.

[d] Only valid votes given.

[e] Relating to registered voters in contested constituencies.

2.3 Abbreviations

BDP	Botswana Democratic Party
BFP	Botswana Freedom Party
BIP	Botswana Independence Party
BLP	Botswana Labour Party
BNP	Botswana National Front
BPP	Botswana People's Party
BPP No. 1	Botswana People's Party No.1
BPU	Botswana Progressive Union
IFP	Independence Freedom Party
LLB	Lesedi la Botswana
UDF	United Democratic Front
USP	United Socialist Party

2.4 Electoral Participation of Parties and Alliances 1965–1994

Party / Alliance	Years	Contested parliamentary elections[a]
BDP	1965, 1969, 1974, 1979, 1984, 1989, 1994	7
BIP	1965, 1969, 1974, 1979, 1984, 1989[b]	6
BPP	1965, 1969, 1974, 1979, 1984, 1989, 1994	7
BPP No.1	1965	1
BNF	1969, 1974, 1979, 1984, 1989, 1994	6
BPU	1984, 1989, 1994	3
BLP	1989, 1994	2
BFP	1989[b]	1
IFP	1994	1
LLB	1994	1
UDF	1994	1
USP	1994	1

[a] There have been six parliamentary elections since independence and one before independence. Indirect presidential elections have been held at the same time as from 1969: at independence in 1966, the then Prime Minister became President without an election. There have been additional indirect elections of a President in 1980 (after the death of the incumbent President) and 1998 (after the voluntary retirement of the incumbent President). In the regular presidential elections, the BDP presented a candidate each time, the BNF five times, the BPP four times and the BPU only once.

[b] BIP and BFP merged into IFP.

2.5 Referendums

Year	1987[a]		1997 (Question 1)[b]	
	Total number	%	Total number	%
Registered voters	–	—	370,173	
Votes cast	—	—	61,873	16.7
Invalid votes	—	—	201	0.3
Valid votes	57,908	—	61,672	99.7
Yes	45,227	78.1	45,122	73.2
No	12,681	21.9	16,550	26.8

[a] The question referred to a constitutional amendment granting a more or less independent status to the office of the Supervisor of Elections.

[b] In the referendum of 1997 three separate questions with regard to a constitutional amendment were asked. Question one referred to a proposal for the establishment of an Independent Electoral Commission.

Year	1997 (Question 2)		1997 (Question 3)[b]	
	Total number	%	Total number	%
Registered voters	370,173	–	370,173	–
Votes cast	62,047	16.8	61,948	16.7
Invalid votes	197	0.3	198	0.3
Valid votes	61,850	99.7	61,750	99.7
Yes	43,555	70.4	36,275	58.7
No	18,295	29.6	25,475	41.3

[a] Decision whether Batswana residing outside the country should be allowed to vote.

[b] Approval of the proposal to lower the voting age from 21 to 18 years.

2.6 Elections for Constitutional Assembly

Elections for Constitutional Assembly have not been held.

2.7 Parliamentary Elections 1965–1994

Year	1965 Total number	%	1969 Total number	%
Registered voters	189,000	–	156,533	–
in contested constit.	175,042		140,428	
Votes cast	—	—	—	—
Invalid votes	—	—	—	—
Valid votes	140,788	80.4	76,858	54.7
BDP	113,167	80.4	52,518	68.3
BIP	6,491	4.6	4,601	6.0
BPP	19,964	14.2	9,329	12.1
BPP No.1	377	0.3	–	–
Independents	789	0.6	–	–
BNF	–	–	10,410	13.5

Year	1974 Total number	%	1979 Total number	%
Registered voters	236,872	–	243,483	–
in contested constit.	205,050		230,321	
Votes cast	—	—	—	—
Invalid votes	—	—	—	—
Valid votes	64,011	31.2	134,496	58.4
BDP	49,047	76.6	101,098	75.2
BIP	3,086	4.8	5,657	4.2
BPP	4,199	6.6	9,983	7.4
BNF	7,358	11.5	17,480	13.0
Independents	321	0.5	278	0.2

Year	1984 Total number	%	1989 Total number	%
Registered voters	301,815	–	367,069	–
in contested constit.	293,571	–	367,069	–
Votes cast	—	—	—	—
Invalid votes	—	—	—	—
Valid votes	227,756	77.6	250,487	68.2
BDP	154,863	68.0	162,277	64.8
BIP	7,288	3.2	6,209	2.5
BPP	14,961	6.6	10,891	4.4
BNF	46,550	20.4	67,513	27.0
BPU	3,036	1.3	2,186	0.9
BFP	–	–	1,363	0.5
BLP	–	–	48	0.0
Independents	1,058	0.5	–	–

Year	1994 Total number	%
Registered voters	370,179	–
Votes cast	—	—
Invalid votes	—	—
Valid votes	283,375	76.6
BDP	154,687	54.7
BPP	11,586	4.1
BNF	104,435	36.9
BPU	3,016	1.1
BLP	23	0.0
IFP	7,658	2.7
LLB	235	0.1
UDF	783	0.3
USP	265	0.1

2.8 Composition of Parliament 1965–1994

Year	1965		1969		1974		1979	
	Seats	%	Seats	%	Seats	%	Seats	%
	31	100	31	100	32	100	32	100
BDP	28	90.3	24	77.4	27	84.4	29	90.6
BIP	–	–	1	3.2	1	3.1	–	–
BPP	3	9.7	3	9.7	2	6.3	1	3.1
BNF	–	–	3	9.7	2	6.3	2	6.3

Year	1984		1989		1994	
	Seats	%	Seats	%	Seats	%
	34	100	34	100	40	100
BDP	28	82.4	31	91.2	27	67.5
BPP	1	2.9	–	–	–	–
BNF	5	14.7	3	8.8	13	32.5

2.9 Presidential Elections

Indirect election: the candidate who commands the support of more than one half of the newly elected members of the National Assembly is declared President.

2.10 List of Power Holders 1966–1998

Head of State and Government	Years	Remarks
Sir Seretse Khama	1966–1980	The then Prime Minister became automatically President on Independence Day (30 September 1966). He died on 13 July 1980.
Sir Ketumile Masire	1980–1998	The then Vice-President Masire was elected President on 17 July 1980. He resigned voluntarily on 31 March 1998.
Festus Mogae	1998–	The then Vice-President Mogae was elected President in April 1998.

3. Bibliography

3.1 Official sources

The Bechuanaland General Elections 1965—Ballot Envelopes and Voting Counters, by George Winstanley, Chief Electoral Officer. Gaborone, including an appendix ('Daily News' Supplement) Bechuanaland General Elections—March 1st, 1965. Results, Majorities, Percentage Polls, Lost Deposits—at a Glance.

'Constitution of Botswana'. *Botswana Independence Order, Schedule 2, Statutory Instrument 1966 No. 1171*, United Kingdom.

'Constitution (Second Amendment) Act 1969 (No. 43 of 1969)'. *Government Gazette,* Vol. VII, suppl. B. 277–279.

'Constitution of Botswana (Amendment) Act 1972 (No. 28 of 1972)'. *Government Gazette*, Vol. X, suppl. A. 165–166.

'Constitution (Amendment) Act 1973 (No. 24 of 1973)'. *Government Gazette*, Vol. XI, suppl. A. 279–280.

'Constitution (Amendment) Act 1983 (No. 1 of 1983)'. *Government Gazette*, Vol. XXI, suppl. A. 1.

'Constitution of Botswana (Amendment) Act 1987 (No. 22 of 1987)'. *Government Gazette*, Vol. XXV, suppl. A. 175–178.

'Constitution (Amendment) Act 1992 (No. 27 of 1992)'. *Government Gazette*, Vol. XXX, suppl. A. 115.

'Constitution (Amendment) Act 1997 (No. 16 of 1997)'. *Government Gazette*, Vol. XXXV, suppl. A. 39–40.

'Constitution (Amendment) Act 1997 (No. 18 of 1997)'. *Government Gazette*, Vol. XXXV, suppl. A. 43–46.

'Electoral Act 1968 (No. 38 of 1968)'. *Government Gazette*, Vol. VI, suppl. B. 219–299.

'Electoral (Amendment) Act 1969 (No. 49 of 1969)'. *Government Gazette*, Vol. VII, suppl. B. 305–310.
'Electoral (Amendment) Act 1974 (No. 8 of 1974)'. *Government Gazette*, Vol. XII, suppl. A. 25.
'Electoral (Amendment) Act 1977 (No. 15 of 1977)'. *Government Gazette*, Vol. XV, suppl. A. 191–193.
'Electoral (Amendment) (No.2) Act 1977 (No. 50 of 1977)'. *Government Gazette*, Vol. XV, suppl. A. 341–342.
'Electoral (Amendment) Act 1981 (No. 29 of 1981)'. *Government Gazette*, Vol. XIX, suppl. A. 139–140.
'Electoral (Amendment) Act 1984 (No. 16 of 1984)'. Government Gazette, Vol. XXII, suppl. A. 35–36.
'Electoral (Amendment) Act 1988 (No. 18 of 1988)'. *Government Gazette*, Vol. XXVI, suppl. A. 85–89.
'Electoral (Amendment) Act 1989 (No. 20 of 1989)'. *Government Gazette*, Vol. XXVII, suppl. A. 129–132.
'Electoral (Amendment) Act 1993 (No. 10 of 1993)'. *Government Gazette*, Vol. XXXI, suppl. A. 35–40.
'Presidential elections (Supplementary Provisions) Act 1969 (No. 41 of 1969)'. *Government Gazette*, Vol. VII, suppl. B. 263–270.
'Presidential elections (Supplementary Provisions) (Amendment) Act 1977 (No. 14 of 1977)'. *Government Gazette*, Vol. XV, suppl. A. 189–190.
'Presidential elections (Supplementary Provisions) (Amendment) Act 1979 (No. 14 of 1979)'. *Government Gazette*, Vol. XVII, suppl. A. 111.
'Referendum Act 1987 (No. 16 of 1987)'. *Government Gazette*, Vol. XXV, suppl. A. 49–61.
'Referendum (Amendment) Act 1987 (No. 17 of 1987)'. *Government Gazette*, Vol. XXV, suppl. A. 63–66.
Republic of Botswana (1970). *Report on the General Elections 1969*. Gaborone: Government Printer.
— (1974). *Report to the Minister of State on the General Elections, 1974*. Gaborone: Government Printer.
— (1979). *Report to the Minister of Public Service and Information on the General Election, 1979*. Gaborone: Government Printer.
— (1984). *Report to the Minister of Public Service and Information on the General Election, 1984*. Gaborone: Government Printer.
— (1989). *Report to the Minister of Presidential Affairs and Public Administration on the General Election, 1989*. Gaborone: Government Printer.
— (1993). *Electoral. Chapter 02:07. Dated 31st December, 1993*. Gaborone: Government Printer.
— (1995). *Report to the Minister of Presidential Affairs and Public Administration on the General Election, 1994*. Gaborone: Government Printer.

'Statute Law (Miscellaneous Amendments) (No. 2) Act 1979 (No. 17 of 1979)'. *Government Gazette*, Vol. XVII, suppl. A. 119–120.

3.2 Books and Articles

Adam, E. (1986). 'Botswana: Parlamentswahlen 1984. Parteienpluralismus in Afrika' *Afrika Spectrum*, 21/2: 189–210.

— (1985). *Botswana: Parlamentswahlen 1984. Parteienpluralismus in Afrika*. Bonn-Bad Godesberg: Forschungsinstitut der Friedrich-Ebert-Stiftung.

Bernard, S. (1990). 'Les elections générales d'octobre 1989 au Botswana. L'apparence de la continuite et de la permanence'. Talence: Centre d'Etudes d'Afrique Noire.

Carlsson, K. (1997). *Politiska Valmanifest i Botswana Inför Valet 1994. Löften, sakfrågor eller lögner?*. Göteborgs universitet: Statsvetenskapliga institutionen.

Charlton, R. (1993). 'The Politics of Elections in Botswana'. *Africa*, 63/3: 330–370.

Cohen, D. L. (1979). 'The Botswana Political Elite: Evidence from the 1974 General Elections'. *Journal of Southern African Affairs*, 4/3: 347–371.

Crowder, M (1988). 'Botswana and the Survival of Liberal Democracy in Africa', in P. Gifford and R. W. Louis (eds.), *Decolonization and African Independence. The Transfers of Power, 1960–1980*. New Haven, Conn.: Yale University Press, 461–476.

Danevad, A. (1995) 'Responsiveness in Botswana Politics: Do Elections Matter?'. *The Journal of Modern African Studies*, 33/3: 381–402.

Darnolf, S. (1997a). *Democratic Electioneering in Southern Africa. The Contrasting Cases of Botswana and Zimbabwe.* Göteborg: Göteborg University Studies in Politics 45.

— (1997b). 'Critics or Megaphones? News Coverage During the Parliamentary Election Campaigns in Botswana 1994 and Zimbabwe 1995'. *Democratization*, 4/2: 167–191.

— (1995a). 'Campaigning in Southern Africa. The Cases of Botswana and Zimbabwe', in T. Negash and L. Rudebeck (eds.), *Dimensions of Development with Emphasis on Africa*. Uppsala University: Nordiska Afrikainstitutet and Forum for Development Studies, 63–75.

— (1995b). *Botswana: En Studie av politiska parties aktiviteter och massmediernas rapportering under valkampanjen 1994*. Göteborgs universitet: Statsvetenskapliga institutionen.

Datta, K. (1990). *A Profile of the Candidates for the Primaries held before the 1989 General Elections in Botswana*. Gaborone: Working paper, Democracy Research Project.

— and Mguni, B. (1990). *A Report on Exit-Polls in the General Elections in Botswana, 1989.* Gaborone: Working paper, Democracy Research Project.

— (1991). *Democracy and Elections in Botswana with some Reference to General Literature on Democracy and Elections in Africa. Bibliography.* Talence: Centre d'Etudes d'Afrique Noire.

Du Toit, P. (1995). *State Building and Democracy in Southern Africa. Botswana, Zimbabwe, and South Africa.* Washington D.C.: United States Institute of Peace Press.

Good, K. (1992). 'Interpreting the Exceptionality of Botswana'. *The Journal of Modern African Studies*, 30/1: 69–95.

— (1996a). 'Towards Popular Participation in Botswana'. *The Journal of Modern African Studies*, 34/1: 53–77.

— (1996b). 'Authoritarian Liberalism: a Defining Characteristic of Botswana'. *Journal of Contemporary African Studies*, 14/1: 29–51.

— (1997). *Realizing Democracy in Botswana, Namibia and South Africa.* Pretoria: Africa Institute.

Högberg, P. (1995). *Political Opposition - The Missing Link in the African Democratization. The Cases of Botswana, Kenya and Zambia.* Uppsala University: Department of Government.

Holm, J. D. (1974). *Dimensions of Mass Involvement in Botswana Politics: A Test of Alternative Theories.* Beverly Hills, Cal.: Sage.

— (1987). 'Elections in Botswana: Institutionalization of a New System of Legitimacy', in F. M. Hayward (ed.), *Elections in Independent Africa.* Boulder, Col.: Westview Press, 121–148.

— (1988). 'Botswana: a Paternalistic Democracy', in L. J. Diamond, J. J. Linz and S. M. Lipset (eds.), *Democracy in Developing Countries. Vol. 2.* Boulder, Col.: Lynne Rienner, 179–215.

— (1989). 'Elections and democracy in Botswana', in J. Holm, and P. Molutsi (eds.), *Democracy in Botswana. The Proceedings of a Symposium held in Gaborone, 1-5 August 1988.* Gaborone: Macmillan Botswana Publishing Company, 189–202.

— (1993). 'Political Culture and Democracy: A Study of Mass Participation in Botswana', in S. J. Stedman (ed.), *The Political Economy of Democratic Development.* Boulder, Col.: Lynne Rienner, 91–111.

— (1994). 'Botswana: one African success story'. *Current History*, 93/583: 198–202.

— and Molutsi, P. (1989). *Democracy in Botswana. The Proceedings of a Symposium held in Gaborone, 1–5 August 1988.* Gaborone: Macmillan Botswana Publishing Company.

— (1992). 'Statesociety Relations in Botswana. Beginning Liberalization', in G. Hyden and M. Bratton (eds.), *Governance and Politics in Africa.* Boulder, Col.: Lynne Rienner, 75–95.

— and Somolekae, G. (1996). 'The Development of Civil Society in a Democratic State: The Botswana Model'. *African Studies Review*, 39/2: 43–69.

Kimble, J., and Molokomme, A. (1985). 'Gender and Politics in Botswana: Some Thoughts of the 1984 Elections', in *Final Report of 1984 General Election in Botswana. Part I.* Gaborone: University of Botswana Election Study Group (mimeo).

Lekorwe, M., and Mgadla, P. T. (1990). *A Report of the 1989 Primaries in Botswana.* Gaborone: Working Paper, Democracy Research Project.

Macartney, W. J. A. (1971). 'The General Elections of 1969'. *Botswana Notes and Records*, 3: 32–36.

Magang, D. N. (1986). 'Democracy in the African Tradition: The Case of Botswana', in D. Ronen (ed.), *Democracy and Pluralism in Africa.* Boulder, Col.: Lynne Rienner, 103–108.

Masale, G. (1985a). 'Ethnicity and Regionalism in Botswana and their Impact on Elections: A Case Study of the North-East and Francistown', in *Final Report of 1984 General Election in Botswana. Part II.* Gaborone: University of Botswana Election Group (mimeo).

— (1985b). 'Who Runs for Office? The Results of Candidates Survey', in *Final Report of 1984 General Election in Botswana. Part I.* Gaborone: University of Botswana Election Group (mimeo).

Molamu, L. (1985a). 'Dimensions of Mass Politics: Result of a Sample Study', in *Final Report of 1984 General Election in Botswana. Part I.* Gaborone: University of Botswana Election Group (mimeo).

— (1985b). 'The Serowe South Constituency Case Study', in *Final Report of 1984 General Election in Botswana. Part II.* Gaborone: University of Botswana Election Group (mimeo).

Molomo, M. G. (1991). 'Botswana's Political Process', in M. G. Molomo and B. T. Mokopakgosi (eds.), *Multiparty Democracy in Botswana*. Harare: Southern Africa Political Economy Series: Trust, State and Democracy Series, 2: 11–22.

— and Mokopakgosi, B. T. (1990). *Mass Mobilisation and Campaign Strategies.* University of Botswana: Democracy Research Project.

Molutsi, P. P. (1991). 'Political Parties and Democracy in Botswana', in M. G. Molomo and B. T. Mokopakgosi (eds.), *Multiparty Democracy in Botswana.* Harare: Southern Africa Political Economy Series: Trust, State and Democracy Series, 2: 5–9.

— and Holm, J. D. (1990). 'Developing Democracy when Civil Society is weak: the Case of Botswana'. *African Affairs*, 89/356: 323–340.

Molutsi, P. P., and Tsie, B. (1990). *Political Mobilisation and Strategies for Elections: A Report of the Study of the 1989 Botswana Elections.* University of Gaborone: Working Paper, Democracy Research Project.

Motswagole, M.T. (1989) 'Election and Democracy in Botswana', in J. Holm and P. Molutsi (eds.), *Democracy in Botswana. The Proceedings of a Symposium held in Gaborone, 1-5 August 1988.* Gaborone: Macmillan Botswana Publishing Company, 182–189.

Nengwekhulu, R. (1985a). 'The 1984 General Election in Gaborone Botswana Constituency', in *Final Report of 1984 General Election in Botswana. Part II.* Gaborone: University of Botswana Election Study Group (mimeo).

— (1985b). 'The 1984 General Election in Lobatse - Barolong Farms Constituency', in *Final Report of 1984 General Election in Botswana. Part II.* Gaborone: University of Botswana Election Study Group (mimeo).

— (1985c). 'Class, State, Politics and Elections in Post Colonial Botswana in the Light of the 1984 Botswana General Election', in *Final Report of 1984 General Election in Botswana. Part I.* Gaborone: University of Botswana Election Study Group (mimeo).

— (1991). 'The Electoral Process', in M. G. Molomo and B. T. Mokopakgosi (eds.), *Multiparty Democracy in Botswana.* Harare: Southern Africa Political Economy Series: Trust, State and Democracy Series, 2: 39–47.

Nuscheler, F. (1978). 'Botswana', in D. Sternberger, B. Vogel, D. Nohlen and K. Landfried (eds.), *Die Wahl der Parlamente und anderer Staatsorgane. Vol. II: Afrika. Politische Organisation und Repräsentation in Afrika,* by Franz Nuscheler, Klaus Ziemer *et al.,* Berlin/ New York: Walter de Gruyter, 543–566.

Otlhogile, B. (1994). 'Judicial Intervention in the Election Process: Botswana's Experience'. *The Comparative and International Law Journal of Southern Africa*, 27: 222–232.

— (1991). 'How free and fair?', in M. G. Molomo and B. T. Mokopakgosi (eds.), *Multiparty Democracy in Botswana.* Harare: Southern Africa Political Economy Series: Trust, State and Democracy Series, 2: 23–28.

— and Molutsi, P. (1993). *Consolidating Democracy: The Electoral Process under Scrutiny. Report of the Workshop on Electoral Law and Administration of Elections in Botswana held on 19-20th February, 1993.* Gaborone: University of Botswana, Democracy Research Project.

Parson, J. D. (1975). 'A Note on the 1974 General Election in Botswana and the UBLS Election Study'. *Botswana Notes and Records*, 7: 73–81.

— (1983). 'The Trajectory of Class and State in Dependent Development. The Consequences of new Wealth for Botswana'. *The Journal of Commonwealth and Comparative Politics,* 21/3: 39–60.

— (1985a). 'Elections and Politics in the Mochudi National Assembly Constituency', in *Final Report of 1984 General Election in Botswana.* Gaborone: University of Botswana Election Study Group (mimeo).

— (1985b). 'The 1984 Botswana General Elections and Results: a Macro-analysis', in *Final Report of 1984 General Election in Botswana. Part I.* Gaborone: University of Botswana Election Study Group (mimeo).

— (1993). 'Liberal Democracy, the Liberal State, and the 1989 General Elections in Botswana', in S. J. Stedman (ed.), *The Political Economy of Democratic Development*. Boulder, Col.: Lynne Rienner, 65–90.

Parsons, N. (1993). 'Botswana: an End to Exceptionality?'. *The Round Table*, 325: 73–82.

Picard, L. A. (1985). 'Bureaucrats, Elections and Political Control: National Politics, the District Administration and the Multi-party System in Botswana', in L. A. Picard (ed.), *The Evolution of Modern Botswana. Politics and Rural Development in Southern Africa*. London: Collings, 176–205, 312–315.

— (1987). *The Politics of Development in Botswana. A Model for Success?* Boulder, Col.: Lynne Rienner.

Polhemus, J. H. (1983). 'Botswana Votes: Parties and Elections in an African Democracy'. *The Journal of Modern African Studies*, 21/3: 397–430.

— (1985a). 'Elections as Administrative Process: A Survey of the 1984 Botswana Elections'. in *Final Report of 1984 General Election in Botswana. Part I.* Gaborone: University of Botswana Election Study Group (mimeo).

— (1985b). 'The 1984 Elections in Selebi-Phikwe: A Preliminary Analysis'. in *Final Report of 1984 General Election in Botswana. Part I.* Gaborone: University of Botswana Election Study Group (mimeo).

Rule, S. P. (1995). 'Electoral Trends in Botswana. A Geographical Perspective'. *Africa Insight*, 25/1: 21–30.

Serema, L. E. (1989). 'Elections and Democracy: How Democratic is the Process?', in J. Holm and P. Molutsi (eds.), *Democracy in Botswana. The Proceedings of a Symposium held in Gaborone, 1-5 August 1988.* Gaborone: Macmillan Botswana Publishing Company, 177–181.

Somolekae, G. (1989). 'Do Batswana Think and Act as Democrats?', in J. Holm and P. Molutsi (eds.), *Democracy in Botswana. The Proceedings of a Symposium held in Gaborone, 1-5 August 1988*. Gaborone: Macmillan Botswana Publishing Company, 75–88.

Stedman, S. J. (ed.) (1993). *Botswana: The Political Economy of Democratic Development*. Boulder, Col.: Lynne Rienner.

Stevens, C., and Speed, J. (1978). 'Multi-partyism in Africa. The Case of Botswana Revisited'. *African Affairs*, 77/304: 381–387.

Tsie, B. (1985a). 'Change and Continuity in Post Colonial Societies: Elections and Politics in Perspective', in *Final Report of 1984 General Election in Botswana. Part I.* Gaborone: University of Botswana Election Study Group (mimeo).

— (1985b). 'Social Classes, Political Parties and Social Change in Kanye', in *Final Report of 1984 General Election in Botswana. Part II.* Gaborone: University of Botswana Election Study Group (mimeo).

— (1991). 'Election, Democracy and Hegemony in Botswana', in M. G. Molomo and B. T. Mokopakgosi (eds.), *Multiparty Democracy in Botswana*. Harare: Southern Africa Political Economy Series: Trust, State and Democracy Series,.2: 49–53.

Winstanley, G. (1966). 'A Note on the Practical Use of the French Voting System in the First Bechuanaland Elections'. *Journal of Administration Overseas*, 5/2: 112–114.

Wiseman, J. (1977). 'Multipartism in Africa: The Case of Botswana'. *African Affairs*, 76/302: 70–79.

— (1980). 'Election and Parliamentary Democracy in Botswana'. *The World Today*, 36/2: 72–78.

— and Charlton, R. (1995). 'The October 1994 Elections in Botswana'. *Electoral Studies*, 14/3: 323–328.

Young, H., and Cohen, D. (1979). *Voters and Candidates in the 1974 General Elections. Two Studies on the Political and Statistical aspects*. Gaborone: National Institute for Development and Cultural Research (N.I.R.). Documentation Unit—University College of Botswana. Working Paper No. 22.

BURKINA FASO

by Florian Grotz*

1. Introduction

1.1 Historical Overview

Since the independence of the former French colony, the political development of Burkina Faso (before 1984: Upper Volta) can be described as a cyclical sequence of authoritarian systems on the one hand and attempts to introduce democratic rule on the other. In all these regime changes the military played an important role.

After a referendum on a constitution draft had been held and a Parliament (*assemblée législative*) had been elected in 1959, Upper Volta became an independent state on 5 August 1960. According to the provisional rules of the new constitution which established a presidential form of government, Maurice Yaméogo was elected as the first President of the state by the *assemblée législative* whose electoral period had been prolonged until 1965. As several of the leaders of the main oppositional *Parti du Regroupement Africain* (PRA) had joined Yaméogo's *Rassemblement Démocratique Africain* (RDA) immediately after the elections of 1959 and other parties had been banned in early 1960, the *Union Démocratique Voltaique—Rassemblement Démocratique Africain* (UDV-RDA), under the leadership of Yaméogo, became the main political institution in a one-party state. Consequently, the parliamentary and presidential elections in 1965 which confirmed Yaméogo and the UDV-RDA were non-competitive.

As Yaméogo lost the support of the Catholic church due to his divorce and remarriage and that of the trade unions because of massive taxation, mass protests against the regime were organized. On 3 January 1966, the military under Lieutenant-Colonel Sangoulé Lamizana took power. In accordance with Lamizana's statements that the military would establish only an interim regime, a liberalization of the Voltaian

---

* The author would like to thank the Embassy of Burkina Faso in Germany and Romila Sudhir (International Foundation for Electoral Systems, Washington, D.C.) for help in the collection of information for the present article.

political system was initiated four years later. In November 1969, political parties were officially re-admitted. In June 1970, the constitution of the Second Republic, which introduced a semi-presidential system similar to that of the French Fifth Republic, was accepted in a referendum. In December of the same year the first competitive parliamentary elections since independence led to a two-third majority of UDV-RDA in the National Assembly. In 1974 Lamizana dissolved the democratic institutions and re-established military rule, because the power struggle between the speaker of the Parliament Joseph Ouédraogo and the Prime Minister Gérard Kango Ouédraogo had escalated in view of the forthcoming presidential elections. This coup d'état, in contrast to that of 1966, was not based on a broad social consensus.

In 1977 the military re-established democracy in a similar way as it had done seven years before. The most important innovation of the Third Republic's constitution consisted in the regulation that only those three parties that gained most of the votes in the first parliamentary elections would be permanently allowed. In these elections of April 1978, the strongest three out of seven parties proved to be the UDV-RDA, the PRA and the *Union Nationale pour la Défense et la Démocratie* (UNDD), which had been founded by Hermann Yaméogo, the son of the first President. The competitive presidential elections held in the same year were won by Lamizana. Three years later, however, the third attempt to democratize Upper Volta failed again, mainly because of personal conflicts between ambitious political leaders and officers, and due to the disastrous economic situation.

In the 1980s, military regimes under different leaders replaced each other regularly (1980, 1983, 1987). The most remarkable political leader in this period remained Captain Thomas Sankara who established a Marxist–Leninist regime in 1983 and initiated revolutionary processes of social transformation that were unique in sub-Saharan Africa. Since his times (5 August 1984), the country is officially named Burkina Faso ('land of the honest people'). As Sankara's political support among the trade unions and the political elite rapidly declined, Blaise Compaoré, a long-time ally of Sankara, finally acceded to power in 1987 after a coup d'état in which Sankara was killed.

In 1989 Compaoré began to liberalize the regime. Parties were officially re-admitted in January 1989. Until the end of 1991, over 40 parties had been founded. The Constitution of the Fourth Republic, which again introduced a semi-presidential form of government was accepted by referendum in June 1991. In the following months, however, the consensus between the opposition alliance *Coordination des Forces*

Démocratique (CFD) and Compaoré's *Organisation pour la Démocratie Populaire—Mouvement de Travail* (ODP-MT), the main successor organization of Sankara's Marxist–Leninist *Front Populaire*, broke down. Thus, the presidential elections of 1991 in which Compaoré was elected as the first President of the Fourth Republic were boycotted by all other parties. In contrast to that, 27 parties participated in the parliamentary elections of May 1992 without preventing the ODP-MT from winning more than two thirds of the seats. In December 1995, the second chamber of the Parliament (*chambre des répresentants*), as stipulated in the constitution, was installed. This institution has consultative functions and consists of 178 members of which 114 are appointed by social groups, 60 by provincial councils and four by the President.

After the ODP-MT had merged with several small opposition parties and re-named itself *Congrès pour la Démocratie et le Progrès* (CDP) in February 1996, it could even increase its hegemonic position in the Burkinabé party system: In the parliamentary elections of May 1997 it got more than 90% of the seats, whereas the main opposition parties (RDA, *Alliance pour la Démocratie et la Féderation* [ADF] of Hermann Yaméogo and the *Parti pour la Démocratie et le Progrès* [PDP] led by Joseph Ki-Zerbo) won only few mandates.

1.2 Evolution of Electoral Provisions

Since 1959 the principles of universal, equal, direct and secret suffrage have been applied. Since independence all citizens who had reached the age of 21 have been entitled to vote. For the elections to the *assemblée nationale* in 1965, candidates had to be aged at least 23. In all parliamentary elections since 1970, every candidate has had to name a person who is called on to replace him, if he should become Secretary of State (as the constitutions of 1970, 1977 and 1991 determined the incompatibility of holding a parliamentary seat and membership in government). For all the presidential elections that have taken place up to now (1965; 1978; 1991), candidates had to be aged at least 35. The electoral law for the first, non-competitive presidential election in 1965 additionally provided that candidates had to be a member of a legally admitted party. Consequently, Yaméogo as the candidate of the sole officially existing party UDV-RDA was the only candidate for President.

As for the presidential electoral system, the first, non-competitive presidential elections in 1965 were formally held under an absolute majority system (with a run-off among the two best places candidates). According to Art. 13 of the Third Republic's constitution, the presidential elections of 1978 were held under the same electoral system, in which the run-off between the two best placed candidates had to be held two weeks after the first round.

For the election to the National Assembly in 1959, which became the first Parliament of the independent Upper Volta, a territorially segmented electoral system was applied. In the north and in the south, traditional RDA-supportive regions, two big electoral districts were established; in these constituencies the deputies (36 in the north, 23 in the south) were elected by a plurality system with party lists. By contrast, in the districts Ouahigouya and Ouagadougou where the PRA supporters were concentrated, there were only eight seats in each of the two constituencies. These were elected by proportional representation. For the non-competitive parliamentary elections of 1965 a plurality system with (one) party list was applied. The electoral law for the parliamentary elections of 1970 provided for a proportional representation list system in constituencies of small and medium size. These constituencies of two to 11 deputies were territorially identical with the administrative districts established in 1965 (*organismes régionaux de développement*). For the parliamentary elections in the Third Republic (1978), the type of electoral system was not changed, but there were only 10 constituencies of four to 10 mandates. The seats were distributed by the d'Hondt method. The first parliamentary elections in the Fourth Republic (1992) were held under the same type of electoral system. The 107 members of the *assemblée des députés du peuple* were elected in 30 constituencies with two to seven seats that were distributed by the simple quota formula and the highest average formula for the the remaining mandates.

1.3 Current Electoral Provisions

Sources: Constitution du Burkina Faso; Loi No. 002/97/ADP du 27 janvier 1997 portant revision de la Constitution (Constitutional Amendments); Loi No. 003/97/ADP du 12 février 1997 portant Code Electoral (Electoral Law).

Elected national institutions: President of Burkina Faso and the first chamber of Parliament (*assemblée nationale,* before 1997: *assemblée des députés du peuple;* 111 elected members). Regular term of office: seven years (for the President), five years (for the *assemblée nationale*).

Suffrage: The principles of universal, equal, direct and secret suffrage are applied. Every citizen who has reached the age of 18 has the right to vote and is entitled to be registered as a voter.

Nomination of candidates
- *presidential elections*: Every candidate for president has to be Burkinabé, has to have parents who are Burkinabé and must be aged at least 35 (Constitution, Art. 38). The original constitutional regulation that a person may not hold office as President for more than two terms (Art. 37) was changed by Parliament in January 1997: Now there is no limit for re-election.
- *parliamentary elections*: Every Burkinabé who has reached the age of 21 is eligible for candidature for Parliament.

Electoral system
- *presidential elections*: Absolute majority system. If no candidate gets more than 50% of the votes cast, the constitution provides for a run-off between the two best placed candidates. This will be held two weeks after the first round. In this second round only a relative majority is required (Art. 89 of the Electoral Law).
- *parliamentary elections*: The Electoral Law provides for an electoral system corresponding to the principle of proportional representation (Art. 112). However, as 45% of the seats are distributed in single-member and two-member districts, the electoral system has rather a majoritarian than a proportional character. Technical elements: *45 constituencies, which are territorially identical with the country's provinces. *Size of the constituencies: one to 11 deputies to be elected (12 single-member; 19 two-member; eight three-member; one four-, three five-, one seven- and one 11-member constituency; average: 2,5). *Closed and blocked party lists. *Simple quota formula and the highest average for the distribution of the remaining seats. If there are two lists with the same highest average remainders, the seat will be allocated to the list that got more votes (Art. 112 of the Electoral Law).

1.4 Comment on the Electoral Statistics

The following electoral statistics are mainly composed on the basis of various secondary sources which contain the relevant official electoral results. The results of the 1991 presidential elections were obtained from the Burkinabé newspaper *Sidwaya* No. 1908 (4 December 1991). The information on the 1992 parliamentary elections obtained from the Embassy of Burkina Faso in Germany includes only those eight out of 27 parties that have got more than 20,000 votes. The results of the 1997 parliamentary elections were taken both from an Election Report (IFES 1997) and from official sources. Regional results are also indicated for all competitive elections except those of 1992. Data for the 1998 presidential elections are based on information from the Independent National Electoral Commission.

Arithmetical errors in the cited electoral reports are corrected as far as possible. With respect to the second round of the presidential elections 1978, the error of two votes in the official statistics that Reuke (1979: 38) remarks is corrected in the respective tables. Concerning decisions between different data for the same elections, the commentaries of Schmitz (1990) were very helpful. With regard to the credibility of the officially edited electoral results, the correctness of the data seems to be uncertain in some cases. This is especially true for the parliamentary elections of 1965 (Ziemer 1978: 1573). In a similar way, Reuke (1979: 27) reports that there were some obvious irregularities in the parliamentary elections of 1978. Although the parliamentary elections in the present Fourth Republic were principally considered as free and fair, there have been serious problems with voter registration in the 1997 parliamentary elections (IFES 1997).

2. Tables

2.1 Dates of National Elections, Referendums and Coups d'Etat

Year	Presidential elections	Parliamentary elections	Elections for Constitutional Assembly	Referendums	Coups d'état
1959		19/04		15/03	
1965	03/10	07/11			
1966					03/01
1970		20/12		14/06	
1974					08/02
1977				27/11	
1978	14/05 (1st) 28/05 (2nd)	30/04			
1980					25/11
1983					04/08
1987					15/10
1991	01/12			02/06	
1992		24/05			
1997		11/05[a]			
1998	15/11				

[a] Because of irregularities the elections were repeated in two provinces (Kouritenga, Oudalan) on 18 June 1997. In these elections, the same results as from the original election were obtained.

2.2 Electoral Body 1958–1998

Year	Type of election[a]	Population[b]	Registered voters		Votes cast		
			Total number	% pop.	Total number	% reg. voters	% pop.
1959	Ref	3,567,000	1,957,732	54.9	1,344,932	68.7	37.7
1959	Pa	3,567,000	1,924,765	54.0	903,290	46.9	25.3
1965	Pr	4,882,000	2,182,425	44.7	2,146,790	98.4	44.0
1965	Pa	4,882,000	2,188,241	44.8	2,132,418	97.4	43.7
1970	Ref	5,384,000	2,351,258	43.7	1,817,341	77.3	33.8
1970	Pa	5,384,000	2,399,468	44.6	1,158,259	48.3	21.5
1977	Ref	6,319,000	2,759,924	43.7	1,972,077	71.5	31.2
1978	Pa	6,728,000	2,927,416	43.5	1,121,799	38.3	16.7
1978	Pr (1st)	6,728,000	2,924,785	43.5	1,028,653	35.2	15.3
1978	Pr (2nd)	6,728,000	2,947,527	43.8	1,283,546	43.5	19.1
1991	Ref	9,242,000	3,403,451	36.8	1,660,321	48.8	18.0
1991	Pr	9,242,000	3,179,053	34.4	868,038	27.3	9.4
1992	Pa	9,682,000	3,727,843	38.5	1,260,107	33.8	13.0
1997	Pa	10,669,000	4,982,621	46.7	2,195,865	44.1	20.6
1998	Pr	11,300,000	4,226,358	37.4	2,369,954	56.1	21.0

[a] Pa = Parliament; Pr = President; Ref = Referendum.

[b] Population data are based on UN estimates. For 1978, the estimations for 1979, for 1992 those for 1993, for 1997 those of 1996 are given.

2.3 Abbreviations

ADES	Alliance pour la Démocratie et l'Emancipation Sociale
ADF	Alliance pour la Démocratie et la Fédération
APL	Alliance pour le Progrès et la Liberté
BSB	Bloc Socialiste Burkinabè
CDP	Congrès pour la Démocratie et le Progrès
CNPP-PSD	Convention Nationale des Patriotes Progressistes - Parti Social-Démocrate
FFS	Front des Forces Sociales
FR	Front de Refus
FU	Forces Unies
GAP	Groupe d'Action Populaire
GDP	Groupes des Démocrates et Patriotes
GDR	Groupe des Démocrates
MDP	Mouvement des Démocrates Progressistes
MDS	Mouvement pour la Démocratie Socialiste
MI-PRA	Mouvement des Indépendants du PRA
MLN	Mouvement de Libération Nationale
MTP	Mouvement pour la Tolérance et le Progrès
NDS	Nouvelle Démocratie Sociale
ODDN	Organisation Prodémocratique pour la Défense de la Nature
ODP-MT	Organisation pour la Démocratie Populaire - Mouvement du Travail
PACT-LS	Parti de l'Action pour le Libéralisme Solidaire
PAI	Parti Africain pour l'Indépendance
PDP	Parti pour la Démocratie et le Progrès
PEP	Parti Ecologiste pour le Progrès
PPDS	Parti pour le Progrès et le Développement Social
PPS	Parti du Progrès Social
PRA	Parti du Regroupement Africain
PSB	Parti Socialiste Burkinabé
PTB	Parti du Travail du Burkina
PVB	Parti des Verts du Burkina Faso
RDA	Rassemblement Démocratique Africain
RSI	Rassemblement des Sociaux-démocrates Indépendants
UDPB	Union des Démocrates et Patriotes du Burkina
UDS	Union des Sociaux-démocrates
UDV-RDA	Union Démocratique Voltaique - Rassemblement Démocratique Africain
UFDP	Union des Forces Démocratiques et Progressistes
UNDD	Union Nationale pour la Défense et la Démocratie
UNI	Union Nationale des Indépendants
UNRV	Union pour la Nouvelle République Voltaique
UPV	Union Progressistes Voltaique
UVDB	Union des Verts pour le Développement du Burkina

2.4 Electoral Participation of Parties and Alliances 1959–1998

Party/Alliance	Years	Elections contested	
		Presidential	Parliamentary
PRA	1959, 1970, 1978	0	3
RDA	1959, 1992, 1997, 1998	3	3
UDV-RDA	1965, 1970, 1978	2	3
MLN	1970	0	1
UNRV	1970	0	1
GAP	1978	0	1
MI-PRA	1978	0	1
UNDD	1978	1	1
UNI	1978	0	1
UPV	1978	1	1
ODP-MT/CDP[a]	1991, 1992, 1997, 1998	2	2
ADES	1992	0	1
ADF	1992, 1997	0	2
APL	1992	0	1
BSB	1992, 1997	0	2
CNPP-PSD	1992	0	1
FR	1992	0	1
FU	1992	0	1
GDP	1992, 1997	0	2
GDR	1992	0	1
MDP	1992	0	1
MDS	1992	0	1
MTB	1992, 1997	0	2
NDS	1992, 1997	0	2
ODDN	1992	0	1
PAI	1992, 1997	0	2
PAKT-LS	1992	0	1
PEP	1992	0	1
PPS	1992	0	1
PSB	1992, 1997	0	2
PSD	1992	0	1
PTB	1992	0	1
RSI	1992	0	1
UDPB	1992	0	1
UDS	1992	0	1
UVDB	1992, 1997	0	2
FFS	1997	0	1
PDP	1997	0	1
PPDS	1997	0	1
PVB	1998	1	0

[a] President Compaoré's majority party changed its name from ODP-MT to CDP in February 1996.

2.5 Referendums

Year	1959		1970	
	Total number	%	Total number	%
Registered voters	1,957,732	–	2,351,258	–
Votes cast	1,344,932	68.7	1,817,341	77.3
Invalid votes	71,753	5.3	34,580	1.9
Valid votes	1,273,179	94.7	1,782,761	98.1
Yes	1,018,936	80.0	1,757,004	98.6
No	254,243	20.0	25,757	1.4

Year	1977		1991	
	Total number	%	Total number	%
Registered voters	2,759,924	–	3,403,451	–
Votes cast	1,972,077	71.5	1,660,321	48.8
Invalid votes	19,108	1.0	39,529	2.4
Valid votes	1,952,969	99.0	1,620,792	97.6
Yes	1,927,691	98.7	1,504,792	92.8
No	25,278	1.3	116,139	7.2

2.6 Elections for Constitutional Assembly

Elections for Constitutional Assembly have not been held.

2.7 Parliamentary Elections

Year	1959		1965	
	Total number	%	Total number	%
Registered voters	1,924,765	–	2,188,241	–
Votes cast	903,290	46.9	2,132,418	97.4
Invalid votes	8,766	1.0	468	0.0
Valid votes	894,524	99.0	2,131,950	100.0
RDA	502,815	56.2	–	–
PRA	391,709	43.8	–	–
UDV-RDA	–	–	2,131,950	100.0

Year	1970		1978	
	Total number	%	Total number	%
Registered voters	2,399,468	–	2,927,416	–
Votes cast	1,158,259	48.3	1,121,799	38.3
Invalid votes	44,373	3.8	51,495	4.6
Valid votes	1,113,886	96.2	1,070,304	95.4
UDV-RDA	754,506	67.7	455,329	42.5
PRA	191,793	17.2	102,335	9.6
MLN	121,668	10.9	–	–
UNDD	–	–	244,754	22.9
UPV	–	–	169,331	15.8
UNI	–	–	79,367	7.4
MI-PRA	–	–	18,361	1.7
GAP	–	–	827	0.1
UNRV and Independ.	45,919	4.1	–	–

Year	1992		1997	
	Total number	%	Total number	%
Registered voters	3,727,843	–	4,982,621	-
Votes cast	1,260,107	33.8	2,195,865	44.1
Invalid votes	40,962	3.3	83,887	3.8
Valid votes	1,219,145	96.7	2,111,978	96.2
ODP-MT/CDP[a]	590,808	48.5	1,449,082	68.6
CNPP-PSD	146,530	12.0	-	-
RDA	138,168	11.3	136,006	6.4
ADF	105,950	8.7	156,325	7.4
PAI	50,418	4.1	31,381	1.5
BSB	28,667	2.4	27,493	1.3
GDP	22,820	1.9	12,652	0.6
MTP	22,050	1.8	7,117	0.3
FFS	-	-	16,597	0.8
NDS	[b]	[b]	2,855	0.1
PDP	-	-	213,620	10.1
PPDS	-	-	11,408	0.5
PSB	[b]	[b]	38,005	1.8
UVDB	[b]	[b]	9,437	0.5

[a] President Compaoré's majority party changed its name from ODP-MT to CDP in February 1996.

[b] The parties concerned participated in the 1992 elections, but got less than 20,000 votes each. The exact results have not been available.

2.7 a) Parliamentary Elections: Regional Results (Absolute Numbers)

1959 Constituency	Registered voters	Votes cast	Invalid votes	Valid votes	RDA	PRA
Constituency I	908,443	370,907	5,403	365,504	247,800	117,704
Constituency II	631,689	308,961	2,007	306,954	227,767	79,187
Constituency III	198,350	148,591	11	148,580	–	148,580
Constituency IV	186,283	74,831	1,345	73,486	27,248	46,238
Total	1,924,765	903,290	8,766	894,524	502,815	391,709

[a] Constituency I = North; Constituency II = South; Constituency III = Ouahigouya; Constituency IV = Ouagadougou.

1970 Constituency	Votes cast	Invalid votes	Valid Votes	UDV-RDA	PRA	MLN	Others
Banfora	47,537	2,036	45,501	26,156	17,867	1,478	–
Bobo	82,498	2,981	79,517	33,545	41,996	3,976	–
Diébougou	71,146	3,783	67,363	18,762	46,053	2,548	–
Fada	80,919	3,874	77,045	46,451	15,838	14,756	–
Kaya	120,645	4,536	116,109	70,031	4,207	11,590	30,281
Koudougou	161,109	4,678	156,431	135,055	9,699	5,138	6,539
Koupéla	75,566	5,240	70,326	51,586	4,787	11,080	2,873
Ouagadougou	211,100	8,259	202,841	173,635	11,551	17,655	–
Sahel	55,170	1,644	53,526	28,088	2,216	23,222	–
Volta Noire	123,200	4,258	118,942	54,429	36,377	28,136	–
Yatenga	129,369	3,084	126,285	116,768	1,202	2,089	6,226
Total	1,158,259	44,373	1,113,886	754,506	191,793	121,668	45,919

1978 Constituency[a]	Valid Votes	UDV-RDA	UNDD	UPV	PRA	UNI	IPRA	GAP
Center	171,093	87,064	40,787	19,493	8,011	11,292	4,446	–
Center-East	81,757	22,226	21,532	17,354	8,436	9,436	2,773	–
Center-North	119,461	54,645	17,526	15,097	4,308	25,612	2,273	–
Center-West	160,795	21,506	116,453	9,946	6,890	6,000	–	–
North	139,301	126,111	1,270	3,024	700	7,369	–	827
East	72,825	30,050	8,815	18,307	11,806	3,847	–	–
Volta Noire	128,843	36,574	19,762	36,772	14,856	12,010	8,869	–
Hauts-Bassins	86,870	35,825	9,744	27,003	12,210	2,088	–	–
South-West	59,703	13,543	5,486	6,865	32,096	1,713	–	–
Sahel	49,656	27,785	3,379	15,470	3,022	–	–	–
Total	1,070,304	455,329	244,754	169,331	102,335	79,367	18,361	827

[a] Center = Ouagadougou; Center-East = Tenkodogo; Center-North = Kaya; Center-West = Koudougou; North = Ouahigouya; East = Fada N'Gorma; Volta Noire = Dédougou; Hauts-Bassins = Bobo-Dioulasso; South-West = Gaoua; Sahel = Dori.

1997 Constituency	Registered voters	Votes cast	Invalid votes	Valid votes	ADF	BSB	CDP	FFS
Bale	80,099	52,527	1,237	51,290	2,555	–	48,735	–
Bam	99,495	47,949	1,188	46,761	2,620	–	32,649	777
Banwa	97,448	38,174	1,885	36,289	–	–	28,298	–
Bazega	100,165	38,409	1,902	36,507	6,517	2,142	18,206	–
Bougouriba	44,062	14,121	807	13,314	1,112	–	8,246	–
Boulgou	199,622	96,645	4,437	92,208	6,554	4,796	67,541	–
Boulkiemde	191,555	84,154	3,266	80,888	19,101	–	51,815	–
Comoe	114,570	48,601	2,004	46,597	7,056	–	30,966	–
Ganzourgou	117,523	56,268	2,395	53,873	1,760	2,029	46,178	–
Gnagna	139,040	57,264	1,930	55,334	3,777	–	39,618	–
Gourma	98,836	35,682	1,527	34,155	–	–	22,211	–
Houet	308,044	90,782	3,103	87,679	7,686	–	47,831	3,571
Ioba	80,914	45,740	1,986	43,754	5,658	–	30,471	–
Kadiogo	538,507	201,515	8,126	193,389	10,267	10,400	122,687	7,378
Kenedougou	102,979	36,392	1,189	35,203	5,796	762	22,593	–
Komondjari	22,469	7,486	193	7,293	–	–	5,902	–
Kompienga	20,258	10,401	409	9,992	–	–	6,080	–
Kossi	120,861	36,178	1,777	34,401	–	–	25,306	–
Koupelgo	87,045	34,554	1,843	32,711	1,664	2,082	23,923	–
Kouritenga	115,116	35,035	1,900	33,135	1,745	–	23,727	–
Kourweogo	53,322	19,552	945	18,607	1,686	–	14,957	665
Leraba	41,210	25,493	666	24,827	–	–	17,028	–
Louroum	50,369	25,493	666	24,827	–	–	17,028	–
Mouhoun	108,452	41,116	1,406	39,710	4,475	–	26,127	–

1997 (cont.) Constituency	Registered voters	Votes cast	Invalid votes	Valid votes	ADF	BSB	CDP	FFS
Nahouri	60,142	28,544	1,547	26,997	2,391	–	19,254	–
Namentenga	134,505	50,608	2,299	48,309	2,309	–	24,080	–
Nayala	63,908	36,069	963	35,106	–	–	20,940	–
Noumbiel	24,331	9,614	553	9,061	3,339	–	4,526	–
Oubritenga	90,868	61,513	1,208	60,305	556	–	58,090	–
Oudalan	74,591	24,650	1,633	23,017	9,327	–	10,740	–
Passore	121,631	64,463	1,925	62,538	–	2,895	43,277	1,912
Poni	92,513	28,821	2,045	26,776	3,031	–	12,516	–
Sanguie	118,282	64,923	2,048	62,875	3,875	–	42,603	–
Sanmatenga	237,745	136,774	4,469	132,305	–	–	93,658	–
Seno	101,173	39,268	1,679	37,589	6,436	1,313	18,810	–
Sissili	68,682	29,023	1,134	27,889	7,482	1,074	18,373	960
Soum	126,505	57,599	1,907	55,692	–	–	43,390	–
Sourou	87,695	43,608	1,562	42,046	1,434	–	31,050	–
Tapoa	103,007	39,009	2,101	36,908	–	–	27,137	–
Tuy	76,065	32,810	1,433	31,377	2,874	–	23,903	–
Yagha	54,595	24,449	1,362	23,087	13,110	–	8,355	–
Yatenga	202,516	141,299	3,748	137,551	–	–	92,686	1,334
Ziro	52,801	18,113	1,049	17,064	3,040	–	13,392	–
Zondoma	59,380	36,832	1,070	35,762	661	–	23,630	–
Zoundweogo	90,566	48,345	1,365	46,980	6,431	–	40,549	–
Total	4,982,621	2,195,865	83,887	2,111,978	156,325	27,493	1,449,082	16,597

1997 (cont.) Constituency	GDP	MTP	NDS	PAI	PDP	PPDS	PSB	RDA	UVDB
Bale	–	–	–	–	–	–	–	–	–
Bam	919	–	1,035	–	4,268	–	1,344	3,149	–
Banwa	–	–	–	–	–	–	–	7,991	–
Bazega	7,013	–	–	–	2,629	–	–	–	–
Bougouriba	–	–	–	1,386	1,737	–	–	833	–
Boulgou	–	–	–	–	13,317	–	–	–	–
Boulkiemde	–	–	–	–	7,709	2,263	–	–	–
Comoe	–	–	–	1,079	1,585	–	–	4,903	1,008
Ganzourgou	–	–	–	–	1,676	1,168	–	1,062	–
Gnagna	–	–	–	–	11,939	–	–	–	–
Gourma	–	–	–	1,205	5,770	3,172	1,797	–	–
Houet	–	–	–	–	9,654	–	3,068	13,566	2,303
Ioba	–	–	–	780	6,845	–	–	–	–
Kadiogo	2,916	6,090	–	–	13,309	2,629	3,182	10,364	4,167
Kenedougou	–	–	–	3,745	861	–	–	1,446	–
Komondjari	–	–	–	–	1,013	378	–	–	–

1997 (cont.) Constituency	GDP	MTP	NDS	PAI	PDP	PPDS	PSB	RDA	UVDB
Kompienga	–	–	–	–	–	–	3,912	–	–
Kossi	–	–	–	–	5,080	–	–	4,015	–
Koupelgo	–	–	–	–	4,159	–	–	883	–
Kouritenga	–	–	–	–	5,865	1,798	–	–	–
Kourweogo	–	543	–	–	756	–	–	–	–
Leraba	–	–	–	–	–	–	–	7,799	–
Louroum	–	–	–	–	–	–	–	7,799	–
Mouhoun	–	–	–	–	6,597	–	–	2,511	–
Nahouri	–	–	–	–	4,955	–	–	397	–
Namentenga	–	–	–	3,875	9,827	–	–	8,218	–
Nayala	–	–	–	–	14,166	–	–	–	–
Noumbiel	–	–	–	–	815	–	–	–	381
Oubritenga	–	484	–	–	814	–	–	361	–
Oudalan	386	–	–	689	1,675	–	–	200	–
Passore	–	–	–	–	–	–	11,777	1,099	1,578
Poni	–	–	–	1,616	5,937	–	–	3,676	–
Sanguie	–	–	–	1,988	12,140	–	1,501	768	–
Sanmatenga	–	–	–	5,759	32,888	–	–	–	–
Seno	–	–	899	8,760	1,371	–	–	–	–
Sissili	–	–	–	–	–	–	–	–	–
Soum	–	–	921	–	3,710	–	–	7,671	–
Sourou	–	–	–	–	7,607	–	–	1,955	–
Tapoa	–	–	–	–	4,584	–	5,187	–	–
Tuy	786	–	–	–	3,814	–	–	–	–
Yagha	–	–	–	–	–	–	–	1,622	–
Yatenga	–	–	–	–	3,366	–	6,237	33,928	–
Ziro	632	–	–	–	–	–	–	–	–
Zondoma	–	–	–	499	1,182	–	–	9,790	–
Zoundweogo	–	–	–	–	–	–	–	–	–
Total	12,652	7,117	2,855	31,381	213,620	11,408	38,005	136,006	9,437

2.7 b) Parliamentary Elections: Regional Results (%)

1959 Constituency	RDA	PRA	Total[a]
Constituency I (North)	68.0	32.0	40.8
Constituency II (South)	74.2	25.8	34.4
Constituency III (Ouahigouya)	–	100.0	16.7
Constituency IV (Ouagadougou)	37.1	62.9	8.2
Nation-wide	56.2	43.8	100.0

[a] Percentages of valid votes cast nation-wide.

1970 Constituency	UDV-RDA	PRA	MLN	Others	Total[a]
Banfora	57.5	39.3	3.2	–	4.1
Bobo-Dioulasso	42.2	52.8	5.0	–	7.1
Diébougou	27.8	68.4	3.8	–	6.0
Fada	60.3	20.6	19.1	–	6.9
Kaya	60.3	3.6	10.0	26.1	10.5
Koudougou	86.3	6.2	3.3	4.2	14.0
Koupéla	73.4	6.8	15.7	4.1	6.3
Ouagadougou	85.6	5.7	8.7	–	18.2
Sahel	52.5	4.1	43.4	–	4.8
Volta Noire	45.8	30.6	23.6	–	10.7
Yatenga	92.5	1.0	1.7	4.9	11.3
Nation-wide	67.7	17.2	10.9	4.1	100.0

[a] Percentages of valid votes cast nation-wide.

1978 Constituency[a]	UDV-RDA	UNDD	UPV	PRA	UNI	MI-PRA	GAP	Total[b]
Center	50.9	23.8	11.4	4.7	6.6	2.6	–	16.0
Centre-East	27.2	26.3	21.2	10.3	11.5	3.4	–	7.6
Center-North	45.7	14.7	12.6	3.6	21.4	1.9	–	11.2
Center-West	13.4	72.4	6.2	4.3	3.7	–	–	15.0
North	90.5	0.9	2.2	0.5	5.3	–	0.6	13.0
East	41.3	12.1	25.1	16.2	5.3	–	–	6.8
Volta Noire	28.4	15.3	28.5	11.5	9.3	6.9	–	12.0
Hauts-Bassins	41.2	11.2	31.1	14.0	2.4	–	–	8.1
South-West	22.7	9.2	11.5	53.8	2.9	–	–	5.6
Sahel	56.0	6.8	31.2	6.1	–	–	–	4.6
Nation-wide	42.5	22.9	15.8	9.6	7.4	1.7	0.1	100.0

[a] Center = Ouagadougou; Center-East = Tenkodogo; Center-North = Kaya; Center-West = Koudougou; North = Ouahigouya; East = Fada N'Gorma; Volta Noire = Dédougou; Hauts-Bassins = Bobo Dioulasso; South-West = Gaoua; Sahel = Dori.

[b] Percentages of valid votes cast nation-wide.

1997 Constituency	ADF	BSB	CDP	FFS	GDP	MTP	NDS
Bale	5.0	–	95.0	–	–	–	–
Bam	5.6	–	69.8	1.7	2.0	–	2.2
Banwa	–	–	78.0	–	–	–	–
Bazega	17.9	5.9	49.9	–	19.2	–	–
Bougouriba	8.4	–	61.9	–	–	–	–
Boulgou	7.1	5.2	73.3	–	–	–	–
Boulkiemde	23.6	–	64.1	–	–	–	–
Comoe	15.1	–	66.5	–	–	–	–
Ganzourgou	3.3	3.8	85.7	–	–	–	–
Gnagna	6.8	–	71.6	–	–	–	–
Gourma	–	–	65.0	–	–	–	–
Houet	8.8	–	54.6	4.1	–	–	–
Ioba	12.9	–	69.6	–	–	–	–
Kadiogo	5.3	5.4	63.4	3.8	1.5	3.2	–
Kenedougou	16.5	2.2	64.2	–	–	–	–
Komondjari	–	–	80.9	–	–	–	–
Kompienga	–	–	60.9	–	–	–	–
Kossi	–	–	73.6	–	–	–	–
Koupelgo	5.1	6.4	73.1	–	–	–	–
Kouritenga	5.3	–	71.6	–	–	–	–
Kourweogo	9.1	–	80.4	3.6	–	2.9	–
Leraba	–	–	68.6	–	–	–	–
Louroum	–	–	68.6	–	–	–	–
Mouhoun	11.3	–	65.8	–	–	–	–
Nahouri	8.9	–	71.3	–	–	–	–
Namentenga	4.8	–	49.9	–	–	–	–
Nayala	–	–	59.7	–	–	–	–
Noumbiel	36.9	–	50.0	–	–	–	–
Oubritenga	0.9	–	96.3	–	–	0.8	–
Oudalan	40.5	–	46.7	–	1.7	–	–
Passore	–	4.6	69.2	3.1	–	–	–
Poni	11.3	–	46.7	–	–	–	–
Sanguie	6.2	–	67.8	–	–	–	–
Sanmatenga	–	–	70.8	–	–	–	–
Seno	17.1	3.5	50.0	–	–	–	2.4
Sissili	26.8	3.9	65.9	3.4	–	–	–
Soum	–	–	77.9	–	–	–	1.7
Sourou	3.4	–	73.9	–	–	–	–
Tapoa	–	–	73.5	–	–	–	–
Tuy	9.2	–	76.2	–	2.5	–	–
Yagha	56.8	–	36.2	–	–	–	–
Yatenga	–	–	67.4	1.0	–	–	–
Ziro	17.8	–	78.5	–	3.7	–	–
Zondoma	1.9	–	66.1	–	–	–	–
Zoundweogo	13.7	–	86.3	–	–	–	–
Nation–wide	7.4	1.3	68.6	0.8	0.6	0.3	0.1

1997 (cont.) Constituency	PAI	PDP	PPDS	PSB	RDA	UVDB	Total[a]
Bale	–	–	–	–	–	–	2.4
Bam	–	9.1	–	2.9	6.7	–	2.2
Banwa	–	–	–	–	22.0	–	1.7
Bazega	–	7.2	–	–	–	–	1.7
Bougouriba	10.4	13.1	–	–	6.3	–	0.6
Boulgou	–	14.4	–	–	–	–	4.4
Boulkiemde	–	9.5	2.8	–	–	–	3.8
Comoe	2.3	3.4	–	–	10.5	2.2	2.2
Ganzourgou	–	3.1	2.2	–	2.0	–	2.6
Gnagna	–	21.6	–	–	–	–	2.6
Gourma	3.5	16.9	9.3	5.3	–	–	1.6
Houet	–	11.0	–	3.5	15.5	2.6	4.2
Ioba	1.8	15.6	–	–	–	–	2.1
Kadiogo	–	6.9	1.4	1.7	5.4	2.2	9.2
Kenedougou	10.6	2.5	–	–	4.1	–	1.7
Komondjari	–	13.9	5.2	–	–	–	0.3
Kompienga	–	–	–	39.2	–	–	0.5
Kossi	–	14.8	–	–	11.7	–	1.6
Koupelgo	–	12.7	–	–	2.7	–	1.5
Kouritenga	–	17.7	5.4	–	–	–	1.6
Kourweogo	–	4.1	–	–	–	–	0.9
Leraba	–	–	–	–	31.4	–	1.2
Louroum	–	–	–	–	31.4	–	1.2
Mouhoun	–	16.6	–	–	6.3	–	1.9
Nahouri	–	18.4	–	–	1.5	–	1.3
Namentenga	8.0	20.3	–	–	17.0	–	2.3
Nayala	–	40.6	–	–	–	–	1.7
Noumbiel	–	9.0	–	–	–	4.2	0.4
Oubritenga	–	1.4	–	–	0.6	–	2.9
Oudalan	3.0	7.3	–	–	0.9	–	1.1
Passore	–	–	–	18.8	1.8	2.5	3.0
Poni	6.0	22.2	–	–	13.7	–	1.3
Sanguie	3.2	19.3	–	2.4	1.2	–	3.0
Sanmatenga	4.4	24.9	–	–	–	–	6.3
Seno	23.3	3.7	–	–	–	–	1.8
Sissili	–	–	–	–	–	–	1.3
Soum	–	6.7	–	–	13.8	–	2.6
Sourou	–	18.1	–	–	4.7	–	2.0
Tapoa	–	12.4	–	14.1	–	–	1.7
Tuy	–	12.2	–	–	–	–	1.5
Yagha	–	–	–	–	7.0	–	1.1
Yatenga	–	2.5	–	4.5	24.7	–	6.5
Ziro	–	–	–	–	–	–	0.8
Zondoma	1.4	3.3	–	–	27.4	–	1.7
Zoundweogo	–	–	–	–	–	–	2.2
Nation–wide	1.5	10.1	0.5	1.8	6.4	0.5	100.0

[a] Percentages of valid votes cast nation-wide.

2.8 Composition of Parliament

Year	1959		1965		1970		1978	
	Seats	%	Seats	%	Seats	%	Seats	%
	75	100	75	100	57	100	57	100
RDA	62	82.7	–	–	–	–	–	–
PRA	13	17.3	–	–	12	21.1	6	10.5
UDV–RDA	–	–	75	100	37	64.9	28	49.1
MLN	–	–	–	–	6	10.5	–	–
UNDD	–	–	–	–	–	–	13	22.8
UPV	–	–	–	–	–	–	9	15.8
UNI	–	–	–	–	–	–	1	1.8
UNRV and Independents	–	–	–	–	2	3.5	–	–

Year	1992		1997	
	Seats	%	Seats	%
	107	99.8[a]	111	100.0
ODP-MT/CDP[b]	78	72.9	101	91.0
CNPP-PSD	12	11.2	–	–
RDA	6	5.6	2	1.8
ADF	4	3.7	2	1.8
PAI	2	1.9	–	–
MDP	1	0.9	–	–
MDS	1	0.9	–	–
PSB	1	0.9	–	–
RSI	1	0.9	–	–
UDS	1	0.9	–	–
PDP	–	–	6	5.4

[a] Due to rounding the sum does not amount to 100.

[b] President Compaoré's majority party changed its name from ODP-MT to CDP in February 1996.

2.8 a) Parliamentary Elections: Regional Distribution of Seats

1959	RDA		PRA		Total	
Constituency	Seats	%	Seats	%	Seats	%[a]
Constituency I (North)	36	100.0	–	–	36	48.0
Constituency II (South)	23	100.0	–	–	23	30.7
Constituency III (Ouahigouya)	–	–	8	100.0	8	10.6
Constituency IV (Ouagadougou)	3	37.5	5	62.5	8	10.6
Nation-wide	62	82.7	13	17.3	75	100.0

[a] Percentages of all parliamentary seats.

1970 Constituency	UDV–RDA Seats	%	PRA Seats	%	MLN Seats	%	Others Seats	%	Total Seats	%[a]
Banfora	1	50.0	1	50.0	–	–	–	–	2	3.5
Bobo–Dioulasso	2	40.0	3	60.0	–	–	–	–	5	8.8
Diébougou	1	25.0	3	75.0	–	–	–	–	4	7.0
Fada	2	50.0	1	25.0	1	25.0	–	–	4	7.0
Kaya	4	57.1	–	–	1	14.3	2	28.6	7	12.3
Koudougou	8	100.0	–	–	–	–	–	–	8	14.0
Koupéla	2	66.7	–	–	1	33.3	–	–	3	5.3
Ouagadougou	9	81.8	1	9.1	1	9.1	–	–	11	19.3
Sahel	2	66.7	–	–	1	33.3	–	–	3	5.3
Volta Noire	2	40.0	2	40.0	1	20.0	–	–	5	8.8
Yatenga	5	100.0	–	–	–	–	–	–	5	8.8
Nation-wide	37	64.9	12	21.1	6	10.5	2	3.5	57	100.0

[a] Percentages of all parliamentary seats.

1978 Constituency[a]	UDV–RDA Seats	%	UNDD Seats	%	UPV Seats	%	PRA Seats	%	Total Seats	%[b]
Center	6	60.0	3	30.0	1	10.0	–	–	10	17.5
Center-East	2	50.0	1	25.0	1	25.0	–	–	4	7.0
Center-North	3	50.0	1	16.7	1	16.7	–	–	6[c]	10.5
Center-West	1	12.5	7	87.5	–	–	–	–	8	14.0
North	5	100.0	–	–	–	–	–	–	5	8.7
East	2	50.0	–	–	1	25.0	1	25.0	4	7.0
Volta Noire	2	33.3	1	16.7	2	33.3	1	16.7	6	10.5
Hauts-Bassins	3	50.0	–	–	2	33.3	1	16.7	6	10.5
South-West	1	25.0	–	–	–	–	3	75.0	4	7.0
Sahel	3	75.0	–	–	1	25.0	–	–	4	7.0
Nation-wide	28	49.1	13	22.8	9	15.8	6	10.5	57	100.0

[a] Center = Ouagadougou; Center-East = Tenkodogo; Center-North = Kaya; Center-West = Koudougou; North = Ouahigouya; East = Fada N'Gorma; Volta Noire = Dédougou; Hauts-Bassins = Bobo Dioulasso; South-West = Gaoua; Sahel = Dori.

[b] Percentages of all parliamentary seats.

[c] In this constituency the UNI gained its only seat.

1997 Constituency	ADF Seats	%[a]	CDP Seats	%[a]	PDP Seats	%[a]	RDA Seats	%[a]	Total Seats	%[b]
Bale	–	–	2	100.0	–	–	–	–	2	1.8
Bam	–	–	2	100.0	–	–	–	–	2	1.8
Banwa	–	–	2	100.0	–	–	–	–	2	1.8
Bazega	–	–	2	100.0	–	–	–	–	2	1.8
Bougouriba	–	–	1	100.0	–	–	–	–	1	0.9
Boulgou	–	–	4	100.0	–	–	–	–	4	3.6
Boulkiemde	1	20.0	4	80.0	–	–	–	–	5	4.5
Comoe	–	–	2	100.0	–	–	–	–	2	1.8
Ganzourgou	–	–	3	100.0	–	–	–	–	3	2.7
Gnagna	–	–	3	100.0	–	–	–	–	3	2.7
Gourma	–	–	2	100.0	–	–	–	–	2	1.8
Houet	–	–	5	71.4	1	14.3	1	14.3	7	6.3
Ioba	–	–	2	100.0	–	–	–	–	2	1.8
Kadiogo	–	–	10	90.9	1	9.1	–	–	11	9.9
Kenedougou	–	–	2	100.0	–	–	–	–	2	1.8
Komondjari	–	–	1	100.0	–	–	–	–	1	0.9
Kompienga	–	–	1	100.0	–	–	–	–	1	0.9
Kossi	–	–	2	100.0	–	–	–	–	2	1.8
Koupelgo	–	–	2	100.0	–	–	–	–	2	1.8
Kouritenga	–	–	3	100.0	–	–	–	–	3	2.7
Kourweogo	–	–	1	100.0	–	–	–	–	1	0.9
Leraba	–	–	1	100.0	–	–	–	–	1	0.9
Louroum	–	–	1	100.0	–	–	–	–	1	0.9
Mouhoun	–	–	2	100.0	–	–	–	–	2	1.8
Nahouri	–	–	1	100.0	–	–	–	–	1	0.9
Namentenga	–	–	2	66.7	1	33.3	–	–	3	2.7
Nayala	–	–	1	50.0	1	50.0	–	–	2	1.8
Noumbiel	–	–	1	100.0	–	–	–	–	1	0.9
Oubritenga	–	–	2	100.0	–	–	–	–	2	1.8
Oudalan	–	–	1	100.0	–	–	–	–	1	0.9
Passore	–	–	3	100.0	–	–	–	–	3	2.7
Poni	–	–	2	66.7	1	33.3	–	–	3	2.7
Sanguie	–	–	3	100.0	–	–	–	–	3	2.7
Sanmatenga	–	–	4	100.0	1	20.0	–	–	5	4.5
Seno	–	–	2	100.0	–	–	–	–	2	1.8
Sissili	–	–	2	100.0	–	–	–	–	2	1.8
Soum	–	–	3	100.0	–	–	–	–	3	2.7
Sourou	–	–	2	100.0	–	–	–	–	2	1.8
Tapoa	–	–	2	100.0	–	–	–	–	2	1.8

1997 (cont.)	ADF		CDP		PDP		RDA		Total	
Constituency	Seats	%[a]	Seats	%[a]	Seats	%[a]	Seats	%[a]	Seats	%[b]
Tuy	–	–	2	100.0	–	–	–	–	2	1.8
Yagha	1	100	–	–	–	–	–	–	1	0.9
Yatenga	–	–	4	80.0	–	–	1	20.0	5	4.5
Ziro	–	–	1	100.0	–	–	–	–	1	0.9
Zondoma	–	–	1	100.0	–	–	–	–	1	0.9
Zoundweogo	–	–	2	100.0	–	–	–	–	2	1.8
Nation–wide	2	1.8	101	91.0	6	5.4	2	1.8	111	100

[a] Percentages of seats in the constituency concerned.
[b] Percentages of total seats.

2.9 Presidential Elections 1965–1998

1965	Total number	%
Registered voters	2,182,425	–
Votes cast	2,146,790	98.4
Invalid votes	309	0.0
Valid votes	2,146,481	100.0
Maurice Yaméogo (UDV-RDA)	2,146,481	100.0

1978 (1st round)	Total number	%
Registered voters	2,924,785	–
Votes cast	1,028,653	35.2
Invalid votes	19,695	1.9
Valid votes	1,008,958	98.1
Sangoulé Lamizana	425,302	42.2
Macaire Ouédraogo (UNDD)	254,467	25.2
Joseph Ouédraogo (faction of UDV-RDA)	167,120	16.6
Joseph Ki-Zerbo (UPV)	162,031	16.1

1978 (2nd round)	Total number	%
Registered voters	2,947,527	–
Votes cast	1,283,546	43.6
Invalid votes	18,870	1.5
Valid votes	1,264,676	98.5
Sangoulé Lamizana	711,722	56.3
Macaire Ouédraogo (UNDD)	552,954	43.7

1991	Total number	%
Registered voters	3,179,053	–
Votes cast	868,038	27.3
Invalid votes	117,892	13.6
Valid votes	750,146	86.4
Blaise Compaoré (ODP-MT)	750,146	100.0

1998	Total number	%
Registered voters	4,226,358	–
Votes cast	2,369,954	56.1
Invalid votes	89,458	3.8
Valid votes	2,280,496[a]	96.2
Blaise Compaoré (CDP)	1,996,151	87.5
Ram Ouedraogo (PVB)	150,796	6.6
Frederic Guirma (RDA)	133,552	5.9

[a] Total sum of candidates' votes is 2,280,499.

2.9 a) Presidential Elections: Regional Distribution of Votes

1978 (1st round) Region[a]	Registered voters	Votes cast	Turnout (in %)	Invalid votes	Valid votes
Ouagadougou	421,322	130,673	31.0	3,160	127,513
Center	58,948	32,636	55.4	269	32,367
Center-East	196,863	71,702	36.4	1,949	69,753
Center-North	333,284	103,665	31.1	2,346	101,321
North	286,731	128,451	44.8	1,090	127,361
Center-West	427,591	166,252	38.9	2,419	163,833
East	190,300	63,192	33.2	1,655	61,528
Volta Noire	317,611	125,289	39.4	1,484	123,805
South-West	201,044	52,490	26.1	1,856	50,634
Hauts-Bassins	288,295	100,518	34.9	2,048	98,470
Sahel	202,796	53,785	26.5	1,410	52,375
Total	2,924,785	1,028,653	35.2	19,686	1,008,960

1978 (continued) Region[a]	Lamizana Votes	%	M. Ouédraogo Votes	%	J. Ouédraogo Votes	%	Ki-Zerbo Votes	%
Ouagadougou	19,347	15.2	25,473	20.0	69,653	54.6	13,040	10.2
Center	5,385	16.6	7,706	23.8	15,106	46.7	4,170	12.9
Center-East	13,503	19.4	22,567	32.4	19,370	27.8	14,313	20.5
Center-North	36,943	36.5	21,383	21.1	26,698	26.4	16,297	16.1
North	120,405	94.5	1,389	1.1	2,060	1.6	3,507	2.8
Center-West	15,056	9.2	131,917	80.5	6,696	4.1	10,164	6.2
East	25,537	41.5	7,960	12.9	9,225	15.0	18,806	30.6
Volta Noire	63,630	51.4	18,572	15.0	5,528	4.5	36,075	29.1
South-West	36,917	72.9	4,079	8.1	3,290	6.5	6,348	12.5
Hauts-Bassins	57,019	57.9	10,098	10.3	5,846	5.9	25,507	25.9
Sahel	31,560	60.3	3,323	6.3	3,688	7.0	13,804	26.4
Total	425,302	42.2	254,467	25.2	167,160	16.6	162,031	16.1

[a] Center = Ouagadougou; Center-East = Tenkodogo; Center-North = Kaya; Center-West = Koudougou; North = Ouahigouya; East = Fada N'Gorma; Volta Noire = Dédougou; Hauts-Bassins = Bobo Dioulasso; South-West = Gaoua; Sahel = Dori.

1978 (2nd round) Region	Registered voters	Votes cast	Invalid votes	Valid votes	Lamizama Votes	%	M. Ouédraogo Votes	%
Ouagadougou	421,597	184,362	2,682	181,680	40,181	22.1	141,499	77.9
Center	65,988	36,179	306	35,873	9,523	26.5	26,350	73.5
Center-East	197,563	77,491	1,350	76,141	23,347	30.7	52,794	69.3
Center-North	333,072	122,271	1,676	120,595	56,767	47.1	63,828	52.9
North	292,616	182,009	1,132	180,877	178,171	98.5	2,706	1.5
Center-West	428,723	216,123	1,955	214,168	26,783	12.5	187,385	87.5
East	189,394	63,245	1,471	61,774	38,309	62.0	23,465	38.0
Volta Noire	318,450	136,580	2,058	134,522	112,235	83.4	22,287	16.6
South-West	295,729	132,186	2,435	129,751	114,696	88.4	15,055	11.6
Hauts-Bassins	201,044	72,813	2,480	70,333	63,909	90.9	6,424	9.1
Sahel	203,351	60,287	1,325	58,962	47,801	81.1	11,161	18.9
Total	2,947,527	1,283,546	18,870	1,264,676	711,722	56.3	552,954	43.7

1991 Region	Registered voters	Votes cast	Turnout in %	Invalid votes	Valid votes[a]
Bam	71,410	23,094	32.3	2,892	20,202
Bazega	120,447	48,393	40.2	4,262	44,131
Bougouriba	68,732	27,308	39.7	5,247	22,061
Boulgou	175,807	40,032	22.8	9,120	30,912
Boukiemde	108,537	22,068	20.3	2,363	19,705
Comoe	108,894	28,454	26.1	4,040	24,414
Ganzourgou	86,227	27,190	31.5	2,980	24,210
Gnagna	62,968	13,460	21.4	3,388	10,072
Gourma	80,971	22,511	27.8	3,587	18,924
Houet	234,798	47,994	20.4	7,767	40,227
Kadiogo	231,171	82,513	35.7	8,370	74,143
Kenedougou	59,653	14,154	23.7	2,161	11,993
Kossi	144,944	26,635	18.4	3,694	22,941
Kouritenga	79,139	7,503	9.5	1,494	6,009
Mouhoun	134,922	25,024	18.5	2,999	22,025
Nahouri	31,375	18,770	59.8	1,402	17,368
Namentenga	60,364	15,208	15.2	4,350	10,858
Oubritenga	64,248	53,831	83.8	2,988	50,843
Oudalan	47,757	13,352	28.0	999	12,353
Passore	93,978	16,227	17.3	2,332	13,895
Poni	90,571	11,212	12.4	3,439	7,773
Sanguie	93,126	25,976	27.9	4,554	21,422
Sanmatenga	160,835	45,255	28.1	5,320	39,935
Seno	114,016	32,444	28.5	7,237	25,207
Sissili	94,052	23,986	25.5	4,444	19,542
Soum	60,163	17,877	29.7	2,413	15,464
Sourou	116,002	38,552	33.2	3,767	34,785
Tapoa	72,542	13,890	19.1	3,870	10,020
Yatenga	248,857	65,616	26.4	4,072	61,544
Zounweogo	62,547	19,509	31.2	2,341	17,168
Total	3,179,053	868,038	27.3	117,892	750,146

[a] The valid votes are identical with those for the only candidate, Blaise Compaoré.

2.10 List of Power Holders 1960–1998

Head of State	Years	Remarks
Maurice Yaméogo	05/08/1960–03/01/1966	President, establishment of a one-party state; 1965 confirmed as President in non-competitive elections.
Sangoulé Lamizana	03/01/1966–29/11/1980	Commander of the army, declared that he intended to be in power only for a transitional period.
Saye Zerbo	25/11/1980–07/11/1982	Coup d'état of military officers under the leadership of Zerbo.
Jean-Baptiste Ouédraogo	7/11/1982–05/08/1983	After a military putsch under Colonel Yorian Somé, Ouédraogo formally became President for a transitional period.
Thomas Sankara	05/08/1983–15/10/1987	Assumption of power by troops of Blaise Compaoré; establishment of a Marxist–Leninist regime.
Blaise Compaoré	15/10/1987–	Violent access to power by Compaoré; after the redemocratization (IV. Republic since 1991) the only candidate in elections (1991), confirmed as President.

Head of Government	Years	Remarks
Maurice Yaméogo	05/08/1960–03/01/1966	Identical with Head of State.
Sangoulé Lamizana	03/01/1966–29/11/1980	Identical with Head of State.
Gérard Kango Ouédraogo	Feb/ 1971–08/02/1974	After referendum on the constitution of the II. Republic and the elections in 1970, Lamizana became President and Ouédraogo became Premier; conflicts between the President of the Parliament and the Premier; Lamizana re-acceded to power, suspension of the constitution.
Joseph Conombo	07/07/1978–25/11/1980	After second attempt to democratize (Third Republic), Lamizana was confirmed as President through elections; after parliamentary elections in 1978, Conombo became Premier.
Thomas Sankara	10/01/1983–17/05/1983	Appointment of Sankara for the newly introduced institution of Premier; after few months, dismissal by Somé and Ouédraogo.
Youssouf Ouédraogo	16/06/1992–16/03/1994	After parliamentary elections of 1992, Y. Ouédraogo became the first Premier of the Fourth Republic.
Roch M. Christian Kabore	20/03/1994–06/02/1996	Resignation of Ouédraogo after unification of oppositional parties with the ODP-MT.
Kadré Desiré Ouédraogo	06/02/1996–	

3. Bibliography

3.1 Official Sources

'Constitution du Burkina Faso', in F.-P. Blanc, A. Lourde and B. Saint-Girons (eds.) (1994), *Constitution et régime politique au Burkina Faso*. Toulouse: Presses de l'Institut d'Études Politiques: 197-232.

Embassy of Burkina Faso in Germany. *Information on Parliamentary Elections of May 1992 and May 1997*. Bonn.

'Loi No. 002/97/ADP du 27 janvier 1997 portant revision de la Constitution'. *Journal Officiel du Burkina Faso*, 39/2 (special issue): 3–10.

'Loi No. 003/97/ADP du 12 février 1997 portant Code Electoral'. *Journal Officiel du Burkina Faso,* 39/2 (special issue): 10–28.

'Ordonnance N 92-18 Pres du 25 mars 1992, portant Code Electoral'. *Journal Officiel du Burkina Faso*, 34/3 (special issue).

3.2 Books, Articles and Electoral Reports

Africa Research Bulletin, 1991 ff.

Ansprenger, F. (1971). 'Wahlen in Obervolta'. *Civitas*, 10: 120–166.

Asche, H. (1993). 'Burkina Faso', in D. Nohlen and F. Nuscheler (eds.), *Handbuch der Dritten Welt, Vol. 4: Westafrika und Zentralafrika*. Bonn: Dietz, 172–191.

Blanc, F.-P., Lourde, A., and Saint-Girons, B. (eds.) (1994). *Constitution et régime politique au Burkina Faso*. Toulouse: Presses de l'Institut d'Études Politiques.

Boudon, L. E. (1997). 'Burkina Faso: The "Rectification" of the Revolution', in J. F. Clark and D. E. Gardinier (eds.), *Political Reform in Francophone Africa*. Boulder/Col.: Westview, 127–144.

Bruchhaus, E.-M. (1992). 'Parlamentarische Demokratie oder Militärdiktatur? Burkina Faso nach den Präsidentschaftswahlen'. *Blätter des iz3w*, 179: 9–12.

Cadenat, P. (1978). 'La constitution voltaique du 27 novembre 1977'. *Revue juridique et politique. Indépendance et Coopération*, 32/4: 1025–1036.

Chérigny, B. (1979). 'La Haute-Volta ou le "luxe" de la démocratie: les élections législatives et présidentielles d'avril-mai 1978'. *Pouvoirs*, 9: 163–181.

Damiba, A. (1970). 'La nouvelle constitution de la Haute-Volta (14 juin 1970)'. *Revue juridique et politique. Indépendance et Coopération*, 25/2: 151–178.

Fauré, Y.-A. (1979). 'L'évolution politique'. *Année Africaine 1977*: 209–243.

Hillebrand, E. (1988). 'Burkina Faso in der Ära Sankara: Eine Bilanz', in Deutsches Übersee-Institut (ed.), *Jahrbuch Dritte Welt 1989. Daten, Übersichten, Analysen*. München: Beck, 248–262.

Institut für Afrikakunde and Hofmeier, R. (1988-1997). *Afrika Jahrbuch. Politik, Wirtschaft und Gesellschaft in Afrika südlich der Sahara*. Opladen: Leske & Budrich.

Institut International pour la Démocratie et l'Assistance Electorale (1998). *La démocratie au Burkina Faso*. Stockolm: International IDEA.

Inter-Parliamentary Union (1993). *Electoral Systems. A World-wide Comparative Study*. Geneva: IPU.

Jaffré, B. (1989). *Burkina Faso. Les années Sankara. De la révolution à la rectification*. Paris: L'Harmattan.

Lavroff, D. G. (1979). 'L'évolution constitutionelle de la République de Haute-Volta: La constitution du 27 novembre 1977'. *Année Africaine 1977*: 170–208.

Otayek, R. (1992). 'The Democratic "Rectification" in Burkina Faso'. *Journal of Communist Studies*, 8/2: 82–104.

Owona, J. (1979). 'La constitution da la IIIéme République voltaique du 21 octobre 1977: retour au parlementarisme rationalisé et au multipartisme limité'. *Penant*, 89/765: 309–328.

Rabl, K. (1973). 'Westafrikanische Verfassungsentwicklungen 1970. Obervolta, Dahomey, Volksrepublik Kongo. Versuch einer vorläufigen Übersicht'. *Verfassung und Recht in Übersee*, 6/2: 191–201.

Reuke, L. (1979). *Obervolta. Demokratisierung—Dritter Versuch*. Bonn: Friedrich-Ebert-Stiftung. Arbeiten aus der Entwicklungsländerforschung No. 79.

Schmitz, E. (1990). *Politische Herrschaft in Burkina Faso*. Freiburg: Arnold-Bergstraesser-Institut.

Sidwaya. Quotidien Burkinabé d'information et de mobilisation du peuple.

Ziemer, K. (1978). 'Obervolta', in D. Sternberger, B. Vogel, D. Nohlen and K. Landfried (eds.), *Die Wahl der Parlamente und anderere Staatsorgane, Band: II: Politische Organisation und Repräsentation in Afrika*, by Franz Nuscheler, Klaus Ziemer *et al.*, Berlin/ New York: Walter de Gruyter, 1555–1596.

BURUNDI

by Matthias Basedau

1. Introduction

1.1 Historical Overview

Burundi, before World War I a German territory in Central Africa, gained full independence from Belgium on 1 July 1962. As in the case of its neighbor Rwanda the country's history has been overshadowed by a severe conflict between the traditionally dominating Tutsi minority (14% of the population) and the Hutu majority (85% of the population) which is additionally intensified by tensions between hard and soft line factions and between various ethnic sub-groups.

Taking into account the large number of military coups, assassinations of major political representatives, and massive bloodshed both among and mainly between the ethnic groups, political parties and elections have played a minor role in political life. The sole (almost) persistently present party, the *Union pour le Progrès National* (UPRONA) was transformed into a single-party and functioned mainly as an organizational framework to maintain Tutsi supremacy. From 1966 to 1992 oppositional parties were banned and balloting in 1982 and 1984 was of strictly non-competitive character. On two occasions (1965 and 1993), however, multi-party elections, resulting in a Hutu victory, led to violent reactions by the Tutsi military and between the ethnic groups.

Independent Burundi entered history as a constitutional parliamentary monarchy that referred to the traditional Tutsi dynasties already in existence before and during the period of German and Belgian colonial rule. By independence Mwami (King) Mwambutsa IV became Head of State. The first nation-wide legislative elections that had taken place before independence in 1961 were won by the pro-monarchical and Tutsi-dominated but (then) principally multi-ethnic UPRONA.

Subsequently, the ethnically integrative powers of the monarchy began to deteriorate gradually. After the assassination of Prime Minister Pierre Ngendandumwe in 1965, the legislative elections of the same year confirmed UPRONA as the dominant party but implied (due to the electoral system) a shift to a two-third Hutu majority in the National Assembly. In the following months, a Hutu uprising and violent reprisals by the Tutsi military led to ethnic bloodshed that left 5,000, mainly Hutu intellectuals, dead.

The power struggle, however, was temporarily ended in 1966 when (then) Cpt. Michel Micombero (Tutsi) overthrew the monarchy and declared himself President of the newly installed Republic. In order to strengthen the minority's supremacy Micombero transformed UPRONA into a strictly Tutsi-dominated single party in the following years. New levels of mayhem were reached in 1972 when in the wake of supposed Hutu coup plots an estimated 100,000 to 250,000 mainly Hutu (among them the entire Hutu elite but also 3,000–10,000 Tutsi moderates) were systematically killed by the Tutsi military and the UPRONA's youth organization, the *Jeunesse Revolutionaire Rwagasore* (JRR).

In November 1976 a new military coup replaced Micombero by Lt. Col. Jean Baptiste Bagaza, a southern Tutsi. He announced socialist policies and efforts to decrease Hutu deprivation. A new constitution approved by referendum in 1981, established single-candidate (and single-party respectively) presidential and parliamentary elections and thus brought almost unanimous support for Bagaza and the still sole legal party, the UPRONA. By the mid-1980s, Bagaza started policies of repression against the Catholic Church which had called for an end to Hutu discrimination but failed to settle domestic turmoil, particularly intra-military rivalries.

As a result, in 1987 another intervention of the military occurred and brought Major Pierre Buyoya (Tutsi) to power. Although maintaining UPRONA as a single party he ended the *Kulturkampf* against the Catholic Church but could not halt another ethnic uprising in 1988 (5,000–20,000 deaths). Subsequently, conceived to give a sustainable perspective to his country and in response to international pressures Buyoya initiated a policy of national reconciliation and 'guided democratization'. In 1991 a Charter of National Unity which named ethnic division as a vital national problem was elaborated and accepted by popular referendum in the same year. A new constitution based on the National Charter providing for a semi-presidential system was approved the following year by referendum. Shortly afterwards, opposition parties were re-authorized but had to be composed of different ethnic groups in order to reflect the spirit of national unity.

Against Buyoya's and UPRONA's expectations the 1993 presidential and legislative elections—internationally observed and judged as extraordinarily free and fair—resulted in a landslide victory of the moderate Hutu-dominated opposition party, the *Front pour la démocratie au Burundi* (FRODEBU). Its presidential candidate, Melchior Ndadaye, became the country's first democratically elected Head of State. Though Buyoya seemed to accept his defeat other factions of the military did not. Conceiving the FRODEBU's triumph as a menace to Tutsi interests President Ndadaye (and a number of government representatives) were killed in an abortive coup d'état by hard line factions of the Tutsi military in October 1993. As a consequence, the country entered into a new period of ethnic violence and growing anarchy (an estimated 50,000 deaths).

In April 1994, while returning from a regional summit in Dar-es-salam (Tanzania) the new President, Cyprien Ntariamyra (FRODEBU), and his Rwandian presidential colleague died when their aircraft was shot down in Kigali (Rwanda) under still unresolved circumstances. Following a special agreement on a government of national unity composed both of UPRONA and FRODEBU in September 1994 ('*convention de gouvernement*'), Sylvestre Ntibantunganya was elected new President by the National Assembly though violating constitutional provisions. However, by mid-1995, due to increased violence between Hutu rebels and Tutsi government forces Ntibantunganya was forced to declare a state of emergency.

Another military coup by (still) Major Buyoya in June 1996 meant a definite return to authoritarian rule. Immediately the neighboring countries agreed to impose full economic sanctions and demanded an instant return to constitutional order. However, despite the formal re-admission of political parties and the rehabilitation of the National Assembly's rights in September 1997 hostilities between government forces and Hutu rebels of the *Conseil National pour la défense de la démocratie* (CNDD), headed by Léonard Nyangoma, a former FRODEBU minister, have not ceased and still (1998) constitute a civil war situation in large parts of the country.

1.2 Evolution of Electoral Provisions

The principles of universal adult suffrage (before 1993 21 years, since: 18 years), introduced already in the last pre-independence elections of 1961, were applied at all subsequent elections.

Under the monarchy (until 1966) only the house of representatives (*Assemblée Nationale*) was directly elected. In 1965 the number of members was reduced from 65 to 33 and the legislative term was extended from four to six years. In addition, an upper chamber composed of 16 senators, partly appointed by the king, partly elected by the National Assembly, was introduced.

The 1981 Constitution under the Bagaza regime provided for 52 out of 65 directly elected members of the unicameral National Assembly to serve a five-year term. The remaining 13 representatives were nominated by the president, who for the first time became himself subject to popular election (five-year term). Under the 1992 constitution the number of deputies to be directly elected (no appointed members) was raised to 81. Their terms were fixed at five years. The President's term was limited to one further renewal.

Concerning the evolution of electoral systems, in 1961 the 65 representatives were elected by proportional representation in multi-member districts. The candidates were nominated by political parties on closed but not blocked lists (preferential voting). The 1965 electoral provisions meant a shift to a relative majority system in 33 one-member districts. Preferential voting, however, was maintained, as the candidates presented themselves on a party list (maximum: four members) in every constituency enabling the voter to choose his favored list member. Every voter had one vote. The candidate with the plurality of votes on the most successful list was declared elected (in case of a tie of two candidates on the same list the deputy was picked by drawing lots, in case of a tie of two lists a second round was held). In consideration of the vast Hutu majority in the ethnic composition of the country this explains—though UPRONA supremacy was clearly maintained in the 1965 balloting—why so many Hutu UPRONA candidates accomplished successful candidacy.

Both the legislative and presidential elections of 1982 and 1984—under the 1981 constitution's provisions—were of a semi and non-competitive character respectively. The parliamentary candidates were put forward by UPRONA's single-party list (104 members and 52 seats) enabling the voters to choose their favored candidate out of two in every constituency. By contrast, electoral provisions under the 1992 constitution met democratic criteria. Deputies of the National Assembly were elected by a proportional representation system (technical elements: *multi-member constituencies, from two to nine seats; *d'Hondt formula; *closed party lists). A 5% nation-wide legal threshold was used. Independent candidates' lists were allowed, but required both the plurality and a quorum of at least 40% of the ballot in their constituencies. The President of the Republic was elected by an absolute majority system. If no candidate succeeded in gaining more than a 50% share of the votes cast a second round was held where the two most successful candidates of the first run-off participated. The candidate that gained the most votes was declared elected.

Regarding the nomination of candidates, in 1965 every registered voter of at least 25 years and two years secondary school or corresponding qualification, having made a caution of 2,500 Francs 30 days before the elections, and presented a list symbol, was eligible for the National assembly. Parliamentary functions were incompatible with the post of Senator, Minister, mayor or communal deputy. Under the Bagaza regime (1976–1987) the legislative candidates were chosen by local UPRONA selection committees and presented on a single list. For the presidential elections, the country's leader Bagaza was the sole candidate in 1984. After being confirmed as UPRONA's chairman in the party's last pre-electoral congress in late July 1984 he became automatically presidential candidate.

The 1992 Constitution required for the candidates for the National Assembly Burundian nationality, age of least 20 years, residence in Burundi at the time the party list was presented, subscription to the Charter of National Unity (which called for fighting ethnicity), and no recent crime conviction or violation of the electoral law. Candidates could be presented either by political parties or as independent candidates. Political parties had to be composed of different ethnic (religious, regional) groups (i.e. above all Hutu and Tutsi). Independents were required to have the support of at least 200 citizens of their constituencies. The mandate of deputy was incompatible with any further public function. Presidential candidates, either presented by a political party or as an independent candidate, had to be of Burundian nationality by birth, aged at least 35 years and resident in the country at the time of candidature, have subscription to the National Charter, and no recent crime conviction. The same incompatibilities as provided for the deputies, applied, including, however, deputy and party chairman functions too.

1.3 Current Electoral Provisions

Since the coup d'état in 1996 the country has been under extra-constitutional rule. Moreover, the political development in Burundi is still marked by the ongoing civil war. Therefore, electoral provisions are currently not in force.

1.4 Comment on the Electoral Statistics

Official data were not available. Thus, the presented data derive entirely from secondary sources (Philipp 1978, Gorvin 1989, *Archiv der Gegenwart* 1981, 1984) which, of course, in turn refer to official information. Only the balloting of 1992 (Ref.) and 1993 (Pr, PA) are well documented (FBIS 11 March 1992, 14 June 1993, 3 July 1993; Hermann 1993; Mehler 1994). In order to complete missing data or to adjust to the standards of the data handbook some figures rely on the author's own calculation (in case, indicated).

2. Tables

2.1 Dates of National Elections, Referendums and Coups d'Etat

Year	Presidential elections	Parliamentary elections	Elections for Constitutional Assembly	Referendums	Coups d'état[a]
1961		18/09			
1965		10/05			
1966					28/11
1976					01/11
1981				18/11	
1982		22/10			
1984	31/08				
1987					03/09
1991				09/02	
1992				09/03	
1993	01/06	29/06			
1996					25/07

[a] Numerous coup attempts not indicated.

2.2 Electoral Body 1961–1993

Year	Type of election[a]	Population[b]	Registered voters		Votes cast		
			Total number	% pop.	Total number	% reg. voters	% pop.
1961	Pa	2,967,000	1,038,653	35.0	783,027	75.4	26.4
1965	Pa	3,131,000	1,300,000[c]	41.5	—	—	—
1981	Ref	4,243,000	1,702,623[d]	40.1	1,604,722	94.3	37.8
1982	Pa	4,362,000	1,578,947[d]	36.2	1,500,000[e]	95.0	34.4
1984	Pr	4,616,000	1,788,493[d]	38.7	1,758,801	98.3	38.1
1991	Ref	5,653,000	2,186,591	38.7	2,103,938	96.2	37.2
1992	Ref	5,812,000	2,287,554	39.4	2,220,033	97.1	38.2
1993	Pr	6,209,000	2,355,126	37.9	2,291,746	97.3	36.9
1993	Pa	6,209,000	2,360,090	38.0	2,156,659	91.4	34.7

[a] Pa = Parliament; Pr = President; Ref = Referendum.

[b] UN figures as reported by Penn World Tables with the exception of the figure for 1992 that is drawn from *Fischer Weltalmanach* 1997.

[c] Estimation taken from Philipp (1978).

[d] Author's calculation (approximate figure; see for details 2.7).

[e] Estimates.

2.3 Abbreviations

FRODEBU	Front pour la Démocratie au Burundi
PDC	Parti Démocrate Chrétien
PP (1961-65)	Parti du Peuple
PP (1993)	Parti Populaire
PRP	Parti pour la Réconciliation du Peuple
RADDES	Ralliement pour la Démocratie et le Développement Economique et Sociale
RPB	Rassemblement du Peuple du Burundi
UPRONA	Union pour le Progrès National/ Parti de l'Unité et du Progrès National[a]

[a] In 1992/93: Parti de l'Unité pour la Démocratie et le Progrès National.

2.4 Electoral Participation of Parties and Alliances 1961–1993

Party / Alliance	Years	Elections contested	
		Presidential	Parliamentary
UPRONA	1961, 1965, 1982, 1984, 1993	2	4
Front Commun	1961	0	1
PP (1)	1961[a], 1965	0	2
PP (2)	1993	0	0
PDC	1961[a]	0	2
FRODEBU	1993	1	1
PRP	1993	1	1
RADDES	1993	0	1
RPB	1993	0	1

[a] In *Front Commun* 1961.

2.5 Referendums

Year	1981		1991	
	Total number	%	Total number	%
Registered voters	1,702,623[a]	–	2,186,591[a]	–
Votes cast	1,604,722[b]	94.3	2,103,938	96.2
Invalid votes	10,393[c]	0.7	13,143[e]	0.6
Valid votes	1,593,783[d]	99.3	2,090,775[d]	99.4
Yes	1,582,244	99.3	1,876,958	89.8
No	11,539	0.7	213,817	10.2

[a] Author's calculation.
[b] Sum of invalid and valid votes.
[c] Abstention votes.
[d] Sum of Yes and No votes.
[e] Original figure was corrected. According to official source invalid votes, composed of 1,327 blank and 11,856 distributed but not balloted votes, add to 13,183 votes.

Year	1992	
	Total number	%
Registered voters	2,287,554	
Votes cast	2,220,033	97.1
Invalid votes	4,337[a]	0.2
Valid votes	2,215,696	96.9
Yes	2,003,411	90.4
No	212,285	9.6

[a] Figure represents the subtraction of valid votes from votes cast; according to the source, however, there were 2,753 'void votes'.

2.6 Elections for Constitutional Assembly

Elections for Constitutional Assembly have not been held.

2.7 Parliamentary Elections 1961–1993

For the elections of 1961, 1965 and 1982 detailed data are not available. Data on voter registration and participation are reported in table 2.2.

Year	1993	
	Total number	%[a]
Registered voters	2,360,090	–
Votes cast	2,156,659	91.4
Invalid votes	45,788[a]	2.1
Valid votes	2,110,871[b]	97.9
UPRONA	461,691	21.9
FRODEBU	1,532,106	72.6
RPB	35,932	1.7
PRP	30,251	1.4
RADDES	26,519	1.3
PP (2)	24,372	1.2

[a] Author's calculation (votes cast minus sum of party votes).
[b] Author's calculation (sum of party votes).

2.8 Composition of Parliament 1961–1993

Year	1961		1965		1982		1993	
	Seats	%	Seats	%	Seats	%	Seats	%
	64	100	33	100	65	100	81	100
UPRONA	58	90.6	21	63.6	65	100	16	19.8
PP	4[a]	6.3[a]	10	30.3	–	–	–	–
PDC	2[a]	3.1[a]	–	–	–	–	–	–
Independents	–	–	2	6.1	–	–	–	–
FRODEBU	–	–	–	–	–	–	65	80.2

[a] In *Front Commun*.

2.9 Presidential Elections 1984 and 1993

1984	Total number[a]	%
Registered voters	1,788,493[b]	–
Votes cast	1,758,804	98.3
Invalid votes	—	—
Valid votes	—	—
Jean-Baptiste Bagaza (UPRONA)	1,752,579	99.6

[a] Figures are inconsistent. According to the given absolute numbers and percentages number of votes cast is too low.
[b] Author's calculation.

1993	Total number	%
Registered voters	2,355,126	–
Votes cast	2,291,746	97.3
Invalid votes	32,410[a]	1.4
Valid votes	2,259,336[b]	98.6
Melchior Ndadaye (FRODEBU)	1,483,904	65.7
Pierre Buyoya (UPRONA)	742,360	32.9
Pierre-Claver Sendegaye (RPB)	33,072	1.5

[a] Author's calculation. According to the original source (FBIS 14/6/1992) there were 21,025 'void votes'.
[b] Author's calculation. According to the original source (FBIS 14/6/1992) there were 2,260,525 voters 'who gave their vote to any one of the three candidates.'

2.9 a) Presidential Elections 1993: Regional Distribution of Votes (in %)

District	Ndadaye (FRODEBU)[a]	Buyoya (UPRONA)[a]	Sendegeya (RPB)[a]	Turnout[b]
Bubanza	84.2	14.2	0.7	97.8
Bujumbura (reg.)	78.0	20.1	0.5	96.3
Bururi	53.6	45.5	0.7	97.3
Cankuzo	30.5	66.0	1.6	98.8
Cibitoke	84.9	13.2	0.8	96.5
Gitega	63.9	33.9	1.3	97.5
Karusi	69.2	26.7	2.1	97.2
Kayanza	61.8	32.5	4.5	97.8
Kirundo	76.7	21.6	0.7	95.6
Makamba	69.3	35.9	0.9	96.0
Muramvya	50.9	47.2	0.8	98.1
Muyinga	67.5	28.3	1.4	98.3
Ngozi	67.3	29.3	2.2	98.0
Rutana	58.3	39.6	1.0	95.6
Ruyigi	70.1	26.1	1.6	96.8
Bujumbura(City)	44.6	53.1	0.8	96.1
Embassies[c]	16.9	80.7	1.4	98.4
Total[d]	64.8	32.4	1.4	97.3

[a] Votes cast as a percentage of valid votes.
[b] Votes cast as a percentage of registered voters.
[c] Votes from Burundians living abroad.
[d] Given percentages refer to votes cast and not to valid votes.

2.10 List of Power Holders 1961–1998

Head of State	Years	Remarks
Mwami Mwambutsa IV. Bangiricemge	1962–1966	King since 1915, overthrown in 8 July 1966.
Mwami Ntare V. Ndizeye	1966	Son of Mwambutsa IV. Inaugurated as King (Mwami) on 1 September 1966; overthrown by Micombero, executed after return from exile in 1972.
Cpt. Michel Micombero	1966–1976	Formerly regularly appointed Prime Minister (see below); overthrew monarchy in military coup on 29 November 1966; dissolved government in 1972.
Lt. Col. Jean-Baptiste Bagaza	1976–1987	Overthrew predecessor in military coup on 1 November 1976; declared himself President on 9 November 1976.

Head of State	Years	Remarks
Major Pierre Buyoya	1987–1993	Overthrew predecessor in military coup on 3 September 1987; declared himself President on 9 September 1987.
Melchior Ndadaye	1993	First democratically elected Head of State (elections on 1 July 1993); inaugurated on 10 July 1993, assassinated during abortive coup d'état on 21 October 1993.
Cyprien Ntaryamira	1994	Elected by National Assembly on 5 February 1994 (constitutional amendment), ending vacancy after Ndadaye's assassination; died on 6 April 1994 with Rwandian President Juvénal Habyarimana when their aircraft was shot down near Kigali while returning from regional summit in Tanzania.
Sylvestre Ntibantunganya	1994–1996	Constitutional successor and transitional President since 8 April 1994 (former President of National Assembly); declared state of emergency on 19 June 1995.
Major Pierre Buyoya	1996–	Overthrew constitutional order in military coup on 25 July 1996; unbanned political parties and restored rights of National Assembly on 12 September 1997; formally sworn in as transitional president on 11 June 1998.

Prime Minister	Years	Remarks
Prince Louis Rwagasore	1961	Assassinated on 13 October 1961.
André Muhirwa	1962–1963	Regularly appointed by Mwami on 1 July 1962.
Pierre Ngendundumwe	1963–1964	Regularly appointed by Mwami on 11 June 1963.
Albib Nyamoya	1964–1965	Regularly appointed by Mwami in May 1964; anti-Western Casablanca-Group partisan; dismissed by the King following Western pressure in January 1965.
Pierre Ngendandumwe	1965	Regularly appointed by Mwami on 11 January 1965; assassinated on 15 January 1965.
Joseph Bamina	1965	Regularly elected on 23 January 1965; dismissed on March 5, 1965; executed in October 1965.

Prime Minister	Years	Remarks
Léopold Biha	1965–1966	Appointed regularly on 13 September 1965; after Hutu uprising in October of 1965 actually powerless; dismissed on 8 July 1966.
Michel Micombero	1966–1972	Appointed on 11 July 1966; became Head of State as well on 29 November 1966;
Adrien Sibomana	1988–1993	Office recreated; appointed by new Head of State on 19 October 1988.
Sylvie Kinigi	1993–1994	Appointed by democratically elected President on 10 July 1993.
Anatole Kanyenkiko	1994–1995	Appointed by Head of State on 7 February 1994.
Antoine Nduwayo	1995–1996	Appointed by Head of State on 15 February 1995; resigned under UPRONA pressures.
Pascal Firmin Ndirmara	1996–	Appointed by new Head of State on 31 July 1996.

3. Bibliography

3.1 Official Sources

Republique du Burundi. Commission Constitutionelle (1991). *Synthese des conclusion du debat national sur le rapport de la Commission Constitutionelle relatif à la démocratisation des institutions et de la vie politique au Burundi*. Bujumbura.

Republique du Burundi. Commission Constitutionelle (1992). *Projet de Constitution de la Republique du Burundi*. Bujumbura.

Republique du Burundi. Cabinet du Président (1993). *Decret loi No. 1/022 du 16 Mars 1993 (portant Code Électoral)*. Bujumburas.

3.2 Books and Articles

Banks, A. S. (1996). *Political Handbook of the World*. New York: CSA.

Chrétien, J.-P. (1987). 'Eglise et état au Burundi: les enjeux politiques'. *Afrique Contemporaine*, 142/2: 63–71.

Cook, C., and Killingray, D. (1991). *African Political Facts since 1945* (2nd edn.). Basingstoke: Macmillan.

Des Forges, A. (1994). 'Burundi: Failed Coup or Creeping Coup?'. *Current History,* 80/5: 202–207.

East, R. (1993). *Political Parties of Africa and the Middle East*. Harlow: Longman.

Eggers, E. K. (1997). *Historical Dictionary of Burundi* (2nd edn.). Metuchen, NJ: Scarecrow Press.

Engel, U. *et al.* (eds.) (1996). *Deutsche Wahlbeobachtung in Afrika* (2nd edn.). Hamburg: Institut für Afrika-Kunde.

Gorvin, I. (1989). *Elections since 1945. A World Wide Compendium*. Harlow: Longman.

Hermann, J. (1993). *Afrika: Wahlen und Abstimmungen 1991–1993*. St. Augustin: Siedler.

International Parliamentary Union (1983). *Chronicle of Parliamentary Elections and Developments* (1 July 1982–30 June 1983). Geneva: International Center of Parliamentary Documentation.

Klingebiel, S. (1993). 'Burundi', in D. Nohlen and F. Nuscheler (1993), *Handbuch Dritte Welt* (3rd edn.).Vol. 5: Ostafrika und Südafrika. Bonn: Dietz, 54–67.

Laely, Th. (1992). *Autorität und Staat in Burundi*. Berlin: Reimer.

Lemarchand, R. (1994). *Ethnocide as Discourse and Practice*. Washington D.C.: Woodrow Wilson Center Press.

— (1994). 'Managing Transition Anarchies: Rwanda, Burundi and South Africa in Comparative Perspective'. *Journal of Modern African Studies* 32/4: 581–604.

Maguire, L. (1995). 'Power Ethnicized: The Pursuit of Protection and Participation in Rwanda and Burundi'. *Buffalo Journal of International Law,* 2/1: 117–132.

Mehler, A. (1994). 'Burundi: Das Scheitern einer Demokratisierung "von oben"', in Institut für Afrika-Kunde and R. Hofmeier (eds.), *Afrika Jahrbuch 1993. Politik, Wirtschaft und Gesellschaft in Afrika südlich der Sahara*. Opladen: Leske&Budrich, 24–34.

— (1995). *Burundi vor einem weiteren Genozid? Zum Hintergrund einer politischen Krise*. Hamburg: Institut für Afrika-Kunde.

— (1996). 'Stammeskriege in Burundi und Ruanda?'. *Jahrbuch Dritte Welt 1995*, München: Beck, 117–132.

Philipp, G. (1978). 'Burundi', in D. Sternberger, B. Vogel, D. Nohlen and K. Landfried (eds.), *Die Wahl der Parlamente und anderer Staatsorgane, Band II: Politische Organisation und Repräsentation in Afrika*, by Franz Nuscheler, Klaus Ziemer *et al.,* Berlin/ New York: Walter de Gruyter, 567–604.

Reyntjens, F. (1996). 'Constitution-making in Situations of Extreme Crisis'. *Journal of African Law*, 40/2: 2034–2042.

Strizek, H. (1996). *Ruanda und Burundi. Von der Unabhängikeit zum Staatszerfall. Studie über eine gescheiterte Demokratie im afrikanischen Zwischenseengebiet*. München/ Köln/ London: Weltforum Verlag.

CAMEROON

by Andreas Mehler

1. Introduction

1.1 Historical Overview

Cameroon, once a German colony (1884–1916), was administered by France and Great Britain in two distinct mandated territories. In the eastern (French) part the violent and efficient repression of the '*maquis*' (1955–1970), an armed revolt by activists of the nationalist *Union des Populations du Cameroun* (UPC) in the Bamiléké and Sanaga Maritime regions, overshadowed the turn to an autonomous status within the *Communauté Française* in 1958. From the very beginning the Cameroonian regime very solidly belonged to the pro-western or pro-French camp.

With the onset of independence of East Cameroon (1 January 1960) liberties were on the wane after an 'Enabling Act' had been bestowed upon Prime Minister Ahmadou Ahidjo as early as October 1959. In view of the '*maquis*' it enabled him to enact emergency laws by ordinances. A new constitution was passed by referendum (21 February 1960),—after the results had been manipulated by a still French dominated administration. In the April elections of the same year, Ahidjo's party *Union Camerounaise* (UC) gained 51 of 100 seats in Parliament by winning 45% of the votes. This result had been enabled by a convenient division of constituencies. It permitted Ahidjo to become elected President by means of indirect parliamentary proceedings on 5 May 1960.

The population of the two British sections of the mandate had to decide whether to join Cameroon or Nigeria. In a plebiscite the 'Northern Cameroons' voted for integration into the Nigerian state, whereas the 'Southern Cameroons' decided to join the Republic of Cameroon on 11 and 12 February 1961. The following constitutional negotiations defined the rules of a federal constitution, which were accepted by the two parliaments. The constitution finally created a presidential regime at the federal level. Both federal states kept their Parliament and Prime Ministers, but not many prerogatives. French and English were declared official languages. West Cameroon's Prime Minister John Ngu Foncha of the *Kamerun National Democratic Party* (KNDP) automatically became Vice-President of State. Both party leaders, Ahidjo and Foncha, could *de facto* appoint all the members of the first Federal Parliament (40 UC and 10 KNDP representatives) for a transitional period (until the last and only partly pluralistic elections on 26 April 1964).

Ahidjo extended his authority continuously by arresting moderate party leaders and finally by forcing the creation of a united party in 1966 (*Union Nationale Camerounaise*, UNC; *Cameroon National Union*, CNU). Elections were henceforth non-competitive and the party hierarchy decided who would represent the people. The 'First Republic' came to a sudden end by the 'Peaceful Revolution' of 20 May 1972: In a referendum—announced only two weeks before—Cameroonians voted for the replacement of the federal by a unitary constitution; all federal institutions were abolished. Governors, who were immediate subjects to Ahidjo's orders, were appointed to the seven newly created provinces. Thus, Ahidjo had reached the peak of his power. In the mid-1970s Cameroon was in fact a centralized police state and functioned in a neo-patrimonial way. Regional quotas were used in respect of state employment in order to obtain nation-wide political support. The introduction of a Prime Minister did not alter the nature of the system.

Ahidjo resigned on 4 November 1982 because of health problems (he did not resign as chairman of UNC, however). Prime Minister Paul Biya was his successor by virtue of a constitutional amendment (1979). Ahidjo engaged in a power struggle with Biya in 1983, lost the party chairmanship, was accused of subversion, assassination plans and libel against the Head of State and sentenced to death *in absentia*. An attempted coup on 6 April 1984 by the presidential guard '*garde républicaine*' loyal to Ahidjo led to numerous executions, political trials and administrative imprisonments for many Cameroonians. Biya's ruling was stabilized during the party congress on 21–24 March 1985 in Bamenda, when the party was renamed RDPC (*Rassemblement Démocratique du Peuple Camerounais; Cameroon People's Democratic Movement*). 'Semi-competitive' elections were held between 1986 and 1988: Limited competition between candidates and lists of candidates of the RDPC had been permitted in elections within the party (1986), communal elections (1987) and parliamentary elections (1988), although the party executive clearly interfered with the arranging of the lists.

The modestly successful economic development since the 1960s turned into a severe crisis after 1985 and Biya had to face the global changes of 1989/90 in a state of weak legitimacy. The reaction to the first two attempts to create an oppositional party in 1990 was repression, but one of them proved to be very popular: the *Social Democratic Front* (SDF) and its leader John Fru Ndi was the most serious challenge to Biya after he had accepted (reluctantly) the return to multi-party politics—claimed by civil society, the Catholic Church and some donor countries. Biya re-introduced the post of Prime Minister (abolished in 1984) to create a scape-goat, but the system remained a presidential one.

The opposition, which at first supported common actions of civil disobedience in a disciplined way (1991), split in view of the elections of 1992 by taking part in legislative elections, e.g. *Union Nationale pour la Démocratie et le Progrès* (UNDP), one wing of the UPC, or boycotting the elections, e.g. SDF, *Union Démocratique du Cameroun* (UDC). The RDPC only won a relative majority of seats and had to rely upon a coalition with a regionalist party, the *Mouvement pour la Défense de la République* (MDR). Five opposition candidates competed for the presidential elections. This facilitated the task of Biya to win by a plurality of votes. A clear regional pattern of voting behavior was most obvious (Biya: South, Center, East and Far North Provinces; Fru Ndi: North West, South West, West and Littoral Provinces; Bello Bouba: North, Adamaoua Provinces). The validity of the official outcome was questioned not only by Fru Ndi, who came in second by a tight margin, but also by international election observers. Violence broke out in the anglophone part of the country, but was controlled by loyal troops. The democratization process was effectively blocked. Only with the partly manipulated municipal elections on 21 January 1996 did the opposition show signs of recovery by winning the majority of urban councils in the bigger cities (exception: Yaoundé). An increasing tribalization 'from above' was the regime's main answer to the multi-party challenge.

New elected institutions, a Senate and Regional Assemblies, were introduced theoretically, though not in practice, by a major constitutional reform, debated and adopted in Parliament in December 1995 (promulgated on 18 January 1996). The scale of the reform raised the question of why the population was not invited to decide on the fundamental text by referendum. Only theoretically did the constitution provide for a semi-presidential system, the Prime Minister being completely dependent on the President's will.

The official results of the 1997 parliamentary elections, once more over-shadowed by allegations of serious fraud, gave a comfortable majority to the CPDM (60% of the seats) and confirmed the regional voting pattern. The SDF is now the strongest opposition party in Parliament, UDC won all seats in Foumban, the home town of its leader

Ndam Njoya. UNDP, UPC and MDR suffered big losses. Presidential elections in October 1997 were boycotted by the main opposition parties (SDF, UNDP, UDC—denouncing the newly amended electoral law). Biya was elected by a large majority of votes reminiscent of results of the one-party era. The official turnout figures seemed grossly overstretched and were in contradiction to independent media reports.

1.2 Evolution of Electoral Provisions

Cameroon has experienced several electoral systems. In the British mandate the plurality system in single-member constituencies was applied in elections to the House of Assembly in 1959 as for the first post-independence vote to the regional parliament. In the French mandate the same system was used in multi-member constituencies before independence. The first post-independence election to the Legislative Assembly saw a mixture of single- and multi-member constituencies, which was clearly designed to favor the ruling party UC (for the most part multi-member constituencies in its regional stronghold in the north, for the most part single-member constituencies to stimulate vote splitting along ethnic lines in the south).

Since 1964 the size of the constituencies has followed the administrative division into so-called *régions administratives* (exclusively multi-member constituencies). The President was now elected by universal suffrage for a five-year term, formally according to plurality system. In fact, only one candidate stood for election. After the 'Peaceful Revolution' in May 1972 legislative elections were held without any reference to constituencies with a national list of UNC candidates.

In 1983 a major change, though only formally, was introduced for presidential elections: Independent candidates could stand for election if they could obtain 500 supporting signatures (50 each in the now 10 provinces) from the rank of elected officials or traditional chiefs and if they had resided in Cameroon for at least the last five years. Another major reform occurred in 1986 and 1987 with semi-competitive elections, which were held first in party and municipal elections, before transferring the same principle to legislative elections (1988). Each 'legally existent party' (the RDPC being the only one) was able to present several lists in each constituency. (The RDPC decided to field a maximum of two lists.) The vote was conducted in 45 multi-member and four single-member constituencies according to plurality rule.

1.3 Current Electoral Provisions

Sources: Constitution of the Republic of Cameroon of 1972, Loi No. 96/06 du 18 janvier 1996 portant révision de la Constitution du 02 juin 1972; Loi No. 91/020 du 16 décembre 1991 fixant les conditions d'élection des députés à l'Assemblée nationale; Loi No. 97/013 du 19 mars 1997 modifiant et complétant certaines dispositions de la Loi No. 91/020; Loi No. 97/020 modifiant certaines dispositions de la Loi No. 92/010 du 17 septembre 1992 fixant les conditions d'élection et de suppléance à la présidence de la République.

Elected national institutions: President of the Republic for a regular term of seven years with one direct re-election being allowed. National Assembly (180 members) for a period of five years (re-eligible). The members of the (*de facto* not yet established) Senate are in part indirectly elected (seven members in each region) and in part appointed by the President (three in each region).

Suffrage: The principles of universal, equal, direct and secret suffrage are postulated by the Constitution. Every citizen who has reached the age of 20 has the right to vote and is entitled to be registered as a voter.

Nomination of candidates
- *presidential elections*: Every citizen of Cameroonian origin aged at least 35 years or over and suffering no restriction of his civic and political rights is eligible, if he or she is a registered voter, a resident for at least one year and is nominated either as a representative of a registered political party or as an independent candidate whose nomination is supported by at least 300 personalities (members of the National Assembly, municipal Councillors, members of consular chambers or first degree traditional chiefs; 30 persons in each region). Candidates shall pay a deposit of F CFA 1.5 million into the public treasury. Nomination papers shall be submitted to the Ministry of Territorial Administration; it is empowered to accept or reject them after verification.
- *elections to the National Assembly*: Every Cameroonian citizen aged at least 23 years is eligible as a member of the National Assembly, if he or she is a registered voter and has the ability to write and read French or English. No person may become a member of the National Assembly if he is in a dependent situation vis-à-vis a foreign country; no military and no security service agent and no civic superior in respective departments

may become members of the National Assembly. No independent candidatures are possible.

Electoral system
- *presidential elections*: Plurality system.
- *elections to the National Assembly*: Plurality system in single-member constituencies and absolute majority system (containing elements of a bonus system and PR) in multi-member constituencies of different size (two to seven seats); constituencies and administration districts, so-called *départements,* are basically identical, several 'special constituencies' were created in 1997 through gerrymandering, though. If a list wins an absolute majority in a multi-member constituency it gets all the seats. If no list wins the absolute majority, the list with a relative majority gets at least half of the seats (to round up), the rest of the seats being distributed proportionally according to Hare quota, greatest remainder) between all the other lists that have passed the electoral threshold of 5%.

1.4 Comment on the Electoral Statistics

The base of the statistics is not completely, but to a large extent reliable, though there are serious doubts whether outcomes and turnout figures were not prefabricated during the 1960s, 1970s and 1980s and heavily manipulated during the 1990s. Information for elections before 1973 are based on Ziemer (1978) basically using official statistics as well as LeVine (1964). LeVines's figures contain some inaccuracy, corrections have been made using Eyinga (1990). Official results of presidential elections are proclaimed by the Supreme Court (in 1997 nominally by the Constitutional Council not yet existing, i.e. still by the Supreme Court) and are reported in the official gazette which was published only irregularly in the 1990s. Official results of parliamentary elections are proclaimed by a national counting commission (and in 1997 by the Constitutional Council) and are usually not reported in the official gazette (exception: parliamentary elections 1988), the figures given are based on the official newspaper *Cameroon Tribune*, cross-checked on international media reports. In some cases national results had to be calculated by the author using official figures from the constituency level. The figure for the registered voters of the 1992 parliamentary elections is the most plausible one given by the UNDP in its request to annul the presidential elections. Figures are not complete for the 1992 parliamentary elections, because *Cameroon Tribune* did not publish the results of the constituency Djérem (one seat, won by UNDP). The 1997 parliamentary elections were invalidated in three out of 73 constituencies, all figures given refer to the 70 remaining constituencies, though 33 of these show tabulation errors.

2. Tables

2.1 Dates of National Elections, Referendums and Coups d'Etat

Year[a]	Presidential elections	Parliamentary elections	Elections for Constitutional Assembly	Referendums	Coups d'état
1964		26/04			
1965	20/03				
1970	28/03	07/06			
1972				20/05	
1973		18/05			
1975	05/04				
1978		28/05			
1980	05/04				
1983		29/05			
1984	14/01				
1988	24/04	24/04			
1992	11/10	01/03			
1997	12/10	17/05			

[a] Nation-wide elections and referendums have been held only since 1964. The referendum to adopt the first Constitution of the independent East Cameroon was held on 21 February 1960, the two referendums about 'reunification' or integration in the two British sections of the mandate were held on 11/12 February 1961. All of them were of national importance and are reported in table 2.5. Legislative elections in the French mandate and later the Republic of Cameroon (East Cameroon) were held on 23 December 1956 and 10 April 1960, see table 2.7.2. Legislative elections in the British mandate and later the state of West Cameroon were held on 24 January 1959 and 30 December 1961 before 'reunification', see table 2.7.3. Further regional elections to the parliaments of each state (in 1965 and 1967) are not reported.

2.2 Electoral Body 1964–1997

Year	Type of election[a]	Population[b]	Registered voters		Votes cast		
			Total number	% pop.	Total number	% reg. voters	% pop.
1964	Pa	—	—	—	2,259,658	—	—
1965	Pr	5,229,000	2,842,515	54.4	2,702,092	95.1	51.7
1970	Pr	6,610,000	3,101,517	46.9	3,030,537	97.7	45.8
1970	Pa	6,610,000	3,094,886	46.8	2,934,923	94.8	44.4
1972	Ref	6,974,000	3,236,280	46.4	3,179,634	98.2	45.6
1973	Pa	7,156,000	3,348,989	46.8	3,295,005	98.4	46.0
1975	Pr	7,520,000	3,501,177	46.6	3,479,186	99.4	46.3
1978	Pa	8,114,000	3,663,358	45.1	3,615,364	98.0	44.6
1980	Pr	8,653,000	3,361,630	38.8	3,329,235	99.0	38.5
1983	Pa	9,361,000	3,657,995	39.1	3,628,579	99.2	38.8
1984	Pr	9,648,000	3,968,673	41.1	3,878,745	97.7	40.2
1988	Pa	10,798,000	3,634,568	33.7	3,282,884	90.3	30.4
1988	Pr	10,798,000	3,634,568	33.7	3,364,090	92.6	31.2
1992	Pa	12,106,000	4,010,062	33.1	2,435,443	60.7	20.1
1992	Pr	12,106,000	4,195,687	34.7	3,015,448	71.9	24.9
1997	Pa	13,937,000	3,844,330[c]	27.6	2,913,186[c]	75.6	20.9
1997	Pr	13,937,000	4,220,136	30.3	3,433,081	81.4	24.6

[a] Pa =Parliament; Pr = President, Ref =Referendum.

[b] Population data are extrapolated from UN estimates and the two censuses of 1976 and 1987.

[c] Registered voters and votes cast in 70 out of 73 constituencies.

2.3 Abbreviations

AMEC	Action pour la Démocratie et l'Egalité des Chances
ANDP	Alliance Nationale pour la Démocratie et le Progrès
CPNC	Cameroons People's National Convention
CUC	Cameroon United Congress
DIC	Démocratie Intégrale du Cameroun
FPUP	Front Populaire pour l'Unité et la Paix
GPC	Groupe des Progressistes du Cameroun
KNC	Kamerun National Congress
KNDP	Kamerun National Democratic Party
KPP	Kamerun People's Party
MANC	Mouvement d'Action Nationale Camerounaise
MDP	Mouvement pour la Démocratie et le Progrès.
MDR	Mouvement pour la Défense de la République
MLJC	Mouvement pour la Libération de la Jeunesse Camerounaise
MP	Mouvement Progressiste
OK	One Kamerun
PDC	Parti des Démocrates Camerounais
PNP	Parti National pour le Progrès
PPD	Parti Populaire pour le Développement
RDPC	Rassemblement Démocratique du Peuple Camerounais
RDPF	Rassemblement du Peuple sans Frontière
RFP	Regroupement des Forces Patriotiques
SDF	Social Democratic Front
UC	Union Camerounaise
UDC	Union Démocratique du Cameroun
UFDC	Union des Forces Démocratiques du Cameroun
UNC	Union Nationale Camerounaise
UNDP	Union Nationale pour la Démocratie et le Progrès
UPC	Union des populations du Cameroun

General note: French names and abbreviations are generally more common for parties competing on a national scale (exception: SDF). The English form of the united party's name (UNC, RDPC) are Cameroon National Union (CNU) and Cameroon People's Democratic Movement (CPDM) respectively. The table does not include smaller parties competing only in the 1992 and 1997 legislative elections (26 and 33 respectively).

2.4 Electoral Participation of Parties and Alliances 1956/59–1997

Party / Alliance	Years	Elections contested Presidential	Parliamentary
MANC	1956	0	1
Paysans Indépendants	1956	0	1
PDC (GDC)[a]	1956–1964, 1992–1997	(1)[c]	5
SFIO	1956	0	1
UC[b]	1956–1965	1	3
KNC/KPP	1959	0	1
KNDP	1959–1965	(1)[d]	3
One Kamerun	1959–1961	0	2
FPUP	1960	0	1
GPC	1960	0	1
UPC	1960, 1992–1997	(1)[e]	3[f]
CPNC	1961–1964	0	2
UNC	1970–1984	4	4
RDPC	1988–1997	2	3
MDR	1992–1997	(1)[c]	2
MP	1992	1	0
PNP	1992	(1)[c]	2
RFP	1992–1997	1	2
SDF	1992–1997	1	1
UDC	1992–1997	1	1
UNDP	1992–1997	1	2
ANDP	1997	(1)[g]	1
MLJC	1997	(1)[g]	1
DIC	1997	1	1
PPD	1997	1	1
RDPF	1997	1	0
AMEC	1997	1	0
UFDC	1997	0	1

General note: Electoral alliances with smaller regional parties in the 1992 presidential elections were important for the candidate John Fru Ndi (SDF). Some of them had a certain audience in 1992 without having contested national elections yet (e.g. the UFDC or the *Mouvement pour la Démocratie et le Progrès*), but were not very active in 1997.

[a] Initially a loose alliance, constituted as a party only in 1958.

[b] Initially a loose alliance, constituted as a party only after the elections of 1956.

[c] Alliance with Biya for the 1992 presidential elections.

[d] John Ngu Foncha (KNDP) was elected Vice-President of State on a ticket with Ahidjo in 1965.

[e] Three different wings of the UPC campaigned for Biya, Bello Bouba or Fru Ndi in the 1992 presidential elections.

[f] Two wings of the UPC fielded candidates in the 1997 elections, only the UPC-K (Kodock) won a single mandate.

[g] Alliance with Biya in the 1997 presidential elections.

2.5 Referendums

Year	1960 (East Cameroon)[a]	
	Total number	%
Registered voters	1,771,969	–
Votes cast	1,338,178	75.5
Invalid votes	9,605	0.7
Valid votes	1,328,573	99.3
Yes	797,498	60.1
No	531,075	39.9

[a] Referendum to adopt the Constitution of the Republic of Cameroon (East Cameroon).

Year	1961 ('Northern Cameroon')[a]		1961 ('Southern Cameroon')[a]	
	Total number	%	Total number	%
Registered voters	292,985	–	349,652	–
Votes cast	—	—	—	—
Invalid votes	—	—	—	—
Valid votes	243,955	83.3	331,312	94.8
Integration into Cameroon	97,659	40.0	233,571	70.5
Integration into Nigeria	146,296	60.0	97,741	29.5

[a] Referendums concerning the integration of the two British sections of the mandate into Cameroon or Nigeria.

Year	1972[a]	
	Total number	%
Registered voters	3,236,280	–
Votes cast	3,179,634	98.2
Invalid votes	1,612	0.1
Valid votes	3,178,022	99.9
Yes	3,177,846	100.0
No	176	0.0

Referendum to adopt the unitary constitution

2.6 Elections for Constitutional Assembly

Elections for Constitutional Assembly have not been held.

2.7 Parliamentary Elections

2.7.1 Territorial Assembly (French Cameroon) and Legislative Assembly (Republic of Cameroon) 1956–1960

Year	1956 Total number	%	1960 Total number	%
Registered voters	1,752,902	–	1,940,438	–
Votes cast	725,000	41.4	1,349,739	69.5
Invalid votes	—	—	—	—
Valid votes	726,817	100.3	1,349,239	100.0
UC	249,693	34.3	606,000	44.9
PDC (GDC)	152,000	20.9	139,780	10.4
Paysans Indépendants	69,457	9.6	–	–
MANC	48,666	6.7	–	–
SFIO	18,001	2.5	–	–
UPC	–	–	151,379	11.2
FPUP	–	–	145,752	10.8
GPC	–	–	60,686	4.5
Independents	–	–	11,853	0.9
Others	189,000	26.0	233,789	17.3

General note: These indications contain evidently some inaccuracy. Percentages calculated differ from those given by LeVine (1964).

2.7.2 House of Assembly (British Cameroon/ West Cameroon) 1959–1961

Year	1959 Total number	%	1961 Total number	%
Registered voters	205,576	–	—	–
Votes cast	—	—	—	—
Invalid votes	—	—	—	—
Valid votes	137,219	–	255,433	100.0
KNDP	73,305	53.4	140,347	54.9
KNC/KPP	51,384	37.4	–	–
CPNC	–	–	68,458	26.8
OK	2,021	1.5	17,733	6.9
Independents	10,509	7.7	27,494	10.8
Others	–	–	1,401	0.6

2.7.3 National Assembly 1964–1997

Year	1964		1970	
	Total number	%	Total number	%
Registered voters	—	–	3,348989	–
Votes cast	2,259,658	—	2,934,923	94.8
Invalid votes	—	—	8,699	0.3
Valid votes	—	—	2,926,224	99.7
East				
UC	1,863,614	93.5	–	–
PDC	129,571	6.5	–	–
West				
KNDP	192,081	76.1	–	–
CPNC	60,485	23.9	–	–
UNC	–	–	2,926,224	100.0

Year	1973		1978	
	Total number	%	Total number	%
Registered voters	3,348,989	–	3,663,358	–
Votes cast	3,295,005	98.4	3,615,364	98.0
Invalid votes	1,577	0.0	596	0.0
Valid votes	3,293,428	100.0	3,614,768	100.0
UNC	3,293,428	100.0	3,614,768	100.0

Year	1983		1988	
	Total number	%	Total number	%
Registered voters	3,657,995	–	3,634,568	–
Votes cast	3,628,579	99.2	3,282,884	90.3
Invalid votes	110	0.0	102,986	3.1
Valid votes	3,628,469	100.0	3,179,898	96.9
UNC	3,628,469	100.0	–	–
RDPC	–	–	3,179,898	100.0

Year	1992		1997[b]	
	Total number	%	Total number	%
Registered voters	4,010,062	–	3,844,330	–
Votes cast	2,435,443	60.7	2,906,186	75.6
Invalid votes	—	–	63,137	2.2
Valid votes	2,173,409[a]	90.2	2,888,716	99.4
RDPC	989,044	45.5	1,399,751	48.0
UNDP	770,586	35.5	392,712	13.5
UPC	189,542	8.7	78,452	2.7
MDR	87,446	4.0	71,762	2.5
PDC	39,758	1.8	3,460	0.1
PNP	17,094	0.8	–	–
SDF	–	–	685,689	23.5
UDC	–	–	76,644	2.6
ANDP	–	–	25,658	0.9
UFDC	–	–	19,824	0.7
MLJC	–	–	12,973	0.4
other	79,939	3.7	121,791	4.2

[a] No information was available for the constituency Djérem (won by UNDP), figures of valid votes and percentages refer to the addition of the other 48 constituencies.

[b] These indications contain evidently some inaccuracy. All figures refer to 70 of 73 constituencies excluding constituencies Mayo-Rey, Mayo-Banyo and Nde, all invalidated by the Constitutional Council. UPC votes is the total of results of both wings competing due to lack of specific information in some constituencies.

2.8 Composition of Parliament

2.8.1 Territorial Assembly (French Cameroon) and Legislative Assembly (Republic of Cameroon) 1956–1960

Year	1956		1960	
	Seats	%	Seats	%
	70	100	100	100
UC	30	42.9	51	51
PDC (GDC)	20	28.6	12	12
Paysans Indépendants	9	12.9	–	–
MANC	8	11.4	–	–
SFIO and other	3	4.3	–	–
FPUP	–	–	19	19
UPC	–	–	8	8
GPC	–	–	7	7
Independent	–	–	3	3

General note: The composition of the legislative Assembly of 1960 changed dramatically after only two years following four by-elections (all won by UC), the integration of FPUP into UC and the arrest of five opposition MPs.

2.8.2 House of Assembly (British Cameroon/West Cameroon) 1959–1961

Year	1959		1961	
	Seats	%	Seats	%
	26	100	37	100
KNDP	14	53.8	24	64.9
KNC	8	30.8	–	–
KPP	4	15.4	–	–
CPNC	–	–	10	27.0
One Kamerun	–	–	1	2.7
Independents	–	–	2	5.4

2.8.3 National Assembly 1964–1997

Year	1964		1970		1973		1978	
	Seats	%	Seats	%	Seats	%	Seats	%
	50	100	50	100	120	100	120	100
UC	40	80	–	–	–	–	–	–
KNDP	10	20	–	–	–	–	–	–
UNC	–	–	50	100	120	100	120	100

Year	1983		1988		1992		1997[a]	
	Seats	%	Seats	%	Seats	%	Seats	%
	120	100	180	100	180	100	180	100
UNC	120	100	–	–	–	–		
RDPC	–	–	180	100	88	48.9	109	60.6
UNDP	–	–	–	–	68	37.8	13	7.2
UPC	–	–	–	–	18	10.0	1	0.6
MDR	–	–	–	–	6	3.3	1	0.6
SDF	–	–	–	–	–	–	43	23.9
UDC	–	–	–	–	–	–	5	2.8
MLJC	–	–	–	–	–	–	1	0.6

[a] All figures refer to 70 out of 73 constituencies (173 seats). By-elections are due to be held in Mayo-Banyo, Mayo-Rey and Nde constituencies.

2.9 Presidential Elections 1965–1997

1965	Total number	%
Registered voters	2,842,515	–
Votes cast	2,702,098	95.1
Invalid votes	1,401	0.1
Valid votes	2,700,697	99.9
Ahmadou Ahidjo/ John Ngu Foncha (UC/KNDP)	2,700,697	100.0

1970	Total number	%
Registered voters	3,501,177	–
Votes cast	3,479,186	99.4
Invalid votes	244	0.0
Valid votes	3,478,942	100.0
Ahmadou Ahidjo (UNC)	3,478,942	100.0

1980	Total number	%
Registered voters	3,361,630	–
Votes cast	3,329,235	99.0
Invalid votes	90	0.0
Valid votes	3,329,145	100.0
Ahmadou Ahidjo (UNC)	3,329,145	100.0

1984	Total number	%
Registered voters	3,968,673	–
Votes cast	3,878,745	97.7
Invalid votes	607	0.0
Valid votes	3,878,138	100.0
Paul Biya (UNC)	3,878,138	100.0

1988	Total number	%
Registered voters	3,634,568	–
Votes cast	3,364,090	92.6
Invalid votes	42,218	1.3
Valid votes	3,321,872	98.7
Paul Biya (UNC)	3,321,872	100.0

1992	Total number	%
Registered voters	4,195,687	–
Votes cast	3,015,448	71.9
Invalid votes	50,012	1.7
Valid votes	2,965,436	98.3
Paul Biya (UNC)	1,185,466	40.0
Ni John Fru Ndi (SDF)	1,066,602	36.0
Bello Bouba Maigari (UNDP)	569,887	19.2
Adamou Ndam Njoya (UDC)	107,411	3.6
Jean-Jacques Ekindi (MP)	23,525	0.8
Emah Otu (RFP)	12,545	0.4

1997	Total number	%
Registered voters	4,220,136	–
Votes cast	3,433,081[a]	81.4[a]
Invalid votes	84,890[b]	2.5[b]
Valid votes	3,422,055	99.7
Paul Biya (UNC)	3,167,820	92.6
Henri Hogbe Nlend (UPC)	85,693	2.5
Samuel Eboua (MDP)	83,506	2.4
Albert Dzongang (PPD)	40,814	1.2
Joachim Tabi Owono (AMEC)	15,817	0.5
Antoine Depadoue Ndemanou (RDPF)	15,490	0.5
Gustave Essaka (DIC)	12,915	0.4

[a] Arithmetically correct calculation as sum of results on provincial level: 3,506,944 votes: 83.1%.

[b] Figure refer to corrected sum of provincial results (instead of the officially given 11,026).

2.10 List of Power Holders 1958–1998

Head of State	Years	Remarks
Ahmadou Ahidjo	1960–1982	Ahidjo was elected President of the Republic of Cameroon by a vote in Parliament. With the *reunification* he became automatically President of the Federal Republic of Cameroon. He was subsequently re-elected by universal suffrage in non-competitive elections in 1965, 1970, 1975 and 1980. He resigned from office on 4 November 1982.
Paul Biya	1982–	As Prime Minister Paul Biya was the designated and constitutional successor since an amendment of the constitution in 1979. He was sworn in on 6 November 1982, elected in non-competitive elections in 1984 and 1988 and re-elected in multi-party elections in 1992 and 1997.

Head of Government	Years	Remarks
Ahmadou Ahidjo	1958–1960	Prime Minister of East Cameroon before Independence.
John Ngu Foncha	1959–1961	Prime Minister of West Cameroon before *reunification* with the Republic of Cameroon.
Sadou Hayatou	1991–1992	The office of the Prime Minister was re-introduced to relieve Biya during the political crisis (23/04/1991). Contrary to the former phase of its existence (1975–1984) the holder of the office was now defined as Head of Government, being responsible to the President (who appointed him) and the National Assembly simultaneously. Sadou Hayatou, a political heavy-weight, was dismissed after the RDPC suffered electoral defeats in his home region in the country's North.
Simon Achidi Achu	1992–1996	Ex-minister under Ahidjo; appointed Prime Minister (09/04/1992) to split the supporters of Fru Ndi in his home region (North West). He failed to do so.
Musonge Mafany	1996–	Musonge Mafany, an anglophone, but from the South West province, was his successor (19/09/1996).

3. Bibliography

3.1 Official Sources

'Loi No. 96/06 du 18 janvier 1996 portant révision de la Constitution du 02 juin 1972'.

'Loi No. 97/013 du 19 mars 1997 modifiant et complétant certaines dispositions de la loi No. 91/020 du 16 décembre 1991 fixant les conditions d'élection des députés à l'Assemblée nationale'. *Cameroon Tribune 6314*, 21/03/1997.

'Loi No. 92/010 du 17 séptembre 1992 fixant les conditions d'élection et de suppléance à la présidence de la République'. *Cameroon Tribune 5218*, 18/09/1992.

'Loi No. 91/020 du 16 décembre 1991 fixant les conditions d'élection des députés à l'Assemblée nationale'. *Cameroon Tribune 5031*, 17/12/1991.

'Loi No. 88/02 du 17 mars 1988 portant modification de l'article 2 de la loi No. 87-16 du 15 juillet 1987 fixant les conditions d'élection des membres de l'Assemblée nationale'. *Journal officiel de la République du Cameroun*, 28, 15/04/1988.

'Loi No. 87/016 du 15 juillet 1987 modifiant certaines dispositions de la loi No. 72-LF-6 du 26 juin 1972 fixant les conditions d'élection des membres de l'Assemblée nationale'. *Journal officiel de la République du Cameroun*, 27, 15/08/1987.

'Loi No. 83/025 du 29 novembre 1983 modifiant et complétant l'article 7 de la Constitution'. *Journal officiel de la République Unie du Cameroun*, 23, 15/12/1983.

'Loi No. 83/026 du 29 november 1983 modifiant les dispositions de la loi No. 73-10 du 7 décembre 1973 relative aux conditions d'élections et de suppléance à la Présidence de la République'. *Journal officiel de la République Unie du Cameroun*, 23, 15/12/1983.

'Loi No. 73/10 du 7 décembre 1973 fixant les conditions d'élections et de suppléance à la présidence de la République, en application des articles 6 et 7 de la Constitution du 2 juin 1972', in J.-P. Guiffo Mopo (1977), *Constitutions du Cameroun. Documents politiques et diplomatiques.* Yaoundé: Editions Stella, 214–226.

'Loi No. 72-LF-6 du 26 juin 1972 fixant les conditions d'élection des membres de l'Assemblée nationale de la République unie du Cameroun en application de l'article 17 de la Constitution du 2 juin 1972'. *Journal officiel de la République Unie du Cameroun*, 12/5 (suppl.), 01/07/1972.

'Décret No. 72-DF-236 du 8 mai 1972 fixant les modalités de déroulement de la campagne du référendum'. *Journal officiel de la République Fédérale du Cameroun*, 12/1 (suppl.), 08/05/1972.

3.2 Books, Articles and Electoral Reports

Bayart, J.-F. (1978*a*). 'Clientelism, Elections and Systems of Inequality and Domination in Cameroun: A Reconsideration of the Notion of Political and Social Control', in G. Hermet, R. Rose and A. Rouquié (eds.), *Elections without choice.* London *et al.*: Macmillan: 66–87.

— (1978*b*). 'Espace électoral et espace social au Cameroun', in CEAN/ CERI, *Aux urnes l'Afrique! Elections et pouvoirs en Afrique noire.* Paris: Pedone: 187–216.

— (1979). *L'Etat au Cameroun.* Paris: Presses de la Fondation nationale des Sciences Politiques.

Collectif 'Changer le Cameroun' (1993). *Le 11 octobre 1992. Autopsie d'une élection présidentielle controversée.* Yaoundé: Les éditions C[3].

Eyinga, A. (1978). *Mandat d'arrêt pour cause d'élections: De la démocatie au Cameroun: 1970–1978.* Paris: L'Harmattan.

— (1990). *Cameroun 1960–1990: La fin des élections. Un cas d'évolution régressive de la démocratie.* Paris: L'Harmattan.

Guiffo Mopo, J.-P. (1977). *Constitutions du Cameroun. Documents politiques et diplomatiques.* Yaoundé: Editions Stella.

Hillebrand, E., and Mehler, A. (1993). 'Kamerun', in D. Nohlen and F. Nuscheler (eds.), *Handbuch der Dritten Welt, Vol. 4: Westafrika und Zentralafrika* (3rd edn.). Bonn: Dietz, 444–460.

Krieger, M. (1994). 'Cameroon's Democratic Crossroads, 1990–4'. *Journal of Modern African Studies*, 32/4: 605–628.

LeVine, V. T. (1964). *The Cameroons from Mandate to Independence.* Berkeley, Cal.: University of California Press.

Mehler, A. (1991–1998). 'Kamerun', in Institut für Afrika-Kunde and R. Hofmeier (eds.), *Afrika Jahrbuch 1990–1997. Politik, Wirtschaft und Gesellschaft in Afrika südlich der Sahara.* Opladen: Leske & Budrich.

— (1993). *Kamerun in der Ära Biya. Bedingungen, erste Schritte und Blockaden einer demokratischen Transition.* Hamburg: Institut für Afrika-Kunde.

— (1996). 'Verfassungsentwicklung in Kamerun'. *Nord-Süd aktuell*, 10/1: 85–92.

— (1997). 'Cameroun: une transition qui n'a pas eu lieu', in J.-P. Daloz and P. Quantin (eds.), *Transitions démocratiques africaines.* Paris: Karthala: 95–138.

Melone, S., Minkoa She, A., and Sindjoun, L. (1996). *La Réforme Constitutionelle du 18 Janvier 1996 au Cameroun. Aspects juridiques et politiques.* Yaoundé: DIHACO.

NDI (National Democratic Institute for International Affairs) (1993). *An Assessment of the October 11, 1992 Election in Cameroon*. Washington, D.C.: NDI.

Schilder, K. (1993). 'La Démocratie aux champs: les présidentielles d'octobre 1992 au Nord-Cameroun'. *Politique Africaine*, 50: 115–122.

Sindjoun, L. (1994). 'La Cour Suprême, la compétition électorale et la continuité politique au Cameroun: La construction de la démocratisation passive'. *Afrique et Développement*, 19/2: 21–69.

Ziemer, K. (1978). 'Kamerun', in D. Sternberger, B. Vogel, D. Nohlen and K. Landfried (eds.), *Die Wahl der Parlamente und anderere Staatsorgane, Band: II: Politische Organisation und Repräsentation in Afrika*, by Franz Nuscheler, Klaus Ziemer *et al.*, Berlin/ New York: Walter de Gruyter, 863–923.

CAPE VERDE

by Ana Catarina Clemente-Kersten

1. Introduction

1.1 Historical Overview

The Republic of Cape Verde was ruled as a single-party system after its independence from Portugal (5 July 1975) until 1991. Following the introduction of multi-party politics, Cape Verde was the first Portuguese speaking African country to achieve a peaceful government change by competitive elections (1991).

Against the background of common colonial rule by Portugal, the liberation struggle of Cape Verde and Guinea-Bissau were closely linked. In 1956 Amílcar Cabral (who was born in Cape Verde) founded the *Partido Africano da Independência da Guiné e Cabo Verde* (PAIGC) in Guinea-Bissau with the aim of liberating Guinea-Bissau and Cape Verde and to create a union between both countries after their independence. From 1963 onwards the PAIGC directed a guerrilla war against colonial rule in Guinea-Bissau and was the strongest liberation movement in both colonies. Cabral was assassinated on 20 January 1973.

During the independence negotiations in 1974–1975 the PAIGC represented Cape Verde and organized the non-competitive elections for the Constitutional Assembly (30 June 1975). Voters were asked to approve or reject the list of candidates proposed by the PAIGC. The elections resulted in a 96% approval of the PAIGC list. The Constitutional Assembly accomplished its mandate on 7 September 1980 with the draft of a Marxist constitution. According to the constitutional provisions the PAIGC was the sole legal party and had the leading political role. New parliamentary elections were set to take place simultaneously in Guinea-Bissau and Cape Verde in 1980. However, Cabral's initial plans for the union between the two countries ended definitely when Cape Verde's government became suspected of involvement in the coup d'état in Guinea-Bissau in November 1980. In the non-competitive elections held in December 1980, the PAIGC candidate list was again approved overwhelmingly. Aristides Pereira, the Secretary-General of the party and Pedro Pires were re-elected by the National People's Assembly, respectively as President and Prime Minister. In January 1981 the Cape Verde wing of the PAICG constituted itself as *Partido Africano da Independência de Cabo Verde* (PAICV), and replaced the PAICG in Cape Verde. The following constitutional revision excluded any reference to the unity with Guinea-Bissau and caused the breakdown of diplomatic relations between the two countries.

In order to guarantee international co-operation with eastern and western countries, the PAICV government conducted a policy strictly following the rules of non-alignment. The 1985 non-competitive elections confirmed the PAICV candidate list once again, maintaining the established power structures with the same political leaders. The parameters of change towards a market economy and democratization of the political system were set on the eve of the breakdown of the communist regimes in Eastern Europe. The 1988 Party Congress initiated a strategy of economic liberalization to enforce the quest for geo-economic advantages. Concerning the political system, the only change consisted in authorizing independents' lists to run for municipal elections.

A new era in Cape Verde's political history since independence began on 28 September 1990 with the approval of the Constitutional Law 2/III/90. Article 4, which had secured the PAICV political leadership, was removed giving way to a new political system based on political pluralism. Institutional conditions were created for the first competitive presidential and legislative elections. The newly founded opposition party *Movimento para a Democracia* (MPD), which was joined by regime critics, former party intellectuals, land owners who had protested in the early 1980s against the land reform, as well as business people, achieved an overwhelming majority in the legislative elections of January 1991. After 15 years of single-party rule the PAICV accepted the results of the elections and adopted its new role as major opposition party. In the following presidential elections the MDP candidate António Mascarenhas Monteiro (a former Supreme Court judge) gained almost three quarters of the valid votes.

The new constitution approved on 5 August 1992 concluded the institutional reforms, giving the country a new framework with strengthened powers for the Prime Minister, a post filled by Carlos Veiga. In December 1995 the MDP gained again the absolute majority of parliamentary seats and Carlos Veiga was re-elected as Prime Minister by Parliament. Running as the only candidate, Mascarenhas Monteiro again won the presidential elections in February 1996. However, the extremely low voter turnout reflected the growing disappointment of the population not used to coping with the market economy and the dismantling of social protections. The young democracy has now to prove its sustainability by creating a new generation of politicians to guarantee the continuity of democracy and a renewal of the political elite.

1.2 Evolution of Electoral Provisions

According to the 1980 constitution the executive President served for a five-year term and was eligible for re-election. Both President and Prime Minister were elected by the unicameral National People's Assembly. The Assembly served for five years and was elected by approving or rejecting a list of candidates proposed by the ruling party. The candidates were not necessarily members of the party. In 1985 the number of deputies was increased from 56 to 83.

The principles of universal, equal, direct and secret suffrage for presidential and legislative elections were only applied after the constitutional reform of 28 September 1990.

1.3 Current Electoral Provisions

Sources: Constitution of the Republic Cape Verde 1992; Boletim Oficial No. 27, Suplemento, 13/07/89; Boletim Oficial, No. 42, 20/12/94; Lei No. 112/IV/94, No. 113/IV/94; No. 116/IV/94; No. 117/IV/94; No. 118/IV/94.

Elected national institutions: President of the Republic, National People's Assembly (72 elected deputies). Regular term of office: five years respectively. The President cannot be re-elected for a third mandate for the following five years after the second consecutive mandate.

Suffrage: The principles of universal, equal, direct and secret suffrage are applied. Every Cape Verdean citizen aged 18 years and over, living in the national territory or abroad, has the right to vote and is entitled to be registered as a voter.

Nomination of candidates

- *presidential elections*: The candidate for presidency must be a native-born Cape Verdean voter, at least 35 years of age at the date of candidacy, and be a permanent resident on the national territory for three years immediately preceding that date. At least 1,000 and a maximum of 4,000 registered voters including a minimum of five residents in at least eight districts have to propose the candidature.
- *parliamentary elections*: Registered Cape Verdean voters of 18 years and more are eligible for candidature as deputy.

Electoral system

- *presidential elections*: The President is elected directly by an absolute majority system. The national territory constitutes one electoral constituency and the countries of the voters with foreign residency constitute another electoral constituency, building each one electoral college. In case the votes cast abroad exceed one fifth of the total of the votes cast on the national territory, there will be considered only a percentage of these votes. If no candidate obtains an absolute majority a second ballot between the two most voted candidates will take place within 15 days of the first scrutiny.
- *parliamentary elections*: Proportional representation system in multi-member constituencies of variable size. Technical elements: *National territory is divided into 19 multi-member constituencies including three constituencies for voters living abroad (African countries, American countries, Europe and other countries). The size of the multi-member constituencies varies (11 constituencies with two seats; one with three seats; four with four seats; one with seven seats; one with 11 seats and one with 13 seats). To the total of the electoral colleges abroad correspond six seats. *Closed party lists. *Single vote. *Seats distributed according to the d'Hondt formula. *No legal threshold.

1.4 Comment on the Electoral Statistics

Only official sources were used in the statistics. Due to the change that has occurred in the political system, the electoral data were collected under different criteria before 1991 and afterwards. Until 1991 only the votes positively cast for the single ruling party were counted and published. Every other vote was counted as null and therefore the positive votes corresponded automatically to the valid votes. Starting with the 1991 elections the electoral data collected were published accurately and completely including absolute and separate figures for the null and the blank votes. All the percentages given in the following tables are calculated by the author according to the standards of the data handbook.

2. Tables

2.1 Dates of National Elections, Referendums and Coups d'Etat

Year	Presidential elections	Parliamentary elections	Elections for Constitutional Assembly	Referendums	Coups d'état
1975			30/06		
1980		07/12			
1985		07/12			
1991	17/02	13/01			
1995		17/12			
1996	18/02				

2.2 Electoral Body 1975–1996

Year	Type of election[a]	Population[b]	Registered voters		Votes cast		
			Total number	% pop.	Total number	% reg. voters	% pop.
1975	CA	250,000	121,724	48.6	105,503	86.7	42.2
1980	Pa	270,000	202,500	75.0	151,875	75.0	56.3
1985	Pa	300,000	143,410	47.8	98,792	68.9	32.9
1991	Pa	371,000	166,818	44.9	125,564	75.3	33.8
1991	Pr[c]	371,000	159,534	43.0	97,922	61.4	26.4
1995	Pa	436,000	207,648	47.6	158,901	76.5	36.4
1996	Pr	436,000	207,146	47.5	90,177	43.5	20.7

[a] CA = Constitutional Assembly; Pa = Parliament; Pr = President.
[b] Estimations of the total population.
[c] Does not include votes of citizens living abroad.

2.3 Abbreviations

MPD	Movimento para a Democracia
PAICV[a]	Partido Africano da Independência de Cabo Verde
PAIGC	Partido Africano da Independência da Guiné e Cabo Verde
PCD	Partido da Convergência Democrática
PSD	Partido Social Democrata
UCID	União Caboverdiana Independente e Democrática

[a] The PAICV is the successor party of the PAIGC (since 1981).

2.4 Electoral Participation of Parties and Alliances 1975–1996

Party / Alliance	Years	Elections contested	
		Presidential	Parliamentary
PAIGC	1975, 1980	0	2
PAICV	1985, 1991, 1995; 1996	1	3
MPD	1991, 1995, 1996	2	2
PCD	1995	0	1
PSD	1995	0	1
UCID	1995	0	1

[a] Seven elections have been held since independence, but only since 1991 in a multi-party system.

2.5 Referendums

No referendum has been held.

2.6 Elections for Constitutional Assembly

1975	Votes		Seats	
	Total number	%	Total (56)	%
Registered voters	121,724	-		
Votes cast	105,503	86.7		
Yes[a]	100,835	95.6		
No[a]	4,668	4.4		
PAIGC			56	100

[a] The election consisted in approving or rejecting the list of candidates proposed by the PAIGC. The Yes votes are officially called 'Positive votes' and are automatically the valid votes. The No votes are officially called 'Null votes' and represent every vote other than Yes.

2.6 a) Elections for the Constitutional Assembly 1975: Regional Distribution of Votes (Absolute Numbers)

1975	Yes[a]	No[b]	Total
N. S. da Graça	12,731	526	13,257
N. S. da Luz/S. Nicolau Tolentino	4,106	122	4,228
SS. Nome de Jesus/S. João Baptista	2,149	73	2,222
Santa Catarina	10,759	346	11,105
S. Salvador do Mundo	3,173	189	3,362
S. Lourenço dos Orgãos/Santiago Maior	6,923	568	7,491
Santo Amaro Abade	3,207	166	3,373
S. Miguel	3,960	287	4,247
N. S. do Livramento/N. S. do Rosário	3,637	181	3,818
Santo Crucifixo/S. Pedro Apóstolo	4,272	68	4,340
Santo António das Pombas	2,532	118	2,650
Santo André	1,287	69	1,356
S. João Baptista	3,217	255	3,472
Cidade do Mindelo	10,409	312	10,721
Bela Vista	2,635	48	2,683
Monte Sossego	2,870	61	2,931
N. S. da Ajuda	3,257	58	3,315
N. S. da Conceição/Santa Catarina	5,230	147	5,377
S. Lourenço	3,485	180	3,665
N. S. do Rosário/N. S. da Lapa	4,576	371	4,947
N. S. da Luz	1,015	305	1,320
S. João Baptista/N. S. do Monte	1,982	18	2,000
N. S. das Dores	2,196	60	2,256
S. João Baptista/Santa Isabel	1,227	140	1,367
Total	100,835	4,668	105,503

[a] Yes votes are officially called Positive votes and are automatically the valid votes.

[b] No votes are officially called Null votes and represent every vote other than Yes.

2.6 b) Elections for the Constitutional Assembly 1975: Regional Distribution of Votes (in %)

1975	Yes[a]	No[b]	Total[c]
N. S. da Graça	96.0	4.0	100
N. S. da Luz/S. Nicolau Tolentino	97.1	2.9	100
SS. Nome de Jesus/S. João Baptista	96.7	3.3	100
Santa Catarina	96.9	3.1	100
S. Salvador do Mundo	94.4	5.6	100
S. Lourenço dos Orgãos/Santiago Maior	92.4	7.6	100
Santo Amaro Abade	95.1	4.9	100
S. Miguel	93.3	6.7	100
N. S. do Livramento/N. S. do Rosário	95.3	4.7	100
Santo Crucifixo/S. Pedro Apóstolo	98.4	1.6	100
Santo António das Pombas	95.6	4.4	100
Santo André	94.9	5.1	100
S. João Baptista	92.7	7.3	100
Cidade do Mindelo	97.1	2.9	100
Bela Vista	98.2	1.8	100
Monte Sossego	97.9	2.1	100
N. S. da Ajuda	98.3	1.7	100
N. S. da Conceição/Santa Catarina	97.3	2.7	100
S. Lourenço	95.1	4.9	100
N. S. do Rosário/N. S. da Lapa	92.5	7.5	100
N. S. da Luz	76.9	23.1	100
S. João Baptista/N. S. do Monte	99.1	0.9	100
N. S. das Dores	97.3	2.7	100
S. João Baptista/Santa Isabel	89.8	10.2	100
Total	95.6	4.4	100

[a] Yes votes are officially called Positive votes and are automatically the valid votes.
[b] No votes are officially called Null votes and represent every vote other than Yes.
[c] Due to rounding the added total of the percentages is not always 100.

2.7 Parliamentary Elections 1980–1995

Year	1980[a]		1985[a]	
	Total number	%	Total number	%
Registered voters	202,500	–	143,410	–
Votes cast	151,875	75.0	98,792	68.9
Yes	141,244	93.0	92,865	94.0
No	10,631	7.0	5,927	6.0

[a] The election consisted in approving or rejecting the list of candidates proposed by the ruling Party (1980 PAIGC and 1985 PAICV). Yes votes were officially called 'Positive votes' and regarded as valid votes. No votes were officially called 'Null votes' and represent every vote other than Yes.

Year	1991		1995	
	Total number	%	Total number	%
Registered voters	166,818	–	207,648	–
Votes cast	125,564	75.3	158,901	76.5
Invalid votes	7,437	5.9	6,779	4.3
Valid votes	118,127	94.1	152,122	95.7
MDP	78,454	66.4	93,249	61.3
PAICV	39,673	33.6	45,263	29.8
PCD	–	–	10,211	6.7
UCID	–	–	2,369	1.6
PSD	–	–	1,030	0.7

2.7 a) Parliamentary Elections: Regional Distribution of Votes (Absolute Numbers)

1995	MPD	PCD	PAICV	UCID	PSD	Total
Paul	2,276	83	915	61	0	3,335
Ribeira Grande	6,490	590	1,408	276	0	8,764
Porto Novo	4,462	361	1,584	0	0	6,407
S. Vicente	15,876	1,245	6,511	703	115	24,450
S. Nicolau	4,160	153	1,466	0	0	5,779
Sal	2,252	222	1,741	0	0	4,215
Boa Vista	678	101	902	27	0	1,708
Maio	1,167	201	801	0	0	2,169
Praia	19,484	2,670	10,870	211	107	33,342
S. Domingos	3,666	222	859	93	20	4,860
Santa Cruz	7,142	685	1,664	118	290	9,899
Santa Catarina	9,803	1,016	2,509	197	414	13,939
Tarrafal	2,264	584	1,771	152	45	8,816
S. Filipe	3,096	917	5,685	59	39	9,796
Mosteiros	1,492	93	1,763	0	0	3,348
Brava	1,652	152	997	0	0	2,801
African countries	1,208	343	1,280	0	0	2,831
American countries	1,094	280	1,651	227	0	3,252
European and other countries	987	293	886	254	0	2,411
Total	93,249	10,211	45,263	2,369	1,030	152,122

2.7 b) Parliamentary Elections: Regional Distribution of Votes (in %)

1995	MPD	PCD	PAICV	UCID	PSD	Total[a]
Paul	68.2	2.5	27.4	1.8	0.0	100
Ribeira Grande	74.1	6.7	16.1	3.1	0.0	100
Porto Novo	69.6	5.6	22.9	0.0	0.0	100
S. Vicente	64.9	5.1	26.6	2.9	0.5	100
S. Nicolau	72.0	2.6	25.4	0.0	0.0	100
Sal	53.4	5.3	41.3	0.0	0.0	100
Boa Vista	39.7	5.9	52.8	1.6	0.0	100
Maio	53.8	9.3	36.9	0.0	0.0	100
Praia	58.4	8.0	32.6	0.6	0.3	100
S. Domingos	75.4	4.6	17.7	1.9	0.4	100
Santa Cruz	72.1	6.9	16.8	1.2	2.9	100
Santa Catarina	70.3	7.3	18.0	1.4	3.0	100
Tarrafal	44.9	4.2	12.7	1.1	0.3	100
S. Filipe	31.6	9.4	58.0	0.6	0.4	100
Mosteiros	44.6	2.8	52.7	0.0	0.0	100
Brava	59.0	5.4	35.6	0.0	0.0	100
African countries	42.7	12.1	45.2	0.0	0.0	100
American countries	33.6	8.2	50.8	7.0	0.0	100
European and other countries	40.9	12.2	36.7	10.2	0.0	100
Total	61.3	6.7	29.8	1.6	0.7	100

[a] Due to rounding the added total of the percentages is not always 100.

2.8 Composition of Parliament 1980–1995

Year	1980		1985		1991		1995	
	Seats	%	Seats	%	Seats	%	Seats	%
	56	100	83	100	79	100	72	100
PAIGC	56	100	–	–	–	–	–	–
PAICV	–	–	83	100	23	29.1	21	29.2
MDP	–	–	–	–	56	70.9	50	69.4
PCD	–	–	–	–	–	–	1	1.4

2.9 Presidential Elections 1991–1996

1991	Total number[a]	%
Registered voters	159,534	–
Votes cast	97,922	61.4
Invalid votes	1,755	1.8
Valid votes	96,167	98.2
António Mascarenhas Monteiro (MDP)	70,623	73.4
Aristides Maria Pereira (PAICV)	25,544	26.6

[a] Does not include votes of citizens living abroad.

1996	Total number	%
Registered voters	207,146	–
Votes cast	90,177	43.5
Invalid votes	1,884	2.1
Valid votes	88,293	97.9
António Mascarenhas Monteiro (MDP)		
Yes	81,281	92.1
No	7,012	7.9

2.9 a) Presidential Elections 1991: Regional Distribution of Votes (Absolute Numbers)

1991[a]	Mascarenhas (MPD)	Pereira (PAICV)	Total
Boa Vista	443	989	1,432
Brava	1,199	853	2,052
Fogo	4,349	6,135	10,484
Maio	664	763	1,427
Sal	1,183	1,191	2,374
Santiago	32,647	9,053	41,700
Santo Antão	13,047	1,938	14,985
S. Nicolau	2,978	1,271	4,249
S. Vicente	14,113	3,351	17,464
Total	70,623	25,544	96,167

[a] The votes of citizens living abroad are not included.

2.9 b) Presidential Elections 1991: Regional Distribution of Votes (*in %*)

1991[a]	Mascarenhas (MPD)	Pereira (PAICV)	Total[b]
Boa Vista	30.9	69.1	100
Brava	58.4	41.6	100
Fogo	41.5	58.5	100
Maio	46.5	53.5	100
Sal	49.8	50.2	100
Santiago	78.3	21.7	100
Santo Antão	87.1	12.9	100
S. Nicolau	70.1	29.9	100
S. Vicente	80.8	19.2	100
Total	73.4	26.6	100

[a] The votes of residents abroad are not included.

[b] Due to rounding the added total of the percentages is not always 100.

2.10 List of Power Holders 1975–1998

Head of State	Years	Remarks
Aristides Maria Pereira	05/07/1975–17/02/1991	Elected by the National People's Assembly, which was elected through non-competitive elections.
António Mascarenhas Monteiro	18/02/1991–	Constitutional President. The constitutional reform of 1990 allowed the direct presidential election and the formation of political parties. Re-elected 1996.

Head of Government	Years	Remarks
Pedro Pires	11/07/1975–25/01/1991	Elected by the National People's Assembly, which was elected through non-competitive elections.
Carlos Veiga	26/01/1991–	Nominated by the President after hearing the political parties seated in the Parliament according to the electoral results.

3. Bibliography

3.1 Official Sources

Constituição da República de Cabo Verde, 1992.
Boletim Oficial, No. 15, 16/04/75.
Boletim Oficial, No. 26, Suplemento, 04/07/75.
Boletim Oficial, No. 52, 31/12/84.
Boletim Oficial, No. 27, Suplemento, 13/07/89, Lei Eleitoral.
Boletim Oficial, No. 29, 21/07/90.
Boletim Oficial, No. 39, Suplemento, 29/09/90, Lei Constitucional No. 2/III/90.
Boletim Oficial, No. 40, 06/10/90.
Boletim Oficial, No. 41, 2° Suplemento, 13/10/90.
Boletim Oficial, No. 3, 25/01/91.
Boletim Oficial, No. 10, 09/03/91, Decreto-Lei No. 8/91, 9/91, 10/91, 11/91, 12/91, 13/91, 14/91.
Boletim Oficial, No. 26, Suplemento, 04/07/91, Lei No. 3/IV/91.
Boletim Oficial, Iª Série, No. 14, 05/10/92.
Boletim Oficial, Iª Série, No. 17, 26/10/92.
Boletim Oficial, Iª Série, No. 19, 16/11/92.
Boletim Oficial, No. 26, Suplemento, 04/07/91
Boletim Oficial, Iª Série, No. 42, 20/12/94, Lei No. 112/IV/94, 113/IV/94, 116/IV/94, 117/IV/94, 118/IV/94.
Boletim Oficial, IIª Série, No. 11, Suplemento, 15/03/96.
I. Encontro Eleitoral (1994): Vol. 2: República de Cabo Verde, Lisbon: MAI/STAPE/Edições 70.

3.2 Books and Articles

Blaustein, A., and Flanz, G. (1994). *Constitutions of The Countries of the World: The Republic of Cape Verde*. New York: Oceana.
Cahen, M. (1991). 'Vent des Iles. La victoire de l'opposition aux Iles du Cap-Vert et à São Tomé et Príncipe'. *Politique Africaine*, 43: 63–78.
Degioanni, B. (1993). 'Le Cap-Vert, terre d'exil'. *Le Monde diplomatique*, May: 15.
Entrevista com o Primeiro-Ministro de Cabo Verde Pedro Pires, *Terra Solidária* 19 (May/August): 1–8.
Gorvin, I. (1989). *Elections since 1945*. Essex: Longman.
Hofmeister, R. (ed.) (1989 ff.): *Afrika-Jahrbuch*. Opladen: Leske&Budrich.
Lima, A. R. (1992). 'Grundzüge des politischen Reformprozesses in Kap Verde', in P. Meyns (ed.), *Demokratie und Strukturreformen im*

portugiesischsprachigen Afrika. Freiburg: Arnold Bergstraesser Institut, 287–303.

Meyns, P. (1993). 'Kap Verde', in D. Nohlen and F. Nuscheler (eds.), *Handbuch der Dritten Welt, Vol. 4: Westafrika und Zentralafrika*, (*3rd edn.*). Bonn: Dietz, 266–277..

PAIGC (1974). *História da Guiné e ilhas de Cabo Verde*. Porto: Afrontamento.

Rios, A. (1989). 'A sociedade caboverdiana', *Terra Solidária*, 19 (May/ August): 17–26.

CENTRAL AFRICAN REPUBLIC

by Andreas Mehler

1. Introduction

1.1 Historical Introduction

The former French territory Oubangui-Chari became independent on 13 August 1960, as Central African Republic (CAR). The founding father and President of the *Conseil de Gouvernement*, Barthélémy Boganda, who dominated pre-colonial politics, died in a mysterious plane accident on 29 March 1959, eight days before the last colonial elections. His closest aide, Abel Goumba, and David Dacko engaged in a power struggle which was won by Dacko who had the backing of the French administration and the Chamber of Commerce. He arrogated the leadership of Boganda's *Mouvement pour l'Evolution Sociale en Afrique Noire* (MESAN) and engaged in legal action against Goumba and his breakaway faction *Mouvement d'Evolution Démocratique de l'Afrique Centrale* (MEDAC). Dacko, who automatically became President of the Republic with the onset of independence, suppressed constitutional liberties in 1960 and forced the creation of a presidential one-party system as soon as 1962. On 31 December 1965, the Dacko regime was toppled by Col Jean-Bédel Bokassa. The Constitution was suspended and the National Assembly dissolved. Bokassa introduced an autocratic rule with some erratic ingredients; two alleged coup attempts in 1969 and 1976 were pretexts for series of executions. Bokassa declared himself President for life in 1972. Ange-Félix Patassé became his Prime Minister in 1976, but the supreme executive power was still in the hands of the autocrat. Finally Bokassa decided to introduce a monarchist constitution with the country's name changing to Central African Empire. In a glamorous act of self-coronation Bokassa became Emperor on 4 December 1977. Only nominally the system was a 'parliamentary monarchy'.

After serious allegations of human rights violations in connection with schoolchildren demonstrations, France, who retained prime importance, *inter alia* by maintaining two military bases, decided to overthrow the Bokassa regime and reinstall Dacko on 21 September 1979. Dacko immediately reintroduced a presidential multi-party system as adopted by a constitutional referendum in 1981. Irregularities in the 1981 presidential elections led to calls for annulment by opposition parties, civil unrest, and finally the postponement of legislative elections. Widespread discontent and the suspension of political parties was the pretext for the bloodless coup d'état of Gen André Kolingba on 1 September 1981. He suspended the constitution again and ruled with a military junta until 1985. In 1986 Kolingba introduced a new presidential constitution, adopted by referendum (only one question was asked concerning approval for the constitution and the prolonging of the President's mandate). Adherence to the new united party, the *Rassemblement Démocratique Centrafricain* (RDC), was voluntary, but the new system was presented as a strong and plebiscitary authoritarianism. Kolingba's rule increasingly relied on members of his own ethnic group, the Yakoma (belonging to the so-called 'river populations'). In 1987 semi-competitive elections to Parliament were held (as were municipal elections in 1988). The two main opponents, Goumba und Patassé, called for a boycott of these elections. But only in 1990 the pro-democracy movement (trade unions, human rights activists, intellectuals and parties) gained force. An open letter of 253 prominent citizens asked for a national conference as it was installed in Benin. Kolingba refused, detained several prominent opponents, named a Prime Minister, and only belatedly accepted the principle of free elections. When several irregularities occurred in some cities like Berbérati the elections of 1992 were suspended by Kolingba and annulled completely by the Supreme Court, probably because of a foreseeable defeat of the incumbent. The international community pressed Kolingba to share power with his main opponents by introducing a collective *Conseil National Politique Provisoire de la République* as an administering body, by appointing one of his rivals (first Timothée Malendoma, later Enoch Dérant Lakoué) Prime Minister and by naming a 'Mixed Electoral Commission' (representatives of all political parties and of the administration). New elections were held in August 1993. Kolingba came in only fourth after Patassé, Goumba and Dacko in the first round and subsequently tried to modify the electoral code as well as to alter the composition of the Supreme Court. But all major donor countries opposed this step firmly and Kolingba gave up his plans. In the second round Patassé was elected President in a largely free and transparent election. His party *Mouvement pour la Libération du Peuple Centrafricain* (MLPC) secured a plurality of seats in Parliament and had to look for coalition partners. The voting behavior showed a clearly regionalist pattern. Patassé and his support came essentially from the neglected but relatively densely populated North-West of the country.

Very soon after the elections Patassé showed no readiness for compromise by pushing forward a unilaterally elaborated constitution (adopted through referendum in December 1994) and by refusing to reinstall a mixed electoral commission for some by-elections as was demanded by the opposition. The Constitution provided for a semi-presidential system with a weak Prime Minister responsible before the President and the National Assembly. Patassé's coalition government was fragile, and Prime Minister Jean-Luc Mandaba had to resign due to corruption accusations in April 1995. In 1996 three army mutinies undermined the country's stability. French troops played an important role in controlling the situation and in engaging in mediation efforts, but finally were considered being a conflict party themselves after engaging in retaliation acts. On 25 January 1997 the Bangui Peace Accord was signed to end a nascent civil war in the capital opposing Patassé's supporters (mainly from the north-western savanna region) and supporters of Kolingba and other opposition supporters (mainly from the southern forest and river populations). The agreement provided for the deployment of an inter-African military mission as a buffer between mutineers and loyalists with logistical support from France. Despite some bloody skirmishes and organizational shortcomings the mission played a constructive role by, *inter alia*, collecting arms. Chief mediator Amadou Toumani Touré brokered the entry of mutineers into the government on 7 April 1997; after a drop-out by the former opposition in May 1997 an inclusive government was re-established on 1 September 1997. But the sudden tribalization of politics in the 1990s will remain a poisonous legacy for the future. During the crisis a tentative ethnic cleansing took place in parts of the capital Bangui. In April 1998 the inter-African military mission was replaced by a UN peace-keeping mission providing security and assistance for the upcoming legislative elections. Due to the co-optation Patassé obtained a slim majority after the 1998 parliamentary elections.

1.2 Evolution of Electoral Provisions

The Central African Republic as an independent state has no tradition of free pluralistic elections. In fact, only the elections of 1993 have met international standards. Following the *loi cadre* of 1956 universal suffrage was applied for the first time for elections to the Territorial Assembly on 31 March 1957. The electoral system used for the last colonial legislative election in 1959 was a plurality system in four multimember constituencies of different size. The Head of Government was elected indirectly by the Legislative Assembly. The same system was used for parliamentary elections in 1964 (the President was elected directly and unopposed). Within the logic of the one-party system the names of all MESAN parliamentary candidates were suggested by the party chairman and then approved by the '*comité directeur*'; the MESAN presidential candidate was nominated by the same committee. There were no elections under Bokassa. For the 1981 presidential elections an absolute majority system with a second round was provided (majority-runoff). Application to candidature could be individual or submitted by a political party. The 1986 'referendum-plus-presidential-election' was a plebiscite with 'yes' and 'no' options. The semi-competitive legislative elections of 1987 were apparently held in 52 single-member constituencies according to the plurality system (no certified information available). The new provisions for the annulled 1992 and then the 1993 elections provided for an absolute majority system in two rounds for President, for parliamentary mandate in 85 single-member constituencies.

1.3 Current Electoral Provisions

Sources: La Constitution de la République Centrafricaine du 14 janvier 1995; Electoral Law: Loi No. 92.012 du 31 juillet 1992 portant Code Electoral de la République Centrafricaine, Décret No. 92.271 du 16 novembre 1992 portant création d'une Commission Electorale Mixte, Ordonnance No. 93.002 du 7 avril 1993 modifiant certaines dispositions du Code Electoral, Ordonnance No. 93.005 du 27 avril 1993 portant suspension de l'application de certaines dispositions du Code Electoral pour les consultations électorales de 1993.

Elected national institutions: President of the Republic and the National Assembly (since 1998: 109 members). Regular term for presidential office: six years, re-eligible once (President); five years without restriction of re-eligibility for members of the National Assembly.

Suffrage: The principle of universal, secret and direct suffrage is postulated for presidential elections; curiously the principle of secret elections for National Assembly elections is not mentioned by the constitution, but the Electoral Law adds the principles of equal and secret elections for both categories. Every citizen who has reached the age of 18 has the right to vote and is not only entitled, but obliged to register as a voter. The constitution mentions an obligation to vote as well.

Nomination of candidates

- *presidential elections*: Every citizen of Central African origin aged 35 years or more is eligible as President, if he is entitled to vote. Application to candidature is individual and not linked to the nomination by a political party.
- *parliamentary elections*: Every citizen aged 25 years is eligible as a member of the National Assembly, if he or she is a (registered) voter. Independent candidatures are possible.

Electoral system

- *presidential elections*: Absolute majority system. Only the two leading candidates of the first round contest a second round, if absolute majority is not achieved in the first round.
- *parliamentary elections*: Absolute majority system in 109 (since 1998) single-member constituencies. Only candidates with at least 10% of valid votes may contest in the second round which has to be held if no candidate wins more than 50% in the first round. A replacement deputy (*suppléant*) is elected along with each deputy.

1.4 Comment on the Electoral Statistics

It is extremely difficult to get exact figures for presidential elections in 1981 and 1986, and even more for parliamentary elections in 1987 and 1993. Information on elections until 1964 are based on Ziemer (1978) basically using official statistics. Official results of presidential and parliamentary elections are proclaimed by the Supreme Court, but the official gazette is not available for long periods of time. The figures given are based on international media reports (*Marchés Tropicaux et Méditerranéens*, *Africa Research Bulletin*) and some research articles (see 3.2). The (incomplete) figures for the 1993 elections are based on personal collections by the author at the Supreme Court in Bangui in 1993. Incomplete figures for the 1998 elections were provided by the Constitutional Court and various media reports.

2. Tables

2.1 Dates of National Elections, Referendums and Coups d'Etat

Year	Presidential elections	Parliamentary elections	Elections for Constitutional Assembly	Referendums	Coups d'état
1959		05/04, 26/04[b]			
1964	15/03				31/12
1979					20/09
1981	15/03			01/02	01/09
1986				21/11	
1987		31/07			
1992	25/10[a]	25/10[a]			
1993	22/08 (1st) 19/09 (2nd)	22/08 (1st) 19/09 (2nd)			
1994				28/12	
1998		22/11 (1st) 13/12 (2nd)			

[a] Elections annulled.

[b] Elections for Territorial Assembly (before independence).

2.2 Electoral Body 1959–1998

Year	Type of election[a]	Population	Registered voters		Votes cast		
			Total number	% pop.	Total number	% reg. voters	% pop.
1959	Pa	1,185,000	631,391	53.3	358,055	56.7	30.2
1964	Pr	1,320,000	732,139	55.5	686,829	93.8	52.0
1964	Pa	1,320,000	728,981	55.2	613,600	84.2	46.5
1981	Ref	2,297,000	928,000	40.4	859,447	92.6	37.4
1981	Pr	2,297,000	971,395	42.3	744,688	76.7	32.4
1986	Ref	2,585,000	871,395	33.7	763,451	87.6	29.5
1987	Pa	2,642,000	900,000	34.1	—	50.0	—
1993	Pr (1st)	2,973,000	1,181,874	39.8	809,298	68.5	27.2
1993	Pa (1st)	2,973,000	1,181,874	39.8	809,298	68.5	27.2
1993	Pr (2nd)	2,973,000	1,235,568	41.6	692,597	56.1	23.3
1993	Pa (2nd)	2,973,000	1,235,568	41.6	—	—	—
1994	Ref	3,028,000	1,247,290	41.2	561,084	45.0	18.5
1998	Pa (1st)	3,376,000	1,471,523	43.6	811,869	55.2	24.0

[a] Pa = Parliament (1959: Territorial Assembly); Pr = President; Ref = Referendum.

2.3 Abbreviations

ADP	Alliance pour la Démocratie et le Progres
CFD	Concertation des Forces Démocratiques
CN	Convention Nationale
FC	Forum Civique
FODEM	Forum Démocratique pour la Modernité
FPO	Front Patriotique Oubanguien
FPP	Front Patriotique pour le Progrès
MDD	Mouvement pour la Démocratie et le Développement
MDREC	Mouvement Démocratique pour la Renaissance et l'Evolution de Centrafrique
MEDAC	Mouvement d'Evolution Démocratique de l'Afrique Centrale
MESAN	Mouvement pour l'Evolution Sociale en Afrique Noire
MLPC	Mouvement de Libération du Peuple Centrafricain
MSA	Mouvement Socialiste Africain
PLD	Parti Libéral Démocrate
PRC	Parti Républicain Centrafricain
PRP	Parti Républicain de Progrès
PSD	Parti Social-Démocrate
PUN	Parti de l'Unité Nationale
RDA	Rassemblement Démocratique Africain
RDC	Rassemblement Démocratique Centrafricain
UDC	Union Démocratique Centrafricain
UPR	Union pour la République

2.4 Electoral Participation of Parties and Alliances 1959–1998

Party / Alliance	Years	Elections contested	
		Presidential	Parliamentary
MESAN	1959, 1964, 1993, 1998	1	4
MSA	1959	0	1
RDA	1959	0	1
FPO	1981	1	0
MLPC	1981, 1993, 1998	2	3
PRD	1981	1	0
UDC	1981	1	0
RDC	1986, 1998	2	3
ADP	1993, 1998	(1)[a]	2
CFD	1993	1	0
CN	1993, 1998	1	2
FC	1993, 1998	1	2
FPP	1993, 1998	(1)[a]	2
MDD[b]	1993, 1998	1	2
MDREC	1993, 1998	(1)[a]	2
PLD	1993, 1998	(1)[a]	2
PRC	1993, 1998	1	2
PSD	1993, 1998	1	2
FODEM	1998	0	1
PUN	1998	0	1
UPR	1998	0	1

[a] Members of the CFD alliance who supported a common candidate (Goumba).
[b] Formed as a party only after the 1993 elections, supporters of Dacko.

2.5 Referendums

Year	1981[a]		1986[b]	
	Total number	%	Total number	%
Registered voters	928,000	–	871,395	–
Votes cast	859,447	92.6	763,451	87.6
Invalid votes	9,463	1.1	8,644	1.1
Valid votes	849,984[c]	98.8	754,807	98.9
Yes	837,410	97.4	696,055	91.2
No	12,360	2.6	58,752	7.7

General note: These indications evidently contain some inaccuracy.
[a] Approval of new constitution.
[b] Approval of new constitution and confirmation of André Kolingba as President (Package vote).
[c] Incomprehensive result: 214 valid votes are not distributed.

Year	1994[a]	
	Total number	%
Registered voters	1,247,290	–
Votes cast	561,084	45.0
Invalid votes	4,340	0.8
Valid votes	556,744	99.2
Yes	460,407	82.1
No	96,337	17.2

[a] Approval of new constitution.

2.6 Elections for Constitutional Assembly

Elections to Constitutional Assembly have not been held.

2.7 Parliamentary Elections 1959–1998

Year	1959		1964	
	Total number	%	Total number	%
Registered voters	631,391	–	728,981	–
Votes cast	358,055	56.7	613,600	84.2
Invalid votes	5,189	1.4	10,636	1.7
Valid votes	352,866	98.6	602,964	98.3
MESAN	344,473	97.6	596,687	99.0
MSA	6,144	1.8	–	–
RDA	2,249	0.6	–	–
against MESAN	–	–	6,227	1.0

For the elections of 1987, 1993 and 1998 detailed data are not available. See table 2.2 for data on voter registration and participation.

2.8 Composition of Parliament 1959–1998

Year	1959		1964		1987		1993		1998	
	Seats	%	Seats	%	Seats	%	Seats	%	Seats	%
	50	100	50	100	52	100	85	100	109	100
MESAN	48[a]	100	50	100	–	–	1	1.2	–	–
RDC	–	–	–	–	52	100	13	15.3	20	18.3
MLPC	–	–	–	–	–	–	34	40.0	47	43.1
FPP	–	–	–	–	–	–	7	8.2	7	6.4
PLD	–	–	–	–	–	–	7	8.2	2	1.8
ADP	–	–	–	–	–	–	6	7.1	5	4.6
MDD	–	–	–	–	–	–	6	7.1	8	7.3
CN	–	–	–	–	–	–	3	3.5	–	–
PSD	–	–	–	–	–	–	3	3.5	6[b]	5.5
PUN	–	–	–	–	–	–	–	–	3	2.8
FODEM	–	–	–	–	–	–	–	–	2	1.8
FC	–	–	–	–	–	–	–	–	1	0.9
UPR	–	–	–	–	–	–	–	–	1	0.9
Others	–	–	–	–	–	–	5	3.5	7[c]	6.4

[a] Two seats were declared vacant until by-elections in 1960 (constituencies of Boganda and another MESAN MP, both victims of a plane crash). Both seats were won by MESAN.

[b] One MP of the PSD declared himself a supporter of President Patassé after the elections and changed the overall electoral outcome (55:54 seats for the presidential camp).

[c] Five independent MPs declared themselves supporters of President Patassé.

2.9 Presidential Elections 1964–1993

1964	Total number	%
Registered voters	732,139	–
Votes cast	686,829	93.8
Invalid votes	4,007	5.8
Valid votes	682,822	94.2
David Dacko (MESAN)	682,607	100.0
Against Dacko	215	0.0

1981	Total number	%
Registered voters	971,395	–
Votes cast	744,688	76.6
Invalid votes	12,742	1.7
Valid votes	731,946	98.3
Daniel Dacko (UDC)	374,027	50.2
Ange-Félix Patassé (MLPC)	283,739	38.1
François Pehoua (Ind.)	39,661	5.3
Henri Maïdou (PRP)	24,007	3.2
Abel Goumba (FPO)	10,512	1.4

In 1986 André Kolingba was confirmed as President through a referendum in which voters decided with the same vote on a new constitution. The results are given in section 2.4.

1993 (1st round)	Total number	%
Registered voters	1,181,874	–
Votes cast	809,298	68.5
Invalid votes	15,317	1.9
Valid votes	793,971[a]	98.1
Ange-Félix Patassé (MLPC)	302,004	37.3
Abel Goumba (CFD)	175,467	21.7
David Dacko (Ind.)	162,721	20.1
André Kolingba (RDC)	97,942	12.1
Enoch Dérant Lakoué (PSD)	19,368	2.4
Timothée Malendoma (CN)	16,400	2.0
François Bozize (Ind.)	12,159	1.5
Ruth Rolland (FC)	8,068	1.0

General note: These indications evidently contain some inaccuracy.

[a] Sum of votes distributed to candidates: 794,129.

1993 (2nd round)	Total number	%
Registered voters	1,235,568	–
Votes cast	692,597	56.1
Invalid votes	13,362	1.9
Valid votes	679,235[a]	98.3
Ange-Félix Patassé (MLPC)	363,297	53.5
Abel Goumba (CFD)	315,935	46.5

General note: These indications evidently contain some inaccuracy.
[a] Sum of votes distributed to candidates: 679,232.

2.10 List of Power Holders 1959–1998

Head of State	Years	Remarks
Daniel Dacko	1960–1965	As acting Head of Government since legislative elections Dacko automatically became President of the Republic after independence (13/08/1960).
Col. Jean-Bédel Bokassa	1965–1979	Seized power in the night of 31/12/1965. At first he used MESAN as power instrument, later he declared himself Emperor of the Central African Empire. Ousted by a French-led military coup (*opération Barracuda*) on 21/09/1979.
Daniel Dacko	1979–1981	Re-installed by the French military operation Dacko initiated a short-lived multiparty era.
Gen. André Kolingba	1981–1993	Seized power on 01/09/1981. Confirmed in the combined referendum of 1986. Created a new one party-system and his own party (RDC) in 1987. Multi-party elections were organized in October 1992, but declared invalid because of some localized irregularities, the main reason, however, was the expected outcome of the elections. Organized new elections in response to pressure from donor countries.
Ange-Félix Patassé	1993–	Agriculturalist and several times minister under Bokassa. Constitutionally elected. Prepared a new constitution, faced criticism of the opposition and three army mutinies.

Head of Government	Years	Remarks
Ange-Félix Patassé	1976–1978	Named Prime Minister on 05/09/1976; theoretically large prerogatives since 14/12/1974 under the imperial constitution. He was forced to step down on 14/07/1978.
Henri Maïdou	1978–1979	Former Minister of Education; took office on 17/07/1978; promoted to the mainly decorative post of Vice-President after the coup of 20/09/1979. Two Prime Ministers with purely administrative functions were appointed in the phase 1979–1981.
Edouard Franck	1991–1992	Former Minister for the Coordination of Government Action; appointed Prime Minister on 15/03/1991 amidst a serious legitimacy crisis.
Gen Timothée Malendoma	1992–1993	Former Minister under Bokassa and Dacko; appointed Prime Minister of an interim government after the failed elections on 05/12/1992 and forced to resign after a dispute with Kolingba on 25/02/1993.
Enoch Dérant Lakoué	1993	PSD candidate for the presidency in 1992 (and 1993), nominated on 26/02/1993 (acting until general elections in August/September 1993).
Jean-Luc Mandaba	1993–1994	Leading MLPC politician; appointed Prime Minister on 24/10/1993; resigned after a vote of no confidence by his own party.
Gabriel Koyambounou	1995–1996	Appointed Prime Minister on 17/04/1995, as a low profile technocrat.
Jean-Paul Ngoupande	1996–1997	Former CAR ambassador to Paris; appointed Prime Minister on 06/06/1996, after two army mutinies; enjoyed some support by the opposition and asked for more prerogatives, which Patassé was not willing to concede.
Michel Gbezerea Bria	1997–1998	Appointed Prime Minister on 30/01/1997; hitherto Minister of Foreign Affairs; formed a government including 11 members of the opposition on 18/02/1997.
Anciet Georges Dologuéle	1999–	Former Finance Minister appointed on 04/01/1999; formed a government with MLPC, PLD and CN members as well as with independent technocrats. The MMD forced three appointed members to step down immediately after their nomination.

3. Bibliography

3.1 Official sources

'Décret Impérial No. 76/001 du 4 décembre 1976 portant promulgation de la Constitution de l'Empire Centrafricain'. *Journal officiel de l'Empire centrafricain*, 18 (spécial), décembre 1976.

'Acte Constitutionnel No 1, du 4 janvier 1966'. *Journal officiel de la République Centrafricaine*, 9/1, 15/01/1966.

'Acte Constitutionnel No 2 du 8 janvier 1966 fixant l'organisation provisoire des pouvoirs de la République'. *Journal officiel de la République Centrafricaine*, 9/1, 15/01/1966.

'Acte Constitutionnel portant organisation provisoire des pouvoirs publics, 21/09/1979'. *Journal officiel de la République Centrafricaine*, 24/1, septembre 1979.

'Ordonnance No 81/001 du 5 janvier 1981 relative à l'élection du Président de la République'. *Journal officiel de la République Centrafricaine*, 24/1, janvier 1981.

'Ordonnance No 81/007 du 21 janvier 1981 modifiant et complétant les dispositions de l'Ordonnance No 79/017 du 26 octobre 1979 autorisant la création des Partis Politiques en République Centrafricaine'. *Journal officiel de la République Centrafricaine*, 24/1, janvier 1981.

'Acte Constitutionnel No 1 du 21 septembre 1985'. reprinted in *Raynal* (1986), 221.

'Constitution de la République Centrafricaine du 28 novembre 1986 (Ordonnance No. 86.065 du 4 novembre 1986 adoptée par le Référendum du 28 novembre 1986, revisée par la Loi No. 91.001 du 8 mars 1991)'. *Journal officiel de la République Centrafricaine*, 33 (Spécial Constitution du 28 novembre 1986), mars 1991.

'Décret No 91.076 du 15 mars 1991 portant nomination du Premier Minister, Chef du Gouvernement'. *Journal officiel de la République Centrafricaine*, 33 (Spécial Constitution du 28 novembre 1986), mars 1991.

'Loi No 92.012 du 31 juillet 1992 portant code électoral de la République Centrafricaine'. (special print with important annexes published by the Commission Electorale Mixte), Bangui.

'Constitution de la République Centrafricaine du 14 janvier 1995'. reprinted in *Afrique Contemporaine*, 175/3, 61–79.

République Centrafricaine and Ministère de l'Economie, du Plan, des Statistiques et de la Coopération Internationale (1992). *Recensement général de la population de décembre 1988*. Bangui.

3.2 Books, Articles and Electoral Reports

Bierschenk, T., and Olivier de Sardan, J.-P. (1997). 'Local Powers and a Distant State in Rural Central African Republic'. *The Journal of Modern African Studies*, 35/3: 441–468.

Bigo, D. (1988). *Pouvoir et obéissance en Centrafrique*. Paris: Karthala.

GOIE (Groupe d'Observateurs Internationaux des Elections) (1993). *Rapport sur les élections présidentielles et législatives. République Centrafricaine, août-septembre 1993*. Bangui, mimeo.

Kalck, P. (1971). *Central African Republic. A Failure in De-Colonisation*. London: Pall Mall Press.

— (1974). *Histoire centrafricaine*. Paris: Berger-Levrault.

Kamto, M. (1983). 'Les nouvelles institutions constitutionelles et politiques de la République Centrafricaine'. *Penant*, 99/793, 7–31.

Knieper, R. (1993). 'Zentralafrikanische Republik', in D. Nohlen and F. Nuscheler (eds.), *Handbuch der Dritten Welt, Vol. 4: Ostafrika und Südafrika*, (3rd edn.). Bonn: Dietz, 523–539.

Koyt, M., M'bringa Takama, M. F., and Decoudras, P.-M. (1995). 'République Centrafricaine. Les vicissitudes du changement', in CEAN (ed.), *L'Afrique Politique 1995*. Paris: Karthala, 235–251.

Leclercq, C. (1987a). 'La Constitution de la RCA du 21 novembre 1986 et les statuts du Rassemblement démocratique centrafricain'. *Afrique Contemporaine*, 26/144, 49–51.

— (1987b). 'La Constitution de la République Centrafricaine du 21 novembre 1986'. *Revue Juridique et Politique*, 26/4: 290–298.

Lique, R.-J. (1993). *Bokassa 1er. La grande mystification*. Paris: Editions Chaka.

Mbeko, M. H. (1993). *Régimes issus des coups d'état militaires et transition démocratique en Afrique noire: Le cas de la République Centrafricaine*. Doctoral dissertation, Université de Laval.

Mehler, A. (1994). 'Präsidentschafts- und Parlamentswahlen in der Zentralafrikanischen Republik (22.8./19.9.1993)', in U. Engel, R. Hofmeier, D. Kohnert and A. Mehler (eds.), *Wahlbeobachtung in Afrika: Erfahrungen deutscher Wahlbeobachter, Analysen und Lehren für die Zukunft (Arbeiten aus dem IAK; Bd. 90)*. Hamburg: Institut für Afrika-Kunde, 195–209.

— (1995). 'Zentralafrikanische Republik', in Institut für Afrika-Kunde and R. Hofmeier (eds.), *Afrika Jahrbuch 1994. Politik, Wirtschaft und Gesellschaft in Afrika südlich der Sahara*. Opladen: Leske & Budrich, 223–226.

— (1996). 'Zentralafrikanische Republik', in Institut für Afrika-Kunde and R. Hofmeier (eds.), *Afrika Jahrbuch 1995. Politik, Wirtschaft und Ge-

sellschaft in Afrika südlich der Sahara. Opladen: Leske & Budrich, 223–226.

— (1999). 'Meuterei der Armee und Tribalisierung von Politik in der "demokratisierten Neokolonie" Zentralafrikanische Republik (ZAR)', in H. Zinecker (ed.), *Unvollendete Demokratisierung in Nichtmarktökonomien*. Amsterdam: Facultas, 193–211.

O'Toole, T. (1986). *The Central African Republic. The Continent's Hidden Heart*. Boulder, Col.: Westview Press.

Owona, J. (1978). 'La nouvelle constitution centrafricaine de 1976: De la "République monocratique" à "l'Empire parlementaire"'. *Penant*, 87/759: 42–57.

Raynal, J.-J. (1983). 'L'évolution politique et constitutionelle de la République Centrafricaine (1958–1983)'. *Revue Juridique et Politique*, 37/4: 795–816.

— (1986). 'Les actes constitutionnels du 21 septembre 1985: La civilisation du régime centrafricain'. *Penant*, 96/791: 221–227.

— (1988). 'La constitution centrafricaine du 28 novembre 1986'. *Penant*, 98/798: 475–482.

Ziemer, K. (1978). 'Zentralafrikanische Republik', in D. Sternberger, B. Vogel, D. Nohlen and K. Landfried (eds.), *Die Wahl der Parlamente und anderer Staatsorgane. Band II: Politische Organisation und Repräsentation in Afrika* by Franz Nuscheler, Klaus Ziemer *et al.*, Berlin/ New York: Walter De Gruyter, 2441–2474.

Zoctizoum, Y. (1983). *Histoire de la Centrafrique*, 2 Vols., Paris: L'Harmattan.

CHAD

by Manuela Römer*

1. Introduction

1.1 Historical Overview

Chad is located in the transition zone between North Africa and sub-Saharan Africa and divided into the northern nomadic Arab and the southern Christian and westernized part, either one being ethnically and tribally highly heterogeneous. During the longest period of its history since independence, Chad experienced an ethno-regional civil war, in which elections played no role in conflict resolution. Since 1990 the country has entered a process of institutionalization that has so far managed to pacify the Chadian society.

Chad was brought under French control in 1900 and became part of French Equatorial Africa in 1910. Designated an autonomous member state of the *Communauté Française* on 28 November 1958, it achieved independence on 11 August 1960. However, the Saharan territory of the North, Borkou-Ennedi-Tibesti, remained under French military administration until 1964. François (later Ngarta) Tombalbaye, a southerner and leader of the *Parti Progressiste du Tchad* (PPT) was elected Prime Minister in March 1959 and became President after independence. He soon transformed the political system into a hierarchical top-down president-centered system that was formalized with the Constitution of 1962. Tombalbaye dissolved all political parties except for the PPT and declared it sole legal party in 1963. Its executive body, the *Bureau Politique National* (BPN) became Chad's supreme political organ. Although the BPN was composed of an equal number of Muslims and southerners, it was dominated by the President. This political monopoly was increasingly opposed by certain northern politicians and after a number of civil disturbances, guerilla war broke out in 1965, focused mainly in the North. The *Front de Libération Nationale du Tchad* (FROLINAT), a

* The Author would like to thank Bernard Lanne, former headmaster of the National School of Administration (ENA) in Chad, for his contribution to election data material and his generous help in clearing up numerous detail questions.

heterogeneous coalition, which was established in Sudan in 1966, soon assumed leadership of the revolt. Despite various initiatives to satisfy the political aspirations of the FROLINAT leaders, the rebellion could not be successfully contained by the government. In order to rebalance his yet destabilized regime, Tombalbaye initiated political reforms to mobilize mass support against the growing opposition within tribal and administrational elites. He changed to direct presidential voting in 1969 and replaced the PPT in 1973 by a *Mouvement National pour la Révolution Culturelle et Sociale* (MNRCS). Nevertheless, a military coup of southerners put an end to his reign (and killed him) on 13 April 1975.

General Felix Malloum was designated chairman of a ruling *Conseil Supérieur Militaire*, but never achieved full authority. Although Malloum's regime gained support within several former opposition groups, fighting continued between the central government and some factions of FROLINAT, the most prominent being FAN (*Forces Armées du Nord*) of Hissène Habré. An initiative for peace came when in 1977 the *Acte fondamentale* was put forward in Karthoum pending the adoption of a permanent constitution and President Malloum co-opted Hissène Habré as Prime Minister. However, a coup on 12 February 1979 by Habré against the President was the starting point of the now called Chadian civil war which escalated with the participation of several other factions of FROLINAT such as FAP (*Forces Armées du Peuple*) of Goukouni Weddeye. In fact, by then Chad was already partitioned in two, the northern part under Libyan military influence and the southern part controlled by the French.

Under international guidance (OAU and neighbor countries) attempts were made to negotiate a truce, but several pacts (Kano I and II in March as well as Lagos in August 1979) failed to establish a consensual government with no less than 11 Chadian political tendencies negotiating for peace. After the Lagos meeting in 1979 Goukouni Weddeye was designated President and head of a transitional government (*Gouvernement d'Union Nationale de Transition, GUNT*). The government contained 22 members, 12 from the northern and 10 from the southern part of the country. However, civil war could not be stopped and Weddeye only held office until 1982, when Habré's FAN gained control over the capital on 7 June 1982 and Habré was sworn in as President on 21 October 1982. In the wake of the installation of an *Acte fondamentale*, Habré formed a 31-member government and a 31-member *Conseil National Consultatif* (CNC) as advisory organ. Habré attempted to consolidate his regime by the first legally recognized political party since the ban of MNRCS in 1975, the *Union Nationale pour l'Independance et la Révolution* (UNIR). In order to gain legitimacy, Chadians were asked on 12 December 1989 to vote for a Constitution to replace the *Acte fondamentale*. The referendum combined support for the new constitution and a National Assembly to be elected in 1990 with the confirmation of President Habré for another seven years. The subsequent parliamentary elections turned out to be the first pluralistic elections since independence, though held on an individual non-party basis (UNIR did not present candidates). The Assembly soon proved to have very little influence within the monolithic structures of Habré's regime, however.

Already five months later on 3 December 1990, various oppositional forces allied under Idriss Déby and his *Mouvement Patriotique du Salut* (MPS) and overthrew the Habré administration. Once again, the constitution was suspended, the Assembly dissolved and Déby was declared President and head of a provisional Council of State on 4 December 1990. An interim National Charter abandoning vice-presidency and introducing the post of Prime Minister was adopted for a 30-month period on 28 February 1991. Although the so-called *Charte Nationale* of 1991 did not differ much from his predecessor's *Acte fondamentale*—MPS was declared state-party—Déby promised further democratization including free media and trade unions, a multi-party system, free elections and a National Conference in order to define Chad's political future. In October 1991 a law concerning political parties was issued. It allowed registration to such parties that could present three representatives in at least 10 of the 15 administrative regions in order to avoid ethnically based groupings. Only MPS was privileged in not having to take part in the formal admission process. About 60 parties registered. Originally announced for May 1992, the National Conference (*Conférence Nationale Souveraine, CNS*) was held in 1993 and adopted a transitional national charter (*Charte de transition*). It replaced the national charter and established a *Conseil Superieur de Transition* (CST) as Parliament and Constitutional Assembly. Its members were indirectly elected by the CNS (a Prime Minister being elected by CST). Finally on 31 March 1996 the new constitution was put on referendum and approved by 60% of the votes cast. Its mixed form of central institutions and regional autonomy was still criticized for lacking federal elements as well as for the President's strong position in relation to the Prime Minister. In the subsequent presidential elections Déby was confirmed as President. Especially in the first round there was suspicion of manipulation, though. Parliamentary elections in January/February 1997 proved that voting still follows regional cleavages: MPS found most of their voters in the North, Center and East of the country, whereas URD (*Union pour le renouvement et la démocratie*) of Kamougué Wadal Abelkader had its strongholds in the South East. Even though the MPS secured a tight absolute majority, the President decided on forming a unity government. By the same time the last guerilla organization of some importance laid down their weapons. The transitional period that ceased with parliamentary elections was by now successful in establishing peace and balancing the North-South conflict, central to any national project in Chad.

1.2 Evolution of Electoral Provisions

Since *Loi Cadre* was introduced in 1956 by the French administration, universal, equal and secret ballot was in force in Chad. Elections were organized by the Ministry of the Interior. With the electoral law of 1989 the electoral commission continued with the Ministry of the Interior. It is independent with the current election law of 1994 (four members designated by the President, two by the President of the National Assembly and two by the President of the Senate).

The Constitution of 1956 of the autonomous Republic of Chad provided for a parliamentary system with the executive lying with a Prime Minister, elected by the National Assembly, while the Head of State remained the President of the French Republic. Parliament consisted of 85 seats, elected for a five-year term. Closed lists in 10 constituencies formed by the state's administrative regions were elected by plurality system. The constitution was changed when independence was gained (*Loi constitutionelle du 28 novembre 1960*) in such a way that the Prime Minister also became Head of State, still being elected by the National Assembly.

However, before the first post-independence elections were held in 1962 a new constitution changed the institutional framework in favor of a presidential system. The President (who had to be at least 30 years old) was elected indirectly for a seven-year term, the electoral body consisting of Parliament, power holders at local level and traditional leaders. The President was elected by a qualified majority system: the first ballot required a two-thirds, second ballot a three-fifths and third ballot absolute majority. The PPT, constitutionally declared state party (§ 4 of the 1959 constitution that provided for free founding and competition of parties was abolished) put forward candidates for the 85 seats on a single list. A plurality system was applied with the whole country forming one electoral district, each region being represented by a certain number of mandates. Until 1975 these provisions were arbitrarily accommodated to necessities of power: The number of seats was reduced to 75 in 1963 (when the President dissolved the assembly) and increased for the 1969 elections (which were two years overdue). The 1969 presidential elections were held directly on the basis of a decree violating the constitution (*Ordonnance du 20 mai 1969*). At the same time the minimum age for voting was reduced from 21 to 20.

After years of civil war and military rule another institutionalization process led to parliamentary, but not presidential elections in 1989. The constitution of 1989 was ratified by referendum combined with the confirmation of the President in power for another seven years. Political parties except for the state party were not legalized by the time of parliamentary elections, which were held on an individual non-party basis. 123 seats were elected by plurality vote in 60 constituencies and five districts of the capital, each constituency sending between one and five representatives according to its size. Seven seats were reserved for women (two were actually elected, five had to be chosen from the nation-wide best losers). Candidates had to pay a deposit of Francs CFA 350,000 in order to register.

In 1993 quasi-legislative elections were held on indirect basis to form a transitional parliament that should also function as Constitutional Assembly. Fifty seven members were elected by the National Conference; three organs were built: a Parliament called *Conseil National de Transition*, a Prime Minister holding executive powers and appointed by Parliament and the President. This transitional government formulated the current electoral provisions and the Constitution of 1996.

1.3 Current Electoral Provisions

Sources: La Constitution du Tchad du 14 avril 1996; Loi No./PR/94 fixant les règles générales applicables au référendum et aux élections présidentielles, législatives, sénatoriales et locales.

Elected national institutions: The President is elected for a five-year term in direct universal suffrage, he is not re-eligible. The 125 members of the National Assembly are elected for a four-year term in direct universal suffrage. A Senate is elected by indirect suffrage; the number of Senators is fixed by an organic law. They are elected for a six-year term, one third is renewed every two years.

Suffrage: Universal, equal, secret, direct and indirect. Requirements: at least 18 years of age, full possession of civil and political rights, registration as voter.

Nomination of candidates
- *presidential elections*: Chadian nationality by birth; no other citizenship, full possession of civil and political rights, at least 35 years, mental and physical health, high moral standards, at least one year of residence in Chad without interruption before registration as a candidate, incompatibility with any other public function. For registration as a candidate a deposit of Francs CFA 10 million is necessary, which is revolved if the candidate receives at least 10% of the votes cast in the first round of balloting.
- *elections to the National Assembly*: Chadian citizenship for at least 10 years, at least 25 years of age, registration as voter, at least one year of residence in Chad without interruption, ability to read and write French or Arabic, incompatibility with any other public function. For registration as a candidate a deposit of Francs CFA 250,000 is necessary; it is revolved when the candidate receives at least 10% of the votes cast in the first round.
- *elections to the Senate*: Chadian citizenship for at least 10 years, at least 40 years of age, registration as voter, at least one year of residence in Chad without interruption, ability to read and write French or Arabic, incompatibility with any other public function.

Electoral system
- *presidential elections*: Absolute majority system. If no candidate achieves absolute majority in the first round, a run-off between the two top candidates is held.
- *elections to the National Assembly*: Absolute majority system in 25 single-member constituencies and 34 multi-member constituencies (closed lists). If no candidate or list achieves absolute majority in the first round, a run-off between the two top candidates or lists is held.
- *elections to the Senate*: Senators are elected indirectly per region, the electoral body is formed by councillors at regional, departmental, municipal and rural level; every region forms a constituency; plurality system is applied.

1.4 Comment on the Electoral Statistics

Election results from 1959 to 1962 follow Le Cornec (1963), who also lists the results of indirect presidential elections in 1962; results of 1969 follow Ziemer (1978); the full list of elected members of parliament 1969 is published in *Annuaire Officiel du Tchad* (1972).

A particularly good source of information is InfoChad, a daily information bulletin by *Agence Tchadienne de Presse*. Laws and election results from 1989 can to be found in InfoChad. Official results of the parliamentary election in 1990 (ATP Bulletin No. 2464 of 23 July 1990) contain a full list of the members of Parliament, but only the winning votes were published. Therefore they could not be calculated. The elections results of the referendum, presidential and parliamentary elections in 1996 and 1997 are presented as published by the *Cour d'Appel* in N'Djaména and *N'Djaména-Hebdo*. The aggregation of parliamentary election results of 1997 had to be calculated on the basis of official results at constituency level partly being incomprehensive or arithmetically wrong.

2. Tables

2.1 Dates of National Elections, Referendums and Coups d'Etat

Year	Presidential elections	Parliamentary elections	Elections for Constitutional Assembly	Referendums	Coups d'état
1959		31/05			
1962		04/03			
1963		22/12			
1969	18/06	14/12			
1975					13/04
1989				10/12	
1990		08/07			03/12
1996	02/06 (1st) 23/06 (2nd)			31/03	
1997		05/01 (1st) 23/02 (2nd)			

2.2 Electoral Body 1959–1997

Year	Type of election[a]	Population[b]	Registered voters		Votes cast		
			Total number	% pop.	Total number	% reg. voters	% pop.
1959	Pa	2,630,000	1,262,985	48.0	582,282	45.0	22.1
1962	Pa	3,254,000	1,297,908	39.9	1,128,503	87.5	34.7
1963	Pa	3,254,000	1,421,520	43.7	1,356,211	95.4	41.7
1969	Pr	3,510,000	1,678,979	47.8	1,562,139	93.0	44.5
1969	Pa	3,510,000	1,664,848	47.4	1,583,422	95.1	45.1
1989	Ref	5,300,000	2,894,825	54.6	2,693,282	93.0	50.8
1990	Pa	6,010,000	2,894,825	48.2	1,622,838	56.1	27.0
1996	Ref	6,261,000	3,260,782	52.1	1,990,669	61.0	31.8
1996	Pr (1st)	6,261,000	3,565,913	56.9	2,406,962	67.5	38.4
1996	Pr (2nd)	6,261,000	3,871,044	61.8	3,007,174	77.7	48.0
1997	Pa (1st)	6,261,000	3,248,333	51.9	1,481,628	45.6	23.7
1997	Pa (2nd)[c]	6,261,000	1,733,931	27.7	784,636	45.3	12.5

[a] Pa = Parliament (*Assemblée Nationale*); Ref = Referendum; Pr = President.

[b] Only two population census were held in Chad since independence. In December 1963: 3,254,000 and in April 1993: 6,158,992. All other numbers are unofficial estimations.

[c] A second round of voting was necessary in 25 of 59 constituencies.

2.3 Abbreviations

ACTUS	Action Tchadienne pour l'Unité et le Socialisme
AND	Action Nationale pour le Développement
ART	Action pour le Renouvellement du Tchad
AST	Action Sociale Tchadienne
CNDS	Convention Nationale des Sociaux - Démocrates Tchadiens
CODE	Convention pour la Démocratie
CSDT	Convention des Social - Démocrates Tchadiens
CSNPD	Comité du Sursaut National pour la Paix et la Démocratie
FAR	Forces des Actions pour la République
FR	Front Républicain
GIRT[a]	Groupement des Indépendants et Ruraux Tchadiens
MDST	Mouvement pour la Démocratie et le Socialisme en Tchad
MESAN	Mouvement pour l'Evolution Sociale de l'Afrique Noire
MNRD	Mouvement National des Rénovateurs Démocratiques
MPDT	Mouvement pour la Démocratie du Tchad
MPS	Mouvement Patriotique du Salut
MSA	Mouvement Socialiste Africain
MSDT	Mouvement Social pour la Démocratie au Tchad
MUDT	Mouvement pour l'Unité et la Démocratie au Tchad

PAP.JS	Parti Africain pour le Progrès et la Justice Sociale
PDT	Parti Démocratique du Tchad
PLD	Parti pour la Liberté et le Développement
PNRD	Parti National du Renouveau Démocratique
PPT-RDA	Parti Progressiste du Tchad - Rassemblement Démocratique Africain
PSDT	Parti Social – Démocrate du Tchad
PUNDDT	Parti d'Union Nationale de Démocratie, de Dialogue et de Développement du Tchad
PUR	Parti pour l'Unité et la Reconstruction
PURN	Parti pour l'Unité et de la Reconstruction Nationale
RDC/PT	Rassemblement Démocratique Culturel pour la Paix et le Travail
RDP	Rassemblement pour la Démocratie et le Progrès
RDR	Rassemblement pour la Démocratie et le Renouveau
RDT	Rassemblement Démocratique du Tchad
RFDT	Rassemblement des Forces Démocratiques du Tchad
RNDA	—
RNDT	Rassemblement National Démocratique du Tchad
RNT	Rassemblement des Nationalistes Tchadiennes
RPJS	Rassemblement pour le Progrès et la Justice Sociale
RPT	Rassemblement du Peuple Tchadien
UCD	—
UDIT	Union des Indépendants du Tchad
UDPT	Union Démocratique pour le Progrès du Tchad
UDR	Union pour la Démocratie et la République
UDT	Union Démocratique Tchadienne
UFD	Union des Forces Démocratiques
UN	Union Nationale
UNCT	Union Nationale pour le Changement du Tchad
UNDD/PC	Union Nationale pour la Démocratie et le Développement
UNDPT	Union Nationale pour la Démocratie et le Progrès Tchadien
UNDR	Union Nationale pour le Développement et la Renouvellement
UNIR	Union Nationale pour l'Indépendance et la Révolution
UNRT	Union Nationale pour le Renouveau du Tchad
UPTRN	Union du Peuple Tchadien pour la Reconstruction Nationale
URD	Union pour le Renouvellement et la Démocratie
VIVA-RNDP	VIVA-Rassemblement National pour la Démocratie et le Progrès

General note: A great number of political parties were founded on the eve of the elections in 1996, did not exercise lasting political activities, and could not establish themselves.

[a] GIRT was not a political party, but a parliamentary faction within the Territorial Assembly installed in 1958.

2.4 Electoral Participation of Parties and Alliances 1959–1997

Party / Alliance	Years	Elections contested	
		Presidential	Parliamentary
AST	1959	0	1
GIRT	1959	0	1
MESAN	1959	0	1
MSA	1959	0	1
PPT-RDA	1959, 1962, 1963, 1969	1	4
UDIT	1959	0	1
MPS	1996, 1997	1	1
RDP	1996, 1997	1	1
UDR	1996, 1997	1	1
UN	1996, 1997	1	0
UNDR	1996	1	0
URD	1996, 1997	1	1
ACTUS	1997	0	1
AND	1997	0	1
ART	1997	0	1
CNDS	1997	0	1
CODE	1997	0	1
CSDT	1997	0	1
CSNDP	1997	0	1
FAR	1997	0	1
FR	1997	0	1
LINGUI	1997	0	1
MDST	1997	0	1
MPDT	1997	0	1
MSDT	1997	0	1
MUDT	1997	0	1
PAP-JS	1997	0	1
PDT	1997	0	1
PLD	1997	0	1
PLUS	1997	0	1
PNRD	1997	0	1
PSDT	1997	0	1
PUNDDT	1997	0	1
PUR	1997	0	1
RDT	1997	0	1
RFDT	1997	0	1
RNDA	1997	0	1
RNDT	1997	0	1
RNT	1997	0	1
RPT	1997	0	1
RPJS	1997	0	1
UCD	1997	0	1

Party / Alliance	Years	Elections contested	
		Presidential	Parliamentary
UDPT	1997	0	1
UDT	1997	0	1
UFD	1997	0	1
UNCT	1997	0	1
UNDP	1997	0	1
UNDD/PC	1997	0	1
UNRT	1997	0	1
VIVA-RNDP	1997	0	1

2.5 Referendums

Year	1989[a]		1996[b]	
	Total number	%	Total number	%
Registered voters	2,894,825	-	3,260,782	
Votes cast	2,693,282	93.0	1,990,669	61.0
Invalid votes	2,997	0.1	88,869	4.5
Valid votes	2,690,285	99.9	1,901,800	95.5
Yes	2,687,352	99.9	1,201,696	63.5
No	1,485	0.1	700,362	36.5

[a] Inconsistent official result: 1,448 valid votes missing. The referendum ratified the Constitution of 1989 and confirmed the President for a seven-year term.

[b] The referendum ratified the Constitution of 1996. The results include votes of Chadians residing abroad.

2.6 Elections for Constitutional Assembly

Elections for Constitutional Assembly have not been held.

2.7 Parliamentary Elections 1959–1997

Year	1959 Total number	%	1962 Total number	%
Registered voters	1,262,985	-	1,297,908	–
Votes cast	582,282	45.0	1,128,503	87.5
Invalid votes	13,340	2.3	4,289	0.4
Valid votes	568,942	97.8	1,124,214	99.6
PPP-RDA	390,377	68.6	–	–
AST	25,597	4.5	–	–
GIRT	44,438	7.8	–	–
UDIT	41,304	7.3	–	–
MSA	55,500	9.8	–	–
MESAN	11,041	1.9	–	–
PPT-RDA	–	–	1,124,214	100.0

Year	1963 Total number	%	1969 Total number	%
Registered voters	1,421,520	–	1,664,848	–
Votes cast	1,356,211	95.4	1,583,422	95.1
Invalid votes	2,434	0.2	2,829	0.2
Valid votes	1,353,777	99.8	1,580,593	99.8
PPT-RDA	1,352,749	99.9	1,580,593	100.0

The parliamentary elections of 1990 were not based on party but only on individual candidates. Therefore detailed results cannot be given. For data on voter registration and participation see table 2.2.

Year	1997 (1st round)[a]		1997 (2nd round)[b]	
	Total number	%	Total number	%
Registered voters	3,248,333	–	1,733,931	–
Votes cast	1,481,628	45.6	784,636	45.3
Invalid votes	106,391	7.2	25,378	3.2
Valid votes	1,028,718	69.4	749,158	95.5
ACTUS	1,915	0.1	19,878	2.6
AND	20,572	1.6	14,732	1.9
ART	4,666	0.4	–	–
CNDS	19,899	1.6	33,574	4.4
CODE	15,226	1.2	–	–
CSDT	15,223	1.2	–	–
CSNDP	354	0.0	–	–
FAR	50,627	4.0	32,274	4.2
FR	678	0.1	–	–
LINGUI	2,096	0.2	18,389	2.4
MDST	21,874	1.7	25,764	3.4
MNRD	2,516	0.2	–	–
MPS	504,045	40.0	262,020	34.4
MPDT	7,026	0.6	–	–
MSDT	8,611	0.7	–	–
MUDT	663	0.1	–	–
PAP-JS	12,875	1.0	–	–
PDT	453	0.0	–	–
PLD	33,344	2.6	–	–
PLUS	14,488	1.1	–	–
PNRD	6,355	0.5	–	–
PSDT	1,417	0.1	5,595	0.7
PUNDDT	2,146	0.2	–	–
PUR	14,909	1.8	1,731	0.2
RDP	84,372	6.7	13,140	1.7
RDT	1,172	0.1	–	–
RFDT	1,502	0.1	–	–
RNDA	5,722	0.4	–	–
RNDT	9,380	0.7	–	–
RNT	2,516	0.2	–	–
RPT	3,891	0.3	–	–
RPJS	6,282	0.5	–	–
UCD	25,603	2.0	18,764	2.5
UDR	48,948	3.9	2,419	0.3
UDPT	5,186	0.4	–	–
UDT	4,324	0.3	–	–
UFD	8,252	0.6	–	–
UN	14,274	1.1	17,133	2.2

Year	1997 (1st round)[a]		1997 (2nd round)[b]	
	Total number	%	Total number	%
UNDP	8,847	0.7	–	–
UNDR	76,156	6.0	63,549	8.3
UNDD/PC	380	0.0	–	–
UNRT	6,242	0.5	–	–
URD	165,639	13.1	214,548	28.2
VIVA RNDP	20,630	1.6	18,345	2.4

[a] As the election results in a number of constituencies are not comprehensive, a consistent aggregation at national level could not be produced. The tables are calculated in the following way: registered, cast, valid and invalid votes are calculated as a sum of the results on constituency level. These are not always comprehensive. As in some constituencies several parties formed common party lists, votes were accorded to the most important party of the alliance, a decision which rested upon the estimation of the author. Percentages per party were calculated on the basis of the sum of votes distributed to all parties (1,261,296).

[b] The result of the second round on national level was calculated in the same way as the first round. Percentages per party were calculated on the basis of the sum of votes distributed to all parties (761,853). Run-off elections were necessary in 25 of 59 constituencies for 69 out of 123 seats. Elections in two constituencies were annulled.

2.8 Composition of Parliament 1959–1997

Year	1959		1962		1963		1969	
	Seats	%	Seats	%	Seats	%	Seats	%
	85[a]	100	85	100	75	100	101	100
PPT-RDA	57	67.0	–	–	–	–	–	–
AST	9	10.5	–	–	–	–	–	–
GIRT	2	2.4	–	–	–	–	–	–
UDIT	16	18.8	–	–	–	–	–	–
MSA	–	–	–	–	–	–	–	–
MESAN	–	–	–	–	–	–	–	–
PPT-RDA	–	–	85	100	75	100	101	100

[a] Inconsistent official result: Only 84 seats are distributed.

Year	1990[a]		1997[b]	
	Seats	%	Seats	%
	123	100	125	100
ACTUS	–	–	1	0.8
AND	–	–	2	1.6
CNDS	–	–	1	0.8
FAR	–	–	1	0.8
MPS	–	–	63	50.4
PLD	–	–	3	2.4
RDP	–	–	3	2.4
UDR	–	–	4	3.2
UNDR	–	–	15	12.0
URD	–.	–	29	23.2

[a] Election on individual non-party-basis.
[b] Composition as of 21 March 1997: Voters were still to elect deputies in the constituency of Borkou in the district of B.E.T and Abougoudoum in the district of Quaddaï on March 29. The two seats were won by MPS, raising their number of seats to 65.

2.8 a) Parliamentary Elections 1997: Regional Distribution of Seats (at the Level of *Prefectures*)

1st round	Batha	B.E.T.	Biltine	Baguirmi	Guera	Kanem
Constituencies	3	4[a]	5	5	4	3
Seats	6	4	5	14	6	5
FAR	–	–	–	–	–	–
MPS	6	3	5	2	5	2
PLD	–	–	–	–	–	–
RDP	–	–	–	–	–	3
UNDR	–	–	–	–	–	–
UNRT	–	–	–	–	–	–
URD	–	–	–	–	–	–
Ballotage	–	–	–	12	1	–

[a] One seat annulled.

1st round	Lac	Logone Occ.	Logone Orient.	Mayo-Kebbi	Moyen Chari	Ouaddai
Constituencies	2	3	4	5	5	5
Seats	4	8	9	17	14	10[a]
FAR	–	–	1	–	–	–
MPS	4	–	–	–	–	6
PLD	–	–	–	–	–	1
RDP	–	–	–	–	–	–
UNDR	–	–	–	6	–	1
UNRT	–	–	–	–	–	1
URD	–	–	2	–	2	–
Ballotage	–	8	6	11	12	–

[a] One seat annulled.

1st round	Salamat	Tandjile	N'Djaména Urbain	Total
Constituencies	3	3	5	59
Seats	4	8	11	125
FAR	–	–	–	1
MPS	4	–	–	37
PLD	–	–	–	1
RDP	–	–	–	3
UNDR	–	–	–	7
UNRT	–	–	–	1
URD	–	–	–	4
Ballotage	–	8	11	69

2nd round	Batha	B.E.T.	Biltine	Baguirmi	Guera	Kanem
Constituencies	3	5	4	5	4	3
Seats	6	5	4	14	6	5
Ballotage	–	–	–	12	1	–
ACTUS	–	–	–	–	–	–
AND	–	–	–	–	–	–
CNDS	–	–	–	–	–	–
FAR	–	–	–	–	–	–
MPS	–	–	–	11	1	–
PLD	–	–	–	–	–	–
RDP	–	–	–	–	–	–
UDR	–	–	–	–	–	–
UNDR	–	–	–	1	–	–
UNRT	–	–	–	–	–	–
URD	–	–	–	–	–	–

2nd round	Lac	Logone Occ.	Logone Orient.	Mayo-Kebbi	Moyen Chari	Ouaddai
Constituencies	2	3	4	5	5	5
Seats	4	8	9	17	14	11
Ballotage	–	8	6	11	12	–
ACTUS	–	–	–	–	–	–
AND	–	2	–	–	–	–
CNDS	–	–	–	–	–	–
FAR	–	–	–	–	–	–
MPS	–	–	–	4	2	–
PLD	–	–	–	–	–	–
RDP	–	–	–	–	–	–
UDR	–	–	–	–	–	–
UNDR	–	–	–	7	–	–
UNRT	–	–	–	–	–	–
URD	–	6	6	–	10	–

2nd round	Salamat	Tandjile	N'Djamé na Urbain	Total 2nd round	Total 1st round	Total
Constituencies	3	3	5	25	34	59
Seats	4	8	11	69	54	125
Ballotage	–	8	11	–	69	–
ACTUS	–	1	–	1	0	1
AND	–	–	–	2	0	2
CNDS	–	–	1	1	0	1
FAR	–	–	–	0	1	1
MPS	–	4	4	26	37	63
PLD	–	–	2	2	1	3
RDP	–	–	–	0	3	3
UDR	–	–	4	4	0	4
UNDR	–	–	–	8	7	15
UNRT	–	–	–	0	1	1
URD	–	3	–	25	4	29

2.9 Presidential Elections 1969–1996

1969	Total number	%
Registered voters	1,678,979	–
Votes cast	1,562,132	93.0
Invalid votes	6,026	0.4
Valid votes	1,556,113	99.6
François Tombalbaye (PPT-RDA)	1,556,113	100.0

1996 (first round)[a]	Total number	%
Registered voters	3,565,913	–
Votes cast	2,406,962	67.5
Invalid votes	88,224	3.7
Valid votes	2,318,738	96.3
Idriss Deby (MPS)	1,016,277	43.8
Kamougué Wadal Abdelkader (URD)	287,512	12.4
Saleh Kebzabo (UNDR)	199,691	8.6
Jean Bawoyeu Alingué (UDR)	192,816	8.3
Lol Mahamat Choua (RDP)	137,612	5.9
Younous Ibedou (CSDT)	76,293	3.3
Adoum Moussa Seif (CNDS)	67,496	2.9
Lamana Abdoulaye (UN)	63,671	2.7
Delwa Kassire Coumakoye (VIVA-RNDS)	53,260	2.2
Yorongar Ngarledjy (independent)	48,407	2.1
Mahamat Abdoulaye (MPDT)	47,830	2.1
Abbas Mahamat Ambadi (independent)	37,568	1.6
Naimbaye Lossimian (independent)	35,420	1.5
Adoum Hassan Issa (UNCT)	28,877	1.2
Elie Romba (UDPT)	26,008	1.1

[a] Election result includes votes of Chadians residing abroad.

1996 (second round)[b]	Total number	%
Registered voters	3,871,044	–
Votes cast	3,007,174	77.7
Invalid votes	69,699	2.3
Valid votes	2,937,475	97.7
Idriss Déby (MPS)	2,102,907	71.6
Komougué Wadal Abdelkader (URD)	834,568	28.4

[a] Election result includes votes of Chadians residing abroad.

2.10 List of Power Holders 1960–1998

Head of State	Years	Remarks
(François) since 1973: Ngarta Tombalbaye	1960–1975	First elected by Parliament prior to independence on 24/03/1959 and 31/05/1959; confirmed as Head of State and Government on 22/04/1962 (indirect elections) and 18/06/1969 (direct elections).
Félix Malloum	1975–1979	Seized power by military coup on 13/04/1975; overthrown by his Prime Minister Hissène Habré on 12/02/1979.
Goukouni Weddeye	1979	Named on 23/03/1979 by a eight-member Provisional State Council after four-party agreement at Kano, Nigeria.
Lol Mahamat Choua	1979	On 29/04/1979 a second provisional government was announced under Choua at a second Kano-Conference where the previous pact broke down.
Goukouni Weddeye	1979–1982	After the fourth conference in Nigeria (Lagos) 20/08/1979 designated as President and head of GUNT (*Gouvernement d'union nationale de transition*) along with Vice-President Kamougue.
Hissène Habré	1982–1990	Seized power by military coup (FAN); sworn in as President on 21/10/1982; confirmed by constitutional referendum of 22/12/1989 for a seven-year term; overthrown by Idriss Déby on 03/12/1990.
Idriss Deby	1990–	Auto-designated on 04/12/1990 after military coup; confirmed on 03/07/1996 in presidential elections.

Head of Government	Years	Remarks
–	1960–1978	Identical with Head of State.
Hissène Habré	1978–1979	Co-opted as Prime Minister by President Malloum on 29/08/78; overthrew the government on 12/02/79.
–	1979–1991	Office of Prime Minister did not exist.
Jean Bawoyen Alingue	1991–1992	04/03/1991–19/05/1992; appointed and dismissed by the President.
Djidingar Dono Ngardoum	1992	Several weeks as Prime Minister in May 1992; appointed and dismissed by the President.
Joseph Yodeyman	1992	Named and dismissed by the President.

Head of Government	Years	Remarks
Fidel Moungar	1993	06/04/1993–28/10/1993, elected by the National Conference, formed first transitional government.
Kassiré Delwa Koumakoye	1993–1995	13/11/1993–08/04/95. Head of the transitional government.
Djimasta Koibla	1995–1997	10/04/1995. Head of the transitional government until parliamentary elections in 1997.
Nassour Ouaïdou	1997–	Since 20/05/97; appointed by the President with a mandate to form a unity government after parliamentary elections in 1997.

3. Bibliography

3.1 Official Sources (Chronological Order)

'Constitution du 31 mars 1959' *Journal Officiel AEF du 1 mai 1959*, 832.

'Loi constitutionelle du 28 novembre 1960'. *Journal Officiel du 15 decembre 1960*, 571.

'Constitution du 16 avril 1962'. *Journal Officiel du 23 mai 1962*, 341.

Ordonnance 15/PG INT du 20 mai 1969 (Electoral Law for Presidential Elections).

Charte Fondamentale du 17 septembre 1977.

Acte Fondamental du 29 septembre 1982.

'Accord sur la réconciliation nationale du 11 novembre 1985'. *Afrique contemporaine*, 138 (1986/2): 62–65.

Constitution du Tchad du 10 décembre 1989.

'Charte Nationale du Tchad du 28 février 1991'. *Afrique contemporaine*, 160 (1991/4): 61–65.

Conférence Nationale Souveraine (1993). *Charte de la Transition de la République du Tchad du 5 avril 1993,* N'Djaména.

'Ordonnance No. 015/PR/91 relative a la création, au fonctionnement et a la dissolution des partis politiques'. *ATP-Bulletin*, 2.678.

Republique du Tchad (1994). *Loi No./PR/94 fixant les règles générales applicables au référendum et aux élections présidentielles, législatives, sénatoriales et locales*.

Republique du Tchad (1996). 'La Constitution du 14 avril 1996'. *Afrique Contemporaine*, 182 (1997/2): 64–88.

3.2. Books, Articles and Electoral Reports

Andriamirado, S. (1992). 'Tchad. L'effrayant bilan d'Hissein Habré.'. *Jeune Afrique*, 1639: 46–49.

Buijtenhuijs, R. (1993). *La conference nationale souveraine du Tchad: un essai d'histoire immediate*. Paris: Karthala.

— (1994). 'Les partis politiques africains ont-ils des projets de société?'. *Politique africaine*, 56: 119–135.

— (1995). 'La situation dans le Sud du Tchad'. *Afrique contemporaine*, 175: 21–30.

— (1996). '"On nous a vole nos voix!" Quelle democratie pour le Tchad?'. *Politique africaine*, 63: 130–135.

— (1996). '"Le Tchad est inclassable". Le referendum constitutionnel du 31 mars 1996'. *Politique Africaine*, 62: 117–123.

Bujumbura Conference (1993). *Democratization in Africa: The Role of the Military*. New York: African American Institute.

Dadi, A. (1987). *Tchad: l'État retrouvé*. Paris: l'Harmattan.

Dadnadji, D. *et al.* (1994). *La democratisation par le haut: de la conference nationale souveraine à la transition*. N'Djaména: CEFOD.

Decalo, S. (1987). *Historical Dictionary of Chad* (2nd edn.). Metuchen, NJ: Scarecrow Press.

Foltz, W. J. (1995). 'Reconstructing the State of Chad', in W. Zartman (ed.), *Collapsed States. The Desintegration and Restoration of Legitimate Authority*. Boulder, Col.: Lynne Rienner, 15–31.

Joffe, G. (1990). 'Turmoil in Chad'. *Current History*, 89/546: 157–160.

Kelley, M. P. (1986). *A State in Dissarray. Conditions of Chad's Survival*. Boulder, Col.: Westview Press.

Khayar, I. H. (1984). *Tchad. Regards sur les élites ouaddaïennes*. Paris: Èditions du Centre National de la Recherche Scientifique.

Killham, T. (1995). 'The unsettled state'. *Africa Report*, 40/5-6: 38–41.

Kotoko, A. (1989). *Le destin de Hamai ou le long chemin vers l'indépendence du Tchad*. Paris: l'Harmattan.

Lanne, B. (1982). *Tchad-Libye. La querelle des frontières*. Paris: Karthala.

— (1987). 'Quinze ans d'ouvrages politiques sur le Tchad'. *Afrique Contemporaine*, 144: 37–47.

Le Cornec, J. (1963). *Histoire politique du Tchad de 1900 à 1962*. Paris: Bibliothèque constitutionelle et de science poltique.

Limane, A. T. (1996). *L'evolution constitutionelle du Tchad: de l'indépendance à nos jours*. Paris: Aresae & PMCT.

Mattes, H.-P. (1993). 'Tschad', in D. Nohlen and F. Nuscheler (eds.), *Handbuch der Dritten Welt, Vol.4., (3rd edn.)*. Bonn: Dietz, 488–502.

Miles, W. F. S. (1995). 'Tragic tradeoffs: democracy and security in Chad'. *The Journal of Modern African Studies*, 33/3: 53–65.

Mouvement patriotique du Salut (1992). *Le Tchad dépuis le 1er decembre 1990*. N'Djamena: Mouvement patriotique du Salut.

Moyrand, A. (1990). *La normalisation constitutionelle au Tchad*. Bordeaux: CEAN.

N'Gangbet, M. (1984). *Peut-on encore sauver le Tchad?*, Paris: Éditions Karthala.

N'Gansop, G. J. (1986). *Tchad. Vingt ans de crise*. Paris: l'Harmattan.

Ngothé Gatta, G. (1985). *Tchad: Guerre civile et desagregation de l'Etat*. Paris: Présence Africaine.

Nolutshungu, S. C. (1996). *Limits of Anarchy; Intervention and State Formation in Chad*. Charlottsville, Virg.: University Press of Virginia.

Thompson, V., and Adloff, R. (1981). *Conflict in Chad*. Berkeley, Calif.: University of California Press.

Triaud, J. L. (1992). 'Au Tchad, la démocratie introuvable'. *Le Monde Diplomatique*, February

Yokabdjim, M. (1995). 'Les vicissitudes de la transition tchadienne'. *Revue juridique et politique (Le Vesinet)*, 49/11–12: 304–321.

Ziemer, K. (1978). 'Tschad', in D. Sternberger, B. Vogel, D. Nohlen and K. Landfried (eds.), *Die Wahl der Parlamente und anderer Staatsorgane, Band II: Politische Organisation und Repräsentation in Afrika,* by Franz Nuscheler, Klaus Ziemer *et al.,* Berlin/ New York: Walter de Gruyter, 2213–2251.

COMOROS

by Bernhard Thibaut

1. Introduction

1.1 Historical Overview

From independence until the early 1990s elections did not play any significant role in the political process of the Comoros. Since then some efforts have been made to establish a democratic regime, but in the context of a political structure marked by conflicts between different traditional clans the effectiveness of formal constitutional rules remains limited and notorious political instability (18 coups or attempted coups since independence) has not been overcome yet. Recent developments indicate once again strong tendencies towards an openly authoritarian regime.

Geographically the Comoros are a group of four islands situated between the African continent and Madagascar: Grande Comore (location of the capital: Moroni), Anjouan, Mohéli and Mayotte. In political terms the independent state of the Comores (official name: Federal Islamic Republic of the Comoros) consists only of the former three islands whereas Mayotte remains *de facto* in the status of an overseas department of France. In recent years separatist tendencies have gained strength on Anjouan and, to a lesser extent, on Mohéli.

Between 1887 and 1909 the Comoros were incorporated step by step into the French colonial regime. Until 1947 the archipelago was administrated by the colonial authorities of Madagascar and then became a French overseas territory of its own. In 1961 the Comoros were granted the right of self administration and in 1968 internal autonomy was achieved.

In the referendum of 1974 an overwhelming majority voted for full independence on Grand Comore, Mohéli and Anjouan. Mayotte with its mainly Christian population opted to stay with France. Building on the result of this referendum, which was not immediately accepted by France, the head of the regional government, Ahmed Abdallah, proclaimed the independent Republic of the Comoros on 7 June 1975. The

Regional Assembly, that had been elected in 1972 renamed itself into Federal Assembly and elected Abdallah for President. One month later Abdallah was ousted in a coup d'état performed by a mercenary force. The newly built 'National Revolutionary Council' appointed Ali Soilih as Head of State and Government in early 1976. The government announced that it would reorganize the state, dismantle the traditional feudal structure of the society and roll back remaining elements of French influence in the Comoros. In practice, none of these goals was achieved.

In May 1978, the Soilih regime was overthrown in a coup d'état, that was again performed by a mercenary force, and Ahmed Abdallah was brought back into power. A constitution was drafted and adopted in a referendum on 1 October 1978. It established the 'Federal Islamic Republic of the Comoros' (*Republique fédérale islamique des Comores)*. However, the inherited centralism remained an important feature of the political structure as well of the development policies pursued by the government which officially propagated a kind of Islamic socialism.

In institutional terms the Constitution of 1978 provided for a presidential system of government with a one-chamber Parliament at the federal level. The presidential elections held in 1978 and 1984 and the parliamentary elections held in 1982 and 1987 were non-competitive in nature, since Abdallah's *Union Comorienne pour le Progrès* (UCP, or Udzima) was the only party allowed to present candidates. As the Constitution of 1978 had established a limit of two consecutive presidential terms a manipulated referendum was held on 5 November 1989 in order to change that article and to allow Abdallah another re-election. In the context of internal power conflicts between the President, the presidential guard (a mercenary force under the leadership of the notorious French Bob Denard) and the army, Abdallah was assassinated three weeks later by the presidential guard. The rebels did not succeed, however, in their effort to install a new regime, and stepped back under external pressure from France and South Africa. The President of the Supreme Court, Said Mohamed Djohar, was appointed as interim President; he subsequently announced the end of the single-party regime and allowed the exiled opposition to return to the country.

The transition to a multi-party regime turned out to be a difficult process marked by serious political instability. Demands of the opposition forces to form a transitional government of national unity and to establish a round table in order to work out a new constitution before the holding of elections were not met by Djohar. The first multi-party presidential elections, which were held on 18 February 1990 had to be nullified on the same day because of severe irregularities. The polls were repeated on 4 March and Djohar was elected in the second round on 11 March 1990. Conflicts over the conditions of the establishment of a new constitutional order remained intense until a National Constitutional Conference could be set up at the beginning of 1992 with the participation of more than 20 political parties and a number of non-governmental organizations.

The new constitution that was approved in a referendum on 7 June 1992 established a semi-presidential system of government based on the model of the Fifth French Republic. The parliamentary elections that were held on 22 and 29 November 1992 were considered free and fair although there were some irregularities and the polls had to be repeated in five constituencies. The highly fragmented parliamentary party system that emerged from the elections, reflecting mainly clan or family based divisions and to some extent regional cleavages between the islands, made it extremely difficult to build a stable and cohesive government. Djohar dissolved the Federal Assembly on 18 June 1993, and new elections were held on 12 and 20 December 1993. They were marked by organizational irregularities and the second round was boycotted by most of the opposition parties. The concentration of the parliamentary party system with Djohar's newly formed party *Rassemblement pour la Démocratie et le Renouveau* (RDR) obtaining an absolute majority of the seats thus did not reflect the political realities of the country.

On 28 September 1995 once again a mercenary force under the leadership of Bob Denard tried to profit from the unstable political conditions on the Comoros. Although military intervention by France prevented the collapse of the constitutional order Djohar was *de facto* deprived of power and sent to exile in Réunion. The presidential elections in March 1996 were won in the second round by Mohamed Taki Abdoulkarim, who had been defeated by Djohar in 1990.

A representative of traditionalist forces and clan interests located in Moroni, Taki began to restructure the political order in the direction of Islamic authoritarianism soon after his inauguration. He dissolved the Federal Assembly on 12 April 1996 and called for a reform of the constitution, which was drafted by a committee boycotted by the opposition parties. The reform, adopted in a referendum on 20 October 1996, restricted the admission of parties to those obtaining at least two seats on each island in the parliamentary elections and enhanced the power of the President in several respects (government formation, appointment of governors, abolition of restrictions to re-election, among others).

Previously, the parties that had supported Taki in the presidential race had joined to build the *Rassemblement National pour le Développement* (RND). The parliamentary elections of December 1996 were again boycotted by nearly all opposition parties (most importantly by the modernist *Forum pour le Redressement National*—FRN of Abbas Djoussouf, who had been defeated in the presidential elections) and marked by violent incidents. As a reaction to the authoritarian and exclusionary politics of Taki, separatist tendencies and demands for reintegration into France gained strength in Anjouan and Mohéli during 1996 and 1997.

1.2 Evolution of Electoral Provisions

Universal suffrage for Comorians older than 21 years was introduced under colonial rule through the *Loi Cadre* of 1956, which was applied for the first time in the elections for the Territorial Assembly *(Assemblée Territoriale)* in 1957. At that time the number of registered voters amounted to 42.9% of the population, raising to 48.5% in the elections to the French National Assembly in 1973.

After independence electoral provisions were laid down in the Constitution of 1978 (promulgated on 5 October, amended by Law No. 82.018 of 5 November 1982 and Law No. 84.14 of 31 December 1984), the Constitution of 1992 (amended in 1996) and an electoral law.

The Constitution of 1978 lowered the minimum age for active suffrage to 18 years and provided for the direct election of the President and the 42 members of the Federal Assembly. The President was to be elected for a six-year period with one consecutive re-election being allowed by absolute majority. *De facto*, in 1978 and 1984 only one candidate was presented to the electorate. Candidates for the presidency had to be at least 40 years old and present signatures of at least five elected officials from each island.

The members of the Federal Assembly were to be elected every five years by absolute majority in single-member districts. Candidates had to be at least 21 years old. The constitution provided that the number of parties allowed to present candidates be fixed by a federal law. From 1982 onwards only the ruling Udzima was allowed to nominate party candidates for the parliamentary elections. In 1987 individual candidates were allowed to compete against the official candidates, but only the 20 constituencies of Grand Comore were contested. The electoral districts were established by federal law, and there had to be at least five in each island. Subject to the foregoing reservation, each district had to contain between 6,000 and 11,000 inhabitants.

In 1989 the number of consecutive re-elections of the President allowed was raised to two through a constitutional referendum. That provision was not applied due to the regime change that followed the assassination of President Abdallah. The Constitution of 1992 went back to the original restriction (one re-election) until the respective provision was abolished in 1996. Before the parliamentary elections of 1996 the number of seats in the Federal Assembly was raised to 43.

The Constitution of 1992 introduced a Senate with 15 members (five from each island) to be elected indirectly by an electoral college for a term of six years. This institution was abolished by the constitutional reform of 1996.

1.3 Current Electoral Provisions

Sources: Constitution of 1992 (electoral law not available).

Suffrage: The principles of universal, equal, direct and secret suffrage are applied. All Comorian citizens with full possession of civil and political rights and a minimum age of 18 years have the right to vote.

Elected national institutions: President of the Republic elected for a term of five years (no restrictions to re-election). 43 members of the Federal Assembly for a term of four years. By-elections are held if vacancies arise.

Nomination of candidates
- *presidential elections*: Candidates must be Comorian citizens with full possession of their civil and political rights and be at least 40 years old. Independent candidacy is allowed.
- *parliamentary elections*: Candidates must be Comorian citizens with full possession of their civil and political rights, be at least 21 years old and be able to read Arabic and French. Each candidate must make a monetary deposit which is reimbursed only to those who obtain at least 10% of the votes in their constituency. The status of a Member of Parliament is incompatible with any other public office.

Electoral system
- *presidential elections*: Absolute majority system. If no candidate obtains the required majority in the first round, a second round takes place between the two candidates who obtained most votes in the first round.
- *parliamentary elections*: Absolute majority system in 43 single-member constituencies. If no candidate obtains an absolute majority in the first round, a second round takes place between the two candidates who obtained most votes in the first round.

1.4 Comment on the Electoral Statistics

Statistical electoral data on the Comoros are difficult to obtain outside the country. Several efforts to establish communication with electoral authorities and to gain access to officially released data sets did not bring about any results. The issue of the establishment of an independent Electoral Commission has been since 1993 one of the main points of conflict between the groups controlling the government and the opposition. For instance, in the chaotic parliamentary elections of 1996 the central administrative building was burned down and ballot boxes as well as other electoral materials were destroyed. Due to these difficulties most of the data presented in the following tables stem from unofficial sources. Results of the 1972 elections were taken from Ziemer (1978). Results of the referendum of 1974 were taken from *Journal Officiel des Comores*, results of the referendum of 1978 from *Africa Research Bulletin*. With regard to the referendums of 1989 and 1996 the results reported below stem from *Marchés Tropicaux*. Less detailed data for the referendum of 1989 which were, however, inconsistent with these were found in the national newspaper *Al-Watwan*. This newspaper was used as a source for the data on the presidential elections of 1990 and the parliamentary elections of 1992 (first round). Results of presidential elections of 1996 were taken from *Marchés Tropicaux*.

2. Tables

2.1 Dates of National Elections, Referendums and Coups d'Etat

Year	Presidential elections	Parliamentary elections	Elections for Constitutional Assembly	Referendums	Coups d'état
1972		03/12[a]			
1974				22/12	
1975					03/08
1978	22/10			01/10	13/05
1982		xx/03			
1984	30/09				
1987		22/03			
1989				05/11	26/11
1990	18/02[b] 04/03 (1st) 11/03 (2nd)				
1992		22/11 (1st) 29/11 (2nd)		07/06	
1993		12/12 (1st) 20/12 (2nd)			
1995					29/09[c]
1996	06/03 (1st) 16/03 (2nd)	01/12 (1st) 08/12 (2nd)		20/10	

[a] Elections to the Chamber of Representatives of the Comore Islands (before independence).
[b] Nullified because of proven manipulations.
[c] Through a military intervention by France on 5 October 1995 the constitutional order was re-established.

2.2 Electoral Body 1972–1996

Year	Type of election[a]	Population[b]	Registered voters		Votes cast		
			Total number	% pop.	Total number	% reg. voters	% pop.
1972	Pa	279,000	129,096	46.3	105,129	81.4	37.7
1974	Ref	292,000	173,179	59.3	161,379	93.2	55.3
1978	Ref	292,000	—	—	187,124	—	—
1978	Pr	316,000	—	—	195,290	98.8	—
1987	Pa	425,000	340,000[c]	80.0	—	65.0[c]	—
1989	Ref	458,000	265,222	57.9	243,770	92.2	53.2
1990	Pr (1st)	475,000	310,925	65.5	198,370	63.7	41.8
1990	Pr (2nd)	475,000	315,391	66.4	190,074	60.2	40.0
1992	Ref	510,000	213,000[c]	41.8	—	63.5	—
1992	Pa (1st)	446,817	214,374	48.0	148,536	69.3	33.2
1992	Pa (2nd)	446,817	—	—	—	—	—
1993	Pa	485,000	—	—	—	—	—
1996	Pr	528,000[d]	—	—	—	—	—
1996	Pa	528,000[d]	—	—	—	—	—

[a] Pa = Parliament; Pr = President; Ref = Referendum
[b] UN estimations as reported by Penn World Tables except for 1992 (1991 census) and 1996.
[c] Estimation.
[d] Estimation for 1997; source: CIA World Fact Book.

2.3 Abbreviations

FDC	Front Démocratique Comorien
FDP	—
FNJ	Front National pour la Justice
FNUC	Front National pour la Unification des Comores
FNUK	Front National Uni des Komores
FPC	Front Populaire Comorien
FRN	Forum pour le Redressement National
MDP	Mouvement pour la Démocratie et le Progrès
MDP/NGDC	Mouvement Démocratique Populaire
PASOCO	Parti Socialiste des Comores
PCDP/Djamnazi	Parti Comorien pour la Démocratie et le Progrès
PCN	—
PDPC/Marouf	—
PEC	Parti de l'Entente Comorienne
PSDC	Parti Social Démocrate des Comores
PSN	—
PUIC	Parti pour l'Indépendance et l'Unité des Comores

RACHADE	Rassemblement pour le Changement et la Démocratie
RDDC	—
RDPC	Rassemblement Démocratique du Peuple Comorien
RDR	Rassemblement pour la Démocratie et le Renouveau
RND	Rassemblement National pour le Développement
SNDC	—
UCP	Union Comorienne pour le Progrès (= Udzima)
UDC	Union Démocratique Comorienne
UDD	Union des Démocrats pour le Développement
UNDC	Union Nationale pour la Démocratie aux Comores
URDC	Union pour une République Démocratique aux Comores

2.4 Electoral Participation of Parties and Alliances 1972–1996

Party / Alliance	Years	Elections contested	
		Presidential	Parliamentary
Mouvement Mahonais	1972	0	1
PASOCO	1972, 1992	0	2
RDPC – UDC	1972	0	1
UMMA	1972	0	1
Udzima	1987, 1993, 1996	1	2
Chuma	1990, 1992, 1993, 1996	2	2
RDR	1990, 1993	1	1
UNDC	1990, 1993, 1996	2	1
FDC	1992	0	1
FDP	1992	0	1
FNJ	1992, 1996	0	2
FPC	1992, 1993[a]	0	2
Maesha Bora	1992	0	1
MDP/NGDC	1992, 1993	0	2
Mourad	1992	0	1
Mwangaza/Shuma	1992	0	1
Nguzo	1992	0	1
PCDP/Djamnazi	1992, 1993	0	2
PCN	1992	0	1
PDPC/Marouf	1992	0	1
PSN	1992	0	1
Rachad	1992	0	1
RDDC	1992	0	1
SNDC	1992	0	1
Toimaya	1992	0	1
Twamaani	1992	0	1
UDD	1992	0	1
Uwezo	1992, 1993[a]	0	2

Party / Alliance	Years	Elections contested	
		Presidential	Parliamentary
Rashad-RTD	1993	0	1
FRN	1996	1	0
RND	1996	0	1

[a] Alliance with RTD.

2.5 *Referendums*

Year	1974[a]		1978	
	Total number	%	Total number	%
Registered voters	173,179	–	—	–
Votes cast	161,379	93.2	187,124	—
Invalid votes	101	0.1	—	—
Valid votes	161,278	93.1	—	—
Yes	153,117	95.0	—	99.3
No	8101	5.0	—	—

[a] The inhabitants of Mayotte voted with a majority of 8,031 to 4,299 votes against independence; there were some irregularities, in three electoral offices the results were nullified.

Year	1989[a]		1992[b]	
	Total number	%	Total number	%
Registered voters	265,222	–	213,000[c]	–
Votes cast	—	94.9	—	63.5
Invalid votes	—	—	—	—
Valid votes	—	—	—	—
Yes	240,281	92.5	—	74.3
No	19,500	7.5	—	23.5

[a] Approve of constitutional reforms (prolongation of the maximum of consecutive presidential terms from two to three).
[b] Approve of a new constitution.

Year	1996[a]	
	Total number	%
Registered voters	—	–
Votes cast	—	64.0
Invalid votes	—	—
Valid votes	—	—
Yes	—	85.0
No	—	15.0

[a] Reform of the constitution, among others: restriction of the number of parties to those that obtain at least two seats in the Federal Assembly; abolition of restrictions to re-election of the President; abolition of the Senate and of the direct election of Governors.

2.6 Elections for Constitutional Assembly

Elections for Constitutional Assembly have not been held.

2.7 Parliamentary Elections 1972–1996

Year	1972[a]		1987	
	Total number	%	Total number	%
Registered voters	129,096	–	340,000[b]	–
Votes cast	105,129	81.5	—	65.0
Invalid votes	267	0.3	—	—
Valid votes	104,862	99.7	—	—
Udzima	–	–	—	—
RDPC-UDC	79,946	76.2	–	–
UMMA	13,021	12.4	–	–
PASOCO	2,352	2.2	–	–
Mouvement Mahonais	9,543	9.1	–	–

[a] Elections for the Territorial Assembly of the Comoros, including Mayotte.

Year	1992[a]	
	Total number	%[a]
Registered voters	214,374	–
Votes cast	148,536	69.3
Invalid votes	2,717[b]	1.8
Valid votes	145,819[c]	98.2
MDP/NGDC	15,194	10.4
UDD	14,961	10.3
Rachad	11,810	8.1
FDC	11,615	8.0
Maesha Bora	9,730	6.7
PCDP/Djamnazi	9,317	6.4
Chuma	9,030	6.2
Mwangaza/Shuma	7,812	5.4
Uwezo	7,674	5.3
FNJ	4,982	3.4
Mourad	4,492	3.1
Nguzo	4,009	2.7
FPC	3,550	2.4
PSN	3,394	2.3
SNDC	3,000	2.1
PDPC/Marouf	2,646	1.8
Twamaani	1,497	1.0
RDDC	1,345	0.9

Year	1992[a]	
	Total number	%[a]
Toimaya	1,239	0.8
FDP	386	0.3
PASOCO	368	0.3
PCN	110	0.1
Independents	13,892	9.5
Others	3,688	2.5

[a] First round. In this round in four of the 42 constituencies a member of the Federal Assembly was elected. In four constituencies the elections were nullified due to irregularities. Results of the second round in the remaining 34 constituencies could not be made available.
[b] The given number corresponds to the subtraction of valid votes *(voix exprimés)* from votes cast.
[c] Official figure. It does not correspond to the sum of the party votes that were calculated on the basis of the constituency results. The difference may result from incomplete reports on constituency results.

For the elections of 1993 and 1996 detailed data are not available.

2.8 Composition of Parliament 1972–1996

Year	1972[a]		1987		1992		1993	
	Seats	%	Seats	%	Seats	%	Seats	%
	39	100	42	100	42	100	42	100
RPDC-UDC	34	87.2	–	–	–	–	–	–
Mouv. Mahorais	5	12.8	–	–	–	–	–	–
Udzima	–	–	42	100	–	–	2	4.8
UDD	–	–	–	–	7	16.7	–	–
Chuma	–	–	–	–	3	7.1	1	2.4
MDP	–	–	–	–	3	7.1	–	–
Mayesha Bora	–	–	–	–	3	7.1	–	–
PCDP	–	–	–	–	3	7.1	–	–
FPC-RTD	–	–	–	–	2[b]	4.8	2	4.8
RDR	–	–	–	–	–	–	28	66.7
UNDC	–	–	–	–	–	–	4	9.5
MDP-NGDC	–	–	–	–	–	–	2	4.8
PSDP-Djamnazi	–	–	–	–	–	–	1	2.4
RASHAD-RTD	–	–	–	–	–	–	1	2.4
UWEZO-RTD	–	–	–	–	–	–	1	2.4
Independents	–	–	–	–	7	16.7	–	–
Others	–	–	–	–	14	33.3	–	–

[a] In 1975 the Regional Assembly renamed itself Federal Assembly and declared itself to be the Parliament of the Federal Republic of the Comoros.
[b] FPC only.

Year	1996	
	Seats	%
	43	100
RND	39	90.7
FNJ	3	7.0
Independents	1	2.3

2.9 Presidential Elections 1978–1996

For the elections of 1978 and 1984 detailed data are not available. On both occasions Ahmed Abdallah Abderamane was the only candidate and according to the official result elected with 99.6% and 98.4% of the valid votes. Data on voter participation are reported in table 2.2.

1990 (first round)	Total number	%
Registered voters	310,925	–
Votes cast	198,370	63.7
Invalid votes	2,753	1.4
Valid votes	194,360	97.9
Mohamed Taki Abdoulkarim (UNDC)	47,329	24.4
Said Mohamed Djohar (RDR)	44,845	23.1
Said Ali Kemal Eddine (Chuma)	26,656	13.7
Abbas Djoussouf	26,379	13.6
Moustoifa Said Cheikh	17,739	9.1
Ali Mroudjaé	8,867	4.6
Mohamed Hassanali	8,867	4.6
Mohamed Ali Mbalia	4,989	2.6

1990 (second round)	Total number	%
Registered voters	315,391	–
Votes cast	190,074	60.2
Invalid votes	2,652	1.4
Valid votes	187,442[a]	98.6
Said Mohamed Djohar (MM)	103,000	55.1
Mohamed Taki (Independent)	84,178	44.9

[a] Official figure which does not correspond to the sum of the votes given for the candidates.

1996 (first round)	Total number	%
Registered voters	—	–
Votes cast	—	64.0
Invalid votes	—	—
Valid votes	—	—
Mohamed Taki Abdoulkarim (UNDC)	38,900	21.3
Abbas Djoussouf (FRN)	28,727	15.7
Omar Tamou (Udzima)	—	13.3
Said Ali Kemal (Chuma)	—	8.7
M. Halifa Houmadi	—	2.3
Others[a]	—	38.7

[a] Ten more candidates.

1996 (second round)	Total number	%
Registered voters	—	–
Votes cast	—	62.0
Invalid votes	—	—
Valid votes	—	—
Mohamed Taki Abdoulkarim	—	64.3
Abbas Djoussouf	—	35.7

2.10 List of Power Holders 1975–1998

Head of State	Years	Remarks
Ahmed Abdallah Abderamane	1975	Elected by the Federal Assembly on 07/07/1975, removed by coup d'état on 03/08/1975.
Said Mohammed Djaffar	1975–1976	Interim.
Ali Soilih	1976–1978	In office since 03/01/1976.
Ahmed Abdallah Abderamane, Mohamed Ahmed	1978	Co-presidency within the military-political council that took power in the coup of 13/05/1978; Mohamed Ahmed left the presidency to Abdallah after the referendum of 01/10/1978.
Ahmed Abdallah Abderamane	1978–1989	Officially inaugurated on 25/10/1978; he was elected twice for six-year terms under the single-party regime introduced by the constitution of 1978 and planned to allow himself another term with the constitutional referendum of 1989; assassinated on 26/11/1989.

Head of State	Years	Remarks
Said Mohamed Djohar	1989–1990	Interim President since 27/11/1989.
Said Mohamed Djohar	1990–1996	Constitutionally elected President, inaugurated on 20/03/1990.
Mohamed Taki Abdulkarim	1996–	Constitutionally elected President, inaugurated on 27/03/1996.

Head of Government	Years	Remarks
	1978–1992	Under the Constitution of 1978 the Prime Minister was appointed and replaced without any parliamentary intervention by the elected President. The office was abolished in 1985.
Mohamed Taki Abdulkarim	1992	Coordinator of the government of national unity; appointed on 06/01/1992, dismissed on 03/07/1992.
M'Chagama	1992	Appointed on 09/07/1992, retreated on 06/11/1992 in order to present himself as candidate in the parliamentary elections.
Halidi Abderamane Ibrahim	1993	Appointed on 01/01/1993, retreated after parliamentary vote of no confidence on 09/05/1993.
Ali Mohamed	1993	Appointed on 25/05/1993.
Ahmed Ben Cheikh	1993	Appointed on 19/06/1993 as coordinator of a caretaker government.
Abdou Madi	1994	Appointed on 02/01/1994, dismissed on 13/10/1994.
Halifa Houmadi	1994–1995	Appointed on 13/10/1994, resigned on 28/04/1995.
Caabi El Yachroutu	1995–1996	Appointed on 28/04/1995.
Tadjidine Ben Said Massonde	1996	Appointed on 27/03/1996; resigned on 27/12/1996.
Ahmed Abdou	1996–	Appointed on 27/12/1996.

3. Bibliography

Chagnoux, H. (1980). *Les Comores*. Paris: Presses universitaires de France.

Charpantier, J. (1984). 'Le regime d'Ali Soilih. Moroni 1975–1978'. *Le Mois en Afrique,* 19/2: 77–87.

Guebourg, J.-L. (1995). *Espace et pouvoirs en Grande Comore.* Paris: L'Harmattan.

Djabir, Abdou (1993). *Les Comores, un Etat en construction*. Paris: L'Harmattan.

Fasquel, J. (1991): *Mayotte, les Comores et la France*. Paris: L'Harmattan.

Lunel, P. (1992). *Bob Denard: le roi de fortune*. Paris: Ed. 1.

Newitt, M. (1984). *The Comoro Islands. Struggle against Dependency in the Indian Ocean*. Boulder, Col.: Westview Press.

Perri, P. (1994). *Comores: les nouveaus mercenaires*. Paris: L'Harmattan.

Jeske, J. (1986). *Die Komoren*. Hamburg: Institut für Afrika-Kunde.

Negrin, J.-P. (1980). 'Le federalisme à la comorienne'. *Annuaire des Pays d l'Ocean Indien,* 7: 131–144.

Ottenheimer, M., and Ottenheimer, H. (eds.) (1994). *Historical Dictionary of the Comoro Islands*. Metuchen, NJ: Scarecrow Press.

Verin, E. N. (1988). *Les Comores dans la tourmente: vie politique de l'archipel de 1976 à 1978*. Paris: Institut des langues et civilisations orientales/ l'Aiglon.

Westenberger, C. (1995). *Komoren*. Kronshagen: Stein.

Mukonoweshuro, E. G. (1990). 'The Politics of Squalor and Dependency in the Comoro Islands'. *African Affairs,* 89/357: 555–577.

CONGO (BRAZZAVILLE)

by Helga Fleischhacker*

1. Introduction

1.1 Historical Overview

Congo's first, if rather short-lived, multi-party experience dates back to the pre-independence period, when the country achieved autonomous status within the *Communauté Française*. The political domination of only one party was enforced rapidly after independence in 1960 and institutionalized in 1963, when the Congo established a socialist, in 1969 a Marxist–Leninist single-party state which would endure for 21 years. Within this institutional framework, however, the political process had been marked by sharp factional conflict. In 1990, on the eve of economic and political collapse a National Conference patterned on the Benin model paved the way for competitive elections. The immediate fruits of this foray into multi-party democracy however, were an accelerated state disintegration and armed conflict. After a protracted period of turmoil, constitutional crisis and civil war, this democratic experiment ended as the country's former autocratic President, Denis Sassou Nguesso, seized military control in October 1997.

Upon the achievement of Congolese independence on 15 August 1960, Abbé Fulbert Youlou was made the new Republic's first President. Fulbert Youlou, who had arisen to prominence within the *Communauté Française* as the first elected Prime Minister of the autonomous Middle Congo, had been the leading political figure during the transition to independence. Upon statehood, he moved to establish a strongly centralized presidential system. Political centralization was, however, not easily imposed over Congo's diverse political forces which, representing the country's ethnic and geographical divisions, now contended for power. While the M'Bochi of the North and their allies coalesced in the *Mouvement Socialiste Africain* (MSA), the southern ethnic Congo groupings (the Bakongo, Basundi and Bavili) affiliated with Youlou's

* The author would like to thank Apolinaire Ngolongolo, Journalist, for the helpful contribution to the collection of data in this chapter.

governing *Union Démocratique de Défense des Intérêts Africains* (UDDIA), which moved increasingly to purge the state administration of oppositional elements, and to eliminate the representation of minority interests within the political process. Growing disapproval reached its peak with strikes and demonstrations organized by the trade unions, the '*Trois Glorieuses*' (13–15 August 1963) that ended Abbé Fulbert Youlou's reign by army intervention.

Alphonse Massamba-Débat followed as President. Initially installed by the military, he was subsequently elected for a five-year term. Under his presidency the political system in 1964 was extensively reorganized on a one-party basis. In this bid to reintegrate all political forces, the existing parties were incorporated into the *Mouvement National de la Révolution* (MNR). The creation of a single party did not signal the end of divisions within the Republic's ruling circles, however. On 4 August 1968 a military coup led by Marien Ngouabi put an end to Massamba-Débat's presidency, while bringing to power the MNR's (northern) Marxist–Leninist wing. The consolidation of this group's power was signaled in late 1969 by the drawing up of a new constitution, and the founding of the elitist avant-garde party *Parti Congolais du Travail* (PCT). Through the new constitution, the Congo was declared a People's Republic on 31 December 1969, with the PCT declared as supreme authority of the land. Upon the assassination of President Ngouabi on 18 March 1977, the PCT—closely tied to the military elites (from the 1968 coup on, all Presidents up to 1990 held high army rank)—transferred the head of state to Jacques-Joachim Yhombi-Opango, who in 1979 was forced to resign due to rising domestic tensions. He was replaced by Denis Sassou Nguesso, who would remain Congo's dominant political figure until the transition to multi-party democracy in 1991.

As deteriorating oil prices drove the government to bankruptcy and undermined the regime's legitimacy at the onset of the 1990s, a wave of strikes and mounting political protest ensued; in response, Sassou Nguesso announced the introduction of a multi-party system and the organization of a National Conference involving 67 parties and 134 associations. This convened in February 1991 and proved successful in wringing a wide range of concessions from the regime. Although President Sassou Nguesso remained formally in office, executive power was effectively transferred to an *interim* Prime Minister, elected by the National Conference, and a transitional parliamentary council, the *Conseil Superieur de la République*. This body was empowered to finish the writing of the new constitution, which was later approved by a wide margin in a referendum held on 15 March 1992.

The new constitution installed a modified presidential system, in which the formation of a government rested upon the consensus of a parliamentary majority. The democratic reform process culminated in the presidential and parliamentary elections of 1992, in which Pascal Lissouba of the *Union Panafricaine pour la Démocratie Sociale* (UPADS) was elected President. A government was formed, resting upon a coalition between UPADS and PCT, while the third political force, the *Mouvement Congolais pour la Démocratie et le Développement Intégral* (MCDDI) of Bernard Kolélas initiated the formation of an oppositional coalition under the banner of *Union pour le Renouveau Démocratique* (URD). Despite organizational problems and postponements, the transitional process had effected an apparently peaceful transfer of power.

But almost immediately after the new government was appointed, its new institutions were deadlocked by conflicting elite interests. A period of political disintegration ensued, punctuated by cyclical outbreaks of (increasingly armed) violence that would ultimately lead to civil war. The party system was undermined by a progressive splintering, with the emergence of approximately 140 registered political parties. These diverse factions tended, however, to operate within an essentially tripolar system, marked by shifting coalitions between the three most important political figures and their movements: Bernard Kolélas (MCDDI) and his URD, Pascal Lissouba (UPADS) and his *Mouvance Présidentielle*, and Denis Sassou Nguesso (PCT) and the *Forces Démocratiques Unies* (FDU). For all the considerable fluctuation of alliances especially on the periphery of this tripolar system, the three movements at its core remained fundamentally opposed to one another, each strategically aiming for ultimate domination. In pursuit of this goal, party elites played upon existing ethno-regional divisions as a means of enhancing their powers of political mobilization. Thus the PCT and MCDDI revived to a certain degree the historical north (M'Bochi) - south (Congo-groups) cleavage, whereas UPADS relied upon strongholds in three regions called the Nibolek.

Within weeks after the new government was installed, the PCT-UPADS coalition was already in tatters, brought to breaking point by dispute over the allocation of Cabinet portfolios. The PCT subsequently formed an anti-government coalition with Kolélas' URD, which insisted upon its own choice for Prime Minister. In response, the President dissolved the National Assembly and called for new elections for December 1992. The opposition thereupon launched a campaign of 'civil disobedience', which soon escalated into wide-scale civil unrest. The military intervened, installing a compromise candidate as Prime Minister and forcing the major parties to rebuild a 'national unity' government. Parliamentary elections were held on 2 May and 3 June 1993. After the first round had brought a majority for the President's coalition, the opposition boycotted the second round, charging election fraud. In a climate of growing violence and turmoil the main political parties formed their own militias, introducing a growing dynamic of armed struggle into an already acute political crisis. International mediators had to be brought in to broker a truce and work out an agreement by all parties to hold a second round of parliamentary elections. The basis for a peaceful solution was subsequently laid by the selective holding of new elections, intended as a corrective to the flawed 1993 elections, and a peace pact signed by the leaders of the most important political parties on 24 December 1995, which included a renunciation of violence, the dissolution of party militias and their partial incorporation into the armed forces. A new round of civil war broke out in June 1997, however, as presidential forces tried to disarm PCT militias in anticipation of presidential elections scheduled for July and August. Peace talks convened in Libreville in September failed to halt the fighting, and after four months of civil war, Denis Sassou Nguesso seized military power on 16 October 1997.

1.2 Evolution of Electoral Provisions

Ever since the implementation of the *Loi Cadre* in 1956, universal suffrage has been in effect for the Congolese. With the establishment, under the Fifth French Republic, of the *Communauté Française* in 1958, France withdrew its jurisdictional rights over member states. Since then, electoral provisions have been rewritten or revised along with the country's erratic constitutional history of no less than seven constitutions: 1959, 1961, 1963, 1969, 1973, 1979 and 1992 as well as the same number of provisional basic laws, including the current *Acte fondamental* of 24 October 1997.

Upon independence the Constitution of 1961 installed a presidential system with universal voting for national office: The (sole) candidate was formally determined by plurality system. Under the Constitution of 1963, indirect presidential elections were held on the basis of an electoral college composed of members of the National Assembly as well as regional and communal office holders. The voting system for parliamentary elections established by the pre-independence constitution of 1959 was formally extended until 1963: parliamentary seats were allocated to party lists by plurality vote in six electoral districts. In reality, in 1963 all parliamentary mandates were filled by a unitary list.

While the constitutions of 1959, 1961 and 1963 had followed the French model, those of 1969, 1973 and 1979 were inspired by the Soviet political system. Political authority now resided within the Central Committee, whose 60 members were determined by the Party Congress, and from which in turn a 10-member Politbureau was selected. The Constitution of 1969 did away completely with state institutions independent of party structures; a National Assembly did not exist until a formally independent Parliament and Minister-President office were reintroduced with the Constitution of 1973. Eligibility for deputies to this National Popular Assembly was restricted to party members, selected by the Central Committee (imperative mandate provided by the state party). The unitary list was ratified by universal suffrage with the whole country forming one electoral district; terms of office were for a five-year period. In 1989 non-members of the PCT were also allowed to run for office. Under the 1970, 1973 and 1979 constitutions, election for presidential office formally transferred to the PCT Party Congress: the head of the Central Committee was *ex officio* President of the Republic.

The Constitution and Election Law of 1992 provided for the following elected national institutions: A President was to be elected for a five-year term (renewable once). In case of vacancy the post was filled by the President of the Senate pending new elections, to be held at least 45, and no more than 90, days afterwards. The 125 members of the National Assembly were elected for a five-year term; alongside each representative, a deputy, authorized to stand in if necessary, was elected on the same ticket. Representatives were re-eligible without limit. The Senate consisted of 60 members, six from each of 10 regional districts and indirectly elected for a six-year term. Every two years one third of all Senate seats were up for election; Senators were re-eligible without limit.

Suffrage was contingent upon Congolese citizenship by birth, a minimum age of 18 years and full possession of civil and political rights as well as registration as a voter. Presidential candidates were required to demonstrate at least 15 years of occupational experience. National Assembly candidates were required to be at least 25 years of age, while candidates to the Senate had to be at least 50 years old.

For presidential elections an absolute majority system was in effect. Absolute majority was required in the first round; if no candidate achieved 50% of the votes cast, a run-off between the two leading candidates had to be held within 15 days of the first round. For elections to the National Assembly an absolute majority system was in effect in 125 single-member constituencies (absolute majority required in the first round, a run-off between the two leading candidates held if no candidate achieved 50% of the votes cast in the first round). Senators were elected through district, local and regional bodies, in which a plurality of votes was required.

1.3 Current Electoral Provisions

Current electoral provisions do not exist.

1.4 Comment on the Electoral Statistics

Parliamentary elections of 1959 are cited from *Semaine Africaine* (21 June 1959). Election results until 1973 follow Ziemer (1978); official election results under the reign of the PCT state party were published in Etumba, the party's central organ. Whereas these elections are well documented but not significant to the political process, it is very difficult to obtain detailed election results for the time from 1992 to 1997. Data had to be collected from different sources such as FBIS (referendum 1992), IFES (presidential elections, first round) and *Marchés tropicaux* (second round). Weissman (1993) lists the regional distribution of votes for presidential elections, but does not present total numbers. Official tallies for parliamentary elections in 1992 and 1993 are not sufficiently detailed; full numbers were not available for both. The distribution of seats for 1992 follows Nkouka-Menga (1997) and *Marchés tropicaux* (3 July 1992), data for 1993 follow the official results given by the *Commission nationale d'organisation et de supervision des éléctions législatives* (only contain the distribution of seats according to electoral coalitions) and *Africa South of the Sahara* (1995).

2. Tables

2.1 Dates of National Elections, Referendums and Coups d'Etat

Year	Presidential elections	Parliamentary elections	Elections for Constitutional Assembly	Referendums	Coups d'état
1959		14/06			
1961	26/03				
1963		08/12		08/12	15/08
1968					31/07
1973		24/06		24/06	
1977					18/03
1979		08/07		08/07	05/02
1984		23/09			
1989		24/09			
1992	02/06 (1st) 16/08 (2nd)	24/06 (1st) 19/07 (2nd)		15/03	
1993		02/05 (1st) 03/06 (2nd) 03/10[a]			

[a] The anticipated parliamentary elections of 1993, carried out only in parts and an atmosphere of civil war, were extremely dubious. After the first round on 2 May 1993 had brought an absolute majority of seats to the *Mouvance présidentielle*, the second round on 3 June 1993 was boycotted by the opposition and later annulled by the supreme court. After a civil war had been stopped by a reconciliation pact the second round was repeated on 3 October 1993. At that time the organization of the ballot was boycotted in two constituencies: Mossaka II and Dongou II. In February 1994 an independent electoral committee annulled the results of the first round in eight constituencies. By-elections for seven seats outstanding since the partially annulled elections of May 1993 were held on 5 May 1995.

2.2 Electoral Body 1959–1993

Year	Type of election[a]	Population[b]	Registered voters		Votes cast		
			Total number	% pop.	Total number	% reg. voters	% pop.
1959	Pa	795,000	420,809	52.9	332,749	79.1	41.9
1961	Pr	815,000	460,270	56.5	415,843	90.3	51.0
1963	Pa	840,000	539,219	64.2	494,279	91.2	58.8
1963	Ref	840,000	539,219	64.2	494,279	91.7	58.8
1973	Ref	1,319,790	673,233	51.8	559,756	83.1	43.1
1973	Pa	1,319,790	662,098	50.2	550,739	83.2	41.7
1979	Ref	1,580,000	826,193	52.3	746,082	90.3	47.2
1979	Pa	1,580,000	826,193	52.3	746,082	90.3	47.2
1984	Pa	1,843,421	927,944	50.3	868,990	93.6	47.1
1989	Pa	2,107,000	1,004,320	47.6	900,357	89.6	42.7
1992	Ref	2,371,000	1,232,581	52.0	874,296	70.9	36.9
1992	Pa	2,371,000	—	—	—	—	—
1992	Pr (1st)	2,371,000	1,332,821	56.2	794,181	59.6	33.5
1992	Pr (2nd)	2,371,000	1,350,241	56.9	831,827	61.6	35.1
1993	Pa	2,443,000	—	—	—	—	—

[a] Pa = Parliament (*Assemblée Nationale*); Pr = President; Ref = Referendum

[b] Population Census of 1974: 1,319,790 and 1984: 1,843,421, all others are estimations.

2.3 Abbreviations

ADENA	Alliance Démocratique Nationale
AMICALE	Union Amicale pour le Changement Intégral
AND[a]	Alliance Nationale pour la Démocratie
CNDD	Comité National pour la Démocratie et le Développement
FDP	Forces Démocratiques et Patriotiques
FDS	Forum pour la Démocratie et la Solidarité
FDU[b]	Forces Démocratiques Unies
MARS	Mouvement Africain pour la Renaissance Sociale
MCDDI	Mouvement Congolais pour la Démocratie et le Développement Intégral
MNR	Mouvement National de la Révolution
MSA	Mouvement Socialiste Africain
PANA	Parti National
PCR	Parti Congolais du Renouvellement
PCT	Parti Congolais du Travail
PRDC	Parti Républicain pour la Défense du Congo
PSDC	Parti Social Démocrate Congolais
PSDL	Parti Social Démocrate Libéral
RDD	Rassemblement pour la Démocratie et le Développement
RDPS	Rassemblement Démocratique pour le Progrès Social
RDPSEL	—
RNDP	Rassemblement National pour la Démocratie et le Progrès
RUDL	Rassemblement pour l'Unité, la Démocratie et la Liberté
UDC	Union pour la Démocratie Chrétienne
UDDIA	Union Démocratique de Défense des Intérêts Africains
UDPS	Union pour le Développement et le Progrès Social
UDR 'Mwinda'	Union pour la Démocratie et la République
UFD	Union des Forces Démocratiques
UNAPAC	Union Nationale des Patriotes Croyants
UNDP	Union Nationale pour la Démocratie et le Progrès
UP	Union pour le Progrès
UPADS	Union Panafricaine pour la Démocratie Sociale
UPDP	Union Patriotique pour la Démocratie et le Progrès
UPRN	Union Patriotique pour la Reconstruction Nationale
UPSD	Union pour le Progrès Social et la Démocratie
URD[c]	Union pour le Renouveau Démocratique
URN	Union pour le Redressement National
URP	Union Républicaine pour le Progrès

[a] Group of approximately 40 parties, coordinated by Stéphane Bongo-Nouarra.

[b] Alliance of six political parties supporting Denis Sassou Nguesso, containing PCT, *Convention pour l'alternative démocratique*, *Parti libéral républicain*, *Union pour le renouveau national*, UNDP and UPRN.

[c] Oppositional parliamentary alliance initiated by MCDDI after 1992 elections in Parliament; initially containing MCDDI, RDPS, UP, PSDC, PANA and UNAPAC.

2.4 Electoral Participation of Parties and Alliances 1959–1993

Party / Alliance	Years	Elections contested Presidential	Parliamentary
MSA	1959	1	1
UDDIA	1959	1	1
MNR	1963	1	1
PCT	1973, 1979, 1984, 1989, 1992, 1993	1	6
AMICALE	1992	1	0
ADENA	1992	0	1
CNDD	1992	0	1
FDP	1992	0	1
FDS	1992	0	1
MARS	1992	0	1
MCDDI	1992, 1993	1	2
PANA	1992	0	1
PRDC	1992	0	1
PSDL	1992	1	0
RDD	1992, 1993	1	2
RDPS	1992, 1993	1	2
RDPSEL	1992	1	0
RNDP	1992	0	1
RUDL	1992	1	0
UDC	1992	0	1
UFD	1992, 1993	1	2
UNDP	1992	0	1
UP	1992	1	1
UPADS	1992, 1993	1	2
UPDP	1992	1	0
UPSD	1992	0	1
URN	1992	1	1
URP	1992, 1993	1	1
PCR	1993	0	1
UDC	1993	0	1
UDPS	1993	0	1
UDR Mwinda	1993	1	1
UPRN	1993	0	1
URD	1993	0	1

2.5 Referendums

Year	1963[a]		1973[b]	
	Total number	%	Total number	%
Registered voters	539,219	–	673,223	–
Votes cast	494,279	91.7	559,756	83.1
Invalid votes	6,561	1.3	30,183	5.4
Valid votes	487,718	98.7	529,573	94.6
Yes	419,893	86.1	411,272	77.7
No	67,825	13.9	188,301	22.3

[a] Constitutional referendum.
[b] Constitutional referendum.

Year	1979[a]		1992[a]	
	Total number	%	Total number	%
Registered voters	826,193	–	1,232,581	–
Votes cast	746,082	90.3	874,296	70.9
Invalid votes	16,277	2.9	10,408	1.2
Valid votes	729,805	97.8	863,889	98.8
Yes	707,421	96.9	832,115	96.3
No	22,284	3.1	31,774	3.7

[a] Constitutional referendum.

2.6 Elections for Constitutional Assembly

Elections for Constitutional Assembly have not been held.

2.7 Parliamentary Elections 1959–1989

Year	1959		1963	
	Total number	%	Total number	%
Registered voters	420,809	–	539,219	–
Votes cast	332,749	79.1	494,279	91.7
Invalid votes	1,486	0.4	54,644	11.1
Valid votes	331,263	99.6	439,635	88.9
UDDIA-RDA	196,985	59.5	–	–
MSA-PPC	134,278	40.5	–	–
MNR	–	–	439,635	100.0

Year	1973		1979	
	Total number	%	Total number	%
Registered voters	662,098	–	826,193	–
Votes cast	550,739	83.2	746,082	90.3
Invalid votes	175,357	31.8	20,101	2.7
Valid votes	375,382	68.2	725,981	97.3
PCT	375,382	100.0	725,981	100.0

Year	1984		1989	
	Total number	%	Total number	%
Registered voters	927,944	–	1,004,320	–
Votes cast	868,990	93.6	900,357	89.6
Invalid votes	15,822	1.8	29,897	3.3
Valid votes	853,168	98.2	870,460	96.7
PCT	853,168	100.0	870,460	100.0

2.7 a) Parliamentary Elections 1959: Regional Distribution of Votes (Absolute Numbers)

Constituency	1[a]	2[b]	3[c]
Registered voters	96,849	34,069	28,430
Votes cast	75,476	27,841	20,978
Invalid votes	364	245	246
Valid votes	75,112	27,596	20,732
UDDIA	51,743	18,925	18,801
MSA	23,369	8,671	1,931

[a] Contains the following administrative units: Pointe Noire, Madingou-Kayes, Mvouti, Dolisie, Kimongo, Loudima, Madingou, Mouyonzi, Boko-Songo. Elected list (16 seats): UDDIA. Head of list: Stéphane Tchichelle.

[b] Contains the following administrative units: Divenié, Kibangou, Mossendjo. Elected list (four seats): UDDIA. Head of list: Hilaire Mavioka

[c] Contains the following administrative units: Komono, Sibiti, Zanaga. Elected list (four seats): UDDIA. Head of list: Pierre Goura.

Constituency	4[a]	5[b]	6[c]
Registered voters	181,762	63,647	16,052
Votes cast	142,970	53,107	12,377
Invalid votes	461	103	67
Valid votes	142,509	53,004	12,310
UDDIA	98,147	3,118	6,251
MSA	44,362	49,886	6,059

[a] Contains the following administrative units: Brazzaville, Boko, Kinkala, Mayama, Mindouli, Abala, Djambala, Gambona, Lékana. Elected list (25 seats): UDDIA. Head of list: Fulbert Youlou.
[b] Contains the following administrative units: Dongou, Epéna; Impfondo, Boundji, Ewo, Fort-Rousset, Kéllé, Makoua, Mossaka. Elected list (10 seats): MSA. Head of list: Jacques Opangault.
[c] Contains the following administrative units: Ouesso, Souanké. Elected list (two seats): UDDIA. Head of list: Germain Samba.

2.7 b) Parliamentary Elections 1959: Regional Distribution of Votes (%)

Constituency	1	2	3	4	5	6
Votes cast	77.9	81.7	73.8	78.7	83.4	77.1
Invalid votes	0.5	0.9	1.2	0.3	0.2	0.5
Valid votes	99.5	99.1	98.8	99.7	99.8	99.5
UDDIA	68.9	68.6	90.7	68.9	5.9	50.8
MSA	31.1	31.4	9.3	31.1	94.1	49.2

General note: For information on the constituencies see table 2.7 a). Percentages refer to: Votes cast in % of registered voters; valid and invalid votes in % of votes cast; party votes in % of valid votes.

2.8 Composition of Parliament 1959–1993

Year	1959		1963		1973		1979	
	Seats	%	Seats	%	Seats	%	Seats	%
	61	100	55	100	115	100	153	100
UDDIA	51	83.6	–	–	–	–	–	–
MSA	10	16.4	–	–	–	–	–	–
MNR	–	–	55	100	–	–	–	–
PCT	–	–	–	–	115	100	153	100

Year	1984		1989[a]		1992[b]		1993[c]	
	Seats	%	Seats	%	Seats	%	Seats	%
	153	100	133	100	125	100	125	100
PCT	153	100	133	100	18	14.4	15	12.0
UPADS	–	–	–	–	39	31.2	47	37.6
MCDDI	–	–	–	–	29	23.2	28	22.4
RDPS	–	–	–	–	9	7.2	10	8.0
RDD	–	–	–	–	5	4	6	4.8
UFD	–	–	–	–	3	2.8	3	2.4
UPSD	–	–	–	–	2	1.6	–	–
MARS	–	–	–	–	1	0.8	–	–
PANA	–	–	–	–	1	0.8	–	–
UDC	–	–	–	–	1	0.8	1	0.8
FDP	–	–	–	–	1	0.8	–	–
RNDP	–	–	–	–	1	0.8	–	–
UP	–	–	–	–	1	0.8	–	–
URN	–	–	–	–	1	0.8	–	–
UNDP	–	–	–	–	1	0.8	–	–
CNDD	–	–	–	–	1	0.8	–	–
PRDC	–	–	–	–	1	0.8	–	–
ADENA	–	–	–	–	1	0.8	–	–
FDS	–	–	–	–	1	0.8	–	–
PCR	–	–	–	–	–	–	2	1.6
UDP–	–	–	–	–	–	–	1	0.8
URD	–	–	–	–	–	–	2	1.6
UDR Mwinda	–	–	–	–	–	–	2	1.6
UPRN	–	–	–	–	–	–	1	0.8
Independents	–	–	–	–	6	4.8	2	1.6

[a] Following the 1989 electoral revision the unitary list contained 74 nominally 'unaffiliated' members drawn from different social organizations along with 59 PCT-members.

[b] In the 1st round 67 seats were distributed: UPADS: 31; MCDDI: 18; PCT: 5; RDPS: 5; RDD: 4; UFD: 4; UPSD: 1; UNDP: 1; MARS: 1; independent: 1. 58 seats remained for ballotage. Elections in two constituencies were annulled.

[c] The elections of 1993 are highly questioned. After the 1st round on 2 May 1993 had brought an absolute majority of seats to the *Mouvance présidentielle*, the 2nd round on 3 June 1993 was boycotted by the opposition and later annulled by the supreme court. Official results for the 1st round showed the following distribution of seats according to *Agence congolaise d'information*: *Mouvance présidentielle*: 65; URD-PCT: 49; UDR-Mwinda 2, UPRN 1. 114 seats were distributed in the 1st round, 11 seats were to be distributed in a 2nd round. The data given above represents the composition of Parliament after the repeated 2nd round on 3 October 1993 (a reconciliation pact had stopped civil war). At that time the organization of the ballot was boycotted in two constituencies: Mossaka II and Dongou II. According to official sources, 123 of 125 seats were distributed. However, we count only 120 seats. In February 1994 an independent electoral committee annulled the results of the 1st round in eight constituencies. At by-elections for seven seats outstanding since the partially annulled elections of May 1993. On 5 May 1995 the PCT won 3 seats while MCDDI and UPADS won two seats each.

2.9 Presidential Elections 1961–1993

Year	1961	
	Total number	%
Registered voters	460,270	–
Votes cast	415,843	90.3
Invalid votes	10,254	2.4
Valid votes	405,589	97.6
Fulbert Youlou (UDDIA)	405,589	100.0

Year	1992 (1st round)[a]	
	Total number	%
Registered voters	1,332,821	–
Votes cast	794,181	59.6
Invalid votes	8,200	1.0
Valid votes	785,981	99.0
Pascal Lissouba (UPADS)	282,020	35.9
Bernard Kolélas (MCDDI)	159,682	20.3
Denis Sassou-Nguesso (PCT)	131,346	16.9
André Milongo (Independent)	79,979	10.2
Jean-Pierre Thystère Tchicaya (RDPS)	45,466	5.8
Joachim Yhombi-Opango (RDD)	27,953	3.5
David Charles Ganao (UFD)	22,514	2.9
Paul Kaya (Independent)	15,277	1.9
Nkoua Gongarad (UPDD)	5,272	0.7
Clément Mierassa (PSDL)	4,298	0.7
Jean Martin Mbemba (UP)	3,558	0.5
Alphonse Souchlaty (URP)	2,378	0.3
Gabriel Bokilo (URN)	2,296	0.3
Agnès Bandou (RDPSEL)	980	0.2
Antoine Makangou (Amicale)	649	0.1
A.C. Kouba (RUDL)	413	0.1

[a] Bokamba-Yangouma and Pierre Nze withdrew the candidacies.

Year	1992 (2nd round)	
	Total number	%
Registered voters	1,350,241	–
Votes cast	831,827	61.6
Invalid votes	6,036	0.6
Valid votes	825,791	99.3
Pascal Lissouba (UPADS)	506,395	61.3
Bernard Kolélas (MCDDI)	319,396	38.7

2.9 a) Presidential Elections 1992: Regional Distribution of Votes (in %)

1st round	Kouilou	Niari	Bouenza	Lékoumou	Pool
Votes cast	51.9	70.9	63.6	71.2	59.4
Valid votes	99.5	99.4	99.0	98.4	99.0
P. Lissouba	40.0	88.8	80.2	91.8	4.8
B. Kolélas	16.3	6.0	6.5	0.9	64.4
D. Sassou-Nguesso	6.0	2.1	1.6	3.9	3.3
A. Milongo	4.7	1.0	1.9	0.5	16.5
J. P. Thystère Tchicaya	27.9	0.7	0.7	0.3	0.4
J. Yhombi-Opango	0.7	0.2	0.3	0.3	0.6
D. C. Ganao	0.6	0.3	0.5	0.5	5.7
P. Kaya	2.1	0.4	7.3	0.7	0.7
N. Gongarad	0.7	0.1	0.1	0.2	0.2
C. Mierassa	0.2	0.1	0.2	0.2	0.6
J. M. Mbemba	0.1	0.1	0.2	0.2	1.9
A. Souchlaty	0.1	0.1	0.1	0.2	0.2
G. Bokilo	0.1	0.0	0.2	0.1	0.2
A. Bandou	0.2	0.1	0.1	0.1	0.2
A. Makangou	0.1	0.1	0.1	0.1	0.2
A. C. Kouba	0.0	0.0	0.1	0.0	0.1

1st round (continued)	Brazzaville	Plateaux	Cuvette	Sangha	Likouala
Votes cast	61.5	65.3	53.9	43.0	44.7
Valid votes	99.2	97.2	98.7	96.5	98.8
P. Lissouba	17.2	10.1	12.8	30.9	24.7
B. Kolélas	30.1	0.9	0.9	3.11	1.1
D. Sassou-Nguesso	20.2	58.9	47.4	41.9	58.5
A. Milongo	21.6	0.7	0.5	2.0	2.4
J. P. Thystère Tchicaya	1.4	0.7	1.1	0.9	0.6
J. Yhombi-Opango	3.3	0.6	29.2	15.7	9.0
D. C. Ganao	3.5	15.3	0.5	0.7	0.6
P. Kaya	1.1	3.4	3.8	0.9	0.6
N. Gongarad	0.3	6.3	0.2	0.2	0.2
C. Mierassa	0.4	4.8	0.5	0.5	0.4
J. M. Mbemba	0.4	0.7	0.5	1.2	0.4
A. Souchlaty	0.2	0.6	0.6	0.7	0.4
G. Bokilo	0.1	0.3	1.5	0.6	0.5
A. Bandou	0.1	0.1	0.3	0.3	0.5
A. Makangou	0.0	0.2	0.2	0.2	0.2
A. C. Kouba	0.0	0.1	0.1	0.2	0.2

2nd round	Kouilou	Niari	Bouenza	Lékoumou	Pool
Votes cast	53.5	73.8	68.4	79.2	67.7
Valid votes	99.7	99.7	99.6	99.6	99.1
P. Lissouba	49.2	92.7	91.2	98.6	13.7
B. Kolélas	50.8	7.3	8.8	1.5	86.3

2nd round (continued)	Brazzaville	Plateaux	Cuvette	Sangha	Likouala
Votes cast	60.7	66.2	54.6	46.2	46.2
Valid votes	99.1	98.9	99.0	98.0	97.9
P. Lissouba	43.2	66.2	94.8	93.4	96.3
B. Kolélas	56.8	98.9	5.4	6.6	3.7

2.10 List of Power Holders 1957–1998

Head of State	Years	Remarks
Abbé Fulbert Youlou	1957–1963	Initially (indirectly) elected Head of State prior to independence; re-elected as President 1961; resigned after mass protests in 1963.
Alphonse Massamba-Débat	1963–1968	Installed by the army and subsequently re-elected for a five-year term; turned out of office by a military coup led by Marien Ngouabi 02/08/1968.
Marien Ngouabi	1968–1977	Army officer. Formally designated Head of State 1969 by the PCT; assassinated 18/03/1977.
Jacques-Joachim Yhombi-Opango	1977–1979	Army officer; head of the military committee to which PCT transferred power in 1977; ousted on 05/02/1979 in reaction to party criticism of his economic policy.
Denis Sassou-Nguesso	1979–1992	Army officer; installed as Interim President by the Central Committee, then re-elected for three terms of office by the PCT Party Congress; turned over power to democratically elected successor in 1992.
Pascal Lissouba	1992–1997	Elected President on 16/08/1992; his mandate expired on 31/08/1997.
Denis Sassou-Nguesso	1997–	Seized military control after four months of civil war on 16/10/1997.

Head of Government	Years	Remarks
	Until 1991	President as Head of Government.
André Milongo	1991–1992	Elected Prime Minister by the National Conference on 08/06/1991; governed until the first parliamentary elections.
Stéphane Bongho-Nouarra	1992	Appointed on 08/09/1992 by President Lissouba; resigned after the UPADS-PCT pact dissolved, on 14/11/1992.
Claude-Antoine Dacosta	1992–1993	Compromise choice as Prime Minister, installed after imposition of a 'national unity' government under military prodding. Named to post on 25/12/1992; governed until parliamentary elections 02/05 and 06/06/1993.

Head of Government	Years	Remarks
Jacques-Joachim Yhombi-Opango	1993–1996	Army Officer, appointed as Prime Minister on 22/06/1993 after riots following legislative elections; resigned in August 1996 after heading three governments, two formed by the *Mouvance Présidentielle*, one formed by a coalition of MCDDI and *Mouvance Présidentielle*.
David Charles Ganao	1996–1997	Appointed in August 1996 to a government of 'electoral campaign'.
Bernard Kolélas	1997	Appointed on 08/09/1997 for a short period during civil war by Pascal Lissouba, whose presidential mandate had already expired on 31 August.

3. Bibliography

3.1 Official Sources

'Accord de Libreville 4/8/93'. *Baniafouna 1995,* 2.

'Acte fondamental de la période de transition politique 4/6/91'. *Baniafouna 1995*, 2.

Acte No. 0015 du 16 septembre 1977 portant organisation et fonctionnement du Parti sur le plan térritorial et sectorial. Brazzaville: Editions du PCT.

Constitution de la République du Congo 1961. Brazzaville: Ministère de l'Information.

'Constitution de la République Populaire du Congo 1979', in A. P. Blaustein and G. H. Flanz (eds.), *Constitutions of the Countries of the World*. Dobbs Ferry, N.Y.: Oceana Publications.

'Constitution de la République du Congo: examinée par le Conseil Supérieur de la République le 20 décembre 1991 et adoptée par référendum le 15 mars 1992'. *Afrique Contemporaine,* 162/2 (1992): 35–59.

Deutsch-Kongolesische Gesellschaft (ed.). *Verfassung der Demokratischen Republik Kongo 1970: Wortlaut und Kommentar*. Köln: Schäuble.

Etumba. Organe Central du Parti Congolais du Travail. Brazzaville: Editions du PCT, several editions.

'Loi No. 001 du 21 Janvier 1992 portant Loi Electorale'. *Baniafouna 1995,* 2.

3.2 Books, Articles and Electoral Reports

Allen, C., and Radu, M. S. (1989). *Congo: Economics, Politics and Society*. New York: Pinter.

Atlas 'Jeune Afrique' République populaire du Congo 1977, Paris: Ed. Jeune Afrique.

Babu-Zalé, R. *et al.* (1996). *Le Congo de Pascal Lissouba*. Paris: L'Harmattan.

Balandier, G. (1985). *Sociologie des Brazzavilles noires* (2nd edn). Paris: Pr. de la Fondation nationale des sciences politiques.

Ball, W. (1963). *Le royaume du Congo aux XVe et XVIe siècles*. Documents d'Histoire, Bruxelles: Présence Africaine.

Ballif, N. (1993). *Le Congo*. Paris: Editions Karthala.

Baniafouna, C. (1995). *Congo Démocratie, 2 Vol.* Paris: L'Harmattan.

Bazenguissa-Ganga, R. (1997). *Les voies du politique au Congo. Essai de sociologie historique.* Paris: Karthala.

Bertrand, H. (1975). *Le Congo: Formation sociale et mode de développement économique*. Paris: Maspero.

Boumankani, B. (1990). 'L'évolution recente de la démocratie au Congo'. *Alternative Democratique, Democratic Alternative*, 2: 177–185.

Breton, J.-M. (1986). 'L'évolution des institutions de la RPC'. *Revue du droit public et de la science politique en France et à l'étranger*, 5: 1327–1352.

— (1987). *Droit public congolais*. Paris: Economica.

— (1991). 'La transition vers la démocratie au Congo'. *Revue Congolaise du Droit*, 10/2: 13–40.

Clark, J. F. (1994:). 'Elections, Leadership and Democracy in Congo'. *Africa Today*, 41/3: 41–60.

— (1996). *Oil and Democratization in the Republic of Congo*. Florida International University, mimeo.

Cornevin, R., and Synge, R. (1991). 'Recent History of the Congo'. *Africa South of the Sahara*, London: Europa Publication, 381–398.

Devesa, J.-M. (1992). 'L'appartenance ethnique contre la conscience nationale. Démocratie et modernité au Congo.' *Le Monde diplomatique*, August: 26.

Dürste, H. (1983). 'Kongo', in S. Mielke (ed.), *Internationales Gewerkschaftshandbuch*. Opladen: Leske & Budrich, 709–713.

EIU (The Economist Intelligence Unit) (1994–1996). *Country Profile. Congo, São Tomé and Príncipe, Guinea-Bissau, Cape Verde*, London: EIU.

Frank, P. (1997). 'Ethnies et partis: Le cas du Congo'. *Afrique Contemporaine,* 182: 3–15.

Gabou, A. (1984). *Les constitutions congolaises*. Paris: Librairie générale de droit et de jurisprudence.

Gauze, R. (1973). *The Politics of Congo-Brazzaville*. Stanford, Cal.: Stanford University Hoover Institute Press.

IFES (1992). *Petit guide des élections démocratiques au Congo*. Brazzaville: Ed. du CSR.

Kolélas, B. (1992). 'Les lignes de force du projet de société du MCDDI'. *Afriques Réalités*, 1131: 8–19.

— (1992). 'Ma pensée politique'. *Le Soleil*, 7:1.

Koudissa, J. (1996). 'Verlorene Hoffnungen. Demokratisierung in der Republik Kongo', in P. Kevenhörster and D. van den Boom (eds.), *Afrika: Stagnation oder Neubeginn? Studien zum politischen Wandel*. Münster: Lit, 29–52.

Kounzilat, A. (1993). *Tribus et éthnies du Congo*. Paris: I.C.E.S.

Lissouba, P. (1992). *Programme du candidat Pascal Lissouba à la présidence de la République du Congo*. Brazzaville: UPADS.

Mankassa, C. (1992). 'De l'Etat-parti à l'Etat-ethno-régional'. *La Semaine africaine*, 1927: 7.

Mbanza, J. (1995). 'La démocratie prise en otage?'. *La Semaine Africaine*, 2027: 4.

Médard, J.-F. (1976). 'Le rapport de clientèle: du phénomène social à l'analyse politique'. *Revue Française de Science Politique*, 25/2: 103–131.

Memorandum sur la rupture de l'alliance UPADS/ PCT, 1992, Brazzaville: Editions du PCT.

Menga, G. (1993). *Congo, La transition escamotée*. Paris: L'Harmattan.

Monkotan, J. B. K. (1991). 'Une nouvelle voie d'accès au pluralisme politique: la conférence nationale souveraine'. *Afrique 2000*, 4ème trimestre: 41–53.

Mouelle Kombi II, N. (1991). 'La conférence nationale africaine: L'émergence d'un mythe politique'. *Afrique 2000*, 4ème trimestre: 35–40.

Ngolongolo, A. (1988). *L'assassinat de Marien Ngouabi, ou, L'histoire d'un pays ensanglanté*. Champigny sur Marne: Autoedition.

— (1993). *Congo. Bravo ou Fiasco? Dépuis la conférence nationale*. Champigny sur Marne: Autoédition.

Nkouka-Menga, J.-M. (1997). *Chronique politique congolaise*. Paris: L'Harmattan.

Nwokedi, E. (1994). *Violence and Democratization in Africa*. Hamburg: Institut für Friedensforschung und Sicherheitspolitik.

Obembe, J.-F. (1987). *Principaux problèmes liés à l'édification du Parti congolais du travail; premier parti marxiste-leniniste au pouvoir en*

Afrique: heritage, naissance, action, bilan, problèmes, perspectives. Brazzaville: PCT.

Ossebi H. (1988). 'Etat et ethnie au Congo: nouvelles situations, vieux démons'. *Revue de l'Institut de sociologie*, 3/4: 211–217.

— (1995). *Ethnicité, logiques partisanes et crises transitionelles en Afrique: Le cas du Congo*. Dakar, Codesria, 8th General Assembly on Crises, Conflicts and Transformations: Responses and Perspectives, Dakar, 26 June–2 July 1995.

Perreira, C. C. (1979). *L'administration congolaise*. Paris: Berger Levrault.

Philippe, C. (1991). 'Congo: L'experience de la conférence nationale'. *Défense Nationale*, 47/11: 115–126.

— (1992). 'La démocratie au Congo: La transition difficile'. *Défense Nationale*, 48/5: 136–140.

Quantin, P. (1994). Congo: Les origines politiques de la décomposition d'un processus de libéralisation, août 1992–décembre 1993. *L'Afrique Politique,* 1994: 167–190.

Sassou-Nguesso, D. (1995). 'Il faut sauver le Congo'. *Jeune Afrique*, 1797: 36–38.

Schmidt, U. (1993). 'Kongo', in D. Nohlen and F. Nuscheler (eds.), *Handbuch der Dritten Welt, Vol.5: Ostafrika und Südafrika* (3rd edn.). Bonn: Dietz, 461–472.

Thompson, V., and Adloff, R. (1984). *Historical Dictionary of the People's Republic of the Congo* (2nd edn.). Metuchen, NJ: Scarecrow Press.

Wadiafwa, H. CSR (1992). 'Le coup d'état de Palais'. *La Rumeur*, 10: 4.

Wagret, J.-M. (1963). *Histoire et sociologie politique de la République du Congo (Brazzaville).* Paris: Pichon & Durand-Auzias.

Weiss, M. (1987). 'Kongo', in R. Hofmeier and M. Schönborn (eds.), *Politisches Lexikon Afrika* (3rd edn.). München: Beck, 174–180.

Weissman, F. (1993). *Election présidentielle de 1992 au Congo: entreprise politique et mobilisation partisane.* Bordeaux: Centre d'Etude d'Afrique Noire.

Ziemer, K. (1978). 'Kongo', in D. Sternberger, B. Vogel, D. Nohlen and K. Landfried (eds.), *Die Wahl der Parlamente und anderer Staatsorgane, Band I: Politische Organisation und Repräsentation in Afrika,* by Franz Nuscheler, Klaus Ziemer *et al.,* Berlin/ New York: Walter de Gruyter, 1014–1060.

CONGO (Democratic Republic)

by Siegmar Schmidt and Daniel Stroux

1. Introduction

1.1 Historical Overview

After 75 years of Belgian colonial rule the Republic of Congo (formerly Belgian Congo or Congo-Leopoldville) and named Zaire from 1971 to 1997, gained independence on 30 June 1960 after mainly non-violent struggle. In the mid-1950s an independence movement of a small elite (the *evolués*) had emerged which had pushed Belgium to concede independence. Political turmoil immediately after independence originated in three main factors: Belgium had kept the country politically unprepared for independence. Since political association had been forbidden until 1957, ethnic association substituted for political formations. The consequence was an ethnically and regionally divided party system. A deep economic crisis in the wake of independence acerbated ethno-regional tensions. A provisional constitution, the *Loi Fondamentale* drafted by a round table conference in Brussels in May 1960, had introduced a federalist parliamentary system headed by a strong double executive which failed to clearly define the function of President and Prime Minister.

Already six days after independence an army mutiny in Kinshasa resulted in the secession of the province Katanga, thus threatening territorial integrity. A UN intervention on 15 July 1960 against Belgian military involvement, requested by Head of State Joseph Kasavubu and charismatic Prime Minister Patrice Lumumba, was realized. Lumumba's unconstitutional dismissal by President Joseph Kasavubu in September 1960, caused by Lumumba's Soviet affiliation at the height of the cold war, and his murder early in 1961 exacerbated political turmoil. Until 1964 separatist movements (Katanga, Kasai, Kivu, Stanleyville (today's Kisangani)) formed parallel governments and fought against central rule. External powers, particularly the USA and Belgium, were involved in the crisis as the control of Congo's vast natural resources was at stake. The UN troops failed to bring stability until their departure in 1964. The first Congolese Constitution of 1 August 1964 prolonged some of the inconsistencies of the *Loi Fondamentale*, but reinforced the power of the President as well as the federal system.

On 24 November 1965, army commander Joseph Désiré Mobutu seized power by military coup. Supported by the USA for geo-strategic reasons, Mobutu established a dictatorship based on an extreme centralization of power and the personalization of political rule. Along with a new Constitution of 26 June 1967, Mobutu assumed executive functions as Head of State and Government as well as Commander-in-Chief of the security forces. The bicameral legislative was replaced by a National Assembly. In December 1970, the *Mouvement Populaire de la Révolution* (MPR) became the single political party. The centralization of power reached its peak with the Constitution of 15 August 1974: the separation of powers was abolished, local and regional autonomy curtailed, the five organs of the MPR became the main bodies of government. A limited political opening in 1977 ensued in the wake of substantial losses in export revenues in the course of declining world market prices and the effects of the ruinous 'zairianization' of the economy in 1973. The rebellion in Shaba in 1977 (and 1978) equally put pressure on the regime. Although the President announced a return to authoritarian rule in 1980, in 1982 former high ranking Mobutu followers launched the oppositional *Union pour la Démocratie et le Progrès Social* (UDPS), headed by Etienne Tshisekedi. However, in the face of the regime's strategy of suppression and co-optation, the opposition remained weak. Corruption, mismanagement, further economic decline and social disaster had reinforced the opposition movement led by (the prohibited) UDPS and civil society groups at the end of the decade. The loss of strategic importance at the end of the cold war, external pressure due to bad human rights records and bad governance as well as the withdrawal of international assistance deprived Mobutu of important power resources. He abolished the one-party state in April 1990.

An extremely fragmented party system of over 100 parties evolved within a year. Three main political camps could be identified: (1) the Mobutu bloc led by the MPR with dozens of parties founded by Mobutu followers; (2) the anti-Mobutu bloc led by the three main opposition parties UDPS, *Union des Féderalistes et Républicains Indépendents* (UFERI) and the Christian-democratic *Parti Démocrat et Social Chrétien* (PDSC); (3) a number of pseudo or small parties without clear-cut political orientation. The anti-Mobutu coalition with broad popular support insisted successfully on the tenure of a National Conference. UDPS, UFERI, PDSC and groups from civil society formed the so-called *Union Sacrée* in July 1991 as a democratic oppositional platform within the National Conference. Headed by archbishop Laurent Monsengwo, the Conference soon became the main arena of the power struggle between the Mobutu camp and the opposition. The election of opposition leader Etienne Tshisekedi (UDPS) as Prime Minister on 15 August 1992 was considered an important step in the democratization process.

A transitional constitution was adopted, which reinstalled the separation of powers, reduced the President's competencies significantly, and strengthened human and civil rights. The Conference also drafted a new federalist constitution to be subject to referendum.

However, President Mobutu, who had been forced to appoint Tshisekedi Prime Minister, dismissed his government illegally in December 1992. Still enjoying the support of the security forces, he managed to remain in power by a subtle strategy of seemingly acquiescing reforms, repression, the instigation of army mutinies, fueling ethnic grievances and the co-optation of prominent opposition leaders e.g. UFERI leader Karl-i-Bond. In 1993 the conflict between pro- and anti-Mobutu forces led to a duplication of political institutions: Two governments (Prime Ministers Tshisekedi and Birindwa), two Parliaments and two currencies coexisted in Zaire. Political deadlock was finally overcome after lengthy negotiations with the two Parliaments merging into one transitional *Haut Conseil de la République—Parlement du Transition* (HCR-PT), which was, in contrast to the National Conference, dominated by pro-Mobutu forces.

In April 1994 the transitional Parliament passed an interim constitution which recognized the principle of separation of powers, and guaranteed basic human and civil rights. It allowed Mobutu to stay in office. Supported by France, Kengo wa Dondo, a compromise candidate and symbol for the 'third way' (which meant neither Tshisekedi nor Birindwa) was elected Prime Minister in June 1994. Although Mobutu had sabotaged fundamental political reform since 1990, freedom of association, opinion and press could be considered as a sign of slow democratization.

In October 1996, Laurent Kabila, a veteran in the fight against Mobutu for over 30 years, formed a four-party military alliance, the *Alliance des Forces pour la Démocratie et la Liberation du Congo-Zaire* (AFDL) supported by Zaire's neighbor countries Rwanda, Uganda and Burundi and by the USA. Within seven months the AFDL controlled the whole country and took over Kinshasa on 17 May 1997. Kabila, who self-proclaimed President, suspended the transitional constitution and electoral law and prohibited all activity of political parties. Only few opposition leaders were included in the new government, which indicated a return to authoritarian rule. The continuous banning of political parties as well as the exclusion of former allies furthermore created a general autocratic atmosphere. In August 1998, a rebellion against Kabila was launched by former Congolese, Rwandan and Ugandan allies in line with former Mobutu supporters. Nevertheless, elections were announced for 1999.

1.2 Evolution of Electoral Provisions

The first elections to the National Assembly subject to universal suffrage in May 1960 were held on the basis of the *Loi Fondamentale*, which was passed by the Belgian Parliament on 19 May 1960. Only male Congolese aged at least 21 years, and citizens of Ruanda-Urundi living more than six years in the country had the right to vote. Belgians living in Congo, who had participated in the first local elections in 1957 and 1959 were excluded from suffrage. In analogy to the Belgian Constitution suffrage was denied to members of the armed forces (police, army). Voting was compulsory.

The 137 members of the National Assembly were elected for a four-year term according to plurality system on open lists (single, preferential vote). The country was divided into 26 constituencies with a varying number of two to 12 mandates depending on the size of the population in the respective constituency. For the allocation of seats the d'Hondt formula was applied. For registration as a candidate to the National Assembly elections 200 signatures (in Leopoldsville, Elisabethville and Jadotville 300 signatures) and a minimum age of 25 years were necessary. The 84 members of the Senate (minimum age: 30) were elected indirectly by the provincial parliaments. The Head of State was to be elected indirectly by Parliament while the Prime Minister was nominated by the Belgish King before independence.

A new constitution approved by referendum in 1964 revised some electoral provisions: The Head of State was now to be elected by an electoral college formed by the National Assembly, the assemblies of the regions and a representation of delegations of Leopoldville. Male Congolese aged at least 18 years elected a 167-member Parliament for a five-year term. Voting was no longer compulsory. The size of the constituencies ranged from one to 14 mandates. For registration as a candidate only 100 signatures supporting the candidacy were necessary.

The Constitution of 24 June 1967 introduced female suffrage and reduced the minimum age to 18 years. According to the electoral law of 1970 (amended 1971 and 1973) electoral campaigns and the electoral procedures e.g. distribution of voter cards, were organized by the newly founded state party. The President was elected for a seven-year term and a Parliament of 217 (National Legislative Council) elected via one single list for a five-year term. For both the plurality system was formally in effect. Candidates to the single party's national list were handpicked by the Political Bureau of the MPR. Inciting for electoral boycott was sanctioned by law, although voting was not mandatory.

The Constitution of 1974 stated that the MPR-President had to be elected by universal suffrage for a five-year term and that the President of the party was *ex officio* Head of State. Mobutu signed a law on 2 April 1975, providing for the legislative elections. A list of 244 candidates for the 244-seat National Assembly was issued by the MPR. The elections were held by 'hand-clap' vote: The names of the candidates were announced in public. Instead of counting ballot papers, the 'level of applause' evaluated by officials, determined the allocation of mandates.

On the eve of the legislative elections in 1977 the secret vote (cabins, envelopes, ballot papers) was re-established. Several candidates were allowed to compete for the same seat in Parliament, however, their nomination had to be confirmed by the MPR. Eligibility for Members of Parliament (*commissaire du peuple*) was tied to a minimum age of 25 years. Campaigning was to be orientated on the ideals of the single part; the articulation of hate, racism or tribalism was explicitly prohibited. While the elections of 1977 provided for a certain degree of competition, legislative elections in 1982 were again based on a single list elaborated by the state party. Formal requirements for a nomination by the Political Bureau were: experience in administrative or political matters, and at least four years of formal education in addition to elementary school.

In 1987 semi-competitive elements for elections to the Parliament were reintroduced. Out of a list of 1,075 candidates produced by the state party, the electorate was to chose 210 Members of Parliament according to plurality system. Voting was mandatory. For the first time, candidates were permitted to send observers to the polling stations in order to control voting and counting. A special committee within the central party for election control was constituted in order to verify the election results and to treat irregularities.

On 31 December 1995 a transitional Parliament installed an Electoral Commission, containing 44 members, 22 each nominated by the opposition and Mobutu-loyal forces (*Loi No. 95-003 du 10 mai 1995 portant organisation et fonctionnement de la Commission nationale des élections*). The draft of an electoral law published in March 1997 proposed an absolute majority run-off system for presidential elections and plurality system for a National Legislative Council. Voters should apply for registration at the local electoral commissions which had to establish a voter's index.

Mobutu's successor Kabila suspended these proposals as well as the Electoral Commission itself. At the end of 1998 the Constitutional Commission presented a draft of a new constitution to the public while the civil war threatened Kabila's reign.

1.3 Current Electoral Provisions

Suspended.

1.4 Comment on the Electoral Statistics

The official results of all elections from 1969 until 1990 reveal the typical characteristics of elections under single-party rule: confirmation of a '*lider maximo*' by high voter turnout, lack of choice, an intimidated electorate and/ or manipulated results. The parliamentary elections differed from this pattern as the regime—under external and internal pressure—allowed competition of several candidates for one mandate.

For the period from independence until the 1970s Philipp (1978) provided most of the necessary information; some completion was necessary, however. Information gathering, especially for elections later than 1970 faced a number of problems. Elections were hardly covered by relevant periodicals such as *Marchés Tropicaux*, *African Contemporary Record* or *Zaire-Afrique* (today *Congo-Afrique*).

Concerning population figures, two Zairian publications proved to be useful: Leon de Saint Moulin's 'adjusted' data (*Cahiers Economiques et Sociaux*, Kinshasa) and Ngondo's references to the elections of 1987 and 1984 presented sufficient material to provide a realistic overview of population figures and voter participation. Elections to the National Assembly in 1977 are documented in detail by *Les Cahiers du CEDAF* (*Centre d'Etudes et de Documentation Africains*) at constituency level; figures were calculated by the author. Hardly any detailed information exists for the 1982 and 1987 elections. Again, *Zaire-Afrique* turned out to be a reliable source concerning details of the electoral process, however, figures on participation were not provided.

Very helpful were the efforts of M. Nsengila Mata, a long-time employee of the Hanns-Seidel-Foundation in Kinshasa/ Brazzaville. His experience with official archives was nearly Kafka-like. Nsengila provided us with election laws, helped with information on Prime Ministers and found some relevant press articles, but could not get hold of details on the 1982 and 1987 elections as administration staff, unpaid for a long time, were not available or refused to provide information without bribe. While under Mobutu documents were not available because of de-motivated staff, the archive of the National Assembly has become part of the presidential administration under Kabila and is inaccessible to the public.

2. Tables

2.1 Dates of National Elections, Referendums and Coups d'Etat

Year	Presidential elections	Parliamentary elections	Elections for Constitutional Assembly	Referendums	Coups d'état
1960		11/05, 25/05			
1964				25/06, 10/07	
1965		18/03, 30/04[a]			24/11
1967				16/06	
1970	01/11	01/11			
1975		02/11[b]			
1977	02/12	15–16/10			
1982		15–19/09			
1984	28–29/07				
1987		06/09			
1997					17/05

[a] These elections were held in four fifths of the territory in a state of civil war. Partial elections were held from 8 to 22 August 1965 in pacified territories.
[b] Election by 'hand clap vote'. No written documentation available.

2.2 Electoral Body 1960–1987

Year	Type of election[a]	Population[b]	Registered voters		Votes cast		
			Total number	% pop.	Total number	% reg. voters	% pop.
1960	Pa	13,569,187	3,390,940	25.0	2,773,595	81.8	20.4
1964	Ref,	16,545,649	—	—	2,404,139	—	14.5
1965	Pa	16,975,580	3,083,683[c]	18.2	2,466,947[d]	80.0	14.5
1967	Ref	17,998,000	—	—	8,404,907	—	46.7
1970	Pr	19,531,722	10,101,330	51.7	10,131,826	100.3[e]	51.9
1970	Pa	19,531,722	10,101,330	51.7	9,854,517	97.6	50.5
1977	Pa	24,100,000	11,177,484	46.4	10,369,259[f]	92.8	43.0
1977	Pr	24,100,000	—	—	10,693,804[g]	—	44.4
1982	Pa	29,193,334	—	—	—	—	—
1984	Pr	30,729,433	—	—	15,012,078	—	48.9
1987	Pa	33,864,891	—	—	—	—	—

[a] Pa = Parliament; Pr = President; Ref = Referendum.

[b] The figure for 1960 is drawn from Philipp (1978), all other figures follow Léon de Saint Moulin (1989) and Ngondo a Pitshandenge Iman (1992).

[c] Figure calculated on the basis of the percentage given by Philipp (1978).

[d] Valid votes without the province of Katanga Oriental.

[e] Philipp (1978) attributes this number to repeated voting.

[f] Drawn from the available figures of votes cast and the percentage of support, see *African Contemporary Record*, 1977-1978, Zaire.

[g] Calculated by the authors on the basis of official tallies on constituency level presented by Van der Steen (1978).

2.3 Abbreviations

ABAKO	Association des Bakongo pour l'Unification, la Conservation et l'Expansion de la langue Kikongo (Alliance de Bakongo)
ABAZI	Alliance de Bayanzi
APR-PRC	Alliance Rurale Progressiste-Alliance Rurale Congolais
ASCCO	—
ASSORESTSHU	—
ATCAR[a]	Association des Tshokwe du Congo Belge, d'Angola et de la Rhodésie
AWALEBO	—
BA-LIKOLO	—
BALUBAKAT[a]	Association Générale des Baluba du Katanga (Association des Baluba)
Cerea	Centre de Regroupement Africain
CONACO[b]	Convention Nationale Congolaise
COAKA	Coalition Kasaienne

CONAKAT	Confédération des Associations Tribales du Katanga
FC-DELVAUX	—
FRONKAT[c]	Front Commun Katangais
FROKONGI	—
LUKA	L'Union Kwangolaise pour l'Indépendance et la Liberté
MEDA	—
MEDERCO	Mouvement pour l'Evolution et le Développement de l'Economie Rurale du Congo
MNC/AMNC-L	Mouvement National Congolais/Alliance des Mouvements Nationalistes Congolais-Lumumba
MNC-K	Mouvement National Congolais-Kalonji
MNC-L	Mouvement national Congolais-Lumumba
MPR[a]	Mouvement Populaire de la Révolution
MPS	—
MUB	Mouvement de l'Unité Basonge
MPR	Mouvement Populaire de la Révolution
PANACO	—
PARECO	—
PDC	Parti Démocratique Congolaise
PRC	—
PNP	Parti National de Progrès: cartel Group of MEDERCO and traditional candidates (coutumier)
PSA[e]	Parti Solidaire Africain
PUNA	Parti de l'Unité Nationale
RADEKO	Rassemblement Démocratique Congolais
RDLK	Rassemblement Démocratique de Lac, Kwango et Kwilu
RECO	Regroupement Congolais
UDA(-Lubaya)	Union Démocratique Africaine
UDECO	Union Démocratique Congolaise
UNC	Union National Congolais
UNEBAFI	—
UNILAC	—
UNIMO	Union des Mongo

General note: Since the political opening of 1990 about 400 political parties have been registered. Although no elections have been held since then, the following political parties have gained major importance: PDSC (*Parti démocrate et social chrétien*), UDI (*Union des démocrates indépendants*), UDPS (*Union pour la démocratie et le progrès social*) and UFERI (*Union des féderalistes et républicains indépendants*), a coalition of lumumbist parties containing PALU (*Parti lumumbiste unifié*), and the mainly Kinshasa based FONUS (*Forces novatrices pour l'union et la solidarité*).

[a] Formed alliance under the banner of Cartel Katangais.

[b] The CONACO-Cartels was an alliance of 49 pro-western parties containing, among others: ATCAR, CTS/UPP, DECO, FNSP, MPS, MUB, PANACO, PARECO, PDC, PDR, RADECO, RAPELU and RECO.

[c] Alliance of parts of CONACAT and BALUBAKAT.

[d] Renamed *Mouvement Populaire pour le Renouveau* on 24 April 1990.

[e] A breakaway of PSA runs as PSA-Kamitatu.

2.4 Electoral Participation of Parties and Alliances 1960–1987

Party / Alliance	Years	Elections contested Presidential	Parliamentary
ABAKO	1960, 1965	0	2
ABAZI	1960	0	1
APR-PRC	1960	0	1
Cartel Katangais	1960	0	1
Cerea	1960	0	1
COAKA	1960	0	1
CONAKAT	1960, 1965	0	2
FC-DELVAUX	1960	0	1
LUKA	1960, 1965	0	2
MNC-L	1960, 1965	0	2
MNC-K	1960	0	1
MUB	1960, 1965	0	2
PNP	1960	0	1
PSA-Kamitatu	1960, 1965	0	2
PUNA	1960, 1965	0	2
RDLK	1960	0	1
RECO	1960	0	1
UNC	1960	0	1
UNEBAFI	1960	0	1
UNIMO	1960	0	1
ASCCO	1965	0	1
ASSORETSHU	1965	0	1
ATCAR	1965	0	1
AWALEBO	1965	0	1
BALUBAKAT	1965	0	1
BA-LIKOLO	1965	0	1
CONACO-Cartels	1965	0	1
FROCONGI	1965	0	1
FRONKAT	1965	0	1
INTERCOUP-Huapa	1965	0	1
MEDA	1965	0	1
Mwinda-Bakongo	1965	0	1
PANACO	1965	0	1
PDC	1965	0	1
PDR	1965	0	1
PRC	1965	0	1
RADEKO	1965	0	1
UDAsLubaya	1965	0	1
UDECO	1965	0	1
MPR	1970, 1977, 1975, 1982, 1984, 1987	3	4

2.5 Referendums

Year	1964[a] Total number	%	1967[a] Total number	%
Registered voters	—	—	—	—
Votes cast	2,404,139	—	—	—
Invalid votes	35,688	1.5	—	—
Valid votes	2,368,451	98.5	8,404,907[b]	—
Yes	2,151,122	90.8	8,220,000	97.8
No	217,329	9.2	184,907	2.2

[a] Approval of Constitution.
[b] Valid votes calculated as a sum of Yes votes and No votes.

2.7 Parliamentary Elections 1960–1977

Year	1960 Total number	%	1965 Total number	%
Registered voters	3,390,940	–	—	–
Votes cast	2,773,595	81.8	2,466,957	—
Invalid votes	549,701	19.8	293,948	11.9
Valid votes	2,223,894[a]	80.2	2,173,009[a]	88.1
ABAKO	210,542	9.5	136,226	6.3
ABAZI	21,024	0.9	–	–
APR-PRC	16,892	0.8	–	–
Cartel Katangais	110,091[b]	4.9	–	–
Cerea	95,721	4.3	–	–
COAKA	47,526	2.1	–	–
CONAKAT	104,821	4.7	178,302	8.2
FC	17,716	0.7	–	–
LUKA	52,612	2.4	62,856	2.8
MNC-L	592,256[c]	26.6	31,874	1.5
MNC-K	161,942[d]	7.3	–	–
PNP	178,237[e]	8.0	–	–
PSA	278,971	12.6	–	–
PUNA	118,661[f]	5.3	82,601	3.8
RDLK	12,761	0.6	–	–
REKO	41,202	1.9	–	–
UNC	63,425	2.9	–	–
UNIMO	16,739	0.8	–	–
Independent	63,333	2.8	12,815	0.6
Regional Groups	19,422	0.9	274,778	12.6
ASCCO	–	–	42,430	2.0
ASSORETSHU	–	–	22,011	1.0
ATCAR	–	–	24,710	1.1

Year	1960 (continued)		1965 (continued)	
	Total number	%	Total number	%
AWALEBO	–	–	104,896	4.8
BA-LIKOLO	–	–	9,634	0.4
BALUBAKAT	–	–	64,866	3.0
CONACO	–	–	227,961	10.5
CONACO-Cartels	–	–	544,483	25.1
FRONKAT	–	–	59,223	2.7
FROKONGI	–	–	19,179	0.9
INTERCOUP-Huapa	–	–	11,645	0.5
MEDA	–	–	36,441	1.7
Mwinda-Bakongo	–	–	68,750	3.1
PANACO	–	–	35,275	1.6
PDC	–	–	15,095[c]	0.7
PRC	–	–	21,861	1.0
PSA-Kamitatu	–	–	79,358	3.7
RADECO	–	–	19,912	0.9
UDA-Lubaya	–	–	64,845	3.0
UDECO	–	–	162,016	7.5
UNILAC	–	–	19,944	0.9
Union Budjala	–	–	32,780	1.5

[a] Valid votes are calculated as a sum of votes distributed to political parties. Official tallies concerning valid and invalid votes were not available.

[b] The votes for the two political parties containing Cartel Katangais are distributed as follows: Balubakat: 80,434; ATCAR: 29,657.

[c] The votes for the MNC-L coalition are distributed as follows: UNEBAFI: 19,324; MUB: 30,280; COAKA: 21,465.

[d] MNC-K contains several independent candidates who contributed a sum of 14,364 votes.

[e] The votes for PNP are distributed as follows: MEDERECO: 27,634; *milieux coutoumiers* (alliance of traditional leaders): 13,408.

[f] The PUNA coalition contained Association Ngwaka (14,364 votes).

Year	1970		1977	
	Total number	%	Total number	%
Registered voters	10,101,330	–	11,177,484	–
Votes cast	9,854,517	97.6	10,369,259	92.8
Invalid votes	91,007	0.9	188,574[a]	1.8
Valid votes	9,763,510	99.1	10,180,685	98.2
MPR (Yes-votes)	9,691,132	99.3	10,180,685	98.2
No-votes	72,378	0.7		

[a] No difference made between invalid votes and No votes.

For the elections of 1982 and 1987 distribution of votes were not available. For data on voter participation see table 2.2.

2.8 Composition of Parliament 1960–1987

Year	1960		Year	1965	
	Seats	%		Seats	%
	137[a]	100		167	100
MNC-L	36[d]	26.3	CONACO-Cartels	42[h]	25.1
PSA	13	9.5	CONACO	38	22.7
ABAKO	12	8.8	ABAKO	10	6.0
Cerea	10	7.3	UDECO	10	6.0
PNP	10[f]	7.3	CONAKAT	9	5.4
PUNA	9[g]	6.6	AWALEBO	7	4.2
CONAKAT	8	5.8	Mwinda-Bakongo	5	3.0
MNC-K	8[e]	5.8	PUNA	4	2.4
Cartel Katangais	7[c]	5.1	LUKA	4	2.4
REKO	4	2.9	PSA-Kamitatu	4	2.4
LUKA	3	2.2	UDA-Lubaya	4	2.4
COAKA	2	1.5	FRONKAT	3	1.8
ABAZI	1	0.7	BALUBAKAT	3	1.8
APRSPRC	1	0.7	ASCCO	3	1.8
FC	1	0.7	PANACO	3	1.8
RDLK	1	0.7	ASSORETSHU	2	1.2
UNC	3	2.1	MNC-L	2	1.2
UNIMO	1	0.7	ATCAR	2	1.2
			MEDA	2	1.2
			BA-LIKOLO	1	0.6
			INTERCOUP-Huapa	1	0.6
			FROKONGI	1	0.6
			PDS	1	0.6
			PRC	1	0.6
			RADECO	1	0.6
			UNILAC	1	0.6
			Union Budjala	1	0.6

[a] According to official tallies only 130 of 137 seats of the National Assembly were allocated.
[b] According to official tallies only 135 of 167 seats of the National Assembly were allocated. The following 32 mandates were annulled by the *Cour d'Appel* on 16 June 1965: ASCCO: 3; ASSORETSHU: 2; CONACO: 4; RECO/CONACO: 4; INTERCOUP-Huapa: 1; PDC: 1; PRC: 1; PANACO: 2; PSA-Kamitatu: 4; UDECO: 10.
[c] Allocation of mandates: Balubakat: 6; ATCAR: 1.
[d] Allocation of mandates: MNC-L: 31; UNEBAFI: 1; MUB: 1; COAKA: 1.
[e] Allocation of mandates: MNC-K: 7; Independents: 1.
[f] Allocation of mandates: PNP: 7; MEDERCO: 2; Coutumier: 1.
[g] Allocation of mandates: PUNA: 7; Association Ngwaka: 2.
[h] Allocation of mandates: Cartels CONACO, ATCAR, CTS/UPP, FNSP: 1; MPS, PDC: 2; MUB: 3; PANACO, PARECO, RADECO, RAPELU: 4; PDR: 5; RECO: 6.

Year	1970		1975[a]		1977		1982	
	Seats	%	Seats	%	Seats	%	Seats	%
	217	100	244	100	289[b]	100	310	100
MPR	217	100	244	100	289	100	310	100

[a] Elected by 'hand clap vote'.

[b] Secondary literature is not consistent concerning the total number of seats in 1977. Van der Steen (1978) presents a number of 289, Legum (*African Contemporary Record*, 1978, B596) gives a number of 327 and *Marchés Tropicaux* (28 October 1977) gives a number of 270 seats.

Year	1987	
	Seats	%
	210	100
MPR	210	100

2.9 Presidential Elections 1970–1984

1970	Total number	%
Registered voters	10,101,330	–
Votes cast	10,131,826	100.3
Invalid votes/ Blanc votes	157	0.1
Valid votes	10,131,669	99.9
Mobutu (MPR)	10,131,669	100.0

1977	Total number	%
Registered voters	—	–
Votes cast	10,693,804	—
Invalid votes/ Blanc votes	201,557	1.8
Valid votes	10,492,247	98.2
Mobutu (MPR)	10,492,247	100.0

1984	Total number	%
Registered voters	—	–
Votes cast	15,012,078	—
Invalid votes/ Blanc votes	126,101	0.8
Valid votes	14,885,977	99.2
Mobutu (MPR)	14,885,977	100.0

2.10 List of Power Holders 1960–1998

Head of State	Years	Remarks
Joseph Kasavubu	1960–1965	Indirectly elected before independence with 159 of 213 votes cast of both chambers of Parliament on 25/06/1960 supported by Prime Minister Patrice Lumumba. Although backed by the West, Kasavubu failed to gain control over the entire territory.
Josef Désiré Mobutu, later Mobutu Sese Seko	1965–1997	Chief of Staff. Mobutu seized power on 24/11/1965; Parliament supported his nomination for a five-year term; a rebellion spreading from the Kivu to the Capital forced him to exile in Morocco on 17/05/1997.
Laurent Désiré Kabila	1997–	Took power on 17/05/1997 as the leader of the AFDL-alliance which ousted Mobutu from power by a military victory; veteran in the fight against Mobutu for over 30 years, supported by neighboring states and the USA.

Head of Government	Years	Remarks
Patrice Lumumba	1960	Appointed on 25/06/1960 by the Belgian King. After the failure to form a government together with President Kasavubu, Lumumba formed his own coalition government. His unconstitutional dismissal on 05/09/1960 was refused by Parliament as were the accusations of 'high treason' of Lumumba's cabinet against Kasavubu. Mobutu, Chief of the Army, ended the political impasse with a military coup, the 'neutralization of Parliament' on 31/12/1960. Lumumba was murdered on 13/02/1961.
Joseph Ileo	1960	Appointed on 09/02/1960 by Kasavubu but not approved by Parliament; his second nomination followed the dissolution of a College of Commissioners, having replaced parliament after the first military coup of Mobutu. He was dismissed on 25/07/1961.

Head of Government	Years	Remarks
Cyril Adoula[a]	1961	Entered office on 02/08/1961 by President Kasavubu and was approved by Parliament, when it opened on 25 June 1961. His centralist concept did collide with federalist and secessionist tendencies.
Moise Tshombe	1964–1965	Tshombe's nomination reflected his reintegration into the central government, after he had led the secessionist government of Katanga from 1960 to 1963. (Parliamentary term was prorogued on 29/09/1963.) Although backed by a broad majority in Parliament (CONACO) he was dismissed on 13/11/1965 by Kasavubu as a potential adversary for the planned presidential elections in 1966.
Evariste Kimba	1965	Appointed on 13/11/1965; the absolute majority of Tshombe's CONACO refused to approve the appointment.
Leonard Mulamba	1965–1966	Upon Mobutu's military coup a new Cabinet under General Mulumba was approved by Parliament on 28/11/1965. Along with the abolition of the office of Prime Minster in October 1966, Mulumba was dismissed.
	1966–1977	No separate office of a Head of government
Mpinga Kasenda	1977–1979	Appointed by Mobutu on 06/07/1977 after the post of a Prime State Commissioner had been introduced in the context of slightly liberalizing politics; dismissed on 06/03/1979.
André Bo-Boliko Lokanga	1979–1980	Labor unionist; appointed by Mobutu on 06/03/1979; dismissed on 18/08/1980.
Nguz Karl-i-Bond	1980–1981	Returned from exile in order to campaign against Mobutu and to denounce bad human rights records; co-opted to the office of Prime Minister on 28/08/1980; dismissed on 17/04/1981.
Joseph Nsinga Udjuu	1981–1982	Appointed by the President on 18/04/1981; dismissed on 07/05/1982.

[a] At this time, various secessionist, regional movements proclaimed their own Head of Government. South Kasai: Kalonij; Katanga: Tshombe; Stanleyville: Gisenga.

Head of Government	Years	Remarks
Kengo-wa-Dondo	1982–1986	Appointed on 05/11/1982; dismissed on 31/10/1986. Kengo was known as chairman for the Judiciary Council for his constant disregard of independence of the magistrates; served as scapegoat to mounting popular discontent with IMF austerity measures.
Mabi Mulumba	1987–1988	One of the main critics of IMF-policies he was appointed on 22/01/1987 after the office had been vacant for several months; dismissed on 07/03/1988.
Sambwa Pidu N'bagui	1988	Governor of the Bank of Zaire, appointed on 07/03/1988 for better cooperation with international donors; dismissed on 26/11/1988.
Kengo-wa-Dondo	1988–1990	Appointed on 26/11/1988. His dismissal on 24/04/1990 was meant to emphasize Mobutu's reform politics together with the abolition of the one-party state.
Vincent de Paul Lunda Bululu	1990–1991	First Prime Minister of the transition period, he was appointed by Mobutu on 25/04/1990; dismissed on 30/03/1991.
Crispin Mulumba Lukodji	1991	Appointed by Mobutu on 30/03/1991. During his tenure, Mobutu unsuccessfully tried to co-opt his opponent Tshisekedi who refused the post of Prime Minister on 22/07/1991.
Etienne Tshisekedi	1991	After the National Conference's failure causing pillages in September 1991, Mobutu agreed to nominate Tshisekedi. However, the latter refused to swear on Mobutu as the 'saviour of the nation' and was dismissed on 21/10/1991, after his Cabinet had remained in front of the Prime Minister's office under trees for one week.
Bernadin Mungul Diaka	1991	Appointed on 30 October; dismissed on 25/11/1991.
Ngunz Karl-i-Bond	1991–1992	Bond's second co-optation on 25/11/1991 weakened the opposition. His membership in the *Union Sacrée* as leader of the Shaba-based UFERI was suspended and an anti-Bond rally followed his appointment. Mounting internal and external pressure led Mobutu to dismiss Bond on 15/08/1992.

Head of Government	Years	Remarks
Etienne Tshisekedi	1992	Elected Prime Minister by an independent institution, the National Conference with a 70% majority of 2,500 delegates on 15/08/1992. His government was illegally dismissed by Mobutu on 01/12/1992, but Tshisekedi remained in office. While Mobutu dismissed the Prime Minister again on 05/02/1993, the *Haut Conseil de la République* confirmed his legitimacy.
Faustin Birindwa	1993	Appointed by Mobutu on 20/03/1993. From 2 April, when a new Cabinet was formed, a 'doubling of institutions' led to the coexistence of two governments and two parliaments until 1994.
Kengo-wa-Dondo	1994–1997	Elected Prime Minister by the merger of the two parliaments HCR-PT (*Haut Conseil de la République - Parlément de Transition*) on 07/07/1994. According to the transitional constitution, the Prime Minister had to represent the opposition and be nominated by consensus; ousted by the HCR-PT on 18/03/1997.
Etienne Tshisekedi	1997	Six weeks before the AFDL forces took over power, the HCR-PT proposed Tshisekedi for the office of Prime Minister. Tshisekedi, appointed on 02/04/1997 caused his removal on 09/04 by dismissing the HCR-PT and trying to introduce a former transitional constitution of 1992.
Likulia Bolongo	1997	General. Immediately after the state of emergency had been declared, Mobutu appointed Likulia Prime Minister of a military government. The function of Prime Minister was abolished when Laurent Désiré Kabila seized power on 17/05/1997.

3. Bibliography

3.1 Official Sources

'Constitution of the Republic of Zaire, June 24, as amended 1971, 1972', in A. J. Peaslee (ed.) (1974), *Constitutions of Nations, Vol.1 Africa*. The Hague: Martinus Nijhoff, 1028–1046.

'Acte Constitutionnel de la Transition'. *Journal Officiel de la République du Zaire*, 35ème Année, Numéro special, avril 1994.

'Loi No. 95-003 du 10 mai 1995 portant organisation et fonctionnement de la Commission Nationale des Elections'. *Journal Officiel de la République du Zaire*, 36ème Année, Numéro special, mai 1995.

Decret No. 0021 du 02 Aout 1996 portant organisation de L'identification des nationaux, du recensement de la population nationale et de l'enrolement du corps electoral en République du Zaire.

Constitution du République Fédérale du Congo. Kinshasa, Novembre 1992.

Projet de Constituion de la IIIème République. Kinshasa, Octobre 1996.

CEPAS (Centre d'Etudes pour l'Action Sociale). Kinshasa, Vol. 1990–1996.

Conférence Nationale Souveraine (1991). 'Le Rapport Final des Traveaux de la Conférence Nationale Souveraine'. *Zaire-Afrique*, 3/273, 135–199.

Loi No. 75-099 du 2 avril 1975 relative à l'organisation des elections législatives.

'Loi No. 77-014 portant l'organisation des elections des membres du Bureau Politique, du Conseil Législative et des Conseils des zones urbaines'. *AZAP* (Agence Zairoise de Presse): Promulgation.

Ordonnance-loi No. 87/002 du 10 janvier 1987.

Ordonnance-loi No. 82 06 du 26 février 1992.

'Organisation et calendrier des élections législatives et municipales, (1987)'. *Elima* (daily), 14 January 1987.

3.2 Books and Articles

Callaghy, T. M. (1984). *The State-Society Struggle: Zaire in Comparative Perspective*. New York: Columbia University Press.

Kaplan, I. (1979). *Zaire—a Country Study*. Washington: Federal Research Division, Area Handbook Series: US Government Printing Office.

Körner, P. (1989–1996). 'Zaire', in Institut für Afrika-Kunde and R. Hofmeier (eds.), *Afrika Jahrbuch 1988–1995*. Opladen: Leske & Budrich.

Kuhn, B. (1992). *Mehrparteiensystem und Opposition in Zaire*. Münster/Hamburg: Lit-Verlag.

Legum, C. *et al.* (1967/68–1987/69). 'Zaire'. *Africa Contemporary Record, Annual Survey and Documents*, Vol. I-XX.

Leslie, W. (1993). *Zaire. Continuity and Change in an Oppressive State*, Boulder, Col.: Westview Press.

Muamba Makomba, J.-M. (1995). 'Les élections au Zaire: expériences et perspectives', in L'Institut de Formation et d'Etudes Politiques and Fondation Konrad Adenauer, sous la direction de J. F. Mutamba Makomba, *L'Organisation des élections démocratiques au Zaire*. Kinshasa.

Ngondo a Pitshandenge Iman (1992). 'Chiffre de population et enjeux politiques sous la 2ème République: les élections législatives de 1987'. *Zaire-Afrique*, 4/264: 227–248.

Philipp, G. (1978). 'Zaire', in D. Sternberger, B. Vogel, D. Nohlen and K. Landfried (eds.), *Die Wahl der Parlamente und anderer Staatsorgane, Band I: Politische Organisation und Repräsentation in Afrika,* by Franz Nuscheler, Klaus Ziemer *et al.*, Berlin/ New York: Walter de Gruyter, 2331–2441.

de Saint Moulin, L. (1989). 'Les statistiques démographiques en République du Zaire'. *Cahiers Economiques et Sociaux,* Université de Kinshasa, 23/1–4: 31.

Schatzberg, M. G. (1988). *The Dialectics of Oppression in Zaire.* Bloomington, Ind.: Indiana UP.

— (1991). *Mobutu or Chaos? The United States and Zaire, 1960-1990.* Lanham, Md.: University Press of America.

Schmidt, S. (1998). 'David gegen Goliath: Blockaden, Selbstblockaden und Chaos des Demokratisierungsprozesses in Zaire', in G. Schubert and R. Tetzlaff (eds.), *Blockierte Demokratien in der Dritten Welt.* Opladen: Leske & Budrich, 197–238.

Stroux, D. (1996). *Zaires sabotierter Systemwechsel. Das Mobutu-Regime zwischen Despotie und Demokratie (1990–1995).* Hamburg: Institut für Afrika-Kunde.

— (1997). *Zaire 1997: vor dem Zusammenbruch oder vor dem Neubeginn?* IAK-Diskussionsbeiträge, 9. Hamburg: Institut für Afrika-Kunde.

Van der Steen, D. (1978). 'Elections et réformes politiques au Zaire en 1977. Analyse de la composition des organes politiques'. *Les Cahiers du CEDAF,* 2–3: 3–98.

Wamba-dia-Wamba, E. (1993). 'Democracy, Multipartism and Emancipative Politics in Africa: The Case of Zaire'. *Africa Development*, 18/4: 95–118.

Willame, J.-C. (1991). 'Zaire, années 90. De la démocratie enrayée (24 Avril–22 Septembre 1991)'. *Les Cahiers du CEDAF*, Centre d´etude et documentation africaines, 6–7.

Young, C., and Turner, T. (1985). *The Rise and Decline of the Zairian State.* Madison, Wi.: University of Wisconsin Press.

CÔTE D'IVOIRE

by Christof Hartmann

1. Introduction

1.1 Historical Overview

Côte d'Ivoire (Ivory Coast) can be considered as a rare example of political and constitutional stability on the African continent. The autocratic President Félix Houphouët-Boigny remained in power for 33 years and the political order he had created was never seriously questioned by the Ivorian population until 1990. The introduction of a multi-party system, the first competitive elections in 1990 and the presidential succession to Henri Konan Bedié in 1993 marked the beginning of an uncertain and turbulent transition to democratic politics.

Côte d'Ivoire achieved its independence on 7 August 1960 with the *Parti Démocratique de la Côte d'Ivoire* (PDCI) as hegemonic political force. Led by Houphouët-Boigny this party, initially formed by indigenous cocoa-planters, had assured almost complete electoral dominance by 1958 when the French colonies were granted internal autonomy. The multi-party elections for the Territorial Assembly in 1957 ended with a devastating defeat for the few remaining opposition parties, which gained only two seats out of 60 in the face of an already working PDCI-electoral machine based on local notables and the ethnic associations of the capital Abidjan. Houphouët-Boigny had applied a shrewd combination of coercion, co-optation of opposition politicians and collaboration with the colonial authorities to impose his party and his leadership. This mixed strategy proved to be a lasting feature of his reign even after independence and up to his death in 1993, with the French continuing to have a say in Ivorian politics.

The constitution of 3 November 1960 which was ratified by the National Assembly shortly after independence calls for a strong presidential system with a directly elected President as Head of Government. The article allowing a multi-party system turned out to be of no importance, since the PDCI-regime did not allow any other party to register. In a similar way the constitutional provisions concerning the national legislature and an independent judiciary did not became effective in a system marked by the personal rule of his President Houphouët-Boigny. The executive was totally dominated by the President, and the PDCI remained throughout all the years important as constant framework for politics, in canalizing political participation and controlling societal activities. The constitution has rarely been amended and never ceased to be in force.

After having consolidated his power against rival contenders in the PDCI in 1963 and crushed a separatist rebellion in the South-East, the President ruled by controlling the party and counting on a very efficient administration which was initially run by French experts. Nobody dared to question the decisions or legitimacy of Houphouët's rule, as the Ivorian economic 'miracle' offered ample opportunities to include and co-opt all major ethnic and social groups into the patrimonial system. Remaining political, ethnic or social protest was regulated not according to formal constitutional procedures but in informal ways which borrowed from the Ivorian traditions. All social groups and interest organizations could address the President with their grievances in a formalized 'dialogue', which established some communication between the President and the people.

The efficiency of this conflict-regulating mechanism is proved by the fact that Houphouët-Boigny had rarely to resort to open repression to secure his dominance and to avoid open or clandestine opposition. It was only the economic crisis of the Ivorian model and growing popular criticism of corrupted PDCI officials at the end of the 1970s that forced the President to innovate by introducing semi-competitive elements on the occasion of the parliamentary elections in 1980. This *démocratie à l'ivoirienne* served, however, only temporarily to counterbalance popular frustrations which led to protests of students and university teachers in 1982 and 1983. The open question of Houphouët-Boigny's presidential succession ensured continuing and bitter conflicts within the PDCI itself.

Against the background of economic and political crisis which was overshadowed by long absences of the aged President, the capital Abidjan was struck in February 1990 by violent protests against new austerity programs. As the demonstrations soon turned political, Houphouët-Boigny decided eventually to reintroduce multi-party politics on 30 April 1990 and to designate a constitutional successor. The emerging party system continued to be characterized by the hegemonic position of the PDCI which prevented widespread defection to the opposition by state-elite, the new opposition parties being able to count only on university students and staff and middle-class professionals. In the light of this balance of forces and resources the presidential and parliamentary elections of 1990, which witnessed the appearance of opposition candidates for the first time since independence but never realized standards of a free and fair competition, ended with a comfortable victory of Houphouët-Boigny and the PDCI.

Since 1990 the political transition has been under way. Neither the introduction of a Prime Minister (who remains completely responsible to the President) nor the presidential succession in December 1993 which opened the way to power for the President of the National Assembly, Henri Konan Bedié, has so far modified the autocratic style of the PDCI and the governing elite. The political system continues to be characterized by a low degree of institutionalization and the predominance of personalistic and informal networks. Lacking the charisma of his predecessor Houphouët-Boigny, President Bedié has not only harassed the opposition and the free press, but alienated a whole part of the population by manipulating the elections in 1995 and provoking social and ethnic conflicts between Northern and Islamic populations and the rest of the country. The rise of this ethnic-religious cleavage led to the formation of a second viable opposition party (the RDR) and to the breakdown of the accommodation process that Houphouët-Boigny had fashioned among ethnic elites to maintain political stability.

1.2 Evolution of Electoral Provisions

The minor importance of elections for the working of the Ivorian political system explains why electoral provisions have traditionally failed to attract the attention of the political actors and observers. Like the Ivorian constitution, the electoral provisions did not evolve until 1980, when the first elements of intra-party competition were introduced at the level of parliamentary elections.

From 1960 onwards presidential and parliamentary elections took place every five years. The principles of universal, equal, direct and secret suffrage were applied. African foreigners living in Côte d'Ivoire were allowed to participate in the elections. Presidential and parliamentary elections were organized in the same day. For the presidency, there were no candidates except for Houphouët-Boigny even though the electoral laws provided for multiple candidatures. The National Assembly was elected on a single list of the PDCI drawn up by the President himself without contest.

This pattern was interrupted by the introduction of elements of intra-party competition for the parliamentary elections in 1980. The new electoral law 80-1039 (1 September 1980) allowed voters to choose between different PDCI candidates in 107 single-member and 19 multi-member constituencies (18 with two seats, one with four seats in Bouaké, closed list, single vote); the number and size of the constituencies was decreed by the President only some weeks before the elections (*decrèt* 80-1099 of 4 October 1980). Absolute majority was required for the candidates or lists (in the multi-member constituencies). The political liberalization initiated by the 1980 parliamentary elections was nevertheless turned back in 1985 when the party and the President organized a pre-selection in every constituency and switched back to a plurality system, resulting in a significantly lower renewal rate.

The reintroduction of multi-partyism in 1990 did not lead to a revision of the electoral provisions (or the electoral calendar). Just for emphasizing the minor variation that represented the presence of other parties from the perspective of the PDCI, the President (and the Parliament) even refused to pass a new *code électoral* and amended the two existing electoral laws from 1985 (Loi No. 85-1073 and No. 85-1074). The regulations with regard to eligibility, candidature and electoral systems (mix of single-member and multi-member constituencies) thus remained essentially the same. Notwithstanding the new opportunities for political parties to present their candidates and lists, independent candidatures were allowed.

President Bedié proposed in 1994 a new *code électoral* combining dispositions for the different elections in one electoral law which was eventually passed by the Parliament in December 1994 and applied in 1995. The new electoral law of 1995 leaves nevertheless a whole range of essential questions to regulation by presidential decree. Opposition claims for an independent electoral commission were rejected.

1.3 Current Electoral Provisions

Sources: Constitution (Loi No. 60-356 du 3 novembre 1960 portant Constitution de la République de Côte d'Ivoire modifiée par les Lois No. 63-1, 75-365, 75-747, 80-1038, 80-1232. 85-1072. 86-90. 90-1529); Electoral Laws: Loi No. 94-642 portant Code électoral; Presidential Decrees No. 95-563-581 du 26 juillet 1995 (concerning the organization of presidential, parliamentary and local elections), Decisions of the Constitutional Court No. E/0005/95 du 27 octobre 1995.

Elected national institutions: President of the Republic and National Assembly (175 members). Regular terms of office: five years (President), five years (Parliament). A constitutional revision in 1998 extended the presidential term to seven years. There are no limitations concerning re-eligibility. The President of the National Assembly is designated as presidential successor. In the case of the National Assembly, by-elections are held.

Suffrage: The principles of universal, equal, direct and secret suffrage are applied. Every citizen who has reached the age of 21 has the right to vote and is entitled to be registered as a voter. Departing from the previous provision, the new electoral law does not allow foreign African citizens to take part in the elections.

Nomination of candidates

- *presidential elections*: Every citizen aged over 40 years, born Ivorian from an Ivorian born mother *and* an Ivorian born father, living in the country during the last five years before the elections, having never renounced his nationality. (This clause was introduced in 1994 to hinder the candidature of the most promising opposition candidate Alassane Ouattara [RDR].) Every candidate has to deposit a caution (F CFA 20 million) and to present a list of 500 supporters for each of the 10 administrative regions.
- *parliamentary elections*: Every citizen who has reached 23 years is eligible if he is born Ivorian from an Ivorian born mother *or* Ivorian born father and has lived the last five years before the elections in the country. (The constitutional court excluded in 1995 an important number of opposition candidates by proving their 'foreign' parenthood.) Every candidate has to deposit a caution (F CFA 100,000) and to be presented by a party or political group. If an elected candidate changes his political affiliation, he will lose his mandate. Independent candidates are admitted if they present a list of 500 supporters in their constituency.

Electoral System

- *presidential elections*: Absolute majority system. If no candidate achieves the absolute majority in the first round, a second round is organized (without limitation of candidates), where plurality is required.
- *parliamentary elections*: Plurality system; 157 constituencies (141 single-member, 15 two-member and one four-member constituency,

(unbalanced) distribution nearly unchanged since first competitive elections 1980); in multi-member constituencies: closed lists/ single vote.

1.4 Comment on the Electoral Statistics

The following tables are generally based on the data of the Ministry of Interior as published in the government-owned daily *Fraternité Matin*. There have never been any officially published and detailed electoral statistics in Côte d'Ivoire. Since the de-linking of parliamentary elections in 1980 and the subsequent fall in participation rates, official publications have completely passed over detailed figures and have contented themselves with enumerating the elected candidates, citing at best an approximate rate of participation. The often incomplete constituency data in *Fraternité Matin* unfortunately do not even allow national percentages or participation rates to be calculated.

As there have not been any free and fair elections in Côte d'Ivoire, the electoral statistics should be regarded with caution; the last presidential and parliamentary elections in 1995 especially have produced results which are questioned by both international and national observers.

2. Tables

2.1 Dates of National Elections, Referendums and Coups d'Etat

Year	Presidential elections	Parliamentary elections	Elections for Constitutional Assembly	Referendums	Coups d'état
1959		12/04			
1960	27/11	27/11			
1965	07/11	07/11			
1970	16/11	16/11			
1975	16/11	16/11			
1980	12/10	09/11 (1st) 23/11 (2nd)			
1985	27/10	10/11			
1990	28/10	25/11			
1995	22/10	26/11			

2.2 Electoral Body 1959–1995

Year	Type of election[a]	Population	Registered voters		Votes cast		
			Total number	% pop.	Total number	% reg. voters	% of pop.
1959	Pa	3,160,000	1,609,345	50.9	1,523,580	94.7	48.2
1960	Pr	3,230,000	1,661,833	51.4	1,641,542	98.8	50.8
1960	Pa	3,230,000	1,661,833	51.4	1,593,135	95.9	49.3
1965	Pr	3,835,000	1,875,547	48.9	1,867,937	99.6	48.7
1965	Pa	3,835,000	1,875,547	48.9	1,867,937	99.6	48.7
1970	Pr	4,310,000	2,020,000	46.9	2,003,714	99.2	46.5
1970	Pa	4,310,000	2,020,000	46.9	1,999,643	99.0	46.4
1975	Pr	6,709,600	2,410,042	35.9	2,405,407	99.8	35.8
1975	Pa	6,709,600	2,410,042	35.9	2,393,019	99.3	35.7
1980	Pr	8,262,300	3,398,056	41.1	2,795,456	82.3	33.8
1980	Pa (1st)	8,262,300	3,398,056	41.1	1,447,572	42.6	17.5
1985	Pr	9,810,000	3,517,259	35.8	3,516,542	99.9	35.8
1985	Pa	9,810,000	3,517,259	35.8	1,606,332	45.7	16.4
1990	Pr	12,233,000	4,408,808[b]	36.0	3,049,133	69.2	24.9
1990	Pa	12,233,000	4,408,808	36.0	1,872,292	40.0	15.3
1995	Pr	14,791,257	3,756,926[c]	25.4	2,109,490[d]	56.2	14.3
1995	Pa	14,791,257	—[e]	—	1,781,503[f]	—	12.0

[a] Pa = Parliament (National Assembly); Pr = President.
[b] The register for the 1990 elections was drawn up in 1987 with the help of a World Bank team.
[c] The fall in registered voters is mainly due to the exclusion of African foreigners who are nevertheless included in the population figure for 1995 (and should amount to some five millions).
[d] Opposition parties decided on an 'active boycott' of their voters.
[e] The revision of the voters' registers between the presidential and parliamentary elections was part of a pact between government and opposition to facilitate the participation of all parties in the parliamentary elections. The election data published in *Fraternité Matin* do indeed reveal different figures of registered voters in nearly every constituency. Total number was not available.
[f] Unofficial figure from *Le Jour* 28/11/1995.

2.3 Abbreviations

FPI	Front Populaire Ivoirien
PDCI	Parti Démocratique de la Côte d'Ivoire
PIT	Parti Ivoirien des Travailleurs
PLCI	Parti Libéral de Côte d'Ivoire
PRCI	Parti Républicain de Côte d'Ivoire
PSI	Parti Socialiste Ivoirien
RDR	Rassemblement des Républicains

UND	Union Nationale pour la Démocratie
USD	Union des Sociaux – Démocrates

General note: Only four parties managed to gain parliamentary seats (in 1990/ 1995). For lack of viable data, all parties are cited which presented candidates in at least 20 constituencies in one of the two elections. In 1995, 27 parties presented candidates, 42 parties were formally registered.

2.4 Electoral Participation of Parties and Alliances 1959–1995

Party / Alliance	Years	Elections contested	
		Presidential	Parliamentary
PDCI	1959, 1960, 1965, 1970, 1975, 1980, 1985, 1990, 1995	8	9
FPI	1990, 1995	1[a]	2
PIT	1990, 1995	1	2
PLCI	1990, 1995	0	2
PRCI	1990	0	1
PSI	1990, 1995	0	2
USD	1990, 1995	0	2
RDR	1995	0[a]	1
UND	1995	0	1

[a] FPI and RDR withdrew their respective candidates in the weeks before the presidential elections 1995.

2.5/ 2.6 Referendums/ Elections for Constitutional Assembly

Referendums and elections for Constitutional Assembly have not been held.

2.7 Parliamentary Elections 1959–1995

Year	1959		1960	
	Total number	%	Total number	%
Registered voters	1,609,345	–	1,661,833	–
Votes cast	1,523,580	94.7	1,593,135	95.9
Invalid votes	1,256	0.1	6,617	0.8
Valid votes	1,522,324	99.9	1,586,518	99.2
PDCI	1,522,324	100.0	1,586,518	100.0

Year	1965 Total number	%	1970 Total number	%
Registered voters	1,875,547	–	2,020,000	–
Votes cast	1,867,937	99.6	1,999,643	98.9
Invalid votes	4,932	0.4	2,083	0.1
Valid votes	1,863,005	99.6	1,997,560	99.9
PDCI	1,863,005	100.0	1,997,560	100.0

Year	1975 Total number	%	1980 Total number	%
Registered voters	2,410,042	–	3,398,056	–
Votes cast	2,393,019	99.3	1,447,572	42.6
Invalid votes	2,453	0.1	—	—
Valid votes	2,390,566	99.9	—	
PDCI	2,390,566	100.0	—	100.0

Year	1985 Total number	%	1990 Total number	%
Registered voters	3,517,259	–	4,408,810	–
Votes cast	1,606,332	45.7	1,872,292	40.0
Invalid votes	—	—	24,480	1.3
Valid votes	—	—	1,847,812	98.7
PDCI	—	100.0	1,324,549	71.7
FPI	–	–	365,999	19.8
Others /Independents	–	–	157,264	8.5

For the 1995 parliamentary elections, no complete data are available. Author's calculations on the base of incomplete figures given in *Fraternité Matin* of 28/ 29 November 1995 (141 out of 158 constituencies) amount to 64.9% for PDCI, 17.9% for FPI, 10.1% for RDR and 1.2% for PIT. Independent candidates gained 2.6% of valid votes.

2.8 Composition of Parliament 1959–1995

Year	1959 Seats	%	1960 Seats	%	1965[a] Seats	%	1970[a] Seats	%
	100	100	70	100	85	100	120	100
PDCI	100	100	70	100	85	100	120	100

[a] Renewal rates 1965: 49/85 outgoing deputies re-elected, 1970: 77/120.

Year	1975		1980[a]		1985[a]	
	Seats	%	Seats	%	Seats	%
	120	100	147	100	175	100
PDCI	120	100	147	100	175	100

[a] Renewal rates: 1980: 27/142 outgoing deputies re-elected; 1985: 61/175

Year	1990		1995/96[a]	
	Seats	%	Seats	%
	175	100	175	100
PDCI	163	93.1	149	85.1
FPI	9	5.1	13	7.4
PIT	1	0.6	–	–
RDR	–	–	13	7.4
Independents	2	1.1	–	–

[a] Elections in four constituencies which had been suspended or invalidated took place on 29 December 1996 (as well as two by-elections). The original results as of November 1995 (including the invalidated mandates) were: PDCI 147, RDR 14, FPI 10.

2.9 Presidential Elections 1960–1995

1960	Total number	%
Registered voters	1,661,833	–
Votes cast	1,641,542	98.8
Invalid votes	190	0.1
Valid votes	1,641,352	99.9
Felix Houphouët-Boigny (PDCI)	1,641,352	100.0

1965	Total number	%
Registered voters	1,875,547	–
Votes cast	1,867,937	99.6
Invalid votes	332	0.1
Valid votes	1,867,605	99.9
Felix Houphouët-Boigny (PDCI)	1,867,605	100.0

1970	Total number	%
Registered voters	2,020,000	–
Votes cast	2,003,714	99.2
Invalid votes	668	0.1
Valid votes	2,003,046	99.9
Felix Houphouët-Boigny (PDCI)	2,003,046	100.0

1975	Total number	%
Registered voters	2,410,042	–
Votes cast	2,405,407	99.8
Invalid votes	502	0.1
Valid votes	2,404,905	99.9
Felix Houphouët-Boigny (PDCI)	2,404,905	100.0

1980	Total number	%
Registered voters	3,398,056	–
Votes cast	2,795,456	82.3
Invalid votes	306	0.1
Valid votes	2,795,150	99.9
Felix Houphouët-Boigny (PDCI)	2,795,150	100.0

1985	Total number	%
Registered voters	3,517,259	–
Votes cast	—	—
Invalid votes	—	—
Valid votes	3,516,542	—
Felix Houphouët-Boigny (PDCI)	3,516,542	100.0

1990	Total number	%
Registered voters	4,408,808	–
Votes cast	3,049,133	69.2
Invalid votes	55,327	1.8
Valid votes	2,993,806	98.2
Felix Houphouët-Boigny (PDCI)	2,445,365	81.7
Laurent Gbagbo (FPI)	548,441	18.3

1995	Total number	%
Registered voters	3,756,926	–
Votes cast	2,109,490	56.2
Invalid votes	52,822	2.5
Annulled votes (Const. Court)	143,845	6.8
Valid votes	1,912,823	90.7
Henri Konan Bedié (PDCI)	1,837,154	96.0
Francis Wodié (PIT)	75,669	4.0

2.10 List of Power Holders 1960–1998

Head of State and Government[a]	Years	Remarks
Felix Houphouët-Boigny	1960–1993	By independence Prime Minister; after coming into effect of the new constitution, declared elected President in December 1960.
Henri Konan Bedié	1993–	Constitutional succession after death of Houphouët-Boigny on 08/12/1993 (as President of the Parliament).

[a] Since November 1990 the President appoints (and dismisses) a Prime Minister (Art. 12, Constitution); the President remains, however, the 'exclusive holder of executive power'.

3. Bibliography

3.1 Official Sources

Loi No. 60-356 du 3 novembre 1960 portant Constitution de la République de Côte d'Ivoire (modifiée par les lois No. 63-1, 75-365, 75-747, 80-1038, 80-1232. 85-1072. 86-90. 90-1529).

Loi No. 85-1074 (du 12 octobre 1985 relative à l'élection des députés à l'Assemblée Nationale, telle que modifiée par la loi No. 90-1392 du 30 octobre 1990).

Loi No. 85-1073 (du 12 octobre 1985 relative à l'élection du Président de la République, telle que modifiée par la loi No. 90-1167 du 10 octobre 1990).

Loi No. 94-642 portant Code électoral.

Decrets No. 95-563-581 du 26 juillet 1995 (portant organisation des élections présidentielles, législatives et municipaux).

Conseil Constitutionnel, Decision No. E/0005/95 du 27 octobre 1995.

LIDHO (Ligue Ivoirienne des Droits de l'Homme): Position de la LIDHO sur la loi portant code electoral, Abidjan Decembre 1994.

3.2 Books and Articles

Amondji, M. (1984). *Félix Houphouët et la Côte d'Ivoire. L'envers de la légende*. Paris: Karthala.

— (1988). *Côte d'Ivoire. La dépendance et l'epreuve des faits*. Paris: L'Harmattan.

Bach, D. (1982). 'L'insertion dans les rapports internationaux', in Y.-A. Fauré and J.-F. Medard (eds.), *Etat et bourgeoisie en Côte d'Ivoire*. Paris: Karthala, 89–121.

Bailly, D. (1995). *La réinstauration du multipartisme en Côte d'Ivoire ou la double mort d'Houphouet-Boigny*. Paris: L'Harmattan.

Bakary Akin, T. (1991a). *Côte d'Ivoire. Une succession impossible? Essai*. Paris: L'Harmattan.

— (1991b). 'Le Retour au pluralisme politique en Côte d'Ivoire'. *Année Africaine 1990–199*, 161–189.

— (1992). *La démocratie par le haut en Côte d'Ivoire*. Paris: L'Harmattan.

Bedié, H. K. (1995). *Discours et Messages de la Campagne Présidentielle 1995*. Abidjan: Editions Neter.

Conte, B., and Lavenue, J.-J. (1992). 'La Côte d'Ivoire un an après les confrontations électorales de 1990: hypothèses et hypothèques'. *Révue Juridique et Politique*, 46/1: 1–27.

Crook, R. C. (1991). 'Les Changements politiques en Cote d'Ivoire: une approche institutionelle'. *Année Africaine 1990–1991*, 87–114.

— (1995). 'Côte d'Ivoire: Multi-party Democracy and Political Change. Surviving the Crisis', in J. A. Wiseman (ed.), *Democracy and Political Change in Sub-Saharan Africa*. London: Routledge, 11–44.

— (1997). 'Winning Coalitions and Ethno-Regional Politics: The Failure of the Opposition in the 1990 and 1995 Elections in Côte d'Ivoire'. *African Affairs*, 96: 215–242.

Dégni-Ségui, R. (1993). 'Evolution politique et constitutionelle en cours et en perspective en Côte d'Ivoire', in G. Conac (ed.), *L'Afrique en transition vers le pluralisme politique*. Paris: Economica, 291–300.

Fauré, Y.-A. (1982). 'Le complexe politico-économique', in Y.-A. Fauré and J.-F. Médard (eds.), *Etat et bourgeoisie en Côte d'Ivoire*. Paris: Karthala, 21–60.

— (1989). 'Côte d'Ivoire: Analysing the Crisis', in D. C. O'Brien, J. Dunn and R. Rathbone (eds.), *Contemporary West African States*. Cambridge: Cambridge UP, 59–74.

— (1991). 'Sur la démocratie en Cote d'Ivoire: passé et present'. *Année Africaine 1990-1991*, 115–160.

Front Populaire Ivorien (1995). *Programme de gouvernement*. Abidjan: Editions DESACI.

Gbagbo, L. (1983). *Côte-d'Ivoire: Pour une alternative démocratique*. Paris: L'Harmattan.

— (1989). *Côte-d'Ivoire. Histoire d'un retour*. Paris: L'Harmattan.

Gombeaud, J.-L., Moutout, C., and Smith, S. (1990). *La Guerre du cacao: Histoire secrète d'un embargo*. Paris: Calmann-Lévy.

Handloff, R. E. (1991). *Côte d'Ivoire. A Country Study*. Washington, D.C.: Federal Research Division, Library of Congress.

Hartmann, C. (1999). *Externe Faktoren im Demokratisierungsprozeß. Eine vergleichende Untersuchung afrikanischer Länder*. Opladen: Leske & Budrich.

Jakobeit, C. (1984). *Die sozio-ökonomische Entwicklung der Elfenbeinküste seit der Unabhängigkeit.* Hamburg: Institut für Afrika-Kunde.

Kalflèche, J.-M. (1991). 'Côte d'Ivoire: Heurs et malheurs des "renovateurs"'. *Géopolitique Africaine,* 14/4: 61–64.

Kamissoko, G. (1996). *L'Après-Houphouet. Bedié, l'heritage et l'avenir*. Abidjan: Editions CEDA/ Fraternité Matin.

Kouassi, L. M. (1996). 'Politischer Wandel in der Côte d'Ivoire: Der steinige Weg vom Einparteistaat zum Mehrparteiensystem'. *Afrika Spectrum*, 31/2: 185–196.

Loucou, J.-N. (1992). *Le multipartisme en Côte d'Ivoire. Essai*. Abidjan: Editions Neter.

Médard, J.-F. (1982). 'La Régulation socio-politique', in Y.-A. Fauré and J.-F. Médard (eds.), *Etat et bourgeoisie en Côte d'Ivoire*. Paris: Karthala, 61–88.

Pimont, Y. (1986). 'A la découverte de la démocratie: les élections présidentielles et législatives d'Octobre-Novembre 1985 en Côte d'Ivoire'. *Revue Juridique et Politique*, 40/3–4: 951–967.

Semi-Bi, Z. (1986). 'Genèse de la démocratie à l'ivorienne. Bilan critique de l'activité parlementaire en Côte d'Ivoire (1980–85)'. *Le Mois en Afrique*, 249–250: 15–30.

Teya Koffi, P. (1985). *Côte d'Ivoire. Le roi est nu*. Paris: L'Harmattan.

Tiemoko, C. (1995). 'Démocratie et surenchères identitaires en Côte d'Ivoire'. *Politique Africaine*, 58: 142–151.

Vidal, C. (1995). 'Côte d'Ivoire: Funérailles présidentielles et devaluation entre décembre 1993 et mars 1994'. *L'Afrique Politique 1995*, 31–46.

Widner, J. A. (1991). 'The 1990 Elections in Côte d'Ivoire'. *Issue*, 20/1: 31–40.

— (1994). 'Two Leadership Styles and Patterns of Political Liberalization'. *African Studies Review,* 37/1: 151–174.

Woods, D. (1996). 'The Politicization of Teachers' Associations in the Côte d'Ivoire'. *African Studies Review*, 39/3: 113–129.

Ziemer, K. (1978). 'Elfenbeinküste', in D. Sternberger, B. Vogel, D. Nohlen and K. Landfried (eds.), *Die Wahl der Parlamente und anderer Staatsorgane. Band II: Politische Organisation und Repräsentation in Afrika,* by Franz Nuscheler, Klaus Ziemer *et al.*, Berlin/ New York: Walter de Gruyter, 643–688.

— (1984). *Demokratisierung in Westafrika*. Paderborn: Schöningh.

Zolberg, A. R. (1969). *One-Party Government in the Ivory Coast.* (rev. edn.) Princeton, N.J.: Princeton UP.

DJIBOUTI

by Bernhard Thibaut

1. Introduction

1.1 Historical Overview

Elections under the conditions of universal suffrage have been held regularly in Djibouti since the second half of the 1950s when the country was still a French colony. From independence (1977) until the early 1990s all elections took place within an authoritarian single-party regime. The return to multi-party politics in 1992 did not bring about substantial democratization of the political system. Due to the common practice of electoral manipulations and favored by an extremely majoritarian electoral system the political hegemony of the former single-party *Rassemblement Populaire pour le Progrès* (RPP) of President Hassan Gouled Aptidon remained untouched.

Djibouti became part of the French colonial empire in 1896 as *Côte Française des Somalis*. From 1945 onwards a relatively small number of natives affiliated with the colonial administration could vote in elections to the French National Assembly where the territory had one representative. In 1956 the *Loi Cadre* introduced universal suffrage and provided for the installation of a directly elected Territorial Assembly. This first step towards political autonomy stimulated the emergence of political parties. The ethnic structure of the population, characterized by the division between the Issa and other groups of Somali origin and the Afar who account for approximately one third of the population (besides which there exist Arab and European minorities), became an important factor of political organization, although parties often relied to some extent on alliances between different ethnic groups. However, most parties were loose and unstable organizations based on the personal ambitions of individual leaders and clientelistic relations.

From 1957 onwards, when elections for the Territorial Assembly were held for the first time, political development was triggered by the controversial question of the future status of the territory. The French authorities shifted their support increasingly from Issa to Afar politicians and parties they perceived to be more loyal to the status quo. Strict control over the register of electors as well as a political culture based on the traditional authority of clan leaders enabled the colonial administration to steer election and referendum results to a considerable extent. Between 1958 and 1965 the number of eligible Issa and other Somali groups increased by 55%, the number of eligible Afar by 195%—without any significant changes in the population structure. These measures raised political representation of the Afar significantly in the 1958 and 1963 elections for Territorial Assembly. In the same way in a referendum held in 1967 on the question of the status of the French Somali Coast the victory of Yes votes opting for the maintenance of the status quo was secured. The territory was renamed *Territoire Français de Afars et Issas* and a new colonial statute slightly enhanced the competence of the territorial legislature (now *Chambre des Députés*) and the government led by Ali Aref Bourhan and his *Regroupement Démocratique Afar* (RDA).

Although the statute prescribed a fair and equitable distribution of political offices among ethnic groups the opposition was seriously handicapped by campaign restrictions and manipulations of the ticket and the polls in the territorial legislative elections of 1968 and 1973. In 1973 all 40 seats in the Chamber of Deputies were won by the government.

The independence process became dynamic when the growing 'parliamentary opposition' emerging from a split of the RDA (renamed *Union National pour l'Indépendance*, UNI) replaced the government in 1976 and gave way to the increasingly popular demands for full independence that had since 1974 been postulated by the main opposition party, the *Ligue Populaire Africaine pour l'Indépendance* (LPAI), representing mainly Issa and other Somali groups. Another independence referendum was held together with legislative elections on 8 May 1977. Almost unanimously, though with rather low participation rates in Afar dominated regions, the electorate voted for independence. In the elections to the National Assembly the LPAI and some minor parties backing the independence process presented a joint single list under the label *Rassemblement Populaire pour l'Indépendance* (RPI) while the Afar parties UNI and *Mouvement pour la Libération de Djibouti* (MLD) boycotted the elections. On 27 June the last French colony in Africa became independent as Republic of Djibouti with a presidential system of government. Already on 24 June the National Assembly had designated LPAI-leader Hassan Gouled as President.

A veteran Issa politician—founder of one of the first political parties of the Somali coast in the 1950s, head of the territorial government for several months in 1958 and 1959 and member of the French National Assembly from 1959 to 1962—Gouled made some efforts to create interethnic loyalties within the RPI. In the course of the independence process institutional rules had been designed to guarantee a proportional representation of ethnic groups in the legislature and in the government. However, many Afar perceived the governments policies (e.g. with regard to education, the labor market, or promotions within the army) as clearly favoring the Issa. Gouled's repressive treatment of the opposition (banning of several parties, detention of leading politicians) as well as terrorist activities of radical groups operating from Somalia and Ethiopia also contributed to political instability.

In 1979 the LPAI merged with several other parties to build the *Rassemblement Populaire pour le Progrès* (RPP) as a multi-ethnic organization. When exiled Afar leaders founded the opposition party *Parti Populaire de Djibouti* (PPD) in August 1981 Djibouti was declared a single-party state through a constitutional amendment. Presidential elections with Gouled as the only candidate had already been held in the same year and were held again in 1987. In the parliamentary elections of 1982 and 1987 a single RPP-list was presented to the voters. Formal mechanisms assuring the political representation of Afar and other non-Somali groups were maintained but did not prevent increasing centralization and personalization of political power in the hands of Gouled and his clan (Mamassa).

In the second half of the 1980s the regime faced growing opposition from clandestine organizations like the *Front Démocratique pour la libération de Djibouti* (FDLD, mainly Afar) and the *Mouvement National de Djibouti pour l'Instauration de la Démocratie* (MNDID, mainly Issa). Both organizations merged in 1990 to build the *Union de Mouvement Démocratique* (UMD). In 1991 the Afar based *Front pour la Restauration de l'Unité et la Démocratie* (FRUD) started to operate as a guerilla movement with the aim of bringing down the 'tribal dictatorship'. Demands for a return to multi-party politics were raised even within the RPP. Besides, pressure to reintroduce political pluralism was exerted at the international level, mainly by France.

At the end of 1991 President Gouled announced a reform of the constitution that would allow for multi-party elections. Approved in a referendum on 4 September 1992, the new chart limited, however, the number of legally registered parties to a maximum of four and was not accepted by the FRUD which boycotted the first multi-party parliamentary elections of December 1992 as well as the presidential elections of 5 May 1993. Both contests were considered fraudulent by the participating opposition parties, which remained without any parliamentary representation, as well as by international observers.

In late 1994 the government and the FRUD signed a peace accord which ended three years of guerilla warfare. The FRUD was legalized as political party, some of its members were assigned Cabinet posts in mid-1995 and it was agreed to work out an electoral reform that would prevent continued manipulations of the electoral register on the part of the government and provide for an effective institutional representation of the political opposition. The agreement between the government and the FRUD resulted in a slight rearrangement of power within the political class rather than enhancing the possibilities for an effective articulation of opposition interests on the bases of a pluralist democracy. In the parliamentary elections of 1997 the RPP and the FRUD presented a joint list that won all 65 seats in the National Assembly leaving the two other participating parties of the opposition, the *Parti pour le Renouveau de la Démocratie* (PRD) and the *Parti National de Djibouti* (PND) once again without any institutional representation.

1.2 Evolution of Electoral Provisions

Universal suffrage was introduced in 1956 by the *Loi Cadre*. All citizens with a minimum age of 21 were entitled to vote. The voting age was reduced to 18 by the Constitution of 1977.

Before independence the electorate of the French Territory of the Afar and Issa voted regularly in elections to the Territorial Parliament (1957, 1958, 1974: 40 seats), in the elections to the National Assembly of France (one representative) and in the French presidential elections. The independence constitution provided for the direct election of the President for a period of six years with a maximum of two terms and of the 65 members of the one-chamber National Parliament *(Assemblée Nationale)* for a period of five years.

The presidential elections of 1981 and 1987 were regulated by Organic Act No. 1/AN/81 of 10 February 1981. Any presidential candidate had to be at least 25 years old, enjoy his full civil and political rights and be supported by a regularly constituted political party represented by at least 25 members of the National Assembly. The President was to be elected under the relative majority formula.

Before independence the elections to the territorial legislature were generally held under a relative majority list system in five multi-member constituencies (size dependent on population). Only in 1958 was a PR system used. The parliamentary elections of 1977 were held with closed list and according to the relative majority formula. The number of candidates per list was equivalent to the number of parliamentary seats to be filled and the country as a whole formed a single constituency. To assure a proportional representation of the different ethnic groups in the National Assembly the lists were required to be composed proportionally of candidates from all districts of the country. The same system was applied in the parliamentary elections of 1982 and 1987 which were regulated by Organic Act No. 2/AN/1981 of 24 October 1981. The minimum age of eligible candidates was set to 23 years; besides, candidates had to have a clean judicial record, be resident in Djibouti for at least five years and able to read, write and speak French or Arabic fluently. Only the RPP was entitled to nominate candidates. Voters could express their disagreement with the RPP list either by abstaining or through casting a blank ballot.

1.3 Current electoral provisions

Sources: Constitution of 1992; electoral law of 1992 *(Loi organique No. 1 /AN /92 relative aux élections)*.

Suffrage: The principles of universal, equal, direct and secret suffrage are applied. Citizens with a minimum age of 18 years who are registered as voters are entitled to vote.

Elected national institutions: President of the Republic for a term of six years (one consecutive re-election being allowed); one-chamber National Parliament (*Chambre de Députés*) with 65 members.

Nomination of candidates
- *presidential elections*: A candidate must be a citizen of Djibouti (any other additional nationality excluded) with full possession of civil and political rights and be at least 40 years old.
- *parliamentary elections*: Candidates have to be a citizen of Djibouti with full possession of civil and political rights and be able to speak French or Arabic fluently. Members of the armed forces, police and

security forces as well as certain public officials and judges are ineligible.

Electoral system
- *presidential elections*: Absolute majority system. If in the first round no candidate receives more than 50% of the votes cast, a second round is held within two weeks between the two strongest candidates of the first round.
- *parliamentary elections*: Plurality system with closed lists in five multi-member constituencies. Any list has to contain as many candidates as seats are to be filled in the respective constituency and be proportionally composed of members of different ethnic groups (parties are constitutionally prohibited from identifying themselves by race, ethnic group, sex, religion, sect, language or region). The list with the relative majority of valid votes wins all seats.

1.4 Comment on the Electoral Statistics

Statistical electoral data for Djibouti are relatively easy to obtain. However, manipulations of the electoral statistics on the part of official authorities have been a common practice since elections have been held, a tradition that was established from the colonial administration.

The data presented in the following tables were taken from Ziemer (1978) with regard to the elections of 1973 and 1977 and the referendums of 1967 and 1977. Data for the elections held during the single-party regime were taken from Keesing's Archives. For the presidential and parliamentary elections since 1991 as well as for the referendum of 1992 data were reported to the author by the French embassy in Djibouti. Generally these data turned out to be more consistent than other, slightly differing and often incomplete data for the same elections that have been reported by sources such as *Marché Tropicaux*, *African Research Bulletin* or the national newspaper *La Nation*.

2. Tables

2.1 Dates of National Elections, Referendums and Coups d'Etat

Year	Presidential elections	Parliamentary elections	Elections for Constitutional Assembly	Referendums	Coups d'état
1967				10/03	
1973		18/11[a]			
1977		08/05	08/05	08/05	
1981	12/06				
1982		21/05			
1987	24/04	24/04			
1992				04/09	
1992		18/12			
1993	07/05				
1997		19/12			

[a] Elections to the Chamber of Representatives of the French Territory of Afar and Issa (pre-independence).

2.2 Electoral Body 1967–1997

Year	Type of election[a]	Population[b]	Registered voters[c]		Votes cast		
			Total number	% pop.	Total number	% reg. voters	% pop.
1967	Ref	125,000	39,312	31.4	37,332	95.0	29.7
1973	Pa[d]	214,000	47,380	22.1	35,841	75.6	16.7
1977	Ref / Pa	270,000	105,962	39.2	81,847	77.7	30.3
1981	Pr	314,000	97,964	31.2	—	—	—
1982	Ref / Pa	332,000	85,870	25.9	79,327	92.4	25.3
1987	Pa	370,000	100,881	27.3	89,475	88.7	24.2
1987	Ref / Pr	370,000	101,946	27.6	—	—	—
1992	Ref	465,000	139,431	30.0	104,804	75.2	22.5
1992	Pa	465,000	151,047	32.5	73,260	48.5	15.8
1993	Pr	570,000	148,742	26.1	76,092	51.2	13.3
1997	Pa	634,000	165,700	26.1	94,304	56.9	14.9

[a] Pa = Parliament; Pr = President; Ref = Referendum.
[b] Figures based on UN sources.
[c] Fluctuations probably result from manipulations of the electoral register on the part of the government, numbers for individual years differ widely between primary and secondary sources.
[d] Pre-independence.

2.3 Abbreviations

FRUD	Front pour la Restauration de l'Unité et la Démocratie
PND	Parti National de Djibouti
PRD	Parti du Renouveau Démocratique
RPI	Rassemblement Populaire pour l'Indépendance
RPP[a]	Rassemblement Populaire pour le Progrès

[a] On 4 March 1979 a number of parties and political groups that had fought for independence (RPI, *Ligue Populaire Africaine pour l'Indépendance, Front Populaire de Libération de la Côte des Somalis, Union Nationale pour l'Indépendance*) merged to build the RPP.

2.4 Electoral Participation of Parties and Alliances 1977–1997

Party / Alliance	Years	Elections contested	
		Presidential	Parliamentary
RPI	1977	0	1
RPP	1981, 1982, 1987, 1992, 1993, 1997	3	4
PND	1993, 1997	1	1
PRD	1992, 1993, 1997	1	2
FRUD	1997[a]	0	1

[a] Alliance with RPP.

2.5 Referendums

Year	1967[a]		1977[b]	
	Total number	%	Total number	%
Registered voters	39,312	–	105,962	-
Votes cast	37,332	95.0	81,847	77.7
Invalid votes	111	0.3	784	1.0
Valid votes	37,221	99.7	81,063	99.0
Yes	22,555	60.6	80,864	99.8
No	14,666	39.4	199	0.2

[a] Referendum on Independence. Yes votes: pro status quo; No votes: pro independence.

[b] Referendum on Independence. Yes votes: pro independence; No votes: against independence.

Year	1992[a] Total number	%	1992[b] Total number	%
Registered voters	139,431	—	139,431	—
Votes cast	104,804	75.2	104,804	75.2
Invalid votes	1,504	1.4	1,504[c]	1.4
Valid votes	103,300	98.6	103,302	98.6
Yes	101,287	98.1	101,125	97.9
No	2,013	1.9	2,177	2.1

[a] Question one: 'Do you approve the new constitution?'
[b] Question two: 'Do you approve the limitation of party politics to four parties?'
[c] Official figure. The valid votes (as a sum of Yes votes and No votes) and the invalid votes reported do not add up to the reported figure of votes cast.

2.6 Elections for Constitutional Assembly

Elections for an assembly with exclusive constituent functions have not been held. The elections of 1977 are sometimes referred to as elections for Constitutional Assembly because it was originally foreseen that the assembly would just work out a constitution before the election of a new Parliament. However, the National Assembly elected in 1977 functioned as the regular legislature until 1981.

2.7 Parliamentary Elections 1973–1997

Year	1973[a] Total number	%	1977[d] Total number	%
Registered voters	47,380	–	105,962	–
Votes cast	35,841	75.6	—	86.3
Invalid votes	443	1.2	—	—
Valid votes	35,398	98.8	—	—
'Majorité'[b]	26,852	75.9	–	–
'Opposition moderée'[c]	5,332	15.1	–	–
'Opposition dure'	3,214	9.0	–	–
RPI	–	–	—	65.8

[a] Elections to the Chamber of Deputies (pre-independence).
[b] Groups supporting the territorial of government Ali Aref Bourhan (mainly Afar).
[c] Groups supporting opposition leader Hassan Gouled Aptidon (mainly Issa and other Somalis).
[d] Electoral boycott by *Union National de Djibouti* and *Mouvement pour la Libération de Djibouti* (both parties mainly representing Afar).

Year	1982 Total number	%	1987 Total number	%
Registered voters	85,870	–	100,881	–
Votes cast	79,327	92.4	89,475	88.7
Invalid votes	1,343	1.7	1,282	1.4
Valid votes	77,984	98.3	88,193	98.6
RPP	77,984	100.0	—	87.3[a]

[a] Share of votes supporting the candidates of the single-party list.

Year	1992[a] Total number	%	1997 Total number	%
Registered voters	151,047	–	165,700	–
Votes cast	73,260	48.5	94,304	56.9
Invalid votes	1,433	2.0	2,556	2.7
Valid votes	71,827	98.0	91,747	97.3
RPP-FRUD[b]	53,578	74.6	72,073	78.6
PRD	18,249	25.4	17,607	16.2
PND	—	—	2,067	2.3

[a] Electoral boycott by FRUD.
[b] In 1992 RPP only.

2.7 a) Parliamentary Elections 1992 and 1997: Regional Results

1992 absolute numbers	Djibouti	Dikhil	Ali-Sabih	Tadjourah	Obock	Total
Registered voters	82,895	26,701	17,454	14,113	9,884	151,047
Votes cast	43,703	12,013	6,636	7,708	3,200	73,260
Invalid votes	977	199	92	97	68	1,433
Valid votes	42,726	11,814	6,544	7,611	3,132	71,827
RPP	29,283	8,623	4,929	7,611	3,132	53,578
PRD	13,443	3,191	1,615	–	–	18,249

1992 percentages	Djibouti	Dikhil	Ali-Sabih	Tadjourah	Obock	Total
Participation rate	52.7	45.1	38.0	54.6	32.4	48.5
RPP	68.5	73.0	75.3	100.0	100.0	74.6
PRD	31.5	27.0	24.7	0.0	0.0	25.4

1997 absolute numbers						
	Djibouti	Dikhil	Ali-Sabih	Tadjourah	Obock	Total
Registered voters	88,248	29,401	17,410	19,366	11,275	165,700
Votes cast	42,204	21,630	5,732	15,153	9,585	94,304
Invalid votes	1,917	140	67	214	218	2,556
Valid votes	40,287	21,490	5,665	14,939	9,366	91,747
RPP-FRUD	25,846	19,405	2,517	14,939	9,366	91,747
PRD	14,441	2,085	1,081	–	–	17,607
PND	–	–	2,067	–	–	2,067

1997 percentages						
	Djibouti	Dikhil	Ali-Sabih	Tadjourah	Obock	Total
Participation rate	47.8	73.6	32.9	78.3	85.0	56.9
RPP-FRUD	64.2	90.3	44.4	100.0	100.0	78.6
PRD	35.9	9.7	19.1	–	–	19.2
PND	–	–	36.5	–	–	2.3

2.8 Composition of Parliament 1977–1997

Year	1977		1982		1987		1992	
	Seats	%	Seats	%	Seats	%	Seats	%
	65	100	65	100	65	100	65	100
RPI	65	100	–	–	–	–	–	–
RPP	–	–	65	100	65	100	65	100

Year	1997	
	Seats	%
	65	100
RPP-FRUD	65[a]	100

[a] RPP: 54 seats, FRUD: 11 seats.

2.9 Presidential Elections 1981–1993

The presidential elections of 1981 and 1987 were not competitive. On both occasions Hassan Gouled Aptidon ran as the only candidate; according to official figures the share of votes supporting him was 84.6% in 1981 and 89.7% in 1987. Figures for registered voters are reported in table 2.2; other data are not available.

1993[a]	Total number	%
Registered voters	148,742	–
Votes cast	76,092	51.2
Invalid votes	1,750[a]	0.3
Valid votes	74,342	97.7
Hassan Gouled Aptidon (RPP)	45,162	60.7
Mohamed Jama Elabe (PRD)	16,386	22.0
Aden Roble Awaleh (PND)	9,143	12.3
Mohamed Musa Ali (Indep.)	2,185	2.9
Ahmed Ibrahim Abdi (Indep.)	1,466	1.9

[a] Electoral boycott by FRUD.
[b] Author's calculation.

2.10 List of Power Holders 1977–1998

Head of State	Years	Remarks
Hassan Gouled Aptidon	1977–	Designated as President of the Republic by the National Assembly (acclamation) on 24/06/1977 (in office since independence on 27/07/1977); confirmed in the presidential elections of 1981 and 1987 (as single candidate) and in the multi-party presidential elections in 1993.

3. Bibliography

Aubry, M.-C. (1990). *Djibouti: bibliographie fondamentale.* Paris: L'Harmattan.

Banque d'information et de documentation de l'ocean Indien (ed.) (1986). *Djibouti, les institutions politiques et militaires*. Paris.

Coubba, A. (1993). *Djibouti: une nation en otage*. Paris : L'Harmattan.

— (1995). *Le mal djiboutien: rivalites ethniques et enjeux politiques*. Paris: L'Harmattan.

Dubois, C. (1997). *Djibouti 1888–1967: héritage ou frustration?* Paris: L'Harmattan.

Farah, G. (1982). *La république de Djibouti: naissance d'un état*. s.l.: Imp. Off. de la Rep. Tun.

Fenet, A. (1983). *Djibouti: 'A Mini-State at the Horn of Africa'*. Analysen aus der Abteilung Entwicklungsländerforschung der Friedrich-Ebert-Stiftung, 106/107. Bonn: FES.

Gouled Aptidon, H. (1990). *Expression d'une jeune republique: discours du President El Hadj Hassan Gouled Aptidon, entre 1977–1989.* Djibouti: Secretariat general a l'information.

Labahn. T. (1993). 'Djibouti', in D. Nohlen and F. Nuscheler (eds.), *Handbuch der Dritten Welt*, *Vol. 5: Ostafrika und Südafrika*, Bonn: Dietz, 68–78.

Laudouze, A. (1989). *Djibouti: nation-carrefour* (2nd edn.). Paris: Karthala.

Matthies, V. (1992). *Äthiopien, Eritrea, Somalia, Djibouti: Das Horn von Afrika.* Munich: Beck.

Oberlé, Ph. (1971). *Afars et Somalis. Le Dossier de Djibouti.* Paris: Présence Africaine.

— and Hugot, P. (1985). *Histoire de Djibouti: des origines à la République.* Paris: Présence Africaine.

Otayek, R. (1985). *Djibouti: construction nationale et contraintes stratégiques.* Bordeaux: CEAN.

Rabeh, O. O. (1984). *Le cercle et la spirale*. Paris: Lettres libres.

— (1985). *Republique de Djibouti, ou, Roue de secours d'Ethiopie?* Ivry/ Paris: Ateliers Silex/ L'Harmattan.

Saint Veran, R. (1981). *Djibouti, pawn of the Horn of Africa*. Metuchen, NJ: Scarecrow Press, 1981 (french orig. Cagnes: R. Tholomier 1977).

Schraeder, P. J. (1991). *Djibouti.* Oxford: Clio Press.

Shehim, K., and Searing, J. (1980). 'Djibouti and the Question of Afar Nationalism'. *African Affairs* 79/315: 209–226.

Territoire francais des Afars et des Issas (1974). *Legislature soixante-treize – soixante-dix-huit.* Djibouti: Service de l'information du Territoire francais des Afars et des Issas.

Thompson, V., and Adloff, R. (1968). *Djibouti and the Horn of Africa.* Stanford, Calif.: Stanford University Press.

Wais, I. (1991). *Dschibuti. Entwicklungsprobleme und Perspektiven kleiner Staaten. Ein Fallbeispiel*. Osnabrück: Verlagscooperative.

Ziemer, K. (1978). 'Djibouti', in D. Sternberger, B. Vogel, D. Nohlen and K. Landfried (eds.), *Die Wahl der Parlamente und anderer Staatsorgane. Band II: Politisch Organisation und Repräsentation in Afrika,* by Franz Nuscheler, Klaus Ziemer *et al*., Berlin/ New York: Walter de Gruyter, 605–642.

EGYPT

by Matthias Ries

1. Introduction

1.1 Historical Overview

In the aftermath of World War I, the 1919 revolution which led Egypt to limited independence from the colonial power Great Britain on 22 February 1922 linked the national question to the establishment of a constitutional monarchy. Although political parties were formed, in the constitution of 1923 political freedoms were not respected either by the kings or by Great Britain, which continued to control Egypt. When parliamentary elections were held in 1950 the *Wafd Party* (WP) won the majority of seats, and in 1951 Prime Minister Mustafa al-Nahhas Pasha repealed the 1936 treaty which gave Britain the right to control the Suez Canal. King Farouk dismissed the Prime Minister, igniting anti-British riots which were put down by the army. This and other reasons compelled the Free Officers to stage a coup d'état on 23 July 1952, and to seize control of Egypt. After the abdication of King Farouk, General Muhammad Ali Nagib, commander of the armed forces, became Prime Minister and later President. But in fact Egypt was ruled by a nine-man Revolutionary Command Council led by Colonel Gamal Abd al-Nasser. The monarchy was abolished, all political parties were banned and the constitution was suspended. On 18 June 1953, the Arab Republic of Egypt was declared. Those involved in political opposition were persecuted, exiled or executed. The Muslim Brothers (MB) which had initially supported the 1952 revolution, were outlawed.

While Nagib was removed from power in 1954, Nasser became acting Head of State and Government. In 1956, almost all registered Egyptians voted for the new constitution and for Nasser as President in the same referendum. In July 1957 a new National Assembly was elected which lasted until February 1958. With the Liberation Rally, the National Union (NU, established in May 1957) and later the Arab Socialist Union (ASU), Nasser's military regime created three political mass organizations. These instruments of mobilization provided the candidates for the

Parliament. Country-wide referendums—with the usual 99% for the regime—and elections within the single mass party were held periodically. Nasser also became the chief advocate and spokesman of the Pan-Arab unity which led to the failed Pan-Arab experiment of the United Arab Republic (UAR) with Syria (1958–1961). In this interim period a provisional constitution for the enlarged Republic replaced the Egyptian Constitution of 1956. While there was no Parliament between 1961 and 1964, in 1962, after the NU had been dissolved, the Charter for National Action was formulated which was meant to lead to Arab Socialism and the 'melting of class differences' in Egypt. The principles of the Charter, comprising an 'alliance of popular working forces' (which included peasants, workers, intellectuals, national capitalists and soldiers) were established in the temporary constitution of 25 March 1964 and the ASU as the new mass instrument served for it. During the period of single-party elections (1957–1976) government control was tight, and candidates were screened for political loyalty by the leading officers who dominated the party. Some choice was permitted between the candidates, who mostly were local notables, and their personal prestige often decided on the outcome of the elections. The dual-member constituency system of the 1960s with the 50%-reservation for workers and peasants was a largely unsuccessful attempt to involve the lower classes in the electoral process. Following the disastrous military defeat against Israel in June 1967 the regime promised more democracy within the ASU by promulgating the Program of 30 March 1968.

After Nasser's death in 1970 Muhammad Anwar al-Sadat assumed control of the government by the 'corrective movement' of 15 May 1971 and the Egyptian Permanent Constitution was established in the same year. Sadat began to reverse the failed socialist policies of his predecessor. Following the 1973 war, he instituted the open door economic policy of 1974 (*Infitah*), and he also moved toward a controlled liberalization. In October 1976 Sadat allowed the establishment of three political forums within the ASU-framework to represent the right, the center and the left. It was the first partly free parliamentary election since 1952. The forums were followed by three parties in 1978 within the National Democratic Party (NDP) as the former center became the ruling party. The President now started to fight the Egyptian left by opting for Islam as political ideology. But Sadat's support for Islam began to backfire as groups like the MB gained wider support and became more vocal in their criticism of government economic policies and the Camp David agreement with Israel. Irritated by the rise of parliamentary criticism in 1979 Sadat dissolved the People's Assembly and called for new elections, in which the regime made sure its main critics like the *New Wafd Party* (NWP) lost their seats. The 1980 constitutional amendment established the Shari'a as the legislative source and a second chamber was added to the system when the Central Committee of the ASU was transformed into the Advisory Council, essentially only a consultative chamber of notables and retired officials in which the ruling NDP kept most of the elected and appointed seats. The confrontation with the opposition reached its peak when Sadat arrested opposition leaders and journalists in the 5 September 1981 crackdown. Although Sadat realized a formal multi-party system and a pluralization of the Egyptian society, the activities of the opposition were very restricted by the party law and by the ban on demonstrations, strikes and assemblies.

After the assassination of Sadat in October 1981 President Hosni Mubarak continued and consolidated Sadat's policy of limited political liberalization. But he first looked for national reconciliation: political prisoners were released, the parties and even the MB became active again. Mubarak allowed the opposition parties to campaign. While the controlled liberalization and the development of the Islamic movement in the 1980s was the most significant change in the political arena, the presidency remained dominant. Although the 1984 election with its proportional electoral system was said to be the first really free election since 1952, all opposition parties complained of government control of the media, vote-rigging, violence and intimidation by the NDP. The Egyptian judiciary was to play a greater role than ever before: the Supreme Constitutional Court annulled the elections of 1984 and 1987 contested by six official parties. Three opposition parties (NWP, SLP and LSP) boycotted the 1990 elections. In the 1995 elections, accompanied by bloody clashes (around 50 people died), 14 official parties were in the running, but the political opposition and human rights groups cried foul while the government's NDP celebrated a landslide victory. The MB, Egypt's most popular but officially outlawed movement, only managed to grab one seat. The increasing violence between militant Islamists and the Egyptian government has left its marks on the 1990s. The state of emergency, established in 1981, is still in force.

1.2 Evolution of Electoral Provisions

A detailed evolution of the electoral provisions until 1976 can be found in Mattes/ Züfle (1978). While there has been ample change in the provisions concerning parliamentary elections, presidential elections have been organized in the same manner since the 1950s.

In 1956 a qualified elector had to be 18 years old enjoying all Egyptian civil and political rights. While voting was compulsory for men who were automatically included in the electoral register, women had to claim for it. Soldiers also had the right to vote. The electoral law of 10 March 1957 regulated the election for the National Assembly: All representatives had to be members of the NU, literate, Egyptian citizens, not less than 30 years old and without any relationship to the royal family. The Republic kept the former majority system with 350 single-member constituencies and thus 350 parliamentary seats.

For the 1964 parliamentary elections a dual-member constituency system was introduced reserving one of two seats for a worker or a peasant as defined in the Charter for National Action. The country was divided into 175 constituencies. In each constituency at least one worker or peasant had to be elected. All representatives had to be members of the ASU for at least one year, literate and over 30 years old (monetary deposit of E£ 20). Civil servants and members of local councils were disqualified from candidature. The electoral law stipulated an absolute majority system with the amended requirement of a relative majority in the second round. For the first time the President appointed 10 additional members to the assembly making a total of 360 in order to include minorities like Beduins and Copts. In 1976, in addition to the nomination of candidates of the three forums, independents were authorized to participate. Officers and soldiers could not stand for election. Then law No. 40 of 1977 was issued which regulated the establishment of political parties in Egypt by imposing the condition on party founders, that 20 parliamentarians had to be among them. In 1979, 30 women-only seats were added, while the country was now divided into 176 constituencies.

Passed by the People's Assembly in August 1983, the new electoral law No. 114 distinguished itself from any electoral system before. A proportional representation system with closed party lists replaced the majority system. Accordingly, the Arab Republic of Egypt was divided into 48 constituencies instead of 176, represented by 448 members in addition to 10 members appointed by the President. The number of seats in each constituency was proportional to the respective numerical weight in the census of 1989. In 31 of the 48 constituencies one seat had to be assigned for women, while independents could no longer stand for election. Most important, the electoral law allowed the majority party to get the votes of the other parties which did not overcome the newly introduced 8%-threshold. Moreover, a party whose list obtained the minimum number of votes and had the right to be represented was still bound to complete the 50% of workers and peasants according to the order shown on the list.

In accordance with the Egyptian Constitution of 1971, which calls for equal political rights for all citizens, the Supreme Constitutional Court ruled in December 1986 that the electoral law ban of independent candidature was unconstitutional. Then Law No. 188 of 1986 amended the electoral system to combine both the PR party list and the individual majority systems, including the same 48 constituencies all over the country, so that each constituency had one member elected by way of the individual majority system and the other representatives by the PR party list system. No one was allowed to stand as a candidate for both channels of representation. There were 458 members in this assembly, 400 of them elected by the party list system, 48 for individual seats (in each constituency with at least 20% of the votes) and 10 members appointed by the President of the Republic. While the proportional representation of seats for women was abolished, the 8%-threshold was maintained. On 5 April 1990, the High Constitutional Court declared the 1987 elections null and void. A resolution was issued by Law No. 201 (30 September 1990) to return to the absolute majority system in two rounds and to abolish the 8%-threshold.

1.3 Current Electoral Provisions

Sources: The Permanent Constitution of the Arab Republic of Egypt issued on 11 September 1971 and amended on 22 May 1980.

Elected national institutions: President of the Republic (six years), People's Assembly (five years, 444 elected members and 10 appointed by the Head of State), Advisory Council (six years, 172 elected and 86 appointed members).

Suffrage: Age: 18 years; Egyptian citizenship (or naturalized for at least five years); disqualifications: among others not rehabilitated persons convicted of a felony, civil servants or employees of the public sector dismissed for dishonorable reasons (in five years preceding election).

Voting is compulsory for men, failure to do so resulting in a fine of E£ 20.

Nomination of candidates

- *presidential elections*: The person to be elected President of the Republic must be a born Egyptian of Egyptian parents enjoying civil and political rights. His age must not be less than 40 years. The People's Assembly nominates the President; the nomination—if the candidate wins two-third of the votes of the Assembly members—shall be referred to the people for a referendum.
- *parliamentary elections*: Qualified electors; age: 30 years; Egyptian citizenship (or naturalized for at least 10 years); descendant of an Egyptian father; proficiency in reading and writing; completion of/or exemption from military service; monetary deposit of E£ 200. No member can hold office in both the People's Assembly and the Advisory Council at the same time.

Electoral system

- *presidential elections*: The candidate shall be considered President of the Republic when he obtains an absolute majority of the votes cast in the presidential referendum. The President of the Republic may be re-elected for other successive terms.
- *elections of the People's Assembly*: 222 (two-seat) constituencies. Individual absolute majority system in two rounds. The elector is obliged to vote for two individual candidates. The electoral law stipulates an absolute majority system with a relative majority in the second round. If the two successful candidates in a constituency are not workers or peasants, the one with the largest number of votes is declared elected and a new plurality poll is held a week later between the two best-placed workers and peasants. If no candidate obtains an absolute majority in a constituency in the first round, a plurality run-off is held a week later between the four best-placed contestants, provided that at least half of them are workers or peasants. The two with the highest vote are declared elected provided that at least one is either worker or a peasant. Vacancies between general elections are filled through by-elections or appointment, according to the case.
- *Advisory Council*: Two thirds of the members are elected by direct balloting in 88 constituencies, at least half of whom must be workers and farmers. The President of the Republic appoints the other third. Renewed elections and appointment of 50% of the total number of members, whether elected or appointed, occur every three years as defined by law.

1.4 Comment on the Electoral Statistics

The results for the period before 1952 can be found in Mattes/ Züfle (1978). From 1952–1976 Egypt was ruled by a single-party system and since then by one dominant party—the NDP. For the lack of official publications of absolute numbers by the Egyptian authorities, most of the following dates and results of the parliamentary and presidential elections in Egypt were taken from secondary literature which was often contradictory (e.g. Aly 1987, Muñoz 1992*a*, Zaki 1994). Population data are based on *Jahrbuch Nahost* (Hamburg) and Statistisches Bundesamt (Wiesbaden).

2. Tables

2.1 Dates of National Elections, Referendums and Coups d'Etat

Year	Presidential referendums	Parliamentary elections	Elections for Constitutional Assembly[a]	Other referendums	Coups d'état
1950		03/01 (1st) 10/01 (2nd)			
1952					23/07
1956	23/06			23/06	
1957		03/07 (1st) 14/07 (2nd)			
1958	21/02			21/02	
1964			10/03 (1st) 19/03 (2nd)		
1965	15/03				
1968				02/05	
1969		08/01 (1st) 13/01 (2nd)			
1970	15/10				
1971		27/10 (1st) 03/11 (2nd)		01/09 11/09	
1974				15/05	
1976	02/10	28/10 (1st) 04/11 (2nd)			
1977				10/02	
1978				21/05	
1979		07/06 (1st) 14/06 (2nd)		19/04	
1980				22/05	
1981	13/10			10/09	
1984		27/05			
1987	05/10	06/04 (1st) 13/04 (2nd)		12/02	
1990		29/11 (1st) 06/12 (2nd)		11/10	
1993	04/10				
1995		29/11 (1st) 06/12 (2nd)			

[a] The National Assembly elected in 1964 was to act as a Constitutional Assembly charged with drafting a permanent constitution for the country.

2.2 Electoral Body 1950–1995

Year	Type of election[a]	Population	Registered voters		Votes cast		
			Total number	% pop.	Total number	% reg. voters	% pop.
1950	Pa	21,470,000	—	—	—	—	—
1956	Pr	23,516,000	5,859,000	24.9	5,508,314	94.0	23.4
1957	Pa	24,225,000	5,697,467	23.5	—	—	—
1958	Pr	24,781,000	6,220,343	25.1	6,104,259	98.1	24.6
1964	Pa	28,750,000	6,900,000	24.0	—	—	—
1965	Pr	29,600,000	7,055,564	23.8	6,950,652	98.5	23.5
1969	Pa	32,501,000	—	—	—	—	—
1970	Pr	33,329,000	8,420,768	22.3	7,157,653	85.0	21.5
1971	Pa	34,130,000	—	—	—	—	—
1976	Pa	37,000,000	—	—	—	40.0	—
1976	Pr	37,000,000	9,500,000	25.7	9,100,000	95.8	24.6
1979	Pa	40,000,000	—	—	—	—	—
1981	Pr	43,470,000	12,028,362	27.7	9,754,766	81.0	22.4
1984	Pa	47,000,000	12,339,417	26.3	5,323,086	43.1	11.3
1987	Pa	52,000,000	—	—	6,824,908	—	13.1
1987	Pr	52,000,000	14,368,247[b]	27.6	12,711,784	88.4	24.4
1990	Pa	56,000,000	17,900,000	32.0	—	45.0	—
1993	Pr	59,500,000	18,897,866	31.8	15,904,512	84.2	26.7
1995	Pa	59,500,000	20,987,453	35.3	10,072,017	47.9[c]	16.9

[a] Pa = Parliament (National Assembly, People's Assembly); Pr = President.

[b] There were around 25 million people eligible to vote in Egypt, but the electoral register contained less than 14 million. The opposition claimed that some 27% of the registered voters were dead, expatriates, registered somewhere else or in the armed forces.

[c] According to NWP only 13%.

2.3 Abbreviations

ADNP	Arab Democratic Nasserist Party
ASU	Arab Socialist Union[a]
DSP	Democratic Socialist Party
DUP	Democratic Unionist Party
EASP	Egypt Arab Socialist Party
GP	Green Party
LCP	Liberal Constitutionalist Party
LSP	Liberal Socialist Party, Liberal Party (former right ASU platform)
MB	Muslim Brothers
MFP	Misr al-Fatah Party
NDP	National Democratic Party (former Misr Party, center ASU platform)
NP	National Party
NPUP	Nationalist Progressive Unionist Party or Tagammu (former left ASU platform)
NU	National Union
NWP	New Wafd Party
PDP	Populist Democratic Party
Sa'dists	Sa'd Party
SJP	Social Justice Party
SLP	Socialist Labor Party
SP	Solidarity Party
UP	Ummah Party
WP	Wafd Party

[a] The ASU was founded in 1962. After the parliamentary elections in 1976 its three election platforms were changed in the independent parties NPUP, LSP and NDP (last one in July 1978). After the first multi-party elections in 1979 the ASU was dissolved and deleted from the constitution in 1980.

2.4 Electoral Participation of Parties and Alliances 1950–1995

Party / Alliance	Years	Elections contested	
		Presidential	Parliamentary
DSP	1950	0	1
LCP	1950	0	1
NP	1950	0	1
Sa'dists	1950	0	1
WP	1950	0	1
NU	1956, 1957, 1958	2	1
ASU	1964, 1965, 1970, 1971, 1976	3	2
LSP[a]	1976, 1979, 1984, 1995	0	4
NDP[b]	1976, 1979, 1981, 1984, 1987, 1990, 1993, 1995	3	6
NPUP[c]	1976, 1979, 1984, 1987, 1990, 1995	0	6
SLP	1979, 1984, 1995	0	3
NWP Alliance[d]	1984	0	1
Islamic Alliance[e]	1987	0	1
NWP	1987, 1995	0	2
UP	1987, 1990, 1995	0	3
DUP	1990, 1995	0	2
EASP	1990, 1995	0	2
GP	1990, 1995	0	2
MFP	1990, 1995	0	2
ADNP	1995	0	1
Party / Alliance	Years	Elections contested	
		Presidential	Parliamentary
PDP	1995	0	1
SJP	1995	0	1
SP	1995	0	1

[a] 1976: ASU-right.
[b] 1976: Misr Party, ASU-center.
[c] 1976: ASU-left.
[d] NWP and MB.
[e] SLP, MB and LSP.

2.5 Referendums

Year	1956[a] Total number	%	1958[b] Total number	%
Registered voters	5,859,000	–	6,220,343	–
Votes cast	5,508,314	94.0	6,104,259	98.1
Invalid votes	10,043	0.2	1,884	0.0
Valid votes	5,498,271	99.8	6,102,375	100.0
Yes	5,488,255	99.8	6,102,128	100.0
No	10,016	0.2	247	0.0

[a] Constitution.
[b] United Arab Republic with Syria.

Year	1968[a] Total number	%	1971[b] Total number	%
Registered voters	7,450,478	–	7,925,297	–
Votes cast	7,317,419	98.2	7,700,000	97.1
Invalid votes	887	0.0	—	
Valid votes	7,316,532	100.0	—	—
Yes	7,315,734	100.0	—	99.9
No	798	0.0	3,404	0.1

[a] Program of 30 March.
[b] Constitution of the Federal Arab Republics.

Year	1971[a] Total number	%	1974[b] Total number	%
Registered voters	8,270,059	–	8,442,122	–
Votes cast	7,867,620	95.1	8,255,554	97.9
Invalid votes	3,640	0.1	4,903	0.1
Valid votes	7,863,980	99.9	8,250,651	99.9
Yes	7,862,617	100.0	8,246,937	99.9
No	1,363	0.0	3,714	0.1

[a] Constitution.
[b] October Paper.

Year	1977[a] Total number	%	1978[b] Total number	%
Registered voters	9,564,482	–	—	–
Votes cast	9,247,737	96.7	—	—
Invalid votes	27,420	0.3	—	—
Valid votes	9,220,317	99.7	—	—
Yes	9,166,179	99.4	—	98.3
No	54,138	0.6	—	1.7

[a] Protection of national unity.
[b] Protection of national unity and social peace.

Year	1979[a] Total number	%	1979[b] Total number	%
Registered voters	10,998,675	–	10,998,675	–
Votes cast	9,920,260	90.2	9,920,260	90.2
Invalid votes	9,772	0.1	9,772	0.1
Valid votes	9,910,488	99.9	9,910,488	99.9
Yes	9,900,271	99.9	9,890,271	99.7
No	10,217	0.1	20,217	0.3

[a] Peace treaty with Israel.
[b] Reforms and dissolution of the Parliament for new elections.

Year	1980[a] Total number	%	1981[b] Total number	%
Registered voters	12,800,000	–	—	–
Votes cast	—	—	—	—
Invalid votes	—	—	—	—
Valid votes	10,447,712	—	—	—
Yes	10,339,055	99.0	—	99.5
No	108,657	1.0	—	0.5

[a] Constitutional amendment.
[b] Protection of national unity.

Year	1987[a] Total number	%	1990[a] Total number	%
Registered voters	14,388,255	–	—	–
Votes cast	—	—	—	—
Invalid votes	—	—	—	—
Valid votes	10,599,438	—	—	—
Yes	9,423,384	88.9	—	94.3
No	1,176,054	11.1	—	5.7

[a] Dissolution of the Parliament for new elections.

2.6 Elections for Constitutional Assembly

The National Assembly elected in 1964 was to act as a Constitutional Assembly charged with drafting a permanent constitution for the country (see table 2.8).

2.7 Parliamentary Elections 1984 and 1987

Year	1984		1987[a]	
	Total number	%	Total number	%
Registered voters	12,339,417	–	—	–
Votes cast	5,323,086	43.1	—	75.0
Invalid votes	176,521	3.3	—	—
Valid votes	5,146,565	96.7	6,824,908	—
NDP	3,756,359	72.9	4,751,758	69.9
NPUP	214,587	4.2	150,570	2.2
LSP	33,448	0.7	–	–
SLP	364,040	7.1	–	–
NWP alliance	778,131	15.1	–	–
NWP	–	–	746,023	10.9
Islamic Alliance	–	–	1,163,525	17.0
UP	–	–	13,031	0.2

[a] The results of the run-off election are not included.

2.8 Composition of Parliament 1950–1995

Year	1950	
	Seats	%
	319	100
WP	225	70.5
Sa'dists	28	8.8
LCP	26	8.1
NP	6	1.9
DSP	1	0.3
Independents	33	10.4

Year	1957[a]		1964[b]		1969[d]		1971	
	Seats	%	Seats	%	Seats	%	Seats	%
	350	100	350[c]	100	350[c]	100	350[c]	100
NU	350	100	–	–	–	–	–	–
ASU	–	–	350	100	350	100	350	100

[a] Over half of the 2,500 candidates were disqualified after screening by the government-appointed National Executive Committee of the NU.
[b] 1,750 candidates contested the 350 seats, over 975 of whom were workers and farmers, and over 25 women. 114 peasants, 75 workers and 114 others (eight women) were elected.
[c] Not all of the 350 seats were filled; excluding the 10 members appointed by the President.
[d] 319 ASU, 11 'independents', 20 seats in final ballot.

Year	1976		1979		1984		1987	
	Seats	%	Seats	%	Seats	%	Seats	%
	350[a]	100	372[a]	100	448[a]	100	448[a]	100
NDP[b]	280	80.0	330	88.7	390[e]	87.3	308	68.8
NPUP[c]	2	0.6	0	0.0	0	0.0	0	0.0
LSP[d]	17	4.9	3	0.9	0	0.0	–	–
SLP	–	–	29	7.7	0	0.0	–	–
NWP Alliance	–	–	–	–	58[f]	12.7	–	–
NWP	–	–	–	–	–	–	36	8.0
Islamic Alliance	–	–	–	–	–	–	56[g]	12.5
UP	–	–	–	–	–	–	–	–
Independents	51	14.5	10	2.7	–	–	48[h]	10.7

[a] Excluding the 10 members appointed by the President.
[b] 1976: ASU-center.
[c] 1976: ASU-left.
[d] 1976: ASU-right.
[e] 31 of these by default; NDP had the majority in all districts, therefore received all the bonus seats.
[f] Among them eight MB.
[g] With the four independents: 37 MB, 20 SLP and 3 LSP.
[h] Most of the independent candidates were affiliated to the NDP.

Year	1990[a]		1995	
	Seats	%	Seats	%
	444[b]	100	444[b]	100
NDP	348	78.4	317	71.6
NPUP	6	1.4	5	1.1
LSP	–	–	1	0.2
SLP	–	–	0	0.0
NWP	–	–	6	1.4
UP	0	0.0	0	0.0
GP	0	0.0	0	0.0
EASP	0	0.0	0	0.0
DUP	0	0.0	0	0.0
ADNP	–	–	1	0.2
PDP	–	–	0	0.0
MFP	0	0.0	0	0.0
SP	–	–	0	0.0
SJP	–	–	0	0.0
Independents	83[c]	18.7	114[d]	25.5

[a] NWP, SLP and LSP boycotted the election. Seven seats remained undecided because of irregularities.
[b] Excluding the 10 members appointed by the President; among them in 1990: three copts and three women
[c] 60 NDP, 14 NWP, eight SLP and one LSP.
[d] Subsequent to the poll, 99 of these reportedly joined the NDP.

2.9 Presidential Referendums

a) Nasser: 1956, 1958 and 1965

Year	1956		1958		1965	
	Total number	%	Total number	%	Total number	%
Registered voters	5,859,000	–	6,220,343	–	7,055,564	–
Votes cast	5,508,314	94.0	6,104,262	98.1	6,950,652	98.5
Invalid votes	3,492	0.1	1,881	0.0	489	0.0
Valid votes	5,504,822	99.9	6,102,381	100.0	6,950,163	100.0
Yes	5,499,555	99.9	6,102,116	100.0	6,950,098	100.0
No	5,267	0.1	265	0.0	65	0.0

b) Sadat: 1970 and 1976

Year	1970 Total number	%	1976 Total number	%
Registered voters	8,420,768	–	9,500,000	–
Votes cast	7,157,653	85.0	9,156,893	96.4
Invalid votes	13,814	0.2	5	0.0
Valid votes	7,143,839	99.8	9,156,888	100.0
Yes	6,432,587	90.0	9,151,288	99.9
No	711,252	10.0	5,600	0.1

c) Mubarak: 1981, 1987 and 1993

Year	1981 Total number	%	1987 Total number	%	1993 Total number	%
Registered voters	12,028,362	–	14,368,247	–	18,897,866	–
Votes cast	9,754,766	81.1	12,711,784	88.5	15,904,512	84.2
Invalid votes	37,212	0.4	266,762	2.1	226,020	1.4
Valid votes	9,717,554	99.6	12,445,022	97.9	15,678,492	98.6
Yes	9,567,904	98.5	12,083,627	97.1	15,095,025	96.3
No	149,650	1.5	361,395	2.9	583,467	3.7

2.10 List of Power Holders 1953–1998

Head of State	Years	Remarks
Ali Muhammad Nagib	1953–1954	Army officer. After the coup d'état of 23/07/1952 imposed as Prime Minister (07/09/1952) and later as President (19/07/1953). He was brought down with being an alleged accessory to the assassination attempt on Nasser in 1954, and he was placed under house arrest for 10 years. In 1971 Nagib was rehabilitated by Sadat.
Gamal Abd al-Nasser	1954–1970	Army officer. Imposed as President and Prime Minister in 1954. 1958–1961 President of the United Arab Republic. Death from heart-attack (28/09/1970).

Head of State	Years	Remarks
Muhammad Anwar al-Sadat	1970–1981	Army officer. Elected President in 1970. When he was killed by Islamist extremists during a military parade (06/10/1981), he held the following positions: President of the Republic, Prime Minister, Supreme Commander of the Armed Forces, Higher Chief of the Judiciary and head of the NDP.
Muhammad Hosni Mubarak	1981–	Army officer. Elected President since 13/10/1981. Third period of office as President since 04/10/1993.

3. Bibliography

3.1 Offical Sources

Al-Ahram [Arabic] 01/11/1976, 17/06/1979, 30/05/1984, 01/06/1984, 01/10/90.

Electoral Law No. 114 of 1983.

Electoral Law No. 188 of 31/12/1986.

Electoral Law No. 201 of 30/09/1990.

The 1980 Constitution of the Arab Republic of Egypt. After the amendments ratified in the May 22, 1980 Referendum. Cairo: State Information Service.

Yearbook 1995. Cairo: State Information Service.

3.2 Books, Articles and Electoral Reports

Abdallah, A. (1992). 'Le cadre de la participation en Egypte'. *Démocratisation dans le Monde Arabe*, Cairo: CEDEJ, 277–282.

Al-Aaal, M. A. (1992). 'Legitimation du pouvoir et démocratisation en Egypte'. *Démocratisation dans le Monde Arabe*, Cairo: CEDEJ, 283–288.

Aly, A.-M. S. (1987). 'Democratization in Egypt'. *American-Arab Affairs*, 27: 11–27.

Amine, N. (1987). 'Women out of Power'. *The Middle East*, 152: 35–36.

Ayubi, N. N. (1987). 'Government and the State in Egypt Today', in C. Tripp and R. Owen (eds.), *Egypt under Mubarak. Papers written for a conference held at the School for Oriental and African Studies in May 1987*, London: Routledge, 1–20.

Badran, W. (1996). *Women and the Parliamentary Elections 1995* [Arabic]. Cairo: University of Cairo/ Friedrich-Ebert Stiftung.

Buccianti, A. (1984). 'Les elections legislatives en Egypte'. *Maghreb/ Machrek*, 106: 54–76.

Büren, R. (1970). *Die Arabische Sozialistische Union. Einheitspartei und Verfassungssystem der Vereinigten Arabischen Republik unter Berücksichtigung der Verfassungsgeschichte von 1840–1968*. Opladen: Deutsches Orientinstitut/ Leske & Budrich.

Büttner, F., and Klostermeier, I. (1991). *Ägypten*. München: Beck.

Büttner, F. (1994). 'Ägypten', in U. Steinbach, R. Hofmeier and M. Schönborn (eds.), *Politisches Lexikon Nahost/Nordafrika* (3rd edn.). München: Beck, 26–47.

— (1996). 'Wahlen am Nil: Ägyptens "Festival der Demokratie"'. *INAMO*, 5/6: 52–54.

Charkaoui, S. al- (1984). 'La loi electorale reglant les elections à l'Assemblée du Peuple'. *Bulletin du Centre de Documentation et d'Etudes Juridiques, Economiques et Sociales*, 13/26: 64–71.

Cooper, M. (1982). *The Transformation of Egypt*. London: Croom Helm.

Darwish, A. (1987). 'Mubarak's Electoral Triumph'. *The Middle East*, 151: 11–14.

'Egypt. Independents Emerge as a Force'. *The Middle East*, 151: 68–69.

Ezzat, D. (1996). 'Election Fever Rages on'. *The Middle East*, 253: 5–7.

Farag, I. (1991). 'Le politique a l'egytienne. Lecture des elections legislatives'. *Monde arabe: Maghreb / Machrek*, 133: 19–33.

Fürtig, H. (1995). 'Die ägyptische Muslimbruderschaft und der nationale Dialog. Eine neue Taktik?'. *Asien, Afrika, Lateinamerika*, 23: 261–284.

Gauch, S. (1991). 'A Flawed Victory'. *The Middle East*, 195: 17–18.

Ghannam, A. A. El- (1968). *Das Regierungssystem des unabhängigen Ägypten 1922–1967*. Thesis (Ph.D.), München.

Hammond, A. (1996). 'A New Political Culture Emerges in Egypt'. *The Middle East*, 255: 5–7.

Harders, C. (1995). *Frauen und Politik in Ägypten. Untersuchungen zur Situation ägyptischer Politikerinnen, Demokratie und Entwicklung*. Münster/ Hamburg: Lit.

Hendriks, B. (1985). 'Egypt's Elections, Mubarak's Bind'. *Middle East Report*, 14/1: 11–18.

Hijab, N. (1984). 'Reform in the Wake of Egypt's Elections'. *The Middle East*, 117: 22–24.

Hilal, A. al-Din (1982). *The Democratic Experiment in Egypt 1970–1981* [Arabic]. Cairo: Center for Political and Strategic Studies.

— (1986*a*). *The Democratic Evolution in Egypt: Issues and Discussions* [Arabic]. Cairo: Maktabat Nahdat al-Sharq.

— (1986*b*). *The People's Assembly Elections 1984. A Study and Analysis* [Arabic]. Cairo: Center for Political and Strategic Studies.

— (1992). *The People's Assembly Elections 1990. A Study and Analysis* [Arabic]. Cairo: Center for Political and Strategic Studies.

Hinnebusch, R. A. (1985). *Egyptian Politics under Sadat*. Cambridge: Cambridge University Press.

Hopkins, N. S. (1995). 'La culture politique et l'Egypte'. *Egypte/Monde arabe*, 24: 29–41.

Howard-Merriam, K. (1990). 'Guaranteed Seats for Political Representation of Women. The Egyptian Example'. *Woman and Politics*, 10/1: 17–42.

Ibn Khaldoun Centre for Development Studies *et al.* (1995). *Report of the National Egyptian Commission for the Observation of the Parliamentary Elections 1995* [Arabic]. Cairo: Ibn Khaldoun Centre for Development Studies.

Ibrahim, F. (1995). *Staat und Zivilgesellschaft in Ägypten.* Münster/ Hamburg: Lit.

Ibrahim, F. N. (1996). *Ägypten; eine geographische Landeskunde*. Darmstadt: Wissenschaftliche Buchgesellschaft.

Ibrahim, S.-E. (1996). 'Reform and Frustration in Egypt'. *Journal of Democracy*, 7/4: 125–135.

Kandil, A. (1995). *The Democratic Transformation in Egypt 1981–1993*. Cairo: Ibn Khaldoun Centre for Development Studies.

Köhler, M. A. (1995). 'Wahlen—Partizipation—Demokratie? Der Einfluß von Wahlen auf die Entwicklung der parlamentarischen Systeme und der politischen Parteien im Nahen und Mittleren Osten', in U. Steinbach and V. Nienhaus (eds.), *Entwicklungszusammenarbeit in Kultur, Recht und Wirtschaft. Grundlagen und Erfahrungen aus Afrika und Nahost.* Opladen: Leske & Budrich, 261–278.

Köndgen, O. (1993). 'Ägypten 1993. Politik, Wirtschaft, Gesellschaft'. *KAS-Auslandsinformationen*, 9/9: 8–19.

— (1994). 'Präsidentschaftsreferendum in Ägypten: Mubarak zu Beginn seiner dritten Amtsperiode'. *KAS-Auslandsinformationen*, 10/3: 81–104.

Koszinowski, T. (1984). 'Der Demokratisierungsprozeß in Ägypten: Die Politik Mubaraks im Lichte der Parlamentswahlen vom Mai 1984'. *Orient*, 25/3: 335–360.

— and Mattes, H. (1984–95). *Nahost-Jahrbuch*. Hamburg: Deutsches Orient-Institut.

Krämer, G. (1984). 'Die Wahl zum ägyptischen Abgeordnetenhaus vom Mai 1984. Parteien, Wahlprogramme und Ergebnisse'. *Orient*, 25/3: 361–375.

— (1986). *Ägypten unter Mubarak. Identität und nationales Interesse.* Baden-Baden: Nomos.

— (1987). *Die Wahl zur ägyptischen Volksversammlung vom April 1987. Legitimation des Präsidenten und Einbindung der islamischen Opposition*. Ebenhausen: Stiftung Wissenschaft und Politik.

— (1992). 'Staat und Zivilgesellschaft im Nahen und Mittleren Osten. Das Beispiel'Ägyptens', in E. Gormsen and A. Thimm (eds.), *Zivilgesellschaft und Staat in der Dritten Welt*. Mainz: University, 115–137.

Landau, J. M. (1953). *Parliaments and Parties in Egypt*. Tel Aviv: Israel Oriental Society.

Leenders, R. (1996). *The Struggle of the State and Civil Society in Egypt. Professional Organizations and Egypt's Careful Steps Towards Democracy*. Amsterdam: MERA.

Makram Ebeid, M. (1989). 'The Role of the Official Opposition', in C. Tripp and R. Owen (eds.), *Egypt under Mubarak. Papers written for a conference held at the School for Oriental and African Studies in May 1987*. London: Routledge, 21–51.

— (1996). 'Egypt's Elections. One Step Forward, Two Steps Back?' *Middle East Policy*, 4/3: 119–136.

Mattes, H., and Züfle, W. (1978). 'Ägypten', in D. Sternberger, B. Vogel, D. Nohlen and K. Landfried (eds.), *Die Wahl der Parlamente und anderer Staatsorgane. Band II: Politische Organisation und Repräsentation in Afrika,* by Franz Nuscheler, Klaus Ziemer *et al.*, Berlin/ New York: Walter de Gruyter, 227–301.

Moench, R. U. (1987). 'The May 1984 Elections in Egypt and the Question of Egypt's Stability', in L. L. Layne (ed.), *Elections in the Middle East*. Boulder, Col.: Westview Press.

Mohsen, A. A. (1979). 'Sadat's Landslide Victory'. *The Middle East*, 57: 17.

Monofy, K. al- (1996). *The Parliamentary Elections 1995* [Arabic]. Cairo: University of Cairo/ Friedrich-Ebert Stiftung.

Muñoz, G. M. (1992*a*). *Politica y elecciones en el Egipto contemporaneo (1922–1990).* Madrid: M.A.E.

— (1992*b*). 'Rencontre avec le pluripartisme. Constants politiques et reflets electoraux de l'Egypte monarchique sur l'Egypte actuelle'. *Démocratisation dans le MondeArabe,* Cairo, CEDEJ: 289–299.

Mustafa, H. (1992). 'Les forces islamistes et l'experience démocratique en Egypte'. *Démocratisation dans le Monde Arabe*, Cairo: CEDEJ, 379–395.

— (1995). 'The Islamist Movement under Mubarak', in L. Guazzone (ed.), *The Islamist Dilemma*. Reading: Ithaca Press.

Najjar, F. (1989). 'Elections and Democracy in Egypt'. *American Arab Affairs*, 29: 96–113.

Neue Zürcher Zeitung 15/07/1957, 18/07/1957, 11/03/1964, 14/05/1964, 16/05/1964, 11/02/1977, 22–23/04/1979, 24/041979, 24–25/05/1980.

Pawelka, P. (1985). *Herrschaft und Entwicklung im Nahen Osten: Ägypten.* Heidelberg: UTB Müller.

Qandil, A. (1994). *The Process of Democratic Change in Egypt 1980–1993.* [Arabic]. Cairo: Ibn Khaldoun Centre for Development Studies/ Konrad-Adenauer Stiftung.

Qazamil, A. (1991). *The Parliamentary Elections of 1990 and the Crisis of Democracy in Egypt* [Arabic]. Cairo: Al-Arabi.

Raj, C. S. (1984). 'Egyptian Election'. *Strategic Analysis*, 8/4: 329–334.

Reid, Ḍ. M. (1979). 'The Return of the Egyptian Wafd 1978'. *International Journal of African Historical Studies*, 12: 389–415.

Robbe, M., and Hösel, J. (1989). *Egypt. The Revolution of July 1952 and Gamal Abdel Nasser (Asien, Afrika, Lateinamerika special issue).* Berlin.

Sarqawi, S. as-, and Nasif, A. (1984). *The Electoral Systems in the World and in Egypt* [Arabic]. Cairo: Dar an-Nahda al Arabiya.

Sayid-Ahmad, M. (1984). *The Future of the Party System in Egypt* [Arabic]. Cairo: Al-Arabi.

Schölch, A., and Mejcher, H. (1992). *Die ägytische Gesellschaft im 20. Jahrhundert*. Hamburg: Deutsches Orient-Institut.

Springborg, R. (1989). *Mubarak's Egypt. Fragmentation of the Political Order*. Boulder, Col.: Westview Press.

Statistisches Bundesamt : *Länderbericht Ägypten 1969, 1972, 1974, 1976, 1977, 1978, 1979, 1980, 1981, 1982, 1984, 1986, 1988, 1993*. Wiesbaden.

Tripp, C., and Owen, R. (1989). *Egypt under Mubarak. Papers written for a conference held at the School for Oriental and African Studies in May 1987*. London: Routledge.

Vatikiotis, P. J. (1969). *The Modern History of Egypt*, London: Weidenfeld and Nicolson.

Waterbury, J. (1983). *The Egypt of Nasser and Sadat*. Princeton, N.J.: Princeton University Press.

Zaki, M. (1994). *Civil Society and Democratization in Egypt*. Cairo: Ibn Khaldoun Centre for Development Studies/ Konrad-Adenauer Stiftung.

EQUATORIAL GUINEA

by Helga Fleischhacker

1. Introduction

1.1 Historical Overview

Ever since Equatorial Guinea's independence, its political life has been dominated by the authoritarian reign of a single family, the Mongomo clan, so-called after the presidential family's home town Mongomo, located in mainland Río Muní. Through a series of regime-metamorphoses and even an intra-familial coup d'état in 1979, the presidential family clan has never lost control of power. Since the regime adopted a more pluralistic style in 1992, with the adoption of a multi-party constitution, a number of political parties have entered Parliament; oppositional forces, however, still face political persecution.

The former territory of Spanish Guinea was granted provincial status in 1959, and, after a referendum of 15 December 1963, granted autonomy over internal affairs in 1964. By the time full independence was achieved by Equatorial Guinea, on 12 October 1968, significant strains had surfaced between the country's two main ethnic groups, the mainland Fang of Río Muní, and the Bubí on the Island of Bioko (former Fernando Poó), in ways that complicated ongoing negotiations with Spain over the terms of independence. The final product of these negotiations was a federal compromise constitution and electoral law, which were submitted for popular approval in a UN-supervised referendum on 11 August 1968. The substantial No votes cast in this referendum underscored the fragility of the settlement, reflecting as it did Bubí fears of mainland domination, and Fang objections to the degree of self-rule conceded to the islanders. In presidential balloting a month later, a mainland Fang, Macías Nguema Biyoyo, supported by a loose alliance, defeated the head of the pre-independence autonomous government.

The Constitution of 1968 was very quickly done away with under the regime of President Macías. He moved swiftly to suppress opposition and to assert his absolute power through a reign of terror. The brutal internal repression of the Macías regime—by the end of his tenure two-thirds of the members of the 1968 National Assembly had disappeared—led to the flight of one-third of the population, including nearly all skilled and educated strata. In 1970 a single-party, the *Partido Unico Nacional de Trabajadores* (PUNT), was established and Macías assumed all legislative, executive and judiciary competencies through a series of decrees. He proclaimed himself President for Life on 29 July 1973, at the same time introducing a new constitution that abolished federal rights and established a centralist, unitary state. The President's omnipotence was extended into the religious realm with the subsequent abolition of the Catholic Church and the proclamation of Macías as 'the unique and indefatigable wonder' of Equatorial Guinea in 1978.

Macías 11-year rule was terminated on 3 August 1979 by a coup d'état (and his assassination). This was led by his nephew, Teodoro Obiang Nguema Mbasogo, who assumed the presidency of a Supreme Military Council, a body in fact dominated by the Mongomo clan. Coincident with the adoption of a new constitution on 15 August 1982, Obiang Nguema was confirmed as President for a seven-year term. Although the regime did away with the most glaring abuses of the Macías era and formally established a number of human and civil rights—the 1982 Constitution provided theoretically for the protection of human rights and a limited right of association—no substantial political reforms were put into effect. Only in late 1987 was a government party, the *Partido Democrático de Guinea Ecuatorial* (PDGE) launched. And like the indirect parliamentary elections on 28 August 1983, the direct elections to the legislature held on 31 July 1988 were strictly *pro forma*. The National Assembly had virtually no independent legislative powers, and neither the constitution, nor the legislature had defined the terms and limits of the single-party's political functions.

Under growing international pressure, Nguema formally conceded the principle of political plurality in August 1989. An extraordinary PDGE congress endorsed the adoption of a multi-party constitution, which was approved in a referendum on 17 November 1991. Two months later, on 23 January 1992, additional laws were passed, setting out ground rules for political parties. A transitional administration was formed and a general amnesty for all political exiles promulgated. Restrictive election and party laws, however, worked to exclude virtually all exiled political opponents from participation in national political life. When legislative elections were held in November 1992, they were boycotted by the eight (out of 14 altogether) legal parties that constituted the opposition alliance, *Plataforma de la Oposición Conjunta* (POC); the opposition forces objected especially to Nguema's refusal to review controversial election law clauses or to permit international observers to inspect voter registration. Indeed, OAU representatives who monitored the elections found widespread violations of electoral procedure.

Local elections in September 1995 were the first truly representative multi-party elections contested by all 14 legal parties; the electoral register had been drafted with UN assistance and the elections were monitored by international observers. But while initial election returns indicated an overwhelming victory for the opposition, later, official tallies awarded victory instead to the ruling party. For the presidential elections of 25 February 1996, the electoral lists drawn up by the UN were discarded in favor of a list produced by the government. Nguema was consequently confirmed for a third term, securing 97.9% of the votes cast.

The legalization of opposition parties in 1992 has produced a sharply divided political landscape: on the one hand, a loose coalition of loyalist parties sits in Parliament—the so-called *multi-nguemismo*—united in its subservience to the government. Against them stands a group of opposition parties facing systematic persecution and intimidation. Alongside this division, the ethnic schism between Fang and Bubí has re-emerged, as signified by the founding of the (as yet illegal) *Movimiento para la Autodeterminación de la Isla de Bioko* (MAIB), which has received strong backing from a majority of the Bubí.

1.2 Evolution of Electoral Provisions

In accordance with the Federal Constitution of 1968, 35 deputies to the National Assembly were elected in single-member districts for five-year terms; 19 of them from Río Muní, 12 from Fernando Poó (today Bioko) and four from smaller islands. Presidential election was based on an absolute majority system. A decree of March 1971 imposed such radical measures upon the Assembly that it ceased to meet, and the President thereupon also assumed legislative powers.

With the 'García Trevijano'-Constitution of 1973, a 60-member Parliament was introduced along with a single governmental party, the PUNT, which enjoyed the right to appoint and dismiss Parliament members (imperative mandate). In 1972 membership of the PUNT became obligatory for all citizens.

After the 1979 coup d'état, the country was ruled by a military council until 1982, when the regime, seeking a more durable institutional basis, adopted a constitution providing for an indirectly installed Parliament. An electorate drawn from the Municipal Councils, estimated at some 50,000 voters, ratified 45 candidates who had been nominated by the President. Age restrictions for parliamentary candidates required that they be between 45 and 60 years of age.

With the 1987 founding of a government party, electoral laws restricted eligibility for office to party members; these were elected by universal suffrage on a single-party list. One hundred and twenty candidates nominated by the President were elected for a five-year term.

1.3 Current Electoral Provisions

Source: Ley Fundamental de Guinea Ecuatorial 1991; Ley No. 3/1993, de fecha 12 de Enero, Reguladora de las Elecciones Legislativas, Municipales y Referendum; Ley No. 7/1995, de fecha 9 de Enero, por que se modifican determinados artículos de la Ley 3/1993; Ley Constitucional número 1/1995, de fecha 17 de Enero por la que se reforma determinados artículos de la Ley fundamental.

Elected national institutions: Single-chamber Parliament (*Asamblea Nacional*), consisting of 80 members directly elected for a five-year term. The President is elected directly, for a seven-year term (renewable once). There is no Vice-President.

Suffrage: Universal, equal, secret and direct. Requirements: at least 18 years of age, Equatorian citizenship; full possession of civil and political rights, registration as voter.

Nomination of candidates
- *presidential elections*: Native Equatorian; full possession of civil and political rights, aged between 40 and 75 years; permanent residence in the country for at least five years, married and secular.
- *parliamentary elections*: Equatorian citizenship, at least 25 years of age, full possession of civil and political rights, permanent residence in the respective electoral district for at least five years; registration as voter; literacy; understanding of the Constitution. Only legal parties are allowed to present candidates; for registration as a political party, a deposit of 30 million CFA is required; the use of funds from abroad for this purpose is prohibited.

Electoral system
- *presidential elections*: Plurality system.

- *parliamentary elections*: Closed list proportional representation system (Hare quota with smallest remainder) in 18 multi-member constituencies corresponding to the country's administrative units. A threshold of 10% at constituency level is applied.

1.4 Comment on the Electoral Statistics

The documentation, for both election laws and election results, is very scarce for Equatorial Guinea. In the country's electoral history, election statistics from the pre-independence period remain the most comprehensive and credible. No official election result since independence can be claimed not to be prefabricated. The only official population census since independence, dating from July 1983, offers what is presumably the estimate of 300,000. The government has never provided systematic information regarding electoral data, procedures and laws. Up until 1992 there was no official gazette; since then a *Boletín Oficial del Estado* has been occasionally published (current electoral laws were published in special numbers). The following tables have therefore been compiled largely from secondary literature, in which documentation for electoral statistics is often incomplete, creating additional problems of verification. Available electoral data, moreover, are not always comprehensive and some vary substantially. Where this was the case, the most complete figures were chosen. The results of the referendums of 1963 and 1968 follow Wagner (1978), whereas those of the presidential elections and the composition of Parliament in 1968 follow Sundiata (1990). Wagner and Liniger Goumaz (1988) each provide different allocations of seats; neither of them reach the total number of 35. Results of the constitu tional referendum in 1982 follow Blaustein/ Flanz (1983); different and less comprehensive figures are given in *African Contemporary Record* 15 (1983) B390.

For parliamentary elections in 1968, only the vote tallies of elected deputies were published, so that tables could not be aggregated (for the distribution of winning votes see Wagner 1978). Results of parliamentary elections of 1993 are given according to the provisional results published by the *Junta Electoral Nacional* on 21 November 1993. The presidential election results of 1996 are presented here as they were announced via state radio *Malabo Radio Nacional de Guinea Ecuatorial* on 8 March 1996. Especially helpful has been the documentation provided by Max Liniger-Goumaz, which includes the full text of some election laws, statistical data and an extensive general bibliography.

2. Tables

2.1 Dates of National Elections, Referendums and Coups d'Etat

Year	Presidential elections	Parliamentary elections	Elections for Constitutional Assembly	Referendums	Coups d'état
1963				15/12	
1968	22/09 (1st) 30/09 (2nd)	22/09		11/08	
1973				29/07	
1979					03/08
1982	15/08			15/08	
1988		31/07			
1989	23/06				
1991				17/11	
1993		21/11			
1996	25/02				

2.2 Electoral Body 1963–1996

Year	Type of election[a]	Population[b]	Registered voters		Votes cast		
			Total number	% pop.	Total number	% reg. voters	% pop.
1963	Ref	240,000	—	—	—	—	—
1968	Ref	246,941	125,253	50.7	113,655	93.7	46.0
1968	Pr	246,941	125,253	50.7	61,900	41.3	25.1
1968	Pa	246,941	125,253	50.7	—	—	—
1982	Ref/Pr	300,000	159,992	53.3	146,545	91.6	48.8
1988	Pa	356,000	—	—	—	—	—
1989	Pr	356,000	—	—	—	—	—
1991	Ref	376,000	—	—	—	—	—
1993	Pa	389,000	116,666	30.0	78,736	67.5	20.2
1996	Pr	389,000	230,238	59.2	183,830	79.8	47.3

[a] Pa = Parliament (*Asamblea Nacional*); Pr = President; Ref = Referendum.

[b] Population census: December 1965: 246,941 and July 1983: 300,000, estimation by UN in the course of the voter registration of 1994: 389,000. All other are unofficial estimations.

2.3 Abbreviations

ADP	Allianza Demócrata y Progresista
AP	Acción Popular
CLD/PL	Convención Liberal Democrática / Partido Liberal
CPDS	Convergencia para la Democracia Social
CSD(P)	Convergencia Socialdemócrata (Popular)
IPGE	Idea Popular de Guinea Ecuatorial
MAIB[a]	Movimiento para la Autodeterminación de la Isla de Bioko
MONALIGE	Movimiento Nacional de Liberación de Guinea Ecuatorial
MUNGE	Movimiento de Unión Nacional de Guinea Ecuatorial
PCSD	Partido Coalición Social Demócrata
PDGE	Partido Democrático de Guinea Ecuatorial
POC[b]	Plataforma de la Oposición Conjunta
PP	Partido Popular
PPGE	Partido del Progreso de Guinea Ecuatorial
PSD	Partido Social Demócrata
PSGE	Partido Socialista de Guinea Ecuatorial
PUNT	Partido Unico Nacional de Trabajadores
UDENA	Unión Demócrata Nacional
UDS	Unión Demócrata Social
UP	Unión Popular

[a] MAIB is not legalized as a party.

[b] Coalition of opposition parties launched in 1992. POC boycotted the 1993 legislative elections. The coalition disintegrated, when it did not manage to present a common candidate for presidential elections in 1996. Its members were: CPDS, ADP, AP, UP, PP and PCSD.

2.4 Electoral Participation of Parties and Alliances 1968–1996

Party / Alliance	Years	Elections contested	
		Presidential	Parliamentary
IPGE	1968	1	1
MONALIGE	1968	1	1
MUNGE	1968	1	1
Unión Bubí	1968	1	1
PDGE	1988, 1989, 1993, 1996	2	2
CLD/PL	1993	0	1
CSD	1993, 1996	1	1
PSD	1993	0	1
PSGE	1993	0	1
UDENA	1993	0	1
UDS	1993	0	1
PP	1996	1	0
UP	1996	1	0

2.5 Referendums

Year	1963[a]		1968[b]	
	Total number	%	Total number	%
Registered voters	—	–	125,253	–
Votes cast	—	—	115,885	92.5
Invalid votes	—	—	2,198	1.9
Valid votes	94,817	—	113,655	98.1
Yes	59,280	62.5	72,458	63.8
No	35,537	37.5	41,197	36.2

[a] Referendum ratified the state of internal autonomy.

[b] Constitutional referendum.

Year	1973[a]		1982[b]	
	Total number	%	Total number	%
Registered voters	—	–	159,992	–
Votes cast	—	—	149,545	93.5
Invalid votes	—	—	3,619	2.4
Valid votes	—	—	145,926	97.6
Yes	—	99.0	139,777	95.8
No	—	1.0	6,149	4.2

[a] Constitutional referendum.

[b] Constitutional referendum. Along with the constitution, the President was confirmed for a seven-year term.

For the constitutional referendum of 1991 detailed results are not available. According to official statements the new constitution was approved with 98.4% of the votes.

2.5 a) Referendums 1963 and 1968: Regional Distribution of Votes

Río Muní

Year	1963		1968	
Yes	53,940	65.5	67,695	65.5
No	28,387	34.5	35,711	34.5

Fernando Poó

Year	1963		1968	
Yes	5,340	42.8	4,763	51.5
No	7,150	57.2	4,486	48.5

2.6 Elections for Constitutional Assembly

Elections for Constitutional Assembly have not been held.

2.7 Parliamentary Elections 1993

For parliamentary elections in 1968 only the winning votes of the deputies elected are documented (see Wagner 1978). Therefore tables could not be aggregated. For parliamentary elections in 1988, only a percentage of 99.2 of valid votes for the state party PDGE could be ascertained.

Year	1993	
	Total number	%
Registered voters	116,666	–
Votes cast	78,736	67.5
Invalid votes	512	0.7
Valid votes	78,224	99.3
PDGE	54,589	69.8
CSDP	8,042	10.3
PL	4,974	6.4
CLD	1,963	2.5
PSD	909	1.2
UDENA	880	1.1
UDS	5,760	7.4
PSGE	1,106	1.4

2.7 a) Parliamentary Elections 1993: Constituency Level

Constituency	Malabo	Annobon	Luba	Bata	Mbini	Kogo
Registered voters	18,113	782	2,757	15,149	3,551	3,404
Votes cast	10,982	465	1,011	12,146	2,367	2,575
Invalid votes	0	6	0	0	56	0
Valid votes	10,982	459	1,011	12,146	2,311	2,575
PDGE	6,394	293	530	7,484	1,467	1,615
CSDP	731	50	122	793	491	540
PL	2,289	25	178	1,668	119	87
CLD	312	41	37	498	72	89
PSD	190	15	38	251	–	162
UDENA	411	11	59	178	–	–
UDS	465	8	47	668	110	81
PSGE	190	16	–	606	52	–

Constituency	Mongomo	Akonibe	Nsork	Akurenam	Niefang	Baney
Registered voters	8,446	3,358	2,538	3,512	9,892	3,173
Votes cast	8,130	3,311	2,386	2,362	4,967	902
Invalid votes	2	0	0	51	390	0
Valid votes	8,128	3,311	2,386	2,311	4,577	902
PDGE	8,126	3,173	2,351	1,707	3,213	477
CSDP	–	138	11	416	388	32
PL	–	–	–	–	187	107
CLD	2	–	6	43	237	58
PSD	–	–	–	–	–	15
UDENA	–	–	–	–	–	201
UDS	–	–	18	110	372	12
PSGE	–	–	–	35	180	–

Constituency	Micomeseng	Añisok	Evinayong	Riaba	Ebebiyin	Nsok-Nsomo
Registered voters	8,657	8,202	8,128	1,038	10,645	5,321
Votes cast	4,507	6,794	5,648	433	6,531	3,219
Invalid votes	0	0	0	7	0	0
Valid votes	4,507	6,794	5,648	426	6,531	3,219
PDGE	2,787	6,122	1,526	319	4,211	2,794
CSDP	253	273	3,758	46	–	–
PL	110	44	–	–	140	20
CLD	75	215	134	8	112	24
PSD	88	–	–	8	142	–
UDENA	–	–	–	20	–	–
UDS	1,194	113	230	25	1,926	381
PSGE	–	27	–	–	–	–

2.8 Composition of Parliament 1968–1993

Year	1968		1988		1993	
	Seats	%	Seats	%	Seats	%
	35	100	120	100	80	100
MONALIGE	10	28.6	–	–	–	–
MUNGE	10	28.6	–	–	–	–
Grupo Macías[a]	8	22.9	–	–	–	–
Unión Bubí	7	20.0	–	–	–	–
PDGE	–	–	120	100	68	85.0
CSD	–	–	–	–	6	7.5
UDS	–	–	–	–	5	6.3
CLD/PL	–	–	–	–	1	1.3

[a] Also referred to as *Secretariado Conjunto*.

2.9 Presidential Elections 1968–1996

1968 (first round)	Total number	%
Registered voters	125,253	–
Votes cast	—	—
Invalid votes	—	—
Valid votes	91,664	—
Macías Nguema (Grupo Macías)	36,716	40.1
Ondo Edu (MUNGE)	31,941	34.8
Ndongo Miyone (MONALIGE)	18,232	19.9
Edmundo Bosio Dioco (Unión Bubí)	4,795	5.2

1968 (second round)	Total number	%
Registered voters	125,253	–
Votes cast	—	—
Invalid votes	—	—
Valid votes	71,400	—
Macías Nguema (Grupo Macías)	47,400	66.4
Ondo Edu Bonifacio (MUNGE)	24,000	33.6

1989	Total number	%
Registered voters	—	–
Votes cast	—	—
Invalid votes	12,000	—
Valid votes	—	100.0
Teodoro Obiang Nguema Mbasosgo	—	100.0

1996	Total number	%
Registered voters	230,238	–
Votes cast	183,830	79.8
Invalid votes[a]	218	0.1
Valid votes[a]	183,544	99.8
Teodoro Obiang Nguema Mbasogo (PDGE)	179,592	97.8
Severo Moto Nsa (PP)	1,017	0.5
Secundino Oyono Awon Ada (CSD)	1,349	0.7
Andres Moses Mbada (UP)	1,135	0.6
Buenaventura Monsue Asumu	451	0.3

[a] Incomprehensive official result: a sum of valid and invalid votes adds to 183,544 of votes cast.

2.10 List of Power Holders 1968–1998

Head of State and Government	Years	Remarks
Macías Nguema Biyoyo	1968–1979	Elected Head of State 1968; turned out of office by a coup led by his nephew Obiang Nguema Mbasogo.
Teodoro Obiang Nguema Mbasogo	1979–	Army officer; assumed power 1979 by military coup; confirmed in office 1982, 1989 and 1996.

3. Bibliography

3.1 Official Sources

'Constitución de la Guinea Equatorial 1968'. *Documentos Políticos*, 10.

'Constitución de la Guinea Equatorial 1973'. *Constitutions of African States, Vol 1*. New York, 233-256.

'Ley fundamental de Guinea Ecuatorial 1982', in F. Reyntjens (ed.) (1988), *Constitutiones Africae*. Brylant: Bruxelles, Vol. I.

'Ley fundamental de Guinea Ecuatorial 1991', in A. P. Blaustein and G. H. Flanz (eds.), *Constitutions of the Countries of the World*. Dobbs Ferry, NY: Oceana Publications.

'Ley Constitucional No. 1/1995, de fecha 17 de Enero, por la que se reforma determinados artículos de la Ley Fundamental'. *Boletín oficial del estado*, 31/01/1995.

'Ley No. 7/1986, de fecha 4 de Julio sobre Partidos Políticos de Guinea Ecuatorial', in M. Liniger Goumaz (1992), *La démocrature, dictature camouflée, démocratie truquée*, 340–342.

'Ley No. 3/1992, de fecha 6 de Enero, de Partidos Políticos de Guinea Ecuatorial', in M. Liniger Goumaz (1992), *La démocrature, dictature camouflée, démocratie truquée*, 351–354.

'Ley No. 4/1992, de fecha 6 de Enero, sobre Libertad de Reunión y Manifestación', in M. Liniger Goumaz (1992), *La démocrature, dictature camouflée, démocratie truquée*, 355–357.

'Ley No. 3/1993, de fecha 12 de Enero, Reguladora de las Elecciones Legislativas, Municipales y Referendum'. *Boletín oficial del estado*, número extraordinario, 14/02/1993.

'Ley No. 7/1995, de fecha 9 de Enero, por la que se modifican determinados artículos de la Ley número 3/1993, de fecha 12 de Enero, Reguladora de las Elecciones Legislativas, Municipales y Referéndum'. *Boletín oficial del estado*, número extraordinario, 10/01/1995.

3.2 Books, Articles and Electoral Reports

Balboa Boneke, J. (1978). *¿Dónde estás Guinea?* Palma de Mallorca: Ed. Cort.

Carrascosa Izquierdo, L. (1970). *Malabo. Ruptura con Guinea*. Madrid: Mayler.

Cronje, S. (1976). *Equatorial Guinea. The Forgotten Dictatorship: Forced Labour and Political Murder in Central Africa*. London: Anti-Slavery Society.

Dilg, K. G. (1969). 'Die Verfassung der Republik Äquatorial-Guinea unter besonderer Berücksichtigung der politischen und verfassungsmäßigen Entwicklung bis zur Unabhängigkeit im Jahr 1968'. *Verfassung und Recht in Übersee*, 2: 291–303.

EIU (The Economist Intelligence Unit) (1986–1987, 1993). *Country Profile. Gabon, Equatorial Guinea*. London: EIU.

Fegley, R. (1989). *Equatorial Guinea: an African Tragedy*. New York: Lang.

— (1991). *Equatorial Guinea*. Oxford: Clio Press.

Fernandez Martin, R. (1976). *Guinea, Materia Reservada*. Madrid: Sedmay.

Jakobeit, C. (1993). 'Äquatorialguinea', in D. Nohlen and F. Nuscheler (eds.), *Handbuch der Dritten Welt. Vol.4: Westafrika und Zentralafrika* (3rd edn). Bonn: Dietz, 420–432.

Klittgard, R. E. (1990). *Tropical Gangsters*. New York: Basic Books.

Kobel, A. (1976). *La République de Guinée Equatoriale, ses ressources potentielles et virtuelles. Possibilités de développement*. Université de Neuchâtel.

Legineche, M. (1996). *La Tribu. Guinea Ecuatorial, 1979–1996*. Madrid: Espasa Calpe.

Liniger-Goumaz, M. (1980). *La Guinée équatoriale. Un pays méconnu*. Paris: L'Harmattan.

— (1986). *Estatisticas de la Guinea Ecuatorial Nguemista. Datos para explicar un desastre político*. Genève: Les Éditions du Temps.

— (1988*a*). *Historical Dictionary of Equatorial Guinea* (2nd edn.). Metuchen, NJ: Scarecrow Press.

— (1988*b*). *Brève histoire de la Guinée Equatoriale*. Paris: L'Harmattan.

— (1989). *Small is not always Beautiful: The Story of Equatorial Guinea*. Totowa, NJ: Barnes and Noble Books.

— (1992). *La démocrature, dictature camouflée, démocratie truquée*. Paris, L'Harmattan

— (1994). *Africa y las democracias desencadenadas: el caso de Guinea Ecuatorial*. La Chaux (Suisse): Les Editions du Temps.

— (1996*a*). *Guinea Ecuatorial. Bibliografía General IX*. Génève: Les Editions du Temps.

— (1996*b*). *Guinea Ecuatorial y el ensayo democrático. La conquista del golfo de Guinea*. Madrid: Editorial claves para el futuro.

Ndongo Bidgoyo, D. (1977). *Historia y tragedia de Guinea Ecuatorial*. Madrid: Ed. Cambio 16.

Nguema, F., and Balboa, J. (1996). *La transición de Guinea Ecuatorial*. Madrid: Labrys 54.

Nsang Andeme, J. A. (1995). *Democracia y derechos humanos en la política de cooperación al desarollo de la Unión Europea y de España. Guinea Ecuatorial*. Master Diss. Madrid: Universidad Complutense.

Ocha'a Mve Bengobesama (1985). *Fuentes archivisticas y bibliotecarias de Guinea Ecuatorial: guía general del administrativo, del investigador y del estudiante*. Malabo: Ediciones Guinea.

Owona, J. (1983). 'La Guinée Equatoriale et la démocratie: l'astucieux recours à un constitutionalisme rédhibitoire'. *Le mois en Afrique*, April-May, 207–208.

Pomponne, M. (1994). 'La Guinée-Equatoriale sous la botte d'un clan'. *Le Monde Diplomatique,* July 1994, 4–5.

Reeves, P. (1996). *1996 Presidential Elections in Equatorial Guinea. Observation Report.* Washington, D.C.: The International Foundation for Elections Systems (IFES).

Ridao, J. M. (1996). 'Guinea Ecuatorial en perspectiva'. *Política Exterior*, 10/54: 136–147.

Roig, J. (1996). 'Guinea Ecuatorial: la dictadura enquistada'. *Cuadernos Bakeaz*, 18: 1–12.

Sundiata, I. K. (1990). *Equatorial Guinea, Colonialism, State Terror and the Search for Stability*. Boulder, Col.: Westview Press.

UNHCR (Commission on Human Rights) (1983). *Une nouvelle constitution en Guinée Equatoriale*. Doc. E/CN.4/1983/NGO/4. Geneva: January 31, 1983.

— *Reports on the Human Rights Situation in Equatorial Guinea*,1989, 1991, 1995, 1996.

Wagner, I. (1978). 'Äquatorialguinea'. in D. Sternberger, B. Vogel, D. Nohlen and K. Landfried (eds.), *Die Wahl der Parlamente und anderer Staatsorgane, Band I: Politische Organisation und Repräsentation in Afrika,* by Franz Nuscheler, Klaus Ziemer *et al.,* Berlin: Walter de Gruyter, 302–318.

de Zaragoza, M. J. (1969). 'La République de Guinée Équatoriale (aperçu sur la constitution et les droits de l'homme)'. *Revue juridique et politique*, 23/2: 213–224.

ERITREA

by Bernhard Thibaut

1. Introduction

1.1 Historical Overview

The Republic of Eritrea emerged in 1993 from the first secession in post-colonial Africa. From 1890 to 1941 the territory of Eritrea was an Italian colony. After Italy had been defeated in World War II Eritrea came under British military administration until in 1950 the UN decided that it was a part of Ethiopia. The guarantee of autonomous self-administration of Eritrea that was part of the agreement between the UN and the Ethiopian Emperor Haile Selassie I was rapidly ignored by the Ethiopian authorities. Even before the complete annexation of Eritrea was proclaimed by Ethiopia in 1962, the Eritrean Liberation Front (ELF) had been formed and engaged in guerrilla warfare with the aim of achieving complete independence. At the time of the Ethiopian revolution of 1974 it controlled important parts of the Eritrean territory. However, after the new Ethiopian regime had overcome internal power struggles as well as external conflicts (Ogaden War against Somalia) in the late 1970s it reacted massively to secessionist movements and forced the Eritrean guerrillas to retreat into the North Western border region. Only in the second half of the 1980s, when the Eritrean People's Liberation Front (EPLF) had emerged from internal conflicts and several splits of the ELF as the strongest guerrilla force, did the independence war regain its dynamism. It ended in May 1991 with the military defeat of the Ethiopian army when EPLF troops took the capital town of Eritrea, Asmara.

The EPLF built a provisional government, headed by its leader Isaias Afwerki, and its 44-member Central Committee functioned as a legislative body. In accordance with the new Ethiopian authorities, which had taken over government after the downfall of the Mengistu regime, a referendum on the question of the future status of Eritrea was organized. The referendum was held under supervision of the UN in April 1993 and resulted in a nearly unanimous approval of the independence option. On

25 May 1993 Eritrea became an independent state. A few months later the provisional legislature (*Hagerawi Baito*—National Assembly) was enlarged by 30 delegates of the councils of the 10 provinces and another 30 newly appointed members.

In early 1994 the EPLF transformed itself into a political party adopting the name Popular Front for Democracy and Justice (PFDJ). In April 1994, the National Assembly appointed a 50-member Constitutional Commission. The draft constitution it presented in mid-1996 after a lengthy process of widespread consultations (it was said that more than half a million people were involved) foresaw a unitary presidential system of government with the President to be elected by the one-chamber National Assembly from within its members. The draft constitution was approved on 23 May 1997 by an assembly composed of the delegates of the different regions of the countries and important social groups.

Politics in Eritrea will in the foreseeable future be marked by the dominant role of the PFDJ. Some important decisions concerning the structure of the political system have already been made during the transitional period, reflecting the concern of the government to insure that the sense of national unity that had marked the independence war be firmly institutionalized. Parties were not allowed to be built upon the basis of ethnicity. In 1995 the administrative structure of Eritrea was reformed in such a way as to make sure that none of the newly created six (instead of formerly 10) regions would be an ethnically homogeneous entity that might bring about regionalist tendencies. In order to assure strict separation of politics and religion a law was passed which states that religious communities must not engage in any political activities (including the management of development projects). Fears that the official commitment of the PFDJ to establish a liberal representative democracy in Eritrea may not easily be reconciled with its desire to control the national political process were nurtured by the border conflict with Ethiopia which turned into open war in summer 1998.

1.2 Evolution of Electoral Provisions

Before 1993, when Eritrea was a part of Ethiopia the Ethiopian electoral provisions applied to the territory and the people of Eritrea.

The legal provisions for the referendum of 1993 were laid down in two proclamations of the transitional government: the Eritrean Nationality Proclamation No. 21/1992 and the Referendum Proclamation No. 22/1992. All Eritrean citizens as defined by the Nationality Proclamation (that is, Eritreans by birth or naturalization) with a minimum age of 18 were entitled to register as voters and participate in the referendum. This applied also to citizens living outside of Eritrea.

1.3 Current Electoral Provisions

Sources: Constitution of Eritrea (23 May 1997).

Elected national institutions: National Assembly (Hagerawi Baito; 150 members) for a five-year term. The President who is Head of State and Head of Government will be elected indirectly from the National Assembly from among its members. No person shall be elected to hold the presidency for more than two terms.

Suffrage: The principles of universal, equal, direct and secret suffrage are applied. Every citizen who has reached the age of 18 has the right to vote.

Nomination of candidates: Norms of ineligibility and concerning the nomination of the deputies will be determined by an electoral law not stipulated yet. The constitution provides for any member of the National Assembly who has citizenship of Eritrea by birth to be elected President.

Electoral System: The procedures for the election of the President and the National Assembly will be laid down in an electoral law that has to be enacted yet.

1.4 Comment on the Electoral Statistics

The statistical data presented in the following tables stem from official and UN-related sources.

2. Tables

2.1 Dates of National Elections, Referenda and Coups d'Etat

Year	Presidential elections	Parliamentary elections	Elections for Constitutional Assembly	Referendums	Coups d'état
1993				23–25/04	

2.2 Electoral Body 1993

Year	Type of election[a]	Population	Registered voters		Votes cast		
			Total number	% pop.	Total number	% reg. voters	% pop.
1993	Ref	2,500,000[b]	1,173,706	46.9	1,156,280	98.5	46.3

[a] Ref = Referendum.

[b] UN-estimation.

2.3 Abbreviations

PFDJ	Popular Front for Democracy and Justice

2.4 Electoral Participation of Parties and Alliances

Elections have not been held yet.

2.5 Referendum 1993

Year	1993[a]	
	Total number	%
Registered voters	1,173,706	–
Votes cast	1,156,280	98.5
Invalid votes	328	0.0
Valid votes	1,155,952	100.0
Yes	1,100,260	95.2
No	1,822	0.2
Tendered ballots	53,878	4.6

[a] Independence referendum.

2.6 Elections for Constitutional Assembly

Elections for Constitutional Assembly have not been held.

2.7 Parliamentary Elections

Parliamentary elections have not yet been held.

2.8 Composition of Parliament

The current legislative is composed of 45 members of the Central Committee of the PFDJ, 30 delegates of the councils of the 10 provinces and another 30 appointed members (party affiliation of non-PFDJ members not available).

2.9 Presidential Elections

Direct presidential elections are not held in Eritrea.

2.10 List of Power Holders 1991–1998

Head of State and Government	Years	Remarks
Isaias Afworki	1993–	Leader of EPLF; from 1991 onwards Head of the provisional government; acting President since independence of Eritrea on 25 May 1993.

3. Bibliography

Cliffe, L., and Davidson, B. (eds.) (1988). *The Long Struggle of Eritrea for Independence and Constructive Peace*. Nottingham: Spokesman.

Eikenberg, K. (1993–1997). 'Eritrea', in Institut für Afrika-Kunde and R. Hofmeier (eds.), *Afrika-Jahrbuch*, Opladen: Leske & Budrich (annually).

Eikenberg, K. (1993). 'Eritrea', in D. Nohlen and F. Nuscheler (eds.), *Handbuch der Dritten Welt*, Vol. 5: Ostafrika und Südafrika (3rd edn.). Bonn: Dietz, 79–87.

Fegley, R. (1995). *Eritrea*. Oxford: Clio Press.

Furrer-Kreski, E. (ed.) (1990). *Handbuch Eritrea: Geschichte und Gegenwart eines Konfliktes*. Zürich: Rio-Verlag.

Gayim, E. (1993). *The Eritrean Question: The Conflict between the Right of Self-Determination and the Interests of States*. Uppsala: Iustus Förlag.

Iyob, R. (1995). *The Eritrean Struggle for Independence: Domination, Resistance, Nationalism 1941–1993*. Cambridge: Cambridge University Press.

Kurdi, N. H. (1994). *L'Érythrée: une identité retrouvée*. Paris: Ed. Karthala.

Markakis, J. (1995). 'Eritrea's National Charter'. *ROAPE* 63 (March), 126–129.

Pateman, R. (1990). *Eritrea. Even the Stones are Burning*. Trenton, NJ: Red Sea Press.

Prouty, C., and Rosenfeld, E. (1994). *Historical Dictionary of Ethiopia and Eritrea* (2nd edn.). Metuchen, NJ: Scarecrow Press.

The African-American Institute (1993). *Eritrea: A Report on the Referendum on Independence, April 23–25, 1993*. Washington, D.C.: The African–American Institute.

Zarembo, A. (1995). 'Controlled Democracy'. *Africa Report*, May–June 1995, 52–55.

Zimmermann, M. (1992). *Eritrea - Aufbruch in die Freiheit*. Essen: Verlag Neuer Weg.

ETHIOPIA

by Michael Meier

1. Introduction

1.1 Historical Overview

When the last Ethiopian king, Emperor Haile Selassie I, was brought down in a military coup d'état in 1974, the end of dynasty thousands of years old which claimed descent from King Solomon and the Queen of Sheba was marked. Except the years between 1935 and 1941, when the Italians occupied Ethiopia, the country was never dominated by external powers.

The beginning of the known Ethiopian history is traced to the famous empire of Axum, the northern part of the country, in 500 BC. Christianity was introduced in 330 AD, Islam arose in the 7th century. By then, Abyssinia (the highlands of Ethiopia) became a closed country. However, only Emperor Tewodros (1855–1868) strengthened the throne and centralized political power after a period of wars and struggles against different enemies. Starting with a military expansion towards the southern, western and eastern territories under Emperor Menelik II in the late 19th century, steps towards a modernization of the feudal Ethiopian society changed the structure of the Abyssinian Kingdom. The Ethiopian-orthodox church included now only about half of the population, the former centers of the kingdom were located on the periphery. But the structure of political power remained basically unchanged for more than another half century. The first constitution of Ethiopia, introduced by Emperor Haile Selassie I in 1931 did not foresee any political participation of the population. Only in 1955 a new constitution introduced universal suffrage and provided for direct elections of one of the two chambers of Parliament. However, political power remained almost unconstrained in the hands of the Emperor.

A coup d'état in 1960 by members of the Imperial Guard failed but marked the beginning of a period of steady state of political unrest until a serious drought which was ignored by the administration led to the dethronement of the Emperor in 1974. The Provisional Military

Government suspended the Constitution of 1955 and dissolved both chambers of the legislature.

The *Derg* (Amharic for committee), which was a group of military leaders, proclaimed under the slogan *Ethiopia Tikdem* (Ethiopia first) a sort of specific Ethiopian socialism. Banks, insurance companies and industries as well as all the land of the feudal class were nationalized. In the period of the so-called 'red terror' the regime killed about 10,000 people only in Addis Abeba between 1977 and 1978. Only in 1987 was a new 'Constitution of the People's Democratic Republic of Ethiopia' established and approved in a referendum held under authoritarian conditions. Non-competitive elections to the National Parliament *(Shengo)* were held in the same year.

From the beginning, the regime had to fight against rebel organizations in Eritrea and Tigray, the two northern provinces. Despite massive support from the Soviet Union and their allies the *Derg* lost step by step first the rural areas and later on the towns in these provinces. In a common action of the Ethiopian Peoples' Revolutionary Democratic Front (EPRDF) and the Eritrean Peoples' Liberation Front (EPLF) they took over the capital Addis Abeba on 28 May 1991.

A national conference was held in July 1991 and a provisional Parliament was formed with members of 33 different organizations or groups. The country was divided into 14 ethnic-based regions (out of which two were town regions) to facilitate the new policy of decentralization. After clashes between the EPRDF and the Oromo Liberation Front (OLF), the OLF decided not to participate in the subsequent elections. A Constitutional Assembly was elected in 1994 and ratified a new constitution that provides for a parliamentary and federal system of government and stipulates freedom of participation in political parties, labor unions and other organizations. Parliamentary elections were held in 1995 and won clearly by the EPRDF as a conglomerate of different parties.

While the new government began with some success to transform the economy (liberalization of the banking sector, privatization of industries, reduction of restrictions in foreign exchange markets) its commitment to political pluralism remained questionable. Still there are journalists in prison and leaders of opposition groups are either in jail or in exile abroad. Important opposition groups are excluded from power at the federal as well as at the regional level. Thus, in the process of decentralization and democratization much remains to be done.

1.2 Evolution of Electoral Provisions

Since 1955 all citizens with a minimum age of 21 years were entitled to vote. Before, only men were allowed to vote and generally only indirect elections had taken place.

The 1955 constitution provided for two legislative chambers, the Senate and the Chamber of Deputies. Whereas the members of the Senate were appointed by the Emperor for six years, the members of the Chamber of Deputies were directly elected for a period of four years. For that purpose the country was divided into electoral districts containing as nearly as possible 200,000 inhabitants. In each district two deputies were elected according to a plurality system. In addition, each town with a population exceeding 30,000 inhabitants elected one deputy and an additional deputy for each additional 50,000 inhabitants. To be eligible as a deputy one had to be 25 years old, Ethiopian by birth, a *bona fide* resident and owner of property in the respective electoral district (land property equivalent to US-$ 400 or other property or income equivalent to US-$ 800).

The 1987 Constitution reduced the minimum age for active suffrage to 18 years. The 835 members of the National *Shengo* were directly elected for five years. To be elected one had to be at least 21 years old and to be nominated by the ruling Workers' Party of Ethiopia, mass organizations or military units. After a multi-staged process of candidate selection, up to three candidates were presented to the voters in each constituency. Though neither the constitution nor the electoral law contained any explicit provisions with respect to the electoral system, it seems that the plurality system in single-member constituencies was applied. The *Shengo* elected the President, the Prime Minister and the other members of government.

1.3 Current Electoral Provisions

Sources: Constitution of the Federal Democratic Republic of Ethiopia of 8 December 1994; Proclamation No. 111/1995 (Proclamation to make the Electoral Law of Ethiopia conform with the Constitution of the Federal Democratic Republic of Ethiopia).

Elected national institutions: National legislature (House of Peoples' Representatives) for a period of five years. The Constitution stipulates that the number of seats in the House of Peoples' Representatives shall not exceed 550; among these minority nationalities shall have at least 20 seats. The members of the second chamber of Parliament ('House of Federations') are elected by the regional parliaments for a period of five years. The Prime Minister is elected by and responsible to the House of Peoples' Representatives from among its members; the (ceremonial) President is elected for a six-year term by both chambers of Parliament.

Suffrage: The principles of universal, equal, direct and secret suffrage are applied. Every citizen who has reached the age of 18 has the right to vote.

Nomination of candidates: To be a candidate one has to be at least 21 years of age, Ethiopian by nationality, versed in the vernacular of the National Region of one's candidature and residing in the constituency for at least five years. A candidate of a political party has to provide not less than 500 endorsement signatures, certified by the local administration to be residents of the constituency. An independent candidate has to provide 1,000 such signatures. The number of candidates in one constituency is limited to 12; if more than 12 candidates are registered, those 12 with the highest number of endorsement signatures will stand for election.

Electoral system: Plurality system in single-member districts (1995: 547). The territory of the country is divided into constituencies based on the *woredas* (counties) without affecting regional boundaries. Each constituency is made up of around 100,000 inhabitants. Minority nationalities are entitled to elect and send their respective representative even if the number of voters in their areas is below 100,000.

1.4 Comment on the Electoral Statistics

There is no official and ready-made statistical abstract on the elections in Ethiopia. During the time of Emperor Haile Selassie all statistics were administered by the National Board of Registration and Elections of the Ministry of Interior whereas during the *Derg's* time the data were distributed among the Ministries of Information, the Prime Minister's Office and the National Election Board. Under the new government there is a trend to centralize the data collection in the hands of the National Election Board. Especially for the period before 1991 the data situation is very difficult. The data and comments presented in the following tables were collected by the National Election Board in cooperation with the Friedrich Ebert Foundation.

2. Tables

2.1 Dates of National Elections, Referendums and Coups d'Etat

Year	Presidential elections	Parliamentary elections	Elections for Constitutional Assembly	Referendums	Coups d'état
1957		12/09–10/10			
1961		17/06–12/07			
1965		23/06–12/07			
1973		23/06–07/07			
1974					12/09
1987		14/06		01/02	
1991					28/05[a]
1994			05/06		
1995		07/05			

[a] Military victory of EPRDF and EPLF over the *Derg* regime.

2.2 Electoral Body 1957–1995

Year	Type of election[a]	Population	Registered voters		Votes cast		
			Total number	% pop.	Total number	% reg. Voters	% pop.
1957	Pa	—	—	—	—	—	—
1961	Pa	23,083,000	—	—	—	—	—
1965	Pa	25,410,000	—	—	—	—	—
1969	Pa	28,193,000	—	—	—	—	—
1973	Pa	31,224,000	—	—	—	—	—
1987	Ref	46,000,000	14,570,011	—	14,035,718	96.3	—
1987	Pa	—	17,768,000	—	13,086,650	73.7	—
1994	CA	54,938,100[b]	16,797,143	30.6	14,698,103	87.5	26.8
1995	Pa	56,677,100	21,337,379	37.6	19,986,179	93.6	35.2

[a] CA = Constitutional Assembly; Pa = Parliament; Pr = President; Ref = Referendum.
[b] Census result (1994).

2.3 Abbreviations

Afar LF	Afar Liberation Front
Afar NLF	Afar National Liberation Front
Afar PDO	Afar People's Democratic Organization
Alaba PDO	Alaba People's Democratic Organization
Alaba PDUO	Alaba People's Democratic Unity Organization
Amhara NDM	Amhara National Democratic Movement
Argoba	Argoba People's Democratic Movement
Argoba NUO	Argoba Nation Unity Organization
Bench PRDO	Bench People's Revolutionary Democratic Organization
Bench, Sheko, Dizi, Meinit PDF	Bench, Sheko, Dizi, Meinit People's Democratic Front
Benishangul Noth-Western Ethiopia PDUP	Benishangul Noth-Western Ethiopia People's Democratic Unity Party
Benshangul PLM	Benshangul People's Liberation Movement
Burji PDO	Burji People's Democratic Organization
Dawro PDO	Dawro People's Democratic Organization
Dawro PRDO	Dawro People's Revolutionary Democratic Organization
Derashe PDO	Derashe People's Democratic Organization
Dizi PRDO	Dizi People's Revolutionary Democratic Organization
ENDP	Ethiopian National Democratic Party
EPRDF	Ethiopian People's Revolutionary Democratic Front
ESDL	Ethiopia Somali Democratic League
Gambella PDUP	Gambella People's Democratic Unity Party
Gambella PLP	Gambella People's Liberation Party
Gamo and Gofa PDO	Gamo and Gofa People's Democratic Organization
Gamo DU	Gamo Democratic Unity
Gideo PRDO	Gideo People's Revolutionary Democratic Organization
Gideo PUDM	Gideo People's Unity Democratic Movement
Gumusz PLM	Gumusz People's Liberation Movement
Gurage PRDM	Gurage People's Revolutionary Democratic Movement
Hadya PDO	Hadya People's Organization
Hareri NL	Hareri National League
Kebena NDO	Kebena Nationality Democratic Organization
Keficho PRDO	Keficho People's Revolutionary Democratic Organization
Kembata PDO	Kembata People's Democratic Organization
Konso PRDO	Konso People's Revolutionary Democratic Organization
Konso PDO	Konso People's Democratic Organization
Kore NUDO	Kore Nationality Unity Democratic Organization
Kore PRDO	Kore People's Revolutionary Democratic Organization
Mareko PDO	Mareko People's Democratic Organization
Mein PRDO	Mein People's Revolutionary Democratic Organization
Ogaden NLF	Ogaden National Liberation Front
Oromo LUF	Oromo Liberation United Front

Oromo PDO	Oromo People's Democratic Organization
SEPDF	Southern Ethiopia People's Democratic Front
Shekecho PDM	Shekecho People's Democratic Movement
Sidama PDO	Sidama People's Democratic Organization
Silti PDUP	Silti People's Democratic Unity Party
Silti, Azernet Berbere, Alicho Worero, Meskan Melga, Wolene Gedebano PDM	Silti, Azernet Berbere, Alicho Worero, Meskan Melga, Wolene Gedebano People's Democratic Movement
Southern Omo PDM	Southern Omo People's Democratic Movement
Tembaro PDO	Tembaro People's Democratic Organization
Tigray PLF	Tigray People's Liberation Front
Wolayta PDO	Wolayta People's Democratic Organization
WSDP	Western Somali Democratic Party
Yem PDF	Yem People's Democratic Front
Zeisei PDO	Zeisei People's Democratic Organization

General note: For most parties the abbreviations given were created by the author for the purposes of this article. With little exceptions the parties/ organizations are generally referred to by their full name.

2.4 Electoral Participation of Parties and Alliances 1987–1995

Party / Alliance	Years	Elections contested[a]
Ethiopian Workers Party	1987	1
Alaba PDO[b]	1994	1
Argoba NUO	1994	1
Benishangul PLM	1994	1
Dawro PDO[c]	1994	1
Gamo DU	1994	1
Gideo PRDO[d]	1994	1
Gumusz PLM	1994	1
Konso PRDO[e]	1994	1
Kore PRDO	1994	1
Mein PRDO	1994	1
Shekecho PDM	1994	1
Silti, Azernet Berbere, Alicho Worero, Meskan Melga, Wolene Gedebano PDM	1994	1
Southern Omo PRDO	1994	1
Afar LF	1994, 1995	2
Afar PDO	1994, 1995	2
Amhara NDM	1994, 1995	2
Bench PRDO	1994, 1995	2
Burji PDO	1994, 1995	2
Dizi PRDO	1994, 1995	2
EPRDF	1994, 1995	2

Party / Alliance	Years	Elections contested[a]
ESDL	1994, 1995	2
Gambella PLP	1994, 1995	2
Gamo and Gofa PDO	1994, 1995	2
Gurage PRDM	1994, 1995	2
Hadya PDO	1994, 1995	2
Hareri NL	1994, 1995	2
Kebena NDO	1994, 1995	2
Keficho PRDO	1994, 1995	2
Kembata PDO	1994, 1995	2
Mareko PDO	1994, 1995	2
Oromo PDO	1994, 1995	2
Sidama PDO	1994, 1995	2
Tembaro PDO	1994, 1995	2
Tigray PLF	1994, 1995	2
Wolayta PDO	1994, 1995	2
WSDP	1994, 1995	2
Yem PDF	1994, 1995	2
Afar NLF	1995	1
Alaba PDUO[c]	1995	1
Argoba PDM	1995	1
Bench, Sheko, Dizi, Meinit PDF	1995	1
Benishangul Noth-Western Ethiopia PDUP	1995	1
Benishangul Western Ethiopia People's Democratic Party	1995	1
Dawro PRDO	1995	1
Derashe PDO	1995	1
ENDP	1995	1
Gambella PDUP	1995	1
Gideo PUDM	1995	1
Konso PDO	1995	1
Kore NUDO	1995	1
Ogaden NLF	1995	1
Oromo LUF	1995	1
SEPDF	1995	1
Silti PDUP	1995	1
Southern Omo PDM	1995	1
Zeisei PDO	1995	1

[a] Parliamentary elections and elections for Constitutional Assembly.
[b] In the 1995 elections the party ran as Alaba PDUO.
[c] In the 1995 elections the party ran as Dawro PRDO.
[d] In the 1995 elections the party ran as Gideo PUDM.
[e] In the 1995 elections the party ran as Konso PDO.

2.5 Referendums

Year	1987[a]	
	Total number	%
Registered voters	14,570,011	
Votes cast	14,035,718	96.3
Invalid votes	—	—
Valid votes	—	—
Yes	—	81
No	—	18

[a] Approval of the new constitution.

2.6 Elections for Constitutional Assembly

1994	Votes		Seats	
	Total number	%	Total (544)	%
Registered voters	16,797,143	–		
Votes cast	14,698,103	87.5		
Invalid votes	329,179	2.2		
Valid votes	14,368,924	97.8		
EPRDF and allied			*463*	*85.1*
Tigray PLF	—	—	37	6.8
Amhara NDM	—	—	134	24.6
Omoro PDO	—	—	179	32.9
Afar PDO	—	—	2	0.4
Gurage PRDM	—	—	12	2.2
Hadya PDO	—	—	8	1.5
Kembata PDO	—	—	5	0.9
Tembaro PDO	—	—	1	0.2
Alaba PDO	—	—	2	0.4
Yem PDF	—	—	1	0.2
Keficho PRDO	—	—	6	1.1
Bench PRDO	—	—	2	0.4
Shekecho PDM	—	—	2	0.4
Sidama PDO	—	—	19	3.5
Wolayta PDO	—	—	13	2.4
Gideo PRDO	—	—	6	1.1
Konso PRDO	—	—	1	0.2
Gamo and Gofa PDO	—	—	13	2.4
Kore PRDO	—	—	1	0.2
Dawro PDO	—	—	4	0.7
Gambella PLP	—	—	2	0.4
EPRDF	—	—	13	2.4

	Votes	%	Seats	%
Parties not allied with EPRDF and Independents	—	—	*81*	*14.9*
Afar LF	—	—	6	1.1
Agoba NUO	—	—	1	0.2
Gumusz PLM	—	—	2	0.4
Benshangul PLM	—	—	5	0.9
Kebena NDO	—	—	1	0.2
Mareko PDO	—	—	1	0.2
Silti, Azernet Berbere, Alicho Worero, Meskan Melga, Wolene Gedebano PDM	—	—	3	0.5
Burji PDO	—	—	1	0.2
Southern Omo PRDO	—	—	7	1.3
Dizi PRDO	—	—	1	0.2
Mein PRDO	—	—	2	0.4
Hareri NL	—	—	1	0.2
Gamo DU	—	—	1	0.2
ESDL	—	—	13	2.4
WSDP	—	—	2	0.4
Independents	—	—	34	6.3

2.7 Parliamentary Elections 1987–1995

Year	1987		1995[a]	
	Total number	%	Total number	%
Registered voters	17,768,000	–	21,337,379	–
Votes cast	16,085,900	90.5	19,986,179	93.7
Invalid votes	2,998,350	18.6	159,889	0.8
Valid votes	13,086,650	81.4	19,826,290	99.2
Workers Party of Ethiopia	12,981,957	99.2	–	–
Independents	104,693	0.8	–	–
EPRDF and allied	–	–	16,429,727	82.9
Parties not allied with EPRDF, independents	–	–	3,369,563	17.1

[a] With some minor exceptions the elections were considered technically correct and reasonably fair but were boycotted by important opposition parties such as All Amhara People's Organization, Oromo Liberation Front, Southern Ethiopian People's Democratic Coalition and Ethiopian Democratic Unity Party. Detailed data of the electoral outcome are not available.

2.8 Composition of Parliament 1987–1995

Year	1987 Seats 835	% 100	1995 Seats 547	% 100
Workers Party of Ethiopia	795	95.2		
Independents	40	4.8		
EPRDF and allied	–	–	*471*	*86.1*
Tigray PLF			38	6.9
Amhara NDM			133	24.3
Oromo PDO			176	32.2
Afar PDO			3	0.6
Gurage PRDM			14	2.6
Hadya PDO			9	1.7
Kembata PDO			4	0.7
Tembaro PDO			1	0.2
Alaba PDO			2	0.4
Yem PDF			1	0.2
Keficho PRDO			6	1.1
Bench PRDO			1	0.2
Sidama PDO			19	3.5
Wolayta PDO			13	2.4
Gideo PUDM			7	1.3
Konso PRDO			1	0.2
Gamo and Gofa PDO			15	2.8
Kore NUDO			1	0.2
Dawro PDO			4	0.7
Gambella PLP			2	0.4
EPRDF			21	3.8
Parties not allied with EPRDF and independents			*75*	*13.9*
Afar LF			3	0.6
Argoba PDM			1	0.2
Benishangul Noth-Western Ethiopia PDUP			5	0.9
Kebena NDO			1	0.2
Mareko PDO			1	0.2
Silti PDUP			1	0.2

Year	1987		1995	
	Seats	%	Seats	%
Burji PDO			1	0.2
Southern Omo PDM			7	1.3
Dizi PRDO			2	0.4
Hareri NL			1	0.2
ESDL			17	3.1
WSDP			1	0.2
Zeisei PDO			1	0.2
Gambella PDUP			1	0.2
Ogaden NLF			3	0.6
Southern Ethiopia PDF			6	1.1
Afar NLF			1	0.2
Derashe PDO			3	0.6
Ethiopian National Democratic Party			1	0.2
Oromo LUF			4	0.4
Bench, Sheko, Dizi, Meinit PDF			2	0.4
Independents			10	1.8

2.9 Presidential Elections

Presidential elections have not been held.

2.10 List of Power Holders 1974–1998

Before 1974 Ethiopia was ruled by Emperor Haile Selassie I (since 1930) in a nearly unconstrained manner. The office of a Prime Minister existed, but he was completely dependent on the Emperor.

Head of State	Years	Remarks
Aman Michael Andom	1974	Military; took office on 13/09/1974; killed by the Derg on 23/11/1974.
Tafari Benti	1974–1977	Military; took office on 26/11/1974; killed by the Derg on 03/02 1977.
Mengistu Haile Mariam	1977–1991	Military; took office on 04/02/1977; constitutional President since 10/09/1987 (elected by the National Shengo); left office on 21/05/1991; in exile in Zimbabwe.
Tesfaye Gabre Kidan	1991	Acting President from 21–27/05/1991; political asylum in the Italian Embassy in Addis Abeba.
Meles Zenawi	1991–1995	Interim President from 02/06/1991 until 22/08/1995.
Negaso Gidada	1995–	Constitutionally elected by the Federal Assembly; took office on 22/08/1995.

Head of Government	Years	Remarks
Aklilu Habtwold	1974	Civilian; in office from 28/02 until 04/03/1974; killed by the Derg.
Indalkachew Mekonnen	1974	Civilian; in office from 04/03 until 22/07/1974; killed by the Derg.
Michael Imeru	1974	In office from 02/08 until 12/09; became Minister of Information under the Derg.
Fikre Selassie Wogderess	1987–1991	Military; left office on 26/04/1991; in prison.
Tesfaye Dinka	1991	Civilian; in office from 26/04 until 27/05; committed suicide in the Italian Embassy.
Tamirat Laynie	1991–1995	Civilian; in office from 05/06/1991 until 22/08/1995; Deputy Prime Minister until his dismissal on 24/10/1996.
Meles Zenawi	1995–	Civilian, constitutional Prime Minister; elected by the House of Peoples' Representatives; in office since 22/08/1995.

3. Bibliography

Abbink, J. (1995). ‘Ethnicité et “democratisation”: le dilemme éthiopien’. *Politique Africaine*, 57: 135–141.

Adelmann, K. (1995). ‘Wahlen in Äthiopien—eine Farce’. *epd-entwicklungspolitik*, 6: 25–27.

Auf, C. (1996). *Staat und Militär in Äthiopien*. Hamburg: Deutsches Übersee-Institut.

Bahru, Z. (1993). *A History of Modern Ethiopia* (2nd edn.). London/ Addis Abeba: Currey.

Brüne, S. (1986). *Äthiopien. Unterentwicklung und radikale Militärherrschaft*. Hamburg: Institut für Afrika-Kunde.

Cayla, F. (1997). ‘Ethiopie. Le nouveau modèle, un réalisme ethnique’. *L'Afrique Politique* 1997, 111–128.

Clapham, C. (1988). *Transformation and Continuity in Revolutionary Ethiopia*. Cambridge: Cambridge University Press.

Eikenberg, K. (1994). ‘Äthiopien’, in D. Nohlen and F. Nuscheler (eds.), *Handbuch der Dritten Welt, Vol. 5: Ostafrika und Südafrika* (3rd edn.). Bonn: Dietz, 32–53.

Engedayehu, W. (1993). ‘Ethiopia: Democracy and the Politics of Ethnicity’. *Africa Today*, 2: 29–52.

Holcomb, B. K., and Ibssa, S. (1990). *The Invention of Ethiopia*. Trenton, NJ: Red Sea Press.

Janssen, V. (1976). *Politische Herrschaft in Äthiopien*. Freiburg: Schwarz.

Lyons, T. (1996). ‘Closing the Transition: the May 1995 Elections in Ethiopia’. *Journal of Modern African Studies*, 34/1: 121–142.

Niggli, P. (1992). *Die verpaßte Chance. Äthiopien nach Mengistu. Die Wahlen vom Juni ’92*. Köln: Heinrich-Böll Stiftung.

Nuscheler, F. (1978). ‘Äthiopien’, in D. Sternberger, B. Vogel, D. Nohlen and K. Landfried (eds.), *Die Wahl der Parlamente und anderer Staatsorgane. Band II: Politische Organisation und Repräsentation in Afrika,* by Franz Nuscheler, Klaus Ziemer *et al.*, Berlin/ New York: Walter de Gruyter, 319–344.

Pankhurst, R. (1990). *A Social History of Ethiopia*. Addis Abeba: Institute of Ethiopian Studies.

Scholler, H. (1996). ‘Die neue äthiopische Verfassung und ihre Auswirkungen auf die Rechtsordnung’. *KAS-Auslandsinformationen*, 12/12: 85–101.

Teferra, D. (1990). *Social History and Theoretical Analyses of the Economy of Ethiopia*. Lewiston: E. Mellen.

Vircoulon, T. (1995). ‘Ethiopie: les risques du fédéralisme’. *Afrique Contemporaine*, 174: 35–50.

GABON

by Helga Fleischhacker*

1. Introduction

1.1 Historical Overview

Gabon's political history is largely distinguished by the ruling elite's success in reshaping government institutions to meet the needs of power conservation. Although essential power structures have shown considerable continuity since independence and plebiscitarian elections have been held regularly, constitutional rules have been subject to continuous change. This pattern, established under the country's first President, Léon M'Ba, was further refined by his successor (and current President), El Hadji Omar Bongo, who followed in the office in 1967.

Buoyed by rapid economic growth by oil revenues a personalist neo-patrimonial system, controlled by an enriched class of state officials and functionaries, the so-called '*système* Bongo' consolidated itself during the 1970s. Lopsided economic development based upon the oil sector created a new set of tensions, however, and these grew more pronounced as economic contraction set in after 1980. Pressed by growing political opposition and social discontent, the regime saw itself forced to inaugurate a phase of gradual liberalization and institutional reform in 1990, however, it managed to maintain its control over the political process and restabilized after the second multi-party elections had been held in 1996.

Gabon gained independence on 17 August 1960, with Léon M'Ba, who had served as Prime Minister under the French constitution of the Fifth Republic, as President. Within the first year of the republic, M'Ba used struggle over the draft of a new constitution in order to discipline the National Assembly. He dissolved Parliament, and forged a unitary list for the subsequent elections. This list, made up of the President's party *Bloc Démocratique Gabonais* (BDG), and the oppositional *Union Démocratique et Sociale Gabonaise* (UDSG) of Jean-Hilaire Aubame. A

* The author would like to thank Fidèle Mengue Me Engouang, Professeur à la Faculté de Droit at Libreville, for his contributions to the documentation of Gabon's vast electoral legislation, V. Obame Emane, Director of Pionniers at Libreville, who drew up the tables of the 1996 parliamentary elections, and the IFES Resource Center.

new constitution, already the country's third, drawn up by the presidency providing the President with far greater power, was quickly approved. As M'Ba and his party consolidated their position under these new arrangements, Aubame and his UDSG were quickly marginalized, and only five UDSG members participated in the new government. In 1963 the long-standing rivalry between the two party leaders led to Aubame's removal from his ministerial post. In 1964, one week before scheduled elections, M'Ba was in turn deposed by a military coup led by Aubame. French military intervention quickly restored M'Ba to office, and multi-party legislative elections were subsequently held under French auspices. These, however, only postponed Gabon's trajectory towards a one-party state. In 1964 opposition forces gathered for the last time under the banner of *Parti de Defense des Institutions Démocratique* (DID). Over the next two years, most members of the opposition would defect to the BDG, and it ran unopposed in the elections of 1967.

M'Ba died in November 1967 and was succeeded by Albert-Bernard (later El Hadji Omar) Bongo, who continued his predecessor's consolidation of power by officially outlawing the opposition. By a decree of 12 March 1968, Bongo dissolved all existing parties into a new unitary party, the *Parti Démocratique Gabonais* (PDG) and formalized the one-party state with the Constitution of 29 July 1972. Additional constitutional amendments in 1975 and 1979 enhanced the powers of the PDG, which was made the country's highest constitutional body, as vested in its Central Committee and Political Bureau. With the constitutional reform of 1975 the governmental post of Vice-President was replaced by that of Prime Minister, but it was not until 1981 that the President actually relinquished his ministerial portfolios, gave up his functions as Head of Government and transferred them to his Prime Minister Léon Mébiame, who had occupied the office since 1975.

In 1981 a clandestine oppositional grouping, the *Mouvement de Redressement National* (MORENA) began to give shape to growing public disapproval with the regime. It accused the '*système* Bongo' of corruption and extravagance and demanded the restoration of multi-party democracy. In response to growing oppositional voices, Bongo introduced a new constitution, which promised broader participation in the National Assembly elections to be held in 1985. He also appealed to exiles to return to Gabon and to participate within a liberalized, though still single-party framework. As a token of his softened stance towards the opposition, he ordered the release from prison of MORENA activists, who had been sentenced in 1981 for belonging to an illegal political organization. In May 1989 Paul M'ba Abessole, the founder of MORENA and the opposition's leading figure, returned from exile.

The reform process took on added urgency after a series of strikes and demonstrations broke out in early 1990, reflecting growing popular discontent with the government's political and economic performance. The PDG central committee set up a 'special commission for democracy', which submitted a report explicitly condemning the one-party state. Bongo reacted by decreeing immediate and substantial political reforms. But his proposal to replace the ruling party with a *Rassemblement Social-Démocrate Gabonais* (RSDG), which would cover a more diverse ideological spectrum, did little to allay public discontent. In March 1990, following a joint session of the Central Committee and the National Assembly, the Political Bureau announced that, after a five-year transitional period, a multi-party system would be introduced. This was, however, rejected by a National Conference of some 2,000 delegates which, convened to draw up a program of transition, voted instead for immediate multi-party elections. Though the conference was not sovereign (unlike similar national conferences in Benin and Congo) and its role only advisory, Bongo acquiesced and appointed a transitional administration headed by a new Prime Minister pending legislative elections. He nonetheless held onto his executive powers, and his mandate (in effect until January 1994) was left intact.

Legislative elections were scheduled for September 1990; their scope was, however, limited by the requirement that only political parties registered at the time of the National Conference would be allowed to field candidates. The first round of the elections, on 16 September, was disrupted by violent protests. Allegations by the opposition of widespread electoral irregularities resulted in the invalidation of election results in 32 constituencies, and the postponement of second round elections until 21 and 28 October. A commission, representing both PDG and oppositional parties, was established to supervise second round polling procedures. Accusations of fraud continued, however, and the final composition of the National Assembly was not determined until March 1991, when a final round of voting was held in five electoral districts, in which allegations of irregularities had persisted. Final vote tallies showed the PDG as having received an absolute majority of National Assembly seats, and PDG members consequently made up two-thirds of the new administration, as attempts to form 'inclusive' governments were rejected by the opposition.

A new draft constitution, promulgated on 22 December incorporated the reforms from the transitional constitution drawn up the previous

May, along with additional measures including the establishment of a Senate. While the government delayed the implementation of the new constitution, opposition parties formed an alliance, to be known as *Coordination de l'Opposition Démocatique* (COD), which announced its withdrawal from the assembly, demanding the full and immediate implementation of the new constitution as well as access to state-controlled media. Political instability continued until presidential elections were held in 1993; these provided Bongo with a first round absolute majority. Despite favorable reports by international observers, the opposition rejected the results and formed a counter-government, *Haut conseil de la résistance* (HCR), that urged its supporters to boycott state institutions.

Finally in mid-1994 the oppositional parties agreed to enter negotiations with the government, to be held in Paris under OAU auspices, to overcome the constitutional deadlock. At the end of September an agreement (*L'accord de Paris*) was reached, which called for the installation of a transitional coalition government, with local elections scheduled to occur after a period of one year, followed by legislative and senatorial elections; a revision of the electoral code; the establishment of an independent electoral commission and a restructuring of the presidential guard. After these constitutional amendments had been ratified by referendum on 25 June 1995, general elections were held in 1996. But although the opposition gained substantial support in the municipal elections which followed, seizing the local governments in Gabon's most important cities, the PDG was able to add to its parliamentary majority in legislative elections in 1996. While dominating both chambers of the National Assembly, the regime was able to reverse substantial restrictions of presidential powers codified in the Paris agreement. The presidential elections of December 1998 resulted in the first-round victory of Bongo. He was thus confirmed as President until 2005.

1.2 Evolution of Electoral Provisions

In Gabon universal suffrage has been in effect since the implementation of the *Loi Cadre* on 23 June 1956 by the French colonial administration. Although Gabon's essential power structures have shown considerable continuity since independence, constitutional and electoral laws have been in state of continuous revision.

The Constitution of 1959 established a 40 seat Parliament, its mandates drawn from eight constituencies, each constituency providing four to eight seats, elected from lists by plurality system. Terms of office were for seven years (when Gabon became a member of the *Communauté Française*, this was reduced to five years; no elections were ever held under this legislation, however).

The Constitution of 1961 introduced compulsory voting, and provided for direct presidential elections, albeit via the single ticket unitary list presented for the so-called National Popular Assembly. Both President and Parliament were elected to seven-year terms. For parliamentary elections a plurality system was in effect, with the whole country forming a single constituency. The President was chosen by the absolute majority system, theoretically providing for a second run-off election. In reality, however, only one presidential candidate stood for election.

For the (French-administered) legislative elections of 1964, the electoral system was revised in order to accommodate opposition candidates. In nine constituencies, conterminous with the country's administrative districts, four to eight seats were allocated to closed party lists according to the plurality system.

In order to formalize succession to the presidency, the post of a Vice-President, elected on the same ticket as the President and the National Assembly, was introduced in 1967 (elections to the vice-presidency were, however, abolished shortly after President Bongo assumed power in December 1967). Although the BDG had in reality already achieved a single-party political monopoly over elections, electoral laws were not revised until 1968, when the new unitary party PDG was founded. Eligibility for office was subsequently restricted to PDG members (Loi No. 12/68, 9 November 1968). A unitary list with candidates chosen by the party's Political Bureau was to be ratified by the whole country, voting as a single constituency, according to plurality rule.

With the revision of the constitution in 1979, the parliamentary mandate was reduced from seven to five years. From that time onwards, presidential and legislative elections were held separately. A new electoral system (Loi No. 19/79 of 20 December 1979) was established, at least nominally designed to provide broader participation. Eighty candidates for the unitary list were selected by the party's sectional bureaus by plurality vote; these were then ratified by universal suffrage on closed lists in each administrative district. Candidates were to be nominated by grass-roots members validated by the party leadership. Nine (one from each administrative district) of 89 Members of Parliament were appointed by the President.

Since the multi-party elections of 1990, electoral laws and procedures have been revised on three occasions. The Code Electoral No. 14/90, in effect during the parliamentary elections of 1990, was replaced by Loi No. 13/92 prior to the presidential elections of 1993. The current revision follows the terms of the 1994 Paris agreement, and was implemented in the elections to the National Assembly and (newly established) Senate in 1996 and 1997. It was amended by the constitutional revision of 1997 (Loi No. 1/97). All of these electoral laws provided for an absolute majority system for both presidential and parliamentary office. With the revision of the electoral law of 1993 the presidential mandate was reduced to a five-year term, with only one term possible through re-election and a maximum age of 70 years. For the nomination of presidential candidates a deposit of 10 million Francs CFA was needed in order to register. The deposit was entirely refunded to the elected candidate, and 50% was returned to all candidates who received at least 5% of the valid votes (Decret No. 000994/PR/MATCLD). The minimum age for candidacy to the National Assembly was reduced from 25 to 18 years, and independent candidates were allowed to run for office. The constitutional revision of 1997 prolonged the presidential term to seven years, lifted the age limit of 70 years and introduced the post of a non-elective Vice-President to be appointed and dismissed by the President.

1.3 Current Electoral Provisions

Sources: Loi No. 3/91 portant Constitution de la République gabonaise, Loi No. 1/97 du 22 avril 1997 portant révision de la Constitution. Le code électoral: Loi No. 7/96 portant dispositions communes à toutes les élections, Loi No. 8/96 du 15 avril 1996 relative à l'élection des sénateurs, Loi No. 10/96 du 15 avril 1996 relative aux conditions d'éligibilité du président de la République, Loi No. 11/96 du 15 avril 1996 relative à l'élection des députés à l'Assemblée nationale, Loi No. 16/96 du 15 avril portant dispositions spéciales relatives à l'élection du président de la République, Loi No. 17/96 du 15 avril 1996 portant dispositions spéciales relatives à l'élection des députés à l'Assemblée nationale, Loi No. 18/96 du 15 avril 1996 portant dispositions spéciales relatives à l'élection des sénateurs, Loi No. 20/96 du 15 avril 1996 relative au référendum.

Elected national institutions: The President is elected for a seven-year term (renewable once). The National Assembly (*Assemblée Nationale*) contains 120 members, elected for a five-year term (renewable). A

Senate is elected indirectly by members of municipal and departmental assemblies (renewable) for a six-year term. It contains 91 seats.

Suffrage: Universal, equal, secret and direct. At least 18 years of age; full possession of civil and political rights; registration as voter.

Nomination of candidates
- *presidential elections*: At least 40 years of age; full possession of civil and political rights. Gabonese nationality by birth in the fourth generation and permanent residence in Gabon. For the nomination of candidates a deposit of five million Francs CFA is needed in order to register. The deposit is refunded to the elected candidate, 50% is returned to the candidates who received at least 10% of the valid votes.
- *elections to the National Assembly*: Full possession of civil and political rights, age of 18. Ineligibility: Certain high officials of the government, members of the armed forces. For the nomination of candidates a deposit of 350,000 Francs CFA is needed in order to register. The deposit is refunded to the elected candidates; 50% is returned to the candidates who received at least 10% of the valid votes.
- *elections to the Senate*: Full possession of civil and political rights, age of 40. Ineligibility: Certain high officials of the government, members of the armed forces. For the nomination of candidates a deposit of 350,000 Francs CFA is needed in order to register. The deposit is refunded to the elected candidates; 50% is returned to the candidates who received at least 10% of the valid votes.

Electoral system
- *presidential elections*: Absolute majority system. If no candidate achieves absolute majority in the first round, a run-off between the two strongest candidates is held.
- *elections to the National Assembly*: Absolute majority system in 120 single-member constituencies. If no candidate achieves absolute majority in the first round, a run-off between the two strongest candidates is held. A replacement deputy (*suppléant*) is elected on one ticket along with each deputy.
- *elections to the Senate*: indirectly elected according to absolute majority system in constituencies formed by the country's administrative districts. If an absolute majority is not achieved in the first round, a second round between the two best finishers is conducted. A replacement Senator is elected on one ticket along with each Senator.

1.4 Comment on the Electoral Statistics

Early data follows Ziemer (1978), election results since 1973 follow the publications in *L'Union*, the government's daily newspaper. Tallies for parliamentary elections in 1996 are drawn from Obame Emane (1998) based on the Rapport de la *Cour Constitutionnelle de la République Gabonaise*. The lists of elected candidates during the reign of the state-party PDG were published in *Annuaire National de la République Gabonaise*, Libreville. Since 1990 results for elections to the National Assembly have been published according to constituency. For these elections the compilation of total figures entailed serious problems. As the initial election results in 1990 were partially invalidated, requiring in some cases as many as five rounds of elections, and because these results were only incompletely published, it was not possible to determine total numbers and correlate these with the actual composition of Parliament. The political affiliations of the candidates for presidential elections in 1993 were not provided, and have had to be assigned. Because some of the politicians involved have changed party affiliations several times, these assignations are not infallible. In the case of the 1998 presidential elections only the party affiliation of the three strongest candidates are given. Electoral data for 1998 are based on information of the *Cour Constitutionnelle*, as kindly provided by the IFES Resource Center.

2. Tables

2.1 Dates of National Elections, Referendums and Coups d'Etat

Year	Presidential elections	Parliamentary elections	Elections for Constitutional Assembly	Referendums	Coups d'état
1957		31/01			
1958				28/09	
1961	12/02	12/02			
1964	12/04	12/04			18/02
1967	19/03	19/03			
1973	04/03	04/03			
1979	30/12				
1980		10/02			
1985		03/03			
1986	09/11				
1990		16/09, 21/10, 28/10, 04/11[a]			
1993	05/12				
1995				23/07	
1996		15/12 (1st) 29/12 (2nd)[b]			
1998	06/12				

[a] Legislative elections were initially scheduled for 16/09 and 23/09. Results of the first round-balloting on 16/09/1990 had to be invalidated in 32 constituencies due to widespread unrest and voting disorder. Following three further rounds on 21/10, 28/10 and 04/11/1990, the Supreme Court invalidated the credentials of five deputies in December 1990. The last partial elections were held in March 1991.

[b] Partial elections were held on 10/08/1997, 24/08/1997.

2.2 Electoral Body 1957–1996

Year	Type of election[a]	Population[b]	Registered voters		Votes cast		
			Total number	% pop.	Total number	% reg. voters	% pop.
1957	Pa	448,564	242,058	55.0	119,916	49.5	29.4
1958	Ref	448,564	265,161	64.9	208,600	78.7	51.2
1961	Pa/Pr	448,564	320,756	71.6	316,679	98.7	70.7
1964	Pa/Pr	549,000	309,049	67.3	262,772	85.0	57.2
1967	Pa/Pr	473,000	348,942	73.8	346,900	99.4	73.3
1973	Pa/Pr	680,000	529,828	77.9	512,932	96.8	75.4
1979	Pr	845,000	—	—	—	—	—
1980	Pa	845,000	651,589	77.1	707,065	108.5[c]	83.7
1985	Pa	950,000	807,241	85.0	771,651	95.6	81.2
1986	Pr	950,000	904,467	95.2	904,039	99.9	95.2
1990	Pa	987,000	—	—	—	—	—
1993	Pr	1,011,710	484,319	47.9	426,594	88.1	42.2
1995	Ref	1,011,710	356,376	35.2	228,169	64.0	22.6
1996	Pa	1,040,000	—	—	—	—	—
1998	Pr	1,207,844	—	—	316,900[d]	—	26.4

[a] Pa = Parliament (*Assemblée Nationale*); Pr = President; Ref = Referendum.
[b] Two censuses were held in Gabon: in May 1961: 448,564 and July 1993: 1,011,710. Population estimates vary widely. All other figures are unofficial estimations.
[c] Registration *a posteriori* was possible on the polling day.
[d] Valid votes only.

2.3 Abbreviations

ADERE	Alliance Démocratique et Républicaine
APSG	Association pour le Socialisme au Gabon
BDG	Bloc Démocratique Gabonais
CDJ	—
CLR[a]	Cercle des Libéraux Réformateurs
COD[b]	Coordination de l'Opposition Démocratiques
CRP	Cercle pour le Renouveau et le Progrès
DID	Parti de Défense des Institutions Démocratique
FAR[c]	Forum d'Action pour le Renouveau
FUNDU	—
MCD	—
MESP	—
MORENA- Bûcherons	Mouvement de Redressement National - Bûcherons
MORENA- Originels	Mouvement de Redressement National - Originels
MORENA-Unionistes	Mouvement de Redressement National - Unionistes
PARI	—

PDG	Parti Démocratique Gabonais
PGCI	Parti Gabonais du Centre Indépendant
PGP	Parti Gabonais du Progrès
PSD	Parti Social – Démocrate
PSG	Parti Socialiste Gabonais
PUP	Parti de l'Unité du Peuple Gabonais
RDI	—
RDP	Rassemblement pour la Démocratie et le Progrès
RDR	—
RNB[d]	Rassemblement National des Bûcherons
UDD	Union pour la Démocratie et le Développement Mayumba
UDG	—
UDS	—
UDSG	Union Démocratique et Sociale Gabonaise
UNDD	Union Nationale pour la Démocratie et le Développement
UPG	Union du Peuple Gabonais
USG	Union Socialiste Gabonais

[a] Founded by a breakaway faction of the PDG in 1993.
[b] Founded 1993 as an informal alliance of eight oppositional presidential candidates.
[c] Founded in 1992 as an alliance of three political parties: MORENA-*Originels*, PSG and USG.
[d] Founded in 1990 as MORENA-*Bûcherons*, changed name in 1992.

2.4 Electoral Participation of Parties and Alliances 1957–1998

Party / Alliance	Years	Elections contested	
		Presidential	Parliamentary[a]
BDG	1957, 1961, 1964, 1967	3	4
UDSG	1957, 1961	0	2
DID	1964	0	1
PDG	1973, 1979, 1980, 1985, 1986, 1990, 1993, 1996, 1998	5	4
APSG[ce]	1990, 1996	0	2
CRP	1990	0	1
MORENA-Bûcheron/RNB[b]	1990, 1993, 1996, 1998	2	2
MORENA-Originels[d]	1990	0	1
PGP	1990, 1993, 1996	1	2
UDD	1990	0	1
USG[cd]	1990, 1996		2
FAR[d]	1993, 1996	1	1
MORENA-Unioniste[e]	1993, 1996	1	1
PSD	1993, 1996	1	1
PGCI[e]	1993, 1996	1	1

Party / Alliance	Years	Elections contested	
		Presidential	Parliamentary[a]
ADERE	1996	0	1
CDJ	1996	0	1
CLR[c]	1996	0	1
RDP	1996	0	1
UPG	1996, 1998	1	1
FUNDU[e]	1996	0	1
IND	1996	0	1
MCD[e]	1996	0	1
MESP[e]	1996	0	1
PARI[e]	1996	0	1
PSG[e]	1996	0	1
PUP	1996	0	1
RDI[e]	1996	0	1
RDR[e]	1996	0	1
UDG[e]	1996	0	1
UDS[e]	1996	0	1

General note: For parliamentary elections in 1990 only parties with parliamentary representation are given, for the 1996 parliamentary elections all parties that presented candidates, for the 1998 presidential elections only the parties of the three strongest candidates.

[a] In bicameral systems only the number of elections for the Lower House is indicated.

[b] MORENA-*Bûcherons* changed its name to RNB in 1991.

[c] APSG, CLR and USG supported Omar Bongo (PDG) in the presidential elections 1993. They formed the *Nouvelle Alliance pour la Démocratie et le Changement* together with PDG and PUP.

[d] In February 1992 MORENA-*Originels*, PSG and USG merged as FAR. USG left in 1993 in order to join the election alliance supporting Omar Bongo.

[e] Political parties which did not gain representation in the National Assembly in 1996.

2.5 Referendums

Year	1958[a]		1995[b]	
	Total number	%	Total number	%
Registered voters	265,161	–	356,376	–
Votes cast	208,600	78.7	228,169	64.0
Invalid votes	3,022	1.4	5,181	2.2
Valid votes	205,578	98.6	222,988	97.7
Yes	190,334	92.6	215,229	96.5
No	15,244	7.4	7,758	3.5

[a] The referendum ratified the status of internal autonomy within the *Communauté Française*.

[b] The referendum ratified the constitutional amendments laid down in the Paris agreements between opposition parties and the government in 1994.

2.6 Elections for Constitutional Assembly

Elections for Constitutional Assembly have not been held.

2.7 Parliamentary Elections 1957–1996

Year	1957[a]		1961	
	Total number	%	Total number	%
Registered voters	242,058	–	320,756	–
Votes cast	119,916	49.5	316,679	98.7
Invalid votes	44,861	37.4	1,344	0.4
Valid votes	75,055	62.6	315,335	99.6
BDG	16,699	22.3	315,335[b]	100.0[b]
UDSG	29,963	39.9	—[b]	—
Others	28,393	37.8	–	–

[a] Valid and invalid votes are calculated on the basis of the sum of party votes and votes cast. The great number of invalid votes results from the difference of votes cast and the sum of party votes.
[b] BDG and UDSG formed a unitary list.

Year	1964		1967	
	Total number	%	Total number	%
Registered voters	309,049	–	348,942	–
Votes cast	262,772	85.0	346,900	99.4
Invalid votes	5,679	2.2	313	0.1
Valid votes	257,093	97.8	346,587	99.9
BDG	142,389	55.4	346,587	100.0
DID	114,704	44.6	–	–

Year	1973		1980	
	Total number	%	Total number	%
Registered voters	529,828	–	651,589	–
Votes cast	517,932	97.8	707,065	108.5
Invalid votes	2,091	0.4	1,061	0.2
Valid votes	515,841	99.6	706,004	99.8
PDG	515,841	100.0	706,004	100.0

Year	1985	
	Total number	%
Registered voters	807,241	–
Votes cast	771,651	95.6
Invalid votes	3,977	0.5
Valid votes	767,674	99.5
PDG	767,674	100.0

For the elections of 1990 and 1996 detailed data are not available.

2.8 Composition of Parliament

Year	1957		1961		1964		1967	
	Seats	%	Seats	%	Seats	%	Seats	%
	40	100	67	100	47	100	67	100
BDG	8	20	67[a]	100	31	66.0	67	100
UDSG	14	35	–[a]	–[a]	16	34.0	–	–
Others	18	45	–	–	–	–	–	–

[a] BDG and UDSG formed a unitary list.

Year	1973		1980		1985[a]		1990[b]	
	Seats	%	Seats	%	Seats	%	Seats	%
	70	100	89	100	120	100	120	100
PDG	70	100	89	100	120	100	63	52.5
MORENA-Bûcherons	–	–	–	–	–	–	20	16.7
PGP	–	–	–	–	–	–	18	15.0
MORENA-Originels	–	–	–	–	–	–	7	5.8
APSG	–	–	–	–	–	–	6	5.0
USG	–	–	–	–	–	–	4	3.3
CRP	–	–	–	–	–	–	1	0.8
UDD	–	–	–	–	–	–	1	0.8

[a] In the 'first round' of elections (selection for unitary list by a restricted electorate) in 1985, 49 of the outgoing deputies were not renominated.

[b] Composition of the National Assembly after 4 November 1990. In partial elections in March 1991 the PDG gained three seats (for a total of 66) and the PGP gained one (for a total of 19), while the *Bûcherons* lost three (for a total of 17) and the USG lost one seat (for a total of three). Subsequent to these elections a number of deputies transferred political affiliations.

Year	1996[a]	
	Seats	%
	120	100[b]
PDG	84	70.0
PGP	10	8.3
RNB	5	4.2
CRL	3	2.5
UPG	2	1.7
USG	1	0.8
ADERE	1	0.8
CDJ	1	0.8
FAR	1	0.8
MORENA-Originels	1	0.8
PSD	1	0.8
PUP	1	0.8
RDP	1	0.8
Independents	7	5.8

[a] Composition of Parliament after elections of 15 and 29/12/1996 plus repeated rounds as published in February 1997.
[b] Calculated on the basis of 120 seats (sum of seats is only 119).

2.8 a) Distribution of Elected Candidates per Province 1996

1st round	1	2	3	4	5	6	7	8	9	Total
PDG	10	15	2	5	4	1	7	3	2	49
RNB	2	–	–	–	–	–	–	–	1	3
PGP	–	–	–	–	–	–	–	2	–	2
CDJ	1	–	–	–	–	–	–	–	–	1
CLR	1	–	–	–	–	–	–	–	–	1
FAR	–	–	–	1	–	–	–	–	–	1
Indep.	–	–	–	–	–	–	–	–	1	1
Total	14	15	2	6	4	1	7	5	4	58

Names of provinces: Estuaire (1); Haut-Ogoué (2); Moyen-Ogooué (3); Ngouniè (4); Nyanga (5); Ogooué Ivindo (6); Ogooué Lolo (7); Ogooué Maritime (8); Woleu-Ntem (9).

2nd round	1	2	3	4	5	6	7	8	9	Total
PDG	4	2	6	5	1	3	3	–	3	27
RNB	–	–	–	–	–	1	–	–	1	2
PGP	–	–	–	1	3	–	–	–	1	4
CLR	–	–	–	1	–	1	–	–	–	2
USG	–	–	1	–	1	–	–	–	–	2
PSD	–	–	–	1	–	–	–	–	–	1
ADERE	–	–	–	–	1	–	–	–	–	1
RDP	–	–	–	–	–	1	–	–	–	1
MOR	–	–	–	–	–	1	–	–	–	1
UPG	–	–	–	1	–	–	–	–	–	1
Indep.	–	–	–	1	–	–	–	–	4	5
Total	4	2	7	11	5	6	3	–	9	47

Names of provinces: Estuaire (1); Haut-Ogoué (2); Moyen-Ogooué (3); Ngouniè (4); Nyanga (5); Ogoouè Ivindo (6); Ogoouè Lolo (7); Ogoouè Maritime (8); Woleu-Ntem (9).

	1	2	3	4	5	6	7	8	9	Total
PDG	–	–	–	–	1	–	–	5	2	8
PGP	–	–	–	–	1	–	–	2	–	3
PUP	–	–	–	–	–	–	–	1	–	1
UPG	–	–	–	–	–	–	–	1	–	1
Indep.	–	–	–	–	–	–	–	–	1	1
Total	–	–	–	–	2	–	–	9	3	14

Names of provinces: Estuaire (1); Haut-Ogoué (2); Moyen-Ogooué (3); Ngouniè (4); Nyanga (5); Ogoouè Ivindo (6); Ogoouè Lolo (7); Ogoouè Maritime (8); Woleu-Ntem (9).

General note: Between 29 December 1996 and 12 January 1997 election were repeated in those 14 constituencies, where irregularities had succeeded.

2.9 Presidential Elections 1961–1998

1961	Total number	%
Registered voters	320,756	–
Votes cast	316,679	98.7
Invalid votes	1,344	0.4
Valid votes	315,335	99.6
Léon M'Ba (BDG)	315,335	100.0

1964	Total number	%
Registered voters	309,049	–
Votes cast	262,772	85.0
Invalid votes	5,679	2.2
Valid votes	257,093	97.8
Léon M'Ba (BDG)[a]	142,389	55.4

[a] The relative weak approval for Léon M'Ba is attributed to the fact that he had to be restored to office by French military intervention after a coup d'état. The subsequent elections were held under French auspices.

1967	Total number	%
Registered voters	348,942	–
Votes cast	346,900	99.4
Invalid votes	313	0.1
Valid votes	346,587	99.9
Léon M'Ba(BDG)[a]	346,587	100.0

[a] A Vice-President, El Hadji Omar Bongo, was elected on the same ticket.

1973	Total number	%
Registered voters	529,828	–
Votes cast	517,932	97.8
Invalid votes / Blank votes	2,091	0.4
Valid votes	515,841	99.6
El Hadj Omar Bongo(PDG)	515,841	100.0

1979	Total number	%
Registered voters	—	–
Votes cast	—	—
Invalid votes / Blank votes	—	—
Valid votes	—	—
El Hadj Omar Bongo (PDG)	—	—

1986	Total number	%
Registered voters	904,467	–
Votes cast	904,039	99.9
Invalid votes / Blank votes	300	0.0
Valid votes	903,739	100.0
El Hadj Omar Bongo (PDG)	903,739	100.0

1993	Total number	%
Registered voters	484,319	–
Votes cast	426,594	88.1
Invalid votes	8,875	2.1
Valid votes	417,719	97.9
Omar Bongo (PDG)[a]	213,793	51.2
Paul Mba Abessole (RNB)	70,747	26.5
Pierre-Louis Agondjo Okawe (PGP)	19,961	4.8
Pierre Claver Maganga-Moussavou (PSD)	15,220	3.6
Jules Bourdes Ogouliguende (indep.)[b]	14,113	3.4
Alexandre Sambat (indep.)[b]	10,819	2.6
Didjob Divungi Di Ndinge[c]	9,203	2.2
Léon Mbou-Yembi (FAR)	7,625	1.8
Jean-Pierre Lemboumba-Lepandou (PGCI)	5,768	1.4
Marc Saturnin Nnang Nguema[c]	3,579	0.9
Simon Oyono Aba'A[c]	3,446	0.9
Adrien Nguema-Ondo (MORENA-Unioniste)	1,842	0.4
Leon Mebiame[c]	1,583	0.4

[a] Omar Bongo was supported by an electoral alliance *Nouvelle alliance pour la démocratie et le changement* containing APSG, PUP, CRL and USG.

[b] Both resigned from the PDG before presidential elections to run as independent candidates.

[c] Party affiliations at the time of presidential elections could not be identified.

1998	Total number	%
Registered voters	—	–
Votes cast	—	—
Invalid votes	—	—
Valid votes	316,900	—
Omar Bongo (PDG)[a]	211,955	66.9
Pierre Mamboundou (UPG)	52,278	16.5
Paul Mba Abessole (RNB)	47,701	13.2
Pierre Andre Kombila	4,847	1.5
Pierre Claver Maganga Moussavou	3,152	1.0
Martin Edzodzomo Ella	1,548	0.5
Alain Engouang Nze	892	0.3
Joseph Adrien Mabicka Maguena	527	0.2

2.10 List of Power Holders 1960–1998

Head of State	Years	Remarks
Léon M'ba	1960–1967	Elected Prime Minister prior to independence (1957). Gained presidency upon Gabon's independence. Re-elected in 1961 and 1967; remained in office until his death on 28 November 1967.
(Albert-Bernard) since 1975 El Hadji Omar Bongo	1967–	Elected Vice-President on 17 March 1967, succeeded to the presidency on 2 December 1967 upon the death of Léon M'ba. Re-elected in 1973, 1979, 1986, 1993, 1998.

Head of Government	Years	Remarks
Léon M'ba	1960–1967	Identical with Head of State.
(Albert-Bernard) since 1975 El Hadji Omar Bongo	1967–1981	Identical with Head of State.
Léon Mébiame	1981–1990	Prime Minister since the post was introduced in 1975, but did not assume role of Head of Government until 1981, when the President finally relinquished these powers. He served until the Government of Transition was established.
Casimir Oyé Mba	1990–1994	Headed the Government of Transition from 29 April 1990 until October 1994.
Paulin Obame-Nguema	1994–	Appointed in October 1994 heading a transitional government after the Paris agreement pending legislative elections. He was reappointed after legislative elections on 28 January 1997.

3. Bibliography

3.1 Official Sources

Annuaire National de la Republique gabonaise (several years). Libreville: Int Afrique.

'Décision No. 16/CC Relative à la Loi No. 13/92 portant Code Electoral, gabonaise'. *Gabon. A Report on the Presidential Elections. December 5, 1993.* New York: The African American Institute 1994, 143–150.

'Décision No. 3-6/CC du 18, 20, 25, 27 mars 1996'. *Hebdo information, Journal Hebdomadaire d'Informations et d'annonces légales*, 334, 30 mars 1996.

'Décision No. 7/CC du 17 avril 1996'. *Hebdo information, Journal Hebdomadaire d'Informations et d'annonces légales*, 336, 27 avril 1996.

'Décision No. 8/CC du avril 1996'. *Hebdo information, Journal Hebdomadaire d'Informations et d'annonces légales*, 336, 27 avril 1996.

'Decret No. 000994/PR/MATCLD'. *Gabon. A Report on the Presidential Elections. December 5, 1993.* New York: The African American Institute 1994, 172–173.

'Loi No. 14/90 du 15 août 1990, portant Code Electoral'. *Supplément du Journal Officiel*, No. 15 du 15 août 1990.

'Loi No. 3/91 portant Constitution de la Republique gabonaise'. *Hebdo information, Journal Hebdomadaire d'Informations et d'annonces légales*, 229, 30 mars 1991.

'Loi No. 4/91 du 3 avril 1991 relative aux partis politiques, gabonaise'. *Gabon. A Report on the Presidential Elections. December 5, 1993.* New York: The African American Institute 1994, 151–159.

'Loi No. 13/92 du 11 mars 1993 portant Code électoral gabonaise'. *Hebdo information, Journal Hebdomadaire d'Informations et d'annonces légales*, 270, 12 mars 1993.

'Loi No. 7/96 portant dispositions communes à toutes les élections'. *Journal officiel de la République gabonaise*, numéro special, mars 1996.

'Loi organique 3/93 du 11 mars 1993, relative à l'élection des députés à l'Assemblée nationale'. *Gabon. A Report on the Presidential Elections. December 5, 1993.* New York: The African American Institute 1994, 133–137.

'Loi organique 4/93 du 11 mars 1993, relative aux conditions d'éligibilité du président de la République'. *Gabon. A Report on the Presidential Elections. December 5, 1993.* New York: The African American Institute 1994, 138–139.

'Loi No. 7/96 du 12 mars 1996 portant dispositions communes à toutes les élections politiques'. *Hebdo information, Journal Hebdomadaire d'Informations et d'annonces légales*, 334, 30 mars 1996.

'Loi No. 8/96 du 15 avril 1996 relative à l'élection des sénateurs'. *Hebdo information, Journal Hebdomadaire d'Informations et d'annonces légales*, 336, 27 avril 1996.

'Loi No. 10/96 du 15 avril 1996 relative aux conditions d'élegibilité du président de la République'. *Hebdo information, Journal Hebdomadaire d'Informations et d'annonces légales*, 336, 27 avril 1996.

'Loi No. 11/96 du 15 avril 1996 relative á l'élection des députés à l'Assemblée nationale'. *Hebdo information, Journal Hebdomadaire d'Informations et d'annonces légales*, 336, 27 avril 1996.

'Loi No. 13/96 du 15 avril 1996 portant création du Conseil National de la Démocratie'. *Hebdo information, Journal Hebdomadaire d'Informations et d'annonces légales*, 336, 27 avril 1996.

'Loi No. 16/96 du 15 avril 1996 portant dispositions spéciales relatives à l'élection du président de la République'. *Hebdo information, Journal Hebdomadaire d'Informations et d'annonces légales*, 336, 27 avril 1996.

'Loi No. 17/96 du 15 avril 1996 portant dispositions spéciales relatives à l'élection des députés à l'Assemblée nationale'. *Hebdo information, Journal Hebdomadaire d'Informations et d'annonces légales*, 336, 27 avril 1996.

'Loi No. 18/96 du 15 avril 1996 portant dispositions spéciales relatives à l'élection des sénateurs'. *Hebdo information, Journal Hebdomadaire d'Informations et d'annonces légales*, 336, 27 avril 1996.

'Loi No. 20/96 du 15 avril 1996 relative au référendum'. *Hebdo information, Journal Hebdomadaire d'Informations et d'annonces légales*, 336, 27 avril 1996.

'Loi No. 21/96 du 15 avril 1996 portant fixation er répartition des sièges de sénateurs'. *Hebdo information, Journal Hebdomadaire d'Informations et d'annonces légales*, 336, 27 avril 1996.

'Loi No. 22/96 du avril 1996 portant fixation et répartition des sièges des députés par Provinces, Département et Commune'. *Hebdo information, Journal Hebdomadaire d'Informations et d'annonces légales*, 336, 27 avril 1996.

3.2 Books, Articles and Electoral Reports

Ajcardi de Saint-Paul, M. (1989). *Gabon: the Development of a Nation*. London: Routledge.

Andriamirado, S. (1992*a*). 'Le Premier ministre gabonais a pris goût à la politique. Casimir Oye Mba joue les troublions'. *Jeune Afrique*, 32/1623: 28–30.

— (1992*b*). 'Energie, prudence, astuce, services secrets. Le système Bongo'. *Jeune Afrique*, 32/1660-61: 44–48.

Assam, A. (1985). *Omar Bongo ou la racine du mal gabonais*. Paris: Pensée universelle.

Bernault, F. (1996). *Démocraties ambiguës en Afrique centrale: Congo-Brazzaville, Gabon 1940–1965*. Paris: Karthala.

Bongo, O. (1987). *El Hadji Omar Bongo/ par lui-même*. Libreville: Editions Multipress.

— (1994). *Confidence d'un Africain*. Paris: A. Michel.

Bouquerel, J. (1970). *Le Gabon*. Paris: Presses universitaires de France.

COD (Coordination de l'opposition démocrate) (1992). *Contre-sommet de Libreville du 4 au 8 octobre 1992* (various papers). Libreville: COD.

Dady Bouchard, J. C. (1992). *La longue marche de la démocratie gabonaise*. Libreville: Gabedip.

Edzodzomo-Ela, M. (1993). *De la démocratie au Gabon: les fondements d'un renouveau national*. Paris: Karthala.

Fall, E. (1993). 'Gabon: démocratie en ballotage'. *Jeune Afrique*, 34/1719: 4–5.

— (1997). 'Gabon: élections législatives des 15 et 29 décembre 1996'. *Jeune Afrique*, 37/1880: 34–35.

Gaulme, F. (1991). 'Le Gabon à la recherche d'un nouvel ethos politique et social'. *Politique Africaine,* 43/10: 50–62.

Hillebrand, E. (1993). 'Demokratisierung als Elitenrecycling: das Beispiel Gabuns'. *Afrika-Spektrum*, 28/1: 73–92.

John-Nambo, J. (1994). 'Parodie d'election présidentielle au Gabon'. *Politique Africaine*, 53/3: 133–138.

Komila-A-Iboanga, F. (1991). 'La résistance du pouvoir à l'instauration de la démocratie pluraliste en Afrique: le cas du Gabon'. *Revue Juridique et Politique*, 45/1: 10–23.

Liman, Z. (1993). 'Peut-on battre Omar Bongo?'. *Jeune Afrique*, 33/1696: 29–30.

Malanda, A.-S. (1996). *Tribus et ethnies du Gabon*. Corbeil-Essonces (France): Editions ICES.

M'Ba, C. (1991). 'La "conférence nationale" gabonaise: du congrès constitutif du Rassemblement Social Démocrate Gabonaise (RSDG) aux assises pour la démocratie pluraliste'. *Afrique 2000*, 7: 75–90.

MORENA-Bûcherons (1989). *Le Gabon et le multipartisme*. Libreville: Morena.

Mengue Me Engouang, F. (1992). 'La transition vers la démocratie pluraliste. L'exemple du Gabon'. *Alternative Démocratique/ Democratic Alternative*, 2: 171–181.

Ndoume Nze, M. (1990). *Elections legislatives gabonaises: septembre-octobre 1990*. Paris: L'Harmattan.

Ndoutoum-Eyi, J. de Dieu (1997*a*). 'Les accords de Paris seront-ils respectés?'. *Le Nouvel Afrique Asie*, 79/4: 17–18.

— (1997*b*). 'Opposition: les raisons d'une débâcle'. *Le Nouvel Afrique Asie*, 96/9: 10–11.

Nguema, I. (1990). *Démocratie gabonaise: droits de l'homme et developpement*. Intervention à la Conference nationale sur la démocratie et le multipartisme, Libreville, 23 mars–11 avril 1990.

Nsoloe Biteghoe, M. (1990). *Echec aux militaires au Gabon*. Paris: Editions Chaka.

Nyonda, V. de Paul (1994). *Autobiographie d'un Gabonais: du villagois au ministre*. Paris: L'Harmattan.

Obame Emane, V. (1998). *Les élections législatives de 1996–1997 au Gabon: Analyse de la distribution des résultats*. Photocopy.

Owondo, J. (1989). *Os direitos humanos na Africa francofona: o caso particular do Gabao*. São Paulo: Thesis (Ph.D.) Universidade de São Paulo.

PDG (Parti démocratique gabonais) (1970). *Méthodologie pratique du militant et organsiation d'un parti*. Libreville: Dialogue.

— (1991). *Congrès extraordinaire du Parti democratique gabonais: Libreville du 3 au 5 août 1991*. Libreville: PDG.

PGP (Parti gabonais du progrès) (1992). *PGP, Parti gabonais du progrès*. Libreville: PGP.

Pochon, J.-F. (1992). 'Ajustement et démocratisation: l'atypisme du Gabon'. *Géopolitique Africaine*, 15/1: 59–70.

Pourtier, R. (1989). *Le Gabon*. Paris: L'Harmattan.

Remondo, M. (1974). *L'administration gabonaise*. Paris: Berger-Levrault.

Rossatanga-Rignault, G. (1993*a*). 'Faut-il avoir peur des Fang? De la démocratisation et de l'ethnique au Gabon'. *Droit et Cultures*, 26: 235–256.

— (1993*b*). 'L'insoutenable condition du clerc gabonais'. *Politique Africaine*, 51/10: 48–60.

— (1993*c*). 'Les partis politiques gabonais: un essai d'analyse'. *Afrique 2000*, 14, july: 107–124.

The African-American Institute (1994). *Gabon. Presidential Elections. December 5, 1993*. New York: The African-American Institute.

Uleri, P. V. (1990). 'Gabon: elezioni, 16 settembre, 21 e 28 ottobre 1990'. *Quaderni dell'Osservatorio elettorale*, 28: 144–145.

USG (Union socialiste gabonaise) (1992). *Contributions a la démocratie gabonaise*. Libreville: USG.

Weinstein, B. (1966). *Gabon: Nation-building on the Ogooue*. Cambridge, Mass.: M.I.T. Press.

Vernet, H. (1995). 'Gabon: que va changer le résultat du réferendum du 23 juillet?'. *Jeune Afrique*, 35/1804: 42.

Yates, D. A. (1994). *The rentier state in Gabon*. Thesis (Ph.D.) Boston University.

Ziemer, K. (1978). 'Gabun', in D. Sternberger, B. Vogel, D. Nohlen and K. Landfried (eds.), *Die Wahl der Parlamente und anderer Staatsorgane. Band II: Politische Organisation und Repräsentation in Afrika,* by Franz Nuscheler, Klaus Ziemer *et al.*, Berlin/ New York: Walter de Gruyter, 689–722.

GAMBIA

by Petra Bendel

1. Introduction

1.1 Historical Overview

Although one of the poorest countries in the world, until 1994 the Gambia was considered unique in disposing of a liberal democratic system in West Africa. Competitive elections were held regularly (1966, 1972, 1977, 1982, 1987 and 1992). From independence (1965) on, a multi-party system was allowed to exist and was maintained after the adoption of a republican constitution in 1970 (Republic in Commonwealth). Since 1994, however, the military has been ruling the country, and Colonel Yayah Jammeh, Junta-leader of the Armed Forces Provisional Ruling Council (AFPRC) after the coup d'état that broke with the democratic tradition, was elected President in non-competitive elections in September 1996. Legislative elections were held in January 1997.

After the country's independence from Great Britain in 1965, the People's Progressive Party (PPP), which had its roots in the 1950s as a supporter of the independence movement, established itself as the predominant political party. Its outstanding position was partly due to its famous leader, Sir Dawda Kairaba Jawara, to traditional identification and partly to patronage and financial backing from big business. The PPP was re-elected five times with a clear majority. The PPP's opposition in the 1970s were the National Convention Party (NCP) and the National Liberation Party (NLP). In the 1980s, the Gambia's Peoples Party (GPP), a splinter group broken away from PPP like the NLP, as well as the People's Democratic Organization for Independence and Socialism (PDOIS) challenged the predominant party. The latter presented an ideological, left-wing alternative in 1987, whereas the other three parties differed only slightly, mostly with regard to personal rather than to ideological questions.

The coup attempt of 1981, a rebellion headed mainly by unemployed young people in the urban center around the capital Banjul and supported by the paramilitary Field Forces, was aborted with the aid of some 3,000 soldiers from Senegal. Following this incident, between 1982 and 1989, the Gambia tightened its relationship with Senegal in the loose confederation of Senegambia. The confederation was unilaterally ended by Senegal, since the Gambia was not willing to give up more and more of its national sovereignty in change for the higher stability won by the unity. In 1991 however, both countries signed a treaty of friendship.

The PPP won the 1982 elections, the first ones with a direct election of the President, which were still held under the state of emergency after the coup attempt. The predominant PPP also defeated its opponents again in 1987 and 1992, although with a descending voter turnout.

A bloodless coup in July 1994 ousted Jawara from power, and dissolved all elective offices, the civilian regime being accused of corruption. When the usurpers announced that they would maintain military rule until 1998, traditional international donors (European Union, Great Britain, USA) condemned the military regime and suspended financial aid for the country. The announcement also engendered adverse reactions within the Gambia. In November 1994, a counter-coup attempt headed by mutinous soldiers was aborted. The military regime set up a two-year transition schedule to restore constitutional rule. Following a referendum that backed a new constitution in August 1996 and substituted the 1970 Constitution (rewritten and re-established in January 1997), the 1996 presidential elections were seriously questioned by international observers: The main opposition parties, including the PPP, had been banned until a few weeks before the presidential elections and all the major pre-coup parties had been banned indefinitely, meetings had been forbidden, and serious irregularities were reported during the campaign and on the election day. Nevertheless, the former military leader Jammeh, who had formally retired from the army to contest the election with his own civilian political party, the Alliance for Patriotic Re-orientation and Construction (APRC), formed only one month before the elections, won the contest and defeated his most important challenger, Ousainou Darboe, of the United Democratic Party (UDP). Although accused of electoral fraud, Jammeh invited the opposition to join his government and announced the dissolution of the Provisional Ruling Council of the Armed Forces, set up in 1994. The APRC again won the 1997 parliamentary elections.

1.2 Evolution of Electoral Provisions

The House of Representatives has been elected regularly since independence. From 1972 to 1977, the President was elected according to the principles of 'parliamentary presidency': The deputy candidates declared their preferences for one of the candidates for the presidency. Without another election round, the candidate who could gather the majority of the elected deputies was elected. This procedure guaranteed a parliamentary majority for the President. The parliamentary elections became a vehicle for the election of the President and his 'ticket'. From 1982 onwards, the President was directly elected according to the plurality system.

Universal, equal, direct and secret suffrage were applied for all the elections since independence. Voting age as well as the age for right to be elected was 21 years for all Gambian citizens. Voters resident for at least six months in the constituency in which they wanted to vote had to register. Head chiefs were explicitly allowed to register (Part II, Section 8 of the Elections Act of 1964).

Candidates to the Parliament (of 21 years at least) had to speak English well enough to make sure that they could take an active part in the proceedings of the House. According to the Constitution of 1965 (Section 35, subsection 6), Parliament could provide that no candidate be qualified to be nominated who was a member of any military force or police force. Employees in the public service could not be candidates for elections to the House of Representatives or the presidency. Candidates nominated for elections to the House of Representatives had to deposit 200 *dalasi*, candidates for the presidency 2,500 *dalasi* (Rule 6, paragraph 4; Section 7 of the Presidential Elections Act, 1982). At least three voters had to nominate a candidate for the House of Representatives (Rule 6, paragraph (2) (a) of the Constituency Election Rules).

The house of representatives included 38 (1987: 50) members: 32 (1987: 36) were directly elected every five years ('elected members') in single-member constituencies; four (1987: five) were indirectly elected by the head chiefs ('head chief representative members'); two (1987: nine) were appointed by the Governor-General in accordance with the advice of the Prime Minister (in fact, he was nominated by the Prime Minister). The speaker was elected by the House of Representatives. The appointed members as well as the Speaker had no voting rights in the legislature in contrast to the chiefs (Section 33, subsection 2 of the Constitution of 1965).

1.3 Current Electoral Provisions

Sources: The Gambia 2nd revised draft Constitution 1996; Elections Decree No.78/1996.

Elected national institutions: President of the Republic and National Assembly. Regular term of office: five years. President and Parliament do not have to be elected on the same day, and, indeed, have not taken place at once up to now. Four out of 49 Members of Parliament are appointed by the President. By-elections in single-member constituencies must be held not later than 90 days after the seat becomes vacant. Holders of the presidency shall be allowed a maximum of two terms.

Suffrage: The principle of secret ballot is established in the constitution. Voting age was lowered in 1996 from 21 to 18 years. Voting is not compulsory.

Nomination of candidates
- *presidential elections*: Candidates for the presidency—restricted to Gambian citizens of at least 30 years and not older than 65—must be nominated by not less than 5,000 voters and not less than 200 from each administrative area. Candidates for the presidency must have completed senior secondary school education. They must leave a deposit returned if they receive not less than 40% of the valid votes cast. They can be either candidates of political parties or independent candidates. Parties formed or organized on an ethnic, sectional, religious or regional basis are not allowed. They are required to encourage tolerance and multi-culturism amongst the inhabitants of the Gambia. The Electoral Commission decides on the admission of candidates, as in the case of parliamentary elections.
- *parliamentary elections*: Candidates for the National Assembly must be at least 21 years old and be able to speak the English language with a degree of proficiency sufficient to enable them to take part in the proceedings of the National Assembly. Members of the armed forces are not eligible. Incompatibility with local administration offices as well as with the functions of district chief or *alkalo* is provided in the constitution. Candidates have to be nominated by not less than 300 voters registered in the constituency. They must present a sworn declaration of his or her assets and a certificate that he or she has paid all taxes. They also have to deposit with the electoral commission a certain sum (prescribed by an act of the National Assembly), returned to them if they receive not less

than 20% of the valid votes cast in their constituency. Incompatibilities: magistrates and judges, members of the armed, police or security forces as well as members of the Independent Electoral Commission.

Electoral system
- *presidential elections*: The President is elected by the absolute majority of the valid votes. If there was only one candidate who failed the required majority, new nomination and election is appointed. If there is no second candidate, the only candidate is declared to have been duly elected. In the case that more than one candidate was nominated in the first ballot and none of those received the absolute majority, a second ballot is held, which decides between the two candidates who received the highest number of votes validly cast at the first ballot. On the second ballot, the candidate who receives the highest number of votes is declared elected President.
- *parliamentary elections*: The Members of Parliament (National Assembly) are elected by plurality system in single-member constituencies. The National Assembly is composed of: 39 members elected from the Chieftaincy Districts, each of which constitutes a constituency, three members elected from the constituencies in Banjul (Banjul North, Banjul South and Banjul Central), three members elected from the constituencies in the Kanifing Municipality, namely: Serrekunda West, Serrekunda East and Bakau.

1.4 Comment on the Electoral Statistics

Due to the extraordinary situation in the Gambia after the 1994 coup, it proved to be very hard to obtain any information on the historical elections from the Gambian authorities. Data on the 1996 and 1997 elections, however, were provided by both national (Chairman of the Provisional Independent Electoral Commission of the Republic of The Gambia) and international sources (see http://www.gambia.com/new/elections/html.). Surprisingly enough, there was also very little detailed information on the elections regularly held between 1965 and 1994 to be found in secondary literature. Data concerning this period were mostly incomplete, and the secondary sources consulted differed strongly. Tables for the period 1960–1970 are mainly based on Nuscheler (1978), for 1987 on different news bulletins (*Africa Research Bulletin*, *Archiv der Gegenwart*) and secondary literature (Arms/Riley 1987, Wiseman

1987). Data on the 1992 elections are lacking. Wherever inconsistencies could not be resolved, it has been indicated in the tables.

2. Tables

2.1 Dates of National Elections, Referendums and Coups d'Etat

Year	Presidential elections	Parliamentary elections	Elections for Constitutional Assembly	Referendums	Coups d'état
1965				27/11	
1966		17–26/05			
1970				24/04	
1972		28–29/03			
1977		04–05/04			
1981					30/07[a]
1982	04/05	04/05			
1987	11/03	11/03			
1992	29/04	29/04			
1994					22–23/07
1996	26/09				
1997		02/01			

[a] Coup attempt.

2.2 Electoral Body 1965–1997

Year	Type of election[a]	Population[b]	Registered voters		Votes cast		
			Total number	% pop.	Total number	% reg. Voters	% pop.
1965	Ref.	300,000	154,626	51.5	93,484[c]	60.5[c]	31.2
1966	Pa	310,000	175,732	56.7	124,992	71.1	40.3
1970	Ref	360,000	135,000	37.5	120,606[c]	89.3[c]	33.5
1972	Pa	490,000	136,521	27.9	103,887	76.1	21.2
1977	Pa	553,000	216,234	39.1	177,781[c]	82.2[c]	32.1
1982	Pa	635,000	—	—	166,102[c]	—	26.2
1987	Pr/Pa	809,000	249,376	30.8	200,000	80.2[c]	24.7
1992	Pr/Pa	878,000	400,000	45.6	223,200[c]	55.8[c]	25.4
1996	Pr	1,204,984	493,171	37.1	394,537	88.4	32.7
1997	Pa	1,155,000	420,507	36.4	307,856	73.2	36.4

[a] Pa = Parliament; Pr = President; Ref. = Referendum.
[b] UN estimations.
[c] Valid votes.

2.3 Abbreviations

APRC	Alliance for Patriotic Reorientation and Construction
DCA	Democratic Congress Alliance
GPP	Gambia People's Party[a]
PPP	People's Progressive Party
NCP	National Convention Party
NLP	National Liberation Party
NRP	National Reconciliation Party
PDOIS	People's Democratic Organization for Independence and Socialism
UDP	United Democratic Party
UP	United Party

[a] Also referred to as Gambian People's Party.

2.4 Electoral Participation of Parties and Alliances 1966–1997

Party / Alliance	Years	Elections contested[a]	
		Presidential	Parliamentary
PPP	1966, 1972, 1977, 1982, 1987	2	5
UP	1966, 1972, 1977	0	3
NCP	1977, 1982, 1987	1	3
NLP/UP	1977	0	1
GPP	1987	0	1
PDOIS	1987,1997	0	2
APRC	1997	1	1
NRP	1997	1	1
UDP	1997	1	1

[a] 1992 elections excluded for lack of data.

2.5 Referendums

Year	1965[a]		1970[a]	
	Total number	%	Total number	%
Registered voters	154,626	–	135,000	–
Votes cast	—	—	—	90
Invalid votes	—	—	—	—
Valid votes	93,484	—	120,606	—
Yes	61,563	65.9	84,968	70.5
No	31,921	34.1	35,638	29.5

[a] Referendum on the question of whether Gambia should become a Republic. Yes/No: for/against the Republic. In 1965, only 758 votes were missing for the necessary 2/3-majority of the votes.

2.6 Elections for Constitutional Assembly

Elections for Constitutional Assembly have not been held.

2.7 Parliamentary Elections 1966–1997

Year	1966		1972	
	Total number	%	Total number	%
Registered voters	175,732	–	136,521	–
Votes cast	124,992	71.1	103,887	76.1
Invalid votes	—	—	—	—
Valid votes	—			
PPP	81,313	65.3	65,388	63.1
Up[a]	—	33.4	17,197	16.6
Independents	1,630	1.3	21,302	20.6

[a] Alliance with GCP in 1966.

Year	1977		1982	
	Total number	%	Total number	%
Registered voters	216,234	–	—	–
Votes cast	—	—	—	—
Invalid votes	—	—	—	—
Valid votes	177,781	—	166,102	—
PPP	123,297	69.4	102,545	61.7
NCP	40,212	22.6	32,634	19.6
UP	5,403	3.0	—	–
NLP/UP	4,095	2.3	—	–
Independents	4,174	2.3	30,923	18.6

Year	1987		1992[a]	
	Total number	%[a]	Total number	%[a]
Registered voters	249,476	–	400,000	–
Votes cast	—	—	—	—
Invalid votes	—	—	—	—
Valid votes	200,000	—	223,200	—
Party / Alliance				
PPP	—	56	—	58.1
NCP	—	27	—	—
GPP	—	16	—	—
PDOIS	—	1	—	—

[a] The Parliament elected in 1992 was dissolved after the military coup d'état. A ban on political rallies was imposed.

Year	1997[a] Total number	%
Registered voters	420,507	–
Votes cast	307,856	73.2
Invalid votes	—[c]	—
Valid votes	307,303	99.8[b]
APRC	160,464	52.2
UDP	104,768	34.1
PDOIS	24,274	7.9
NRP	5,890	1.9
Independents	11,907	3.9

[a] Differing data according to different sources.
[b] As a result of a very simple balloting system, very few invalid votes are reported. The voter is given a marble, which has to be dropped into the ballot box in a voting enclosure that corresponds to the candidate of his choice, the ballot being indicated by a photo, a symbol and his party colors. (cf. *Elections Today* 1996, 6/4: 27.) Nevertheless, the numbers given for each party do not sum up to the number of the votes cast. This indicates that there are still some invalid votes left, which are not reported in the official election results.

2.8 Composition of Parliament 1966–1997

Year	1966		1972		1977		1982	
	Seats	%	Seats	%	Seats	%	Seats	%
	32	100	35	100	34[b]	100	35	100
PPP	24	75.0	24[a]	—	27	79.4	27	77.1
Up[c]	8	25.0	3	—	–	–	—	
NCP	–	–	–	–	5	14.7	3	8.6
Independents	–	–	1	—	–	–	5	14.3

[a] Seven candidates were elected in 'silent elections'.
[b] In one constituency, there had to be by-elections because of the death of one candidate.
[c] 1966 in alliance with GCP.

Year	1987		1992		1997[b]	
	Seats	%	Seats	%	Seats	%
	36[a]	100	36[a]	100	45	100
PPP	31	86.1	25	69.4	–	–
NCP	5	13.9	6	16.6	–	–
PPG	–	–	2	5.5	–	–
APRC	–	–	–	–	33	77.3
UP	–	–	–	–	7	15.5
NRP	–	–	–	–	2	4.4
PDOIS	–	–	–	–	1	2.2
Independents	–	–	3	8.3	2	4.4

[a] 36 seats out of 50: elected members only.
[b] The ruling APRC contested all the constituencies, whereas the main opposition UPD fielded 34 constituencies.

2.9 Presidential Elections 1982–1996

1982	Total number	%[a]
Registered voters	—	–
Votes cast	—	—
Invalid votes	—	—
Valid votes	189,156	—
Sir Dawda Jawara (PPP)	137,202	72.4
Sherif Dibba	52,136	27.6

1987	Total number	%[a]
Registered voters	249,376	–
Votes cast	—	—
Invalid votes	—	—
Valid votes	—	—
Sir Dawda Jawara (PPP)	—	59.2
Sherif Dibba (NCP)	—	27.5
Assan Musa Camara (GPP)	—	13.3

1992	Total number	%[a]
Registered voters	—	–
Votes cast	201,017	—
Invalid votes	—	—
Valid votes	—	—
Sir Dawda Jawara (PPP)	117,549	58.5
M. Sherif Mustapha Dibba	44,639	22.2

1996	Total number	%[a]
Registered voters	493,171	
Votes cast	394,537	80.0
Invalid votes	43	0.9
Valid votes	394,494	99.1
Yahya A. J. J. Jammeh (APRC)	220,011	55.8
Ousano Darbo (UDP)	141,387	35.8
Hamat N. K. Bah (NRP)	21,759	5.5
Sidia Jatta (PDOIS)	11,337	2.9

2.10 List of Power Holders 1965–1998

Head of State and Government	Years	Remarks
Sir Dawda Kairaba Jawara	1965–1994	Went into exile after the coup of 1994.
Capt Yaya Jammeh	1994–	Declared himself Head of State (26/07) after the coup d'état of 23/07/1994; chairman of the Armed Forces Provisional Ruling Council; elected President in 1996.

3. Bibliography

3.1. Official sources

'Elections Act 1964 (Amendment of Eighth Schedule) Rulesí. 17 december 1986'. Supplement A to *The Gambian Gazette,* No. 51 of 26 December.

The Gambian 2nd revised draft Constitution, August 1996.

3.2. Books, Articles and Electoral Reports

Arms, T. E., and Riley, E. (1987). *World Elections on File, Vol.2.* New York: Facts on File.

Gailey, H. (1987). *Historical Dictionary of the Gambia* (2nd edn.). Metuchen, NJ: Scarecrow Press.

Hughes, A., and Perfect, D. (1993). *Political History of the Gambia, 1816–1992.* London: Hurst.

Nuscheler, F. (1978). 'Gambia', in D. Sternberger, B. Vogel, D. Nohlen and K. Landfried (eds.), *Die Wahl der Parlamente und anderer Staatsor-*

gane. Vol.II: Afrika: Politische Organisation und Repräsentation in Afrika, by Franz Nuscheler, Klaus Ziemer *et al.*, Berlin: Walter de Gruyter, 723–759.

Nyang, S. S. (1984). 'The Impact of US Constitutionalism in Africa: A Gambian Case Study', in K. W. Thompson (ed.), *The US Constitution and Constitutionalism in Africa*. Lanham: University Press of America, 77–100.

PDOIS (The Central Committee of The People's Democratic Organization For Independence and Socialism) (1992). *Analysis of the Present Electoral System in The Gambia*. 1 January 1992.

Sall, E. (1995). 'Gambie: le coup d'Etat de juillet 1994'. *L'Afrique Politique 1995*, 181–192.

— and Sallah, H. (1995). *The Military and the Crisis of Governance: The Gambian Case*. Dakar: CODESRIA, 8th General Assembly on Crises, Conflicts and Transformations: Responses and Perspectives, Dakar, 26 June–2 July 1995.

Schmittlein, C., and Meier, M. (1995), 'Gambia', in D. Nohlen and F. Nuscheler (eds.), *Handbuch der Dritten Welt, Bd.4: Westafrika und Zentralafrika*. Bonn: Dietz, 212–226.

Wiese, B., and Block, D. (1995). *Senegal, Gambia: Länder der Sahel-Sudan-Zone*. Gotha: Perthes.

Wiseman, J. A. (1987). 'The Gambian Presidential and Parliamentary Elections of 1987'. *Electoral Studies*, 6/3: 286–288.

— (1996). 'Military Rule in The Gambia: an Interim Assessment'. *Third World Quarterly*, 17/5: 917–940.

—(1998). 'The Gambia: From Coup to Elections'. *Journal of Democracy*, 9/2:64–75.

— and Vidler, E. (1995). 'The July 1994 Coup d'Etat in The Gambia: The End of an Era?'. *The Round Table*, 333: 53–66.

GHANA

by Michael Krennerich*

1. Introduction

1.1 Historical Overview

Ghana's political history since independence has been marked by frequent alternations of civil and military rule. Although authoritarianism was the rule rather than the exception, repeated attempts to install liberal democracy were made, and electoral processes became a fixture in politics. Before its fourth return to multi-party rule in the 1990s, independent Ghana had experienced, apart from several (rigged) referendums (1960, 1964, 1978), two competitive elections in 1969 and 1979, which had demonstrated the ongoing faith of many Ghanaians in democratic procedures on the one hand and the elitist nature of electoral politics on the other. Electoral politics proceeded along group, ethno-regional, personalist and paternalistic lines.

At the end of the British colonial rule, power gradually passed over to the hands of the Ghanaians. In the domestic power struggles on the eve of independence, the populist movement Convention People's Party (CPP) and its charismatic leader Kwame Nkrumah gained control of the colonial state, winning the pre-independence parliamentary elections of 1951, 1954 and 1956 against parties that represented the more conservative British-oriented Ghanaian establishment as well as particularistic interests. Under the prime ministership of Nkrumah, the British colony of the Gold Coast became an independent nation within the Commonwealth under the name of Ghana on 6 March 1957. Prior to the 1956 elections, the voters of British Togoland approved unification with the Gold Coast in a plebiscite of 9 May 1956.

The Constitution of 1957 established a unitary government with the British Queen as Head of State, represented by a Governor-General. Executive power lay with the Prime Minister and its Cabinet of ministers, responsible to the unicameral legislature. Following a referendum on a

* The author would like to thank Dr Peter Mayer, Resident Director of the Friederich Ebert Foundation in Ghana, for his helpful contribution on data research.

new constitution and the presidency (Nkrumah versus Danquah), the First Republic (1960–1966) was inaugurated with Nkrumah as the first elected President on 1 July 1960. The office of the Governor-General and the post of the Prime Minister had been abolished in favor of a powerful executive President. Nkrumah and his CPP came to dominate the political arena completely and established a socialist one-party state, which was officially approved by a national referendum in 1964. The CPP candidates for the 1965 parliamentary elections were declared elected without elections being held. In the face of repression, internal mismanagement and severe economic problems, the Nkrumah regime gradually lost the popular support that it had carefully nurtured during decolonization. On 24 February 1966, a military coup toppled the regime and suspended the constitution. The National Assembly was dissolved, and political parties were proscribed. A National Liberation Council (NLC), composed of army and police officers, assumed power and legislated by decree. NLC members justified the coup, denouncing the dictatorial and corrupt character of the Nkrumah regime, and promised to restore democratic rule as soon as possible. The ban on political parties was lifted on 1 May 1969, and competitive elections were held, which saw the victory of the Western-oriented Progress Party (PP), led by Kofi A. Busia.

On 30 September 1969, Ghana officially returned to civilian rule. The constitution of the Second Republic (1969–1972), promulgated on 22 August 1969, provided for a unicameral parliamentary system with a President as Head of State. Presidential functions were exercised provisionally by a presidential commission until 31 August 1970. In the face of rapidly deteriorating economic conditions, however, the government of Busia was ousted by a military coup that ended the Second Republic on 13 January 1972.

A National Redemption Council (NRC), consisting mainly of army officers and led by Lt-Col. (later General) Ignatius Kutu Acheampong, took over government power and ruled by decree. Initially, the NRC did not outline any plan for a return to democratic rule and sought to institutionalize military rule. The NRC was replaced by a Supreme Military Council (SMC) as the highest legislative and executive organ of the state on 9 October 1975. As popular opposition increased in the wake of economic hardship, the SMC conceded to form a 'Union Government', to be composed of elected civilians and appointed military members. The plan was approved in the March 1978 referendum. In response to political pressure for further change, however, Acheampong was forced to resign on 5 July 1978. He was replaced by Lt-Gen. Frederick W. K.

Akuffo. The reorganized SMC was explicitly transitional and promised to hand over political power to a civilian government to be elected on 1 July 1979.

Shortly before the elections, the SMC was ousted in a coup d'état led by junior officers on 4 June 1979. An Armed Forces Revolutionary Council (AFRC) was formed under the chairmanship of Flgt-Lt. Jerry John Rawlings. Despite the coup and the subsequent executions of ex-members of military governments, including three former Heads of State (Afrifa, Acheampong, Akuffo), the scheduled multi-party elections took place, and Ghana returned to civilian rule with the inauguration of the elected President Hilla Limann on 24 September 1979. The constitution of the Third Republic (1979–1982) provided for a presidential system and a unicameral Parliament. In practice, however, it was a rule on probation under the auspices of officers associated with the former AFRC, many of whom were retired by the Limann government. As the economy continued to decline and the limited support of the civilian government eroded, Rawlings led another coup on 31 December 1981 and suspended the Constitution.

Rawlings again became Head of State as chairman of the military-civilian Provisional National Defense Council (PNDC), which was invested with full executive and legislative powers. Accompanied by radical populist rhetoric, the PNDC pushed a form of 'participatory democracy', restructuring the state and creating mass organizations, while political parties were prohibited and political opposition was silenced by systematic repression. Despite its initial revolutionary self-image, Ghana became Africa's showcase example of structural adjustment from 1983 onwards. A political opening began under strict control from above, starting with the non-party district elections of 1988/89 in order to mobilize rural support for the regime. Under increasing foreign and domestic pressure, the PNDC conceded to return Ghana to civilian rule in 1991. A new constitution was approved by a referendum held on 28 April 1992. Following the lifting of the party-ban on 18 May 1992, presidential elections were held in November 1992, which led to the victory of Rawlings. While international observers declared the elections as generally free and fair, major political parties alleged vote rigging and withdrew from the parliamentary elections of the same year. Thus, Rawlings' National Democratic Congress (NDC) won almost all the seats in the largely uncontested parliamentary elections of December 1992.

The Fourth Republic was inaugurated on 7 January 1993. The 1992 Constitution provided for a presidential system with a unicameral

Parliament. Despite the lack of parliamentary representation, opposition parties managed to play a constructive role outside Parliament and to form the Great Alliance, which brought together the two main opposition parties representing the political traditions both of Nkrumah and of Danquah–Busia. The competitive elections of 1996, however, were won by Rawlings and his NDC. For the first time in Ghana's history, an elected government had completed its term of office and was re-elected in competitive elections.

1.2 Evolution of Electoral Provisions

In the pre-independence elections, voters were bound to meet certain tax requirements. Since independence, as far as elections have taken place, all adult citizens have had the right to vote and have been entitled to be registered, the minimum voting age being 21 years until 1979, and 18 years thereafter. The principles of equal and secret voting have been applied since independence.

The President was directly elected in 1960, 1979 and, after the return to civilian rule, in the 1990s. The 1960 referendum only provided for the competition between two presidential candidates, and the candidate with the most votes was elected. In 1979 and 1992 an absolute majority system was applied. In the case that none of the candidates obtained an absolute majority of votes, a run-off had to be held between the two leading candidates of the first poll.

Parliamentary elections have been held on the basis of the plurality system in single-member constituencies since 1956. There were 104 constituencies in 1956, 196 in 1965 (when candidates were declared elected unopposed without elections being held), 140 in 1969 and 1979, and 200 in 1992.

The constitutional term of office of elected institutions varied between four and five years, but until recently, elected Presidents and Parliaments did not finish their regular term of office.

1.3 Current Electoral Provisions

Sources: Constitution of the Republic of Ghana, 1992; Public Elections Regulations, 1996; Public Elections (Presidential & Parliamentary elections), 1996 (see 3.1).

Elected national institutions: President of the Republic (together with Vice-President as his/her running mate) and unicameral Parliament (200 elected members). President and Parliament are elected on the same day, but with different votes and on different ballot papers. Regular term of office: four years. A person shall not be elected to hold office as President for more than two terms.

Suffrage: The principles of universal, equal, direct and secret suffrage are applied. Every citizen who has reached the age of 18 years has the right to vote. To use this right, citizens have to be registered voters and be resident in the electoral area where they intend to vote. Their names have to be included on the voters' list of their respective polling station. Special arrangements are made to allow removed citizens to vote in their new resident constituency (transferred voters' list) and to allow persons to vote who by reason of their duties on the polling day are unable to present themselves at the polling station where they are registered (special voters' list). Registration and voting are non-compulsory.

Nomination of candidates
A candidate may stand for presidential and parliamentary elections either on the ticket of a political party or as an independent candidate. Political parties based on ethnic, religious, regional or other sectional divisions are prohibited.
- *presidential elections*: A presidential candidate must be of at least 40 years of age. The nomination must be supported by two registered voters from each of the country's 110 districts. The nomination paper must include the name of the vice-presidential candidate, who must satisfy the same qualifications required from the presidential candidate. The candidate has to pay a deposit (five million cedis) which is refunded in the case that he/she obtains a minimum of 25% of the total valid votes cast.
- *parliamentary elections*: A parliamentary candidate must be of at least 21 years of age. The nomination must be supported by 20 registered voters resident in the constituency where he/she stands for election. The candidate has to pay a deposit (200,000 cedis) which is refunded in the case that he/she obtains a minimum of 12.5% of the valid votes cast in the constituency.

Electoral system
- *presidential elections*: Absolute majority system. The candidate who receives more than 50% of the valid votes is declared elected. If no

candidate obtains more than 50% of the valid votes cast, a run-off election will be held for the two candidates with the highest number of votes within 21 days.

- *parliamentary elections*: Plurality system in 200 single-member constituencies. The candidate who gets the highest number of valid votes cast in the respective constituency is elected.

1.4 Comment on the Electoral Statistics

Although there is a large number of publications on Ghanaian politics, the data situation is not satisfactory, since data sheets offered by secondary literature differ considerably. Recently, the Electoral Commission of Ghana and the Friedrich Ebert Foundation have published a booklet (Afriyie-Badu/ Larvie 1996), which compiles data regarding Ghana's referendums and elections until 1992, backed by the statistic department of the Electoral Commission. The data in our handbook is largely based on this useful booklet, except for the following elections: As Afriyie-Badu/ Larvie (1996) do not offer data on the distribution of votes for the 1956 parliamentary elections and the 1960 referendum, we have taken the data presented by Langer (1978). For the 1969 parliamentary elections, different authors (among others, Austin 1970, Langer 1978, Afriyie-Badu/ Larvie 1996) offer the same data on the composition of Parliament, but different data with regard to the distribution of votes per party; we decided to take the data presented by Langer (1978), who also worked with official sources. In the case of the 1979 presidential elections, for which different data sheets are also offered in the literature, however, we preferred to use the data compiled by Afriyie-Badu/ Larvie (1996), completed by the data on registered voters which are not included in that source. Besides the composition of Parliament, no data have been available for the parliamentary elections of 1979. Finally, the results of the presidential elections of 1996 are based on the official data sheet presented by IFES and have been preferred to the data given by Ayee (1997), which are inconsistent in themselves. In the case of the parliamentary elections, the IFES data indicate only the votes obtained by the elected representatives. So far results of the 1996 parliamentary elections have only been available in disaggregated and incomplete form. We used the data set published by the *Daily Graphic* of 11 December 1996. All the percentages given in the following tables are calculated by the author according to the standards of the data handbook.

2. Tables

2.1 Dates of National Elections, Referendums and Coups d'Etat

Year	Presidential elections	Parliamentary elections	Elections for Constitutional Assembly	Referendums	Coups d'état
1956		17/07		09/05	
1960	19, 23, 27/04			19, 23, 27/04	
1961[a]					
1964				23–31/01	
1965		(09/06)[b]			
1966					24/02
1969		29/08			
1972					13/01
1978				30/03	
1979	18/06 (1st) 09/07 (2nd)	18/06			
1981					31/12
1992	03/11	29/12		28/04	
1996	07/12	07/12			

[a] There were no elections in 1961. The parliamentary mandate was extended for another five years without elections.
[b] All the CPP candidates were declared elected unopposed without the scheduled elections being held.

2.2 Electoral Body 1956–1996

Year	Type of election[a]	Population[b]	Registered voters Total number	% pop.	Votes cast Total number	% reg. voters	% pop.
1956	Pa	4,676,000	1,392,874[c]	29.8	697,498[d]	50.1	14.9
1960	Ref (Pr)	6,726,800	2,098,651	31.2	1,140,699[d]	54.4	17.0
1964	Ref	7,540,000	—	—	2,776,372[d]	—	—
1969	Pa	8,383,000	2,362,665[e]	28.2	1,493,281[d]	63.2	17.8
1978	Ref	11,000,000	4,497,803	40.9	2,282,813[d]	50.8	20.8
1979	Pr (1st)	11,300,000	5,070,000[f]	44.9	1,788,209[d]	35.3	17.0
1992	Ref	15,800,000	—	—	3,680,974[d]	—	23.3
1992	Pr	15,800,000	8,229,902	52.1	4,127,876	50.2	26.1
1992[g]	Pa	15,800,000	8,229,902	52.1	1,962,543[d]	23.8	12.4
1996[h]	Pr	17,900,000	9,279,605	51.8	7,266,693	78.3	40.6

[a] Pa = Parliament; Pr = President; Ref = Referendum.

[b] Unofficial estimations. Official population census: 1960: 6,726,815, 1970: 8,559,313; 1984: 12,296,081. As for the 1964 population data, only an estimation for 1963 is given.

[c] With regard to the registered voters, differing data are given in the literature: 1,459,743. Total electorate (estimated adult population): 2,450,224.

[d] Valid votes only.

[e] Total electorate (estimated adult population): 3,179,234.

[f] Differing data given: 5,022,369 registered voters.

[g] The main opposition parties boycotted the elections.

[h] Only for presidential elections, data are given. As for parliamentary elections, no complete data are available (see table 2.7). In the face of irregularities in the voter register in 1992, an entirely new voter register was compiled for the 1996 elections.

2.3 Abbreviations

ACP	Action Congress Party
APRP	All People's Republican Party
CPP	Convention People's Party
DPP	Democratic People's Party
EGLE Party	Every Ghanaian Living Everywhere (EGLE) Party
FYO	Federation of Youth Organisations
GCP	Ghana Congress
GCPP	Great Consolidated Popular Party
MAP	Muslim Association Party
NAL	National Alliance of Liberals
NCP	National Convention Party
NDC	National Democratic Congress
NIP	National Independence Party
NLM	National Liberation Movement

NPP[a]	New Patriotic Party
NPP[a]	Northern People's Party
PAP	People's Action Party
PCP	People's Convention Party
PFP	Popular Front Party
PHP	People's Heritage Party
PNC	People's National Convention
PNP	People's National Party
PP	Progress Party
SDF	Social Democratic Front
TC	Togoland Congress
TFP	Third Force Party
UNC	United National Convention
UNP	United Nationalist Party
UP	United Party

[a] The New Patriotic Party participated in the elections of 1992 and of 1996. The Northern People's Party took part in those of 1956.

2.4 Electoral Participation of Parties and Alliances 1956–1996

Party / Alliance	Years	Elections contested	
		Presidential	Parliamentary
CPP	1956, 1960, (1965)	1	2
FYO	1956	0	1
MAP	1956	0	1
NLM	1956	0	1
NPP	1956	0	1
TC	1956	0	1
UP	1960	1	0
APRP	1969	0	1
NAL	1969	0	1
PAP	1969	0	1
PP	1969	0	1
UNP	1969	0	1
ACP	1979	1	1
PFP[a]	1979	1	1
PNP[b]	1979	1	1
SDF	1979	1	1
TFP	1979	1	1
UNC	1979	1	1
EGLE Party[c e]	1992, 1996	2	2
NCP[c]	1992, 1996	1	1
NDC[c e]	1992, 1996	2	2
NIP[d]	1992	1	0

Party / Alliance	Years	Elections contested Presidential	Parliamentary
NPP[d f]	1992, 1996	2	1
PHP[d]	1992	1	0
PNC[d]	1992, 1996	2	1
DPP[e]	1996	1	1
GCPP	1996	0	1
PCP[f]	1996	1	1

[a] The PFP was a direct continuation of the former PP.
[b] The PNP was based on the old networks of the CPP but presented a large number of young parliamentary candidates.
[c] In the presidential elections of 1992, NDC, NCP and EGLE Party formed the Progressive Alliance which supported the candidacy of Rawlings.
[d] NIP, NPP, PHP and PNC boycotted the parliamentary elections of 1992.
[e] In the 1996 elections, NDC, EGLE Party and DPP formed the Progressive Alliance which supported the candidacy of Rawlings.
[f] In the 1996 elections, NPP and PCP formed the Great Alliance.

2.5 Referendums

Year	1956[a] Total number	%	1960[b] Total number	%
Registered voters	272,663	–	2,098,651	–
Votes cast	—	—	—	—
Invalid votes	—	—	—	—
Valid votes	224,413	—	1,140,165 1,140,699	—
Yes	142,214	63.9	1,008,740	88.5
No	80,199	36.1	131,425	11.5
K. Nkrumah (CPP)	–	–	1,016,076	89.1
J. B. Danquah (UP)	–	–	124,623	10.9

[a] Plebiscite held in British Togoland under Kingdom Trusteeship. Voters were asked whether they were in favor of integrating the territory into the Gold Coast or not.
[b] Voters were asked a) whether they were in favor of or against the new constitution and b) whether Nkrumah or Danquah should be the first President of the New Republic.

Year	1964[a]		1978[b]	
	Total number	%	Total number	%
Registered voters	—	–	4,497,803	–
Votes cast	—	—	—	—
Invalid votes	—	—	—	—
Valid votes	2,776,372	—	2,282,813	—
Yes	2,773,920	99.9	1,372,427	60.1
No	2,452	0.1	910,386	39.9

[a] Referendum on the constitutional amendments (new national flag, introduction of a one-party system; presidential power to dismiss judges).
[b] Referendum on the suitability of a military–civilian government system, the so-called Union Government.

Year	1992[a]	
	Total number	%
Registered voters	—	–
Votes cast	—	—
Invalid votes	—	—
Valid votes	3,680,974	—
Yes	3,408,119	92.6
No	272,855	7.4

[a] Referendum on the draft constitution. The required turn-out was 35%. The required share of Yes votes was 70%.

2.6 Elections for Constitutional Assembly

Elections for Constitutional Assembly have not been held.

2.7 Parliamentary Elections 1956–1996

Year	1956 Total number	%	1969[a] Total number	%
Registered voters	1,392,874	–	2,351,658	–
Votes cast	—	—	—	
Invalid votes	—	—	—	
Valid votes	697,257	—	1,493,371	—
CPP	398,141	57.1	–	–
NLM	145,657	20.9	–	–
NPP	72,440	10.4	–	–
TC	20,352	2.9	–	–
MAP	11,111	1.6	–	–
FYO	10,745	1.5	–	–
PP	–	–	876,378	58.7
NAL	–	–	454,646	30.4
Other Parties[b]/ Independents	–	–	162,347	10.9
Independents	38,811	5.6	–	–

[a] In 1969 two out of 140 seats were unopposed, one taken by PP, the other by NAL. There were 479 candidates in the 138 contested constituencies: 138 of each PP and NAL, 86 of UPP, 52 of PAP, 45 of APRP and 20 independent candidates.
[b] UNP, APRP and PAP.

Year[a]	1992 Total number	%	1996[b] Total number	%
Registered voters	8,229,902	–	—	—
Votes cast	—	—	—	—
Invalid votes	—	—	—	—
Valid votes	1,962,543	—	6,947,762[c]	—
NDC	1,521,629	77.5	3,679,985	53.0
NCP	377,673	19.2	51,919	0.7
EGLE Party	10,098	0.5	6,979	0.1
NPP	–	–	2,346,791	33.8
PCP	–	–	420,192	6.0
PNC	–	–	226,643	3.3
DPP	–	–	8,247	0.1
GCPP	–	–	1,485	0.0
Independents	53,143	2.7	205,521	3.0

[a] Data for the 1979 parliamentary elections are not available. In 1979, there were 799 candidates: PNP: 140, PFP: 139 (one out of 140 was disqualified), UNC: 140, ACP: 131, TFP: 125, SDF: 113, and 11 independent candidates.
[b] In 1996, there were 780 candidates: NDC: 199, NPP: 179, PNC: 127; PCP: 116, NCP: 71, DPP: 22, EGLE-Party: 8, GCPP: 1, independent candidates: 57.
[c] Incomplete results, indicating only the general tendency of the elections. The results of two constituencies and one independent candidate are missing.

2.8 Composition of Parliament 1956–1996

Year	1956[a]		1965[b]		1969[c]		1979[d]	
	Seats	%	Seats	%	Seats	%	Seats	%
	104	100	198	100	140	100	140	100
CPP	71	68.3	198	100	–	–	–	–
NPP	15	14.4	–	–	–	–	–	–
NLM	12	11.5	–	–	–	–	–	–
TC	2	1.9	–	–	–	–	–	–
MAP	1	1.0	–	–	–	–	–	–
FYO	1	1.0	–	–	–	–	–	–
PP	–	–	–	–	105	75.0	–	–
NAL	–	–	–	–	29	20.7	–	–
UNP	–	–	–	–	2	1.4	–	–
PAP	–	–	–	–	2	1.4	–	–
APRP	–	–	–	–	1	0.7	–	–
PNP	–	–	–	–	–	–	71	50.7
PFP	–	–	–	–	–	–	47	33.6
ACP	–	–	–	–	–	–	10	7.1
UNC	–	–	–	–	–	–	8	5.7
SDF	–	–	–	–	–	–	4	2.9
Independents	2	1.9	–	–	1	0.7	–	–

[a] In 1957 opposition parties amalgamated to form the UP. Many politicians of the opposition, however, crossed the floor, and joined the CPP after the elections. There were no elections in 1961. The parliamentary mandate was extended for another five years without elections being held. Until 1963 the parliamentary opposition disappeared. By-elections (1957–1963: 33) were usually won by the CPP.

[b] All the candidates of the CCP were declared elected unopposed without elections being held.

[c] Two out of 140 seats were unopposed, one taken by PP, the other seat by NAL. PP and NAL each presented 138 candidates, UPP 86, PAP 52 and APRP 45.

[d] Differing data are given in the literature with regard to PFP (42 seats), UNC (13 seats), SDF (three seats) and independents (one seat).

Year	1992		1996	
	Seats	%	Seats	%
	200	100	200	100
NDC	189	94.5	133	66.5
NCP	8	4.0	–	–
EGLE Party	1	0.5	–	–
NPP	–	–	61	30.5
PCP	–	–	5	2.5
PNC	–	–	1	0.5
Independents	2	1.0	–	–

2.8 a) Regional Distribution of Seats 1969–1996

1969	PP	NAL	UNP	PAP	APRP	Independ.	Total
Ashanti	22	0	0	0	0	0	22
B. Ahafo	13	0	0	0	0	0	13
Central	15	0	0	0	0	0	15
Eastern	18	4	0	0	0	0	22
G. Accra	3	3	2	0	0	1	9
Northern	9	5	0	0	0	0	14
Upper	13	3	0	0	0	0	16
Volta	2	14	0	0	0	0	16
Western	10	0	0	2	1	0	13
Total	105	29	2	2	1	1	140

1979	PNP	PFP	UNC	ACP	SDF	Independ.	Total
Ashanti	2	19	1	0	0	0	22
B. Ahafo	2	10	0	0	0	0	12
Central	8	0	0	7	0	0	15
Eastern	11	6	4	0	0	0	21
G. Accra	6	1	3	0	1	0	11
Northern	7	4	0	0	3	0	14
Upper	15	1	0	0	0	0	16
Volta	11	5	0	0	0	0	16
Western	9	1	0	3	0	0	13
Total	71	47	8	10	4	0	140

1992	NDC	NCP	EGLE-Party	Independents	Total
Ashanti	33	0	0	0	33
B. Ahafo	20	0	0	1	21
Central	16	1	0	0	17
Eastern	22	3	1	0	26
G. Accra	22	0	0	0	22
Northern	23	0	0	0	23
Upper East	11	0	0	1	12
Upper West	8	0	0	0	8
Volta	18	1	0	0	19
Western	16	3	0	0	19
Total	189	8	1	2	200

1996	NDC	NPP	PCP	PNC	Total
Ashanti	5	27	0	0	32
B. Ahafo	17	4	0	0	21
Central	14	3	0	0	17
Eastern	15	11	0	0	26
G. Accra	13	9	0	0	22
Northern	18	3	1	1	23
Upper East	12	0	0	0	12
Upper West	8	0	0	0	8
Volta	19	0	0	0	19
Western	12	3	4	0	19
Total	133	60	5	1	199[a]

[a] Distribution of only 199 seats (out of 200).

2.9 Presidential Elections 1979–1996

For the results of the presidential elections of 1960 see table 2.5.

1979 (1st round)	Total number	%
Registered voters	5,070,000	–
Votes cast	—	—
Invalid votes	—	—
Valid votes	1,788,209	—
Hilla Limann (PNP)[a]	631,559	35.3
Victor Owusu (PFP)	533,928	29.9
William Ofori-Atta (UNC)	311,265	17.4
Frank George Bernasko (ACP)	167,775	9.4
Alhaji Ibrahim Mahama (SDF)	66,445	3.7
John Bilson (TFP)	49,104	2.7
R. P. Baffour (Independent)	8,812	0.5
Kwame Nyanthe (Independent)	8,490	0.5
Diamond Nii Addy (Independent)	5,957	0.3
Alhaji Imoro Ayannah (Independent)	4,874	0.3

[a] The anticipated presidential candidate of the PNP, Imoru Egala, was debarred from standing for election since he was found guilty of using public office for private gain. However, Egala was able to secure the candidacy of his nephew, the virtually unknown Hilla Limann.

1979 (2nd round)	Total number	%
Registered voters	5,070,000	–
Votes cast	—	—
Invalid votes	—	—
Valid votes	1,804,402	—
Hilla Limann (PNP)	1,118,305	62.0
Victor Owusu (PFP)	686,097	38.0

1992	Total number	%
Registered voters	8,229,902	–
Votes cast	4,127,876	50.2
Invalid votes	149,811	3.6
Valid votes	3,978,065	96.4
Jerry John Rawlings (Progressive Alliance)[b]	2,323,135	58.4
Adu Boahen (NPP)	1,204,764	30.3
Hilla Limann (PNC)	266,710	6.7
Kwabena Darko (NIP)	113,629	2.9
E. A. Erskine (PHP)	69,827	1.8

[a] Alliance of Rawlings' NDC, the NCP and the EGLE Party.

1996	Total number	%
Registered voters	9,279,605	–
Votes cast	7,266,693	78.3
Rejected	120,921	1.7
Valid votes	7,145,772	98.3
Jerry John Rawlings (Progressive Alliance)[a]	4,099,758	57.4
John Agyekum Kufour (Great Alliance)[b]	2,834,878	39.7
Edward Nasigrie Mahama (PNC)	211,136	3.0

[a] Alliance of Rawlings' NDC, the EGLE-Party and the DPP. However, only the symbol of NDC was printed on the ballot paper.

[b] Alliance of NPP and PCP. However, only the symbol of NPP was printed on the ballot paper.

2.9 a) Presidential Elections. Regional Results. 1992 and 1996

1992 (absolute numbers)	Rawlings	Boahen	Limann	Darko	Erskine	Valid votes
Volta	446,365	17,295	7,431	3,534	4,105	478,730
Upper West	66,049	11,535	48,075	2,329	1,612	129,600
Western	239,477	89,800	33,760	21,924	9,325	394,286
Ashanti	234,237	431,380	17,620	25,298	4,049	712,584
Northern	203,004	52,539	35,452	4,682	26,715	322,392
Upper East	108,999	21,164	65,644	2,791	3,348	201,946
Central	222,092	86,683	6,308	11,631	7,312	334,026
Gt. Accra	270,825	188,000	22,027	20,731	5,861	507,444
Eastern	288,726	190,327	9,747	11,730	3,663	504,193
B. Ahafo	243,361	116,041	20,646	8,979	3,837	392,864
Total	2,323,135	1,204,764	266,710	113,629	69,827	3,978,065

1992 (percentages)	Rawlings	Boahen	Limann	Darko	Erskine	Valid votes[a]
Volta	93.2	3.6	1.6	0.7	0.9	100
Upper West	51.0	8.9	37.1	1.8	1.2	100
Western	60.7	22.8	8.6	5.6	2.4	100
Ashanti	32.9	60.5	2.5	3.6	0.6	100
Northern	63.0	16.3	11.0	1.5	8.3	100
Upper East	54.0	10.5	32.5	1.4	1.7	100
Central	66.5	26.0	1.9	3.5	2.2	100
Gt. Accra	53.4	37.0	4.3	4.1	1.2	100
Eastern	57.3	37.7	1.9	2.3	0.7	100
B. Ahafo	61.9	29.5	5.3	2.3	1.0	100
Total	58.4	30.3	6.7	2.9	1.8	100

[a] Due to rounding the added total of the percentages is not always 100.

1996 (absolute numbers and percentages)							
	Rawlings	%	Kuffour	%	Mahama	%	Valid votes
Volta	690,421	94.5	34,538	4.7	5,292	0.7	730,251
Upper West	145,812	74.6	21,871	11.2	27,754	14.2	195,437
Western	405,992	57.3	289,730	40.9	12,862	1.8	708,584
Ashanti	459,090	53.8	384,597	45.0	10,251	1.2	853,938
Northern	370,330	61.2	199,801	33.0	35,472	5.9	605,603
Upper East	230,791	69.0	58,041	17.4	45,696	13.7	334,528
Central	330,841	55.2	259,555	43.3	8,715	1.5	599,111
Gt. Accra	658,626	54.0	528,484	43.3	32,723	2.7	1,219,833
Eastern	412,474	32.8	827,804	65.8	17,736	1.4	1,258,014
Brong Ahafo	395,381	61.7	230,457	36.0	14,635	2.3	640,473
Total	4,099,758	57.4	2,834,878	39.7	211,136	3.0	7,145,772

2.10 List of Power Holders 1957–1998

Head of State	Years	Remarks
Elizabeth II	1957–1960	Represented by the Governor-General: Charles N. Arden-Clarke (1957) and Lord William Francis Hare, Earl of Listowel (1957–1960).
Kwame Nkrumah	1960–1966	On 01/07/1960, the First Republic was established with the inauguration of Nkrumah as the first President. On 07/09/1962, Nkrumah was named President for Life by Parliament, but he never formally accepted the designation. Nkrumah was overthrown by a military coup on 22/02/1966 while he was on a state visit in China. He took up asylum in Guinea, where he remained until his death in 1972.
Jospeh Arthur Ankrah	1966–1969	As the chairman of the National Liberation Council (NLC), Lt Gen. Ankrah became Head of State after the coup. On 02/04/1969, he was forced to resign after admitting that he had received money for political purposes.
Akwasi Amankwaa Afrifa	1969	Brig. (later Lt Gen.) Afrifa became the new chairman of the NLC and Head of State.

Head of State	Years	Remarks
Presidential Commission	1969–1970	The functions of the President were exercised by a three-member Presidential Commission, which was set up by the Constitution of 1969 for a maximum period of three years. The Presidential Commission, which consisted of Akwasi A. Afrifa, John Willie Kofi Harlley and A.K. Ocran, took office on 03/09/1969.
Edward Akuffo-Addo	1970–1972	Akuffo-Addo was elected as President of the Second Republic by a presidential electoral college on 28/08/1970. A military coup ended the Second Republic on 13/01/1972.
Ignatius Kutu Acheampong	1972–1978	As the chairman of the National Redemption Council (NRC), Lt Col. (later: General) Acheampong became Head of State. He was forced to resign on 05/07/1978 by his military colleagues. Achempong was executed under the Rawlings regime on 16/06/1979.
Frederick W. K. Akuffo	1978–1979	Lt Gen. Akuffo who had replaced Achampong was ousted by a coup d'état on 04/06/1979. Akuffo was executed (together with the former Head of State Afrifa) under the Rawlings regime on 26/06/1979.
Jerry John Rawlings	1979	As chairman of the Armed Forces Revolutionary Council, Flgt-Lt Rawlings became *de facto* Head of State until the return to civilian rule.
Hilla Limann	1979–1981	Limann was inaugurated as elected President of the Third Republic on 24/09/1979. A coup d'état ended the Third Republic on 31/12/1981.
Jerry John Rawlings	1981–1993	As the chairman of the PNDC, Rawlings again became Head of State.
	1993–	President of the Fourth Republic, elected in the multi-party elections of 1992 and inaugurated on 07/01/1993. Rawlings was re-elected in 1996.

Head of Government	Years	Remarks
Kwame Nkrumah	1957–1966	Ghana gained independence on 06/03/1957 with Nkrumah as the Prime Minister. As the executive President, Nkrumah was both Head of State and Head of Government in the First Republic (1960–1966).
National Liberation Council (NLC)	1966–1969	The NLC took government power after the coup d'état.
Kofi Abrefa Busia	1969–1972	Following the competitive elections of 1969, Busia was sworn in as Prime Minister on 03/09/1969.
National Redemption Council (NRC)	1972–1975	Military coup of 13/01/1972.
Supreme Military Council (SMC)	1975–1979	The seven-member SMC, led initially by Achaempong, later by Akuffo, was established on 09/10/1975.
Armed Foreces Revolutionary Council	1979	Military coup of 04/06/1979.
Hilla Limann	1979–1981	Identical with Head of State.
Provisional National Defense Council (PNDC)	1981–1993	Coup d'état of 31/12/1981.
Jerry John Rawlings	1993–	Identical with Head of State.

3. Bibliography

3.1 Official Sources (chronological order)

The Constitution of the Republic of Ghana (1979). Accra: Ghana Publishing.

Republic of Ghana (1991). *Report of the Committee of Experts (Constitution) on Proposals for a Draft Constitution of Ghana*, July 31.

The Constitution of the Republic of Ghana (1992). Accra: Ghana Publishing.

Public and Political Party Office Holders Law, 1992 (PNDCL 280).

Political Parties Law, 1992 (PNDCL 281).

Political Parties (Amendment) Law, 1992 (PNDCL 283).

Representation of the People Law, 1992 (PNDCL 284).

Presidential Elections Laws, 1992 (PNDCL 285).

Public Elections (Parliament) Regulations, 1992 (L.I. 1537)

Public Elections (Parliament) (Amendment) Regulations, 1992 (L.I. 1544).

Representation of the People (Parliamentary Constituencies) Instrument (L.I. 1538).
Interim National Electoral Commission: *A Guide to the Voter: Presidential—Parliamentary '92*. Accra.
The Electoral Commission Act, 1993 (Act 451).
Public Elections (Registration of Voters) Regulations, 1995 (C.I. 12)
Public Elections (Presidential and Parliamentary Elections), 1996 (C.I. 12).
Public Elections Regulations, 1996 (C.I. 15).
Electoral Commission: *Public Elections Regulations, 1996*. Accra.
Electoral Commission: *A Guide to the Voter, Presidential—Parliamentary '96*. Accra.

3.2 Books, Articles and Electoral Reports

Afari-Gyan, K. (1995). *The Making of the Fourth Republican Constitution of Ghana*. Accra: Friedrich Ebert Foundation.
Afriyie-Badu, K., and Larvie, J. (1996). *Elections in Ghana 1996, Part I*. Accra: Electoral Commission of Ghana/ Friedrich Ebert Foundation.
Ansprenger, F., Traeder, H., and Tetzlaff, R. (1972). *Die politische Entwicklung Ghanas von Nkrumah bis Busia*. München: Weltforum.
Apter, D. E. (1972). *Ghana in Transition*. Princeton: Princeton University Press.
Austin, D. (1964). *Politics in Ghana 1946–1960*. London/ New York: Oxford University Press for the Royal Institute for International Affairs.
— (1967). 'Opposition in Ghana, 1947–67'. *Government and Opposition*, 2/4:539–555.
— (1970). *Elections in Ghana, 1969*. New Delhi: Indian Council for Africa.
— and Luckham, R. (1975). *Politicians and Soldiers in Ghana, 1966–1972*. London: Frank Cass.
Awoonar, K. N. (1990). *Ghana. A Political History*. Accra: Sedco/ Woeli.
Ayee, J. R. A. (1997). 'The December 1996 General Elections in Ghana'. *Electoral Studies*, 16/3: 416–427.
Baynham, S. (1988). *The Military and the Politics in Nkrumah's Ghana*. Boulder, Col.: Westview Press.
Boahen, A. A. (1989). *The Ghananian Sphinx: Reflections on the Contemporary History of Ghana, 1972–1987*. Accra/ New York: Ghana Democratic Movement.
— (1995). 'A Note on the Ghanaian Elections'. *African Affairs*, 94/375: 277–280.
Bretton, H. L. (1966). *The Rise and Fall of Kwame Nkrumah: A Study of Personal Rule in Africa*. New York: Praeger.

Chazan, N. (1983). *An Anatomy of Ghanaian Politics: Managing Political Recession, 1969–82*. Boulder, Col.: Westview Press.

— (1987). 'The Anomalies of Continuity: Perspectives on Ghanaian Elections Since Independence', in F. M. Hayward (ed.), *Elections in Independent Africa*. Boulder, Col./ London: Westview Press, 61–86.

— (1992). 'Liberalization, Governance and Political Space in Ghana', in G. Hyden and M. Bratton (eds.), *Governance and Politics in Africa*. Boulder, Col.: Lynne Rienner Publishers, 121–141.

— and Le Vine, V. (1979). 'Politics in a "Non-Political System": the March 30, 1978 Referendum in Ghana'. *African Studies Review*, 22/1: 177–207.

COG (Commonwealth Observer Group) (1992). *The Presidential Election in Ghana, 3 November, 1992. The Report of the Commonwealth Observer Group*. London: Commonwealth Secretariat.

— (1997). *The Presidential and Parliamentary Elections in Ghana, 7 December, 1996. The Report of the Commonwealth Observer Group*. London: Commonwealth Secretariat.

Crook, R. (1987). 'Legitimacy, Authority and the Transfer of Power in Ghana'. *Political Studies*, 35: 552–572.

Gyimah-Boadi, E. (1993). *Ghana Under PNDC Rule, 1982–1989*. Dakar: Codesria.

— (1994). 'Ghana's Uncertain Political Opening'. *Journal of Democracy*, 5/2: 75–86.

— (1997). 'Ghana's Encouraging Elections: The Challenges Ahead'. *Journal of Democracy*, 8/2: 78–91.

Hansen, E. (1991). *Ghana Under Rawlings*. Oxford: Malthouse.

— and Ninsin, K. A. (1989). *The State, Development, and Politics in Ghana*. London: Codesria.

Haynes, J. (1993). 'Sustainable Democracy in Ghana? Problems and Prospects'. *Third World Quarterly*, 14/3: 451–467.

— (1995). 'Ghana: From Personalistic to Democratic Rule', in J. A. Wiseman (ed.), *Democracy and Political Change in Sub-Saharan Africa*. London/ New York: Routledge, 92–115.

Herbst, J. (1993) *The Politics of Reform in Ghana, 1982–1991*. Berkeley, Cal.: University of California Press.

— (1994). 'The Dilemmas of Explaining Political Upheaval: Ghana in Comparative Perspective', in J. A. Widner (ed.), *Economic Change and Political Liberalization in Sub-Saharan Africa*. Baltimore, Md: Johns Hopkins University Press, 182–198.

IFES (International Foundation for Electoral Systems) (1996). *Supporting the Electoral Process in Ghana. Results of the Presidential and Parliamentary Elections. 7 December 1996*. Washington, D.C.: IFES.

Jeffries, R. (1980). 'The Ghanaian Elections of 1979'. *African Affairs*, 79/316: 397–414.

— (1998). 'The Ghanaian Elections of 1996: Towards the Consolidation of Democracy? *African Affairs*, 97: 189–208.

— and Thomas, C. (1993). 'The Ghanaian Elections of 1992'. *African Affairs*, 92/368: 331–366.

Koomson, B. (1995). *Handbook on Electoral Coverage*. Accra: Friedrich Ebert Foundation.

Kumado, K. (1996). 'Financing of Political Parties in Ghana: The Case for Public Funding', in K. Kumado (ed.), *Funding Political Parties in West Africa*. Accra: The Electoral Commission of Ghana/ Friedrich Ebert Foundation, 8–23.

Langer, P. (1978). 'Ghana', in D. Sternberger, B. Vogel, D. Nohlen and K. Landfried (eds.), *Die Wahl der Parlamente und anderer Staatsorgane. Band II: Politische Organisation und Repräsentation in Afrika*, by Franz Nuscheler, Klaus Ziemer *et al.*, Berlin/ New York: Walter de Gruyter, 749–798.

La Verle, B. (1995). *Ghana: A Country Study* (3rd edn.). Washington, D.C.

Lyons, T. (1997). 'Ghana's Encouraging Elections. A Major Step Forward'. *Journal of Democracy*, 8/2: 65–77.

Massing, A. W. (1994). *Local Government Reform in Ghana: Democratic Renewal or Autocratic Revival?* (Cologne Development Studies, Vol. 21), Saarbrücken: Breitenbach.

Ninsin, K. A., and Drah, F. K. (1991). *Ghana's Transition to Constitutional Rule*. Accra: Ghana University Press.

— (1993). *Political Parties and Democracy in Ghana's Fourth Republic*. Accra: Woeli.

NPP (New Patriotic Party) (1993). *The Stolen Verdict: Ghana, November 1992 Presidential Elections*. Accra: New Patriotic Party.

Nugent, P. (1993). *The Flight-Lieutenant and the Professor: The Road to Ghana's Fourth Republic (including election statistics)*. Edinburgh: Centre of African Studies.

Oquaye, M. (1980). *Politics in Ghana, 1972–1979*. Accra: Tornado Publishers.

— (1995). 'The Ghanaian Elections of 1992. A Dissenting View'. *African Affairs*, 94/375: 259–275.

Owusu, M. (1970). *Uses and Abuses of Political Power: A Case Study of Continuity and Change in the Politics of Ghana*. Chicago: University of Chicago Press.

— (1979). 'Politics without Parties: Reflections on the Union Government Proposals in Ghana'. *African Studies Review*, 22/1: 89–108.

— (1989). 'Rebellion, Revolution, and Tradition: Re-Interpreting Coups in Ghana'. *Comparative Studies in Society and History*, 31/2: 372–397.

Owusu-Ansah, D., and McFarland, D. M. (1995). *Historical Dictionary of Ghana* (2nd edn.). Metuchen, NJ/ London: Scarecrow Press.

Pellow, D., and Chazan, N. (1986). *Ghana: Coping with Uncertainty*. Boulder, Col./ London: Westview Press/ Gower.

Ray, D. I. (1986). *Ghana: Politics, Economics, and Society*. Boulder, Col.: Lynne Rienner.

Rothchild, D. (1980). 'Military Regime Performance: An Appraisal of the Ghana Experience, 1972–1978'. *Comparative Politics*, 12/4: 459–479.

— (ed.) (1991). *Ghana. The Political Economy of Recovery*. Baltimore, Md: Johns Hopkins University Press.

— (1995). 'Rawlings and the Engineering of Legitimacy in Ghana', in I. W. Zartman (ed.), *Collapsed States: The Desintegration and Restoration of Legitimate Authority*. Boulder, Col.: Lynne Rienner, 49–65.

Shillington, K. (1992). *Ghana and the Rawlings Factor*. New York: St Martin's Press.

Tetzlaff, R. (1969). 'Wahl und Stammespluralismus am Beispiel des Regierungswechsels in Ghana'. *Internationales Afrikaforum*, 5/11: 690–694.

Waldenhof, B. (1996). 'Ghana: Politischer "Modellfall"? Ein Image auf dem Prüfstand', in P. Kevenhörster and D. van den Boom (eds.), *Afrika: Stagnation oder Neubeginn? Studien zum politischen Wandel*. Münster: Lit, 4–28.

GUINEA

by Stefan Brüne

1. Introduction

1.1 Historical Overview

Formerly French Guinea, part of French West-Africa, the Republic of Guinea became independent on 2 October 1958. In a 'historical' referendum held on 28 September 95% of voters rejected membership of a proposed community of self-governing French overseas territories to be established under the constitution of the new French republic. Guinea was the only French colony to reject the proposal. Punitive economic reprisals were taken by the departing French authorities and French aid and investment were suspended. Sekou Touré, the Secretary-General of the *Parti Démocratique de Guinée—Rassemblement Démocratique Africain* (PDG-RDA), which had won 58 of the 60 seats in the Territorial Assembly in 1957, became the country's first President, and the PDG-RDA was constitutionally established in November 1958 as a single party.

In the initial euphoria of independence the party state was remarkably cohesive and well organized. Initially obtaining assistance from the USSR, Guinea withdrew from the Franc Zone in 1960. Sékou Touré who made repeated allegations of foreign plots to overthrow him ruled the country until his sudden death in March 1984. Ruthlessly suppressing any opposition, his survival in office was mainly attributable to his dominance of all central governmental activities, reliance on a group of close collaborators and his ability to balance the authority of the armed forces against that of the PDG-RDA's people's militia. Some 2,000,000 (sic!) opponents were forced into exile. A few days after Sékou Touré's death the army staged a coup d'état on 5 April 1984, and a *Comité de Redressement National* (CMRN) composed mainly of middle and lower ranking officers seized power. Its principal leaders, Col. (later Gen.) Lansana Conté and Col. Diarra Traoré, who had both held senior positions for some years, became President and Prime Minister respectively. The constitution of the Popular and Revolutionary Republic of Guinea, adopted in May 1982, was suspended and the National Assembly dissolved. A semi-civilian government trying to improve regional relations was appointed and Sékou Touré's 'party state' was dismantled under a Second Republic (1984–1991). In December 1984 Conté abolished the office of Prime Minister, a measure which led to an abortive coup, mainly supported by members of the police force, in July 1985. Party political activities officially ceased until April 1992.

Adopted in a national referendum (23 December 1990) the constitution of the Third Republic was promulgated on 23 December 1991. Under the new constitution a *Comité National de Transition*, comprised of military and civilian representatives, replaced the military *Comité de Redressement National* and presided over a controversial transition period leading to the election of a unicameral Parliament in 1995. An 'organic law' of 3 April 1992 provided for the immediate establishment of an unlimited number of political parties and countermanded the constitution's provision of a two-party system. In December 1992 the government announced the indefinite postponement of the legislative elections which were (contrary to the preference of most opposition parties) preceded by presidential elections in December 1993. General Lansana Conté of the Party of Unity and Progress (PUP) who, in accordance with the constitution, resigned from the army in order to contest the presidency as a civilian was re-elected in a controversial contest which led to widespread doubts about the country's democratic system and the neutrality of the electoral commission under the jurisdiction of the powerful Ministry of Interior and Security. In March 1995 elections to the new National Assembly were announced to take place on 11 June. At the elections—the first multi-party contest in the history of the country with each voter having two votes—a total of 846 candidates from 21 parties contested with the PUP winning an overwhelming majority. At the municipal elections in late June 1995 the PUP won control of 20 of the country's 36 municipalities, while the major opposition parties *Rassemblement du peuple guinéen* (RPG), *Parti du renouveau et du progrès* (PRP) and *Union pour la nouvelle république* (UNR), which had presented a coordinated campaign, took 10. On all occasions electoral behavior largely followed the ethnic structure of the country with its main divisions between Peuhl (40% of the population), Malinke (30%), Soussou (20%) and some smaller ethnic groups (10%).

The CTRN was dissolved following the legislative and municipal elections of June 1995. Despite opposition protests of electoral fraud the inaugural session of the National Assembly, on 30 August 1995, was attended by representatives of all elected parties. In early February 1996 spontaneous demonstrations by some 2,000 disaffected soldiers demanding increased pay evolved into a coup attempt. Conté was reportedly seized and held by the rebels until he made concessions including a doubling of salaries. In early July 1996 the President—for the first time under the Third Republic—announced the appointment of a Prime Minister. The presidential elections of December 1998, once more overshadowed by allegations of serious fraud, took place in a climate of extreme political tension and were accompanied by acts of repression. Conté was re-elected in the first round.

1.2 Evolution of Electoral Provisions

Universal suffrage was introduced by the French *Loi Cadre* in 1956 for citizens with a minimum age of 21.

Under the 1958 Constitution presidential candidates had to be at least 35 years old; for parliamentary candidates the minimum age was set at 25 years by the electoral law of 1963. According to the constitution the President was to be elected under the absolute majority system for a term of seven years. However, in all four presidential elections from 1961 to 1982 only one candidate (Sékou Touré) was presented to the voters. Constitutionally the regular term of office for the National Assembly was set to five years. The members of the National Assembly (1963 and 1968: 75; 1974: 150) were elected on a single national list nominated by the PDG-RDA although the electoral law formally allowed for the candidacy of different parties.

1.3 Current Electoral Provisions

Sources: Loi fondamentale, Préambule, 23 decembre 1991; Loi organique No. 91/02/CTRN—Loi organique portant charte des partis politiques, 23 decembre 1991; Loi organique No. 91/012/CTRN portant Code Electoral, 23 decembre 1991, modifiée par la Loi organique N-L 93/039/CTRN (20 août 1993); Décret No. 91/263/PRG/SGG du 27 decembre 91 portant dispositions réglementaires du Code Electoral, 27 decembre 1991; Décret No. 93/228/PRG/SGG rectifiant le décret No. D/93/196/PRG/SGG portant création, organisation et fonctionnement de la Commission Nationale Electorale, 8 decembre 1993.

Elected national institutions: President of the Republic (no Vice-President) and National Assembly (114 elected members). Regular term of office: five years respectively. A person shall hold office as President for not more than two terms. In the single-member constituencies, by-elections are held.

Suffrage: The principals of universal, direct, equal and secret suffrage are applied. Every citizen who has reached the minimum age of 18 years and is registered as voter is entitled to vote. Registration is compulsory. Foreign residents may vote if there exists an 'agreement of reciprocity' *(accord de reciprocité)* with their respective country of origin.

Nomination of candidates
– *presidential elections*: Every Guinean-born citizen between 40 (minimum) and 70 (maximum) years is eligible. Candidates are appointed by parties only. Candidates have to deposit a fixed amount of money determined by a Financial Commission, which is reimbursed if the candidate obtains 5% of the votes cast.
– *parliamentary elections*: Candidature is open to every Guinean citizen of at least 25 years and, in case of naturalization, 10 years of residence and citizenship in Guinea. Independent candidature is not admitted. Besides, standard incompatibilities apply. Candidates have to deposit a fixed amount of money determined by a Financial Commission, which is reimbursed if the candidate/party obtains 5% of the votes cast in the respective constituency.

Electoral system
– *presidential elections*: Absolute majority system (majority run-off). If no candidate receives the absolute majority of the votes cast a second round is being held between the two candidates with the most votes in the first round.
– *parliamentary elections*: Out of the 114 members of the National Assembly, 38 (one third) are elected in single-member constituencies under the plurality system. The constituencies correspond to the 33 *préfectures* and the five *communes* of the capital Conakry. In the 1995 elections the number of voters per constituency varied between 34,000 and 162,000. The other 76 representatives are elected under a proportional system. Technical elements: *National constituency; *Closed lists; *Single vote; *Hare quota and largest remainder formula; *No legal threshold.

1.4 Comment on the Electoral Statistics

It is difficult to obtain valid and detailed electoral data for Guinea. With regard to the elections held from independence until 1984 the significance of the (incomplete) official data is clearly limited by the fact that all elections were held under the conditions of an autocratic single-party state. As to the first multi-party presidential elections of 1993, according to the International Foundation for Electoral Systems (IFES) the official results were 'fraudulent' and did not 'reflect the real electoral outcome' (*Rapport de l'IFES sur les élections présidentielles en Guinée*, December 1993, p.3). With respect to the period before 1974 the data reported in the following tables were drawn from Ziemer (1978). For the more recent elections and referendums official data as published by national newspapers and international newsletters such as *Marchés Tropicaux et Méditerranéens* were used.

2. Tables

2.1 Dates of National Elections, Referendums and Coups d'Etat

Year	Presidential elections	Parliamentary elections	Elections for Constitutional Assembly	Referendums	Coups d'état
1957		31/03[a]			
1958				28/09	
1961	27/01				
1963		01/01			
1968	01/01	01/01			
1974	27/12	27/12			
1982	09/05				
1985					05/04
1990				23/12	
1993	19/12				
1995		11/06			
1998	14/12				

[a] Elections for Territorial Assembly.

2.2 Electoral Body 1958–1995

Year[a]	Type of election[b]	Population[c]	Registered voters Total number	% pop.	Votes cast Total number	% reg. voters	% Pop.
1957	TA	—	1,270,847	—	765,798	60.2	—
1958	Ref	3,765,000[d]	1,408,500	37.4	1,203,875	85.5	32.0
1961	Pr	3,905,000	1,586,544	40.6	1,567,747	98.8	40.1
1963	Pa	4,020,000	—	—	—	—	—
1968	Pr / Pa	4,345,000	1,996,926	46.0	1,990,829	99.7	45.8
1974	Pr / Pa	4,091,000	2,436,485	59.6	2,432,129[g]	99.8	59.5
1982	Pr	4,643,000[e]	3,100,110	66.8	3,063,700	98.8	66.0
1990	Ref	5,880,000[f]	3,004,961	51.1	2,926,968	97.4	49.8
1993	Pr	6,306,000	2,850,394	45.2	2,236,426	78.5	35.5
1995	Pa	6,591,000	3,049,262	46.3	1,887,902	61.9	28.6

[a] Data for the presidential elections of December 1998 have not been available yet.
[b] Pa = Parliamentary Elections; Pr = Presidential elections; Ref = Referendum; TA = Elections for Territorial Assembly.
[c] Data from Penn World Tables database (http://cansim.epas.utoronto.ca:5680/pwt/pwt.html).
[d] The given number refers to 1959.
[e] Official census of 4 February 1983: 4,533,240.
[f] Official census of 1992: 5,600,000.
[g] Votes obtained by the official candidate for the presidency, Sékou Touré.

2.3 Abbreviations

ANP	Alliance Nationale pour le Progrès
LCC	La Cause Commune
PDG	Parti Démocratique de Guinée
PDG-RDA	Parti Démocratique de Guinée - Rassemblement Démocratique Africain
PDG-AST	Parti Démocratique de Guinée - Ahmed Sékou Touré[a]
PEG	Parti des Ecologistes Guinéens
PGP	Parti Guinéen do Progrès
PLD	Parti Libéral Démocrate
PND	Parti National pour le Développement
PPG	Parti du Peuple de Guinée
PRP	Parti du Renouveau et du Progrès
PUP	Parti de l'Unité et du Progrès
RPD	Rassemblement pour la Paix et le Développement
RPG	Rassemblement du Peuple Guinéen
UFR	Union des Forces Républicaines
UNP	Union National pour la Prospérité[b]
UNPG	Union National pour la Prospérité en Guinée

UNR	Union pour la Nouvelle République
UPG	Union pour le Progrès en Guinée
UPN	Union pour le Progrès National

[a] Founded in 1994 as a breakaway from the PDG-RDA.

[b] Founded as a breakaway from the UNPG before the presidential elections of 1993.

2.4 Electoral Participation of Parties and Alliances 1961–1998

Party / Alliance	Years	Elections contested	
		Presidential	Parliamentary
PDG-RDA	1961, 1968, 1974, 1982, 1993	5	3
Djama	1993	1	1[b]
PDG	1993	1	1[b]
PRP	1993	1	1[b]
PUP	1993, 1998	2	1[b]
RPG	1993, 1998	2	1[b]
UNPG	1993	1	1[a]
UNR	1993, 1998	2	1[b]
UPG	1993, 1998	2	1[b]
ANP	1995	0	1[a]
LCC	1995	0	1[a]
PDG	1995	0	1[b]
PDG-AST	1995	0	1[a]
PEG	1995	0	1[a]
PGP	1995	0	1[a]
PPG	1995, 1998	1	1[a]
RPD	1995	0	1[a]
UFR	1995	0	1[a]
UNP	1995	0	1[b]
UPN	1995	0	1[a]

General note: The *Coordination de l'opposition démocratique* (CODEM) was established in July 1995 as an alliance of 12 opposition groups. Other than the UNR, leading members include the PRP and the PRG. The UPG withdrew from the alliance in May 1996.

[a] National list only.

[b] National list and single-member constituencies.

2.5 Referendums

Year	1958[a]		1990[b]	
	Total number	%	Total number	%
Registered voters	1,408,500	–	3,004,961	–
Votes cast	1,203,875	85.5	2,926,968	97.4
Invalid votes	10,570	0.9	5,234	0.2
Valid votes	1,193,305	99.1	2,921,734	99.8
Yes	56,981	4.8	2,883,156	98.7
No	1,136,324	95.2	38,578	1.3

[a] The referendum referred to the constitution of the Fifth Republic of France and to the offer of 'independence within the community' (*indépendance dans la communauté*). Guinea was the only French colony to reject this offer in favor of the demand for full independence.
[b] Approval of the constitution of the 'Popular and Revolutionary Republic of Guinea', adopted in May 1992. This constitution was suspended in April 1994 by the Military Committee for National Recovery.

2.6 Elections for Constitutional Assembly

Elections for Constitutional Assembly have not been held.

2.7 Parliamentary Elections 1957–1995

	1957[b]	
	Total number	%
Registered voters	1,270,847	
Votes cast	765,789	60.3
Invalid votes	10,569	1.4
Valid votes	755,220	98.6
PDG-RDA	584,438	77.4
BAG	45,489	6.0
DSG	77,643	10.3
Others	47,650	6.3

[a] Elections to the Territorial Assembly. The 60 seats in the Assembly were distributed as follows: PDG-RDA: 56; DSG: 3; Others: 1.

In 1963, 1968 and 1974 parliamentary elections were held under the conditions of the one-party state. Detailed data are available only for the 1968 and 1974 elections. On both occasions the number of votes obtained by the PDG was according to the official result identical with the number of valid votes (see table 2.2 for the respective figures).

	1995 Total number	%
Registered voters	3,049,262	–
Votes cast	1,887,902	61.9
Invalid votes	39,330	2.1
Valid votes	1,849,983	97.9
PRP	170,806	9.2
RPG	354,927	19.2
PDG-RDA	36,709	1.9
Dyama	20,696	1.1
PDG	21,233	1.1
UNR	178,692	9.6
UNP	31,295	1.6
PUP	990,184	53.5
UPG	44,441	2.4

[a] Votes for national lists only (proportional representation).

2.8 Composition of Parliament 1963–1995

In the legislatures from 1963 until 1974 all seats in the National Assembly were held by the single-party.

Year	1995 Seats	%
	114	100
PUP	71[a]	62.2
RPG	19[b]	16.6
PRP	9[c]	7.9
UNR	9[c]	7.9
UPG	1[d]	0.9
Dyama	1[d]	0.9
PDG-AST	1[d]	0.9
PDG-RDA	1[d]	0.9
UNP	1[d]	0.9

[a] Single-member constituencies: 30; national list: 41.

[b] Single-member constituencies: 4; national list: 15.

[c] Single-member constituencies: 2; national list: 7.

[d] National list.

2.9 Presidential Elections 1961–1998

The presidential elections held in 1961, 1968, 1974 and 1982 were non-competitive elections, the only running candidate being the leader of the single-party PDG-RDA, Sékou Touré. In these elections valid votes by definition were identical with the votes for Touré. Detailed data are available only for the 1961, 1968 and 1982 elections.

1961	Total number	%
Registered voters	1,586,544	–
Votes cast	1,576,747	98.8
Invalid votes	167[a]	0.1
Valid votes	1,576,580	99.9
Sékou Touré (PDG)	1,576,580	100.0

[a] The number given corresponds to the subtraction of valid votes from votes cast. Author's calculation.

1968	Total number	%
Registered voters	1,996,926	–
Votes cast	1,990,829	99.7
Invalid votes	103[a]	0.0
Valid votes	1,990,726	100.0
Sékou Touré (PDG)	1,990,726	100.0

[a] The number given corresponds to the subtraction of valid votes from votes cast. Author's calculation.

1982	Total number	%
Registered voters	3,100,110	–
Votes cast	3,063,700	98.8
Invalid votes	8	0.0
Valid votes	3,063,692	100.0
Sékou Touré (PDG)	3,063,692	100.0

1993	Total number	%
Registered voters	2,850,394	–
Votes cast	2,236,426	78.5
Invalid votes	153,586	6.9
Valid votes	2,082,840[b]	93.1
Lansana Conté (PUP)[c]	1,077,017	51.7
Alpha Condé (RPG)	407,221	19.6
Mamadou Boye Ba (UNR)	278,638	13.4
Siradiou Diallo (PRP)	247,100	11.9
Faciné Touré (UNPG)	29,266	1.4
Jean-Marie Doré (UPG)	19,007	0.9
Mohamed Mansour Kaba (Djama)	12,890	0.6
Ismael Mohamed Gassim Gushein (PDG-RDA)	11,696	0.6

[a] The votes for the different candidates add up to 2,082,835.

[b] The supreme court had nullified the electoral results of Kankan and Siguiri prefectures in both of which opposition parties had won more than 90% of the votes.

For the elections of December 1998 no detailed data have been available yet. According to the *Cour suprême* Lansana Contè (PUP) was elected with 1,455,007 votes (56.1%). Mamadou Boye Bâ (UNR) obtained 24.6% of the valid votes, Alpha Condé (RPG) 16.6%, Jean Marie Doré (UPG) 1.7%, and Charles Pascal Tolno (PPG) 1.0%.

2.10 List of Power Holders 1958–1998

Head of State	Years	Remarks
Sékou Touré	1958–1984	Took office on 02/19/1958 following a referendum held in French Guinea which led to complete independence from France.
Lansana Conté	1984–	Military (colonel, later general); took office on 04/04/1984 in an army staged coup d'état after the sudden death of Sékou Touré; constitutionally elected on 19/12/1993 and 14/12/1998.

Head of Government	Years	Remarks
Diarra Traoré	1984	April–December.
Sidya Touré	1996–	Appointed on 09/07/1996 as the First Prime minister of the Third Republic.

3. Bibliography

3.1. Official Sources

'Loi No. 113 AN-63, sur l'élection des députés à l'Assemblée Nationale'. *Journal officiel de la Republique de Guinée*, 15 Octubre 1996, 258–260.

'Loi fondamentale, lois organiques 1992'. *Journal officiel de la Republiqe de Guinée* (Numero special), Conakry.

Ministère de l'Interieur et la Securité (Guinée) (1993*a*). *Guide de bureau de vote*. Conakry.

— (1993*b*). *Guide des scrutateurs*. Conakry.

— (1993*c*). *Guide du delegué de parti au niveau des bureaux de vote*. Conakry.

Recueil de textes à l'intention des observateurs des elections législatives de la République de Guinée du 11 Juin 1995. Conakry 1995

3.2. Books, Articles and Electoral Reports

Alao, S. A. (1994). 'The Role of Elections and Electoral Systems in the Process of Democratization in Africa', in S. Brüne, J. Betz and W. Kühne (eds.), *Africa and Europe: Relations of Two Continents in Transition*. Hamburg: Lit, 225–247.

Amnesty International (1992). *Guinea: Amnesty International's Concerns since 1984*. Hagen: WARAN-Koordination Guinea (AI Index AFR 29/03/91).

Bah, M. (1990). *Construire la Guinée apres Sékou Touré*. Paris: L'Harmattan.

Brüne, S., and Maltzan, O. von (1995). 'Demokratische Transition: Wahlen und Wahlbeobachtung in Guinea', in J. Betz and S. Brüne (eds.), *Jahrbuch Dritte Welt 1996*. München: Beck, 53–62.

Brüne, S., Maltzan, O. von, and Rossum, T. van (1996). 'Parlamentswahlen in Guinea (11.6.1995)', in U. Engel, R. Hofmeier, D. Kohnert and A. Mehler (eds.), *Deutsche Wahlbeobachtung in Afrika* (2nd edn.). Hamburg: Institut für Afrika-Kunde, 143–154.

Caire, G. (1988). 'Guinée: deuxieme gouvernement de la République, an deux'. *Mondes en développement*, 16/62-63: 15–33.

Charles, B. (1989). 'Quadrillages politiques et administratif des militaires?'. *Politique africaine*, 36: 9–21.

Devey, M. (1996). 'La Guinée apres la tentative de Coup d'état. Une passe difficile'. *Marchés Tropicaux et Méditerranéens*, 51/2640: 1184–1187.

Dubresson, A. et al. (1989). 'Guinée: apres Sékou Touré'. *Politique africaine*, 39: 2–96.

'Guinea'. *Africa South of the Sahara 1971 ff.* London: Europa Publications.

Gaud, M. (1995). 'Guinée: au-dela de Conakry'. *Afrique contemporaine*, 173: 3–13.

Gaulme, F. *et al.* (1989). 'Guinée 1989'. *Marchés Tropicaux et Méditerranéens*, 45/2275: 1629–1705.

'Guinea turns to democracy 1992'. *The Courier*, 135: 8–22.

Hemstedt, K. (1988–1996). 'Guinea', in Institut für Afrika-Kunde and R. Hofmeier (eds.), *Afrika Jahrbuch 1988–1996*. Opladen: Leske & Budrich.

IFES (International Foundation for Electoral Systems) (1994). *Rapport de l'IFES sur les élections presidentielles en Guinée Decembre 1993*. Washington, D.C.: IFES.

— (1993). *Rapport de L'IFES sur les elections presidentielles en Guinée Decembre 1993*. Washington, D.C.: IFES.

Ingham, K. (1990). *Politics in Modern Africa: The Uneven Tribal Dimension*. London: Routledge.

Kaba, L. (1988). 'From Colonialism to Autocracy. Guinea under Sékou Touré', in P. Gifford (ed.), *Decolonization and African Independence. The Transfers of Power, 1960–1980*. New Haven, Conn.: Yale University Press, 225–244.

Kobele-Keita, S. (1993). *Y a-t-il eu des complots contre la Guinée entre 1958 et 1984? Compte rendu de lecture*. Conakry: Les Ed. Universitaires.

— (1993). *Qui a organisé l' agression du 22 novembre 1970 contre la Guinée et comment?* Conakry: Les Ed. Universitaires.

L'exception guinéene (1996). 'Dossier realisé sous la direction de Jean-Louis Buchet et François Soudan'. *Jeune Afrique Plus*, 36/2: 63–103.

Liste des partis politiques 1992, Conakry.

Lootvoet, B. (1996). 'Guinée: les tentations du passé. Elements d'analyse de la scene politique', in Centre d'Étude d'Afrique Noire (ed.), *Afrique politique 1996. Democratisation: arret sur images*. Paris: Karthala, 85–108

O'Tole, T. E. (1988). *Historical Dictionary of Guinea*. Metuchen, NJ: Scarecrow Pess.

Parti des Ecologistes Guinéens (Guinée) (1992). *Parti des Ecologistes Guinéens*. Conakry.

Parti Dyama (Guinée) (1992). *Assemblee generale constitutive des 19 et 20 avril 1992 à Conakry*. Conakry.

Parti Social-Democrate de Guinée (1992). *Documents*. Conakry.

Placca, J. B. (1989). 'Guinée: comment oublier Sékou Touré?' *Jeune Afrique*, 29/1478: 30–33.

Rassemblement pour la Paix et le Developpement (Guinée) (1992). *Documents*. Conkary.

Rassemblement Guinéen pour le Développement (1991). *Documents*. Conakry.

Rassemblement National pour le Progres (Guinée) (1992). *Documents*. Conakry.

Raulin, A. de (1992). 'La constitution guinéenne du decembre 1990'. *Revue juridique et politique*, 46/2: 182–190.

— (1993). 'La transition democratique en Guinée', in G. Conac (ed.), *L'Afrique en transition vers le pluralisme politique*. Paris: Economica, 311–329.

— (1994). 'A partir du régime constitutionnel guinéen. Reflexion sur les institutions futures de l'Afrique'. *Revue juridique et politique*, 48/2: 126–147.

Roy, P. (1992). 'La Guinee à l'aube de l'Etat de droit'. *Penant*, 102/809, 133–155.

Schmidt, U. (1993). 'Guinea', in D. Nohlen and F. Nuscheler (eds.), *Handbuch der Dritten Welt, Vol. 4: West- und Zentralafrika*. Bonn: Dietz, 243–252.

Shivji, I. G. (1991). *An African Debate on Democracy*. Harare: Southern Africa Political Economy series (SAPES).

'Special Guinée 1995'. *Marchés Tropicaux et Mediteranéens*, 50/2584: 1137–1087.

Siradiou, D. (1991). 'Les jours comptes de Lansana.La revolte en Guinée'. *Jeune Afrique*, 31/1587: 16–20.

Topouzis, D. (1989). 'Conté's Challenges'. *Africa Report*, 34/6: 38–41.

Union Democratique de Guinée (1992). *Documents*. Conakry.

Union des Forces Democratiques (Guinée) (1991). *L' U.D.F., un espoir pour la Guinée*. Conakry.

Union Nationale pour la Prosperité (Guinée) (1992). *Documents*. Conakry.

Voss, J. (1971). *Der progressistische Entwicklungsstaat. Das Beispiel der Republik Guinea (Schriftenreihe des Forschungsinstituts der Friedrich-Ebert-Stiftung)*. Hannover: Verlag für Literatur und Zeitgeschehen.

GUINEA-BISSAU

by Ana Catarina Clemente-Kersten

1. Introduction

1.1 Historical Overview

Amilcar Cabral founded in 1956 the *Partido Africano da Independência da Guiné e Cabo y Verde* (PAIGC) with the aim of liberating African countries from Portuguese colonial rule and building a union between Guinea-Bissau and Cape Verde. As the leading political movement, the PAIGC directed the guerrilla war against the Portuguese army. The *Frente de Libertação para a Independência da Guiné* (FLING) acted in parallel with the PAIGC, but wanted independence without Cape Verde. In 1972—during the colonial war—elections for 15 Regional Councils were organized and held in the territories controlled by the PAIGC (75% of the territory). The candidate list proposed by the PAIGC was approved and the newly constituted Regional Councils elected the delegates to the Constitutional Assembly. The foundations of the Republic of Guinea-Bissau were laid with the draft of a Marxist constitution, and the PAIGC declared the independence of Guinea-Bissau on 24 September 1973. The Constitutional Assembly elected the Vice-Secretary General of the PAIGC, Luis Cabral, Head of State and Francisco Mendes Head of Government. Real decision-making power, however, was concentrated in the eight-member Permanent Commission which administered the party and directed government policy. Guinea-Bissau was the first Portuguese African colony to become recognized as a sovereign country on 10 September 1974.

As the constitutionally sole legal political force in society and state the PAIGC ruled the country under a single-party system. The non-competitive elections for the Regional Councils, held in December 1976, guaranteed the PAIGC's maintenance of power through the approval of the proposed candidate list. Following Francisco Mendes' death in July 1978, João Bernardo Vieira was nominated Prime Minister. In November 1980 a new constitution was approved, which allowed a Cape Verdian to become President (the Cape Verdian constitution did not include such a possibility for a Guinean candidate) and strengthened the powers of the President by eliminating the post of Prime Minister. This led to the overthrow of President Luiz Cabral by Vieira's supporters. After the coup d'état the PAIGC section of Cape Verde changed its name into *Partido Africano da Independência de Cabo Verde* (PAICV) and cancelled the union project between the two countries. In Guinea-Bissau, however, the PAIGC kept its former name. President Vieira centralized all governmental bodies, formed a military Revolutionary Council, banned the National People's Assembly and formed an interim government headed by Victor Saúde Maria in May 1981. With the approval of a new constitution (May 1984) the Revolutionary Council was replaced by a predominantly civilian State Council and, simultaneously, the office of Prime Minister was abolished again. Elections to the Regional Councils (now reduced to eight), held in 1984, endorsed the PAIGC party lists. The councilors elected 150 delegates to the re-established National People's Assembly.

The summary execution of the two regime critics Paulo Correia and Viriato Pan in 1986, and the arrests of 52 supporters accused of instigating three coup attempts, led to growing opposition against the regime, headed by FLING and the Bafatá Movement. Only after the breakdown of the communist regimes in Eastern Europe and the concomitant pressure from international financial institutions, however, did the PAIGC start economic liberalization and allow the establishment of a multiparty system. The PAIGC's political monopoly was constitutionally abolished in May 1991 and the principles of free party registration, freedom of the press, free union choice and market economy were admitted. Further institutional barriers were only reluctantly removed through pressure from the civil society and from emerging political forces. The amendment of the Party Law (August 1991) enabled the registration of opposition parties.

In December 1991 the office of Prime Minister was reintroduced with the nomination of Carlos Correia and presidential as well as parliamentary elections were set to take place in 1992. President Vieira, also running as candidate, postponed them twice by decree and they were finally held in July 1994. The PAIGC gained the majority of seats in the National People's Assembly and the presidential elections gave the incumbent President Vieira (PAIGC) a bare majority in the second ballot. His opponent Koumba Yala, chairman of the *Partido da Renovação Social* (PRS), did not accept the results immediately, as organizational shortcomings, the extension of suffrage for two days and the late announcement of the results had raised some doubts concerning the validity of

Vieira's victory. When the UN Election Observer Commission declared the elections fair and free, Yala resigned in his role as opposition leader. Manuel Saturnino da Costa was nominated to the office of Prime Minister succeeding Carlos Correia.

The expected political change has not really been achieved, since the former leaders have retained their power, but the foundations for a transition to democracy have been laid. The opposition, though immature and lacking in political tradition, is legally organized and represented in the National People's Assembly and the Marxist constitution is undergoing revision to cope with the new political reality.

1.2 Evolution of Electoral Provisions

The indirect election for the Constitutional Assembly in 1972 set the procedures for the next elections. Fifteen Regional Councils were elected by universal, equal, direct and secret elections by approving or rejecting a closed candidate list proposed by the PAIGC. The sole activity of the Regional Councillors was to elect two thirds of the 120 delegates to the Constitutional Assembly (later National People's Assembly) from within its members. The remaining one third was chosen by the PAIGC. The candidates were required to have a minimum age of 18 years, not having collaborated with the Portuguese army, not having committed any crimes and having a good reputation. Every Guinean of at least 15 years was entitled to be registered as a voter.

With the Electoral Law of 1976 the right to vote was limited to Guineans aged at least 18 years. Every Guinean aged at least 21 years, not having served in the colonial administration, was eligible. The Head of State was elected by the National People's Assembly. Furthermore the number of delegates to the National People's Assembly was increased to 150. A later constitutional reform in 1984 reduced the Regional Councils to a total of eight.

1.3 Current Electoral Provisions

Sources: Constitution of the Republic of Guinea-Bissau, 1984; amended 1991 and 1993; Boletim Oficial No. 4, 28/01/93, Suplemento: Lei 2/93, Lei 3/93; Boletim Oficial No. 8, 24/02/93, Suplemento: Lei 4/93.

Elected national institutions: President of the Republic, National People's Assembly (102 members). Regular term of office: five and four years respectively. The President cannot be re-elected for a third mandate for the following five years after the second consecutive term.

Suffrage: The principles of universal, equal, direct and secret suffrage are applied. Every citizen of at least 18 years has the right to vote and is entitled to be registered as a voter. Citizens living abroad can register and vote in the respective consular representations of Guinea-Bissau.

Nomination of candidates
- *presidential elections*: The candidates for the presidency have to be Guinean citizens of Guinean descent and over 35 years old. Candidates have to be nominated by parties, coalitions or by 5,000 voters, with at least 50 of them resident in five of the nine regions.
- *parliamentary elections*: Registered voters, of Guinea-Bissauan descent and of at least 21 years are eligible for candidature as deputy. Independent candidatures are not admitted.

Electoral system
- *presidential elections*: The President is directly elected by absolute majority. If no candidate obtains the absolute majority in the first ballot a second ballot will be held between the two most voted candidates within 21 days.
- *parliamentary elections*: 100 Members of Parliament are elected according to a proportional representation system. Technical elements: *27 multi-member constituencies with varying size (14 constituencies with three seats, eight with four seats, four with five seats and one with six seats); *Closed party lists; *Single vote; *d'Hondt formula; *No legal threshold. Two Members of Parliament are elected by plurality system in two single-member constituencies (for emigration circles).

1.4 Comment on the Electoral Statistics

It is extremely difficult to obtain electoral data from Guinea-Bissau. Data from 1972–1989 was mostly extracted from secondary literature (Rudebeck 1974, Witzel/ Nohlen 1978). The official statistics from 1994 are complete. The absolute figures are taken from official documents. The percentages were calculated by the author according to the standards of the data handbook.

2. Tables

2.1 Dates of National Elections, Referendums and Coups d'Etat

Year	Presidential elections	Parliamentary elections	Elections for Constitutional Assembly	Referendums	Coups d'état
1972			Jan./Feb.		
1976		19–21/12			
1980					14/11
1984		31/03, 18/04			
1989		01/06			
1994	03/07 (1st) 07/08 (2nd)	03/07			

2.2 Electoral Body 1972–1994

Year	Type of election[a]	Population[b]	Registered voters		Votes cast		
			Total number	% pop.	Total number	% reg. voters	% pop.
1972	CA	630,000	83,000	13.2	77,515	93.4	12.3
1976	Pa	—	—	—	—	—	—
1984	Pa	—	—	—	—	—	—
1989	Pa	921,000	420,285	45.6	223,592	53.2	24.3
1994	Pa	1,000,000	400,417	40.0	355,992	88.9	35.6
1994	Pr	1,000,000	400,417	40.0	357,682	89.3	35.8

[a] CA = Constitutional Assembly; Pa= Parliament; Pr = President.

[b] UN estimations.

2.3 Abbreviations

FCG	Forum Cívico Guineense
FD	Frente Democrática
FDS	Frente Democrática Social
FLING	Frente de Libertação para a Independência da Guiné
MUDE	Movimento para a Unidade e a Democracia
PAIGC	Partido Africano da Independência da Guiné e Cabo Verde
PCD	Partido da Convergência Democrática
PDP	Partido Democrático do Progresso
PRD	Partido da Renovação e Desenvolvimento
PRS	Partido da Renovação Social
PS	Partido Socialista
PUSD	Partido Unido Social Democrático
RGB-MB	Resistência da Guiné-Bissau - Movimento Bafatá
UM	União para a Mudança
UNIDO	União Democrática da Oposição

General note: The table also includes non-registered parties which took part in electoral alliances. Four parties (PCD, FDS, PUSD and RGB-MB) formed the *Forum Democrático* on 22 January 1992. In November 1992 there was a split in the *Forum Democrático*; FLING, PCD, PDP and PRS formed the UNIDO. The parties constituted in exile are: *Movimento Bafatá*, PDP, MUDE, *Forum Cívico Guineense* and PS.

2.4 Electoral Participation of Parties and Alliances 1972–1994

Party / Alliance	Years	Elections contested	
		Presidential	Parliamentary
PAIGC	1972, 1976, 1984, 1989, 1994	1	5
FCG	1994	0	1
FLING	1994	1	1
PCD	1994	1	1
PDP	1994	0	1
PRS	1994	1	1
PUSD	1994	0	1
RGB-MB	1994	1	1
UM	1994	1	1

General note: Six elections have been held since independence, but only since 1991 in a multi-party system.

2.5 Referendums

Referendums have not been held.

2.6 Elections for Constitutional Assembly

1972	Votes Total number	%	Seats Total (120)	%
Registered voters	83,000	–		
Votes cast	77,515	93.4		
Yes[a]	75,163	97.0		
No[a]	2,352	3.0		
PAIGC	—	—	120	100

[a] The election consisted in approving or rejecting the list of candidates proposed by the PAIGC. This election was held during the anti-colonial war.

2.7 Parliamentary Elections 1976–1994

The elections of 1976, 1984 and 1989 were non-competitive elections, in which voters could only approve or reject the list of candidates proposed by the PAICV. In 1976 the list was approved with 81.0% of the valid votes according to official statements. For the elections of 1984 there are no data available.

Year	1989 Total number	%	1994[b] Total number	%
Registered voters	420,285	–	400,417	–
Votes cast	223,592	53.2	355,992	88.9
Invalid votes	—	—	65,024	18.3
Valid votes	—	—	290,968	81.7
PAIGC	214,201[a]	95.8	134,982	46.4
RGB-MB	–	–	57,566	19.8
UM	–	–	36,797	12.6
PRS	–	–	29,957	10.3
PCD	–	–	15,411	5.3
PUSD	–	–	8,286	2.8
FLING	–	–	7,475	2.6
FCG	–	–	494	0.2

[a] There were 9,390 No votes (4.2%).

[b] Only national territory; the electoral constituencies 22 and 23 for the emigration circles Africa and Europe are not considered.

2.7 a) Parliamentary Elections 1994: Regional Distribution of Votes

1994	PAICG	RGB	PUSD	FLING	FCG	PCD	PRS	UM	Total[a]
Catio	3,575	2,596	350	175	–	304	2,634	743	10,377
Bandanda	5,779	1,999	388	597	–	482	–	2,668	11,913
Buba	5,047	570	100	–	–	325	595	536	7,173
Fulacunda	2,914	1,237	137	126	–	186	1,669	686	6,955
Bissorã	2,106	1,601	322	289	–	403	7,013	1,181	12,915
Farim	4,091	1,385	331	–	–	724	–	1,876	8,407
Mansaba	4,440	930	167	371	–	554	–	1,428	7,890
Mansoa	3,460	5,655	527	–	–	330	4,947	1,650	16,569
Quinhamel	7,490	648	107	–	–	159	–	893	9,297
Safim	5,186	1,568	223	–	–	157	–	1,626	8,760
Bolama	9,836	698	109	–	–	154	–	507	11,304
Bafatá	7,896	3,789	374	639	–	1,122	–	2,517	16,337
Bambadinca	4,779	1,902	282	–	–	517	1,303	1,127	9,910
Contuboel	6,599	2,104	692	485	–	997	–	1,490	12,367
Boé	5,323	1,367	311	–	–	1,189	–	1,747	9,937
Gabú	6,508	2,591	338	–	–	872	–	1,854	12,163
Pirada	2,504	1,139	159	–	–	584	–	900	5,286
Sonaco	3,598	1,243	179	246	–	882	–	967	7,115
Bigene	3,131	1,559	703	338	–	345	4,147	1,229	11,452
Caió	4,002	1,175	278	2,241	–	409	–	1,767	9,872
Cacheu	3,782	1,289	272	1,073	–	677	–	1,670	8,763
Achada	5,914	3,747	394	–	180	1,120	–	1,232	12,587
Sta. Luzia	4,331	2,375	202	–	–	441	5,099	949	13,397
Mindará	5,996	2,572	161	434	130	601	–	985	10,879
Pefine	6,292	5,862	569	–	–	837	–	1,976	15,536
Belém	6,106	4,203	420	461	184	650	–	1,632	13,656
Penha	4,297	1,762	191	–	–	390	2,550	961	10,151
Total	134,982	57,566	8,286	7,475	494	15,411	29,957	36,797	290,968

[a] Only the national territory is counted, the electoral constituencies 22 and 23 for the emigration circles Africa and Europe are not considered.

2.7 b) Parliamentary Elections 1994: Regional Distribution of Votes (%)

1994	PAICG	RGB	PUSD	FLING	FCG	PCD	PRS	UM	Total[a]
Catio	34.5	25.0	3.4	1.7	–	2.9	25.4	7.2	100
Bandanda	48.5	16.8	3.3	5.0	–	4.0	–	22.4	100
Buba	70.4	7.9	1.4	–	–	4.5	8.3	7.5	100
Fulacunda	41.9	17.8	2.0	1.8	–	2.7	24.0	9.9	100
Bissorã	16.3	12.4	2.5	2.2	–	3.1	54.3	9.1	100
Farim	48.7	16.5	3.9	–	–	8.6	–	22.3	100
Mansaba	56.3	11.8	2.1	4.7	–	7.0	–	18.1	100
Mansoa	20.9	34.1	3.2	–	–	2.0	29.9	10.0	100
Quinhamel	80.6	7.0	1.2	–	–	1.7	–	9.6	100
Safim	59.2	17.9	2.5	–	–	1.8	–	18.6	100
Bolama	87.0	6.2	1.0	–	–	1.4	–	4.5	100
Bafatá	48.3	23.2	2.3	3.9	–	6.9	–	15.4	100
Bambadinca	48.2	19.2	2.8	–	–	5.2	13.1	11.4	100
Contuboel	53.4	17.0	5.6	3.9	–	8.1	–	12.0	100
Boé	53.6	13.8	3.1	–	–	12.0	–	17.6	100
Gabú	53.5	21.3	2.8	–	–	7.2	–	15.2	100
Pirada	47.4	21.5	3.0	–	–	11.0	–	17.0	100
Sonaco	50.6	17.5	2.5	3.5	–	12.4	–	13.6	100
Bigene	27.3	13.6	6.1	3.0	–	3.0	36.2	10.7	100
Caió	40.5	11.9	2.8	22.7	–	4.1	–	17.9	100
Cacheu	43.2	14.7	3.1	12.2	–	7.7	–	19.1	100
Achada	47.0	29.8	3.1	–	1.4	8.9	–	9.8	100
Sta Luzia	32.3	17.7	1.5	–	–	3.3	38.1	7.1	100
Mindará	55.1	23.7	1.5	4.0	1.2	5.5	–	9.1	100
Pefine	40.5	37.7	3.7	–	–	5.4	–	12.7	100
Belém	44.7	30.8	3.1	3.4	1.3	4.8	–	12.0	100
Penha	42.3	17.4	1.9	–	–	3.8	25.1	9.5	100
Total	46.4	19.8	2.8	2.6	0.2	5.3	10.3	12.6	100

[a] Only the national territory is counted, the electoral constituencies 22 and 23 for the emigration circles Africa and Europe are not considered. Due to rounding the added total of the percentages is not always 100.

2.8 Composition of Parliament 1976–1994

Year	1976		1984		1989		1994	
	Seats	%	Seats	%	Seats	%	Seats	%
	150	100	150	100	150	100	100[a]	100
PAIGC	150	100	150	100	150	100	62	62.0
RGB/MB	–	–	–	–	–	–	19	19.0
PRS	–	–	–	–	–	–	12	12.0
UM	–	–	–	–	–	–	6	6.0
FLING	–	–	–	–	–	–	1	1.0

[a] The two seats for the emigration constituencies are not considered.

2.9 Presidential Elections 1994

1994 (1st round)	Total number	%
Registered voters	400,417	–
Votes cast	357,682	89.3
Invalid votes	49,059	13.7
Valid votes	308,623	86.3
João Bernardo Vieira (PAIGC)	142,577	46.2
Koumba Yala (PRS)	67,518	21.9
Fernando Domingos Gomes (RGB-MB)	53,825	17.4
Carlos Domingos Gomes (PCD)	15,645	5.1
François Kankola Mendy (FLING)	8,655	2.8
Bubacar Djalo (UM)	8,506	2.8
Victor Saúde Maria (PUSD)	6,388	2.1
Antonieta Rosa Gomes (PDP)	5,509	1.8

1994 (2nd round)	Total number	%
Registered voters	400,417	–
Votes cast	326,615	81.6
Invalid votes	16,868	5.2
Valid votes	309,747	94.8
João Bernardo Vieira (PAIGC)	161,083	52.0
Koumba Yala (PRS)	148,664	48.0

2.9 a) Presidential Elections, 1994: Regional Distribution of Votes

1994	A. R. Gomes PDP	Yala PRS	C. D. Gomes PCD	Vieira PAICG	F. D. Gomes RGB-MB	Saúde PUSD	Djalo UM	Mendy FLING	Total[a]
Catio	114	4,394	245	3,423	2,140	184	164	71	10,735
Bandanda	194	3,941	622	5,394	753	264	1,206	354	12,728
Buba	194	1,017	378	5,051	440	51	220	69	7,420
Fulacunda	103	3,362	268	2,659	845	76	167	35	7,515
Bissorã	155	9,722	458	1,680	985	248	268	165	13,681
Farim	212	716	1,006	5,234	1,741	238	249	173	9,569
Mansaba	146	944	965	4,805	914	232	313	163	8,482
Mansoa	226	7,717	384	3,486	5,042	203	220	123	17,401
Quinhamel	129	928	297	7,646	496	78	42	54	9,670
Safim	169	2,541	220	5,280	778	102	59	109	9,258
Bolama	145	268	159	10,156	577	66	55	54	11,480
Bafatá	351	1,359	1,191	8,986	4,437	370	776	248	17,718
Bambadinca	311	2,241	641	4,838	1,989	151	218	180	10,569
Contuboel	386	571	1,497	6,910	2,729	304	264	274	12,935
Boé	375	316	1,208	5,947	2,012	302	445	271	10,876
Gabú	283	456	860	6,940	3,106	282	500	171	12,598
Pirada	223	112	599	2,893	1,533	166	174	110	5,810
Sonaco	211	162	845	4,052	1,853	311	263	129	7,826
Bigene	220	6,110	594	2,677	1,143	783	117	245	11,889
Caió	204	1,106	510	4,354	1,201	203	209	3,057	10,844
Cacheu	305	1,217	869	3,785	1,293	353	142	1,372	9,336
Achada	148	1,640	352	6,858	3,382	230	400	108	13,118
Sta. Luzia	132	6,112	269	4,326	2,217	147	214	93	13,510
Mindará	135	1,620	291	6,903	2,236	199	235	282	11,901
Pefine	133	3,605	301	6,835	4,442	362	587	223	16,488
Belém	128	1,911	281	6,848	3,707	310	566	338	14,089
Penha	177	3,430	335	4,611	1,834	173	433	184	11,177
Total	5,509	67,518	15,645	142,577	53,825	6,388	8,506	8,655	308,623

[a] Only the national territory is counted, the electoral constituencies 22 and 23 for the emigration circles Africa and Europe are not considered.

2.9 b) Presidential Elections 1994: Regional Distribution of Votes (%)

1994	A. R. Gomes PDP	Yala PRS	C. D. Gomes PCD	Vieira PAICG	F. D. Gomes RGB-MB	Saúde PUSD	Djalo UM	Mendy FLING	Total[a]
Catio	1.1	40.9	2.3	31.9	19.9	1.7	1.5	0.7	100
Bandanda	1.5	31.0	4.9	42.4	5.9	2.1	9.5	2.8	100
Buba	2.6	13.7	5.1	68.1	5.9	0.7	3.0	0.9	100
Fulacunda	1.4	44.7	3.6	35.4	11.2	1.0	2.2	0.5	100
Bissorã	1.1	71.1	3.3	12.3	7.2	1.8	2.0	1.2	100
Farim	2.2	7.5	10.5	54.7	18.2	2.5	2.6	1.8	100
Mansaba	1.7	11.1	11.4	56.6	10.8	2.7	3.7	1.9	100
Mansoa	1.3	44.3	2.2	20.0	29.0	1.2	1.3	0.7	100
Quinhamel	1.3	9.6	3.1	79.1	5.1	0.8	0.4	0.6	100
Safim	1.8	27.4	2.4	57.0	8.4	1.1	0.6	1.2	100
Bolama	1.3	2.3	1.4	88.5	5.0	0.6	0.5	0.5	100
Bafatá	2.0	7.7	6.7	50.7	25.0	2.1	4.4	1.4	100
Bambadinca	2.9	21.2	6.1	45.8	18.8	1.4	2.1	1.7	100
Contuboel	3.0	4.4	11.6	53.4	21.1	2.4	2.0	2.1	100
Boé	3.4	2.9	11.1	54.7	18.5	2.8	4.1	2.5	100
Gabú	2.2	3.6	6.8	55.1	24.7	2.2	4.0	1.4	100
Pirada	3.8	1.9	10.3	49.8	26.4	2.9	3.0	1.9	100
Sonaco	2.7	2.1	10.8	51.8	23.7	4.0	3.4	1.6	100
Bigene	1.9	51.4	5.0	22.5	9.6	6.6	1.0	2.1	100
Caió	1.9	10.2	4.7	40.2	11.1	1.9	1.9	28.2	100
Cacheu	3.3	13.0	9.3	40.5	13.8	3.8	1.5	14.7	100
Achada	1.1	12.5	2.7	52.3	25.8	1.8	3.0	0.8	100
Sta. Luzia	1.0	45.2	2.0	32.0	16.4	1.1	1.6	0.7	100
Mindará	1.1	13.6	2.4	58.0	18.8	1.7	2.0	2.4	100
Pefine	0.8	21.9	1.8	41.5	26.9	2.2	3.6	1.4	100
Belém	0.9	13.6	2.0	48.6	26.3	2.2	4.0	2.4	100
Penha	1.6	30.7	3.0	41.3	16.4	1.5	3.9	1.6	100
Total	1.8	21.9	5.1	46.2	17.4	2.1	2.8	2.8	100

[a] Only the national territory is counted, the electoral constituencies 22 and 23 for the emigration circles Africa and Europe are not considered. Due to rounding the added total of the percentages is not always 100.

2.10 List of Power Holders 1973–1998

Head of State	Years	Remarks
Luiz de Almeida Cabral	24/09/1973–14/11/1980	Elected by the Constitutional Assembly. 13/03/1977 elected by the National People's Assembly and deposed by Vieira in a coup d'état.
João Bernardo Vieira	15/11/1980–	João Bernardo Vieira overthrew the President Luiz de Almeida Cabral. Since 29/09/1994 constitutionally direct elected President.

Head of Government	Years	Remarks
Francisco Mendes	24/09/1973–07/07/1978	Elected by the Constitutional Assembly; re-elected by the National People's Assembly on 13/03/1977.
Constantino Teixeira	15/07/1978–27/09/1978	Appointed by the President to succeed Mendes after his death.
João Bernardo Vieira	28/09/1978–14/11/1980	Appointed by the President; lead the coup d'état that overthrew Cabral.
Victor Saúde Maria	17/05/1981–11/03/1984	After the coup d'état Vieira institutionalized a military Revolution Council, banned the National People's Assembly. In May 1981 a provisory government headed by Victor Saúde Maria took place. The office of the Prime Minister was abolished with the constitution of 1984.
Carlos Correia	27/12/1991–24/10/1994	The office of the Prime Minister was institutionalized following institutional reforms aiming the introduction of direct and competitive elections. Correia was nominated by the President.
Manuel Saturnino da Costa	25/10/1994–07/05/1997	Nominated by the President after hearing the political parties seated in the Parliament according to the electoral results.
Carlos Correia	08/05/1997–	Appointed by the President.

3. Bibliography

3.1 Official Sources

Boletim Oficial, No. 48, Suplemento, 01/12/1976, Decisão No. 11/76.
Boletim Oficial, No. 48, Suplemento, 01/12/1976, Decreto Nos. 36–37/76.
Boletim Oficial, No. 4, Suplemento, 28/01/1993, Lei 2/93, Lei 3/93.
Boletim Oficial, No. 8, Suplemento, 24/02/1993, Lei 4/93.
Boletim Oficial, No. 28, 2°Suplemento, 18/07/1994.
Boletim Oficial, No. 35, Suplemento, 30/08/1994.
Constituição da República da Guiné-Bissau, 1991.

3.2 Books, Articles and Electoral Reports

Achinger, G. (1993). 'Guinea-Bissau', in D. Nohlen and F. Nuscheler (eds.), *Handbuch der Dritten Welt, Vol. 4: Westafrika und Zentralafrika*. Bonn: Dietz, 253–265.

Augel, J. (1994). 'Bitterer Reis. Zum ersten Mal demokratische Wahlen in Guinea-Bissau'. *Der Überblick*, 1: 73–76.

Blaustein, A. P., and Flanz, G. H. (1994). *Constitutions of the Countries of the World: The Republic of Guinea-Bissau*. New York: Oceana.

Cardoso, C. (1994). 'A transição democrática na Guiné-Bissau: Um parto difícil'. *Saounda. Revista de Estudos Guineenses*, 17: 5–30.

I. Encontro Eleitoral (1994), Vol. 3: Guiné-Bissau. Lisbon: MAI *et al.*

Forrest, J. B. (1992). *Guinea-Bissau.* Boulder, Col.: Westview.

Gorvin, I. (1989). *Elections Since 1945.* Harlow: Longman.

Institut für Afrika-Kunde and Hofmeier, R. (eds.). *Afrika-Jahrbuch*. Opladen: Leske & Budrich, various years.

Mendes Fernandes, R. (1994*a*). 'Processo democrático na Guiné-Bissau'. *Saounda. Revista de Estudos Guineenses*, 17: 31–44.

— (1994*b*). 'Guinée-Bissau. Transition Démocratique?' *L'Afrique Politique, 1994*, 81–91

PAIGC (1974). *História da Guiné e ilhas de Cabo Verde*. Porto: Afrontamento.

Rudebeck, L. (1974). *Guinea-Bissau*. Uppsala: SIAS.

Witzel, R., and Nohlen, D. (1978), 'Guinea-Bissau', in D. Sternberger, B. Vogel, D. Nohlen and K. Landfried (eds.), *Die Wahl der Parlamente und anderer Staatsorgane. Band II: Politische Organisation und Repräsentation in Afrika,* by Franz Nuscheler, Klaus Ziemer *et al.*, Berlin/ New York: Walter de Gruyter, 847–862.

KENYA

by Dirk Hartmann

1. Introduction

1.1 Historical Overview

Kenya's political history since independence has been characterized by the single-party rule of the Kenya African National Union (KANU), first under the regime of Jomo Kenyatta, and, since 1978, under the presidency of Daniel arap Moi. In stark contrast to the experience in other authoritarian African states, elections have always been an institutionalized and important feature of national political life. The re-introduction of multi-party politics in December 1991 has significantly altered electoral politics and the contours of the political system, but so far failed to menace the dominance of President Moi and the former single-party KANU.

Pre-independence politics had seen the splitting of the nationalist movement into two rival parties, the KANU and the Kenya African Democratic Union (KADU), representing the two largest ethnic groups, the Kikuyu (of Central Province) and the Luo (from Nyanza) and the most productive farm areas on the one side (KANU) and the remaining, less numerous ethnic groups of the Rift Valley and the coast on the other (KADU). During the constitutional negotiations preceding independence on 12 December 1963, the KADU, concerned at the prospect of domination by the Kikuyu, and the strong white settler community, which had exerted substantial control over the colonial state, pressed for a federal constitution (*majimbo*-system), which would have made Regional Assemblies responsible for wide areas of policy. The KANU and its leader Kenyatta, having won the May 1963 general elections, did not succeed in imposing a strong central state and eventually agreed to a federal constitution and a bicameral legislature.

Having obtained formal independence Prime Minister Kenyatta moved rapidly to consolidate his position within KANU and over the state. The constitution was amended to return to a unitary form of government. The office of President was created, which Kenyatta himself assumed at the end of 1964. The Senate was merged with the House of Representatives in 1967 to form one National Assembly. By 1968 the executive powers of the Regional Assemblies had been abolished. Nor did the multi-party system survive for long. The KADU Members of Parliament who had initially resisted crossing the floor, joined KANU by December 1964, creating a *de facto* single-party state, where all ethnic groups and different socioeconomic interests were supposed to be represented in the governing coalition.

This fragile coalition, however, fell apart in 1966 when the intra-party defeat of the radical KANU-wing under Oginga Odinga led to the formation of the new opposition party Kenya People's Union (KPU), which was joined by 29 Members of Parliament. The government eventually passed a constitutional amendment requiring all defecting MPs to seek confirmation from their constituents in by-elections. The control over the political and administrative process which KANU had reached by 1966 rendered a level playing field for the KPU illusory. As in other parts of Africa, the strategy of 'ethnicizing' political opposition proved a successful weapon, confirmed by the nine seats won by KPU (out of 29), virtually all Luos from Nyanza, on the occasion of the 'little general election' in 1966. Following the assassination of Tom Mboya, KANU's Secretary-General, and the ensuing riots by Luo youths, the KPU was formally banned on 30 October 1969 and its leaders detained. Odinga and other KPU leaders subsequently returned to the KANU fold during the 1970s. Until the 1990s KANU was to remain the sole political party.

Even after the the suppression of multi-party competition, national elections were regularly held from 1969 onwards. Parliamentary elections remained open contests that allowed multiple candidature, but limited competition to those who did not challenge KANU's and Kenyatta's monopoly of power. The ruling party's primary became the key stage in the electoral process, where any number of candidates, cleared by the KANU headquarters, could compete. Winning the primary signified election to Parliament, since the formal parliamentary election three weeks later only confirmed the victors of the KANU elections. Semi-competitive elections in single-member constituencies were thus transformed into a series of local referendums on the ability of individual leaders to secure state resources for their ethnic followings. Electoral politics provided a mechanism by which the regime could facilitate the circulation of individual leaders into and out of positions of power, deal with local discontent, and thus endow the regime with a considerable degree of political legitimacy and support, as proved by the rising voter turn-out during the 1970s. Instead of being transformed into a powerful political machine, KANU remained a loose coalition of local and regional clientelist networks that were mono-ethnic in character.

Kenyatta was succeeded after his death on 22 August 1978 by his Vice-President Daniel arap Moi. This constitutional succession which initially seemed to guarantee continuity led to profound changes in the political and electoral system Kenyatta had built since independence. After having successfully won over open Luo and Kikuyu political resistance (formalization of the single-party regime through constitutional amendment and failed coup of the Air Force in 1982, dismissal of influential Kikuyu minister Njonjo in 1983), Moi not only began to rebuild the former KADU ethno-political alliance to counterbalance the political and economic influence of the Kikuyu (reallocating vast resources to the hitherto neglected peripheral regions), but strengthened the control of the KANU over the political process and societal activities. Elections continued to take place regularly, but were increasingly controlled and manipulated by the presidential office and the regional administration. At the same time Moi reduced the freedom of intra-party lobbies, of lawyers and religious actors as well as farmers' associations which had maintained a relatively autonomous status in the Kenyatta era.

Against a deteriorating social and economic background and in the face of growing discontent in the still Kikuyu-dominated economic elite over corruption and mismanagement, the grossly rigged and widely boycotted 1988 elections revealed the narrowing power base of the government and the decline of electoral politics in Kenya. Still, Moi managed to silence Kikuyu heavy-weights such as Kenneth Matiba by excluding them from the single-party KANU. Only when foreign donors joined by 1990 the rang of the opposition, the President was forced to install a KANU Review Commission and to hold a Party Conference, which, in December 1990, cancelled the restrictions Moi had forced upon the party since the mid-1980s, such as the non-secret ballot (queue-voting) and the expulsion of dissenting party members from KANU. These concessions, however, came too late and could not stop the growing mobilization of civil society and opposition groups. The failure to suppress demonstrations in Nairobi eventually led Moi in December 1991 to revoke Article 2 (a) of the Constitution and to re-introduce a multi-party system.

The first multi-party contest for presidency and Parliament since independence in December 1992 did not bring the expected victory for the opposition, which had split along inter- and intra-ethnic lines. As Moi and KANU managed to maintain control over electoral legislation and administration and even instigated 'ethnic clashes' in oppositional regions—depriving hundreds of thousands of their right to vote—it was not the disagreement between the opposition leaders but the non-competitive setting that has to be regarded as the principal reason for their defeat. Moi was finally elected President with barely one-third of the votes cast, KANU won a absolute majority of seats with 30% of the votes.

Political developments since the 1992 elections have demonstrated that the control of nearly half of Parliament did not enhance the influence of a splintered opposition on the political decision-making process. MPs continued to view the single-member constituencies as local battlefields between contenders now carrying different party colors but without linking their competition to national politics. It was again civil society which pushed for democratization and institutional reforms and threatened to boycott the elections. Their battle for constitutional changes, once again buttressed by donor institutions, was, however, compromised by a last-minute parliamentary alliance of opposition parties and KANU agreeing on some minor constitutional and political concessions in October 1997 (ignoring the question of presidential powers and the design of the electoral system). The victory of Moi (with 41% of the votes cast) and KANU (with 38%) at the presidential and parliamentary elections of December 1997 thus came as no surprise.

1.2 Evolution of Electoral Provisions

The elections for the Legislative Assembly of 18 to 26 May 1963 were the first that were held under the conditions of universal, direct and equal suffrage (secret suffrage was introduced *de iure* in 1966). Every citizen with a minimum age of 21 years had the right to register as a voter. In 1974 the voting age was lowered to 18 years.

Direct parliamentary elections have been held regularly since independence. Until 1966 the national Parliament consisted of two houses: the House of Representatives with 117 elected members (plus 12 members elected by these 117 forming an electoral college) serving a regular period of five years (re-election being allowed), and the Senate with 41 members (one for every district and for Nairobi) elected for a six-year term (one third renewal every two years). Candidates for both chambers had to be at least 21 years old and be able to speak and read English. Senatorial candidates additionally had to meet certain tax requirements and to show a record of residency in their respective constituency for the previous five years.

In 1966 both houses were amalgamated to form the National Assembly with 158 directly elected members, 12 members appointed by the President and two *ex officio* members. Between 1986 and 1988 the number of directly elected members was increased from 158 to 188 and again in 1997 to 210.

From 1969 onwards the parliamentary elections were semi-competitive elections within a *de facto* single-party system which was constitutionally established on 25 June 1982. In 1969 electoral regulations set the bases for a pre-selection of parliamentary candidates by KANU authorities. Candidates had to pay a nomination fee of £50, be members of the KANU for at least six months (extended to three years in 1974 for ex-prisoners; a measure to disadvantage former KPU members), and the party leaders had the right to reject candidates. In 1986 open primary elections to select the official KANU candidates were introduced. On the day of the primaries KANU members (around 3.5 million out of 5.5 million registered voters) could demonstrate their support for a specific candidate within their constituency by lining up behind him or his image ('queuing'). If one of the candidates was supported in this way by more than 70% of the voters present the parliamentary seat was assigned to him right away. In 1988 this was the case in 65 out of 188 constituencies. The system of queue voting in the KANU primaries was abolished in December 1990. In December 1991 the multi-party system was legalized again.

Since independence all parliamentary elections took place in single-member constituencies under the plurality formula.

Since 1969 the President has been elected for a period of five years without any restrictions of re-election. Candidates had to be at least 35 years old and Kenyan citizens with full civil and political rights. Parliamentary and presidential elections were held with a single ballot, and for the presidential elections an absolute majority system was applied. Parliamentary candidates had to declare on the ballot their support for one of the presidential candidates. To win the elections a presidential candidate had to win himself a seat in Parliament and the parliamentary candidates supporting him had to win at least 50% of the seats in the National Assembly. An additional requirement which is currently in force (see 1.3) was introduced 1992.

After sporadic electoral law changes in 1992, brokered initially by the lobby group, the National Convention Executive Council and later prepared by the Inter-Party Parliamentary Group (IPPG: 36 Opposition and 38 KANU legislators) the constitution is about to be fundamentally reviewed in 1999. Parliament is yet to pass the Constitution of Kenya Review Commission Bill and Constitution of Kenya Amendment Bill, which should prepare the way for extended democratic changes.

1.3. Current Electoral Provisions

Sources: Constitution of Kenya of 10 April 1969 with amendments until April 1998, National Assembly and Presidential Elections Act of 1969 (amended several times) and Presidential and Parliamentary Election Regulations. Most of the legal provisions regulating the elections are laid down in the constitution.

Suffrage: The principles of universal, equal, direct and secret suffrage are applied. All Kenyan citizens with full possession of civil and political rights and a minimum age of 18 years are entitled to register as voters.

Elected national institutions: President of the Republic for a term of five years (two successive re-elections being allowed); 210 members of the one-chamber Parliament (National Assembly) for a regular term of five years (additionally there are 12 members who are appointed by the President upon nomination of the parties in accordance with their parliamentary strength; the Speaker and the Attorney-General as *ex officio* members of the National Assembly).

Nomination of candidates
- *presidential elections*: A candidate must be a Kenyan citizen with full possession of civil and political rights and a minimum age of 35 years. He must be a registered voter and has to be nominated by a political party. Additionally the support of 1,000 registered voters is required.

- *parliamentary elections*: Candidates must be Kenyan citizens of at least 21 years with full possession of civil and political rights and be able (unless incapacitated by blindness or other physical cause) to speak and read English and Swahili. They must be nominated by a political party and be supported by seven to eighteen citizens of the constituency they want to represent. All candidates are required to make a deposit of Kenyan Shilling 5,000 before the elections. Candidates who are in the service of the government or the East African Community or any local government authority have to resign their post six months before the election.

Electoral system

The voter has a single vote for the candidate of his preference in the parliamentary elections and for the presidential candidate of the same party.

- *presidential elections*: Qualified majority system; the winning candidate is required to win the plurality of votes and to have obtained at least 25% of the valid votes cast in at least five of the eight provinces. He also must have won a parliamentary seat himself. If no candidate meets all these requirements a second ballot ('re-run election') is held between the two candidates with the highest number of valid votes cast. In this election again the threshold of 25% of the vote in at least five of the eight provinces is applied.
- *parliamentary elections*: Plurality system in single-member constituencies. By-elections are held continually.

1.4 Commentary on the Electoral Statistics

The election results of 1992 and 1997 have been published and detailed documented in the independent newspapers *Daily Nation* and *Weekly Review*. The data are also well documented by NGO's like the National Election Monitoring Unit. In contrast official institutions such as the Electoral Commission have not been willing to give away any electoral information. Because the counting of votes can take up to one year the data differ between the various sources. Newspaper publications of election results rely mostly on provisional countings. Electoral data are therefore rarely consistent. Because of the common practice of bribery, election rigging and other manipulations the results cannot be regarded as reliable. Apart from the newspaper sources electoral data have been taken from Nuscheler (1978) and Peters (1998).

The percentages have been calculated by the author. They may differ from other sources insofar as the respective candidate's/ party's share of votes is not calculated on the basis of all the votes cast (valid and invalid votes), but, in accordance with international standards, on the basis of the valid votes cast.

2. Tables

2.1 Dates of National Elections, Referendums and Coups d'Etat

Year	Presidential elections	Parliamentary elections	Elections for Constitutional Assembly	Referendums	Coups d'état
1963		26/05[a]			
1966		11/06[a]			
1969	06/12	06/12			
1974	14/10	14/10			
1979	08/11	08/11			
1983	26/09	26/09			
1988	21/03	21/03			
1992	29/12	29/12			
1997	29/12	29/12			

[a] Elections to the upper and lower house of the then two-chamber National Parliament.

2.2 Electoral Body 1963–1997

Year	Type of election[a]	Population	Registered voters		Votes cast		
			Total number	% pop.	Total number	% reg. voters	% pop.
1963	R	8,847,000	2,583,000	29.2	1,843,879[f]	71.3	20.8
1963	S	8,847,000	2,583,000	29.2	1,746,388	67.6	19.7
1966	R[b]	9,780,000	482,300	4.9	159,170[f]	33.0	1.6
1966	S[b]	9,780,000	482,300	4.9	140,971[f]	29.2	1.4
1969	NA/Pr	10,880,000	3,784,276	34.8	1,687,734[f]	44.6	15.5
1974	NA/Pr	12,912,000	4,654,465	36.0	2,627,308[f]	56.5	20.3
1979	NA/Pr	15,922,000	5,529,571	34.7	3,721,514[f]	67.3	23.4
1983	NA/Pr	18,744,000	7,269,586	38.8	3,338,394[f]	45.9	17.8
1988	NA[c]/Pr	22,550,000	6,091,798	27.0	1,980,501	32.5	8.8
1988	NA[d]	22,500,000	6,091,798	27.0	2,241,962	36.8	9.9
1992	NA/Pr	25,669,000	7,956,354	31.0	5,270,516[g]	66.2	20.5
1997	NA/Pr	30,522,000[e]	9,063,390	29.5	4,277,942[f]	47.2	14.0

[a] NA = National Assembly, R = House of Representatives, S = Senate, Pr = President.
[b] 'Little general elections' (by-elections).
[c] First round.
[d] Second round.
[e] Official estimation 1995.
[f] Number of valid votes
[g] Number of valid votes, corrected by the author on the basis of the provincial results.

2.3 Abbreviations

APP	African Peoples' Party
BPU	Baluhya Political Union
CPP	Coast People's Party
DAP	Democratic Assistance Party
DP	Democratic Party
EIP	Economic Independence Party
FORD-A	Forum for the Restoration of Democracy – Asili
FORD-K	Forum for the Restoration of Democracy – Kenya
FORD-P	Forum for the Restoration of Democracy – People
GAP	Green African Party
KADU	Kenya African Democratic Union
KANU	Kenya African National Union
KENDA	Kenyan National Democratic Alliance
KNC	Kenyan National Congress
KSC	Kenyan Social Congress
KPU	Kenyan Peoples' Union
LP	Liberal Party
LPD	Labour Party Democracy
NDP	National Democratic Party
NPUA	Nyanza Province African Union
PICK	Party of Independent Candidates for Kenya
RRP	Republican Reformed Party
Safina	(Kiswahili for 'Arc')
SDP	Social Democratic Party
SPK	Shirikisho Party of Kenya
UPP	Umma Patriotic Party
UPPK	United Patriotic Party of Kenya

2.4 Electoral Participation of Parties and Alliances 1963–1997

Party / Alliance	Years	Elections contested	
		Presidential	Parliamentary
APP	1963	1	1
BPU	1963	1	1
CPP	1963	1	1
KADU	1963	1	1
KANU	1963, 1966, 1969, 1974, 1979, 1983, 1988, 1992, 1997	8	9
NPUA	1963	1	1
KPU	1966	0	1[a]
FORD - Asili	1992, 1997	2	2
FORD - Kenya	1992, 1997	2	2

Party / Alliance	Years	Elections contested	
		Presidential	parliamentary
KENDA	1992, 1997	2	2
KNC	1992, 1997	2	2
KSC	1992, 1997	2	2
PICK	1992, 1997	1	2
SDP	1992, 1997	2	2
DAP	1997	1	1
DP	1997	1	1
EIP	1997	1	1
FORD-People	1997	1	1
GAP	1997	1	1
LP	1997	1	1
LPD	1997	1	1
NDP	1997	1	1
RRP	1997	1	1
Safina	1997	1	1
Shirikisho	1997	1	1
SPK	1997	1	1
UPP	1997	1	1
UPPK	1997	1	1

[a] 'Little general elections'.

2.5 Referendums

Referendums have not been held.

2.6 Elections for Constitutional Assembly

Elections for Constitutional Assembly have not been held.

2.7 Parliamentary Elections

2.7.1 House of Representatives 1963–1966

Year	1963 Total number	%	1966[a] Total number	%
Registered voters	2,583,000	–	482,300	–
Votes cast	1,843,879[a]	71.3	159,170[a]	33.0
Invalid votes	—	—	—	—
Valid votes	—	—	—	—
KANU	988,311	53.6	72,584	45.6
KADU	476,218	25.8	–	–
APP	137,008	7.4	–	–
BPU	14,896	0.8	–	–
CPP	9,135	0.5	–	–
KPU	–	–	86,334	54.3
Independents	218,311	11.8	252	0.1

[a] Votes cast correspond to valid votes.

2.7.2 Senate 1963–1966

Year	1963 Total number	%	1966 Total number	%
Registered voters	2,583,000	–	482,300	–
Votes cast	1,746,388	67.6	140,971	29.2
Invalid votes	7,662	0.3	—	—
Valid votes	1,738,726	99.7	—	—
KANU	1,028,906	59.2	61,698	43.8
KADU	474,933	27.3	–	–
APP	147,039	8.5	–	–
BPU	5,520	0.3	–	–
KPU	–	–	78,288	55.5
Independents	82,328	4.7	985	0.7

2.7.3 National Assembly 1969–1997

Year	1969		1974	
	Total number	%	Total number	%
Registered voters	3,784,276	–	4,654,465	–
Votes cast	1,687,734[a]	44.6	2,627,308[a]	56.5
Invalid votes	—	—	—	—
Valid votes	—	—	—	—
KANU	1,687,734	100.0	2,627,308[b]	100.0

[a] Votes cast correspond to valid votes.
[b] Incumbents received 13.7% votes less than in the previous election

Year	1979		1983	
	Total number	%	Total number	%
Registered voters	5,529,571	–	7,269,586	–
Votes cast	3,721,514[a]	67.3	3,338,394[a]	45.9
Invalid votes	—	—	—	—
Valid votes	—	—	—	—
KANU	3,721,514[b]	100.0	3,338,394[c]	100.0

[a] Votes cast correspond to valid votes.
[b] Incumbents received 10.6% votes less than in the previous election.
[c] Incumbents received 6.8% votes less than in the previous election.

Year	1988		1992	
	Total number	%	Total number	%
Registered voters	6,091,798	–	7,900,366	–
Votes cast	1,980,501 (1st) 2,241,962 (2nd)	 36.8	5,486,768	69.4
Invalid votes	—		61,173	1.1
Valid votes	—		5,425,595	98.9
KANU	1,980,501 (1st) 2,241,962 (2nd)	100.0 100.0	1,327,691[a]	24.5
FORD-Asili	–		1,118,247	20.6
DP	–		1,016,049	18.7
FORD-Kenya	–		928,364	17.1
KNC	–		81,788	1.5
PICK	–		42,109	0.8
KSC	–		17,133	0.3
KENDA	–		771	0.0
SDP	–		177	0.0

[a] KANU won unopposed in 16 constituencies, for 11 constituencies the data were not available.

Detailed data for the elections of 1997 (absolute numbers of party votes at national level) have not been published.

2.8 Composition of Parliament

2.8.1 Lower Chamber (House of Representatives) 1963–1966

	House of Representatives				Senate			
Year	1963		1966		1963		1966	
	Seats	%	Seats	%	Seats	%	Seats	%
	129[a]		129[b]		41[d]		41[e]	
KANU	83[c]	64.3	12	9.3	18[f]	43.9	8	19.5
KADU	33[c]	25.6	–	–	16[f]	39.0	–	–
APP	8	6.2	–	–	2	4.9	–	–
KPU	–	–	7	5.9	–	–	2	4.9
NPUA	–	–	–	–	1	2.4	–	–
Independents	–	–	–	–	1	2.4	–	–

[a] Five seats remained vacant because of the Shifta war.
[b] Re-election.
[c] Because of cross defections the proportions were in 1964 KANU: 104/ KADU 23.
[d] Three seats remained vacant because of the Shifta war.
[e] Re-election.
[f] Because of cross defections the proportions were in 1964 KANU: 27/ KADU 14.

2.8.2 National Assembly 1969–1997

Year	1969		1974		1979		1983	
	Seats	%	Seats	%	Seats	%	Seats	%
	172	100	172	100	172	100	172	100
KANU	172	100	172	100	172	100	172[a]	100

[a] Because in five constituencies there was only one candidate, only 153 seats were to be filled.

Year	1988		1992		1997[a]	
	Seats	%	Seats	%	Seats	%
	202	100	202	100	210	100
KANU	202	100	100	49.5	108	51.4
NDP	–	–	–	–	21	10.0
FORD-K	–	–	31	15.3	17	8.1
SDP	–	–	–	–	15	7.1
FORD-A	–	–	31	15.3	1	0.5
DP	–	–	23	11.4	39	18.6
Safina	–	–	–	–	4	1.9
KSC	–	–	1	0.5	1	0.5
KNC	–	–	1	0.5	–	–
PICK	–	–	1	0.5	–	–
FORD-P	–	–	–	–	1	0.5
Shirikisho	–	–	–	–	1	0.5

[a] Only elected members. Additionally 12 members were nominated by the parties in accordance with their parliamentary strength (KANU: 6; DP: 2; NDP: 1; FORD-K: 1; SDP: 1; Safina: 1).

2.9 Presidential Elections 1969–1997

In all presidential elections before 1992 the KANU candidates Jomo Kenyatta (1969, 1974) and Daniel T. arap Moi (1979, 1983 and 1988) were elected unopposed. Detailed data for these elections are not available. Data on voter registration are reported in table 2.2.

1992	Total number	%
Registered voters	7,956,354	–
Votes cast	—	—
Invalid votes	—	—
Valid votes	5,270,516[a]	66.2[a]
Daniel T. arap Moi (KANU)	1,927,645	36.6
Kenneth Matiba (FORD-Asili)	1,354,856	25.8
Mwai Kibaki (DP)	1,035,507	19.6
Oginga Odinga (FORD-Kenya)	903,886	17.1
Chibule wa Tsuma (KNC)	15,393	0.3
George Anyona (KSC)	14,253	0.3
John Harun Mwau (PICK)	10,449	0.2
Mukaru Ng'ang'a (KENDA)	8,527	0.2

[a] Data as published in Weekly Review 01/01/1993, number of valid votes corrected by author (total of candidates' votes).

1997	Total number	%
Registered voters	9,063,390	–
Votes cast	—	—
Invalid votes	—	—
Valid votes	4,277,942	47.5
Daniel T. arap Moi (KANU)	2,500,865	40.4
Mwai Kibaki (DP)	1,911,742	30.9
Raila Odinga (NDP)	667,886	10.8
Michael Wamalwa (FORD-Kenya)	505,704	8.2
Charity Ngilu (SDP)	488,600	7.9
Joseph M. Shikuku (FORD-Asili)	36,512	0.6
Katama Mkangi (KNC)	23,554	0.4
George Anyona (KSC)	16,428	0.3
Nyoike Wa Kimani (FORD-People)	8,306	0.1
Koigi Wa Wamwere (KENDA)	7,745	0.1
Munyua Waiyaki (UPPK)	6,194	0.1
Godfrey M'Mwereria (GAP)	4,627	0.1
Wangari Maathai (LPK)	4,246	0.1
Stephen Oludhe (EIP)	3,691	0.1
Stephen Ngethe (UPP)	3,584	0.1

2.9 a) Presidential Elections: Regional Distribution of Votes

1992[a]	Moi	Matiba	Kibaki	Odinga	Valid votes
Nairobi	62,410	165,553	69,715	75,888	375,510
Coast	188,296	33,399	32,201	42,796	303,345
N/Eastern	46,420	7,188	3,259	5,084	62,024
Eastern	290,372	79,436	392,481	13,673	784,781
Central	21,918	630,194	373,147	10,668	1,042,872
Rift Valley	981,488	214,727	98,302	75,465	1,373,517
Western	219,187	214,060	14,404	98,822	557,319
Nyanza	117,554	10,299	51,998	581,490	771,148
Total	1,927,640	1,354,856	1,035,507	903,886	5,270,516

[a] Only the four best-placed candidates are listed, as other candidates reached no more than 0.3% nationwide. Total valid votes includes the votes of other candidates.

1997[a]	Moi	Kibaki	Odinga	Wamalwa	Ngilu	Valid votes
Nairobi	75,272	160,124	59,415	24,971	39,707	366,049
Coast	257,065	51,909	24,844	11,306	38,089	407,449
N/Eastern	70,506	20,404	311	4,431	440	96,636
Eastern	370,954	296,335	7,787	7,017	349,754	1,047,894
Central	56,367	891,484	6,869	3,058	30,535	1,005,757
Rift Valley	1,140,109	343,529	36,022	102,178	11,345	1,643,416
Western	314,669	9,755	13,458	338,120	3,429	704,750
Nyanza	215,923	138,202	519,180	14,623	15,301	918,003
Total	2,500,865	1,911,742	667,886	505,704	488,600	4,277,942

[a] Only the five best-placed candidates are listed. Total valid votes includes the votes of the other candidates.

2.9 b) Presidential Elections: Regional Distribution of Votes (%)

1992	Moi	Matiba	Kibaki	Odinga	Total[a]
Nairobi	16.6	44.0	18.6	20.2	100.0
Coast	62.1	11.0	10.6	14.1	100.0
N/Eastern	74.8	11.6	5.3	8.2	100.0
Eastern	37.0	10.1	50.0	1.7	100.0
Central	2.1	60.4	35.8	1.0	100.0
Rift Valley	71.5	15.6	7.2	5.5	100.0
Western	39.3	38.4	2.6	1.8	100.0
Nyanza	15.2	1.3	6.7	75.4	100.0
Total	36.6	25.8	19.6	17.1	100.0

[a] Total turnout includes percentages of other four candidates.

1997	Moi	Kibaki	Odinga	Wamalwa	Ngilu	Total[a]
Nairobi	20.6	43.7	16.2	6.8	10.9	100.0
Coast	63.1	12.7	6.1	2.8	9.4	100.0
N/Eastern	73.0	21.1	0.3	4.6	0.5	100.0
Eastern	35.4	28.3	0.7	0.7	33.4	100.0
Central	5.6	88.6	0.7	0.3	3.0	100.0
Rift Valley	69.4	20.1	2.2	6.2	0.7	100.0
Western	44.7	1.4	1.9	48.0	0.5	100.0
Nyanza	23.5	15.1	56.6	1.6	1.7	100.0
Total	40.4	30.1	10.8	8.2	7.8	100.0

[a] Total turnout includes percentages of other 10 candidates.

2.10 List of Power Holders 1963–1998

Head of State	Years	Remarks
Jomo Kenyatta	1963–1978	Prime Minister of independent Kenya after the victory of KANU in the parliamentary elections of 1963. The office of Prime Minister was abolished in 1964 when Kenya became a republic and Kenyatta became President; confirmed in the office in single-party elections in 1969 and 1974; died on 22/08/1978.
Daniel Toroitich arap Moi	1978–	When Kenyatta died in 1978 Vice-President Moi became his constitutional successor; confirmed in the office three times in one-party elections and twice in multi-party elections.

3. Bibliography

Ajulu, R. (1995). 'The Left and the Question of Democratic Transition in Kenya: A Reply to Mwakenya'. *Review of African Political Economy*, 64: 229–235.

Barkan, J. D. (1984). *Legislators, Elections and Political Linkage. Politics and Public Policy in Kenya and Tanzania*, New York: Praeger.

— (1987). 'The Electoral Process and Peasant State Relations in Kenya', in F. Hayward (ed.), *Elections in Independent Africa*. Boulder: Westview, 213–238.

— (1992). 'The Rise and Fall of a Governance Realm in Kenya', in G. Hyden and M. Bratton (eds.), *Governance and Politics in Africa*. Boulder, Col.: Rienner, 167–192.

— (1993). 'Kenya: Lessons from a Flawed Election'. *Journal of Democracy*, 4/3: 85–99.

— and Ng'ethe, N. (1998). 'Kenya Tries Again'. *Journal of Democracy*, 9/2: 32–48.

Berg-Schlosser, D. (1978). 'Soziale Differenzierung und Klassenbildung in Kenia'. *Politische Vierteljahresschrift*, 20/4: 313–329.

— (1985). 'Elements of Consociational Democracy in Kenya'. *European Journal of Political Research*, 13: 95–109.

— (1989). 'Democracy and the One-Party State in Kenya', in P. Meyns and D. Nabudere (eds.), *Democracy and One-Party State in Africa*. Hamburg: Institut für Afrika-Kunde, 111–130.

Bratton, M. (1994). 'Civil Society and Political Transitions in Africa', in J. W. Harbeson, D. Rothchild and N. Chazan (eds.), *Civil society and the state in Africa*. Boulder: Lynne Rienner, 51–82.

Bourmaud, D. (1985). 'Elections et autoritarisme: la crise de la régulation politique au Kenya'. *Revue française de science politique*, 35/2: 206–234.

Chege, M. (1994). 'The Return of Multiparty Politics', in J. D. Barkan (ed.), *Beyond Capitalism vs. Socialism in Kenya and Tanzania*. Boulder: Lynne Rienner, 47–74.

Commonwealth Observer Group (1993). *The Presidential, Parliamentary and Civic Elections in Kenya: 29.12.1992*. London: Commonwealth Secretary.

Daily Nation (Nairobi), 28 May 1963, 29 May 1963, 28 June 1966, 4 January 1993.

Erdmann, G. (1993). 'Ethnizität und Wahlen. Weshalb die Opposition verloren hat'. *blätter des iz3w,* 190: 37–42.

Geisler, G. (1993). 'Fair? What has Fairness Got to Do with It? Vagaries of Election Observations and Democratic Standards'. *Journal of Modern African Studies*, 31/4: 613–637.

Gertzel, C. (1970). *The Politics of Independent Kenya*. Evanston: Northwestern University Press.

Gicheru, N. H. B. (1976). *Parliamentary Practice in Kenya*. Nairobi: Transafrica Publishers.

Grosh, B., and Orvis, S. (1997). 'Democracy, Confusion, or Chaos: Political Conditionality in Kenya'. *Studies in Comparative International Development*, 31/4: 46–65.

Harnischfeger, J. (1994). 'Ethnische Säuberungen in Kenia'. *Internationales Afrikaforum*, 30/3: 261–273.

Haugerud, A. (1995). *The Culture of Politics in Modern Kenya*. New York: Cambridge University Press.

Hofmeister, W. (1995). 'Zwischen Beharrung und Wandel. Zur politischen Entwicklung in Kenia, Uganda und Tansania'. *Aus Politik und Zeitgeschichte,* B 44–45: 24–37.

Holmquist, F., and Ford, M. (1992). 'Kenya: Slouching Toward Democracy'. *Africa Today*, 39/3: 97–111.

— (1994). 'Kenya: State and Civil Society the First Year after the Election'. *Africa Today*, 41/4: 5–25.

Hornsby, C. P., and Throup, D. W. (1992). 'Elections and Political Change in Kenya'. *The Journal of Commonwealth and Comparative Politics*, 30/2: 172–199.

Human Rights Watch Africa (1994). *Kenya. Multipartyism Betrayed in Kenya*. New York: Human Rights Watch.

Hyden, G., and Leys, C. (1972). 'Elections and Politics in Single-Party Systems: The Case of Kenya and Tanzania'. *British Journal of Political Science,* 2: 250–265.

Imanyara, G. (1993). 'Anfänge für den Liberalismus in Kenya'. *liberal*, 35/2: 32–35.

Kenya Institute of Administration (1963/ 1969). *A Guide to the Constitutional Development of Kenya*. Nairobi.

Kibwana, K. (1996). 'One Year After Multi-party Elections: Wither Patriotism, Democracy and Kenya?', in K. Kibwana, P. Maina and J. Oloka-Onyango (eds.), *In Search of Freedom and Prosperity*. Nairobi: Clairpress, 311–339.

— Maina, P., and Oloka-Onyango, J. (eds.) (1996). *In Search of Freedom and Prosperity*. Nairobi: Clairpress.

Kuria, G. K. (1991). 'Confronting Dictatorship in Kenya'. *Journal of Democracy*, 2/4: 115–126.

Lafargue, J. (1994). 'Une lecture (nécessairement) politique des troubles ethno-régionaux'. *L'Afrique politique* 1994, 281–304.

Leys, C. (1971). 'Politics in Kenya: The Development of Peasant Society'. *British Journal of Political Science*, 1: 307–337.

— (1994). 'Learning from the Kenya Debate', in D. E. Apter and C. G. Rosberg (eds.), *Political Development and the New Realism in Sub-Saharan Africa*. Charlottesville, Virg.: University Press of Virginia, 220–243.

Mair, S. (1994). *Kenias Weg in die Mehrparteiendemokratie*. Baden-Baden: Nomos.

— (1996). *Politischer Wandel in Ostafrika. Kenia, Tansania und Uganda auf dem Weg zur Demokratie?*. Ebenhausen: SWP.

— (1998). 'Kenia—Eine blockierte Demokratie trotz starker Opposition', in G. Schubert and R. Tetzlaff (eds.), *Blockierte Demokratien in der 'Dritten Welt'*. Opladen: Leske & Budrich, 239–265.

Makinda, S. M. (1992). 'Kenya: Out of the Straitjacket, Slowly'. *The World Today*, October, 188–192.

Muigai, G. (1995). 'Ethnicity and Renewal of Competitive Politics in Kenya', in H. Glickman (ed.), *Ethnic Conflict and Democratisation in Africa*. Atlanta: ASA Press, 161–196.

Muriuki, G. (1974). *A History of the Kikuyu 1500–1900*. Oxford: Oxford University Press.

Mwakenya (1994). 'Democratisation in Kenya: Should the Left Participate or Not?' *Review of African Political Economy*, 61: 475–478.

Ngunyi, M. G., and Gathiaka, K. (1993). 'State-Civil Institutions in Kenya in the 1980's', in P. Gibbon (ed.), *Social Change and Economic Reform in Africa*. Uppsala: Nordiska Afrikainstitutet, 28–52.

Nuscheler, F. (1978). 'Kenia', in D. Sternberger, B. Vogel, D. Nohlen and K. Landfried (eds.), *Die Wahl der Parlamente und anderer Staatsorgane. Band II: Politische Organisation und Repräsentation in Afrika,* by Franz Nuscheler, Klaus Ziemer *et al.*, Berlin/ New York: Walter de Gruyter, 935–978.

Nwokedi, E. (1995). *Politics of Democratisation Changing Authoritarian Regimes in sub-Saharan Africa*. Münster/ Hamburg: Lit.

Nyong'o, P. A. (1989). 'State and Society in Kenya. The Disintegration of the Nationalist Coalitions and the Rise of Presidential Authoritarianism, 1963–78'. *African Affairs*, 88/2 (351): 229–252.

Nzomo, M. (1994). 'The 1992 Multi-Party-Elections and Democratic Transition in Kenya–A Review', in W. Jung and S. Krieger (eds.), *Culture and Democracy in Africa South of the Sahara.* Mainz: von Hase & Koehler, 171–196.

Ochieng, W. (1989). *A Modern History of Kenya*. London/ Nairobi/ Ibadan: Evans Brothers.

Ogot, B., and Zeleza, T. (1988). 'Kenya: The Road to Independence and After', in P. Gifford and W. Louis (eds.), *Decolonization and African Independence: The Transfer of Power*. New Haven, Conn.: Yale University Press, 406–426.

Ojwang, J. B. (1990). *Constitutional Development in Kenya*. Nairobi: Acts Press, African Studies for Technology Studies.

Oyugi, W. O. (1997). 'Ethnicity in the Electoral Process: The 1992 General Elections in Kenya'. *African Journal of Political Science*, 2/1: 41–69.

Peters, R.-M. (1996). *Zivile und politische Gesellschaft in Kenya*. Hamburg: Institut für Afrika-Kunde.

— (1998). *Die Präsidentschafts- und Parlamentswahlen in Kenya 1997*. Hamburg. Institut für Afrika-Kunde.

Schatzberg, M. G. (ed.) (1987). *The Political Economy of Kenya.* New York: Praeger.

Southall, R., and Wood, G. (1996). 'Local Government and the Return to Multi-Partyism in Kenya'. *African Affairs*, 95/4: 501–527.

Throup, D. (1993). 'Elections and political legitimacy in Kenya'. *Africa*, 63/3: 371–398.

— and Hornsby, C. (1998). *Multiparty–Politics. The Kenyatta and Moi States and the Triumph of the System in the 1992 Elections.* London: James Currey.

Weekly Review (Nairobi), 1 January 1993.

Widner, J. A. (1992). *The Rise of a Party-state in Kenya: From 'Harambee' to 'Nyayo'!* Berkeley, Cal.: University of California.

LESOTHO

by Ulf Engel

1. Introduction

1.1 Historical Overview

Since independence from Great Britain (4 October 1966) the political history of the Kingdom of Lesotho has been dominated by the unsuccessful quest of the late King Moshoeshoe II (Constantine Bereng Seeiso) for direct executive power on the one hand and party rivalry between the Basutoland Congress Party (BCP, founded by Ntsu Mokhele in 1952) and the Basotho National Party (BNP, founded by Chief Leabua Jonathan in 1958) on the other. Basically, this represented a structural conflict between Protestants and Catholics, between 'Africanists' and traditional authorities. Tactically the BNP allied with the Marematlou Freedom Party (MFP) which was founded in 1957 to rally support for the Principal Chiefs. In addition, Lesotho experienced several political, economic and military interventions by its dominant neighbor South Africa.

In the elections of 1965 held before independence the BNP won slightly over the BCP. As a result of the strictly applied Westminster model with single-member constituencies the BNP occupied a manufactured absolute majority of the Legislative Council's seats. Chief Jonathan became the first Prime Minister of the constitutional monarchy. However, in 1970 the BNP did not accept defeat at the polls. Instead, Chief Jonathan annulled the election, declared a state of emergency and established a government by decree on 30 January 1970. Political parties were banned and the King, after a brief exile, was forced to accept a proclamation which prohibited him from playing an active part in politics. Although a non-elected 86-member interim National Assembly was installed and the state of emergency was lifted on 24–25 July 1973, no real progress was made towards the re-establishment of democracy. A coup attempt on 7–8 January 1974 was attributed to the BCP and resulted in severe government reactions. Political violence has featured prominently since, with the military wing of the BCP's 'external' faction, the Lesotho Liberation Army, playing an important part. Additionally, new parties were formed inside the country, representing growing internal opposition. The government tried to ease the pressure by announcing forthcoming elections. The National Assembly was dissolved, yet elections were boycotted by the internal parties because the BNP refused to publish the electoral roll. Subsequently, the BNP candidates were declared elected unopposed on 14 August 1985.

Following intense conflicts with South Africa on questions of the apartheid regime's regional security policy and indications that Chief Jonathan was prepared to accept Soviet economic assistance, South Africa closed the borders, thus effectively sealing off the land-locked country from all vital imports. Encouraged by the South African apartheid regime the Lesotho army took over power and replaced Chief Jonathan's government by a Military Council led by Maj.-Gen. Justin M. Lekhanya on 20 January 1986. While internal opposition was effectively silenced, the monarch's political ambitions again caused conflict, leading to King Moshoeshoe's being exiled (10 March 1990) and deposed by the Military Council. He was replaced by his son Mohato Bereng Seeiso, who was elected Paramount Chief and became King Letsie III on 6 November 1990. Lekhanya in turn was ousted by Col. Phitsoana Ramaema on 30 April 1991. Apart from a conflict over personalities within the Military Council rather than politics, South African fears concerning a possible lack of political stability with regard to a major power project, the envisaged Lesotho Highland Water Scheme, were the main reasons for this internal coup.

In 1993 the Military Council finally allowed for the re-establishment of democracy through free and fair elections (27–29 March 1993) which resulted in an overwhelming victory of the previously outlawed BCP under Ntsu Mokhele which secured all parliamentary seats, both General Lekhanya and BNP leader Evaristus Sekhonyana being defeated.

King Moshoeshoe's political ambitions remained a problem. His son reigned from 1990 to 1995 as King Letsie III. After a short-lived coup (14 August–14 September 1994), however, he gave way to the second enthronement of Moshoeshoe II on 25 January 1995. After his death on 15 January 1996 King Letsie III succeeded to the throne.

Democracy was restored in autumn 1994 through the forceful mediation of a South Africa-led SADC troika that later served as guarantee powers (incl. Botswana and Zimbabwe). As a result of the internal strive, in June 1997 the BCP split in two with Prime Minister Mokhele leading the new Lesotho Congress for Democracy (LCD). He was joined by all Cabinet Ministers and 40 out of 65 former BCP MPs. Prior to polling on 23 May 1998 Mokhele passed the party leadership over to Deputy Prime Minister Pakalitha Mosisili. The results, however, remained heavily contested by the opposition, leading to rising tension and, ultimately, public unrest. The SADC troika then brokered an agreement which led to the establishment of a Commission of Inquiry into the election results. Though the Langa Commissions's report acknowledged some irregularities, it clearly dismissed the opposition's view that the elections were rigged. In the meantime junior officers forced their superiors to resign. Subsequently the Prime Minister called the guarantee powers of 1994 for help. On 20 September 1998 troops from South Africa and Botswana intervened and, after meeting some initial heavy resistance, restored a fragile order. On 15 October 1998 the government, the opposition and SADC agreed on the formation of an Independent Political Authority. Along the South African transitional model (1993) this parallel structure was set-up in order to prepare for new elections to be held within 18 months (co-chairs: Lekheto Rakuane, Deborah Raditapole).

1.2 Evolution of Electoral Provisions

For the first time the principles of universal, equal, direct and secret suffrage were applied in the election held before independence in 1965. Since then the plurality system has been applied in single-member constituencies. The number of constituencies has been increased from 60 (1965 and 1970 elections) to 65 (1993) and 80 (1998).

1.3 Current Electoral Provisions

Sources: The revised draft of the Constitution for Lesotho (Government Notice No. 12 of 1993); National Assembly Election Order, 1992 (Order No. 10 of 1992); and National Assembly Election (Amendment) (No. 2) Order, 1993 (Order No. 10 of 1993) as at 31 December 1997.

Elected national institutions: Parliament comprises the King (named by a Council of Chiefs according to customary law), the Senate and the National Assembly. Only the latter is elected. The second chamber is made up of 22 Principal Chiefs and 11 other Senators nominated by the King (i.e. the Paramount Chief) acting in accordance with the advice of the Council of State which was established through the 1993 constitution. The leader of the National Assembly's majority party or coalition is appointed Prime Minister by the King.

Suffrage: The principles of universal, equal, direct and secret suffrage are applied. Every citizen who has reached the age of 18 (until 1997: 21) has the right to vote and is entitled to be registered as a voter. Parliament may declare a person who has been convicted in connection with elections or a person who holds or is acting in any office which is related to the organization or conduct of elections in any constituency as not entitled to vote for a period not exceeding five years or not to vote in that election in that constituency.

Nomination of candidates: Every citizen who has reached the age of 21, is registered as a voter and has sufficient ability to communicate in either Sesotho or English is eligible for candidature as a member of the National Assembly. Parliament may exclude certain professionals from their right to stand for election, such as members of the security forces, the secret service or the prison service. Principal Chiefs and Senators do not qualify for election as a member of the National Assembly. In order to register as a candidate the support of two electors of his constituency and a deposit of 200 Maluti (Lesotho currency) is required. The deposit is reimbursed if the candidate obtains at least 10% of the votes cast in his constituency.

Electoral system: Plurality system in 80 single-member constituencies.

1.4 Comment on the Electoral Statistics

Documentation of the 1965 and 1970 elections is poor, particularly of the latter because the official announcement of results was stopped after the counting of 46 of the 60 constituencies. Figures quoted in the literature differ; reference is to Leeman (1985). 1993 results are based on official figures as certified by the Chief Electoral Officer. For 1998 the official provisional results of 27 May 1998 are drawn up.

2. Tables

2.1 Dates of National Elections, Referendums and Coups d'Etat

Year	Presidential elections	Parliamentary elections	Elections for Constitutional Assembly	Referendums	Coups d'état
1965		29/04			
1970		27, 28/01			30/01
1986					20/01
1993		27, 29/03			
1994					17/08[a]
1998		23/05			

[a] Civilian rule was restored on 14 September 1994.

2.2 Electoral Body 1965–1998

Year	Type of election[a]	Population[b]	Registered voters		Votes cast[c]		
			Total number	% pop.	Total number	% reg. Voters	% pop.
1965	LC	838,000	416,952	49.8	261,824	62.8	31.2
1970	NA	1,040,000	—	—	305,033	—	29.3
1993	NA	1,700,000	736,930	43.3	532,678	72.3	31.3
1998	NA	1,980,000	1,017,753[d]	51.4	—	—	—

[a] LC = (Pre-independence) Legislative Council; NA = National Assembly.

[b] UN estimates.

[c] Counting of the 1970 election vote was discontinued and the election suspended on 30 January 1970. Official results have never been published. Figures based on observer reports partly close to the BCP.

[d] Registered votes and votes cast are not presented by the provisional results of 27 May 1998. Registered votes are summed up on the basis of Legal Notice No. 38 OF 1998: The National Assembly Election Order 1992; Constituency Delimitation Order.

2.3 Abbreviations

BCP[a]	Basutoland Congress Party
BNP	Basotho National Party
CDP	Congress for Democracy Party
HB	Ha-Re-Eeng Basotho Party
KB	Kapanang Basotho Party
LCD[a]	Lesotho Congress for Democracy
LCP	Lesotho Communist Party

LEP	Lesotho Educational Party
LLP	Lesotho Labour Party
LPL	Liberal Party of Lesotho
MFP	Marematlou Freedom Party
MTP	Marema Tlou Party
NIP	National Independent Party
NPP	National Progressive Party
PFD	Patriotic Front for Democracy
SDU	Sefate Democratic Union
UDP	United Democratic Party
UP	United Party

[a] The ruling BCP was split in June 1997 with Prime Minister Ntsu Mokhele leading the new formation called LCD. The latter has governed since then.

2.4 Electoral Participation of Parties and Alliances 1965–1998

Party / Alliance	Years	Parliamentary elections contested
BCP[a]	1965, 1970, 1993, 1998	4
BNP	1965, 1970, 1993, 1998	4
MFP	1965, 1970, 1993, 1998	4
MTP	1965	1
LCP	1970	1
UDP	1970, 1993, 1998	3
HB	1993	1
KB	1993, 1998	2
PFD	1993, 1998	2
LEP	1993, 1998	2
LLP	1993, 1998	2
LPL	1993	1
NIP	1993, 1998	2
UP	1993	1
CDP	1998	1
LCD[a]	1998	1
NPP	1998	1
SDU	1998	1

2.5/ 2.6 Referendums/ Elections for Constitutional Assembly

Referendums and Elections for Constitutional Assemblies have not been held.

2.7 Parliamentary Elections 1965–1970, 1993–1998

Year	1965		1970[a]	
	Total number	%	Total number	%
Registered voters	416,952	–	—	–
Votes cast	261,824	62.8	305,033	—
Invalid votes	4,426	1.7	6,435	2.1
Valid votes	257,398	98.3	298,598	97.9
BCP	103,068	40.0	151,883	50.9
BNP	108,140	42.0	104,537	42.7
MFP	40,414	15.7	12,666	5.3
MTP	5,697	2.2	–	–
UDP	–	–	668	0.2
Independents	79	0.0	861	0.3

[a] Counting of the 1970 election vote was discontinued and the election suspended on 30 January 1970. Official results have never been published. Figures based on observer reports partly close to the BCP.

Year	1993		1998[a]	
	Total number	%	Total number	%
Registered voters	736,930	–	1,017,753	–
Votes cast	—	—	—	—
Invalid votes	—	—	—	—
Valid votes	532,678	—	593,955	—
BCP	398,355	74.8	62,313	10.5
BNP	120,686	22.7	145,210	24.5
MFP	7,650	1.4	7,546	1.3
PFD	947	0.2	3,077[b]	0.5
KB	417	0.0	174	0.0
HB	646	0.1	–	–
UDP	582	0.1	357[c]	0.1
LLP	244	0.0	–[c]	–
NIP	241	0.0	1,644	0.3
LEP	63	0.0	92	0.0
UP	51	0.0	–	–
LPL	43	0.0	–	–
LCD	–	–	359,764	60.6
NPP	–	–	2,897	0.5
SDU	–	–	3,160	0.5
CDP	–	–	1,185	0.2
Independents	2,753	0.5	6,536	1.1

[a] Registered votes and votes cast are not presented by the provisional results of 27 May 1998 as presented here. Registered votes are summed up on the basis of Legal Notice No.38 OF 1998: The National Assembly Election Order 1992; Constituency Delimitation order.

[b] Formed alliance with KHOEETSA.

[c] UDP and LLP formed an electoral alliance.

2.7 a) Distribution of Votes/Party per District 1998

1998	1 (5)	2 (13)	3 (10)	4 (18)	5 (9)	6 (8)	7 (5)	8 (3)	9 (5)	10 (4)
LCD	20,901	60,409	50,701	79,375	42,519	37,706	17,458	16,049	24,439	10,207
BNP	7,188	27,457	13,836	33,533	13,478	13,778	9,906	5,832	13,729	6,473
BCP	3,982	10,916	6,006	15,936	6,434	4,893	1,357	2,321	2,068	8,400
MFP	326	1,085	1,614	1,947	617	446	433	121	202	755
SDU	–	39	238	2,564	254	65	–	–	–	–
PFD[a]	353	227	43	825	129	196	115	115	1,074	–
NPP	142	513	1,444	510	757	129	–	–	84	–
NIP	–	925	–	719	–	–	–	–	–	–
CDP	–	–	–	1,185	–	–	–	–	–	–
LLP[b]	–	31	–	176	–	–	150	–	–	–
KBP	–	–	–	138	–	36	–	–	–	–
LEP	–	–	–	–	–	92	–	–	–	–
Ind.	169	1,349	85	1,618	611	2,110	–	–	594	–

General note: The districts are enumerated as follows (number of constituencies indicated in parentheses): 1: Butha-Buthe (constituencies 1–5); 2: Leribe (constituencies 6–18); 3: Berea (constituencies 19–28); 4: Maseru (constituencies 29–46); 5: Mafetang (constituencies 47–55); 6: Mohales'Hoek (constituencies 56–63); 7: Quithing (constituencies 64–68); 8: Qacha's Nek (constituencies 69–71); 9: Thaba-Tseka (constituencies 72–76); 10: Mokkotlong (constituencies 77–80).

[a] Full name of the alliance: KHOEETSA/ PFD.

[b] Full name of the alliance: LLP/ UDP.

2.8 Composition of Parliament 1965–1970; 1993–1998

Year	1965		1970[a]		1993		1998	
	Seats	%	Seats	%	Seats	%	Seats	%
	60	100	60	100	60	100	80[b]	100
BCP	25	41.7	36	60.0	65	100	–	–
BNP	31	51.7	23	38.3	0	0	1	1.3
MFP	4	5.7	1	1.7	0	0	–	–
LCD	–	–	–	–	–	–	78	97.5

[a] Counting of the 1970 election vote was discontinued and the election suspended on 30 January 1970. Official results have never been published. Figures based on observer reports partly close to the BCP.

[b] One seat is vacant.

2.9 Presidential Elections

In Lesotho's parliamentary system no presidential elections have been held.

2.10 List of Power Holders 1966–1998

Head of State	Years	Remarks
King Moshoeshoe II	1966–1990	Assumed kingship (executive powers being vested in the post of Prime Minister) at independence until 31/03/1970 when he had to leave into exile until 04/11/1970 after Chief Jonathan had annulled the 1970 elections. He was exiled by the then ruling military council on 10/03/1990 until 20/07/1992.
King Letsie III	1990–1995	After King Moshoeshoe II was deposed on 06/11/1990 his son was elected Paramount Chief and became King Letsie III. His formal coronation, however, was only on 02/04/1993.
King Moshoeshoe II	1995–1996	The accord on the re-establishment of civilian rule also provided for the replacement of Letsie III by his father who assumed the throne on 25/01/1995. The King died in a (apparently genuine) car accident on 15/01/1996.
King Letsie III	1996–	King Letsie III was confirmed by the College of Chiefs on 16/01 and enthroned on 07/02/1996.

Head of Government	Years	Remarks
Chief Leabua Jonathan	1966–1986	Party leader of BNP which had gained legislative majority in 1965. Became Prime Minister at independence in 1966.
Maj.-Gen. Justin M. Lekhanya	1986–1991	Lekhanya ousted Chief Jonathan on 20/01/1986 and was head of the ruling Military Council until he was himself ousted in a bloodless coup on 30/04/1991.
Col. Phitsoana E. Ramaema	1991–1993	Replaced Lekhanya as chairman of the Military Council until legislative elections were held on 27/03/1993.
Prime Minister Ntsu Mokhehle	1993–1998	Party leader of the previously outlawed BCP, which secured all legislative mandates in the 1993 elections, was installed as Head of Government on 02/04/1993. His mandate was interrupted by a short-lived coup in which King Letsie III suspended both the Parliament and the constitution on 14/08/1994. Civilian rule was re-established on 14/09/1994 after joint pressure had been exerted by the governments of South Africa, Zimbabwe and Botswana.
Prime Minister Pakalitha Mosisili	1998–	On the eve of elections in 1998 Mokhele yielded his place as party leader of the LDC (the officialist breakaway of BCP) to Mosisili and retired from political life. Mosisili was elected Prime Minister on 28/05/1998.

3. Bibliography

3.1 Official Sources

Electoral Codes. 1993, Maseru.

The Lesotho Independence Order, 1966 (Statutory Instrument No. 1172 of 1966). Maseru: Government Printer.

National Assembly Election Order, 1992 (Order No. 10 of 1992) as at 31st December 1997. Maseru: Government Printer.

National Assembly Election Order, 1992. Description of the Constituency Boundaries (Legal Notice No. 1 of 1993). Maseru: Government Printer.

National Assembly Election (Amendment) (No. 2) Order (Order No. 10 of 1993), 1993. Maseru: Government Printer.

National Constituent Assembly 1992: Report of the National Constitutional Commission 1991/1992. Maseru: Government Printer.
The Revised Draft of the Constitution for Lesotho (Government Notice No. 12 of 1993). Maseru: Government Printer (as amended by Government Notice No. 28 of 1993).
National Assembly Elections Regulations 1998 (Legal Notice No. 16 of 1998). *Lesotho Government Gazette Extraordinary*, 26 February 1998.
National Assembly Election Order, 1992 (Legal Notice No. 38 OF 1998, 15th April 1998) Constituency Delimitation Order. Maseru: Government Printer.

3.2 Books and Articles

Baumhögger, G. (1988 ff.), 'Lesotho', in Institut für Afrika-Kunde and R. Hofmeier (eds.), *Afrika Jahrbuch. Politik, Wirtschaft und Gesellschaft in Afrika südlich der Sahara*. Opladen: Budrich & Leske (annually).
Engel, U. (1994). 'Parlamentswahlen in Lesotho (27.3.1993)', in U. Engel, R. Hofmeier, D. Kohnert and M. Mehler (eds.), *Wahlbeobachtung in Afrika: Erfahrungen deutscher Wahlbeobachter. Analysen und Lehren für die Zukunft. Arbeiten aus dem Institut für Afrika-Kunde No.90*. Hamburg: Institut für Afrika-Kunde, 109–123.
Ferguson, J. (1990). *The Anti-Politics Machine. Development, Depolitization and Bureaucratic State Power in Lesotho*. Cambridge: Cambridge University Press.
Leeman, B. (1985). *Lesotho and the Struggle for Azania, 3 vol*. [London].
Macartney, W.J.A. (1970). 'African Westminster? The Parliament Of Lesotho'. *Parliamentary Affairs*, 23/2: 121–140.
Matlosa, K. (1993). *The 1993 Elections in Lesotho and the Challenges for the New Government, Southern African Perspectives No. 27*. Bellville: Centre for Southern African Studies.
— (1997). 'The 1993 Elections in Lesotho and the Nature of the BCP Victory'. *African Journal of Political Science*, 2/1: 140–151.
Neocosmos, M. (1994). 'Lesotho. Political Liberalization. Recent Developments'. *L'Afrique Politique*, 1994: 269–280
Nuscheler, F. (1978). 'Lesotho', in D. Sternberger, B. Vogel, D. Nohlen and K. Landfried (eds.), *Die Wahl der Parlamente und anderer Staatsorgane. Band II: Politische Organisation und Repräsentation in Afrika,* by Franz Nuscheler, Klaus Ziemer *et al.,* Berlin/New York: Walter de Gruyter, 1061–1083.
Southall, R. (1994). 'The 1993 Lesotho Election'. *Review of African Political Economy*, 21/59: 110–118.

— and Petlane, T. (1995). *Democratisation and Demilitarisation in Lesotho: The General Election of 1993 and its Aftermath*. Pretoria: Africa Institute of South Africa.

Spence, J. E. (1968). *Lesotho. The Politics of Dependence*. London: Oxford University Press.

Weisfelder, R. (1992). 'Lesotho and the Inner Periphery in the New South Africa'. *Journal of Modern African Studies*, 30/4: 643–668.

van Wyk, A. J. (1967). *Lesotho: a Political Study*. Pretoria: Africa Institute of South Africa.

LIBERIA

by Matthias Basedau

1. Introduction

1.1 Historical Overview

Liberia, one of the oldest states in sub-Saharan Africa, experienced decades of stability, though under *de facto* single-party rule. A military coup in 1980 was followed by a period of repression and decay, which led to a seven-year civil war from 1989 on. In 1996, finally, an internationally and regionally imposed plan succeeded in restoring peace. The conduct of competitive elections in 1997—won by the civil war's initiator—meant a substantial step towards democracy. Its consolidation and thus the country's future, however, remains uncertain.

Liberia was founded by freed black slaves from the US and the West Indies, known as Americo-Liberians, in 1822. Formal independence from the rule of the American Colonization Society (ACS) was gained on 29 July 1847. Except for some federal elements Liberia's first constitution was modeled on that of the USA with a strong President and a bicameral Congress.

Internal politics were characterized by relative stability under the guidance of the True Whig Party (TWP), which had ruled continuously for more than a century after coming to power in 1878. Although a number of other parties contested several elections during that period, they failed to present a risk to the TWP's presidential candidates or even to gain seats in the Congress. The TWP's domination of the country's political system, resulting in *de facto* one-party government, also reflected the supremacy of the Americo-Liberian minority (up to 5% of the population).

William V. S. Tubman, who served as chief executive from 1944 to 1971, strongly centralized political authority but called also for unification by integrating the Americo-Liberian and indigenous ethnic groups. After Tubman's death in 1971, his successor as President, William R. Tolbert tried to maintain these policies but his failure to cope with widespread bad governance and corruption raised domestic unrest.

As a result, the unchallenged supremacy of the Americo-Liberians ended when the Tolbert government was overthrown by a coup d'état in 1980 and its leader (then) Master Sergeant Samuel K. Doe became Liberia's first indigenous President. Backed by his ethnic group, the Krahn, Doe's regime, both repressive and ruinous, accelerated the political crisis. Doe's efforts to legitimize his rule—by the establishment of a new constitution in 1984 (approved by referendum), and general elections in 1985 (in questionable conditions)—did not reduce ethnic tensions and resulted in open violence.

The civil war, caused by repression and ineffective economic policies, started in 1989, when a then small rebel force, the National Patriotic Front of Liberia (NPFL), infiltrated into Liberia from neighboring Côte d'Ivoire. Following increasingly intense fighting, the rebels reached the capital's suburbs only months later. By mid 1990, members of the Economic Organization of the West African States (ECOWAS), guided and dominated by its most powerful member Nigeria, sent an armed monitoring group (ECOMOG) in order to defend what was left of the government in Monrovia. However, the ECOWAS intervention failed to settle the conflict, and in July 1990, Doe was killed by members of the INPFL (Independent National Front of Liberia), an offshoot of the NPFL. Hostilities continued all over the country, the number of war factions increased dramatically (1996: more than five) and, as a consequence, the country became effectively divided into several parts controlled by regional warlords lacking any credible political goals apart from personal power and enrichment. Subsequently, various international efforts by both the ECOWAS and the United Nations (UN) brought the civil war factions to the negotiation table, but proved incapable of providing a sustainable solution to the conflict. Although a large number of peace agreements were signed, the civil war reached new levels of mayhem and devastation every year. An estimated 150,000 persons were killed, and great parts of the population were forced to flee their homes. However, in August 1996 another peace plan, including the conduct of general elections and the disarmament of the war factions, was signed in Abuja (Nigeria). General elections, held on 19 July 1997, saw the overwhelming triumph of Charles Taylor (the most powerful warlord, leader of the NPFL and initiator of the civil war) and his party, the National Patriotic Party (NPP), gaining a three to one majority in both presidential and legislative elections. Despite some irregularities in preparing the vote international monitors judged the balloting itself to be free and fair.

Future developments in Liberia's politics will depend on the willingness of both President Taylor and the representatives of the former warring factions to give up violent policy options and to step back in favor of the rules of democracy.

1.2 Evolution of Electoral Provisions

Until the coup d'état in 1980 there had always been direct elections to the bicameral Congress (House of Representatives and Senate), the President and the Vice-President. The President's (and Vice-President's) term was gradually extended. After having been raised from two to four years in 1907 the term was extended again to eight years in 1935. Under this provision re-eligibility was possible without limitation (similar to previous provisions), but in the case of being re-elected the President served only a reduced four-year term. The members of the Senate (originally six, in 1955 18 and finally 26 members) served a six-year term, the Representatives (in 1922: 22, 1955: 29 and finally 64 members) a four-year term (1847–1907: two years).

Suffrage, originally, was limited to male adult (21 years) Americo-Liberians and Congo (liberated African slaves who chose to settle in Liberia) having regular income. In 1907 tax-paying indigenous male Liberians were added, and universal adult suffrage was completed, when the vote for women was established in 1947. In 1971 the age required to vote was lowered to 18 years. Eligibility was limited by age, previous Liberian citizenship and personal property. Every Liberian of 35 years or older, at least 15 years of citizenship (1847–1927: five years) and a personal property of 2,500 Liberian $ (1847–1927: 600 L$) was eligible for the presidency. Candidates for the Senate (House of Representatives) were required to be at least 25 (23) years old, three (two) years of citizenship and property of 1,200 L$ (1847–1927: 200 and 150 respectively).

With regard to electoral systems, the Senators, two of them representing a county or territory of the republic, were elected by plurality system in two-member constituencies. The representatives were also elected by plurality system, but the number of seats varied according to demographic weight of the constituencies from one to five. The President was elected by absolute majority system. If no candidate gained the necessary number of votes to fulfil the quorum the Chambers of Congress served as electoral body choosing the future Head of State from the two most successful candidates of the regular balloting (this provision was applied only once, in 1859).

The constitution of the Doe regime did not differ significantly from its predecessor concerning electoral provisions: Universal, equal, direct and secret suffrage was re-established. Again, there was a bicameral Congress consisting of a House of Representatives (64 members) and a Senate (26 members). Members of the former served a six-year term, the Senators a nine-year term. Both were elected by a plurality system, the Senators in 13 two-member electoral districts, the Representatives in 13 multi-member constituencies (Article 83b of the Constitution, however, provided for all elections to be determined by an absolute majority system). Candidates for the Congress were required to be a certain age (Senate: 30, House of Representatives: 25 years), to have one year of residency in the country and had to be tax payers. The President (together with a Vice-President), elected by absolute majority vote, had a term of six years and could only be re-elected once. Before being re-eligible again he had to stand down for one term. Candidates had to be at least 35 years, and have Liberian citizenship by birth, residency of at least 10 years in the country, and a fixed amount of real property (25,000 L$). In 1985, presidential and congressional elections were technically linked. Every voter had one vote only.

1.3 Current Electoral Provisions

Source: Republic of Liberia/ Independent Elections Commission: Special Elections Law for the 1997 Elections, approved by the Ministerial Committee of Nine of the Economic Community of West African States (ECOWAS) on 21 May 1997.

Elected national institutions
The President (six-year term, once renewable), the House of Representatives (64 members, six-year term) and the Senate (26 members, nine-year term) are directly elected. By-elections are held within 90 days, except in the last 90 days before a general election.

Suffrage: The principles of universal adult suffrage (18 years) are applied. Liberian citizenship is obligatory. Norms of ineligibility concern insanity and judicially declared incompetence. Voting is not compulsory. Liberian refugees and citizens living abroad have to return on the national territory for registration.

Nomination of candidates
- *presidential elections*: Presidential candidates must be natural born Liberian citizens and 35 years of age or above. Independent candidature is not admitted. Candidates must reside in the country during the period of convention and campaigning.
- *parliamentary elections*: Candidates for the House of Representatives are required to be at least 25 years of age and original Liberian citizenship. Candidates for the Senate must be of at least 30 years and of original Liberian citizenship as well. Candidates for both chambers have to be nominated by political parties, coalitions or alliances on lists which have to contain 26 (Senate) and 64 (HoR) names respectively. Party candidates must reside in the country during the period of convention and campaigning. In the case of the 1997 elections former government officials had to resign their posts before 28 February 1997.

Electoral system
In 1997 presidential and parliamentary elections were technically linked, and parliamentary and the first round of presidential elections were held on the same day. Every voter had one single ballot for both elections.
- *presidential elections*: The President of the Republic is elected by an absolute majority system. If no candidate gains more than 50% of the valid votes cast, a run-off has to be held where the two most successful candidates in the first election will participate.
- *parliamentary elections*: Representatives and Senators are elected by proportional representation. Technical elements: *One nation-wide constituency; *Closed party lists; *Single vote; *Hare quota and largest remainder formula. *The electoral law fixed an 'artificial' threshold for representation; which actually coincides with the natural threshold for winning seats (1.56% of the national vote for the House and 3.84% for the Senate).

1.4 Comment on the Electoral Statistics

Official data were not available; the following tables are based on secondary sources which refer to official information. Partly, data were completed by author's calculations according to the standards of the data handbook. Documentation of the numerous elections under TWP rule (1878–1980) are highly deficient. For the period since 1955, data are given by Philipp (1978). Complete data were available for the 1985 general elections. However, the competitive character of these elections is rather questionable. Regarding inconsistencies, priority has been given to Givens (1986). For the 1997 general elections data were drawn from the Independent Elections Commission.

2. Tables

2.1 Dates of National Elections, Referendums and Coups d'Etat

Year	Presidential elections	Parliamentary elections[a]	Elections for Constitutional Assembly	Referendums	Coups d'état
1955	03/05				
1959	05/05				
1963	07/05				
1967	xx/05				
1971	04/05				
1975	07/10				
1980					12/04
1984				03/07	
1985	15/10	15/10			
1997	19/07	19/07			

[a] Parliamentary elections are not indicated before 1985. They were usually held together with presidential elections. For further details see 1.2.

2.2 Electoral Body 1955–1985

Year	Type of election[a]	Population	Registered voters		Votes cast		
			Total number	% pop.	Total number	% reg. Voters	% pop.
1955	Pr	930,000	—	—	246,071[d]	—	26.3
1959	Pr	1,125,000[c]	—	—	530,621[d]	—	47.2
1963	Pr	1,016,443[b]	—	—	565,044[d]	—	55.6
1971	Pr	1,170,000[b]	—	—	714,005[d]	—	61.0
1975	Pr	1,503,368[c]	—	—	—	—	—
1984	Ref.	2,101,628[c]	689,929	32.8	566,891	82.2	27.0
1985	Pr/Pa	2,101,628[c]	977,862	46.5	518,872[d]	53.1	24.7
1997	Pr/Pa	2,760,000[b]	751,430	35.8	621,880[c]	82.8	22.5

[a] Pr = President; Pa = Parliament.
[b] UN estimations; figure for 1959 refers to 1956; figure for 1997 refers to 1995.
[c] Census; figure for 1963 refers to 1962, figure for 1975 to 1974, and figure for 1985 to 1984.
[d] Valid votes.

2.3 Abbreviations

ALCOP	All Liberian Coalition Party
DP	Democratic Party
FDP	Free Democratic Party
IPP	Independent Presidential Party
ITWP	Independent True Whig Party
LAP	Liberia Action Party
LINU	Liberia National Union
LLP	Liberian Liberal Party
LPP	Liberian People's Party
LUP	Liberian Unification Party
NDPL	National Democratic Party of Liberia
NPP	National Patriotic Party
NRP	National Reformation Party
PDPL	People's Democratic Party of Liberia
PP	People's Party
PPP	Progressive People's Party
RAP	Reformation Alliance Party
RP	Reformation Party
TWP	True Whig Party
UP	Unity Party
UPP	United People's Party
UTW	United True Whigs

2.4 Electoral Participation of Parties and Alliances 1955–1985

Party / Alliance	Years	Elections contested	
		Presidential	Parliamentary[a]
TWP	1927, 1931, 1935, 1943, 1951, 1955, 1959, 1963, 1967, 1971, 1975	11	—
PP	1927, 1931, 1935	3	—
UTW	1935	1	—
DP	1943	1	—
RP	1951, 1955	2	—
ITWP	1955	1	—
LAP	1985, 1997[b]	2	2
LUP	1985	1	1
NDPL	1985, 1997	2	2
UP	1985, 1997	2	2
ALCOP	1997	1	1
Alliance of Political Parties	1997	1	1

Party / Alliance	Years	Elections contested	
		Presidential	parliamentary
LPP	1997	1	1
NPP	1997	1	1
NRP	1997	1	1
PDPL	1997	1	1
PPP	1997	1	1
RAP	1997	1	1
UPP	1997	1	1

[b] Not indicated before 1985.

[a] 1997 in Alliance of Political Parties.

2.5 Referendum 1984

Year	1984	
	Total number	%[d]
Registered voters	689,929	–
Votes cast	566,891[a]	82.2
Invalid votes	19,007[b]	3.4
Valid votes	547,884[c]	96.6
Yes	540,113	98.6
No	7,771	1.4

[a] Author's calculation. Figure represents sum of invalid votes and valid votes.

[b] Author's calculation. Figure represents sum of 'abstention ballots' (14,759) and 'questioned ballots'(4,248) .

[c] Author's calculation. Figure represents sum of Yes votes and No votes.

[d] Author's calculations.

2.6. Elections for Constitutional Assembly

Elections for Constitutional Assembly have not been held.

2.7 Parliamentary Elections 1985–1997

Figures for House of Assembly and Senate elections are identical as one single ballot was used. For the parliamentary elections until 1975 no data are available.

Year	1985 Total number	%	1997 Total number	%
Registered voters	977,862	–	751,430	–
Votes cast	—	—	—	—
Invalid votes	—	—	—	—
Valid votes	518,872	—	621,880	—
NPP	—	—	468,443	75.3
NDLP	264,364	50.9	—	—
LAP	137,270	26.5	—	—
LUP	59,965	11.6	—	—
UP	57,273	11.0	59,557	9.6
ALCOP	—	—	25,059	4.0
Alliance of Political Parties	—	—	15,969	2.6
UPP	—	—	15,604	2.5
LPP	—	—	10,010	1.6
NDPL	—	—	7,843	1.3
LINU	—	—	6,708	1.1
PDPL	—	—	3,497	0.6
NRP	—	—	2,965	0.5
PPP	—	—	2,142	0.3
RAP	—	—	2,067	0.3
FDP	—	—	2,016	0.3

2.7 a) Parliamentary Elections 1997: Results by County

Absolute numbers	NPP	UP	ALCOP	Alliance	UPP	Others	Total
Bomi	11,248	511	612	120	52	468	13,011
Bong	87,938	932	1,597	844	89	873	92,273
Grand Bassa	39,258	889	424	276	960	755	42,562
Cape Mount	12,862	1,296	622	408	81	2,115	17,384
Grand Gedeh	5,352	166	100	329	69	3,716	9,732
Grand Kru	5,897	204	57	159	99	1,736	8,152
Lofa	36,078	1,385	8,846	929	203	4,502	51,943
Margibi	30,985	1,338	392	175	312	463	33,665
Maryland	14,562	322	207	77	15	323	15,506
Montserrado	125,948	49,931	10,360	10,732	11,724	19,556	228,251
Nimba	86,544	366	1,642	700	115	296	89,663
Rivercess	5,378	339	65	81	743	265	6,871
Sinoe	6,393	1,878	135	1,067	1,142	2,252	12,867
Total	468,443	59,557	25,059	15,969	15,604	37,242[a]	621,880

[a] Official figure; sum of votes per county: 37,248.

Percentages							
	NPP	UP	ALCOP	Alliance	UPP	Others	Total
Bomi	86.5	3.9	4.7	0.9	0.4	3.6	100
Bong	95.3	1.0	1.7	0.9	0.1	1.0	100
Grand Bassa	92.2	2.1	1.0	0.7	2.3	1.7	100
Cape Mount	74.0	7.5	3.6	2.8	0.5	11.6[b]	100
Grand Gedeh	55.0	1.7	1.0	3.4	0.7	38.2[c]	100
Grand Kru	72.3	2.5	0.7	2.0	1.2	21.3[d]	100
Lofa	70.0	2.7	17.0	1.8	0.4	8.1	100
Margibi	92.0	4.0	1.2	0.5	0.9	1.4	100
Maryland	93.9	2.1	1.3	0.6	0.1	2.0	100
Montserrado	55.2	21.9	4.5	4.7	5.1	8.6	100
Nimba	96.5	0.4	1.8	0.8	0.1	0.4	100
Rivercess	78.3	4.9	1.0	1.2	10.8	3.9	100
Sinoe	49.7	14.6	1.0	8.3	8.9	17.5[e]	100
Total	75.3	9.5	4.0	2.6	2.5	6.0	100

[a] Parties that gained less than 2% of the vote nation-wide.
[b] NRP: 7.4%.
[c] NDLP: 35.1%.
[d] PDLP: 9.0%; LPP:10.0%.
[e] LPP: 10.8%.

2.8 Composition of Parliament

2.8.1 House of Representatives 1955, 1985 and 1997

Year	1955		1985		1997	
	Seats	%	Seats	%	Seats	%
	29	100	64	100	64	100
TWP	29	100	–	–	–	–
NDLP	–	–	51	79.7	–	–
LAP	–	–	8	12.5	–	–
LUP	–	–	3	4.7	–	–
UP	–	–	2	3.1	7	10.9
NPP	–	–	–	–	49	76.6
ALCOP	–	–	–	–	3	4.7
Others	–	–	–	–	5	7.8

2.8.2 Senate 1955, 1985 and 1997

Year	1955		1985		1997	
	Seats	%	Seats	%	Seats	%
	10	100	26	100	26	100
TWP	10	100	–	–	–	–
NDLP	–	–	22	84.6	–	–
LAP	–	–	2	7.7	–	–
LUP	–	–	1	3.9	–	–
UP	–	–	1	3.9	3	11.5
NPP	–	–	–	–	21	80.8
ALCOP	–	–	–	–	2	7.7

2.9 Presidential Elections 1955–1997

1955	Total number	%
Registered voters	—	–
Votes cast	—	—
Invalid votes	—	—
Valid votes	246,071	—
William V. S. Tubman (TWP)	244,873	99.5
Edwin J. Barclay (RP)	1,182	0.5
W. O. Davies-Bright (Independent)	16	0.0

1959	Total number	%
Registered voters	—	–
Votes cast	—	—
Invalid votes	—	–
Valid votes	530,621	—
William V. S. Tubman (TWP)	530,566	100.0
W. O. Davies-Bright (Independent)	55	0.0

Detailed data for the presidential elections 1963, 1967, 1971 and 1975 are not available. For the number of valid votes see table 2.2.

1985	Total number	%
Registered voters	977,862	–
Votes cast	—	—
Invalid votes	—	—
Valid votes	518,872	—
Samuel K. Doe (NDPL)	264,364	50.9
Jackson F. Doe (LAP)	137,270	26.5
William G. Kpolleh ((LUP)	59,965	11.6
Edward B. Kessely (UP)	57,443	11.1

1997	Total number	%
Registered voters	751,430	–
Votes cast	—	—
Invalid votes	—	—
Valid votes	621,880	—
Charles Taylor (NPP)	468,443	75.3
Ellen Johnson-Sirleaf (UP)	59,557	9.6
Alhaji V. A.Kromah (ALCOP)	25,059	4.0
Cletus Wotorson (Alliance of Political Parties)	15,969	2.6
Baccus Matthwes (UPP)	15,604	2.5
Togba-Nah Tipoteh (LPP)	10,010	1.6
George Boley (NDPL)	7,843	1.3
Henry Moniba (LINU)	6,708	1.1
Fiyah Gbolie (PDPL)	3,497	0.6
Martin Sherif (NRP)	2,965	0.5
Chea Cheapo (PPP)	2,142	0.3
Henry Fahnbulleh (RAP)	2,067	0.3
George T. Washington (FDP)	2,016	0.3

2.9 a) Presidential Elections 1997: Regional Results

Absolute numbers	Taylor	Johnson-Sirleaf	Kromah	Wotorson	Matthews	Others[a]	Total
Bomi	11,248	511	612	120	52	468	13,011
Bong	87,938	932	1,597	844	89	873	92,273
Grand Bassa	39,258	889	424	276	960	755	42,562
Cape Mount	12,862	1,296	622	408	81	2,115	17,384
Grand Gedeh	5,352	166	100	329	69	3,716	9,732
Grand Kru	5,897	204	57	159	99	1,736	8,152
Lofa	36,078	1,385	8,846	929	203	4,502	51,943
Margibi	30,985	1,338	392	175	312	463	33,665
Maryland	14,562	322	207	77	15	323	15,506
Montserrado	125,948	49,931	10,360	10,732	11,724	19,556	228,251
Nimba	86,544	366	1,642	700	115	296	89,663
Rivercess	5,378	339	65	81	743	265	6,871
Sinoe	6,393	1,878	135	1,067	1,142	2,252	12,867
Total	468,443	59,557	25,059	15,969	15,604	37,242[b]	621,880

[a] Candidates that gained less than 2% of the national vote.
[b] Official figure; sum of votes per region: 37,248.

Percentages	Taylor	Johnson-Sirleaf	Kromah	Wotorson	Matthews	Others[a]	Total
Bomi	86.5	3.9	4.7	0.9	0.4	3.6	100
Bong	95.3	1.0	1.7	0.9	0.1	1.0	100
Grand Bassa	92.2	2.1	1.0	0.7	2.3	1.7	100
Cape Mount	74.0	7.5	3.6	2.8	0.5	11.6[b]	100
Grand Gedeh	55.0	1.7	1.0	3.4	0.7	38.2[c]	100
Grand Kru	72.3	2.5	0.7	2.0	1.2	21.3[d]	100
Lofa	70.0	2.7	17.0	1.8	0.4	8.1	100
Margibi	92.0	4.0	1.2	0.5	0.9	1.4	100
Maryland	93.9	2.1	1.3	0.6	0.1	2.0	100
Montserrado	55.2	21.9	4.5	4.7	5.1	8.6	100
Nimba	96.5	0.4	1.8	0.8	0.1	0.4	100
Rivercess	78.3	4.9	1.0	1.2	10.8	3.9	100
Sinoe	49.7	14.6	1.0	8.3	8.9	17.5[e]	100
Total	75.3	9.5	4.0	2.6	2.5	6.0	100

[a] Candidates that gained less than 2% of the national vote.
[b] Sherif (NRP): 7.4%.
[c] Boley (NDLP): 35.1%.
[d] Gbolie (PDLP): 9.0%; Tipoteh (LPP):10.0%.
[e] Tipoteh (LPP): 10.8%.

2.10 List of Power Holders 1931–1998

Head of State and Government	Years	Remarks
Edwin James Barclay	1931–1944	1931; regularly elected.
William V. S. Tubman	1944–1971	04/01/1944; regularly elected (death during term on 23/07/1971.
William R. Tolbert	1971–1980	23/07/1971; constitutional successor of late predecessor (himself killed in coup of successor in 1980).
Samuel K. Doe	1980–1990	12/04/1980; coup d'état (killed by rebel troops in civil war).
Amos Sawyer	1990–1993	22/11/1990; appointed by transitional government.
Bismarck Kuyon	1993	17/08/1993; appointed by transitional government.
Phillip Banks	1993	13/11/1993; appointed by transitional government.
David Kpormakpor	1994–1995	07/03/1994; appointed by transitional government.
Willton Sankawulo	1995–1996	01/09/1995; appointed by transitional government.
Ruth Perry	1996–1997	03/09/1996; appointed by transitional government.
Charles Taylor	1997–	directly and democratically elected on 19/07/1997.

3. Bibliography

Banks, A. S. (1995). *Political Handbook of the World, 1994–1995*. Binghampton, N.Y.: CSA Publications.

Boom, Dirk van den (1993). *Bürgerkrieg in Liberia. Chronologie—Protagonisten—Prognose.* Münster: Lit.

Burrowes, C.P. (1989). *The Americo-Liberian Ruling Class and Other Myths*. Philadelphia: Temple University, Institute of African and African-American Affairs.

Constitution of the Republic of Liberia, January 6, 1986, Monrovia.

Cook, C., and Killingray, D. (1991). *African Political Facts since 1945* (2nd edn.). Basingstoke, Hampshire: Macmillan.

Dunn, D. E., and Holsoe, S. E. (1985). *Historical Dictionary of Liberia*. Metuchen, NJ: Scarecrow Press.

Dunn, D. E., and Tarr, S. B. (1988). *Liberia. A National Polity in Transition*. Metuchen, NJ: Scarecrow Press.
East, R. (1993). *Political Parties of Africa and the Middle East*. Harlow: Longman.
Givens, W. A. (1986). *Liberia. The Road to Democracy under the Leadership of Samuel Kanyon Doe*. Abbotsbrook: Kensal Press.
Gorvin, I. (1989). *Elections Since 1945. A Worldwide Compendium*. Harlow: Longman.
Guannu, J. S. (1982). *An Introduction to Liberian Government. The First Republic and the People's Redemption Council*. Smithtown, N.Y.: Exposition Press.
— (1985). *A Short History of the First Liberian Republic*. Pampona Beach, Florida: Exposition Press.
Hermann, J. (1993). *Afrika. Wahlen und Abstimmungen 1991–1993*. St. Augustin: Siedler.
Hlophem, S. S. (1979). *Class, Ethnicity and Politics in Liberia*. Washington, D.C.: University Press of America.
Kappel R., and Korte, W. (1990*a*). '10 Jahre Militärherrschaft in Liberia'. *Afrika Spektrum*, 25/1: 35–63.
— (1990*b*). *Human Rights Violations in Liberia, A Documentation*. Bremen. Informationszentrum Afrika, Liberia Working Group.
— (1992). 'Liberia: Der Zerfall eines Landes und die Schwierigkeiten einer afrikanischen Intervention', in R. Hofmeier and V. Matthies (eds.), *Vergessene Kriege in Afrika*. Göttingen: Lamuv, 319–346.
— (1993). 'Liberia', in D. Nohlen and F. Nuscheler (eds.), *Handbuch Dritte Welt, Band 4: Westafrika und Zentralafrika* (3rd edn.). Bonn: Dietz, 278–297.
— and Mascher, F. (1986). *Liberia. Unterentwicklung und politische Herrschaft in einer peripheren Gesellschaft* (Arbeiten aus dem Institut für Afrika-Kunde, No. 50). Hamburg: Institut für Afrika-Kunde.
Lavroff, D.-G., and Peiser, G. (1964). *Les constitutions Africaines. États anglophones*. Paris: Editions A. Pérone.
'Liberia Special Report (1997)'. *New African*, 31/358.
Liebenow, J. G. (1987). *Liberia: The Quest for Democracy*. Bloomington, Indianapolis: Indiana University Press.
Lowenkopf, M. (1976). *Politics in Liberia. The Conservative Road to Development*. Stanford, Calif.: Hoover Institution Press.
Lyons, T. (1998*a*). 'Liberia's Path from Anarchy to Elections'. *Current History*, May, 229–234.
— (1998*b*). 'Peace and Elections in Liberia', in K. Kumar (ed.), *Postconflict Elections, Democratization and International Assistence*. Boulder, Col.: Lynne Rienner, 177–194.

Philipp, G. (1978). 'Liberia', in D. Sternberger, B. Vogel, D. Nohlen and K. Landfried (eds.), *Die Wahl der Parlamente und anderer Staatsorgane. Band II: Politische Organisation und Repräsentation in Afrika,* by Franz Nuscheler, Klaus Ziemer *et al.,* Berlin/ New York: Walter de Gruyter, 1085–1121.

Reno, W. (1995). 'Reinvention of an African Patrimonial State. Charles Taylor's Liberia'. *Third World Quarterly,* 16: 109–120.

Sawyer, A. (1987*a*). *Effective Immediately. Dictatorship in Liberia, 1980–1986*. Bremen.

— (1987*b*). *The Emergence of Autocracy in Liberia. Tragedy and Challenge.* San Francisco, Calif.: ICS Press.

Wegemund, R. (1997). 'Wahlbeobachtung in Liberia: Präsidentschafts- und Parlamentswahlen am 19.7.1997'. *Afrika Spectrum,* 32/2: 217–223.

— (1998). 'Liberia. Durch Wahlen zum Frieden?'. *Afrika Spectrum*, 33/3.

LIBYA

by Hanspeter Mattes

1. Introduction

1.1 Historical Overview

In December 1951, Libya became an independent state. It had already lost its status as an Italian colony during World War II, when it came under British and French military administration. In 1949, after the Allied Forces had turned over the decision about Libya's political future to the United Nations, the deadline for its independence was fixed for 1 January 1952 and a UN commissioner was nominated in order to observe the institution-building process. In the summer of 1950, the National Constituent Assembly of Libya was established. Its 60 members were selected by renowned regional leaders, with 20 from each of the three main provinces (Cyrenaika, Tripolitania, Fezzan). Before it proclaimed Libya's independence on 24 December 1951, the Assembly named Emir Idris al-Sanusi King of the new state (2 December 1950) and passed a constitution (7 October 1951) that established a parliamentary form of government and a federal system consisting of the three provinces.

From the beginning the domestic political development of the Kingdom of Libya was afflicted both by high expenses for executive institutions such as the King, the federal and provincial governments and by the dominance of the traditional elite. Rivalries between provincial and federal institutions, conflicts between monarchists and republicans as well as between federalists and those favoring a unitary state constituted the main obstacles for the functioning of the parliamentary system. The only party that participated in the first national elections of 1952, the National Congress Party (NCP), could not assert itself against the alliance of the governmental elite and local leaders: The NCP chairman was banished immediately after the elections; some months later all parties were banned by the government. The parliamentary elections of 1956 and 1960 did not change the rule of the King's camarilla. Even the constitutional reform of 1963 that established a unitary state with 10 administrative districts and introduced the women's franchise could not improve the situation. Due to supposed irregularities the King annulled the parliamentary elections of October 1964 which were dominated by moderate candidates (repeat elections were held in May 1965).

In view of increasing political and socioeconomic problems, as protests by civil movements and trade unions remained unsuccessful, the military undertook a coup d'état. On 1 September 1969, the Revolutionary Command Council lead by Lieutenant Mu'ammar al-Qaddafi deposed King Sanusi and proclaimed the Libyan Arab Republic. This event initiated a period of institutional change which continues up to now. Throughout this process, however, some features of the regime remained permanent: (1) revolutionary legitimacy of political leadership (as opposed to legitimacy through elections); (2) rejection of parties, except for the pan-Arabic state party Arab Socialist Union (ASU) in the period 1971–1975, and party pluralism; (3) instead of competitive elections, selection of representatives (with imperative mandate) within the structures of direct participation of the 'masses' (in Arabic: *jamahir*).

The institutional development of the revolutionary regime took place in two steps: While the Revolutionary Command Council's Constitutional Proclamation of 1969 had merely transitory character, the formal institutionalization of the regime began only in 1975, when Qaddafi published his 'Green Book' with quasi-constitutional character. According to the first part of this book, People's Congresses serve as 'legislative' organs at local level, selecting local 'executive' organs (People's Committees) and delegating representatives to the General People's Congress at the national level. Members of the national government (General People's Committee) are elected by the General People's Congress which has always accepted to Qaddafi's suggestions of candidates. This institutional framework was confirmed by the Proclamation of People's Power in March 1977. Since then, the country is officially named Socialist People's Libyan Arab Jamahiriya (*jamahiriya*= state of the masses).

Since 1978, in addition to the institutions established in the 'Green Book', Qaddafi formed so-called Revolutionary Committees all over the country (under the motto: *lijan fi kulli makan* = committees everywhere). Apart from increasing mass participation, the main purpose of these organizations has been to stabilize the regime by liquidating the 'enemies of the Revolution abroad' (especially in the campaigns of 1980/81 and 1984). Due to the powerful range of these committees, political dominance shifted from the governmental institutions to the 'revolutionary sector'. This process culminated in Qaddafi's 'Proclamation of the

Separation of Governmental Rule and Revolution' in March 1979, which gave to the Revolutionary Committees quasi-constitutional status. Whereas the political influence of the Revolutionary Committees varied (deprivation of power due to political liberalization in 1987; revaluation after escalating conflicts with militant Islamists since 1992), the functioning of the Jamahiriya institutions has remained unchanged in the 1990s.

1.2 Evolution of Electoral Provisions

The Constitution of 1951 and the Electoral Law of 6 November 1951 (with slight modifications in 1959 and 1963) formed the legal basis for parliamentary elections in the independent Kingdom of Libya. The Parliament consisted of two chambers: The House of Representatives was elected directly every four years. According to the provision that about 20,000 inhabitants should be represented by one deputy, this chamber had 55 members (1964: 103; 1968: 99). The 24 members of the Senate (since 1968: 42) were elected for eight years. Each province contributed eight Senators half of which were appointed by the King. After 1963, all Senators were appointed by the King.

All male citizens who had reached the age of 21 were entitled to vote. Candidates for the House of Representatives had to be aged at least 30, candidates for the Senate had to be at least 40 years old. Since the constitutional amendment of 1963, women were also entitled to vote and were allowed to stand as candidates in the 1964 and 1965 elections.

For all the elections between 1952 and 1965, the plurality system in single-member districts was applied.

1.3 Current Electoral Provisions

After Qaddafi had acceded to power in 1969, both the Constitution of the Kingdom and the Electoral Law were suspended. Since then, no new electoral law has been established. The legal regulations concerning the functioning of the revolutionary regime can be found in various laws and decrees of the Revolutionary Command Council and the General People's Congress.

From 1969 to 1971, political participation of the population was not possible. With the foundation of the state party Arab Socialist Union (ASU) in June 1971, all Libyan citizens were allowed to participate in the 'revolutionary transformation' of the country by engagement in the local, regional and national institutions of the ASU. Since the organizational integration of the ASU into the system of the People's Committees in 1976, political participation in the Libyan state model is regulated as follows:

The fundamental institutions of political participation are the local Basic People's Congresses in which 'the Arabic-Libyan people are organized' (Law No. 9/1984; No. 2/1423 [1994]; Law No. 1/1425 [1996]). Since the municipal reform of 1994, there are 1,500 of these assemblies (one for each municipality). All Libyan citizens who have reached the age of 18 have the right to participate in the Congresses (between 1984 and 1994 this threshold was lowered to 16 years).

The local executive organs, the People's Committees, are elected by the respective People's Congresses every three years. For the validity of this vote, at least 50% of its members have to participate.

1.4 Comment on the Electoral Statistics

As no statistical data have been available for the parliamentary elections of 1952, 1956, 1960 and 1965 and neither presidential nor parliamentary elections have been held since the proclamation of the Libyan Arab Republic, the following electoral statistics include only the results of the 1971 referendum concerning the foundation of the Federation of Arab Republics between Egypt, Libya and Syria.

2. Tables

2.1 Dates of National Elections, Referendums and Coups d'Etat

Year	Presidential elections	Parliamentary elections	Elections for Constitutional Assembly	Referendums	Coups d'état
1952		19/02			
1956		07/01			
1960		17/01			
1964		10/10[a]			
1965		08/05			
1969					01/09
1971				01/09	
1975					05/08[b]

[a] Invalidated.
[b] Failed.

2.2 Electoral Body 1971

Year	Type of election[a]	Population	Registered voters		Votes cast		
			Total number	% pop.	Total number	% reg. voters	% of pop.
1971	Ref	2,010,000[b]	511,803	25.5	484,231	94.6	24.1

[a] Ref = Referendum.
[b] Estimate for 1970.

2.3 Abbreviations

See explanatory note in 1.4.

2.4 Electoral Participation of Parties and Alliances

See explanatory note in 1.4.

2.5 Referendum 1971

Year	1971	
	Total number	%
Registered voters	511,803	–
Votes cast	484,231	94.6
Invalid votes	–	–
Valid votes	484,231	100.0
Yes	477,490	98.6
No	6,741	1.4

2.6 Elections for Constitutional Assembly

Elections for Constitutional Assembly have not been held.

2.7 Parliamentary Elections

For the parliamentary elections of 1952, 1956, 1960, 1964, and 1965 no results are available; since then no direct parliamentary elections in the sense established for the purpose of this handbook have been held.

2.8 Composition of Parliament

See explanatory note to 2.7.

2.10 List of Power Holders 1951–1998

Head of State	Years	Remarks
Idris al-Sanusi	24/12/1951–01/09/1969	Proclaimed as the King of independent Libya by the National Constituent Assembly; deposed after a coup d'état lead by al-Qaddafi.
Mu'ammar al-Qaddafi	01/09/1969–	01/09/1969–02/03/1977: President of the Revolutionary Command Council; 02/03/1977–02/03/1979: General Secretary of the General People's Congress; since 02/03/1979: Leader of the Revolution.

3. Bibliography

3.1. Official Sources

Mu'ammar al Qathafi (1986). *The Green Book, Part I–III.* Tripolis: Public Establishment for Publishing.

'Constitution of the United Kingdom of Libya as promulgated by the National Constituent Assembly on 7 October 1951', in A. Pelt (1970), *Libyan Independence and the United Nations. A Case of Planned Decolonization.* New Haven, Conn./ London: Yale University Press, 902–921.

'Elections du 9 mai 1965. Liste des députés de la cinquième législature'. *Annuaire de l'Afrique du Nord 1965*, Paris: CNRS 1966, 662–666.

'The Electoral Law (of 1951) for the Election of the Libyan Federal House of Representation', in A. Pelt (1970), *Libyan Independence and the United Nations. A Case of Planned Decolonization.* New Haven, Conn./ London: Yale University Press, 922–940.

'Gesetz zum Schutz der Revolution vom 11. Dezember 1969', in H. Mattes (1982), *Die Volksrevolution in der Sozialistischen Libyschen Arabischen Volksgamahiriyya.* Heidelberg: Kivouvou-Verlag, 49.

'Gesetz Nr. 78/15.10.1973 bzgl. der Verwaltungsverantwortlichkeiten der Volkskomitees', in H. Mattes (1982), *Die Volksrevolution in der Sozialistischen Libyschen Arabischen Volksgamahiriyya*. Heidelberg: Kivouvou-Verlag, 393–396.

'Law No. 1 for the Year 1425 (1996) Concerning the Rules of the Procedure of the People's Congresses and the People's Committees'. *Summary of World Broadcasts*, London: BBC, 18/02/1996, MED/19–22.

'Proklamation der Volksmacht (vom 2.3.1977)', in R. Falk and P. Wahl (1980), *Befreiungsbewegungen in Afrika. Politische Programme, Grundsätze und Ziele von 1945 bis zur Gegenwart*. Köln: Pahl-Rugenstein, 256–258.

3.2 Books and Articles

Badry, R. (1986). *Die Entwicklung der Dritten Universaltheorie (DUT) Mu'ammar al-Qadafis in Theorie und Praxis.* Frankfurt/M.: Peter Lang Verlag.

Bleuchot, H., and Monastiri, T. (1979). 'Libye. L'évolution des institutions politiques (1969-1978)'. *Annuaire de l'Afrique du Nord*, Paris: CNRS, 141–187.

Bryde, B.-O. (1970). 'Die libysche Verfassungsproklamation vom 11. Dezember 1969'. *Verfassung und Recht in Übersee*, 3/3: 383–384

(English text of the Proclamation of the Constitution of December 11th, 1969, see pp. 395–389).

Djaziri, M. (1996). *Etat et société en Libye*. Paris: L'Harmattan.

Ebert, H.-G. (1995), 'Libyen', in H. Baumann and M. Ebert (eds.), *Die Verfassungen der Mitgliedsländer der Liga der Arabischen Staaten*. Berlin: Arno Spitz, 435–451.

El Fathaly, O. I. *et al*. (1977). *Political Development and Bureaucracy in Libya*. Lexington/ Toronto: Lexington Books.

Hayford, E. R. (1970). *The Politics of the Kingdom of Libya in Historical Perspective*. Ph.D. Diss., Tufts University.

Khadduri, M. (1963). *Modern Libya. A Study in Political Development*. Baltimore, MD: The Johns Hopkins Press.

Landfried, K., and Abdel Ghaffar, A. A. (1978). 'Libyen', in D. Sternberger, B. Vogel, D. Nohlen and K. Landfried (eds.), *Die Wahl der Parlamente und anderer Staatsorgane. Band II: Politische Organisation und Repräsentation in Afrika*, by Franz Nuscheler, Klaus Ziemer *et al*., Berlin/ New York: Walter de Gruyter, 1123–1151.

'Libye. Chronique'. *Annuaire de l'Afrique du Nord 1962ff*., Paris: CNRS 1963ff.

Mattes, H. (1982). *Die Volksrevolution in der Sozialistischen Libyschen Arabischen Volksgamahiriyya*. Heidelberg: Kivouvou-Verlag.

— (1987ff.). 'Libyen', in T. Koszinowski and H. Mattes (eds.), *Nahost-Jahrbuch 1986ff*., Opladen: Leske & Budrich.

— (1992). 'Demokratie und Menschenrechte in Libyen zwischen Ideologie und Pragmatismus 1969–1991', in S. Faath and H. Mattes (eds.), *Demokratie und Menschenrechte in Nordafrika*. Hamburg: Edition Wuquf, 289–364.

Pelt, A. (1970). *Libyan Independence and the United Nations. A Case of Planned Decolonization*. New Haven, Conn./ London: Yale University Press.

MADAGASCAR

by Bernhard Thibaut*

1. Introduction

1.1 Historical Overview

Madagascar gained independence from French colonial rule on 26 June 1960. Solid state structures had existed already in the second half of the 19th century when the Merina-monarchy, originally based at the center of the island, controlled over two thirds of the territory. In the course of French intervention beginning in the 1880s Madagascar had become a French protectorate in 1896. Nationalist opposition to colonial domination remained intense with violent explosions in 1913, 1917 and 1947.

Since the 1950s political development has been influenced by conflict structures that trace back to the 19th century but were reinforced by colonial politics of 'divide and rule'. Already before independence the cleavage between the Merina living in the highlands in the interior of the island and the inhabitants of the coastal regions translated itself into the political system, dividing the two camps of the 'nationalists' (with strongholds in the central region) and the more moderate 'provincialists' (coastal region), the latter being clearly favored by France. The provincial elections of 1957 were won by 'Union of Malagasy Social Democrats' (*Union de Démocrates Sociaux Malgaches*—UDSM) and 'Social Democratic Party' (*Parti Social Démocrate*—PSD). Both held an affirmative position towards the French offer of 'independence within the community' whereas the opposition forces of the 'Congress for the Independence of Madagascar' (later transformed into the 'Congress Party for the Independence of Madagascar'—*Antokon'ny Kongresy Fahaleovantenan'i Madagasikara*—AKFM) demanded full independence. The moderate position was approved in a referendum in 1958 and the PSD as a leading force of the decolonialization process transformed

---

* I am indebted to Bernhard Barth (Friedrich Ebert Foundation, Antananarivo) and to Olivier Ramahadison (Ministry of the Interior, Antananarivo) for their helpfulness in the collection of data presented in this chapter.

itself rapidly from a regionally oriented organization into a hegemonic party.

The constitution of the First Republic provided for a system of government framed after the model of the Fifth French Republic with the President, however, being the unconstrained head of the executive. Politics were dominated by the PSD under its leader Philibert Tsiranana, who followed a pragmatic socialist ideology. The parliamentary elections of 1965 and 1970 could scarcely be regarded as free and fair as the government used the administrative apparatus to manipulate the electoral process. Besides, majoritarian effects of the electoral system secured the hegemonic position of the PSD within the National Assembly.

At the beginning of the 1970s and against the background of serious economic difficulties societal opposition to the autocratic regime of Tsiranana increased. In 1971 a rebellion in the southern province of Tuléar led by radical nationalists was brutally suppressed. In 1972 massive political protest mainly organized by students forced Tsiranana to resign. His submission of executive power to General Gabriel Ramanantsoa constituted the breakdown of the First Republic and gave way to a period of transitional government (Parliament was dissolved) which was foreseen to take five years and legitimized as such in a referendum.

Politically the government under Ramanantsoa represented a shift toward more radical nationalist positions. Madagascar left the monetary union with France, French troops had to leave the country and development policies followed a more explicit state-interventionist approach. In terms of the party system support for the government stemmed mainly from the AKFM. However, within the Cabinet conflicts with regard to the overall development strategy soon gained importance. In January 1975 Ramanantsoa resigned and turned power over to Colonel Richard Ratsimandrava. Six days after taking office, Ratsimandrava was assassinated. After a short interregnum a Military Council appointed Captain Didier Ratsiraka (formerly Minister of International Affairs) as chief of the executive. Ratsiraka's program of a 'true socialist revolution' together with a new constitution was approved in a referendum held under authoritarian conditions in December of the same year.

The Second Republic combined formal elements of constitutional government (direct election of the President and the National Assembly) and revolutionary institutions (Supreme Council of the Revolution) within an authoritarian political order. Only parties loyal to the regime were allowed to organize within the 'National Front for the Defense of the Revolution' (*Front National pour la Défense de la Révolution—*

FNDR) dominated by Ratsiraka's 'Avantgarde of the Malagasy Revolution' (*Avantgarde de la Révolution Malgache*—AREMA). In at best semi-competitive elections Rastiraka was confirmed as President in 1982 and 1989 and AREMA held hegemonic majorities in the National Assembly. Membership of the regime party stemmed mainly from the former PSD. With regard to development policies the approach of the early 1970s was continued with emphasis on the rural sector and efforts to revitalize traditional structures of communal organization (*Fokonolona*).

In 1990 and 1991 the severe economic crisis which had plagued Madagascar since the early 1980s as well as general tendencies of political change in Africa led to an opening up of the regime that eventually resulted in a negotiated democratic transition. In 1990 the government and opposition forces which had left the FNDR and allied under the label 'Committee of the Living Forces' (*Comité des Forces Vives*—CFV) agreed to build a transitional government and to suspend the official organs of the Second Republic. A new democratic constitution, providing for a semi-presidential system of government, was elaborated and approved in a referendum in August 1992. The presidential elections held in February 1993 completed the transition when opposition leader Albert Zafy won in the second round against Ratsiraka. However, internal heterogeneity of the *Forces Vives* made it difficult to form a stable governing majority. In 1995 intense conflicts between the President and the Prime Minister were resolved through a referendum called by Zafy in order to enhance his constitutional powers. His proposal was approved that the President should be allowed to choose the Prime Minister out of three candidates presented to him by the National Assembly. In 1996 Zafy was impeached by a two-thirds vote of the National Assembly and had to resign. In the following (regular) presidential elections he ran again but was defeated by former dictator Ratsiraka. New parliamentary elections constitutionally should have taken place in June 1997 but due to organizational problems (issuance of obligatory identity cards to all voters) the High Constitutional Court extended the term of representatives. The elections were finally held in May 1998. The successor organization of AREMA, Ratsiraka's *Avantgarde pour le Redressement Economique et Social* (ARES), emerged as the strongest party but failed to get an absolute majority.

The new democracy still faces many problems at the organizational level of the party system as well as at the level of elite behavior. However, on various occasions since 1993 severe political conflicts were resolved within the established institutional framework. In this respect, the High Constitutional Court has several times played a major role.

1.2 Evolution of Electoral Provisions

Universal suffrage was introduced under colonial rule, that is, when Madagascar was a French *Territoire d'Outre-Mer*. The *Loi Cadre* of 1956 was applied for the first time in the provincial elections (elections to provincial assemblies) of 1957. Following the rules established by the *Loi Cadre* the independence constitution of 29 April 1959 granted active suffrage to all Malagasy citizens elder than 21 years. In 1972 the voting age was reduced to 18.

With respect to passive suffrage, candidates for the National Assembly had to be at least 25 years old and to be able to speak one of the two official languages. The usual norms of ineligibility were laid down in the Electoral Law of 1959 (Art.7).

The President was elected indirectly by an electoral college until 1962. Since then he has been elected directly under the absolute majority system for a period of seven years. Candidates for presidency had to be at least 40 years old.

After independence, members of the National Assembly were directly elected on closed party lists in multi-member constituencies built by the provinces. Towns bigger than 50,000 inhabitants built separate constituencies. The number of seats per constituency depended on the population size of the respective province (one MP for every 50,000 inhabitants with a residual of 30,000). If one party list got more than 55% of the valid votes, the party gained all the seats of the constituency; in the other cases seats were distributed proportionally between parties that had surpassed the electoral threshold of 5% at the constituency level.

In 1973 the transitional government built a 'Popular National Council for Development' (*Conseil National Populaire de Développement* CNPD) as a quasi-parliamentarian institution that did not, however, perform any significant decisional or control functions. Of the 162 members of the CNDP 52 were directly elected, the others being in part indirectly elected and in part designated by the President.

In the Second Republic, from 1975 onwards, candidacy for both presidential and parliamentary elections was restricted to parties organized within the FNDR which meant a strong limitation of political pluralism. In the parliamentary elections of 1977 only a single FNDR list was presented to the electorate, which could only be approved or disapproved; in 1983 and 1989 slightly more possibilities for political competition were allowed without putting the dominant position of the regime party AREMA at any risk. The number of seats in the National Assembly varied from 137 in 1977 to 134 in 1983 and 138 in 1989.

The first parliamentary elections in the Third Republic of 1993 took place under proportional representation with closed party lists in 57 multi-member constituencies of varying size (dependent on the number of inhabitants of the respective constituency); for the allocation of seats the Hare quota with the largest remainder was applied.

The Constitution of 1992 (Art. 77) originally foresaw a Senate as an organ of functional and regional representation, whose members would have been in part appointed by the President and in part indirectly elected by regional assemblies. However, the Senate was never constituted and the respective provisions of the constitution were canceled by the referendum of 1998.

1.3 Current Electoral Provisions

Sources: Constitution of the Republic of Madagascar of 19 August 1992 (amended 1995 and 1998); electoral law not available.

Suffrage: The principles of universal, equal, direct and secret suffrage are applied. All Malagasy citizens with a minimum age of 18 years, who are registered as voters and live in the country are entitled to vote. Voter registration is compulsory.

Elected national institutions: President of the Republic *(Ray amandreny)* for a term of five years (one immediate re-election being allowed); 150 members (*deputés)* of the National Assembly *(Antenimieram Pirenena)* for a term of four years.

Nomination of candidates
- *presidential elections*: Candidates must have a minimum age of 40 years. A President who wants to run again for the office has to resign one day before the beginning of the electoral campaign (that is, 21 days before the elections) in order to present himself as a candidate.
- *parliamentary elections*: Candidates must have a minimum age of 21 years. Naturalized citizens can be parliamentary candidates only 10 years after having achieved citizen status. The right to run as a candidate is restricted to those who never have been condemned of a crime or a

penalty and have paid all due taxes and fees regularly for at least four consecutive years before the elections.

Electoral system
- *presidential elections*: Absolute majority system. If in the first round no candidate receives more than 50% of the valid votes cast a second round is held within 30 days. In this round only the two most voted candidates of the first round can run.
- *parliamentary elections*: In the 1998 parliamentary elections 82 of the 150 seats in the National Assembly were allocated in single-member districts by plurality. The other 78 seats were allocated in two-member districts under a party list system with Hare quota and the rule of the highest average (binominal system).

1.4 Comment on the Electoral Statistics

Most of the statistical data presented in the following sections are based on the official publications of electoral results in the *Journal Officiel de la République de Madagascar* (JORM). Lack of data is due to the fact that the results have not been published for all elections. An attempt has been made to fill gaps and eliminate inconsistencies, as far as possible, by reference to secondary literature listed in the bibliography. For the 1995 referendum the official results announced by the Supreme Constitutional Court as published by *Marchés Tropicaux et Méditerranéens* are reported.

2. Tables

2.1 Dates of National Elections, Referendums and Coups d'Etat

Year	Presidential elections	Parliamentary elections	Elections for Constitutional Assembly	Referendums	Coups d'état
1960		04/09			
1965	30/03	08/08			
1970		04/09			
1972	30/01			08/10	18/05[a]
1975				21/12	
1977		30/06			
1982	07/10				
1983		28/08			
1989	06/04	06/04			
1992	25/11 (1st)			19/08	
1993	10/02 (2nd)	16/06			
1995				17/09	
1996	03/11 (1st) 24/12 (2nd)				
1998		17/05		15/03	

[a] The transfer of power from Prime Minister Tsiranana to General Ramanantsoa did not follow constitutional rules although Tsiranana was not ousted by a military coup.

2.2 Electoral Body 1960–1998

Year[a]	Type of election[b]	Population	Registered voters		Votes cast		
			Total number	% pop.	Total number	% reg. voters	% pop.
1960	NA	5,393,000	2,412,828	44.7	1,890,541	78.4	35.1
1965	NA	6,420,000	2,610,930	40.7	2,465,536	94.4	38.4
1970	NA	6,750,000	2,756,978	40.8	2,612,956	94.8	38.7
1972	Ref	7,198,640	3,448,203	47.9	2,906,469	84.3	40.4
1975	Ref	7,400,000	3,698,541	50.0	3,394,115	91.8	45.9
1977	NA	8,471,814	—	—	—	—	—
1982	Pr	9,607,000[c]	4,749,054	49.4	4,119,596	86.7	42.8
1983	NA	9,851,000[c]	4,838,279	49.1	3,519,997	72.7	35.7
1989	Pr	11,151,000[c]	5,823,778	52.2	4,719,618	81.0	42.3
1989	NA	11,151,000[c]	5,723,927	51.3	4,191,477	73.2	37.6
1992	Ref	12,028,000	5,467,031	45.5	3,554,596	65.0	29.6
1992	Pr (1st)	12,028,000[c]	6,054,966	50.3	4,506,993	74.4	37.5
1993	Pr (2nd)	12,421,000	6,282,564	50.6	4,302,663	68.5	34.6
1993	NA	12,421,000	6,317,974	50.9	3,454,847	54.7	27.8
1995	Ref	13,101,000[c]	5,894,982	45.0	3,854,982	65.4	29.4
1996	Pr (1st)	13,397,000[c]	6,453,612	48.2	3,769,623	58.4	28.1
1996	Pr (2nd)	13,397,000[c]	6,667,192	49.8	3,310,902	49.7	24.7
1998	NA	14,462,500[c]	5,234,198	36.2	3,147,368	60.1	21.8

[a] For the referendum of 1998 data have not been available yet.
[b] NA = National Assembly; Pr = President; Ref = Referendum.
[c] Estimation.

2.3 Abbreviations

AKFM	Antokon'ny Kongresy Fahaleovantenan'i Madagasikara (Parti du Congrès de l'Indépendance de Madagascar)
AKFM-F	Antokon'ny Kongresin'ny Faaleovantenan'ni—Fanavaozana (Parti du Congrès de Madagascar—Renouveau)
AKFM-KDRSM	Parti du Congrès de Madagascar—Socialisme Scientifique
AREMA	Avantgarde de la Révolution Malgache
ARES[a]	Avantgarde pour le Redressement Economique et Social
AVI	Asa Vita Ifampitsanara
CFV	Comité des Forces Vives
CSDDM	Comité pour le Support de Démocratie et Développement au Madagascar
FAMIMA	Faritra Miara-Mamindra (Association des Malgaches Unifié)

GRAD-Iloafo	Groupe de Réflexion et d'Action pour le Développement de Madagascar
LEADER-Fanilo	Libéralisme Economique et Action Démocratique pour la Reconstruction Nationale
MONIMA / KM	Mouvement pour l'Indépendance de Madagascar/ Ka Miviombio
PMDM	Parti Militant pour le Développement de Madagascar
PSD	Parti Social Démocrate
RNM	Rassemblée Nationale de Madagascar
RPSD	Rassemblement pour le Socialisme et la Démocratie
UDSM	Union des Démocrates Sociaux Malgaches
UNDD	Union Nationale pour le Développement et la Démocratie
UNDD-R	Union Nationale pour le Développement et la Démocratie—Rasalama
VITM	Vonjy Iray Tsy Mivaky—Rassemblement des Modérés

General note: With regard the following abbreviations, full party names can not be given: AFFA, Cartel HVR, GLM, MFM/MFT, MM/HVR, PRM, RCM, UDECMA/KMTP.
[a] Successor organization of AREMA.
[b] Alliance of several parties in opposition to the Ratsiraka regime such as Rasalama, Fihaonana, AKFM-F, Farimbona, UNDD, CSDDM, Vatomizana, GRAD-Iloafo.

2.4 Electoral Participation of Parties and Alliances 1960–1998

Party / Alliance	Years	Elections contested	
		Presidential	Parliamentary
AKFM	1960, 1965, 1970, 1977	0	4
PSD	1960, 1965, 1970, 1977	2	3
RCM	1960	0	1
RNM	1960	0	1
UDSM	1960, 1983	1	1
AREMA / ARES	1977, 1983, 1989, 1993, 1996, 1998	4	5
Vonjy	1977	0	1
UDECMA / KMTP	1977	0	1
AKFM / KDRSM	1983, 1989, 1993, 1998	—	4
M(K)FM / MFT	1983, 1989, 1993, 1998	1	4
MONIMA / KM	1983, 1989	1	2
VITM	1983, 1989, 1993	3	3
AKFM-F	1989, 1993, 1998	—	3
Accord	1993	0	1
Cartel HVR	1993	0	1
CFV	1993	1	0
CSDDM	1993	0	1
FAMIMA	1993	0	1
FARIMBONA	1993	0	1

Party / Alliance	Years	Elections contested	
		Presidential	Parliamentary
Fihaonana	1993, 1998	—	2
Filongoa	1993	—	1
Fivoarana	1993	0	1
Forces Vives Rasalama	1993	—	1
GLM	1993	0	1
GRAD-Iloafo	1993, 1998	0	2
Leader Fanilo	1993, 1998	0	2
Mahaolona	1993	—	1
MM / HVR	1993	—	1
PMDM	1993	0	1
PRM	1993	0	1
PRS	1993	0	1
PSD-RPSD	1993, 1998	—	2
Tsy miankina amin'Antoko	1993	—	1
UNDD	1993, 1996	2	1
UNDD-R	1993	—	1
Vatomizana	1993	0	1
AFFA	1998	0	1
AVI	1998	0	1

2.5 Referendums

Year	1972[a]		1975[b]	
	Total number	%	Total number	%
Registered voters	3,448,203	–	3,698,541	–
Votes cast	2,906,469	84.3	3,394,115	91.8
Invalid votes	18,567	0.6	32,101	0.9
Valid votes	2,887,902	99.4	3,362,014	99.1
Yes	2,784,687	96.4	3,213,146	95.6
No	103,215	3.6	148,868	4.4

[a] Approval of a 'project of constitutional law' and confirmation of General Ramanantsoa as President for a term of five years under special conditions with wide ranging executive and legislative powers.

[b] Approval of the Charter of the Socialist Republic ('Red Book') and confirmation of Didier Ratsiraka as President for a seven-year term.

Year	1992[a]		1995[b]	
	Total number	%	Total number	%
Registered voters	5,467,031	–	5,894,982	–
Votes cast	3,554,596	65.0	3,854,982[c]	65.4
Invalid votes	348,470	9.8	489,128	12.7
Valid votes	3,206,126	90.2	3,365,665[d]	87.3
Yes	2,330,641	72.7	2,139,378	63.6
No	875,485	27.3	1,226,286	36.4

[a] Approval of the new constitution.
[b] Approval of several suggestions of President Zafy to amend the constitution; most importantly the President's prerogatives with regard to the appointment of the Prime Minister were enhanced.
[c] Official figure. Invalid votes and valid votes add up to 3,854,793.
[d] Official figure. Yes and No votes add up to 3,365,664.

For the referendum of 1998 detailed data have not been available yet.

2.6 Elections for Constitutional Assembly

Elections for Constitutional Assembly have not been held.

2.7 Parliamentary Elections

Year	1960		1965	
	Total number	%	Total number	%
Registered voters	2,444,269	–	2,610,930	–
Votes cast	1,893,469	77.5	2,465,536	94.4
Invalid votes	16,883	0.9	33,649	1.4
Valid votes[a]	1,876,586	99.1	2,431,887	98.6
PSD	1,156,684	61.6	2,277,055	93.6
AKFM	220,640	10.7	68,794	2.8
Others	499,298	26.6	61,775	2.5

[a] The numbers given correspond to the subtraction of invalid votes from votes cast. This result does not correspond to the sum of party votes. Therefore the percentages of party votes given do not add up to 100.

Year	1970 Total number	%	1977[a] Total number	%
Registered voters	2,756,978	–	—	—
Votes cast	2,612,956	94.8	—	—
Invalid votes	11,528	0.4	—	—
Valid votes	2,601,428	99.6	—	—
PSD	2,413,421	92.8	—	—
AKFM	186,626	7.2	—	—
Others	3,381	0.0	—	—

[a] Results of the 1977 elections were not published.

Year	1983 Total number	%	1989 Total number	%
Registered voters	4,838,279	–	5,723,927	–
Votes cast	3,519,997	72.7	4,191,477	73.2
Invalid votes	87,734	2.5	114,628	2.7
Valid votes	3,432,263	97.5	4,076,849	97.3
AREMA	2,239,770	65.2	227,378	66.9
VITM	425,996	12.4	382,242	6.2
MFM/MFT	372,847	10.9	455,922	13.3
AKFM-KDRSM	300,809	8.8	251,366	6.2
Others	140,030	4.1	259,935	6.4

For the 1993 and 1998 parliamentary elections detailed data have not been available yet.

2.8 Composition of Parliament 1960–1998

Year	1960 Seats	%	1965 Seats	%	1970 Seats	%	1977 Seats	%
	127	100	107	100	107	100	137	100
PSD	76	59.8	104	97.2	104	97.2	–	–
AKFM	9	7.1	3	2.8	3	2.8	16	11.7
RNM	5	3.9	–	–	–	–	–	–
RCM	3	2.4	–	–	–	–	–	–
UDSM	1	0.8	–	–	–	–	–	–
AREMA	–	–	–	–	–	–	112	81.8
VONJY	–	–	–	–	–	–	7	5.1
UDECMA/KMTP	–	–	–	–	–	–	2	1.5
Others	33	26.0	–	–	–	–	–	–

Year	1983 Seats	%	1989 Seats	%	1993 Seats	%	1998 Seats	%
	134	100	136	100	138	100	150	100
AKFM-F	–	–	3	2.2	5	3.6	3	2.0
AKFM-KDRSM	8	5.9	3	2.2	–	–	–	–
AREMA / ARES	115	85.8	118	86.8	–	–	63	42.0
VITM	6	4.5	4	2.9	2	1.4	–	–
MFM / MFT	3	2.2	7	5.1	15	10.9	3	2.0
MONIMA / KM	2	1.5	1	0.7	–	–	–	–
Cartel HVR	–	–	–	–	47	34.1	–	–
Leader Fanilo	–	–	–	–	14	10.1	16	10.7
FAMIMA	–	–	–	–	11	8.0	–	–
PSD-RPSD	–	–	–	–	8	5.8	11	7.3
UNDD-R	–	–	–	–	6	4.3	–	–
Accord	–	–	–	–	2	1.4	–	–
CSDDM	–	–	–	–	2	1.4	–	–
Farimbona	–	–	–	–	2	1.4	–	–
Fihaonana	–	–	–	–	2	1.4	1	0.6
Fivoarana	–	–	–	–	2	1.4	–	–
UNDD	–	–	–	–	2	1.4	–	–
Filongoa	–	–	–	–	1	0.7	–	–
GRAD Iloafo	–	–	–	–	1	0.7	1	0.6
GLM	–	–	–	–	1	0.7	–	–
Maha olona	–	–	–	–	1	0.7	–	–
MM / HVR	–	–	–	–	1	0.7	–	–
PRM	–	–	–	–	1	0.7	–	–
Tsy miankina amin'Antoko	–	–	–	–	1	0.7	–	–
Vatomizana	–	–	–	–	1	0.7	–	–
AVI	–	–	–	–	–	–	14	9.3
AFFA	–	–	–	–	–	–	6	4.0
Others / Independents	–	–	–	–	4	2.9	32	21.3

2.9 Presidential Elections 1965–1996

The presidential elections of 1965 and 1972 were not competitive. Philibert Tsiranana (PSD) was the only candidate and according to official statements was elected with 97.8% and 99.7% respectively. Detailed results are not available. For data on voter registration and participation see table 2.2.

1982	Total number	%
Registered voters	4,749,054	49.4
Votes cast	4,119,596	86.7
Invalid votes	137,571	3.4
Valid votes	3,982,025	96.6
Jaona Monja (—)	789,869	19.8
Didier Ratsiraka (AREMA)	3,192,156	80.2

1989	Total number	%
Registered voters	5,823,778	52.2
Votes cast	4,719,618	81.0
Invalid votes	108,994	2.3
Valid votes	4,610,624	97.7
Didier Ratsiraka (AREMA)	2,891,333	62.7
Manadafy Rakotonirina (MFM/MFT)	891,161	19.3
Marojama Jerome Razanabahiny (VITM)	688,345	14.9
Jaona Monja (MONIMA-KM)	139,735	3.0

1992 (first round)[a]	Total number	%
Registered voters	6,054,966	50.3
Votes cast	4,506,993	74.4
Invalid votes	99,595	2.2
Valid votes	4,407,398	97.8
Albert Zafy (CFV)	2,024,841	45.9
Didier Ratsiraka (AREMA)	1,260,193	28.6
Manandafy Rakotonirina	444,288	10.1
Evariste Marson	205,204	4.7
Ruffine Tsirana	152,952	3.5
Jacques Rabemananjara	124,901	2.8
Tovonanahary Rabetsitonta	96,445	2.2
R. Andriamanalina	98,574	2.2

[a] Available sources do not indicate the party labels for all candidates.

1993 (second round)	Total number	%
Registered voters	6,282,564	50.6
Votes cast	4,302,663	68.5
Invalid votes	157,319	3.6
Valid votes	4,145,344	96.4
Albert Zafy (CFV)	2,766,704	66.7
Didier Ratsiraka (AREMA)	1,378,640	33.3

1996 (first round)[a]	Total number	%
Registered voters	6,453,612	–
Votes cast	3,769,623	58.4
Invalid votes	159,834	4.2
Valid votes	3,609,789	95.8
Didier Ratsiraka (ARES)	1,321,388	36.6
Albert Zafy (UNDD)	844,459	23.4
Herizo Razafimahelo	546,211	15.1
Norbert L. Ratsirahonana	365,896	10.1
Richard Andriamanjato	178,352	4.9
Jean E. Voninahitsy	100,652	2.8
Alain Ramaroson	55,930	1.6
Guy W. Razanamasy	42,873	1.2
Marojama J. Razanabahiny	32,812	0.9
Tovonanahary Rabetsitonta	32,518	0.9
Philippe Rakotovao	28,777	0.8
Evariste Vazaha	16,071	0.5
Albert Andriamanana	15,202	0.4
Charles Ramantsoa	15,160	0.4
Désiré Rakotoarijoana	13,488	0.3

[a] Unfortunately available sources do not indicate the party labels for all candidates.

1996 (second round)	Total number	%
Registered voters	6,667,192	–
Votes cast	3,310,902	49.7
Invalid votes	139,444	4.2
Valid votes	3,171,458	95.8
Didier Ratsiraka (ARES)	1,608,321	50.7
Albert Zafy (UNDD)	1,563,137	49.3

2.10 List of Power Holders 1960–1998

Head of State	Years	Remarks
Philibert Tsiranana	1961–1972	Constitutionally elected by the National Assembly; re-elected in direct elections in 1965 and 1972; resigned due to popular unrest born out of the student movement of 1972 on 18/05/1972.
Gabriel Ramanantsoa	1972–1975	Military; established a transitional government with extraordinarily executive and legislative powers which was foreseen to last five years; resigned on 05/02/1975.

Richard Ratsimandrava	1975	Military; assassinated on 11/02/1975.
Military Council ('Comité National')	1975	Transitional Government.
Didier Ratsiraka	1975–1993	Military and former Minister of External Affairs: took office on 15/06/1997; confirmed as Head of State in a referendum held in 1975; twice re-elected in semi-competitive elections.
Albert Zafy	1993–1996	Constitutionally elected; took office on 27/03/1993; after a parliamentary impeachment approved by the Constitutional Court he had to resign on 05/09/1996.
Norbert Ratsirahonana	1996–1997	The Prime Minister was appointed as transitional President after Zafy's impeachment.
Didier Ratsiraka	1997–	Constitutionally elected; took office on 27/02/1997.

Head of Government	Years	Remarks
Francisque Ravony	1993–1995	Appointed on 09/08/1993; resigned on 13/10/1995 after a referendum had confirmed Zafy's position in the institutional conflict between President and Prime Minister/ Parliament.
Emmanuel Rakotovahiny	1995–1996	Appointed on 30/10/1995; submitted to a parliamentary motion of censure in May 1996.
Norbert Ratsirahonana	1996–1997	Appointed on 28/05/1996; before, Ratsirahona had been chief of the High Constitutional Court.
Pascal Rakotomavo	1997–1998	Appointed on 27/02/1997; no party affiliation.
Tantely Andrianarivo	1998–	Appointed on 23/07/1998.

3. Bibliography

3.1. Official sources

'Constitution de la République Malgache de 29/04/1959'. *Journal Officiel de la République Malgache (JORM)*, 29/04/1959, 54–71.

'Constitutional Amendment of 28/06/1960'. *JORM*, 18/06/1960.

'Loi organique No. 4 de 09/06/1959 (Election of the President)'. *JORM*, 13/06/1959, 1353.

'Loi organique No. 5 de 09/01/1959 (Election of the National Assembly)'. *JORM*, 13/06/1959, 1354.
'Code Electoral, Ordonnance No. 92-041', 05/10/1993.
'Ordonnance No. 93-007', modified by 'Ordonnance No 93-915', 23/04/1993 and by 'Ordonnance NO. 93-020', 30/04/1993 (Election of the National Assembly).

3.2 Books, Articles and Electoral Reports

Allen, P. M. (1995). *Madagascar: Conflicts of Authority in the Great Island*. Boulder, Col.: Westview Press.
Andriambelomiadana, R. (1992). *Liberalisme et développement à Madagascar*. Antananarivo: Foi et justice.
Archer, R. (1976). *Madagascar depuis 1972: la marche d'une revolution*. Paris: L'Harmattan.
Backler, D., Belanger, S., Kraemer, C., and Pharaon, L. (1992). *A Pre-Election Assessment Report*. Washington, D.C.: IFES.
Brown, M. (1995). *A History of Madagascar*. Cambridge: Damien Tunacliffe.
Cadoux, C. (1969). *La République malgache*. Paris: Berger-Levrault.
Chaigneau, P. (1985). *Rivalités politiques et socialisme à Madagascar*. Paris: CHEAM.
Covell, M. (1987). *Madagascar: Politics, Economics and Society*. London/New York: Pinter.
Deleris, F. (1986). *Ratsiraka: socialisme et misère à Madagascar*. Paris: L'Harmattan.
Deschamps, H. (1972). *Histoire de Madagscar* (4th edn.). Paris.
Kottak, C. P. (1986). *Madagascar: Society and History*. Durham, NC: Carolina Academic Press.
Kuhn, W. S. III, Massicotte, L., and Owen, B. (1992). *Training National Election Observer Trainers: Report on Referendum and Post Referendum Experiences*. Washington, D.C.: International Foundation for Electoral Systems.
Massiot, M. (1967). *Les institutions politiques et administratives de la République malgache*. Tananarive.
Raison, J. P. (1993). 'Une esquisse de géographie électorale malgache'. *Politique Africaine*, 52: 67–75.
Raison-Jourde, F. (1993). 'Une transition achevée ou amorcée?'. *Politique Africaine,* 52: 6–18.
Rakontrondrabe, D. T. (1993). 'Beyond the Ethnic Group: Ethnic Groups, Nation State and Democracy in Madagascar'. *Transformation*, 22.

Ramamonjisoa, S. (1993). 'Empowerment of Women and Democracy in Madagscar'. *Review of African Political Economy*, 58: 118–123.

Randrianarisoa, P. (1991). *Madagascar. D'une république à l'autre*. Fandriana, Madagascar.

Ravaloson, J. (1994). *Transition démocratique à Madagascar*. Paris: L'Harmattan.

Revel, E. (1994). *Madagascar: L'île rouge: les remords d'un président déchu, Didier Ratsiraka, 1976–1993*. Paris: Editions Balland.

Sick, W.-D. (1979). *Madagaskar. Tropisches Entwicklungsland zwischen den Kontinenten*. Darmstadt: Wissenschaftliche Buchgesellschaft.

Wachendorfer, A. (1978), 'Madagaskar', in D. Sternberger, B. Vogel, D. Nohlen and K. Landfried (eds.), *Die Wahl der Parlamente und anderer Staatsorgane. Band II: Politische Organisation und Repräsentation in Afrika*, by Franz Nuscheler, Klaus Ziemer *et al.*, Berlin/ New York: Walter de Gruyter, 1153–1196.

MALAWI

by Heiko Meinhardt

1. Introduction

1.1 Historical Overview

Malawi, the former British Protectorate Nyasaland, achieved independence on 6 July 1964. The Western trained medical practitioner Dr Hastings Kamuzu Banda, since 1960 Life President of the Malawi Congress Party (MCP), was appointed Prime Minister on 1 February 1963 after Malawi gained self-governance. After independence Malawi remained a member of the Commonwealth with the British Queen as Head of State, represented by the British Governor Glyn Jones. Due to the landslide victory of the MCP in the 1961 elections to the Legislative Council, Malawi was a *de facto* one-party state when it gained independence. The elections to the unicameral National Assembly scheduled for May 1964 did not take place because only the MCP had nominated candidates which were all elected unopposed.

On 6 July 1966 Malawi became a Republic within the Commonwealth, and Parliament nominated Banda unanimously as President. In the republican constitution the one-party system was established. The President who also was Head of Government and Commander-in-Chief of the armed forces had a wide range of constitutional powers including the right to dissolve Parliament at any time. Banda ruled the state in a most autocratic way. This system of personal rule culminated in the fact that Banda was elected life President by acclamation at the MCP Convention in 1970 and was sworn in on 6 July 1971. Parliamentary elections in 1971 and 1976 did not take place. Instead Banda in his capacity as President of the MCP nominated one candidate for each constituency who was automatically elected unopposed. In the parliamentary elections of 1978, 1983, 1987 and 1992 a limited contest took place. In most of the constituencies, Banda nominated from the names proposed by the local party machinery between two and five candidates—all members of the MCP—while in other constituencies only one candidate or in a few cases no one at all was nominated. Unpopular ministers often returned unopposed in order to avoid the embarrassment of a defeat although, for example, in the 1992 elections one defeated minister and four deputy ministers were appointed as nominated Members of Parliament by the President. Campaigning was prohibited. The fact that all candidates were handpicked made manipulations or rigging in the elections unnecessary.

From 1992 on Banda's regime came under considerable pressure from western donors to introduce democratic reforms and to improve the disastrous human rights situation. In order to legitimize the one-party system, Banda called for a referendum on the question of whether a multi-party system of government should be introduced (14 June 1993). After the for him unexpected results—two thirds of the voters favored the multi-party system—Banda legalized political parties other than the MCP and paved the way for major constitutional reforms including the abolition of the life presidency. In the first democratically organized competitive presidential and parliamentary elections on 17 May 1994, the electorate voted along ethnic–regional lines. While Banda and the MCP dominated the Central Region (the residence of the Chewa tribe which Banda himself belongs to), the UDF candidate Bakili Muluzi won most parts of the southern region, the home of the Yao, and Chakufwa Chihana won the entire but thinly populated northern region, the main settlement area of the Tumbuka. Banda was defeated in the elections which were by and large free and fair.

Since 21 May 1994 Malawi has been ruled by Bakili Muluzi as elected executive President. Since the UDF failed to win a majority of seats in Parliament, the government needs to cooperate with members of other parties. A democratic constitution, which is based on the principle of checks and balances and in which the human and basic freedom rights are guaranteed, was passed by the old one-party Parliament on 16 May 1994 as a provisional constitution and was adopted with some minor changes by the democratically elected Parliament and came into effect on 17 May 1995.

1.2 Evolution of Electoral Provisions

In the 1961 elections to the Legislative Council, voters were bound to meet certain preconditions. The voters on the lower roll had to meet some income, wealth or tax requirements while the qualifications for the higher roll (income, wealth, educational standards) were stricter. Under these circumstances only a few people qualified to vote.

Prior to the achievement of independence the franchise was extended to all Malawian citizens over 21 years of age with continuous residence in the country for two years. A candidate in the parliamentary elections had to be 25 years of age or over while for a presidential candidate a minimum age of 40 years was required. Every candidate for the parliamentary elections had to be a member of the MCP and had to be approved by the party president himself. Each registered voter was entitled to vote by secret ballot. The candidates were elected in single-member constituencies. A relative majority of valid votes was sufficient for the victory (plurality system).

The special representation for the European minority in the country (in the 1964 elections three seats and since 1966 five seats were reserved for their representatives) was abolished in 1973.

At the end of 1992 Parliament amended the constitution in order to allow for the implementation of referendums. The right to call for a referendum was a privilege of the President. He was, however, not bound by the outcome of the poll.

1.3 Current Electoral Provisions

Sources: Constitution of the Republic of Malawi (1994); Parliamentary and Presidential Elections Act (No. 31 of 1993).

Elected National Institutions: President of the Republic and his running mate for the office of first Vice-President and the National Assembly (177 elected members, no nominated members). Regular term of office: five years respectively. Presidential and parliamentary elections are carried out on the same day but with different votes and on different ballot papers. A person shall not hold the presidency for more than two consecutive terms.

In case of death, resignation or any other case of vacancy of office of the President, the first Vice-President will serve as President until the end of the regular term. The President has the right to appoint at any time a second Vice-President if he wishes to. The post of second Vice-President can only be filled by a member of a political party other than the party to which the President belongs. Vacancies in the National Assembly are filled through by-elections. The establishment of a Senate as a second chamber of Parliament has been postponed until 1999.

Suffrage: Universal, equal, direct and secret suffrage is applied. Every citizen of Malawi residing in Malawi and having been ordinarily resident in Malawi for seven years and who shall have attained on or before polling day the age of 18 years qualifies as a voter.

Nomination of candidates
- *presidential elections*: Every citizen of Malawi by birth or descent who has attained the age of 35 years, who is not a serving member of the defense forces or police force and meets the requirements for parliamentary candidates (see below) can stand in presidential elections. The candidate can either stand for a political party or as an independent whose nomination is supported by at least 10 registered voters in each of the 24 districts. Each candidate has to deposit a certain amount fixed by the electoral commission (in 1994: Kwacha 5,000 = US$ 568) which is refundable if the candidate gains at least 5% of the valid votes cast.
- *parliamentary elections*: Every Malawian citizen who has attained the age of 21 years is eligible for candidature as Member of Parliament if he or she is a registered voter and able to read and speak English. No person shall be qualified as a candidate who belongs to and is serving in the armed forces or police force, or who has, within the last seven years, been convicted by a competent court of a crime involving dishonesty or moral turpitude or who had gone bankrupt. This last requirement was highly disputed between the political parties during the drafting of the electoral law because of the fact that the presidential candidate of UDF, the serving President Bakili Muluzi was once convicted in a theft case. However, the seven-year provision, which was in the beginning disputed by the other political parties, saved him from disqualification. A candidate can stand either for a political party or as an independent. His nomination has to be supported by 10 voters in the respective constituency. The candidate has to deposit a certain amount of money (1994: Kwacha 250 = US$ 28) which is refundable if he gains at least 5% of the valid votes cast. The seat of a Member of Parliament who crosses the floor to another political party is to be declared vacant.

Electoral system
- *presidential elections*: Plurality system.
- *parliamentary elections*: Plurality system in 177 single-member constituencies.

1.4 Comment on the Electoral Statistics

The availability of data for the 1993 referendum and 1994 presidential and parliamentary elections is excellent. The data are based on official sources. The documentation of the parliamentary elections in the one-party system is incomplete because the figures were treated as a secret. The information given is based on confidential official sources. For the 1978 elections no figures at all were available. Most of the official statistical material got lost after the respective elections. The documentation of the 1961 elections is quite fair although information on the votes cast and valid votes is not available. The data are based on official sources and secondary literature. For the purpose of this book data based on official sources were converted using the standard of the data handbook.

2. Tables

2.1 Dates of National Elections, Referendums and Coups d'Etat

Year	Presidential elections	Parliamentary elections[a]	Elections for Constitutional Assembly	Referendums	Coups d'état
1961		15/08			
1964		28/04			
1971		17/04			
1976		22/05			
1978		29/06			
1983		27–28/06			
1987		27–28/05			
1992		26/06			
1993				14/06	
1994	17/05	17/05			

[a] In the elections of 1964, 1971 and 1976 there was only one candidate in each constituency which made voting unnecessary. In 1978, 1983, 1978 and 1992 voters had a choice between up to five candidates, all of them members of the single party MCP.

2.2 Electoral Body 1961–1994

Year[a]	Type of election[b]	Population	Registered voters		Votes cast		
			Total number	% pop.	Total number	% reg. voters	% pop.
1961	Pa	2,900,000	80,108[c]	2.8	76,263[d]	95.2	2.6
1983	Pa	6,600,000	3,278,907	49.7	—	—	—
1987	Pa	7,988,500	3,278,907[e]	41.0	—	—	—
1992	Pa	9,280,000	2,203,103	23.7	859,318	39.0	9.3
1993	Ref	9,500,000	4,699,526[f]	49.5	3,153,448	67.1	33.2
1994	Pr	9,500,000	3,775,256	39.7	3,040,665	80.5	32.0
1994	Pa	9,500,000	3,775,256	39.7	3,004,835	79.6	31.6

[a] The elections of 1964, 1971 and 1976 were left out because registration and voting did not take place. For 1978 no figures are available.

[b] Pa = Parliament; Pr = President; Ref = Referendum.

[c] The total number of registered voters was 111,477 but in five constituencies voting did not take place since there was a single candidate.

[d] Valid votes.

[e] The official figures of registered voters remained unchanged in the 1987 elections.

[f] This official number of registered voters is exaggerated due to many cases of double registration. The real number should be about 3.8 million.

2.3 Abbreviations

AFORD	Alliance for Democracy
CLP	Congress Liberation Party
CSR	Congress for the Second Republic of Malawi
MCP	Malawi Congress Party
MDP	Malawi Democratic Party
MDU	Malawi Democratic Union
MNDP	Malawi National Democratic Party
UDF	United Democratic Front
UFMD	United Front for Multiparty Democracy
UFP	United Federal Party

2.4 Electoral Participation of Parties and Alliances 1961–1994

Party / Alliance	Years	Elections contested	
		Presidential	Parliamentary
CLP	1961	0	1
MCP	1961, 1964, 1971, 1976, 1978, 1983, 1987, 1992, 1994	1	9[a]
UFP	1961	0	1
AFORD	1994	1	1
CSR	1994	0	1
MDP	1994	1	1
MDU	1994	0	1
MNDP	1994	0	1
UDF	1994	1	1
UFMD	1994	0	1

[a] Including seven elections in the one-party system (1964–1992).

2.5 Referendum 1993

Year	1993[a]	
	Total number	%
Registered voters	4,699,526	–
Votes cast	3,153,448	67.1
Invalid votes	70,979	2.3
Valid votes	3,082,469	97.7
Yes (multi-party system)	1,993,996	64.7
No (one-party system)	1,088,473	35.3

[a] Referendum on the question of whether a multi-party system should be introduced or the one-party system should remain.

2.5 a) Referendum 1993: Regional Distribution of Votes

District	Registered voters	Votes cast	Invalid votes	Valid votes	Multi-party system	One-party system
North	629,339	444,196	4,526	439,670	392,569	47,101
Chitipa	58,404	41,073	305	40,768	37,165	3,603
Karonga	110,603	65,376	539	64,837	61,038	3,799
Rumphi	59,300	51,342	712	50,630	43,943	6,687
Nkhata Bay	129,514	60,211	822	59,389	54,990	4,399
Mzimba	271,518	226,194	2,148	224,046	195,433	28,613
Central	1,833,820	1,270,881	38,436	1,232,445	400,032	832,413
Kasungu	232,276	179,542	4,982	174,560	48,960	125,600
Nkhotakota	133,866	79,336	2,856	76,480	35,965	40,515
Ntchisi	64,204	52,053	883	51,170	11,224	39,946
Dowa	194,010	139,732	3,429	136,303	20,345	115,958
Mchinji	196,393	116,425	6,854	109,571	34,559	75,012
Lilongwe	591,460	384,790	12,512	372,278	105,110	267,168
Salima	94,472	78,592	1,859	76,733	34,586	42,147
Dedza	184,589	139,440	3,972	135,468	34,628	100,840
Ntcheu	142,550	100,971	1,089	99,882	74,655	25,227
South	2,236,367	1,438,371	28,017	1,410,354	1,201,395	208,959
Mangochi	352,263	201,319	3,711	197,608	179,697	17,911
Machinga	344,753	201,239	2,813	198,426	181,186	17,240
Zomba	260,163	170,731	1,603	169,128	146,632	22,496
Mulanje	347,006	191,366	8,480	182,886	145,111	37,775
Chiradzulu	98,605	82,572	3,455	79,117	70,578	8,539
Blantyre	271,152	230,408	2,107	228,301	197,938	30,363
Mwanza	74,890	41,525	749	40,776	29,137	11,639
Thyolo	186,262	153,485	2,403	151,082	122,823	28,259
Chikwawa	194,987	106,873	1,878	104,995	80,364	24,631
Nsanje	106,287	58,853	818	58,035	47,929	10,106
Total	4,699,526	3,153,448	70,979	3,082,469	1,993,996	1,088,473

2.5 b) Referendum 1993: Regional Distribution of Votes (%)

District	Votes cast	Invalid votes	Valid votes	Multi-party system	One-party system
North	70.6	1.0	99.0	89.3	10.7
Chitipa	70.3	0.7	99.3	91.2	8.8
Karonga	59.1	0.8	99.2	94.1	5.9
Rumphi	86.6	1.4	98.6	86.8	13.2
Nkhata Bay	46.5	1.4	98.6	92.6	7.4
Mzimba	83.3	1.0	99.0	87.2	12.8
Central	69.3	3.0	97.0	32.5	67.5
Kasungu	77.3	2.7	97.3	28.0	72.0
Nkhotakota	59.3	3.6	96.4	47.0	53.0
Ntchisi	81.1	1.7	98.3	21.9	78.1
Dowa	72.0	2.5	97.5	14.9	85.1
Mchinji	59.3	5.9	94.1	31.5	68.5
Lilongwe	65.1	3.3	96.7	28.2	71.8
Salima	83.2	2.4	97.6	45.1	54.9
Dedza	75.5	2.9	97.1	25.6	74.4
Ntcheu	70.8	1.1	98.9	74.7	25.3
South	64.4	2.0	98.0	85.2	14.8
Mangochi	57.2	1.8	98.2	90.9	9.1
Machinga	58.4	1.4	98.6	91.3	8.7
Zomba	65.6	0.9	99.1	86.7	13.3
Mulanje	55.2	4.4	95.6	79.3	20.7
Chiradzulu	83.7	4.2	95.8	89.2	10.8
Blantyre	85.0	0.9	99.1	86.7	13.3
Mwanza	55.5	1.8	98.2	71.5	28.5
Thyolo	82.4	1.6	98.4	81.3	18.7
Chikwawa	54.8	1.8	98.2	76.5	23.5
Nsanje	55.4	1.4	98.6	82.6	17.4
Total	67.1	2.3	97.7	64.7	35.3

2. 6 Elections for Constitutional Assembly

Elections for Constitutional Assembly were not held.

2.7 Parliamentary Elections 1961–1994

1961[a]	Lower roll Total number	%	Upper roll Total number	%
Registered voters	75,707[b]	—	4,401	—
Votes cast	—	—	—	—
Invalid votes	—	—	—	—
Valid votes	72,538	95.8	3,725	84.6
MCP	71,659	98.8	385	10.3
UFP	607	0.8	2,108	56.6
CLP	272	0.4	–	–
Independents	–	–	1,232	33.0

[a] In the 1961 election to the Legislative Council, 20 members were elected on the lower and eight members on the higher roll.

[b] The total number of registered voters (lower roll) was 107,076, but in five constituencies voting did not take place due to the fact that only one candidate was standing. These candidates were elected unopposed.

Year	1994 Total number	%
Registered voters	3,775,256	–
Votes cast	3,004,835	79.6
Invalid votes	70,550	2.3
Valid votes	2,934,285	97.7
UDF	1,360,460	46.4
MCP	988,172	33.7
AFORD	557,353	19.0
UFMD	9,859	0.3
MDP	6,980	0.2
MNDP	2,913	0.1
CSR	2,118	0.1
MDU	323	0.0
Independents[a]	6,159	0.2

[a] There were 13 independent candidates.

2.7 a) Parliamentary Elections 1994: Regional Distribution of Votes (%)

District	Votes cast	UDF	MCP	AFORD[a]
Chitipa	89.2	3.2	8.4	87.7
Karonga	85.7	2.2	7.6	87.4
Rumphi	86.8	5.0	4.9	89.1
Nkhata Bay	80.6	12.1	8.7	72.6
Mzimba	83.4	4.6	9.0	86.0
Kasungu	80.5	19.1	62.9	21.8
Nkhotakota	85.2	41.4	44.7	12.6
Ntchisi	80.2	33.2	62.6	4.3
Dowa	82.9	15.1	78.8	4.9
Salima	77.3	42.0	52.2	5.1
Mchinji	74.7	26.2	70.4	3.2
Lilongwe	82.8	19.7	74.0	6.1
Dedza	70.7	24.9	72.2	2.5
Ntcheu	77.3	69.0	24.9	4.3
Mangochi	78.2	85.3	8.3	6.0
Machinga	82.2	90.3	7.9	1.0
Zomba	80.4	81.1	10.0	5.9
Chiradzulu	84.4	86.4	9.9	3.0
Blantyre	73.5	75.0	15.8	7.6
Mwanza	79.6	68.7	24.8	3.9
Thyolo	75.4	68.2	21.0	9.4
Mulanje	78.6	62.4	20.6	15.8
Chikwawa	74.9	56.2	38.7	4.4
Nsanje	67.1	46.3	52.8	0.7
Total[b]	79.6	46.4	33.7	19.0

[a] In the following districts AFORD presented a candidate only in some constituencies: Nkhotakota (two out of five constituencies), Lilongwe (16 out of 17), Dedza (seven out of eight), Machinga (three out of 10), Zomba (seven out of eight), Thyolo (seven out of eight), Nsanje (one out of five).

[b] Differences to 100% are due to the share of small parties.

2.8 Composition of Parliament 1961–1994

Year[a]	1961		1978[b]		1983[c]		1987[d]	
	Seats	%	Seats	%	Seats	%	Seats	%
Total seats[e]	28	100	87	100	101	100	112	100
MCP	22	78.6	87	100	101	100	112	100
UFP	5	17.9	–	–	–	–	–	–
Independents	1	3.5	–	–	–	–	–	–

[a] In 1987, 1983 and 1987 not all constituencies were contested. In a considerable number of constituencies the candidate was elected unopposed while in a small number of constituencies no candidate at all was nominated.

[b] In 1978 33 Members of Parliament returned unopposed. 31 Members were defeated.

[c] In 1983 21 sitting Members were elected unopposed. 34 Members were re-elected, and 64 new Members were elected. Three constituencies remained vacant.

[d] In 1987 38 Members were elected unopposed. 53 sitting Members lost their seat.

[e] The number of seats was extended to 50 (+ 3 seats reserved for Europeans) in 1964, in 1970 to 60, in 1973 to 63, and in 1976 to 87.

Year	1992[a]		1994	
	Seats	%	Seats	%
	141	100	177	100
MCP	141	100	56	31.6
UDF	–	–	85	48.0
AFORD	–	–	36	20.3

[a] In the 1992 elections 45 Members of Parliament were elected unopposed. Only 37 out of 106 former Members were re-elected (six seats were vacant). In the new and enlarged Parliament (141 seats) there were 78 new and 58 old Members (five seats remained vacant).

2.8 a) Composition of Parliament 1994: Regional Distribution of Seats

District	UDP	MCP	AFORD
Chitipa	0	0	5
Karonga	0	0	5
Rumphi	0	0	4
Nkhata Bay	0	0	7
Mzimba	0	0	12
Kasungu	0	7	2
Nkhotakota	2	2	1
Ntchisi	0	4	0
Dowa	0	7	0
Salima	2	3	0
Mchinji	0	6	0
Lilongwe	3	14	0
Dedza	1	7	0
Ntcheu	6	1	0
Mangochi	10	0	0
Machinga	10	0	0
Zomba	8	0	0
Chiradzulu	5	0	0
Blantyre	10	0	0
Mwanza	4	0	0
Thyolo	7	0	0
Mulanje	11	0	0
Chikwawa	5	1	0
Nsanje	1	4	0
Total	85	56	36

2.9 Presidential Elections 1994

1994	Total number	%
Registered voters	3,775,256	–
Votes cast	3,040,665	80.5
Invalid votes	61,780	2.0
Valid votes	2,978,885	98.0
Bakili Muluzi (UDF)	1,404,754	47.2
Hastings Kamuzu Banda (MCP)	996,353	33.5
Chakufwa Chihana (AFORD)	562,862	18.9
Kamlepo Kalua (MDP)	15,624	0.5

2.9 a) Presidential Elections 1994: Regional Distribution of Votes (%)

District	Votes cast	Invalid votes	Valid votes	Muluzi	Banda	Chihana	Kalua
Chitipa	86.0	1.0	99.0	1.8	9.6	88.3	0.3
Karonga	84.6	2.1	97.9	2.9	5.2	91.6	0.4
Rumphi	86.7	1.1	98.9	4.7	5.6	89.4	0.4
Nkhata Bay	83.3	1.6	98.4	8.5	6.2	84.7	0.7
Mzimba	86.5	1.2	98.8	4.5	8.2	87.0	0.3
Kasungu	81.3	2.0	98.0	15.1	65.5	18.9	0.4
Nkhotakota	84.8	2.3	97.7	37.9	46.6	15.2	0.4
Ntchisi	80.0	3.4	96.6	30.9	65.2	3.5	0.5
Dowa	81.9	2.5	97.5	15.0	80.5	3.8	0.7
Salima	77.4	2.9	97.1	47.7	47.3	4.4	0.6
Mchinji	79.5	2.3	97.7	26.8	69.5	3.3	0.4
Lilongwe	85.6	2.1	97.9	20.2	71.7	7.8	0.3
Dedza	74.0	3.5	96.5	26.3	71.6	2.3	0.4
Ntcheu	76.6	2.5	97.5	72.0	23.8	3.7	0.6
Mangochi	81.1	1.9	98.1	88.7	7.5	3.3	0.5
Machinga	84.3	1.9	98.1	91.2	7.0	1.5	0.4
Zomba	82.5	1.8	98.2	84.1	11.2	4.1	0.6
Chiradzulu	70.0	1.9	98.1	89.1	9.0	1.5	0.4
Blantyre	82.7	1.5	98.5	78.4	13.2	7.9	0.6
Mwanza	79.8	3.2	96.8	69.1	25.1	4.6	1.2
Thyolo	77.3	2.6	97.4	71.4	19.9	7.7	0.5
Mulanje	66.4	3.4	96.6	66.7	20.8	11.8	0.6
Chikwawa	75.9	2.4	97.6	56.8	38.5	3.4	1.3
Nsanje	81.4	3.4	96.6	42.6	52.9	2.9	1.6
Total	80.5	2.0	98.0	47.2	33.5	18.9	0.5

2.10 List of Power Holders 1964–1998

Head of State	Years	Remarks
Elizabeth II	1964–1966	After independence Malawi remained a member of the Commonwealth with the British Queen as Head of State, represented by the British Governor Glyn Jones.
Hastings Kamuzu Banda	1966–1994	On 06/07/1966 Malawi became a Republic and Parliament unanimously elected Banda as President. On 06/07/1971 Banda was sworn in as President for Life. On 17/11/1993 Parliament repealed the life presidency. Banda was voted out in the presidential elections of 17/05/1994.
Bakili Muluzi	1994–	Elected President in direct elections on 17/05/1994; sworn in on 21/05/1994.

Head of Government	Years	Remarks
Hastings Kamuzu Banda	1964–1966	Parliament elected Banda as Prime Minister after the achievement of self-government on 01/02/1963. Malawi gained independence under the prime ministership of Banda on 06/07/1964. On 06/07/1966 Malawi became as Republic. Since then, the President has been Head of both State and Government.

3. Bibliography

3.1. Official Sources

Constitution of the Republic of Malawi, 1966.

Constitution (Referendum on Malawi's Political System) Regulations, 1993, Zomba.

Constitution of the Republic of Malawi, 1994, Zomba.

Department of Information (1987). *Parliamentary General Elections 1987*. Blantyre.

Electoral Commission (1982). *The Fifth Report of the Electoral Commission on Delimitation of Constituencies 1982*. Zomba.

— (1987). *The Sixth Report of the Electoral Commission on Delimitation of Constituencies 1987*. Zomba.

— (1992). *The Seventh Report of the Electoral Commission on Delimitation of Constituencies 1992*. Zomba.

— (1994). *Report to Parliament by the Electoral Commission. The Number of Parliamentary Constituencies and the Boundaries of each Constituency*. Blantyre.

— (1994). *1994 Parliamentary and Presidential Elections Report*. Blantyre.

— (1997). *Parliamentary By-elections: An update 1994–1997*. Blantyre.

Information Department (1996). *Biographies/ Profiles of the Malawi Cabinet and Members of the Parliament*. Blantyre.

Laws of Malawi (1968). *Presidential Elections* (Chapter 2:01).

Laws of Malawi (1970). *Parliamentary Elections* (Chapter 2:02).

Laws of Malawi (1993). *Parliamentary and Presidential Elections Act* (No. 31 of 1993).

Nyasaland Protectorate (1961). *Legislative Council Proceedings* (76th Session). Zomba.

Referendum Commission (1993). *Referendum on Malawi's Political System, 14th June, 1993. Report of the National Referendum Commission*. o.O.

Republic of Malawi (1986). *Parliament: Biographies*. Blantyre.

— (1992). *Parliamentary General Elections 1987 and 1992 Results of Poll*. Zomba (confidential document).

3.2. Books, Articles and Electoral Reports

Africa Research Bulletin, London.

Commonwealth Observer Group (1994). *The Parliamentary and Presidential Elections in Malawi, 17 May 1994*. London: Commonwealth Secretariat.

Crosby, C. A. (1993). *Historical Dictionary of Malawi* (2nd edn.). Metuchen, NJ/ London: The Scarecrow Press.

Cullen, T. (1994). *Malawi. A Turning Point*. Edinburgh *et al.*: Pentland Press.

Dzimbiri, L.B. (1993). 'The Malawi Referendum of June 1993'. *Electoral Studies*, 13/3: 229–234.

Glagow, M., and Ruffert, M. (1993). *Non-governmental Organizations in Malawi. Societal Self-guidance in the Process of Democratization and Development*. Eschborn: GTZ.

Joint International Observer Group (1993). *Report on the Malawi National Referendum (14 June 1993)* (Lilongwe).

Kalipeni, E. (1997). 'Regional Polarisation in Voting Pattern: Malawi's 1994 Election'. *African Journal of Political Science*, 2/1: 152–167.

Kaspin, D. (1995). 'The Politics of Ethnicity in Malawi's Democratic Transition'. *Journal of Modern African Studies*, 33/4: 595–620.

Kees van Donge, J. (1995). 'Kamuzu's Legacy: The Democratization of Malawi'. *African Affairs*, 94: 227–257.

L'Hoiry, P. (1988). *Le Malawi*. Paris and Nairobi: Karthala and Credu.

Lwanda, J. L. (1993). *Kamuzu Banda of Malawi. A Study in Promise, Power and Paralysis*. Glasgow: Dudu Nsomba Publications.
— (1996). *Promises, Power, Politics and Poverty. Democratic Transition in Malawi*. Glasgow: Dudu Nsomba Publications.
Mair, L. (1962). *The Nyasaland Elections of 1961*. London: Athlone Press.
Mair, S. (1994). 'Malawi - Bericht über die Beobachtung der Vorreferendum-Periode und Abschlußbericht der Beobachtergruppe', in U. Engel *et al.* (eds.), *Wahlbeobachtung in Afrika: Erfahrungen deutscher Wahlbeobachter, Analysen und Lehren für die Zukunft (Arbeiten aus dem Institut für Afrika-Kunde, Bd.90)*. Hamburg: Institut für Afrika-Kunde, 147–165.
McMaster, C. (1974). *Malawi Foreign Policy and Development*. London: Julian Friedman.
Meinhardt, H. (1990). 'Parlamentarismus in Malawi'. *Afrika Spectrum*, 25/3: 313–328.
— (1993). *Das Parlament im autoritären Malawi*. Hamburg: Institut für Afrika-Kunde.
— (1994). 'Malawi auf dem Weg zur Demokratie? Das Referendum und seine Folgen'. *Verfassung und Recht in Übersee*, 27/1: 45–65.
— (1996). 'Externe Einflüsse auf den Demokratisierungsprozeß in Malawi', in R. Hanisch (ed.), *Demokratieexport in die Länder des Südens?* Hamburg: Deutsches Übersee-Institut, 405–430.
— (1997). *Politische Transition und Demokratisierung in Malawi*. Hamburg: Institut für Afrika-Kunde.
Mhone, G. C. Z. (1992). *Malawi at the Crossroads. The Post-Colonial Political Economy*. Harare: SAPES.
Mtewa, M. (1986). *Malawi. Democratic Theory and Public Policy*. Cambridge, Mass.: Schenkman Books.
Newell, J. (1995). 'A Moment of Truth'? The Church and Political Change in Malawi'. *Journal of Modern African Studies*, 33/2: 243–262.
Ng'ong'ola, C. (1996). 'Managing the Transition to Political Pluralism in Malawi: Legal and Constitutional Arrangements'. *The Journal of Commonwealth & Comparative Politics*, 34/2: 85–110.
Nuscheler, F. (1978). 'Malawi', in D. Sternberger, B. Vogel, D. Nohlen and K. Landfried (eds.), *Die Wahl der Parlamente und anderer Staatsorgane. Band II: Politische Organisation und Repräsentation in Afrika*, by Franz Nuscheler, Klaus Ziemer *et al.*, Berlin/ New York: Walter de Gruyter, 1197–1217.
Nzunda, M., and Ross, K. R. (1995). *Church, Law and Political Transition in Malawi 1992–94*. Gweru: Mambo Press.
Posner, D. N. (1995). 'Malawi's New Dawn'. *Journal of Democracy*, 6/1: 131–145.

Ross, K. R. (1996). *God, People and Power in Malawi*. Blantyre: Christian Literature Association.

Taube, G. (1993). 'Malawi', in D. Nohlen and F. Nuscheler (eds.), *Handbuch der Dritten Welt*, Vol. 5: *Ostafrika und Südafrika*. Bonn: Dietz, 368–383.

Venter, D. (1995). 'The Transition to Multi-Party Politics', in J. A. Wiseman (ed.), *Democracy and Political Change*. London/ New York: Routledge, 152–192.

Williams, T. D. (1978). *Malawi. The Politics of Despair*. Ithaca, N.Y.: Cornell University Press.

MALI

by Shaheen Mozaffar*

1. Introduction

1.1 Historical Overview

Mali became an independent country on 22 February 1960 after 65 years of French colonial rule. In the first half of the 20th century, there were almost no institutional opportunities for African political participation. In 1946, the Constitution of the Fourth French Republic established Territorial Assemblies and granted a limited number of Africans the right to directly elect deputies to the French National Assembly. In 1951, the French National Assembly legislated electoral reforms that for the first time extended voting rights to eligible women and created a rural majority in the electorate. And in 1956, the comprehensive *Loi Cadre* reforms devolved substantial powers to the Territorial Assemblies, gave African leaders the authority to constitute territorial executives and established universal suffrage, thus pushing the Malian electorate from less than 1% before 1951 to more than 60%.

Between 1946 and 1958, Malian voters voted in four referendums, directly elected deputies to the French Constituent and National Assemblies five times and representatives to the Territorial Assembly three times, and indirectly elected Senators to the French Council of the Republic three times. These elections stimulated the birth of political parties for the purpose of organizing the competing interests of established and newly mobilized African groups. The first party to emerge was the *Parti Soudanais Progressiste* (PSP), which articulated and pursued the conservative pro-French policy of its founder, Fily Diabo Sissoko, a schoolteacher and canton chief, and drew its support largely from the traditional segments of Malian society. Opposing the PSP was the *Union Soudanais—Rassemblement Démocratique Africain* (US-RDA), which was co-founded by Modibo Keita, the future first President of independent Mali. The US began as an independent party in the

* I thank the National Science Foundation for financial support and the Boston University African Studies Center for continued research support. I am responsible for the article.

French Soudan, but became the Soudanese branch of the RDA. The RDA was formed in Bamako (the Malian capital) in 1946 as a loose union of French West African and French Equatorial African parties. From the very beginning, the US-RDA possessed a strong administrative infrastructure and articulated a coherent policy of ending colonial rule.

The PSP–US-RDA rivalry dominated electoral politics in Mali between 1946 and 1958. In this period, the PSP, because of its narrow traditional political base and the support of the French colonial administration, steadily lost its political dominance to the US-RDA, which emerged as the dominant party in the first general election to be held under universal franchise in 1957. Sissoko made a futile attempt to revive the PSP under a new name, the *Parti du Regroupement Soudanais* (PRS), before joining the US-RDA. The US-RDA led Mali to independence.

At independence in 1960, Mali established a constitutional democracy with a French-style presidential-premier form of government. Modibo Keita became the country's first President. His tenure was marked by the centralization of executive power, economic mismanagement and the cooptation and occasional suppression of political opposition. With the US-RDA controlling all seats, the Malian National Assembly reconfirmed Keita as President with extensive executive powers. Keita used these powers to rapidly africanize the civil service and, consistent with official socialist ideology, establish large parastatals, thus creating employment opportunities for a growing urban population as well as a core base of political support in the public sector. In the absence of a viable opposition, the US-RDA was deployed as a mass mobilization party to co-opt regional leaders and voluntary organization (teachers and labor unions, students, women's groups, farmers and peasant associations, etc.) who could potentially threaten the regime.

The socialist policies, however, produced severe shortages of food and consumer goods instead of the promised economic prosperity. And Keita's ill-conceived withdrawal of Mali from the French West African Monetary Union and the issuance of a non-convertible currency destroyed the profitable commercial sector. As political opposition began to build as a result, the regime reacted repressively. The National Political Bureau of the US-RDA, a venue of ideological debate in the party, was abolished, and the National Assembly forced to dissolve itself. The CNDR was created to reorganize Malian politics and economy along rigid socialist lines and a paramilitary militia was launched to transform Malian society along the lines of the Cultural Revolution in China. This militia directly threatened the autonomy and integrity of the army, which launched a pre-emptive coup overthrowing the Keita regime in November 1968.

The military regime, headed by a collective executive *Comité Militaire de Liberation Nationale* (CMLN) with Moussa Traoré as the President, abolished the US-RDA and the *Comité National de Défense de la Révolution* (CNDR), disbanded the militia and replaced the 1960 constitution with a Fundamental Law by which Mali was governed until the promulgation of a new constitution in 1974. This constitution, which was approved in a national referendum, returned the country to civilian, but not liberal democratic, rule by establishing a single-party regime. The *Union Démocratique du Peuple Malien* (UDPM) was launched accordingly in 1975, and governed Mali for the next 17 years. In this period elections to the National Assembly were held four times. However, more than one candidate was allowed to run on the UDPM ticket for each National Assembly seat, thus allowing voters a semblance of electoral choice albeit within the single-party framework. That 42% of the incumbents in the 1979 election and half of the incumbents in the 1985 and 1988 elections were defeated attests to the fact that voters were able to exercise this choice as an expression of their dissatisfaction with the UDPM government. Traoré was confirmed twice as President in non-competitive elections.

Like its US-RDA predecessor, the UDPM also pursued a corporatist strategy to encompass, control and accommodate a wide range of regional leaders, civic organizations, and public sector employee unions. While this strategy facilitated control of political dissent, it also enabled these very groups to mobilize anti-regime demonstrations by reducing the organizational costs of collective action. This is precisely what happened in 1991, when continued economic decline, eroding living standards, the fall of communism and the Berlin Wall, and growing international support for democracy combined to precipitate violent anti-regime demonstrations that quickly transformed into full-fledged demands for comprehensive political reforms, signaling Mali's democratic transition.

The failure of the UDPM government to accommodate the pro-democratic forces led to its overthrow by a military coup in March 1991. After quickly abrogating the 1974 Constitution and dissolving the UDPM and the National Assembly, Lt. Col. Amadou Touré, the new military ruler, formed the *Conseil de Reconciliation Nationale* (CRN) to negotiate with the pro-democracy forces. These forces, however, bolstered by strong international support, demanded direct participation in the government. The CRN was replaced with the *Comité de Transition pour le Salut du Peuple* (CTSP), comprising 15 civilian and 10 military members and chaired by Touré. Soumana Sacko, a widely respected former finance minister, was appointed as Prime Minister. The legalization of political parties and civic organizations prompted the immediate registration of 22 political parties and 1,070 civic organizations. An additional 25 parties registered later. Between 29 July and 12 August 1991, members of the widely-representative National Conference called by the CSTP wrote a new constitution, formulated a new electoral code, and produced a charter for political parties.

The new constitution was approved by an overwhelming majority in a referendum in January 1992. It established presidential-premier form of government. The *Alliance pour la Démocratie au Mali* (ADEMA), which was founded in 1990 as a pro-democracy pressure group by Alpha Konaré, director of a publishing house, successfully transformed itself into a political party and won a plurality of votes and seats in the municipal elections held one week after the adoption of the new constitution and an absolute majority of seats in the National Assembly in the subsequent legislative elections. In the first round of the presidential election, which was contested by candidates from eight parties, including the revived US-RDA, Konaré won a plurality. In the second round, he defeated the US-RDA candidate and was officially installed as President on 8 June 1992, ushering in Mali's Third Republic.

The 1997 elections were held under a revised electoral code produced after extensive negotiations between the government and the opposition parties. This revision created the *Commission Electorale Nationale Indépendante* (CENI), a key opposition demand, increased the number of constituencies to accommodate population differentials, authorized independent candidates, and introduced a mixed majoritarian–proportional representation formula for allocating legislative seats (a provision that was declared unconstitutional by the Constitutional Court). In existence only two months, CENI's lack of experience in election management led to severe administrative problems in the legislative elections of 13 April 1997. Because of these problems, which were widely acknowledged by both the government and the opposition, the Constitutional Court annulled the elections. The main opposition parties held the Konaré government responsible for these problems, and, after a futile demand for its resignation, boycotted the new round of legislative elections held on 20 July. As a result, only ADEMA and seven minor parties contested this election. ADEMA won an overwhelming majority of votes and seats. In the presidential elections held on 11 May 1997, Konaré was re-elected in a decisive victory over nine other candidates.

1.2 Evolution of Electoral Provisions

Prior to independence, the electoral provisions for Mali were incorporated in legislation passed by the French National Assembly. Until 1957, the electoral provisions created two separate electoral rolls, one African and one French. The two voted separately to elect representatives to the Territorial Assembly, but voted jointly in a common roll to elect deputies to the French National Assembly. Members of the Territorial Assembly voted by each roll also voted separately to elect Senators to the French Council of the Republic, but voted jointly to elect members to the Grand Council of French West Africa and the Assembly of the French Union. The 1956 *Loi Cadre* reforms abolished the separate rolls and introduced universal adult franchise with a minimum voting age of 21 years.

For electoral purposes, Mali was divided into multi-member constituencies. Political parties were required to submit lists of candidates equal to the number of available seats. Each list receiving a plurality of votes won all the seats in the constituency. This system was retained through the 1964 general election, in which only the US-RDA submitted candidate lists, although other political parties were not legally proscribed.

The 1974 Constitution, which established a single-party regime, also established multi-member constituencies, a party-list system in which the officially authorized party was required to submit a list of candidates equal to the number of available seats, and plurality voting formula. The minimum voting age remained at 21 years.

The 1991 electoral code formulated by the National Conference was issued as a decree by the CTSP, and established the current basic legal framework for elections. This law was superseded by Loi electorale, No. 96-46 (27 September 1996), which established the *Commission Electorale National Independante* (CENI). Previously, the Ministry of Territorial Administration was responsible for the management and administration of all elections. Additional modifications were made by Loi electorale No. 97-001 (8 January 1997). Finally, Loi electorale No. 97-008 (14 January 1997) and Loi electorale No. 97-011 (12 February 1997) introduced changes in the number of seats in several constituencies, increased the number of seats in the National Assembly from 129 to 147, and authorized independent candidates.

1.3 Current Electoral Provisions

Sources: Loi electorale, No. 96-46 du 27 septembre 1996, Loi electorale No. 97-001 du 8 janvier 1997; Loi electorale No. 97-008 du 14 janvier 1997; Loi electorale 97-011 du 12 fevrier 1997.

Elected national institutions: The President is directly elected for five years. The unicameral National Assembly is also elected for five years. The National Assembly initially comprised 129 seats, of which 116 were elected by the domestic electorate and 13 by Malians residing overseas. The number of seats elected by the domestic electorate was increased to 147 in 1997.

Suffrage: Mali has universal adult suffrage. Minimum voting age is 18 years. Voting is not compulsory.

Nomination of candidates
- *presidential elections*: Nominated by political parties. Self-nomination of independent candidates without party affiliation is also permitted. The minimum age for candidacy is 35 years.
- *parliamentary elections*: Nominated by political parties. Self-nomination of independent candidates without party affiliation is also permitted. The minimum age for candidacy for 21 years.

Electoral system
- *presidential elections*: Absolute majority system. If no candidate wins an absolute majority in the first round, the top two first-round finishers compete in the second round in which the majority determines the winner.
- *parliamentary elections*: Two-round absolute majority system with closed party lists in 55 multi-member constituencies spread between the country's eight administrative regions and the six Bamako communes (plus overseas constituencies). If no party list or candidate wins an absolute majority in the first-round, the top two first round finishers compete in the second round in which the majority determines the winner.

1.4 Comment on the Electoral Statistics

Election results as well as information on electoral codes for Mali are available but difficult to retrieve in a cost-effective way. Pre-independence results are available in a number of secondary sources (e.g. Snyder 1965), the most useful of which is Morgenthau (1964). If available, old issues of *L'Essor*, the paper of the US-RDA, also contain detailed results of elections through 1964.

For the Third Republic, the *Journal Officiel de la République du Mali* is a very useful source for original electoral codes and changes to them, for detailed information on the party lists nominated for election in each constituency, as well as for detailed information on the size of the population, the size of the electorate, and the number of polling stations in each constituency. The problem with this source, however, is that it is not readily available in all research libraries, except in highly specialized law libraries.

Therefore an eclectic, multi-faceted research strategy was utilized that relied on a variety of sources such as: *Africa Research Bulletin*; *Economic Intelligence Unit Country Report*; *Keesing's Record of World Events*; *Chronicle of Parliamentary Elections and Development* (published by the Geneva-based Inter-parliamentary Union); *AFPress Clips*; *Africa Confidential*; *Africa International*; *Africa News*; *FBIS Daily Reports*; *Marches Tropicaux et Mediterranéens; Jeune Afrique; Politique Africaine*; and *West Africa*.

In addition, reports on technical assistance and election observation of international non-governmental organizations as The African–American Institute (AAI); The International Foundation for Election Systems (IFES); and the National Democratic Institute (NDI) were consulted.

2. Tables

2.1 Dates of National Elections, Referendums and Coups d'Etat

Year	Presidential elections	Parliamentary elections	Elections for Constitutional Assembly	Referendums	Coups d'Etat
1957		21/03[a]			
1959		08/03[b]			
1964		12/04			
1968					19/11
1974				02/06	
1979	19/06	19/06			
1982		13/06			
1985	09/06	09/06			
1988		26/06			
1991					26/03
1992	12/04 (1st) 26/04 (2nd)	24/02 (1st) 08/03 (2nd)		12/01	
1997	11/05	13/04[c]			
1997		20/07 (1st) 03/08 (2nd)			

[a] Territorial Assembly.
[b] Legislative Assembly.
[c] Annulled.

2.2 Electoral Body 1957–1997

Year	Type of election[a]	Population	Registered voters		Votes cast		
			Total number	% pop.	Total number	% reg. voters	% pop.
1957	TA	3,347,000	2,090,048	62.5	710,616	34.0	21.2
1958	Ref	3,708,000	2,142,266	57.8	972,197	45.4	26.2
1959	LA	3,708,000	2,148,667	58.0	693,335	32.3	18.7
1964	NA	4,449,000	2,419,054	54.4	2,150,539	88.9	48.3
1974	Ref	—	—	—	—	—	—
1979	NA	6,446,000	3,283,985	51.0	3,185,258	97.0	49.4
1979	Pr	6,446,000	3,397,250	52.7	3,302,251	97.2	51.2
1982	NA	6,883,000	3,591,716	52.2	3,453,068	96.1	50.2
1985	NA	7,389,000	—	—	—	—	—
1985	Pr	7,389,000	—	—	—	—	—
1988	NA	7,994,000	3,701,006	46.3	3,620,474	97.8	45.3
1992	Ref	8,160,000	5,233,432[b]	64.1	2,276,291	43.5	27.9
1992	NA	8,160,000	4,780,416	58.6	1,017,019	21.3	12.5
1992	Pr	8,160,000	4,780,416	58.6	1,075,594	22.5	13.2
1997	Pr	10,203,383	5,830,824[b]	57.2	1,692,282	29.0	16.6
1997	NA	10,203,383	5,253,299	51.5	1,133,767	21.6	11.1

[a] TA = Territorial Assembly; LA = Legislative Assembly; NA = National Assembly; Pr = President; Ref = Referendum.

[b] Includes Malians residing overseas.

2.3 Abbreviations

ADEMA	Alliance pour la Démocratie au Mali
CNID	Congres National d'Initiative Démocratique
FSD	Front Sauvegarde de la Démocratie
PDP	Parti pour la Démocratie et le Progrès
PMD	Parti Malien pour le Développement
PRS	Parti du Regroupment Soudanais
PSP	Parti Soudanais Progressiste
PUDP	Parti pour l'Unite la Démocratie et le Progrès
RDA	Rassemblement Démocratique Africain
RDP	Rassemblement pour la Démocratie et le Progrès
RDT	Rassemblement pour le Démocratie et le Travail
UDD	Union pour la Démocratie et le Développement
UDPM	Union Démocratique du Peuple Malien
UFD	Union des Forces Démocratiques
UFDP	Union des Forces Démocratiques pour le Progrès
UMDD	Union Malien pour la Démocratie et le Développement
US	Union Soudanais
US-RDA	Union Soudanais—Rassemblement Démocratique Africain

2.4 Electoral Participation of Parties and Alliances 1957–1997

Party / Alliance	Years	Elections contested	
		Presidential	Parliamentary
US-RDA	1957	1	0
PSA	1957, 1959, 1992	3	0
US-RDA	1959, 1964, 1992, 1997	4	4
PRS	1959	1	0
UDPM	1979, 1982, 1985, 1988	4	2
ADEMA	1992, 1997	2	2
CNID	1992, 1997	2	1
PDP	1992, 1997	2	1
PMD	1992, 1997	2	0
PUDP	1992, 1997	2	2
RDP	1992, 1997	2	1
RDT	1992, 1997	1	1
UDD	1992, 1997	1	1
UFD	1992, 1997	0	1
UFDP	1992, 1997	1	1
UMDD	1992, 1997	1	2

2.5 Referendums

Year	1974[a]		1992[b]	
	Total number	%	Total number	%
Registered voters	—	–	5,233,432	–
Votes cast	—	—	2,276,291	43.5
Invalid votes	—	—	41,590	1.8
Valid votes	—	—	2,234,701	98.2
Yes	—	99.0	2,212,354	99.0
No	—	1.0	22,347	1.0

[a] Approval of the constitution of the Second Republic.
[b] Approval of the constitution of the Third Republic.

2.6 Elections for Constitutional Assembly

Elections for Constitutional Assembly have not been held.

2.7 Parliamentary Elections 1957–1997

Year	1957[a] Total number	%	1959[d] Total number	%
Registered voters	2,090,048	–	2,148,667	–
Votes cast	710,616	34.0	693,335	32.3
Invalid votes	11,370	1.6	14,560	2.1
Valid votes	699,246	98.4	678,775	97.9
US-RDA	468,494	67.0	515,869	76.0
PSP	216,766	31.0	–	–
PRS[b]	–	–	162,906	24.0
Others[c]	13,985	2.0	–	–

[a] Territorial Assembly.
[b] Successor to PSP.
[c] Includes three minor parties all of which merged with the US-RDA after the election.
[d] Legislative Assembly.

Year	1964 Total number	%
Registered voters	2,419,054	–
Votes cast	2,150,539	88.9
Invalid votes	2,470	1.0
Valid votes	2,128,069	99.0
US-RDA	2,106,788	99.0

Year	1979 Total number	%	1982 Total number	%
Registered voters	3,283,985	–	3,591,716	–
Votes cast	3,185,258	97.0	3,453,068	96.0
Invalid votes	—	—	9,364	0.3
Valid votes	—	—	3,443,704	99.7
UDPM	3,180,565	99.9	3,437,505	99.9

Year	1985 Total number	%	1988 Total number	%
Registered voters	—	–	3,701,006	–
Votes cast	—	—	3,620,474	98.0
Invalid votes	—	—	—	—
Valid votes	—	99.0	—	—
UDPM	—	100.0	3,615,779	99.9

Year	1992		1997[a]	
	Total number	%	Total number	%
Registered voters	4,780,416	–	5,253,299	–
Votes cast	1,017,019	21.3	1,133,767	21.6
Invalid votes	33,388	3.3	22,010	1.9
Valid votes	983,631	96.7	1,111,757	98.1
ADEMA	476,254	48.4	837,389	75.3
US-RDA	172,998	17.6	–[b]	–
CNID	54,623	5.6	–[b]	–
PDP	50,335	5.1	–[b]	–
RDP	43,658	4.4	–[b]	–
UDD	43,313	4.4	–[b]	–
RDT	36,946	3.8	–[b]	–
PMD	26,676	2.7	–[b]	–
PSP	16,901	1.7	–[b]	–
UFDP	15,888	1.6	–[b]	–
UMDD	4,252	0.4	–[b]	–
Others[c]	41,787	4.3	274,368	24.7

[a] The Constitutional Court, citing violations of four articles of the electoral code by CENI, annulled the results of the elections held on 13 April 1997. The new elections held on 20 July 1997 were boycotted by major opposition parties amidst violent expression of dissatisfaction with the government in Bamako. Only ADEMA and nine minor parties contested these elections.
[b] Boycotted the elections.
[c] Include 11 minor parties for the 1992 elections and seven minor parties for the 1997 elections.

2.8 Composition of Parliament 1957–1997

Year[a]	1957[a]		1959		1964	
	Seats	%	Seats	%	Seats	%
	70	100	80	100	80	100
US-RDA	64[b]	91.4	80	100	80	100
PSP	6	8.6	–	–	–	–

[a] For 1957 and 1959 the data refer to the composition of the Territorial Assembly and the Legislative Assembly respectively, for 1964 they refer to the composition of the National Assembly of independent Mali.
[b] Includes seven seats won by minor parties all of which merged with the US-RDA after the elections.

Year	1979[a]		1982[a]		1985[a]		1988[a]	
	Seats	%	Seats	%	Seats	%	Seats	%
	80	100	80	100	80	100	80	100
UPDM	80	100	80	100	80	100	80	100

[a] Single-party regime. Only the UPDM, the officially sanctioned party, was permitted to nominate candidates.

Year	1992		1997	
	Seats	%	Seats	%
	116[a]	100	147[a]	100
ADEMA	76	65.5	128	87.1
USRDA	8	6.9	–[b]	–
CNID	9	7.8	–[b]	–
PDP	2	1.7	–[b]	–
RDP	4	3.5	–[b]	–
UDD	4	3.5	–[b]	–
RDT	3	2.6	–[b]	–
PMD	6	5.2	–[b]	–
UFDP	3	2.6	–[b]	–
UMDD	1	0.9	–[b]	–
Others[c]	–	–	19	12.9

[a] Thirteen additional seats were elected by Malians residing overseas.

[b] Boycotted the elections.

[c] Includes seven minor parties.

2.9 Presidential Elections 1979–1997

1979	Total number	%
Registered voters	3,397,250	–
Votes cast	3,302,251	97.2
Invalid votes	3,774	0.1
Valid votes	3,298,477	99.9
Moussa Traoré (UPDM)	3,298,477	100.0

1985	Total number	%
Registered voters	—	–
Votes cast	—	—
Invalid votes	—	—
Valid votes	—	99.9
Moussa Traoré (UPDM)	—	100.0

1992 (first round)	Total number	%
Registered voters	4,780,416	–
Votes cast	1,128,178	23.6
Invalid votes	30,461	2.7
Valid votes	1,097,717	97.3
Alpha Konaré (ADEMA)	493,973	45.0
Tiéoulé M. Konate (USRDA)[a]	159,169	14.5
Mountaga Tall (CNID)	125,140	11.4
Almamy Sylla (RDP)	103,185	9.4
Baba A. Haidara (USRDA)[a]	76,840	7.0
Idrisa Traoré (PDP)	77,938	7.1
Amadou A. Niangadou (RDT	43,909	4.0
Mamadou Diaby (PUDP)	24,150	2.2
Bamba M. Diallo	21,954	2.0

[a] The USRDA split into two factions just before the elections and ran two candidates.

1992 (second round)	Total number	%
Registered voters	4,780,416	–
Votes cast	969,468	20.9
Invalid votes	19,389	2.0
Valid votes	950,079	98.0
Alpha O. Konaré (ADEMA)	655,555	69.0
Tiéoulé M. Konate (USRDA)	294,524	31.0

1997	Total number	%
Registered voters	5,830,824	–
Votes cast	1,692,282	29.0
Invalid votes	38,054	2.2
Valid votes	1,654,228	97.8
Alpha O. Konaré (ADEMA)	1,395,581	84.4
Mamdou M. Diaby (PUDP)	59,001	3.6
Mountaga Tall (CNID)	30,195	1.8
Soumana Sako (CPP)	30,060	1.8
Choguel K. Maiga (MPR)	29,259	1.8
Seydou B. Kouyate (US-RDA)	26,565	1.6
Abdoul W. Berthe (PMDR)	21,860	1.3
Idrissa Traore (PDP)	19,437	1.2
Almamy Sylla (RDP)	16,115	1.0
Mamdou L. Traoré (MIRIA)	15,030	0.9

2.10 List of Power Holders 1960–1998

Head of State	Years	Remarks
Modibo Keita	1960–1968	Became President of the Republic of Mali on 22/09/1960; overthrown by coup on 19/11/1968.
Moussa Traoré	1968–1991	Co-leader of the 1968 coup; became President of CMLN on 19/11/1968; introduced the 1974 constitution, establishing Mali's Second Republic; founded the UDPM; elected President in 1979 and 1985 as the sole legal candidate; overthrown by military coup on 26/03/1991 in the face of violent pro-democracy demonstrations.
Amadou Touré	1991–1992	Led the 1991 coup. Established the CRN on 26/03/1991 and replaced it with the CTSP four days later under pressure from pro-democracy forces strongly supported by the international community; chaired the CTSP which negotiated with pro-democracy forces and managed democratic transition to Mali's Third Republic.
Alpha Konaré	1992–	Elected President on 26/04/1992 and officially installed on 08/06/1992 as President of Mali's Third Republic. Re-elected on 11/05/1997.

Head of Government	Years	Remarks
Soumana Sacko	1991–1992	Appointed Prime Minister on 02/04/1991 to oversee the democratic transition.
Younoussi Touré	1992–1993	Appointed Prime Minister on 08/06/1992; resigned on 09/04/1993 amidst student demonstrations and political differences within the ruling ADEMA-CNID-USRDA coalition.
Abdulaye Sou	1993–1994	Appointed Prime Minister on 13/04/1993, resigned on 02/02/1994 amidst ideological differences with radical cabinet members of ADEMA.
Ibrahim Keita	1994–	Appointed Prime Minister on 05/02/1994; remained Prime Minister until the constitutional dissolution of the government; re-appointed after the 1997 elections on 14/09/1997.

3. Bibliography

3.1 Official Sources

Constitution de la Republique du Mali, 1992.
Loi electoral, No. 96-46, 27 September 1996.
Loi electoral, 97-008, 14 January 1997.
Loi electoral, 97-011, 12 February 1997.

3.2 Books, Articles and Electoral Reports

Fay, C. (1995). 'La démocratie au Mali ou le pouvoir en pâtue'. *Cahiers d'Etudes Africaines* 137: 19–53.

Foltz, W. J. (1965). *From French West Africa to the Mali Federation*. New Haven, Con.: Yale University Press.

Hanke, S. (1997). 'Möglichkeiten und Grenzen unabhängiger Wahlkomissionen im Demokratisierungsprozeß: Das Beispiel der Commission Electorale Independante in Mali'. *Afrika Spectrum* 32: 225–240.

Hodgkin, T., and Schachter Morgenthau, R. (1964). 'Mali', in J. S. Coleman and C. G. Rosberg (eds.), *Political Parties and National Integration in Tropical Africa*. Berkeley, Cal.: University of California Press, 216–258.

Imperato, J. P. (1989). *Mali: A Search for Direction*. Boulder, Col.: Westview Press.

— (1997). *Historical Dictionary of Mali* (3rd edn.). London: Scarecrow Press.

International Foundation for Election Systems (ed.) (1998): *Serie Internationale: Les Lois Electorales, Tome 1: L' Afrique Francophone*. Washington D.C.: IFES.

Mozaffar, S. (1997). 'Mali: A Two-Round System in Africa', in A. Reynolds and B. Reilly (eds.), *The International IDEA Handbook of Electoral System Design*. Stockholm: International Institute for Democracy and Electoral Assistance, 45–47.

Nzouankeu, J. M. (1993). 'The Role of the National Conference in the Transition to Democracy in Africa. The Cases of Benin and Mali'. *Issue* 21/1-2: 44–50

Robinson, K. (1955). 'Political Development in French West Africa', in C. W. Stillman (ed.), *Africa in the Modern World*. Chicago, Ill.: University of Chicago Press, 140–181.

Schachter Morgenthau, R. (1964). *Political Parties in French-Speaking West Africa*. Oxford: Clarendon Press.

Snyder, F. G. (1965). *One-Party Government in Mali: Transition Toward Control*. New Haven, Con.: Yale University Press.

Vengroff, R. (1993). 'Governance and the Transition to Democracy: Political Parties and the Party System in Africa'. *The Journal of Modern African Studies*, 31/4: 541–562.

— (1994). 'The Impact of Electoral System on the Transition to Democracy in Africa: The Case of Mali'. *Electoral Studies*, 13/1: 29–37.

MAURITANIA

by Regina Wegemund

1. Introduction

1.1 Historical Overview

The Islamic Republic of Mauritania gained independence (1960) as an autonomous part of the *communauté française*, the successor organization to the French colonial empire. Political discussions concentrated on the demand for independence, symbolized differences between traditional authorities and modern administration and produced first frictions between the black and white populations, forced to live together on the territory of the new state. The difference between a northern desert region without modern infrastructure, inhabited by nomads, and the south with its agricultural potential, oriented towards the southern neighbor Senegal, proved to be the lasting feature of post-colonial politics.

After independence, political power was gradually concentrated in the hands of President Mokhtar Ould Daddah, Head of Government since 1957, and the *Parti du Peuple Mauritanien* (PPM). In February 1965, a one-party system was officially established. Ould Daddah initially managed to use the single-party as an effective way to control and canalize traditional and tribal influences. However, a disastrous drought at the end of the 1960s and the involvement in the Western Saharan War (since 1975) led to a rapid delegitimization of the regime.

The First Republic ended with the coup d'état of 1978 triggering off 14 years of military rule by the *Comité militaire du salut national* (CMSN). Initially military leadership was characterized by the absence of a coherent political and economic program, differences concerning the ongoing Western Saharan War between Morocco and the independence movement POLISARIO—Mauritania now tried to remain neutral in the conflict—, and the reorganization of tribal and traditional authorities ('retribalization' of the political system). Consolidation of political power first occurred under President Khouna Ould Haidallah. But his growing political isolation caused by economic difficulties and his position in favor of POLISARIO, led to another coup d'état in 1984 and the seizure of power by Maaouiya Ould Sid' Ahmed Taya'.

His leadership saw the escalation of the ethnic conflict between the white, Arab and black Mauritania populations. Increasing unemployment and growing desertification had profoundly changed the conditions and the way of life of the Mauritianian population since the times of independence. The policy of *arabization*, meaning the preferential treatment of the Arab part of the population, which had been started already at the time of independence, escalated under the reign of Taya', and culminated in 1989–90 in pogroms, the expulsion of about 65,000 blacks to Senegal and Mali and in a bilateral conflict with Senegal (avoiding a war with difficulty), followed by economic decline since Senegal was still one of the biggest economic partners of the country.

Another outbreak of the ethnic conflict in December 1990, the ongoing strained relations with Senegal and the support of the Iraqi position in the Gulf War II aggravated the political situation of the regime. Now, the growing opposition in the country demanded the examination of alleged cases of torture relating to the ethnic conflict, and real democratic change. The President, still refusing any cooperation with the opposition, eventually introduced a multi-party system (in 1996 21 parties existed, most of them, however, only nominally). In July 1991 a new constitution, inspired by the model of the French Fifth Republic, was approved by popular referendum. On 24 January 1992 the first contest for the presidency since independence took place: The strongest contender to Ould Taya' was Ahmed Ould Daddah, half-brother of the former president, who represented the opposition coalition. As the opposition called the elections manipulated and decided to boycott the parliamentary elections in March, the elected National Assembly was consequently dominated by the presidential *Parti Républicain Democratique et Social* (PRDS).

These elections did not augur well for the democratization of the political system. The following years were characterized by a rather harsh confrontation between the President and his strongest contender Ould Daddah (relating to the speed and contents of democratic change, to the social problems caused by the implementation of structural adjustment programs and the rehabilitation of and compensation for the victims of the ethnic conflict) and by growing splits within the opposition: their members either crossed the floor to the PRDS or founded their own parties. Black Africans who had conceived the democratization process as a key to the solution to the ethnic conflict were especially disappointed with the behavior of the predominantly Arab members of the oppositional *Union des Forces Démocratiques-Ere Nouvelle* (UFD-EN) of Ahmed Ould Daddah.

The second elections in 1996/97 did not change the basic parameters of political life. Parliamentary elections in October 1996 confirmed the hegemonic position of the ruling party in the National Assembly. The opposition competed separately and thus facilitated the overwhelming 7/8 victory of the PRDS. The radical *Action pour le Changement* (AC), a party dominated by former slaves and blacks, developed as one of the most important opposition forces. The biggest challenge to PRDS came, however, from independent candidates who had failed to be considered for nomination by the PRDS. Even though the voting day proceeded without any direct interferences, the elections were faced with structural obstacles (lacking population registers, an administration controlled by the PRDS) which constrained severely the competitiveness of the poll. The presidential election in December 1997 was boycotted by the now united opposition. President Ould Taya' was re-elected but the turnout revealed growing rejection of governmental policies in the political and economic centers Nouakchott and Nouadhibou, and even in Northern Mauritania.

1.2 Evolution of Electoral Provisions

Except in the years of the military regime (1978–1991), electoral provisions were based on the principles of universal, equal, direct and secret suffrage. Nevertheless, the political will to implement these principles remained strongly hampered by the existing traditional social structures, i.e. existence of slavery and tribal bindings and the failure of sufficient developed administrative structures.

In the First Republic (1960–1978), the President and the National Assembly were directly elected in non-competitive elections. Since the introduction of a multi-party system in the 1990s, the President has been elected according to an absolute majority system and the National Assembly by a plurality system described below in detail (1.3).

1.3 Current Electoral Provisions

Sources: Constitution of the Islamic Republic of Mauritania of 20 July 1991; Décret No. 86-130 (13 August 1986) on the organization of the electoral campaign and of the voting process; Ordonnance No. 91-027 (7

October 1991) on the election of the President of the Republic; Décret No. 91-140 (13 November 1991) on the organization of the electoral campaign and the voting process of the presidential elections; Ordonnance No. 91-028 (7 October 1991) on the election of the members of the National Assembly; Décret No. 91-141 (13 November 1991) on the organization of the electoral campaign and the material organization of the election of the members of the National Assembly; Ordonnance No. 91-029 (7 October 1991) on the election of the Senators; Loi organique No. 94-011 (15 February 1994) on the election of the Senators representing Mauritanians living abroad; Décret No. 91-142 (13 November 1991) on the organization of the electoral campaign and the material organization of the elections of the Senators; Ordonnance No. 92-04 (18 February 1992) on the Constitutional Council; Réglement No. 001 (10 March 1994) on the procedure before the Constitutional Council in cases of appeals against the elections of Deputies and Senators.

Elected national institutions: President of the Republic (no Vice-President) and National Assembly (79 members) which is part of the Parliament consisting of the National Assembly and the Senate. The Senate is elected indirectly for six years (one third every two years) representing the districts of the country and Mauritanians living abroad. Regular term of office: President: six years with no restriction of re-election, National Assembly: five years. No by-elections are held.

Suffrage: The principles of universal, equal, direct and secret suffrage are applied. Every adult citizen of either sex with full civil and political rights has the right to vote and is entitled to be registered as a voter.

Nomination of candidates
- *presidential election*: Every citizen born Mauritanian and of Islamic faith with full civil and political rights aged at least 40 years at the date of candidature is eligible if the candidature is presented by at least 50 councillors of whom only 20% must belong to the same constituency of the same district. Political parties are not involved in the nomination of presidential candidates.
- *parliamentary election*: Every citizen of either sex aged at least 25 years can be elected, excluding: citizens without full civil and political rights; citizens who have been judged because of corruption or electoral manipulations; citizens who have been declared bankrupt without rehabilitation or who are in the process of settlement *sub judice*; citizens who have not been of Mauritanian nationality for at least 10 years. Partial in-

compatibilities apply to members of the armed and of the security forces in active service; court officials or administrative personal serving in the territory in which their constituency is situated; persons having not regulated their tax duties; parliamentarians who have been dismissed because of not fulfilling their obligations (they can not be elected for 10 years). Each candidate has to deposit 50,000 Ouguiya which will only be reimbursed if he has received more than 10% of the votes cast. Independent candidature is allowed.

Electoral system
- *presidential elections*: Absolute majority system. If no candidate has reached a majority of the votes cast in the first ballot, the two candidates with most of the votes compete in a second round.
- *parliamentary elections*: 53 constituencies with one or two seats. The number of the seats for each constituency is fixed by law and depends on the number of inhabitants of the constituencies concerned: Up to 31,000 inhabitants = one seat; more than 31,000 inhabitants = two seats. In constituencies with one seat an absolute majority system is applied. If no candidate has received at least 50% of the vote, a second round will be held between the two strongest candidates. In constituencies with two seats a majoritarian system is used with the following characteristics: Candidates are presented in closed party lists; each voter has a single vote. If one list has received at least 50% there will be only one round; after having eliminated the lists below 10%, the seats are distributed according to an electoral quotient (not specified in the electoral law), the remaining seat is given to the majority list. In the constituencies where no list has obtained the absolute majority in the first round, the two lists with most of the votes will proceed into a second round. The seats are distributed according to a quota formula, the remaining seat is attributed to the list with most of the votes. (Thus, it is almost impossible that two parties win a seat in the same two-member constituency.) Due to the small sizes of the constituencies and the rule of converting votes into seats, the electoral system has a strongly majoritarian effect, and favors the majority party.

1.4 Comment on the Electoral Statistics

Due to the lack of administrative structures data (especially for the First Republic) are often scarce, official figures can not be regarded as reliable. Tables for the elections until 1976 are based on secondary sources (Ziemer 1978). The elections of the 1990s have not significantly improved the data situation, as information given by the administration or the opposition differ. The complete results for all constituencies, publicized in the Mauritanian newspapers (the 'official' *Horizons* of 09/03/1992, 16/10/1996 and 20/12/1997, and the private *L'Eveil Hebdo* of 15/12/1997, *Mauritanie Nouvelles* of 10/11/1996 and *Nouakchott info* of 10/12/1997) lack reliability. The *Journal Officiel de la RIM* gives only incomplete figures for the presidential elections.

2. Tables

2.1 Dates of National Elections, Referendums and Coups d'Etat

Year	Presidential elections	Parliamentary elections[a]	Elections for Constitutional Assembly	Referendums	Coups d'état
1959		17/05			
1961	20/08				
1965		09/05[b]			
1966	07/08				
1971	08/08	08/08[c]			
1975		26/10			
1976	08/08	08/08			
1978					10/07
1980					04/01
1984					12/12
1991				12/07	
1992	24/01	06/03 (1st) 13/03 (2nd)			
1996		11/10 (1st) 18/10 (2nd)			
1997	12/12				

[a] Only the lower chamber, the National Assembly, was elected directly whereas the upper chamber, the Senate, was elected indirectly by the municipalities.

[b] Prolongation of the legislative period to enable Parliament to declare the PPM as single-party.

[c] Prolongation of the legislative period so that presidential and parliamentary elections could be held simultaneously.

2.2 Electoral Body 1959–1997

Year	Type of election[a]	Population[b]	Registered voters		Votes cast		
			Total number	% pop.	Total number	% reg. voters	% pop.
1959	Pa	730,000	387,829	53.1	352,851	90.3	48.3
1961	Pr	980,000	397,588	40.6	371,808	93.6	37.9
1965	Pa	1,028,900	482,305[c]	46.9	447,660	92.8	43.5
1966	Pr	1,070,000	491,320	45.9	472,657	96.2	44.2
1971	Pa	1,200,000	534,994	44.6	511,414	95.6	42.6
1971	Pr	1,200,000	534,994	44.6	515,121	96.3	42.9
1975	Pa	1,320,000	661,416	50.1	578,201	87.4	43.8
1976	Pr	1,338,830	648,876	48.5	634,936	97.9	47.4
1976	Pa	1,338,830	648,876	48.5	—	—	—
1991	Ref.	2,027,770	857,121	42.3	731,512	85.4	36.1
1992	Pr	2,086,585	1,183,892	56.7	560,796	47.4	26.9
1992	Pa (1st)	2,086,585	1,174,087	56.3	456,237	38.5	21.9
1996	Pa (1st)	2,270,000	1,040,855	45.9	541,849	52.1	23.9
1997	Pr	2,500,000	1,203,668	48.1	899,444	74.7	36.0

[a] Pr = President; Pa = Parliament (House of Representatives); Ref = Referendum.

[b] Population data are based on World Bank data (for the 1960s), official sources (*Office National de la Statistique*) for the 1970s, 1991, 1992; and estimations of Economist Intelligence Unit (1996, No.4) and *Marchés Tropicaux* (March 1998) for 1996 and 1997.

[c] Provisional results published by the Minister of Interior on 12 May 1965.

2.3 Abbreviations

AC	Action pour le Changement
APP	Alliance Populaire Progressiste
PAN	Parti de l'Avant-Garde Nationale—At-Taalia
PCD	Parti pour la Coopération Démocratique
PCDM	Parti du Centre Démocratique Mauritanien
PLEJ	Parti pour la Liberté, l'Egalité et la Justice
PMR	Parti Mauritanien du Renouveau
PPM	Parti du Peuple Mauritanien
PRDS	Parti Républicain Démocratique et Social
PRM	Parti du Regroupement Mauritanien
PTUN	Parti du Travail et de l'Unité Nationale
PUD	Parti Unioniste Démocratique
RDU	Rassemblement pour la Démocratie et l'Unité
RNLDJ	Rassemblement National pour la Liberté, la Démocratie et la Justice
UDP	Union pour la Démocratie et le Progrès
UDP (2)[a]	Union pour la Démocratie et le Progrès[a]
UFD/EN[b]	Union des Forces Démocratiques/ Ere Nouvelle[b]
UPC	Union pour la Planification et la Construction
UPSD	Union Populaire Sociale et Démocratique

[a] UDP(2) consists of former members of the UDP and was registered under the same name as the 'mother party' by the Minster of Interior in 1996.

[b] Until June 1992: UFD. The name was changed after Ahmed Ould Daddah, the presidential candidate of 1992 supported by the UFD, became member and Secretary-General of the party.

2.4 Electoral Participation of Parties and Alliances 1959-1997

Party / Alliance	Years	Elections contested	
		Presidential	Parliamentary
PRM	1959	0	1
PPM	1961, 1965, 1966, 1971, 1975, 1976	4	4
PAN	1992, 1996	0	2[a]
PCDM	1992, 1996	0	2[b]
PMR	1992, 1997	1	1
PRDS	1992, 1996, 1997	2[c]	2[d]
PTUN	1992, 1996	0	2
RDU	1992, 1996	0	2[e]
UFD/ EN	1992, 1996	1[f]	1[g]
UPC	1992	0	1
UPSD	1992, 1996, 1997	2	2[h]
AC	1996	0	1[i]
APP	1996	0	1[j]
PCD	1996	0	1
PUDS	1996	0	1
RNLDJ	1996	0	1
UDP	1996	0	1[k]
UDP(2)	1996	0	1[l]
PLEJ	1997	1	0

[a] Alliances also with UFD and UDP.
[b] Boycott of the parliamentary elections in 1992, but two of its members (one of them the Secretary-General) were independent candidates.
[c] The candidate of the PRDS was supported by PAN and PTUN.
[d] In 1996, an alliance also with RDU.
[e] 1992: boycott of the second round. 1996: alliances also with PRDS.
[f] Candidature as UFD, comprising the following parties in 1996: UFD/ EN, AC, UDP, UDP(2). The candidature was also supported by PCDM.
[g] 1992: boycott. In 1996, also alliances with PAN, AC, APP and independent candidates.
[h] In 1996 alliances also with UFD/ EN.
[i] Alliances also with UDP, UFD/ EN, APP and Talia.
[j] Alliances also with UFD/ EN.
[k] Alliances also with AC, PAN and UPSD.
[l] Alliances also with UPSD.

2.5 Referendums

Year	1991[a]	
	Total number	%
Registered voters	857,121	–
Votes cast	731,512	85.3
Invalid votes	3,020	0.4
Valid votes	728,492	99.6
Yes	713,493	97.9
No	14,998	2.1

[a] Constitutional Referendum.

2.6 Elections for Constitutional Assembly

Elections for Constitutional Assembly have not been held.

2.7 Parliamentary Elections 1959–1996

Year	1959		1965	
	Total number	%	Total number	%
Registered voters	387,829	–	482,305	–
Votes cast	352,851	90.3	447,660	92.8
Invalid votes	2,725	0.8	1,816	0.4
Valid votes	350,126	99.2	445,844	99.6
PRM	350,126	100.0	–	–
PPM	–	–	445,844	100.0

Year	1971		1975	
	Total number	%	Total number	%
Registered voters	534,994	–	661,416	–
Votes cast	511,414	95.6	578,201	87.4
Invalid votes	7,008	1.2	3,443	0.6
Valid votes	504,406	98.6	574,758	99.4
PPM	504,406	100.0	574,758	100.0

For the 1976 parliamentary elections no data were available.

Year	1992[a] Total number	%	1996[a] Total number	%
Registered voters	1,174,087	–	1,040,855	–
Votes cast	456,237	38.9	541,849	52.1
Invalid votes	10,912[b]	2.4	—	—
Valid votes	445,325	97.6	—	—
PRDS	301,349	67.7	352,482	67.6
RDU[d]	32,841	7.4	7,392	1.4
UFD/EN	–	–	27,779	5.3
AC	–	–	26,295	5.3
UDP	–	–	8,666	1.7
RDU / PAGN	5,090	1.1	–	–
PAN[e]	4,504	1.0	–	–
PMR	3,203	0.7	–	–
PMR - C / UPC	319	0.1	–	–
UPSD	1,553	0.3	707	0.1
UPC	382	0.1	–	–
PCDM	357	0.1	159	0.1
PTUN	83	0.0	360	0.1
APP	–	–	370	0.1
UDP2	–	–	109	0.0
PCD	–	–	107	0.0
Independents	95,644	21.5	66,234	12.7

[a] Results of first round.
[b] Sum of *bulletins nuls* (5,670) and *bulletins neutres* (5,242). Contrary to Mauritanian electoral statistics but according to international standards, the *bulletins neutres* are not regarded as valid votes in this data handbook.
[c] Results of alliances: PRDS-RDU: 6,244 votes (1.2%); UFD/EN-PAN: 9,411 (1.8%); UFD/EN-Independents: 7,757 (1.5%); PAN-UFD/EN: 1,574 (0.3%); UDP-AC: 1,499 (0.3%); UFD/EN-AC-APP: 932 (0.2%); UDP-PAN: 615 (0.1%); UPSD-UD: 576 (0.1%); UFD/EN-Independent El Islah: 508 (0.1%); UDP2-UPSD: 248 (0.1%).
[d] Boycott of the second round in 1992.
[e] In 1996 PAN presented candidates only in alliances with other parties; see above c.

2.8 Composition of Parliament 1959–1996

Year	1959 Seats	%	1965 Seats	%	1971 Seats	%	1975 Seats	%
	40	100	40	100	50	100	70	100
PRM	40	100	–	–	–	–	–	–
PPM	–	–	40	100	50	100	70	100

Year	1976[a]		1992		1996	
	Seats	%	Seats	%	Seats	%
	–	100	79	100	79	100
PPM	–	–	–	–	–	–
PRDS	–	–	67	84.8	70	88.6
PMR	–	–	1	1.3	–	–
RDU	–	–	1	1.3	1	1.3
AC	–	–	–	–	1	1.3
Independents	–	–	10	12.7	7	8.9

[a] No data available.

2.9 Presidential Elections 1961–1997

1961	Total number	%
Registered voters	397,588	–
Votes cast	371,808	93.6
Invalid votes	838	0.2
Valid votes	370,970	99.8
Mokhtar Ould Daddah (PPM)	370,970	100.0

1966	Total number	%
Registered voters	491,320	–
Votes cast	472,657	96.2
Invalid votes	1,080	0.2
Valid votes	471,577	99.8
Mokhtar Ould Daddah (PPM)	471,577	100.0

1971	Total number	%
Registered voters	534,994	–
Votes cast	515,121	96.3
Invalid votes	2,413	0.5
Valid votes	512,708	99.5
Mokhtar Ould Daddah (PPM)	512,708	100.0

1976	Total number	%
Registered voters	648,876	–
Votes cast	634,936	97.9
Invalid votes	4,301	0.7
Valid votes	630,635	99.3
Mokhtar Ould Daddah (PPM)	630,635	100.0

1992	Total number	%
Registered voters	1,183,892	–
Votes cast	560,796	47.4
Invalid votes	11,314[a]	2.0
Valid votes	549,482	98.0
Maaouiya Ould Sid'Ahmed Taya' (PRDS)	345,583	62.7
Ahmed Ould Daddah (UFD)	180,658	32.8
El Moustapha Ould Mohammed El Saleck (Independent)	15,735	2.9
Mohamed Mahmoud Ould Mah (UPDS)	7,506	1.4

[a] Corrected by the author according to the standards of the handbook. Includes '*suffrages nuls*' and '*suffrages neutres*'.

1997	Total number	%
Registered voters	1,203,668	–
Votes cast	899,444	74.7
Invalid votes	19,643[a]	2.2
Valid votes	879,801[a]	97.8
Maaouiya Ould Sid'Ahmed Taya' (PRDS)	800,333	91.0
Mohamed Lemine Chbih Ould Cheikh Mailainine	62,138	7.1
Moulaye Ould Jiyid (PMR)	7,652	0.9
Mohamed Mahmoud Ould Mah (UPSD)	6,352	0.7
Amadou Moctar Kane (PLEJ)	3,326	0.4

[a] Author's calculation. Contrary to Mauritanian electoral statistics but according to international standards, the *bulletins neutres* are not regarded as valid votes in this data handbook. Accordingly, the percentages differ from Mauritanian electoral statistics. Mauritanian newspapers give inconsistent data concerning total sum of invalid votes.

2.9 a) Presidential Elections 1992 and 1997: Results per *Moughataa*

1992 (absolute numbers)					
	Sid' Ahmed Taya'	Ahmed Ould Daddah	Mahmoud Ould Mah	Moustapha Ould Sack	Valid votes
Hodh el-Sharqui	52,440	5,285	795	2,771	61,291
Hodh el-Gharbi	54,342	7,507	618	1,903	64,370
Assaba	31,304	9,014	516	1,948	42,782
Gorgol	16,179	16,888	348	360	33,775
Brakna	30,248	17,443	556	1,001	49,248
Trarza	32,083	30,739	1,003	1,012	64,837
Adrar	17,182	1,787	228	1,003	20,200
Dakhlet Nouad.	17,092	15,356	606	1,320	34,374
Tagant	18,089	3,407	233	425	22,154
Guidimakha	12,713	13,608	321	441	27,083
Tiris Zemmour	7,506	3,598	127	460	11,691
Inchiri	2,926	823	109	168	4,026
Nouakchott	53,479	55,203	2,046	2,923	113,651
Total	345,583	180,658	7,506	15,735	549,482

1992 (percentages)					
	Sid' Ahmed Taya'	Ahmed Ould Daddah	Mahmoud Ould Mah	Moustapha Ould Sack	Valid votes
Hodh el-Sharqui	85.6	8.6	1.3	4.5	100
Hodh el-Gharbi	84.4	11.7	1.0	3.0	100
Assaba	73.2	21.1	1.2	4.6	100
Gorgol	48.0	50.0	1.0	1.0	100
Brakna	61.4	35.4	1.1	2.0	100
Trarza	49.5	47.4	1.5	1.6	100
Adrar	85.0	8.8	1.1	5.0	100
Dakhlet Nouad.	49.7	44.7	1.8	3.8	100
Tagant	81.7	15.4	1.1	1.9	100
Guidimakha	46.9	50.2	1.2	1.6	100
Tiris Zemmour	64.2	30.8	1.1	3.9	100
Inchiri	72.7	20.4	2.7	4.2	100
Nouakchott	47.1	48.6	1.8	2.6	100
Total	62.9	32.9	1.4	2.9	100

1997 (absolute numbers)						
	S. A. Taya'	Chbih	Jiyed	Ould Mah	Kane	Valid votes
Hodh el-Sharqui	191,708	1,608	341	472	129	194,258
Hodh el-Gharbi	112,060	4,186	513	788	165	117,712
Assaba	97,947	3,836	544	605	183	103,115
Gorgol	39,872	2,558	269	452	323	43,474
Brakna	58,802	3,064	335	559	223	62,983
Trarza	120,099	4,018	281	539	299	125,236
Adrar	21,579	2,980	612	200	93	25,464
Dakhlet Nouad.	12,996	10,155	406	229	164	23,950
Tagant	31,236	784	844	172	169	33,205
Guidimakha	30,675	1,667	283	397	276	33,298
Tiris Zemmour	7,431	3,962	889	133	89	12,504
Inchiri	12,439	557	21	67	23	13,107
Nouakchott	63,489	22,763	2,314	1,739	1,190	91,495
Total	800,333	62,138	7,652	6,352	3,326	879,801

1997 (percentages)						
	S. A. Taya'	Chbih	Jiyed	Ould Mah	Kane	Valid votes[a]
Hodh el-Sharqui	98.7	0.8	0.2	0.2	0.1	100
Hodh el-Gharbi	95.2	3.6	0.4	0.7	0.1	100
Assaba	95.0	3.7	0.5	0.6	0.2	100
Gorgol	91.7	5.9	0.6	1.0	0.7	100
Brakna	93.4	4.9	0.5	0.9	0.4	100
Trarza	95.9	3.2	0.2	0.4	0.2	100
Adrar	84.7	11.7	2.4	0.8	0.4	100
Dakhlet Nouad.	54.3	42.4	1.7	1.0	0.7	100
Tagant	94.1	2.4	2.5	0.5	0.5	100
Guidimakha	92.1	5.0	0.8	1.2	0.8	100
Tiris Zemmour	59.4	31.7	7.1	1.1	0.7	100
Inchiri	94.9	4.2	0.2	0.5	0.2	100
Nouakchott	69.4	24.9	2.5	1.9	1.3	100
Total	91.0	7.1	0.9	0.7	0.4	100

[a] Due to rounding the total of the percentages shown does not always amount to 100.

2.10 List of Power Holders 1959–1998

Head of State and Government	Years	Remarks
Mokhtar Ould Daddah	1959–1978	Elected; overthrown by a coup d'état (10/07/1978); Head of Government and State.
El Moustapha Ould Mohamed El Saleck	1978–1979	Head of military government.
Mohamed Mahmoud Ould Ahmed Louly	1979–1980	Head of military government, 27/05/1979-04/01/1980.
Mohamed Khouna Ould Haidallah	1980–1984	Head of military government, 12/12/1980-12/12/1984.
Maaouiya Ould Sid'Ahmed Taya'	1984–	Head of a military government from 12/12/1984 to 18/04/1992; since then elected President.

The new Constitution (1991) provides for a Prime Minister who shall direct and coordinate the action of government. He is exclusively appointed and dismissed by the President of the Republic who exercises the executive power and presides over the Council of Ministers. Since 1992 the President has appointed four Prime Ministers (Sidi Mohamed Ould Boubacar 1992–1996; Cheikh el Afia Ould Mohamed Khouna 1996–1997; Mohamed Lemine Ould Guig 1997–1998; Cheikh el Afia Ould Mohamed Khouna since 1998).

3. Bibliography

3.1 Official Sources

Islamic Republic of Mauritania (1991). Constitution, approved by referendum on 12 July 1991, in A. P. Blaustein and G. H. Flanz (eds.), *Constitutions of the Countries of the World*. Dobbs Ferry: Oceana, Release 93–95.

RIM. *Journal Officiel de la République Islamique de Mauritanie (JORIM)*, 75 (30/01/1992).

RIM, Ministère de l'Intérieur, des Postes et Télécommunications. Direction de la Traduction, de la Législation et de la Documentation (1996). *Recueil de textes législatifs et réglementaires relatifs au processus démocratique et aux libertés publiques.*

RIM, Ministère du Plan et de l'Aménagement du Territoire (1983). *Recensement général de la population 1977.*

RIM, Ministère du Plan. Office National de la Statistique (1995). *Annuaire Statistique de Mauritanie*, Année 1993.

3.2 Books and Articles

Calderini, S. (comp.) (1992). *Mauritania*. Oxford: Clio Press.

Clausen, U. (1993). *Demokratisierung in Mauretanien. Einführung und Dokumente*. Hamburg: Deutsches Orient-Institut.

— (1994). *Mauretanien. Eine Einführung.* Mitteilungen des Deutschen Orient-Instituts No. 50. Hamburg: Deutsches Orient-Institut.

— (published annually). 'Mauretanien', in Institut für Afrika-Kunde and R. Hofmeier (eds.), *Afrika Jahrbuch*. Opladen: Leske & Budrich.

Commission of the European Community (1978). *ACP: Statistical Yearbook 1970–1976.* Bruxelles: CEC.

CRESM (Centre de Recherches et d'Etudes sur les Sociétes Méditerranéennes. Centre d'Etudes d'Afrique Noire) (1979). *Introduction à la Mauritanie*. Paris: CRESM.

EIU (Economic Intelligence Unit) (1996). *Country Report. Senegal, The Gambia, Mauritania*. No. 4, London: EIU.

Marchesin, P. (1992). *Tribus, ethnies et pouvoir en Mauritanie.* Paris: Karthala.

Mohamedou, M.-M. (1995). *Social Transition to Democracy in Mauritania.* Cairo: Ibn-Khaldoun Center for Development Studies.

Moore, C. H. (1965). 'One-Partyism in Mauritania'. *Journal of Modern African Studies* 3/3: 409–420.

Ould-Mey, M. (1998). 'Structural Adjustment Programs and Democratization in Africa: The Case of Mauritania', in J. M. Mbaku and J. O. Ihonvbere (eds.), *Multiparty Democracy and Political Change. Constraints to Democratization in Africa*. Aldershot: Ashgate, 33–63.

Pazzanita, A. G. (1996). *Historical Dictionary of Mauritania*. Metuchen, NJ: Scarecrow Press.

Sordet, M., and Milcent, E. (1969). 'Le Parti Mauritanien du Peuple'. *Revue Francaise des Etudes Politiques Africaines* 45: 36–44.

Wegemund, R. (1988). 'Die Militärregierung in Mauretanien. Zwischenbilanz nach zehn Jahren'. *Afrika Spectrum*, 23/3: 293–314.

— (1991). *Politisierte Ethnizität in Mauretanien und Senegal. Fallstudien zu ethnisch-sozialen Konflikten, zur Konfliktentstehung und zum Konfliktmanagement im postkolonialen Afrika.* Arbeiten aus dem Institut für Afrika-Kunde No. 79. Hamburg: Institut für Afrika-Kunde.

— (1993). 'Mauretanien', in D. Nohlen and F. Nuscheler (eds.), *Handbuch der Dritten Welt, Bd.4: Westafrika und Zentralafrika*. Bonn: Dietz, 315–327.

World Bank (1976). *World Bank Tables 1976*. Washington, D.C.

Ziemer, K. (1978). 'Mauretanien', in D. Sternberger, B. Vogel, D. Nohlen and K. Landfried (eds.), *Die Wahl der Parlamente und anderer Staatsorgane. Band II: Politische Organisation und Repräsentation in Afrika,* by Franz Nuscheler, Klaus Ziemer *et al.*, Berlin/ New York: Walter de Gruyter, 1359–1390.

MAURITIUS

by Michael Krennerich

1. Introduction

1.1 Historical Overview

Mauritius is one of the few African countries in which a multi-party system has been maintained since independence (12 March 1968), and where competitive elections have been held almost regularly. Party politics have been influenced by inter-related ethnic and class conflicts as well as by personal rivalries of charismatic party leaders, party breakaways and tactical alliances which up to now have been indispensable to form parliamentary majorities.

After having introduced internal self-government under the pressure of the Mauritius Labour Party and its trade unions, the British government decided on the London Constitutional Conference of 1965 to grant independence to Mauritius, and provided general elections (instead of a referendum) to sanction it. However, the elections of 1967 were almost a referendum on the issue of independence, which had raised intense conflict within the country. The elections were won narrowly by the Independence Party, a pro-independence alliance formed by Sir Seewoosagur Ramgoolam's Labour Party and two smaller groups (Muslim Action Committee, MAC; Independent Forward Bloc, IFB), against the *Parti Mauricien Social Democrate* (PMSD), then led by Sir Gaëtan Duval, and other small parties which campaigned for an association or integration formula with the United Kingdom, arguing that Mauritius was too small, isolated and economically too vulnerable to be viable as an independent country. They also claimed that independence would mean 'Hindu hegemony'. On 12 March 1968, Mauritius gained independence within the Commonwealth under the prime ministership of Sir Ramgoolam. Until 1992, it constituted a parliamentary monarchy with the British Queen as Head of State, represented by a Mauritian Governor-General.

Due to the existence of different communities (Hindus, Muslims, Sino-Mauritians and the so-called General Population), 'communalism' has always existed in the heterogeneous Mauritian society. However, it rarely reached a critical level. Escalating ethnic conflicts seriously threatened the country's political and social stability only in 1963 and 1968. In response to communal riots, a grand coalition (Labour Party, PMSD, MAC) was formed shortly after independence. The opposition vacuum was filled by a new left-wing extra-parliamentary party, the *Mouvement Militant Mauricien* (MMM), led by Paul Berénger. From its very inception in 1969, the MMM focussed its attention on class struggle rather than on ethnic politics, advocated by the traditional parties in the 1950s and 1960s. It formed several militant trade unions and gained strong support among the youth. Alarmed by the growing strength of the MMM, which had won seats in by-elections for the Legislative Assembly and Municipal Councils in 1970 and 1971, and by a wave of strikes, generally acknowledged to have been stirred up by MMM members, the government not only abolished by-elections and passed a repressive Public Order Act, but also refused to hold general elections in 1972 and declared a state of emergency in December 1971, which was renewed several times. MMM leaders were held in continuous detention and the government maintained strict control over the party's activities. However, the MMM was allowed to participate in the election of 1976, characterized by a three-cornered competition between the Labour-led Independence Party, the PMSD and the MMM, the latter promising radical reforms. The MMM's strengthening of leftist and nationalist ideologies did not replace communalism as the basis of politics, but helped to weaken and modify it. At least since 1976, all national political parties have ensured the representation of various communities and of various economic substrata within each community in the selection of candidates. In the 1976 elections, the MMM won almost an absolute majority of seats. Nevertheless, the Labour Party was able to form a new coalition government with the PMSD.

It was not until 1982 that elections brought a drastic political change. The results of the 1982 elections showed a total swing towards the MMM and its small alliance partner *Parti Socialiste Mauricien* (PSM), a breakaway from Labour. Except for the two seats of the island of Rodrigues, MMM/PSM won all directly elected seats. The candidates of the traditional parties—Labour, MAC and PMSD—which had dominated the Mauritian political scene up to then, suffered stunning defeats. The new coalition government with MMM president Sir Anerood Jugnauth as its Prime Minister was much less radical than assumed, influenced by the conditions set by the IMF and the World Bank for much-needed loans. Within a year, however, the coalition broke up due to a split within the MMM. Bérenger led the MMM into opposition while Jugnauth continued as Prime Minister and founded the *Mouvement Socialiste Mauricien* (MSM) around his loyal MMM wing and PMS supporters. Unable to command a parliamentary majority, Jugnauth called for new elections in 1983. He managed to continue as Prime Minister on the basis of an alliance formed by MSM, PMSD and Labour. Favored by the electoral system, Jugnauth's alliance won comfortable majorities of parliamentary seats in 1983 and 1987. In the face of an impending electoral pact between Labour and the opposition party MMM, Jugnauth successfully negotiated an alliance of MSM and MMM before the elections of 1991. The election resulted in a resounding victory for the MSM/MMM alliance with Jugnauth remaining Prime Minister. As part of the alliance agreement, at the MMM's insistence, Mauritius became a republic by constitutional change on 12 March 1992. Since the office of President is essentially a ceremonial one, however, the replacement of the post of the Governor-General by a President has not led to any significant changes in national politics.

In 1993 the MMM suffered another split: While the breakaway MMM, led once again by Bérenger, joined the opposition, the loyal MMM wing stayed within the MSM-led coalition government and formed a new party, the *Renouveau Militant Mauricien* (RMM). The 1995 elections were won overwhelmingly by the opposition alliance Labour/MMM, thus marking the second transfer of power to the opposition *via* elections since independence.

1.2 Evolution of Electoral Provisions

Since independence, the principles of universal, equal, direct and secret suffrage have been applied to the parliamentary elections. The electoral provisions have remained essentially unchanged until today (see 1.3). The most important change was the lowering of the voting age to 18, one year before the 1976 election.

As for the electoral system, a British commission presided by Sir Harold Banwell was appointed to devise an electoral system for Mauritius before granting independence. The Banwell Commission was subject to strong pressure from political players within Mauritius. It proposed a form of proportional representation which was favored by the PMSD and other anti-independence parties who thrived on 'ethnic politics'. The two biggest pro-independence parties, Labour and IFB, however, opposed the PR proposal vehemently and organized public protests until the Banwell Commission shelved the plan for proportional representation. It was replaced by the majority representation system which is still in use (see 1.3). As a concession to the anti-independence parties, however, an additional best loser system was implemented as a constitutional guarantee against the under-representation of ethnic groups and parties in Parliament. The eight best loser seats (out of 70 Members of Parliament) constitute a device to assure a better representation of ethnic groups, but cannot compensate for the disproportionality effect that stems from the majority system applied for the election of the other 62 seats.

1.3 Current Electoral Provisions

Sources: Constitution of the Republic of Mauritius, especially Chapter V, Part I: The National Assembly, and the First Schedule: Election of Members of National Assembly.

Elected national institution: Unicameral Parliament (National Assembly), consisting of 62 members, directly elected in 21 constituencies, and a maximum of eight additional members ('best losers'), nominated on the basis of the election results. The ordinary parliamentary term is five years.

Suffrage: Persons are entitled to be registered as electors if they are Commonwealth citizens of not less than 18 years, and either have resided in Mauritius for a period of not less than two years or are domiciled in Mauritius and are residents there. No person may be entitled to be registered as an elector in more than one constituency or in any constituency in which he/ she is not resident. Registered persons who are returning officers or have been concerned in any offence connected with elections are prohibited from voting. No person may vote at any election for any constituency who is not registered as an elector in that constituency.

Nomination of candidates: Every candidate may at nomination declare that he/ she belongs to a registered party. In such a case, the name of that party is stated on the ballot paper. Otherwise, he/ she is regarded as an independent candidate. Every candidate must declare which community he/ she belongs to. The respective community is stated in a published notice of his/ her nomination. The population of Mauritius is regarded as including a Hindu community, a Muslim community and a Sino-Mauritian community; every person who does not appear, 'from his way of life', to belong to one or other of those three communities is regarded as belonging to the General Population, which is itself regarded as a fourth community.

Electoral system
- *direct elections of 62 representatives*: The plurality system is applied in 20 three-member constituencies (island of Mauritius) and in one two-member constituency (island of Rodrigues). There are no party lists, but individual candidacies. There can be several candidates of the same party (in practice, usually, there are not more candidates of the same party than there are representatives to be elected in the constituency). Multiple vote: Each voter must cast as many votes as there are representatives to be elected in his/ her constituency, that is, three votes in three-member constituencies or two votes in the two-member constituency of Rodrigues. No vote cast by any elector is counted unless he has cast as many valid votes as there are representatives to be elected in the constituency in which he is registered. Accumulation is not allowed.
- *allocation of eight additional seats ('best losers')*: In order to ensure 'a fair and adequate representation of each community', eight seats are allocated to unelected candidates. The allocation of additional seats is restricted to candidates belonging to a political party.

The first four best loser seats are allocated on a purely community basis to the most under-represented communities, irrespective of party affiliation. The under-representation of a community for the first seat is determined by dividing the population of each community by the number of seats obtained by it plus one. The community with the highest quotient is regarded as the under-represented one. The first seat goes to the candidate who has failed to get elected but has got the highest score amongst the defeated candidates of the under-represented community, regardless of the party he/ she belongs to. The exercise is repeated to allocate the other three seats. In order to determine the under-represented community for each seat, however, the seats already obtained (including best loser seats) by each community, are considered in the calculation.

The second four best loser seats are awarded on a party and community basis: When the first four seats have been allocated to candidates belonging to parties other than the most successful party (e.g. the party with most seats won in the direct elections), then an equal number of seats is allocated to the most successful unelected candidates belonging both to the most successful party and to the under-represented community. (As shown above, the latter is determined by dividing the population of each community by the seats which it has already obtained plus one.) In the case that any of the seats remains unfilled, the next seat is be allocated to the most successful non-elected candidate belonging both to the most successful party that has not received any of the eight seats and to the under-represented community, and the next seat (if any) is allocated to the most successful candidate of the second most successful party and to the under-represented community, and so on.

1.4 Comment on the Electoral Statistics

Except for the 1967 elections, taken from Mathur (1991), the following electoral results are based on official sources (*Government Gazette* or information given by the Electoral Commissioner Office), accessible on the island of Mauritius. However, the official results indicate only the votes cast for each candidate, but neither the candidate's party affiliation nor the votes cast for each party at the constituency or the national level. Hence, a laborious procedure was necessary to calculate the national votes cast for each party: (1) Each candidate's party affiliation had to be identified on the basis of the nomination lists. (2) The votes won by the candidates of the same party in the respective constituencies had to be summed up. (3) The constituency votes of each party had to be summed up in order to obtain the national results. Such a complex calculation procedure is likely to produce errors. Although the calculations have been done very carefully and have been checked several times, the electoral data should be handled with care. Differing data are given by Mathur (1991).

2. Tables

2.1 Dates of National Elections, Referendums and Coups d'Etat

Year	Presidential elections	Parliamentary elections	Elections for Constitutional Assembly	Referendums	Coups d'état
1967		07/08			
1976		20/12			
1982		15/06			
1983		21/08[a]			
1987		30/08			
1991		15/09			
1995		20/12			

[a] After the split of the MMM as the major partner of the government alliance in March 1983, the Prime Minister called for new elections in August 1983.

2.2 Electoral Body 1967–1995

Year	Type of election[a]	Population[b]	Registered voters		Valid ballot papers[c]		
			Total number	% pop.	Total number	% reg. voters	% pop.
1967	Pa	774,000	324,358	41.9	273,579	84.3	35.3
1976	Pa	898,000	462,034	51.5	407,526	88.2	45.4
1982	Pa	995,000	540,000	54.3	483,810	89.6	48.6
1983	Pa	1,000,432	551,708	55.1	464,465	84.2	46.4
1987	Pa	1,040,000	639,491	61.5	561,058	87.7	53.9
1991	Pa	1,077,800	680,836	63.2	573,419	84.2	53.2
1995	Pa	1,104,000[d]	715,179	64.8	559,005	78.2	50.6

[a] Pa = Parliament.

[b] Population census: 1,000,432 (1983) and 1,065,988 (1990). Population data of 1987 and 1991 are based on official estimations. Other data are unofficial estimations.

[c] One ballot paper for each voter. Each voter had to cast as many votes on the ballot paper as there were representatives to be elected in his or her constituency (three votes in the 21 three-member constituencies of Mauritius and two votes in the two-member constituency of Rodrigues); otherwise, the ballot paper was regarded as invalid.

[d] Unofficial estimation for 1994.

2.3 Abbreviations

FTS	Front Travailleurs Socialistes
IFB	Independent Forward Bloc
MLP	Mauritius Labour Party (= Parti Travailliste)
MAC	Muslim Action Committee (= Comité d'Action Musulman)
MMM	Mouvement Militant Mauricien
MMMSP	Mouvement Militant Mauricien Socialiste et Progressiste
MMSM	Mouvement Militant Socialiste Mauricien
MR	Mouvement Rodriguais
MSM	Mouvement Socialiste Militant
MTD	Mouvement Travailliste Démocrates
OPR	Organisation du Peuple Rodriguais
PAN	Parti de l'Alliance Nationale
PGD	Parti Gaëtan Duval
PMSD	Parti Mauricien Social Démocrate
PR	Parti Rodriguais
PSM	Parti Socialiste Mauricien
RMM	Renouveau Militant Mauricien
RPR	Regroupement du Peuple de Rodrigues
UDM	Union Démocratique Mauricienne
UTL	Unité des Travaillistes Libéraux

General note: Abbreviations are only indicated when they have been used in official sources or secondary literature.

2.4 Electoral Participation of Parties and Alliances 1967–1995

Party / Alliance	Years	Elections contested[a]
All Mauritius Hindu Congress	1967	1
Independence Party	1967, 1976	2[b]
IFB	1967, 1976, 1982, 1995	4[c]
MLP	1967, 1976, 1982, 1983, 1987, 1991, 1995	7[d]
Mauritius Liberation Font	1967	1
Mauritius Workers' Party	1967	1
Mauritius Young Communist League	1967	1
MAC	1967, 1976, 1982	3[e]
National Socialist Workers' Party	1967	1
PR	1967	1
PMSD	1967, 1976, 1982, 1983, 1987, 1991	6[f]
Communist Party of Mauritius	1976, 1983, 1991	3
Mauritius Muslim Democratic League	1976	1

Party / Alliance	Years	Elections contested[a]
Mauritius Muslim Rights	1976, 1983	2
Mauritius People's Progressive Party	1976	1
Mauritius United Party	1976, 1987, 1991, 1995	4
MMM	1976, 1982, 1983, 1987, 1991, 1995	6[g]
MMMSP	1976	1
Mouvement et la Jeunesse Socialiste Mauricienne	1976	1
OPR	1976, 1982, 1983, 1987, 1991, 1995	6
Parti du Centre Republicain	1976, 1982	2
Parti du Sud	1976	1
Parti Socialiste Progressiste	1976	1
People's Democratic Party	1976, 1987, 1991	3
Union de la Population Générale	1976	1
UDM[h]	1976, 1982	2
UTL	1976	1
Dhravediennes United Party	1982	1
Fraternité Tamoule de l'Île Maurice	1982, 1987, 1991	3
Front Libération National	1982	1
Independent Democratic Movement	1982	1
Mauritius National Party	1982	1
Mauritius Socialist Congress	1982	1
Mauritius Young Labour Movement	1982	1
Mouvement Liberal du Nord	1982, 1983	2
Mouvement Radical Mauricien	1982	1
Organisation du Peuple Mauricien	1982	1
PAN[i]	1982	1
Parti Islamique Mauricien	1982	1
PSM	1982	1[j]
Zenes Socialiste	1982	1
Front Mauricien Indépendant	1983	1
Groupement Mauricien	1983	1
Groupement Progressiste	1983	1
Groupement Socialiste du Sud	1983	1
Lalit Travayer	1983, 1987	2
Mouvement Démocrate Mauricien	1983	1
MSM	1983, 1987, 1991, 1995	4[k]
Parti du Peuple Mauricien	1983, 1987, 1991, 1995	4
Parti Ouvrier Progressiste	1983	1
L'Avenir Mauricien	1987	1
FTS	1987, 1991	2[m]
Groupement Mario Fabien	1987	1

Party / Alliance	Years	Elections contested[a]
MEM/PE	1987	1
Mouvement Planteurs Mauricien	1987	1
Mouvement Socialiste Progressiste	1987	1
Mouvement Socialiste du Sud	1987, 1991, 1995	3
MTD	1987	1[n]
MTS	1987	1
National Mauritius Muslim Rights	1987	1
OMT-FNAS	1987	1
Organisation de l'Unité Mauricienne	1987	1
Parti National Mauricien	1987	1
Rassemblement pour l'Economie et le Développement	1987	1
RPR	1987, 1991	2
Hizbullah	1991, 1995	2
Mauritius Party Rights	1991, 1995	2
Parti Action Libéral	1991, 1995	2
Parti Militant Travailler	1991	1
Démocratie Mauricienne	1995	1
Front Populaire Musulman	1995	1
Hindu Ekta Andolan Dul	1995	1
MMP / HP	1995	1
MMSM	1995	1
Mouvement Democratique Mauricien	1995	1
Mouvement des Démocrates Libéraux	1995	1
Mouvement Mauricien Pour la Paix	1995	1
Mouvement pour la Justice	1995	1
Mouvement Rodriguais	1995	1
Mouvement Travailleurs Mauritien	1995	1
PGD	1995	1
Parti de la Loi Naturelle	1995	1
Parti Républicain	1995	1
RMM	1995	1[o]

[a] Parliamentary elections; total number: 7.

[b] In 1967, alliance made up of three separate parties: MLP as the major partner, the MAC and the IFB. In 1976, the IFB was no longer formal part of the alliance.

[c] In 1967, the IFB was part of the alliance that formed the Independence Party.

[d] In 1967 and 1976, the MLP was the major partner in the alliance that formed the Independence Party; in 1982, the MLP led the PAN. It formed alliances with: the MSM in 1983 and 1987, the PMSD in 1991 and the MMM in 1995.

[e] In 1967 and 1976, the MAC was part of the alliance that formed the Independence Party. In 1982 it entered the PAN, led by the MLP.

[f] Originally, a dissident movement from the MLP. In the 1991 elections it formed an alliance with the MLP.

[g] In alliance with PSM (1982), MMT and FTS (1987), with MSM (1991) and with MLP (1995).

[h] The party was formed by a wing that broke away from the PMSD.
[i] Alliance led by the MLP as the major partner with the MAC and dissidents of the PMSD.
[j] The PSM was originally founded by MLP dissidents. It formed an electoral alliance with MMM in 1982. The PSM dissolved itself in 1983 when it was integrated into the MSM.
[k] After the split of the MMM in March 1983, the wing which stayed loyal to Prime Minister A. Jugnauth formed the MSM with the help of the PSM. The MSM formed an alliance with the MLP in 1983 and 1987, with the MMM in 1991 and with the RMM in 1995.
[m] In 1987 in alliance with MMM and MTD.
[n] In alliance with MMM and FTS.
[o] Originally known as the Nababsingh faction of the MMM, the RMM was founded in June 1994. Electoral alliance with MSM in 1995.

2.5 Referendums

Referendums have not been held.

2.6 Elections for Constitutional Assembly

Elections for Constitutional Assembly have not been held.

2.7 Parliamentary Elections

Year	1967 Total number	%	1976[a] Total number	%
Registered voters	324,358	–	462,034	–
Ballot papers cast	—	—	—	—
Invalid ballot papers	—	—	—	—
Valid ballot papers	273,579	—	407,526	—
Valid votes[b]	813,917	–	1,213,160	–
Independence Party[c]	444,262	54.6	461,949	38.1
PMSD	354,196	43.5	200,559	16.5
MMM	–	–	469,420	40.9
Independent Forward Bloc	–	–	26,902	2.2
UDM	–	–	12,505	1.0
Parti Socialiste Progressiste	–	–	9,807	0.8
OPR	–	–	6,376	0.5
MMM-Socialiste Progressiste	–	–	5,372	0.4
Parti du Sud	–	–	2,223	0.2
Parti du Centre Republicain	–	–	1,636	0.1
Other Parties	15,459	1.9[d]	2,390[e]	0.2
Independents	–	–	14,021	1.2

[a] 369 candidates in 21 constituencies. MMM: 60 candidates in 20 constituencies; Independence Party: 62/21; PMSD: 59/20; IFB: 30/10; UDM: 35/13; Parti Socialiste Progressiste: 13/8; OPR: 2/1; MMMSP: 15/5; Parti du Sud: 6/3; Parti du Centre Republicain: 13/6. 22 candidates of other parties and 52 independent candidates.

[b] Voter must cast as many votes as there were representatives to be elected in the respective constituency (see 1.3 for further details).

[c] In 1967 the Independence Party consisted of the MLP as the major partner, the IFB and the MAC. In 1976 the Independence Party was an alliance of MLP (major partner) and MAC.

[d] All Mauritius Hindu Congress, Mauritius Liberation Front, Mauritius Workers Party, Mauritius Young Communist League, National Socialist Workers Party and PR.

[e] All parties with less than 1,000 votes: UTL (800 votes), Mauritius Muslim Democratic League (266), Mauritius People's Progressive Party (249), Communist Party of Mauritius (244), Mauritius Muslim Rights (236), Mauritius United Party (186), Mouvement et la Jeunesse Socialiste Mauricienne (174), People's Democratic Party (143), Unión de la Population Générale (92).

Year	1982[a]		1983[b]	
	Total number	%	Total number	%
Registered voters	540,000	–	551,708	–
Ballot papers cast	—	—	470,008	
Invalid ballot papers	—	—	5,543	
Valid ballot papers	483,810	—	464,465	
Valid votes[c]	1,438,816	–	1,381,151	–
MMM / PSM	906,800	63.0	–	–
MMM	–	–	629,528	45.6
MSM / MLP	–	–	575,996	41.7
PAN[d]	357,385	24.8	–	–
PMSD	120,214	8.4	140,864	10.2
OPR	16,129	1.1	15,981	1.2
Parti Islamique Mauricien	9,334	0.6	–	–
IFB	6,134	0.4	–	–
Lalit	–	–	3,116	0.2
Front Mauricien Independant	–	–	2,637	0.2
Parti Ouvrier Progressiste	–	–	2,143	0.2
UDM	1,558	0.1	–	–
Front Libération National	1,325	0.1	–	–
Mauritius National Party	1,285	0.1	–	
Mouv. Démocrate Mauricien	–	–	1,036	0.1
Other parties	3,259[e]	0.2	3,192[f]	0.2
Independents	15,393	1.1	6,658	0.5

[a] 311 candidates in 21 constituencies: MMM/PSM: 60 candidates in 20 constituencies; PAN: 59/20; PMSD: 59/21; OPR: 2/1; Parti Islamique Mauricien: 10/4; IFB: 1/1; UDM: 7/3; Front Libération National: 8/5; Mauritius National Party: 5/3; 27 candidates of other parties and 73 independent candidates.

[b] 281 candidates in 21 constituencies: MMM: 60/20; MSM/MLP: 48/16; PMSD: 14/5; OPR: 2/1; Lalit: 15/5; Front Mauricien Independant: 38/12; Parti Ouvrier Progressiste: 35/11; Mouvement Démocrate Mauricien: 8/5. 28 candidates of other parties and 33 independent candidates.

[c] Voter must cast as many votes as there were representatives to be elected in the respective constituency (see 1.3 for further details).

[d] The alliance consisted in MLP as the major partner, MAC and dissidents of the PMSD.

[e] Parties with less than 1,000 votes. Mouvement Liberal du Nord (910 votes), Mauritius Young Labour Movment (523), Parti du Centre Republicain (454), Independent Democratic Movement (334), Zenes Socialiste (265), Mouvement Radical Mauricien (255), l'Organisation du Peuple Mauricien (189), Fraternité Tamoule de l'Île Maurice et Mouvement Progressiste Hindou (118), Mauritius Socialist Congress (115), Dhravediennes United Party (96).

[f] Parties with less than 1,000 votes: Groupement Mauricen (735 votes), Communist Party of Mauritius (704), Mouvement Liberal du Nord (572), Mouvement Progressiste (426), Parti du Peuple Mauricien (358), Groupement Socialiste du Sud (241), Mauritius Muslim Rights (156).

Year	1987[a]		1991[b]	
	Total number	%	Total number	%
Registered voters	639,491	–	680,836	–
Ballot papers cast	—	—	—	—
Invalid ballot papers	—	—	—	—
Valid ballot papers	561,058		573,419	
Valid votes[c]	1,668,739	–	1,706,240	
MSM / MMM	–	–	944,521	55.4
L'Union (MMM /MTD / FTS)	789,268	47.3	–	–
Alliance (MSM / Labour)	675,757	40.5	–	–
Labour / PMSD	–	–	670,631	39.3
PMSD	141,878	8.5	–	–
OPR	17,044	1.0	16,080	0.9
FTS	–	–	12,162	0.7
RPR	11,826	0.7	11,646	0.7
Lalit	8,723	0.5	–	–
Parti Action Liberal	–	–	6,053	0.4
Parti du Peuple Mauricien	3,794	0.2	5,696	0.3
Hizbullah	–	–	5,550	0.3
Parti Militan Travayer	–	–	2,137	0.1
MTS	2,077	0.1	–	–
OMT / FNAS	1,529	0.1	–	–
Other parties	4,916[d]	0.3	1,759[e]	0.1
Independents	11,927	0.7	30,005	1.8

[a] 359 candidates in 21 constituencies: L'Union (MMM/MTD/FTS): 62 candidates in 20 constituencies; Alliance (MSM/MLP): 48/16; PMSD: 12/4; OPR: 2/1; RPR: 2/1; Lalit: 42/14; Parti du Peuple Mauricien: 22/12; Mouvement Travailliste Socialiste: 3/1; OMT/FNAS: 30/10. 61 candidates of other parties and 75 independent candidates.

[b] 331 candidates in 21 constituencies. MSM/MMM: 60 candidates in 20 constituencies; MLP/PMSD: 61/21; OPR: 2/1; FTS: 30/11; RPR: 2/1; Parti Action Liberal: 5/2; Parti du Peuple Mauricien: 27/14; Hizbullah: 3/1; Parti Militan Travayer: 6/2. 11 candidates of other parties and 124 independent candidates.

[c] Voter must cast as many votes as there were representatives to be elected in the respective constituency (see 1.3 for further details).

[d] Parties with less than 1,000 votes: MEM/PE (678 votes), l'Avenir Mauricien (676), National Mauritius Muslim Rights (606), Mouvement Socialiste Progressiste (590), Mouvement Planteurs Mauricien (524), Rassamblement pour l'Economie et le Développement (512), Mouvement Socialiste du Sud (459), Groupement Mario Fabien (362), Fraternité Tamoule de l'Île Maurice (240), People's Democratic Party (117), Parti National Mauricien (57), Mauritius United Party (54), Organisation de l'Unité Mauricienne (41).

[e] Parties with less than 1,000 votes: Mouvement Socialiste du Sud (686 votes), Communist Party of Mauritius (358), Mauritius Party Rights (243), Fraternité Tamoule de Maurice (191), Mauritius United Party (160), People Democratic Party (121).

Year	1995[a] Total number	%
Registered voters	715,179	
Ballot papers cast	—	—
Invalid ballot papers	—	—
Valid ballot papers	559,005	—
Valid votes[b]	1,663,816	–
Labour / MMM	1,084,236	65.2
MSM / RMM	330,219	19.8
PGD	105,282	6.3
MMP / HP	28,749	1.7
MMSM	25,472	1.5
OPR	16,631	1.0
MR	9,529	0.6
Front Populaire Musulman	8,233	0.5
Mouv. Des Democrats Liberaux	6,848	0.4
Parti de la Loi Naturelle	4,074	0.2
Parti Action Liberal	3,332	0.2
Parti du Peuple Mauricien	2,505	0.2
Mouv. Mauricien Pour la Paix	1,630	0.1
Hizbullah	1,375	0.1
Mouvement pour la Justice	1,149	0.1
Other parties	2,545[c]	0.2
Independents	32,007	1.9

[a] 481 candidates in 21 constituencies: MLP/MMM: 60 candidates in 20 constituencies; MSM/RMM: 60/20; PGD: 53/18; MMP/HP: 9/3; MMSM: 26/9; OPR: 2/1; MR: 2/1; Front Populaire Musulman: 30/10; Mouvement des Démocrates Liberaux: 3/1; Parti de la Loi Naturelle: 21/17; Parti Action Liberal: 2/2; Parti du Peuple Mauricien: 15/7; Mouvement Mauricien Pour la Paix: 2/1; Hizbullah: 1/1; Mouvement pour la Justice: 4/3. 19 candidates of other parties and 172 independent candidates.

[b] Voter must cast as many votes as there were representatives to be elected in the respective constituency (see 1.3 for further details).

[c] Parties with less than 1,000 votes: Mouvement Democratique Mauricien (859 votes), Mouvement Socialiste du Sud (342), Hindu Ekta Andolan Dul (307), Parti Republicain (281), Democratie Mauricienne (259), Mouvement Travailleurs Mauritien (212), Mauritius United Party (185), Mauritius Party Rights (100).

2.8 Composition of Parliament

Year	1967		1976		1982		1983	
	Seats	%	Seats	%	Seats	%	Seats	%
	70[a]	100	70[b]	100	66[c]	100	70[e]	100
Independence Party	43	61.4	28	40.0	–	–	–	–
PMSD	27	38.6	8	11.4	2	3.0	–	–
MSM/Labour/ PMSD	–	–	–	–	–	–	46	65.7
MMM	–	–	34	48.6	–	–	22	31.4
MMM/PSM	–	–	–	–	60[d]	90.9	–	–
PAN	–	–	–	–	2	3.0	–	–
OPR	–	–	–	–	2	3.0	2	2.9

[a] 62 constituency seats (Independence Party: 39, PMSD: 23) and eight best loser seats (Independence Party: 4, PMSD: 4).

[b] 62 constituency seats (MMM: 30, Independence Party: 25, PMSD: 7) and eight best loser seats (MMM: 4, Independence Party: 3, PMSD: 1).

[c] Exceptionally, the Parliament was made up of only 66 members: 62 constituency seats (MMM/PSM: 60, OPR: 2) and four best loser seats (PAN: 2, PMSD: 2). The second batch for best losers could not be assigned, since all the MMM/PSM constituencies candidates had been elected.

[d] Within the MMM/PSM alliance the MMM won 42 seats and the PSM 18.

[e] 62 constituency seats (MSM/MLP/PMSD: 41, MMM: 19, OPR: 2) and eight best loser seats (MSM/MLP/PMSD: 5, MMM: 3).

Year	1987		1991		1995	
	Seats	%	Seats	%	Seats	%
	70[a]	100	66[b]	100	66[c]	100
MSM / MLP / PMSD	44	62.9	–	–	–	–
MSM	–	–	30	45.5	–	–
MLP	–	–	6	9.1	–	–
PMSD	–	–	1	1.5	–	–
MMM	24	34.3	27	40.9	–	–
MLP / MMM	–	–	–	–	60[d]	90.9
OPR	2	2.9	2	3.0	2	3.0
MR	–	–	–	–	2	3.0
PDG	–	–	–	–	1	1.5
Hizbullah	–	–	–	–	1	1.5

[a] 62 constituency seats (MSM/MLP/PMSD: 39, MMM: 21, OPR: 2) and eight best loser seats (MSM/MLP: 4, PMSD: 1, MMM: 3).

[b] 62 constituency seats and four best loser seats. Only four best loser seats were allocated.

[c] 62 constituency seats (MLP/MMM: 60, OPR: 2) and only four best loser seats (MR: 2, PDG: 1, Hizbullah: 1).

[d] Within the MLP/MMM alliance, the MLP won 35 seats and the MMM 25.

2.9 Presidential Elections

No direct presidential elections have been held.

2.10 List of Power Holders 1968–1998

Head of State	Years	Remarks
Queen Elizabeth II	1968–1992	Mauritius became independent on 12/03/1968, with the British Queen as symbolic Head of State, represented by the following Governors-General: Sir Arthur Leonard Williams (1969–74), Sir A. O. Osman (1974–78), Sir Dayendranath (1978–83), Sir Seewoosagur Ramgoolam (1983–85), Sir Veerasamy Ringadoo (1986–92).
Sir Veerasamy Ringadoo	1992	Mauritius became a republic on 12/03/1992. The former Governor-General Ringadoo became President of the Republic until the nomination to the presidency of Cassam Uteem.
Sir Cassam Uteem	1992–	President Uteem (since 01/07/1992) was elected for a five-year term by the National Assembly on 30/06/1992; re-elected 1997.

Head of Government	Years	Remarks
Sir Seewoosagur Ramgoolam	1968–1982	After having been Chief Minister (1961–64) and Premier (1965–68) under British rule, Ramgoolam became Prime Minister when Mauritius achieved independence on 12/03/1968. He was defeated in the 1982 elections.
Sir Aneerood Jugnauth	1982–1995	After the June 1982 elections, Jugnauth (MMM) was elected Prime Minister by Parliament and led a coalition government. He managed to continue as Prime Minster on the basis of coalition governments formed after the elections of 1983, 1987 and 1991.
Navin Ramgoolam	1995–	After the December 1995 elections, Ramgooglam (MLP) assumed the office of Prime Minister on 27/12/1995.

3. Bibliography

3.1 Official Sources

Electoral Commissioner's Office (1987). *Results of the General Elections*, 1987 (mimeo).

La Constitution de la République de Maurice 1993, Port Louis: Best Graphics.

The Government Gazette of the Colony of Mauritius, 11th July, 1967: General Notices No. 673-693 of 1967.

The Government Gazette of the Colony of Mauritius, 10th August 1967: General Notice No. 793 of 1967: Results of the General Election 1967.

The Government Gazette of Mauritius, Extraordinary, 6th December, 1976: General Notices No. 1230ff. of 1976 (Notice of Taking of Poll).

The Government Gazette of Mauritius, Extraordinary, 23th December, 1976: General Notice No. 1310 of 1976: Results of the General Elections, 1976.

The Government Gazette of Mauritius, Extraordinary, 21th May, 1982, General Notices No. 562ff. of 1982 (Notice of Taking of Poll).

The Government Gazette of Mauritius, Extraordinary, 15th June 1992, General Notice No. 728 of 1982: Results of the General Election, 1982.

The Government Gazette of Mauritius, Extraordinary, 15th and 25th July, 1983: General Notices No. 1011ff. (Notice of Taking of Poll).

The Government Gazette of Mauritius, Extraordinary, 24th August, 1983: General Notice No. 1144 of 1983: Results of the General Elections, 1983.

The Government Gazette of Mauritius, Extraordinary, 10th August 1987: General Notices No. 944ff. (Notice of Taking of Poll).

The Government Gazette of Mauritius, Extraordinary, 2nd September, 1991: General Notices No. 1160-1180 of 1991 (Notice of Taking of Poll).

The Government Gazette of Mauritius, Extraordinary, 18th September, 1991: General Notice No. 1240 of 1991: Results of the General Election, 1991.

The Government Gazette of Mauritius, Extraordinary, 12 December 1995: General Notices No. 1538-1588 of 1995 (Notice of Taking of Poll).

The Government Gazette of Mauritius, Extraordinary, 23 December 1995: General Notice No. 1586 of 1995: Results of the General Election, 1995.

3.2 Books, Articles and Electoral Reports

Addison, J., and Hazareesingh, K. (1993). *A New History of Mauritius* (rev. edn). Stanley, Rose Hill: Editions de l'Océan Indien.

Allen, P. M. (1975). 'Mauritius—The Ile de France Returns', in J. M. Ostheimer (ed.), *The Politics of the Western Indian Ocean Islands*. New York: Praeger, 195–227.

Boisson, J.-M., and Louit, C. (1978). 'Les élections législatives du 20 décembre 1976 à l'île Maurice: l'enjeu économique et politique'. *Annuaire des pays de l'Océan Indien*, 3: 215–267.

Bowman, L. W. (1991). *Mauritius. Democracy and Development in the Indian Ocean*. Boulder, Col.: Westview Press.

Bräutigam, D. (1997). 'Institutions, Economic Reform, and Democratic Consolidation in Mauritius'. *Comparative Politics*, 30/1, 45–62.

Caroll, B. W. (1997). 'State and Ethnicity in Botswana and Mauritius: A Democratic Route to Development'. *The Journal of Development Studies*, 33/4: 464–486.

Commonwealth Office (1967). *Mauritius General Election 1967*. Reports by Commonwealth Observers, London: HMSO.

Durand, J. P. (1977). 'Le Mouvement Militant Mauricien'. *Revue Française d'Études Politiques Africaines*, 138/139: 77–93.

Houbert, J. (1981). 'Mauritius: Independence and Dependence'. *The Journal of Modern African Studies*, 19/1: 75–105.

Keller, S., and Nuscheler, F. (1993). 'Mauritius', in D. Nohlen and F. Nuscheler (eds.), *Handbuch der Dritten Welt, Band 5: Ostafrika und Südafrika*. Bonn: Dietz, 257–272.

Leffler, U. (1988). *Mauritius. Abhängigkeit und Entwicklung einer Inselökonomie.* (Hamburger Beiträge zur Afrika-Kunde 33). Hamburg: Institut für Afrika-Kunde.

Livet, P., and Oraison, A. (1979). 'Le Mouvement Militant Mauricien'. *Annuaire des pays de L'Océan Indien*, 4: 40–93.

Louit, C. (1984). 'Les élections législatives de juin 1982', in Centre d'Études et des Recherches sur les Sociétés de l'Océan Indien (ed.), *L'île Maurice. Sociale, économique et politique (1974–1980).* Aix-en-Provence: CERSOI, 425–430.

Mathur, H. (1991). *Parliament in Mauritius*. Rose Hill: Editions de L'Océan Indien.

Nuscheler, F. (1978). 'Mauritius', in D. Sternberger, B. Vogel, D. Nohlen and K. Landfried (eds.), *Die Wahl der Parlamente und anderer Staatsorgane. Bd.II: Politische Organisation und Repräsentation in Africa*, by Franz Nuscheler, Klaus Ziemer *et al.*, Berlin/ New York: Walter de Gruyter, 1391–1409.

Obeegadoo, S. (1984). *From Revolution to Reformism. The Political Dynamics of Mauritian Society and the Evolution of the Mauritius Militant Movement*. Rose Hill: Editions de L'Océan Indien.

Prosper, J.-G. (without year). *Indépendance et République*. Vacoas: Editions Le Printemps.

Ramgoolam, S. (presented by Anand Mulloo) (1982). *Our Struggle. 20th Century Mauritius*. New Delhi: Vision Books.

Selvon, S. (1986). *Ramgoolam*. Mauritius: Editions de l'Océan Indien.

— (1991). *Historical Dictionary of Mauritius* (2nd edn). Metuchen, NJ: Scarecrow Press.

Simmons, A. S. (1982). *Modern Mauritius. The Politics of Decolonization*. Bloomington, IN: Indiana University Press.

MOROCCO

by Juan Montabes Pereira and María A. Parejo Fernández

1. Introduction

1.1 Historical Overview

From 1912 to 1956 Morocco was subject to *de facto* French and Spanish control, but the internal authority of the Sultan was nominally respected. Under pressure from Morrocan nationalists, who organized within the Istiqlal party in 1944, the French and Spanish relinquished their protectorates on 2 March and 7 April 1956 and the country was unified under Mohamed V. Since then Morocco's political system has been defined and colored by the Crown. The royal protagonism within the political system, laid down in the first constitution negotiated between Mohamed V and France on the eve of independence and even more so the political ubiquity of his successor King Hassan II have shaped Morocco's political landscape. According to the constitutions of 1962, 1970, 1972 and the revisions of 1992 and 1996, the Monarch personifies the center of political power. He symbolizes the country's unity and guarantees the continuity of the state. As *Emir al Mouminin* (prince of the believers) he unifies religious and political power. The principles of a constitutional and democratic monarchy laid down in the first article of the constitution collide with this concentration of power: The Monarch assumes legislative competencies between the parliamentary sessions, he disposes of a right to veto and to dissolve Parliament; he can submit any law project to referendum, he nominates the Prime Minister and he heads the *Conseil Superieur de la Magistrature*.

Within this institutional framework the competencies, as well as the composition of the National Assembly—only a part of the seats had been allocated by direct vote from 1970 to 1993 (the bicameral system adopted in 1996 has its predecessor in a similar but short-lived constitutional arrangement from 1963 to 1965)—collide with the principles of representative democracy. Moreover, the electoral process controlled by the state administration, has often intervened manipulating and even violating electoral provisions. Although this has not completely demolished the legitimacy of electoral outcomes, it has certainly devalued them. Due to the Monarch's political privileges, elections to the National Assembly do not have direct effects on the composition of the government. Thus electoral participation provides for a legitimating impulse to the political system and especially to the Monarchy.

Nonetheless, Morocco's uninterrupted history of constitutionally obligatory multi-party elections stands alone within the Arab world. The constitutional prohibition of the one-party state (Article 3), originally installed by the monarchy in order to contain the dynamics of the nationalist Istiqlal party, provided for a rather broad integration of political élites in the long run. The four important opposition parties today, Istiqlal, *Union des Socialistes des Forces Populaires* (USFP), *Parti du Progrès et du Socialisme* (PPS) and *Organisation de l'Action Démocratique et Populaire* (OADP), have maintained diverse relations with the regime over the years, but have generally explicitly or implicitly contributed to the consensus about fundamental forms and questions of Moroccan politics. The pro-governmental parties, which were constructed around the Crown and its administrative apparatus, *Union Constitutionelle* (UC), *Rassemblement National des Indépendants* (RNI) *Parti National Démocratique* (PND) and *Mouvement Populaire* (MP) have formed a pro-governmental coalition since 1984.

Those eight political parties, formally and factually recognized by the regime, are being consulted, informed and heard by the Crown, depending on the case. In a broader view, the approximately 14 parties existing today coalesce into the rather stable formations of a tripolar system of the leftist Koutla bloc, the Center bloc and the conservative Wifaq bloc.

From the first municipal elections in 1960, the country's political history was marked by continuous negotiations on institutional arrangements between the Crown and the major political forces. The constitutional and electoral history shows a long, gradual and open (1962–1996) process of national construction paved with ruptures, violence and reconciliation between the opposed actors: On the one side the *Majzen* (government), trying to maintain its predominance; on the other hand the opposition, engaged in a struggle for greater freedom of action. The inclination to constitutionalize political conflict (three constitutions and three constitutional reforms) as well as frequent elections (16) reveal the society's search for the definition of political protagonism, liberty and justice via the primacy of the law.

Thus the Crown could enforce its favorite constitutional arrangements and electoral system (uninominal majority system in small constituencies) against the main oppositional force of Istiqlal in 1962, but already three years later dissatisfaction with the economic and social policies of the regime led to rioting in Casablanca. Three months later, on 6 June 1965, the King assumed legislative and executive powers proclaiming a state of emergency. In June 1967, the King again relinquished the post of Prime Minister, but continued hostility of oppositional forces led to frequent government changes.

A new constitution, approved in July 1970, provided for a partial presumption of parliamentary government, a strengthening of royal powers and a limited role for political parties. Despite the opposition of major political groups, an election for a new Assembly of Representatives was held in August 1970 yielding a pro-government majority. However, the King's failure to unify the political class behind his programs was dramatically illustrated by abortive military revolts in 1971 and 1972 (attempting the King's assassination). A new constitution was approved by popular referendum in March 1972, but legislative elections in order to reconstitute the Assembly of Representatives were not held until June 1977. On 30 May 1980 a Constitutional Amendment extending the term of the Assembly of Representatives from four to six years was approved by referendum, thus postponing new elections until 1983, which were further postponed pending the results of an OAU sponsored referendum in the Western Sahara. Elections were finally held on 14 September 1984. A national referendum on 1 December 1989 approved the King's proposal to postpone legislative elections until 1990 in order to permit participation by Western Saharans following a self-determination vote in the disputed territory. In mid-1992 amid indications that the referendum might be delayed indefinitely or even abandoned, the government announced that forthcoming local and national elections would include the residents of Western Sahara as participants.

In May 1992 the opposition parties, which had experienced a progressive electoral marginalization of 53% of the votes cast in 1965, 40% in 1977 and 25% in 1984, launched an oppositional bloc under the banner of Koutla or Democratic bloc, aiming for greater democratization of the political system.

New constitutional provisions considered as insufficient by the opposition were approved on 4 September 1992 by a national referendum under boycott of some oppositional political parties. However, the subsequent balloting for directly elective assembly seats on 25 June 1993 was hailed as a victory for the Koutla bloc. It secured 99 of 222 seats in the direct poll, but only 15 seats of 111 seats in the second indirect round in electoral colleges made up of local officials, trade unionists and representatives of professional associations.

Due to the Koutla bloc's considerable strength, the subsequent legislative term from 1993 to 1996 was marked by weakened relations between executive and parliamentary majority and difficulties in forming stable governments. Parliament, however, gained importance as a national forum of demands for institutional reform. Political consensus over Koutla's claim for democratic reform and the extension of the direct vote to all seats of the House of Representatives was achieved in a process of negotiation, political blockade and re-negotiation. The long-awaited reform was presented by the King and approved by referendum on 13 September 1996 with 99.6% of the valid votes supported by all political parties. The subsequent parliamentary elections on 14 November 1997 could not fulfil the opposition's hopes for a majority in the National Assembly. However, for the first time for 40 years, elections broke the ritual of forming government; a socialist, Abderahman Youssoufi, was appointed Prime Minister, thus transforming the majority of votes cast into a governmental majority.

1.2 Evolution of Electoral Provisions

In Morocco electoral provisions were never integrated into one coherent electoral code, but have developed through a great number of organic laws, decrees, directives and so-called Dahirs (see official sources), which have made electoral provisions often incoherent, even contradictory and facilitated oblivion. This tremendous disparity and important judicial and political obstacle was—insufficiently—resolved with the current *code électoral Dahir No. 1-97-83 du 2 avril 1997*.

Since 1956 King Mohamed V had installed indirectly elected Advisory Councils by law of *Dahir 1-56-162*, which did not cement an electoral system. Municipal elections in May 1960 were the first elections subject to universal and direct suffrage. Plurality rule in single-member constituencies was applied, an electoral formula which remains unaltered until today. The minimum age for voters was then 21 years; it was reduced to 20 years of age with the reform of electoral laws in 1993.

The Constitution of 14 December 1962 provided for a bicameral system with a *Chambre de Représentants* of 144 seats directly elected for a four-year term. A *Chambre des Conseillers* of 120 seats was indirectly elected for a six-year term by an electorate consisting of officials at local, province and prefectorial level (for 80 seats) and of corporate organizations (for 40 seats). Members of the *Chambre des Conseillers* had to be at least 35 years of age, half of the Chamber being renewed every three years. Each province was represented by closed lists of one to 13 members elected according to proportional rule.

The Constitution was suspended from June 1965 to July 1970, when the Constitution of 20 March 1970 paved the way for the restitution of Parliament. A unicameral system was then introduced emphasizing corporate representation and indirect election. Of the 240 members of Parliament 90 were directly elected, while 90 seats were installed by an electorate of municipal councils and 60 seats by professional associations and factory committee members according to closed lists and proportional rule. The parliamentary term was extended to six years. Due to the fact that Parliament was widely regarded as non-representative and therefore boycotted by almost all political parties a new constitution was put into effect on 10 March 1972 which extended the number of directly installed seats to 160 of a total of 240 seats elected for a four-year term. The proportion of two thirds directly and one third indirectly installed mandates was not altered until 1996 when a bicameral Parliament was installed: In 1977 Parliament contained 267 seats of which 178 were directly and 89 indirectly elected; in 1984 of a total of 306 seats 204 were directly and 102 were indirectly elected; in 1993 of a total of 333 seats 222 were directly and 111 were indirectly elected. The parliamentary term was extended from four to six years by referendum on 30 May 1980. The duration of the parliamentary term as the constitutionally fixed six years was prolonged for two years by referendum on 1 December 1989 because of the Sahara conflict.

The normative base of the electoral system existing today is the *Dahir No. 1-77-177 de 9 mai 1977*. The amendments of 1982, 1984, 1992 and 1993 updated its contents in view of upcoming elections. The *Dahir* of 1977 and its reforms were completed by decrees creating and listing the respective constituencies. This made gerrymandering comparatively easy for the Ministry of the Interior, which was repeatedly complained about by the opposition. In 1997 the House of Representatives abolished the Dahir of 1977 with the *loi organique No. 31-97 art 86*.

The current electoral law *Dahir No. 1-97-83 de 2 avril 1997* is the product of a negotiation process which started in 1992 when the Koutla bloc achieved the installation of a National Commission concerned with the formulation of an electoral law.

1.3 Current Electoral Provisions

Sources: Constitution, adopted by referendum on 13 September 1996, Dahir No. 1-97-83, 23 kaada 1417 of 2 April 1997; Dahir No. 1-97-83 du 2 avril 1997 portant promulgation de la loi No. 9-97 formant code électoral BO 3-VI-1997; Dahir No. 1-97-187 du 1er joumada I 1418 (4 septembre 1997) portant promulgation de la loi organique No. 31-97 relative à la Chambre des Répresentants BO 18-IX-97; Dahir No. 1-97-186 du 1er joumada I 1418 (4 septembre 1997) portant promulgation de la loi organique No. 32-97 relative à la Chambre des Conseillers BO 18-IX-97.

Elected national institutions: A bicameral Parliament consisting of a directly elected Assembly of Representatives (*Majlis al-Nuwab*) and a indirectly elected Assembly of Councillors *(Maijlis al-Mustasharin*). The Assembly of Representatives contains 325 members and is elected for a five-year term. The Assembly of Councillors contains 270 members and is elected for a nine-year term (partially renewed every three years) with three-fifths (162 members) being elected by local councils at the community, prefectorial, provincial and regional level and two-fifths (81 members) being elected by an electoral college representing the professional chambers and labor organizations. The professional chambers send 33 members of the agricultural sector, 24 of the commercial, industrial and service sector, 21 of the artisan and three of the maritime fishery sector. A number of 27 labor representatives are sent by an electoral college consisting of all labor organizations.

Suffrage: Universal, equal, secret and direct. Requirements: at least 20 years of age, Morrocan citizenship, voter registration is compulsory.

Nomination of candidates
- elections to the Assembly of Representatives: Qualified electors, 23 years of age, Moroccan citizenship. Ineligibilities: Naturalized citizens, persons restricted by court order, six months after having held the following functions: judges and public prosecutors, governors on local and district level and members of the armed and police forces. This temporal ineligibility extends to a period of two years for the same functions when the candidate is presented in the same constituency where he had held one of the positions mentioned. Candidatures must be submitted at least 14 days prior to the polling day; a compulsory monetary deposit of

2,000 Dirhams is reimbursed if the candidate obtains at least 5% of the votes cast in the constituency concerned.
- *elections to the Assembly of Councillors*: Qualified electors, 30 years of age, Moroccan citizenship. Candidates have to be members of their electoral colleges. Ineligibilities: Naturalized citizens, persons restricted by court order. Candidatures must be submitted at least eight days prior to the polling day; a compulsory monetary deposit is reimbursed if the candidate or list of candidates obtains at least 5% of the votes cast in the constituency concerned.

Electoral system
- *elections to the Assembly of Representatives*: Plurality system in 325 single-member constituencies. In case of stalemate the older candidate is elected; in case of equal age the lot decides. Vacancies arising between general elections are filled through by-elections within three months of the annulment of the mandate.
- *elections to the Assembly of Councillors*: Proportional system, single vote, closed lists and Hare quota (greatest remainder). In the case of only one candidate to be elected plurality system is in effect.

1.4 Comment on the Electoral Statistics

Moroccan elections were at any time initiated, supervised and controlled by the Crown via the Ministry of the Interior, which constructed and deconstructed electoral provisions according to current political intentions. The monarchical administration's ubiquity within the electoral process has devalued the electoral system and has also aroused doubts concerning the credibility of official statistics published by the Ministry of the Interior. Official tallies have shown differing quality; sometimes of arbitrary content, sometimes extensively detailed. The full results of the 1970 parliamentary elections were not published.

For a complete picture secondary literature was consulted. Until 1977 electoral data follow Philipp (1978); for later the following publications were consulted: Azerdane (1977), Bamchameo (1982), Miege (1986), Santucci (1977), Sehmi (1978, 1985), *Le Matin du Sahara et du Maghreb* (6 December 1989, 20 September 1993, 20 September 1995, 17 September 1996), *Al-Bayane* (30 June 1993). For the 1996 elections information was drawn from IFES and the IPU website (www.ipu.org). Population data given in table 2.2 are estimations by World Bank and UNESCO.

2. Tables

2.1 Dates of National Elections, Referendums and Coups d'Etat

Year	Presidential elections	Parliamentary elections	Elections for Constitutional Assembly	Referendums	Coups d'état
1962				07/12	
1963		17/05			
1970		28/08		24/07	
1972				01/03	
1977		03/06			
1980				23/05, 30/05	
1984		02/10		31/08	
1989				01/12	
1992				04/09	
1993		25/06			
1995				15/09	
1996				13/09	
1997		14/11			

2.2 Electoral Body 1962–1997

Year	Type of election[a]	Population	Registered voters		Votes cast		
			Total number	% pop.	Total number	% reg. voters	% pop.
1962	Ref	11,649,393	4,654,955	40.0	3,919,733	84.2	33.6
1963	Pa	12,665,000	4,803,654	37.9	3,448,539	71.8	27.2
1970	Ref	15,400,000	4,847,310	31.5	4,515,743	93.2	29.3
1970	Pa	15,400,000	4,874,598	31.6	4,160,001	85.3	27.0
1972	Ref	15,825,000	4,862,009	30.7	4,519,923	93.0	28.6
1977	Pa	17,899,000	6,519,301	36.4	5,369,431	82.3	30.0
1980	Ref	19,332,000	7,130,703	36.9	6,902,717	96.8	35.7
1980	Ref	19,332,000	7,079,518	36.6	6,429,477	90.8	33.3
1984	Ref	21,331,000	7,742,908	36.3	7,514,344	97.0	35.2
1984	Pa	21,331,000	7,414,846	34.8	4,999,646	67.4	23.4
1989	Ref	23,951,000	9,960,578	41.6	9,844,189	98.0	41.1
1992	Ref	26,300,000	11,804,038	44.9	11,483,623	97.3	43.7
1993	Pa	27,600,000	11,398,987	41.1	7,153,211	62.7	25.9
1995	Ref	29,720,000	11,613,119	39.0	8,155,359	70.2	27.4
1996	Ref	—	12,287,651	—	10,443,112	85.0	—
1997	Pa	—	12,790,631	—	7,456,996	58.3	—

[a] CA = Constitutional Assembly; Pa = Parliament; Pr = President, Ref = Referendums.

2.3 Abbreviations

FDIC	Front pour la Défense des Institutions Constitutionnelles
FFD	Front des Forces Démocratiques
MD	Mouvement pour la Démocratie
MDS[a]	Mouvement Démocratique et Social
MNP[a]	Mouvement National Populaire
MP[b]	Mouvement Populaire
MPCD[a]	Mouvement Populaire Constitutionnel et Démocratique
OADP[d]	Organisation de l'Action Démocratique et Populaire
PA	Parti de l'Action
PCM[c]	Parti Communiste Marocain
PDI	Parti Démocratique de l'Indépendance
PI-Istiqlal[d]	Parti de l'Indépendance – Istiqlal
PND[b]	Parti National Démocratique
PPS[c]	Parti du Progrès et du Socialisme
PNUS	Parti National pour l'Unité et la Solidarité
PRP[cd]	Partie du Renouveau du Progrès
PSD	Partie Social et Démocratique
RNI[a]	Rassemblement National des Indépendants
SAP	Sans Appartenance Politique
UC[b]	Union Constitutionnelle
UMT	Union Marocaine du Travail
UNFP	Union Nationale des Forces Populaires
USFP[d]	Union Socialiste des Forces Populaires

[a] Member of the Center bloc.
[b] Member of the Wifaq bloc.
[c] The Morrocan Communist Party ran in parliamentary elections in 1963 under the banner of PCM, in 1977, 1984 and 1993 under the banner of PPS and in 1997 of PRP.
[d] Member of the Koutla bloc.

2.4 Electoral Participation of Parties and Alliances 1963–1997

Party / Alliance	Years	Elections contested
FDIC	1963	1
PCM[a]	1963	1
PI	1963, 1977, 1984, 1993, 1997	5
MP	1963, 1977, 1984, 1993, 1997	5
UNFP	1963	1
MPCD	1977, 1984, 1997	3
PA	1977, 1984, 1993, 1997	4
PPS[a]	1977, 1984, 1993	3
USFP	1977, 1984, 1993, 1997	4
OADP	1984, 1993, 1997	3

Party / Alliance	Years	Elections contested
PDI	1984, 1993, 1997	3
PND	1984, 1993, 1997	3
PUSN-PCS	1984	1
RNI	1984, 1993, 1997	3
UC	1984, 1993, 1997	3
MNP	1993, 1997	1
PRP[a]	1997	1
MDS	1997	1
FFD	1997	1
PSD	1997	1
MD	1997	1

[a] The Moroccan Communist Party has run in all elections since independence under the banners of PCM, PPS and PRP in succession.

2.5 Referendums

Year	1962[a]		1970[a]	
	Total number	%	Total number	%
Registered voters	4,654,955	–	4,847,310	–
Votes cast	3,919,737	84.2	4,515,743	93.2
Invalid votes	72,720	1.9	36,008	0.8
Valid votes	3,847,017	98.1	4,479,735	99.2
Yes	3,733,816	97.0	4,424,393	98.8
No	113,199	3.0	55,342	1.2

[a] Constitutional referendum.

Year	1972[a]		1980[b]	
	Total number	%	Total number	%
Registered voters	4,862,009	–	7,130,703	–
Votes cast	4,519,923	93.0	6,902,717	96.8
Invalid votes	29,276	0.6	27,013	0.4
Valid votes	4,490,647	99.4	6,875,704	99.6
Yes	4,434,859	98.8	6,849,813	99.6
No	55,737	1.2	25,891	0.4

[a] Constitutional referendum.

[b] Referendum on constitutional reform: Reduction of the heir to the throne's age of majority from 18 to 16. The electorate included Western Saharans, but not Moroccan citizens abroad.

Year	1980[a]		1984[b]	
	Total number	%	Total number	%
Registered voters	7,079,518	–	7,742,908	–
Votes cast	6,429,477	90.8	7,514,344	97.0
Invalid votes	58,683	0.9	21,700	0.3
Valid votes	6,370,794	99.1	7,492,644	99.7
Yes	6,158,369	96.7	7,490,914	100.0
No	212,425	3.3	2,134	0.0

[a] Referendum on the revision of articles 43 and 95 of the constitution: The parliamentary term is extended from four to six years, the term of the President of Parliament is extended from one to three years.

[b] Referendum on the treaty of a projected union with Libya signed by Hassan II and Mohamad al-Qaddafi on 13 August 1984.

Year	1989[a]		1992[b]	
	Total number	%	Total number	%
Registered voters	9,960,578	–	11,804,038	–
Votes cast	9,844,189	98.8	11,483,623	97.3
Invalid votes	6,568	0.1	17,309	0.2
Valid votes	9,837,621	99.9	11,466,314	99.8
Yes	9,836,260	100.0	11,461,470	100.0
No	1,361	0.0	4,844	0.0

[a] Referendum on the extension of the legislative term for two years to permit the participation by Western Saharans following a self-determination vote in the disputed territory.

[b] Referendum on the revision of the constitution.

Year	1995[a]		1996[b]	
	Total number	%	Total number	%
Registered voters	11,613,119	–	12,287,651	–
Votes cast	8,155,359	70.2	10,443,112	85.0
Invalid votes	42,199	0.5	110,201	1.0
Valid votes	8,113,160	99.5	10,380,911	99.0
Yes	8,080,866	99.6	10,332,469	99.5
No	32,294	0.4	48,442	0.5

[a] Referendum on the bringing forward of the annual budget debate from September to April.

[b] Referendum on constitutional reform: Direct election of a lower chamber, introduction of a upper chamber, reform of the Supreme Court and the financial court.

2.6 Elections for Constitutional Assembly

Elections for Constitutional Assembly have not been held.

2.7 Parliamentary Elections 1963–1997

Year	1963		1970[a]	
	Total number	%	Total number	%
Registered voters	4,803,654	–	4,874,598	–
Votes cast	3,448,539	71.8	4,160,001	85.3
Invalid votes	113,221	3.3	54,181	1.3
Valid votes	3,335,318	96.7	4,105,820	98.7
FDIC	1,159,932	34.8	–	–
PI	1,000,506	30.0	–	–
UNFP	751,056	22.5	–	–
PCM	2,345	0.1	–	–
MP	–	–	—	—
Independents	421,479	12.6	—	—

[a] 90 of a total of 240 deputies were elected by universal and direct vote. These have been one of the most irregular elections in Morrocan history; probably full official tallies never left the Ministry of the Interior in charge. The only official tallies available figure the number of votes obtained by the two best finishers in each constituency. The political parties belonging to Koutla (PI, UNFP and PCM) as well as MPD and PDI boycotted the elections. Only MP fielded candidates and some members of PI and UNFP ran as independents. The PDC could register its candidates officially and left it to their decision to run as independents.

Year	1977[a]		1984[b]	
	Total number	%	Total number	%
Registered voters	6,519,301	–	7,414,846	–
Votes cast	5,369,431	82.3	4,999,646	67.4
Invalid votes	324,063	6.0	556,642	11.1
Valid votes	5,019,252	93.5	4,443,004	88.9
PI	1,090,960	21.7	681,083	15.3
USFP	738,541	14.7	550,291	12.9
PPS	116,470	2.3	102,314	2.8
PA	90,840	1.8	20,126	0.5
MPDC	102,358	2.0	69,862	1.6
MP	625,786	12.5	695,020	15.6
Independents	2,254,297	44.9	–	–
UC	–	–	1,101,502	24.8
RNI	–	–	763,395	17.2
PND	–	–	396,370	8.9
OADP	–	–	32,766	0.7
PDI	–	–	20,126	0.5
PUSN-PCS	–	–	9,810	0.2

[a] 176 of a total of 264 deputies were elected by universal and direct vote.
[b] 199 of a total of 306 deputies were elected by universal and direct vote.

Year	1993[a] Total number	%	1997 Total number	%
Registered voters	11,398,987	–	12,790,631	–
Votes cast	7,153,211	62.7	7,456,996	58.3
Invalid votes	930,993	13.0	1,085,366	14.6
Valid votes	6,222,218	87.0	6,371,630	85.4
UC	769,149	12.8	647,746	10.2
RNI	824,117	13.2	705,397	11.1
PI	760,082	12.2	840,315	13.8
MP	751,864	12.1	659,331	10.3
USFP	820,641	13.2	884,061	13.9
PND	500,253	8.0	270,425	4.2
MNP	662,214	10.6	431,651	6.8
PPS	245,064	3.9	–	–
OADP	196,268	3.2	184,009	2.9
PA	145,981	2.4	89,614	1.4
PDI	257,372	4.1	76,176	1.2
SAP[c]	259,213	4.2	–	–
PRP	–	–	274,862	4.3
MDS	–	–	603,156	9.5
MPCD	–	–	264,324	4.1
FFD	–	–	243,275	3.8
PSD	–	–	188,520	3.0
MD	–	–	8,768	0.1

[a] 222 of a total of 333 deputies were elected by universal and direct vote.

[b] Non-obedience candidates. Candidates without party affiliation which ran under the label of SAP, because independent candidates were not authorized.

2.8 Composition of Parliament 1963–1997

Year	1963 Seats	%
	144	100
FDIC	69	47.9
PI	41	28.5
UNFP	28	19.4
Independents	6	4.2

[a] One seat is missing, the three seats of the Saharan provinces are not included.

Year	1970 Seats 90[a]	% 100	1970 Seats 240[b]	% 100	1977 Seats 176[a]	% 100	1977 Seats 264[b]	% 100
MP	21	23.3	60	25.0	29	16.5	44	16.4
PI	4	4.4	8	3.3	45	25.6	50	18.7
UNFP/PC	1	1.1	1	0.4	–	–	–	–
PDC	–	–	2	0.8	–	–	–	–
Independents	64	71.1	159	66.0	81	46.0	141	52.8
Labor organizations	–	–	10	4.1	–	–	–	–
USFP	–	–	–	–	16	9.1	15	5.6
UMT	–	–	–	–	–	–	7	2.6
MPDC	–	–	–	–	2	1.1	3	1.1
PA	–	–	–	–	2	1.1	2	0.7
PPS	–	–	–	–	1	0.6	1	0.3

[a] Seats filled by universal and direct vote.
[b] Composition of Parliament including indirectly installed deputies.

Year	1984 Seats 199[a]	% 100	1984 Seats 306[b]	% 100	1993 Seats 222[a]	% 100	1993 Seats 333[b]	% 100
UC	55	27.6	83	27.1	27	12.2	54	16.2
RNI	38	19.1	61	19.9	28	12.6	41	12.3
USFP	34	17.1	39	12.7	48	21.6	56	16.2
MP	31	15.6	47	15.3	33	14.9	51	15.3
PI	23	11.6	42	14.1	43	19.4	52	15.6
PND	15	7.5	24	7.8	14	6.3	24	7.2
PPS	2	1.0	2	0.6	6	2.7	10	3.0
OADP	1	0.5	1	0.3	2	0.9	2	0.6
PUSN/PCS	–	–	1	0.3	–	–	–	–
UMT	–	–	5	1.6	–	–	3	0.9
MNP	–	–	–	–	14	6.3	25	7.5
PDI	–	–	–	–	3	1.4	9	2.7
PA	–	–	–	–	2	0.9	2	0.6
SAP	–	–	–	–	2	0.9	4	1.2

[a] Seats filled by universal and direct vote.
[b] Composition of Parliament including indirectly installed deputies.

Year	1997	
	Seats	%
	325	100
USFP[a]	57	17.6
Pi[a]	32	9.8
PRP[a]	9	2.8
OADP[a]	4	2.8
Uc[b]	50	15.4
MP[b]	40	12.3
PND[b]	10	3.0
RNI[c]	46	14.2
MDS[c]	32	9.8
MNP[c]	19	5.8
MPCD[c]	9	2.8
FFD	9	2.8
PSD	5	1.5
Pa[c]	2	0.6
PDI[c]	1	0.3
MD	–	–

[a] Parties pertaining to the Koutla bloc (102 seats).
[b] Parties pertaining to the Wifaq bloc (100 seats).
[c] Parties pertaining to the Center bloc (83 seats).

2.9 Presidential Elections

As Morocco is a constitutional monarchy no presidential elections have been held.

2.10 List of Power Holders 1961–1998

Head of State	Years	Remarks
Mohamed V	1956–1961	Morocco gained independence and was unified under the reign of Sultan Mohamed V on 02/03/1956.
Hassan II	1961–	Followed his father on 03/03/1961. Constitutional monarchy was established in 1962. Heir to the throne: Crown Prince Sidi Mohamad.

Head of Government	Years	Remarks
El Hbil Bekkai	1955–1958	07/12/1955 until 16/04/1958.
Ahmed Balafrej	1958	12/05 until 03/12/1958.
Abdallah Ibrahim	1958–1960	24/12/1958 until 20/05/1960. Headed an ultra-left government.
Mohamed V	1960–1961	The Monarch headed government from 25/05/1960 until 26/02/1961.
Hassan II	1961–1963	From 26/02/1961 until 13/11/1963 Hassan II headed three governments.
Ahmed Bahnini	1963–1965	13/11/1963 until 08/06/1965.
Hassan II	1965–1967	The King assumed all legislative and executive powers, the constitution was suspended from 07/06/1965 until 1970.
Mohamed Benhima	1967–1969	06/07/1967 until 07/10/1969.
Ahmed Laraki	1969–1971	07/10/1969 until 04/08/1971.
Mohamed Karim Lamrani	1971–1972	06/08/1971 until 20/11/1972.
Ahmed Osman	1972–1979	Appointed 20/11/1972, dismissed on 27/03/1979.
Maati Bouabi	1979–1983	Appointed on 27/03/1979, dismissed on 30/09/1983.
Mohamed Karim Lamrani	1983–1986	Appointed on 30/11/1983 heading a coalition government of five parties, resigned for health reasons on 30/09/1986.
Azzedine Laraki	1986–1992	Appointed on 30/09/1986, dismissed on 11/08/1992.
Mohamed Karim Lamrani	1992–1994	On 11/08/1992 the King reappointed Lamrani, he formed a new non-party government after the democratic bloc won the parliamentary elections of 1993. He was dismissed on 25/05/1994.
Abdellatif Filali	1994–1998	Appointed on 26/05/1994, on 27/02/1995 the King presented a new Cabinet, with the Prime Minister staying in office.
Abderrahman Youssoufi	1998–	Appointed on 05/02/1998.

3. Bibliography

3.1 Official Sources

Arrêté ministériel No. 3-82-92 du 28 septembre 1992 fixant le montant de la participation de l'Etat au financement de la campagne électorale menée par les partis politiques à l'occasion des élections générales communales et législatives. BO 28 septembre 1998.

Dahir No. 1-77-177 du 9 mai 1977 portant loi organique relative á la composition et l'élection de la Chambre de Répresentants. BO 10 mai 1977.

Dahir No. 1-79-303 du 8 novembre 1979 portant promulgation de la loi organique No. 16-79 modifiant et completant l'article 1 du dahir No. 1-77-177 du 9 mai 1977 portant loi organique relative à la composition et l'élections de la Chambre des Représentants. BO 21 novembre 1979.

Dahir No. 1-81-379 du mai 1982 portant promulgation de la loi organique No. 31-80 modifiant le dahir No. 1-77-177 du 9 mai 1977 portant loi organique relative à la composition et l'élections de la Chambre des Représentants. BO 16 juin 1982.

Dahir No. 1-83-267 du 27 janvier 1984 portant promulgation de la loi organique No. 27-83 modifiant et completant le dahir No. 1-77-177 du 9 mai 1977 portant loi organique relative à la composition et l'élections de la Chambre des Représentants. BO 1 février 1984.

Dahir No. 1-92-90 du 11 juin 1992 portant promulgation de la loi No. 12-92 relative à l'etablissement et à la révision des listes électorales générales et à l'organisation des élections des conseils communaux. BO 17 juin 1992.

Dahir No. 1-92-143 du 7 décembre 1992 portant promulgation de la loi No. 25-92 soumettant les fonctionnaires et agents de l'Etat, des collectivités locales et des établissements publics ainsi que les membres du gouvernements, de la Chambre des Représentants, des conseils des collectivités locales et des chambres professionelles, à la déclaration des biens immobiliers et valeurs mobilières leur appartenant ou appartenant à leurs enfants mineurs. BO 16 janvier 1993.

Dahir portant loi No. 1-93-91 du 28 avril 1993 relatif à l'adaption des listes électorales générales suite à leur informatisation. BO 5 mai 1993.

Dahir No. 1-93-93 du 27 avril 1993 portant loi organique modifiant le dahir No. 1-77-177 du 9 mai 1977 portant loi organique relative à la composition et l'élections de la Chambre des Représentants. BO 5 mai 1993.

Dahir No. 1-97-83 du 2 avril 1997 portant promulgation de la loi No. 9-97 formant code électoral. BO 3 avril 1997.

Dahir No. 1-97-83 du 2 avril 1997 portant promulgation de la loi organique No. 31-97 relative à la Chambre des Représentants. BO 4 septembre 1997.

Dahir No. 1-97-186 du 4 septembre 1997 portant promulgation de la loi organique No. 32-97 relative à la Chambre des Conseillers. BO 4 septembre 1997.

Décret No. 1-77-319 du 9 mai 1977 créant et énumerant les circonscriptions pour l'élection des répresentants au suffrage direct. BO 10 mai 1977.

Décret No. 2-84-515 du 15 août créant et énumerant les circonscriptions électorales pour l'élection des représentants au suffrage universel direct hors du territoire du Royaume. BO 15 août 1984.

Décret No. 1-92-129 du 13 août 1992 portant promulgation de la loi No. 23-92 modifiant les articles 3 et 30 de la loi No. 12-92 relative à l'etablissement et à la revision des listes électorales générales et à l'organisation des élections des conseils communaux. BO 19 août 1992.

Décret No. 2-92-721 du 28 septembre 1992 relative à la participation de l'Etat au financement des campagnes électorales menées par les partis politiques à l'occasion des élections générales communales et législatives. BO 28 septembre 1992.

Décret No. 2-93-3 du 29 avril fixant les délais et formes de production des justifications d'utilisation des subventions accordées par l'Etat aux partis politiques au titre de participation au financement de leurs campagnes électorales à l'occasion des élections générales communales et législatives. BO 5 mai 1993.

Décret No. 2-93-255 du 12 mai 1993 portant répartition, entre les préfectures et provinces, des sièges des représentants à élire par le college des conseillers communaux. BO 19 mai 1993.

Décret No. 2-93-254 du 12 mai 1993 créant et délimitant les circonscriptions électorales pour l'élection des représentants au suffrage universel direct. BO 19 mai 1993.

Décret No. 2-97-786 du 24 septembre 1997 concernant la création des circonscriptions électorales pris en application de la loi organique No. 31-97 relative à la Chambre des Représentants. BO 24 septembre 1997.

'Le Nouveau droit électoral 1997'. *Publications de la Revue Marocaine d'Administration Locale et de Développement*, Rabat.

3.2 Books, Articles and Electoral Reports

Azerdane, A. (1977). 'Le nouveau parlement marocaine: La première année de législature'. *Annuaire de l'Afrique du Nord.* Paris: CNRS.

Balta, P. (1990). *Le Grand Maghreb. Des indépendances à l'an 2000*. Paris: La Découverte/ Essais.

Bamchameo, N. (1982). *Le Parlement dans le système politique marocain.* Thèse d'Etat (Diss.), Université de Lille.

Basri, D., Rousset, M., and Vedel, G. (1992). *Revision de la constitution marocaine. Analyses et commentaires*. Rabat: Imprimerie Royale.

Chambergeat, P. (1966). 'Observations sur le système électoral marocain'. *Annuaire de l'Afrique du Nord*, 99–110.

Claisse, A., and Conac, G. (1988). *Le Grand Maghreb. Données socio-politiques et facteurs d'integration des Etats du Maghreb*. Paris: Economica.

Clement, J. F. (1990). 'Maroc: les atouts et les defis de la monarchie', in B. Kodmany-Darwish and M. Chartouni-Dubarry (eds.), *Maghreb: les années de transition*. Paris: Masson.

Commission Nationale chargée de superviser les operations électorales (1993). *Documents de la Commission Nationale chargée de superviser les opérations électorales*. Rabat: Royaume du Maroc.

Del Pino, D. (1983). *El Parlamento marroquí: ¿Una institución marginal?*, Paper presented at the colloquium of the Faculty of Law of Rabat on Parliament in Morocco, Rabat, 23 June 1983.

— (1990). *Marruecos, entre la tradición y el modernismo. Biblioteca de Ciencias Políticas y Sociología*. Granada: Universidad de Granada.

El Malki, H., and Santucci, J.-C. (1990). *Etat et développement dans le monde arabe. Crises et mutations au Maghreb*. Paris: Editions du CNRS.

Flory, M., Korany, B., Mantran, R., Camau, M., and Agate, P. (1990). *Les régimes politiques arabes*. Paris: Presses Universitaires de France.

Gellner, E. (1991). 'Studies on North Africa—Introduction to a New Series'. *Government and Opposition*, 26/3: 329–330.

Hudson, M. C. (1977). *Arab Politics. The Search for Legitimacy*. New Haven, Conn.: Yale University Press.

Ihrai, S. (1986). *Pouvoir et influence. Etat, partis et politique étrangère au Maroc*. Rabat: Edino.

Información comercial española (1991). *Argelia, Marruecos, Túnez* (monographical number). Publicación de la Secretaría de Estado de Comercio, No. 2283, 10–16 June 1991.

IFES (International Foundation for Electoral Systems) (1994). *Maroc. Elections legislatives directes 25 juin 1993. Rapport des delegations responsables du suivi et d'observateurs de l'IFES*. Washington, D.C.: IFES.

Kodmany-Darwish, B., and Chartouni-Dubarry, M. (1990). *Maghreb: Les années de transition*. Masson. Paris.

Korany, B. (1994). 'Arab Democratization: A poor cousin?'. *Political Science & Politics*, 27/3: 511–513.

Lamghari Moubarrad, A. (1996). 'La nouvelle constitution marocaine de 1996'. *Publications de la Revue Marocaine d'Administration Locale et de Développement*, No. 10.

Leca, J. (1994). 'La démocratisation dans le monde arabe: incertitude, vulnerabilité et legitimité', in G. Salamé (ed.), *Démocraties sans democrates. Politiques d'ouverture dans le monde arabe et islamique.* Paris: Fayard.

Lacoste, C., and Lacoste, Y. (1991). *L'Etat du Maghreb*. La Découverte, Paris.

Lewis, B. (1990). *El lenguaje político del Islam*. Madrid: Taurus.

López Garcia, B. (1981). 'Elecciones parciales y crisis política en Marruecos'. *Revista de Estadios Políticos*, 22: 251–262.

— (1985). 'Las elecciones legislativas del 14 de Septiembre de 1984 en Marruecos'. *Revista Española de Investigaciones Scociológicas*, 30: 245–292.

— (1990). 'Transiciones políticas en el Magreb'. *Razón y Fé*, 222: 289–304.

— (1991). 'Leyes electorales, artimañas legales. La legislación Magrebí a la hora del pluripartidismo', in B. López Garcia, G. Martin Muñoz and M. H. De Larramendi (eds.), *Elecciones, participación y transiciones políticas en el Norte de Africa*. Ministerio de Asuntos Exteriores/ICMA Madrid.

— (1996). 'Marruecos:Un referéndum no como los otros'. *El País*. 11 October 1996.

— (1997). 'Marruecos, Tierra De Trance'. *El País*. 13 June 1997.

López Garcia, B., Martin Muñoz, G., and H. de Larramendi, M. (1991). *Elecciones, Participación y Transiciones Políticas En El Norte De Africa*. Madrid: Ministerio de Asuntos Exteriores/ICMA.

López Garcia, B., and Fernández Suzor, C. (1985). *Introducción a los Regímenes y Constituciones Arabes*. Madrid: Centro de Estudios Constitucionales.

Mackenzie, W. J. M. (1962). *Elecciones libres*. Madrid: Tecnos.

Martín Muñoz, G. (1996). 'Marruecos ¿Cambio o continuidad?'. *Política Exterior*, 54.

Miege, Jean-Louis 1986: *Le Maroc*. Paris: Presses Universitaires de France.

Montabes, J., and López Garcia, B. (1995). *El Magreb tras la Crisis del Golfo: Transformaciones políticas y orden internacional*. Universidad De Granada: Agencia Española de Cooperación Internacional.

Munson, H. Jr. (1991). 'Morocco's Fundamentalists'. *Government and Opposition*, 26/3: 331–344.

Najib Ba, M. (1990). 'Constitutions et changements en Tunisie et en Algerie: Sur la question pluripartite'. *Al Mayadine, Revue Universitaire des Etudes Juridiques Economiques et Politiques*, 6: 9–20.

Nohlen, D. (1981). *Sistemas electorales del mundo*. Madrid: Centro de Estudios Constitucionales.

— (1991). 'Transiciones políticas y regímenes electorales', in B. López Garcia, G. Martin Muñoz and M. H. De Larramendi (eds.), *Elecciones, participación y transiciones políticas en el Norte de Africa*. Madrid: Ministerio de Asuntos Exteriores/ICMA.

Parejo Fernández, M. A. (1999). *Aproximación a la función de control en el parlamento Marroquí*. VI Jornadas de Derecho Parlamentario, Congreso de los Diputados, Madrid; in press.

— (1997). *Las élites políticas marroquíes. Los parlamentarios 1977–1993*. Thesis: Universidad de Granada.

Philipp, G. (1978). 'Marokko', in D. Sternberger, B. Vogel, D. Nohlen and K. Landfried (eds.), *Die Wahl der Parlamente und anderer Staatsorgane. Band II: Politische Organisation und Repräsentation in Afrika,* by Franz Nuscheler, Klaus Ziemer *et al.*, Berlin/ New York: Walter de Gruyter, 1263–1357.

Purtschet, C., and Valentino, A. (1966). *Sociologie electorale en Afrique du Nord*. Paris: Presses Universitaires de France.

Rousset, M. (1992). 'Maroc 1972–1992. Une constitution immuable ou changeante'. *Monde Arabe, Maghreb-Mahrek*, 137: 15–24.

Saaf, A. (1987). *La politique juridique au Maroc*. Paper presented at: Coloquio de la fundación Ibn Saoud, Casablanca.

— (1996). *Sobre el sistema político marroquí. Sistemas políticos del Magreb Contemporáneo*. Madrid: Mapfre.

Salamé, G. (ed.) (1994). *Démocraties sans démocrates. Politiques d'ouverture dans le monde arabe et islamique*. Paris: Fayard.

Santucci, J.-C. (1977). 'Les élections législatives marocaine du juin 1977'. *L'Annuaire de l'Afrique du Nord 1977*.

— (1985). *Chroniques politiques Marocaines 1971–1982*. Paris: Editions Du CNRS.

— (1991). 'Processus électoraux et legitimation du pouvoir: Réflexions sur l'experiénce marocaine', in B. López Garcia, G. Martin Muñoz and M. H. De Larramendi (eds.), *Elecciones, participación y transiciones políticas en el Norte de Africa*. Madrid: Ministerio de Asuntos Exteriores/ ICMA.

Segura I Mas, A. (1994). *El Magreb: Del colonialismo al islamismo*. Barcelona: Universitat de Barcelona.

Sehimi, M. (1978). *Etude des élections législatives au Maroc, Juin 1977*. Rabat: FSJES.

— (1984). 'La préponderance du pouvoir royal dans la constitution marocaine'. *Revue du Droit Public et de la Science Politique en France et à l'Etranger*, 4: 971–990.

— (1985). 'Les élections législatives au Maroc'. *Monde Arabe, Maghreb-Machrek*, 107: 23–51.

— (ed.) (1986). *La grande encyclopédie du Maroc. Vol.I: Les institutions politiques, administratives et judiciaires*. Rabat: GEI.

Tozy, M. (1992) 'Islam et Etat au Maghreb'. *Monde Arabe, Maghreb Machrek*, 126 (Special Number).

V.V.A.A. (1990). 'North Africa. The Other Border of Europe'. *Middle East Report,* 163.

Wickham, C. R. (1994). 'Beyond Democratization. Political Change in the Arab World'. *Political Science & Politics*, 27/3: 507–509.

MOZAMBIQUE

by Michael Krennerich*

1. Introduction

1.1 Historical Overview

Mozambique has suffered three decades of war. After an 11-year armed struggle (1964–1974) for liberation led by the *Frente de Libertação de Moçambique* (FRELIMO) against colonial rule by Portugal, independent Mozambique enjoyed only a short period of relative peace. The external destabilization policy of neighboring countries—firstly, the former Rhodesia, later the South African apartheid regime—and dissatisfaction within the Mozambican population, soon involved the FRELIMO government in a civil war with the *Resistencia Naçional Moçambicana* (RENAMO), which lasted for 16 years (1976 to 1992). Not until the end of the war, did the country experience its first multi-party election (1994).

Following the Portuguese revolution of 1974, the Portuguese government transferred power to FRELIMO under the terms of the Lusaka Agreement of 7 September 1974, almost unconditionally. Neither elections nor a referendum were held. After a nine-month period of transitional government under a FRELIMO appointed Prime Minister, Joaquim Chissano, the Independence Constitution was proclaimed by FRELIMO's Central Committee on 25 June 1975. The party's President, Samora Machel, became the first President of the People's Republic of Mozambique. The general principles of the constitution laid down that power belongs to the workers and peasants united and led by FRELIMO, and exercised through the organs of people's power. Constitutionally, the Republic was to be guided by the political line defined by FRELIMO as the leading force of state and society.

In the years immediately after independence, FRELIMO established a single-party socialist system and declared itself as a Marxist–Leninist Party at its Third Congress in 1977. Steps were taken to transform

* The author would like to thank Mr Peter Häussler, representative of the Friedrich Ebert Foundation in Maputo, Mozambique, for his helpful contribution on data research.

FRELIMO from a front to a vanguard party and to reorganize it throughout the country. The so-called dynamizing groups (*grupos dinamizadores*), which formerly had carried out the work of mobilization and organization under the slogans of unity, work and vigilance, were successively abolished in the countryside. Mass organizations helped to strengthen the linkage between state/ party and society. In the face of the concentration of power in the hands of the FRELIMO party and its President, who was automatically President of the People's Republic, the People's Assembly, indirectly elected in 1977 and 1986, was only of secondary political importance. It was the apex of the pyramid which consisted of popular assemblies at the local, city, district, provincial and national level. Having been established according to the principles of 'democratic centralism', in practice, this system of '*poder popular*' functioned mainly as a channel for central directives downwards.

Despite some significant improvements in education and health, the legitimacy of the FRELIMO government was severely challenged by several factors. This was in the first instance a long-lasting brutal civil war that devastated the country—leaving a sad legacy in the form of landmines. Furthermore, the extension of party control and rural collectivization programs—in the context of a radical socialist policy approach—violated traditional community structures, cultures and beliefs and alienated large parts of the rural population, especially if accompanied by forced resettlement. Finally, Mozambique faced severe economic problems as the result, among others, of structural deficits of the inherited colonial economy, the mass exodus of white settlers and skilled personal in 1974/75, natural disasters (flood, droughts), problems of highly centralized development planning, internal mismanagement and massive, but uneconomic investment in the modern sectors of the economy under state control as well as by external destabilization and the civil war. Even though the FRELIMO governments of President Machel (1975–1986) and, after his death, of President Chissano (from 1986 onwards) initiated campaigns to combat inefficiency, bureaucracy, corruption and incompetence in the state/ party apparatus and to increase production, even by economic liberalization steps, by the end of the 1980s the economy was devastated. The central government lost control over large areas of the countryside. Despite military assistance from the former Soviet Union and its allies, the capacity of the government to defend the state and its population was severely restricted. In the 1980s, RENAMO, strongly supported by South Africa and by right-wing political activists in the United States and Europe, was increasingly based inside Mozambique itself and, while not abandoning its tactics of destruction and crude terror, exploited the rural opposition to FRELIMO in order to nurture the civil war.

Throughout the 1980s efforts to end the war showed little effect. The Nkomati Accord, signed by the governments of Mozambique and South Africa on 16 March 1984, provided that both sides did not support armed insurrection in each other's countries. However, RENAMO still received support from South Africa. It was not until 1990, after FRELIMO and RENAMO had lost much of their foreign support due to a changing international context, that the first direct talks between the government and RENAMO took place in Rome. In the same year, a new constitution came into force (30 November 1990).

The Constitution of 1990 represented the abandonment of the socialist terrain, eliminating the leading role of the FRELIMO party in state and society and introducing multi-party politics and the direct election of President and Parliament. Proposals to make the Prime Minister (a powerless post introduced in 1986) the Head of Government were rejected. Mozambique's system still remains a strongly presidential one. The official name of the country has been changed to 'The Republic of Mozambique'.

On 4 October 1992, the General Peace Agreement (GPA) was signed by the President of the Republic, Joaquim Chissano and the President of RENAMO, Afonso Dhlakama. The United Nations Operation in Mozambique (ONUMOZ), which was established in the same year, monitored and mediated the difficult processes of implementing the peace agreement and democratizing the country. Not without postponements, the peace and democratization processes culminated in the multi-party elections of 1994, that, despite the large number of participating parties, were characterized by the two-party competition between FRELIMO and RENAMO. Unlike in Angola, where the two rival armies continued in existence and resumed fighting after elections, the UN mission was able to demobilize a substantial number of former combatants before the election, and the electoral results have been accepted by both sides. The elections saw a clear victory for the old and new President Chissano, and FRELIMO gained (with 44% of the vote) an absolute majority of seats in Parliament.

However, the consolidation of democracy and peace is by no means assured. The political future of the Third Republic depends largely on the willingness of FRELIMO and RENAMO to conduct their conflicts democratically and on the capacity of the government to tackle the severe economic, social and political problems of a post-war society.

1.2 Evolution of Electoral Provisions

Until 1994, no direct presidential and parliamentary elections had been held. Under the single-party socialist system (until 1990), the President of the FRELIMO party was by virtue automatically declared President of the People's Republic of Mozambique. The supreme legislative body, the People's Assembly, was indirectly elected in 1977 and 1986. According to the model of the *poder popular*, the structure of the entire electoral process was a pyramidal one: At local level, elections to the local assemblies and the administrative post assemblies were direct and public, by show of hands at mass meetings. At subsequent levels, the metropolitan assemblies, the district assemblies, the provincial assemblies and, finally, the People's Assembly were elected indirectly. Lower assemblies elected higher ones, through an electoral college mechanism. The People's Assembly was the apex of the pyramid. The 250 members of the People's Assembly were elected by the provincial assemblies. In 1977, the members of the provincial assemblies voted for or against an entire national list proposed by the Central Committee of the FRELIMO party. In 1986, they voted for a provincial list that contained more candidates (299) than deputies (250), also proposed by the Central Committee. (However, candidates only had to be approved by FRELIMO, but did not have to be members of the party and could be chosen by the provincial assemblies.) If electors agreed with the official proposal, they left the ballot paper unmarked. If they disagreed they could delete a certain number of names from the list. While in 1977 only the People's Assembly was elected by secret ballot, in 1986 the secret ballot was used not only at the national level, but also at the provincial, urban and district levels.

1.3 Current Electoral Provisions

Sources: Constitution of 1990, General Peace Agreement (Law 13/92 of 14 October 1992), Electoral Law (Law 4/93 of 28 December 1993).

Elected national institutions: President and Assembly of the Republic (250 elected members). Regular term of office: five years respectively. President and Assembly are elected simultaneously on two consecutive days (authorized extension for a third day in 1994), but with different votes and on different ballot papers. According to Art. 118 of the constitution, a President who has been re-elected on two consecutive elections may only stand for presidential elections five years after the end of his last term of office.

Suffrage: Universal, equal, direct and secret suffrage. Every citizen, aged 18 years or over, duly registered as a voter and not affected by any of common incapacities (insanity, sentenced to imprisonment for a malicious common-law crime etc.) is allowed to vote. According to the Electoral Law, citizens resident abroad may in principle exercise the right to vote in the parliamentary elections. However, the electoral acts will not take place outside Mozambique if no consensus is reached in the National Electoral Commission on the existence of the necessary material conditions and mechanisms for control, administration and inspection of voter registration and polling abroad. Due to the lack of such a consensus, citizens abroad were not allowed to register and vote in 1994. The exercise of the right to vote is defined as a 'civic duty'. Non-voting is not punished.

Nomination of candidates
- *presidential elections*: Every citizen with original nationality, aged 35 years or over who is duly registered as voter, is eligible for the office of President of the Republic, with a few exceptions: Citizens who have been affected by any of the common incapacities (e.g. having been sentenced to imprisonment for certain crimes etc.) and who have not resided ordinarily in the national territory for at least six months prior to the date of the elections are not eligible. The nominations for the office of President may be presented by the legally constituted political parties and coalitions of parties with the support of at least 10,000 electors. It may also be presented by groups of electors, with a minimum of 10,000 signatures.
- *parliamentary elections*: All registered Mozambican citizens (who have not been affected by common incapacities) are eligible to stand for the Assembly of the Republic, with a few exceptions: Magistrates of the judiciary or the Department of Public Prosecution, professional army and militarized personnel and career diplomats are not eligible if they are still on active duty. The mandate of Deputy is incompatible with the functions of member of government and with paid employment by foreign states or international organizations.

Electoral system
- *presidential elections*: Absolute majority system. The candidate who receives more than half of the validly cast votes is elected. If no candidate obtains the absolute majority of votes, a second ballot will be held (between the 7th and 21st day after the publication of the results of the first ballot), in which only the two candidates with the highest number of votes compete. In the run-off election, the candidate with the majority of votes is elected.
- *parliamentary elections*: Proportional representation system in multi-member constituencies of variable size. Technical elements (as applied in the 1994 elections): *11 constituencies (constituency sizes: 11, 13, 13, 15, 16, 18, 18, 21, 22, 49 and 54 Members of Parliament to be elected in the respective constituencies). *Closed party lists at the constituency level. *Each voter has one vote (single vote). *Conversion of votes into seats in accordance with the d'Hondt method. Legal threshold: 5% of the votes cast nation-wide.

1.4 Comment on the Electoral Statistics

The first direct presidential and parliamentary elections (1994) in Mozambique's history are well documented. Comprehensive information and detailed data on the elections are presented, among others, by the Final Report of the National Elections Commission (1995) and by Mazula *et al.* (1995). The data in our handbook are largely based on these useful sources. Further information is taken from a series of official and unofficial sources, which are indicated in the bibliography. All the percentages given in the following tables are calculated by the author according to the standards of the data handbook.

2. Tables

2.1 Dates of National Elections, Referendums and Coups d'Etat

Year	Presidential elections	Parliamentary elections	Elections for Constitutional Assembly	Referendums	Coups d'état
1977		(04/12)[a]			
1986		(15/12)[a]			
1994	27–29/10[b]	27–29/10[b]			

[a] Date of the indirect elections of the People's Assembly which constituted the last step in the multi-staged electoral process. The electoral process of 1986 proved impossible to organize in some parts of the country due to guerilla activities.
[b] Mozambique's first direct and first multi-party elections at the national level.

2.2 Electoral Body 1994

Year	Type of election[a]	Population	Registered voters		Votes cast		
			Total number	% pop.	Total number	% reg. voters	% pop.
1994	Pr	16,614,000[b]	6,148,842[c]	37.0	5,402,940	87.9	32.5
1994	Pa	16,614,000[b]	6,148,842[c]	37.0	5,404,199	87.9	32.5

[a] Pa = Parliament; Pr = President.
[b] Estimation. Latest population census (1 August 1980): 12,130,000.
[c] The voters' roll only contained a total of 6,148,842 names, 257,219 less than the number of registered voters (as reported during registration: 6,396,061). The estimated voter population was 7,894,850 in 1994.

2.3 Abbreviations

AP	Coligação Aliança Patriotica
FAP	Frente de Acção Patriotica
FRELIMO	Frente de Libertação de Moçambique
FUMO	Frente Unida de Moçambique
MONAMO	Movimiento Nacionalista Moçambicano
PACODE	Partido de Congresso Democrático
PADEMO	Partido Democrático de Moçambique
PALMO	Partido Democrático e Liberal de Moçambique
PANADE	Partido Nacional Democrático
PANAMO	Partido Nacional de Moçambique
PCD	Partido de Convergência Democrática
PCN	Partido de Convenção Nacional

PIMO	Partido Independente de Moçambique
PMSD	Partido Moçambicano da Social Democracia
PPPM	Partido do Progresso do Povo de Moçambique
PRD	Partido Renovador Democrático
PT	Partido Trabalhista
RENAMO	Resistência Nacional Moçambicana
SOL	Partido Social Liberal e Democrático
UD	União Democrática
UNAMO	União Nacional Moçambicana

2.4 Electoral Participation of Parties and Alliances 1994

Party / Alliance	Years	Elections contested	
		Presidential	Parliamentary
AP (MONAMO / FAP)	1994	1	1
FRELIMO	1994	1	1
FUMO/ PCD	1994	1	1
PACODE	1994	1	1
PADEMO	1994	1	1
PCN	1994	0	1
PIMO	1994	1	1
PPPM	1994	1	1
PRD	1994	0	1
PT	1994	0	1
RENAMO	1994	1	1
SOL	1994	1	1
UD[a]	1994	0	1
UNAMO	1994	1	1

[a] Alliance of PALMO, PANADE and PANAMO.

2.5 Referendums

Referendums have not been held.

2.6 Elections for Constitutional Assembly

Elections for Constitutional Assembly have not been held.

2.7 Parliamentary Elections 1994

1994	Total number	%
Registered voters	6,148,842	–
Votes cast	5,404,199	87.9
Invalid votes	630,974[a]	11.7
Valid votes	4,773,225	88.3
FRELIMO	2,115,793	44.3
RENAMO	1,803,506	37.8
DU	245,793	5.1
AP (MONAMO / FAP)	93,031	1.9
SOL	79,622	1.7
FUMO/ PCD	66,527	1.4
PCN	60,635	1.3
PIMO	58,590	1.2
PACODE	52,446	1.1
PPPM	50,793	1.1
PRD	48,030	1.0
PADEMO	36,689	0.8
UNAMO	34,809	0.7
PT	26,961	0.6

[a] Sum of 457,382 blank ballot sheets (*votos em branco*) and 173,592 invalid votes (*votos nulos*).

2.7 a) Parliamentary Elections 1994: Regional Distribution of Votes

	FRELIMO	RENAMO	U.D.	Others	Total
Cabo Delgado	250,436	98,180	25,041	56,223	429,880
Gaza	259,868	8,513	21,861	28,161	318,403
Inhambane	192,659	42,018	38,255	50,025	322,957
Mancia	63,620	134,176	9,347	24,801	231,944
Maputo	198,429	17,749	15,055	23,197	254,430
Maputo (City)	293,511	33,436	10,361	34,296	371,604
Nampula	300,933	472,638	43,445	151,060	968,076
Niassa	97,169	68,531	12,343	26,698	204,741
Sofala	53,667	284,495	5,340	27,132	370,634
Tete	83,838	131,444	15,749	36,761	267,792
Zambézia	278,559	463,844	39,489	102,446	884,338
Sub-total	2,072,689	1,755,024	236,286	560,800	4,624,799
Reassessed invalid votes	43,104	48,482	9,507	47,333	148,426
Total	2,115,793	1,803,506	245,793	608,133	4,773,225

2.7 b) Parliamentary Elections 1994: Regional Distribution of Votes (%)

	FRELIMO	RENAMO	U.D.	Others	Total
Cabo Delgado	58.3	22.8	5.8	13.1	100
Gaza	81.6	2.7	6.9	8.8	100
Inhambane	59.7	13.0	11.8	15.5	100
Mancia	27.4	57.8	4.0	10.7	100
Maputo	78.0	7.0	5.9	9.1	100
Maputo (City)	79.0	9.0	2.8	9.2	100
Nampula	31.1	48.8	4.5	15.6	100
Niassa	47.5	33.5	6.0	13.0	100
Sofala	14.5	76.8	1.4	7.3	100
Tete	31.3	49.1	5.9	13.7	100
Zambézia	31.5	52.5	4.5	11.6	100
Sub-total	44.8	37.9	5.1	12.1	100
Reassessed invalid votes	29.0	32.7	6.4	31.9	100
Total	44.3	37.8	5.1	12.7	100

[a] Due to rounding the added total of the percentages is not always 100.

2.8 Composition of Parliament 1994

1994	Seats	%
	250	100
FRELIMO	129	51.6
RENAMO	112	44.8
UD	9	3.6

2.8 a) Regional Distribution of Seats 1994

Constituencies[a]	FRELIMO	RENAMO	UD	Total
Maputo (city)	17	1	0	18
Maputo (province)	12	1	0	13
Gaza	15	0	1	16
Inhambane	13	3	2	18
Sofala	3	18	0	21
Manica	4	9	0	13
Tete	5	9	1	15
Zambézia	18	29	2	49
Nampula	20	32	2	54
Cabo Delgado	15	6	1	22
Niassa	7	4	0	11
Total	129	112	9	250

[a] Each of the 10 provinces and the City of Maputo comprise a multi-member constituency.

2.9 Presidential Elections 1994

1994	Total number	%
Registered voters	6,148,842	–
Votes cast	5,402,940	87.9
Invalid votes	461,425[a]	8.5
Valid votes	4,941,515	91.5
Joaquim Alberto Chissano (FRELIMO)	2,633,740	53.3
Afonso Macacho Marceta Dhlakama (RENAMO)	1,666,965	33.7
Wehia Monakacho Ripua (PADEMO)	141,905	2.9
Carlos Alexandre dos Reis (UNAMO)	120,708	2.4
Máximo Diogo José Dias (MONAMO / FAP)	115,442	2.3
Vasco Campira Momboya Alfazema (PACODE)	58,848	1.2
Jacob Neves Salomão Sibindy (PIMO)	51,070	1.0
Domingos António Mascarenhas Arouca (FUMO/ PCD)	37,767	0.8
Carlos José Maria Jeque (Independent)	34,588	0.7
Casimiro Miguel Nhamithambo (SOL)	32,036	0.6
Mário Fernando Carlos Machele (Independent)	24,238	0.5
Padimbe Mahose Kamati Andrea (PPPM)	24,208	0.5

[a] Sum of 312,143 blank ballot sheets (*votos em branco*) and 149,282 invalid votes (*votos nulos*).

2.10 List of Power Holders 1975–1998

Head of State and Government	Years	Remarks
Samora Machel	1975–1986	Mozambique gained independence on 25/06/1975, and FRELIMO's president Machel was sworn in as President of the People's Republic of Mozambique. He died in an aircraft accident on 20/10/1986.
Joaquim Chissano	1986–	On 03/11/1986, the foreign minister, Chissano, was elected by the FRELIMO Central Committee to succeed President Machel. After eight years of presidency, Chissano won the presidential elections of 1994 and was sworn in as the first directly elected President on 09/12/1994.

3. Bibliography

3.1 Official Sources

Assambleia da República (1990). *Constituição*. Maputo: Imprensa Nacional de Moçambique.

Lei Eleitoral (No. 4/93, de 28 de Dezembro). Maputo: Imprensa Nacional de Moçambique.

'Lei Eleitoral para as eleições das Assambleias do Povo na República Popular de Moçambique em 1977 (Lei No. 1/77 de 1 de Setembro)'. *Boletim da República. Publição Oficial da República Popular de Moçambique*, I serie, número 101, 01/09/1977.

National Elections Commission (1995). *Final Report*. Maputo: National Elections Commission.

3.2 Books, Articles and Electoral Reports

Adam, E. (1992). 'Reform in Mosambik—eine Rückkehr zu den "wahren" Zielen der Befreiung?', in P. Meyns (ed.), *Demokratie und Strukturreformen im portugiesischsprachigen Afrika*. Freiburg: Arnold Bergstraesser Institut, 76–94.

— (1993). 'Mozambique', in D. Nohlen and F. Nuschler (eds.), *Handbuch der Dritten Welt, Bd.5: Ostafrika und Südafrika*. Bonn: Dietz, 384–400.

Africa Research Bulletin, 23/7: 11–12.

AIM (Agência de Informação de Moçambique) Information Bulletin, No. 125 (December 1986), No. 126 (January 1987) and No. 127 (February 1987).

Alden, C. (1995). 'The UN and the Resolution of Conflict in Mozambique'. *Journal of Modern African Studies*, 33/1: 103–128.

AWEPA (African-European Institute) (1994). *Electoral Law of Mozambique 1993*. Amsterdam: AWEPA.

Azevedo, M. J. (1991). *Historical Dictionary of Mozambique*. Metuchen, NJ: Scarecrow Press.

Birmingham, D. (1992). *Frontline Nationalism in Angola & Mozambique*. London: James Currey.

Braathen, E. (1994). *Voting for Peace: Mozambique Presidential and Legislative Elections*. Bergen: The Norwegian Institute of Human Rights.

Chingono, M. F. (1996). *The State, Violence and Development: The Political Economy of War in Mozambique, 1975–1992*. Aldershot: Avebury.

De Brito, L. (1995). 'Des élections pour la paix au Mozambique'. *Politique Africaine*, 56: 144–146.

Diario de Moçambique, 17 December 1986.

Fandrych, S., and Weimer, B. (1994). *Mosambik vor den Wahlen*. Maputo: Friedrich Ebert Foundation.

Finnegan, W. (1992). *A Complicated War: The Harrowing of Mozambique*. Berkeley, Cal.: University of California Press.

Haines, R., and Wood, G. (1995). 'The 1994 Election and Mozambique's Democratic Transition'. *Democratization*, 2/3: 362–376.

Hall, M., and Young, T. (1991). 'Recent Constitutional Developments in Mozambique'. *Journal of African Law*, 35/1-2: 102–115.

Hanlon, J. (1984). *Mozambique: The Revolution Under Fire*. London: Zed.

— (1991). *Mozambique: Who Calls the Shots?* London: James Currey.

Henriksen, T. H. (1978). *Mozambique. A History*. London: Collings/ Cape Town: Philip.

ISSA (Informationsdienst südliches Afrika), various issues.

Jett, D. (1996). 'Cementing Democracy: Institution-Building in Mozambique'. *The South African Journal of International Affairs*, 3/2: 1–12.

Küppers, H. (1996). *RENAMO: Über den Wandel der mosambikanischen Rebellenbewegung zu einer politischen Partei*. Münster/ Hamburg: Lit.

Lloyd, R. B. (1995). 'Mozambique: The Terror of War, the Tensions of Peace'. *Current History*, 94/591: 152–155.

Mazula, B. (1995). *Moçambique, Eleições, Democracia e Desenvolvimiento*. Maputo: Inter Africa-Group.

Morgan, G. (1990). 'Violence in Mozambique: Towards an Understanding of Renamo'. *Journal of Modern African Studies*, 28/4: 603–619.

Mozamibque Peace Process Bulletin. Special Political Parties Supplement, August 1994.

Meyns, P. (1979). *Befreiung und nationaler Wiederaufbau von Mozambique—Studien zu Politik und Wirtschaft 1960–1978*. Arbeiten aus dem Institut für Afrika-Kunde, 18. Hamburg: Institut für Afrika-Kunde.

— (1996). 'Parlaments- und Präsidentschaftswahlen in Moçambique (27–29.10.1994)', in U. Engel, R. Hofmeier, D. Kohnert and A. Mehler (eds.), *Deutsche Wahlbeobachtung in Afrika*. Hamburg: Institut für Afrika-Kunde, 132–144.

Munslow, B. (1983). *Mozambique: The Revolution and its Origins*. London: Longman.

Nelson, H. D. (1985). *Mozambique: A Country Study*. Washington, D.C.: US Gov. Pr. Office.

Newitt, M. (1995). *A History of Mozambique*. London: Hurst.

Schutz, B. (1995). 'The Heritage of Revolution and the Struggle for Government Legitimacy in Mozambique', in W. Zartman (ed.), *Collapsed States. The Disintegration and Restoration of Legitimate Authority*. Boulder, Col.: Lynne Rienner, 109–124.

südliches Afrika, No. 12/77 (December 1977).

Turner, J. M., Nelson, S., and Mahling-Clark, K. (1998). 'Mozambique's Vote for Democratic Governance', in: K. Kumar (ed.), *Postconflict Elections, Democratization, and International Assistance*. Boulder, Col.: Lynne Rienner, 153–175.

UN (United Nations) (1995). *The United Nations and Mozambique, 1992–1995*. New York: United Nations.

— (1996). *Elections in the Peace Process in Mozambique. Record of an Experience*. New York: United Nations.

Vines, A. (1994). *No Democracy without Money. The Road to Peace in Mozambique (1982–1992)*. London: Catholic Institute for International Relations.

Wagner, I., and Witzel, R. (1978). 'Mozambique', in D. Sternberger, B. Vogel, D. Nohlen and K. Landfried (eds.), *Die Wahl der Parlamente und anderer Staatsorgane. Band II: Politische Organisation und Repräsentation in Africa,* by Franz Nuscheler, Klaus Ziemer *et al.,* Berlin/ New York: Walter de Gruyter, 1411–1435.

Weimer, B. (1994). *Vom Bürgerkrieg zum Wiederaufbau. Mosambik nach den Wahlen*. Maputo: Friedrich Ebert Foundation.

— (1995). 'Mosambik hat gewählt: Analyse der Wahlergebnisse und Perspektiven des Wiederaufbaus'. *afrika spektrum*, 30/1: 5–33.

Wood, G., and Haines, R. (1998). 'Tentative Steps Towards Multi-Partyism in Mozambique'. *Party Politics*, 4/1, 107–117.

NAMIBIA

by Michael Krennerich

1. Introduction

1.1 Historical Overview

After a prolonged independence struggle against South African apartheid rule, Namibia gained independence on 21 March 1990. Following the competitive pre-independence elections to the Constituent Assembly (1989) and the adoption of a most liberal constitution (1990), Namibia's multi-party democracy had a promising start and saw further competitive elections not only at the national level (1994), but also at the regional (1992) and at the local level (1992, 1998). Against the background of a predominant party system and the lack of an efficient political opposition, however, the democracy is still far from being consolidated.

Namibia experienced a century of colonial rule, first by Germany from 1884 to 1915 followed by South Africa from 1915 onwards. Initially, the South African Union administered the territory on the basis of a mandate conferred upon it by the League of Nations in 1920. From 1946 onwards, however, the South African governments opposed all efforts of the United Nations (UN) to place its mandated territories in the UN-trusteeship system. Despite the obvious violation of international law, South Africa continued encouraging the integration of the territory into the South African apartheid state, even when the UN General Assembly terminated the mandate for South West Africa (renamed 'Namibia' in a 1968 resolution) and declared that the territory be placed under the interim administration of the UN in 1966. Meanwhile, black nationalist politicians had formed the South West African People's Organization (SWAPO), which initiated an armed liberation struggle against South African rule in 1966 and was recognized as the 'sole and authentic representative of the Namibian people' by the UN General Assembly in 1973.

In response to the increasing pressure for independence, South Africa pursued a policy of 'internal solution' in Namibia. The Constitutional Conference ('Turnhalle Conference'), established in 1975, announced plans for a multi-racial government to lead the territory to independence. Delegates of 'internal' political parties and organizations representing different 'ethnic' groups set up a draft constitution. It was, however, never to be implemented, a crucial factor being the international rejection of the effort to maintain a reformed version of apartheid rule. South Africa refused to implement the UN Security Council Resolution (UNSCR) 435 of 1978, which laid down the procedure for an internationally recognized move towards independence by holding UN-supervised elections for a Constituent Assembly. Instead, unsupervised elections took place from 4 to 8 December 1978, which were boycotted by the SWAPO and declared as 'null and void' by the UN Security Council. The Democratic Turnhalle Alliance (DTA), a heterogeneous alliance made up of 'ethnically' structured parties emerged from the election as the winning faction. The newly established National Assembly and Council of Ministers, both dominated by the DTA, were granted certain legislative and administrative powers, subject to the South African Administrator-General's right of veto. On 18 January 1983 South Africa reassumed direct rule over Namibia.

Due to international mediation talks, however, all the political players, including the SWAPO and South Africa, committed themselves to uphold the 'Principles concerning the Constituent Assembly and the constitution for an independent Namibia' (1982), which stated that a yet to be elected Constituent Assembly was to draw up a constitution based on Western democratic principles and to approve it with a two-thirds majority. Nevertheless, South Africa (supported by the USA) linked the Namibian independence process to a withdrawal of Cuban troops from Angola ('Cuban Linkage'). Only the Tripartite Agreement, signed by Angola, Cuba and South Africa in consequence of the east–west rapprochement on 22 December 1988, gave the process the decisive impetus. In accordance with the UNSCR 435 of 1978, UN-supervised elections were held for a Namibian Constituent Assembly on 7–11 November 1989. The elections were certified as having been free and fair by the UN, although they did not proceed without difficulty. They were characterized by a competition between the two main political forces: the SWAPO, identified most strongly with the armed struggle for liberation, and the DTA, which was unable to give up its image as a collaborationist and racially oriented alliance. The SWAPO gained the absolute majority in the Assembly. The SWAPO's failure, however, to win a two-thirds majority emphasized the consensual and compromising aspects of the young democracy and strengthened the inclusive character of the constitution building process.

On the basis of the constitutional principles of 1982, within a matter of three months the Assembly unanimously adopted a constitution (1990), which is considered one of the most liberal in Africa. It comprises an extensive catalogue of human rights and creates a classical tripartite government (with an independent ombudsman). The executive power is vested in a popularly elected, powerful President, who is the Head of both State and Government as well as the Commander-in-Chief of the defense forces, and the Cabinet. The National Assembly constitutes the principal legislative authority. Though its legislative power is subject to certain checks by the National Council (a second house made up of delegates from the Regional Councils first elected in 1992), the President and the Supreme Court, all but the latter can be overcome by sufficient majorities. The National Assembly has the power to remove the President from office by means of impeachment as well as Cabinet members by vote of no confidence. The Assembly can be dissolved by the President, but only at the cost of ending his own term.

The political fortune of independent Namibia depends largely upon the SWAPO, which provides the government and dominates the political landscape. Due to its strong ties with the largest ethnic (albeit heterogeneous) group of the population—the Ovambo—the SWAPO benefits from a structural 'in-built majority', but also enjoys a great deal of support in other parts of the country and amongst other ethnic groups. In the 1994 presidential and parliamentary elections the SWAPO, led by the charismatic 'father figure' of President Sam Nujoma, increased its supremacy still further and received the two-thirds majority in the National Assembly required for constitutional reforms. In view of the structural supremacy of the SWAPO and the weakness of the political opposition, the democratic development will largely depend on whether the former liberation movement will continue to obey democratic principles and to promote a political culture of tolerance and reconciliation.

1.2 Evolution of Electoral Provisions

The principles of universal, equal, direct and secret suffrage were applied for the founding elections of 1989. Every person of 18 years or over who was a) born in the territory, b) the natural child of a person born in the territory or c) ordinarily resident in the territory for a continuous period of no less than four years was eligible for voter registration. The application for registration of a political party had to be signed by 2,000 registered voters and to be accompanied by a monetary deposit

(R 10,000). The Constituent Assembly was elected by a proportional representation system at the national level (pure proportional representation).

1.3 Current Electoral Provisions

Sources: Constitution of the Republic of Namibia, 1990; Electoral Act, 1992; Electoral Amendment Act 1994.

Elected national institutions: President of the Republic (no Vice-President) and National Assembly (72 elected members). Regular term of office: five years respectively. President and National Assembly are elected on the same day, but with different votes and on different ballot papers. In the case of the National Assembly, no by-elections are held. Vacant seats are filled through appointments from the respective party list. A person shall not hold office as President for more than two terms. (However, it is likely that President Nujoma will be allowed to stand for a third mandate since he has been directly elected in 1994 only). No prohibition of re-election exists for Members of Parliament.

Suffrage: The principles of universal, equal, direct and secret suffrage are applied. Every citizen who has reached the age of 18 has the right to vote and is entitled to be registered as a voter.

Nomination of candidates
- *presidential elections*: Every citizen aged 35 years or over is eligible for candidature as President, if he or she is a registered voter and is nominated either as a representative of a registered political party or as an independent candidate whose nomination is supported by at least 300 registered voters, from each of at least 10 regions in Namibia. Incompatibilities are the same as for parliamentary candidates.
- *parliamentary elections*: Every Namibian citizen who has reached the age of 21 is eligible for candidature as a member of the National Assembly, if he or she is a registered voter and is a member of the political party submitting the list of candidates in question. No person may become a member of the National Assembly if he/ she is a remunerated member of the Public Service or a member of the National Council, regional councils or local authorities.

Electoral system
- *presidential elections*: Absolute majority system. The constitution provides that no person shall be elected as President unless he or she has received more than 50% of the votes cast. The ballots shall be conducted until such a result is reached.
- *parliamentary elections*: Proportional representation list system at the national level (pure proportional representation). Technical elements: *National constituency (the 23 so-called 'constituencies' merely have the function of voting/ polling districts). *Closed national party lists. *Single vote (for National Assembly). *Hare quota and greatest remainder. No legal electoral threshold exists.

1.4 Comment on the Electoral Statistics

Election results as well as information on elections are easily available in a number of secondary sources. One of the most useful among them is Tötemeyer/ Wehmhörner/ Weiland (1996). As for the 1994 elections, we took the data of that secondary source. With regard to the regional distribution of the 1989 elections, however, we preferred to use the data published by Harneit-Sievers (1990) on the basis of *The Namibian* (15 November 1989), since the number of the so-called tendered votes are presented separately there. The national results of both sources, however, are identical. The percentages have been calculated by us. They may differ from other sources insofar as the respective candidate's/ party's share of votes is not calculated on the basis of all the votes cast (valid and invalid votes), but, in accordance with international standards, on the basis of the valid votes cast.

2. Tables

2.1 Dates of National Elections, Referendums and Coups d'Etat

Year	Presidential elections	Parliamentary elections	Elections for Constitutional Assembly	Referendums	Coups d'état
1989			07–11/11[a]		
1994	07–08/12	07–08/12			

[a] The Constituent Assembly declared itself National Assembly on February 16 of 1990. After Independence Day (21 March 1990), it served as Namibia's first legislature.

2.2 Electoral Body 1989–1994

Year	Type of election[a]	Population[b]	Registered voters		Votes cast		
			Total number	% pop.	Total number	% reg. voters	% pop.
1989	CA	1,288,000	701,483	54.5	682,787	97.3	53.0
1994	Pr	1,500,000	654,189	43.6	497,508	76.0	33.2
1994	Pa	1,500,000	654,189	43.6	497,508	76.0	33.2

[a] CA = Constitutional Assembly; Pa = Parliament (National Assembly); Pr = President.
[b] Estimates of the total population.

2.3 Abbreviations

ACN	Aksie Christelik Nasionaal
ANS	Action National Settlement
BA	Bushmen Alliance
BC	Bondelswarts Council
CANU	Caprivi African National Union
CDA	Christian Democratic Action for Social Justice
CDP-DTA	Christian Democratic Party - DTA
DAN	Democratic Action for Namas
DEC	Damara Executive Council
DC	Damara Council
DCN	Democratic Coalition of Namibia
DCP	Damara Christian Party
DP	Democratic Party
DTA	Democratic Turnhallen Alliance
DTPN	Democratic Turnhalle Party of Namibia
FCN	Federal Convention of Namibia
LP	Labour Party

LP	Liberal Party
MAG	Monitor Action Group
MPP	Mmabatho People's Party
NCDP	Namibia Christian Democratic Party
NDP	National Democratic Party
NDUP	National Democratic Unity Party
NIP	Namibian Independence Party
NNDP	Namibia National Democratic Party
NNF	Namibia National Front
NPF	National Patriotic Front of Namibia
NPLF	National People's Liberation Front
NPP	Namibia People's Party
NPP	National Progressive Party
NUDO	National Unity Democratic Organization
NUDO-PP	NUDO-Progressive Party
NUDU	Nation Unity Democratic Union
OPPN	Original People's Party of Namibia
PUM	Patriotic Unity Movement
RDTAP	Rehoboth Democratic Turnhalle Alliance Party
RFDP	Rehoboth Free Democratic Party
RP	Republican Party
RUP	Riemvasmaak United Party
RVP	Rehoboth Volksparty
SDS	Students for Democratic Society
SP	Seoponsengive Party
SWANU	South West African National Union
SWANU-P	SWANU-Progressives
SWAPO	South West Africa People's Organization
SWAPO-D	SWAPO-Democrats
UDF	United Democratic Front of Namibia
UDP	United Democratic Party
ULM	United Liberation Movement
UNPP	United People's Party
UP	United Party of Namibia
VP	Voice of the People
WRP	Workers' Revolutionary Party

General note: The table also includes the non-registered parties which took part in electoral alliances.

2.4 Electoral Participation of Parties and Alliances 1989–1994

Party / Alliance	Years	Elections contested	
		Presidential	Parliamentary
ACN	1989	0	1
CDA	1989	0	1
DTA[a]	1989, 1994	1	2
FCN[b]	1989, 1994	0	2
NNDP	1989	0	1
NNF[c]	1989	0	1
NPF[d]	1989	0	1
SWAPO	1989, 1994	1	2
SWAPO-D	1989	0	1
SWANU[e]	1989, 1994	0	2
UDF[f]	1989, 1994	0	2
WRP[g]	1989, 1994	0	2
DCN[h]	1994	0	1
MAG	1994	0	1

General note: In this table, only those parties and alliances are indicated that participated at least in one election under their own name.

[a] In 1989, alliance of the following parties (in alphabetical order): BA, CDP-DTA, DTPN, NDP, NDUP, NUDO, NUDU, RDTAP, RP, SP, UDP, UP.

[b] In 1989, alliance of the NPP (National Progressive Party) and BC, DAN, DCP, DEC, DP, LP (Liberal Party), NCDP, NPLF, NPP (Namibia People's Party), NUDO-PP, RFDP, RUP, SDS, ULM, VP.

[c] In 1989, alliance of SWANU-P and MPP, NIP, RVP, UNPP.

[d] In 1989, alliance of ANS, CANU and SWANU.

[e] SWANU participated in the elections of 1989 within the alliance NPF.

[f] In 1989, alliance of DC, LP (Labour Party), OPPN, PUM and WRP.

[g] The WRP took part in the elections of 1989 within the alliance UDF.

[h] The DCN is the successor party of the NPF.

2.5 Referendums

National referendums have not been held.

2.6 Elections for Constitutional Assembly

1989	Votes Total number	%	Seats Total (72)	%
Registered voters	701,438	–		
Votes cast	682,787	97.3		
Invalid votes	11,957	1.8		
Valid votes	670,830	98.2		
SWAPO	384,567	57.3	41	56.9
DTA	191,532	28.6	21[a]	29.2
UDF	37,874	5.6	4[b]	5.6
ACN	23,728	3.5	3	4.2
NPF	10,693	1.6	1[c]	1.4
FCN	10,452	1.6	1[d]	1.4
NNF	5,344	0.8	1[e]	1.4
SWAPO-D	3,161	0.5	0	0.0
CDA	2,495	0.4	0	0.0
NNDP	984	0.1	0	0.0

[a] All the 12 parties of the alliance obtained seats.
[b] Seats filled by DC, LP and OPPN.
[c] Seat filled by SWANU.
[d] Seat filled by NPP.
[e] Seat filled by SWANU-P.

2.6 a) Elections for Constitutional Assembly 1989: Regional Distribution of Votes (Absolute Numbers)

	SWAPO	DTA	UDF	ACN	NPF	FCN	Others[a]	Total
Northern Namibia								
Ovambo	197,100	9,200	4,674	247	428	107	1,880	213,636
Kavango	27,256	22,046	1,202	407	455	356	987	52,709
Caprivi	9,350	12,782	514	86	649	411	312	24,104
Kaokoland	1,025	6,699	41	33	2,152	83	173	10,206
Central Namibia								
Windhoek	39,060	30,475	6,147	4,153	1,554	1,208	2120	84,717
Swakopmund	11,479	4,998	1,400	1,020	119	318	284	19,618
Grootfontein	5,336	7,226	1,094	1,418	323	198	201	15,796
Gobabis	2,119	10,539	374	1,801	320	137	533	15,823
Hereroland	1,835	8,440	58	44	1,573	147	609	12,706
Damaraland	3,407	2,040	6,944	140	39	26	119	12,715
Tsumeb	6,476	3,452	1,085	848	45	78	124	12,108
Otjiwarongo	3,194	4,274	1,540	626	79	56	163	9,932
Okahandja	3,256	3,672	993	611	283	30	114	8,959
Outjo	984	2,658	1,186	719	39	73	64	5,723
Omaruru	1,022	2,538	499	198	280	30	211	4,778
Southern Namibia								
Keetmanshoop	4,778	8,229	1,314	1,312	192	284	643	16,752
Karasburg	1,830	7,727	651	3,588	111	323	126	14,356
Rehoboth	2,460	6,590	326	96	196	4,499	416	14,583
Mariental	2,411	6,584	878	1,319	78	307	173	11,750
Lüderitz	5,422	1,890	342	453	56	56	247	8,466
Karibib	1,932	1,637	1,289	344	139	47	79	5,467
Maltahöhe	758	579	334	355	10	128	40	2,204
Bethanien	398	1,153	69	258	8	51	53	1,990
Tendered votes[b]	51,679	26,104	4,920	3,652	1,565	1,499	2,313	91,732
Total votes	384,567	191,532	37,874	23,728	10,693	10,452	11,984	670,830

[a] NNF, SWAPO-D, CDA, NNDP.

[b] If voters did not vote in the same district they were registered in or if the voter's registration card or identity document did not comply with the formal requirements, these citizens had to vote by 'tendered ballots'.

2.6 b) Elections for Constitutional Assembly 1989: Regional Distribution of Votes (in %)

	SWAPO	DTA	UDF	ACN	NPF	FCN	Others[a]	Total[b]
Northern Namibia								
Ovambo	92.3	4.3	2.2	0.1	0.2	0.1	0.9	100
Kavango	51.7	41.8	2.3	0.8	0.9	0.7	1.9	100
Caprivi	38.8	53.0	2.1	0.6	2.7	1.7	1.3	100
Kaokoland	10.0	65.6	0.4	0.7	21.1	0.8	1.7	100
Central Namibia								
Windhoek	46.1	36.0	7.3	4.9	1.8	1.4	2.5	100
Swakopmund	58.5	25.5	7.1	5.2	0.6	1.6	1.4	100
Grootfontein	33.8	45.7	6.9	9.0	2.0	1.3	1.3	100
Gobabis	13.4	66.6	2.4	11.4	2.0	0.9	3.4	100
Hereroland	14.4	66.4	0.5	0.3	12.4	1.2	4.8	100
Damaraland	26.8	16.0	54.6	1.1	0.3	0.2	0.9	100
Tsumeb	53.5	28.5	9.0	7.0	0.4	0.6	1.0	100
Otjiwarongo	32.2	43.0	15.5	6.3	0.8	0.6	1.6	100
Okahandja	36.3	41.0	11.1	6.8	3.2	0.3	1.3	100
Outjo	17.2	46.4	20.7	12.6	0.7	1.3	1.1	100
Omaruru	21.4	53.1	10.4	4.1	5.9	0.6	4.4	100
Southern Namibia								
Keetmanshoop	28.5	49.1	7.8	7.8	1.1	1.7	3.8	100
Karasburg	12.7	53.8	4.5	25.0	0.8	2.2	0.9	100
Rehoboth	16.9	45.2	2.2	0.7	1.3	30.9	2.9	100
Mariental	20.5	56.0	7.5	11.2	0.7	2.6	1.5	100
Lüderitz	64.0	22.3	4.0	5.4	0.7	0.7	2.9	100
Karibib	35.3	29.9	23.6	6.3	2.5	0.9	1.4	100
Maltahöhe	34.4	26.3	15.2	16.1	0.5	5.8	1.8	100
Bethanien	20.0	57.9	3.5	13.0	0.4	2.6	2.7	100
Tendered votes	56.3	28.5	5.4	4.0	1.7	1.6	2.5	100
Total votes	57.3	28.6	5.6	3.5	1.6	1.6	1.8	100

General note: Percentages refer to party votes in % of valid votes.

[a] NNF, SWAPO-D, CDA, NNDP.

[b] Due to rounding the total of the percentages shown does not always amount to 100.

2.7 Parliamentary Elections 1994

Year	Total number	%
Registered voters	654,189	–
Votes cast	497,508	76.0
Invalid votes	7,863	1.6
Valid votes	489,645	98.4
SWAPO	361,809	73.9
DTA	101,748	20.8
UDF	13,309	2.7
FCN	1,166	0.2
DCN	4,058	0.8
MAG	4,005	0.8
SWANU	2,598	0.5
WRP	952	0.2

2.7 a) Parliamentary Elections 1994: Regional Distribution of Votes (Absolute Numbers)

	SWAPO	DTA	UDF	DCN	MAG	Swanu	FCN	WRP	Total
Caprivi	11,765	11,868	183	125	25	37	44	30	24,077
Okavango	19,884	3,570	162	98	23	82	37	74	23,930
Ohengwena	58,797	285	145	53	11	106	32	86	59,515
Omusati	70,573	179	189	31	12	139	15	86	71,224
Oshana	50,722	1,509	171	146	14	116	28	57	52,763
Oshikoto	43,275	2,412	591	80	128	160	38	92	46,776
Kunene	5,480	6,883	3,484	635	267	69	62	34	16,914
Erongo	18,955	8,138	3,200	297	546	268	75	41	31,520
Otjozondjupa	15,137	15,870	1,839	825	657	240	130	92	34,790
Omaheke	6,054	10,562	194	328	432	435	69	35	18,109
Khomas	33,269	19,609	2,124	935	793	555	192	169	57,646
Hardap	7,385	9,613	325	206	465	122	255	68	18,439
Karas	12,362	8,630	421	191	530	178	157	60	22,529
Unspecified[b]	8,151	2,620	281	108	102	91	32	28	11,413
Total votes	361,809	101,748	13,309	4,058	4,005	2,598	1,166	952	489,645

[a] Unspecified votes are those 'tendered votes' without indication of the electoral district/ region for which the vote had been cast.

2.7 b) Parliamentary Elections 1994: Regional Distribution of Votes (in %)

	SWAPO	DTA	UDF	DCN	MAG	Swanu	FCN	WRP	Total
Caprivi	48.9	49.3	0.8	0.5	0.1	0.2	0.2	0.1	100
Okavango	83.1	14.9	0.7	0.4	0.1	0.3	0.2	0.3	100
Ohengwena	98.8	0.5	0.2	0.1	0.0	0.2	0.1	0.1	100
Omusati	99.1	0.3	0.3	0.0	0.0	0.2	0.0	0.1	100
Oshana	96.1	2.9	0.3	0.3	0.0	0.2	0.1	0.1	100
Oshikoto	92.5	5.2	1.3	0.2	0.3	0.3	0.1	0.2	100
Kunene	32.4	40.7	20.6	3.8	1.6	0.4	0.4	0.2	100
Erongo	60.1	25.8	10.2	0.9	1.7	0.9	0.2	0.1	100
Otjozondjupa	43.4	45.5	5.3	2.4	1.9	0.7	0.4	0.3	100
Omaheke	33.4	58.2	1.1	1.8	2.4	2.4	0.4	0.2	100
Khomas	57.7	34.0	3.7	1.6	1.4	1.0	0.3	0.3	100
Hardap	40.1	52.1	1.8	1.1	2.5	0.7	1.4	0.4	100
Karas	54.9	38.3	1.9	0.8	2.4	0.8	0.7	0.3	100
Unspecified[b]	71.4	23.0	2.5	0.9	0.9	0.8	0.3	0.2	100
Total votes	73.9	20.8	2.7	0.8	0.8	0.5	0.2	0.2	100

General note: Percentages refer to party votes in % of valid votes.

[a] Due to rounding the total of the percentages shown does not always amount to 100.

2.8 Composition of Parliament 1994

Year	1994	
	Seats	%
	72	100
SWAPO	53	73.6
DTA	15	20.8
UDF	2	2.8
DCN	1	1.4
MAG	1	1.4

2.9 Presidential Elections 1994

1994	Total number	%
Registered voters	654,189	–
Votes cast	497,508	76.0
Invalid votes	12,213	2.4
Valid votes	485,295	97.5
Sam Nujoma (SWAPO)	370,452	76.3
Mishake Muyongo (DTA)	114,843	23.7

2.9 a) Presidential Elections 1994: Regional Distribution of Votes

1994	Registered voters	Votes cast	Invalid votes	Valid votes	Sam Nujoma	in %[a]	Mishake Muyongo	in %[a]
Caprivi	36,734	22,671	222	22,449	11,120	49.5	11,329	50.5
Okavango	41,533	24,474	886	23,588	19,986	84.7	3,602	15.3
Ohengwena	69,488	60,169	895	59,274	58,789	99.2	485	0.8
Omusati	82,273	73,185	2,452	70,733	70,433	99.6	300	0.4
Oshana	65,353	53,227	1,135	52,092	50,496	96.9	1,596	3.1
Oshikoto	58,266	47,749	815	46,934	44,037	93.8	2,897	6.2
Kunene	27,586	16,962	1,158	15,804	7,102	44.9	8,702	55.1
Erongo	47,929	31,690	576	31,114	21,054	67.7	10,060	32.3
Otjozondjupa	51,409	35,344	1,128	34,216	16,144	47.2	18,072	52.8
Omaheke	26,731	18,200	511	17,689	6,460	36.5	11,229	63.5
Khomas	83,487	58,738	935	57,803	34,907	60.4	22,896	39.6
Hardap	29,632	18,958	552	18,406	7,686	41.8	10,720	58.2
Karas	33,768	22,851	609	22,242	12,657	56.9	9,585	43.1
Unspecified[b]	–	13,290	339	12,951	9,581	74.0	3,370	26.0
Total Votes	654,189	497,508	12,213	485,295	370,452	76.3	114,843	23.7

[a] Votes per candidate in % of valid votes.

[b] Unspecified votes are those 'tendered votes' without indication of the electoral district/region for which the vote had been cast for.

2.10 List of Power Holders 1989–1998

Head of State and Government	Years	Remarks
Sam Nujoma	1989–	On 16/02/1990, the Constituent Assembly unanimously elected Sam Nujoma as President of the Republic Namibia, to be sworn in on Independence Day (21/03/1990) by the UN Secretary-General. Nujoma was re-elected in direct elections in 1994.

3. Bibliography

3.1 Official Sources

Agreement Among the People's Republic of Angola, the Republic of Cuba, and the Republic of South Africa. Tripartite agreement on the implementation of UN Security Council Resolution 435 and withdrawal of Cuban troops from Angola. 22 December 1988.

Constitution of the Republic of Namibia, adopted by the Constituent Assembly in Windhoek. Namibia, 9 February 1990.

'Electoral Act, 1992 (Act 24 of 1992), of the National Assembly'. *Government Gazette of the Republic of Namibia*, No. 471, 31 August 1992.

'Electoral Amendment Act, 1994 (Act No. 23, 1994), of the Parliament'. *Government Gazette of the Republic of Namibia*, No. 957, 21 October 1994.

Parliament, Republic of Namibia (1997). *Namibian Parliamentary Directory 1996/97*. Windhoek: New Namibian Books.

Republic of Namibia, National Planing Commission, Central Statistics Office (1993). *1991 Population and Housing Census*. Windhoek.

South West Africa, Administrator General (1989*a*). *Constituent Assembly Proclamation*. No. 91 of 1989.

— (1989*b*). *Election (Constituent Assembly) Proclamation*. No. 49 of 1989.

— (1989*c*). *Registration of Political Organizations (Constituent Assembly) Proclamation*. No. 49 of 1989.

— (1989*d*). *Registration of Voters (Constituent Assembly) Proclamations*. No. 58 of 1989.

UN Security Council Resolution 435, September 1978.

UN Security Council Document s/15287: Constitutional Principles, 12 July 1982.

3.2 Books, Articles and Electoral Reports

African–European Institute (1995). *Consolidation of Democracy in Namibia. AWEPA Electoral Observer Mission December 1994*. Amsterdam: African–European Institute.

Alcardi de Saint-Paul, M. (1990). 'Les élections namibiennes (7–11 novembre 1989)'. *Afrique Contemporaine*, 153: 64–67.

Ansprenger, F. (1991*a*). *Freie Wahlen in Namibia. Der Übergang zur staatlichen Unabhängigkeit*. Frankfurt a.M.: Peter Lang.

— (1991*b*). 'Die Verfassung Namibias'. *KAS-Auslandsinformationen*, 7/12: 14–22.

Blaustein, A. P. (1990). 'Republic of Namibia', in A. P. Blaustein and G. H. Flanz (eds.), *Constitutions of the Countries of the World*. New York: Oceana Publications.

Cliffe, L. *et al.* (1994). *The Transition to Independence in Namibia*. Boulder, Col.: Lynne Rienner.

Commonwealth Secretariat (1989). *Preparing for a Free Namibia: Elections, Transition and Independence. The Report of the Commonwealth Observer Group on Namibia.* Windhoek.

Commonwealth Secretariat (1995) *The Presidential and National Assembly Elections in Namibia, 7–8 December 1994. The Report of the Commonwealth Observer Group*. London: Commonwealth Secretariat.

Diescho, J. (1994). *The Namibian Constitution in Perspective*. Windhoek: Gamsberg Macmillan.

Du Pisani, A. (1995). 'Limited Choice: The 1994 National and Presidential Elections in Namibia'. *Africa Institute Bulletin*, 35/1, 1–4.

Fiamingo, C. (1997). *Namibia (Africa del Sud Ovest). Itinerari bibliografici ed orientamenti di ricerca*. Bologna: Il Nove.

Forrest, J. B. (1994). 'Namibia—the First Postapartheid Democracy'. *Journal of Democracy*, 5/3: 88–100.

Foundation for Democracy in Namibia (1989). *Coming of Age: Choices for Namibian Voters*. Windhoek.

Grotpeter, J. J. (1994). *Historical Dictionary of Namibia*. Metuchen, NJ: Scarecrow Press.

Harneit-Sievers, A. (1990). *Namibia: Wahlen zur Verfassunggebenden Versammlung 1989. Analyse und Dokumentation.* Arbeiten aus dem Institut für Afrika-Kunde, 69. Hamburg: Institut für Afrika-Kunde.

International Parliamentary Observer Mission to Namibia (1989). *Report of the International Parliamentary Observer Mission to Namibia, 1–12 November 1989*. London: International Freedom Foundation.

Keulder, Ch. (1998). *Voting Behaviour in Namibia. A Report on the Voters*. Windhoek: University of Namibia.

Kießwetter, A. (1993). *Die Verfassungsentwicklung in Namibia.* Schriften zum Staats- und Völkerrecht, 51. Frankfurt a.M.: Peter Lang.

Kößler, R. (1992). *Towards Greater Participation and Equality? Some Findings of the 1992 Regional and Local Elections in Namibia.* NEPRU Working Paper, 57. Windhoek: The Namibian Economic Policy Research Unit.

Leys, C., and Saul, J. S. *et al.* (1995). *Namibia's Liberation Struggle. The Two-Edged Sword*. London: James Currey/ Athens: Ohio University Press.

Leistner, E., and Esterhuysen, P. (1991). *Namibia 1990: An Africa Institute Country Survey*. Pretoria: Africa Institute of South Africa.

Lindeke, W. A. (1995). 'Democratization in Namibia: Soft State, Hard Choices'. *Studies in Comparative International Development*, 30/1: 3–29.

— Wanzala, W., and Tonchi, V. (1992). 'Namibia's Election Revisited'. *Politikon*, 18/2: 121–138.

Marias, C. *et al.* (1996). *Southern Africa after Elections: Towards a Culture of Democracy*. Windhoek: Friedrich-Ebert-Foundation.

Möckli, S. (1995). 'Wahlhilfe durch die UN. Am Beispiel Namibia 1989 und Südafrika 1994'. *Österreichische Zeitschrift für Politikwissenschaft*, 24/4: 457–464.

Namibia Institute for Democracy (1996). *Building Democracy: Perceptions and Performances of Government and Opposition in Namibia*. Windhoek: NID.

National Democratic Institute for International Affairs (1995). *Comments on the Namibian Presidential and National Assembly Elections*. Washington, D.C.: National Democratic Institute for International Affairs.

Nuscheler, F. (1978). 'Rhodesien', in D. Sternberger, B. Vogel, D. Nohlen and K. Landfried (eds.), *Die Wahl der Parlamente und anderer Staatsorgane, Bd. II: Politische Organisation und Representation in Afrika*, by Franz Nuscheler, Klaus Ziemer *et al.*, Berlin/ New York: Walter de Gruyter, 1627–1690.

Pendelton, W. *et al.* (1993). *A Study of Voting Behaviour in the 1992 Namibian Regional and Local Government Elections plus Elections Statistics*. Windhoek: University of Namibia.

Potgieter, P. J. J. S. (1991). 'The Resolution 435 Election in Namibia'. *Politikon*, 18/2: 26–48.

Saxena, S. C. (1991). *Namibia and the World: The Story of the Birth of a Nation*. Delhi: Kalinga.

Schuhmacher, U., and Naudascher, K. (without year). *Die Wahlen zur Verfassunggebenden Versammlung in Namibia vom 7. bis 11.11.1989*. Kiel: Institut für Sicherheitspolitik an der Christian-Albrechts-Universität Kiel.

Simon, D. (1995). 'Namibia: SWAPO Wins Two-Thirds Majority'. *Review of African Political Economics*, 63: 107–114.

Soiri, I. (1998). *Why the 1997 Local Authority Elections in Namibia were Postponed.* Working Paper 1/98. Helsinki: Institute for Development Sudies, University of Helsinki.

Tötemeyer, G. K. H., Wehmhörner, A., and Weiland, H. (1996). *Elections in Namibia*. Friedrich-Ebert-Foundation. Windhoek: Gamsberg Macmillan Publishers.

United Nations Institute for Namibia (1989). *Comparative Electoral Systems and Political Consequences: Options for Namibia*. Lusaka.

Weiland, H. (1995*a*). 'Wahlen in Namibia: Lackmustest der Demokratisierung?' *Africa Spektrum*, 30/1: 63–76.

— (1995*b*). 'Landslide Victory for SWAPO in 1994: Many Seats But Few New Votes'. *Journal of Modern African Studies*, 33/2: 349–357.

— (1996). 'Verfassung und Verfassungsgrenzen in der Dritten Welt: der Fall Namibia'. *Nord-Süd aktuell*, 10/1: 93–102.

— and Braham, M. (1994). *The Namibian Peace Process: Implications and Lessons for the Future*. Freiburg: Arnold Bergstraesser Institut.

NIGER

by Matthias Basedau

1. Introduction

1.1 Historical Overview

Since independence politics in Niger, one of the least developed countries in the world, has been to a great extent of strongly authoritarian character. After a period of one-party government (1960–1974) the military took over the country and stayed in power until 1987 when Niger returned to formal civilian rule. Initially successful efforts to establish democracy in the early 1990s, completed by the conduct of competitive elections, failed when following a government crisis a military coup in 1996 meant an end to democratic rule. Despite international and domestic pressures democracy has not been restored so far.

Niger gained independence from France on 3 August 1960. From 1960 until 1974 it experienced one-party rule by the PPN-RDA (*Parti progressiste Nigérien-Rassemblement démocratique africaine*), the Nigerian section of the pre-independence movement RDA in French West Africa which had won the last election under French Rule in 1958. The PPN-RDA's head Diori Hamani, a member of the southern Djerma ethnic group, became the country's first President.

Although other parties were not explicitly banned by the 1959 Constitution the PPN-RDA candidates in the general elections of 1965 and 1970 actually ran unopposed. In both elections the Diori government was re-elected by overwhelming majorities but proved incapable of coping with the effects of both the prolonged Sahelian drought and the enduring corruption in the country.

A coup d'état led by (then) Lt. Col. Seyni Kountché overthrew the one-party government in 1974 and resulted in 13 years of military rule. In 1987, after Kountché's death, the supreme military council chose Ali Saibou as the Head of State. In a move to re-establish civilian rule the military council disbanded, naming Saibou as President. The MNSD (*Mouvement national pour la societé et le developpement*), backed by the military, was authorized as the only legal party and consequently triumphed in the 1989 elections.

In 1990, continuing harsh economic problems and the 'wind of change' from Eastern Europe inspired mass protest demanding democratization. Saibou responded by announcing the holding of a National Conference to discuss political reforms. The National Conference (more than 1,200 members), however, declared itself 'sovereign', stripped Saibou of all but ceremonial powers, and paved the way for the new—democratic—Constitution of the Third Republic, which was conceived as a semi-presidential model and approved by referendum in December 1992.

Shortly after the country's first multi-party parliamentary elections, held in early 1993 and internationally judged as free and fair, a number of opposition parties formed the *Alliance des forces de changement* (AFC) in order to block the MNSD's return to power and to obtain a majority in the National Assembly. The following month, Mahamane Ousmane (*Convention démocratique et sociale*—CDS), backed by the AFC, won the presidential elections and became Niger's first democratically elected President. He subsequently nominated Mahamadou Issoufou, a member of the AFC ally *Parti Nigérien pour la démocratie et le progrès* (PNDS), for the post of Prime Minister. Naming his government 'war cabinet' Issoufou immediately called for a decisive response to the continuing Tuareg rebellion (since 1991), which had been stimulated by feelings of economic and political deprivation among the members of the Tuareg ethnic minority (10% of the population). Following increased violence in early 1994 and 1995, however, government authorities and rebels entered into negotiations and a peace agreement was signed in April 1995.

During that period, domestic politics were marked by an institutional crisis between President and Prime Minister. In September 1994, accusing its hitherto allies of 'betrayal', the PNDS left the AFC government coalition and PM Issoufou resigned his post. President Ousmane had to call new legislative elections in January 1995, which, taking place under competitive conditions, were lost by the parties of the presidential majority. As a turn for the worse, Ousmane was forced to nominate Amadou Hama from the former single and now majoritarian party MNSD, as Prime Minister. Subsequently, Ousmane's and Amadou's disagreement resulted in a situation of institutional deadlock and open enmity, and eventually provoked another intervention by the military on 27 January 1996. Whereas the population seemed to approve the coup's leader Col. Ibrahim Mainassara Baré, leading Western countries suspended their financial (and in the case of France its military) support. In order to regain international aid Mainassara immediately announced a plan for redemocratization including the organization of elections. In an apparent effort to avoid another paralysis of the government a new constitution strengthening the President's position was prepared and approved by referendum in May 1996. Presidential and parliamentary elections of July and November of the same year were won by Mainassara and allied parties respectively, notwithstanding the severe domestic and international critics concerning the doubtful democratic standards of both elections. The current situation in Niger must thus be considered as a breakdown of democracy.

1.2 Evolution of Electoral Provisions

Since independence Niger has experienced five constitutions (1959; 1987; 1989; 1992; 1996) and different electoral provisions. The Constitution of 1987 was never put into practice and will not be considered below.

Except for the period of military rule (1974–1987), the national bodies to be directly elected have always been the President (no Vice-President) and the unicameral National Assembly, roughly similar to the constitutional model of the Fifth French Republic. While the terms of the Deputies never changed (constantly five years) the number of Deputies varied from 50 to 93 (1958: 60, 1965: 50, 1989: 93, 1992: 83). With the exception of the 1989 Constitution, when the term was extended to seven years, the President has served a five-year term. Previously unrestricted, the President may only serve for a maximum of two consecutive terms since 1989.

The 1959 Constitution, in force until 1974, provided for adult, universal, equal, direct and secret suffrage. When the country returned to civilian rule in 1987 these principles were re-established and are still in force.

As for the nomination of candidates, from 1959 to 1974, presidential candidates had to be at least 41 years and to be born of Nigerian parents. Candidates for the National Assembly were required to be at least 23 years and to master the French language. The 1989 provisions demanded that both the President and the Deputies were put forward from the single-list of the ruling MNSD thus emphasizing their non-competitive character. Since the 1992 Constitution came into effect every qualified voter of at least 25 years (President 40 years) has been eligible.

Furthermore, candidates had to be nominated by a political party. Parties built on regionalist, ethnic or religious terms were prohibited.

With regard to the electoral system, from 1959 to 1974 the President was elected by an absolute majority system. If no candidate gained more than 50% of the votes in the first round the National Assembly would have had to choose between the two most successful candidates. Members of the legislative chamber were elected by the plurality system in 16 variable-member constituencies, the number of seats varying according to their demographic weight. Every voter had one vote in the parliamentary elections. Under the 1989 constitution both the President and the Deputies nominated on a single list by the MNSD were elected at the same time in 56 variable-member constituencies. The 1992 constitution re-established an absolute majority system for the presidential elections, as had applied until 1974. Concerning the parliamentary elections the same constitution provided, in contrast to previous provisions, for 75 out of 83 deputies for a proportional representation system in eight multi-member districts of different size (closed party lists, single vote, Hare quota and largest remainder). The remaining eight seats were distributed in special national minority districts by relative majority vote. When the 1996 Constitution came into effect these principles were re-established (see below).

1.3 Current Electoral Provisions

Sources: Constitution of the Republic of Niger 1996; Ordonnance 96-014 (16 April 1996) portant Code Electoral.

Elected national institutions: The President (no Vice-President) and the (unicameral) National Assembly are directly elected. In both cases the regular term is five years. The President is re-eligible only once.

Suffrage: The principles of adult (18 years or married) universal, direct, equal and secret suffrage are applied.

Nomination of candidates

- presidential elections: Every Nigerian of 40 years and older is eligible. Incompatibilities apply for: members of the government, the Supreme Court, the electoral office and the armed forces. Every candidate has to deposit CFA 10 million (until 1996: 2 million). Independent candidature is allowed.

- *parliamentary elections*: Every qualified voter of 25 years or older is eligible. Incompatibilities apply for members of the government, civil servants, employees of foreign states or international organizations. The provision banning independent and non-partisan candidates has been abolished, but independent candidates have to present a list representing 1% of registered voters in the relevant constituency. Independent candidates may present common lists with political parties in the multi-member constituencies. Additional requirements: deposit of CFA 100,000 reimbursed when candidate wins at least 5% in the constituency.

Electoral system
- *presidential elections*: The President is directly elected by an absolute majority system. If no candidate gains more than 50% of the votes cast in the first round, a second one is held, where the two most successful candidates compete.
- *parliamentary elections*: The National Assembly has 83 members. Seventy five Deputies are elected according to a proportional representation system. Technical elements: *eight variable-member constituencies according to their demographic weight (three constituencies with four seats, one with 10 seats, three with 13 seats, one with 14 seats); *closed party lists; *single vote; *Hare quota and highest average formula; *no artificial threshold. The remaining eight deputies are elected in relatively small single-member 'national minority' constituencies by relative majority.

1.4 Comment on the Electoral Statistics

Documentation of three out of 14 elections and referendums remained incomplete. Official data were not available. As a result, information derives entirely from secondary sources, which in turn rely on official figures. Data are generally reliable, inconsistencies are indicated. To a certain extent data were completed by author's calculation.

Elections under the Diori regime (1960–1974), completely covered but short of detailed information, were taken from Ziemer (1978). Except for the elections of 1995 (Grégoire 1995), the balloting of the Second Republic (1987–1992), and the Third Republic (1992–1996) data are documented according to Raynal (1993). Detailed information covering both national and regional results were available for the 1996 presidential elections (Boubacar 1996 and the newspapers *Alternative* and *Le Sahel*). This is not the case for the referendum and parliamentary elections of the same year, where information is drawn from newspaper (*Archiv der Gegenwart*) and internet sources (IPU Website) respectively.

2. Tables

2.1 Dates of National Elections, Referendums and Coups d'Etat

Year	Presidential elections	Parliamentary elections	Elections for Constitutional Assembly	Referendums	Coups d'état
1958		14/12			
1965	30/09	21/10[a]			
1970	01/10	22/10[a]			
1974					15/04
1987				14/06	
1989				24/09	
1989	10/12	10/12			
1992				16/12	
1993	27/02 (1st) 27/03 (2nd)	14/02			
1995		12/01			
1996	07-08/07	23/11		12/05	27/01

[a] Single-party elections.

2.2 Electoral Body 1965–1996

Year	Type of election[a]	Population	Registered voters		Votes cast		
			Total number	% pop.	Total number	% reg. voters	% pop.
1965	Pr	3,328,000	1,707,044	51.3	1,680,570	98.5	50.4
1965	Pa	3,328,000	1,708,605	51.2	1,679,196	98.2	50.4
1970	Pr	4,016,000	1,942,774	48.4	1,910,626	98.3	47.6
1970	Pa	4,016,000	1,906,283	47.4	1,851,146	97.1	46.0
1987	Ref	7,249,596[b]	3,370,000[c]	46.8	3,292,200	96.8	45.4
1989	Ref	7,249,596[b]	3,477,874	48.0	3,306,875	94.9	45.6
1989	Pr/Pa	7,249,596	3,508,204	48.4	3,334,913	95.1	46.0
1992	Ref	8,171,000[c]	3,900,881	47.7	2,207,220	56.6	24.8
1993	Pa	8,171,000[c]	3,995,751	48.9	1,307,682	32.7	16.0
1993	Pr	8,171,000[c]	4,069,333	49.8	1,433,393	35.5	17.5
1995	Pa	8,846,000[c]	—	—	—	—	—
1996	Ref	8,846,000[c]	—	—	—	35.1	—
1996	Pr	8,846,000[c]	3,804,750	43.0	2,525,019	66.4	28.5
1996	Pa	8,846,000[c]	3,939,101	44.5	1,535,963	39.0	17.4

[a] Pa = Parliament (National Assembly); Pr = President; Ref = Referendum.
[b] Census 1988.
[c] UN estimations, figure for 1995 and 1996 refers to 1994.

2.3 Abbreviations

AFC	Alliance des Forces de Changement
ANDP	Alliance Nigérienne pour la Démocratie et le Progrès
CDS	Convention Démocratique et Sociale
FNN	Front National du Niger
MDP	Mouvement pour la Démocratie et le Progrès
MNSD	Mouvement national pour la Société et le Développement
PDP	Parti pour la Dignité du Peuple Daraja
PMT	Parti du Mouvement des Travailleurs
PNDS	Parti Nigérien pour la Démocratie et le Socialisme
PPN-RDA	Parti Progressiste Nigérien—Rassemblement Démocratique Africain
PSDN	Parti Social Démocrate du Niger
PUND	Parti pour l'Unité et la Démocratie
UND	Union Démocratique Nigérien
UDP	Union pour la Démocratie et le Progrès
UDPS	Union pour la Démocratie et le Progrès Social
UDFP	Union Démocratique des Forces Progressistes
UNIRD	Union Nationale des Indépendants pour le Renouveau Démocratique
UPDP	Union des Patriotes Démocrates et Progressistes

2.4 Electoral Participation of Parties and Alliances 1958–1996

Party / Alliance	Years	Elections contested	
		Presidential	Parliamentary[a]
PPN-RDA[b, c]	1958, 1965, 1970, 1993, 1995	3	5
Sawaba	1958	0	1
MNSD	1989, 1993, 1995, 1996	3	3
ANDP[b]	1993, 1995, 1996	2	3
CDS[b]	1993, 1995, 1996	2	2
PNDS	1993, 1995, 1996	2	2
PSDN[b]	1993, 1995, 1996	1	2
UDPS[b]	1993, 1995, 1996	0	3
UDFP	1993	1	1
UPDP	1993, 1995, 1996	1	3
PUND[b]	1995	0	1
MDP	1996	0	1
PDP	1996	0	1
PMT	1996	0	1
UNIRD	1996	0	1

[a] For parliamentary elections only parties are indicated that actually won seats.
[b] In 1993 part of AFC. Not all parties that constitute the AFC participated in the parliamentary elections of 1993 and not all that participated gained seats.
[c] In 1958 the PPN-RDA contested as UCFA.

2.5 Referendums

Year	1987[a]		1989[a]	
	Total number	%	Total number	%
Registered voters	3,370,000	–	3,477,874	–
Votes cast	3,262,314[b]	96.8	3,306,875	94.9
Invalid votes	6,991[c]	0.2	7,425[e]	0.2
Valid votes	3,255,323	99.8	3,299,450	99.8
Yes	3,241,589	99.6	3,275,737	99.3
No	13,734[d]	0.4	23,713	0.7

[a] Approval of a new constitution.
[b] Figure represents sum of valid votes and invalid votes.
[c] *Blank votes*.
[d] Author's calculation (valid votes minus 'Yes' votes); according to source (*Africa Research Bulletin* 8531) there were 11,734 No votes.
[e] Author's calculation (votes cast minus valid votes); figure given by source (Raynal 1993) is 7,445.

Year	1992[a] Total number	%	1996[a] Total number	%
Registered voters	3,900,881	–	—	–
Votes cast	2,207,220	56.6	—	35.1
Invalid votes	40,300	1.9	—	–
Valid votes	2,166,920	98.4	—	–
Yes	1,945,653	89.8	—	92.3
No	221,267	10.2	—	7.7

[a] Approval of a new constitution.

2.6 Elections for Constitutional Assembly

Elections for Constitutional Assembly have not been held.

2.7 Parliamentary Elections 1965–1996

Year	1965 Total number	%	1970 Total number	%
Registered voters	1,709,605	–	1,906,283	–
Votes cast	1,679,196	98.2	1,851,146	97.1
Invalid votes	1,433	0.1	178	0.0
Valid votes	1,677,763	99.9	1,850,968	100.0
PPN- RDA	1,677,763	100.0	1,850,968	100.0

Year	1989 Total number	%	1993 Total number	%
Registered voters	3,508,204	–	3,995,751	–
Votes cast	3,334,913	95.1	1,307,682	32.7
Invalid votes	5,259	0.2	55,425	4.2
Valid votes	3,329,654	99.8	1,252,257	95.8
MNSD	3,316,182[a]	99.6	383,758	30.7
CDS	–	–	341,576	27.3
ANDP	–	–	191,112	15.3
PNDS	–	–	183,085	14.6
UDFP	–	–	39,270	3.1
UPDP	–	–	36,189	2.9
PPN-RDA	–	–	32,735	2.6
PSDN	–	–	18,604	1.5
UDPS	–	–	463	0.0
Others	–	–	22,564	1.8

[a] No votes: 13,472 (0.4%).

Year	1995		1996[a]	
	Total number	%	Total number	%
Registered voters	—	–	3,939,101	–
Votes cast	—	35.1	1,535,963	39.0
Invalid votes	—	—	36,151[b]	—
Valid votes	—	—	—	—
MNSD	—	—	–[c]	–[c]
CDS	—	—	–[c]	–[c]
ANDP	—	—	123,957	10.1
PNDS	—	—	–[c]	–[c]
UDFP	—	—	–	–
UPDP	—	—	91,944	2.5
PPN-RDA	—	—	–[c]	–[c]
PSDN	—	—	–[c]	–[c]
UDPS	—	—	36,899	3.7
PUND	—	—	–[c]	–[c]
UNIRD	–	–	990,308	56.7
Daraja	–	–	21,475	5.3
PMT	—	—	107,000	4.2
MDP	—	—	7,562	1.5
Independents	–	–	46,805	6.1

[a] Highly inconsistent figures as reported by IPU, *Parline Database*.
[b] Blank and null votes.
[c] Electoral boycott.

2.7 a) Parliamentary Elections 1993: Regional Results

Absolute numbers								
District[a]	Agadez	Diffa	Dosso	Maradi	Tohoua	Tillabéry	Zinder	Niamey
ANDP	2,701	815	64,228	10,750	8,186	65,885	5,934	29,174
CDS	6,938	2,782	32,642	91,658	48,565	13,434	124,304	20,675
MDP	–	–	4,486	–	–	–	–	1,481
MNSD	9,092	15,281	28,733	63,529	82,334	98,209	31,830	40,183
PMT	–	–	1,721	5,891	–	2,965	3,933	789
PNDS	3,771	2,957	12,560	29,464	91,424	16,181	10,349	11,349
PPN-RDA	558	1,105	6,285	6,736	–	9,737	3,910	4,404
PSDN	–	7,649	–	5,490	–	–	4,650	660
PUND	1,153	–	–	–	–	–	–	–
UDFP	–	1,214	3,112	11,490	6,175	6,975	7,392	2,333
UDPS	–	–	–	–	–	–	–	–
UPDP	–	–	4,523	18,835	–	–	11,326	1,483
Total	24,213	31,803	158,950[b]	243,840[c]	236,684	213,386	203,628	112,527[d]

[a] Number of seats to be distributed: Agadez: 4, Diffa: 4. Dosso: 10, Maradi: 13, Tohoua: 13, Tillabéry: 13, Zinder: 14, Niamey: 4.

[b] Official figure; sum of party votes: 158,290.

[c] Official figure; sum of party votes: 243,843.

[d] Official figure; sum of party votes: 112,531.

Percentages								
District[a]	Agadez	Diffa	Dosso	Maradi	Tohoua	Tillabéry	Zinder	Niamey
ANDP	11.2	2.6	40.6	4.4	3.5	30.9	2.9	25.9
CDS	28.7	8.6	20.6	37.6	20.5	6.3	61.0	18.4
MDP	–	–	2.8	–	–	–	–	1.3
MNSD	37.6	48.1	18.2	26.1	34.8	46.0	15.6	35.7
PMT	–	–	1.1	2.4	–	1.4	1.9	0.7
PNDS	15.6	9.3	7.9	12.1	38.6	7.6	5.1	10.1
PPN-RDA	2.3	3.5	4.0	2.8	–	4.5	1.9	3.9
PSDN	–	24.1	–	2.3	–	–	2.3	0.6
PUND	4.8	–	–	–	–	–	–	–
UDFP	–	3.8	2.0	4.7	2.6	3.3	3.6	2.1
UDPS	–	–	–	–	–	–	–	–
UPDP	–	–	2.9	7.7	–	–	5.6	1.3
Total	23.5	24.9	30.6	34.0	31.7	32.3	25.1	61.7

[a] Number of seats to be distributed: Agadez: 4, Diffa: 4. Dosso: 10, Maradi: 13, Tohoua: 13, Tillabéry: 13, Zinder: 14, Niamey: 4.

2.7 b) Parliamentary Elections 1993: Special Electoral Districts

Absolute numbers	Banibangou	Bankilaré	Bermo	Bilma	N'Gourti	Tassara	Tesker[a]	Torodi
ANDP	319	1,796	23	77	127	1,097[b]	–	2,789
CDS	–	–	128	223	–	226	–	–
MNSD	3,509[b]	2,343[b]	190	1,121[b]	1,288[b]	1,030	348	4,738[b]
PMT	–	–	–	–	–	–	145	–
PNDS	132	785	247	838	649	8	900[b]	1,481
PSDN	–	–	–	34	121	–	–	–
UDFP	28	–	–	251	–	–	7	293
UDPS	–	–	463[b]	–	–	–	–	–
UPDP	–	–	–	–	–	–	22	–
Total	3,988	4,924	1,051	2,594[c]	2,185	2,361	1,422	9,301

[a] Original results annulled by Supreme Court. Results presented derive from 11 April 1993.
[b] Seat gained.
[c] Official figure; sum of party votes: 2,544.

Percentages	Banibangou	Bankilaré	Bermo	Bilma	N'Gourti	Tassara	Tesker[a]	Torodi
ANDP	8.0	36.5	2.1	3.0	5.8	46.5[b]	–	30.0
CDS	–	–	12.2	8.6	–	9.6	–	–
MNSD	88.0[b]	47.6[b]	18.1	43.2[b]	59.0[b]	43.6	24.5	50.9[b]
PMT	–	–	–	–	–	–	10.2	–
PNDS	3.3	15.9	23.5	34.2	29.7	0.3	63.3	15.9
PSDN	–	–	–	1.3	5.5	–	–	–
UDFP	0.7	–	–	9.7	–	–	0.5	3.2
UDPS	–	–	44.1[b]	–	–	–	–	–
UPDP	–	–	–	–	–	–	1.6	–
Total	26.6	15.6	11.4	42.9	14.3	29.7	16.2	29.0

[a] Original results annulled by Supreme Court. Results presented derive from 11 April 1993.
[b] Seat gained.

2.8 Composition of Parliament 1958–1996

Year	1958		1965		1970		1989	
	Seats	%	Seats	%	Seats	%	Seats	%
	60	100	50	100	50	100	93	100
PPN- RDA	49	81.7	50	100	50	100	–	–
Sawaba	11	18.3	–	–	–	–	–	–
MNSD	–	–	–	–	–	–	93	100

Year	1993		1995		1996	
	Seats	%	Seats	%	Seats	%
	83	100	83	100	83	100
MNSD	29	34.9	29	34.9	–	–
CDS	22	26.5	24	28.9	–	–
PNDS	13	15.7	12	14.5	–	–
ANDP	11	13.3	9	10.8	8	9.6
PPN-RDA	2	2.4	1	1.2	–	–
UDFP	2	2.4	0	0	–	–
UPDP	2	2.4	1	1.2	4	4.8
PSDN	1	1.2	2	2.4	–	–
UDPS	1	1.2	2	2.4	3	3.6
PUND	0	0	3	3.6	–	–
UNIRD	–	–	–	–	59	71.1
PDP	–	–	–	–	3	3.6
PMT	–	–	–	–	2	2.4
MDP	–	–	–	–	1	1.2
Independents	–	–	–	–	3	3.6

2.9 Presidential Elections 1965–1996

1965	Total number	%
Registered voters	1,707,044	–
Votes cast	1,680,570	98.5
Invalid votes	1,658	0.1
Valid votes	1,678,912	99.9
Diori Hamani (PPN-RDA)	1,678,912	100.0

1970	Total number	%
Registered voters	1,942,774	–
Votes cast	1,910,626	98.,3
Invalid votes	2,953	0.2
Valid votes	1,907,673	99.8
Diori Hamani (PPN-RDA)	1,907,673	100.0

1989	Total number	%
Registered voters	3,508,204	–
Votes cast	3,334,913	95.1
Invalid votes	5,259	0.2
Valid votes	3,329,654	99.8
Ali Saibou (MNSD)	3,316,182	99.6
No votes	13,417	0.4

1993 (1st round)	Total number	%
Registered voters	4,082,076	–
Votes cast	1,328,152	32.5
Invalid votes	35,695	2.7
Valid votes	1,292,457	97.3
Tandja Mamadou (MNSD)	443,223	34.3
Mahamane Ousmane (CDS)	343,261	26.6
Mahamadou Issoufou (PNDS)	205,707	15.9
Adamou Moumouni Djermakoye (ANDP)	196,949	15.2
Illa Kane (UPDP)	32,951	2.6
Oumaru Garba Youssouffou (PPN-RDA)	25,769	2.0
Katzelma Omar Mahaman Taya (PSDN)	23,565	1.8
Djibo Bakary (UDFP)	21,662	1.7

1993 (2nd round)	Total number	%
Registered voters	4,069,333	–
Votes cast	1,433,393	35.2
Invalid votes	30,499	2.1
Valid votes	1,402,894	97.9
Mahamane Ousmane (CDS/ AFC)	763,476	54.4
Mamadou Tandja (MNSD)	639,418	45.6

1996	Total number	%
Registered voters	3,804,750	–
Votes cast	2,525,019[a]	66.4[b]
Invalid votes	—	—
Valid votes	—	—
Ibrahim Mainassara Baré	1,262,308	52.2
Mahamane Ousmane (CDS)	477,826	19.8
Tanja Mamadou (MNSD)	378,322	15.7
Mahamadou Issoufou (PNDS)	187,826	7.6
Adamou Moumouni Djermakoye (ANDP)	115,302	4.8

[a] Official figure which according to source (Boubacar 1996) is not reliable. Votes given for candidates add up to 2,721,620.

2.9 a) Presidential Elections 1993: Regional Results

First round: absolute numbers

	Tandja (MSND)	Ousmane (CDS)	Issoufou (PNDS)	Djermakoyé (ANDP)	Kané (UPDP)	Others[a]	Total
Agadez	11,026	9,955	4,649	2,542	539	842	29,553
Diffa	17,948	2,607	3,819	761	887	7,527[b]	33,549
Dosso	37,818	28,973	14,459	71,889	1,960	10,546	165,645
Maradi	85,188	90,212	32,522	8,097	11,696	15,918	243,633
C.U. Niamey	46,326	20,100	9,474	29,994	725	3,504	110,123
Tahoua	81,125	46,122	100,495	4,441	6,736	7,240	246,159
Tillabéry	119,791	11,001	18,967	67,167	4,275	13,671	234,872[c]
Zinder	38,916	129,499	12,419	4,991	6,028	11,339	203,192
Embassies	4,875	5,152	8,903	7,063	105	408	25,730[d]
Total	443,233[e]	343,261[f]	205,707	196,949[g]	32,951	70,996	1,292,457

[a] Candidates that gained less than 2% of the vote nation-wide.

[b] Katzelma Omar M. Taya: 6,416.

[c] Official figure; sum of given votes for candidates: 234,873.

[d] Official figure; sum of given votes for candidates: 26,506.

[e] Official figure; sum of given votes per region: 443,014.

[f] Official figure; sum of given votes per region: 343,621.

[g] Official figure; sum of given votes per region: 196,945.

First round: percentages

	Tandja (MSND)	Ousmane (CDS)	Issoufou (PNDS)	Djermakoyé (ANDP)	Kané (UPDP)	Others	Total
Agadez	37.3	33.7	15.7	8.6	1.8	2.9	100
Diffa	53.5	7.8	11.4	2.3	2.6	22.4[a]	100
Dosso	22.8	17.5	8.7	43.4	1.2	6.4	100
Maradi	35.0	37.0	13.4	3.3	4.8	6.5	100
C.U. Niamey	42.0	18.2	8.6	27.4	0.6	3.2	100
Tahoua	33.0	18.7	40.8	1.8	2.7	2.9	100
Tillabéry	51.0	4.7	8.1	28.6	1.8	5.8	100
Zinder	19.2	63.7	6.1	2.5	3.0	5.6	100
Embassies	15.9	20.0	34.6	27.5	0.4	1.5	100
Total	34.3	26.6	15.9	15.2	2.5	5.5	100

[a] Katzelma M. Taya: 19.1%.

Second round								
	Reg. voters	Votes cast		Valid votes	Ousmane (CDS)		Tandja (MNSD)	
		abs.	%		abs.	%	abs.	%
Agadez	106,254	35,066	33.0	34,672[a]	22,095	60.5	14,456	39.6
Diffa	141,821	41,975	29.6	40,557	15,760	38.9	24,797	61.1
Dosso	515,783	168,800	32.7	165,365	107,077	64.8	58,288	35.3
Maradi	724,544	272,692	37.6	264,870	143,194	54.1	121,676	45.9
Tahoua	742,460	263,271	35.5	257,444	142,749	55.5	114,695	44.6
Tillabéri	707,542	254,402	36.4	252,943[a]	84,772	32.6	175,180	67.4
Zinder	823,485	243,334	29.4	237,423	178,091	75.0	59,332	25.0
Niamey	181,976	111,415	61.2	110,599	48,589	43.9	62,010	56.1
Embassies	116,468	26,449	22.7	26,033	21,149	70.2	4,884	29.8

[a] Official figure; sum of votes for candidates: 259,952.
[b] Official figure; sum of votes for candidates: 36,551.

2.9 b) Presidential Elections 1996: Regional Results

Absolute numbers					
	Mainassara	Ousmane (CDS)	Tandja (MNSD)	Issoufou (PNDS)	Djermakoyé (ANDP)
Agadez	26,034	10,618	13,858	6,817	941
Diffa	11,196	7,226	21,092	5,635	815
Dosso	269,854	18,979	28,815	18,643	52,455
Maradi	165,042	76,484	49,454	16,881	5,571
Niamey	46,828	11,656	28,148	6,001	7,640
Tahoua	160,705	75,023	85,122	96,084	6,926
Tillabéry	465,420	16,406	112,237	17,512	35,376
Zinder	117,220	261,039	39,596	16,253	5,578
Total	1,262,308[a]	477,826[b]	378,322	187,826	115,302

[a] Official figure; sum of votes per region: 1,262,299.
[b] Official figure; sum of votes per region: 477,431.

Percentages	Mainassara	Ousmane (CDS)	Tandja (MNSD)	Issoufou (PNDS)	Djermakoyé (ANDP)
Agadez	44.7	18.2	23.8	11.7	1.6
Diffa	24.4	15.7	45.9	12.3	1.8
Dosso	69.4	4.9	7.4	4.8	13.5
Maradi	52.7	24.4	15.8	5.4	1.8
Niamey	46.7	11.6	28.1	6.0	7.6
Tahoua	37.9	17.7	20.1	22.7	1.6
Tillabéry	71.9	2.5	17.4	2.7	5.5
Zinder	26.7	59.4	9.0	3.7	1.3
Total	52.2	19.8	15.7	7.6	4.8

2.10 List of Power Holders 1960–1998

Head of State	Years	Remarks
Diori Hamani	1960–1974	Constitutionally elected on 03/08/1960; ousted on 15/04/1974.
Seyni Kountché	1974–1987	Leader of the coup d'état of 15/04/1974.
Ali Saibou	1987–1993	Appointed by military council after the death of Kountché on 14/11/1987.
Mahamane Ousmane	1993–1996	Constitutionally elected; assumed office on 16/04/1993; ousted on 27/01/1996.
Ibrahim Mainassara Baré	1996–	Leader of the coup d'état of 27/01/1996.

Prime Minister	Years	Remarks
Oumarou Mamane	1983	Appointed on 21/01/1983 when the post of Prime Minister was newly created.
Hamid Algabid	1983–1988	Appointed by military council on 14/11/1983
Oumarou Mamane	1988–1989	On 02/08/1989 the office of Prime Minister was eliminated.
Aliou Mahamidou	1990–1991	On 02/03/1990 the office was reestablished.
Amadou Cheiffou	1991–1993	Appointed by National Conference on 24/10/1991.
Mahamadou Issoufou	1993–1994	Regularly appointed by the President on 17/04/1993.
Souley Aboulayé	1994–1995	From 28/09 to 16/10/1994 regularly appointed Prime Minister; afterwards: acting holder of the office.
Amadou Cissés	1995	Regularly appointed on 07/02/1995.
Amadou Hama	1995–1996	Regularly appointed on 21/02/1995.

Prime Minister	Years	Remarks
Boukari Adji	1996	Appointed on 30/01/1996 by Mainassara Baré; acting Prime Minister.
Boubacar Amadou Cisse	1996–1997	Appointed on 21/12/1996 by Mainassara Baré; dismissed on 24/11/1997 due to 'incompetence and bad governance of his cabinet'.
Ibrahim Hassane Mayaki	1997–	Formerly secretary of foreign affairs; appointed on 27/11/1997 by Mainassara Baré.

3. Bibliography

Alhada, A. (1995). *Evolution politique et constitutionelle du Niger (1974–1995)*. Paris, Diss., Univ. de Paris XII.

Amadou, T. (1997). 'La constitution de la Republique du Niger du 12 mai 1996. *Revue juridique et politique*, 51/2: 82–102.

Banks, A. S. (1996). *Political Handbook of the World*. New York: CSA Publications.

Baré Mainassara, I. (1997). *Mon ambition pour le Niger*. Paris: Jeune Afrique Livres

Beuchelt, E. (1968). *Niger*. Bonn: Schroeder.

Blankmeister, B. (1994). 'Der Islam in Niger—Eine Gefahr für die Demokratie?' *KAS-Auslandsinformationen*, 10/10: 32–39.

Charlick, R. B. (1990). *Niger-Personal Rule and Survival in the Sahel*. Boulder, Col.: Westview Press.

Commission Electorale Nationale Indépendante (1996). *Code Electoral. Edition 1996*. ('Ordonnance 96-014 du 16 Avril 1996 portant Code Electoral').

Cook, C., and Killingray, D. (1991). *African Political Facts since 1945* (2nd edn.). Basingstoke (Hampshire): Macmillan.

Decalo, S. (1997). *Historical Dictionary of Niger* (3rd. edn.). Metuchen, NJ: Scarecrow Press.

Decoudras, P. (1994). 'Niger. Démocratisation réussie, avenir en suspens'. *L'Afrique Politique* 1994, 45–58.

Dodo Mindaoudou, A. (1995). 'Les élections démocratiques au Niger'. *Verfassung und Recht in Übersee*, 28/3: 339–357.

East, R. (1993). *Political Parties of Africa and the Middle East*. Harlow: Longman.

Grégoire, E. (1995). 'Cohabitation au Niger'. *Afrique Contemporaine*, 175/3: 43–51.

Hermann, J. (1993). *Afrika: Wahlen und Abstimmungen 1991–1993*. St. Augustin: Siedler.

Higgott, R., and Fuglestad, F. (1975). 'The 1974 Coup d'Etat in Niger: Towards an Explanation'. *Journal of Modern African Studies* 13/3: 383–398.

Ibrahim, J. (1994). 'Political Exclusion, Democratisation, and Dynamics of Ethnicity in Niger'. *Africa Today,* 41/3: 15–39

Illiasou, A., and Tidjani Alou, M. (1994). 'Le processus électoral et démocratisation au Niger'. *Politique Africaine,* 53: 128–132.

Issa Abdourhamane, B. (1996). *Crise institutionelle et démocratisation au Niger.* Talence: Institut d'Etudes Politiques de Bordeaux.

Jouve, E. (1978). 'Du Niger de Diori Hamani au gouvernement des militaires (1974–1977)'. *Revue Française d'Etudes Politiques Africaines*, 13/199: 19–44.

Lohse, V. (1993). 'Niger: Die neue Verfassung der III. Republik'. *Verfassung und Recht in Übersee*, 26/2: 162–180.

Morgenthau, R. S. (1964). *Political Parties in French-Speaking West Africa.* Oxford: Clarendon Press.

Olivier de Sardin, J.-P., and Gazobo, M. (1996). 'Niger. Démocratie ambigue. Chronique d'un coup annoncé'. *L'Afrique politique* 1997, 155–170.

'Ordonnance No. 92-058 du 9 December 1992 portant fixation et repartition des sièges des députés à l'Assemblée Nationale par circonscription électorale'.

Raulin, A de. (1997). 'Le processus de démocratisation en Afrique et au Niger: espoir ou désillusion'. *Revue juridique et politique*, 51/2: 82–102.

Raynal, J.-J. (1990). 'De la démocratisation à la démocratie? La constitution nigérienne du 24 septembre 1989'. *Afrique Contemporaine*, 155/3: 68–79.

— (1993). *Les institutions politiques du Niger*. Saint-Maur: Sepia.

Raynaut, C *et al.* (1990). 'Le Niger—Chronique d'un Etat'. *Politique Africaine*, 38: 1–110.

Republique du Niger (1996). *Code électoral* (Commission Electorale Nationale independante).

Robert, D. (1993). 'Niger', in D. Nohlen and F. Nuscheler (eds.), *Handbuch Dritte Welt, Band 4: Westafrika und Zentralafrika* (3rd edn.). Bonn: Dietz, 328–343.

Rosenberg, D. (1992). 'Le peuple Touareg—Du silence à l'autodétermination'. *Revue Belge du droit international*, 23/1: 5–39.

Thompson, V. (1966). 'Niger', in G. M. Carter (ed.), *National Unity in Eight African States*. Ithaca, N.Y.: Cornell University Press, 151–230.

Zamponi, L. F. (1994). *Niger (World Bibliographical Series).* Oxford: Clio Press.

Ziemer, K. (1978). 'Niger', in D. Sternberger, B. Vogel, D. Nohlen and K. Landfried (eds.), *Die Wahl der Parlamente und anderer Staatsorgane. Band II: Politische Organisation und Repräsentation in Afrika,* by Franz Nuscheler, Klaus Ziemer *et al*., Berlin/ New York: Walter de Gruyter, 1455–1492.

NIGERIA

by Petra Bendel

1. Introduction

1.1 Historical Overview

Since Nigeria's independence from Great Britain (1 October 1960), the military has ruled the country except for the periods 1960 to 1966 and 1979 to 1983. A third effort of democratization, initiated by the military rulers in the 1980s, was regarded as another failure, at least until President Abacha's death in 1998. Whereas political representatives legitimized by national elections in 1966, 1983 and 1993 were hindered from taking office by military coups d'état, local elections in December 1998 and Governor's elections in January 1999 were considered a prelude to the fourth transition to democracy at the end of the 1990s.

The Independence Constitution of the First Republic (1960–1966) was based on the British Westminster system. With its tri-regional federal arrangement, it expressed the will to overcome the regionally based conflicts between the conservative, traditionalist Islamic North and the 'modern' South of the country. Nevertheless, integrative political institutions or mediating organizations did not emerge. The military overthrew the government of Nnamdi Azikiwe in 1966, which had been legitimized by (controversial) elections and justified the coup with the violent conflicts that accompanied the electoral campaign for the House of Representatives in 1964 and the Parliament of the Western Region in 1965.

The military suspended the constitution, abolished the country's fragile federative structure and prohibited political parties. While the first coup of 1966 had been backed principally by the ethnic group of the Igbos, a second coup in July of the same year was upraised mainly by the Hausa-Fulani. An attempted secession of the Eastern region, rich in oil resources and mainly Igbo-inhabited, as the 'Republic of Biafra' in 1967 led Nigeria to civil war that was not ended until 1970 by the non-conditioned capitulation of Biafra. The nationalization of oil revenues strengthened the central government and led to the creation of a rentier-state which nurtured a military-bureaucratic alliance that cemented its power by corruption and clientelistic structures. Nevertheless, the military under Brigadier Mohammed Murtala (1975–1976) and his successor General Olusegun Obasanjo (1976–79) understood its role as a temporary solution to the country's problems (concept of 'corrective government'). It initiated a transition program to civil rule containing the reformation of the federal states, local administration and elections for Local Government Councils in 1976, amendment of a new constitution in 1978, legalization of political parties and elections for state legislatures, national House of Representative and President in 1979. The 1979 Constitution, following the US system, strengthened the President's role, introduced 19 federal states (instead of the 12 created in 1966), whose boundaries cut across the geographical and cultural redoubts of 'majority' ethnic groups, and changed the capital to Abuja in the country's center. The Constitutional Assembly opted for a multi-party system supposedly to take into account Nigeria's social heterogeneity, at the same time trying to prevent ethnic and regional parties from resurgence. The 1979 elections, in which only five out of more than 30 parties were able to fulfil the condition of national organization to participate, were generally characterized as free and fair. They brought the civilian Shehu Shagari of the National Party of Nigeria (NPN) to power.

This second experiment with civil rule entered into history as one of the country's most unstable, socially polarized and corrupt phases. The governing NPN was re-elected in 1983 on the basis of manipulation and clientelism. Great parts of the army capitalized on the population's discontent with economic mismanagement, which showed its effect in a harsh financial crisis in 1982–1983, and headed another coup. The military's repressive and highly unpopular regime under General Major Muhummadu Buhari (1983–1985) was overthrown by a palace revolt under Ibrahim Badamasi Babangida in August 1985.

In opposition to the preceding authoritarian regime, Babangida renewed the concept of 'corrective government' and committed himself to a political transition. But his initial politics of dialogue and consensus once again gave way to corruption, repression and the violation of human rights. The transition program provided for the creation of several new political institutions. The 1989 Constitution was once again inspired by the US model. Two political parties were designed 'from above': The center-left Social Democratic Party (SDP) and the center-right National Republican Convention (NRC). Although Governors' and state legislatures' elections in 1991 and 1992 eventually handed over power to civilians (the number of states being increased to 21 in 1987 and to 30 in 1991), the 1993 presidential elections were interrupted and annulled in the course of the vote-counting process, when, for the first time in the country's history, a Southerner, Moshood Abiola (SDP), emerged as the presumable winning candidate. Babangida, trying to dam public protests against the fraud, nominated Ernest Shonekan as an interim-President, who subsequently was overthrown by a coup d'état headed by General Sani Abacha.

Abacha's extremely repressive regime brought the transition process to an abrupt end. It suspended the Constitution, dissolved the elected state legislatures, suppressed political parties and social organizations and filled political institutions with military representatives. Neither international sanctions nor national protests were able to exercise sufficient pressure on the regime to fulfil the promise for democratic transition which was supposed to culminate in presidential elections in August 1998. The 1979 Constitution and its 1984 amendments were declared valid again. On 27 June 1995, the prohibition of political parties was lifted, and first, municipal elections were held in 1996. New parties were created, but only five of them legalized: The United Nigerian Congress Party (UNCP), the Committee for National Consensus, the National Centre Party of Nigeria, the Democratic Party of Nigeria (DPN), and the Grassroot Democratic Movement. In 1997 state legislatures' elections were held, in which the two Abacha-near parties, UNCP and DPN, were victorious. The 1998 parliamentary elections, which gave the UNCP a very high percentage of the vote, were boycotted by the opposition, and several Western governments warned that they would extend their sanctions if Nigeria did not establish democratic rule. All the five parties adopted Abacha as their presidential candidate for the announced August elections of 1998.

After Abacha's unforeseen death in June 1998, the Military Council named Abdusalam Abubakar as his successor. The military government scheduled new parliamentary and presidential elections for February 1999, once again declaring its will to open the way to democracy.

1. 2 Evolution of Electoral Provisions

Institutions elected at national level include President and Vice-President (combined in a single ballot), Federal Representatives and Senators elected in single-member constituencies for a four-year term.

Universal, equal, direct and secret suffrage was gradually introduced. The 1959 Constitution provided for universal suffrage throughout the country; nevertheless, women in the Islamic North of Nigeria were legally disqualified from voting until 1979, when female suffrage came into effect on the basis of the 1977 Electoral Decree. According to the provisions of 1989 (Basic Constitutional and Transitional Provisions, Decree No. 15 of 1989), voting required Nigerian citizenship and a minimum age of 18 years. The voter had to register in the ward or constituency of his regular residence in order to obtain a registration card. Section 87 (2) of Decree No. 50 of 1991 explicitly stipulated that 'voting shall be by open ballot'. Voters were requested to queue up in front of the poster of their candidate's choice. This so-called 'open ballot system' was applied in the 1993 presidential election. Voters thumbmarked their cards in secret corners, but still voted in the full view of all present.

For the 1979 elections (1977 Electoral Decree and the 1978 Constitution) ineligibility was provided for: candidates found guilty of corruption, unjust enrichment or abuse of office by any tribunal or inquiry held since 15 January 1966. Civil servants, academics and school teachers had to resign from their posts at least four months prior to the election. In the 1982 Electoral Act, former legal incapacities such as imprisonment or criminal record were no longer accepted as reasons for disenfranchisement. Only functionaries of the National Electoral Commission (NEC) were statutorily excluded from voting. Ineligibility referred to non-Nigerians or persons with more than one nationality as well as members of the Armed Forces and traditional (Paramount) rulers. The Participation in Politics and Elections (Prohibition) Decree (Decree No. 25 of 1987) excluded those persons from the politics of the 'transition period', who had held offices at the federal or state level in the civilian governments between 1960 and 1966 and from 1979 to 1983 'for the purpose of ensuring a clean break with the past', former or serving Military Governor Administrators, Service Chiefs in the Armed Forces and Police, including former military Heads of State and the President in office as well as those persons who 'either collectively or individually, had been liable or indicted and found guilty of acts of unjust enrichment, corruption, fraud, embezzlement of public funds, elections malpractices or contributed in one way or the other to the economic adversity of the nation such persons who exercised corrupt influence on public office holders.'

In 1989 eligibility was tied to a minimum age of 21 years for state legislatures or Federal House of Representatives and 35 years for all other elective positions at the state or federal level (1979: 30 years). For the presidency, the minimum age of 35 years and Nigerian citizenship by birth was required, for Senators Nigerian citizenship and a minimum age of 30 years, for the House of Representatives 25 years, were required. Presidents of the last two tenures were not qualified for candidacy. All candidates had to be educated up to School Certificate level or its equivalent. Apart from current exclusions of eligibility, neither persons employed in the public services of the federation or of any state nor members of secret societies or undischarged bankrupts could be elected. Decision on the eligibility in 1979 was up to the Federal Electoral Commission (FEDECO), first established in 1976 by the Military Government. It is important to remark that the National Electoral Commission (NEC), which replaced the defunct FEDECO (Decree No. 23 of September 1987) was not assured of independence. Instead, the military government was permitted to give the Commission directives; the NEC (Amendment) Decree No. 8 of February 1989 deprived the NEC of the power to register political parties, which was instead transferred to the Armed Forces Ruling Council.

From 1979 on, candidates at any election had to be nominated by political parties. In 1979, political parties had to be nation-wide and democratically organized. Each party had to demonstrate organizational structures in at least two-thirds of the states and a delegative assembly had to confirm its manifesto and the party's leadership. Parties were not allowed to use regional, ethnic or religious signs and had to have their main domicile in Abuja. A minimum of ethnic mix within the party structures was also prescribed. In the 1989 elections, only the National Republican Convention (NRC) and the Social Democratic Party (SDP) were accepted to contest for political power in 1989.

As for the electoral system, in the 1979 elections, the President had not only to obtain the relative majority of votes, but also one quarter of the vote in at least two-thirds of the states or, if only two candidates contested the election, a majority of votes in more than half of the states. Failing that, he had to be selected by an electoral college involving all the national and state representative legislative bodies. The 1989 Constitution required, if possible, the nomination of more than one candidate for the presidency. In the case of one single candidate, the latter had to receive a majority of Yes over No votes cast at the election and to obtain not less than one-third of the votes cast in each of at least two-thirds of all the states in the federation. In the case that a single candidate failed to be elected in accordance with these conditions, there had to be fresh nominations. If there were two candidates for the election (only two parties were permitted in 1993), the President had to obtain a relative majority of votes cast, but not less than one-third in each of at least two-thirds of all the states of the federation. Failing this, the 1989

Constitution provided for a second election in which a successful candidate must obtain one-third of the votes in only a majority of the states or, in default of a conclusive second election, the selection of the President by a relative majority of votes cast in an electoral college comprising all members of the national and state legislatures. With regard to the parliamentary electoral system, the plurality system in single-member districts was retained until 1993 from the First and Second Republics.

1.3 Current Electoral Provisions

Since the 1993 abolition of the Constitution and annulment of the elections, elections have taken place in 1997 (state legislatures) and 1998 (National Parliament). Information was not available. The President, appointed by the military rulers, should have been elected in August 1998, according to the time-table before Abacha's death in June of the same year. The military government under Abubakar again announced presidential elections for 27 February and parliamentary elections for 20 February 1999.

1.4 Comment on the Electoral Statistics

The following tables are based on both official, and, where official data could not be acquired, on historiographical and sociological sources as well as on newspapers. Nevertheless and probably more than for other African countries, the existing data are often very inconsistent and incomplete. They often differ both within one single source and between different sources. Many of these inconsistencies could not be resolved and have been commented on in footnotes.

Data for elections in 1959, 1963 and 1964 follow Adam/ Beckett (1978) and, partly, Whitaker (1991), data for 1979 follow Tyoden (1978), Adamu/ Ogunsanwo (1980), Nigeria's Elections (1981), Kurfi (1985), Joseph (1987), Miles (1988) and Whitaker (1991), for 1983 the *Daily Times* (1983). Deviating data for presidential elections in 1983 are presented in Joseph (1987). For 1992, data are drawn from Nigerian newspapers (*The Guardian*, 6 July 1992; *Nigerian Tribune*, 6 and 7 July 1992). Results of the interrupted presidential elections in 1993 at national level are drawn from Fawchinmi (1993), the regional distribution of votes follows *African Concord* No. 6, 28 June 1993. Slightly different numbers are provided by *Newswatch*, 28 June 1993. 'Votes cast' evidently is used in the Nigerian terminology as the number of valid votes cast on the candidates. In Nigeria, there is no information on valid and invalid votes.

2. Tables

2.1 Dates of National Elections, Referendums and Coups d'Etat

Year	Presidential elections	Parliamentary elections		Elections for Constitutional Assembly	Referendums	Coups d'état
		Lower house	Upper house			
1959		12/12				
1964		30/12				
1966						15/01
						28/07
1975						29/07
1976						13/02
1977				31/08[a]		
1979	11/07	07/07	07/07			
1983	06/08	20/08[b]	27/08			31/12
1985						27/08
1992		04/07[d]	04/07			
1993[c]	12/06					17/11
1994				23/05[e]		
1998[f]		25/04				

General note: Local Government Councils elected in: December 1976 (203 members elected, 20 nominated by military government) on a no-party basis, December 1987, also on a no-party basis (50,000 people were hindered from participating in any political activity on 23 September 1987), 1990 and April 1996 on party basis.

[a] Annulled; election results were not announced.

[b] Federal elections: Governors' elections in the states on 14 August 1983; State Assembly elections in September (delayed only in Ondo and Oyo States because of violence accompanying the Governors' elections)

[c] Annulment announced by the military regime on 22 June 1993. Elections had been initially planned for 5 December 1992. They were delayed several times due to 'danger for stability', according to President Babangida. All the 23 candidates who had participated in the primaries were excluded, and the SDP and NRC leadership was suspended.

[d] Governors' elections were held the same day.

[e] The opposition movement NADECO called for abstention.

[f] Presidential elections scheduled for August 1998 were not held because President Abacha died suddenly in June 1998. As for the parliamentary elections, no data could be obtained.

2.2 Electoral Body 1959–1993

Year[a]	Type of election[b]	Population[c]	Registered voters		Votes cast		
			Total number	% pop.	Total number	% reg. Voters	% pop.
1959	R	30,400,000	9,043,404[d]	29.7	7,628,847[e]	79.5	23.7
1964	R	55,600,000	—	—	5,761,483[e]	—	10.4
1979	Pr	78,800,000	48,633,782[f]	61.7	16,846,533[e]	34.6	21.4
1979	R	78,800,000	48,633,782[f]	61.7	14,941,555	30.7	19.0
1979	S	78,800,000	48,633,782[f]	61.7	12,532,195	25.8	15.0
1983	Pr/R/S	89,022,000	65,304,818[g]	73.4	25,430,096[e]	54.0	28.6
1992	R/S	88,514,501	38,866,336	43.9	16,909,871[h]	43.5	19.1
1993	Pr	88,514,501	39,000,000[i]	44.1	14,293,396	36.6	16.1

[a] For the 1977 and 1984 CA elections and the 1998 parliamentary elections no data were available.

[b] CA = Constitutional Assembly; R = House of Representatives (lower chamber); S = Senate (upper chamber); Pr = President.

[c] For 1959 estimation according to census of 1952. For 1964 estimation according to census of 1963; the census of 1962 was annulled. Probably, the number was lower in reality: each region tried to push up the number of its inhabitants, because representation in the Federal Parliament was based on the population. For 1979 according to census 1973 (not reliable). For 1992 and 1993 according to the census, published 19 March 1991.

[d] The estimated numbers of persons fulfilling the requirements for registration as voters were: Total: 10,244,000; Northern Region: 3,885,000 (male only), Eastern Region: 2,759,000, Lagos: 177,000.

[e] Valid votes.

[f] Census of 14 January to 28 February 1979. For the first time, female suffrage was applied in the Islamic North.

[g] Serious doubts announced by observers with regard to the revised register of 1983. Observers felt the figures were deliberately inflated to give room for phantom voters.

[h] Valid votes, figure for lower house elections. Senate: 15,803,776.

[i] The number of voters given for the governors' elections was officially given as 35,280,300.

2.3 Abbreviations

AG	Action Group
DP	Dynamic Party
DPN	Democratic Party of Nigeria
GDM	Grassroots Democratic Movement
GNPP	Great Nigerian People's Party
MDF	Midwestern Democratic Front
NAP	Nigerian Advance Party
NCNC	National Council of Nigeria Citizens
NCPN	National Center Party of Nigeria
NDC	Niger Delta Congress
NEPU	Northern Elements Progressive Union
NNA	Nigerian National Alliance
NNDP	Nigerian National Democratic Party
NPC	Northern People's Congress[a]
NPF	Northern Progressive Front
NPN	National Party of Nigeria
NPP	Nigerian People's Party
NRC	National Republican Convention
PRP	People's Redemption Party
SDP	Social Democratic Party
UMBC	United Middle Belt Congress
UNCP	United Nigerian Congress Party
UNIP	United National Independence Party
UPGA	United Progressive Grand Alliance[b]
UPN	United Party of Nigeria
UPP	United People's Party

[a] Coalition of four parties from the Middle Belt and North-Central Nigeria.
[b] NCNC, NEPU, AG, UNPC and, according to some sources, UMBC.

2.4 Electoral Participation of Parties and Alliances 1959–1993

Party / Alliance	Years	Elections Contested Presidential	Parliamentary[a]
AG	1959, 1964	0	2[b]
NCNC	1959, 1964	0	2[b]
NEPU	1959, 1964	0	2[b]
NPC	1959, 1964	0	2
NNA	1964	0	1
UPGA	1964	0	1
NNDP	1964	0	1
NCNC	1964	0	1
NPF	1964	0	1
GNPP	1979, 1983	2	1
UPN	1979, 1983	2	1
NPN	1979, 1983	2	1
PRP	1979, 1983	1	1
NPP	1979, 1983	1	1
NAP	1983	1	1
SDP	1992, 1993	1	1
NRC	1992, 1993	1	1

[a] Number of elections for the House of Representatives.
[b] In 1964 as part of the UPGA-alliance.

2.5 Referendums

Referendums have not been held.

2.6 Elections for Constitutional Assembly

Elections for Constitutional Assembly have been held in 1977 and 1994. No data were available.

2.7 Parliamentary Elections 1959–1992

2.7.1 House of Representatives 1959–1992

Year	1959[a]		1964[b]	
	Total number	%	Total number	%
Registered voters	9,043,404	–	–	–
Votes cast	—	—	—	—
Invalid votes	—	—	—	—
Valid votes	7,628,847	—	5,761,483	—
NCNC	2,594,577	34.0	1,640,700	28.5
AG	1,992,364	26.1	494,730	37.6
NPC	1,922,179	25.2	2,168,007	8.6
NEPU	509,050	6.7	–	
NNDP	–	–	870,833	15.1
NPF	–	–	258,913	4.5
MDF	–	–	93,161	1.6
DP	–	–	42,834	0.7
RP	–	–	25,831	0.4
SWAFP	–	–	20,347	0.4
NDC	–	–	17,798	0.3
Others	610,677	8.0	–	
Independents	–	–	128,329	2.2

[a] Serious inconsistencies in some sources. Percentages refer to a total of 7,628,847 valid votes.
[b] Massive electoral manipulation and violence. UPGA called for electoral abstention, which was followed only partly in the West and ignored completely in the Mid-West. In the eastern part of the country, elections did not take place at all.

Year	1979		1992	
	Total number	%	Total number	%
Registered voters	48,633,782	–	38,866,336	–
Votes cast	14,941,555	30.7	—	—
Invalid votes	—	—	—	—
Valid votes	—	—	16,909,871	43.5[a]
NPN	5,325,680	35.6	–	–
UPN	3,691,553	24.6	–	–
NPP	2,391,279	16.0	–	–
NRC	–	–	8,551,080	50.6
SDP	–	–	8,358,791	49.4

[a] Valid votes as a % of registered votes.

For the elections of 1983 detailed data are not available. See table 2.2 for data on voter registration and participation.

2.7.1 a) House of Representatives: Regional Results

1959[a]	North		West		East	
	Total number	%	Total number	%	Total number	%
NCNC/NEPU[b]	18,685	0.6	758,462	40.2	1,246,984	64.6
NEPU[c]	509,050	15.6	–	–	–	–
NPC	1,994,045	61.2	32,960	1.7	–	–
AG[d]	559,878	17.2	933,680	49.5	445,144	23.1
Others[e]	179,022	5.5	162,107	8.6	237,626	12.3

[a] Serious inconsistencies in comparison with national data which rely on other sources.
[b] Alliance of both parties in the Western and Eastern Region; in the Northern region NCNC only.
[c] In alliance with NCNC in the Western and Eastern region.
[d] In alliance with UMBC in the Northern region.
[e] Minor parties and independents.

1964	North	West	Mid West	East	Total
NPC	2,065,392	–	–	102,615	2,168,007
NPF	258,913	–	–	–	258,913
AG	4,803	389,941	–	99,986	494,730
NCNC	1,103	155,777	315,318	1,168,502	1,640,700
NDC	–	–	1,424	16,374	17,798
SWAFP	–	1,530	676	18,141	20,347
NNDP	–	870,833	–	–	870,833
DP	–	–	–	42,834	42,834
RP	–	–	–	25,831	25,831
MDF	–	–	93,161	–	93,831
Independents	33,343	19,348	262	75,376	128,329
Total	2,363,554	1,437,430	410,841	1,549,659	5,761,483

1979	Total votes cast	NPN	%	UPN	%
Anambra	1,108,771	253,979	22.9	18,535	1.7
Bauchi	807,201	481,581	59.7	27,049	3.4
Bendel	903,140	426,859	47.3	371,033	4.1
Benue	513,359	353,551	68.9	13,728	2.7
Borno	736,327	260,762	35.4	31,558	4.3
Cross River	729,667	388,354	53.2	94,443	12.9
Gongola	668,381	231,126	34.6	142,326	21.3
Imo	1,162,689	223,456	19.2	16,585	1.4
Kaduna	1,256,780	497,931	39.6	87,947	7.0
Kano	1,045	235,489	22.5	10,804	1.0
Kwara	340,692	167,737	49.2	138,359	40.6
Lagos	595,149	56,559	9.5	528,629	88.8
Niger	299,712	212,944	71.0	13,003	4.3
Ogun	612,454	53,297	8.7	557,316	91.0
Ondo	824,759	55,688	6.8	755,696	91.6
Oyo	1,011,233	199,972	19.8	790,580	78.2
Plateau	584,167	190,562	32.6	22,693	3.9
Rivers	491,264	287,575	58.5	25,542	5.2
Sokoto	1,250,647	748,262	36.4	25,727	2.1
Total	14,941,555	5,325,684	35.6	3,691,553	24.6

1979 (cont.)	NPP	%	GNPP	%	PRP	%
Anambra	787,359	71.0	33,944	3.1	14,954	1.3
Bauchi	33,082	4.1	196,967	24.4	68,531	8.5
Bendel	72,661	8.0	30,420	3.7	2,167	0.0
Benue	79,571	15.5	59,538	12.0	6,971	1.4
Borno	7,440	1.0	390,365	53.0	46,202	6.3
Cross River	85,829	11.8	157,975	21.7	3,066	0.4
Gongola	27,408	0.4	237,548	35.5	29,973	4.5
Imo	804,254	69.2	103,993	8.9	14,128	1.2
Kaduna	55,365	4.4	253,536	20.2	362,001	28.8
Kano	–	–	26,378	2.5	772,483	73.9
Kwara	731	0.2	33,024	9.7	841	0.2
Lagos	1,072	0.2	5,703	1.0	3,186	0.5
Niger	3,268	1.1	60,597	20.2	9,900	3.3
Ogun	–	–	1,841	0.3	–	–
Ondo	9,798	1.2	2,569	0.3	1,008	0.1
Oyo	7,012	0.7	10,579	1.0	3,090	0.3
Plateau	299,136	51.2	53,329	9.1	18,447	3.2
Rivers	117,293	23.9	56,480	11.5	4,374	0.9
Sokoto	–	–	455,268	36.4	21,390	1.7
Total	2,391,279	16.0	2,170,054	14.5	1,382,712	9.3

1992	Registered voters	Valid votes	%	NRC	%	SDP	%
Abia	991,469	342,485	34.5	191,992	56.1	150,493	43.9
Adamawa	955,822	451,022	47.2	267,785	59.4	183,237	40.6
Akwa Ibom	1,032,955	526,566	51.0	343,307	65.2	183,259	34.8
Anambra	1,248,226	409,759	32.8	164,380	40.1	245,379	59.9
Bauchi	2,048,627	1,163,897	56.8	834,443	71.7	329,454	28.3
Benue	1,296,331	661,115	51.0	230,912	34.9	430,203	65.1
Borno	1,222,533	402,081	32.9	178,597	44.4	223,484	55.6
Cross River	876,599	523,548[a]	59.7	311,726	59.5	211,822	40.5
Delta	1,154,563	535,628	48.1	231,663	43.2	323,965	56.8
Edo	912,680	440,011	48.2	167,130	38.0	272,881	62.0
Enugu	1,110,430	670,433	60.4	353,085	52.7	317,348	47.3
Imo	1,141,364	375,145	32.9	191,207	51.0	183,938	49.0
Jigawa	1,350,151[a]	284,882[a]	21.1	116,504	40.9	168,378	59.1
Kaduna	1,621,211	863,633	53.3	408,336	47.3	455,297	52.7
Kano	2,583,057	336,244	13.0	168,328	50.1	167,916	49.9
Katsina	1,661,132	470,993	28.4	262,387	55.7	208,606	44.3
Kebbi	824,254	416,544	50.5	365,447	87.7	51,097	12.3
Kogi	973,019	459,606[a]	47.2	256,183	55.7	203,423	44.3
Kwara	664,625	376,910	56.7	106,839	28.3	270,071	71.7
Lagos	2,327,239	827,030[a]	35.6	240,120	29.0	586,910	71.0
Niger	1,022,173	451,035	44.1	321,948	71.4	129,087	28.6
Ogun	941,939	397,121[a]	42.1	110,096	27.7	287,025	72.3
Ondo	1,774,666	841,303[a]	47.4	254,806	30.3	586,497	69.7
Osun	1,056,690	420,852[a]	39.8	134,885	32.0	285,967	68.0
Oyo	1,583,049	595,800	37.6	175,283	29.4	420,517	70.6
Plateau	1,503,001	917,878	61.1	386,977	42.2	530,901	57.8
Rivers	1,902,873	1,364,835	71.7	926,257	67.9	438,578	32.1
Sokoto	1,636,119	594,380[a]	36.3	526,746	88.6	67,634	11.4
Taraba	701,327	672,545	95.9	205,673	30.6	466,872	69.4
Yobe	665,299	220,265	33.1	92,947	42.2	127,318	57.8
Abuja FCT	153,450	55,632	36.3	25,091	45.1	30,541	54.9
Total	38,866,336[a]	16,909,871[a]	43.5	8,551,080	50.6	8,358,791	49.4

[a] Serious inconsistencies (within the same source as well as between the sources) with regard to voter turnout and sum of NRC and SDP could not be resolved. Neither could those referring to total registered voters.

2.7.2 Senate 1979–1992

Year[a]	1979		1992	
	Total number	%	Total number	%
Registered voters	48,633,782	–	38,866,336	–
Votes cast	12,532,195	—	—	—
Invalid votes	—	—	—	—
Valid votes	12,314,107	—	15,803,776	40.7
NPN	4,032,329	32.7	–	–
UPN	2,835,362	23.0	–	–
NPP	2,145,859	17.4	–	–
GNPP	1,847,019	15.0	–	–
PRP	1,453,538	11.8	–	–
NRC	–	–	8,309,548	52.6
SDP	–	–	7,494,228	47.4

[a] No detailed data available for the 1983 elections. For 1979 and 1992, serious inconsistencies with regard to absolute numbers given for each party.

2.7.2 a) Senate: Regional Results

1979	NPN	UPN	NPP	GNPP	PRP	Total
Anambra	210,101	10,932	699,157	12,832	19,574	952,596
Bauchi	323,392	28,959	39,868	188,819	127,279	708,317
Bendel	250,194	316,511	60,639	38,332	2,055	667,731
Benue	332,967	14,769	75,523	46,452	–	469,711
Borno	184,633	22,145	–	278,352	31,508	516,638
Cross River	310,071	77,479	68,203	161,353	–	617,106
Gongola	203,226	124,707	17,830	223,121	30,708	599,592
Imo	145,508	7,533	750,518	101,184	8,609	1,013,352
Kaduna	410,888	85,094	61,807	233,824	278,305	1,069,918
Kano	233,985	13,831	–	35,430	683,367	966,613
Kwara	54,282	126,065	1,020	32,383	328	214,078
Lagos	35,730	428,573	52,738	14,480	2,556	534,077
Niger	175,597	13,860	1207	71,498	8,139	270,301
Ogun	31,963	230,411	119	1,018	–	263,511
Ondo	49,612	501,522	6,417	4,905	–	562,456
Oyo	200,372	758,696	4,397	9,472	2,497	975,434
Plateau	154,792	20,024	220,278	41,287	220,278	656,659
Rivers	153,454	20,106	86,138	46,985	30	306,713
Sokoto	571,562	34,145	–	305,292	38,305	949,304
Total	4,032,329	2,835,362	2,145,859	1,847,019	1,453,538	12,314,107

[a] Different data according to different sources.

1992[a]	Reg. voters	Valid votes	%[b]	NRC	%	SDP	%
Abia	991,469	340,334	34.3	177,267	52.1	163,067	47.9
Adamawa	955,822	447,313	46.8	258,742	57.8	188,571	42.2
Akwa Ibom	1,032,955	560,362[a]	54.3	343,307	61.3	183,259	38.7
Anambra	1,248,226	388,502[a]	31.1	139,748	36.0	245,754	64.0
Bauchi	2,048,627	719,138[a]	35.1	590,033	82.0	126,050	18.0
Benue	1,296,331	662,883	51.1	272,216	41.1	390,667	58.9
Borno	1,222,533	402,520[a]	32.9	132,727	33.0	219,793	67.0
Cross River	876,599	518,229	59.1	303,601	58.6	214,628	41.4
Delta	1,154,563	561,025[a]	48.6	221,873	39.5	339,147	60.5
Edo	912,680	439,549[a]	48.1	157,902	35.9	270,902	64.1
Enugu	1,110,430	555,786	50.1	327,155	58.9	228,631	41.1
Imo	1,141,364	472,554	41.4	275,178	58.2	197,376	41.8
Jigawa	1,621,211[a]	283,044	22.8	121,780	43.0	161,264	57.0
Kaduna	1,621,211	851,172	53.0	429,723	50.5	421,449	49.5
Kano	2,583,057	329,018	12.7	159,759	48.6	153,759	41.4
Katsina	1,661,132	346,083	20.8	185,611	53.6	160,472	46.4
Kebbi	824,254	391,784[a]	48.0	343,254	87.6	48,172	12.4
Kogi	973,019	458,745	47.1	259,621	56.6	199,124	43.4
Kwara	664,625	374,772	56.4	134,056	35.8	240,716	64.2
Lagos	2,327,239	801,563[a]	33.7	227,377	28.4	580,186	71.6
Niger	1,022,173	336,055[a]	33.5	274,203	81.6	61,857	18.4
Ogun	941,939	296,070	42.1	106,033	35.8	190,037	64.2
Ondo	1,774,666	651,621	36.7	222,960	34.2	428,661	63.8
Osun	1,056,690	418,621[a]	39.6	45,621	10.9	273,000	89.1
Oyo	1,583,049	591,606	37.4	154,301	26.1	437,305	73.9
Plateau	1,503,001	902,518	59.8	383,834	42.5	518,684	57.5
Rivers	1,902,873	1,354,609	72.0	1,023,103	75.5	326,506	24.5
Sokoto	1,636,119	599,998[a]	36.7	543,659	90.6	56,349	9.4
Taraba	701,327	463,544	66.1	185,954	40.1	277,590	49.9
Yobe	665,299	227,385[a]	34.2	37,726	16.6	129,659	73.4
Abuja FCT	153,450	55,373	36.1	23,583	42.6	31,790	47.4
Total	38,866,336[a]	15,803,776[a]	40.7	8,309,548[a]	52.6	7,494,228	47.4

[a] Serious inconsistencies within source could not be resolved.

[b] Valid votes as a percentage of registered voters.

2.8 Composition of Parliament

2.8.1 House of Representatives 1959–1992

Year	1959		1964		1979		1983	
	Seats	%	Seats	%	Seats	%	Seats	%
	312	100	469	100	449	100	386[a]	100
NPC	134	42.9	162	34.5	–	–	–	–
NCNC	81	26.0	–	–	–	–	–	–
AG	73	23.4	–	–	–	–	–	–
NEPU	8	2.6	–	–	–	–	–	–
MABOLAJE	6	1.9	–	–	–	–	–	–
IGALA Union	4	1.3	–	–	–	–	–	–
IGBIRRA Tribal Union	1	0.3	–	–	–	–	–	–
Niger Delta Congress	1	0.3	–	–	–	–	–	–
NNA	–	–	198	42.2	–	–	–	–
UPGA	–	–	109	23.2	–	–	–	–
NPN	–	–	–	–	168	37.4	264	68.4
UPN	–	–	–	–	111	24.7	33	8.5
NPP	–	–	–	–	78[b]	17.4	48	12.4
PRP	–	–	–	–	49	10.9	41	10.6
GNPP	–	–	–	–	43[b]	9.6	–	–
Independents	4	1.3	–	–	–	–	–	–

[a] Does not include Oyo and Ondo states (64 seats), where elections were delayed due to violence.
[b] According to other sources, NPP gained 79 and GNPP 48 seats which would sum up to 455 instead of 449 seats.

Year	1992	
	Seats	%
	589	100
SDP	312[a]	—
NRC	275[a]	—

[a] According to some sources, SDP gained 315, NRC 260 seats. Neither set of data gives the complete 589 seats.

2.8.1 a) House of Representatives: Regional Distribution of Seats

1959	North		West & Lagos		East		Total
	Seats	%	Seats	%	Seats	%	Seats
NCNC	–	–	21[a]	33.9	58	79.5	81
NPC	134	77.0	–	–	–	–	134
AG	25	14.4	33[a]	53.2	14	19.2	73
NEPU	8	4.6	–	–	–	–	8
Others	7	4.0	8	12.9	1	1.4	16
Total	174	100	62	100	73	100	312

[a] Different data on NCNC (23) and AG (34) found in Kurfi (1983: 173).

1979	NPN	UPN	NPP	GNPP	PRP	Total
Anambra	3	–	26	–	–	29
Bauchi	18	–	1	1	–	20
Bendel	6	12	2	–	–	20
Benue	18	–	1	–	–	19
Borno	2	–	–	22	–	24
Cross River	22	2	–	4	–	28
Gongola	5	7	1	8	–	21
Imo	2	–	28	–	–	30
Kaduna	19	1	2	1	10	33
Kano	7	–	–	–	39	46
Kwara	8	5	–	1	–	14
Lagos	–	12	–	–	–	12
Niger	10	–	–	–	–	10
Ogun	–	12	–	–	–	12
Ondo	–	22	–	–	–	22
Oyo	4	38	–	–	–	42
Plateau	3	–	13	–	–	16
Rivers	10	–	4	–	–	14
Sokoto	31	–	–	6	–	37
Total	168	111	78	43	49	449

1983	NPN	UPN	NPP	PRP	Total
Anambra	15	–	14	–	29
Bauchi	20	–	–	–	20
Bendel	18	2	–	–	20
Benue	15	–	4	–	19
Borno	24	–	–	–	24
Cross River	26	2	–	–	28
Gongola	21	–	–	–	21
Imo	10	–	20	–	30
Kaduna	33	–	–	–	33
Kano	33	–	3	41	46
Kwara	9	5	–	–	14
Lagos	–	12	–	–	12
Niger	8	–	2	–	10
Ogun	–	12	–	–	12
Ondo	–	–	–	–	22
Oyo	–	–	–	–	42
Plateau	10	–	6	–	16
Rivers	14	–	–	–	14
Sokoto	37	–	–	–	37
Abuja	1	–	–	–	1
Total	264	33	48	41	450

2.8.2 Senate 1979–1992

Year	1979		1983		1992	
	Seats	%	Seats	%	Seats	%
	95	100	85[a]	100	91[b]	100
NPN	36	37.9	55	64.7	–	–
UPN	28	29.5	12	14.1	–	–
NPP	16	16.8	12	14.1	–	–
GNPP	8	8.4	1	1.2	–	–
PRP	7	7.4	5	5.9	–	–
NAP	–	–	0	0.0	–	–
SDP	–	–	–	–	52	58.4
NRC	–	–	–	–	37	41.6

[a] Does not include Oyo and Ondo states (10 seats), where elections were delayed due to violence.

[b] Three Senators from each of the 30 States, one Senator from Abuja, according to electoral provisions. Nevertheless, available data does not sum up to 92.

2.9 Presidential Elections 1979–1993

1979	Total number	%
Registered voters	48,633,782	–
Votes cast	—	—
Invalid votes	—	—
Valid votes	16,846,533	34.6
Shehu Shagari (NPN)	5,688,857	33.8
Obafemi Awolowo (UPN)	4,916,551	29.2
Nnamdi Azikiwe (NPP)	2,822,523	16.8
Aminu Kano (PRP)	1,732,113	10.3
Waziri Ibrahim (GNPP)	1,686,489	10.0

1983[a]	Total number	%
Registered voters	65,304,818	–
Votes cast	—	—
Invalid votes	—	—
Valid votes	25,430,097	54.0
Alhaji Shehu Shagari (NPN)	12,081,471	47.5
Chief Obafemi Awolowo (UPN)	7,907,209	31.2
Nnamdi Azikiwe (NPP)	3,557,113	14.0
Yusuf (PRP)	968,974	3.8
Alhaji Ibrahim Waziri (GNPP)	643,806	2.5
Tunji Braithwaite (NAP)	271,524	1.0

[a] The 1983 elections were disputed in a violent manner and the results were seriously questioned. Correspondingly, different sources provide very different data.

1993[a]	Total number	%
Registered voters	39,000,000[b]	–
Votes cast	—	—
Invalid votes	—	—
Valid votes	14,293,396	36.6
Kashimawo Olawale Abiola (SDP)	8,341,309	58.4
Alhaji Bashir Othman (NRC)	5,952,087	41.6

[a] The elections were interrupted when Abiola emerged as a winner in 14 of 30 states. Abiola declared himself winner of the elections on 18 June 1993. The military regime officially declared the elections null and void on 12 June 1993. Abiola nominated a counter-government to General Abacha's military regime on 11 June 1994. The data were taken from Fawhindmi 1993: 143–144.

[b] Estimation.

2.9 b) Presidential Elections: Regional Results

1979[a] (absolute numbers)

State	Waziri GNPP	Awolowo UPN	Shagari NPN	Kano PRP	Azikive NPP	Total votes cast
Anambra	20,228	9,063	163,164	14,500	1,002,083	1,209,038
Bauchi	154,218	29,960	623,989	143,202	47,314	998,683
Bendel	8,242	356,381	242,320	4,939	57,629	669,511
Benue	42,993	13,864	411,648	7,277	63,097	538,879
Borno	384,278	23,885	246,778	46,385	9,642	710,968
Cross-River	100,105	77,775	425,815	6,737	50,671	661,103
Gongola	217,914	138,561	227,057	27,750	27,856	639,138
Imo	34,616	7,335	101,516	10,252	99,636	1,153,355
Kaduna	190,936	92,382	596,302	437,771	65,321	1,382,642
Kano	18,482	14,873	243,423	932,803	11,082	1,220,691
Kwara	20,251	140,006	190,142	2,376	1,830	354,605
Lagos	3,943	681,762	59,515	3,874	79,320	828,414
Niger	63,273	14,155	287,072	14,555	4,292	383,347
Ogun	23,974	689,655	46,358	2,338	2,343	744,668
Ondo	3,561	1,294,666	57,361	2,509	11,752	1,369,849
Oyo	8,029	1,197,983	177,999	4,804	7,732	1,396,547
Plateau	37,400	29,029	190,458	21,852	269,666	548,405
Rivers	15,025	71,114	499,846	3,212	98,754	687,951
Sokoto	359,021	34,102	898,094	44,977	12,503	1,348,697
Total	1,706,509	4,833,407	7,158,857	1,732,113	1,922,523	16,846,491

[a] Data for regional distribution do not coincide with data at national level.

1979 (in %)						
State	GNPP	UPN	NPN[a]	PRP	NPP	Total
Anambra	1.7	0.7	13.5	1.2	82.9	100.0
Bauchi	15.4	3.0	62.5	14.3	4.7	100.0
Bendel	1.2	53.2	36.2	0.7	8.6	100.0
Benue	8.0	2.6	76.4	1.4	11.7	100.0
Borno	54.0	3.3	34.7	6.5	1.4	100.0
Cross-River	15.1	11.8	64.4	1.0	7.7	100.0
Gongola	34.1	21.7	35.5	4.3	4.4	100.0
Imo	3.0	0.6	8.8	0.6	86.7	100.0
Kaduna	13.8	6.7	43.1	31.7	4.7	100.0
Kano	1.5	1.2	19.9	76.4	0.9	100.0
Kwara	5.7	39.5	53.6	0.7	0.5	100.0
Lagos	0.5	82.3	7.2	0.5	9.6	100.0
Niger	16.5	3.7	74.9	3.8	1.1	100.0
Ogun	0.5	93.6	6.2	0.3	0.3	100.0
Ondo	0.3	94.5	4.2	0.2	0.9	100.0
Oyo	0.6	85.8	12.7	0.3	0.6	100.0
Plateau	6.8	5.3	34.7	4.0	49.2	100.0
Rivers	2.2	12.3	72.7	0.5	14.4	100.0
Sokoto	26.6	2.5	66.6	3.3	0.9	100.0

[a] The FEDECO decided that there was no need for a run-off election, although Shagari had not reached 25% of the votes in two-thirds of the states, but only 25% in 12 states and 20% in 13 (= two-thirds) states. The decision aroused protests from the other parties, especially from the second strongest candidate, Awolowo of UPN, who challenged the ruling in the courts. However, the Special Election Tribunal (10 September 1979) and the Supreme Court (27 September 1979) confirmed FEDECO´s interpretation, according to which the constitutional requirement meant that 25% of the vote in two-thirds of the states meant in practice not 13 states, but 12 2/3 states.

1983 (absolute numbers)							
State	GNPP	NAP	NPN	NPP	PRP	UPN	Total vote
Anambra	36,163	27,511	385,297	669,348	16,103	23,859	1,158,283
Benue	19,897	10,573	384,045	152,209	6,381	79,690	652,795
Bendel	11,723	8,653	452,776	53,306	7,358	566,035	1,099,851
Borno	179,265	15,698	348,974	26,972	26,996	120,138	718,043
Bauchi	37,203	18,979	1,507,144	65,258	54,564	98,974	1,782,122
Cross River	16,582	10,967	696,592	46,418	8,229	606,922	1,285,710
Niger	12,984	8,182	272,086	112,971	8,736	15,772	430,731
Kwara	7,670	6,056	299,654	16,215	3,693	275,134	608,422
Ogun	6,874	2,862	43,821	5,022	4,449	1,118,033	1,261,061
Ondo	11,629	10,566	366,217	20,340	7,052	1,412,539	1,828,343
Oyo	15,732	9,891	885,127	34,852	9,174	1,396,226	2,351,000
Plateau	18,612	10,490	292,606	280,803	11,581	38,210	652,302
Imo	52,364	32,684	398,463	1,064,436	18,370	22,648	1,588,975
Gongola	25,530	37,318	282,820	148,055	81,205	160,720	735,648
Sokoto	46,752	22,152	2,605,935	63,238	24,280	75,428	2,837,786
Kaduna	80,862	37,396	1,266,894	225,919	300,476	225,878	2,137,398
Kano	35,252	14,209	383,998	274,102	436,997	48,494	1,193,050
FCT	1,103	977	127,372	4,156	641	1,102	135,351
Rivers	12,981	15,061	921,664	151,558	4,626	251,825	1,357,715
Lagos	11,748	8,636	126,165	119,455	6,570	1,367,807	1,640,381

[a] Data for regional distribution do not coincide with data at national level.

1983 (in %)[a]							
State	GNPP	NAP	NPN	NPP	PRP	UPN	Total vote
Anambra	3.1	2.3	33.3	57.8	1.4	2.1	100.0
Benue	3.0	1.6	58.8	23.3	1.0	12.2	100.0
Bendel	1.1	0.8	41.2	4.8	0.7	51.5	100.0
Borno	25.0	2.2	48.6	3.8	3.8	26.7	100.0
Bauchi	2.1	1.1	84.6	3.7	3.1	5.6	100.0
Cross River	1.3	0.9	54.2	3.6	0.6	47.2	107.8[a]
Niger	3.2	1.9	63.2	26.2	2.0	3.7	100.0
Kwara	1.3	1.0	49.3	2.7	0.6	45.2	100.0
Ogun	0.5	0.2	3.5	0.4	0.4	88.7	93.7[a]
Ondo	0.6	0.6	20.0	1.1	0.4	77.3	100.0
Oyo	0.7	0.4	37.6	1.5	0.4	59.4	100.0
Plateau	2.9	1.6	44.9	43.0	1.8	5.6	100.0
Imo	3.3	2.1	25.1	67.0	1.2	1.4	100.0
Gongola	3.5	5.1	38.4	20.1	11.0	21.8	100.0
Sokoto	1.6	0.8	91.8	2.3	0.9	2.7	100.0
Kaduna	3.8	1.7	59.3	10.6	14.1	10.6	100.0
Kano	3.0	1.2	32.2	23.0	36.6	4.1	100.0
FCT	0.8	0.7	94.1	3.1	0.5	0.8	100.0
Rivers	1.0	1.1	67.9	11.2	0.3	18.5	100.0
Lagos	0.7	0.5	7.7	7.3	0.4	83.4	100.0

[a] In some cases, data do not sum up to 100; faults could not be resolved. For Cross River, Joseph (1991: 220) gives 39.4% with the same absolute number as in the table above. For Ogun, he gives UPN 95% with the same absolute number.

1993[a]							
State	Registered voters	Total votes cast	Turnout %	SDP Votes	%	NRC Votes	%
Abia	991,569	256,500	25.9	105,273	41.0	151,227	59.0
Adamawa	954,680	308,114	32.3	155,525	46.5	178,805[a]	53.5
Akwa Ibom	1,032,955	414,129	40.1	214,787	51.9	199,342	48.1
Anambra	1,248,226	347,053	27.8	212,024	61.1	135,029	38.9
Bauchi	2,048,627	847,274	41.4	334,197	39.4	513,077	60.6
Benue	1,297,072	433,132	33.4	246,830	57.0	186,302	43.0
Borno	1,222,533	282,180	23.1	153,496	54.4	128,684	45.6
Cross River	876,599	342,755	39.1	189,303	55.2	153,452	44.8
Delta	1,155,182	472,278	40.9	327,277	69.3	145,001	30.7
Edo	912,680	308,979	33.9	205,407	66.5	103,572	33.5
Enugu	1,291,750	427,250	33.1	193,969	45.4	233,281	54.6
Imo	1,441,630	350,402	30.7	156,700	44.7	193,702[a]	55.3
Jigawa	1,230,215	228,388	18.6	138,652	60.7	89,836	39.3
Kaduna	1,614,258	726,573	45.0	389,713	53.6	336,860	46.4
Kano	2,583,057	324,428	12.6	169,619	52.3	154,809	47.7
Katsina	1,661,132	442,246	26.6	171,169	26.6	271,077	38.7
Kebbi	824,254	215,027	26.1	77,102	38.7	209,872	61.3
Kogi	978,019	488,492	50.0	222,760	45.6	265,732	54.4
Kwara	669,625	368,479	55.0	288,270	78.2	80,209	21.8
Lagos	2,397,421	953,297	39.8	883,965	84.3	149,432	15.7
Niger	1,002,173	357,787	35.7	136,350	38.1	221437	61.9
Ogun	941,889	464,971	51.5	425,725	87.8	59,246	12.2
Ondo	1,767,896	964,018	54.5	803,024	83.3	160,994	16.7
Osun	1,056,690	437,334	41.4	365,266	83.5	72,068	16.5
Oyo	1,579,280	641,799	40.6	536,011	83.5	105,788	15.5
Plateau	1,518,186	676,959	44.7	417,656	61.7	259,391	38.3
Rivers	1,908,878	996,824	53.8	379,872	37.0	616,952	63.0
Sokoto	1,636,119	469,976	28.7	97,726	20.8	372,250	79.2
Taraba	769,912	228,393	21.5	138,557	60.7	89,836	39.3
Yobe	665,299	176,054	26.5	110,921	63.0	65,133	37.0
FCT-Abuja	152,086	38,218	25.1	110,921	52.1	65,133	47.8
Total	39,125,492	13,976,976	36.3	8,128,720	58.3	5,848,247	41.6

[a]Again, serious inconsistencies between the sources as well as within one source (for instance, for: Anambra, Bauchi, Enugu, Imo, Kaduna, Katsina, Kwara, Lagos, Ondo, Rivers, Taraba Yobe and FCT-Abuja). The source underlying here is *African Concord* (1993); differing data are given in *Newswatch* (28 June 1993), Fawchinmi (1993: 143–144).

2.10 List of Power Holders 1960–1998

Head of State and Government	Years	Remarks
Abubakar Tafawa balewa	1960–1963	Federal Prime Minister.
Nnamdii Azikiwe[a]	1963–1966	Federal Prime Minister.
Aguiyi Ironsi	1966	Military ruler (Major General). Seized power on 15 January by coup d'état, assassinated during counter-coup on 29 July 1966.
Yakubu Gowon	1966–1975	Military ruler (Lieutenant Corporal, later General). Named Supreme Commander of State and Army, seized power by a counter-coup on 29 July 1966, ousted by military coup in 1975.
Murtala Rufai Mohamed	1975–1976	Military ruler (Brigadier, later General). Seized power by a coup d'état on 29 July 1975; assassinated in 1976 during a failed coup.
Olusegun Obasanjo	1976–1979	Military ruler. Succeeded to the presidency upon the assassination of Murtala Rufai Mohamed.
M. Alhadji Shehu Shagari	1979–1983	Elected President on 11 June 1979; ousted on 31 December 1983.
Muhammadu Buhari	1983–1985	Military ruler (General). Seized power on 31 December 1983, overthrown on 27 August 1985.
Ibrahim Badamasi Babangida[b]	1985–1993	Military ruler (Major General). Seized power on 27 August 1985 by coup d'état.
Sani Abacha	1993–1998	Military ruler (General). Seized power by coup d'état on 17 November 1993.
Abdusalam Abubakar	1998–	Military ruler (General). Nominated by Military Council on 8 June 1998 after Abacha's death.

[a] Azikiwe appointed Sir Abubakar Tafawa Balewa Prime Minister on 31 March 1965. He was in office until the military coup on 15 January 1966.

[b] Babangida, a Northern Muslim, appointed a Yoruba Christian as Head of Government and chairman of a 26-member Transitional (Ministerial) Council in 1992.

3. Bibliography

3.1 Official Sources

The Constitution of The Federal Republic of Nigeria 1979. (Federal Ministry of Information, Printing Division, Lagos).

Transition to Civil Rule (Lifting of Ban on Politics) Decree 1989, authorized and published by The Federal Military Government of Nigeria, and printed by the Ministry of Information and Culture, Printing Division, Lagos.

The Constitution of the Federal Republic of Nigeria (Promulgation) 1989. published and authorized by The Federal Military Government of Nigeria, and printed by the Ministry of Information and Culture, Printing Division, Lagos, Federal Republic of Nigeria, (Official Gazette, No. 29, Vol. 76), Lagos 3rd May, 1989.

3.2 Books, Articles and Electoral Reports

Agboola, A.T. (1983). *Nigerian Elections: A Bibliography.* Yaba/ Lagos: University of Lagos Library.

Adam, E., and Beckett, P. A. (1978). 'Nigeria', in D. Sternberger, B. Vogel, D. Nohlen and K. Landfried (eds.), *Die Wahl der Parlamente und anderer Staatsorgane. Band II: Politische Organisation und Repräsentation in Afrika,* by Franz Nuscheler, Klaus Ziemer *et al.*, Berlin/ New York: Walter de Gruyter, 1493–1554.

Aké, C. (1992). *The Feasibility of Democracy in Africa.* Keynote Address at the Symposium on Democratic Transition in Africa (Centre de Recherches, d' Echanges et de Documentation Universitaire, Occasional Publication No. 1, 1992), University of Ibadan, 16–19 June 1992.

Azinge, E. (1994). 'The Right to Vote in Nigeria: A Critical Commentary on the Open Ballot System'. *Journal of African Law*, 38/2: 173–180.

Bergstresser, H. (1988). 'Wirtschaft und Politik in Nigeria'. *afrika spectrum*, 23/2: 183–200.

— (1993). 'Nigeria', in D. Nohlen and F. Nuscheler (eds.), *Handbuch der Dritten Welt, Band 4: Westafrika und Zentralafrika*. Bonn: Dietz, 344–363.

— (1994). 'Nigeria: Militärherrschaft ohne Ende?', in Deutsches Übersee-Institut (ed.), *Jahrbuch Dritte Welt 1995*. München: Beck.

— and Pohly-Bergstresser, S. (1991). *Nigeria*. München: Beck.

Bienen, H. (1987): 'Nigeria', in M. Weiner and E. Özbudun (eds), *Competitive Elections in Developing Countries.* Durham N.C.: Duke University Press, 201–247.

Campbell, I. (1994). 'Nigeria's Failed Transition. The 1993 Presidential Election'. *Journal of Contemporary African Studies*, 12/2: 179–200.

Caron, B., Gboyega, A., and Osaghae, E. (1992). *Democratic Transition in Africa*. (CREDU Documents in Social Sciences and the Humanities, Series No. 1,), Ibadan (Centre de Recherches d'Echanges et de Documentation Universitaire).

Coleman, J. S. (1958). *Nigeria: Background to Nationalism*. Berkeley, Calif.: University of California Press.

Crowder, M. (1978). *The Story of Nigeria*. London: Faber and Faber.

Diamond, L. (1988*a*). 'Nigeria: Pluralism, Statism, and the Struggle for Democracy', in L. Diamond, J. Linz and S. M. Lipset (eds.), *Democracy in Developing Countries: Africa*. Boulder, Col.: Lynne Rienner.

— (1988*b*). *Class, Ethnicity and Democracy in Nigeria. The Failure of the First Republic*. Syracuse, N.Y.: Syracuse University Press.

— (1991). 'Nigeria's Search for a New Political Order'. *Journal of Democracy*, 2/2: 54–69.

— Kirk-Greene, A., Oyediran, O., and Biersteker, T. (eds.) (1997). *Transition without End: Nigerian Politics and Civil Society under Babangida*. Boulder, Col.: Lynne Rienner.

Elias, J. T. O. (1967). *Nigeria—The Development of Its Laws and Constitution*. London: Stevens.

Falola, T., and Ihonvbere, J. (1985). *The Rise and the Fall of the Second Republic 1979–1984*. London: Zed Books.

Fawchinmi, G. (1993). *June 12 Crisis: The Illegality of Shonekan's Government*. Lagos: Nigerian Law Publications.

Graf, W. D. (1988). *The Nigerian State*. London: James Currey.

Hart, C. (1983). 'The Nigerian Elections of 1983'. *Africa*, 63/3: 397–418.

Hauck, G. (1995). 'Die Konsolidierungschancen der afrikanischen Demokratie am Beispiel Nigerias. Zum Verhältnis von Staat, Ethnoparteien und konfliktfähigen Gruppen', in R. Tetzlaff, U. Engel and A. Mehler (eds.), *Afrika zwischen Dekolonisation, Staatsversagen und Demokratisierung* (Hamburger Beiträge zur Afrika-Kunde, Bd. 45). Hamburg: Institut für Afrika-Kunde, 189–298.

Ihonvbere, J., and Vaughan, O. (1995). 'Nigeria: Democracy and Civil Society. The Nigerian Transition Programme, 1985–1993', in J. A. Wiseman (ed.), *Democracy and Political Change in Sub-Saharan Africa*. London: Routledge.

Joseph, R. A. (1987). *Democracy and Prebendal Politics in Nigeria. The Rise and Fall of the Second Republic*. Cambridge: Cambridge University Press.

Kirk-Greene, A. H. M. (1971). *Crisis and Conflict in Nigeria*. London: Oxford University Press.

Koehn, P. (1989). 'Competitive Transition to Civilian Rule: Nigeria's First and Second Experiments'. *The Journal of Modern African Studies*, 27/3: 401–430.

König, C.-D. (1994). *Zivilgesellschaft und Demokratisierung in Nigeria.* Münster/ Hamburg: Lit.

Kurfi, A. (1983). *The Nigerian General Elections 1959 and 1979.* Lagos: Macmillan Nigeria.

Lewis, P. M. (1994). 'Endgame in Nigeria? The Politics of a Failed Democratic Transition'. *African Affairs*, 93: 323–340.

— (1999). 'Nigeria: An End to the Permanent Transition?'. *Journal of Democracy*, 10/1: 141–156.

— and Rubin, B. R., and Robinson, P. T. (1998). *Stabilizing Nigeria: Sanctions, Incentives, and Support for Civil Society.* New York: The Council on Foreign Relations and The Century Foundation.

Miles, W. (1988). *Elections in Nigeria. A Grassroots Perspective.* Boulder, Col.: Lynne Rienner.

Montclos, M.-A. de (1994). *Le Nigeria.* Institut français de recherche en Afrique, University of Ibadan, Nigeria.

Nwokedi, E. (1994). 'Nigeria's Democratic Transition: Explaining the Annulled 1993 Presidential Elections'. *The Round Table*, 330: 189–204

Odinkalu, C. A. (1996). *The Management of Transition to Civil Rule by the Military in Nigeria (1966–1996).* Reference Paper prepared for the International Workshop on 'The Nigerian Democratization Process and the European Union', Centre d'Etude d'Afrique Noire, Bordeaux, 12–14 September 1996.

Olagunju, T., Jinadu, A., and Oyuvbaire, S. (1993). *Transition to Democracy in Nigeria (1985–1993).* St. Helier/Jersey, Channel Islands (UK)/Ibadan, Nigeria: Safari Books/ Spectrum Books.

Ollawa, P. E. (1976). 'Militärherrschaft und politische Stabilität: Der Fall Nigeria'. *Aus Politik und Zeitgeschichte*, 22: 15–29.

Olugbade, K. (1992). 'The Nigerian State and the Quest for a Stable Polity'. *Comparative Politics*, 24: 293–316.

Oluwafemi Mimiko, N. (1995). *Crises and Contradictions in Nigeria's Democratization Programme, 1986–93.* Akure: Stabak Ventures Ltd.

Oyediran, O., and Agbaje, A. (1991). 'Two-Partyism and Democratic Transition in Nigeria'. *The Journal of Modern African Studies*, 29/2: 213–235.

Panter-Brick, K. (1979). 'Nigeria: The 1979 Elections'. *afrika spektrum*, 79/3: 317–336.

Phillips, C. S. (1980). 'Nigeria's New Political Institutions'. *The Journal of Modern African Studies*, 18/2: 1–22.

Read, J. S. (1979). 'The New Constitution of Nigeria, 1979: "The Washington Model"?'. *Journal of African Law*, 23/2: 131–169.

Suberu, R. T. (1993). 'The Travails of Federalism in Nigeria'. *Journal of Democracy*, 4/4: 39–53.
— (1994). *1991 State and Local Government Reorganizations in Nigeria.* (Centre d'Etude d'Afrique Noire/ Institut Français de Recherche en Afrique; Travaux et Documents No. 41), Bordeaux/ Ibadan.
Traub, R. (1990). *Strukturanpassung und Demokratisierung*. Bonn: Friedrich Ebert Foundation—Länderanalyse Nigeria.
Tyoden, S. W. (1978). 'Continuity and Change in Nigeria's Political Evolution: The 1979 Elections'. *The African Review*, 8/3-4: 77–89.
Uwazurike, P. C. (1990). 'Confronting Potential Breakdown. The Nigerian Redemocratisation Process in Critical Perspective'. *Journal of Modern African Studies*, 28/1: 55–77.
Weber, H. (1979). *Nigeria: Demokratisierung—Bildung von Parteien—politische Hintergründe*. Forschungsinstitut der Friedrich-Ebert-Stiftung, Arbeiten aus der Abteilung Entwicklungsländerforschung, No. 73.
Whitaker, C. S. (1991). 'Second Beginnings: The New Political Framework in Nigeria', in R. L. Sklar and C. S. Whitaker (eds.), *African Politics and Problems in Development*. Boulder, Col.: Lynne Rienner.

RWANDA

by Tilo Stolz

1. Introduction

1.1 Historical Overview

Since Rwanda became independent on 1 July 1962, political development has been shaped by tensions between the two major ethnic groups, the Hutu majority and the Tutsi minority. Both colonial powers (first Germany, then Belgium) monopolized political power in the hands of the Tutsi and reinforced ethnic identities. Thus the dynamic of the transition from colonial rule to independence was determined in large part by conflicts between the two groups. In the Bahutu Manifesto of 24 March 1957 the Hutu demanded political and social rights and subsequently formed two parties with different regional bases, the *Association pour la promotion sociale de la masse* (APROSOMA) and the *Parti du mouvement de l'émancipation Hutu* (PARMEHUTU). The Tutsi chiefs and other conservative Tutsi rejected the political demands of the Hutu and formed the *Union national rwandaise* (UNAR) which supported the monarchy and demanded immediate independence.

Between 1959 and 1961 Rwanda was transformed from a Tutsi-dominated monarchy to a Hutu-led republic. The fierce anti-colonial position of the Tutsi elite led the Belgian authorities to shift their support to the Hutu majority. The subsequent prosecution of Tutsi and widespread ethnic violence caused a mass exodus of approximately 130,000 Tutsi into neighboring countries. On 28 January 1961 an emergency meeting of *bourgemestres* and municipal councillors in Gitarama declared the 'sovereign democratic Republic of Rwanda', adopted a republican constitution and elected a President. After this legal coup that gave Rwanda *de facto* independence the United Nations organized a referendum on the question of the Mwami (king) of Rwanda as well as parliamentary elections on 25 September 1961. A clear majority voted for the abolition of the monarchy. PARMEHUTU under Grégoire Kayibanda emerged as the dominant political party and he was elected President by the National Assembly on 26 October 1961.

The Constitution of 24 November 1962 provided for a unitary republic with a central administration and a presidential form of government. The first years of the government of President Kayibanda were characterized by severe violent ethnic conflicts which led to further political marginalization of the Tutsi. By 1965, when legislative and presidential elections were held, Rwanda had become *de facto* a single-party state.

On 5 July 1973, the First Republic was ended through a military coup conducted by senior army commander Major-General Juvénal Habyarimana. The new civilian–military government suspended parts of the 1962 Constitution, dissolved MDR-PARMEHUTU as well as the legislature, and further centralized the administrative system. In July 1975, Habyarimana founded the *Mouvement révolutionnaire national pour le développement* (MRND). In 1978 a new constitution was adopted by a national referendum. The constitution established a centralized presidential system and enshrined single-party rule. While presidential elections in 1978, 1983 and 1988 were of a non-competitive nature (in every occasion Habyarimana was confirmed as the only candidate) a restricted form of competition was allowed in the elections to the legislative body (*Conseil National de Développement*—CND) in 1981, 1983 and 1988. Within the MRND there was a choice between two candidates for each seat. Through the introduction of a quota system that regulated the access to education and public offices for the two major ethnic groups of Rwanda further, severe ethnic conflicts between Hutu and Tutsi were prevented between 1973 and 1990. However, the quota system institutionalized previous practices of ethnic discrimination and increased the importance of ethnicity as the determining factor in the social and political life of the country.

In the early 1990s Rwanda embarked on a process of political liberalization as a result of internal and external pressure. In July 1990 the drafting of a National Charter as the basis for the establishment of a multi-party system was announced. The launching of an attack by fighters of the Rwandese Patriotic Front (RPF) from Uganda on 1 October 1990, with the aim to overthrow the authoritarian regime of President Habyarimana and to enable the refugees living abroad to return, was a violent external catalyst to the process of political liberalization. On 10 June 1991, a new constitution formally put an end to the one-party system. By June 1992 more than 10 parties had been registered. Four opposition parties gained political significance: *Mouvement démocratique républicain* (MDR), *Parti social-démocrate* (PSD), *Parti libéral* (PL), *Parti démocrate-chrétien* (PDC). In early 1992 President Habyarimana announced multi-party elections within one year's time.

However, the increased political and ethnic polarization of the Rwandese society and renewed fighting put insurmountable obstacles to the democratization process. A Peace Agreement between the government and the RPF which was signed at Arusha, Tanzania on 4 August 1993, foresaw the formation of a transitional government and the holding of multi-party elections after a 22-month period. Due to the fierce opposition of Hutu radicals, political differences within and between various political parties and escalating political violence, the fulfillment of the agreement was postponed several times. After President Habyarimana was killed on 6 April 1994 when his plane was shot down, members of the presidential Guard and Hutu militias started to kill Tutsi and moderate Hutu. The killings were planed in advance and fueled by radio broadcasts of hate propaganda. Between April and July 1994 more than 800,000 people were killed in a genocide that was ethnically as well as politically motivated. Up to two million persons fled into neighboring countries and another one million persons became internally displaced. The RPF responded to the killings by launching an offensive in the North of the country on 8 April 1994. Its troops controlled large parts of the country by June 1994.

On 19 July 1994 a new Government of National Unity was sworn in. On the basis of a multi-party protocol of understanding a 70-member National Transitional Assembly was inaugurated on 12 December 1994, comprised of representatives of the RPF as well as of other parties except those involved in the genocide. On 5 May 1995 the Assembly announced the adoption of a new constitution based on parts of the 1991 Constitution, the 1993 Arusha Accord, the victory declaration of RPF of July 1994 and the multi-party protocol of understanding of November 1994. A Supreme Court was established on 10 October 1995. In 1998 members of the government, MPs, prefecture heads, respected elders and church leaders began to discuss the political future of Rwanda. A date for the next parliamentary and presidential elections has not yet been set.

1.2 Evolution of Electoral Provisions

Electoral provisions were set down in the constitutions of 1962 and 1978 as well as in the electoral laws of 20 May 1963, 5 July 1967 and subsequent changes which took place on 19 May 1969, 22 August 1981 and 27 August 1983.

Since the elections of 1961 all citizens of Rwanda (men and women) with a minimum age of 18 years were entitled to vote.

In 1965 and 1969, the President and the members of the National Assembly were elected for a four-year term. The 1978 Constitution extended the mandate of the President as well as of the Members of Parliament (now called *Conseil National de Developpement—CND*) to five years.

Until the 1978 Constitution the candidate for the office of the President had to be masculine and a member of PARMEHUTU. According to Art. 40 of the Constitution of 1978 the president of the *Mouvement révolutionnaire national pour le developpement* (MRND) was the only candidate for the presidential elections. All candidates for the election to the CND had to be members of MRND. Parliamentary candidates generally had to be at least 21 years old; for presidential candidates the minimum age was set to 35 years, the maximum age to 60 years (maximum age restrictions only in the 1960s).

Since 1965 the President was elected by a plurality system. The National Assembly inherited the Belgian system of proportional representation in multi-member districts which was applied until the elections of 1969. The number of seats in the National Assembly was increased from 44 to 47 in 1965. The candidates were nominated by political parties on closed but not blocked lists (preferential voting). Every voter had one vote. The d'Hondt formula was applied at constituency level.

When the CND was elected for the first time in 1981 it had 64 members. This number was increased to 70 in August 1983. According to law No. 18 of 1983 the territory of Rwanda was divided into 10 electoral districts in which parliamentarians were to be elected proportionally to population size: Kigali (nine representatives), Gitarama (nine), Butare (nine), Gikongoro (six), Cyangugu (five), Kibuye (five), Gisenyi (seven), Ruhengeri (eight), Byumba (seven), Kibungo (five).

1.3 Current Electoral Provisions

Neither the current President (in office since 19 July 1994) of Rwanda, Pasteur Bizimungu, nor the 70 members of the current Parliament called National Transitional Assembly which was inaugurated on 12 December 1994 have been elected. The composition of the National Transitional Assembly is mainly based on the Arusha Agreement of 4 August 1993 which gave all major political parties a certain number of seats. The seats of the MRND (now renamed MRNDD) which was not allowed to send deputies to the National Transitional Assembly because of its involvement in the genocide were shared out among the remaining parties. The Arusha Agreement provides the basis for the setting up of an Electoral Commission that shall be responsible for the organization of local, parliamentary and presidential elections. The modalities of the next presidential and parliamentary elections have not yet been determined.

1.4 Comment on the Electoral Statistics

The only parliamentary election for which detailed figures are available is the 1961 election which was organized by the UN. There are few figures available for the 1965 and the 1969 elections. Data are drawn from Philipp (1978), except for the 1961 parliamentary elections (corrigendum of the UN report of 1963) and the number of registered voters in 1981 (Décret-Loi No. 27/81). There are almost no figures available which are relevant for the following tables in the case of the three parliamentary elections that took place in the 1980s.

2. Tables

2.1 Dates of National Elections, Referendums and Coups d'Etat

Year	Presidential elections	Parliamentary elections	Elections for Constitutional Assembly	Referendums	Coups d'état
1961		25/09		25/09	
1965	03/10	03/10			
1969	28/09	28/09			
1973					05/07
1978	24/12			17/12	
1981		28/12			
1983	19/12	26/12			
1988	19/12	26/12			

2.2 Electoral Body 1961–1988

Year	Type of election[a]	Population[b]	Registered voters Total number	% pop.	Votes cast Total number	% reg. voters	% pop.
1961	Pa	2,750,000	1,337,096	48.6	1,278,144	95.6	46.5
1961	Ref	2,750,000	1,337,342	48.6	1,274,631[c]	95.3	46.4
					1,273,691[d]	95.2	46.3
1965	Pa	3,130,000	—	—	—	—	—
1965	Pr	3,130,000	1,440,440	46.0	1,261,458	87.6	40.3
1969	Pa	3,570,000	—	—	—	—	—
1969	Pr	3,570,000	1,578,704	44.2	1,434,977	90.9	40.2
1978	Ref	4,800,433[e]	—	—	—	—	—
1978	Pr	4,800,433[e]	—	—	—	—	—
1981	Pa	5,353,000	2,244,547	41.9	—	—	—
1983	Pa	5,757,000	—	—	—	—	—
1983	Pr	5,757,000	—	—	—	—	—
1988	Pa	6,611,000	—	—	—	—	—
1988	Pr	6,611,000	—	—	—	—	—

[a] Pa = Parliament; Pr = President; Ref = Referendum.
[b] Unless otherwise indicated these figures are midyear estimates of the population. Source: Demographic Yearbook of the United Nations.
[c] Number of votes cast regarding question 1 of the referendum.
[d] Number of votes cast regarding question 2 of the referendum.
[e] Census result (15–16 August 1978). Census of 15 August 1991: 7,142,755.

2.3 Abbreviations

ABAKI	Alliance des Abakiga
APADEC	Parti Démocrate Chrétien
APROFER	Association pour la Promotion des Femmes Rwandaises
APROSOMA	Association pour la Promotion Sociale de la Masse
AREDETWA	Association pour le Relèvement Démocratique des Batwa
ASSERU	Association des Eleveurs du Rwanda
CDR	Coalition pour la Défense de la République
FPR / RPF	Front Patriotique Rwandais / Rwandese Patriotic Front
FRD	Forces de Résistance pour la Démocratie
MDR	Mouvement Démocratique Républicain
MMFBP	Mouvement des Femmes et du Bas—peuple
MOMOR	Mouvement Monarchiste Rwandais
MRND	Mouvement Révolutionnaire Nationale pour le Développement
MRNDD[a]	Mouvement Républicain Nationale pour la Démocratie et le Développement
MUR	Mouvement pour l'Union Rwandaise

PADE	Parti Démocrate
PADER	Parti Démocrate Rwandais
PAMOPRO	Parti Monarchiste du Progrès
PARERWA	Parti Républicain
PARMEHUTU	Parti du Mouvement de l'Emancipation Hutu
PDC[b]	Parti Démocrate Chrétien
PDI	Parti Démocratique Islamique
PECO	Parti des Ecologistes
PL	Parti Libéral
PPJR	Parti Progressiste de la Jeunesse Rwandaise—RAMA
PSD	Parti Social Démocrate
PSR	Parti Socialiste Rwandais
RADER	Rassemblement Démocratique Rwandais
RPA	Rwandese Patriotic Army
RTD	Rassemblement des Travaillistes pour la Démocratie
UAARU	Union des Aborozi africaines du Ruanda-Urundi
UDPR	Union Démocratique du Peuple Rwandais
UMAR	Union des Masses Rwandaise
UNAR	Union Nationale Rwandaise
UNISODEL	Union Sociale des Démocrates Chrétiens

General note: About half of the parties listed above have been founded in the early 1990s and have not yet participated in any elections.

[a] During an extraordinary party congress in April 1991 the MRND changed its name to MRNDD.

[b] In 1998 the PDC changed its name from *Parti Démocrate Chrétien* to *Parti Démocrate Centriste*.

2.4 Electoral Participation of Parties and Alliances 1961–1988

Party / Alliance	Years	Elections contested	
		Presidential	Parliamentary
APROSOMA	1961	0	1
PARMEHUTU/ MDR[a]	1961, 1965, 1969	2	3
RADER	1961	0	1
UNAR	1961	0	1
MRND	1978, 1981, 1983, 1988	3	3

[a] After its foundation PARMEHUTU adopted the name *Mouvement Démocratique Républicain*. The party is often referred to as MDR-*Parmehutu*.

2.5 Referendum 1961

1961	Question 1[a] Total number	%	Question 2[b] Total number	%
Registered voters	1,337,342	–	1,337,342	–
Votes cast	1,274,631	95.3	1,273,691	95.2
Invalid votes	14,329	1.1	11,526	0.9
Valid votes	1,260,302	98.9	1,262,165	99.1
Yes	253,963	20.2	257,510	20.4
No	1,006,339	79.9	1,004,655	79.6

General note: For the 1978 referendum no detailed data are available. Supposedly, the constitution was approved by approximately 90% of the electorate.

[a] 'Do you wish to retain the institution of the Mwami in Rwanda?'

[b] 'If so, do you wish Kigeli V to continue as the Mwami of Rwanda?'

2.6 Elections for Constitutional Assembly

Elections for Constitutional Assembly have not been held.

2.7 Parliamentary Elections 1961–1988

Year	1961 Total number	%
Registered voters	1,337,096	–
Votes cast	1,278,144	95.6
Invalid votes	22,248	1.7
Valid votes	1,255,896	98.3
PARMEHUTU	974,329	77.6
UNAR	211,929	16.9
APROSOMA	45,740	3.6
RADER	4,172	0.3
Others	19,726	1.6

For the parliamentary elections of 1965, 1969, 1981, 1983 and 1988 detailed data are not available. All these elections took place under a one-party regime (1965 and 1969: PARMEHUTU; 1981–1988: MRND respectively).

2.8 Composition of Parliament 1961–1988

Year	1961 Seats	%	1965 Seats	%	1969 Seats	%
	44	100.0	47	100.0	64	100.0
APROSOMA	2	4.6	–	–	–	–
PARMEHUTU	35	79.6	47	100.0	64	100.0
UNAR	7	15.9	–	–	–	–

Year	1981 Seats	%	1983 Seats	%	1988 Seats	%
	64	100.0	70	100.0	70	100.0
MRND	64	100.0	70	100.0	70	100.0

General note: The composition of the National Transitional Assembly which was inaugurated on 12 December 1994 is as follows: FPR: 13 seats, PSD: 13, PL: 13, MDR: 13, PDC: 6, PSR: 2, PDI: 2, UDPR: 2, RPA: 6.

2.9 Presidential Elections 1965–1988

Year	1965 Total number	%
Registered voters	1,440,440	–
Votes cast	1,261,458	87.6
Invalid votes	24,804	2.0
Valid votes	1,236,654	98.0
Grégoire Kayibanda (PARMEHUTU-MRD)	1,236,654	100.0

Year	1969 Total number	%
Registered voters	1,578,704	–
Votes cast	1,434,977	90.9
Invalid votes	8,276	0.4
Valid votes	1,426,701	99.4
Grégoire Kayibanda (PARMEHUTU-MRD)	1,426,159	100.0

During the Second Republic presidential elections were held in 1978, 1983 and 1988. For these elections, detailed data are not available. However, in every occasion President Juvenal Habyarimana (MRND) was the only candidate and according to official statements confirmed by 99% to 100% of the voter turnout.

2.10 List of Power Holders 1961–1998

Head of State	Years	Remarks
Grégoire Kayibanda	1961–1973	Constitutionally elected by the National Assembly on 26/10/1961; ousted in a bloodless coup d'état by General Juvénal Habyarimana on 05/07/1973.
Juvénal Habyarimana	1973–1994	Killed on 06/04/1994 when his plane was shot down.
Théodore Sindikubwabo	1994	As Speaker of the CND Sindikubwabo declared himself interim President of Rwanda on 08/04/1994.
Pasteur Bizimungu	1994–	Inaugurated as President for a five-year term on 19/07/1994.

Head of Government	Years	Remarks
	1961–1991	Until 1991 when the post of a Prime Minister was created the President was also Head of Government.
Sylvestre Nsanzimana	1991–1992	Appointed to the newly established post of Prime Minister by the President on 13/10/1991.
Dismas Nsengiyareme	1992–1993	Appointed as Prime Minister by the President on 02/04/1992.
Agathe Uwilingiyimana	1993–1994	Appointed as Prime Minister by the President on 17/07/1993; killed in April 1994.
Jean Kambanda	1994	Appointed as Prime Minister by the five remaining political parties of the government. However, his authority was challenged by the FPR.
Faustin Twagiramungu	1994–1995	Took office on 19/07/1994 as Prime Minister of a New Government of National Unity. Resigned on 28/08/1995 as a consequence of a political crisis.
Pierre Célestin Rwigyema	1995–	Took office on 30/08/1995.

3. Bibliography

Bakinahe, D. (1993). *Les élections législatives au Rwanda de 1981 à 1988.* Kigali.

Becker, P. (1994). 'Rwanda', in D. Nohlen and F. Nuscheler (eds.), *Handbuch der Dritten Welt, Vol. 5, Ostafrika und Südafrika* (3rd edn.). Bonn: Dietz, 114–133.

Braeckman, C. (1994). *Rwanda: histoire d'un génocide.* Paris: Fayard.

'Decret-Loi, No.27/81. 30 Octobre 1981'. *Journal Officiel*, 1981, 977.

Destexhe, A. (1995). *Rwanda and Genocide in the Twentieth Century.* New York: New York University Press.

Dießenbacher, H. (1994). 'Bürgerkrieg und Völkermord in Ruanda', *Aus Politik und Zeitgeschichte*, B31: 14–23.

Dorsey, L. (1994). *Historical Dictionary of Rwanda.* Metuchen: Scarecrow Press.

Gasore-Rukara, P. (1992). *Les partis politiques au Rwanda. Idéologies, stratégies et pesanteurs sociologiques*. Kigali.

Keane, F. (1995). *Season of Blood. A Rwandan Journey*. London/ New York: Penguin Books.

Lemarchand, R. (1970). *Rwanda and Burundi.* New York/ Washington/ London: Praeger Publishers.

Minear, L., and Guillot, P. (1996). *Soldiers to the Rescue. Humanitarian Lessons from Rwanda*. Paris: Development Centre of the Organisation for Economic Cooperation and Develpment.

Molt, P. (1994). 'Zerfall von Staat und Gesellschaft in Ruanda', *KAS-Auslandsinformationen*, 10/5: 3–38.

Muyombano, C. (1995). *Ruanda. Die historischen Ursachen des Bürgerkrieges*. Stuttgart: Verlag Stephanie Nagelschmid.

Nyankanzi, E. L. (1994). *Genocide. Rwanda & Burundi.* New York: AAIC International.

Philipp, G. (1978). 'Rwanda', in D. Sternberger, B. Vogel, D. Nohlen and K. Landfried (eds.), *Die Wahl der Parlamente und anderer Staatsorgane, Bd. II: Politische Organisation und Repräsentation in Afrika,* by Franz Nuscheler, Klaus Ziemer *et al.*, Berlin/ New York: Walter De Gruyter, 1691–1730.

Prunier, G. (1995). *The Rwanda Crisis. History of a Genocide.* New York: Columbia University Press.

Rake, A. (1997). 'Rwanda', in A. Rake (ed.), *New African Yearbook 1997-98*. London: IC Publications, 371–377.

Republique Rwandaise (1989). *Recueil des textes relatifs au pouvoir législatif au Rwanda de 1960 à nos jours*. Kigali: Conseil National de Développement.

Reyntjens, F. (1985). *Pouvoir et droit au Rwanda. Droit public et évolution politique, 1916–1973*. Butare: Institut National de Recherche Scientifique, Publication No. 28.

— and Gorus, J. (1979–1984). *Codes et lois du Rwanda*, Volume 1–4. Butare: Faculté de Droit, Université Nationale du Rwanda.

'Ruanda-Burundi'. *Yearbook of the United Nations 1961*, New York 1963: United Nations, Office of Public Information, 484–494.

'Rwanda'. *Africa South of the Sahara 1999* (28th edn.). London: Europa Publications Limited, 847–868.

'Rwanda'. *World Bibliographical Series* (Volume 154). Oxford *et al.*: Clio Press.

Schürings, H. (1994). *Ein Volk verläßt sein Land. Krieg und Völkermord in Ruanda*. Köln: Neuer ISP Verlag.

Sellström, T., and Wohlgemuth, L. (1996). *The International Response to Conflict and Genocide: Lessons from the Rwanda Experience. Study 1, Historical Perspective: Some Explanatory Factors*. Copenhagen: Steering Committee of Joint Evaluation of Emergency Assistance to Rwanda.

Strizek, H. (1996). *Ruanda und Burundi von der Unabhängigkeit zum Staatszerfall. Studie über eine gescheiterte Demokratie im afrikanischen Zwischenseengebiet*. München/ Köln/ London: Weltforum.

UN (United Nations) (1960). 'Resolution 1605: Question of the future of Ruanda-Urundi', in *Resolutions adopted by the General Assembly during its Fourth Emergency Special Session 17–19 September 1960*. New York: General Assembly, Official Records, Supplement No. 1 (A/4510), 8–9.

— (1963). 'Report of the United Nations Commission for Ruanda-Urundi', in *General Assembly 16th Session*, Official Records, Annexes, Document A/4994, 1–81 and Corrigendum, 1: 1–3.

— (1996). *The United Nations and Rwanda 1993–1996, Blue Books Series (Volume X)*. New York: United Nations, Department of Public Information.

Vanderlinden, J. (1970). *Encyclopédie politique et constitutionelle. La République Rwandaise*. Paris: Berger-Levrault.

Webster, J. B. (1964). *The Constitutions of Burundi, Malagasy and Rwanda. A Comparison and Explanation of East African French Language Constitutions*. Syracuse: Maxwell Graduate School of Citizenship and Public Affairs.

— (1966). *The Political Development of Rwanda and Burundi*. Syracuse: Maxwell Graduate School of Citizenship and Public Affairs.

SÃO TOMÉ AND PRÍNCIPE

by Helga Fleischhacker

1. Introduction

1.1 Historical Overview

The islands of São Tomé and Príncipe form a micro-state with a small and ethnically homogeneous population. The country's politics for long remained the sole preserve of a narrow political elite, which, constituted as the *Movimento de Libertação de São Tomé e Príncipe* (MLSTP), had led the campaign for national independence. By the mid-1980s, the failure of its socialist development strategies led the MLSTP government to initiate a political reform process, one of the first African governments to do so. In 1990 this process had yielded a multi-party democracy which, largely sustained by the political and administrative elite which had inhabited the former state-party structures, has enjoyed a comparatively successful consolidation.

Discovered by Portuguese explorers in 1471, São Tomé and Príncipe was made a Portuguese territory in 1522, and an Overseas Province of Portugal in 1951. A nationalist movement founded by Manuel Pinto da Costa in 1960, the MLSTP, quickly became the leading advocate of independence from Portugal. It was not until the 1974 military coup in Lisbon, however, that negotiations over independence began between the Portuguese government and the MLSTP, which was recognized as sole official spokesman for the islands. The two parties agreed that independence would be proclaimed on 12 July 1975, and that a transitional government council would be formed under MLSTP leadership pending elections on 7 July 1975.

Unopposed by any other political force the MLSTP put into effect a constitution that closely intertwined state and party structures, and invested absolute authority in the hands of the President and the Political Bureau of the MLSTP. The Prime Minister was thus left with few effective powers. Radical socialist policies were soon introduced and any activity opposing the presidential branch's directives was disregarded. Serious ideological and personal divisions arose within the MLSTP, and up through the mid-1980s a number of prominent members, who favored a more moderate approach to social and economic reforms, were forced into exile. One of these was the country's popular Prime Minister, Miguel Trovoada, whose post was abolished after he departed.

In 1985, confronted with the threat of economic collapse, the President began to abandon the country's ties to the Eastern bloc and pursue an internal strategy of political reconciliation. From 1985 onwards a wider range of ideological views were represented in the (indirectly elected) National Popular Assembly. In October 1987 the Central Committee of the MLSTP announced a major constitutional reform, including universal adult suffrage; in January 1988 the Assembly approved a constitutional amendment providing for the re-establishment of the office of Prime Minister. Increasingly alarmed by economic crisis and encouraged by the reformist faction within the MLSTP, the regime embarked, after a National Party Conference in late 1989, on a transition to full multi-party democracy. In a referendum held in August 1990 the electorate ratified the new constitution proposed by the MLSTP Central Committee.

After a general amnesty decreed by the President in April 1990, oppositional political groupings returning from exile mainly coalesced into two small parties: *Coligação Democrática da Oposição* (CODO), a merger of three exile parties, and *Frente Democrata Cristã* (FDC). But the major challenge to the former state party came from the local opposition among young MLSTP cadres, professionals and independents, who formed the *Partido da Convergência Democrática—Grupa de Reflexão* (PCD-GR). In the National Assembly elections of January 1991, the PCD-GR outdistanced all other political forces, gaining an absolute majority of parliamentary seats and formed a transitional government pending presidential elections. These served, in effect, as a plebiscite regarding Miguel Trovoada, who ran as an independent candidate supported by PCD-GR and CODO. Thus the newly emerging party system not only reintegrated former MLSTP dissidents, but gave space to a new generation of politicians who had claimed personnel and institutional renovation. With the country's first competitive elections, held on the basis of universal suffrage, power switched from the unitary power to the representatives of the moderate and reformist factions which had taken shape outside of it.

These forces have nonetheless experienced considerable difficulty in building and maintaining government consensus; problems in this respect have been aggravated by tensions among government branches, and the need to forge and sustain majority coalitions in Parliament. By early 1992, a growing lack of cooperation between the presidency and government broke out in political crisis, leading to prolonged institutional conflict.

After the President had dismissed three different administrations over two years, continued institutional deadlock prompted him to dissolve Parliament and announce legislative elections for October 1994. These, however, provided the President with no parliamentary majority, resulting instead in a decisive advance for the MLSTP-PSD, which now found itself only one seat short of holding an absolute majority. Efforts by the newly appointed Prime Minister to form a coalition government failed, and the institutional crisis persisted. In the midst of rising popular discontent with the government's political and economic performance, a group of officers carried out a short-lived coup d'état, in which they seized control of the presidential palace and placed the Prime Minister under arrest. But their lack of internal support, along with mounting international pressures, quickly led them to begin negotiations with the President, which resulted in the rapid restoration of constitutional rule.

Since December 1994 several attempts have been made to form a Government of National Unity capable of combining political consensus with effective action. However, the conflictive state of cohabitation was prolonged by the electorate, when President Trovoada was re-elected in 1996. Yet, the fact that all important political forces continue to rely on the constitutional framework as the basis for their political activity and contention can be seen as evidence for ongoing democratic consolidation.

1.2 Evolution of Electoral Provisions

The 1975 Constitution, as revised in 1982, identified the socialist single-party MLSTP as the country's 'directing political force' and provided for an indirectly elected National Popular Assembly with 40 seats subject to re-election every five years. Such elections were held in fact in 1975, 1980 and 1985. Candidates nominated by an MLSTP Candidature Commission were elected by the People's District Assemblies. The President was thereupon named by the National Popular Assembly for a five-year term.

Constitutional changes introduced in October 1987 provided for direct election of the President and the deputies to the National Popular Assembly. Independent candidates were to be allowed, in addition to candidates chosen by the party and such 'recognized organizations' as trade unions and youth groups. The President was to be elected by universal suffrage; however, eligibility was restricted to the MLSTP party president (elected by secret ballot at the Party Congress). These reforms, however, were never enacted; they were superceded in 1990 by the fourth and current revision of the constitution.

1.3 Current Electoral Provisions

Sources: Lei No. 7/90, Constitução política; Lei No. 11/90, Lei eleitoral da República Democrática de São Tomé e Príncipe; Lei No. 8/90, Lei dos partidos políticos; Lei No. 2/90 Lei do direito de sufrágio e do recenseamento eleitoral; Lei No. 3/90, Lei do referendo.

Elected national institutions: The President is elected for a five-year term, renewable twice. In the case of the President's death, permanent incapacity or resignation, his functions are assumed by the President of the National Assembly until a new President is elected. The election of a new President is to occur 90 days afterwards, at which point a new tenure begins. The unicameral National Assembly is to contain no less than 45, no more than 55 members; in the event of a deputy stepping down, he is to be replaced by the next candidate on the same party list.

Suffrage: Universal, equal, secret and direct. Requirements: At least 18 years of age, voter registration is compulsory.

Nomination of candidates
- *presidential elections*: Registration as voter, must hold exclusively São Tomé and Príncipe citizenship and be older than 35 years; all candidates for presidential office must produce at least 250, and no more than 500 signatures from registered voters.
- *elections to the National Assembly*: Registration as voter; São Tomé and Príncipe citizenship; candidacy is determined by the election lists drawn up by parties or citizen groups; these must produce signatures from 100 registered voters.

Electoral system
- *presidential elections*: Absolute majority system. Absolute majority is required in the first round; if no candidate achieves the required majority, a run-off election is held between the two top finishers of the first round.
- *elections to the National Assembly*: Proportional representation system in multi-member constituencies of variable size. Technical elements (as applied in the 1998 elections): *Seven constituencies (constituency

sizes: 5, 5, 6, 6, 7, 13, 13 Members of Parliament to be elected in the respective constituencies). *Closed party lists at the constituency level. *Each voter has one vote (single vote). *Conversion of votes into seats in accordance with the d'Hondt method. There is no legal threshold.

1.4 Comment on the Electoral Statistics

Official election results as well as all laws and provisions are published (since 1836) in the fortnightly official gazette *Diário da República São Tomé e Príncipe* which remains the most important and also exhaustive source (although it is not easy to obtain outside of São Tomé and Príncipe). Electoral data are presented according to the official gazette, even where the given calculations are not strictly comprehensive. Invalid votes were calculated as a sum of blank and null votes. Valid votes do not figure in the official tables and were calculated as a sum of all votes distributed to candidates. Presidential elections include votes of São Tomé and Príncipe citizens abroad (Gabon, Angola, Portugal and Equatorial Guinea). Data for the 1998 parliamentary elections stem from the National Electoral Commission, as provided by the IFES Resource Center.

2. Tables

2.1 Dates of National Elections, Referendums and Coups d'Etat

Year	Presidential elections	Parliamentary elections	Elections for Constitutional Assembly	Referendums	Coups d'état
1990				22/08	
1991	03/03	20/01			
1994		19/02			
1995					15/08
1996	30/06 (1st) 21/07 (2nd)				
1998		12/11			

2.2 Electoral Body 1990–1998

Year	Type of election[a]	Population[b]	Registered voters		Votes cast		
			Total number	% pop.	Total number	% reg. voters	% pop.
1990	Ref	117,505	52,917	45.1	42,333	80.0	36.0
1991	Pa	117,505	51,610	43.9	39,605	76.7	33.7
1991	Pr[c]	117,505	52,618	44.8	32,523	60.0	27.7
1994	Pa	125,000	55,862	44.7	29,100	52.1	23.3
1996	Pr (1st)[c]	135,000	50,256	37.2	38,841	77.3	28.8
1996	Pr (2nd)[c]	135,000	49,606	36.7	39,024	78.7	28.9
1998	Pa	150,123	49,639	33.1	32,034	64.5	21.3

[a] Pa = Parliament; Pr = President; Ref = Referendum.
[b] Census of 04/08/1991: 117,505. Unofficial estimations for 1994, 1996 and 1998.
[c] Presidential elections include São Tomé and Príncipe citizens residing abroad.

2.3 Abbreviations

ADI	Ação Democrática Independente
AP	Aliança Popular
CODO	Coligação Democrática da Oposição
FDC	Frente Democrata Cristã
MLSTP	Movimento de Libertação de São Tomé e Príncipe
MLSTP-PSD	Movimento de Libertação de São Tomé e Príncipe—Parti Social Democrate
PCD-GR	Partido da Convergência Democrática—Grupa de Reflexão

General note: Full name of PPP and UNDP can not be given.

2.4 Electoral Participation of Parties and Alliances 1990–1998

Party / Alliance	Years	Elections contested	
		Presidential	Parliamentary
CODO	1991, 1994, 1998	0	3
FDC	1991, 1994, 1998	0	3
MLSTP-PSD	1991, 1994, 1996, 1998	1	3
PCD-GR	1991, 1994, 1996, 1998	1	3
ADI	1994, 1996, 1998	1	2
AP	1994, 1998	0	2
PPP	1998	0	1
UNDP	1998	0	1

2.5 Referendum 1990

1990	Total number	%
Registered voters	52,917	–
Votes cast	42,333	80.0
Invalid votes	2,381	5.6
Valid votes	39952	94.4
Yes	38,100	95.3
No	1,852	4.7

2.6 Elections to the Constitutional Assembly

Elections to the Constitutional Assembly have not been held.

2.7 Parliamentary Elections 1991–1998

Year	1991 Total number	%	1994 Total number	%	1998 Total number	%
Registered voters	51,610	–	55,862	–	49,639	–
Votes cast	39,605	77.1	29,100	52.1	32,034	64.5
Invalid votes	3,171	8.0	3,748	12.9	2,951	9.2
Valid votes	36,434	92.0	25,352	87.1	29,083	90.8
MLSTP-PSD	12,090	30.5	10,782	42.5	14,785	50.8
ADI	–	–	6,660	26.3	8,222	28.3
PCD-GR	21,535	54.4	6,235	24.6	4,667	16.0
CODO	2,071	5.2	1,152	4.5	483	1.7
AP	–	–	342	1.4	183	0.6
FDC	598	1.5	181	0.7	156	0.5
UNDP	–	–	–	–	363	1.2
PPP	–	–	–	–	334	1.1

2.7 a) Distribution of Votes per Electoral District

1991	Água Grande	Mé-Zóchi	Cantagalo	Lobata
Registered voters	17,003	17,075	4,754	4,573
Votes cast	13,980	10,880	4,197	3,970
Invalid votes	1,038	848	472	293
Valid votes	12,942	10,032	3,725	3,677
MLSTP-PSD	4,074	2,107	727	1,863
PCD-GR	7,866	7,350	2,707	1,622
CODO	729	472	229	149
FDC	273	103	62	43

1991 (continued)	Lembà	Pagué	Caué	Total
Registered voters	3,830	2,261	2,114	51,610
Votes cast	2,899	1,879	1,800	39,605
Invalid votes	247	133	180	3,171
Valid votes	2,552	1,746	1,620	36,294
MLSTP-PSD	1,006	1,333	980	12,090
PCD-GR	1,297	358	335	21,535
CODO	215	14	263	2,071
FDC	34	41	42	598

1994	Água Grande	Mé-Zóchi	Cantagalo	Lobata
Registered voters	19,032	17,843	5,297	4,908
Votes cast	9,482	7,439	3,484	3,080
Invalid votes	991	1,035	597	1912
Valid votes	8,491	6,406	2,887	2,721
MLSTP-PSD	3,584	2,184	797	1,422
ADI	2,339	1,956	922	768
PCD-GR	2,098	1,709	854	453
CODO	315	401	223	50
AP	115	110	59	20
FDC	40	46	32	8

1994 (continued)	Lembá	Pagué	Caué	Total
Registered voters	4,295	2,084	2,403	55,862
Votes cast	2,417	1,598	1,600	29,100
Invalid votes	357	170	141	2,748
Valid votes	2,060	1,428	1,359	25,352
MLSTP-PSD	1,169	965	661	10,782
ADI	421	98	156	6,660
PCD-GR	325	340	456	6,235
CODO	114	11	38	1,152
AP	21	8	9	342
FDC	10	6	39	181

2.8 Composition of Parliament 1991–1998

Year	1991		1994		1998	
	Seats	%	Seats	%	Seats	%
	55	100	55	100	55	100
MLSTP-PSD	21	38.2	27	49.0	31	56.4
PCD-GR	33	60.0	14	25.5	8	14.5
CODO	1	1.8	–	–	–	–
ADI	–	–	14	25.5	16	29.1

2.9 Presidential Elections 1991–1996

1991	Total number	%
Registered voters	52,618	–
Votes cast	32,523	60.0
Invalid votes	5,919	18.2
Valid votes	26,604	81.8
Miguel Trovoada (indep.)[a]	26,604	100.0

[a] Miguel Trovoada was supported by PCD-GR and CODO. The two other candidates listed on the election ballots, Afonso dos Santos (FDC) and João Vieiga Guadeloupe de Ceita (independent), withdrew two days before the elections. The MLSTP had publicly recommended abstention from the elections and did not field candidates.

1996 (1st round)	Total number	%
Registered voters	50,256	–
Votes cast	38,841	77.3
Invalid votes	1,764	4.5
Valid votes	37,082	95.5
Miguel Trovoada (indep.)[a]	15,344	41.4
Manuel Pinto da Costa (MLSTP-PSD)	13,627	37.7
Alda Bandeira (PCD-GR)	5,970	16.1
Carlos da Graça (indep.)[b]	1,973	5.3
Armindo Tomba	163	0.5

[a] Trovoada's candidacy was supported by ADI and CODO.

[b] Carlos da Graça is a member of the MLSTP-PSD, but his candidacy was not supported by his party.

1996 (2nd round)	Total number	%
Registered voters	49,606	–
Votes cast	39,024	78.7
Invalid votes	1,317	3.4
Valid votes	37,703	96.4
Miguel Trovoada (indep.)[a]	19,887	52.7
Manuel Pinto da Costa (MLSTP-PSD)	17,820	47.3

[a] Trovoada's candidacy was supported by ADI and-CODO.

2.9 a) Distribution of Votes per Electoral District

1991	Água Grande	Mé-Zóchi	Cantagalo	Lobata	Lembá	Pagué
Reg. voters	17,078	17,350	4,793	4,586	3,595	2,337
Votes cast	10,779	9,190	3,728	2,802	2,469	1,546
Invalid votes	1,907	1,110	492	685	435	849
Valid votes	8,872	8,080	3,236	2,117	2,034	697
M. Trovoada	8,872	8,080	3,236	2,117	2,034	697

1991 (continued)	Caué	Angola	Gabon	Portugal	Equatorial Guinea	Total
Reg. voters	2,107	1,293	660	369	–	54,168
Votes cast	1,688	73	196	52	–	32,523
Invalid votes	387	14	22	18	–	5,919
Valid votes	1,301	59	174	34	–	26,604
M. Trovoada	1,301	59	174	34	–	26,604

1996, 1st round	Água Grande	Mé-Zóchi	Cantagalo	Lobata	Lembá	Pagué
Reg. voters	20,034	12,663	4,120	3,989	3,145	1,835
Votes cast	14,342	10,369	3,325	3,445	2,719	1,642
Invalid votes	619	415	194	112	193	39
Valid votes	13,723	9,954	3,181	3,333	2,526	1,599
M. Trovoada	5,100	5,217	1,801	1,100	1,071	192
M. Pinto da Costa	5,264	2,680	679	1,598	992	1,003
A. Bandeira	2,543	1,627	527	424	217	344
C. da Graça	749	396	156	201	238	53
A. Tomba	67	34	18	10	8	7

1996, 1st round (continued)	Caué	Angola	Gabon	Portugal	Equatorial Guinea	Total
Reg. voters	2,012	439	959	967	93	50,256
Votes cast	1,705	184	733	243	84	38,841
Invalid votes	120	9	38	19	6	1,764
Valid votes	1,585	175	695	224	78	37,077
M. Trovoada	309	19	423	77	35	15,344
M. Pinto da Costa	957	108	209	94	42	13,627
A. Bandeira	195	41	9	42	1	5,970
C. da Graça	110	6	54	7	0	1,973
A. Tomba	14	1	0	4	0	163

1996, 2nd round	Água Grande	Mé-Zóchi	Cantagalo	Lobata	Lembá	Pagué
Reg. voters	19,362	12,659	4,136	3,950	3,147	1,833
Votes cast	14,657	10,351	3,338	3,435	2,745	1,620
Invalid votes	444	303	124	110	136	51
Valid votes	14,213	10,048	3,214	3,325	2,609	1,569
M. Trovoada	7,165	6,573	2,107	1,403	1,062	462
M. Pinto da Costa	7,048	3,475	1,107	1,922	1,547	1,107

1996, 2nd round (continued)	Caué	Angola	Gabon	Portugal	Equatorial Guinea	Total
Reg. voters	2,012	485	961	968	93	49,606
Votes cast	1,661	182	714	243	78	39,024
Invalid votes	95	3	22	20	9	1,317
Valid votes	1,566	179	692	223	69	37,707
M. Trovoada	447	44	475	102	47	19,887
M. Pinto da Costa	1,119	135	217	121	22	17,820

2.10 List of Power Holders 1975–1998

Head of State	Years	Remarks
Manuel Pinto da Costa	1975–1991	Elected and re-elected indirectly 1975, 1979, 1983, 1985.
Miguel Trovoada	1991–	Elected President; assumed office on 04/04/1991; re-elected 1996.

Head of Government	Years	Remarks
Miguel Trovoada	1975–1979	Named Prime Minister upon independence; dismissed in April 1979; arrested and accused of complicity in a coup attempt.
	1979–1987	The President assumed the function of Head of Government.
Celestino Rocha da Costa	1988–1991	Appointed by the President in January 1988 after the constitutional revision of 1987.
Daniel Lima dos Santos Daio (PCD-GR)	1991–1992	Elected by Parliament after the first direct parliamentary elections on 03/03/1991, dismissed by President citing 'institutional disloyalty' on 22/04/1992.
Norberto José d'Alva Costa Alegre (PCD-GR)	1992–1994	Named on 16/05/1992 and dismissed by the President citing 'institutional conflict' on 02/07/1994.
Evaristo do Espirito Santo Cavalho (PCD-GR)	1994	Named by the President on 02/07/1994; dismissed upon his subsequent expulsion from his party.
	1994	An interim government comprising eight ministers took office on 09/07/1994 pending legislative elections in October. No Prime Minister was appointed.
Carlos da Graça (MLSTP)	1994	Named after parliamentary elections on 25/10/1994; dismissed after 'Government of National Unity' failed on 30/12/1994.
Armindo Vaz d'Almeida (MLSTP)	1994–1996	Appointed to conciliate between MLSTP-PSD, ADI and CODO on 30/12/1994; dismissed after motion of no-confidence on 20/09/1996 pending in office as in a caretaker capacity.
Raúl Bragança Neto (MLSTP)	1996–	Appointed by decree in November 1996.

3. Bibliography

3.1. Official Sources

'Acta da Assamblea de apuramento geral da eleições legislativas'. *Diária de la República São Tomé e Príncipe*, 11/02/1991.

'Acta da Assamblea de apuramento geral as eleições presidenciais'. *Diária de la República São Tomé e Príncipe*, 27/03/1991.

'Acta da Assamblea de apuramento geral da eleição legislativa'. *Diária de la República São Tomé e Príncipe*, 02/10/1994.

'Acta da Assamblea de apuramento geral as eleições presidenciais'. *Diária de la República São Tomé e Príncipe*, 20/08/1996.

Constitução política. Aprovado pela Lei No. 7/90, São Tomé: Empresa de artes gráficas.

Government of São Tomé and Príncipe (1990). *Country Presentation*. United Nations Conference on the Least Developed Countries, Paris: 3–14/09/1990.

'Lei No. 11/90 Lei eleitoral'. *Diária de la República São Tomé e Príncipe*, 17–26/11/1990.

'Lei No. 8/90 Lei dos partidos políticos'. *Diária de la República São Tomé e Príncipe*, 21/09/1990.

'Lei No. 2/90 Lei do direito de sufrágio e do recenseamento eleitoral'. *Diária de la República São Tomé e Príncipe*, 14/05/1990.

'Lei No. 3/90 Lei do referendo'. *Diária de la República São Tomé e Príncipe*, 01/06/1990.

3.2 Books, Articles and Electoral Reports

A comprensão do processo democrático: seminário, 25 de novembro a 1 de dezembro 1992: patrocinado pelo Governo dos Estados Unidos. São Tomé e Príncipe: Centro Cultural Portugues, CPL Consultoria e projectos, LDA.

Barraza, H. V. (1979). 'Análisis histórico-político del estado en Africa: el caso der la República de São Tomé e Príncipe'. *Estudios del Tercer Mundo*, 2/1: 115–154.

Brito, P. (1988). *Um estudo sobre as relações economicas externas da República Democrática de São Tomé e Príncipe*. Lisboa: Fundação de Relações Internacionais, Tendências e Perspectivas das Relações Económicas entre Portugal e os PALOP.

Cahen, M. (1991). 'Vent des Iles. La victoire de l'opposition aux Iles du Cap-Vert et à São Tomé et Príncipe'. *Politique Africaine*, 43: 63–78.

Costa, M. P. da (1979). *Discursos.* São Tomé e Príncipe: Arquivo Histórico de São Tomé e Príncipe.

Da Cruz, C. B. (1975). *São Tomé e Príncipe. Do colonialismo á independência.* Lisbon: Moraes.

Clarence-Smith, G. (1985). *The Third Portuguese Empire 1825–1975. A Study in Economic Imperialism.* Manchester: Manchester UP.

Espirito Santo, C. (1979). *Contribução para a história de São Tomé e Príncipe.* Lisbon.

Gaye, A. (1996*a*). 'São Tomé et Príncipe: l'élection du 30 juin 1996 verra s'affronter le président sortant et son prédécesseur'. *Jeune Afrique,* 36/1846: 34–35.

— (1996*b*). 'São Tomé et Príncipe: Le bon exemple'. *Jeune Afrique,* 36/1856: 29

Hodges, T., and Newitt, M. (1988). *São Tomé and Príncipe: From Plantation Colony to Microstate.* Boulder, Col.: Westview Press

Kpatindé, F. (1993). 'São Tomé et Príncipe: Libertés et chrysanthèmes'. *Jeune Afrique,* 33/1701–1702: 30–31.

IMF (International Monetary Fund) (1986). *São Tomé and Príncipe, Staff Report for the 1986 Article IV Consultation.* Washington, D.C.: IMF.

Newitt, M. (1989). *On the Perils of Being a Microstate, Conference on the Political Economy of Small Tropical Islands.* University of Exeter, 05–07/09/1989.

Pélissier, R. (1979). *Le nauvrage des caravelles. Études sur la fin de l'empire portugais (1961–1975).* Montamets: Ed. Pélissier.

São Tomé and Príncipe 1970: A Brief Survey. Lisbon: Agência-general do ultramar

Sebastião, A. J. (1971). *Para um futuro melhor. Discursos e mensagens no governo de São Tomé e Príncipe 1963–67, 1967–71.* São Tomé e Príncipe: Cámera Municipal.

Schümer, M. (1987). *São Tomé und Príncipe: Ausbruch aus der Isolation.* Bonn: Europa-Union Verlag.

— (1992). 'Demokratisierung in São Tomé und Príncipe', in P. Meyns (ed.), *Demokratie und Strukturreformen im portugiesischsprachigen Afrika. Die Suche nach einem Neuanfang.* Freiburg: Arnold Bergstraesser Institut, 208–234.

— (1993). 'São Tomé und Príncipe', in D. Nohlen and F. Nuscheler (eds.), *Handbuch der Dritten Welt, Vol. 5, Westafrika und Zentralafrika* (3rd edn.). Bonn: Dietz, 473–487.

Seibert, G. (1991). 'Demokratische Transformation in São Tomé und Príncipe'. *DASP-Hefte,* 29.

— (1992). 'Strukturanpassung in São Tomé und Príncipe—Programme und Probleme', in P. Meyns (ed.), *Demokratie und Strukturreformen im portugiesischsprachigen Afrika. Die Suche nach einem Neuanfang.* Freiburg: Arnold Bergstraesser Institut, 189–207.

Separação de poderes o papel dos parlamentos na consolidação da democracia: Semiário de CPL Consultoria e Projectos. LDA in São Tomé and Príncipe from April 20 to 26, 1994.

Torp, J. E., Denny, L. M., and Ray, D. I. (1989). *Mozambique / São Tomé and Príncipe: Economics, Politics and Society*. London *et al.*: Pinter.

SENEGAL

by Petra Bendel*

1. Introduction

1.1 Historical Overview

For more than 30 years since independence in 1960, Senegal was considered one of the few stable regimes in Western Africa. Due to its electoral tradition, it even seemed to stand apart from most other African countries. However, Senegal was, in fact, long ruled by a one-party system. Multi-party competition was only allowed to exist from the 1980s onwards. However, most multi-party elections were characterized by violent incidents during the voting processes. Democratic legitimacy and public credibility of the political class remain important problems.

Senegal had a single-party system from 1966 to 1976. It was dominated by the *Union Progressiste Sénégalaise* (UPS) with its founder and leader, Léopold Sédar Senghor, who was re-elected four times as the Republic's President. According to the First Constitution (oriented on the example of the Constitution of the Fifth French Republic), the President was clearly superior to the Prime Minister. Only as the result of a power conflict between Senghor and his party-mate, Mamadou Dia, who was nominated as the first Prime Minister, was the constitution changed in 1962/63, providing a pure presidential system. In 1970, a referendum sanctioned the constitutional reintroduction of the Prime Minister (Abdou Diouf being the first Prime Minister), whose role, nevertheless, was lowered in comparison with the 1960 Constitution: Nominated by the President, he could be recalled both by Parliament and by the President. The President also maintained some central areas of policy (*domaines privilégiés*) as his own competencies, such as foreign policy and the formulation of his party's theory. The 1983 Constitutional Amendment abolished the post of the Prime Minister again, directly

---

* The author would like to thank the Friedrich Ebert Foundation's Representation in Dakar, Senegal, for helpful contribution on data research, kindly elaborated by Mr Moussa Sidi BA, Journalist.

subordinating the executive to the President and thus returning to a pure presidential system.

The predominant UPS had emerged from the strongest independence movement as an integrative political force, the *Bloc Démocratique Sénégalais* (BDS), which, based on the African values of *négritude,* had long campaigned for better living conditions for the population. It had, in fact, proved able to absorb or integrate the most influential regional and other small national political parties as well as the Socialist Party. Programmatically, it campaigned for a democratic African socialism, which integrated elements of Marxist theory without at the same time accepting an atheist approach. The UPS assured its dominance by introducing electoral provisions that practically either excluded opposition parties or did at least not allow them to win seats in the National Assembly. It also tried to co-opt opposition parties such as the *PRA-Sénégal,* offering them high political posts within the UPS. Although a certain pluralism was guaranteed, the UPS partly prohibited opposition parties (as, for instance, the *Parti Africain de l'Indépendance*, PAI, in 1960 and the *Front National Sénégalais*, FNS in 1964).

Opposition parties such as the *Parti Démocratique Sénégalais* (PDS), founded in 1974 by Abdoulaye Wade, were only recognized from the 1970s onwards. Through changes in the party law in 1975 and 1976 and constitutional amendments in 1976 and 1978, the foundation of three political parties was legalized. Those were supposed to represent the essential ideological currents such as liberal democratic, socialist democratic and Marxist–Leninist. As the UPS itself claimed the position of democratic socialism, the PDS had to 'choose' the liberal democratic role. In 1976, the UPS, renamed *Parti Socialiste* (PS), was accepted as the first African party in the Socialist International. The *Rassemblement National Démocratique* (RND), which refused to accept Marxist–Leninist ideology as the only position left to be represented, was therefore not recognized until 1981. In 1978, a Conservative Party was accepted. The same year, the opposition parties joined together around 18% of the vote cast.

After Senghor's voluntary retreat from the presidency in 1980/81, his Prime Minister and nominated successor, Abdou Diouf, further continued the democratic opening, allowing a multi-party system to emerge successively, this time without ideological restrictions (Constitutional Amendment of 24 April 1981). Only parties based on regional, ethnic or religious cleavages were not allowed. Although many parties have been created, up to date, only the PS and PDS have emerged as nationally important political forces and no change of government has as yet been achieved. Elections held in the 1980s (1983, 1988) were not wholly free and fair: Voting was partly public, since the use of polling booths was not obligatory, and thus strongly favored the ruling PS. Protesting against supposed electoral fraud and irregularities, opposition deputies at first refused to take over their parliamentary seats in 1983. Religious loyalties towards the governmental party from Muslim brotherhoods of the Mourides, the most powerful organization of the country, also strongly supported the PS. Although there had been rumors of a planned military coup at the end of the 1980s, the army proved loyal to the political leadership. Still, rebellions against the worsening living conditions and dissatisfaction with the ruling PS were repressed, and the opposition was accused of menacing national security. Negotiations between government and opposition, the integration of political opposition leaders into a newly formed cabinet in 1991, law and constitutional amendments eventually succeeded in calming down the manifestations of political and social unrest. Thus, the figure of a political mediator (*médiateur*) was created to arbitrate conflicts between society and the state, the parliamentary competencies were amplified, and parties' accession to the media was newly regulated. After the elaboration of a new, amply recognized Electoral Law (1992), which responded to the concerns of the political opposition parties who had long claimed that the electoral provisions had been open to fraud and partisan influence, secret presidential and parliamentary elections were held for the first time in 1993. The contest, which concentrated on two candidates only, Abdou Diouf (PS) and Abdoulaye Wade (PDS), was applauded by international observers as well developed, but still protested against by opposition parties which did not immediately acknowledge the election once more of President Diouf. Opposition parties also accused the ruling Socialist Party after the parliamentary elections of 1998, won again by the PS, of having committed massive fraud.

1.2 Evolution of Electoral Provisions

Universal suffrage was introduced in 1946, when the Senegalese population, still under French domination, elected four communes. Then already, Senegal could look back to a long tradition of electoral competition, which had culminated in 1914, when Blaise Diagne had become the first Black African deputy to the French National Assembly. Universal suffrage was provided, too, in the First Constitution of 1960. The President and the *Assemblée Nationale* were elected in universal and direct suffrage from 1963 on (Constitution of 1963). Voting age was of 21 years. In the multi-party elections of 1983, the use of the secret ballot was declared to be 'optional' (the voter could make use of a voting booth or *isoloir*), but rarely ever used. These regulations opened the possibility for voter intimidation.

According to the Constitution of 1960, the President was elected for a seven-year term (re-elections being allowed) by two thirds of the 'Congress', which was constituted (similar to the Fifth French Republic) of the *Assemblée Nationale* and one member of each regional and municipal assembly. If in the two first rounds the required majority could not be gained, he would be elected with absolute majority of the Congress members. In contrast to the Constitution of 1960, from 1963 on, the President was elected in general elections by absolute majority or, in the case that no candidate received an absolute majority, by relative majority in the second round for a four-year term. In 1970, the re-election of the President was reduced to one time of office. As this regulation became valid only in 1970, President Senghor was allowed to stand in 1973 and again in 1978 and could be in office until 1983.

According to the provisions of 1963, for presidential elections, a candidate who had completed at least 35 years, had to present the signatures of 50 registered voters, 10 of whom had to be deputies of the National Assembly. Since with the exception of one deputy all the deputies belonged to the UPS, the sole candidate could be Senghor. In 1967, it was sufficient to present either a nomination by an officially recognized political party *or* the 50 signatures of 50 registered voters, 10 of whom had to be deputies. From 1973 on, the candidate could be nominated also by any officially recognized party, but still had to show the 50 signatures including the 10 deputies' signatures.

The Party Law of 1975 (and additions of 6 April 1976) provided only for three official political parties, each of which had to 'opt for' a different ideology (liberal democratic, democratic socialism, Marxism–Leninism). Parties which departed too much from the chosen ideology, however, could be dissolved. That way, the executive had the final control over the parties. It was not until April 1981 that the law banning new political parties was abolished.

From 1963 on, deputies, elected for a four-year term (in 1960: at least five years) by universal and direct suffrage, as well as the President (from 1967 on: five years for both), could not be members of government. Since possible ministers also lanced candidacies, party lists included an additional list with 20 substitutes apart from the 80 regular candidates. This regulation was abolished in the constitutional reform of

1967. From then on, members of government could maintain their deputy; accordingly, the electoral law abolished the 20 replacement candidates on the reserve list. A modification of the *Loi organique* augmented the number of deputies from 80 to 100 in 1972 (and to 120 in 1988); also, the number of deputies re-nominated in 1972 was 35 out of the former 80 (1968: 52 out of 80).

As for the electoral system, the Electoral Law of 1963 created one sole national constituency instead of the several existing before, aiming at removing opportunities for regionally concentrated opposition parties (for instance in the Casamance), as well as at reducing the power of regional networks within the UPS. Instead of absolute majority in plural constituencies, it provided for a sole national list. The list that was victorious according to relative majority, would win all the seats in the National Assembly. Since 1977, seats were proportionally distributed under the three existing parties.

1.3 Current Electoral Provisions

Sources: Constitution of 1963, amended in 1991 and 1992 (Constitutional Acts No. 91-46 and No. 92-14, promulgated respectively on 6 October 1991 and 15 January 1992), Electoral Law of 1992 (laws No. 92-15 and 92-16, 7 February 1992, modified by laws No. 92-23 (30 May 1992), No. 92-55 and 92-56 (3 September 1992), No. 93-08 (21 April 1993), No. 93-09 (23 April 1993), No. 94-70 (22 August 1994), No. 96-08 (22 March 1996), No. 96-12 (19 August 1996), 96-16 and 96-17 (28 August 1996) and two further amendments of 2 March 1998; Decree No. 98-239 (12 March 1998). The Electoral Law of 1992, elaborated in several months of negotiations involving 15 out of 17 political parties, was the first one to be accepted by all parties since the introduction of a multi-party system. The Court of Appeals, in charge of overseeing the legality of electoral operations until 1993, was substituted in 1997 by the *Observatoire National des Elections* (O.N.E.L.) by Law No. 97-15 of 8 September 1997.

Elected national institutions: The President is elected directly for seven years (before: five years), re-election is not prohibited. The 140 deputies of the Parliament are elected for a five-year term. The electoral law provides that presidential and parliamentary elections must not take place the same day. No by-elections for Parliament are held.

Suffrage: Voting age was lowered to 18 years in 1992. The secret ballot is now mandatory. Voting is not compulsory. Soldiers and police officers do not vote. All Senegalese citizens living abroad have the right to vote, if at least 500 of them register with the Senegalese diplomatic representation of the respective country. Voting conditions for Senegalese citizens living abroad are laid down in Electoral Law No. 92-55 and have to be put in practice by decree.

Nomination of candidates: Presidential candidates have to be Senegalese citizens by birth and aged at least 35 years. Parliamentary candidates have to be at least 25 years old and Senegalese citizens for at least 10 years, double nationality being excluded. Soldiers, constables and police officers on active service are not eligible. Candidates have to deposit a caution provided for by law and reimbursed if the party or list receives at least one seat in the National Assembly.

Presidential and parliamentary candidates are nominated by legally recognized political parties and party coalitions. Independent candidature is allowed. Independents (and independent lists) have to present at least 10,000 signatures of registered voters in six (of the 10) regions (500 minimum per region) for presidential as well as for parliamentary nomination. Parties or independents lists do not have to nominate candidates in all constituencies. Parliamentary candidates have to decide if they are to be nominated in the departmental constituencies or on the national list.

Electoral system
- *presidential elections*: The President is elected in the first round by an absolute majority. (Until August 1998, the winning candidate had also to be supported by one-fourth of the total number of registered voters). If no candidate obtains the required majority, the second ballot is held on the Sunday following the first ballot. At the second ballot, a relative majority will suffice.
- *parliamentary elections*: 70 deputies (until 1998: 50) are elected by a plurality system in 30 constituencies under the department's jurisdiction. The number of deputies to be elected by department is set by decree (for the 1998 elections Decree No. 98-239) based on the respective demographic size of each department and varies between a maximum of five and a minimum of one (two five-member constituencies, eight three-member, 16 two-member and four single-member constituencies). In the 26 multi-member constituencies lists are closed. The remaining 70 deputies are elected by a proportional election system using the national

list. Hare quota system is applied, distribution of the remaining votes according to the method of the greatest remainder. There is no legal threshold. Only one ballot is used for both the election at departmental (plurality) and at national level (proportional representation). Every voter has one vote which is first used to determine the winner or winning list in the departmental constituency and subsequently to calculate the national quota.

1.4 Comment on the Electoral Statistics

Official results could be obtained for most of the elections. Where secondary literature had to be consulted, results differ slightly, but nevertheless do not change the outcome. Most data based on secondary literature follow Ziemer (1978 and 1983) with regard to the elections up to 1973. 1978 presidential election data are the officially announced final results as they were published in the *Journal Officiel* (1 March 1978). They differ slightly from those given by Ziemer (1983) and by Sidi (1997). 1978 parliamentary election data also refer to the official results. Slight variation with regard to regional results could not be resolved; they rely on *Le Soleil* (Dakar) as quoted by Ziemer (1983). Data for 1983 (also Nzouankeu 1983), 1988 (also Zuccarelli 1988) and 1993 (also Kanté 1994) are fundamentally based on Sidi (1997), whose data differ slightly from those given by Villalón (1994). Data for 1998 are drawn from the internet site of *Le Soleil* (Dakar) at *www.primature.sn/lesolei/lg_res_p.htm*. The data refer to the official results; slight variation with regard to regional results could not be resolved.

2. Tables

2.1 Dates of National Elections, Referendums and Coups d'Etat

Year	Presidential elections	Parliamentary elections	Elections for Constitutional Assembly	Referendums	Coups d'état
1958				28/09	
1959		22/03			
1963	01/12	01/12		03/03	
1968	25/02	25/02			
1970				22/02	
1973	28/01	28/01			
1978	26/02	26/02			
1983	27/02	27/02			
1988	28/02	28/02			
1993	21/02	09/05			
1998		25/05			

2.2 Electoral Body 1958–1998

Year	Type of election[a]	Population	Registered voters		Votes cast		
			Total number	% pop.	Total number	% reg. voters	% pop.
1958	Ref.	—	1,106,828	—	893,369	80.7	—
1959	Pa	2,648,000	1,107,057	41.8	824,229	74.5	31.1
1963	Ref	3,326,000	1,232,479	37.1	1,162,060	94.3	34.9
1963	Pr	3,326,000	1,339,679	40.3	1,156,059	86.2	34.8
1963	Pa	3,326,000	1,339,679	40.3	1,203,783	89.9	36.2
1968	Pr	3,685,000	1,306,791	35.5	1,237,431	94.6	33.6
1968	Pa	3,685,000	1,306,791	35.5	1,215,730	93.0	33.0
1970	Ref	—	1,329,701	—	1,266,381	99.0	—
1973	Pr	4,122,000	1,399,433	34.0	1,357,359	97.0	32.9
1973	Pa	4,122,000	1,399,433	34.0	1,356,099	96.9	32.9
1978	Pr	5,397,000	1,556,250	28.8	988,566	63.5	18.3
1978	Pa	5,397,000	1,556,250	28.8	974,825	62.6	18.1
1983	Pr/Pa	6,316,000	1,928,257	30.5	1,083,681	56.2	17.2
1988	Pr	7,101,000	1,932,269	27.2	1,135,501	58.8	16.0
1988	Pa	7,101,000	1,932,265	27.2	1,118,245	57.9	15.7
1993	Pr	8,152,000	2,549,699	31.3	1,312,154	51.5	16.1
1993	Pa	8,152,000	2,613,028	32.1	1,070,539	41.0	13.1
1998	Pa	—	3,180,857	—	1,234,274	38.8	—

[a] Pa = Parliament; Pr = President. Ref = Referendum.

2.3 Abbreviations

AJ/PADS	And Jëf / Parti Africain pour la Démocratie et le Socialisme
CDP-Garab-gi	Convention des Démocrates et des Patriotes / Garab-gi
DUS[a]	Défense de l'Unité Sénégalaise
FSD/BJ	Front pour le Socialisme et la Démocratie Benno Jubël
LD/MPT	Ligue Démocratique / Mouvement pour le Parti du Travail
MDP	Mouvement Démocratique Populaire
MRS	Mouvement Républicain Sénégalais
PAI	Parti Africain de l'Indépendance
PDS	Parti Démocratique Sénégalais
PDS/R	Parti Démocratique Sénégalais / Rénovation
PIT	Parti de l'Indépendance et du Travail
PLP	Parti pour la Libération du Peuple
PPS	Parti Populaire Sénégalais
PRA	Parti du Regroupement Africain
PS[b]	Parti Socialiste
RND	Rassemblement National Démocratique
UDS/R	Union Démocratique Sénégalaise / Rénovation
UPS[b]	Union Populaire Sénégalaise
URD	Union pour le Renouveau Démocratique

[a] Alliance including *PRA-Sénégal*, PAI and *Bloc des masses sénégalaises* (BMS).
[b] UPS changed name to PS in 1976.

2.4 Electoral Participation of Parties and Alliances 1959–1998

Party / Alliance	Years	Elections contested	
		Presidential	Parliamentary
PRA-Sénégal	1959, 1963	0	2
PSS	1959	0	1
(U)PS	1959, 1963, 1968, 1973, 1978, 1983, 1988, 1993, 1998	7	9
PAI	1978, 1983, 1988	1	3
PDS	1978, 1983, 1988, 1993, 1998	4	5
LD/MDT	1983, 1988, 1993, 1998	1	4
MDP	1983	1	1
PIT	1983, 1988, 1993,1998	0	4
PPS	1983	0	1
RND	1983, 1993, 1998	1	2

Party / Alliance	Years	Elections contested	
		Presidential	Parliamentary
PLP	1988	2	1
AJ/PADS	1993, 1998	1	1
CDP-Garabg-i	1993, 1998	1	1
Jappo Liggeeyal Senegal[a]	1993	0	1
UDS/R	1993, 1998	0	2
Action pour le Développement National	1998	0	1
Alliance Jëf-Jël-USD	1998	0	1
Bloc des Centristes Gaïndé	1998	0	1
FSD/BJ	1998	0	1
Mouvement pour le Socialisme et l'Unité	1998	0	1
MRS	1998	0	1
Parti Africain pour l'Indépendance des Masses	1998	0	1
Rassemblement Patriotique Sénégalais Jammi Rewmi	1998	0	1
Rassemblement pour le Progrès, la Justice et le Socialisme	1998	0	1
Union pour la Démocratie et le Fédéralisme/Mbooloo Mi	1998	0	1
URD	1998	0	1

[a] Electoral coalition formed by: *And-Jëf/ Parti Africain pour la démocratie et le socialisme*, CDP-Garab-gi, Indepedents of Mamadou Lô, and RND.

2.5 Referendums

Year	1958[a]	
	Total number	%
Registered voters	1,106,828	–
Votes cast	893,369	80.7
Invalid votes	2,527	0.3
Valid votes	890,842	99.7
Yes	869,061	97.6
No	21,781	2.4

[a] The 1958 Referendum approved the project of the French Constitution of the Fourth Republic, according to which the African colonies formed a state to be self-governed within the community.

Year	1963[a]		1970[b]	
	Total number	%	Total number	%
Registered voters	1,232,479	–	1,329,701	–
Votes cast	1,162,060	94.3	1,266,381	90.5
Invalid votes	634	0.1	1,488	0.2
Valid votes	1,161,426	99.9	1,262,122	99.7
Yes	1,155,077	99.5	1,261,580	100.0
No	6,349	0.5	542	0.0

[a] Constitution of the so-called 'Second Republic' (strong presidential system).

[b] Referendum for Constitutional Amendment (among others, introduction of the post of the Prime Minister). Low credibility of voter turnout and result. According to electoral observers, voter turnout was probably lower in reality than reported officially; cf. Ziemer (1978).

2.6 Elections for Constitutional Assembly

Elections for Constitutional Assembly have not been held.

2.7 Parliamentary Elections 1959–1998

Year	1959		1963	
	Total number	%	Total number	%
Registered voters	1,107,057	–	1,339,679	–
Votes cast	824,229	74.5	1,203,783	89.9
Invalid votes	1,417	0.2	1,488	0.2
Valid votes	822,812	99.8	1,202,294	99.8
UPS	682,365	83.0	1,132,518	94.2
PSS	99,332	12.1	–	–
PRA-Sénégal	40,270	4.9	–	–
DUS	–	–	69,773	5.8

Year	1968		1973[b]	
	Total number	%	Total number	%
Registered voters	1,306,791	–	1,399,433	–
Votes cast	1,215,730[a]	93.0[a]	1,356,099	96.9
Invalid votes	5,746	0.5	793	0.1
Valid votes	1,209,984	99.5	1,355,306	99.9
(U)PS	1,209,984	100.0	1,355,306	100.0

[a] According to electoral observers, voter turnout was probably lower in reality than officially reported; cf. Ziemer (1978).

[b] Data differ slightly between available secondary sources. Sidi (1997) gives the following data: Registered voters: 1,145,466; votes cast: 1,115,256; invalid votes: 218; valid votes: 1,115,038; UPS: 1,115,038. Data reported here follow Ziemer (1983).

Year	1978[a] Total number	%	1983[b] Total number	%
Registered voters	1,556,250	–	1,928,257	–
Votes cast	974,825	62.6	1,083,681	56.2
Invalid votes	7,344	0.8	4,511	0.4
Valid votes	967,481	99.2	1,079,170	99.6
(U)PS	790,799	81.7	862,713	75.9
PDS	172,948	17.9	150,785	14.0
PAI	3,734	0.4	3,269	0.3
RND	–	–	29,271	2.7
MDP	–	–	13,030	1.2
LD/MDT	–	–	12,053	1.1
PIT	–	–	5,910	0.6
PPS	–	–	2,139	0.2

[a] 1978 elections (first multi-party elections) harshly criticized by the PDS opposition.
[b] Electoral observers regarded fraud and electoral handicaps of the opposition to have enlarged the size of the PS majority, but did not change the result.

Year	1988[a] Total number	%	1993 Total number	%
Registered voters	1,932,269	–	2,613,028	–
Votes cast	1,118,245	57.9	1,070,539	41.0
Invalid votes	4,499	0.4	5,967	0.6
Valid votes	1,113,746	99.6	1,064,582	99.4
PS	794,559	71.0	602,171	56.6
PDS	275,532	24.6	321,585	30.2
Jappoo Ligeeyal Senegal	–	–	52,189[b]	4.9
LD/MDT	15,664	1.4	43,950	4.1
PLP	13,184	1.2	–	–
PIT	9,304	0.8	32,348	3.0
UDS/R	–	–	12,339	1.2
PDS/R	5,481	0.4	–	–

[a] Electoral observers regarded fraud and electoral handicaps of the opposition to have enlarged the size of the PS majority, but did not change the result.
[b] Author's calculation. Jappoo Ligeeyal Senegal, an electoral alliance, was dissolved shortly after the elections.

Year	1998[a]	
	Total number	%
Registered voters	3,180,857	
Votes cast	1,234,274	38.8
Invalid votes	13,845	1.1
Valid votes	1,220,429	98.0
PS	612,559	50.2
PDS	233,287	19.1
URD[b]	161,320	13.2
AJ/PADS	60,673	5.0
LD/MPT	48,097	3.9
CDP-Garab-gi	24,405	2.0
FSD/BJ	16,282	1.3
PDS/R	12,928	1.1
PIT	10,764	0.9
RND	8,171	0.7
Bloc des Centristes Gaïndé	7,468	0.6
Rassemblement Patriotique Sénégalais Jammi Rewmi	4,616	0.4
Mouvement pour le Socialisme et l'Unité	3,656	0.3
Mouvement Républicain Sénégalais	3,597	0.3
Parti Africain pour l'Indépendance des Masses	3,439	0.3
Rassemblement pour le Progrès, la Justice et le Socialisme	3,397	0.3
Action pour le Développement National	2,962	0.2
Union pour la Démocratie et le Fédéralisme / Mbooloo Mi	2,808	0.2

[a] Results only for national list and without votes cast from foreign embassies.
[b] According to some sources alliance Jëf-Jël/UDS.

2.7 a) Parliamentary Elections 1959: Regional Distribution of Votes

Absolute numbers	Cap-Vert	Thiès	Diourbel-Louga-Linguère	Bas-Sénégal-Podor-Matam	Tamba-counda-Bakel-Kédougou	Kaolack
Reg.voters	90,087	164,553	189,133	141,290	53,802	185,637
Votes cast	66,957	131,804	161,868	101,851	33,004	141,813
Invalid votes	1,079	148	146	203	113	96
Valid votes	65,878	131,656	161,722	101,648	32,891	141,717
UPS	59,124	107,751	150,586	75,748	26,876	117,124
PSS	5,348	23,905	11,136	23,329	6,015	23,899
PRA	1,316	–	–	2,247	–	660
Independents	90	–	–	–	–	–

[a] UPS presented candidates in seven constituencies, PSS in all the constituencies except in Ziguinchor, whereas PRA presented candidates only in four constituencies. Due to the electoral system, only UPS gained representation in the *Assemblée Nationale.*

Percentages	Cap-Vert	Thiès	Diourbel-Louga-Linguère	Bas-Sénégal-Podor-Matam	Tamba-counda-Bakel-Kédougou	Kaolack
Votes cast	73.3	80.1	85.5	72.0	61.3	76.4
Invalid votes	1.7	0.1	0.1	0.0	0.3	0.1
Valid votes	98.4	99.9	99.9	100	99.7	99.9
UPS	89.8	81.8	93.1	74.3	81.7	82.6
PSS	8.1	18.2	6.9	23.0	18.3	16.9
PRA	2.0	–	–	2.2	–	0.5
Independents	0.1	–	–	–	–	–

2.7 b) Parliamentary elections 1978: Regional Distribution of Votes

Absolute numbers	Registered voters	Votes cast	Valid votes	PS	PDS	PAI
Cap Vert	168,068	106,573	105,494	75,982	27,113	2,399
Casamance	245,217	168,923	168,261	145,745	22,224	292
Diourbel	163,331	105,490	104,836	83,919	20,826	91
Fleuve	152,391	970,238	97,048	91,740	5,262	46
Sénégal-Oriental	91,348	60,636	60,355	55,803	4,463	89
Sine-Saloum	341,691	203,852	202,582	155,171	47,254	157
Thiès	223,233	130,064	129,343	107,349	21,926	68
Louga	149,044	85,097	84,812	69,321	15,457	34
Total	1,534,323	957,773	952,731	785,030	164,525	3,176

Percentages					
	Votes cast	Valid votes	PS	PDS	PAI
Cap Vert	63.4	98.9	72.0	25.7	2.3
Casamance	68.9	99.6	87.0	13.0	0.0
Diourbel	64.6	99.4	80.0	19.9	0.0
Fleuve	63.8	99.8	94.5	5.4	0.0
Sénégal-Oriental	66.4	99.5	92.5	7.4	1.1
Sine-Saloum	59.7	99.4	76.6	23.3	0.1
Thiès	58.3	99.4	83.0	16.9	0.0
Louga	57.1	99.7	81.7	18.2	0.0
Total	62.4	99.5	82.5	17.3	0.3

2.8 Composition of Parliament 1963–1998

Year	1963		1968		1973		1978	
	Seats	%	Seats	%	Seats	%	Seats	%
	80	100	80	100	100	100	100	100
(U)PS	80	100	80	100	100	100	83	83
PDS	–	–	–	–	–	–	17	17

Year	1983[a]		1988		1993		1998	
	Seats	%	Seats	%	Seats	%	Seats	%
	120	100	120	100	120	100	140	100
PS	111	92.5	103	85.8	84	70.0	93	66.4
PDS	8	6.7	17	14.2	27	22.5	23	16.4
RND	1	0.8	–	–	–	–	1	0.7
Jappo Liggeeyal Sénégal[b]	–	–	–	–	3	2.5	–	–
LD/MPT	–	–	–	–	3	2.5	3	2.1
PIT	–	–	–	–	2	1.7	1	0.7
UPS/R	–	–	–	–	1	0.8	–	–
URD[c]	–	–	–	–	–	–	11	7.9
AJ/PADS	–	–	–	–	–	–	4	2.9
CDP-Garab-gi	–	–	–	–	–	–	1	0.7
PDS/R	–	–	–	–	–	–	1	0.7
FSD/BJ	–	–	–	–	–	–	1	0.7
Bloc Centr.	–	–	–	–	–	–	1	0.7

[a] The opposition refused to take their seats in the National Assembly in protest against election fraud.

[b] Electoral alliance, dissolved shortly after the elections.

[c] According to some sources: Jëf-Jël/UDS.

2.9 Presidential Elections 1963–1993

1963	Total number	%
Registered voters	1,339,679	–
Votes cast	1,156,059	86.2
Invalid votes	6,124	0.5
Valid votes	1,149,935	99.5
Léopold Sédar Senghor (UPS)	1,149,935	100.0

1968	Total number	%
Registered voters	1,306,791	–
Votes cast	1,237,431	94.6
Invalid votes	7,504	0.6
Valid votes	1,229,927	99.4
Léopold Sédar Senghor (UPS)	1,229,927	100.0

1973[a]	Total number	%
Registered voters	1,399,433	–
Votes cast	1,357,359	97.0
Invalid votes	303	0.0
Valid votes	1,357,056	100.0
Léopold Sédar Senghor (UPS)	1,357,056	100.0

[a] Data given by Sidi (1997) differ slightly: Registered voters: 1,049,614; votes cast: 1,024,514; invalid votes: 138; valid votes: 1,024,386; Senghor: 1,024,386.

1978	Total number	%
Registered voters	1,566,250	–
Votes cast	988,566	63.5
Invalid votes	6,234	0.4
Valid votes	982,332	99.4
Léopold Sédar Senghor (PS)	807,515	82.2
Abdoulaye Wade (PDS)	174,817	17.8

1983[a]	Total number	%
Registered voters	1,928,257	–
Votes cast	1,083,681	56.2
Invalid votes	4,511	0.5
Valid votes	1,079,170	99.5
Abdou Diouf (PS)	908,879	84.2
Abdoulaye Wade (PDS)	161,067	14.9
Mamadou Dia (MDP)	15,150	1.4
Oumar Wone (PPS)	2,145	0.2
Mahjmout Diop (PAI)	1,833	0.2

[a] The opposition protested against fraud and manipulation of vote tabulation process.

[b] RND did not present any presidential candidate nor did it support any other candidacy. LD/MPT supported Mamadou Dia, and PIT Abdoulaye Wade.

1988	Total number	%
Registered voters	1,932,269	–
Votes cast	1,135,501	58.8
Invalid votes	4,033	0.4
Valid votes	1,131,468	99.6
Abdou Diouf (PS)	826,301	73.2
Abdoulaye Wade (PDS)	291,869	25.8
Babacar Niang (PLP)	8,449	0.8
Landing Savané (Mouvement Révolutionnaire pour la Démocratie Nouvelle)	2,849	0.3

1993	Total number	%
Registered voters	2,549,699	–
Votes cast	1,312,154	51.5
Invalid votes	15,499[a]	1.2[a]
Valid votes	1,296,665	96.5
Abdou Diouf (PS)	757,311	58.4
Abdoulaye Wade (PDS)	415,295	32.0
Landing Savané (And-Jëf/Parti africain pour la démocratie et le socialisme)	37,787	2.9
Abdoulaye Bathily (LD/MPT)	31,279	2.4
Iba Der Thiam (CDP Garab-gi)	20,840	1.6
Madior Diouf (RND)	12,635	1.0
Mamadou Lô (Independent)	11,058	0.9
Babacar Niang (PLP)	10,450	0.8

[a] For the difference between votes cast and valid votes, there are 10 votes missing with respect to invalid votes.

2.9 a) Presidential Elections 1978: Regional Distribution of Votes

Absolute numbers	Registered voters	Votes Cast	Valid votes	Senghor	Wade
Cap Vert	168,068	108,369	106,658	75,249	31,409
Casamance	245,217	170,210	169,800	146,107	23,693
Diourbel	163,331	107,038	106,627	85,308	21,319
Fleuve	152,391	97,353	97,135	91,866	5,269
Sénégal-Oriental	91,348	58,179	58,018	54,351	3,667
Sine-Saloum	341,691	205,699	204,908	158,046	46,862
Thiès	223,233	129,803	129,110	107,623	21,487
Louga	149,044	85,391	85,094	69,618	15,476
Total	1,534,323	962,042	957,350	788,168	169,182

Percentages	Votes Cast	Valid votes	Senghor	Wade
Cap Vert	64.5	98.4	70.6	29.4
Casamance	69.4	99.8	86.0	14.1
Diourbel	65.5	99.6	80.0	20.0
Fleuve	63.9	99.8	94.6	5.4
Sénégal-Oriental	63.7	99.7	93.7	6.3
Sine-Saloum	60.2	99.6	77.1	22.9
Thiès	58.1	99.5	83.4	16.6
Louga	57.3	99.7	81.8	18.2
Total	62.7	99.5	82.3	17.7

2.10 List of Power Holders 1960–1998

Head of State	Years	Remarks
Léopold Sédar Senghor	1960–1981	Elected President on 5 September 1960 by an electoral college established by the constitution; re-elected in general elections in 1963 and 1968 (as the only candidate); retired on 01/01/1981 because of age.
Abdou Diouf	1981–	Former Prime Minister; nominated as Senghor's successor on 01/01/1981.The corresponding constitutional provision that allowed this accession to the presidency was crafted by Senghor himself. Diouf was re-elected in 1983, 1988 and 1993.

Head of Government	Years	Remarks
Mamadou Dia	1960–1962	Prime Minister. After a having been questioned by the National Assembly because of his authoritarian style of governance and having reduced the Parliament's competencies, conflicts over the legitimacy of the Prime Minister's acting between Senghor and Dia were decided by military intervention. Dia was imprisoned and in 1963 judged to lifelong imprisonment. The post of Prime Minister was abolished until 1970.
Abdou Diouf	1970–1980	Nominated as President on 01/01/1981. The post of the Prime Minister was finally abolished in 1983.

3. Bibliography

3.1 Official Sources

République du Senegal. Ministère de l'Interieur (1996). *Code Electoral.*

Lois No. 92-15 et 92-16 du 07 Février 1992 portant code électoral (Partie Legislative).

Decret No. 92-267 du 15 Février 1992 (Partie Réglementaire).

3.2 Books and Articles

Beck, L. (1997). 'Senegal's Patrimonial Democrats: Incremental Reform and Obstacles to the Consolidation of Democracy'. *Canadian Journal of African Studies*, 31: 1–31.

Collin, F. (1993). 'Les elections présidentielles du 21 février 1993 au Sénégal'. *Alternative Démocratique*, 7: 25–44.

Colvin, L. G. (1981). *Historical Dictionary of Senegal.* Metuchen, NJ: Scarecrow Press.

Coulon, C. (1988). Senegal. Development and Fragility of a Semi-Democracy, in L. Diamond, J. Linz and S. M. Lipset (eds.), *Democracy in Developing Countries: Africa*. Boulder, Col.: Lynne Rienner, 411–448.

Diouf, M. (1993). 'Senegal's February Elections: New Factors in the Political Arena'. *CODESRIA Bulletin*, 20: 4–7.

Fatton, R. Jr. (1987). *The Making of a Liberal Democracy: Senegal's Passive Revolution 1975–1985*. Boulder, Col.: Lynne Rienner.

Hayward, F. M., and Grovogui, S. N. (1987). 'Persistence and Change in Senegalese Electoral Processes', in F. M. Hayward (ed.), *Elections in Independent Africa*. Boulder, Col.: Westview.

Hesseling, G. (1985). *Histoire politique du Sénégal: Institutions, droit et société*. Paris: Karthala.

Kanté, B. (1994). 'Senegal's Empty Elections'. *Journal of Democracy*, 5/1: 96–108.

Mbodj, El H. (1992). 'La Democratie mulipartisane sénégalaise a la lumière du nouveau Code Electoral'. *Alternative Démocratique*, 6: 73–91.

Nzouankeu, J. M. (1983). *Les partis politiques sénégalais*. Dakar: Editions Clairafrique.

O'Brien, D. B. C. (1978). 'Senegal', in J. Dunn (ed.), *West African States: Failure and Promise. A Study in Comparative Politics*. Cambridge: Cambridge University Press, 173–188.

Sidi, M. (1997). *Données statistiques sur les elections au Senegal de 1959 à 1993*. Dakar: Fondation Friedrich Ebert- Dakar.

Stetter, E., and Voll, K. (1983). 'Stabilität und Legitimationskrise: Präsidentschafts- und Parlamentswahlen 1983 im Senegal'. *Afrika Spektrum*, 18/3: 241–255.

— (1988). 'Senegal: Mehrparteiensystem zwischen Bewährung und Krise. Präsidentschafts- und Parlamentswahlen 1988'. *Afrika Spektrum*, 23/1: 43–53.

Vengroff, R. (1998). 'The Impact of Electoral Reform at the Local Level in Africa: the Case of Senegal's 1996 Local Elections'. *Electoral Studies*, 17/4: 463–482.

— and Creevey, L. (1997). 'Senegal: the Evolution of a Semi-Democracy', in J. Clark and D. Gardinier (eds.), *Political Reform in Francophone Africa*. Boulder, Col.: Westview, 204–222.

Villalón, L. A. (1994). 'Democratizing a (Quasi) Democracy: The Senegalese Elections of 1993'. *African Affairs*, 93: 163–193.

Weiß, M., Stetter, E., and Voll, K. (1983). *Senegal. Mehrparteiensystem und Wahlen 1983*. Hamburg: Institut für Afrika-Kunde.

Young, C., and Kanté, B. (1992). 'Governance. Democracy and the 1988 Senegalese Elections', in G. Hyden and M. Bratton (eds.), *Governance and Democracy in Africa*. Boulder, Col.: Lynne Rienner.

Ziemer, K. (1978). 'Senegal', in D. Sternberger, B. Vogel, D. Nohlen and K. Landfried (eds.), *Die Wahl der Parlamente und anderer Staatsorgane. Band II: Politische Organisation und Repräsentation in Afrika,* by Franz Nuscheler, Klaus Ziemer *et al.*, Berlin/ New York: Walter de Gruyter, 1809–1870.

— (1983). *Demokratisierung in Westafrika?* Paderborn: Schöningh.

Zuccarelli, F. (1988). *La vie politique sénégalaise (1940–1988)*. Paris: CHEAM.

SEYCHELLES

by Bernhard Thibaut*

1. Introduction

1.1 Historical Overview

Elections under conditions of universal suffrage have been held in the Seychelles almost regularly since the late 1960s, but from 1979 until the early 1990s all elections had a non-, or, at best, semi-competitive character. Between 1991 and 1993 the Seychelles experienced a relatively smooth transition from a single-party regime to a multi-party democracy within which, however, the former official party, the Seychelles People's Progressive Front (SPPF) of President France A. René maintained a dominant or even hegemonic political position.

The Seychelles became part of the British Empire in 1814 and a crown colony in 1903. Until the 1960s there were no significant demands for political self-determination but in the larger context of the African movement towards independence this became an issue of growing importance. In 1964, within two weeks, two parties were organized that took different positions on how to define the relations to the colonial power for the future. The Seychelles People's Unity Party (SPUP), founded by René, demanded social reforms and full independence whereas the Seychelles Democratic Party (SDP) of James R. Mancham, representing the interests of the land owner and commercial establishment, wanted to maintain close ties with Britain and achieve for the Seychelles a similar legal status to that of the Canal islands (a proposition that was soon rejected by Britain).

All three elections held with the participation of both parties before independence (1967: Governing Council, 1970 and 1974: Legislative Council) were won by the SDP. Mainly due to the inherited plurality system, in 1970 and 1974 the SDP's vote-share of 52.8% and 52.4% (against the SPUP's 44.1% and 47.6%) was transformed into a hegemonic parliamentary majority with 10 of 15 elected seats in 1970 and 13 of 15 seats in 1974. At a conference held in London in January 1975 in

* Many thanks to Sonja Horchler for her assistance in the preparation of this chapter.

order to lay down constitutional rules within the independence process SDP and SPUP agreed to soften the existing imbalances of representation. In addition to the elected members of the Legislative Council 10 new members were appointed, five upon nomination of the Chief Minister (Mancham) and five upon nomination of the leader of the opposition (René). Shortly after the conference the two parties built a coalition government. Since third parties hardly had a chance of significant electoral success a stable arrangement of power sharing seemed to have emerged. A second conference in January 1976 scheduled the decolonization process. On the basis of a constitutional compromise between the SDP and the SPUP the Seychelles became an independent republic with a semi-presidential system of government on 28 June 1976. For a transitional period that was foreseen to last until the holding of new elections in 1979 the coalition government was prolonged with Mancham as President of the Republic and René as Prime Minister.

The consociational politics that had characterized the independence process lasted only one year. On 4 June 1977, when Mancham was abroad to participate in the Commonwealth Conference in London, supporters of the SPUP staged an armed coup d'état and René took the presidency. In June 1979 the SPUP was renamed the Seychelles People's Progressive Front (SPPF) and declared the only legal party under the new Constitution of 5 June 1979. Though adherent to a rhetoric of socialist transformation of the social and economic system René followed a rather pragmatic political course in order to secure foreign investment in the tourism industry which had become the main source of economic growth since the early 1970s. Presidential elections were held in 1979, 1984 and 1989 with René as the only candidate and the parliamentary elections of 1979, 1983 and 1987 took place under conditions of limited competition within the SPPF. Low rates of voter turnout indicated, however, that the single-party system relied more on passive toleration than on active support.

The wave of regime changes in Africa in the aftermath of the breakdown of communism in the Soviet Union and Eastern Europe also reached the Seychelles. Already in 1989 some leaders of the SPPF (e.g. J. Michel, Minister of Finance) were openly considering the merits of multi-partyism, not least in order to alleviate public identification of the party with the state apparatus that was criticized as a source of bureaucratization and corruption. During 1990 and most of 1991 President René rejected any demands to allow for multi-party elections. Instead, he announced that internal processes of decision making and nomination of candidates for public office would be made more transparent and democratic, administrative reforms would be introduced, and called for a constitutional referendum. However, this proved not to be sufficient to keep control over the opposition movement, which gained strength not only within the Seychelles, where the demands for free elections were supported by leaders of the Anglican and Catholic Churches and by some prominent SPPF dissidents, but also abroad, where exiled politicians such as Mancham and their organizations found increasing attention and support.

In the local elections of December 1991 more than 40% of the votes cast were blank ballots expressing dissatisfaction with the political status quo. Faced with this apparent loss of legitimacy René gave way to the growing internal and external pressure and on 3 December 1991 an Extraordinary Congress of the SPPF decided to introduce a multi-party system. Political parties were allowed to register from 27 January 1992 on, and in the following weeks seven opposition parties appeared on the political stage. Some of them were founded on the bases of rather personal career motives by former SPPF politicians (e.g. the *Mouvement Seychellois pour la Démocratie*—MSD, and the Seychelles Liberal Party—SLP), others had deeper historical roots, the most important one being the successor organization to the SDP, the Democratic Party (DP) of Mancham, who returned from exile in April 1992.

On 26 July 1992 the first multi-party elections since independence were held to form a 'Constitutional Commission' that would draft a new constitution. They took place under the presence of various international observer groups and were widely applauded as free and fair and well organized. The result was disappointing for the opposition, though, since the SPPF won an absolute majority of the votes and 14 of 22 seats. The DP with a vote-share of 33% turned out to be the only opposition party represented in the Commission. The country seemed to have returned to the same basic structures of political organization and representation (though with exchanged roles) that had existed before 1977. In spite of the fact that both parties announced that they would follow a course of political cooperation (*'cohabitation'*) they were not able to reconcile their positions with regard to the institutional structure to be established by the new constitution. Whereas the SPPF favored a presidential system, the DP preferred the mixed system of the Independence Constitution. Finally, the draft constitution was elaborated and adopted only by the representatives of the SPPF (on several occasions the DP members had left the Commission under protest) and was submitted to referendum on 15 November 1992. Unanimously rejected by all opposition parties the proposal failed to achieve the required majority of 60%. In January

1993 René and Mancham agreed on another joint effort to elaborate a constitution. The Constitutional Commission was once again set into notion open to consultation by social and political organizations. The final result of the negotiations that was presented to the public on 7 May reflected above all a consensus of the two parties represented in the Commission and was again rejected by the other opposition parties. However, the new constitution was approved by a majority of nearly 75% in a referendum held from 15 to 18 June 1993. In institutional terms it established a presidential system of government and a segmented electoral system for the parliamentary elections.

The general elections held on 25 July 1993—again evaluated as free and fair by international observer groups—confirmed the dominant position of the SPPF. President René was re-elected in the first round with 59.5% of the votes and the SPPF easily won an absolute majority in the parliamentary elections. Apart from the SPPF and the DP only the United Opposition (UO), an electoral alliance of the National Alliance Party (NAP), the *Parti Seselwa* (PS) and the Seychelles National Movement (SNM), had been able to present candidates. In the following years René's government combined majoritarian politics with cooperative decision making, searching for agreements above all with the DP in order not to feed possible perceptions that nothing had changed in the Seychelles. Substantial measures of economic liberalization and privatization were applied with the consent of both parties whereas the UO took the role of an advocate of social compensation and reform in favor of the lower classes. In the elections of 20 to 22 March 1998 René was re-elected with a two-thirds majority and the SPPF, favored by the segmented electoral system, gained 80% of the seats whereas the DP lost ground to the UO.

1.2 Evolution of Electoral Provisions

The first elections held under the conditions of universal, equal, direct and secret suffrage were the elections for the Governing Council (an organ with limited executive and legislative functions with eight half, its 15 members being elected) on 11–12 December 1967. All citizens with a minimum age of 21 who had registered as voters could cast their vote. Until that time illiterates were excluded from the suffrage. In 1979 the new constitution lowered the voting age from 21 to 18.

The 'Seychelles Order 1970' established a Legislative Assembly with 15 directly elected members (plus three members appointed by the

Governor himself) serving for a regular term of four years. Under the 'Seychelles Order 1975', which was to serve as an interim constitution for a transitional period that would last until 6 June 1979, the Parliament (House of Assembly) consisted of 15 legislators elected in 1974 and 10 appointed members (five to be nominated by the Prime Minister and five by the leader of the opposition). The 1970 and 1974 legislative elections were held in seven two-member constituencies and one single-member constituency and the plurality system was applied.

The Independence Constitution provided for direct election of all 25 members of the National Assembly as well as the direct election of the President. Eight of the 25 members of the National Assembly were to be elected in single-member districts under the plurality system, the other 17 seats would be distributed proportionally at the national level according to the Hare quota. The President was to be elected together with the members of the National Assembly on the same ballot (single vote). Every parliamentary candidate had to declare his support for one of the presidential candidates and the one with the highest number of supporters elected to Parliament would be declared winner of the presidential elections. Due to the coup of 4 June 1977 the provisions of the Independence Constitution were never applied.

Under the 1979 Constitution 23 members of the national Parliament ('Peoples Assembly') were to be elected for a term of four years in single-member districts by simple majority vote (two additional members were appointed by the President to represent migrant people of the outer islands). The parliamentary mandate was incompatible with the offices of President of the Republic and Minister of the Government. Candidates had to be qualified as voters and be nominated by the SPPF, the only legal party.

The President was to be directly elected for a term of five years (limit of three consecutive terms) with an absolute majority of the national vote. In the presidential elections of 1979, 1984 and 1989 René was the only candidate.

In the elections to the Constitutional Commission of July 1992 (regulated by Act 2, 1992) all residents with Seychellois identity older the 18 years were allowed to vote and to be nominated as members of the Commission. (Seychellois living abroad were thus excluded from active and passive suffrage.) Every party surpassing the legal threshold of 5% of the national vote was entitled to nominate one member of the Constitutional Commission (the number of seats had to be determined by the elections, between 20 and 25) for every 4% of the votes cast in its favor.

In the 1993 parliamentary elections 22 members of the National Assembly were elected in single-member constituencies. Another 11 seats were distributed at national level between the parties that had passed a legal threshold of 8%. The number of proportional members each party could nominate was determined according to the Hare–Niemeyer formula.

1.3 Current Electoral Provisions

Sources: Constitution of the Third Republic of Seychelles of 18 June 1993 with amendments until 1 August 1996; Elections Act, 1995; Elections (Amendment) Act, 1996 (Act 19 of 1996).

Suffrage: The principles of universal, equal, direct and secret suffrage are applied. All Seychellois citizens aged a minimum of 18 years who are registered as voters and live in the country are entitled to vote.

Elected national institutions: President of the Republic for a term of five years with three consecutive re-elections being allowed (the Vice-President is assigned by the President); 34 members of the National Assembly elected for a five-year term.

Nomination of candidates
- *presidential elections*: A candidate must be a citizen of the Seychelles and must not be disqualified from registration as a voter. Candidates must be supported by a certain number of registered voters and they must deposit a certain sum of money with the Electoral Commissioner. Both the numbers of supporters and the sum of money to be deposited have to be fixed by the Electoral Commissioner at least 21 days prior to the election. The deposited sum is reimbursed only to candidates who receive more than 5% of the votes cast in the elections.
- *parliamentary elections*: Candidates have to be registered voters and may not perform any official function in connection with the conduct of the elections nor for the compilation or revision of an electoral register for the respective election. Independent candidacy is possible.

Electoral system
- *presidential elections*: Absolute majority system. If in the first round no candidate receives more than 50% of the votes cast, a second round is being held within not less than seven days and not more than 14 days after the first ballot. In this round the two strongest candidates of the first round can run. A third candidate is allowed if one candidate receives the highest number of votes and two, equally, the second highest number.
- *parliamentary elections*: Segmented system; 25 members of the National Assembly are elected in single-member districts by plurality vote (by-elections are held within 30 days after a seat has become vacant). A maximum of 10 additional seats is distributed at national level between the parties that have passed a legal threshold of 10% of the national vote. For the distribution of seats the Hare quota is applied, resting seats are not filled.

1.4 Comment on the Electoral Statistics

Elections that were hold before independence are documented in Nuscheler (1978). For the non-competitive elections under the single-party-system period between 1979 and 1991 detailed results are not reported in the secondary literature nor are official reports available. For these elections the statistical data reported below stem from periodical issues of the *African Research Bulletin* and of *African Contemporary Records*. In contrast, the elections that were held after the return to the multi-party system are very well documented. Results of the parliamentary and presidential elections of 1993 and 1998 have been published by the independent Electoral Commissioner of the Republic of Seychelles. Moreover, the reports of the Commonwealth Observer Group on the elections for the Constitutional Commission of 1992 and on the general elections of 1993 provide detailed election results that are consistent with the respective publications of the Electoral Commissioner. Some minor internal inconsistencies—e.g. the number of registered voters differs between aggregated data and the sum of the numbers for electoral districts—could not be clarified but do not indicate unreliability of the data.

2. Tables

2.1 Dates of National Elections, Referendums and Coups d'Etat

Year	Presidential elections	Parliamentary elections	Elections for Constitutional Assembly	Referendums	Coups d'état
1974		25/04[a]			
1977					05/06
1979	27/06	27/06			
1983		07/08			
1984	xx/06				
1987		06/12			
1989	12/06				
1992			26/07	12–15/11	
1993	23/07	23/07		15–18/06	
1998	22/03	22/03			

[a] Elections for Legislative Assembly (pre-independence).

2.2 Electoral Body 1974–1998

Year	Type of election[a]	Population	Registered voters		Votes cast		
			Total number	% pop.	Total number	% reg. voters	% pop.
1974	TA	58,000	—	—	41,822[a]	84.0	72.1
1979	Pr	62,000	—	—	29,931	—	48.3
1983	Pa	64,000	34,908	54.5	20,705	59.3	32.4
1984	Pr	65,000	—	—	—	—	—
1987	Pa	66,000	43,051	65.2	28,410	66.0	43.0
1989	Pr	67,000	—	—	—	91.0	—
1992	CA	69,000	49,975	72.4	42,648	85.3	61.8
1992	Ref	69,000	—	—	—	—	—
1993	Ref	70,000	—	—	—	—	—
1993	Pa	70,000	50,370	72.0	43,579	86.5	62.3
1993	Pr	70,000	50,370	72.0	43,584	86.5	62.3
1998	Pa	78,000[c]	54,847	70.3	47,563	86.7	61.0
1998	Pr	78,000[c]	54,847	70.3	47,550	86.7	61.0

[a] CA = Constitutional Assembly; Pa = Parliament; Pr = President; Ref = Referendum; TA = Territorial Assembly.

[b] Valid votes.

[c] Estimate at July 1997.

2.3 Abbreviations

DP[a]	Democratic Party
MSD	Mouvement Seychellois pour la Démocratie
NAP	National Alliance Party
PS	Parti Seselwa
SCD	Seychelles Christian Democrats
SDP	Seychelles Democratic Party
SLP	Seychelles Liberal Party
SNM	Seychellois National Movement
SPPF[b]	Seychelles People's Progressive Front
SPUP[b]	Seychelles People's Unity Party
UO[c]	United Opposition

[a] Successor of SDP.
[b] In 1978 the SPUP was renamed SPPF.
[c] Alliance of NAP, PS and SNM.

2.4 Electoral Participation of Parties and Alliances 1974–1998

Party / Alliance	Years	Elections contested	
		Presidential	Parliamentary
SDP	1974	0	1
SPUP	1974	0	1
SPPF	1983, 1984, 1987, 1989, 1993, 1998	4	4
DP	1993, 1998	2	2
UO	1993, 1998	2	2
MSD	1993, 1998	0	2[a]
SLP	1993, 1998	0	2[a]

[a] Electoral alliance with the DP.

2.5 Referendums

Year	1992[a]		1993[b]	
	Total number	%	Total number	%
Registered voters	—	–	—	–
Votes cast	—	—	—	—
Invalid votes	—	—	—	—
Valid votes	—	—	—	—
Yes	—	53.7	—	73.9
No	—	44.6	—	24.1

[a] Proposal of a new constitution. The proposal was rejected because the number of Yes votes remained below the necessary quorum of 60%.
[b] Approval of the new constitution.

2.6 Elections for Constitutional Assembly

1992	Votes		Seats	
	Total number	%	Total (22)	%
Registered voters	49,975			
Votes cast	42,648	85.3		
Invalid votes	623	1.5		
Valid votes	42,025	98.5		
SPPF	24,538	58.4	14	63.6
DP	14,150	33.7	8	36.4
PS	1,829	4.4	–	–
NAP	672	1.6	–	–
MSD	322	0.8	–	–
SNM	259	0.6	–	–
SLP	201	0.5	–	–
SCD	54	0.1	–	–

2.7 Parliamentary Elections 1974–1998

Year	1974		1979	
	Total number	%	Total number	%
Registered voters	—	–	—	–
Votes cast	—	—	27,920	96.4
Invalid votes	—	—	—	—
Valid votes	41,822	—	—	—
SDP	21,902	52.4	—	–
SPUP	19,920	47.6	—	–
SPPF	–	–	—	98.0

The parliamentary elections of 1979, 1983 and 1987 were not competitive. Only the SPPF was allowed to present candidates. In 1983 candidates had to obtain at least 20% of the votes in local district primaries to be nominated. Thirty candidates ran in the elections, 17 of them unopposed. In 1987 there were 36 candidates and 10 constituencies were uncontested. For data on electoral participation see table 2.2.

Year	1993		1998	
	Total number	%	Total number	%
Registered voters	50,370	–	54,847	–
Votes cast	43,579	86.5	47,563	86.7
Invalid votes	713	1.6	1,205	2.5
Valid votes	42,866	98.4	46,363	97.5
SPPF	24,642	56.6	28,610	61.7
DP (alliance with MSD and SLP)	14,062	32.3	5,069	12.1
UO	4,163	9.7	12,084	26.1

2.8 Composition of Parliament 1974–1998

Year	1974		1979		1983		1987	
	Seats	%	Seats	%	Seats	%	Seats	%
	15	100	25[a]	100	25[a]	100	25[a]	100
SDP	13	86.7	–	–	–	–	–	–
SPUP	2	13.3	–	–	–	–	–	–
SPPF	–	–	25	100	25[b]	100	25[c]	100

[a] Elected: 23, appointed by the President: 2.
[b] 17 seats were won uncontested.
[c] 10 seats were won uncontested.

Year	1993		1998	
	Seats	%	Seats	%
	33	100	34	100
SPPF	27[a]	81.8	30[c]	88.2
DP	5[b]	15.2	1	2.9
UO	1	3.0	3[d]	8.8

[a] Directly elected: 22.
[b] Directly elected: 1.
[c] Directly elected: 24.
[d] Directly elected: 1.

2.9 Presidential Elections 1979–1998

In 1979, 1984 and 1989 René was elected President in non-competitive elections. On all occasions he was the only candidate presented to the electorate and obtained, according to official statements, 98%, 92.6% and 86% of the valid votes. For data on electoral participation see table 2.2.

1993	Total number	%
Registered voters	50,370	–
Votes cast	43,584	86.9
Invalid votes	513	1.2
Valid votes	43,071	98.8
France A. René (SPPF)	25,627	58.8
James R. Mancham (DP)	15,815	36.3
P. J. R. Boullé (UO)	1,631	3.7

1998	Total number	%
Registered voters	56,409	–
Votes cast	47,550	84.3
Invalid votes	977	2.1
Valid votes	46,573	97.9
France A. René (SPPS)	31,048	66.7
Wavel Ramkawalan (UO)	9,098	19.5
James R. Mancham (DP)	6,427	13.8

2.10 List of Power Holders 1976–1998

Head of State	Years	Remarks
James Mancham	1976–1977	First President of the Independent Republic of the Seychelles on 18/06/1976; ousted by coup d'état on 04/06/1977.
France A. René	1977–	Assumed the presidency as a consequence of the coup staged by armed supporters of the SPUP; constitutionally elected in non-competitive elections in 1979, 1984 and 1989; after the return to a multi-party system in 1991 he was re-elected in competitive elections in 1993 and 1998.

Head of Government	Years	Remarks
France A. René	1976–1979	Prime Minister of the independence coalition government of SDP and SPUP that came to an end with the coup of 1977. The Constitution of 1979 abolished the institution of Prime Minister.

3. Bibliography

3.1. Official Sources

Constitution of the Republic of Seychelles. *Supplement to Official Gazette*, 21 June 1993, 285–445.

Constitution of the Republic of Seychelles (First Amendment) Act, 1994. *Supplement to Official Gazette*, 11 July 1994, 33–40.

Constitution of the Republic of Seychelles (Second Amendment) Act, 1995. *Supplement to Official Gazette*, 20 March 1995, 83–274.

Constitution of the Republic of Seychelles (Fourth Amendment) Act, 1996. *Supplement to Official Gazette*, 1 August 1996, 141–157.

Elections Act, 1996. *Supplement to Official Gazette*, 20 November 1996, 209–265.

Elections (Amendment) Act, 1996 (Act. No. 19 of 1996). *Supplement to Official Gazette*, 2 December 1996, 189–199.

Political Parties (Registration and Regulation) Act, 1991. *Supplement to Official Gazette*, 30 December 1991, 249–256.

3.2. Books, Articles and Electoral Reports

Bennet, G. B., and Bennet, P. R. (1993). *Seychelles*. Oxford: Clio Press.

Bulbeck, C. (1984). 'Socialism in the Seychelles'. *Australian Outlook,* 38/1: 40–44.

Commonwealth Secretariat (1992). *Elections to the Constitutional Commission in Seychelles*. The Report of the Commonwealth Observer Group.

Commonwealth Secretariat (1993). *The Presidential and National Assembly Elections in Seychelles, 20–23 July 1993*. The Report of the Commonwealth Observer Group.

Filliot, J. M. (1982). *Histoire des Seychelles*. Paris: Ministère des Relations Exterieures.

Franda, M. (1982). *The Seychelles: Unquiet Islands*. Boulder, Col: Westview.

Hatchard, J. (1993). 'Re-establishing a Multi-Party State: Some Constitutional Lessons from the Seychelles'. *Journal of Modern African Studies*, 31/4: 601–612.

Hofmeyer, R. (1993), 'Seychellen', in D. Nohlen and F. Nuscheler (eds.), *Handbuch der Dritten Welt. Vol.5: Ostafrika und Südafrika*. Bonn: Dietz, 273–288.

Leffler, U. (1988 ff.). 'Seychellen', in Institut für Afrika-Kunde and R. Hofmeyer (eds.), *Afrika Jahrbuch*. Opladen: Leske & Budrich (annually).

MacGregor, F. (1997). 'The Seychelles Experience'. *Parliamentarian,* 78/2: 331–333.

Mukonoweshuro, E. G. (1991). 'Radicalism and the Struggle for Affluence in the Seychelles'. *Scandinavian Journal of Development Alternatives,* 10/1–2: 139–171.

Nuscheler, F. (1978). 'Seychellen', in D. Sternberger, B. Vogel, D. Nohlen and K. Landfried (eds.), *Die Wahl der Parlamente und anderer Staatsorgane. Band II: Politische Organisation und Repräsentation in Afrika,* by Franz Nuscheler, Klaus Ziemer *et al.*, Berlin/ New York: Walter de Gruyter, 1871–1880.

SIERRA LEONE

by Andrew Reynolds

1. Introduction

1.1 Historical Overview

The West African nation of Sierra Leone has never had the opportunity to develop under a stable and safe political environment. As such, it joins Liberia as one of those West African 'basket cases' in which every step towards constitutional democracy is countered by three steps back towards authoritarianism and each new dawn for peace seems to be crushed by military leaders driven by greed and delusions of power. Since political independence from British colonial rule (27 April 1961) the citizens of Sierra Leone have endured five military coups which interrupted three separate experiments with multi-party democracy.

Settled by freed British slaves in the late 18th century, Sierra Leone remained under British colonial rule for over 150 years, from 1808 to 1961. As in neighboring Liberia the descendants of freed slaves, known as 'Creoles', enjoyed a special status throughout the colonial period. Competitive electoral politics were first ushered into the country through restricted pre-independence elections in 1951 for a Legislative Council, and in 1957 universal franchise elections were held. These multi-party elections, for a national House of Representatives, were won by the Sierra Leone People's Party (SLPP), led by Sir Milton Margai, which relied on a patronage network of chiefs and kinship ties for support. In 1957 the SLPP won almost two-thirds of the directly elected seats with 46% of the popular vote. As in many African nations preparing for independence in the 1950s Sierra Leone's first multi-party elections offered the hope that 'Westminster democracy' would flourish in Freetown in much the same way that it worked in other former British colonies (i.e. Canada, New Zealand, India and Australia).

After three years of SLPP rule a breakaway faction of the party, led by Siaka Stevens and other eminent Northerners, named itself the All-People's Congress (APC). The new party became the official opposition in the first post-independence elections of 1962. The SLPP won 28 seats in the 62-member Parliament in those elections with 35% of the vote while Stevens' APC took 16 seats and independents 14 seats. At this stage multi-party electoral politics was viewed as being rigorous and open, although not without worrying symptoms of authoritarian intolerance. Nevertheless, a robust and relatively independent judicial system meant that the Electoral Commission dealt severely with candidates whose supporters violated the electoral law.

SLPP Prime Minister Milton Margai was replaced upon his death in 1964 by his brother Albert Margai and a legislative attempt by the SLPP in 1965 to make the country a one-party state was defeated by negative popular reaction. The APC campaigned forcefully on the issue of political pluralism in the 1967 elections and, with 44% of the vote, 48% of the seats and the aid of sympathetic independent MPs, were able to build a governing majority in Parliament. This was perhaps the brightest day for electoral politics in the fledgling democracy. However, this democratic hand-over between government and opposition was short-lived as elements of the defeated SLPP conspired with the upper echelons of the army and police to oust Stevens from the position of Prime Minister only hours after his swearing in. Nevertheless, within a year a counter-coup had resulted in the return of Stevens at the head of an APC civilian-led government. In 1971 Stevens declared Sierra Leone a Republic, with himself as the first President.

From 1968 to 1973 political violence became increasingly endemic within the electoral process culminating in an attempt on the life of SLPP leader, Salia Jusu-Sheriff, which prompted the SLPP to withdraw from the 1973 general election, leaving the APC to dominate Parliament in the face of almost non-existent electoral competition. After 1968 'free and fair' elections became an increasingly fading memory in Sierra Leone. With the SLPP effectively driven underground, Stevens was the sole candidate in the 1976 presidential elections. However, the SLPP returned to the fray in 1977 and were able to win 15 seats in parliamentary elections even though the battle for votes was fought on a grossly uneven playing field. In 1978 the APC, perhaps pricked by the re-emergence of a parliamentary opposition, called a referendum on moving to a one-party state—in which a 'reported' 95% of the electorate supported Stevens bid for unopposed power. As a result, all non-APC MPs in Parliament were either forced to resign or join the ruling party.

Stevens was sworn in for a seven-year presidential term as leader of the new one-party state and in 1985 his nominated successor, Major-General Joseph Saidu Momoh, was returned unopposed to the presidency. Single-party elections in 1982 and 1986 were characterized by violence, voter apathy and allegations of widespread fraud but in 1991 President Momoh announced that Sierra Leone would return to multi-party competitive politics. It was at about the same time that the rebel Revolutionary United Front (RUF), under the leadership of former military officer Foday Sankoh intensified their attacks on government troops, villages and economic installations in the rural South and East. Nevertheless, Momoh pressed forward with democratization and a new constitution was approved by the electorate in 1991 with elections scheduled for May 1992.

However, before the May 1992 elections could take place Momoh himself was overthrown by junior army officers led by Valentine Strasser and the legislature was replaced with a 22-member National Provisional Ruling Council. Strasser incongruously stated that he too wished to step down in favor of a democratically elected civilian government and set January 1996 as the target date for the installation of a new government. Surprisingly, against the backdrop of an intensifying civil war, he followed the announced time-scale and presidential and parliamentary elections were scheduled for early 1996. Strasser never survived in office to resign as, on the eve of the elections, he was the victim of Sierra Leone's fourth military coup since independence. The coup leader's, Brigadier Maada Bio, justification was that Strasser wanted to manipulate the transition to remain in power and someone had to step in to allow the multi-party elections to be held as planned—and Bio did let the elections go ahead as planned in February–March 1996.

The first multi-party elections held in the country for nearly two decades were contested by 15 political parties led by 15 presidential candidates. Unlike previous elections they were conducted on the basis of a proportional representation system. Six parties won seats in the 80-member Parliament with no party gaining a majority. In the presidential elections no single candidate won the required 55% share of the vote in the first round. In the run-off Ahmad Tejan Kabbah (SLPP) secured the presidency against John Karefa-Smart (UNPP). The elections were certified as 'free and fair' and signaled a return to competitive multi-party politics which was warmly greeted by the Commonwealth and the West.

Sierra Leone's third experiment with multi-partyism proved to be even more fleeting than their first two experiences as the SLPP coalition government was overthrown by yet another military coup in May 1997. Major Johnny Paul Koroma led a group of 20 heavily armed men who forced Kabbah into exile in neighboring Guinea, rounded up Cabinet members of his civilian government, and clashed violently with the Nigerian troops lent to protect the presidential palace. The following month Koroma announced that he was forming a ruling alliance with Foday Sankoh and the RUF, but that he would return the country to democratic government within 18 months. Over the next four months civil order degenerated further with sporadic but intense fighting between Nigerian troops, forces loyal to President Kabbah and RUF militiamen. In October 1997 Koroma agreed to a West African peace plan which would reinstall Kabbah in power in April 1998 and guarantee immunity to the coup leaders. However, in February 1998, when Koroma appeared to be backing away from the deal, the Nigerian-led West African forces overwhelmed the force loyal to the military junta and thus paved the way for the return of President Kabbah on 10 March 1998.

1.2 Evolution of Electoral Provisions

Under British colonial rule pre-independence elections were held in 1951 for a Legislative Council on the basis of the plurality system. The franchise was restricted to property owners and tribal leaders. The principles of universal, equal, direct and secret suffrage began to be applied in the elections of 1957. The six multi-party legislative elections since 1957 have all been held on the basis of the plurality system in single-member constituencies with voting eligibility at age 18. The number of contested seats in the legislature has risen from 39 in 1957 to 80 in 1996. There remain 12 seats reserved for 'paramount chiefs' elected separately through a restricted franchise.

According to the Constitution of June 1978 the President was elected by members of the National Delegates' Conference of the single party (APC). In 1985 he was elected by popular vote. His term was seven years, his presidency being restricted to two consecutive terms. The minimum age for presidency was reduced by constitutional amendment in 1985 from 50 to 45 years.

1.3 Current Electoral Provisions

Sources: The Constitution of Sierra Leone, 1991; The Electoral Provisions (Consolidation) Decree, 1995; The Franchise and Electoral Registration (Consolidation) Decree, 1995.

Elected national institutions: President and Vice-President of the Republic and Parliament of Sierra Leone (80 members—68 ordinary members and 12 paramount chiefs). Regular term of office: five years respectively. Parliamentary and the first round of presidential elections are held on the same day, but with different votes and on different ballot papers. By-elections are held to fill vacancies which arise between general elections. A person shall hold office as President for not more than two terms of five years, whether or not these terms were consecutive.

Suffrage: The principles of universal, equal, direct and secret suffrage are applied for elections for the presidency and ordinary members of the Parliament of Sierra Leone. Every citizen who has reached the age of 18 has the right to vote and is entitled to be registered as a voter. The franchise for election of paramount chiefs is limited to: the Chiefdom Councillors' list which is comprised of paramount chiefs, section chiefs and section speakers, heads of villages, town chiefs and customary officials.

Nomination of candidates
- *presidential elections*: Every citizen aged 40 years or over who is eligible to be elected to office as a member of the Parliament is eligible for candidature as President, if he or she is a registered voter, nominated by a registered political party, and able to speak and read English. Vice-presidential candidates must fulfill the same requirements and are nominated by parties along with their presidential candidate.
- *parliamentary elections*: Every Sierra Leone citizen who has reached the age of 21 is eligible for candidature as an 'ordinary' member of the Parliament, if he or she is a registered voter, is a member of the political party submitting the list of candidates in question, and is proficient in spoken and written English. No persons may become Members of Parliament if they have allegiance to a foreign state, have a sentence of imprisonment exceeding 12 months, or have been disqualified from practicing a profession. Candidates for the 12 paramount chief seats must be 'substantive paramount chiefs'.

Electoral system
- *presidential elections*: Absolute majority system. The constitution provides that no person shall be elected as President unless he or she has received more than 55% of the votes cast. If no single candidate achieves the required majority on the first ballot, a second ballot shall be held, no more than 14 days after the announcement of the results from

the first ballot, between the top two candidates from the first round. The plurality winner in this election is deemed to be elected.

- *parliamentary elections*: Proportional representation system at the national level (pure PR system) for the 68 'ordinary' members. Technical elements: *National constituency (the 12 'constituencies' have only the function of polling districts). *Closed national party lists. *Single vote (for Parliament). *Hare quota with largest remainders. *A threshold of 5% is imposed before a party may be awarded seats (however, a 'rounding-up' principle applies for parties which have polled between 4.51% and 4.99% of the popular vote. The 12 paramount chief members are elected according to plurality system in single-member districts.

1.4 Comment on the Electoral Statistics

Primary source electoral data is notoriously difficult to find for Sierra Leone. A consequence of the country's troubled and turbulent history was that official records were rarely kept safely and distributed widely, if they were kept at all. The following electoral statistics should be treated as the best approximations of reality that we have, as they are drawn from secondary sources which occasionally disagree. While the reader should have confidence in the parliamentary seat totals, the party vote percentages may be slightly inaccurate. Data for 1957 is drawn from Cartwright (1970) and Scott (1960), data for 1962 and 1967 is from Cartwright (1970), Allen (1968) and Hayward and Kandeh (1987), for 1973 from Keesing's Contemporary Archives, for 1977 from Hayward and Kandeh (1987), and for 1996 from Riley (1996) and Keesing's Record of World Events.

2. Tables

2.1 Dates of National Elections, Referendums and Coups d'Etat

Year	Presidential elections	Parliamentary elections	Elections for Constitutional Assembly	Referendums	Coups d'état
1957		03/05[a]			
1962		25/05[b]			
1967		17/03[c]			23/03
1968					18/04
1973		11/05[d]			
1977		06/05			
1978				05–12/06	
1982		01/05			
1985	01/10				
1986		30/05			
1991				23–30/08	
1992					29/04
1996	26–27/02 (1st) 15/03 (2nd)	26–27/02			16/01
1997					25/05

[a] In some parts of the country elections were held on 8 May and 13 May 1957.
[b] Elections for the 62 directly elected seats were hold on 25 May 1962. The 12 paramount chiefs were elected on 23 May.
[c] Elections for the 66 directly elected seats took place on 17 March 1967. The 12 paramount chiefs were elected by the District Councils on 21 March.
[d] Chiefs were elected on 9 March 1973.

2.2 Electoral Body 1957–1996

Year	Type of election[a]	Population[b]	Registered voters		Votes cast		
			Total number	% pop.	Total number	% reg. voters	% pop.
1957	Pa	2,113,000	494,917	23.7	165,479	33.4	7.8
1962	Pa	2,180,000	—	—	663,674[c]	—	30.4
1967	Pa	2,439,000	—	—	622,650[c]	—	25.5
1973	Pa	2,815,000	—	—	—	—	—
1977	Pa	3,058,000	—	—	686,810	—	22.4
1978	Ref	3,124,000	2,235,004	71.5	2,215,646	99.1	70.9
1982	Pa	3,411,000	—	—	—	—	—
1985	Pr	3,515,812	—	—	2,784,591	—	79.2
1986	Pa	3,743,000	—	—	—	—	—
1991	Ref	4,243,000	—	—	—	—	—
1996	Pa[d]	4,613,000	1,500,000	32.5	750,858	50.1	16.3
1996	Pr (1st)	4,613,000	1,500,000	32.5	748,846	49.9	16.2
1996	Pr (2nd)	4,613,000	1,500,000	32.5	1,028,851[c]	68.6	22.3

[a] Pa = Parliament; Pr = President, Ref = Referendum.

[b] World Bank data as reported by Penn World Tables (www.datacentre.chass.utoronto.ca:5680); last census on 15 March 1985 (3,515,812).

[c] Valid votes.

[d] IDEA reports the following tallies (only for parliamentary elections): Registered voters: 1,244,601; votes cast: 746,764.

2.3 Abbreviations

APC	All People's Congress
CPP	Coalition for Progress Party
DCP	Democratic Center Party
KPM	Kono Progressive Movement
LP	Labour Party
NADP	National Alliance Democratic Party
NC	National Council
NDA	National Democratic Alliance
NPP	National Peoples Party
NRP	National Republican Party
NUM	National Unity Movement
NUP	National Unity Party
PDP	People's Democratic Party (Sorbeh)
PNC	People's National Convention
PNP	People's National Party
PPP	People's Progressive Party
SDP	Social Democratic Party

SLIM	Sierra Leone Independence Movement
SLPIM	Sierra Leone Progressive Independence Movement
SLPP	Sierra Leone People's Party
UNPP	United National Peoples Party
UPP	United Sierra Leone Progressive Party

2.4 Electoral Participation of Parties and Alliances 1957–1996

Party / Alliance	Years	Elections contested	
		Presidential	Parliamentary
KPM[a]	1957	0	1
LP	1957	0	1
NC	1957	0	1
SLIM	1957	0	1
SLPP	1957–1996	1	5
UPP	1957–1962	0	2
APC	1962–1996	3	5
SLPIM[a]	1962	0	1
CPP	1996	1	1
DCP	1996	1	1
NADP	1996	1	1
NDA	1996	1	1
NPP	1996	1	1
NRP	1996	1	1
NUM	1996	1	1
NUP	1996	1	1
PDP	1996	1	1
PNC	1996	1	1
PNP	1996	1	1
PPP	1996	1	1
SDP	1996	1	1
UNPP	1996	1	1

[a] Successor party of the KPM.

2.5 Referendum 1978

1978[a]	Total number	%
Registered voters	2,235,004	–
Votes cast	2,215,646	99.1
Invalid votes	—	—
Valid votes	2,215,646—	—
Yes	2,152,460	97.1
No	63,186	2.9

[a] Referendum on a one-party constitution.

No data are available for the constitutional referendum of August 1991. Reportedly 60% of the population approved the new multi-party constitution.

2.6 Elections for Constitutional Assembly

Elections for Constitutional Assembly have not been held.

2.7 Parliamentary Elections 1957–1996

Year	1957 Total number	%	1962 Total number	%
Registered voters	494,917	–	—	–
Votes cast	—	—	—	—
Invalid votes	—	—	—	—
Valid votes	165,479	33.4	663,674	—
SLPP	75,575	45.7	230,118	34.7
UPP	20,935	12.6	1,660	0.3
NC	2,984	1.8	–	–
LP	1,128	0.7	–	–
SLIM	1,126	0.7	–	–
APC	–	–	114,333	17.2
SLPIM			34,839	5.2
Independents	62,086	37.5	282,724	42.6

Year[a]	1967 Total number	%	1996 Total number	%
Registered voters	—	—	1,500,000	—
Votes cast	—	—	—	—
Invalid votes	—	—	—	—
Valid votes	622,650	—	750,858[b]	50.1
SLPP	230,999	37.1	269,888	35.9
APC	279,715	44.9	42,467	5.7
UNPP	–	–	165,219	22.0
PDP	–	–	114,429	15.2
NUP	–	–	39,285	5.2
DCP	–	–	35,632	4.8
Others	–	–	79,282	10.5
Independents	111,936	18.0	–	–

[a] No data were available for the 1973, 1977, 1982 and 1986 elections.
[b] The sum of votes distributed (746,202) is closer to the number of valid votes presented by IDEA (746,764).

2.8 Composition of Parliament 1957–1996

Year	1957 Seats	%	1962 Seats	%	1967 Seats	%	1973 Seats	%
	39	100	62	100	66	100	85	100
SLPP	24	61.5	28	45.2	28	42.4	–	–
UPP	5	12.8	–	–	–	–	–	–
APC	–	–	16	25.8	32	48.5	84	98.8
SLPIM	–	–	4	6.4	–	–	–	–
Independents	10	25.6	14	22.6	6	9.1	1	1.2

Year	1977 Seats	%	1982 Seats	%	1986 Seats	%	1996 Seats	%
	87	100	85	100	105	100	68	100
APC	72	82.8	85	100	105	100	5	7.3
SLPP	15	17.2	–	–	–	–	27	39.7
UNPP	–	–	–	–	–	–	17	25.0
PDP	–	–	–	–	–	–	12	17.6
NUP	–	–	–	–	–	–	4	5.9
DCP	–	–	–	–	–	–	3	4.4

2.9 Presidential Elections 1985–1996

1985	Total number	%
Registered voters	—	–
Votes cast	—	—
Invalid votes	—	—
Valid votes	2,784,591	—
Joseph Saidu Momoh	2,780,495	99.9
Opposing votes	4,096	0.1

1996 (first round)	Total number	%
Registered voters	1,500,000	–
Votes cast	748,846	—
Invalid votes	—	—
Valid votes	741,586[a]	—
Ahmad Tejan Kabbah (SLPP)	266,893	35.8
John Karefa Smart (UNPP)	168,666	22.6
Thaimu Bangura (PDP)	119,782	16.1
John Karimu (NUP)	39,617	5.3
Edward Mohammed Turay (APC)	38,316	5.1
Adu Aiah Koroma (DCP)	36,779	4.9
Abass Chernon Bundu (PPP)	21,557	3.5
Amandu M.B. Jalloh (NDA)	17,335	2.3
Edward John Kargbo (PNC)	15,798	2.1
Desmond Luke (NUM)	7,918	1.1
Andrew Victor Lungay (SDP)	5,202	0.7
Mohamed Yahya Sillah (NADP)	3,723	0.5

[a] Sum of votes for candidates (author's calculation).

1996 (second round)	Total number	%
Registered voters	1,500,000	–
Votes cast	—	—
Invalid votes	—	—
Valid votes	1,028,851	—
Alhaji Ahmad Tejan Kabbah (SLPP)	612,166	59.5
John Karefa-Smart (UNPP)	416,685	40.5

2.10 List of Power Holders 1957–1998

Head of Government	Years	Remarks
Sir Milton Margai	1957–1964	Prime Minister; died on 28/04/1964.
Sir Albert Margai	1964–1967	Prime Minister.
Siaka Probyn Stevens	1967	Appointed Prime Minister by the General Governor on 21/03/1967; overthrown by a coup d'état on 23/03/1967.
National Reformation Council	1967–1968	The NRC, led by Col. Andrew Juxon-Smith, was overthrown by another coup d'état in April 1968.
National Interim Council	1968	The NIC, led by Col. John Bangura, took power after the coup of April 1968.
Siaka Probyn Stevens	1968–1971	Re-appointed Prime Minister by the NIC on 26/04/1968.

Head of State and Government	Years	Remarks
Saika Probyn Stevens	1971–1985	Elected President of the Republic by the Parliament after the proclamation of the Republic of Sierra Leone on 21/04/1971; re-elected by Parliament on 26/03/1976; on the basis of a new constitution, which provided a single-party system sworn in as President for a seven-year period on 14/06/1978.
Joseph Saidu Momoh	1985–1992	Elected President in non-competitive elections of 1985; sworn in on 28/11/1985; ousted by a military coup on 29/04/1992.
Valentine Strasser	1992–1996	Head of the National Provisional Ruling Council after the military coup of 29/04/1992; sworn in as President of the Republic on 06/05/1992; overthrown by a bloodless military coup on 16/01/1996.
Julius Maada Bio	1996	Following the military coup, Captain (then self-appointed General) Bio was sworn in as President on 17/01/1996.
Alhaji Ahmad Tejan Kabbah	1996–1997	Inauguration as elected President on 29/03/1996. Overthrown by a military coup d'état on 25/04/1997
Johnny Paul Koroma	1997–1998	Declared President after the military coup on 26/04/1997.
Alhaji Ahmad Tejan Kabbah	1998–	Reintroduced as President after the successful military intervention of ECOWAS on 10/03/1998.

3. Bibliography

3.1 Official Sources

The Constitution of Sierra Leone, 1991.
The Electoral Provisions (Consolidation) Decree, 1995.
The Franchise and Electoral Registration (Consolidation) Decree, 1995.

3.2 Books, Articles and Electoral Reports

Alie, J. A. (1990). *A New History of Sierra Leone.* London: Macmillan.

Allen, C. (1968). 'Sierra Leone Politics Since Independence'. *African Affairs*, 67, 305–329.

Commonwealth Secretariat (1996). *The Presidential and Parliamentary Elections in Sierra Leone: 27–28 February 1996*. Report of the Commonwealth Observer Group on Sierra Leone.

Cartwright, J. (1970). *Politics in Sierra Leone 1947–67*. Toronto: University of Toronto Press.

— (1978). *Political Leadership in Sierra Leone*. London: Croom Helm.

Clapham, C. (1976). *Liberia and Sierra Leone: An Essay in Comparative Politics*. Cambridge: Cambridge University Press.

Collier, G. (1970). *Sierra Leone: Experiment in Democracy in an African Nation*. New York: New York University Press.

Fischer, H. J. (1969). 'Elections and Coups in Sierra Leone'. *The Journal of Modern African Studies*, 7/4: 611–636.

Hayward, F., and Kandeh, J. D. (1987). 'Perspectives on Twenty-Five Years of Elections in Sierra Leone', in F. M. Hayward (ed.), *Elections in Independent Africa*. Boulder, Col./ London: Westview Press, 25–59.

Langer, P. (1978). 'Sierra Leone'. in D. Sternberger, B. Vogel, D. Nohlen, and K. Landfried (eds). *Die Wahl der Parlamente und anderer Staatsorgane, Band II: Politische Organisation und Repräsentation in Afrika*, by Franz Nuscheler, Klaus Ziemer *et al.*, Berlin/ New York: Walter de Gruyter, 1881–1907.

Riley, S. P. (1996). 'The 1996 Presidential and Parliamentary Elections in Sierra Leone'. *Electoral Studies*, 15/4: 537–545.

Scott, D. J. R. (1960). 'The Sierra Leone Election, May 1957', in W. J. M. MacKenzie and K. Robinson (eds.), *Five Elections in Africa*. Oxford, Clarendon Press, 168–280.

Thompson, B. (1997). *The Constitutional History and Law of Sierra Leone (1961–1995).* Lanham: University Press of America.

SOMALIA

by Michael Krennerich

1. Introduction

1.1 Historical Overview

Even though the Somali society is quite homogeneous as far as language, religion and culture is concerned, politics is strongly influenced by clan interests. Animosities and conflicts between clan-families (Darood, Hawiye, Isaaq, Digil and Reyanweyn, Dir), clans and sub-clans can be regarded as a major obstacle to establishing an effective central government since independence. In order not to fail, each government, democratic or autocratic by nature, has so far been obliged to accommodate clan interests. Political institutions have served *inter alia* as negotiating forums of clan representatives competing about state resources.

The Somali Republic was established on 1 July 1960. Its territory comprised both the former British protectorate of Somaliland, which under the name of State of Somaliland gained independence on 26 June 1960 (and became the Northern Region of the Somali Republic), and the former United Nations Trust Territory (until 1950, Italian Somalia) which became independent on 1 July 1960 (Southern Region of the Republic). Upon unification, the National Assembly of the new Republic was formed by the legislatures of both territories with 33 members from the North and 90 members from the South. The Southern Legislature President, Aden Abdullah Osman, became provisional President of the Republic, until he was formally elected President by the National Assembly in July 1961. The constitution of the former Trust Territory became the constitution of the entire nation, approved by a popular referendum on 20 June 1961. It provided for a semi-presidential system. The executive power was vested in the government, led by a Prime Minister who was not only responsible to Parliament, but also to the President. The President was empowered to appoint and dismiss the Prime Minister and to authorize draft laws originated within the government. Elected by Parliament for a six-year term, he had the power to dissolve the National

Assembly and to veto legislation. However, the presidential veto could be overridden by a two-thirds majority in Parliament.

The unification was accompanied by strong emotive pan-Somali sentiments, which dominated public opinion within Somalia and, thus, the international policies of the government in the first years after independence. The Somalian government actively supported the irredentist efforts of Somalis living in northern Kenya, eastern Ethiopia and French Somaliland (Djibouti), provoking open hostilities with neighboring countries. The pan-Somali issue, however, temporarily lost some of its intensity after 1967 when the government began to pursue the issue by peaceful means and gave priority to the republic's internal development.

Internal problems resulted initially from regional cleavages between the North and the South, reflecting different colonial legacies, disparate administrative, legal and educational systems and totally disintegrated economies. Moreover, due to the uneven distribution of the clan-families throughout the country, the delicate clan balance was disturbed by the unification and had to be re-established under changed terms. Particularly, the then predominant clan-family in the North (Isaaq) lost much of its political importance by the unification. A strong sense of Northern resentment soon replaced the euphoria of the unification process. Dissatisfaction found its political expression in the constitutional referendum of 1961, approved by a majority only in the South but not in the North, as well as in the abortive military coup of December 1961 and the rupture (1963) of the uneasy government coalition between the leading party of the First Republic (1960–1969)—the Somali Youth League (SYL)—and the two predominant parties of the North, the Somali National League (SNL) and the United Somali Party (USP).

The rupture of the coalition left three main parties in the field that came to operate nation-wide: the SYL; the Somali National Congress (SNC), which was formed in 1963 and absorbed most of the SNL-USP and of SYL dissidents; the Social Democratic Union, founded in 1962 on the basis of the Greater Somali League and of several splinter groups. In the 1964 National Assembly elections the SYL won an absolute majority of seats, and subsequent floor-crossing by a number of other parties' representatives increased its parliamentary strength. However, as President Osman nominated Abdirizak Haji Hussein as Prime Minister against the resistance of the SYL caucus (which preferred the former Prime Minister Shermarke), a governmental crisis broke out, resulting in changing intra- and interparty alliances supporting the government. The crisis was overcome when Shermarke was elected President by the National Assembly in the presidential elections of 1967 and Mohammed

Ibrahim Egal became Prime Minister. In the light of a high proliferation of parties, the SYL won an absolute majority of seats in the subsequent 1969 parliamentary elections. The disintegration of the multi-party system became evident and the SYL predominance became overwhelming as nearly all elected representatives joined the SYL after the elections. However, the *de facto* single-party system did not imply stability since the SYL government was in fact an extremely heterogeneous assemblage of competing personal and clan interests. Furthermore, faced with serious allegations of government rigging, the elections intensified intra- and inter-elite conflicts.

On 15 October 1969, President Shermarke was assassinated by a member of his bodyguard. Only a few days later, on 21 October, Somali's parliamentary government was overthrown in a bloodless military coup. A Supreme Revolutionary Council (SRC), composed of 25 senior military and police officers and led by the commander of the army, Major General Mohammed Siyad Barre, took power. The coup leaders initially justified their coup by widespread corruption, nepotism and 'tribalism' and by the leadership crisis that followed the assassination of President Shermarke. Ideologically characterized by a mélange of socialism, nationalism and Islam, the revolutionary regime began to transform state and society (suspension of the constitution; abolition of Parliament and parties; nationalization of large farms and industries; promotion of self-help development programs; adoption of a standard written form of Somali as the official language etc.). Despite its avowed intention to fight tribalism, however, the regime was not able to eliminate clan particularism and, from its very inception, rested itself on clan loyalities (particularily from the Darood clan-family). Within the SRC, Siyad Barre continuously consolidated his power and managed to install a personal autocratic rulership, promoting a cult mystification around his person. While real power remained in the hands of Siyad Barre and a small group of loyal officers, military rule had formally been replaced by a socialist avant-garde party, the Somali Revolutionary Socialist Party (SRSP) in 1976. The decision to establish a one-party state was influenced by the Soviet Union which sent substantial military and economic aid to the regime. However, as the Soviet Union and Cuba supported the Marxist Ethiopian military regime in the Ogaden War between Somalia and Ethiopia (1977–1978), relations deteriorated rapidly, and Barre switched to the USA and other Western states in search of military support.

The military defeat in the Ogaden War resulted in a legitimacy crisis of the Siyad Barre regime and provoked unsuccessful coup attempts and political unrest. Combining liberalization steps (constitutional referendum 1979; direct, albeit non-competitive parliamentary and presidential elections) and repression (State of Emergency etc.), Siyad Barre managed to hold power until the regime broke down in the context of an escalating civil war mainly in the northern region at the end of the decade. The state apparatus collapsed, the national army fell apart, and the dictator fled the country in January 1991. The downfall of the dictator resulted in open clashes between clans and subclans which centered on power and resources. Due to widespread hostilities and the resulting famine, hundreds of thousands of people died or were forced to leave their homes, causing a dire need for emergency humanitarian assistance. In accordance with the 'Agreement on the Implementation of a Cease-Fire' (3 March 1992) signed by the then main protagonists of the civil war, the UN Security Council established the United Nations Operation in Somalia (UNOSOM) to monitor the cease-fire and to protect humanitarian supplies. As, however, the delivery of humanitarian supplies was severely hindered by political chaos, a deteriorating security situation and by widespread banditry of rival militias, the UN Security Council (acting under Chapter VII of the UN Charter) authorized the use 'of all necessary means to establish as soon as possible a secure environment for humanitarian relief operations in Somalia' (Resolution 794 of 3 December 1992), resulting in a humanitarian intervention by the international United Task Force (UNITAF) under the leadership of the USA. In May 1993 UNITAF was transformed into the peace-keeping force UNOSOM II. While the UN intervention was able to establish a relatively secure environment for urgent humanitarian assistance in Somalia for a short period of time, the political situation was still chaotic when the last UNOSOM II troops left the country in March 1995. Notwithstanding several reconciliation initiatives, Somalia is still torn by the power struggle of competing clans and subclan factions and lacks functioning government and state structures.

The northern part of the country (Somaliland) has even proclaimed its independence on 18 May 1991. Though armed conflicts mainly between the various Isaaq (sub)clans hampered the state building process in 1992 and 1994/95, the 'Republic of Somaliland' successively has built up its own functioning government and state structures. Following the first 'National Conference' that had proclaimed independence, Mohammed Ibrahim Egal was elected President of Somaliland by a second 'National Conference' on 15 May 1993. The third 'National Conference' (1996) drew up a constitution that created a two chamber assembly (Parliament; 'Senate of clans') and a supreme court and formalized governmental structures. President Egal was reconfirmed for a five-year term on 23 February 1997. Nevertheless, the 'Republic of Somaliland' is still not recognized as independent state by the international community.

1.2 Evolution of Electoral Provisions

The first National Assembly of the independent and unified Somali Republic consisted of 123 members: 90 members came from the Legislative Assembly of the former Somalia (Southern Region), having been elected in 1959 by universal suffrage on the basis of a PR system; the other 33 members came from the Legislative Assembly of the former Somaliland (Northern Region), having been elected in 1960 by male suffrage, on the basis of a majority system in single-member constituencies.

The Electoral Law of 1964 extended female suffrage and the PR system to the whole country. In the first post-independence elections (1964) the 123 members of the National Assembly were elected by universal, equal, direct and secret suffrage for a five-year term, the minimum voting age being 21 years. Candidates had to be at least 25 years old and able to read and write. A PR system in constituencies of variable sizes was applied (47 constituencies—35 in the Southern Region and 12 in the North— ranging from one to seven seats; closed party lists; single vote; Hare quota and largest remainder).

Against the background of the proliferation of small, locally based parties, the Electoral Law of 1968 slightly modified the electoral system, changing the access to the distribution of remaining seats in trying to hit the small parties (see Nuscheler 1978). Shortly after the March 1969 elections, the parliamentary government was overthrown in a military coup and the National Assembly was dissolved.

Not until the adoption of a new constitution, which was approved in the referendum of 1979, did direct parliamentary elections (1979, 1985) and direct presidential elections (1986) take place. They were, however, non-competitive in nature. Voters were permitted only to vote 'yes' or 'no' for the single candidate (presidential elections) or for the entire list of 171 candidates (parliamentary elections). The other six of the 177 members of the People's Assembly were appointed by the President.

Since the breakdown of the Siyad Barre regime, no national elections have been held.

1.3 Current Electoral Provisions

Due to the lack of functioning government and state structures in Somalia, no electoral provisions exist.

1.4 Comment on the Electoral Statistics

Different secondary sources provide information and data on the pre-independence elections and on the elections of the First Republic. For this time period, the electoral data in this handbook are largely based on Nuscheler (1978) who himself worked with secondary sources, among them also Somali newspapers.

As for the non-competitive elections under the Siyad Barre, the data situation is extremely poor. Almost no details were given by the government on the elections, and officially announced voter turnout figures and elections results seem to be highly exaggerated. The little information given for the elections in the 1970s and 1980s are based on secondary sources (e.g. *Africa Research Bulletin*; Nelson 1982) which, however, do not pay much attention to the elections due to their restricted political importance.

2. Tables

2.1 Dates of National Elections, Referendums and Coups d'Etat

Year	Presidential elections	Parliamentary elections	Elections for Constitutional Assembly	Referendums	Coups d'état
1959		08/03			
1960		17/02			
1961				20/06	
1964		30/03			
1969		24–26/03			21/10
1979		30/12		25/08	
1985		01/01			
1986	23/12				
1991					27/01

2.2 Electoral Body 1959–1986

Year	Type of election[a]	Population[b]	Registered voters		Votes cast		
			Total number	% pop.	Total number	% reg. voters	% pop.
1959	Pa[c]	1,330,000[e]	—	—	313,760[f]	—	23.9
1960	Pa[d]	650,000[e]	—	—	81,366[f]	—	12.5
1961	Ref	2,030,000	—	—	1,943,451	—	95.7
1964	Pa	2,450,000	—	—	913,069	—	37.3
1969	Pa	2,730,000	—	—	879,554	—	32.2
1979	Ref	5,578,000	—	—	3,605,590[e]	—	64.4
1979	Pa	5,578,000	—	—	4,000,000[g]	—	71.7
1985	Pa	6,686,000	—	—	3,000,000[g]	—	44.9
1986	Pr	6,896,000	—	—	4,800,000[g]	—	69.6

[a] Pa = Parliament; Pr = President; Ref = Referendum.
[b] Not until February 1975, the first nationwide population census (3.25 million) was carried out. The census undercounted the nomadic population severely. In 1986/87 another census occurred, according to which the population amounted to 7,114,431 inhabitants.
[c] Pre-independence elections to the Legislative Council of the Trust Territory of Somalia (later: Southern Region of the Republic).
[d] Pre-independence elections to the Legislative Council of British Somaliland (later: Northern Region of the Republic).
[e] UN estimations for 1958.
[f] Valid votes only.
[g] Rough approximations. According to official announcements nearly 4 million voters went to the polls in 1979. Reportingly, there were around 3 million voters in 1985 and about 4.8 million voters in 1986. Based on official announcements of the autocratic regime, all the data seem to be exaggerated.

2.3 Abbreviations

HDMS	Hisbia Destour Mustaquil Somali
LP	Liberal Party
NUF	National United Front
SANU	Somali African National Union
SDU	Somali Democratic Union
SNC	Socialist National Congress
SNL	Somali National League
SRSP	Somali Revolutionary Socialist Party
SYL	Somali Youth League
USP	United Somali Party

2.4 Electoral Participation of Parties and Alliances 1959–1986

Party / Alliance	Years	Elections contested	
		Presidential	Parliamentary
HDMS	1959, 1964, 1969	0	3
LP	1959	0	1
SYL	1959, 1960, 1964, 1969	0	4
NUF	1960	0	1
SNL	1960, 1964, 1969	0	3
USP	1960, 1964, 1969	0	3
Partito Liberal Giovani S.	1964, 1969	0	2
SANU	1964, 1969	0	2
SDU	1964, 1969	0	2
SNC	1964, 1969	0	2
SRSP	1979, 1985, 1986	1	2

General note: The table includes only parties with parliamentary representation.

2.5 Referendums

Year	1961		1979[a]	
	Total number	%	Total number	%
Registered voters	—	—	—	—
Votes cast	—	—	—	—
Invalid votes	—	—	—	—
Valid votes	1,943,451	—	3,605,590	—
Yes	1,760,540	90.6	3,597,692	99.8
No	182,911	9.4	7,898	0.2

[a] Referendum of the draft constitution adopted at the extraordinary congress of the SRSP. The officially announced voting results should not be regarded as reliable.

2.6 Elections for Constitutional Assembly

Elections for Constitutional Assembly have not been held.

2.7 Parliamentary Elections 1959–1985

Year	1959[a]		1960[b]	
	Total number	%	Total number	%
Registered voters	—	–	—	–
Votes cast	—	—	—	—
Invalid votes	—	—	—	—
Valid votes	313,760	—	81,366	—
SYL	237,134	75.6	4,626	5.7
HDMS	40,857	13.0	–	–
LP	35,769	11.4	–	–
SNL	–	–	42,395	52.1
NUF	–	–	20,249	24.9
USP	–	–	13,350	16.4
Others	–	–	746	0.9

[a] Electoral boycott of GSL, SNU and most of the HDMS.
[b] Electoral alliances between SNL and USP on the one hand, and NUF and SYL on the other.

Year	1964[a]		1969[b]	
	Total number	%	Total number	%
Registered voters	—	–	—	–
Votes cast	—	—	—	—
Invalid votes	—	—	—	—
Valid votes	914,069	—	—	—
SYL	472,296	51.7	—	—
SNC	186,208	20.4	—	—
SDU	95,707	10.5	—	—
HDMS	80,173	8.8	—	—
USP	7,552	0.8	—	—
Partito Liberale	6,766	0.7	—	—
Giovani S.				
SNL	4,354	0.5	—	—
SANU	3,930	0.4	—	—
Others	57,083	6.2	—	—

[a] A total of 21 parties (973 candidates) contested the elections
[b] Data not available. A total of 62 parties (1,200 candidates) took part in the elections.

Year	1979[a]		1985	
	Total number	%	Total number	%[a]
Registered voters	—	—	—	–
Votes cast	4,000,000	—	—	—
Invalid votes	1,480	—	—	—
Valid votes	—	—	—	—
Yes votes	—	100.0	—	—
No votes	1,826	0.0	—	—

[a] Voters had to vote 'yes' or 'no' to the entire list of 171 candidates. The officially announced voting results can not been considered as reliable with regard to the number of voters, invalid votes and negative votes.

2.8 Composition of Parliament 1959–1985

Year	1959[a]		1960[b]		1964[c]		1969[d]	
	Seats	%	Seats	%	Seats	%	Seats	%
	90	100	33	100	123	100	123	100
SYL	83	92.2	–	–	69	56.1	73	59.3
HDMS	5	5.6	–	–	9	7.3	3	2.4
LP	2	2.2	–	–	–	–	–	–
SNL	–	–	20	60.6	1	0.8	1	0.8
USP	–	–	12	36.4	1	0.8	1	0.8
NUF	–	–	1	3.0	–	–	–	–
SNC	–	–	–	–	22	17.9	11	8.9
SDU	–	–	–	–	15	12.2	2	1.6
Partito Liberale Giovani S.	–	–	–	–	1	0.8	3	2.4
SANU	–	–	–	–	1	0.8	6	4.9
Others	–	–	–	–	4	3.3	23	18.7

[a] Pre-independence elections to the Legislative Council of the Trust Territory of Somalia (later: Southern Region of the Republic).

[b] Pre-independence elections to the Legislative Council of British Somaliland (later: Northern Region of the Republic).

[c] Composition according to the electoral results. Soon after the elections, 21 members elected under other party banners crossed the floor and joined the SYL.

[d] Composition according to the electoral results. After elections, almost all Members of Parliament joined the SYL.

Year	1979		1985	
	Seats	%	Seats	%
	171	100	171	100
SRSP[a]	171	100	171	100

[a] All 171 candidates were nominated by the SRSP.

2.9 Presidential Elections 1986

1986	Total number	%
Registered voters	—	–
Votes cast	—	—
Invalid votes	—	—
Valid votes	4,889,078	—
Siyad Barre (Yes votes)	4,887,592	100.0
No votes	1,486	0.0

2.10 List of Power Holders 1960–1998

Head of State	Years	Remarks
Aden Abdullah Osman	06/07/1960–30/06/1967	After unification Osman became provisional President until he was elected by the National Assembly in the presidential elections of July 1961.
Abdirashid Ali Shermarke	01/07/1967–15/10/1969	Elected by the National Assembly in 1967. Shermarke was assassinated by one of his bodyguards on 15 October 1969.
Mohammed Siyad Barre	21/10/1969–27/01/1991	Following the military coup of 1969, Major General Siyad Barre was declared President of the Republic. He was elected to a six-year term by the People's Assembly in January 1980 and by non-competitive popular elections in December 1986.
No clear authority	1991–	The overthrow of President Siyad Barre and the breakdown of existing state structures have left Somalia with no clear central authority.

Head of Government	Years	Remarks
Abdirashid Ali Shermarke	1960–1964	Nominated as Prime Minister after the National Assembly elections of 1960.
Abdirizak Haji Hussein	1964–1967	Nominated as Prime Minister by President Osman after the National Assembly elections of 1964.
Mohammed Haji Ibrahim Egal	1967–1969	Nominated as Prime Minister by the new President Shermarke and confirmed by the National Assembly in August 1967
Mohammed Siyad Barre	1969–1991	*De facto* identical with Head of State.

Head of Government	Years	Remarks
No clear authority	1991–	The overthrow of President Siyad Barre and the breakdown of existing state structures have left Somalia with no clear central authority.

3. Bibliography

Adam, H. M. (1995). 'Somalia: A Terrible Beauty Being Born?', in W. Zartman (ed.), *Collapsed States. The Desintegration and Restoration of Legitimate Authority*. London, 69–90.

Ahmed, A. J. (ed.) (1995). *The Intervention of Somalia.* Lawrenceville, NJ: Red Sea Press.

Aves, A. M., and Bechthold, K.-H. (eds.) (1987). *Somalia im Wandel.* Tübingen: Inst. für Wiss. Zusammenarbeit.

Bongartz, M. (1991). *Somalia im Bürgerkrieg. Ursachen und Perspektiven des innenpolitischen Konflikts*. Hamburg: Institut für Afrika-Kunde.

Brons, M. (1993). *Somaliland. Zwei Jahre nach der Unabhängigkeit.* Hamburg: Institut für Afrika-Kunde.

Castagno, M. (1975). *Historical Dictionary of Somalia*. Metuchen, NJ: Scarecrow Press.

Clarke, W. L. (1997). *Learning from Somalia: The Lessons of Armed Humanitarian Intervention*. Boulder, Col.: Westview Press.

Contini, P. (1969). *The Somali Republic: An Experiment in Legal Integration*. London: Frank Cass.

Drysdale, J. (1994). *Whatever Happened to Somalia?* London: Haan.

Elmi Salad, O. (1993). *The Somali Conflict and the Undercurrent Causes.* Mogadishu.

Herrmann, R. H. (1997). *Der kriegerische Konflikt in Somalia und die internationale Intervention 1992–1995.* Frankfurt a.M. *et al.*: Peter Lang.

Laitin, D. D. (1976). 'The Political Economy of Military Rule in Somalia'. *Journal of Modern African Studies*, 14: 449–468.

— and Samatar, S. S. (1987). *Somalia. Nation in Search of a State.* Boulder, Col./ London: Westview Press.

Lewis, I. M. (1961). *A Pastoral Democracy*. London: Oxford University Press.

— (1972) 'The Politics of the 1969 Somali Coup'. *Journal of Modern African Studies*, 10: 382–408.

— (1988). *A Modern History of Somalia: Nation and State in the Horn of Africa, revised, updated and expanded version*. Boulder, Col.: Westview Press.

Lyons, T., and Samatar, A. S. (1995). *Somalia: State Collapse, Multilateral Intervention and Strategies for Political Reconstruction.* Washington, D.C.: Brookings Inst.

Makinda, S. M. (1993). *Seeking Peace from Chaos: Humanitarian Intervention in Somalia*. Boulder, Col.: Lynne Rienner.

Martin, C. J. (1966). 'The Somali Republic'. *The British Survey*, 203: 1–20.

Matthies, V. (1994). *Ähiopien, Eritrea, Somalia, Dschibuti: das Horn von Afrika* (2nd edn.). München: Beck.

Mayall, J. (ed.) (1996). *The New Interventionism, 1991–1994: United Nations Experience in Cambodia, former Yugoslavia and Somalia.* Cambridge: Cambridge University Press.

Menkhaus, K. (1998). 'Somalia: Political Order in a Stateless Society'. *Current History*, May, 220–224.

Michaelson, M. (1993). 'Somalia—The Painful Road to Reconciliation'. *Africa Today*, 2: 53–73.

Michler, W. (1993). *Somalia. Ein Volk stirbt. Der Bürgerkrieg und das Versagen des Auslands*. Bonn: Dietz.

Mubarak, J. A. (1996). *From Bad Policy to Chaos in Somalia.* Westport, Conn.: Praeger.

Nuscheler, F. (1978). 'Somalia', in D. Sternberger, B. Vogel, D. Nohlen and K. Landfried (eds.), *Die Wahl der Parlamente und anderer Staatsorgane. Band II: Politische Organisation und Repräsentation in Afrika,* by Franz Nuscheler, Klaus Ziemer *et al.*, Berlin/ New York: Walter de Gruyter, 1909–1943.

Omar, M. O. (1996). *Somalia: A Nation Driven to Despair. A Case of Leadership Failure.* New Delhi: Somali Publ.

Petrucci, P. (1993). *Mogadiscio*. Torino: Nuovo Ed.

Potholm, C. P. (1979). *The Theory and Practice of African Politics*. Englewood Cliffs: Prentice Hall.

Prunier, G. (1998). 'Somaliland Goes it Alone'. *Current History*, May, 225–228.

Saideman, S. M. (1997/1998). 'Inconsistent Irredentism? Political Competition, Ethnic Ties, and the Foreign Policies of Somalia and Serbia'. *Security Studies*, 7/3: 51–93.

Samatar, A. I. (1988). *Socialist Somalia. Rhetoric and Reality*. London: Zed.

— (1992). 'Destruction of the State and Society in Somalia: Beyond the Tribal Convention'. *The Journal of Modern African Studies*, 30/4: 625–641.

— (1994). *The Somali Challenge. From Catastrophe to Renewal?* Boulder, Col.: Lynne Rienner.

Samatar, S. S. (1995). *Somalia: A Nation in Turmoil*. London: Minority Rights Group.

Torrenzano, A. (1995). *L'imbroglio somalien. Histoire d'une crise de succession.* Paris: L'Harmattan.

Touati, J. (1997). *Politik und Gesellschaft in Somalia (1890–1991).* Hamburg: Institut für Afrika-Kunde.

UN (United Nations) (1995). *The United Nations and the Situation in Somalia. Reference Paper, April 1995.* New York: United Nations Department of Public Information.

SOUTH AFRICA

by Ulf Engel

1. Introduction

1.1 Historical Introduction

South Africa's first democratic elections were held in 1994, although the country is looking back at a comparatively long history of multi-party elections. However, from 1910 to 1994 the right to vote was granted exclusively to citizens of European decent and, to some extent and in some regions only, to people of so-called Colored or Indian origin. The political history of South Africa has been totally dominated by the European settler's attempts to defend their colonial gains through political control of and over other population groups, mainly the African majority.

After the Anglo-Boer War (1899–1902) and an interregnum of British control the former British colonies Cape and Natal and the former Boer republics Transvaal and Orange Free State merged to form the Union of South Africa (31 March 1910). According to the South Africa Act, 1909, political power was vested in a Prime Minister, with certain powers held by a Governor-General (for the British crown). On 5 October 1961 the Europeans decided by referendum on a constitutional change from union to republican status, thus preventing continued membership of the Commonwealth. In 1978 a *de facto* parallel system of government was installed through management committees which were controlled by a state security council and the military. With the Republic of South Africa Constitution Act, 1983, the basically Westminster-type model of government was replaced by an executive President and a tricameral Parliament which gave representation to Europeans (House of Assembly), so-called Coloureds (House of Representatives) and so-called Indians (House of Delegates).

Though the politics of racial segregation originated from the period before 1948, the system was perfected and extended under the name apartheid by the National Party (NP) governments after 1948: The population was classified into racial categories (1950) and non-Europeans were deprived of their remaining political rights. Specific acts were passed to cover all areas of life (education, housing, labor etc.). Geographical segregation was introduced through the Group Area Act (1950 and 1957 as amended). Starting in 1949 a system of homelands was introduced, finally providing for the internationally non-recognized 'independent' TBVC states (Transkei, Bophuthatswana, Venda, Ciskei) and 'semi-autonomous' territories (Gazankulu, kwaNdebele, kaNgwane, kwaZulu, Lebowa und QwaQwa). This process was accompanied by a series of measures aiming at suppression of African political activity, leading to the banning of all African organizations in 1960.

Throughout the century European party politics had been dominated by Afrikaner nationalism and a strong anti-British sentiment. In contrast, the original rift between Boer Afrikaners, represented by the South African Party (SAP), and English-speaking Europeans, represented by the Unionist Party, was soon overcome by marginalization of the Unionists and their subsequent merger with the SAP (1920). Opposition to the SAP governments of Louis Botha (1915–1919) and Jan Smuts (1919–1924) emerged from within the Afrikanerdom: the NP of James Hertzog was founded in 1914 to rally Afrikaner opposition against SAP support for Britain in World War I. Together with the South African Labour Party (SALP) it managed to supersede the SAP, starting the 'Pact Government' period (1924–1932). From 1932 to 1934 Hertzog ruled on the basis of a NP-SAP coalition, when the two parties merged to form the United Party (UP) and the extremist wings formed the 'Purified' NP and the small Dominion Party respectively. Another split in Afrikanerdom occurred when Hertzog failed to plead for South African neutrality in World War II. While Vice-Premier Smuts managed to form a UP-DP-SALP coalition government (1939–1948), the NP reunited as Herenigde Nasionale of Volksparty (HNP 1940). Supported by inequalities in the delimitation of constituencies which favored rural over urban ones, in 1948 the NP managed to gain a majority of seats on a minority of votes (in coalition with the Afrikaner Party, AP). Under successive leaders–Johannes G. Strijdom (1954–1958), Hendrik F. Verwoerd (1958–1966), Balthazar John Vorster (1966–1978), Pieter W. Botha (1978–1989) and Frederik W. de Klerk (1989–1994)—the NP held power until 1994. Political dissent within the Afrikanerdom led to the formation of the Herstigte Nasionale Party (HNP 1969) and the Conservative Party (CP 1982) respectively. The UP was dissolved in 1977. A limited 'liberal' opposition to the politics of apartheid was articulated by the Liberal Party (founded 1953) and its successors (*inter alia* Progressive Party 1959, Progressive Federal Party 1977 and Democratic Party 1989).

The removal of apartheid was a complex and inter-linked process of internal revolt, failed controlled change from above and pressure exerted by parts of the international community. With the enactment of the 1983 Constitution and the attempted co-optation of non-Africans, South Africa entered a circle of increased political protest, repression and violence (1983–1989). Historically, basic opposition to the politics of apartheid had been organized by a Charterist and an 'Africanist' spectrum of organizations. While the former were led by the African National Congress (ANC, founded 1912) and its ally, the South African Communist Party (SACP 1921), both of whom acted on the basis of the 'Freedom Charter' (1955), the 'Africanists' and black consciousness forces were dominated by the Pan-Africanist Congress of Azania (PAC) who had split from the ANC in 1959. As repression increased and a country-wide state of emergency was introduced (8 June 1986), the opposition rallied increasingly around positions of the exiled ANC and the internal 'Mass Democratic Movement'. Subsequently, conflicts over regional hegemony arose in kwaZulu and Natal between ANC-led forces and Inkatha (since 15 July 1990: Inkatha Freedom Party, IFP).

The transitional period (1989–1994) started with the change from President Botha to de Klerk (15 August 1989). Reforms led to the unbanning of political parties and the release of remaining political prisoners, among them Nelson Mandela (February 1990). The following 'negotiated revolution' was characterized mainly by hegemonial bilateral NP/ANC negotiations, accompanied by increased levels of political violence and resistance to substantial change by different political actors, such as IFP, CP and some homeland-leaders. Finally, an Interim Constitution was agreed on 22 December 1993. It favored ANC positions on a strong central state over NP/IFP positions on strong federal states and provided for an elected executive President based on a Government of National Unity (for five years) and a Constitutional Assembly (i.e. National Assembly plus Senate). The final phase of the transition to majority rule (1993–1994) was controlled by a dual structure of government and joint committees under a Transitional Executive Council (TEC, constituted on 7 December 1993). With the exception of the CP, all important political players (even the pragmatic Boers forming the Freedom Front and the late-coming IFP) participated in the elections of May 1994. The elections were organized by an Independent Electoral Commission (IEC) and monitored by national and international observers, declaring the elections as substantially 'free and fair', though the general political climate of violence and intolerance remained unconducive to the elections and major logistical and technical problems occurred.

After the final constitution had been passed by the elected Constitutional Assembly (8 May 1996), amended and finally validated by the Constitutional Court (4 December 1996) it came into force on 3 February 1997. The new constitution, too, provides for a presidential system, based on a two-chamber Parliament (National Assembly plus National Council of Provinces).

1.2 Evolution of Electoral Provisions

The principles of universal, equal, direct and secret suffrage were applied for the first time in 1994 when an elected Constitutional Assembly replaced the tricameral system of 1983 with its separate parliamentary representation for Europeans, Coloureds and Indians. The period 1910 to 1989 was dominated by a dual process of granting franchise to all Europeans on the one hand, and depriving non-Europeans in the Cape Province of their respective rights as laid down in the South Africa Act, 1909, on the other. European women were granted the right to vote in 1930 (Women's Enfranchisement Act, No. 18 of 1930); equal, direct and secret suffrage was extended to all male Europeans in Natal and the Cape in 1931 (Franchise Laws Amendment Act, No. 41 of 1931). The voting age was lowered from 21 to 18 in 1958 (Electoral Law Amendment Act, No. 30 of 1958).

In contrast to this gradual extension of voting rights for Europeans, the rights of non-Europeans were restricted and then abolished altogether. In 1936 the African Cape population was placed on a separate roll (Representation of Natives Act, No. 12 of 1936). As of 1946 the Indian population in Natal and Transvaal was allowed a limited parliamentary representation through Europeans (Asian Land Tenure and Indian Representation Act, No. 28 of 1946) which, however, was boycotted and repealed in 1948. In a first attempt to scrap the common roll voting rights of Cape Coloureds which these had enjoyed since 1853 and prevent further registration of non-Europeans in Natal, the Separate Representation of Voters Act (No. 46 of 1951) was passed. Though the Act was subsequently declared invalid by the Supreme Court of South Africa (because it contravened the entrenched clauses of the South Africa Act), it was revalidated five years later by the South Africa Act Amendment Act (No. 9 of 1956). The remaining representation of Africans by Europeans was abolished through the Promotion of Bantu Self-

Government Act (No. 46 of 1959), which *inter alia* outlined the homeland project on the basis of the 1936 reserves. Representation of the Cape Coloureds was finally abolished in 1968 (Separate Representation of Voters Amendment Act, No. 50 of 1968), and instead they were given a partly elected, partly nominated Colored Persons Representative Council (Act 52 of 1968). For Indians a body established in 1964 was given statutory authority, though the Council remained wholly nominated (Acts 31 of 1968 and 67 of 1972). After these councils had failed politically, the 1983 Constitution replaced them with two chambers of Parliament, the House of Representatives and the House of Delegates, which co-existed with the European-only House of Assembly, but held no real power within the constitutional dispensation (Electoral Act, No. 45 of 1979, and Registration and Elections Amendment Act, No. 103 of 1983). The House of Assembly was elected on the basis of a plurality system in single-member constituencies.

1.3 Current Electoral Provisions

Sources: Final Constitution of the Republic of South Africa (Act 108 of 1996), replacing the Constitution of the Republic of South Africa Act (No. 200 of 1993) and the Constitution of the Republic of South Africa Amendment Act (No. 2 of 1994); The Electoral Act, 1993 (No. 202 of 1993), and Electoral Amendment Act, 1994 (No. 1 of 1994), as amended by Proclamations No. 45 (16 March 1994), No. 69 (20 April 1994), No. 73 and No. 85 of 1994 (both 21 April 1994); related Electoral Regulations: Government Notice R310 (17 February 1994) and R809 of 1994 (20 April 1994); Independent Electoral Commission Act (No. 150 of 1993); Amendment of the Independent Electoral Commission Act, 1993 (Proclamation No. 46 of 1993), 16 March 1994; Independent Electoral Commission Amendment Act, 1994 (No. 5 of 1994); and related Government Notice No. 198 of 1994 (3 March 1994).

Elected national institutions: National Assembly (currently with 400 members; as of 30 April 1999 there shall be no fewer than 350 and no more than 400 members). Additionally Parliament comprises a second chamber, the Senate (as of 6 February 1997: National Council of Provinces) whose members are representatives of the Provinces.

Suffrage: The principles of universal, equal, direct and secret suffrage have been applied since 1994. Every citizen who has reached the age of

18 and is in possession of a voter's eligibility document has the right to vote. In 1994 different documents were recognized, ranging from various forms of passes to temporary voter IDs. The right for prisoners to vote—except those convicted of murder, robbery with aggravating circumstances and rape—was granted after heated discussions within the TEC (Proclamation No. 85 of 1994).

Nomination of candidates: Every citizen who is qualified to vote may be nominated as a candidate, except (a) anyone who is appointed by, or is in the service of, the state and receives renumeration for that appointment or service (other than the President, Deputy President, Ministers and Deputy Ministers, as well as other office-bearers whose functions are compatible with the functions of a MP and have been declared compatible with those functions by national legislation); (b) permanent delegates to the Senate (or National Council of Provinces), or members of a provincial legislature or a municipal council; (c) unrehabilated insolvents; (d) anyone declared to be of unsound mind by a court of the RSA; and (e) anyone who, after 1 January 1997, has been convicted of an offence and sentenced to more than 12 months imprisonment without the option of a fine (disqualified for five years).

Electoral system: Proportional representation system. Technical elements (as applied in 1994): *Nine multi-member constituencies of variable size, corresponding to the nine provinces of the country. However, the primary basis for the allocation of the 400 seats is the votes cast for each party in the country as a whole (national constituency). *National and/or regional party lists. Parties can decide whether to submit only regional lists or to submit both regional and a national list, provided that the list of candidates does not in total contain the names of more than 400 candidates. The list form is closed. *Each voter has one vote (for National Assembly).*Allocation of seats: a) 200 seats are distributed proportionately in nine multi-member constituencies at provincial level according to the STV-Droop quota (quota = votes divided by (seats + 1) +1), in conjunction with the largest remainder formula. b) The total number of seats for each party is calculated proportionately on the basis of the votes cast for each party in the country as a whole, applying the STV-Droop quota at the national level. No legal threshold exists. c) The number of seats allocated to a given party at constituency level is subtracted from the total number of seats that the party obtained from the votes cast at national level. The difference is filled by the national party list. If a particular party did not submit a national list, the difference is filled by the regional party lists (in the same proportion as set out in the first step).

1.4 Comment on the Electoral Statistics

Documentation of election results and the distribution of seats is far less sophisticated than one would expect from a country with these historical experiences. For reason of standardization reference has been made to the only complete list of voting figures and distribution of seats (1910–1987) as published in the Official Yearbook of the Republic of South Africa (15th edn., 1989/90). However, sometimes figures within this list are obviously wrong. For 1910–1970 competing data has been offered by Noller (1978), though he did not always work with official figures. For 1943–1970 Heard (1974) has offered data based on results as published in Government Gazettes. Without reference to respective data it is, however, not possible to explain differences between the Official Yearbook and Heard or Noller respectively (*inter alia*, inconsistencies occurred when delayed elections or by-elections were added to original results). Election results of the tricameral Parliament are based on the Official Yearbook (1989/90), too, and government figures (1989). 1994 election results are based on the final report of the Independent Electoral Commission (1994). Results of the referendum 1978 have been taken from *The Times*, 04/11/1983, results of the referendum 1992 from *S. A. Barometer*, 27/03/1992. Composition of Parliament 1989 according to written communication by RSA Government to the author (03/02/1990).

2. Tables

2.1 Dates of National Elections, Referendums and Coups d'Etat[a]

Year	Presidential elections	Parliamentary elections	Elections for Constitutional Assembly	Referendums	Coups d'état
1910		15/09			
1915		20/10			
1920		20/03			
1921		08/02			
1924		17/06			
1929		12/06			
1933		17/05			
1938		18/05			
1943		07/07			
1948		26/05			
1953		15/04			
1958		16/04			
1960				05/10	
1961		18/10			
1966		30/03			
1970		22/04			
1974		24/04			
1977		30/11			
1981		29/04			
1983				02/11	
1984[b]		22/08			
1987[c]		06/05			
1989[d]		06/09			
1992				17/03	
1994			26–29/04		

[a] All elections and referendums 1910 to 1989 based on racial criteria, with the exclusion of the African majority population.

[b] Elections to the 'Coloured' House of Representatives and the 'Indian' House of Delegates only. Earlier, regional elections were held for a (Cape) Coloured Persons Representative Council (24/09/1969, 19/03/1975).

[c] House of Assembly elections only.

[d] Elections to all Houses of the tricameral Parliament.

2.2 Electoral Body 1910–1994

Year	Type of election[a]	Population[b]	Registered voters		Votes cast		
			Total number	% of Pop.	Total number	% reg. voters	% of pop.
1910	HoA	1,117,000	—	—	—	—	—
1915	HoA	—	365,307	—	261,433	71.6	—
1920	HoA	—	421,790	—	282,361	66.9	—
1921	HoA	1,521,000	449,531	29.6	277,742	55.6	18.3
1924	HoA	—	413,136	—	319,047	77.2	—
1929	HoA	—	461,820	—	347,924	75.3	—
1933	HoA	—	957,636	—	323,417	33.8	—
1938	HoA	2,003,334	1,052,652	52.5	835,378	79.4	41.7
1943	HoA	—	1,114,110	—	885,623	79.5	—
1948	HoA	2,372,044	1,337,543	56.4	1,073,364	80.2	45.3
1953	HoA	2,641,689	1,385,591	52.5	1,218,631	88.0	46.1
1958	HoA	—	1,563,426	—	1,162,576	74.4	—
1961	HoA	3,080,159	1,800,426	58.5	802,079	44.5	26.0
1966	HoA	—	1,901,479	—	1,302,151	68.5	—
1970	HoA	3,751,328	2,161,234	57.6	1,507,634	69.8	40.2
1974	HoA	—	2,332,623	—	1,158,074	51.9	—
1977	HoA	—	2,193,635	—	1,054,400	48.5	—
1981	HoA	4,528,000	2,290,626	50.6	1,349,933	58.9	29.8
1984	HoR	2,832,705	881,984	31.1	272,854	30.9	9.6
1984	HoD	821,361	411,901	50.1	83,613	20.3	10.2
1987	HoA	4,568,739	3,031,414	66.4	2,056,627	67.8	45.0
1989	HoA	—	3,120,104	—	2,167,929	69.5	—
1989	HoR	—	1,439,112	—	261,047	18.1	—
1989	HoD	—	663,604	—	154,524	23.3	—
1994	CA	—	22,754,152	—	19,726,579	86.7	—

[a] CA = Constitutional Assembly; HoA = House of Assembly (Europeans); HoR = House of Representatives (Coloureds); HoD = House of Delegates (Indians).

[b] Due to the application of 'racial' criteria and the fact that up to 1968 Cape Coloureds were allowed a limited parliamentary representation census figures for 1910–1968 can not be strictly applied. Figures refer to 'White' (i.e. European) population only. 1910 based on census 1911, 1938 on census 1936, 1948 on census 1946, 1953 on census 1951, 1961 on census 1960, 1981 based on 1980 census, and 1984 based on 1985 census. According to the 1991 census (without TVBC states) there were 4,521,873 Europeans, 2,929,323 Coloureds and 863,874 Indians in South Africa.

2.3 Abbreviations

1910–1989	
AP	Afrikaner Party
CP	Conservative Party
DP	Democratic Party
HNP	Herstigte [Re-constituted] Nasionale Party
HNP/V	Herenigde [Re-united] Nasionale of Volksparty
NCP	National Conservative Party
NP	National Party
NRP	New Republic Party
NUP	National Union Party
PFP	Progressive Federal Party
PP	Progressive Party
PRP	Progressive Reform Party
SAP	South African Party
SALP	South Africa Labour Party
UP	United (South African National) Party
Since 1994	
ACDP	African Christian Democratic Party
ADM	African Democratic Movement
AMCP	African Moderates Congress Party
AMP	African Muslim Party
ANC	African National Congress
DP	Democratic Party
DPSA	Dikwankwetla Party of South Africa
FF	Freedom Front
FP	Federal Party
GRP	The Green Party
IFP	Inkatha Freedom Party
IP	Islamic Party
KISS	The Keep it Straight and Simple Party
LSAP	Luso-South African Party
MF	Minority Front
NP	National Party (since 1998: New National Party)
PAC	Pan-Africanist Congress of Azania
RP	Right Party
SAWP	South African Women's Party
SOCCER	Sports Organisation for Collective Contribution and Equal Rights
UDF	United People's Front
WI	Workers International to Rebuild the Fourth International (SA)
WKFP	Wees-Kaap Federalse Party
WLP	Workers' List Party
WRPP	Women's Rights Peace Party
XPP	Ximoko Progressive Party

2.4 Electoral Participation of Parties and Alliances

Party / Alliance	Years	Elections contested (1910–1989)
SAP	1910, 1915, 1920, 1921, 1924,1929, 1933	7
SALP	1910, 1915, 1920, 1921, 1924,1929, 1933, 1938, 1943, 1948, 1953, 1958, 1961	13
Unionist Party	1910, 1915, 1920	3
NP	1915, 1920, 1921, 1924, 1929, 1933, 1948, 1953, 1958, 1961, 1966, 1970, 1974, 1977, 1981, 1984, 1987, 1989	18
Socialist Party	1915, 1920, 1938, 1943, 1948	5
Home Rule	1933	1
Roos Party	1933	1
Dominion Party	1938, 1943	2
HNP/V	1938, 1943	2
UP	1938, 1943, 1948, 1953, 1958, 1961, 1966, 1970, 1974, 1977	10
AP	1943, 1948	2
Liberal Party	1958, 1961	2
NUP	1961	1
PP	1961, 1966, 1970, 1974	4
HNP	1970, 1974, 1977, 1981, 1984, 1987, 1989	7
PFP	1977, 1981, 1984, 1987	4
NRP	1977, 1981, 1984, 1987	4
SAP	1977	1
NCP	1981	1
CP	1987, 1989	2
DP	1989	1

Party / Alliance	Years	Elections contested
ACDP	1994	1
ANC	1994	1
DP	1994	1
FF	1994	1
IFP	1994	1
NP	1994	1
PAC	1994	1

2.5 Referendums

Year	1960[a]		1983[b]	
	Total number	%	Total number	%
Registered voters	1,800,426	–	—	–
Votes cast	1,634,240	90.8	2,062,469	75.5
Invalid votes	7,904	0.5	10,669	0.5
Valid votes	1,626,336	99.5	2,051,800	99.5
Yes	850,458	52.3	1,360,223	66.0
No	775,878	47.7	691,577	33.5

[a] On the question of South Africa becoming a Republic (votes incl. Namibia).
[b] On the introduction of the tricameral Parliament, i.e. co-optation of Coloureds and Indians.

Year	1992[a]	
	Total number	%
Registered voters	3,296,800	
Votes cast	2,804,947	85.1
Invalid votes	5,142	0.2
Valid votes	2,799,805	99.8
Yes	1,924,186	68.7
No	875,619	31.2

[a] On a continuation of the government's reform strategy which aimed at a new constitution through negotiations.

2.6 Elections for Constitutional Assembly

1994	Votes Total number	%	Seats Total (400)	%
Registered voters	22,754,152[a]			
Votes cast	19,726,579	86.7		
Invalid votes	193,081	0.1		
Valid votes	19,533,498	99.9		
ANC	12,237,665	62.6	252	63.0
NP	3,983,690	20.4	82	20.5
IFP	2,058,294	10.5	43	10.8
FF	424,555	2.2	9	2.3
DP	338,426	1.7	7	1.8
PAC	243,478	1.2	5	1.3
ACDP	88,104	0.5	2	0.5
Others[b]	—	0.8	0	0.0
AMP	34,446			
AMCP	27,690			
DPSA	19,451			
FP / RP	17,663			
MF	13,433			
SOCCER	10,575			
ADM	9,886			
WRPP	6,434			
XPP	6,320			
KISS	5,916			
WLP	4,169			
LSAP	3,293			

[a] IEC estimate.

[b] Other parties than those named here contested at provincial level only.

2.7 Parliamentary Elections

2.7.1 House of Assembly ('Europeans') 1910–1989

Year	1910 Total number	%	1915 Total number	%
Registered voters	—	–	365,307	–
Votes cast	—	—	261,433	71.6
Invalid votes	—	—	4,330	1.7
Valid votes	105,623	—	257,103	98.3
NP	—	—	75,623	29.4
SAP	30,052	28.4	94,285	36.7
Unionist Party	39,765	37.6	49,917	19.4
Labour Party	11,549	10.9	24,755	9.6
Socialist Party	448	0.4	140	0.0
Independents	23,808	22.7	12,383	4.8

Year	1920 Total number	%	1921 Total number	%
Registered voters	421,790	–	499,531	–
Votes cast	282,361	66.9	277,742	55.6
Invalid votes	4,876	1.7	—	—
Valid votes	277,485[a]	98.3	285,219[b]	—
NP	101,227	36.5	105,039	36.8
SAP	90,152	32.5	137,389	48.7
Unionist Party	38,946	14.1	–	–
SALP	40,639	14.7	39,406	13.8
Socialist Party	202	0.0	–	–
Independents	5,986	2.2	3,385	1.2

[a] Total party votes and spoilt papers (277,152) differ from the official number of valid votes as given by the Official Yearbook. Party share of votes is given as a % of party votes.
[b] Total party votes (authors calculation); higher than official figure for votes cast (277,742).

Year	1924 Total number	%	1929 Total number	%
Registered voters	413,136	–	461,820	–
Votes cast	319,047	72.1	347,924	75.3
Invalid votes	—	—	—	—
Valid votes	316,242[a]	—	343,897[a]	—
NP	111,483	35.3	141,579	41.2
SAP	148,769	47.0	159,896	46.5
SALP	45,380	14.3	33,919	9.9
Independents	10,610	3.4	8,503	2.5

[a] Total party votes add up to 316,242 and 343,897 respectively. Party share of vote is given as a % of added party votes.

Year	1933 Total number	%	1938 Total number	%
Registered voters	957,636	–	1,052,652	–
Votes cast	323,417	33.8	835,378	79.4
Invalid votes	3,406	1.0	5,481	0.7
Valid votes	320,011	99.0	828,897[a]	99.3
NP (1938: HNP/V)	101,159	31.6	259,543	31.3
SAP	71,486	22.3	–	–
UP	–	–	446,032	53.8
SALP	20,276	6.3	48,641	5.9
Roos Party	27,441	8.6	–	–
Home Rule Party	12,328	3.9	–	–
Dominion Party	–	–	52,356	6.3
Socialist Party	–	–	4,963	0.6
Independents	87,321	27.3	17,362	2.1

[a] According to the Official Yearbook, votes cast minus invalid votes is 830,897. Reference, however, is to party votes as percentage of added valid votes.

Year	1943 Total number	%	1948 Total number	%
Registered voters	1,114,110	–	1,338,543	–
Votes cast	885,623	79.5	1,073,364	80.2
Invalid votes	9,360	1.1	7,393	0.7
Valid votes	876,263	98.9	1,065,971	99.3
NP (1943: HNP/V)	321,601	36.7	401,834	37.7
AP	15,601	1.8	41,885	3.9
UP	435,297	49.7	524,230	49.2
SALP	38,206	4.3	27,360	2.6
Dominion Party	29,023	3.3	–	–
Socialist Party	6,350	0.7	–	–
Independents	30,185	3.4	70,662	6.6

Year	1953 Total number	%[a]	1958 Total number	%[a]
Registered voters	1,385,591	–	1,563,426	–
Votes cast	1,218,631	88.0	1,162,576	74.4
Invalid votes	8,709	0.7	7,573	0.7
Valid votes	1,209,922	99.3	(1,155,403)[b]	99.3
NP	598,718	49.5	642,006	(55.6)
UP	576,474	47.6	503,648	(43.6)
SALP	34,730	2.9	2,070	(0.2)
Liberal Party	–	–	2,934	(0.3)
Others	–	–	1,193	(0.1)
Independents	–	–	3,552	(0.3)

Year	1961 Total number	%	1966 Total number	%
Registered voters	1,800,426	–	1,901,479	–
Votes cast	802,079	44.5	1,302,151	68.5
Invalid votes	4,518	—	7,494	—
Valid votes	803,268[a]	—	1,302,151[b]	—
NP	370,395	46.1	759,331	58.3
UP	288,217	35.9	486,629	37.4
SALP	2,461	0.3	–	–
PP	69,045	8.6	39,717	3.1
NUP	50,279	6.2	–	–
Others	17,164	2.1	10,674	0.8
Independents	5,707	0.7	5,800	0.4

[a] Total party votes are higher than votes cast. Reference is to party votes as percentage of added valid votes.

[b] Total party votes equal votes cast although there are invalid votes. Reference is to party votes as percentage of added valid votes.

Year	1970 Total number	%	1974 Total number	%
Registered voters	2,161,234	-	2,332,623	-
Votes cast	1,507,634	69.8	1,158,074	51.9
Invalid votes	9,982	0.7	20,923	1.8
Valid votes	1,497,652	99.3	1,137,151	98.2
NP	822,034	54.9	638,424	56.1
UP	561,676	37.5	363,478	32.0
PP	51,742	3.5	72,479	6.4
HNP	53,735	3.6	44,717	3.9
DP	–	–	10,500	0.9
Others	5,336	0.4	5,471	0.5
Independents	3,129	0.2	2,532	0.2

Year	1977 Total number	%	1981 Total number	%
Registered voters	2,193,635	–	2,290,626	–
Votes cast	1,064,400[a]	48.5	1,349,933	58.9
Invalid votes	15,930	1.5	22,086	1.6
Valid votes	1,048,420[b]	98.5	1,327,847	98.4
NP	685,035	65.3	778,371	58.6
PFP	177,705	16.9	265,297	20.0
HNP	34,159	3.3	191,249	14.4
NRP	127,335	12.1	93,603	7.0
SAP	17,915	1.7	–	–
NCP	–	–	19,149	1.4
Independents / others	6,271	0.6	2,264	0.2

[a] Excluding one constituency.
[b] Total party votes plus invalid votes are less than votes cast given (1,064,350). Reference is to party votes as percentage of added valid votes.

Year	1987 Total number	%	1989 Total number	%
Registered voters	3,031,414	–	3,120,104	–
Votes cast	2,056,627	67.8	2,167,929	69.5
Invalid votes	15,890	0.6	10,336	0.5
Valid votes	2,040,737	99.4	2,157,593	99.5
NP	1,075,505	52.7	1,039,704	48.2
CP	547,559	26.8	680,131	31.5
PFP	288,574	14.1	–	–
NRP	40,494	2.0	–	–
DP	–	–	431,444	20.0
HNP	61,456	3.3	5,416	0.3
Independents	27,149	1.3	898	0.0

2.7.2 (Cape) Coloured Persons Representative Council 1969–1975

Year	1969		1975	
	Total number	%	Total number	%
Registered voters	614,865	–	521,557	–
Votes cast	300,918	48.9	251,631	48.2
Invalid votes	1,128	0.4	4,895	1.9
Valid votes	299,790[b]	99.6	246,736	98.0
Labour Party	135,202	46.1	151,410	61.2
Federal Coloured People's Party	90,025	30.7	75,851	30.1
Republican Coloured People's Party of SA & SWA	30,238	10.3	–	–
Republican Party	–		2,934	1.2
National Coloured People's Party	23,260	7.9	–	–
Social Democratic Party	–		2,736	1.1
Conservative Party	3,216	1.0	–	–
Independents	11,407	3.9	13,805	5.6

[a] Total valid votes differ from the figure given (293,348 instead of 299,790). Reference is to party votes as percentage of added valid votes.

2.7.3 House of Representatives ('Coloreds') 1984–1989

Year	1984		1989	
	Total number	%	Total number	%
Registered voters	881,984	–	1,439,112	–
Votes cast	272,854	30.9	261,047	18.1
Invalid votes	(5,477)	2.0	2,861	1.1
Valid votes	267,377	98.0	258,186	98.9
Labour Party	200,335	74.9	171,930	66.6
Democratic Reform Party	–	–	39,741	15.4
United Democratic Party	–	–	19,861	7.7
Freedom Party	13,505	5.1	1,949	0.8
People's Congress Party	31,701	11.9	–	–
Reformed Freedom Party	2,632	1.0	–	–
Independents	19,204	7.2	24,705	9.6

2.7.4 House of Delegates ('Indians') 1984–1989

Year[a]	1989 Total number	%
Registered voters	663,604	–
Votes cast	154,524	23.3
Invalid votes	1,388	0.9
Valid votes	153,136	99.1
Solidarity	58,216	38.0
National People's Party	38,523	25.2
Democratic Party	10,427	6.8
National Federal Party	8,058	5.3
People's Party of SA	6,064	4.0
United Party	2,712	1.8
Merit People's Party	2,078	1.3
Progressive Independent Party	1,497	1.0
Freedom Party of SA	703	0.5
Republican Party of SA	701	0.5
Independents	24,157	15.8

[a] For the 1984 elections no data are given.

2.8 Composition of Parliament

2.8.1 House of Assembly ('Europeans') 1910–1989

Year[a]	1910 Seats		1915 Seats		1920 Seats		1921 Seats	
	Seats	%	Seats	%	Seats	%	Seats	%
	121	100	130	100	133	100	134	100
NP	–	–	27	20.8	44	32.8	45	33.6
SAP	66	54.6	54	41.5	41	30.6	79	59.0
Unionist Party	36	29.8	39	30.0	25	18.7	–	–
SALP	3	2.4	4	3.1	21	15.7	9	6.7
Independents	16	13.2	6	4.6	3	2.2	1	0.7

[a] 1938–1958 three additional European MPs representing the Cape African population. 1953–1977 six additional MPs representing SWA/Namibia. 1958–1961 four additional European MPs representing the Coloured population. Directly elected seats only. Through a system of indirect election by elected MPs and additional nominations by the State President the actual number of seats was higher, i.e. in 1989 178 (as opposed to 166).

Year	1924		1929		1933		1938	
	Seats	%	Seats	%	Seats	%	Seats	%
	135	100	148	100	150	100	150	100
NP	63	39.3	78	52.7	75	50.0	27	18.0
SAP	53	46.7	61	41.2	61	40.7	–	
UP	–	–	–	–	–	–	111	74.0
SALP	18	13.3	8	5.4	2	1.3	3	2.0
Dominion Party	–	–	–	–	–	–	8	5.3
Socialist Party	–	–	–	–	–	–	1	0.7
Central	–	–	–	–	2	1.3	–	
Home Rule Party	–	–	–	–	2	1.3	–	–
Independents	1	0.7	1	0.7	8	5.3	–	–

Year	1943		1948		1953		1958	
	Seats	%	Seats	%	Seats	%	Seats	%
	150	100	150	100	156	100	156	100
NP	–	–	–	–	94	60.3	103	66.0
HNP/V	43	28.7	70	46.7	–	–	–	–
UP	89	59.3	65	43.3	57	36.5	53	34.0
SALP	9	6.0	6	4.0	5	–	–	–
Dominion Party	7	4.7	–	–	–	–	–	–
AP	–	–	9	9.0	–	–	–	–
Independents	2	1.3	–	–	–	–	–	–

Year	1961		1966		1970		1974	
	Seats	%	Seats	%	Seats	%	Seats	%
	156	100	166	100	165	100	171	100
NP	105	67.3	126	75.9	117	70.9	120	70.2
UP	49	31.4	39	23.5	47	28.5	44	25.7
PFP	1	0.6	1	0.6	1	0.6	7	4.1
NUP	1	0.6	–	–	–	–	–	–

Year	1977		1981		1987		1989	
	Seats	%	Seats	%	Seats	%	Seats	%
	164	100	165	100	166	100	166	100
NP	134	81.7	131	79.4	123	74.1	94	56.6
PFP	17	8.5	26	15.8	19	11.4	–	–
NRP	10	6.1	8	4.9	1	0.6	–	–
DP	–	–	–	–	–	–	33	19.9
CP	–	–	–	–	22	13.3	39	23.5
SAP	3	1.8	–	–	–	–	–	–
Independents / others	–	–	–	–	1	0.6	–	–

2.8.2 Cape Coloreds Representative Council 1969–1975

Year	1969		1974	
	Seats	%	Seats	%
	40	100	40	100
Labour Party	26	65.0	31	77.5
Federal Coloured People's Party	11	27.5	8	20.0
Republican Coloured People's P. of SA & SWA	1	2.5	–	–
National Coloured People's Party	1	2.5	–	–
Independents	1	2.5	1	2.5

2.8.3 House of Representatives ('Coloureds') 1984–1989

Year	1984		1989	
	Seats	%	Seats	%
	80[a]	100	81[a]	100
Labour Party	76	95.0	69	85.2
Democratic Reform Party	–	–	5	6.3
United Democratic Party	–	–	3	3.7
Freedom Party of South Africa	–	–	1	1.2
Democratic Party	–	–	–	–
Independents	2	2.5	3	3.7

[a] Elected seats. Five additional non-elected seats.

2.8.4 House of Delegates ('Indians') 1984–1989

Year	1984		1989	
	Seats	%	Seats	%
	40[a]	100	40[a]	100
National People's Party	18	45.0	8	20.0
Solidarity	17	42.5	16	40.0
Democratic Party	–	–	3	7.5
Merit People's Party	–	–	3	7.5
United Party	–	–	2	5.0
People's Party of South Africa	–	–	1	2.5
Progressive Independent Party	1	2.5	–	–
National Federal Party of South Africa	–	–	1	2.5
Independents	4	10.0	6	15.0

[a] Elected seats only. Five additional non-elected seats.

2.9 Presidential Elections

Presidential elections have not been held.

2.10 List of Power Holders 1910–1998

Head of State	Years	Remarks
British Monarch	1910–1961	Exercised through Governors-General: Viscount Gladstone 1910–1914, Viscount Buxton 1914–1920, Prince Arthur of Connaught 1920–1924, Earl of Athlone 1924–1931, Earl of Clarendon 1931–1937, Sir Patrick Duncan 1937–1943, N. J. de Wet (acting) 1943–1945, Gideon van Zyl 1946–1950, Ernest G. Jansen 1951–1959 and C. R. Swart 1960–1961.
C. R. Swart	1961–1967	–
N. Diederichs	1975–1978	–
Balthazar J. Vorster	1978–1979	–
Marais Viljoen	1979–1984	–
Pieter W. Botha	1984–1989	After promulgation of the 1983 Constitution as executive President and tricameral Parliament (co-optation of Coloureds and Indians) and Head of State; 08/06/1986 until 07/06/1990: countrywide State of Emergency.

Head of State	Years	Remarks
Frederick W. de Klerk	1989–1994	Until 1993 as acting Head of State and Government
Nelson R. Mandela	1994–	Executive President

Head of Government	Years	Remarks
Gen. Loius Botha	1910–1919	Based on an Act of the British Parliament (South Africa Act, 20/09/1909) the four territories Cape, Natal, Transvaal and Orange Free State formed the Union of South Africa (31/05/1910). 1915–1919 SAP-government tolerated by Unionist Party.
Gen. Jan C. Smuts	1919–1924	1920 coalition government with Unionists who joined the SAP.
Gen. James B.M. Hertzog	1924–1939	'Pact Government' between NP and SAP. 1928 split within SALP, with the Creswell faction joining a coalition with the NP in 1929. 1931 reunion of SALP, with one of five MPs disobeying orders to leave the government. 1932–1934 NP-SAP coalition government, joined by Creswell faction of SALP. 1934 merger of NP and SAP, forming the UP. 1939 split over participation in World War II.
Gen. Jan C. Smuts	1939–1948	UP-DP-SALP coalition government. 1940 union of NP and Gesuiwerde NP, forming HNP/V. 1948 NP-AP election pact.
Daniel F. Malan	1948–1954	NP-AP coalition government. 1951 NP-AP union.
Johannes G. Strijdom	1954–1958	—
Hendrik F. Verwoerd	1958–1966	31/05/1961 change from Union to Republic of South Africa; 1962 Merger of NP and NUP.
Balthazar John Vorster	1966–1978	Assumed power after assassination of Verwoerd 06/09/1966; 1969 NP split, formation of HNP; 1977 UP dissolved.
Pieter W. Botha	1978–1984	*De facto* 'parallel' rule by 'securocrats' dominated State Security Council.
Transitional government	1993–1994	Parallel rule by committees dominated by NP and ANC until the 1994 elections (with a non-racial franchise).

General note: Heads of Government are listed only insofar they differ from the Head of State.

3. Bibliography

3.1 Official Sources

Constitution of the Republic of South Africa Act, 1993 (No. 200 of 1993). Pretoria: Government Printer.

Constitution of the Republic of South Africa Amendment Act (No. 2 of 1994). Pretoria: Government Printer.

Electoral Amendment Act, 1994 (No. 1 of 1994). Pretoria: Government Printer.

Government Notice R310 of 1994. Pretoria: Government Printer.

Government Notice R809 of 1994. Pretoria: Government Printer.

Government Notice No. 198 of 1994. Pretoria: Government Printer.

Independent Electoral Commission Act (No. 150 of 1993). Pretoria: Government Printer.

Independent Electoral Commission Amendment Act, 1994 (No. 5 of 1994). Pretoria: Government Printer.

Proclamation No. 46 of 1993. Pretoria: Government Printer.

Proclamation No. 45 of 1994. Pretoria: Government Printer.

Proclamation No. 69 of 1994. Pretoria: Government Printer.

Proclamation No. 73 of 1994. Pretoria: Government Printer.

Proclamation No. 85 of 1994. Pretoria: Government Printer.

Republic of South Africa and Bureau for Information (on behalf of the Department of Foreign Affairs) (1989). *South Africa 1989–90. Official Yearbook of the Republic of South Africa* (15th edn.). Cape Town.

— (1983). *South Africa 1983. Official Yearbook of the Republic of South Africa*. Pretoria.

The Constitution of the Republic of South Africa (Act 108 of 1996). Pretoria: Government Printer.

The Electoral Act, 1993 (No. 202 of 1993). Pretoria: Government Printer.

3.2 Books, Articles and Election Reports

Anglin, D. G. (1995). 'International Monitoring of the Transition to Democracy In South Africa, 1992–1994'. *African Affairs*, 94/377: 519–543.

Association of European Parliamentarians for (Southern) Africa (1994). *South Africa Between Yesterday and Tomorrow. AWEPA Electoral Observing in South Africa*. Amsterdam: African European Forum.

Christopher, A. J. (1983). 'Parliamentary Delimitation in South Africa, 1910–1980'. *Political Geography Quarterly*, 2/3: 205–217.

Commonwealth (1994). *The End of Apartheid. The Report of the Commonwealth Observer Group to the South African Elections 26–29 April 1994*. London: Commonwealth Secretariat.

Eldridge, M., and Seekings, J. (1996). 'Mandela's Lost Province: The African National Congress and the Western Cape Electorate in the 1994 South African Elections'. *Journal of Southern African Studies*, 22/4: 517–540.

Engel, U. (1990–1997). 'Südafrika', in Institut für Afrika-Kunde and R. Hofmeier (eds.), *Afrika Jahrbuch. Politik, Wirtschaft und Gesellschaft in Afrika südlich der Sahara*. Opladen: Leske & Budrich (annually).

— (1994). *Demokratische Transition in Südafrika (Focus Afrika. IAK-Diskussionsbeiträge, 2)*. Hamburg: Institut für Afrika-Kunde.

EU (European Union) (1994). *Observing South Africa's 1994 National and Provincial Elections. Final Report to the European Commission from the European Union Election Unit*. Johannesburg.

Hanf, T. (1994). 'Konfliktregelung durch Wahlen', in Deutsches Übersee-Institut (ed.), *Jahrbuch Dritte Welt 1995*. München: Beck, 88–116.

Heard, K. A. (1974). *General Elections in South Africa 1943–1970*. London etc.: Oxford University Press.

Horowitz, D. L. (1991). *A Democratic South Africa? Constitutional Engineering in a Divided Society*. Berkeley, Cal.: University of California Press.

Independent Electoral Commission (1994). *Report of the Independent Electoral Commission: The South African Elections of April 1994*. Johannesburg: Independent Electoral Commission.

Johnstone, A. (1994). 'South Africa: The Election and the Emerging Party System'. *International Affairs*, 70/4: 721–736.

de Kock, C. *et al.* (1993). *The Prospects for a Free, Democratic Election: Inhibiting And Facilitating Factors in Voting Intention*. Pretoria: Human Sciences Research Council.

Krennerich, M., and de Ville, J. (1997). 'A Systematic View on the Electoral Reform Debate in South Africa'. *Verfassung und Recht in Übersee*, 30/1: 26–41.

Lemon, A. (1982). 'Issues and Campaigns in the South African General Election of 1981'. *African Affairs*, 81/325: 511–526.

Lodge, T. (1995). 'The South African General Election, April 1994. Results, Analysis and Implications'. *African Affairs*, 94/377: 471–500.

MacDonald, M. (1982). 'The Siren's Song: The Political Logic of Power-Sharing in South Africa'. *Journal of Southern African Studies*, 18/4: 709–725.

Midlane, M. (1979). 'The South African General Election of 1977'. *African Affairs*, 78/312, 371–387.

National Democratic Institute for International Affairs and O'Malley, P. (1994). *The Point of No Return: The Politics of South Africa on Election Day. April 1994*. Washington, D.C.: National Democratic Institute for International Affairs.

Noller, J. F. (1978). 'Südafrika', in D. Sternberger, B. Vogel, D. Nohlen and K. Landfried (eds.). *Die Wahl der Parlamente und anderer Staatsorgane. Bd. II: Politische Organisation und Repräsentation in Afrika*, by Franz Nuscheler, Klaus Ziemer *et al.*, Berlin/ New York: Walter de Gruyter, 1995–2100.

Pakendorf, H. (1987). 'The National Party: Challenged by a Changed Support Base'. *Africa Insight*, 17/3: 188–191.

Reynolds, A. (ed.) (1994). *Election '94 South Africa: An Analysis of the Campaigns, Results and Future Prospects*. Cape Town: David Philip.

Schoeman, B. M. (1977). *Parlementere verkiesings in Suid-Afrika 1910–1976*. Pretoria: Aktuele Publikasies.

Sisk, T. D. (1993). 'Choosing an Electoral System. South Africa Seeks New Ground Rules'. *Journal of Democracy*, 4/1: 79–91.

Southall, R. (1994*a*). 'The South African Elections of 1994: The Remaking of a Dominant-Party State'. *Journal of Modern African Studies*, 32/4: 629–655.

— (1994*b*). 'South Africa's 1994 Election in an African perspective'. *Africa Insight*, 24/2: 86-98.

Stadler, A. W. (1975). 'The 1974 General Election In South Africa'. *African Affairs*, 74/295: 209–218.

Strauss, A. (1993). 'The 1992 Referendum in South Africa'. *Journal of Modern African Studies*, 31/2: 339–360.

Szeftel, M. (1994). 'Negotiated Elections in South Africa, 1994'. *Review of African Political Economy*, 61: 457–470.

UN (United Nations) (1994). *Report of the Secretary-General on the Question of South Africa*. UN S/1994/717, 16 June 1994.

de Ville, J., and Steytler, N. (eds.) (1996). *Voting in 1999: Choosing an Electoral System*. Durban: Butterworths.

Welsh, D. (1984). 'Constitutional Changes in South Africa'. *African Affairs*, 83/331: 147–163.

SUDAN

by Helga Fleischhacker and Curtis F. Doebbler

1. Introduction

1.1 Historical Overview

Sudan's political history is marked by repeated efforts to impose stable government over a country divided by numerous religious, linguistic, ethnographic and political differences. These have led to 30 years of civil war in the 42 years of Sudan's existence.

Within the Northern political forces religion plays a major role. Although the Sudanese Communist Party was a substantial force from independence in 1956 until about 1975, the party was almost complete routed by a violent purge conducted by President Ja'faar Muhammad Nimeiri. Since then three religious-based parties have effectively functioned as the leading political parties in Sudan. The party that appears to have the largest following is the Umma Party. Originally founded in 1945, the Umma Party is based on the Islamic teachings of the Ansar movement, which dates back to the 19th century. The Ansar centers of power are in the rural west of the country and in the capital, Khartoum. The second of the three prominent religious-based parties is the Democracy Union Party (DUP), formerly the National Union Party (NUP) and then later the Peoples' Democratic Party (PDP). It was established in 1943 when the Khatmiyya or Mirghaniyya Islamic sect joined political forces with the Ashigga Party. Its original founder was Muhammad Osman al-Mirghani and it is still today led by his descendent. Although enjoying widespread support throughout Northern Sudan, the DUP has always been overshadowed by the political success of the Umma Party and had limited political effectiveness because of its internal divisions. The third religious-based party is the National Islamic Front (NIF). This party originated from the Muslim Brotherhood in Egypt sometime between 1949 and the early 1970s. Since the late 1970s it has been led by Hassan Abdallah al-Turabi. It contested the 1986 election earning 17% of the vote before orchestrating the 1989 coup. Although supported by diverse Islamic groups, the NIF has been characterized by a mix of modernist and extremist political policies. Al-Turabi, the real force behind the official regime, has preferred to remain in the background until recently.

Sudan became self-governing in 1954 and fully independent on 1 January 1956 under a transitional constitution providing for an elected Parliament. It led to two civilian governments under first Ismail al-Azhari (NUP) and then Abdullah Khalil (Umma). This brief flirtation with democracy was soon interrupted by the military regime of General Ibrahim Abboud, but the dictatorial repression of this regime brought about its downfall in 1964. In 1964 a transitional government was formed, headed by non-partisan Sirr al-Khatim. In elections that same year, Muhammad Ahmed Mahjoub, an independent, became Prime Minister. In 1965, Sadiq El-Mahdi succeeded when he won a challenge for leadership of the Umma Party. El-Mahdi retained this post through the 1968 elections for the Constitutional Assembly. Throughout this initial period, the NUP and the Umma party dominated the other political parties as the increasingly deadly civil war in the South dominated the political agenda of all parties.

On 25 May 1969, General Ja'faar Muhammad Nimeiri seized power in a military coup supported by the Sudanese Communist Party (SCP). As self-proclaimed President, Nimeiri immediately announced that Sudan would henceforth be a socialist state. After a failed coup by the SCP in July 1971, Nimeiri reorganized the state structure and issued a new constitution. Elections were held at the end of 1972 and Nimeiri was elected President. During his next 14 years in power Nimeiri fluctuated from communist (1969–1971) to vague pan-Arabist positions within the framework of a single-party regime based on the repressive Sudan Socialist Union (SSU) (1971–1977), to the postulation of 'National Reconciliation' whereby parties previously in opposition (DUP, Umma and NIF) were invited to join a coalition (1977), and finally, of a strong Islamic leadership (after 1977). In April 1973, Sudan adopted a National Constitution declaring Sudan a one-party state and creating a strong presidential form of government. This agreement was complemented by a negotiated end to the civil war.

In 1980, Nimeiri embarked upon a comprehensive de-centralization program dividing the North into five new administrative regions with greater local autonomy. In 1981, he dissolved both the National People's Assembly and the Southern Regional Assembly in favor of new bodies with more devolved authority. And in May 1983, he unilaterally abrogated the Southern Regional Constitution by dividing the South into three separate administrative regions. This made the South more manageable, but led to widespread discontent and eventually to his downfall.

The strongest opposition to Nimeiri came from the Islamic NIF. In an apparent attempt to co-opt this party, and also probably due to his increased faith in the Islamic religion, Nimeiri entered into a close alliance with the NIF which cumulated in September 1983 when he announced that Islamic law would be introduced throughout Sudan. By the end of the year, the civil war had been renewed by the SPLA/SPLM and the Northern parties were becoming increasingly critical of Nimeiri's government. After a severe famine in the South and a series of widespread strikes and demonstrations in the North, Nimeiri was overthrown by a non-violent military coup while abroad on an official visit to the United States on 6 April 1985.

General Abd al-Rahman Sawr al-Dahab assumed power after the coup. He formed a 14-member Transitional Military Council, announced that elections would be held within one year and suspended the 1973 Constitution. The Sharia laws remained in effect and an interim constitution was enacted. In April 1986, elections were held and Sadiq El-Mahdi became Prime Minister of a Umma–DUP coalition government. The election was marred by violence in 43 of the Southern constituencies and voting was cancelled in these constituencies. The NIF acquired 17% of the vote to place itself as the third party in Sudan.

In January 1987, in an effort to end the conflict in the South El-Mahdi's government announced the formation of a new Southern Administrative Council based on the Koka Dam Agreement that the Umma Party had negotiated with the SPLA/SPLM in March 1986. The Council was to comprise representatives from six Southern political parties and the governors of the three Southern administrative regions. As the agreement did not have the support of the DUP and the NIF, the Southern Council was unable to function and it was dissolved in January 1988 with the signing of a Transitional Charter that was more agreeable to all three Northern parties. While the DUP had initially opposed the Umma Party's attempts to negotiate an end to the civil war by November 1988, the DUP was convinced that ending the conflict was necessary and it signed an agreement with the SPLA. The agreement called for a freeze in the implementation of Sharia laws, a cease-fire and the lifting of the State of Emergency. The Umma Party's failure to condemn the DUP-SPLA agreement caused the NIF to cease its cooperation with government and the DUP to rejoin the coalition in early 1989. By mid-1989 it appeared that a consensus had been reached between the Northern

Umma and DUP parties and the SPLA and that the war might be brought to an end.

However, a 1989 coup brought Lt-General Omar Hassan Ahmad al-Beshir to power with the backing of the NIF. One of the government's first moves was to ban all political parties and impose a State of Emergency and subsequently to launch a reign of terror, arresting and executing many of its opponents. In 1991, a 'national political conference' was convened, but the main opposition parties did not attend. Nevertheless, this conference endorsed the government's proposal for decentralized government based on 281 popularly elected local councils, and 66 indirectly elected provincial councils, nine state governments and the federal government. In 1993, President al-Beshir appointed a 300-member Transitional National Assembly until the permanent National Assembly could be elected. Around the same time, the Revolutionary Command Council (RCC) confirmed al-Beshir as President and dissolved itself. Most of the RCC members reappeared as Cabinet Ministers in al-Beshir's government.

In 1996, elections were held for both the National Assembly and the presidency. While al-Beshir's closest competitor acquired less than 3% of the votes, the National Assembly was filled by a number of directly elected independents, mostly from among those sympathetic to the policies of the NIF and the Muslim Brotherhood Movement, the more extreme Islamists. The elections did not include large parts of Southern Sudan and were widely criticized as having been staged.

On 1 July 1998, a new constitution came into force for Sudan. It was marred by controversy from its beginning because it was negotiated during an on-going civil war and without the participation of any opposition representatives. Nevertheless, it appeared to offer a ray of hope in the mist of deteriorating living standards and increasingly uncontrolled security operations. The drafting had begun with the National Constitutional Committee and passed through the Office of the President and the National Assembly before being submitted to the people for a referendum, which was characterized by government oppression and suppression of opinion.

The Constitution of 1998 establishes a government where the primary legislative power remains with the National Assembly, the President is given broad powers in times of emergency and the right to form political parties may be re-instituted. It is ambiguous about whether political parties will again be allowed to operate because of the vague language of article 26 which appears to allow only traditional Islamic parties to operate and the statements of the President declaring that no party that offended Islam would be tolerated.

1.2 The Evolution of Electoral Provisions

The first legislative elections were held while Sudan was still a British–Egyptian condominium in 1953 under the electoral law of the same year. All male Sudanese above the age of 21 years were entitled to vote. Of the 97 members of the first legislative chamber, 24 were indirectly elected and 68 were directly elected in single-member constituencies according to the plurality system. Candidates were required to have been resident in their constituency for at least six months prior to the elections. Indirectly elected members of the legislature were chosen in two rounds of elections. First, an electoral college was elected. Second, the members or this electoral college elected the 24 members of the legislature. The second chamber was composed of 20 members appointed by the British Governor-General and 30 members chosen by representatives of provincial and local councils, graduates, teachers, and the representatives of the first chamber. Any Sudanese male over 30 years of age could be a candidate.

The Electoral Law of 1953 was revised on the eve of the legislative elections in 1958. A single National Assembly of 173 directly elected legislators was created and suffrage was extended to all male Sudanese with a minimum age of 30 years. The government of General Abboud implemented a system of provincial councils, that were elected by the directly elected local council members following the 'basic democracy model' that had become known in Pakistan in 1961. The transitional government, which came to power in 1964, called for elections of a single-chamber legislature. The voting age was lowered to 18 years and suffrage was extended to women. Of the total 233 seats, 218 were elected in single-member constituencies according to the plurality system, while another 15 were elected by the 12,584 registered graduates according to a plurality rule based on a list (preferential vote). Every voter had 15 votes, which had to be cast for different candidates. The same electoral systems applied to the 1968 elections.

After Nimeiri came to power in 1969, several different forms of election took place. First, Nimeiri confirmed his position as Head of State in a plebiscite in 1971. One year later, a National People's Council of 207 members was indirectly elected by local councils (voting for 175 seats) and representatives of youth groups, women's groups and cooperatives (voting for 32 seats). The Constitution of 1973 provided for the President to be nominated by the state-party and confirmed by a referendum for a six-year term, a Vice-President from Southern Sudan and a single-chamber legislature elected every four years. Every Sudanese minimum age 21 years who was of 'sane mind' had the right to vote. In order to stand for election to the National Assembly one had to be a member of the SSU. Of the 250 seats in the legislature, 125 were directly elected in single-member constituencies according to the plurality system. For each seat at least two candidates had to compete. Youth, women's, village and professional organizations and the state governments chose the other 125 indirectly elected members. The size of the Peoples' Assembly was changed several times under Nimeiri and only the legislatures elected in 1974 served their full four-year term.

When Nimeiri was overthrown in 1985, all existing legislative bodies were dissolved and a Transitional Military Council assumed power. The transitional constitution that it introduced provided for a National Assembly which was duly chosen in 1986. Of the 301 seats, 264 were directly elected in single-member constituencies. In 37 of these constituencies voting had to be indefinitely postponed because of the continuing civil war. The al-Beshir government dissolved the National Assembly, which was elected in 1986, when it came to power in 1989.

On 13 February 1992, President al-Beshir appointed a 300-member Transitional National Assembly consisting of all the members of his Cabinet (the former members of the RCC), a number of advisors to the President, all state governors, representatives of the army, trade unions and former political parties. As this government ruled principally through presidential decrees, the form of government was established in these decrees. The Twelfth Constitutional Decree divided the country into 26 states, each with an elected assembly. The Thirteenth Constitutional Decree in 1995 created a system that looked very much like that found in the American constitution in terms of the balance of powers. A directly elected President and single-chamber legislature was foreseen. This constitutional system was tested between 6 and 18 March 1996 when both presidential and legislative elections were held. The President was elected according to the absolute majority system for a five-year term, the National Assembly contained 400 members elected for a four-year term: 125 seats were filled by the members of the National Conference, which had been nominated by the President and 275 seats were filled by direct universal suffrage in single-member constituencies according to the plurality system. On 1 July 1998, the new Constitution of Sudan confirmed that Sudan was a Federal Republic and provided a constitutional basis for most of the existing organs of state. In doing so, it continued the terms of both the President and members of the National Assembly. The President was henceforth entitled to be re-elected once (Article 41). For the first time, a woman may be elected President. In 1997 a Fourteenth Constitutional Decree implemented the Peace Agreement of 21 April 1997 that the government of al-Beshir had signed with some rebels who had defected from the Southern resistance movement. This decree created a Southern States Co-ordinating Council appointed by President al-Beshir. This decree remains in force under the new Constitution of 1998 until the expiry of the four-year transitional period in 2001.

1.3 Current Electoral Provisions

Sources: Constitution of the Republic of Sudan 1998 and forthcoming Electoral Law.

Suffrage: Universal, secret, direct and indirect. Sudanese, at least 18 years of age, resident in the constituency for three months before voting and registered as a voter (can be done at time of voting).

Elected national institutions: The President, elected for a five-year term by direct universal suffrage (one consecutive re-election being allowed). In the case of vacancy, the first Vice-President assumes office temporarily until new elections are held within a period of 60 days. A unicameral National Assembly is constituted of an undefined number of members elected through direct and indirect elections for a term of four years.

Nomination of candidates
- *presidential elections*: Sudanese citizens who are of at least 40 years of age, of sound mind and who have not been convicted of 'an offence involving honor or honesty' in the seven preceding years (Art. 37 of the 1998 Constitution).
- *elections to the National Assembly*: Sudanese of at least 21 years of age and who have not been convicted of 'an offence involving honor or honesty' in the seven preceding years (Art. 68 of the 1998 Constitution).

Electoral system
- *presidential elections*: Absolute majority. If no candidate achieves an absolute majority a second round run-off election is held between the

two candidates receiving the most votes, unless the other candidates withdraw after the first round, in which case the remaining candidate is elected without a second round of elections.
- *elections to the National Assembly*: Seventy-five percent of the membership is elected through direct general elections from geographic constituencies, while 25% is elected through indirect elections by the representatives of women's, scientific and trade organizations and state and national electoral colleges established according to law.

1.4 Comment on the Electoral Statistics

The results of the 1953, 1958 and 1965 to the legislature and the 1971 presidential elections are based on figures supplied by Klaus Landfried and Abdelgadir A. Abdel Ghaffar (1978) crosschecked with Ibrahim Mohammed Hag Musa (1970). Other figures are based on unofficial statistics released by the government of Sudan or based on estimates.

In general electoral statistics are found differ substantially from one another and are often incomprehensive. Figures released by the government except for those of 1986 have been highly disputed and are generally considered unreliable. Even the pre-independence election in 1953 was heavily interfered with by the Egyptians and the British according to Fabunmi (1960). Although the 1996 elections were observed by delegates from the Organization of African Unity who said they had been conducted without extensive irregularities, the majority of the international community as well as the opposition groups criticized the elections as rigged and invalid.

2. Tables

2.1 Dates of National Elections, Referendums and Coups d'Etat

Year	Presidential elections	Parliamentary elections		Elections for Constitutional Assembly	Referen-dums	Coups d'état
		Lower Chamber	Upper Chamber			
1953		02/11; 25/11	02/11; 25/11			
1958		27/02; 8/03	27/02; 8/03			17/11
1965				21/04; 8/05[a]		
1968				21/04–02/05		
1969						25/05
1971	15/09					
1972				22/09–04/10[b]		
1974		15/08				
1977	10–20/04					
1981		xx/12[c]				
1983	14–25/04					
1985						06/04
1986				01–12/04[d]		
1989						30/06
1996	06–17/03	06/03–17/03				
1998					01-20/05	

[a] Elections in the South were held two years later in 1967 on 8 March and 18 April.
[b] Indirectly elected.
[c] Supposedly another parliamentary election was held in 1978, however, neither the exact date nor statistics could be provided.
[d] Elected as a constituent and legislative assembly.

2.2 Electoral Body 1953–1998

Year	Type of election[a]	Population[b]	Registered voters		Votes cast		
			Total number	% pop.	Total number	% reg. Voters	% pop.
1953	R	8,500,000	1,687,000	19.8	—	—	—
1958	R	10,200,000	1,582,909	15.5	—	—	—
1965	CA	12,500,000	2,257,854	18.0	1,269,584	56.2	10.2
1968	CA	14,800,000	3,051,118	20.6	1,862,911	61.0	12.6
1971	P	16,000,000	4,191,747	26.2	3,895,688	92.9	24.3
1977	P	—	—	—	5,672,506	98.3	—
1986	CA	—	5,851,000[b]	—	3,948,544	67.5	—
1996	R	28,100,000	8,110,650	28.9	5,525,280	69.0	19.7
1996	Pr	28,100,000	8,110,650	28.9	5,525,280	69.0	19.7
1998	Ref	28,100,000	11,900,000[b]	42.3	10,900,000[b]	91.6	38.8

[a] CA = Constitutional Assembly; R = House of Representatives (Lower Chamber); Pr = President, Ref = Referendum.

[b] Rounded numbers as given by Reuters on 24 July 1998.

2.3 Abbreviations

DUP[a]	Democratic Unionist Party
ICF	Islamic Charter Front
NIF	National Islamic Front
NUP	National Union Party
PDP	People's Democratic Party
PPP	People's Progressive Party
SAC	Sudanese African Congress
SANU	Sudan African National Union
SAPCO	Sudan African People's Congress
SCP	Sudanese Communist Party
SLP[b]	Southern Liberal Party
SNP	Sudanese National Party
SPFP	Sudanese People's Federal Party
SPLM[c]	Sudanese Popular Liberation Movement
SRP	Southern Regional Party
SSPA	Southern Sudan Political Association
SSU	Sudan Socialist Union

[a] NUP and PDP fad combined to form DUP since the 1969 elections.

[b] Ran under the name of Liberal Party in 1953.

[c] Also referred to as SPLA: Sudanese Popular Liberation Army.

2.4 Electoral Participation of Parties and Alliances 1953–1986

Party / Alliance	Years	Elections contested	
		Presidential	Parliamentary[a]
Liberal Party[b]	1953	0	1
NUP	1953, 1958,1965, 1968	0	4
SRP	1953	0	1
Umma	1953, 1958, 1965, 1968,1986	0	5
PDP	1958	0	1
SLP	1958	0	1
ICF	1965, 1968	0	2
Nuba Mountain Federation	1965, 1968	0	2
SANU	1965, 1968	0	2
SCP[c]	1965, 1986	0	3
SLP	1965	0	1
Unity Party	1965, 1968	0	2
Beja Congress	1968	0	1
Congress of New Forces	1968	0	1
Democratic South	1968	0	1
DUP	1968, 1986	0	2
Free	1968	0	1
Islamic	1968	0	1
Nile	1968	0	1
Peace	1968	0	1
Socialist Democrats	1968	0	1
Socialist Front	1968	0	1
Socialists	1968	0	1
Southern Front	1968	0	1
Tenants Union	1968	0	1
Western Sudan Union[d]	1968	0	1
Workers Federation	1968	0	1
Workers Force	1968	0	1
SSU[e]	1974, 1977, 1978, 1982, 1983 supposed number	2	3
NIF	1986	0	1
PPP	1986	0	1
SAC	1986	0	1
SAPCO	1986	0	1
SNP	1986	0	1

Party / Alliance	Years	Elections contested	
		Presidential	Parliamentary[a]
SPFP	1986	0	1
SSPA	1986	0	1

[a] Elections to Constitutional Assemblies are included.
[b] Changed name to SLP in 1958.
[c] The SCP participated in the elections before 1965 as the Front against Colonization (1953) and the Independents (1958 and 1968)
[d] According to Hag Musa (1970) the Western Sudan Union also participated in the 1965 election.
[e] Supposedly there have been parliamentary elections in 1978 and 1981, however, no exact data were available.

2.5 Referendums

1998[a]	Total number	%
Registered voters	11,935,029[b]	–
Votes cast	10,427,888[b]	91.9
Invalid votes	—	—
Valid votes	—	—
Yes	10,472,888	96.7
No	326,732	3.3

[a] Referendum on the constitution ratified by Parliament on 28 March 1998 and signed into law on 30 June 1998. Throughout the referendum, it seemed unlikely that more than 50% of the population would vote. However, the electoral commission announced that the constitution had been adopted by the percentages presented above. The official government statement concerning invalid and valid votes is that there are no invalid votes. These figures were immediately met by skepticism by observers inside and outside Sudan.
[b] Results were taken from *Marchés Tropicaux*, 3 July 1998.

2.6 Elections for Constitutional Assembly

1965[a]	Votes		Seats	
	Total number	%	Total (207)	%
Registered voters	1,959,880			
Votes cast	1,126,229	58.1		
Invalid votes	—	—		
Valid votes	—	—		
Umma	—	—	90	43.5
NUP	—	—	59	28.5
Independents	—	—	21	10.1
Beja-Congress	—	—	10	4.8

1965[a]	Votes		Seats	
	Total number	%	Total (207)	%
Southern Sudan African Union	—	—	10	4.8
SCP	—	—	8	3.9
ICF	—	—	5	2.4
PDP	—	—	3	1.4
Southern Sudan Liberals	—	—	1	0.5

[a] Distribution of seats after by-elections in the South in 1967.

1968	Votes		Seats	
	Total number	%	Total (218)	%
Registered voters	3,051,118	–		
Votes cast	1,862,911	61.0		
Invalid votes	43,139	2.3		
Valid votes	1,819,772	97.7		
DUP	742,226	40.8	101	46.3
Umma (Sadiq)	384,986	21.2	36	16.5
Umma (Imam)	329,952	18.1	30	13.8
Umma	43,288	2.4	6	2.8
SANU	60,493	3.3	15	6.9
Southern Front	39,822	2.2	10	4.6
Independents	70,047	3.9	9	4.1
ICF	44,552	2.5	3	1.4
Beja Congress	15,382	0.9	3	1.4
Nuba Mountains Fed.	3,171	0.2	2	0.9
Nile	2,704	0.2	1	0.5
Workers Force	5,204	0.3	1	0.5
Unidentified	8,264	0.5	1	0.5
Socialist Front	21,814	1.2	–	–
Socialists	19,690	1.1	–	–
NUP	10,159	0.6	–	–
Tenants Union	6,661	0.4	–	–
Free	1,844	0.1	–	–
Islamic	1,772	0.1	–	–
Western Sudan Union	1,695	0.1	–	–
SCP	1,652	0.1	–	–
Democratic South	1,535	0.1	–	–
Unity	1,478	0.1	–	–
Workers Federation	668	0.0	–	–
Peace	387	0.0	–	–
Socialist Democrats	220	0.0	–	–
NUP-Sadiq wing	63	0.0	–	–
Congress of New Forces	33	0.0	–	–

1986	Votes		Seats	
	Total number	%	Total (301)	%
Registered voters	5,851,000	–		
Votes cast	3,948,544	67.5		
Invalid votes	—	—		
Valid votes	—	—		
Umma	—	—	101	33.6
DUP	—	—	63	20.9
NIF	—	—	51	16.9
PPP	—	—	11	3.7
SNP	—	—	8	2.7
SSPA	—	—	8	2.7
SAPCO	—	—	7	2.3
Independents	—	—	5	1.7
SCP	—	—	3	1.0
SAC	—	—	2	0.7
SPFP	—	—	1	0.3

General note: According to official sources, in 37 of a total of 68 constituencies in the South there were not enough voters registered for the holding of elections due to the election boycott of SPLA. 1,100 candidates were fielded by more than 30 parties in those 264 constituencies, where elections were held.

2.7 Parliamentary Elections

For parliamentary elections no detailed results has been available.

2.8 Composition of Parliament

2.8.1 Lower Chamber (House of Representatives) 1953–1996

Year	1953		1958		1974		1996	
	Seats	%	Seats	%	Seats	%	Seats	%
	97	100	173	100	151[a]	100	400[b]	100
NUP	51	52.6	45	26.0	–	–	–	–
Umma	22	22.7	63	36.4	–	–	–	–
SRP	3	3.0	–	–	–	–	–	–
Southern Party	9	9.3	–	–	–	–	–	–
Independents	12	12.8	–	–	–	–	–	–
PDP	–	–	27	15.6	–	–	–	–
Southern Liberal Party	–	–	38	22.0	–	–	–	–
SSU	–	–	–	–	151	100	–	–

[a] Presumably consecutive parliamentary elections were held under SSU rule in 1978 and 1981. Unfortunately no information on the date or the number of seats installed could be provided.

[b] Of the 400 seats, 275 were directly elected, 125 were indirectly elected by the preceding 'national conference'. Although according to law political parties do not exist, it can be stated that the Assembly is dominated by the National Islamic Front and other fundamentalist Islamic members. The elections were boycotted by the main opposition parties.

2.8.2 Upper Chamber (Senate) 1953–1958

Year	1953		1958	
	Seats	%	Seats	%
	50[a]	100	30[b]	100
NUP	31(10)	62.0	5	16.7
Umma	8 (4)	16.0	14	46.6
SRP	1 (0)	2.0	–	–
Southern Party	6 (3)	12.0	–	–
Independents	4 (3)	8.0	–	–
PDP	–	–	5	16.7
Others[c]	–	–	6	20.0

[a] Of 50 Senators 30 were indirectly elected by local and province councils and 20 were appointed by the British Governor-General. The number of nominated Senators is indicated in parentheses.

[b] Directly elected.

[c] Representatives of the Southern provinces.

2.9 Presidential Elections 1971–1996

1971	Total number	%
Registered voters	4,191,784	–
Votes cast	3,895,688	92.9
Invalid votes	—	—
Valid votes	—	38.0
Ja'faar Nimeiri	3,839,374	98.6
No votes	56,314	1.4

1977	Total number	%
Registered voters	—	–
Votes cast	5,672,506	98.3
Invalid votes	—	—
Valid votes	—	—
Ja'faar Nimeiri	—	99.1
No votes	48,378	0.9

1983	Total number	%
Registered voters	—	—
Votes cast	—	—
Invalid votes	—	—
Valid votes	—	—
Ja'faar Nimeiri	—	99.6
No votes		—

1996	Total number	%
Registered voters	8,110,650	–
Votes cast	5,525,082	72.2
Invalid votes	—	—
Valid votes	—	—
Omar Hassan Ahmad al-Beshir	4,181,784	75.7
Abd al-Majid Sultan Kijab	133,032	2.4

General note: 41 candidates took part in the presidential election as independents due to the ban for political parties.

2.10 List of Power Holders 1953–1998

Head of State	Years	Remarks
Council of Sovereignty	1956–1958	After the British Governor-General had been withdrawn along with independence on 1 January 1956, a Council of Sovereignty was established as Head of State. It contained five members elected by Parliament; chairmanship changed monthly.
Ibrahim Abboud	1958–1964	On 17 November 1958 the army ousted the government and a transitional High Council made up 13 army officers transferred all executive, legislative and judicative powers to Ibrahim Abboud, who proclaimed himself President. The military regime retreated after protest demonstrations in October 1964. A civilian government assumed office on 1 November 1964; President Abboud resigned 15 days later.
Council of Sovereignty	1964–1969	Along with civilian rule the Council of Sovereignty was re-established in 1964.
Ja'faar Muhammad Nimeiri	1969–1985	Coup d'état on 25 May 1969 organized by a group of nationalist, left-wing officers led by Nimeiri, who headed a 10-member Revolutionary Council. The regime institutionalized in 1971 with a transitional constitution, presidential elections, a national constitution in 1973 and parliamentary elections in 1974. The President was confirmed on two occasions in 1977 and 1983.
Abd al-Rahman Sawr al-Dahab	1985–1986	A group of army officers led by al-Dahab seized power on 6 April 1985; a 14-member Transitional Military Council was formed until elections to a constituent and legislative assembly on 1–12 April 1986.
Supreme Council	1986–1989	A Supreme (Presidential) Council appointed by Parliament was meant to function as Head of State; however, the Assembly was unable to agree on its composition. The Prime Minister *de facto* assumed the functions of Head of State.

Head of State	Years	Remarks
Omar Hassan Ahmad al-Beshir	1989–	Assumed power by military coup as chairman of a Revolution Command Council (RCC) on 30 June 1989. The RCC dissolved itself on 16 October 1993 along with a formal return to civilian rule after declaring al-Beshir President and his acclamation by elections in 1996. On 1 July 1998 a new constitution entered into force by which al-Beshir remained President.

Head of Government	Years	Remarks
Ismail al-Azhari	1954–1956	Elected Prime Minister by a NUP majority in the House of Representatives for a transitional period to independence of three years under the trusteeship of the British Governor-General.
Abdullah Khalil	1956–1958	After the break-away of a faction of 18 MPs within NUP a new coalition government was formed in June 1956 under Khalil containing all political parties represented in the House of Representatives except for NUP. This coalition was continued after elections in February and March 1958, but ousted on 17 November 1958 by military coup after mass demonstrations.
	1958–1964	Under the reign of Ibrahim Abboud the Head of Government and Head of State were identical.
al-Khatim Khalifa	1964–1965	Assumed office on 1 November 1964 as head of a coalition government formed by all former political parties including the Communist Party.
Muhammad Ahmed Mahjoub	1965–1966	After parliamentary elections in 1965, which were only held in the North of the country due to civil war, a new coalition government was formed by Umma and NUP under Mahgub (Umma) while NUP-leader Azhari was granted the chairmanship of the Council of Sovereignty.
Sadiq al-Mahdi	1966–1967	After the Umma Party had splintered into a conservative (Imam al-Mahdi) and a progressive (Sadiq al-Mahdi) faction, the latter formed a coalition government together with NUP on 15 July 1966 which would endure only for nine months.

Head of Government	Years	Remarks
Muhammad Ahmed Mahjoub	1967–1969	In April 1967 Umma's Imam-faction under Mahjoub again coalesced with NUP. After elections in April and May 1968 this coalition was continued until its ouster by military coup on 25 May 1969.
	1969–1985	Under the reign of Ja'faar Nimeiri Head of Government and Head of State were identical.
al-Gizouli Dafallah	1985–1986	Named to head of an Interim Council of Ministers until legislative elections (April 1986) by Sawr al-Dahab on 22 April 1985.
Sadiq al-Mahdi	1986–1989	Assumed the post of Prime Minister with a coalition government based mainly on his Umma Party and DUP. The Mahdi regime was overthrown by military coup on 30 June 1989.
	1989–	Under the reign of al-Beshir Head of Government and Head of State are identical. Under the new Constitution of 1998 the situation remains the same.

3. Bibliography

Abdel-Rahim, M. (ed.) (1986). *Sudan Since Independence: Studies of the Political Development since 1956.* Aldershot: Gower.

Alier, A. (1990). *Southern Sudan: Too Many Agreements Dishonoured.* Exeter: Ithaca Press.

Al-Shahi, A. (1979). *La republique du Soudan.* Paris: Berger-Levrault.

Bechthold, P. (1976): *Politics in Sudan. Parliamentary and Military Rule in an Emerging African Nation*. New York: Praeger.

Beshir, M. O. (1974). *Revolution and Nationalism in the Sudan.* New York: Barnes & Noble Books.

— (1975). *The Southern Sudan: From Conflict to Peace.* Khartoum: The Khartoum Bookshop.

Daly, M. W., and Sikainga, A. A. (eds.) (1993). *Civil War in the Sudan.* London/ New York: British Academic Press.

Deng, F. (1995). *War of Visions*. Washington, D.C.: Brookings Institute.

El Badrawi, A. M. (1971). *Die Entwicklung der Demokratie im Sudan von 1936 bis 1968.* Doctoral Dissertation, University of Bonn.

Fabunmi, L. A. (1960). *The Sudan and Anglo–Egyptian Relations 1800–1956.* London: Longmans.

Flory, M. *et al.* (eds.) (1990). *Les régimes politiques arabes*. Paris: Presses universitaires de France.

Garang, J. (1992). *The Call for Democracy in Sudan.* London/ New York: Kegan Paul International.

Giovanninni, P. (1988). *Der Sudan zwischen Krieg und Frieden.* Wien: Afro Publ.

Gundlach, R. *et al.* (eds.) 1996. *Der Sudan in Vergangenheit und Gegenwart.* Frankfurt/M.: Lang.

Gurdon, C. (1984). *Sudan at the Crossroads.* Wisbech: Middle East & North African Studies Press.

Hag Musa, I. M. (1970). *The Democratic Experience and the System of Government in Sudan: The Elections of 1953, 1958, 1965 and 1968.*

Hamid, M. B. (1984). *The Politics of National Reconciliation in the Sudan: the Numayri Regime and the National Front Opposition.* Washington, D.C.: Center for Contemporary Arab Studies, Georgetown University.

Kalid, M. (1985). *Nimeiri and the Revolution of dis-May.* London/ Boston: KPI.

— (1990). *The Government they Deserve: The Role of the Elite in Sudan's Political Evolution.* London/ New York: Kegan Paul International.

Malwal, B. (1981). *People and Power in Sudan.* London: Ithaca.

Niblock, T. (1987). *Class and Power in Sudan: The Dynamics of Sudanese Politics, 1898–1985*. Albany: State University of New York Press.

Nok, P. N. (1996). *Governance and Conflict in Sudan, 1985–1995.* Hamburg: Deutsches Orient-Institut.

Sharma, B. S. (1966/67). Elections in the Sudan during the Military Regime. *Parliamentary Affairs,* 20: 274–280.

Sidahmed, A. S. 1997. *Politics and Islam in Contemporary Sudan.* Richmond: Curzon.

Sylvester, A. (1977). *Sudan under Nimeiri.* London: Bodley Head.

Tetzlaff, R. (1993). *Staatswerdung im Sudan.* Münster/ Hamburg: Lit.

Thomas, G. F. (1993). *Sudan: Struggle for Survival.* London: Darf.

Voll, J. O. (ed.) (1991). *Sudan: State and Society in Crisis.* Bloomington: Middle East Institute/ Indiana University Press.

Wauschkuhn, M., and Wohlmuth, K. (eds.) (1995). *Die Sudanforschung in der Bundesrepublik Deutschland.* Münster/ Hamburg: Lit.

Woodward, P. (1990). *Sudan, 1989–1989. The Unstable State.* London: L. Crook Academic Publ.

— (ed.) (1991): *Sudan after Nimeiri.* London/ New York: Routledge.

Zwier, L. J. (1998). *Sudan: North against South.* Minneapolis, Minn.: Lerner Publications Co.

SWAZILAND

by Matthias Basedau

1. Introduction

1.1 Historical Overview

A brief summary of Swaziland's history since independence illustrates the minor role of elections in its politics. The small British protectorate in South Africa's neighborhood became independent on 6 September 1968. Like most of the former British colonies she adopted a Westminster-style constitution, with a Prime Minister being responsible to a bicameral Parliament and a King (Sobhuza II) as Head of State. The first elections held several months before the advent of independence in 1967 saw the unopposed victory of the King's party, the Imbokodvo National Movement (INM). In the 1972 elections the Ngwane National Liberatory Congress (NNLC), an opposition party backed by the labor unions, won a few seats in the National Assembly, which was considered as a serious threat to the hitherto unchallenged supremacy of the Swazi-establishment, the Dlamini clan.

As a result, King Sobhuza II dissolved Parliament in 1973 and suspended the post-independence Constitution accusing it of being the major cause of 'growing unrest, insecurity' and responsible for the failure 'to provide the machinery for good government'. Basic civil rights were denied and all party activity was banned. Subsequently, the King ruled by decree until a new (unwritten) constitution, the so-called *Tinkhundla*-system, was established in October 1978. It confirmed the King's powers and was based on regional traditional assemblies (*Tinkhundlas*). The bicameral Parliament (*Libandla*) consisting of a House of Assembly and a Senate was confined to debating government proposals and advising the King. Political parties and campaigning were condemned as alien to traditional Swazi custom, were prohibited. Accordingly the *Tinkhundla*-system can be described as 'absolute monarchy plus Parliament minus political parties'.

The period after the death of Sobhuza II in 1982 until the coronation of his son and successor four years later ('Interregnum') was characterized by a power struggle between the members of the ruling Dlamini clan. Following Sobhuza's death authority was—according to traditional custom—transferred to the Queen Mother (Indlovukazi) Dzeliwe, who also took the title of Queen Regent. In August 1983 she was replaced as both Queen Mother and Regent by Indlovukazi Ntombi, the mother of the young heir to the throne, Prince Makhosetive. In an apparent effort to halt the power struggle that had followed his father's death, the Prince assumed the title of King Mswati III on 25 April 1986, two years earlier than originally planned. Conceived as a move to strengthen his personal authority he dissolved Parliament one year before schedule and elections were held in November 1987.

In recent years the *Tinkhundla*-system, faced with domestic, regional and international pressures, has been severely criticized and has become more difficult to sustain. Since 1991 the King has initiated public discussions and a review of the *Tinkhundla*-system. Several Tinkhundla Review Commissions were established (also known as Vusela I–III) but proved unable or unwilling to accomplish essential reforms. Although 55 out of 65 members of the lower chamber were directly elected for the first time since 1972, the 1993 elections were held without the participation of parties again. Still prohibited, a number of parties (e.g. the People's United Democratic Movement, Pudemo) are operating underground.

However, in the latter half of 1996 Mswati III announced the work-out of a new constitution as an adequate answer to the country's current problems and challenges. In accounts of current mass protest and domestic unrest future developments in the constitutional field and general politics—democratization not excluded—will have to be under careful observation.

1.2 Evolution of Electoral Provisions

The sole national body to be directly elected in Swaziland has always been the House of Assembly (since 1978: *Libandla*). In the years 1978–1987 members of the House of Assembly were elected indirectly (see below). The number of members has varied from 24 (1967 and 1972) to 65 (1978–1987: 50: 1992: 65). The term has always been five years. Except for the period 1973–1978, when no elections were held, the principles of universal, equal, direct and secret suffrage were applied.

Concerning the nomination of candidates, in the elections of 1967 and 1972 candidates were required to be qualified voters and have a three-year residency in the country. During the period 1978–1987 candidates additionally qualifying by special 'knowledge and merit' were nominated by an 80-member Electoral College, which was elected by the people by the plurality system in 40 two-member constituencies (single vote). In order to avoid 'domestic unrest' caused by political campaigning the candidates' names were kept secret until National Nomination Day ('vote at first sight'). A major cut in Swaziland's electoral evolution was made when in 1973 all party activity was banned after the suspension of the post-independence Constitution. Since then only non-partisans have been eligible. In 1992 the Electoral College was abolished and the number of the then three-member constituencies in the pre-elections raised to 50 (further details see below).

With regard to the electoral system, in the legislative elections of 1967 and 1972 a plurality system in eight three-member constituencies (three votes) was applied. From 1978 to 1987 40 out of 50 members were appointed by an 80-member Electoral College. Since 1993 50 out of 65 Members of Parliament have been elected by the plurality system (number of candidates limited to three, single vote) in 50 single-member constituencies (further details see below). Moreover, since 1978 10 members of the House of Assembly have been nominated by the King.

1.3 Current Electoral Provisions

Sources: Electoral Order 1992.

Elected national institutions: The sole national body to be directly elected is the House of Assembly. (The 30 members of the Senate are by one third elected by the House of Assembly and by two thirds appointed by the King). The regular term is five years.

Suffrage: The principles of adult (18 years) universal, equal, direct and secret suffrage are applied.

Nomination of candidates: Every qualified voter additionally qualifying by special personal merit, knowledge and substantial contribution 'to the good government in Swaziland' is eligible as a non-partisan candidate. Furthermore, a pre-election system is applied to nominate the three candidates to contest the direct balloting. On National Nomination Day the candidates go through a primary election at the level of each of the *Tinkhundlas* which correspond with the 55 single-member constituencies of the second round. The first three most successful candidates then proceed to the secondary and direct election (see below).

Electoral system: The plurality system is applied in single-member constituencies: Three candidates, elected in the primary elections, compete in each of the 55 constituencies (one vote per voter). Ten are appointed by the King.

1.4 Comment on the Electoral Statistics

The data situation can be described as relatively satisfactory. Information derives in the first place from secondary sources (*Archiv der Gegenwart*, Interparliamentary Union, Boloro 1994, http://www.swazinews.co.sz), but was completed by official information, kindly put at the author's disposal by the Embassy of Swaziland, Brussels. Election results for 1967 and 1972 were obtained from Nuscheler (1978). The indirect character of the subsequent elections did not allow the application of conventional principles of statistical documentation, with the exception of the electoral body.

2. Tables

2.1 Dates of National Elections, Referendums and Coups d'Etat

Year	Presidential elections	Parliamentary elections[a]	Elections for Constitutional Assembly	Referendums	Coups d'état
1967		19–20/04			
1972		16–17/05			
1973					12/04[b]
1978		27/10			
1983		28/10			
1987		16/11			
1993		21/08, 12/10			
1998		14–28/10			

[a] Lower chamber; upper chamber (Senate) not directly elected.
[b] Constitution suspended by King Sobhuza II.

2.2 Electoral Body 1967–1998

Year	Type of election[a]	Population	Registered voters		Votes cast		
			Total number	% pop.	Total number	% reg. voters	% pop.
1967	Pa	385,000	106,121	27.6	83,620[b]	79.8	22.0
1972	Pa	430,000	—	—	71,307[b]	74.0	16.6
1978	Pa	499,046[c]	—	—	—	55.0[d]	—
1983	Pa	494,534[c]	—	—	—	—	—
1987	Pa	681,059[c]	359,120	52.4	—	—	—
1993	Pa	825,000	283,693	34.4	173,053	61.0	21.0
1998	Pa	944,462	198,445	21.0	119,845	60.4	12.7

[a] Pa = Parliaments (House of Assembly).
[b] Author's calculation.
[c] UN estimations as reported in the UN Statistical Yearbook. The figure of 1983 refers to 1984.
[d] Official estimation.

2.3 Abbreviations

INM	Imbokodvo National Movement
NNLC	Ngwane National Liberatory Congress
SPP	Swaziland Progressive Party
SUF	Swaziland United Front

General note: Since 1973 all parties have been banned.

2.4 Electoral Participation of Parties and Alliances 1967–1972

Party / Alliance[a]	Years	Elections contested
INM	1967, 1972	2
NNLC (Zwane)	1967, 1972	2
SPP	1967, 1972	2
SUP	1967, 1972	2
NNLC (Samketti)	1972	1

[a] Since 1973 all parties have been banned.

2.5 Referendums

Referendums have not been held.

2.6 Elections for Constitutional Assembly

Elections for Constitutional Assembly have not been held.

2.7 Parliamentary Elections (House of Assembly) 1967–1972

Year	1967		1972	
	Total number	%	Total number	%
Registered voters	106,121	–	—	–
Ballot papers cast[a]	84,685[b]	79.8	71,307	74.0
Invalid ballot papers[a]	3,888	4.5	1,034	1.5
Valid ballot papers[a]	80,314[b]	95.5	70,273	98.5
INM	191,160	79.3	164,493	78.0
NNLC (Zwane)	48,744	20.2	38,554	18.3
NNLC (Samketti)	–	–	6,393	3.0
SUF	681	0.3	797	0.4
SPP	356	0.2	582	0.3

[a] Three votes per ballot paper.
[b] Author's calculation (approximate figure; sum of votes per party: 240,941; divided by three: 80,314, rounded).

The indirect character of the elections in 1978, 1983, 1987 and 1993 precludes statistical documentation.

2.8 Composition of House of Assembly 1967–1972

Year[a]	1967		1972	
	Seats	%	Seats	%
	24	100	24	100
INM	24	100	21	87.5
NNLC	0	0	3	12.5

[a] All parties banned since 1973: In 1978, 1983, 1987 and 1993 all members of the House of Assembly were non-partisans.

2.9 Presidential Elections

Presidential elections have not been held.

2.10 List of Power Holders 1968–1998

Head of State	Years	Remarks
King Sobhuza II	1968–1982	Regular inauguration on 06/09/1968.
Queen Mother Dzeliwe	1982–1983	Assumed office on 21/08/1982 after death of Sobhuza II; Interregnum.
Queen Mother Ntombi	1983–1986	Assumed office on 10/08/1983.
King Mswati III	1986–	Coronation on 25/04/1986.

Head of Government	Years	Remarks
Prince Makohosini Dlamini	1968–1976	Appointed on 06/09/1968.
Maphevu Dlamini	1976–1979	Appointed by the King on 19/01/1976.
Benjamin Nsibandze	1979	Assumed office on 25/10/1979 as acting Prime Minister after the death of Maphevu Dlamini.
Prince Mbandla Dlamini	1979–1983	Appointed on 23/11/1979.
Prince Bhekimpi Dlamini	1983–1986	Appointed on 23/03/1983.
Sotsha Dlamini	1986–1989	Appointed on 04/10/1986.
Obed Mfanyana Dlamini	1989–1993	Appointed in July 1989.
Jameson Mblini Dlamini	1993–1996	Appointed on 12/11/1993; dismissed on 08/05/1996.
Sibusiso Barnabas Dlamini	1996–	Appointed on 26/07/1996.

3. Bibliography

Ayee, J. R. A. (1991). 'Swaziland and the International Monetary Fund'. *Verfassung und Recht in Übersee*, 24/1: 52–75.

Baloro, J. (1994). 'The Development of Swaziland's Constitution: Monarchial Responses to Modern Challenges'. *Journal of African Law*, 38/1: 19–34.

Banks, A. S. (1996). *Political Handbook of the World*. Binghampton, New York: CSA Publications.

Bischoff, P.-H. (1986). 'Swaziland - A Small State in International Relations'. *Afrika Spektrum*, 2: 175–189.

Boehmer, G. von (1967). 'London entläßt Swaziland aus dem Protektorat'. *Aussenpolitik,* 18/3: 166–170.

Booth, A. R. (1983). *Swaziland. Tradition and Change in a Southern African Kingdom*. Boulder, Col.: Westview Press.

Cook, C., and Killingray, D. (1991). *African Political Facts since 1945* (2nd edn.). Basingstoke, Hampshire: Macmillan.

Daniel, J., and Vilane, J. (1986). 'Swaziland: Political Crisis, Regional Dilemma'. *Review of African Political Economy*, 35: 54–67.

Davies, R.H., O'Meara, D., and Dlamini, S. (1985). *The Kingdom of Swaziland—A Profile*. London: Zed Books.

East, R. (1993). *Political Parties of Africa and the Middle East*. Harlow: Longman.

Fornara, P. (1978). 'Swaziland—Dieci anni di indipendenzia'. *Relaz. Internaz.*, 42/38: 836–837.

Gorvin, I. (1989). *Elections since 1945. A World Wide Compendium*. Harlow: Longman.

Griffith, L. I., and Funell, D. C. (1991). 'The Abortive Swaziland Deal'. *African Affairs*, 90: 51–64.

Matlosa, K. (1998). 'Democracy and Conflict in Post-Apartheid Southern Africa. Dilemmas of Social Change in Small States.' *International Affairs* 74/2: 319–337

Matselbula, J. S. M. (1988). *A History of Swaziland* (3rd edn.). Cape Town: Longman.

Mayer, H. (1993). 'Swaziland', in D. Nohlen and F. Nuscheler (eds.), *Handbuch Dritte Welt, Band 5: Ostfrika und Südafrika* (3rd edn.). Bonn: Dietz, 464–476.

Nuscheler, F. (1978). 'Swaziland', in D. Sternberger, B. Vogel, D. Nohlen and K. Landfried (eds.), *Die Wahl der Parlamente und anderer Staatsorgane, Bd. II: Politische Organisation und Repräsentation in Afrika*, by Franz Nuscheler, Klaus Ziemer *et al.*, Berlin/ New York: Walter de Gruyter, 2101–2124.

Potholm, C. P. (1977). 'Ngwemyama of Swaziland. The Dynamics of Political Adaption', in R. Lemarchand (ed.), *African Kingdoms in Perspective. Political Change and Modernization in Monarchial Settings*. London: Frank Cass.

Report of the Tinkhundla Review Commission. Nkhanini, June 1992.

Swaziland Government Gazette Extraordinary. Mbanane, August 26th, 1996.

The Kingdom of Swaziland (1996). *Report on the Elections to the House of a Assembly Held on 21st August and 12th October 1993*. Nkhanini (March 1996).

University of Swaziland and Social Science Research Unit (1983). *The Swaziland Rural Homestead*.

TANZANIA

by Wolfgang Fengler

1. Introduction

1.1. Historical Overview

Tanzania was founded on 26 April 1964 by the independent states of Tanganyika and Zanzibar. Since colonial times the two states had gone through very different processes of political development. In Tanganyika there was a strong liberation movement, the Tanganyika African National Union (TANU), with its leader Julius K. Nyerere opposing the British, who had held Tanganyika as a League of Nations and United Nations trusteeship since 1919. TANU constituted a united movement supported by all racial and ethnic groups in Tanganyika. Its broad support was demonstrated by overwhelming victories in the multi-party elections of 1958/59 and 1960, which were held under the supervision of the British colonial government.

TANU's success underlined its dominant position during and after independence. After the parliamentary elections of 1960 Nyerere was appointed Prime Minister of a transitional government preparing the last steps of Tanganyikan independence. The resolution of the United Nations on 21 April 1961 declared Tanganyika's self-governance for 1 May 1961. Independence was achieved on 9 December 1961 with Nyerere as the first Prime Minister of independent Tanganyika. The presidential elections of 1 November 1962 marked Tanganyika's transformation into a republic.

On the basis of the broad support of the population, the TANU government decided to transform the multi-party system into a one-party state. In order to sustain the democratic character of Tanganyika's political system a competition between candidates of the single party was established at parliamentary elections. After an inner-party selection process two candidates of TANU competed in each of the constituencies. Therefore Tanganyika—and later on Tanzania—can be considered an example of semi-competitive elections.

In contrast to Tanganyika, Zanzibar experienced a troublesome and violent transition to independence. In Zanzibar two parties were competing for political power. While the Afro-Shirazi-Party (ASP) represented the predominantly black lower class, Zanzibar National Party (ZNP) and its smaller coalition partner Zanzibar and Pemba People's Party (ZPPP) was backed by the Arabian upper class and the majority of Zanzibar's mixed population, the Swahili.

Although ASP won five of six seats in the first election in 1957 it could not repeat its victories in the following three elections between 1961 and 1963 due to the bias of the majoritarian electoral system. ASP did not obtain a majority of seats although it won the popular vote in all elections. It did not participate in any of these governments either. However, in January 1964 ASP took over power in a coup d'état. A Revolutionary Council chaired by the leader of ASP, Abeid Karume, was established and served as the legislative and executive body. Karume announced the end of democratic elections for the next 60 years.

Due to Zanzibar's instability and external pressure Nyerere and Karume decided eventually to unite both countries and founded the United Republic of Tanzania on 26 April 1964. Nyerere took over presidency while Karume became his deputy and remained President of the then semi-autonomous Zanzibar. Since 1965 Tanzania has regularly conducted national elections under the framework of the democratic one-party state. Parliamentary elections, however, were conducted only on the Tanzania mainland.

On 5 February 1977, the two regional parties, TANU and ASP, merged to found *Chama Cha Mapinduzi* (CCM, Party of Revolution) and the concept of a democratic one-party state was extended to Zanzibar. At the same time party supremacy was established with CCM as the fourth constitutional authority, which was superior to government and Parliament. As a consequence of the new political structure Zanzibar, which remained semi-autonomous, has conducted its own parliamentary and presidential elections since 1980.

Tanzanian one-party elections guaranteed a relatively high rate of elite circulation. The opportunity to choose the local candidate for the Parliament was another reason for the high level of acceptance of the Tanzanian one-party state. However, the democratic wave that swept over Africa in the early 1990s forced the Tanzanian government to reintroduce multi-partyism in July 1992. Thirteen parties were eligible to participate in Tanzania's first multi-party election after the formation of the union. Due to limited capacities and resources the new parties were not able to challenge CCM. The CCM demonstrated its organizational superiority since in three decades of single rule CCM had created a dense net of national party structures at the grassroots level.

However, chaotic organization of the elections and obvious rigging of Zanzibar's regional elections overshadowed CCM's clear victory in the presidential and parliamentary elections of October 1995.

1.2 Evolution of Electoral Provisions

Universal franchise was introduced shortly before Tanganyika's and Zanzibar's independence gradually. The first elections in Tanganyika were based on a parity system with strong restrictions on voters' eligibility (minimum income of 30,000 Tanzanian Shillings or higher education). In eight constituencies each voter had to choose one candidate from the three communities (African, Asian, European), respectively. In 1960, when parliamentary elections were held to prepare for independence, restrictions on voters' eligibility were reduced significantly; hence participation increased by more than 14-fold. The presidential elections of 1962 were the first without any artificial restrictions on universal suffrage. In Zanzibar's 1957 election only men with a certain level of income and education were allowed to participate. In 1960 women were eligible and since 1963 all Zanzibaris—just as with Tanganyikans—above the age of 18 were adjudged universal suffrage. Additional reasons for exclusion were mental illness and high treason.

Under the framework of the one-party system the elections of 1965 to 1990 can be described as semi-competitive. In each constituency two candidates, chosen in inner-party primaries of the (single) party, contested the elections. At the end of the 1970s a substantial change in the electoral process occurred due to an increase in nominated and indirectly elected Members of Parliament. From 1977 to 1985 especially the proportion of those two groups was heavily biased toward indirect representation: 111 elected parliamentarians were elected whereas 128 did not have a direct legitimization through the electorate.

All parliamentary elections in Tanganyika, Zanzibar and Tanzania were decided by the plurality system in single-member constituencies. In the presidential elections the electoral system was not an issue until 1995. Except in 1962, when Nyerere contested against Mtemvu (ANC), only one candidate was nominated, who could only be confirmed or rejected by the electorate. The constitution provided for the 1962 elections a plurality system. In the one-party state the candidates for presidency had to achieve at least 50% plus one of the valid votes. No minimum turnout was required.

1.3. Current Electoral Provisions

Sources: Constitution of the United Republic of Tanzania (Katiba ya Jamhuri ya Mwungano wa Tanzania ya Mwaka 1977, 1995); United Republic of Tanzania, Elections Act, 1985; United Republic of Tanzania, Political Parties Act, 1992. Details of the electoral process itself are regulated by the electoral law. The party law defines the functions of parties with regard to the electoral process and is therefore also of some importance.

Elected national institutions: Parliament with 232 elected (of a total of 275) members, elected for five years; President elected for five years, consecutive re-election being allowed twice.

Suffrage: Tanzanian citizens with a minimum age of 18 years, who must be registered in order to vote. Voter registration is voluntary.

Nomination of candidates: Candidates for both types of elections must hold Tanzanian citizenship and be members of parties with full registration; independent candidacy is not possible. The Political Parties Act provides that newly founded parties have the status of a temporarily registered party for six months. Within this period they must fulfil the requirements for full registration. Parliamentary candidates must have a minimum age of 21 years; presidential candidates of 40 years.

Electoral system
- *presidential elections*: Absolute majority system (majority run-off). If no candidate receives the absolute majority a second round is held between the two candidates with the most votes in the first round.
- *parliamentary elections*: Plurality system in 232 single-member districts. Besides the elected representatives there are co-opted Members of Parliament: 37 women, five members of the House of Representatives of Zanzibar and the Attorney-General. With exception of the latter all co-opted seats must be assigned to the parties proportionally to the representation they have achieved due to the election results.

1.4 Comment on the Electoral Statistics

Availability of official data is limited. The results of the October 1995 elections have been published by the National Electoral Committee. However, it has to be said that the *University of Dar es Salaam* has regularly conducted studies on national elections based on official data (Cliffe 1967; Election Study Committee 1974; Othman/Bavu/Okema 1990; Mukandala/Othman 1994), but analyses of the 1975 and 1980 elections have not been published. A very useful collection of election results can be found in the *Chronicle of Parliamentary Elections and Developments* published by the Inter-Parliamentary Union. As complementary sources Nuscheler (1978), Samoff (1987) and Othman (1990, 1995) were consulted.

2. Tables

2.1 Dates of National Elections, Referendums and Coups d'Etat

2.1.1 Tanganyika 1958–1962

Year	Presidential elections	Parliamentary elections	Elections for Constitutional Assembly	Referendums	Coups d'état
1958		08/09, 12/09			
1959		09/02, 15/02			
1960		30/08			
1962	01/11, 05/11				

2.1.2 Zanzibar 1957–1963

Year	Presidential elections	Parliamentary elections	Elections for Constitutional Assembly	Referendums	Coups d'état
1957		22/07			
1961		17/01			
1961		01/06			
1963		08/07, 15/07			
1964					12/01

2.1.3 Tanzania 1965–1995

Year	Presidential elections	Parliamentary elections	Elections for Constitutional Assembly	Referendums	Coups d'état
1965	30/09	30/09			
1970	30/10	30/10			
1975	26/10	26/10			
1980	26/10	26/10			
1985	27/10	27/10			
1990	28/10	28/10			
1995	29/10	29/10			

2.2 Electoral Body 1957–1995

2.2.1 Tanganyika 1958–1962

Year	Type of election[a]	Population	Registered voters		Votes cast		
			Total number	% pop.	Total number[c]	% reg. voters	% pop.
1958	Pa	9,076,000	40,567	0.4	63,204[d]	—	—
1960	Pa	9,238,000	885,000[b]	9.6	121,445	13.7[b]	1.3[b]
1962	Pr	9,559,000	1,800,000[b]	18.8	1,149,254	63.8	12.0

[a] Pa = Parliament; Pr = President.
[b] Estimation.
[c] Valid votes. Data on votes cast were not available.
[d] The total of votes extends the registered voters because each voter could have voted for a maximum of three candidates (tripartite roll).

2.2.2 Zanzibar 1957–1963

Year	Type of election[a]	Population	Registered voters		Votes cast		
			Total number	% pop.	Total number	% reg. voters	% pop.
1957	Pa	296,000	39,873	13.5	35,361	90.2	11.9
1961	Pa	315,000	90,000[b]	28.6[b]	84,963[c]	94.4[b]	26.9[b]
1961	Pa	315,000	93,918	29.8	90,595	99.6	28.8
1963	Pa	320,000	165,000[b]	51.6[b]	163,511	99.1[b]	51.1[b]

[a] Pa = Parliament.
[b] Estimation.
[c] Valid votes.

2.2.3 Tanzania 1965–1995

Year	Type of election[a]	Population	Registered voters		Votes cast		
			Total number	% pop.	Total number	% reg. voters	% pop.
1965	Pa	11,673,000	3,187,215	27.3	2,289,602	71.8	19.6
1965	Pr	11,673,000	3,187,215	27.3	2,636,040	82.7	22.6
1970	Pa	13,273,000	4,860,456	36.6	3,360,881	69.2	25.3
1970	Pr	13,273,000	5,051,938	38.1	3,649,789	72.3	27.5
1975	Pa	15,310,000	5,577,569	36.4	4,557,595	81.7	29.8
1975	Pr	15,310,000	5,577,566	36.4	4,557,595	81.7	29.8
1980	Pa	18,500,000	6,604,408	35.7	5,594,342	84.7	30.2
1980	Pr	18,500,000	6,969,803	37.7	5,986,942	85.9	32.4
1985	Pa	21,733,000	6,736,863[b]	31.0[b]	4,983,321[b]	74.0[b]	22.9[b]
1985	Pr	21,733,000	6,910,555	31.8	5,181,999	75.0	23.8
1990	Pa	25,635,000	7,296,553	28.5	5,425,282	74.4	21.2
1990	Pr	25,635,000	7,296,553	28.5	5,425,282	74.4	21.2
1995	Pa	30,337,000	8,928,816	29.4	6,831,578	76.5	22.5
1995	Pr	30,337,000	8,929,969	29.4	6,512,745	72.9	21.5

[a] Pa = Parliament; Pr = President.
[b] Estimation.

2.3 Abbreviations

ANC	African National Congress
ASP	Afro-Shirazi Party
CCM	Chama Cha Mapinduzi (Swahili: Party of the Revolution)
CHADEMA	Chama Cha Demokrasia na Maendeleo (Swahili: Party of Democracy and Development)
CUF	Civic United Front
NCCR	National Committee for Constitutional Reform
NLD	National League for Democracy
NPSS	National Party of the Subjects of the Sultan of Zanzibar
NRA	National Reconstruction Alliance
PONA	Popular National Party
TADEA	Tanzania Democratic Alliance Party
TANU	Tanganyika African National Union
TLP	Tanzania Labour Party
TPP	Tanzania People's Party
UDP	United Democratic Party
UMD	Union for Multiparty Democracy
UPDP	United People's Democracy Party
UTP	United Tanganyika Party

ZNP	Zanzibar Nationalist Party
ZPPP	Zanzibar and Pemba People's Party

2.4 Electoral Participation of Parties and Alliances 1957–1995

2.4.1 Tanganyika 1958–1962

Party / Alliance	Years	Elections contested	
		Presidential	Parliamentary
ANC	1958–1962	1	2
TANU	1958–1962	1	2
UTP	1958–1960	0	1

2.4.2 Zanzibar 1957–1963

Party / Alliance	Years	Elections contested	
		Presidential	Parliamentary
ASP	1957–1963	0	4
ZNP	1957–1963	0	4
ZPPP	1961–1963	0	3

General note: From 1980 onwards regional elections have been held in Zanzibar.

2.4.3 Tanzania 1965–1995

Party / Alliance	Years	Elections contested	
		Presidential	Parliamentary
TANU	1965, 1970, 1975	3	3
CCM	1980, 1985, 1990, 1995	4	4
CHADEMA	1995	0	1
CUF	1995	1	1
NCCR-Mageuzi	1995	1	1
NLD	1995	0	1
NRA	1995	0	1
PONA	1995	0	1
TADEA	1995	0	1
TLP	1995	0	1
TPP	1995	0	1
UDP	1995	1	1
UMD	1995	0	1
UDPD	1995	0	1

2.5 Referendums

Referendums have not been held.

2.6 Elections for Constitutional Assembly

Elections for Constitutional Assembly have not been held.

2.7 Parliamentary Elections 1957–1995

2.7.1 Tanganyika 1958–1962

Year	1958/59[a] Total number	%	1960 Total number	%
Registered voters	40,567	–	885,000	–
Votes cast	—	—	—	—
Invalid votes	—	—	—	—
Valid votes	63,204	—	121,445	—
TANU	47,685	75.4	100,581	82.8
UTP	6,909	10.9	–	–
ANC	53	0.0	337	0.3
Independents	8,557	13.6	20,527	16.9

[a] The elections were organized in two phases and took place in 10 constituencies. In September 1958 five constituencies elected their representatives. The remaining five constituencies held elections in February 1959. The total of votes extends the registered voters because each voter could have voted for a maximum of three candidates (tripartite roll).

2.7.2 Zanzibar 1957–1963

Year	1957 Total number	%	January 1961 Total number	%
Registered voters	39,873	–	90,000[a]	–
Votes cast	35,980	90.2	—	—
Invalid votes	619	1.7	—	—
Valid votes	35,361	98.3	84,963	—
ASP	21,632	61.2	36,698	43.2
ZNP	7,761	21.9	32,724	38.5
ZPPP	–	–	15,541	18.3
Others[b]	5,968	16.9	–	–

[a] Estimation.

[b] Candidates of Indian, Muslim or Comorian associations.

Year	June 1961		1963	
	Total number	%	Total number	%
Registered voters	93,918	–	165,000[a]	–
Votes cast	90,595	99.6	163,510	99.1[a]
Invalid votes	1,331	1.4	2,866	1.8
Valid votes	89,264	98.6	160,644	98.2
Party / Alliance				
ASP	45,172	50.6	87,085	54.2
ZNP	31,681	35.3	47,950	29.9
ZPPP	12,411	13.9	25,609	15.9

[a] Estimation.

2.7.3 Tanzania 1965–1995

Year	1965		1970	
	Total number	%	Total number	%
Registered voters	3,187,215	–	4,860,456	–
Votes cast	2,289,602	71.8	3,237,255	66.6
Invalid votes	25,772	1.1	—	—
Valid votes	2,263,830	98.9	—	—
TANU/ASP	2,263,830	100.0	—	—

Year	1975		1980	
	Total number	%	Total number	%
Registered voters	5,577,569	–	6,604,408	–
Votes cast	4,557,595	81.7	5,594,342	84.7
Invalid votes	83,328	1.8	177,243	3.2
Valid votes	4,474,267	98.2	5,417,099	96.8
TANU/ASP	–	–	–	–
CCM	4,474,267	100.0	5,417,099	100.0

Year	1985[a]		1990[b]	
	Total number	%	Total number	%
Registered voters	6,736,863	–	7,296,553	–
Votes cast	4,983,321	74.0	5,425,282	74.4
Invalid votes	214,324	4.3	418255[c]	7.7
Valid votes	4,768,997	95.7	5,007,027[c]	92.3
CCM	4,768,997	100.0	5,007,027[c]	100.0

[a] The numbers are calculated by the author. They represent an estimate based on data for constituencies (Othman *et al.* 1990: 219–232). In five constituencies the candidate of CCM was unopposed; in four constituencies the data was incomplete but could be estimated.
[b] In the 1990 elections 68 out of 180 Members of Parliament were elected the first time; 36 out of 148 incumbent Members of Parliament lost their seat.
[c] The numbers are calculated by the author. The calculation was based on the data for constituencies from Othman *et al.* 1990: 219–232 (Mukandala/Othman 1994: 295–319).

Year	1995	
	Total number	%
Registered voters	8,928,816	–
Votes cast	6,831,578	76.5
Invalid votes	390,665	5.7
Valid votes	6,440,913	94.3
CCM	3,814,125	59.2
NCCR-Mageuzi	1,406,343	21.8
CHADEMA	396,825	6.2
CUF	323,432	5.0
UDP	213,481	3.3
TADEA	76,639	1.2
NRA	60,707	0.9
UMD	41,257	0.6
TLP	27,963	0.4
NLD	26,666	0.4
UPDP	19,841	0.3
PONA	18,155	0.3
TPP	15,335	0.2

2.8 Composition of Parliament 1960–1995

2.8.1 Tanganyika 1958–1962

Year	1958/59		1960	
	Seats	%	Seats	%
	12	100	71	100
TANU	12	100	70	98.6
UTP	0	0	–	–
ANC	0	0	0	0
Independent	–	–	1	1.4

2.8.2 Zanzibar 1957–1962

Year	1957		1961 (January)		1961 (June)		1963	
	Seats	%	Seats	%	Seats	%	Seats	%
	6	100	22	100	23	100	31	100
ASP	5	83.3	10	45.5	10	43.5	13	41.9
ZNP	0	0.0	9	40.9	10	43.5	12	38.7
ZPPP	–	–	3	13.6	3	13.0	6	19.4
Others	1	17.7	–	–	–	–	–	–

2.8.3 Tanzania 1965–1995

Year	1965[a]		1970[a]		1975[a]	
	Seats	%	Seats	%	Seats	%
	188	100	195	100	223	100
TANU	188	100	195	100	223	100

[a] Including national members, appointees by the President and the Attorney-General.

Year	1980		1985		1990		1995	
	Seats	%	Seats	%	Seats	%	Seats	%
	264[a]	100	274[a]	100	284[a]	100	275[b]	100
CCM	264	100	274	100	284	100	214[c]	79.6
CUF	–	–	–	–	–	–	28[d]	10.4
NCCR-Mageuzi	–	–	–	–	–	–	19[e]	7.1
CHADEMA	–	–	–	–	–	–	4[f]	1.5
UDP	–	–	–	–	–	–	4[g]	1.5

[a] Including national members, appointees by the President and the Attorney-General.
[b] Including five deputies from the Zanzibar National Assembly, the Attorney-General as member *ex officio* and 37 appointed members (women). The Deputies from Zanzibar and the Attorney-General are not included in the figures of the distribution of seats by parties which therefore adds up only to 269.
[c] Elected: 186, appointed: 28.
[d] Elected: 24, appointed: 4.
[e] Elected: 16, appointed: 3.
[f] Elected: 3, appointed: 1.
[g] Elected: 3, appointed: 1.

2.9 Presidential Elections 1962–1995

2.9.1 Tanganyika 1962

1962	Total number	%
Registered voters	1,800,000[a]	–
Votes cast	—	—
Invalid votes	—	—
Valid votes	1,149,254	—
Julius K. Nyerere (TANU)	1,127,987	99.2
Zuberi Mtemvu (ANC)	21,276	0.8

[a] Estimation.

2.9.2 Zanzibar

Presidential elections were not held in Zanzibar.

2.9.3 Tanzania 1965–1995

1965	Total number	%
Registered voters	3,187,215	–
Votes cast	2,636,041	82.7
Invalid votes	26,537	1.0
Valid votes	2,609,504	99.0
Julius K. Nyerere (CCM)	2,520,904	96.6
No votes	88,600	3.4

1970	Total number	%
Registered voters	4,860,456	–
Votes cast	3,407,083	70.1
Invalid votes	77,491	2.2
Valid votes	3,329,592	97.8
Julius K. Nyerere (CCM)	3,220,636	96.7
No votes	108,956	3.3

1975	Total number	%
Registered voters	5,577,566	–
Votes cast	4,557,595	81.7
Invalid votes	83,323	1.8
Valid votes	4,474,272	98.2
Julius K. Nyerere (CCM)	4,172,267	93.3
No votes	302,005	6.7

1980	Total number	%
Registered voters	6,969,803	–
Votes cast	5,986,942	85.9
Invalid votes	157,019	2.6
Valid votes	5,829,923	97.4
Julius K. Nyerere (CCM)	5,570,883	95.5
No votes	259,040	4.5

1985	Total number	%
Registered voters	6,910,555	–
Votes cast	5,181,999	75.0
Invalid votes	188,259	3.6
Valid votes	4,993,740	96.4
Ali Hassan Mwinyi (CCM)	4,778,114	95.7
No votes	215,626	4.3

1990	Total number	%
Registered voters	7,296,553	–
Votes cast	5,425,282	74.4
Invalid votes	109,796	2.0
Valid votes	5,315,486	98.0
Ali Hassan Mwinyi (CCM)	5,198,120	97.8
No votes	117,366	2.2

1995	Total number	%
Registered voters	8,929,969	–
Votes cast	6,846,681	76.7
Invalid votes	333,936	4.9
Valid votes	6,512,745	95.1
Benjamin William Mkapa (CCM)	4,026,422	61.8
Augustino Lyatonga Mrema (NCCR)	1,808,616	27.8
Ibrahim Aruna Lipumba (CUF)	418,973	6.4
John Momose Cheyo (UDP)	258,734	4.0

2.10 List of Power Holders 1961–1998

Head of State and Government	Years	Remarks
Julius Nyerere	1962–1985	Assumed office on 09/12/1962; four times constitutionally re-elected in one-party elections; resigned in 1985.
Ali Hassan Mwinyi	1985–1995	Assumed office on 05/11/1985; twice constitutionally elected in one-party elections. The constitution prohibited a third term.
Benjamin William Mkapa	1995–	Assumed office on 23/11/1995; constitutionally elected in multi-party-elections.

3. Bibliography

3.1. Official Sources

Elected Candidates in Constituencies (1995). Dar es Salaam: National Electoral Commission.

Elections Act (1985). Dar es Salaam: Government Printer.

Political Parties Act (1992). Dar es Salaam: Government Printer.

3.2. Books, Articles and Electoral Reports

Aumüller, I. (1980). *Dekolonisation und Nationwerdung in Sansibar. Prozesse zur Unabhängigkeit und territorialen Integration*. München: Weltforum.

Ayany, S. G. (1970). *A History of Zanzibar. A Study in Constitutional Development 1934–1964*. Nairobi/ Dar es Salaam/ Kampala: East African Literature Bureau.

Babu, A. M. (1991). 'The 1964 Revolution: Lumpen or Vanguard', in A. Sheriff and E. Ferguson (eds.), *Zanzibar under Colonial Rule*. Ohio: Ohio University Press, 220–247.

Barkan, J. D. (1994). *Beyond Capitalism and Socialism in Kenya and Tanzania*. Boulder, Col.: Lynne Rienner.

Berg-Schlosser, D., and Siegler, R. (1988). *Politische Stabilität und Entwicklung. Eine vergleichende Analyse der Bestimmungsfaktoren und Interaktionsmuster in Kenya, Tansania und Uganda*. München: Weltforum.

Bienen, H. (1967). *Tanzania: Party Transformation and Economic Development* (2nd edn.). Princeton: Princeton University Press

Boesen, J. (1986). *Tanzania Crisis and Struggle for Survival*. Uppsala: Nordiska Afrikainstitutet.

Cliffe, L. (1967). *One Party Democracy. The 1965 Tanzanian General Elections*. Nairobi: East African Publishing House

— (1972). 'Democracy in a One-Party State: The Tanzanian Experience', in L. Cliffe and J. Saul (eds.), *Socialism in Tanzania: An Interdisciplinary Reader, Volume 1*. Nairobi: East African Publishing House.

Donner-Reichle, C. (1988). *Ujamaadörfer in Tanzania. Politik und Reaktionen der Bäuerinnen* (Arbeiten aus dem Institut für Afrika-Kunde, 58). Hamburg: Institut für Afrika-Kunde.

Election Study Committee (University of Dar es Salaam) (1974). *Socialism and Participation: Tanzania's 1970 National Elections*. Dar es Salaam: Tanzania Publishing House.

Erdmann, G. (1995). *Tanzania vor den Wahlen. Legitimität und Probleme einer gesteuerten Demokratisierung* (Aktuelle Informations-Papiere zu Entwicklung und Politik, 19). Freiburg: Arnold-Bergstraesser-Institut

Fengler, W. (1997). *Konfliktformationen und Zukunftsperspektiven der Tanzanischen Union* (Arbeiten aus dem Institut für Afrika-Kunde, 95). Hamburg: Institut für Afrika-Kunde.

— and Kabudi, J. (1996). *Tanzania 1995: Wie unschuldig sind Wahlsysteme? Hintergründe und Simulationen zu den Mehrparteienwahlen* (Focus Africa. IAK-Diskussionsbeiträge, 7). Hamburg: Institut für Afrika-Kunde.

— and Mair, S. (1996). 'Zur Wahlbeobachtung der Präsidentschafts- und Parlamentswahlen in Tanzania vom Oktober 1995'. *Afrika Spectrum*, 31/1: 93–100.

Havnevik, K. J. (1993). *Tanzania: The Limits to Development from Above*. Stockholm: Almqvist & Wiksell.

Hodd, M. (1988). *Tanzania after Nyerere*. London: Pinter.

Hofmeier, R. (1993), 'Tansania', in D. Nohlen and F. Nuscheler (eds.), *Handbuch der Dritten Welt, Vol. 5: Ostafrika und Südafrika* (3rd edn.). Bonn: Dietz, 178–200.

— (1994). 'Tansania: Neue Freiheiten, neue Konflikte'. *Der Überblick*, 30/4: 88–91.

— (1995). 'Tanzania', in Institut für Afrika-Kunde and R. Hofmeier (eds.). *Afrika Jahrbuch 1994*. Opladen: Leske & Budrich, 304–312.

— (1996). 'Tanzania', in Institut für Afrika-Kunde and R. Hofmeier (eds.), *Afrika Jahrbuch 1995*. Opladen: Leske & Budrich, 310–319.

Hofmeister, W. (1995). 'Zwischen Beharrung und Wandel: Zur politischen Entwicklung in Kenia, Uganda und Tansania'. *Aus Politik und Zeitgeschichte*, 44–45: 24–37.

Inter-Parliamentary Union (1976). *Chronicle of Parliamentary Elections and Developments*. Geneva: IPU.

— (1981). *Chronicle of Parliamentary Elections and Developments*. Geneva: IPU.

— (1986). *Chronicle of Parliamentary Elections and Developments*. Geneva: IPU.

— (1991). *Chronicle of Parliamentary Elections and Developments*. Geneva: IPU.

Kabudi, J. (1993). 'The United Republic of Tanzania after a Quarter of a Century: A Legal Appraisal of the State of the Union of Tanganyika and Zanzibar'. *The African Journal of International and Comparative Law*, 5/2: 311–339.

Keesing's Contemporary Archives (1958). *Weekly Diary of Important World Events, Vol. No. XI (1957–1958)*. London: Keesing's Publications Limited.

— (1960). *Weekly Diary of Important World Events, Vol. No. XI (1959–1960)*. London: Keesing's Publications Limited.

— (1962). *Weekly Diary of Important World Events, Vol. No. XI (1961–1962)*. London: Keesing's Publications Limited.

Klein, K., and Reeves, P. R. (1995). *Republic in Transition: 1995 Elections in Tanzania and Zanzibar* (IFES Observation Report). Washington, D.C.

Luanda, N. N. (1994). '1990 Parliamentary Elections: Continuity in Change', in R. Mukandala and H. Othman (eds.), *Liberalization and Politics. The 1990 Election in Tanzania*. Dar es Salaam: Dar es Salaam University Press, 257–268.

Martin, D. C. (1978). 'The 1975 Tanzanian Elections: The Disturbing Six Per Cent', in G. Hermet, R. Rose and A. Rouquié (eds.), *Elections without Choice*. London/ Basingstoke: The Macmillan Press, 108–128.

— (1993).'La Tanzanie et le multipartisme'. *Afrique Contemporaine* 167: 3–13.

Mmuya, M. (1993). *The Anticlimax in Kwahani Zanzibar. Partizipation and Multipartism in Tanzania*. Dar es Salaam: Dar es Salaam University Press.

— (1994). *The Political Parties and Democracy in Tanzania*. Dar es Salaam: Dar es Salaam University Press.

— and Chaligha, A. (1992). *Towards Multiparty Politics in Tanzania. A Spectrum of the Current Opposition and the CCM Response*. Dar es Salaam: Dar es Salaam University Press.

Mwakyembe, H. G. (1985). 'The Parliament and the Electoral Process', in I. G. Shivji (ed.), *The State and the Working People in Tanzania*. Dakar: CODESRIA.

— (1995). *Tanzania's Eighth Constitutional Amendment and its Implications on Constitutionalism, Democracy and the Union Question*. Münster: Lit.

Mwapachu, J. (1994). *A Proposal for a new Parliamentary Electoral System. Discussion Paper, Symposium of the Society for International Development (Tanzania Chapter): Towards 1995: Proposals for a new Constitutional, Electoral and Union Order*. 11–12/10/1994, Dar es Salaam.

Mukandala, R., and Othman, H. (1994). *Liberalization and Politics. The 1990 Election in Tanzania*. Dar es Salaam: Dar es Salaam University Press.

Nuscheler, F. (1978). 'Tanzania', in D. Sternberger, B. Vogel, D. Nohlen and K. Landfried (eds.), *Die Wahl der Parlamente und anderer Staatsorgane, Bd. II: Politische Organisation und Repräsentation in Afrika*, by Franz Nuscheler, Klaus Ziemer *et al.*, Berlin/ New York: Walter de Gruyter, 2125–2175.

Nyerere, J. K. (1967). *Freedom and Unity—Uhuru na Umoja. A Selection from Writings and Speeches 1962–1965*. London.

— (1995). *Our Leadership and the Destiny of Tanzania*. Harare: African Publishing Group.

Othman, H. (1994). 'Succesion Politics and the Union Presidential Elections', in R. Mukandala and H. Othman (eds.), *Liberalization and Politics. The 1990 Election in Tanzania*. Dar es Salaam: Dar es Salaam University Press, 134–145.

— and Mlimuka, A. (1990*a*). 'The 1985 Zanzibar Presidential Elections', in H. Othman, I. K. Bavu and M. Okema (eds.), *Tanzania: Democracy in Transition*. Dar es Salaam: Dar es Salaam University Press, 58–64.

— (1990*b*). 'The Political and Constitutional Development of Zanzibar and the Case Studies of the 1985 Zanzibar General Elections', in H. Othman, I. K. Bavu and M. Okema (eds.), *Tanzania: Democracy in Transition*. Dar es Salaam: Dar es Salaam University Press, 150–181.

Richey, L., and Ponte, S. (1996). 'The 1995 Tanzania Union Elections'. *Review of African Political Economy*, 67: 80–87.

Samoff, J. (1987). 'Single-Party Competitive Elections in Tanzania', in F. Hayward (ed.), *Elections in Independent Africa*. Boulder, Col.: Westview Press, 149–186.

Sheriff, A., and Ferguson, E. (1991). *Zanzibar under Colonial Rule*. Ohio: Ohio University Press.

Shivij, I. G. (1986). *Law, State and the Working Class in Tanzania*. London: Currey.

— (1990). *The Legal Foundations of the Union in Tanzania's Union and Zanzibar Constitutions*. Dar es Salaam: Dar es Salaam University Press.

Tambila, I. K. (1995). 'The Tranistion to Multiparty Democracy in Tanzania: Some History and Missed Opportunities'. *Verfassung und Recht in Übersee*, 28/4: 468–521.

UN (United Nations) (1982). *Demographic Yearbook 1980*. New York: United Nations Publications.

TOGO

by Daniel Stroux

1. Introduction

1.1 Historical Overview

Togo became an autonomous republic under French administration in 1956 and achieved internal sovereignty on 22 February 1958, when the legislative chamber was granted the right to elect a Prime Minister. The first elections after independence on 27 April 1960 were already undemocratic in character, since Prime Minister Sylvanus Olympio prevented an oppositional coalition of *Union Démocratique des Populations Togolaises* (UDPT) and *Juvento* from fielding a common list. As a consequence Olympio was elected President unopposed and his *Parti de l'Unité Togolaise* (PUT) secured all seats in the National Assembly. A new constitution was introduced in 1961 replacing the parliamentary with a semi-presidential system. The President was granted superordinate authority by a seven-year term, a right to veto to be rejected by a two-thirds parliamentary majority, and the right to dissolve the Parliament. Political parties were prohibited in 1962. Olympio's autocratic reign, which excluded the country's Northern political elite (the President stemmed from the Southern commercial elite which had been privileged by colonial rule) and oppressed extra-parliamentary opposition, was ended by military coup on 13 January 1963.

An interim government headed by UDPT leader Nicolas Grunitzky legalized political parties and prepared a draft constitution providing the President with the right to accumulate the office of President and Prime Minister, thus placing him in the very center of power structures. Parliamentary elections in 1963 proved to be non-competitive as the four existing parties, *Juvento*, UDPT, PUT and *Mouvement Populaire Togolais* (MPT) presented a joint electoral list based on the agreement that each party would be provided with 25% of the parliamentary seats, regardless of their individual political strength. However, Grunitzky failed to forge a cohesive single party integrating all important political tendencies, and was ousted by the army on 13 January 1967.

A transitional commission, the *Conseil de la Réconciliation Nationale* (CRN) composed of members of the armed forces as well as civilians was installed in order to prepare the return to civil rule within three months. However, chief of the army Gnassingbé Eyadéma, who had already participated in the overthrow of Olympio and had initiated the second coup d'état, seized power on 15 April 1967, dissolved the CRN, outlawed political parties, and designated himself President. For the following 13 years Eyadéma governed without any constitutional framework. In 1969 a state party, the *Rassemblement du Peuple Togolais* (RPT) was launched, dominating all spheres of politics and society. Only in 1972 did Eyadéma seek legitimation of his presidency by referendum. A relatively successful economic policy, considerable foreign investments, co-optation and inclusion of (potential) opposition forces as for example the Southern elite, and the traditional '*chefferie*', stabilized his regime. During the first half of the 1970s Eyadéma's popularity profited from economic growth based on a boom in the phosphate sector.

However, the drop in world market prices soon impeded public spending, thus provoking popular discontent and the reformation of the Southern elite's opposition. In reaction to rising criticism Eyadéma decided to institutionalize his reign; the new constitution provided him with far-reaching powers such as the right to appoint the government, to preside over all governmental institutions and to dissolve the National Assembly. It confirmed the predominance of the state party, also headed by the President. Thus, the National Assembly could only play a minor role. The constitution was ratified by referendum, the President and a National Assembly were elected on 30 December 1979. But the institutionalization of Eyadéma's regime signaled the end of his inclusive style of politics, which was increasingly replaced by the promotion of family and ethnic ties within the regime. Corruption and human rights abuses increased, up to the point that Togo had one of Africa's worst human rights records. In the mid-1980s internal and external political pressure led to a slight political opening, exacerbated by economic collapse. Liberalized electoral provisions, though within the framework of the state party, brought a drastic rejuvenation of the National Assembly and the replacement of 71% of its members in 1985.

The erosion of Eyadéma's power, however, did not lead to political opening until 1991, when the oppositional movement *Front des Associations pour le Renouveau* (FAR), later *Front de l'Opposition Démocratique* (FOD), broadly supported by waves of strikes by the urban classes, succeeded in holding a National Conference in July and August.

The conference discussed human rights abuses, abolished the Constitution of 1979, introduced a High Council of the Republic (HCR), and decided on a time-table for the promulgation of a constitution and multiparty elections. Finally a transitional government was formed under the moderate opposition leader Kokou Koffigoh.

Three coups d'état by the army, one of Eyadéma's strongholds, reversed the democratization process: In October 1991, the military occupied the High Council, the members of the government were forced to resign and the National Assembly was taken hostage. Koffigoh, still Prime Minister, had no choice but to give way for a partial return to authoritarian rule. In 1992, several prominent opposition politicians were murdered, in October the army occupied the National Assembly once again. A general strike of eight months followed. In spite of the obviously regime-provoked insecurity in 1992, the political class supported unanimously a constitutional project prepared during the National Conference, which was ratified by referendum on 27 September 1992. The new constitution strengthened the position of the Prime Minister, although this nomination from the parliamentary majority was left with the President. The latter also appointed the ministers proposed by the Prime Minister and could dissolve the legislative body after consultation with the Prime Minister and the President of the National Assembly, except during the first year of its existence. After a demonstration had been brutally suppressed leading to a refugee flow of 250,000 to 300,000 people in January 1993, the oppositional coalition and the government agreed on holding presidential and parliamentary elections (*Accord de Ouagadougou III*) under international pressure (mainly Germany, France and the United States) in July 1993.

Eyadéma's manipulated re-election in August 1993 was boycotted by the opposition. Except for France, all donor countries withdrew their election observers. International mediators had to convince moderate opposition parties such as *Comité d'Action pour le Renouveau* (CAR) and *Union Togolaise pour la Démocratie* (UTD) to participate in the parliamentary election of February 1994. In rather fair and transparent elections the alliance of CAR and UTD could have won an absolute majority of seats in the National Assembly. However, the High Court, loyal to Eyadéma, deprived the opposition of their success by annulling the results in three constituencies gained by the oppositional coalition and Eyadéma managed to split up the oppositional coalition by the co-optation of UTD party leader Edem Kodjo as Prime Minister. The by-election in August 1996, boycotted by CAR, was won by the RPT. Thus provided with an absolute majority in Parliament (coalition with UJD and CFN), Eyadéma regained control over all key positions in government making the loyal Kwassi Klutse Prime Minister. Newly installed institutions such as the Constitutional Court, the Human Rights Commission and the High Authority of the Media were almost exclusively filled with RPT members, which led the opposition to boycott the nominations in Parliament. Thus, in spite of the creation of formally democratic institutions, the transition process that had begun in 1991 has not resulted in an effective democratization of the political system.

The autocratic character of the Eyadéma regime was revealed with the presidential election of 1998. Counting was stopped by forces loyal to the President on realizing the possibility of a landslide victory of Gilchrist Olympio, son of Togo's first President and Eyadéma's main rival. Under enormous pressure, the regime-appointed members of the Electoral Commission including its President stepped down the day after the election. Opposition members were hindered by soldiers from saving the existing results. The Interior Minister, loyal to Eyadéma, proclaimed detailed results only two days later and declared the incumbent as elected with 52%, although the count had been stopped. Results were confirmed by the Constitutional Court (again loyal to Eyadéma). The population protested with road blocks at the 'stolen election'. The European Union (EU), which had closely monitored and supported the election process, insisted on transparent elections for the resumption of the frozen cooperation. Due to the refusal of the Togo government to meet the demands for effective democratization, the suspension of the cooperation has not been lifted by the end of 1998.

1.2 Evolution of Electoral Provisions

Universal suffrage for all Togolese citizens was introduced under French administration by the *Loi Cadre* in June 1956. The Election Law of 1958 provided for a 46-member Parliament elected for a five-year term in single-member constituencies according to plurality system. In order to register as a candidate a minimum age of 23 years, at least two years residence in the country and sufficient knowledge of French was required. A deposit of 50,000 F was needed in order to register as a candidate. The deposit was refunded to those candidates who secured at least 10% of the valid votes.

Upon assuming independence the Constitution of 1961 introduced direct election to the presidency (minimum age of 40 years) by plurality system. The President was elected for a seven-year term, while a

National Assembly of 51 members was elected for a five-year term. The whole country formed one single constituency with closed lists being elected according to plurality system, thus abolishing parliamentarian opposition.

The Constitution of 1963 reduced the presidential mandate to five years and introduced the post of Vice-President, elected on one ticket with the President according to plurality system. Both had to be at least 35 years old. An Electoral Law provided for elections to a 56-member Parliament by formally national lists according to plurality system. However, only one single list was presented containing candidates of the four most important political parties UDPT, *Juvento*, MPT and PUT. Following the so-called concept of '*pluralisme non concurrentiel*' each party was provided with 25% of the seats.

During the period of extra-constitutional rule between 1967 and 1979 no elections were held except for one referendum in 1972 confirming Eyadéma as President. The Constitution of 1980 laid down a seven-year term for the presidency. The 67 members of the National Assembly were elected for a period of five years. A single national list presented by the state party was to be ratified by plurality rule. The minimum age for suffrage was reduced to 18 years. In 1985 competitive elements were introduced for elections to Parliament (77 members): 216 candidates presented by the state party's list were elected by single preferential vote and plurality system. (Of those, 85 candidates withdrew before the election.) Eligible were Togolese citizens aged at least 25 years. A total of 233 candidates competed on the list of the single party.

Current electoral provisions were defined by the Constitution of 1992 and fixed in an Electoral Law which was modified in 1993 in view of presidential elections. Special provisions for the first elections under the new constitution were negotiated in the '*Accord de Ouagadougou III*', a transitional pact which formally expired with the by-elections in 1996. It modified the Electoral Law concerning electoral organization and the composition of the Electoral Commission. The Electoral Commission consisting of nine persons was filled with three members of the presidential camp and three members of the three oppositional camps; two were chosen in a common accord. Special safety regulations were assured by foreign military observers supervising the electoral process together with an international committee. After the '*Accord de Ouagadougou*' had expired in 1996 further modifications to the Electoral Law were made in 1997. The composition of the Electoral Commission changed to four members of the ruling party and four members of the opposition and its position was weakened: Special provisions for the candidates' and the electorate's safety were abolished and the Ministry of the Interior explicitly organized the elections, whereas equal access to state media during the campaign was supervised by the Electoral Commission. The accreditation of election observers resides with the government, while the Electoral Commission is left with the right to propose observers. The new provisions were ratified by the National Assembly in a vote boycotted by the opposition.

1.3 Current Electoral Provisions

Sources: Constitution de la IVème République, adoptée par référendum le 27 septembre 1992 et promulgée le 14 octobre 1992; Code Electoral, Loi 92-003/PM du 8 Juillet 1992, Loi 92-003/PM du 8 Juillet 1992, modifié par ordonnance No. 93-02/PR on 16 avril 1993; Loi 97-15.

Elected national institutions: President and National Assembly are both directly elected for a five-year term. The re-election of the President is allowed for one consecutive term only, the re-election of currently 81 members of the National Assembly is not restricted.

Suffrage: The principles of universal, equal, direct and secret suffrage are applied (Article 1, Electoral Law). Every Togolese aged at least 18 years and in possession of full civil and political rights has the right to vote. He must be registered in the electoral list. Togolese living outside the country have a right to vote but must get registered regularly in the list of the respective embassy. Registration as a voter is not obligatory.

Nomination of candidates
- *presidential elections*: A candidate must be Togolese by birth and be at least 45 years old when applying for candidature. His good state of health must be confirmed by three Togolese doctors selected by the Constitutional Court (Article 62, Constitution). In order to register, candidates must resign from duties within the military or police. A candidate nominated by a party or a party coalition needs a declaration of the respective group or party supporting his candidature. Independent candidates must present a list of 2,000 signatures of registered voters in 10 (of 34) different prefectures (and sub-prefectures). The Constitutional Court decides in case of dispute over the right of candidature.
- *parliamentary elections*: Parliamentary candidates have to be at least 25 years old on the day of the election. Candidates can be nominated by

a political party or run as independents. Each candidate has to present a substitute candidate subject to the same requests as the candidate. The imperative mandate is explicitly excluded. The Constitutional Court decides in case of dispute over the right of candidature.

Electoral system
- *presidential elections*: Absolute majority system (majority run-off). If in the first round no candidate obtains more than 50 % of the valid votes, a run-off between the two best finishers of the first round is held two weeks later (Sunday).
- *parliamentary elections*: Absolute majority system in 81 single-member constituencies. If in the first round no candidate obtains more than 50% of the valid votes, a run-off between the two best finishers of the first round is held. After a dissolution of the National Assembly, elections must be held within 60 days. (There are enormous differences between the number of voters in rural constituencies with a minimum of 6,000 voters, compared to the biggest constituency in the capital with 111,000 voters in one of five in Lomé. Lomé which is representing about 17% of the voters has a representation in the National Assembly of 6.25%.)

1.4 Comment on the Electoral Statistics

After the political opening in 1991 the Eyadéma régime attempted to continue a tradition of prefabricated electoral results mainly by the means of extended voter registers: The number of registered voters in the 1993 and 1994 elections show an electorate too big compared with the estimate of population growth and age. The electoral participation of 39% for presidential elections in 1993 (boycotted by the opposition) was generally regarded as exaggerated. Unofficial estimates figured percentages between 25 and 30. A revision of the voters' register on the eve of legislative elections in 1994 on the basis of the 1992 register drawn up before the constitutional referendum showed only partial effects and is still considered to be blown up. However, since control of the electoral process was granted by an independent Electoral Commission installed by the '*Accord de Ouagadougou*', the electoral outcomes of legislative elections in 1994 can be considered the most reliable in the country's electoral history.

Very few publications cover Togolese elections in detail. The main publication for the 1960s is Ziemer (1978). Ziemer (1984) fills the gap between the first elections and the time after military rule in 1979. Main sources for the 1980s are *Africa Contemporary Records*, *Marchés Tropicaux*, *Africa Research Bulletin* and Toulabor (1990) although sometimes not sufficiently detailed. Sufficient official material particularly about the 1993 and 1994 elections was available during the author's several stays in Togo since 1993 (election observer, consulting member of the Electoral Commission 1994). A Togolese journalist, Tata Houncali, put official sources on the by-elections of 1996 and lacking details on the presidential and parliamentary elections of 1993 and 1994 at the author's disposal.

2. Tables

2.1 Dates of National Elections, Referendums and Coups d'Etat

Year	Presidential elections	Parliamentary elections	Elections for Constitutional Assembly	Referendums	Coups d'état
1958		27/04			
1961	09/04	09/04		09/04	
1963	05/05	05/05		05/05	13/01
1967					13/01
1972				09/01	
1979	30/12	30/12		30/12	
1985		24/03			
1986	21/12				
1990		04/03 (1st) 18/03 (2nd)			
1992				27/09	
1993	25/08				
1994		06/02 (1st) 20/02 (2nd)[a]			
1998	14/06[b]				

[a] By-elections were held on 4 and 18 August 1996.
[b] Counting was stopped and was not resumed.

2.2 Electoral Body 1958–1998

Year	Type of election[a]	Population[b]	Registered voters[c]		Votes cast		
			Total number	% pop.	Total number	% reg. voters	% pop.
1958	Pa	1,284,000	489,519	38.1	317,669	64.9	24.7
1961	Ref/Pr/Pa	1,480,000	627,688	42.4	564,617	90.0	38.1
1963	Ref/Pr/Pa	1,559,000	639,524	41.0	582,309	91.1	37.4
1972	Ref	2,100,000	880,890	41.9	868,989	98.6	41.4
1979	Ref	2,570,000	1,303,970	50.7	1,295,609	99.4	50.4
1979	Pr	2,570,000	1,303,970	50.7	1,296,851	99.5	50.5
1979	Pa	2,570,000	1,303,970	50.7	1,294,243	99.3	50.4
1985	Pa	3,062,000	1,318,979	43.0	1,036,975	78.6	33.2
1986	Pr	3,160,000	1,757,426	55.6	1,738,611	98.9	55.0
1990	Pa	3,508,000	1,522,491	43.4	1,197,754	78.7	34.1
1992	Ref	3,752,000	1,972,676	52.6	1,464,479	74.2	39.0
1993	Pr	3,880,000	2,038,937	52.5	737,237	36.2	18.5
1994	Pa (1st)	4,012,000	1,998,051	49.8	1,300,741	65.1	32.4
1998	Pr	4,406,000	2,319,203	52.6	—	—	—

[a] Pa = Parliament, Pr = President; Ref = Referendum.

[b] Figures on the population are based on UNDP estimations. The provisional result of a population census in 1981 figured 2,705,250 (*Africa South of the Sahara*, London: 1993). Official Togolese estimations generally lie slightly above UNDP estimations: For 1996 the UNDP estimates 4.26 million, the Togolese official estimate presents a number of 4.4 million.

[c] From 1979 on, the fact that 50% of the population of Togo was younger than 15 years of age indicates that either the population was underestimated at that time, or, more probably, the voter register was blown up (*African Contemporary Records* 1979–1980, B646). Although the register was purified of voters being registered twice, three or even five times in 1994, opposition forces still estimated the Togolese electorate as a presumable 1.6 million.

2.3 Abbreviations

ADDI	Alliance des Démocrates pour le Développement Intégral (O)
ADI[b]	— (R)
ADR	Alliance des Démocrates pour la République (R)
AJD	—
ARENA[c]	Alliance pour le Renouveau National (R)
ATD[a]	Alliance Togolaise pour la Démocratie (I)
CAR	Comité d'Action pour le Renouveau (O)
CDPA	Convention Démocratique du Peuple Africain (O)
CFN	Coordination des Forces Nouvelles (R)
CSD / TOGO	Convention des Sociaux - Démocrates / Togo (O)
CUT	Comité de l'Union Togolaise
Juvento	Justice, Union, Vigilance, Education, Nationalisme, Tenacité, Optimisme
MOCEP[b]	Mouvement des Croyants pour l'Egalité et la Paix (R)
MPT	Mouvement Populaire Togolais
PAD	Parti d'Action pour le Développement (O)
PADEC	Parti d'Action pour le Développement (I)
PDC	Parti des Démocrates Centristes (I)
PDR	— (O)
PDU	Parti des Démocrates pour l'Unité (O)
PRI	Parti Républicain Indépendant (O)
PST[c]	Parti du Salut du Togo (R)
PTP	Parti Togolais du Progrès
PUT	Parti de l'Unité Togolaise
RJT	Rassemblement des Jeunes Togolais
RPT	Rassemblement du Peuple Togolais (R)
SOLITO[c]	Parti Social Libéral du Togolais (R)
UCPN	Union des Chefs et des Populations du Nord
UDPT[d]	Union Démocratique des Populations Togolaises
UDR	Union des Démocrates pour le Renouveau (R)
UDR[c]	Union des Démocrates pour le Renouveau (R)
UDS	Union pour la Démocratie et la Solidarité (O)
UFC	Union des Forces pour le Changement (O)
UJD	Union pour la Justice et le Développement
ULI	Union des Libéraux Indépendants
UTD	Union Togolaise pour la Démocratie (O)
UTJ[b]	Union pour le Travail et la Justice (R)

General note: (I) = Independent; (O) = Opposition; (R) = Regime; validity of information: December 1993.

[a] Ife Adani ran for presidency under the banner of ATD in 1993.

[b] Joined the party coalition CDL.

[c] Joined the party coalition CFN, which formed a government coalition with UDR under Prime Minister Koffigoh (1991–1994).

[d] In an opposition coalition with *Juvento*.

2.4 Electoral Participation of Parties and Alliances 1958–1998

Party / Alliance	Years	Elections contested	
		Presidential	Parliamentary
CUT	1958	0	1
Juvento	1958, 1963	0	2
MPT	1958, 1963	0	2
PTP	1958	0	1
RJT	1958	0	1
UCPN	1958	0	1
PUT	1961, 1963	1	2
UDPT	1963	0	1
RPT	1979, 1985, 1986, 1990, 1993, 1994, 1998	4	3[a]
ATD	1993	1	0
ADDI	1994	0	1
ADI[c]	1994	0	1
ADR	1994	0	1
AJD	1994	0	1
ARENA[b]	1994	0	1
ATD	1994	0	1
CAR	1994, 1998	1	1
CDL	1994	0	1
CSD / TOGO	1994	0	1
MOCEP[c]	1994	0	1
PAD	1994	0	1
PADEC	1994	0	1
PDC	1994	0	1
PDU	1994	0	1
PRI	1994	0	1
PST[b]	1994	0	1
SOLITO[b]	1994	0	1
UDR	1994	0	1
UDR[b]	1994	0	1
UDS	1994	0	1
UJD	1994	0	1
ULI	1994	0	1
UTD	1994, 1998	1	1[a]
UTJ[c]	1994	0	1
CDPA	1998	1	0
PDR	1998	1	0
UFC	1998	1	0
ULI	1998	1	0

[a] Only RPT, ADR and UTD ran in the by-election of 1996, CAR boycotted the election.
[b] Member of CFN.
[c] Member of CDL.

2.5 Referendums

Year	1961[a] Total number	%	1963[b] Total number	%
Registered voters	627,688	–	639,524	–
Votes cast	564,617	90.0	582,309	91.0
Invalid votes	2,245	0.4	5,423	0.9
Valid votes	562,372	99.6	576,886	99.1
Yes	560,258	99.6	568,402	98.5
No	2,114	0.4	8,484	1.5

[a] Approval of constitution.
[b] Approval of constitution.

Year	1972[b] Total number	%	1979[c] Total number	%
Registered voters	880,890	–	1,303,970	–
Votes cast	868,989	98.6	1,295,609	99.4
Invalid votes	170	0.1	44	0.0
Valid votes	868,819	99.9	1,295,565	100.0
Yes	967,941	99.9	1,293,872	100.0
No	878	0.1	1,693	0.0

[b] Approval of presidential mandate.
[c] Approval of constitution.

Year	1992[a] Total number	%
Registered voters	1,972,676	–
Votes cast	1,464,479	74.2
Invalid votes	15,679	1.1
Valid votes	1,448,800	98.2
Yes	1,436,858	98.2
No	11,942	0.8

[a] Approval of constitution.

2.6 Elections for Constitutional Assembly

Elections for Constitutional Assembly have not been held.

2.7 Parliamentary Elections 1958–1994

Year	1958		1961	
	Total number	%	Total number	%
Registered voters	489,519	–	627,688	–
Votes cast	317,669	64.9	564,617	90.0
Invalid votes	6,481	2.0	3,779	0.7
Valid votes	311,019	98.0	560,938	99.3
CUT	190,098	61.2	–	–
Juvento[a]	510	0.2	–	–
MPT	842	0.3	–	–
RJT	6	0.0	–	–
PTP	40,486	13.0	–	–
UCPN	56,281	18.1	–	–
Independent	22,753	7.2	–	–
PUT	–	–	560,938	100.0

[a] Dissident breakaway. The majority of *Juvento* participated in the CUT list.

Year	1963		1979	
	Total number	%	Total number	%
Registered voters	639,524	–	1,303,970	–
Votes cast	582,309	91.1	1,294,243	99.6
Invalid votes	5,423	0.9	43,301	3.4
Valid votes	576,886	99.1	1,250,942	96.6
Réconciliation et Union Nationale[a]	568,893	98.6	–	–
RPT	–	–	1,250,942	100.0

[a] Single list containing candidacies of the following political parties: PUT, *Juvento*, UDPT and MPT.

Year	1985		1990	
	Total number	%	Total number	%
Registered voters	1,319,439	–	1,522,491	–
Votes cast	1,036,975	78.6	1,197,754	78.7
Invalid votes/ Blank votes	12,422	1.2	22,152	1.8
Valid votes	1,024,553	98.8	1,175,602	98.2
RPT	1,024,533	100.0	1,175,602	100.0

Year	1994[a]	
	Total number	%
Registered voters	1,998,051	–
Votes cast	1,300,741	65.1
Invalid votes	37,407	2.9
Valid votes	1,263,334	97.1
RPT	—	—
CAR	—	—
UTD	—	—
CFN	—	—
RPT	—	—
UJD	—	—

[a] Results of the first round. Results of the second round were not available. For by-elections on 4 and 18 August 1996 for three parliamentary mandates results were presented as follows: Registered voters: 65,788; Votes cast: 34,540; Invalid votes: 1,097; Valid votes: 33,565. The RPT won all three mandates. Officially available figures after the election day differ from those received after the count. 1996 officially received figures are: Registered voters: 1,964,709; Votes cast: 1,279,480 (65.1%); Valid votes: 1,242,816 (97.1%).

2.8 Composition of Parliament 1958–1994

Year	1958		1961		1963		1979	
	Seats	%	Seats	%	Seats	%	Seats	%
	46	100		100		100		100
CUT	29	63.0	–	–	–	–	–	–
PTP	3	6.5	–	–	–	–	–	–
UCPN	10	21.7	–	–	–	–	–	–
Independent	4	8.7	–	–	–	–	–	–
PUT	–	–	51	100	14	25.0	–	–
Juvento	–	–	–	–	14	25.0	–	–
MPT	–	–	–	–	14	25.0	–	–
UDPT	–	–	–	–	14	25.0	–	–
RPT	–	–	–	–	–	–	67	100

Year	1985		1990		1994[a]	
	Seats	%	Seats	%	Seats	%
	77	100	77	100	81	100
RPT	77	100	77	100	35	43.2
CAR	–	–	–	–	35	43.2
UTD	–	–	–	–	5	6.2
UJD	–	–	–	–	2	2.5
CFN	–	–	–	–	1	1.2

[a] Three seats were invalidated by the Constitutional Court. CAR and UTD formed a coalition. During the first two years of political impasse, at least two parliamentarians of CAR defected to the RPT. The RPT won by-elections for three seats in 1996, which were boycotted by CAR. Since August 1996 the coalition of RPT, UJD and CFN holds an absolute majority in the National Assembly.

2.9 Presidential Elections 1961–1998

1961	Total number	%
Registered voters	627,688	–
Votes cast	564,617	90.0
Invalid votes	3,779	0.7
Valid votes	560,938	99.3
Sylvanus Olympio (PUT)	560,938	100.0

1963	Total number	%
Registered voters	639,524	–
Votes cast	582,309	91.1
Invalid votes	13,416	2.3
Valid votes	568,893	97.7
Nicolas Grunitzky/ Antoine Méatchi	568,893	100.0

1979	Total number	%
Registered voters	1,303,970	–
Votes cast	1,296,851	99.5
Invalid votes[a]	267	0.0
Valid votes	1,296,584	100.0
Gnassingbé Eyadéma (RPT)	1,296,584	100.0

[a] Including blank votes.

1986	Total number	%
Registered voters	1,757,426	–
Votes cast	1,738,611	99.0
Invalid votes[a]	840	0.0
Valid votes	1,737,771	100.0
Gnassingbé Eyadéma (RPT)	1,737,771	100.0

[a] Including blank votes.

1993[a]	Total number	%
Registered voters	2,038,937	–
Votes cast	737,237	36.2
Invalid votes[b]	32,948	4.5
Valid votes	704,592	97.3
Gnassingbé Eyadéma (RPT)	691,485	96.5
Jacques Amouzou (Independent)	13,168	1.6
Ife Adani (ATD)	11,584	1.9

[a] The presidential election was boycotted by the major opposition parties on the grounds that they lacked preparation and gave obvious possibilities for manipulation. Eyadéma ran against candidates of minor political importance, which were fielded in order to pseudo-legitimize the election. However, the low participation rate of 36.2% was still believed to be manipulated.

[b] Incomprehensive official result: the number of invalid votes does not correspond to the difference between cast votes and valid votes.

For the presidential elections of 1998 no detailed data can be reported. President Gnassingbé Eyadéma (PRT) was officially declared elected with 52.1% of the votes. Other candidates: Gilchrist Olympio (UFC): 34.1%, Yaovi Agboyigbo (CAR): 9.5%, Zarifou Ayewa (PDR); 3.0%, Leopold Messan Gnininvi (CDPA): 0.8%, Jacques Amouzou (ULI): 0.3. (see 1.1 for further details).

2.10 List of Power Holders 1960–1998

Head of State	Years	Remarks
Sylvanus Olympio	1961–1963	Prime Minister from May 1958 to April 1961 under French trusteeship; elected President upon independence on 09/04/1961; assassinated on 13/01/1963 in a coup d'état.
Nicolas Grunitzky	1963–1967	Headed an interim government as Prime Minister from 16/01/1963 until presidential elections on 05/05/1963, when he was elected for a five-year term together with Vice-President Antoine Méatchi. Méatchi was dismissed by the President in November 1966; the President's rule was ended by coup d'état on 13/01/1967.
Kléber Dadjo	1967	Headed a military government while a *Conseil de la Réconciliation Nationale* (CRN) was installed in order to prepare the return to civilian rule within three months.
Gnassingbé Eyadéma	1967–	Lieutenant-Colonel; chief of the army; designated himself President on 15/04/1967. Confirmed by referendum on 09/01/1972; re-elected in 1979, 1986 and 1993.

Head of Government	Years	Remarks
	1963–1991	Identical with Head of State.
Joseph Kokou Koffigoh	1991–1994	Headed the first transitional government after the end of one-party rule on 26/08/1991. Under political and physical pressure from the army, his far-reaching concessions discredited him as Eyadéma's puppet. Until 23/05/1994 he formed three transitional governments and a '*cabinet de crise*'.
Edem Kodjo	1994–1996	Appointed by Eyadéma on 23/05/1994 in order to split up the parliamentary coalition of CAR (Agboyigbo) and UTD (Kodjo); resigned on 19/08/1996, when RPT (Eyadéma) won three seats at by-elections.
Kwassi Klutse	1996–	Former Planning Minister and reputed technocrat; appointed on 20/08/1996.

3. Bibliography

3.1. Official Sources

Accord de Ouagadougou III, 11 Juillet 1993.

Code Electoral, Loi 92-003/PM du 8 Juillet 1992, modifié par Ordonnance No. 93-02/PR du 16 Avril 1993.

Constitution de la IVe République Togolaise, adoptée par Référendum le 27 Septembre 1992 et promulgée le 14 Octobre 1992.

3.2. Books, Articles and Electoral Reports

'Abschlußbericht der Beobachtergruppe: Präsidentschaftswahlen in Togo (25.8.1993)', in U. Engel, D. Hofmeier and A. Mehler (eds.), *Deutsche Wahlbeobachtung in Afrika*. Hamburg: Institut für Afrika-Kunde, 178–187.

Adick, C. (1993). 'Togo', in D. Nohlen and F. Nuscheler (eds.), *Handbuch der Dritten Welt, Vol.4: Westafrika und Zentralafrika*. Bonn: Dietz, 404–419.

Apedo-Amah, A. T. (1997). 'Togo. Le ventre mou d'une démocratisation'. *L'Afrique Politique 1997*, 255–270.

CNDH (Commission Nationale des Droits de l'Homme) *et al.* (1990/1993). *Togo; La stratégie de la terreur. 3 ans de violations des droits de l'homme* (5 Octobre 1990–5 Octobre 1993).

Cornevin, R. (1987). 'Le Togo, 20e anniversaire'. *Afrique Contemporaine*, 142/2: 41–60.

Gräbener, J., van Rossum, T., and Schäfer, M. (1996). 'Wahlbeobachterbericht—Togo. Nachwahlen zum Parlament in den Bezirken Haho, Oti und Wawa (1. Wahlrunde) vom 4. August 1996'. *Africa Spectrum*, 2: 211–219.

Heilbrunn, J. R., and Toulabor, C. (1995). 'Une si petite démocratisation pour le Togo'. *Politique Africaine*, 58: 85–100.

Kohnert, D. (1990–1996). 'Togo', Institut für Afrika-Kunde and R. Hofmeier (eds.), *Afrika Jahrbuch. Politik, Wirtschaft und Gesellschaft in Afrika südlich der Sahara*. Hamburg: Institut für Afrika-Kunde.

Legum, C. *et al.* (1967/68–1987/88). 'Togo'. *Africa Contemporary Record. Annual Survey and Documents. Vols. I–XX.*

Stroux, D. (1994). 'Wahlen gewonnen—Einfluß verloren. Die Opposition in Togo kann sich nicht durchsetzen'. *Der Überblick*, 3/30: 113–115.

— (1996). 'Erster Wahlgang der Parlamentswahlen in Togo (6.2.1994)', in U. Engel, D. Hofmeier and A. Mehler (eds.), *Deutsche Wahlbeobachtung in Afrika*. Hamburg: Institut für Afrika-Kunde, 69–76.

Toulabor, C. M. (1986). *Le Togo sous Eyadéma.* Paris: Karthala.

— (1990). 'Dix ans de "démocratisation" au Togo, les faussaires de la démocratie'. *Année Africaine 1989*, Bordeaux: Centre d'Etude d'Afrique Noir et Centre de Recherche et d'Etude sur les Pays d'Afrique Orientale, 287–310.

von Trotha, T. (1993). 'Beobachtungen eines Wahlbeobachters: Togo', *Nord-Süd-Aktuell*, 9: 624–639.

Voss, H. (1987–1989), 'Togo'. in Institut für Afrika-Kunde and R. Hofmeier (eds.), *Afrika Jahrbuch. Politik, Wirtschaft und Gesellschaft in Afrika südlich der Sahara*. Hamburg: Institut für Afrika-Kunde.

Ziemer, K. (1978). 'Togo', in D. Sternberger, B. Vogel, D. Nohlen and K. Landfried (eds.), *Die Wahl der Parlamente und anderer Staatsorgane, Band II: Politische Organisation und Repräsentation in Afrika*, by Franz Nuscheler, Klaus Ziemer *et al.*, Berlin/ New York: Walter de Gruyter, 2177–2212.

— (1984). *Demokratisierung in Westafrika, Die politischen Systeme von Senegal, Elfenbeinküste und Togo nach zwei Jahrzehnten Unabhängigkeit*. Paderborn: Ferdinand Schönigh Verlag.

TUNISIA

by Juan Montabes Pereira

1. Introduction

1.1 Historical Introduction

Occupied by France in 1881 Tunisia became a French protectorate under a line of native rulers in 1883. Pressure for political reforms began after World War I and in 1934 resulted in the establishment of the nationalist Neo-Destour (New Constitution) Party, which became the spearhead of a movement for independence under the charismatic leadership of Habib Bourguiba.

The transition to independence began on 31 August 1955 when France conceded internal autonomy and Tunisia gained independence on 20 March 1956. A national Constituent Assembly controlled by the Neo-Destour Party voted on 25 July 1957 to abolish the monarchy and establish a republic with Bourguiba as President. A new constitution was adopted on 1 July 1959, while Bourguiba's leadership and that of the party were overwhelmingly confirmed in presidential and legislative elections in 1959 and 1964.

Since that time Tunisia has been organized as a centralist presidential system backed by the dominant position of the Neo-Destour Party (since 1988 *Rassemblement Constitutionnel Démocratique*, RCD). The President enjoys exceptionally broad powers including the right to rule by decree during legislative adjournments. The country's long unquestioned leader, President Bourguiba who shaped the political system by personal rule, was granted life tenure under a 1975 amendment to the constitution.

Bourguiba's reign was ended in 1987, when he was forced to step down, after a panel of doctors had declared the aged President medically unfit. General Zine El-Abdine Ben Ali who had been appointed Prime Minister five weeks before, succeeded to the office on 2 October 1987. Although widely termed a 'bloodless coup', the ouster of Bourguiba was in accord with relevant constitutional provisions. Since then President Ben Ali who immediately after assuming the presidency had announced his commitment to pluralism, has pursued policies of gradual political and economic liberalization.

Although constitutionally not mandated, Tunisia had been effectively a one-party state from the time the *Parti Communiste Tunisien* (PCT) was banned in January 1963 until its return to legal status in July 1981. A month earlier in 1981 the government had announced that recognition would be extended to all parties obtaining at least 5% of the valid votes in legislative balloting in 1981. In the case of the PCT the 5% requirement was not be imposed and in 1983 recognition was extended to two other parties, the *Parti de l'Union Populaire* (PUP) and *Mouvement des Démocrates Socialistes* (MDS). However, all three boycotted the 1986 legislative elections because of the rejection of a number their candidate lists.

The Ben Ali government endorsed the current party law in 1987, which legalizes any political party that consents to certain conditions, the most important of those aimed to serve as a barrier to the legalization of growing Islamic groups: 'No party has the right to refer in its principles, objectives and activities to religion, language, race or a regime'. The subsequent elections, originally scheduled for 1991, were moved forward to 2 April 1989, Ben Ali declaring they would serve as an indication of the public's satisfaction with the recent changes. Ben Ali was not challenged in the presidential poll, but several legalized opposition parties and independent Islamist candidates contested the parliamentary elections. However, none of the oppositional forces gained representation in the Chamber of Deputies.

This is caused by an electoral system which systematically marginalizes smaller parties who lack strong organization and implementation at national level. With its concentrating effect it has always sanctioned the President's party's officialist role by creating unanimous election results. Until 1994, no other political organization was ever represented in Parliament: If the electoral formula applied in the 1989 and 1994 parliamentary elections had been proportional, Islamist groups would have secured 24, MDS between two and three of the 141 seats.

Apparently in response to criticism that the government's enthusiasm for democratization had waned as its anti-fundamentalist fervor had surged, electoral law changes were adopted in late 1993 to assure opposition parties some legislative representation in the upcoming general election. Nevertheless the RCD, officially credited with 97.7% of the votes, won all 144 seats for which it was eligible in the balloting for a 163-member house on 20 March 1993. Almost symbolically some opposition parties entered the Chamber of Deputies via the recently introduced minority clause. Moreover, Ben Ali was re-elected with a reported 99%, two potential independent challengers having been prevented from appearing on the ballot paper by their failure to receive the required endorsement of at least 30 national legislators or municipal council presidents.

Since 1989 both electoral rules and the monolithic structure of the Tunisian party system have fueled a steady process of political polarization between two essentially authoritarian antagonists: On the one side the dominant officialist catch-all party orchestrated by the President, and on the other the politically excluded Islamist groups, represented by the (now outlawed) *Mouvement de la Tendence Islamique* (MTI) and the *Ennahda* (Renaissance) movement. Within this rather immovable binary framework persist a number of liberal, nationalist and social democratic parties searching for an independent political standing.

1.2 Evolution of Electoral Provisions

The Constitution of 1 June 1959 has been revised on six occasions: 1 July 1965, 30 June 1967, 31 December 1969, 19 March 1975, 8 April 1976 and July 1988.

Electoral provisions were first laid down in the *Loi Electoral* of 30 July 1959. The current *Code Electoral* was reformulated on 8 April 1969 and has been revised on several occasions since then.

From independence on, universal and direct suffrage was in effect for the elected office of President and a unicameral House of Representatives, both elected for a five-year term. Conditions for the right to vote were a minimum age of 20 years, Tunisian citizenship for at least five years and full possession of civil and political rights.

Under the *Loi Electoral* of 30 July 1959 candidates to the presidency had to be at least 30 years of age and be born of a Tunisian father. The President was elected by plurality system (renewable once). Deputies to the House of Representatives were elected in 17 constituencies providing for four to seven mandates. Closed lists and the plurality system were applied.

While the *Code Electoral* of 8 April 1969 continued the basic features of the electoral system, in 1974 Bourguiba assumed presidency for life which was granted by the 1975 Amendment to the Constitution. The constitutional reform of 1976 stated that the Prime Minister succeeds in the office of President in the case of the latter's fallacy. In 1989 the presidency returned to subjection to universal vote (renewable twice).

Since the last revision of 1993 Tunisians residing outside the country enjoy the right to vote in presidential elections.

The electoral system for the House of Representatives was reformed to its current status in 1993 (*loi organique No. 93/118 du 27 décembre 1993*).

1.3 Current Electoral Provisions

Sources: Loi No. 69-25 du 8 avril 1969, portant Code Electoral, modifiée par la loi organique No. 74-60 du 2 juillet 1974; loi organique No. 75-25 du 31 mars 1975; loi organique No. 76-66 du 11 août 1976; loi organique No. 79-35 du 15 août 1979; loi organique No. 81-71 du 9 août 1981; loi organique No. 88-79 du 24 septembre 1988; loi organique No. 88-144 du 29 décembre 1988; loi organique No. 90-48 du 4 mai 1990; loi organique No. 93-118 du 27 décembre 1993.

Elected national institutions: The President is elected for a five-year term, renewable twice. The House of Representatives, also referred to as Chamber of Deputies, is elected for a five-year term. The number of seats is fixed by presidential decree.

Suffrage: Universal, equal, secret and direct. The vote is not compulsory. Requirements: at least 20 years of age, Tunisian citizenship for at least five years and full possession of civil and political rights. Army members and Tunisians during their military service are excluded from the right to vote.

Nomination of candidates
- *presidential elections*: Qualified electors, Islamic religion, Tunisian citizenship by birth and without interruption, Tunisian father and mother by birth and without interruption, minimum age of 40 years. Candidates for presidential office must produce at least 30 signatures of members of the House of Representatives or presidents of municipal councils declaring their support for the candidacy.
- *elections to the House of Representatives (Chamber of Deputies)*: Qualified electors, at least 25 years of age, Tunisian Citizenship, born of a Tunisian father. Ineligibility: The presidents of the Constitutional Council and the economic and social council; governors, magistrates, ambassadors, international employees as well as first delegates,

delegates or heads of sector (regional public functions) can not be nominated.

Electoral system
- *presidential elections*: Plurality system.
- *elections to the House of Representatives* (Chamber of Deputies): The number of seats fixed by decree is based on the calculation of 52,500 inhabitants being represented by one parliamentary seat (Article 104, Reform of the Electoral Law, 1993). The resulting number of seats is distributed between 25 multi-member constituencies (2–10 seats) at one seat per 60,000 inhabitants. The remaining seats are supplementary seats at national level. In the last general election 163 deputies were elected: 144 in 25 constituencies and the remaining 19 seats at national level. In the 25 multi-member constituencies (2–10 seats) closed lists are elected according to the plurality system. The remaining supplementary seats are allocated at national level by the highest average formula including the votes of all unsuccessful lists at constituency level (Article 105, Reform of 1993). Vacancies are filled by by-elections within 12 months. During the last 12 months of a parliamentary term, no by-elections are held.

1.4 Comment on the Electoral Statistics

From 1959, the year in which elections were held for the first time, until 1989 legislative elections constituted a plebiscitarian element within the political system. Since 1989 elections have seemingly become competitive and plural; however, their function has essentially remained the same.

The overall electoral results were usually published only several years later by the state administration. The only up-to-date information stemmed from mass media also supervised by the government.

The main source of information used in this article is provided by the *Centre de Documentation Nationale* located at the Ministry of Information, earlier tallies being cross-checked with Raulf (1978). For the last parliamentary and presidential elections in 1994 detailed information was available at the Inter Parliamentary Union website (www.ipu.org).

2. Tables

2.1 Dates of National Elections, Referendums and Coups d'Etat

Year	Presidential elections	Parliamentary elections	Elections for Constitutional Assembly	Referendums	Coups d'état
1956			24/03		
1959	08/11	08/11			
1964	08/11	08/11			
1969	02/11	02/11			
1974	03/11	03/11			
1979		04/11			
1981		01/11			
1986		02/11			
1989	02/04	02/04			
1994	20/03	20/03			

2.2 Electoral Body 1956–1994

Year	Type of election[a]	Population[b]	Registered voters		Votes cast		
			Total number	% pop.	Total number	% reg. voters	% pop.
1956	CA	3,783,169	726,128[c]	19.2	606,899	83.6	16.0
1959	Pa/Pr	4,107,000	1,099,577	26.8	1,007,959	91.7	24.5
1964	Pa/Pr	4,565,000	1,301,534	28.5	1,257,947	96.6	27.6
1969	Pa/Pr	5,030,000	1,443,347	28.7	1,367,122	94.7	27.2
1974	Pa/Pr	5,650,000	—	—	1,573,291	96.8	27.8
1979	Pa	6,225,000	2,013,581	32.3	1,621,975	80.6	26.1
1981	Pa	6,354,000	2,311,031	36.4	1,962,127	84.9	30.9
1986	Pa	7,068,000	2,622,482	37.1	2,175,093	82.9	30.8
1989	Pa/Pr	7,481,000	2,711,925	36.2	2,073,719	76.5	27.7
1994	Pa	8,405,000	2,976,366	35.4	2,841,557	99.7	33.8
1994	Pr[d]	8,405,000	3,150,612	37.5	2,989,880	99.9	35.6

[a] CA = Constitutional Assembly; Pa = Parliament; Pr = President.
[b] Estimations by the World Bank and UNESCO.
[c] In 1956 women did not yet enjoy the right to vote.
[d] Including Tunisians residing abroad.

2.3 Abbreviations

MDS	Mouvement des Démocrates Socialistes
MR	Mouvement de la Rénovation (Harakat Ettajdid)
MTI[a]	Mouvement de la Tendence Islamique
MUP[a]	Mouvement de l'Unité Populaire
PCT[b]	Parti Communiste Tunisien
PSD[c]	Parti Socialiste Destourien
PSL	Parti Social Libéral
PSP	Parti Social pour le Progrès
PUP	Parti de l'Union Populaire
RCD[c]	Rassemblement Constitutionnel Démocratique
RSP[a]	Rassemblement Socialiste Progressiste
UDU	Union Démocratique Unioniste

[a] Tolerated, but not formally legalized political parties.
[b] The PCT was banned in January 1963 until its return to legal status in July 1981.
[c] Usually referred to as Neo-Destour Party. Founded in 1934, it was renamed RCD in 1988.

2.4 Electoral Participation of Parties and Alliances 1956–1994

Party / Alliance	Years	Elections contested	
		Presidential	Parliamentary
PSD	1956, 1959, 1964, 1969, 1974, 1979, 1981, 1986	4	8
PCT	1956, 1959	0	2
RCD	1989, 1994	2	2
MDS	1994	0	1
MR	1994	0	1
MDU	1994	0	1
PUP	1994	0	1
PSL	1994	0	1
PPS	1994	0	1

2.5 Referendums

Referendums have not been held.

2.6 Elections for Constitutional Assembly

1956	Votes Total number	%	Seats Total (98)	%
Registered voters	726,168	–		
Votes cast	606,899	83.6		
Invalid votes	1,447	0.2		
Valid votes	605,452	99.8		
PSD	597,763	98.7	98	100
PCT	7,352	1.2	–	–
Independents	235	0.1	–	–

2.7 Parliamentary Elections 1959–1994

Year	1959 Total number	%	1964 Total number	%
Registered voters	1,099,577	–	1,301,534	–
Votes cast	1,007,959	91.7	1,257,947	96.8
Invalid votes	2,190	0.2	2,794	0.2
Valid votes	1,005,769	99.8	1,255,153	99.8
PSD	1,002,298	99.7	1,255,153	100.0
PCT	3,471	0.3	–	–

Year	1969 Total number	%	1974 Total number	%
Registered voters	1,443,347	–	–	–
Votes cast	1,367,122	94.7	1,573,291	96.8
Invalid votes	3,183	0.2	2,337	0.1
Valid votes	1,363,939	99.8	1,570,954	99.9
PSD	1,363,939	100.0	1,570,954	100.0

Year	1979 Total number	%	1981 Total number	%
Registered voters	2,013,581	–	2,311,031	–
Votes cast	1,621,975	80.1	1,962,127	84.9
Invalid votes	61,222	3.8	20,269	1.0
Valid votes	1,560,753	96.2	1,941,858	99.0
PSD	1,560,753	100.0	1,828,363	94.2
MSD	–	–	63,234	3.3
MUP	–	–	18,755	1.0
PCT	–	–	14,677	0.8
Independents	–	–	7,966	0.4

Year	1986[a]		1989	
	Total number	%	Total number	%
Registered voters	2,622,482	–	2,711,925	–
Votes cast	2,175,093	82.9	2,073,719	76.5
Invalid votes	10,036	0.5	31,836	1.6
Valid votes	2,165,057	99.5	2,041,883	98.4
PSD[b]	—[c]	—	–	–
RCD[b]	–	–	1,633,004	80.6
MDS	–	–	76,520	3.8
PUP	–	–	13,956	0.7
UDU	–	–	7,912	0.4
Leftist Coalition	–	–	7,619	0.4
PSP	–	–	5,270	0.3
RSP	–	–	4,054	0.2
IRSP	–	–	1,224	0.1
Independents	—	—	277,155	13.7

[a] The elections were boycotted by MSD, PUP and PCT because a number of their candidate lists were rejected.
[b] The PSD was renamed RCD in 1988.
[c] Two independent lists presented candidates of which one gained 1.4% of the votes cast in the constituency of Ben-Arous, a suburb of the capital, the other one gained 2.7% in the constituency of Sfax.

Year	1994	
	Total number	%
Registered voters	2,976,366	–
Votes cast	2,841,557	95.5
Invalid votes	8,686	0.3
Valid votes	2,832,871	99.7
RCD	2,768,667	97.7
MDS	30,660	1.1
MR (Ettajdid)	11,299	0.4
MDU	9,152	0.3
PUP	8,391	0.3
PSL	1,892	0.1
PPS	1,749	0.1
Independents[a]	1,061	0.0

[a] The independent list was fielded in the Tunis-2 constituency.

2.8 Composition of Parliament 1959–1994

Year	1959		1964		1969		1974	
	Seats	%	Seats	%	Seats	%	Seats	%
	90	100	101	100	101	100	112	100
PSD	90	100	101	100	101	100	112	100

Year	1979		1981		1986		1989	
	Seats	%	Seats	%	Seats	%	Seats	%
	121	100	136	100	125	100	141	100
PSD	121	100	136	100	125	100	–	–
RCD	–	–	–	–	–	–	141	100

Year	1994	
	Seats	%
	163	100
RCD	144	88,3
MDS	10	6,1
MR Ettajdid	4	2,5
MDU	3	1,8
PUP	2	1,2

2.9 Presidential Elections 1959–1994

Presidential elections in 1959, 1964, 1969 and 1974 which affirmed Habib Bourguiba equal parliamentary elections.

1989	Total number	%
Registered voters	2,762,109	–
Votes cast	2,102,351	76.1
Invalid votes	15,348	0.7
Valid votes	2,087,028	99.3
Zine El-Abdine Ben Ali (RCD)	2,087,028	100.0

1989	Total number	%
Registered voters	2,711,925	–
Votes cast	2,073,719	76.5
Invalid votes	31,836	1.6
Valid votes	2,041,883	98.5
Zine El-Abdine Ben Ali (RCD)	—	100.0

1994	Total number	%
Registered voters	3,150,612	–
Votes cast	2,989,880	94.9
Invalid votes	2,505	0.1
Valid votes	2,987,375	99.9
Zine El-Abdine Ben Ali (RCD)	2,987,375	100.0

2.10 List of Power Holders 1956–1998

Head of State	Years	Remarks
Habib Bourguiba	1957–1987	Acceded to the presidency by vote of the Constitutional Assembly in 1957; relinquished the post of Head of Government and was re-elected in 1969; named President for Life in 02/11/1974; forced to step down in favor of Ben Ali on 07/11/1987 after a panel of doctors had declared him medically unfit.
Zine El-Abdine Ben Ali	1987–	General; former Prime Minister; acceded to the presidency upon the deposition of Habib Bourguiba on 07/11/1987; returned to office unopposed at elections of 1989 and 1994.

Head of Government	Years	Remarks
Bahi Ladgham	1969–1970	Designated on 07/11/1969; dismissed in 1970.
Hedi Nouira	1970–1980	Designated on 06/11/1970; in office until 23/04/1980, when he suffered a stroke.
Mohamed Mzâli	1980–1986	Designated on 24/04/1980; reappointed after general elections in 1981; dismissed on 08/07/1986.
Rachid Sfar	1986–1987	Designated on 08/07/1986; dismissed on 02/10/1987.
Zine El-Abdine Ben Ali	1987	Designated on 02/10/1987; acceded to the presidency five weeks later on 07/11/1987.
Hedi Baccouche	1987–1989	Designated on 07/11/1987, dismissed on 27/09/1989.
Hamad Karoui	1989–	Designated on 27/09/1989.

3. Bibliography

3.1 Official Sources

Centre de Documentation Nationale. Ministère de l'Information (1982). *Les élections législatives tunisiennes 1956–1981*. République Tunisienne.

'Code Electoral. République Tunisienne'. *Journal Officiel de la République Tunisienne*. Agence Tunisienne de Communication Extérieure. Février 1994.

'Organisation des élections présidentielles et législatives, 20 mars 1994. Textes législatives'. *Journal Officiel de la République Tunisienne*.

Recueil des textes relatif à l'organisation politique et aux libertés publiques. Publications de l'imprimerie Officielle de la République Tunisienne. 1989.

3.2 Books, Articles and Electoral Reports

Anderson, L. (1991). 'Political Pacts, Liberalism, and Democracy. The Tunisian National Pact of 1988'. *Government and Opposition*, 26/2: 244–260.

Astié, P., and Breillat, D. (1994). 'Repères étrangeres: Tunesie—20 mars 1994: élections présidentielles et législatives'. *Pouvoirs*, 18: 180–181.

Association Tunisienne de Droit Constitutionnel (1987). *Les experiences constitutionnelles maghrebines*. Publications du Centre d'Etudes de Recherches et de Publications de Tunis.

Ben Hammed, M. R. (1987). *Rapport introductif, en association Tunisienne de droit constitutionnel: Les experiences constitutionnelles maghrebines*.

Bras, J. P. (1996). 'Túnez', in M. Y. Hernando de Larramendi and B. López García (eds.), *Sistemas politicos de maghreb actual*. Madrid: Editorial Mapfre.

Burgat, F. (1990) 'Points de repère sur l'islamisme au Maghreb', in B. Kodmany-Darwish and M. Chartouni-Dubarry (eds.), *Maghreb: les années de transition*. Paris: Masson, 206–216.

Camau, M. (1979). 'Caractère et role du constitutionnalisme dans les Etats maghrebins'. *Développements politiques au Maghreb*, Paris: Editions du CNRS.

— (1991). *Changements politiques au Maghreb*. Paris: Editions du CNRS.

Claisse, A., and Conac, G. (1988). *Le Grand Maghreb. Données socio-politiques et facteurs d'integration des Etats du Maghreb*. Paris: Economica.

Denoeux, G. (1994). 'Tunesie: les élections présidentielles et législatives'. *Maghreb*, 145, 49–72.

El Malki, H., and Santucci, J.-C. (1990). *Etat et développement dans le monde arabe. Crises et mutations au Maghreb*. Paris: Editions du CNRS.

Elbaji El-Hermassi, M. (1990). 'Le système politique tunisien et le 7 novembre', in B. Kodmany-Darwish and M. Chartouni-Dubarry (eds.), *Maghreb: les années de transition*. Paris: Masson, 97–106.

Flory, M. *et al.* (1990). *Les régimes politiques arabes*. Paris: PUF.

Gellner, E. (1991). 'Studies on North Africa—Introduction to a New Series'. *Government and Opposition*, 26/3: 329–330.

Hernando de Larramendi, M. (1991). 'Frontismo electoral y democracia en Túnez 1956–1989', in B. López Garcia, G. Martin Muñoz and M. Hernando de Larramendi (eds.), *Elecciones, participación y transiciones políticas en el Norte de Africa*. Madrid: Ministerio de Asuntos Exteriores/ ICMA.

Hudson, M.C. (1977). *Arab Politics. The Search for Legitimacy*. New Haven, Conn.: Yale University Press.

Informacion Comercial Española (1991). 'Argelia, Marruecos, Túnez (monographical number)'. *Publicación de la Secretaría de Estado de Comercio*, 2283, 10–16 June 1991.

Kodmany-Darwish, B., and Chartouni-Dubarry, M. (1990). *Maghreb: les années de transition*. Paris: Masson.

Korany, B. (1994). 'Arab Democratization: A Poor Cousin?' *Political Science & Politics*, 27/3: 511–513.

Leca, J. (1994). 'La démocratisation dans le monde arabe: Incertitude, vulneralité et legitimité', in G. Salamé (ed.), *Démocraties sans democrates. Politiques d'ouverture dans le monde arabe et islamique*. Paris: Fayard.

Lacoste, C., and Lacoste, Y. (1991). *L'Etat du Maghreb*. Paris: La Découverte.

Lewis, B. (1990). *El lenguaje político del Islam*. Madrid: Taurus.

López Garcia, B. (1982). 'Las elecciones tunecinas del 1 de noviembre de 1981'. *Revista de Estudios Políticos Nueva Época*, 25: 193–220.

— (1990). 'Transiciones políticas en el Magreb'. *Razón y Fé*, 222: 289–304.

— (1991). 'Leyes electorales, artimañas legales. La legislación magrebí a la hora del pluripartidismo', in B. López Garcia, G. Martin Muñoz and M. Hernando de Larramendi (eds.), *Elecciones, participación y transiciones políticas en el Norte de Africa*. Madrid: Ministerio de Asuntos Exteriores/ ICMA.

— and Fernández Suzor, C. (1985). *Introducción a los regímenes y Constituciones arabes*. Madrid: Centro de Estudios Constitucionales.

Mackenzie, W. J. M. (1962). *Elecciones libres*. Madrid: Tecnos.

Montabes, J., and López Garcia, B. (1995). *El Magreb tras la crisis del Golfo: Transformaciones políticas y orden intranacional*. Universidad de Granada: Agencia Española de Cooperación Internacional.

Najib Ba (1990). 'Constitutions et changements en Tunisie et en Algerie: Sur la question pluripartite'. *Al Mayadine. Revue Universitaire des Etudes Juridiques Economiques et Politiques*, 6: 9–20.

Nohlen, D. (1981). *Sistemas electorales del mundo*. Madrid: Centro de Estudios Constitucionales.

— (1991). 'Transiciones políticas y regímenes electorales', in B. López Garcia, G. Martin Muñoz and M. Hernando de Larramendi (eds.). *Elecciones, participación y transiciones políticas en el Norte de Africa*. Madrid: Ministerio de Asuntos Exteriores/ ICMA.

Raulf, H. (1978). 'Tunesien', in D. Sternberger, B. Vogel, D. Nohlen and K. Landfried, (eds.), *Die Wahl der Parlamente und anderer Staatsorgane, Band II: Politische Organisation und Repräsentation in Afrika*, by Franz Nuscheler, Klaus Ziemer *et al.*, Berlin/ New York: Walter de Gruyter, 2253–2298.

Santucci, J. C. (1991). 'Processus électoraux et legitimation du pouvoir: réflexions sur l'experiénce marocaine'. in B. López Garcia, G. Martin Muñoz, and M. Hernando de Larramendi (eds.), *Elecciones, participación y transiciones políticas en el Norte de Africa*. Madrid: Ministerio de Asuntos Exteriores/ ICMA.

Segura I Mas, A. (1994). *El Magreb: del colonialismo al islamismo*. Barcelona: Universitat de Barcelona.

Wickham, C. R. (1994). 'Beyond Democratization: Political Change in the Arab World'. *Political Science & Politics*, 27/3: 507–509.

UGANDA

by Siegmar Schmidt

1. Introduction

1.1 Historical Overview

After over 60 years under British colonial rule Uganda gained independence through a smooth transition on 9 October 1962. The legacy of British colonialism was a Westminster-style parliamentary system which was not in line with the realities of the heterogeneous society. Postcolonial political development was strongly influenced by deep rooted socio-economic and ethnic (over 40 tribes) cleavages. Most important were the differences between the economically marginalized North (a recruitment basis for the colonial army) and the South which became the economic powerhouse and developed more sophisticated political structures. Already under colonial rule the societal heterogeneity was translated into the party system. The Democratic Party (DP, founded in 1954) especially organized small catholic farmers, the *Kabaka Yekka* ('the king only', founded in 1961) was the party of the (mainly Protestant) Baganda, the largest ethnic group and the royalists. The Uganda People's Congress (UPC, 1960) had its strongholds among the Protestants in the northern and north-eastern parts of the country. The elections of 1961 and 1962 (before independence) saw the rise of two political camps and shaped the political landscape for the following four years. The UPC won and formed a fragile coalition government with the *Kabaka Yekka* which gained an overwhelming majority in the 1962 elections for the regional Parliament of Buganda (Lukiko). Due to continuous efforts from the Buganda kingdom for greater self-determination a power struggle between King (Kabaka) Mutesa II and Prime Minister Milton Obote escalated into armed conflict in 1966. Mutesa II was ousted from power, Buganda autonomy was severely limited and in 1967 a new constitution introduced a highly centralized regime with Milton Obote as President. By 1969 all political parties with the exception of UPC were forbidden and constitutionally provided elections were postponed. In 1971 the Commander-in-Chief of the armed forces, the Muslim Idi Amin, performed a coup d'état and installed himself as Head of State. All democratic institutions were abolished and in the following years Amin's reign of terror took the life of hundreds of thousands of Ugandans. The expulsion in 1972 of 50,000 to 100,000 Asians, who had dominated the Ugandan economy, led to total economic deterioration.

In 1979, military intervention by Tanzanian forces ended the brutal Amin dictatorship. Because of lack of political support (especially from the army) the two interim governments of Yusufu K. Lule and Godfrey Binaisa were only short-lived. Despite a political climate close to civil war, elections were held in December 1980. The official result was a victory of Obote's UPC. Despite the elections having been rigged the DP decided to form the parliamentary opposition. In contrast, the Uganda People's Movement (UPM) of Yoweri Museveni (formerly a leading member of the United National Liberation Front that had fought against the regime of Idi Amin) decided among other groups to 'go into the bush' starting with guerilla warfare. During the second Obote regime (1980–1985) the terror Ugandans had experienced under Idi Amin continued and nearly half a million people were killed by the security forces. In 1986, shortly after Obote was overthrown by General Lutwa Okello, Museveni's National Resistance Movement (NRM) with its military wing, the National Resistance Army, gained control over the country. Museveni's military victory was welcomed by the population as an act of liberalization. He declared himself President and formed a broad based government including (a few) members from the DP and from the Buganda royal family.

Instead of restoring pluralist democracy Museveni's NRM government established a system of Resistance Councils (RC) based on the premise that political participation should not be realized within multiparty politics. At the lowest administrative level all inhabitants of a village elected nine delegates (RC1) who together with other delegates elected the RC2 level and so on. At the top the National Resistance Council (until 1989 40 members without any democratic legitimation; then expanded to 278 members indirectly elected at county level) functioned as a quasi-Parliament but without the right of controlling the executive. RC elections took place in 1989 and 1992. Although at best half-democratic the RC system gained a certain amount of legitimacy within Uganda since basic goods were delivered to the population in that war-torn country. It was also tolerated and more or less supported by African states and the international donor community. Significant improvements of the human rights situation and the restoration of economic stability and growth through the adoption of structural adjustment policies recommended by the IMF and the World Bank helped the regime to maintain internal and external political support.

Under (relatively) mild pressure from the donor community the NRM in 1988 began a process of constitutional engineering. On the basis of over 25,000 grass-roots proposals a draft constitution was written and discussed and modified by a directly elected (though not in competitive multi-party elections) Constitutional Assembly from 1994 on. On 8 October 1995 a new constitution (the fourth since independence) was adopted. It improved the protection of human rights, strengthened—unprecedentedly in Uganda—the status of women, reintroduced the rule of law and restored the powers of Parliament. In sum, however, the democratic character of the political regime remains ambivalent: The powers of the President are still overwhelming, severe restrictions on party activities remain and demands of the opposition parties for greater federalism were not met. In the presidential and parliamentary elections in May and in June 1996, respectively, candidates were not allowed to run under party labels. On both occasions the NRM, who still claims not to be a party, maintained a dominant position. According to the transitional provisions of the Constitution a referendum is scheduled for 2000 giving the electorate the chance to reintroduce multi-party politics. Besides, the future of the party system will depend on the one hand on the evolution of the NRM as a catch-all party (up to now, the movement has been able to avoid factionalism), and, on the other hand, on developments within the main opposition parties, UPC and DP, both of which face serious internal conflicts and organizational problems.

1.2 Evolution of Electoral Provisions

Constitutional and legal electoral provisions of Uganda are characterized by great continuity. The colonial legislation of 1957 was maintained with only marginal additions by all subsequent governments after independence for four decades. All elections after 1962 were held under the provisions of the Constitution of 1967 which provided for universal suffrage for all Ugandans above the age of 18. Direct elections were proscribed for the National Assembly whereas the President was elected indirectly. Members of the National Assembly had to be able to speak and read English. Elections were to be held every five years according to plurality system in single-member districts. The number of seats in the

National Assembly was increased from 82 in 1967 to 96 in 1970, and finally to 126 in 1980.
According to Article 45 (2) of the 1967 Constitution the Electoral Commission should play a crucial role in supervising the whole electoral process. The Electoral Commission had the authority to review the boundaries of the constituencies and to nominate election officers. Since the President was given the right to appoint the Chairman and the two members of the Commission the door for political manipulations was left wide open. Whenever elections were held in Uganda the government of the day used the Commission for the purpose of its own interests.

1.3 Current Electoral Provisions

Sources: Constitution of the Republic of Uganda, 1995; The Presidential Elections (Interim Provisions) Statute, 1996; The Parliamentary Elections, (Interim Provisions) Statute, 1996.

Elected national institutions: President of the State of Uganda and 214 (out of a total of 276) Members of the Parliament of Uganda are elected for a five-year term. The President may serve for a maximum of two consecutive terms.

Suffrage: The principles of universal, equal, direct and secret suffrage are applied. Every Ugandan citizen with a minimum age of 18 who is registered as a voter is entitled to vote. A national register of voters is administered by the Interim Electoral Commission. Voters have to apply for registration in a polling division.

Nominations of candidates
- *presidential elections*: Candidates have to be Ugandan citizens by birth, aged between 35 and 75 years and must have obtained a minimum of formal education of Advanced Level standard. Additionally, a list of 100 registered voters supporting the candidate of two thirds of the districts has to be presented. Only individual candidates without a direct and open affiliation to a political party are allowed.
- *parliamentary elections*: Candidates have to be Ugandan citizens with a minimum age of 18, obtain a minimum of formal education and pay a nomination fee of 200,000 Ugandan shillings. Furthermore 10 registered voters of the respective constituency must support the candidacy.

Traditional leaders are not eligible. Only individual candidates without a direct and open affiliation to a political party are allowed.

Electoral system

- *presidential elections*: Absolute majority system. If no candidate obtains the required majority, a second ballot is held within 30 days between the two most voted candidates of the first round.
- *parliamentary elections*: Plurality system in single-member constituencies. The Electoral Commission defines the boundaries of the constituencies. The number of constituencies in the 39 administrative districts of the country ranges from two to 11. Beside the directly elected Members of Parliament there are 10 representatives from the army, three from the trade unions, five from youth organizations and five from the organizations of the disabled (all elected by delegates of the respective organizations). Additionally, each of the 39 districts of Uganda delegates one woman representative to Parliament. Furthermore, the constitution states that all members of the Cabinet, including the Vice-President shall become Members of Parliament automatically.

1.4 Comment on the Electoral Statistics

Most of the figures given in the following tables are problematic, since the data basis is insufficient. Due to poor statistics (no registration of citizens exists), the civil wars and hundred of thousands of refugees from neighboring countries (Sudan, Rwanda) even population estimations are questionable. For the elections held before 1978 the data were drawn from the standard analysis of Nuscheler (1978). With respect to the elections of 1994 and 1996 the official results as published by Uganda's most reliable *The New Vision* are reported. Inconsistencies of several of the calculations in this country profile could not be avoided.

2. Tables

2.1 Dates of National Elections, Referendums and Coups d'Etat

Year	Presidential elections	Parliamentary elections	Elections for Constitutional Assembly	Referendums	Coups d'état
1961		23/03[a]			
1962		22/02[b]			
1962		25/04[c]			
1966					24/05
1971					25/01
1979					11/04[d]
1979					21/06[e]
1980		06–10/12			18/05[f]
1985					27/07
1994			28/03		
1996	09/05	27/06			

[a] Legislative Council of Uganda (without Buganda).
[b] Parliament (Lukiko) of Buganda.
[c] National Assembly of Uganda (without Buganda).
[d] Military intervention by Tanzanian forces led to the fall of Idi Amin.
[e] Non-violent overthrow of President Lule.
[f] Non-violent overthrow of President Binaisa by army officers.

2.2 Electoral Body 1961–1996

Year	Type of election[a]	Population	Registered voters		Votes cast		
			Total number	% pop.	Total number	% reg. voters	% pop.
1961[b]	Pa	6,845,000	1,336,115	19.5	1,005,394	77.4	14.7
1962[c]	Pa	—	805,092	—	733,992[e]	91.2	—
1962[d]	Pa	—	1,553,233	—	1,052,544[e]	67.7	—
1980	Pa	12,636,200	4,898,117	38.8	4,174,382	85.2	33.0
1994	CA	18,600,000	7,180,514	38.6	6,197,525	86.3	33.3
1996	Pr	18,590,000	8,492,154	45.7	6,163,678	72.3	33.2
1996	Pa	18,590,000	8,492,154	45.7	4,665,185[e]	60.7[f]	25.1

[a] CA = Constitutional Assembly; Pa = Parliament; Pr = President.
[b] Uganda only (without Buganda, where only 22,190 votes were cast due to a boycott).
[c] Parliament of Buganda (Lukiko) only.
[d] National Assembly of Uganda (without Buganda).
[e] Valid votes.
[f] The fact that in 15 out of 214 constituencies seats were not contested probably reduced voter participation.

2.3 Abbreviations

CP	Conservative Party
DP	Democratic Party
IPC	Inter-Party Committee
NCD	National Caucus for Democracy
NLP	National Liberal Party
NRM	National Resistance Movement
UNC	Uganda National Congress
UNM	Uganda National Movement
UPC	Uganda People's Congress
UPM	Uganda Patriotic Movement

2.4 Electoral Participation of Parties and Alliances

Party / Alliance	Years[a]	Elections contested	
		Presidential	Parliamentary
DP	1961–1980	0	5
UNC	1961	0	2
UPC	1961–1980	0	3
CP	1980	0	1
UPM	1980	0	1
IPC[b]	1996	1	0
NRM	1996	1	1[c]

[a] In 1996 parties were not allowed to participate in the elections.
[b] Alliance of DP, UPC and NLP.
[c] The RC elections of 1989 and 1992 not included.

2.5 Referendums

Up to 1996 no referendums have been held in Uganda. According to the Constitution of 1994 a referendum for the purpose of a change of the political system may be held on request of (a) the absolute majority of Parliament, or (b) the total membership of the majority of district councils, or (c) of a tenth of the registered voters of two thirds of the districts.

2.6 Elections for Constitutional Assembly

1994	Votes		Seats[a]	
	Total number	%	Total (214)	%
Registered voters	7,180,514			
Votes cast	6,197,525	86.3		
Invalid votes	213,493	3.4		
Valid votes	5,964,797	83.1		
NRM	—	—	—	—
DP	—	—	—	—
UPC	—	—	—	—
CP	—	—	—	—
NLP	—	—	—	—
UPM[b]	—	—	—	—

[a] The Constituent Assembly Election Rules allowed only individual candidates. Therefore no exact figures of the parties' shares can be given. According to estimations from Uganda's sources the following numbers seem plausible: Since 68 elected members of the CA formed the National Caucus for Democracy within the CA, it could be estimated that the opposition parties together (UPC, DP CP, NLP) won 68 mandates. The NRM won 146 from the 214 total number of mandates. In addition 70 CA members were appointed: All parties delegated two, the army 10, the National Youth Council four, National Organizations of Trade Unions two, the National Union of Disabled People one and each of the 39 districts one woman. The President delegated 10 members on the advice of the Cabinet.

[b] The UPM declared that the party integrated itself into the NRM.

2.7 Parliamentary Elections 1961–1996

Year	1961[a]	
	Total number	%
Registered voters	1,336,115	–
Votes cast	1,227,524	91.9
Invalid votes	—	—
Valid votes	1,027,051[b]	83.7
UNC	40,134	4.0
UPC	495,909	49.2
DP	436,420	41.3
Independent	45,473	4.5
Other	9,115	0.9

[a] Elections to the Legislative Council (without Buganda).

[b] The given number corresponds to the sum of party votes (author's calculation).

Year	1962[a] Total number	%	1962[b] Total number	%
Registered voters	805,092	—	1,553,233	–
Votes cast	—	—	—	—
Invalid votes	—	—	—	—
Valid votes	733,992	—	1,052,544	—
UPC	155	0.0	545,324	51.8
DP	–	–	484,933	46.1
UNC	103,180	14.0	2,565	0.2
Bataga Party of Busoga	629,310	85.7	2,375	0.2
Uganda National Union	1,072	0.1	39	0.0
Independents	275	0.0	17,308	1.6

[a] Elections to the Parliament of Buganda (*Lukiko*) only.
[b] Elections to the National Assembly of Uganda (without Buganda). The results of two constituencies in Toro, where the elections could be held only one week after the official election day, are included.

Year	1980[a] Total number	%	1996[c] Total number	%
Registered voters	4,898,117	–	8,492,154	–
Votes cast	4,174,328	85.2	4,752,570	60.7
Invalid votes	2,419	0.1	87,385	1.8
Valid votes	4,171,909[b]	99.9	4,665,185	98.2
DP	1,966,244	47.1	–	–
UPC	1,963,679	47.1	–	–
UPM	171,785	4.1	–	–
CP	70,181	1.6	–	–

[a] Electoral results were manipulated by the government. The numbers given are official figures.
[b] The number given corresponds to the sum of party votes; author's calculation.
[c] Candidates could only participate as individuals without any open party affiliation. The number of seats per party can only be roughly estimated. Because of irregularities in the presidential elections a few weeks before, the DP recommended 'their' candidates to boycott the elections. The majority of candidates followed this recommendation. Candidates who, according to estimations, were supporters of UPC and DP were successful especially in constituencies in Northern districts.

2.8 Composition of the National Assembly 1961–1996

Year	1961[a]		1962[b]		1980		1996	
	Seats	%	Seats	%	Seats	%	Seats	%
	82	100	82		126[e]	100	214[f]	100
UPC	35	49.2	37[c]	45.1	75	59.5	–	–
DP	44	41.3	24[c]	29.3	50	39.7	–	–
UNC	1	4.0	–	–	–	–	–	–
UPM	–	–	–	–	1	0.8	–	–
Kabaka Yekka	–	–	21[d]	25.9	–	–	–	–
Independents	2	4.5	–	–	–	–	–	–

[a] Legislative Council of Uganda.

[b] National Assembly of Uganda including delegated members from the Parliament of Buganda (*Lukiko*). *Kabaka Yekka* held 65 of 68 seats of the *Lukiko*, the three remaining seats were held by the DP.

[c] Directly elected members.

[d] Delegated Members from the Parliament of Buganda.

[e] Elected seats only according to (manipulated) electoral results as reported by the Electoral Commission. Additionally, MPs were appointed by the President and social organizations. Seventeen seats were won unopposed by the UPC (all in Northern constituencies).

[f] Elected seats only. Additionally, 69 MPs were appointed by the President and social organizations. Because candidates were not allowed to run under party labels the composition of Parliament with regard to political forces can not be given. However, due to the DP boycott only 6–10% (author's estimate) of the MPs are supporters of the opposition parties.

2.9 Presidential Elections 1996

	Total number	%
Registered voters	8,492,154	–
Votes cast	6,163,678	72.3
Invalid votes	196,130	3.2
Valid votes	5,967,548	96.8
Yoweri Museveni (NRM)[a]	4,428,119	74.2
Paul Ssemogerere (IPC)[a]	1,416,139	23.7
Muhammed Mayanja (Independent)	123,290	2.1

[a] Candidates were not allowed to run under party labels. The NRM claims not to be a party. The IPC was formed by the DP, the UPC and the NLC. The electoral process was, according to electoral observers, acceptable. The term 'free and fair' was avoided because of the discrimination against opposition parties. In contrast to electoral observers the DP first declared that the elections were rigged, but later spoke of irregularities. The IPC's candidate, DP-leader Ssemogerere won only seven out of 39 districts. With one exception these strongholds of the opposition lie in the North of the country, an area which is shaken by civil war. Additionally, the North is the traditional base of the UPC. Because of the coalition with the UPC the DP failed to get the majority of Baganda votes. Until now the Baganda are still traumatized by their historical experience with UPC terror.

2.10 List of Power Holders 1962–1998

Head of Government	Years	Remarks
Milton Obote	1962–1971	Took office on 09/10/1962 as Prime Minister in the Westminster System which was a heritage from British colonial rule; from 1966 to 25/01/1971 Obote held both offices, President and Prime Minister. From 1971 onwards the center of political power has been the presidency.

Head of State	Years	Remarks
Sir Edward Muteesa II	1963–1966	Kabaka (king) of the Buganda kingdom (formed by the largest ethnic group – Baganda) since 09/11/1963, leader of the Kabaka Yekka/ UPC alliance; overthrown by his Prime Minister Milton Obote on 24/05/1966; died in London in exile shortly afterwards.
Milton Obote	1966–1971	Took office on 24/05/1966; leader of the UPC; political scientist; pillars of his autocratic rule were a centralization of the decision-making process and the militarization of society; overthrown by coup of his army commander, Idi Amin on 25/01/1971.
Idi Amin	1971–1979	Despotic reign with uncontrolled violent atrocities; 'Africanization' of state and economy through expulsion of the Asians; overthrown by a military intervention of Tanzanian forces on 11/04/1979.
Yusufu Lule	1979	Appointed on 11/04/1979; ex-Chancellor of Makerere University and a 'neutral' political figure without support of key groups. Had to resign on 21/06/1979 after faction fighting within his weak party alliance.
Godfrey Binaisa	1979–1980	Appointed on 21/06/1979; former Attorney-General in Obote's Cabinet; more or less a puppet of Obote; resigned on 18/05/1980.
Milton Obote	1980–1985	Returned after nine years in Tanzanian exile; manipulated the elections of 1980 and took government on 25/12/1980; his brutal dictatorship was weakened by increasing success of several militant rebel groups; ousted on 27/07/1985.

Head of State	Years	Remarks
Lutwa Okello	1985–1986	Army officer; continued dictatorship; military defeat against the National Resistance Army led by Museveni on 26/01/1986.
Yoweri Museveni	1986–	Took office on 26/01/1986; had started guerilla activities in 1980 with only 27 supporters; a well-educated intellectual, who studied Economics and Politics in Dar es Saalam; installed a moderate autocratic system which restructured the economy successfully; in addition political reforms led to a gradual, democratization process; constitutionally elected as President in May 1996 in 'half-democratic' (non-party based) elections.

3. Bibliography

3.1 Official sources

Constitution of the Republic of Uganda (1995). Entebbe.

Report of the Electoral Commission 1980. Kampala.

The Constitution of Uganda (1962). Entebbe.

The Constitution of Uganda (1967). Entebbe.

The Parliamentary Elections, (Interim Provisions) Statute, 1996, Statute No.4. Entebbe, 11 March 1996.

The Presidential Elections (Interim Provisions) Statute, 1996, Statute No.3. Entebbe, 26 February 1996.

3.2 Books, Articles and Electoral Reports

Africa Contemporary Record (yearly editions since 1968). London/ New York: Holms and Meier.

Berg-Schlosser, D., and Siegler, R. (1988). *Politische Stabilität und Entwicklung. Eine vergleichende Analyse der Bestimmungsfaktoren und Interanktionsmuster in Kenia, Tansania und Uganda*. Münster/ Köln: Weltforum-Verlag.

Bossert, A. (1994). 'Uganda auf dem Weg zu einer neuen Verfassung'. *KAS-Auslandsinformationen*, 10/1: 63–74.

— (1995). 'Zur aktuellen Situation der Democratic Party in Uganda'. *KAS-Auslandsinformationen*, 11/4: 46–51.

— (1996). 'Ugandas neue Verfassung'. *KAS-Auslandsinformationen*, 12/1: 31–54.

Bwengye, F. A. W. (1985). *The Agony of Uganda*. London: Regency Press.

Byrnes, R. M. (1992). *Uganda: a Country Study* (2nd edn.). Washington, Federal Research Division, Area Handbook Series: US Government Printing Office.

Calas, B., and Prunier, G. (1994). *L'Ouganda contemporain*. Paris: Karthala.

Cooper, L., and Stroux, D. (1996). 'International Election Observation in Uganda. Compromise of the Expense of Substance'. *Afrika Spektrum*, 31: 201–209.

Furley, O. (1986). 'Uganda's Retreat from Turmoil?' *Conflict Studies*, 196. London: The Centre for Security and Conflict Studies.

— and Katalikawe, J. (1997). 'Constitutional Reform in Uganda: The New Approach'. *African Affairs*, 96: 243–260.

Hansen, H. B., and Twaddle, M. (1995). 'Uganda: The Advent of No-Party Democracy', in J. A. Wiseman (ed.), *Democracy and Political Change in Sub-Saharan Africa*. London: Routledge, 137–151.

— (eds.) (1996). *From Chaos to Order: The Politics of Constitution Making in Uganda*. Kampala/ London: Fountain Publ. and James Currey.

Hartmann, C. (1999). *Externe Faktoren im Demokratisierungsprozeß. Eine vergleichende Untersuchung afrikanischer Länder*. Opladen: Leske & Budrich.

Hofmeier, R. (1988–1997). 'Uganda', in Institut für Afrika-Kunde and R. Hofmeier (eds.), *Afrika-Jahrbuch*. Opladen: Leske & Budrich, annually.

Kabwegyere, T. B. (1995). *The Politics of State Formation and Destruction in Uganda* (3rd edn.). Kampala: Fountain Publ.

Khadiagala, G. M. (1995). 'State Collapse and Reconstruction in Uganda', in W. I. Zartman (ed.), *Collapsed States*. Boulder, Col.: Westview, 33–47.

Khiddu-Makubuya, E. (1996). 'The Law and Practice of Elections in Uganda: Prospects for the Future', in K. Kibwaba, J. Oloka-Onyango and C. M. Peter (eds.), *Law and the Struggle for Democracy in East Africa*. Nairobi: Claripress, 545–584.

Kokole, O., and Mazrui, A. A. (1988). 'Uganda: The Dual Polity and the Plural Society', in L. Diamond, J. J. Linz and S. M. Lipset (eds.), *Democracy in Development Countries, Vol. 2: Africa*. Boulder, Col.: Lynne Rienner, 259–299.

Low, D. A. (1962). *Political Parties in Uganda, 1949–1962*. London: Atholone Press.

Nuscheler, F. (1978), 'Uganda', in D. Sternberger, B. Vogel, D. Nohlen and K. Landfried (eds.), *Die Wahl der Parlamente und anderer Staatsorgane. Band II: Politische Organisation und Repräsentation in Afrika*, by Franz Nuscheler, Klaus Ziemer *et al.*, Berlin/ New York: Walter de Gruyter, 2299–2329.

Omara-Otunu, A. (1987). *Politics and the Military in Uganda, 1895–1985*. New York: St Martin's Press.

— (1995). 'The Dynamics of Conflict in Uganda', in O. Furley (ed.), *Conflict in Africa*. London/ New York: Tauris Publ., 223–236.

Tidermand, P. (1994). 'Le système des conseils de résistance', in B. Calas and G. Prunier (eds.), *L'Ouganda contemporain*. Paris: Karthala, 193–209.

The New Vision, daily newspaper, Kampala.

ZAMBIA

by Michael Krennerich*

1. Introduction

1.1 Historical Overview

Between 1964 and 1991 independent Zambia was ruled by President Kenneth Kaunda and his United National Independence Party (UNIP), from 1972 onwards under one-party rule. In the 1990s, Zambia was the first English-speaking African country to re-introduce multi-party politics. The electoral victory of the opposition leader Frederick Chiluba and his Movement for Multiparty Democracy (MMD) in 1991 made Zambia an internationally heralded model for a peaceful transition to democracy in Africa. However, the democratic transition was soon undermined by the non-democratic measures of the new government to concentrate power and to silence criticism. The 1996 elections, which saw another victory for Chiluba and his MMD, can not be regarded as being free and fair.

Zambia, formerly Northern Rhodesia, became a sovereign and independent country within the Commonwealth on 24 October 1964. With significant departures from the British Westminster model, the new constitution established a predominantly presidential system. In his function as incumbent Prime Minister, Kenneth Kaunda, 1964 was declared President of the First Republic, vested with wide-ranging executive power. Since Kaunda's UNIP had played a leading role in the last years of the independence struggle and held an overwhelming majority in the National Assembly, elected in January 1964, it instantly played a dominant part in the multi-party system of the First Republic (1964–1972). The ruling party faced only a small, but persistent regionally based opposition, the African National Congress (ANC), which had also played an active part in the independence struggle. Due to a great disparity in resources and levels of activities between the two running parties, UNIP overwhelmingly won the first post-independence elections for both

---

* The author would like to thank Dr Heiko Meinhardt (Hamburg) for his very helpful contribution on data research, particularly with regard to the single-party elections.

President and National Assembly (1968), but failed to realize its goal of a 'peaceful transition to a one-party system through the ballot-box'. However, the most important arena of political conflict was within the UNIP itself. President Kaunda used both his personal legitimacy and his presidential authority to manage intra-party dissension, resulting in further concentration of power into the presidency and an increasing control of the ruling party by Kaunda. In the face of the continuing factionalism within the UNIP and the formation of splinter parties (as the United Progressive Party, UPP), Kaunda finally adopted a one-party system with limited intra-party competition, officially designated as a 'one-party participatory democracy', in December 1972. In line with his efforts to solidify 'one Zambia, one nation', he envisaged being able to structure political competition and to counter the centrifugal forces operating (partly along ethnic lines) within the nation. Zambia thus followed, although some years later, the one-party trend which had characterized the politics of independent African states since the early 1960s, and to which the ruling UNIP had been committed since 1964.

On 13 December 1972, the Second Republic was inaugurated with Kaunda as President. The new Constitution of Zambia and the new party constitution of UNIP, both promulgated in 1973, transformed the political system by giving UNIP the sole right to organize and to act as a political party and by stipulating the supremacy of the party over the government. The highest executive body of the party, i.e. the Central Committee, was meant to be the supreme decision making body of the state. In practice, however, as President both of the Republic and, since 1973, of the UNIP, Kaunda dominated 'The Party and its Government'. The President was chief executive as well as Head of State. He appointed *de facto* all senior party and government officials as well as heads of state companies. As part of the Parliament, the President also shared the legislative role with the weak National Assembly. As in the First Republic, he had the power to dissolve the National Assembly, at the cost of ending his own term, but he himself was not subject to a vote of no-confidence. Initially, the one-party system received only limited resistance. UNIP soon co-opted former opposition leaders. Trade unions and business groups protected their corporate interests by participating in the one-party system. Elections for both President and National Assembly were, in general, trouble-free and peaceful. While they did not provide for inter-party competition, intra-party competition was allowed to some extent in the elections to the National Assembly. However, the one-party system was beset with several problems which eventually undermined its legitimacy. The official ideology of 'Humanism', already adopted in 1967, expressed Kaunda's vision of an egalitarian society, but in practice failed to be a coherent guiding principle for economic and political government actions. The 'one-party participatory democracy', officially envisioned by the President, also remained unfulfilled since decisions were made at the top and not at the bottom. In fact, the over-concentration of power in the hands of the President increasingly restricted the openness of intra-party participation and severely limited the policy capacities of party and state organs other than the President and his State House. Finally, related to the principle of party supremacy over the state, a huge inefficient party bureaucracy emerged, accompanied by increasing abuse of office by paid party functionaries.

Confronted by severe economic and social problems, increasing protest against the one-party rule and a changing international context, President Kaunda finally announced that a referendum on whether to continue the one-party system would be held on 17 October 1990. Under further pressure, however, Kaunda called off the planned referendum and appointed a Commission to draft a new constitution that would provide for multi-party elections to be held before the end of 1991. The new constitution, which took effect on 24 August 1991, represented a constitutional break with the previous one-party state by de-linking ruling party and state and by re-introducing multi-party democracy—and, consequently, ended the Second Republic. Along the lines of the Independence Constitution of 1964, it provided for a directly elected President vested with wide, though reduced and more circumscribed, powers as Head of State and Government. Elections for both President and the National Assembly were held on 31 October 1991, resulting in a resounding victory of the main opposition party MMD and its leader Chiluba against incumbent President Kenneth Kaunda and the UNIP. The MMD was supported by the Zambia Congress of Trade Unions, led by Chiluba for nearly two decades. After the elections, the MMD, formerly a broad-based protest group against the one-party state, transformed itself into a ruling party that held a substantial majority of seats in the National Assembly. In power, it liberalized the economy and privatized a huge number of state-owned companies, but had severe problems with keeping up with democratic principles. Politically, the distinction between state and ruling party continued to be blurred, and government institutions have still been used to harass opposition parties, critical non-governmental organizations and the independent press. State intimidation of the opposition even increased after Kaunda had announced a formal return to politics in 1995. In spite of widespread protest from the international community, selected candidates, including Kaunda, were not allowed to contest the elections of 18 November 1996 due to constitutional maneuvering. Consequently, UNIP and five minor opposition parties boycotted the elections. With no viable opponents in the race, Chiluba once again won the presidency and his MMD gained almost all parliamentary seats.

1.2 Evolution of Electoral Provisions

After independence, direct parliamentary and presidential elections took place almost regularly, however, between 1973 and 1988 under one-party rule. The number of elected Members of Parliament successively increased (1964: 75; 1968: 105; 1973–1988: 125; since 1991: 150). Parliamentary and presidential elections were held simultaneously, but usually with different votes. Only in 1968, were both elections combined.

The principles of universal, equal, direct and secret suffrage were introduced in 1963. However, in the last pre-independence elections (1964) there had been separate voters rolls, which were abolished after independence. In 1967, the minimum voting age was lowered from 21 to 18 years. For the multi-party elections of 1968, presidential and parliamentary candidates were required to pay a deposit and needed to be supported by a certain number of registered voters (presidential candidate: 1,000; parliamentary candidate: two resident in the constituency). For being nominated each parliamentary candidate (even an independent one) had to indicate his/her preference for a particular presidential candidate. The presidential candidate who received the relative majority of votes was declared President. For the parliamentary elections, the plurality system was applied in 105 single-member constituencies.

As for the presidential elections under one-party rule (1973, 1978, 1983, 1988), the person elected UNIP President at the General Conference of the party automatically became the sole presidential candidate. Before the 1978 elections, several amendments to the party constitution were made in order to prevent former opposition leaders (then co-opted into the ruling party) to stand for the office of UNIP President against Kaunda. To qualify as candidate for the party presidency—and, thus, indirectly for the sole candidature to the Republic's presidency—one had to be UNIP member for at least five years. Furthermore, the candidature had to be approved by the party's National Council and had to be supported by 20 delegates from each of the provinces that attended the party's General Conference.

As for parliamentary candidates, primary elections were held in 1973 and 1977, in which the party (via electoral colleges) selected up to three candidates to stand in the respective constituency. In 1982, primary elections were abolished. Instead of contesting primaries, prospective candidates had to seek approval to stand as parliamentary candidate from the UNIP Central Committee. In the parliamentary elections, the plurality system was applied to determine the winner in the single-member constituencies.

Since the re-introduction of the multi-party system in 1991, the plurality system has been maintained for parliamentary elections. As for the 1991 presidential elections, however, an absolute majority system was used. If not presidential candidate received more than 50% of the valid votes cast, a second round would take place. If, at the second poll, still no candidate achieved the absolute majority, the Parliament would elect the President.

1.3 Current Electoral Provisions

Sources: Constitution of Zambia (Amendment) Act, 1996; Electoral Act as amended by Act No.23 of 1996.

Elected national institutions: The President and 150 members of the National Assembly are elected directly. Regular term of office: five years respectively. The Vice-President is appointed by the President from amongst the members of the National Assembly. In the case of vacancy of parliamentary seats, by-elections are held. No person who has twice been elected as President is eligible for re-election to the presidency.

Suffrage: The principles of universal, equal, direct and secret suffrage are applied. Every citizen who has reached the age of 18 years is entitled to be registered as a voter.

Nomination of candidates
- *presidential elections*: Every citizen of the age of 35 years or above who is qualified to be elected as a member of the National Assembly is qualified to be a candidate for election as President, a) if he/she is a member of, or is sponsored by, a political party, and b) if his/her parents are Zambians by birth or descent, and c) if he/she has been domiciled in Zambia for a period of at least 20 years. The last two conditions—as

well as the clause that a presidential candidate must not already have been elected twice to office—were introduced by the Constitutional Amendment Act of 1996, which appeared to be designed to exclude selected opposition leaders from the election, including former President Kaunda. A presidential candidate shall not be entitled to take part in an election unless he/she has paid an election fee and his/her nomination is supported by not less than 200 registered voters.

- *parliamentary elections*: Every citizen of the age of 21 years or above is qualified to be elected if he or she is literate and conversant with the official language of Zambia (English). Chiefs are only qualified to do so if they have abdicated the chieftainship before lodging their nomination. A person holding or acting in any post, office of appointment in the defense and police forces, in the Public Service, the Teaching Service or 'in any statutory body or any company or institution in which the government has any interest' are not allowed to be elected as a Member of Parliament either.

Electoral system

- *presidential elections*: Plurality system.
- *parliamentary elections*: Plurality system in 150 single-member districts. The candidate who gets the highest number of valid votes cast in the respective constituency is elected.

1.4 Comment on Electoral Statistics

Although the electoral data given in the following tables are mainly based on official sources (indicated in the bibliography, see 3.1), the data situation can not be regarded as good. Official results of the single-party elections are extremely difficult to get. Sometimes they contain mathematical errors, which in the following tables have been eliminated by the author as far as possible. Interestingly enough, even after the re-introduction of multi-party politics, the documentation of electoral results is not satisfactory. No official final report of the 1991 and the 1996 elections has so far been published and approved by Parliament. Thus, all official results are still declared 'provisional'. Moreover, provisional results from one and the same official source—the Electoral Commission—may differ considerably. This is true with regard to both the 1991 and the 1996 elections (see e.g. Kabwe 1997, CCC 1996). Not surprisingly, different data are given by different secondary sources. The data presented in the following tables are based on the most recent official results. As for the 1991 elections, the national votes cast for each candidate/party were re-calculated by ourselves on the basis of the official constituency data. For the number of registered voters in 1991, however, ZIMT data has been used. With regard to the 1996 elections the data coincide with the results given to the author by the Electoral Commission in 1998.

2. Tables

2.1 Dates of National Elections, Referenda and Coups d'Etat

Year	Presidential elections	Parliamentary elections	Elections for Constitutional Assembly	Referendums	Coups d'état
1964		20–21/01			
1968	19/12	19/12			
1969				17/06	
1973	05/12	05/12			
1978	12/12	12/12			
1983	27/10	27/10[a]			
1988	26/10	26/10			
1991	31/10	31/10			
1996	18/11	18/11			

[a] Due to the death of adopted candidates, parliamentary elections took place on 22 November and 8 December in two constituencies (Chasefu, Mbabala).

2.2 Electoral Body 1964–1996

Year	Type of election[a]	Population[b]	Registered voters		Votes cast		
			Total number	% pop.	Total number	% reg. Voters	% pop.
1964	Pa	3,600,000	876,212[c]	24.3	830,415	94.8	23.1
			23,981[d]	0.7	17,758	74.1	0.5
1968	Pr	4,010,000	1,587,966	39.6	1,383,479	87.1	34.5
1968	Pa	4,010,000	1,166,637[e]	29.1	962,150	82.5	24.0
1969	Ref	4,057,000	1,584,574	39.1	1,103,352	69.6	27.2
1973	Pr	4,420,000	1,746,107	39.5	688,686	39.4	15.6
1978	Pr	5,356,000	1,971,881	36.8	1,315,609	66.7	24.6
1978	Pa	5,356,000	1,884,399[f]	35.2	1,273,462	67.6	23.8
1983	Pr	6,240,000	2,377,610	38.1	1,558,063[g]	65.5	25.0
1983	Pa	6,240,000	2,377,610	38.1	1,572,333[g]	66.1	25.2
1988	Pr	7,563,000[h]	2,600,000[i]	34.4	1,529,000[i]	58.8	20.2
1991	Pr	8,760,000	2,917,338	33.3	1,325,155	45.4	15.1
1991	Pa	8,760,000	2,917,338	33.3	1,320,397	45.3	15.1
1996	Pr	9,456,000	2,267,383[j]	24.0	1,325,053	58.4	14.0
1996	Pa	9,456,000	2,267,382[j]	24.0	1,331,047	58.7	14.1

[a] Pa = Parliament; Pr = President; Ref = Referendum.

[b] Population census: August 1969: 4,056,995; September 1980: 5,679,808; August 1990: 7,818,447. Except the data of 1969 (census) and 1996 (official estimation), population data are based on unofficial estimations mainly from UN sources. The UN estimation for 1991 is explicitly not in accordance with the latest census.

[c] Common roll.

[d] Reserved districts.

[e] This figure represents the total number of registered voters only in those 75 constituencies where elections were contested.

[f] Excluding the number of the registered voters (87,482) in those six constituencies where no voting took place as candidates were returned unopposed.

[g] Provisional results. Mathematical error of the official figure (1,558,551).

[h] Estimation for 1987.

[i] Approximations.

[j] Out of an electorate of estimated 4,596,000 adult citizens.

2.3 Abbreviations

ANC	African National Congress
AZ	Agenda for Zambia
DP	Democratic Party
GWP	Grassroots Welfare Party
IDF	Independent Democratic Front
LP	Labour Party
LPF	Liberal Progressive Front
MDP	Movement for Democratic Process
MMD	Movement for Multi-Party Democracy
NADA	National Democratic Alliance
NC	National Congress
NDP	National Democratic Party
NLP	National Lima Party
NP	National Party
NPD	National Party for Democracy
NPP	National Progressive Party
NSP	National Salvation Party
PPP	Party for Poor People
RDP	Real Democracy Party
UFP	United Federal Party
UNIP	United National Independence Party
ZDC	Zambia Democratic Congress

2.4 Electoral Participation of Parties and Alliances 1964–1996

Party / Alliance	Years[a]	Elections contested	
		Presidential[b]	Parliamentary
ANC	1964, 1968	1	2
UNIP	1964, 1968, 1973, 1978, 1983, 1988, 1991	6	7
NPP	1964	0	1
DP	1991	0	1
MMD	1991, 1996	2	2
NADA	1991	0	1
NPD	1991	0	1
AZ	1996	1	1
MDP	1996	1	1
NC	1996	0	1
NLP	1996	0	1
NP	1996	1	1
PPP	1996	0	1
RDP	1996	0	1
ZDC	1996	1	1

[a] The following parties boycotted the 1996 elections: UNIP, LPF, NDP, NSP, GWP, IDF and LP. However, two UNIP candidates and one LPF candidate took part in the parliamentary elections.
[b] Not including the indirect presidential elections of 1964.

2.5 Referendum 1969

Year	1969	
	Total number	%
Registered voters	1,584,574	–
Votes cast	1,103,352	69.6
Invalid votes	39,667	3.6
Valid votes	1,063,685	96.4
Yes	904,337	85.0
No	159,348	15.0

[a] Voters were asked: 'Do you support the provision of the Constitution (Amendment) (No 3) Act, 1969?'.

2.5 a) Referendum 1969, Provincial Results

Province	Yes	%[a]	No	%[a]	Valid votes	Invalid votes	Total votes
Barotse	23,225	39.2	36,094	60.8	59,319	3,463	62,782
Central	126,224	84.9	22,414	15.1	148,638	7,703	156,341
Eastern	168,399	97.5	4,398	2.5	172,797	6,587	179,384
Luapula	121,923	99.6	532	0.4	122,455	2,526	124,981
Northern	165,040	99.6	683	0.4	165,723	4,097	169,820
N.Western	36,209	72.9	13,479	27.1	49,688	2,921	52,609
Southern	30,709	32.9	62,541	67.1	93,250	5,258	98,508
Western	232,608	92.4	19,207	7.6	251,815	7,112	258,927
Totals	904,337	85.0	159,348	15.0	1,063,685	39,667	1,103,352

[a] % of valid votes (rejected ballot papers are excluded).

2.5 Referendums

Referendums have not been held.

2.6 Elections for Constitutional Assembly

Elections for Constitutional Assembly have not been held.

2.7 Multi-Party Parliamentary Elections 1964–1996

1964	Main roll		Reserved roll	
	Total number	%	Total number	%
Registered voters	876,212	–	23,981	–
Votes cast	830,415	94.8	17,758	74.1
Invalid votes	4,178	0.5	224	1.3
Valid votes	826,237	99.5	17,534	98.7
UNIP	570,612	69.1	6,177	35.2
ANC	251,963	30.5	165	0.9
NPP	–	–	11,157	63.6
Independents	3,662	0.4	35	0.2

	1968 Total number	%	1991[b] Total number	%
Registered voters	1,166,637	–	2,917,338	–
Votes cast	962,150	82.5	1,320,397	45.3
Invalid votes	63,490	6.6	44,609	3.4
Valid votes	898,660	93.4	1,275,788	96.6
UNIP	657,764	73.2	314,726	24.7
ANC	228,277	25.4	–	–
MMD	–	–	947,777	74.3
NADA	–	–	1,695	0.1
NPD	–	–	803	0.1
DP	–	–	120	0.0
Independents	12,619	1.4	10,667	0.8

[a] UNIP presented candidates in all 150 constituencies, MMD in 149, NPD in five, NADA in three and DP in only one constituency. 21 independent candidates obtained votes.

Year	1996[a] Total number	%
Registered voters	2,267,382	–
Votes cast	1,331,047	58.7
Invalid votes	53,462	4.0
Valid votes	1,277,585	96.0
MMD	778,989	61.0
ZDC	176,521	13.8
NP	90,823	7.1
NLP	81,876	6.4
AZ	18,982	1.5
NC	2,214	0.2
LPF	759	0.1
MDP	632	0.0
UNIP	477	0.0
PPP	293	0.0
RDP	182	0.0
Independents	125,837	9.8

[a] Only MMD presented candidates in all constituencies. Number of candidates per party: MMD: 150, ZDC: 143, NP: 99, NLP: 83, AZ: 11, NC: 4, UNIP: 2, MDP: 2, LPF: 1, RDP: 1, PPP: 1. There were 96 independent candidates.

2.7 a) Parliamentary Elections 1991–1996: Provincial Results

1991 (absolute numbers)							
	MMD	UNIP	NADA	NPD	DP	Indep.	Valid votes
Central	70,547	26,059	–	234	–	–	96,840
Copperbelt	265,040	30,991	489	158	120	608	297,406
Eastern	41,257	124,089	–	–	–	3,380	168,726
Luapula	80,306	11,497	–	–	–	–	91,803
Lusaka	130,830	39,073	1,206	352	–	1,259	172,720
Northern	116,828	22,144	–	–	–	750	139,722
N.-Western	43,529	19,506	–	–	–	2,563	65,598
Southern	125,372	23,601	–	59	–	1,265	150,297
Western	74,068	17,766	–	–	–	842	92,676
Total	947,777	314,726	1,695	803	120	10,667	1,275,788

1991 (percentages)							
	MMD	UNIP	NADA	NPD	DP	Indep.	Total[a]
Central	72.8	26.9	–	0.2	–	–	100
Copperbelt	89.1	10.4	0.2	0.1	0.0	0.2	100
Eastern	24.5	73.5	–	–	–	2.0	100
Luapula	87.5	12.5	–	–	–	–	100
Lusaka	75.7	22.6	0.7	0.2	–	0.7	100
Northern	83.6	15.8	–	–	–	0.5	100
N.-Western	66.4	29.7	–	–	–	3.9	100
Southern	83.4	15.7	–	0.0	–	0.8	100
Western	79.9	19.2	–	–	–	0.9	100
Total	74.3	24.7	0.1	0.1	0.0	0.8	100

[a] Due to rounding the added total of the percentages is not always 100.

1996 (absolute numbers)							
	MMD	ZDC	NP	NLP	Others	Indep.	Valid votes
Central	50,739	9,847	4,070	12,681	182	24,344	101,863
Copperbelt	194,215	25,769	14,601	20,062	632	20,350	275,629
Eastern	68,571	26,956	7,131	4,406	1,136	2,529	110,729
Luapula	75,489	11,433	2,592	6,765	100	11,221	107,600
Lusaka	105,042	25,433	7,254	8,779	615	16,260	163,383
Northern	93,795	19,267	5,287	4,146	–	26,315	148,810
N.-Western	40,730	7,085	32,840	3,507	–	7,660	91,822
Southern	95,434	32,718	5,965	20,946	4,332	7,990	167,385
Western	54,974	18,013	11,083	584	16,542	9,168	110,364
Total	778,989	176,521	90,823	81,876	23,539	125,837	1,277,585

1996 (percentages)							
	MMD	ZDC	NP	NLP	Others	Indep.	Total[a]
Central	49.8	9.7	4.0	12.4	0.2	23.9	100
Copperbelt	70.5	9.3	5.3	7.3	0.2	7.4	100
Eastern	61.9	24.3	6.4	4.0	1.0	2.3	100
Luapula	70.2	10.6	2.4	6.3	0.1	10.4	100
Lusaka	64.3	15.6	4.4	5.4	0.4	10.0	100
Northern	63.0	12.9	3.6	2.8	–	17.7	100
N.-Western	44.4	7.7	35.8	3.8	–	8.3	100
Southern	57.0	19.5	3.6	12.5	2.6	4.8	100
Western	49.8	16.3	10.0	0.5	15.0	8.3	100
Total	61.0	13.8	7.1	6.4	1.8	9.8	100

[a] Due to rounding the added total of the percentages is not always 100.

2.8 Composition of Parliament 1964–1996

Year	1964 common roll		1964 special const.[b]		1968	
	Seats	%	Seats	%	Seats	%
	65	100	10	100	105	100
UNIP	55[a]	84.6	–	–	81[c]	77.1
ANC	10	15.4	–	–	23	21.9
NPP	–	–	10	100	–	–
Independents	–	–	–	–	1	1.0

[a] 25 out of 55 seats were won unopposed (without holding elections).
[b] Reserved for white minority.
[c] 51 seats contested, 30 seats unopposed (without holding elections).

Year	1973		1978		1983	
	Seats	%	Seats	%	Seats	%
	125	100	125	100	125	100
UNIP	125[a]	100	125[b]	100	125	100

[a] Up to three UNIP candidates contested the elections. 14 seats were uncontested.
[b] Up to three UNIP candidates contested the elections. Six seats were uncontested.

Year	1988		1991		1996	
	Seats	%	Seats	%	Seats	%
	125	100	150	100	150	100
UNIP	125	100	25	16.7	–	–
MMD	–	–	125	83.3	131[a]	87.3
NP	–	–	–	–	5	3.3
AZ	–	–	–	–	2	1.3
ZDC	–	–	–	–	2	1.3
Independents	–	–	–	–	10	6.7

[a] Three candidates were elected unopposed.

2.9 Presidential Elections 1968–1996

1968	Total number	%
Registered voters	1,587,966	–
Votes cast	1,383,477	87.1
Invalid votes	63,490	4.6
Valid votes	1,319,987	95.4
Kenneth Kaunda (UNIP)	1,079,970[a]	81.8
Harry Nkumbula (ANC)	240,017	18.2

[a] Figure slightly corrected on the basis of results at the constituency level (official figure: 1,079,972).

1973	Total number	%
Registered voters	1,746,107	–
Votes cast	688,686	39.4
Invalid votes	34,326	5.0
Valid votes	654,360	95.0
Kenneth Kaunda (UNIP)		
Yes	581,245	88.8
No	73,115	11.2

1978	Total number	%
Registered voters	1,971,881	–
Votes cast	1,315,609	66.7
Invalid votes	44,763	3.4
Valid votes	1,270,846	96.6
Kenneth Kaunda (UNIP)		
Yes	1,026,127	80.7
No	244,719	19.3

1983	Total number	%
Registered voters	2,377,610	–
Votes Cast	1,558,063[a]	65.5
Invalid votes	34,679	2.2
Valid votes	1,523,384	97.8
Kenneth Kaunda (UNIP)		
Yes	1,453,029	95.4
No	70,355	4.6

[a] Mathematical error of the official figure (1,558,551).

1988	Total number[a]	%
Registered voters	2,600,000	–
Votes cast	1,529,000	58.8
Invalid votes	48,000	3.1
Valid votes	1,481,000	96.9
Kenneth Kaunda (UNIP)		
Yes	1,414,000	95.5
No	67,000	4.5

[a] Approximations.

1991	Total number	%
Registered voters	2,917,338	–
Votes cast	1,325,155	45.4
Invalid votes	41,641	3.1
Valid votes	1,283,514	96.9
Frederick Chiluba (MMD)	972,753	75.8
Kenneth Kaunda (UNIP)	310,761	24.2

1996	Total number	%
Registered voters	2,267,383	–
Votes cast	1,325,053	58.4
Invalid votes	66,248	5.0
Valid votes	1,258,805	95.0
Frederick Chiluba (MMD)	913,770	72.6
Dean Mung'omba (ZDC)	160,439	12.7
Humphrey Mulemba (NP)	83,875	6.7
Akashambatwa Mbikusita-Lewanika (AZ)	59,250	4.7
Chama Chakomboka (MDP)	41,471	3.3

2.9 a) Presidential Elections 1968–1996: Provincial Results

1968	Kaunda (UNIP)	Nkumbula (ANC)	Valid votes	Invalid votes	Votes cast	Registered voters
Central	142,651	52,522[a]	195,173	17,660	212,833	259,494
Copperbelt	247,025	20,750	267,775	11,826	279,601	305,954
Eastern	198,737	4,951	203,688	6,061	209,749	227,753
Luapula	131,455[b]	278	131,733	835	132,568[c]	134,893
Northern	190,412	341	190,753	1,937	192,690[d]	202,725
N.Western	89,799	3,161	92,960	2,023	94,983	103,184
Southern	34,425	106,394	140,819	13,783	154,602	190,673
Barotse	45,466	51,620	97,086	9,365	106,451	163,290
Total	1,079,970	240,017	1,319,987	63,490	1,384,477	1,587,966

[a] Figure corrected by the author on the basis of constituencies results (official figure: 53,401).
[b] Figure corrected by the author on the basis of constituencies results (official figure: 132,355).
[c] Figure corrected by the author on the basis of constituencies results (official figure: 133,468).
[d] Figure corrected by the author on the basis of constituencies results (official figure: 192,384).

1973	Yes votes (Kaunda)	No votes	Valid votes	Invalid votes	Votes cast	Registered voters
Central	37,393	3,932	41,325	2,136	43,461	135,033
Copperbelt	126,626	16,231	142,857	8,351	151,208	323,700
Eastern	113,063	2,545	115,608	4,266	119,874	245,697
Luapula	76,840	1,016	77,856	2,812	80,668	149,588
Lusaka	53,552	6,398	59,950	3,262	63,212	158,432
Northern	69,384	12,153	81,537	2,647	84,184	219,394
N.Western	39,224	1,121	40,345	3,403	43,748	115,778
Southern	33,882	20,589	54,471	4,735	59,206	202,722
Western	31,281	9,130	40,411	2,714	43,125	195,763
Total	581,245	73,115	654,360	34,326	688,686	1,746,107

1978	Yes votes (Kaunda)	No votes	Valid votes	Invalid votes	Votes cast	Registered voters
Central	88,432	16,994	105,426	3,351	108,777	164,295
Copperbelt	227,279	55,621	282,900	12,623	295,523	411,980
Eastern	166,324	6,206	172,530	3,829	176,359	251,744
Luapula	84,516	18,567	103,083	3,086	106,169	150,656
Lusaka	131,557	22,104	153,661	7,693	161,354	222,062
Northern	111,765	38,916	150,681	3,342	154,023	224,506
N.Western	81,391	3,427	84,818	2,361	87,179	120,282
Southern	70,025	66,818	136,843	5,393	142,236	237,728
Western	64,838	16,066	80,904	3,085	83,989	188,628
Total	1,026,127	244,719	1,270,846	44,763	1,315,609	1,971,881

1983	Yes votes (Kaunda)	No votes	Valid votes	Invalid votes	Votes cast	Registered voters
Central	125,140	6,055	131,195	2,896	134,091	214,260
Copperbelt	329,509	27,437	356,946	9,978	366,924	508,257
Eastern	184,001	4,174	188,175	3,685	191,860	272,823
Luapula	97,586	3,754	101,340	1,967	103,307	163,721
Lusaka	214,499	9,411	223,910	6,234	230,144	320,787
Northern	159,177	3,462	162,639	2,565	165,204	265,647
N.Western	83,845	1,504	85,349	1,306	86,655	133,903
Southern	168,539	11,518	180,057	4,217	184,274[a]	293,907
Western	90,733	3,040	93,773	1,831	95,604	204,305
Total	1,453,029	70,355	1,523,384	34,679	1,558,063[b]	2,377,610

[a] Mathematical error in the official figure (184,768).
[b] Mathematical error in the official figure (1,558,557).

1991	Kaunda (UNIP)	Chiluba (MMD)	Valid votes	Invalid votes	Votes cast	Registered voters
Central	25,575	74,355	99,930	3,247	103,177	272,051
Copperbelt	28,085	271,252	299,337	7,547	306,884	604,541
Eastern	126,961	44,483	171,444	8,699	180,143	364,941
Luapula	10,189	83,039	93,228	2,556	95,784	203,381
Lusaka	39,466	129,249	168,715	4,665	173,380	394,563
Northern	21,038	119,686	140,724	5,412	146,136	329,190
N.Western	19,941	46,950	66,891	1,796	68,687	160,977
Southern	22,299	128,589	150,888	4,619	155,507	356,774
Western	17,207	75,150	92,357	3,100	95,457	230,920
Total	310,761	972,753	1,283,514	41,641	1,325,155	2,917,338

1996	Chiluba (MMD)	Mung'omba (ZDC)	Mulemba (NP)	Mbikusita (AZ)	Chakom-boka (MDP)	Valid Votes
Central	73,718	14,370	5,212	2,185	5,291	100,776
Copperbelt	234,580	20,900	8,947	2,636	4,601	271,664
Eastern	69,897	21,364	7,477	3,788	6,616	109,142
Luapula	91,414	6,397	1,786	5,272	2,153	107,022
Lusaka	121,734	27,915	6,047	4,612	3,267	163,575
Northern	120,392	17,840	3,686	1,851	5,831	149,600
N.Western	46,933	5,685	33,883	1,362	2,049	89,912
Southern	111,560	30,466	8,638	7,780	7,747	166,191
Western	43,542	15,502	8,199	29,764	3,916	100,923
Total	913,770	160,439	83,875	59,250	41,471	1,258,805

2. 9 b) Presidential Elections 1968–1996: Provincial Results (in %)

1968[a]	Kaunda (UNIP)	Nkumbula (ANC)	Valid votes	Invalid votes	Votes cast
Central	73.1	26.9	91.7	8.3	82.0
Copperbelt	92.3	7.7	95.8	4.2	91.4
Eastern	97.6	2.4	97.1	2.9	92.1
Luapula	99.8	0.2	99.4	0.6	98.3
Northern	99.8	0.2	99.0	1.0	95.0
N.Western	96.6	3.4	97.9	2.1	92.1
Southern	24.4	75.6	91.1	8.9	81.1
Barotse	46.8	53.2	91.2	8.8	65.2
Total	81.8	18.2	95.3	4.6	87.2

[a] The percentages given refer to: votes per candidate in % of valid votes; valid votes and invalid votes in % of total votes cast; votes cast in % of registered voters.

1973[a]	Yes votes (Kaunda)	No votes	Valid votes	Invalid votes	Votes cast
Central	90.5	9.5	95.1	4.9	32.2
Copperbelt	88.6	11.4	94.5	5.5	46.7
Eastern	97.8	2.2	96.4	3.6	48.8
Luapula	98.7	1.3	96.5	3.5	53.9
Lusaka	89.3	10.7	94.8	5.2	39.9
Northern	85.1	14.9	96.9	3.1	38.4
N.Western	97.2	2.8	92.2	7.8	37.8
Southern	62.2	37.8	92.0	8.0	29.2
Western	77.4	22.6	93.7	6.3	22.0
Total	88.8	11.2	95.0	5.0	39.4

[a] The percentages given refer to: votes per candidate in % of valid votes; valid votes and invalid votes in % of total votes cast; votes cast in % of registered voters.

1978[a]	Yes votes (Kaunda)	No votes	Valid votes	Invalid votes	Votes cast
Central	83.9	16.1	96.9	3.1	66.2
Copperbelt	80.3	19.7	95.7	4.3	71.7
Eastern	96.4	3.6	97.8	2.2	70.1
Luapula	82.0	18.0	97.1	2.9	70.5
Lusaka	85.6	14.4	95.2	4.8	72.7
Northern	74.2	25.8	97.8	2.2	68.6
N.Western	96.0	4.0	97.3	2.7	72.5
Southern	51.2	48.8	96.2	3.8	59.8
Western	80.1	19.9	96.3	3.7	44.5
Total	80.7	19.3	96.6	3.4	66.7

[a] The percentages given refer to: votes per candidate in % of valid votes; valid votes and invalid votes in % of total votes cast; votes cast in % of registered voters.

1983[a]	Yes votes (Kaunda)	No votes	Valid votes	Invalid votes	Votes cast
Central	95.4	4.6	97.8	2.2	62.6
Copperbelt	92.3	7.7	97.3	2.7	72.2
Eastern	97.8	2.2	98.1	1.9	70.3
Luapula	96.3	3.7	98.1	1.9	63.1
Lusaka	95.8	4.2	97.3	2.7	71.7
Northern	97.9	2.1	98.4	1.6	62.2
N.Western	98.2	1.8	98.5	1.5	64.7
Southern	93.6	6.4	97.7	2.3	62.7
Western	96.8	3.2	98.1	1.9	46.8
Total	95.4	4.6	97.8	2.2	65.5

[a] The percentages given refer to: votes per candidate in % of valid votes; valid votes and invalid votes in % of total votes cast; votes cast in % of registered voters.

For the presidential elections of 1988 no provincial results are available.

1991[a]	Kaunda (UNIP)	Chiluba (MMD)	Valid votes	Invalid votes	Votes cast
Central	25.6	74.4	96.9	3.1	37.9
Copperbelt	9.4	90.6	97.5	2.5	50.8
Eastern	74.1	25.9	95.2	4.8	49.4
Luapula	10.9	89.1	97.3	2.7	47.1
Lusaka	23.4	76.6	97.3	2.7	43.9
Northern	14.9	85.1	96.3	3.7	44.4
N.Western	29.8	70.2	97.4	2.6	42.7
Southern	14.8	85.2	97.0	3.0	43.6
Western	18.6	81.4	96.8	3.2	41.3
Total	24.2	75.8	96.9	3.1	45.4

[a] The percentages given refer to: votes per candidate in % of valid votes; valid votes and invalid votes in % of total votes cast; votes cast in % of registered voters.

1996	Chiluba (MMD)	Mung'omba (ZDC)	Mulemba (NP)	Mbikusita (AZ)	Chakom-boka (MDP)	Valid Votes[a]
Central	73.2	14.3	5.2	2.2	5.3	100
Copperbelt	86.3	7.7	3.3	1.0	1.7	100
Eastern	64.0	19.6	6.9	3.5	6.1	100
Luapula	85.4	6.0	1.7	4.9	2.0	100
Lusaka	74.4	17.1	3.7	2.8	2.0	100
Northern	80.5	11.9	2.5	1.2	3.9	100
N.Western	52.2	6.3	37.7	1.5	2.3	100
Southern	67.1	18.3	5.2	4.7	4.7	100
Western	43.1	15.4	8.1	29.5	3.9	100
Total	72.6	12.7	6.7	4.7	3.3	100

[a] Due to rounding the added total of the percentages is not always 100.

2.10 List of Power Holders 1964–1998

Head of State and Government	Years	Remarks
Kenneth Kaunda	1964–1991	Sworn in as President of the Republic of Zambia on 24/10/1964. Directly elected in Zambia's first post-independence election (1968); re-elected in non-competitive elections in 1973, 1978, 1983 and 1988; defeated in the 1991 elections.
Frederick Chiluba	1991–	Sworn in as elected President on 02/11/1991; re-elected in 1996.

3. Bibliography

3.1 Official Sources

Constitution of Zambia Act 1973.

Constitution of Zambia (Amendment) Act 1990 (Act No. 20 of 1990).

Constitution of Zambia Act 1991 (Act No. 1 of 1991).

Constitution of Zambia (Amendment) Act 1996 (Act No. 18 of 1996), Lusaka: Government Printer.

Electoral Commission of Zambia (1996*a*). *Presidential and Parliamentary General Elections 1996. Provisional Results*. 25 November 1996, Lusaka.

Electoral Commission of Zambia (1996*b*). *Summary of Provisional Presidential Election Results (1996).* 26 November 1996, Lusaka.

Elections Office (without year). *Presidential and Parliamentary Elections. Summary of Elections Results 1962 and 1964.*

Elections Office (1964). *Analysis of Polling—Northern Rhodesia. General Election 1964.*

Elections Office (without year). *Presidential and Parliamentary Elections. Summary of Elections Results 1968 and the Referendum—1969*. Lusaka.

Elections Office (1979). *Presidential and Parliamentary General Elections Results 1978.* Lusaka.

Elections Office (1984). *Presidential and Parliamentary General Elections Results 1983*. Lusaka.

Electoral Acts (Acts No. 1 and 2 of 1991), Lusaka.

Electoral (Amendment) Act 1996, Lusaka.

Republic of Zamiba (without year). *1991 Presidential and Parliamentary Election. Provisional Official Election Results*. Lusaka.

3.2 Books, Articles and Electoral Reports

Andreassen, B.-A., Geisler, G., and Tostensen, A. (1992). *Setting a Standard for Africa? Lessons from the 1991 Zambian Elections*. Bergen: Chr. Michelsen Institute.

Baylies, C., and Szeftel, M. (1992). 'The Fall and Rise of Multi-Party Politics in Zambia'. *Review of African Political Economy*, 54: 75–92.

Baumhögger, G. (1988–1997). 'Zambia', in Institut für Afrika-Kunde and R. Hofmeier (eds.), *Afrika-Jahrbuch*. Opladen: Leske & Budrich (annually).

Bjornlund, E., Bratton, M., and Gibson, C. (1992). 'Observing Multiparty Elections in Africa: Lessons from Zambia'. *African Affairs*, 91/364: 405–431.

Bratton, M. (1992). 'Zambia Starts Over'. *Journal of Democracy*, 3/2: 81–94.

Burnell, P. (1995). 'Building on the Past? Party Politics in Zambia's Third Republic'. *Party Politics*, 1/3: 397–405.

— (1997). 'Whither Zambia? The Zambian Presidential and Parliamentary Elections of November 1996'. *Electoral Studies*, 16/3: 407–416.

Chanda, A. W. (1996) 'Zambia's Fledgling Democracy: Prospects for the Future'. *Zambia Law Journal*, 25–28: 125–154.

Chanda, D. (ed.) (without year). *Democracy in Zambia. Key Speeches of President Chiluba 1991/92*. Lusaka: Africa Press Trust.

Chikulo, B. C. (1986). *Electoral Politics in Zambia's Second Republic*. Lusaka: Department of Political Science and Administrative Studies.

— (1988). 'The Impact of Elections in Zambia's One Party Second Republic'. *Africa Today*, 35/2: 37–49.

— (1993). 'End of an Era: An Analysis of the 1991 Zambian Presidential and Parliamentary Elections'. *Politikon*, 20/1: 87–104.

Committee for a Clean Campaign (1996). *Presidential and Parliamentary Elections in Zambia. November 18th 1996. A Report by the Committee for a Clean Campaign (CCC)*. Lusaka: Multimedia Zambia.

Commonwealth Observer Group (1992). *Presidential and National Assembly Elections in Zambia, 31 October 1991. The Report of the Commonwealth Observer Group*. London: Commonwealth Secretariat.

Daloz, J. P. (1994). 'Zambia. Analyse d'une dérive prévisible'. *L'Afrique Politique*, 231–244.

Donge, J. K. van (1995). 'Zambia: Kaunda and Chiluba. Enduring Patterns of Political Culture', in J. Wiseman (ed.), *Democracy and Political Change in Sub-Saharan Africa*, London: Routledge, 193–219.

— (1998). 'Reflections on Donors, Opposition and Popular Will in the 1996 Zambian General Elections'. *Journal of Modern African Studies*, 36/1: 71–99.

FODEP (Foundation for Democratic Process) (1996). *Final Election Monitoring Report. Zambia's November 18, 1996 Presidential and Parliamentary Elections*. Lusaka: FODEP.

Gertzel, C., Baylies, C., and Szeftel, M. (1984). *The Dynamics of the One-Party-State in Zambia*. Manchester: Manchester University Press.

Hinz, B. (1992). 'Ein Land im Aufbruch: Sambia nach den Präsidentschafts- und Parlamentswahlen vom 31. Oktober 1991'. *KAS-Auslandsinformationen*, 8: 18–25.

Ihonvbere, J. O. (1996). *Economic Crisis, Civil Society and Democratization: The Case of Zambia*. Lawrenceville: Africa World Press.

— (1998). 'How not to Consolidate a Democracy: the Experience of the Movement for Multiparty Democracy (MMD) in Zambia', in J. M. Mbaku and J. O. Ihonvbere (eds.), *Multiparty Democracy and Political Change*. Aldershot: Ashgate, 219–240.

Kaplan, I. (1979). *Zambia. A Country Study*. Washington, D.C.

Kabwe, T. Ch. (ed.) (1997). *Kenneth David Kaunda. Founder President of the Republic of Zambia (Perspectives on His Exit from Office)*. Harare: SAPES Books.

Meyns, P. (1989). 'The Road to One-Party Rule in Zambia and Zimbabwe: A Comparative View', in P. Meyns and D. W. Nabudere (eds.), *Democracy and the One-Party State in Africa*. Hamburg: Institut für Afrika-Kunde, 179–202.

— (1995). *Zambia in der 3. Republik. Demokratische Transition und politische Kontinuität. Analyse und Dokumentation*. Hamburg: Institut für Afrika-Kunde.

— (1996). 'Zambia in der 3.Republik—Elitenkonflikte und eine schwache Opposition', in P. Meyns (ed.), *Staat und Gesellschaft in Afrika. Erosions- und Reformprozesse*. Münster/Hamburg: Lit, 46–59.

Milimo, J. T. (1993). 'Multiparty Democracy in Africa. Lessons from Zambia'. *International Journal on World Peace*, 10/1: 35–42.

Molteno, R. (1972). 'Zambia and the One-Party State'. *East Africa Journal*, 9/2: 22–35.

— and Scott, I. (1974). 'The 1968 General Elections and the Political System', in W. Tordoff (ed.), *1974: Politics in Zambia*. Manchester: Manchester University Press, 155–196.

Mphaisha, C. J. J. (1996). 'Retreat from Democracy in Post One-Party State Zambia'. *The Journal of Commonwealth and Comparative Politics*, 34/2: 65–84.

— (1997). 'Rituals of Constitution-Making in Zambia: The Role of Public Commissions'. *Zango. Zambian Journal of Contemporary Issues*, 21/11: 1–19.

Mwanakatwe, J. M. (1994). *End of Kaunda Era*. Zambia: Multimedia Publications.

Mulford, D. C. (1964). *The Northern Rhodesian General Elections, 1962*. Nairobi: Oxford University Press.

— (1967). *Zambia. The Politics of Independence, 1957–1964*. London: Oxford University Press.

NDI (National Democratic Institute) and Carter Center of Emory University (1992). *The October 31 1991 National Elections in Zambia*. Washington, D.C./ Atlanta, Geo.

Nuscheler, F. (1978). 'Sambia', in D. Sternberger, B. Vogel, D. Nohlen and K. Landfried (eds.), *Die Wahl der Parlamente und anderere Staatsorgane, Band II: Politische Organisation und Repräsentation in Afrika*, by Franz Nuscheler, Klaus Ziemer *et al.*, Berlin/ New York: Walter de Gruyter, 1749–1800.

Nzerem, R. C. (1992). 'A Fresh Start: Zambia's Third Republican Constitution'. *Commonwealth Law Bulletin*, 18/3: 1188–1194.

Panter-Brick, K. (1994). 'Prospects for Democracy in Zambia'. *Government and Opposition*, 29/2: 231–247.

Peters, W.-C. (1989). 'Politische Stabilität im wirtschaftlichen Niedergang. Eine Untersuchung zum zambischen Wahlsystem'. *Afrika-Spektrum*, 24/1: 47–69.

Pettman, J. (1974). *Zambia: Security and Conflict*. Lewies: Julian Friedmann.

Randall, V., and Scarritt, J.R. (1996). 'Cautionary Notes on Democratization: Lessons from India and Zambia'. *The Journal of Commonwealth and Comparative Politics*, 34/2: 19–45.

Scarritt, J. R. (1996). 'Measuring Political Change: The Quantity and Effectiveness of Electoral and Party Participation in the Zambian One-Party State, 1973–1991'. *British Journal of Political Science*, 26/2: 283–297.

Sichone, O. (1989). 'One-Party Participatory Democracy and Socialist Orientation. The De-Politicization of the Masses in Post-Colonial Zambia', in P. Meyns and D. W. Nabudere (eds.), *Democracy and the One-Party State in Africa*. Hamburg: Institut für Afrika-Kunde, 131–147.

Tetzlaff, R. (1971). 'Opposition in Zambia: Echte Alternative oder sinnloser Widerstand'. *Internationales Afrika Forum*, 7/2: 187–196.

Weber, U. (1997). 'Zu den Parlaments- und Präsidentschaftswahlen in Sambia'. *KAS-Auslandsinformationen*, 2: 72–81.

United National Independence Party (1983). *Statistical Summary of Presidential and General Elections Results 1983*. Lusaka: Elections and Publicity Committee, Freedom House.

Zambian Elections Monitoring Coordinating Committee (1991). *Setting a Standard for Africa: Free and Fair Elections*. Final Report, Lusaka, 7 November 1991.

ZIMT (Zambia Independent Monitoring Team) (1997). *Presidential and Parliamentary Elections in Zambia 18th November 1996*. Lusaka: ZIMT.

ZIMBABWE

by Goswin Baumhögger

1. Introduction

1.1 Historical Overview

At independence (18 April 1980) a coalition government came to power consisting of the two main African nationalist movements originally known as Zimbabwe African National Union (ZANU) and Zimbabwe African People's Union (ZAPU), led by Robert Mugabe and Joshua Nkomo respectively. Because of the ban imposed on them during the preceding years, both parties had been forced to operate in exile. They had become liberation movements fighting an armed guerilla warfare directed against the white settler minority regime under Prime Minister Ian Smith after its internationally unrecognized Unilateral Declaration of Independence (UDI, 11 November 1965) from Britain.

Due to the pressure exerted by the guerilla warfare as well as by international attempts—including economic sanctions—at resolving the crisis, the settler regime finally agreed to what was termed an Internal Settlement (3 March 1978). This allowed for some kind of participation of collaborating African parties under Abel Muzorewa (United African National Council, UANC) and the expelled founding President of ZANU, Ndabaningi Sithole, whose party was then known as ZANU Sithole (and later ZANU Ndonga). Under a new constitutional set-up providing for African majority rule while at the same time safeguarding real power for the white minority, the subsequent elections (17–21 April 1979) ushered in a new government on 1 June 1979 under the leadership of Muzorewa. This being little else but a black puppet regime at Smith's will and because the elections had been held without the still banned liberation movements and had also been rigged extensively, the Internal Settlement partners failed to achieve the international acceptance deemed crucial for their political survival.

This finally prompted Britain as the former colonial power to take the initiative again, in conjunction with the Commonwealth, which resulted in bringing together the Internal Settlement partners as well as the liberation movements—since 1976 cooperating under the umbrella of the Patriotic Front—at the Lancaster House Conference in London (10 September–12 December 1979). A constitutional settlement plus a cease-fire as well as transitional arrangements were finally negotiated under considerable pressure from the British side which then resumed responsibility for the country during a short transitional period (as from 13 December 1979). Much to the surprise not only of Britain, the liberation movements won almost all the 'common roll' seats at the following general elections (27–29 February 1980) whereas Smith's Rhodesian Front won all the seats reserved for the electorate of the 'white roll'.

Just before the elections, the Patriotic Front had—at the instigation of Mugabe's ZANU—split again into the original components which now used the Patriotic Front (PF) label in addition to the parties' names, i.e. ZANU (PF) and PF-ZAPU. This ultimately facilitated a determination of the real strength of each component, resulting in a profound shock for PF-ZAPU which, due to its leading role in the formation of African nationalist parties since the late 1950s, had until then still nurtured the notion of being the bigger one of the two liberation movements. This position, however, had obviously been passed on to ZANU (PF). Making the most of its overwhelming victory, the ZANU (PF) leadership pushed its coalition partner PF-ZAPU to the side through a number of harsh and insensitive actions. The coalition led by Prime Minister Mugabe was called off at the beginning of 1982, leaving ZANU (PF) as the sole ruling party, although a few ministers from PF-ZAPU stayed on until November 1984. The ensuing menace of numerous indiscriminate acts of violence perpetrated in the southwestern parts of the country by former members of PF-ZAPU's guerilla army as well as some deserters from the new national army led to a military overreaction by the government which feared South African involvement within the framework of that country's regional destabilization policy. These military actions caused a considerable number of additional deaths among the civilian population and alienated the mainly Ndebele-speaking population in PF-ZAPU's political stronghold in the southwestern area, thereby underpinning the power conflict with a seemingly ethnic undertone.

The first post-independence elections (1985) were, therefore, held in an atmosphere of widespread repression and intimidation, with many of PF-ZAPU's politicians having been detained although the party had maintained its denial of any involvement with the bandits who were misleadingly labeled 'dissidents'. Thus, the elections were characterized by a sharp polarization between ZANU (PF) and PF-ZAPU, with the smaller opposition parties becoming totally marginalized. ZANU (PF) won an overwhelming victory, but PF-ZAPU was able to entrench its position in the Matabeleland provinces in the southwest even more forcefully than in 1980. The obvious inability of ZANU (PF) to make any inroads into PF-ZAPU's strongholds was one of the reasons for a revision of the confrontational policy. After protracted negotiations the Unity Agreement was signed (22 December 1987), followed by a merger of both parties into ZANU PF precisely two years later.

Meanwhile, constitutional amendments had replaced the Westminster system with an executive presidency (31 December 1987), preceded by the abolition of the 20% reserved parliamentary seats (21 September 1987) and followed by the abolition of the Senate, the second parliamentary chamber with 25% of the seats reserved for the electorate of the 'white roll'. Both the Senate and the House of Assembly were replaced by an enlarged Parliament with 150 seats at the end of the parliamentary period. The subsequent elections of 1990 were overwhelmingly won by the united party ZANU PF, but a new challenger—the Zimbabwe Unity Movement (ZUM) led by Edgar Tekere, the expelled former Secretary-General of ZANU (PF)—was able to win almost one fifth of the votes which indicated the existence of a considerable opposition potential. Due to the plurality system ZUM could not, however, reap the benefits and ended up with less than 2% of the seats. Likewise, in the first direct presidential election Tekere scored 17% against the incumbent President Mugabe who was thus re-elected.

While the 1990 election remained controversial because of a lot of pre-election violence and intimidation, the 1995 parliamentary elections were conducted in considerably less controversial circumstances. But several opposition parties, claiming an uneven battle ground and demanding constitutional changes as well as the repeal of the Electoral Act of 1990, boycotted the elections, which resulted in ZANU PF winning almost half of the seats without being challenged. Of the remaining seats only two were not won by ZANU PF in the election contest. The presidential elections that followed in 1996 were characterized by the last-minute—and legally invalid—withdrawal of the two candidates Abel Muzorewa and Ndabaningi Sithole. President Mugabe was re-elected, but as there had been no real contest, voter participation reached an embarrassing all-time low.

1.2 Evolution of Electoral Provisions

The pre-independence elections (1980) and the first post-independence elections (1985) were held under a system of separate electoral rolls. 20% of the parliamentary seats were reserved for the electorate of the so-called 'white roll' including not only the white population but also—without their consent—the so-called coloured population of mixed origin as well as the 'Asian' population originating from the Indian sub-continent. The remainder of the population, supposed to be on a 'common roll' (although a valid electoral roll was in existence only in 1985), elected the remaining 80 members of the House of Assembly. Under this arrangement, the 'white roll' MPs elected 10 and the 'common roll' MPs 14 members of the Senate, the second parliamentary chamber. Six Senators were appointed by the President acting on the advice of the Prime Minister, while the remaining 10 Senators were elected by electoral colleges of the Chiefs, evenly but disproportionately split between Mashonaland (which contained the bulk of the population) and Matabeleland.

Whereas single-member constituencies were already in existence for the 'white roll' electorate, these were introduced for the 80 'common roll' seats only in 1985, together with the plurality system. Previously, in 1980, the 'common roll' electorate had to choose a pre-determined number of members of the House of Assembly for each of the eight provinces by way of provincial party lists, while the following system of seat allocation was applied: The combined number of valid votes of all those parties polling less than 10% of the total vote in a given province were 'eliminated' from the total valid votes cast and the resulting sum was divided by the number of seats allocated to that particular province. The resulting figure served as a divisor for the results of those parties not yet 'eliminated', with the final result being rounded up or down respectively. Also in the 'white roll' elections of 1985 a particular system was in use in such cases where there were more than two candidates, with none of them getting the absolute majority; in such cases, second preferences indicated on the ballot paper were added while the weakest candidate was struck off. This procedure was even repeated for another round in three cases.

As soon as it was possible to get rid of the provisions of separate voters' rolls and reserved seats entrenched for seven years in the clauses of the new constitution (which had been more or less imposed by the outgoing British colonial power), the constitutional changes of 21 September 1987 abolished all notions of separate voters' rolls based on racial criteria and scrapped the reserved parliamentary seats as well. The principles of universal as well as equal, direct and secret suffrage have, therefore, been fully applied only since the general elections of 1990. For a short transitional period, the 20 abolished reserved seats were filled through by-elections (23 October 1987) with the remaining 80 members of the House of Assembly sitting as an electoral college.

With the expiry of the parliamentary term 1985–1990, a totally new system was installed; the Senate was abolished, and the newly constituted Parliament had 150 seats with 120 seats for members elected in single-member constituencies. The replacement of the imposed Westminster system (ceremonial President and executive Prime Minister) with an executive presidency system inaugurated direct elections to this office by the population as from 1990. Only in 1987, when the executive presidency was introduced, was the President elected indirectly, with members of the House of Assembly and the then still existing Senate sitting together as an electoral college.

1.3 Current Electoral Provisions

Sources: Constitution of 1980 and amendments relating to electoral provisions: Constitution of Zimbabwe Amendment No. 3 Act (No. 1 of 1983), Amendment No. 5 Act (No. 4 of 1985), Amendment No. 6 Act (No. 15 of 1987), Amendment No. 7 Act (No. 23 of 1987), Amendment No. 8 Act (No. 4 of 1989), Amendment No. 9 Act (No. 31 of 1989), Amendment No. 10 Act (No. 15 of 1990), Amendment No. 11 Act (No. 30 of 1990), Amendment No. 14 Act of 1997, Electoral Act, 1990 (No. 7 of 1990), amended by the Electoral (Amendment) Act, 1992 (No. 7 of 1992) and the Electoral Act (Modification) Notice, 1995. Electoral Regulations, 1992, amended by the Electoral (Amendment) Regulations, 1995 (No. 1), 1995 (No. 2), 1996 (No. 3), and 1996 (No. 4). Electoral (Applications, Appeals and Petitions) Rules, 1995.

Elected national institutions: Parliament (120 directly elected members) and President. Regular terms of office: five years (Parliament), six years (President), so far without restrictions as to the number of terms possible. Besides the 120 directly elected members, Parliament embraces eight Provincial Governors as *ex-officio* members, up to 12 members appointed by the President and 10 traditional Chiefs. Two of the Chiefs are elected by the Council of Chiefs sitting as an electoral college, while the other eight are elected by provincial assemblies of Chiefs sitting as electoral colleges and electing one Chief each to be a Member of Parliament. In addition, the Attorney-General is also an *ex-officio* Member of Parliament (without voting rights), but the Speaker and the President are not Members of Parliament.

Suffrage: The principles of universal, equal, direct and secret suffrage are applied. All those accepted as registered voters are entitled to vote. Any person who has attained the age of 18 years and is a citizen of Zimbabwe or, since 31 December 1985, has been regarded by virtue of a written law as permanently resident in Zimbabwe qualifies for registration as a voter. Besides usual disqualifications (mental disorder etc.), expelled Members of Parliament are disqualified from voting for five years.

Nomination of candidates

- *presidential elections*: Candidates must be citizens of Zimbabwe by birth or descent and be ordinarily resident in Zimbabwe and must have attained the age of 40 years. Requirements for the nomination are not fewer than 10 registered voters in each of the 10 provinces and a money deposit to which the same rules apply as in the case of parliamentary candidates.
- *parliamentary elections*: Candidates must have attained the age of 21 years, must have been registered as a voter and must have been ordinarily resident in Zimbabwe for not less than five years during the period of 20 years immediately preceding the nomination. Disqualified are those holding public office (exemptions: Vice-Presidents, Ministers, Deputy Ministers, Provincial Governors, members of statutory bodies, and some other persons). A candidate's nomination must be supported by no fewer than 10 persons registered on the voters' roll for that particular constituency. The candidate must pay a monetary deposit which is forfeited if the candidate withdraws or wins less than 20% of the valid votes of the winning candidate.

Electoral system

- *presidential elections*: Absolute majority system. If no candidate receives an absolute majority of the total number of valid votes cast, a second election has to be held within 21 days in which only the two candidates who received the highest number of valid votes at the previous election are eligible to contest.
- *parliamentary elections*: Plurality system in 120 single-member constituencies.

1.4 Comment on the Electoral Statistics

Figures of election results are usually published extensively in the local print media. On account of occasional omissions without bad intent and because of printing errors, the necessary precision is not ensured so that the calculation of sums is often rather trying. Although the Electoral Supervisory Commission, whose duty it is to supervise the registration of voters and the conduct of elections, may submit a report to the President concerning the matters under its supervision, such reports—which have to be laid before Parliament (for the 1990 election this was done only on 6 December 1994)—do not contain any results. Thus, the only authoritative source with regard to precise figures is the office of the Registrar General whose report on the 1985 elections (published on 13 September 1985) has been made use of; however, no subsequent reports have been published so far. Therefore, for the elections of 1990 and 1995 the figures as published in the local print media have been used and corrected where necessary. With regard to the 1990 election, Moyo (1992) provides a full set of election results, which unfortunately contains some serious errors as the sources—the reports by the local print media—have not been sufficiently scrutinized. As to the 1980 elections, documents No. 1113 and No. 1142 of Baumhögger (1984) give the full sets of results.

2. Tables

2.1 Dates of National Elections, Referendums and Coups d'Etat

Year	Presidential elections	Parliamentary elections[c]	Elections for Constitutional Assembly	Referendums	Coups d'état
1980		14/02[a]			
		27–29/02[b]			
1985		27/06[a]			
		01–02/07[b]			
1990	28–30/03	28–30/03			
1995		08–09/04			
1996	16–17/03				

[a] White roll.

[b] Common roll.

[c] National Assembly; there have been no elections to the Senate (abolished in 1990) since independence.

2.2 Electoral Body 1980–1996

Year	Type of election[a]	Population[b]	Registered voters		Votes cast		
			Total number	% pop.	Total number	% reg. voters	% pop.
1980	HA (wr)	—	97,379	—			—
			29,566[c]		16,497	55.8[d]	
	HA (cr)	7,000,000	—	—	2,702,275	—	38.6
1985	HA (wr)	—	—	—	35,753	—	—
	HA (cr)	8,200,000	2,989,369	36.5	2,971,242	99.4	36.2
1990	Pa	9,600,000	4,799,324	50.0			23.3
			4,222,892[c]		2,237,846	53.0[d]	
	Pr	9,600,000	4,799,324	50.0	2,587,204	53.9	27.0
1995	Pa	11,200,000	4,803,866	42.9			13.1
			2,589,508[c]		1,468,191	56.7[d]	
1996	Pr	11,500,000	—	—	1,514,061[e]	—	13.2

[a] HA = House of Assembly - white roll (wr), common roll (cr); Pa = Parliament; Pr = President.
[b] Estimates according to census figures of 1982 and 1992, adjusted to the date of the elections.
[c] Second file: registered voters in contested constituencies.
[d] In relation to registered voters in contested constituencies.
[e] Valid votes only.

2.3 Abbreviations of Names of Parties and Alliances

ANP	African National Party
CAZ	Conservative Alliance of Zimbabwe
FPZ	Forum Party of Zimbabwe
IZG	Independent Zimbabwe Group
NDU	National Democratic Union
NFZ	National Front of Zimbabwe
PF-ZAPU	Patriotic Front - Zimbabwe African People's Union[a]
RF	Rhodesian Front[b]
UANC	United African National Council[c]
UNFP	United National Federal Party
UP	United Parties
UPAM	United People's Association of Matabeleland
ZA	Zimbabwe Aristocrats
ZANU	Zimbabwe African National Union
ZANU (PF)	Zimbabwe African National Union (Patriotic Front)[a]
ZANU PF	Zimbabwe African National Union - Patriotic Front
ZCP	Zimbabwe Congress Party
ZDP	Zimbabwe Democratic Party
ZFP	Zimbabwe Federal Party
ZUM	Zimbabwe Unity Movement

[a] Patriotic Front - Zimbabwe African People's Union and Zimbabwe African National Union (Patriotic Front) merged into Zimbabwe African National Union - Patriotic Front.
[b] Changed its name into Conservative Alliance of Zimbabwe.
[c] Became the dominant partner of the United Parties.

2.4 Electoral Participation of Parties and Alliances 1980–1996

Party / Alliance	Years	Elections contested	
		Presidential	Parliamentary
NDU	1980, 1985, 1990	0	3
NFZ	1980, 1985	0	2
PF-ZAPU	1980, 1985	0	2
RF	1980	0	1
UANC	1980, 1985, 1990	0	3
UNFP	1980	0	1
UPAM	1980	0	1
ZANU	1980, 1985, 1990, 1995, 1996	1	4
ZANU (PF)	1980, 1985	0	2
ZANU PF	1990, 1995, 1996	2	2
ZDP	1980	0	1
CAZ	1985	0	1
IZG	1985	0	1
ZUM	1990	1	1
ANP	1995	0	1
FPZ	1995	0	1
ZA	1995	0	1
ZCP	1995	0	1
ZFP	1995	0	1
UP	1996	1	0

General note: Three parliamentary elections have been held since 1980. Presidential elections were held at the same time as the parliamentary elections in 1990 and separately in 1996.

2.5 Referendums

Since independence there have not been any referendums.

2.6 Elections for Constitutional Assembly

Elections for Constitutional Assembly have not been held.

2.7 Parliamentary Elections

2.7.1 House of Assembly 1980–1985

a) White roll

Year	1980		1985	
	Total number	%	Total number	%
Registered voters	97,379	–	32,502[c]	–
In contested const.[a]	29,566	30.4	—	—
Votes cast	—	—	35,753	—
Invalid votes	—	—	1,712	4.8
Valid votes	16,402	55.5[b]	34,041	95.2
RF	13,621	83.0	–	–
Independents	2,781	17.0	1,486	4.4
CAZ	–	–	18,731	55.0
IZG	–	–	13,513	39.7
PF-ZAPU	–	–	311	0.9

[a] Registered voters in contested constituencies, percentages relating to the total number of registered voters.
[b] In relation to registered voters in contested constituencies.
[c] At the time of the publication of the Delimitation Commission report in May 1985.

b) Common (i.e. African) roll

Year	1980[a]		1985[b]	
	Total number	%	Total number	%
Registered voters	—	–	2,989,369[c]	–
Votes cast	—	—	2,972,146	99.4
Invalid votes	—	—	78,861	2.7
Valid votes	2,649,529		2,893,285	97.3
NDU	15,056	0.6	295	0.0
NFZ	18,794	0.7	81	0.0
PF-ZAPU	638,879	24.1	558,771	19.3
UANC	219,307	8.3	64,764	2.2
UNFP	5,796	0.2	–	–
UPAM	1,181	0.0	–	–
ZANU	53,343	2.0	36,054	1.2
ZANU (PF)	1,668,992	63.0	2,233,320	77.2
ZDP	28,181	1.1	–	–

[a] No valid voters roll in existence.
[b] Figures as supplied by the Registrar General's report of 13 September 1985 which differ slightly from the figures originally published in the media (votes cast: – 904, invalid votes: – 33, valid votes: – 871, PF-ZAPU: – 1,875, UANC: + 1,578, ZANU: – 574).
[c] Including one constituency where polling was postponed to 2 August 1985, but where no contest took place. The number of registered voters is according to the Registrar General, whereas at the time of the publication of the Delimitation Commission report in May 1985 it was given as 2,970,146.

2.7.2 House of Assembly 1990–1995 (common roll)

Year	1990[a] Total number	%	1995 Total number	%
Registered voters	4,799,324	–	4,803,866[b]	–
in contested const.[c]	4,222,892	88.0	2,589,508	53.9
Votes cast	2,237,846	53.0[d]	1,468,191	56.7[d]
Invalid votes	139,653	6.2	63,173	4.3
Valid votes	2,098,193	93.8	1,405,018	95.7
NDU	498	0.0	–	–
UANC	11,191	0.5	–	–
ZANU	19,448	0.9	97,470	6.9
ZANU PF	1,690,071	80.5	1,143,349	81.4
Independents	7,954	0.4	70,818	5.0
ZUM	369,031	17.6	–	–
ANP	–	–	431	0.0
FPZ	–	–	84,219	6.0
ZA	–	–	1,571	0.1
ZCP	–	–	3,779	0.3
ZFP	–	–	3,381	0.2

[a] Including the results of one constituency where polling was postponed to 29–30 May 1990.

[b] The voters' rolls were grossly inflated at this time; after an election petition with regard to one constituency they were purged of more than 300,000 registered voters who had died since 1982 without having been removed from the rolls.

[c] Registered voters in contested constituencies, percentages relating to total number of registered voters.

[d] In relation to registered voters in contested constituencies. .

2.8 Composition of Parliament 1980–1995

Year	1980 Seats	%	1985 Seats	%	1990 Seats	%	1995 Seats	%
	100	100	100	100	120	100	120	100
RF	20	20.0	–	–	–	–	–	–
PF-ZAPU	20	20.0	15	15.0	–	–	–	–
UANC	3	3.0	–	–	–	–	–	–
ZANU (PF)	57	57.0	64[a]	64.0	–	–	–	–
ZANU PF	–	–	–	–	117[b]	97.5	118[c]	98.3
CAZ	–	–	15	15.0	–	–	–	–
IZG	–	–	4	4.0	–	–	–	–
Independents	–	–	1	1.0	–	–	–	–
ZANU	–	–	1	1.0	1	0.8	2	1.7
ZUM	–	–	–	–	2	1.7	–	–

[a] Including one constituency where polling was postponed to 2 August 1985, but where no contest took place.

[b] Including one constituency where polling was postponed to 29–30 May 1990.
[c] After a by-election on 25–26 November 1995 following a successful election petition, ZANU PF lost one seat to an independent candidate.

2.9 Presidential Elections 1990–1996

1990	Total number	%
Registered voters	4,799,324	–
Votes cast	2,587,204	53.9
Invalid votes	146,388	5.7
Valid votes	2,440,816	94.3
Robert Mugabe (ZANU PF)	2,026,976	83.0
Edgar Tekere (ZUM)	413,840	17.0

1996	Total number	%
Registered voters	4,902,244	–
Votes cast	1,557,558	31.8
Invalid votes	43,497	2.8
Valid votes	1,514,061	97.2
Robert Mugabe (ZANU PF)	1,404,501	92.7
Abel Muzorewa (United Parties)[a]	72,600	4.8
Ndabaningi Sithole (ZANU)[a]	36,960	2.4

[a] Candidates withdrew a few days before the contest which was, however, no longer possible in legal terms.

2.10 List of Power Holders 1980–1998

Head of State	Years	Remarks
Canaan Banana	1980–1987	Ceremonial President.
Robert Mugabe	1987–	On 31/12/87 the post of an executive President was created by a constitutional amendment; since then Mugabe has been Head of State and Government.

Head of Government	Years	Remarks
Robert Mugabe	1980–1987	Executive Prime Minister after independence.

3. Bibliography

3.1. Official sources

'Constitution of Zimbabwe Amendment (No. 3) Act, 1983 (No. 1 of 1983)'. *Government Gazette*, Vol. LXI, suppl. (Acts) 1–5.

'Constitution of Zimbabwe Amendment (No. 5) Act, 1985 (No. 4 of 1985)'. *Government Gazette*, Vol. LXIII, suppl. (Acts) 25–28.

'Constitution of Zimbabwe Amendment (No. 6) Act, 1987 (No. 15 of 1987)'. *Government Gazette*, Vol. LXV, suppl. (Acts) 333–335.

'Constitution of Zimbabwe Amendment (No. 7) Act, 1987 (No. 23 of 1987)'. *Government Gazette*, Vol. LXV, suppl. (Acts) 331–352.

'Constitution of Zimbabwe Amendment (No. 8) Act, 1989 (No. 4 of 1989)'. *Government Gazette*, Vol. LXVII, suppl. (Acts) 13–16.

'Constitution of Zimbabwe Amendment (No. 9) Act, 1989 (No. 31 of 1989)'. *Government Gazette*, Vol. LXVIII, suppl. (Acts) 167–180.

'Constitution of Zimbabwe Amendment (No. 10) Act, 1990 (No. 15 of 1990)'. *Government Gazette*, Vol. LXVIII, suppl. (Acts) 299–302.

'Constitution of Zimbabwe Amendment (No. 11) Act, 1990 (No. 30 of 1990'. *Government Gazette*, Vol. LXIX, suppl. (Acts) 395–400.

'Constitution of Zimbabwe Amendment (No.14) Act, 1997. *Government Gazette*, Vol. LXXIV, suppl. (Acts).

'Electoral Act, 1990 (No. 7 of 1990)'. *Government Gazette*, Vol. LXVIII, suppl. (Acts) 109–197.

'Electoral (Amendment) Act (No. 7 of 1992)'. *Government Gazette*, Vol. LXXI, suppl. (Acts) 91–95.

'Electoral Act (Modification) Notice, 1995, Statutory Instrument 72 B of 1995'. *Government Gazette*, Vol. LXXIII, suppl. (SI) 508 G–M.

'Electoral (Applications, Appeals and Petitions) Rules, 1995, Statutory Instrument 74 A of 1995'. *Government Gazette*, Vol. LXXIII, suppl. (SI) 518 A–P.

'Electoral Regulations, 1992, Statutory Instrument 58 of 1992'. *Government Gazette*, Vol. LXX, suppl. (SI) 345–410.

'Electoral (Amendment) Regulations, 1995 (No. 1), Statutory Instrument 70 of 1995'. *Government Gazette*, Vol. LXXIII, suppl. (SI) 503–504.

'Electoral (Amendment) Regulations, 1995 (No. 2), Statutory Instrument 89 A of 1995'. *Government Gazette*, Vol. LXXIII, suppl. (SI) 614 A–B.

'Electoral (Amendment) Regulations, 1996 (No. 3), Statutory Instrument 34 B of 1996'. *Government Gazette*, Vol. LXXIV, suppl. (SI) 342 C–M.

'Electoral (Amendment) Regulations, 1996 (No. 4), Statutory Instrument 38 A of 1996'. *Government Gazette*, Vol. LXXIV, suppl. (SI) 352 A–B.

3.2. Books, Articles and Electoral Reports

Baker, C. (1982). 'Conducting the Elections in Zimbabwe 1980'. *Public Administration and Development*, 2/1: 45–58.

Banana, C. S. (1989). *Turmoil and Tenacity. Zimbabwe 1890–1990*. Harare: The College Press.

Baumhögger, G. (1987). 'Verfassungsänderungen in Zimbabwe'. *Informationsdienst Südliches Afrika*, 8: 22–24.

— (1988). 'Aussöhnungspolitik unter Beweis gestellt. Zu den Nachwahlen in Zimbabwe'. *Informationsdienst Südliches Afrika*, 1: 33–35.

— (1996*a*). 'Sprengsatz Kandidatenkür. Konfliktlinien im Umfeld der Parlaments- und Kommunalwahlen in Zimbabwe'. *Afrika Süd*, 1: 23–26.

— (1996*b*). *Zimbabwe 1995–96: Wahlboykott, Demokratie und Reputation*. (Focus Afrika 6, IAK-Diskussionsbeiträge). Hamburg: Institut für Afrika-Kunde.

Baynham, S. (1992). *Zimbabwe in Transition*. Stockholm (in co-operation with the Africa Institute of South Africa, Pretoria).

Chitopo, P. (1993). 'Electoral Law and Administration in Zimbabwe', in B. Otlhogile and P. Molutsi (eds.), *Consolidating Democracy: The Electoral Process under Scrutiny: Report of the Workshop on Electoral Law and Administration of Elections in Botswana held on 19–20th February, 1993*. Gaborone: Democracy Research Project, University of Botswana.

Cliffe, L. (1980). 'The Zimbabwe Elections'. *Review of African Political Economy*, 15–16: 124–130.

—, Mpofu, J., and Munslow, B. (1980). 'Nationalist Politics in Zimbabwe: The 1980 Elections and Beyond'. *Review of African Political Economy*, 18: 44–67.

Cokorinos, L. (1984). 'The Political Economy of State and Party Formation in Zimbabwe', in M. Schatzberg (ed.), *The Political Economy of Zimbabwe*. New York: Praeger, 8–54.

Darnolf, S. (1995). 'Campaigning in Southern Africa. The Cases of Botswana and Zimbabwe', in T. Negash and L. Rudebeck (eds.), *Dimensions of Development. With Emphasis on Africa*. Uppsala University: Nordiska Afrikainstitutet and Forum for Development Studies, 63–75.

— (1997*a*). *Democratic Electioneering in Southern Africa. The Contrasting Cases of Botswana and Zimbabwe*. (Göteborg Studies in Politics 45 Göteborg). University: Department of Political Science.

— (1997*b*). 'Critics or Megaphones? News Coverage During the Parliamentary Election Campaigns in Botswana 1994 and Zimbabwe 1995'. *Democratization*, 4/2: 167–191.

Electoral Supervisory Commission (1995). *The Conduct of General Elections in Zimbabwe*. Harare: Electoral Supervisory Commission.

Gregory, M. (1981). 'Politicisation through Armed Struggle and Electoral Mobilization'. *The Journal of Commonwealth and Comparative Politics*, 19/1: 63–94.

Herbst, J. I. (1990). *State Politics in Zimbabwe*. Harare: University of Zimbabwe Publications.

Kongwa, S. (1990). 'Zimbabwe's 1990 General Election and the Search for Direction'. *AI Bulletin*, 30/3: 6–8.

Kreuz, L. (1985). 'Parlamentswahlen in Zimbabwe'. *KAS-Auslandsinformationen*, 1/7: 55–71.

Laakso, L. (1994). 'Voting without Choosing. State and Democratization in Zimbabwe', in *Thirty-Seventh Annual Meeting of the African Studies Association, Toronto, November 3-6, 1994*. Toronto: ASA, 1–22.

— (1996). 'Relationship Between the State and Civil Society in the Zimbabwean Elections 1995'. *The Journal of Commonwealth and Comparative Politics*, 34/3: 218–234.

— (1997). 'Why are Elections not Democratic in Africa? Comparisons Between the Recent Multi-Party Elections in Zimbabwe and Tanzania'. *Nordic Journal of African Studies*, 6/1: 18–35.

Lemelle, T. J. (1980). 'Winning Against a Stacked Deck: The Elections in Zimbabwe'. *Africa Today*, 27/1: 5–16.

Lemon, A. (1988). *The Zimbabwe General Election of 1985*. Africa Seminar, 23 March 1988. Cape Town: Centre for African Studies.

— (1988). 'The Zimbabwe General Election of 1985'. *The Journal of Commonwealth and Comparative Politics*, 26/1: 3–21.

Linington, G. (1996). 'The 1995 Parliamentary Elections: A Legal Perspective'. *Legal Forum*, 8/1: 51–58, and 8/2: 25–38.

Makumbe, J. (1991*a*). 'The 1990 Zimbabwe Elections: Implication for Democracy', in I. Mandaza and L. Sachikonye (eds.), *The One-Party State and Democracy. The Zimbabwe Debate*. Harare, 179–188.

— (1991*b*). *Zimbabwe Elections 1990: An Overview*. Harare: University of Zimbabwe, Department of Political and Administrative Studies, Election Studies Project, Occasional Paper Series, 1/3.

— (1995). 'Has the President Lost Support?'. *Southern Africa Political and Economic Monthly*, 9/7: 20–24.

Mandaza, I. (1986). *Zimbabwe: The Political Economy of Transition*. Dakar: Codesria.

— and Sachikonye, L. (1991). *The One-Party State and Democracy. The Zimbabwe Debate*. Harare, Southern Africa Political Economy Series Trust. State and Democracy Series, 1.

Mhlaba, L. (1991). *Report on the 1990 General and Presidential Elections: Mashonaland Central, Mashonaland East, Midlands, Matabeleland South Provinces*. Harare: University of Zimbabwe, Department of

Political and Administrative Studies, Election Studies Project, Occasional Paper Series, 1/1.

Moyo, J. N. (1992*a*). *Voting for Democracy. A Study of Electoral Politics in Zimbabwe*. Harare: University of Zimbabwe Publications.

— (1992*b*). 'State Politics and Social Domination in Zimbabwe'. *The Journal of Modern African Studies*, 30/2: 305–330.

Mpofu, J. M. (1980). *The February 1980 Zimbabwe Elections: The Matabeleland North and South Provinces*. Conference on Zimbabwe. University of Leeds, 21 June 1980.

Ncube, W. (1991). *Report on the 1990 General and Presidential Elections: Midlands, Mashonaland West and Mashonaland East Provinces*. Harare: University of Zimbabwe, Department of Political and Administrative Studies, Election Studies Project, Occasional Paper Series, 1/2.

— (1994). 'Review of Electoral Laws and Institutions in Zimbabwe'. *Legal Forum*, 6/3: 17–27.

Olsson, P. (1996). *Löften, sakfrågor eller lögner? En studie av patiernas politiska budskap till väljarna i Zimbabwe 1995*. Göteborgs universitet: Statsvetenskapliga institutionen.

Patel, H. H. (1990). 'The March 1990 Elections: Some Comments'. *Southern Africa Political and Economic Monthly*, 3/6: 3–4.

Quantin, P. (1992). 'The 1990 General Elections in Zimbabwe: Step Towards a One-Party State?', in S. Baynham (ed.), *Zimbabwe in Transition*. Stockholm, 24–44.

Raftopoulus, B. (1992). 'Beyond the House of Hunger: Democratic Struggle in Zimbabwe'. *Review of African Political Economy*, 54: 59–74.

Rich, T. (1980). *The Internal Elections. Differentiation of Support in Zimbabwe—Rhodesia, April 1979*. Conference on Zimbabwe. University of Leeds, 21 June 1980.

— (1982). 'Legacies of the Past. The Results of the 1980 Election in Midlands Province, Zimbabwe'. *Africa*, 52/3: 42–55.

Sachikonye, L. M. (1989). 'The Debate on Democracy in Contemporary Zimbabwe'. *Review of African Political Economy*, 45–46: 117–125.

— (1990). 'The 1990 Zimbabwe elections: a post-mortem'. *Review of African Political Economy*, 48: 92–99.

Sithole, M. (1986). 'The General Elections: 1979–1985', in I. Mandaza (ed.), *Zimbabwe: The Political Economy of Transition*. Dakar: Codesria, 73–97.

— (1988). 'Zimbabwe: In Search of a Stable Democracy', in L. Diamond, J. J. Linz and S. M. Lipset (eds.), *Democracy in Developing Countries: Vol.2: Africa*. Boulder, Col.: Lynne Rienner, 217–257.

—, Chitopo, P., and Masendeke, A. (1991). *Report on the 1990 General and Presidential Elections: Masvingo and Manicaland Provinces*. Harare:

University of Zimbabwe, Department of Political and Administrative Studies, Election Studies Project, Occasional Paper Series, 1/4.

Spengler, F. (1990). 'Zimbabwische Parlaments- und Präsidentschaftswahlen vom März 1990'. *KAS-Auslandsinformationen*, 6/4: 15–20.

Stenberg, S. (1997). *TV-Valdebatt i Zimbabwe till någon nytta? En studie av TV-valdebatten inför parlamentsvalet 1995*. Göteborg universitet: Statsvetenskapliga institutionen.

Stoneman, C. (ed.) (1988). *Zimbabwe's Prospects. Issues of Race, Class, State and Capitalism in Southern Africa*. London: Macmillan.

— and Cliffe, L. (1989). *Zimbabwe: Politics, Economics and Society*. London: Pinter Publishers

Sylvester, C. (1986). 'Zimbabwe's 1985 Elections. A Search for National Mythology'. *The Journal of Modern African Studies*, 24/1: 229–255.

— (1990). 'Unities and Disunities in Zimbabwe's 1990 Election'. *The Journal of Modern African Studies*, 28/3: 375–400.

— (1991). *Zimbabwe. The Terrain of Contradictory Development*. Boulder, Col.: Westview Press.

— (1995). 'Whither Opposition in Zimbabwe?'. *The Journal of Modern African Studies*, 33/3: 403–423.

Tshuma, L. (1991). *Background to Electoral Law*. Harare: University of Zimbabwe, Department of Political and Administrative Studies, Election Studies Project, Occasional Paper Series, 1/5.

Tsanga, A. S. (1994). 'Women and Elections in Zimbabwe'. *Legal Forum*, 6/4: 16–21.

ZimRights (1994). 'Report and Resolutions of the National Consultative Conference on Electoral Laws and General Elections in Zimbabwe. Held in Harare 25–26 July 1994'. *Legal Forum*, 6/3: 13–17.

— (1995*a*). *Election Monitoring Report*. Harare: Zimbabwe Human Rights Association.

— (1995*b*). 'Zimbabwe: Beyond the Elections'. *Southern Africa Political and Economic Monthly*, 8/6: 5–9.

— (1996). 'Presidential Elections: An Assured Victory'. *Southern Africa Political and Economic Monthly*, 9/6: 5–8.

Glossary

Candidacy: The sphere of candidacy is particularly important because the voter representative relationship can be influenced by different arrangements. A fundamental distinction must be drawn between individual candidacies and party lists, i.e., the idea of voting for certain candidates or personalities, or for the so-called impersonal lists of individuals. Contrary to many assumptions, the personality of the candidate can play a larger role on party lists than in individual candidacies, given that there are different forms of lists and some are open to personal votes (see *Forms of lists*).

Closed and blocked list: A list system (also referred to as simply *closed list*) which allows the voter to cast his/her vote only for one strictly structured list of party candidates, without the possibility to express preferences within this list. See *Forms of lists*.

Closed and non-blocked list: A list system which permits the voter to decide who should represent the party in Parliament by the possibility to choose between the candidates within one list. See *Forms of lists*

d'Hondt method: A highest average formula with the sequence of divisors 1, 2, 3, 4, 5, etc. Favours larger parties. See *Electoral formulae*.

Droop quota: The total number of valid votes cast (V), divided by the district magnitude (M) plus one (V/M + 1). Identical with *Hagenbach–Bischoff quota*.

Electoral formulae: Where seats are distributed in accordance with proportional representation (see *Principle of decision*), a specific method of calculation has to be used. Although there exists a whole series of such procedures, most of them can be classified into two basic categories, those based on average formula and those based on a quota. The typical feature of the *highest average formula*—the best known example is the *d'Hondt formula*—is as follows: The votes gained by the various political parties are divided by series of divisors (1, 2, 3, 4, 5, etc.) so that decreasing numerical series emerge for each party. The allocations of seats correspond to the highest numbers of quotients. The advantages of this kind of distribution method lie in its simplicity as well as in the fact that all seats will be distributed in just one procedure. Under quota systems, a certain quota is established. The parties will gain as many seats as their number of votes can be divided by the quota. Examples are the *Hare, Droop* or *Hagenbach–Bischoff quota,* gained by the division of the number of total votes cast by a divisor that can be differently established. These methods cannot allocate all seats in just one operation so that the remaining seats have to be distributed in a second operation, usually by the largest remainder of votes. In comparison to the average formula systems, the quota systems normally produce a more proportional outcome, therefore small parties are favored.

Electoral system: Set of formal rules according to which the voters may express their political preferences in elections and according to which it is possible to convert votes into parliamentary seats (in the case of parliamentary elections) or into executive positions (in the case of elections for President, governors, mayors, etc.). These rules refer to the following dimensions: districts, candidates, voting and conversion from votes into seats.

Forms of lists: The forms of party lists deal mainly with the relationship between the voter and the candidates or between the candidates and their parties. The strict *closed and blocked list* only permits voting *en bloc* for a political party. Party committees decide about the sequence of the candidates of the lists. Strict party lists increase the dependence of the representatives on the political parties. On the other hand, the parties can plan the composition of the party in Parliament (experts, minorities, women, etc.). In contrast to this, preferential voting within a *closed, but non-blocked* list permits voters to decide who should represent the party in Parliament. This decision is only ‘pre-structured’ by the party committees. The representative therefore feels less dependent on his party. The *open (i.e., non-closed and non-blocked) list* allows voters to cross party lines and enables them to compile their own lists. The lists only possess the significance of a proposal.

Gerrymandering: Gerrymandering is the practice of drawing electoral district boundaries with political parties’ interests in mind. In this case, the political manipulation is of a deliberate nature. The varying spatial distribution of support for the various political parties is exploited. The manipulative tactic is named after a Mr Gerry, who cut out a safe salamander-shaped district for himself in the city of Boston.

Greatest average: Method for the allocation of remaining seats. Seats that can not be distributed under the electoral quota used are allocated successively to those parties with the highest average number of votes per seat (votes of a party distributed by seats gained under the electoral quota).

Hagenbach–Bischoff quota: The total number of valid votes cast (V), divided by the district magnitude (M) plus one (V/M + 1). Identical with *Droop quota*. See *Electoral formulae*.

Hare quota: The total number of valid votes cast (V), divided by the district magnitude (M): V/M. See *Electoral formulae*.

Highest average formula: see *Electoral formulae*.

Largest remainder: Formula used for the allocation of remaining seats. Seats that can not be distributed under the electoral quota used are allocated successively to those parties with the largest remainder (total votes of the respective party minus its successful votes).

Malapportionment: Term to describe a situation in which imbalances in the population density between different constituencies are systematically related to the relative strengths of different parties, that is some parties are favored over others.

Majority principle: see *Principle of decision*.

Majority representation: see *Principle of representation*.

Open (i.e., non-closed and non-blocked) lists: A list system which allows voters to cross party lines and enables them to compile their own list. See *Forms of lists*.

Principle of decision: The decision principle represents the formula according to which the winners and losers in an election are to be determined. The majority formula as a decision principle means that the majority of the votes cast decides who wins the election (*majoritiy principle*). The proportional formula as a decision principle means that the result of an election is decided according to the proportion of votes cast that is obtained by each candidate or party (*proportional principle*).

Principle of representation: There are two basic principles for classifying electoral systems according to the impact they have on the votes/seats relationship: *majority representation* and *proportional representation*. With majority representation, the objective is to produce a parliamentary majority for one party or for a coalition of parties, which is achieved by the disproportion between votes and seats inherent in majority electoral systems. With proportional representation, the objective is to reflect the existing social forces and political groups in a given country as accurately as intended, i.e. a more or less proportional relation between votes and seats.

Proportional principle: see *Principle of decision*.

Proportional representation (PR): see *Principle of representation.*

Quota systems: see *Electoral formulae* and *Droop, Hagenbach–Bischoff* and *Hare quota.*

STV Droop quota: The total number of valid votes cast (V), divided by the district magnitude (M) plus one and then add one [(V/M+1) +1].

Thresholds of representation: Legal threshold (or hurdle) of representation means that political parties have to obtain a certain, legally fixed number of votes or seats in order to be able to participate in the allocation of seats. This does not refer to the individual candidate of the party who keeps his seat when he has won it, for example, for having reached the plurality in a single-member district.